THE WILLS
OF
AMHERST COUNTY, VIRGINIA

1761-1865

SOUTHERN HISTORICAL PRESS
INC

Book Publishers

By
THE REV. BAILEY FULTON DAVIS

Please direct all correspondence and orders to:

www.southernhistoricalpress.com
or
SOUTHERN HISTORICAL PRESS, Inc.
PO BOX 1267
375 West Broad Street
Greenville, SC   29601
southernhistoricalpress@gmail.com

ISBN #0-89308-302-X

Printed in the United States of America

AMHERST COUNTY, VIRGINIA, WILLS

1761 - 1865

by

Rev. Bailey Davis

-A-

DANIEL AARON -- Administrator's Bond, Book 1, Page 55 -- April 1, 1765; Administrator: ANNE AARON; Bondsman: JOHN SYNDOR. Inventory, Book 1, Page 72 -- Total: L 36-15-0 -- June 2, 1766. Commissioners: HENRY KEY, THOS. JOPLING, HENRY ROBARDS.

EZEKIEL E. ADCOCK - Book 8, Page 200 -- Administrator's Bond, April 17, 1832. Administrator: CHAMOE CARTER; Bondsman: JNO. THOMPSON, JR. (Note: This is one of the numerous errors found by the compiler. This item is indexed for ELIZ. ALLCOCK and the name of EZEKIEL ADCOCK does not appear in the index.)

ELIZABETH ADKINSON (Note variations inspelling) -- Guardian Bond, Book 3, Page 214 -- December 5, 1791. Guardian: JAMES McALEXANDER; Bondsman: JNO. HENDERSON; Parent: HEZIAH ADKINSON, deceased; Ward: ELIZ. ATKINSON.

HEZEKIAH ADKINSON (Note variations in spelling) -- Book 1, Page 370 -- Administrator's Bond, September 1, 1777. Administrator: WILLIAM ADKINSON; Bondsmen: CHAS. ASHLEY, WM. OGLESBY. Book 1, Page 384 -- Inventory of HEZEKIAH ATKINS (sic) -- September 3, 1777. Total: L 75-7-0; Commissioners: LEE HARRIS, JAS. HALLYBURTON, DAVID SHELTON.

WALKER ADKINSON -- Book 4, Page 264 -- Will, Written: May 24, 1806; Probated: September 15, 1806. Wife: RACHEL. My sister: MOLLY ADKINSON. Executors: Wife and WALTER SANDIDGE. Witnesses: JNO. SANDIDGE, STEPHEN CARTER, NELSON CARTER. Book 4, Page 268 -- Inventory, December 13, 1806. Total: L 241-15-6; Commissioners: BENJ. HIGGINBOTHAM, JOSEPH HIGGINBOTHAM, HENRY BALLEN-GER. Book 4, Page 434 -- Administrator's Bond, September 15, 1806. Adminis-trator: RACHEL ADKINSON; Bondsmen: JOHN and WALTER SANDIDGE; Wit-nesses: S. GARLAND, D. Clk.

WILLIAM AKERS -- Book 9, Page 322 -- Constable's Bond, June 19, 1837, appointed for two years. Bondsmen: JNO. H. GOODWIN and JNO. S. GOOD-WIN. Book 10, Page 134 -- Constable's Bond -- June 27, 1839 -- to GOV. DAVID CAMPBELL. Appointed for two years. Bondsmen: THOS. R. TERRY; THOS. HUTCHESON. Book 10, Page 357 -- Constable's Bond -- June 23, 1841, for two years. Bondsmen: JNO. L. GOODWIN and THOS. HUTCHESON. Book 11, Page 151 -- Constable's Bond, June 19, 1843, to GOV. JAS. McDOWELL, for two years appointed. Bondsmen: THOS. HUTCHESON and JAS. C. BECK Book 11, Page 317 -- Constable's Bond, June 16, 1845, appointed for two years. Bondsmen: PETER G. AKERS and THOS. BARBER (BARBOUR)(?) Book 11, Page 524 -- (Indexed as 324) Constable's Bond for two years appointed. June 21, 1847. Bondsmen: THOS. BARBOUT and PETER G. AKERS. Book 12, Page 236 -- Constable's Bond, June 18, 1849, for two years appointed. Bondsmen: JNO. H. AKERS and THOS. BARBOUR.

ANNE ALDRIDGE (Indexed for JANE ALDRIDGE) -- Book 5, Page 672 -- Guardian Bond, July 21, 1816. Guardian: JAS. S. PENDLETON; Ward: ANNE ALDRIDGE; Parent: ADAM ALDRIDGE, deceased; Bondsmen: JAS. WARE and REUBEN PENDLETON.

1

JANE ALDRIDGE -- Book 13, Page 348 -- Will, Written: July 25, 1848; Probated: May 15, 1854. Nephew: ROBT. A. COGHILL -- gets Glebe on left hand of the Main Stage road from New Glasgow to Amherst Courthouse. Many slaves named. Niece: ADELAIDE PENDLETON. Nephew: ROBT. A. PENDLETON. WM. G. PENDLETON -- slave and COGHILL Trustee thereof. JAS. S. PENDLETON, JR. -- same. Same to WM. H. ROSE during lifetime of ELIZA JANE ROSE and children living at her death, or descendants thereof. Upon event of death of any of my nices and nephews -- children of my sister, CATHERINE PENDLETON, before my death. ELIZA JANE DAWSON -- COGHILL trustee for her until 21, or married. Children of my sister, CATHERINE PENDLETON: ROBT. A., ADELAIDE PENDLETON. E. A. ROSE (E. J. previously mentioned) -- W. H. ROSE, trustee. JAS. S. PENDLETON and WM. G. PENDLETON -- Coghill trustee for them. Executor: ROBT. A. COGHILL. Witnesses: V. McGINNIS and A. B. McDANIEL. Codicil: Revokes item pertaining to ELIZA JANE DAWSON and sets up another type of trust for her. One slave to ADELAIDE PENDLETON has died and another given to her. Glebe has been sold, but residue of estate to COGHILL.
Book 13, Page 351 and Page 354 -- May 15, 1854 -- Executor: ROBT. A. COGHILL; Bondsmen: SAML. M. GARLAND, H. S. BROWN, WM. S. CLAIBORNE, ROBT. A. PENDLETON, W. H. ROSE, SAML. HEISKELL.

ROBERT ALDRIDGE -- Book 5, Page 564 -- Guardian Bond, February 19, 1816. Guardian: JAS. S. PENDLETON; Ward: ROBT. ALDRIDGE; Parent: ADAM ALDRIDGE, deceased; Bondsmen: REUBEN PENDLETON, THOS. ALDRIDGE.
Book 6, Page 61 -- Administrator's Bond, April 19, 1819. Administrator: JAS. S. PENDLETON; Bondsman: STERLING CLAIBORNE.
Book 6, Page 537 -- Administrator's Account, Recorded May 15, 1824. JAS. C. PENDLETON. From May 15, 1819. Payments to MRS. FRANCES GLASSCOCK, MISS JANE ALDRIDGE, PEACHY FRANKLIN, THOS. ALDRIDGE, but not stipulated as legatees. Paid to HEZEKIAH FULCHER for expenses to Martinsburg on estate business and for trip "over the mountain"; taxes "over the mountain." Some vouchers not submitted and rejected. Commissioners: EDMUND PENN, CHAS. S. BARRET, JOSEPH STAPLES.

PRISCILLA ALFORD -- Book 3, Page 583 -- Inventory, October 20, 1800, record date. Total: L 54-9-1; Commissioners: JOSEPH LOVING, CHAS. EDMONDS, DAVID PROFFITT.
Book 4, Page 323 -- Administrator's Bond, September 15, 1800. Administrator: WILLIAM ALFORD; Bondsman: DAVID PROFFITT.

ALEXANDER T. ALIFF -- Book 11, Page 537 -- Guardian Bond, August 16, 1847. Guardian: WILLIAM LAWHORNE; Parent: Not given -- figure "5" is written in by someone by "11," but I found nothing on Page 5 or Book 5; Bondsman: GEO. SHRADER.

JOHN ALICOCK -- Book B, Page 43 -- Circuit Court on Friday, March 21, 1851. Motion by JAS. W. COPPEDGE and JAS. H. JOINER to commit estate to sheriff, JNO. D. DAVIS, since ALLCOCK has been dead more than three months and no one has applied as administrator.

JOSEPH B. ALLCOCK -- Book 7, Page 210 -- Guardian Bond, February 16, 1829. Guardian: IRA ALLCOCK; Parent: "Orphan of the said IRA ALLCOCK." Bondsman: JOHN ALLCOCK.

RICHARD ALLCOCK -- Book 3, Page 515 -- Tobacco Inspector's Bond, November 20, 1797. Camden's Warehouse; Bondsman: NATHAN HALL.
Book 3, Page 521 -- Tobacco Inspector's Bond, September 17, 1798. Camden's Warehouse; Bondsman: JOSEPH BURRUS.
Book 4, Page 240 -- Tobacco Inspector's Bond, September 16, 1799. Governor's commission of 179--, Camden's Warehouse; JOSIAS WINGFIELD.
Book 4, Page 243 -- Same on September 15, 1800. Bondsman: JOEL CAMPBELL.
Book 4, Page 250 -- Same, September 20, 1802. Bondsman: MICAJAH CAMDEN.
Book 4, Page 254 -- Same, September 19, 1803. Bondsman: JOEL CAMPBELL.
Book 4, Page 279 -- Same, September --, 1805. Bondsman: WM. CAMDEN.
Book 4, Page 283 -- Same, September 15, 1805. Bondsman: JOSEPH ALLCOCK.
Book 6, Page 167 -- Inventory, September 18, 1820. Total: $729.00;

Commissioners: THOS. APPLIN, LEWIS LAYNE, JOS. KENADY.
Book A, Page 25 -- Executor's Bond, April 25, 1820. Executor: JOHN
ALLCOCK; Bondsmen: MICAJAH PENDLETON and WILLIAM HORSLEY.
Book A, Page 26f -- Will written: April 10, 1810; Probated: April 26,
1820. Wife: FRANCES -- land next to KENNEDY and HIGGINBOTHAM. My
two youngest daughters: ELIZABETH H. ALLCOCK and NANCY TILLER -- if
without issue. Son: JOHN ALLCOCK. My six (?) children; my there (sic)
sons are to be executors. Witnesses: P. (?) DAWSON; MICAJAH PENDLE-
TON; GEO. PENN. JOHN ALLCOCK qualified on probate date as executor.
Bondsmen: MICAJAH PENDLETON and WILLIAM HORSLEY.
Book A, Page 64 -- Estate Administration, JOHN ALLCOCK, executor, from
September 1, 1814. Sugar and coffee for the family for four years,
1816-1820 -- $70.00; Salt for same period -- $16.00. Recorded
September 22, 1823. Commissioners: THOS. APPLING, MOSES PHILLIPS,
LEWIS LAYNE.

GRACEY ANN ALLEN -- Book 6, Page 612 -- Guardian Bond, August 15,
1825. Guardian: WILLIAM DUNCAN; Wards: GRACEY ALLEN, WILLIAM STAN-
TON ALLEN, MARGARET A. ALLEN, MARY E. ALLEN, MARTHA JANE ALLEN, and
ROBT. FIELDS ALLEN (Note: I have supplied some of the middle names
for they show up in other items later.) Parent: ROBT. ALLEN, deceased; Bondsmen: HILL CARTER and JAS. W. SMITH.

JESSE ALLEN -- Book 2, Page 61 -- Will, Written: July 27, 1780;
Probated: June 3, 1782. JESSE ALLEN of Buckingham County, Virginia --
To JESSE JOPLING, son of ALSEY JOPLING -- unless he dies before 21.
Children of SAMUEL ALLEN. JESSE ALLEN, son of SAML. and HANNAH ALLEN --
Buckingham land. GEO. ALLEN, same, gets Buckingham land. LUCY ALLEN,
daughter of same couple -- If any legatee dies before 21 or marries.
Executors: My brother, SAMUEL ALLEN; and friend, GEO. HILTON. Wit-
nesses: THOS. JOPLING, SR.; and THOS. JOPLING, JR.; and BETHENIAH
HILTON.
Book 2, Page 63 -- Executor's Bond, June 3, 1782. Exeuctor: SAML.
ALLEN and GEO. HILTON; Bondsmen: WM. SPENCER and THOS. JOPLING, JR.
Book 2, Page 80 -- Inventory, September 20, 1782 -- Total: L 565-13-6;
Commissioners: JAS. PAMPLIN, ROBT. HORSLEY, JNO. HORSLEY.

MARGARET AMANDA ALLEN -- Book 8, Page 74 -- Guardian Bond, December 20,
1830. Guardian: JOHN (H. or B.) (?) DUFF; Parent: ROBERT ALLEN,
deceased; Bondsman: JULIUS SIMPSON.

MARTHA JANE ALLEN -- Book 9, Page 217 -- Administrator's Bond,
February 15, 1836. Administrator: PEYTON KEITH; Bondsman: JAS. W.
KEITH.
Book 9, Page 354 -- Administrator's Account, Recorded Nov. 22, 1837 --
PEYTON KEITH, administrator -- from April 18, 1836 - Attorney for
JNO. D. BOWLING or BOLLING and share of ROBT. ALLEN estate. WM. LOGAN
and wife -- share; JNO. F. DUFF -- Share; WM. STANTON ALLEN; MARY E.
ALLEN; ROBT. F. ALLEN, JR. -- PEYTON KEITH, guardian for them --
$4803 to each -- confusing for some are ROBT. ALLEN estate shares and
others are for interest in MARTHA JANE ALLEN's estate. Commissioners:
W. S. CRAWFORD, WM. H. KNIGHT, GEO. CALLOWAY.

MARY F. ALLEN -- Book 9, Page 352 -- Guardian's Account, Recorded
November 22, 1837 -- PEYTON KEITH, guardian -- from January 1, 1835 --
her share of ROBT. ALLEN's estate; H. CARTER for tuition -- $5.00.
Total: $275.71. Commissioners: W. S. CRAWFORD, WM. H. KNIGH, GEO.
CALLOWAY.
Book 14, Page 582 -- Will, Written: December 1, 1856; Probated:
June 21, 1858. For several years she has had care of SARAH MILDREN
LYNN, orphan of MARY LYNN, deceased, and has formed attachment for
her. Estate to be held in trust for her by JOS. C. BROWN, son of
MARTIN BROWN, at her death it goes to her children or children born
of lawful wedlock. If no issue, then to JOS. C. BROWN and his brother,
JAMES W. BROWN, or heirs. Witnesses: JNO. H. WATTS; AUGUSTUS D.
WHITTEN. JOS. S. (C. in body of will) BROWN, qualified on probate
date. Bondsmen: SAML. R. IRVINE, CHAS. M. WATTS, JAS. W. BROWN.
Book 15, Page 44 -- Inventory, November 18, 1858. Total: $4,529.50.
Commissioners: LEWIS S. CAMPBELL; WILKERSON D. TUCKER; B. T. (or Y.)
HENLEY.

Book 15, Page 581 -- Inventory and Account -- JOE S. BROWN, administrator -- Recorded November 19, 1860. Interest of WILLIAM LOGAN, SR.
(?) -- gold spectacles retained for MRS. LOGAN (Note: ROBT. ALLEN
data shows that ROBT. ALLEN's widow married WM. LOGAN so this is mother
of MARY E. ALLEN.) Burial fee of $25.00 paid to SYLVESTER L. BURFORD.
Book 16, Page 314 -- Administrator's Account, Recorded May --, 1863.
From June 20, 1859 -- SARAH MILDRED LYNN, legatee -- October 9, 1959.
Tuition fee of $20.00 Mention of LOGAN's administrator. Tuition fees
paid on November 15, 1860.

ROBERT ALLEN (Note: His son is called ROBT. FIELDS ALLEN, JR., in
one item) -- Book 6, Page 483 -- Administrator's Bond, September 20,
1824. Administrator: ELIZ. ALLEN and FIELDING BROWN; Bondsmen: WM.
DUNCAN and PEYTON KEITH.
Book 6, Page 613 -- Administrator's Bond, August 25, 1825. Adminis-
trator: FIELDING BROWN; Bondsmen: WM. DUNCAN and JAS. WOOD.
Book 6, Page 628 -- Inventory, October 19, 1825. Total: $2,110.48.
Commissioners: MICAJAH CAMDEN, PETER G. CAMDEN, ST. GEO. TUCKER.
Book 6, Page 661 -- Administrator's Account. FIELDING BROWN, administrator. Recorded April 17, 1826. Rent paid MICAJAH CAMDEN. RO. TINS-
LEY, trustee for M. CAMDEN, intestate bond. Witnesses paid: JNO.
MASTERS, WM. B. JACOBS. Paid H. S. FULCHER, constable. Paid to
S. CLAIBORN's executors. To H. M. GARLAND, constable. R. RIVES'
administrators. Ticker for clerk to Court of Appeals. RICHESON TAYLOR
paid for making coat for STANTON -- $2.00. Tuition for four scholars
to S. G. HARRIS and JNO. B. DUNCAN -- $20.00 in 1824 -- and $11.65 to
each one. JOHN FLOYD for making four pairs of double solid shoes --
$2.00. Two pairs of fine shoes: $1.50 six pairs of small shoes --
$1.50. To SAML. WOOD for services rendered in the plantation in 1824
to save the crop -- $10.00. Same paid to WM. LOGAN. Coroner's fee
to CHAS. P. TALIAFERRO. Sixteen yards of calico furnished to the
children. Nelson county law suit, but style not given -- April and
September terms, 1825. To WM. DUNCAN, guardian of the children, for
slave division. AMANDA LEE for tuition for four scholars for three
months -- $12.00. To WM. LOGAN part of his distributive share -- two
slaves are not in distribution pending suit to determine title. To
WM. LOGAN, who married ELIZ. ALLEN, widow of decedent. Children of
ROBT. ALLEN -- slaves -- and children are set forth as follows:
GRACEY ANN ALLEN, WM. STANTON ALLEN, MARGARET AMANDA ALLEN, MARY EMILY
ALLEN, MARTHA JANE ALLEN, ROBERT FIELDS ALLEN -- all infants, and WM.
DUNCAN, guardian. Commissioners: LYNSE S. TALIAFERRO, WM. TUCKER,
CORNELIUS SALE.
Book 8, Page 84 -- Slave division: To JNO. D. BOLLING, who married
GRACEY ANN ALLEN; To JOHN DUFF who married MARGARET AMANDA ALLEN; To
WM. S. ALLEN; MARY E. ALLEN; and ROBT. F. ALLEN -- PEYTON KEITH,
guardian, and when they come of age. Representatives of MARTH J.
ALLEN, deceased, and her mother. Reported March 22, 1831. Commis-
sioners: WM. HENLEY, WM. TUCKER, R. HENLEY.
Book 9, Page 351 -- Estate Division with PEYTON KEITH's guardian
accounts. November 22, 1837. Legatees: WM. S. ALLEN; MARY E. ALLEN;
ROBT. F. ALLEN; MARTHA JANE ALLEN estate, PEYTON KEITH, administrator;
Attorneys of JNO. D. BOWLING; WM. LOGAN's share; JOHN F. DUFF's share.
Commissioners: W. S. CRAWFORD, WM. H. KNIGHT, GEO. CALLOWAY.
Book 14, Page 495 (Incorrectly indexed as Book 14, Page 401, but index
in front of book is correct) -- Administrator's Account, Recorded
February 28, 1856. Administrator: JAS. W. BROWN. $607.36 in Savings
Bank at Lunchburg on January 5, 1855. Cash paid to C. DABNEY and
amount received of JOHN THOMPSON, JR. Balance due legatees from
balance in bank.
Book 15, Page 175 -- Administrator's Account, April term, 1859. Ad-
ministrator: JAS. W. BROWN. Widow's share paid to WM. LOGAN. MARY
E. ALLEN -- amount deposited in Central Savings Bank to credit of
JNO. D. BOXLEY. To legatees: WM. S. ALLEN and JOHN DUFF.

ROBERT FIELDS ALLEN -- Book 9, Page 352 -- See #26 above -- Book 9,
Page 351f.
Book 10, Page 99 -- Administrator's Bond, April 15, 1839. Administra-
tor: PEYTON KEITH; Bondsman: JOS. K. (or R.) IRVING.
Book 10, Page 139 -- App. Recorded June 17, 1839. Two slaves and Lot
of "Lattin books and platting instruments." Commissioners: JNO. W.
BROADDUS, DANL. L. COLEMEN, ROBERT PAGE.

Book 10, Page 156 -- PEYTON KEITH as guardian reports on his accounts for the ward. May 2, 1839. Several tutor items; amount received from WM. S. ALLEN to equalize slave division.
Book 10, Page 297 -- PEYTON KEITH gives Administrator's Account, December 21, 1840. Refers to the Latin books in appraisal. Amounts of $84.89 paid to following: WM. LOGAN; WM. S. ALLEN; JOHN DUFF; MARY E. ALLEN; Child of GRACY BOLING (sic), formerly GRACY ALLEN.

SAMUEL ALLEN -- Book 3, Page 557 -- Will Written: January 30, 1799; Probated: January 20, 1800. Wife: HANNAH ALLEN. Son, GEORGE ALLEN - one-fifth and land in Buckingham -- 216 acres bought from JESSE STRANGE and where GEO. now lives. Daughter: LUCY TINDALL. Son: JESSE ALLEN. Daughter: MARTHA ALLEN. Daughter: BETHENIAH ALLEN. Son: SAML. H. ALLEN. Son: JOHN ALLEN. Witnesses: DANL. PERROW; GUENEMT (?) PERROW; DRURY HUDSON.
Book 4, Page 118 -- Administrator's Account, Order of January court, 1802. GEO. ALLEN, administrator. Recorded October 15, 1802. Paid for executions on estate to JNO. C. CHRISTIAN, JR., and LEWIS TINDAL. Commissioners: JNO. HORSLEY, MICAJAH PENDLETON, WM. JORDAN. Reported June 20, 1803.
Book 4, Page 303 -- Administrator's Bond, December 16, 1799. Administrator: JNO. CHRISTIAN, JR.; Bondsman: JNO. CHRISTIAN, B (So inserted in document and so signed). (Note: There are discrepancies here for probate date was January 20, 1800, and this qualification bears date of 1799 -- unless there were two SAML. ALLENS. Again, GEO. ALLEN was administrator in 1802 and there is no record of his having qualified.)
Book 5, Page 37 -- Inventory -- so indexed, but nothing is there and nothing in book index nor in Book 4.

DAVID ANDERSON -- Book 11, Page 145 -- Slave division -- January court order, 1842. Done: January 18, 1842. Motion of WM. G. RUCKER and wife, MARY F., late MARY F. LEE -- to divide slaves of DAVID ANDERSON, late of Prince Edward County, deceased, and bequeathed to grandchildren: MARY F.; CATHERINE A. LEE; and MARTHA J. LEE. (WM. RUCKER is called WM. F. and WM. G. in various places). Commissioners: WM. KENT; ROBT. RIDGWAY; CHAS. WINGFIELD; THOS. A. EDWARDS. (Note: For data on MARTHA J. LEE -- daughter of JAMES and KATHARINE (ANDERSON) LEE -- who married in Amherst, February 14, 1849, DR. POWHATAN C. SUTPHIN -- see PERRIN, BATTLE, and KNIFFIN - History of Kentucky, 3rd edition -- Hart County, Page 1030.)

ELIZABETH ANDERSON & C -- Book 9, Page 332 -- Trustee Bond. August 21, 1837. Trustee: HENRY F. BEAMONT. For: ELIZABETH ANDERSON and Children. Bondsman: STERLING C. ANDERSON -- attorney-in-fact.

SAMUEL ANDERSON -- Book 6, Page 83 -- Administrator's Bond, August 16, 1819; Administrator: JESSE BECK; Bondsman: CHAS. WINGFIELD.
Book 6, Page 97 -- Inventory, October 4, 1819. Total: $411.42-1/2. Items: Wheelwright and cabinet maker tools, blacksmith tools, stock, etc.; Commissioners: WM. TURNER, HENRY TURNER, WM. DAY, SOLOMON DAY.

WILLIAM ANDREWS -- Book 6, Page 231 -- Constable's Bond, June 18, 1821. For First Hundred for two years. Bondsman: WM. ANDREWS, SR.

SARAH C. A. APPLING -- Book 16, Page 101 -- Guardian Bond, December 16, 1861. Guardian: AMERICAN V. WATTS; Bondsmen: DAVID APPLING, JAS. M. WATTS; Parent: Not set forth.

THOMAS APPLING -- Book 9, Page 126 -- Will, Written: February 13, 1835; Probated: September 21, 1835. Wife: ELIZABETH APPLING -- land, etc. Remaining two-thirds to my children. One-ninth to each of these children: Son, JOEL; lawful heirs of my daughter, NANCY CHRISTIAN, wife of WM. CHRISTIAN; to my daughter, SUSAN, wife of JOSIAH LEEK, and to lawful heirs at her death; to my son, WM. APPLING and heirs; to my son, THOMAS APPLING; to my son, AUSTIN M. APPLING; to my daughter, ELIZABETH, wife of CLAIBORNE STILL and to lawful heirs at her death; to my son, JAMES R. APPLING; to my son, DAVID APPLING -- to remain with his mother for her life and is permitted to work own hands on the plantation and gets land at Mother's death. Executors: Sons: AUSTIN M. and DAVID APPLING. Witnesses: JAS. D. WATTS, WM. WRIGHT, ASAHEL FRENCH.

5

Book 9, Page 127 -- Administrator's Bond, September 21, 1835. Administrator: DAVID APPLING; Bondsmen: WM. H. TYLER, JOS. KYLE, AUSTIN M. APPLING.

Book 9, Page 179 -- Inventory, Commissioner appointed September termand done October 24, 1835. Total: $8,045.85. Commissioners: MOSES PHILLIPS, PEYTON KEITH, JAS. G. CHRISTIAN.

Book 9, Page 182 -- Sales, December 4, 1835 -- DAVID APPLING, administrator; Commissioners: JOSHIAH LEAKE (LEEK in will), WM. S. CHRISTIAN. $432.21 after deducting one-third for widow's dower, and $100.00 for overseer in 1835.

Book 9, Page 260 (Indexed as 160) -- Division, December 2, 1835. Executor: DAVID APPLING. Widow's share of one-third. Commissioners: PEYTON KEITH; JAS. W. KEITH; J. PIERCE, J.P.

Book 10, Page 170 -- Executor's Account (Indexed as 169), October 21, 1839. Administrator: DAVID APPLING; Blacksmith account of DRURY CHRISTIAN; Commissioners: PEYTON KEITH and MOSES PHILLIPS.

Book 11, Page 6 (Indexed as 7) -- Executor's Account, November 15, 1841. Executor: DAVID APPLING; Blacksmith account of D. and ROBT. ARNOLD; JNO. SMOOT for making shoes. Commissioners: JAS. W. and PEYTON KEITH.

Book 11, Page 190 -- Executor's Account, Order of October Court, 1843; Recorded Nov. 26, 1843. DAVID APPLING, executor. Commissioners: JAS. W. KEITH, WM. L. WATTS, WM. S. TURNER.

Book 11, Page 356 (Indexed as 350) -- Executor's Account, October term, 1845; Recorded: November 17, 1845. DAVID APPLING, executor; account from August 12, 1843. Commissioners: JOS. KYLE, JAS. W. KEITH, WM. S. TURNER, HOWEL S. BROWN (did not sign report.)

Book 12, Page 109 -- Executor's Account, Recorded December 18, 1848. DAVID APPLING, executor. From August 10, 1845. Commissioners: JAS. D. WATTS and JAS. W. KEITH.

Book 12, Page 403 -- Executor's Account, Recorded April 21, 1851. DAVID APPLING, executor. From September 8, 1839 -- ELIZ. APPLING bought a colt.

Book 13, Page 102 -- Executor's Account, Recorded June 18, 1852. DAVID APPLING, executor. From January 3, 1851, but note that December 31, 1850, items are listed, too. To JUDITH F. WOODSON, midwife -- $3.00.

Book 13, Page 302 -- Final report recorded July 16, 1853. Herein it is cited that WM. H. TYLER and JOS. KYLE were bondsmen for DAVID APPLING on September 21, 1835, and they are now released from bond since the final distribution has been made.

SARAH H. ARMISTEAD -- Book 7, Page 251 -- Will, Written: December 30, 1838; Probated: June 16, 1829. My niece: JANE MEREDITH COBBS -- 192-3/4 acres in Amherst County which was assigned to me by Commissioners as my fifth part of land of my late father, COL. SAML. MEREDITH -- next to land deeded to COL. WILLIAM ARMISTEAD. My niece: SARAH A. WALLER. My niece: JANE HENRY GARLAND. My niece: ELIZ. BRECKINRIDGE COLEMAN. My nephew: WILLIAM H. GARLAND. Nephew by marriage: DR. JNO. P. COBBS. My nephew: SAML. M. GARLAND. Executors: DAVIS S. GARLAND and DR. JNO. P. COBBS; Witnesses: JAS. L. NEVIL, PAUL C. BOWLES; Codicil: Slaves to my brother-in-law, DAVID S. GARLAND, who married my sister, JANE H. GARLAND.

Book 7, Page 263 -- Executor's Bond, June 16, 1829. Executtor: DAVID S. GARLAND; Bondsman: WILLIAM M. WALLER.

WILLIAM ARMISTEAD -- Book B, Page 31 -- Estate Commitment to Sheriff, Friday, March 31, 1848. Motion by RODERICK WAUGH to commit estate to sheriff, JAS. S. LAMKIN, since ARMISTEAD has been dead more than three months -- intestate -- and no applicant to administer.

THOMAS ARNY (Indexed as 368, but it is 388) -- Book 10, Page 388 -- Administrator's Bond, September 20, 1840 (1841, see below). Administrator: DAVID STAPLES; Bondsman: WM. KENT. (Note: The document has 1840 as date of bond, but at the bottom it is recorded on September 20, 1841, so probably clerk's error.)

ANDREW J. ARRINGTON -- Book 12, Page 71 -- Refunding Bond, December 19, 1848. Bondsmen: JAS. M. DILLARD, ROBT. L. BROWN. Executed by ARRINGTON to ROBERT MITCHELL and RUFUS HIGGINBOTHAM, executors of will of RANDOLPH CASH -- $2,500.00 -- ANDREW J. ARRINGTON has married LUCY MITCHELL, daughter of ROBERT MITCHELL, and one of legatees of RANDOLPH CASH, but MITCHELL has refused to deliver to her slaves and other bequests until refunding bond is executed. Witnesses: WARNER JONES and JNO. SHIPMAN. LUCY ARRINGTON appends note stating that she desires her husband, ANDREW J. ARRINGTON, to take possession of her legacy -- including slave and his hire from time that she is entitled to same -- under the will of "my Grandfather CASH's will." Written: December 16, 1848. Witnesses: JNO. J. STEVENS and GEORGE S. STEVENS.

WILLIAM BOLLING ASBURY (Indexed as ASHBURY) -- Book 1, Page 273 -- Guardian Bond, November 7, 1774. Guardian: WILLIAM GARRISON; Ward: WM. BOLLING ASBURY, orphan; Parent: JOHN ASBURY; Bondsman: JOSEPH MAYS and JNO. DAVIS.

CHARLES ASHLEY -- Book 1, Page 273 -- Administrator's Bond, June 19, 1815. Administrator: JAMES BAILEY; Bondsman: HUGH NORVELL. Book 5, Page 537 -- Inventory, August 3, 1815. Shoemaker or cobbler inventory of $49.25. Commissioners: DAVID TINSLEY, SR.; WM. McDANIEL; REUBEN NORVELL.

JAMES B. ATKINS -- Book 11, Page 129 -- Estate Commitment to Sheriff, March court, 1843. Motion of GARLAND (?) STOUT to commit to sheriff, JAMES DOWELL, since ATKINS has been dead more than three months and no one has applied to admr.

ISAIAH ATKINSON -- Book 6, Page 168 -- Will, Written: October 20, 1818; Probated: August --, 1820. WILLIAM and PATSEY ATKINSON are to keep control of land whereon I now live until marriage of PATSEY and WILLIAM's arrival at age. Sons and daughters of ISAIAH ATKINSON: WILLIAM, PATSEY, and ELIZABETH BURRUS. Executors: My nephew, ALEXD(?) ATKINSON and my children, WILLIAM and PATSEY. Witnesses: ISAAC RUCKER; ROBERT WINGFIELD; WILEY CAMPBELL; ROBT. WINGFIELD, JR. (Note: This book contains the poorest writing of the books and some of it is quite hard to decipher.)
Book 6, Page 165 -- Inventory, August 22, 1820. Total: $2,575.84. Commissioners: WILEY CAMPBELL; ROBT. WINGFIELD, JR.; CHAS. MORE. Book 6, Page 174 -- Executor's Bond, August 20, 1820. Executor: WILLIAM ATKINSON; Bondsmen: BENAJAH FREELAND; CHAS. MOORE; WM. DUNCAN; ISAAC RUCKER. (Signature of what appears to be M. I. ATKINSON)

THOMAS AUSTIN -- Book 4, Page 175 -- Inventory, March 1, 1805. Total: L 80-7-0. Commissioners: ZACHARIAH ROBERTS; JOHN MOSBY; WM. H. MOSBY. Book 4, Page 387 -- Administrator's Bond, July 16, 1804. Administrator: REBECCA AUSTIN; Bondsmen: JOHN TURNER; JAMES TURNER, JR.

COSBY AYERS -- Book 1, Page 271 -- Noncupative will, August 5, 1774; Probated: November 7, 1774. JOSIAH and JONATHAN CHEATHAM state that two days before COSBY AYERS died, LEONARD PHILIPS, JR., asked him "who he would leave his estate to and he told him he would leave it to him - everything that he had." Certified by ALEX. REID, JR., on August 5, 1774.
Book 1, Page 272 -- Administrator's Bond, November 7, 1774. Administrator: LEONARD PHILIPS, JR.; Bondsman: WILLIAM HARRIS. Book 1, Page 289 -- Inventory, October 2, 1775. Total: L 13-17-10. Commissioners: JAS. TURNER, JOHN DAWSON, WM. HARRIS.

SAMUEL AYERS -- Book 2, Page 169 -- Will, Written: February 10, 1784; Probated: May 3, 1784. WILLIAM AYERS, son and heir of THOMAS AYERS, deceased, and wife, MARY, of Essex County. My wife, RACHEL AYERS. Estate to be equally divided between: EVE LACKEY; JOSEPH HIGGINBOTHAM MORRISON; EZRA MORRISON; TERZA DAVIS; and JOHN LACKEY, son of EVE LACKEY (if he dies before 21). Executors: Wife and JOSEPH HIGGINBOTHAM MORRISON; Witnesses: WM. BARNETT, JAS. BARNETT, JNO. CLARK, WM. MORRISON.

Book 2, Page 170 -- Exeuctor's Bond, May 3, 1784. Executor: RACHEL
AYERS; Bondsmen: JOSEPH HIGGINBOTHAM MORRISON and JOHN BARNETT.
Book 2, Page 193 -- Inventory, No total, August 3, 1784 -- 8 slaves.
Commissioners: NATHAN CRAWFORD; ALEX. REID, JR.; WM. BARNETT.

-B-

JOHN BAGBY (Some items appear to be BAGLEY) -- Book 3, Page 392 --
Tobacco Inspector -- Warminister -- September 19, 1796. Bondsmen:
CHAS. STATHAM, JAS. WILLIS.
Book 3, Page 511 -- Tobacco Inspector -- Swan's Creek Warehouse;
September 18, 1787. Bondsman: R. RIVES.
Book 4, Page 223 -- Tobacco Inspector -- Swan's Creek, September 16,
1799. Bondsman: GEO. LOVING.

JOHN G. BAGWELL -- Book 3, Page 568 -- Inventory, L 52-4-0 -- June 17,
1799. WILLIS WILLS, RO. RIVES, JNO. JOHNSON.

PATSY BALDOCK -- Book 12, Page 419 -- Administrator's Bond -- WYATT
COX and JNO. S. TURNER, June 16, 1851 for WYATT COX.
Book 12, Page 439 -- Inventory, $836.50 -- October 20, 1851 -- WM.
TUCKER, GEO. W. OLD, WM. P. SCOTT.

REUBEN BALDOCK -- Book 9, Page 423 -- Administrator's Bond -- PATSY
BALDOCK and REUBEN COX, March 19, 1838, for PATSY BALDOCK.

RICHARD BALDOCK -- Book 1, Page 408 -- Administrator's Bond -- ELIZ.
BALDOCK, ROBT. CHRISTIAN, JAS. PAMPLIN, JNO. CHRISTIAN, & HENRY BELL,
March 2, 1778, for Executor's Bond.
Book 1, Page 410 -- Inventory -- L 70-18-0, March 12, 1779. JAS. &
DRURY CHRISTIAN and LARKIN GATEWOOD.

WILLIAM BALDOCK -- Book 11, Page 11 -- Administrator's Bond -- ROB. H.
MAYS & GUSTAVUS A. EDWARDS, February 21, 1842, for ROB. H.
MAYS.
Book 11, Page 21 -- Inventory, $98.50 -- April 18, 1842. CHAS. L. BROWN,
JNO. MEHONE, THOS. HUTCHESON.
Book 13, Page 50 (Indexed in Master Index as Book 12, Page 50) --
Administrator's Bond -- ROBT. A. COGHILL & WM. CABELL, March 22,
1853, for ROBT. A. COGHILL.
Book 14, Page 177 -- Administrator's Account -- RO. A. COGHILL -- from
April 14, 1854 -- $11,277.00. Recorded November 1, 1854.

ELIZABETH BALL -- Book 9, Page 125 -- Estate Commitment to Sheriff --
September 21, 1835 -- dead more than three months and no one has
applied to administrator. Motion of THWING & REYNOLDS. Sheriff:
THOS. N. EUBANK.

JOHN BALL -- Book 5, Page 660 -- May 9, 1817, written; August 18, 1817,
probated. Witnesses: JAS. W. SMITH, WM. M. WALLER, GABL. PAGE.
Us, ELIZ. - house and 5 slaves; granddaughter SALLY PROPET (Note two
spellings of name; probably PROFFITT). Son, JAMES; daughter, KESEAH
PROPHET; daughter, RACHEL EDMONDS - my three children above mentioned;
granddaughters, JUDITH and COATNEY PROPHET - children of my daughter,
ELIZ. PROPHET, deceased. Property not to go out of Virginia, but
may be moved to Nelson County. My three grandchildren, JOHN, JANE, and
MILLY ANN, children of daughter, MILLY PROPHET, deceased, when of age.
Sons: WILLIAM & SAMUEL. Executors: Friends: WM. DUNCAN; JOHN SMITH,
SR.; and BARTLETT CASH. (Note: This book is fading fast in spots.)
Book 5, Page 694 -- Administrator's Bond -- JAMES BALL; ELIZ. BALL;
REUBIN PROPHET; and FLEMING EDWARDS, October 20, 1817, for JOHN BALL.

VALENTINE BALL -- Book 1, Page 155 -- January 12, 1769, written;
March 5, 1770, probated. Witnesses: MARY KEY, JUDITH TOLLEY, WM.
BISHNELL. Planter; us, SUSANNA; one shilling to each of these, but
relationship not stated: JAMES BALL, LEWIS BALL, ALICE WRIGHT, SARAH
BOWMAN, SUSAN HAIGHS, ELIZ. HUGHES, JOHN BALL, and MARY HARGROVE. My
son, WILLIAM, and my daughter, JANE BALL. Executors: CAPT. HENRY
KEY and my ux.

Book 1, Page 157 -- Administrator's Bond -- HENRY KEY; SUSANNA BALL; MOSES HUGHES; JOHN KEY, JR.; March 5, 1770, for HENRY KEY and SUSANNA BALL.
Book 1, Page 179 -- Inventory, L 31-13-11, July 2, 1770. WM. WALTON; PETER HENDRIX; JOHN HARPER.
Book 1, Page 255 -- Administrator's Account -- HENRY KEY. Committee: JAS. NEVIL, CORNL. THOMAS, WM. MARTIN. From April 25, 1771; JOHN BALL mentioned; Recorded December 6, 1773.

HENRY BALLENGER -- Book 5, Page 92 -- This is an incomplete item, but indexed for HENRY BALLENGER. It merely sets forth that he and MICAJAH CAMDEN were bonded on February 12, 1812, for BALLENGER to serve as guardian, but no wards named.
Book 5, Page 379 -- Ordinary Bond, May 17, 1813; Bondsman: ANSALEM CLARKSON.
Book 5, Page 447 -- Constable's Bond, April 18, 1814. Bondsman: JESSE RICHESON.

JOSEPH BALLENGER -- Book 4, Page 31 -- February 3, 1802, written; February 15, 1802, probated. Witnesses: THOS. POWELL, HUGH CAMPBELL, ELIZ. CAMPBELL. Ux; stock of black cattle on home plantation where WM. HICKS lives; my three sons: ECHILLES, JAMES, & RICHARD. My daughter, PEGGY HENSLEY gravel (six) -- 80 acres on Brown Mt. with a mill; 90 acres where WM. HICKMAN lives; 27 acres on Pedlar bought from WM. HICKS; my other children: MILLEY WHITE, ELIZ. JOHNSTON, CHARITY COX TARRENCE, and PHEBY TUCKER. Administrators: JOEL FRANKLIN, HENRY BALLENGER, JNO. WARE.
Book 4, Page 342 -- Administrator Bond -- JOEL FRANKLIN; HENRY BALLEN-GER; February 15, 1802. Bondsmen: JNO. WARWICK, HUGH CAMPBELL.
Book 4, Page 38 -- Inventory -- March 9, 1802. L 1744-9-0. CHAS. TALIAFERRO; NELSON CRAWFORD; BENJ. TALIAFERRO. (See Deed Book 1, Page 454).
    Additional comment on this man, Order Book 1782-1784; Page 113: REV. JOSEPH BALLENGER made return for marriage of WM. CRUTCHER and ELIZ. POLLARD, January 10, 1784. Deed Book A, Page 36, JOSEPH BALLEN-GER and ux, SARAH, and RICH. BALLENGER to JOSEPH MAYS, July 15, 1762. BALLENGER's Mt. mentioned therein. April 3, 1782, REV. BENJ. COLEMAN made return on marriage of JOSEPH BALLENGER and TABITHA BALLOWE. TABITHA BALLOWE is named as mother of ELIZ. CAMPBELL, natural daughter of NEILL CAMPBELL, in CAMOBELL's will. Therein he thanks her for nursing him through illness and names her natural daughter, ELIZ. In Deed Book I, Page 419, April 26, 1802, ACHILLES, RICH., and JAMES BALLINGER waive all claims against TABITHA under the wills of NEILL CAMPBELL and JOSEPH BALLINGER. Some of these BALLINGER descendants went to my native Kentucky.

RICHARD BALLINGER -- Book 5, Page 203 -- Constable's Bond -- January 31, 1803. Bondsmen: HENRY BALLENGER & HENRY HICKS.

FANNIE E. BALLOWE -- Book 24, Page 164 -- February 18, 1911, written; April 15, 1914, probated. Witnesses: F. N. HICKS, T. W. COX -- both of JAMES RIVER and Elon District. Daughter, VIRGIE; one-third to these after VIRGIE's part paid -- her sisters and brothers -- JNO. T., WILLARD, and EDNA. Grandchildren: JAMES, WM., and DABNEY RAGLAND BALLOWE -- all minor heirs of JAMES SHELTON BALLOW -- where he lived prior to his death. My son, JNO. T., is to guardian for them. WILLARD ROBT. BALLOWE is to administer. He is styled WM. ROBT. BALLOWE in qualification.

GERARD BANKS -- Book 1, Page 515 -- March 20, 1776, written; February 7, 1780, probated. Witnesses: DAVID SHEPHERD, GABL. PENN, GEO. PENN, HENRY GILBERT. Codicil: December 22, 1779. Witnesses: GABL. PENN, LAWRENCE CAMPBELL, ELIZ. HOWELL. Ux; son, WILLIAM; land on Bly's Path that empties into Buffalo above Cabell's Mill. Sons: REUBEN, THOS., and daughters, MARY and SARAH BANKS -- if without issue. Sons: LINN, ADAM; daughters: ELIZ. HUME and RACHEL HIGGINBOTHAM; grandson, GERARD BANKS, to get good schooling. Executors: Sons: WM. and REUBEN. Codicil: Considerable losses sustained as sons WM. and THOS. to get slaves after death of my ux. Part of estate to be sold and proceeds to WM., THOS., REUBEN, MARY, and SARY.

Book 1, Page 517 -- Administrator's Bond -- WM. BANKS, WM. SPENCER, &
LINDSEY COLEMAN, February 7, 1780, for WM. BANKS.
Book 1, Page 525 -- Inventory -- April 20, 1780 -- L 12056-5-0.
JNO. WIATT, GEO. PENN. & LINDSEY COLEMAN.
Book 3, Page 260 -- Administrator's Account -- WM. BANKS from 1780 --
to SAML. MEREDITH for 24 Dist. Militia; legacy to SAML. CAMP, to SARAH
BANKS, GERARD BANKS the Younger, THOS. BANKS, REUBEN BANKS. Sale
L 9344 HUGH ROSE, JAMES HIGGINBOTHAM, GABL. PENN, Recorded October 15,
1792.
Book 5, Page 213 -- Administrator's Account -- WM. BANKS. Recorded
May 17, 1813.

THOMAS BARBOUR -- Book 12, Page 465 -- Constable's Bond -- so indexed,
but not there.
Book 14, Page 572 -- Constable -- June 21, 1858. Bondsmen: WM. HIX,
JACOB SMITH, SAML M. GARLAND.

JOHN BARKER -- Book 4, Page 620 -- Inventory -- March 28, 1810.
ABRAM CARTER, WM. PRYOR, HENRY BROWN.
Book 5, Page 17 -- Administrator' Bond -- ELIZ. BARKER, WM. SALE,
JESSE JONES, March 19, 1810, for ELIZ. BARKER.

PERMELIA BARNES (So indexed, but it is BURRUS -- Guardian Bond).

JOHN BARNETT -- Book 4, Page 452 -- Constable's Bond -- June 20, 1803.
Bondsmen: DANL. McDONAL, JESSE CLARKSON.
Book 4, Page 459 -- Constable's Bond -- October 23, 1805. Bondsman:
JESSE CLARKSON.
Book 4, Page 463 -- Constable's Bond -- June 15, 1807. Bondsmen:
NATHAN BARNETT, JAS. MONTGOMERY.

ROBERT BARNETT -- Book 1, Page 417 -- Guardian Bond, May 4, 1778 --
ALEX. REID, miner (sic) and ALEX. REID for ALEX. REID, minor, as
guardian of RO. BARNETT, orphan of JOSEPH BARNETT.
Book 2, Page 69 -- Guardian's Account -- ALEX. REID; Recorded
August 5, 1782.
Book 3, Page 35 -- September 16, 1786, written; June 4, 1787, probated.
Witnesses: CHAS. JONES, JNO. SHIELDS, PATRICK HIGHT, THOS. JONES.
Son, JOHN -- land devised to me by will of REV. ROBT. ROSE. Ux,
MARY; son, JAMES; daughter, JANE; daughter, MARY; daughter, REBECCA
MOORE; son, ALEX.; daughter, RACHEL; daughters, ELIZ. and ANNE.
Executors: Son, JOHN, and assistants -- my friends -- JOHN ROSE
and ZACH. TALIAFERRO.
Book 3, Page 37 -- Administrator's Bond -- JOHN BARNETT, JNO. SHIELDS,
JOSEPH MONTGOMERY, on probate date, for JOHN BARNETT.
Book 3, Page 50 -- Inventory -- August 18, 1787 -- L 348-13-6. JAS.
WILLS, NICHL. WREN.

ELIJAH BARNS -- Book 7, Page 266 -- June 25, 1829, written; August 17,
1829, probated. Witnesses: JAS. T. TOLER, MARGARET C. DUNCAN, CHARI-
TY GILLESPIE. My interest in estate of WM. MOORE, deceased; UNION
MILLS; my stills. Land to ux, FRANKY; my children: WM. HENRY, ELIJAH
WADE, LUCY WOOD BARNS, PULHELY (?) BARNS, SALLY BARNS, MILDRED AMANDY
MELINEY BARNES -- my 6 children.
Book 7, Page 267 -- Administrator's Bond -- GODFREY TOLLER and
PETER RUCKER on probate date for GODFREY TOLLER.
Book 7, Page 334 -- Inventory -- October 22, 1829 -- $1,162.05.
ABRAM CARTER, JNO. RUSSELL, JNO. F. HALL.
Book 7, Page 338 -- Refunding Bond -- December 4, 1827, ELIJAH
BARNES & DABNEY HILL to HILL CARTER, administrator of WM. MOORE, de-
ceased. BARNES in right of ux has received slaves valued at $750.00.
Book 8, Page 47 -- Administrator's Account -- GODFREY TOLER from
September 21, 1829. To LUCY GILLESPIE for Tobacco crop in 1828;
to widow. Recorded November 22, 1831. J. D. TURPIN, CHAS. L. BARRETT.

CHAS. L. BARRETT -- Book 9, Page 398 -- Estate Commitment to Sheriff --
November court, 1837. Motion of THOS. N. LUBANK. Sheriff: JNO.
COLEMAN.

JAMES BARRETT -- Book 4, Page 301 -- Guardian Bond, April 18, 1797 --
HUGH CAMPBELL & NELSON CRAWFORD for HUGH CAMPBELL as guardian of
CHARLES, JAMES, and ANN BARROTT (sic) orphans of THOMAS BARROTT (sic),
deceased.
Book 4, Page 432 -- Guarduan Bond -- CHAS. L. BARRETT and PETER P.
THORNTON, July 21, 1796, for CHAS. L. BARRETT as guardian of JAMES
BARRETT, orphan of THOS. BARROTT (sic), deceased.

JOHN G. BARRETT -- Book 19, Page 373 -- Administrator's Bond --
December 16, 1787; NC. KEITH and W. L. VAUGHAN for NC. KEITH.

LUCY A. BARRETT -- Book 14, Page 347 -- Guardian Bond -- WM. F. BARRETT
and RO. A. COGHILL, March 16, 1857, for WM. F. BARRETT as guardian of
LUCY A. BARRETT, infant daughter of WM. F. BARRETT.

SARAH BARRETT, MRS. -- Book 17, Page 23 -- Administrator's Bond --
ROBT. W. SNEAD and RO. A. PENDLETON, February 20, 1865, for ROBT.
SNEAD.
Book 17, Page 24 -- Inventory -- RUFUS A. HIGGINBOTHAN, JNO. E.
McDANIEL, and JNO. W. JENNINGS, recorded, March 6, 1865.
Book 17, Page 25 -- Sale by ROBT. W. SNEAD, administrator, Monday,
March 6, 1865. Family buyers: MATTHEW and R. L. BARRETT. $12,587.80.

THOMAS BARRETT -- Book 3, Page 308 -- Administrator's Bond -- ELIZ.
and WM. BARRETT, September 15 (?), 1794, for ELIZ. BARRETT.
Book 3, Page 336 -- Inventory -- L 12-0-3, March 21, 1795. CHRISTO-
PHER SMITH, CHAS. & ROBT. BARROTT (sic).

REUBEN E. BATES -- Book 16, Page 104 -- Administrator's Bond --
ELVIRA W. BATES and ANDREW J. EVERETT, December 16, 1861, for ELVIRA
W. BATES.

WILLIAM BATES -- Book 11, Page 449 -- Administrator's Bond -- ELVIRA
W. BATES and M. C. GOODWIN, October 19, 1846, for ELVIRA BATES.
Book 11, Page 507 -- Inventory -- December 23, 1846 -- $576.00. JAS.
S. RICHESON, CHAS. H. (?) RUCKER, GEO. MARKHAM.
Book 11, Page 508 -- Sale by ELVIRA W. BATES, admrs. December 23,
1846.

MITCHELL BAUGHAN -- Book 1, Page 71 -- Administrator's Bond -- SAML.
BAUGHAN, PEARCE WADE, and JNO. HARDWICK, June 2, 1776, for SAML.
BAUGHAN.
Book 1, Page 81 -- Inventory -- September 1, 1776 - L 59-13-10. GEO.
McDANIEL and AMBROSE RUCKER.

JOSEPH F. BAXTER (Indexed for JAMES N. BAXTER) -- Book 11, Page 433 --
Administrator's Bond -- THORNTON O. ROGERS and WM. A. ROGERS (by
THORNTON O. ROGERS attorney); July 20, 1845, for THORNTON O. ROGERS.
Book B, Page 23 -- Administrator's Bond -- JNO. H. ROBERTS and
SIDNEY S. BAXTER, March 31, 1845, for JNO. ROBERTS.

(I think that I stated in beginning that the Master Index covers
24 numbered books and A and B of old Circuit wills. I have found
some unindexed deeds in one of the two circuit books and hope to
index them and put them in the office.)
Book B, Page 28 -- Administrator's Bond -- THORNTON O. ROGERS and
WM. A. ROGERS, August 29, 1846, for THORNTON ROGERS. ROBT. TINSLEY
attorney for WM. A. ROGERS and power granted in Albemarle on
August 27, 1846.
Book B, Page 33 -- Inventory in Albemarle on order of Amherst Court,
August 1846. Returned December 30, 1848. JAS. HART, STEPHEN F.
SAMPSON, PETER MERIWETHER. THOS. J. RANDOLPH, J.P., in Albemarle.

JOHN BEAREFORD (BERRFORD; BERASFORD) -- Book 1, Page 11 -- -----;
March 7, 1763. Witnesses: CHAS. TULEY, SARAH SMITH, HANNAH ELLIS.
Land in Augusta - when youngest child is of age or married. Daughters:
MARY, MARGARET, CATRON, ANN, LIDDY, FRANCES, JEANE. My ux, MARY.
Exrs.: Friends: JAS. TRIMBLE, ARCHIBALD ALEXANDER. Ux and others
refused to qualify & bond made by MARY BERRFORD, the Younger. Bonds-
man: NATHANIEL EVANS.
Book 1, Page 39 -- Inventory of JOHN BERASFORD -- L 80-3-9, December 5,
1763. JAS. EDMISTON, JNO. POUGE, JNO. MATTAHUS.

CAROLINE BEAUFORD -- Book 6, Page 179 -- Guardian Bond -- so indexed in Master, but not there. However, there is a CAROLINE BURFORD in Book 4; see.

ANN BECK -- Book 11, Page 446 -- Administrator's Bond -- September 21, 1846, JAS. C. BECK and NATHAN GUTHRIE for JAS. C. BECK. Indexed in Master as Page 448.

JAMES C. BECK (Middle initial is garbles in data) -- Book 10, Page 395 - Refunding Bond -- November 16, 1841 -- JAS. C. BECK and CHAS. PALMER to JESSE BECK, deceased. JAS. C. BECK has received legacy.
Book 11, Page 238 -- Guardian Bond -- JAS. C. BECK and JNO. RHOADES, September 16, 1847, for JAS. C. BECK as guardian of JAS. D., JNO. B., and ANDREW B. BECK, orphans of JOHN BECK. In recapitulation clerk garbles them and refers to them as JAS. B. and JOHN R. BECK.
Book 11, Page 240 -- Refunding Bond -- September 16, 1844 -- JAS. C. BECK, guardian of JAS. B., JOHN R., and ANDREW B. BECK, orphans of JOHN BECK, deceased, and infant heirs of JESSE BECK -- to JESSE MUNDY, administrator of JESSE BECK, have received legacies from estate of their grandfather, JESSE BECK, as children of JOHN BECK. JOHN RHODES, bondsman.

JESSE BECK -- Book 10, Page 348 -- June 22, 1838, written; May 17, 1841, probated. Witnesses: BENJ. WATTS, SAML. MAYS, WM. A. BURFORD. JESSE and CHAS. MUNDY qualified on probate date for JESSE MUNDY to administrator. My ux, lands on south side of road to Lunchburg to Muster Spring; daughter, FRANCES PALMORE and heirs; sons, ELIHU, JESSE, JOHN, REUBEN, and heirs; daughter, ANN BECK and heirs; son, JAMES and heirs; daughter, LUCY TERRY and heirs; granddaughter, LUCY LAIN; grand-children: RICHARD and MARY ANDERSON, children of deceased; daughter, SUSANNAH ANDERSON, and heirs. Executor: Friend, JESSE MUNDY.
Book 10, Page 360 -- Inventory -- 550 acres at $6,265.50; order of May, 1841. DANIEL DAY, NICHL. GUTHRIE, THOS. HUTCHESON. Recorded June 21, 1841.
Book 11, Page 30 -- Administrator's Account -- JESSE MUNDY - from November 8, 1841. Widow out of share of C. PALMORE; WM. BECK; DAVID H. TERRY; JAMES C. BECK; to ANN BECK, and account of ANN BECK SMITH; legacy to JESSE BECK. Legatees: ELIHU BECK, CHAS. PALMER (PALMORE in places), JOHN BECK's heirs, REUBEN BECK, WM. BECK who married LUCY BECK, legatee; SAM'L. ANDERSON's heirs. Commissioners: GRANVILLE LAIN, JOHN RHOADS, RICH. ANDERSON. Recorded November 15, 1841.
Book 11, Page 336 -- Rfunding Bond, March 21, 1843 -- JESSE BECK, JR.; WM. J. BECK; ELIHU BECK; JOHN C. BECK; and WM. BECK to JESSEY MUNDY, administrator of JESSE BECK, for JESSE BECK, JR., who has received legacy. Witnesses: JNO. D. ALEXANDER and JOS. W. GRIGG. Receipt below which is hard to decipher for it appears to be signed by SUE BECK, but will shows that only one by that name mentioned is dead. It states that amount has been received from administrator, JESSE MUNDY, through "my brother, ELIHU BECK." Same date as above.
Book 12, Page 103 -- Administrator's Account -- JESSE MUNDY from November, 1841. Cash from JAS. LAIN et als. Name of RICH. ANDERSON appears. REUBEN BECK bought a slave on October 20, 1847. Recorded December 18, 1848.

WILLIAM BECKHAM -- Book 7, Page 31 -- Administrator's Bond -- JNO. & WM. PUGH, August 21, 1827, for JNO. PUGH.

JOHN BECKLEY (BICELEY) -- Book 3, Page 278 -- November 25, 1792, written; September 16, 1793, probated. Witnesses: CHAS. ELLIS, JR.; RICH. SHELTON ELLIS; JOSIAH ELLIS, JR. Ux, SUSANNAH, my children: CHAS. BICLEY, WM. JOSEPH, ELIZ. COLEMAN, MARY CARTER, and son, JOHN CARTER, JANE HOLLAND HUMPHREY BICELEY, METILDA BICLEY, HANNAH, JAMES, and FRANCES. Executors: CHAS. BICLEY and RICH. SHELTON.
Book 3, Page 281 -- Administrator's Bond -- RICH. SHELTON and ISAAC RUCKER, October 21, 1793, for RICH. SHELTON.
Book 3, Page 295 -- Inventory -- December 13, 1793 -- L 325-17-6; CHAS. BURKS, JNO. EUBANK, JNO. BURKS.

SUSANNAH BECKLEY -- Book 6, Page 51 -- Administrator's Bond -- JNO. ELLIS & THOS. EUBANK, December 21, 1818 (this date is patently an error on part of clerk for her will was not probated until 1819) -- both to administrator. Bondsman: JNO. WARWICK.
Book 6, Page 59 -- June 17, 1796, written; March 17, 1819, probated. Witnesses: THOS. MOORE, SALLY MOORE, JNO. GOODRICH and proved by both MOORES. My nine children: HANNAH HAYNES, ELIZ. GILLIAM, SUSANNAH WRIGHT, JOSIAH ELLIS, MARIANN CARTER, CHAS. ELLIS, SALLY HARRISON, BETHENA LEFTWICH, ROSEY (?) DAVIES - my daughters and their daughters. Executors: Son, JOSIAH ELLIS, RODERICK McCULLOCH, and JNO. BURKE. (Note by compiler: Just how many of her children were by ELLIS is a moot question. She was a widow when she married JOHN BECKLEY, December 21, 1767. WM. HORSLEY was bondsman and she gave her own consent. ROSEY is probably oOSANNAH ELLIS who married CHAS. DAVIS, July 1, 1782. JOSIAH ELLIS was surety and it is certified that she was of age. The marriage return is in Order Book, 1782-84, Page 107, by REV. CHAS. CLAY.)

ANN E. BELL -- Book 19, Page 112 -- Guardian Bond, February 21, 1876 -- ANN E. BELL, J. N GORDON, and WM. F. BELL for ANN E. BELL as guardian of her infant children: MARY V., JNO. P., PATRICK M., DELILAH S., and FRANK LEE BELL.

DAVID BELL -- Book 3, Page 179 -- Administrator's Bond -- MARY DUKE BELL, HENRY BELL, and CHAS. CHRISTIAN, June 6, 1791, for MARY DUKE BELL.
Book 3, Page 264 -- Inventory -- L 54-15-7 -- STEPHEN WATTS, JNO. CHRISTIAN, and NOTLEY W. (?) MADDOX, June 28, 1791.

DRURY BELL, CAPT. -- Book 5, Page 74 -- This is a SAML. BELL item, so See, but indexed for DRURY.
Book 9, Page 292 -- Administrator's Bond -- ROBT. BELL and EDWARD A. CABELL, March 20, 1837, for ROBT. BELL.
Book 9, Page 310 -- Inventory, $172.25 taken at late residence of CAPT. D. BELL, March 23, 1837.

GEORGE BELL -- Book 2, Page 242 -- Administrator's Bond -- HANNAH BELL, NICHL. WREN, and JAS. CAMPBELL, August 1, 1785, for HANNAH BELL.
Book 3, Page 15 -- Inventory Order of November 12, 1785 -- no total -- ABRAHAM SMITH, JAS. TILFORD, JAS. CAMPBELL, July 3, 1786.
Book 3, Page 55 -- Administrator's Account -- HANNAH BELL for 1786 -- L 24-17-5-1/2. JNO. ROSE, ZACH. TALIAFERRO. Recorded September 1, 1787.

HENRY BELL -- Book 3, Page 286 -- Guardian Bond -- JNO. JOHNSON & JAS. DILLARD, October 22, 1793, for J. J. as guardian of HENRY, SARAH, and CHAS. BELL, orphans of DAVID BELL.
Book 3, Page 548 -- September 15, 1797, written; September 16, 1799, probated. Witnesses: LINDSEY COLEMAN, JEREMIAH FRANKLIN, DAVID S. GARLAND, and WM. EDMUNDS, JR. Sons, SAML. and DRURY - my mill seat and land where DRURY and I live; daughters: MARY PHILLIPS, MARTHA WATTS, ANN PHELPS. Three children of my deceased son, DAVID: HENRY DUKE BELL, CHAS. CHRISTIAN BELL, and SALLY WARE (?) BELL. Executors: STEPHEN WATTS, SAML. BELL, & DRURY BELL. WATTS and DRURY BELL qualified on probate date. Recorded on Book 4, Page 305. Bondsmen: GEO. DILLARD and JNO. CHRISTIAN.

HENRY DUKE BELL -- Book 4, Page 406 -- Guardian Bond (Indexed as Book 4, Page 416 in Master). DRURY BELL and MOSES PHILLIPS, June 17, 1805, for DRURY BELL as guardian of HENRY D. BELL, orphan of DAVID BELL, deceased.

SAMUEL BELL -- Book 5, Page 74 -- Administrator's Bond -- DRURY BELL & MICAJAH PENDLETON, August 19, 1811, for DRURY BELL and indexed for him in Master.
Book 5, Page 206 -- February 13, 1811, written; June 17, 1811, probated. Witnesses: JEREMIAH TAYLOR, ABNER CHRISTIAN, JAS. CHRISTIAN. Proved by ABNER CHRISTIAN on probate date and August 19, 1811, by JAS. CHRISTIAN. My ux, and my two sons: GEO. H. and BOLLING BELL;

my daughters: SOPHIA BELL, STILEY BELL, ELIZ. BELL, and ELIZ. ANDREW(S).
Executors: Ux and DRURY BELL and DRURY CHRISTIAN.
Book 5, Page 454 -- Inventory, $430.50, September 19, 1814 -- DRURY
CHRISTIAN, ABNER CHRISTIAN, JER. TAYLOR.
Book 8, Page 339 -- Administrator's de bonis non Bond -- BENJ. P.
WALKER and JNO. HORSLEY, JR., August 19, 1833, for BENJ. WALKER.
Book 8, Page 362 -- Administrator's Account -- DRURY BELL from 1812 -
to SALLY BELL; WM. L. (S.) BELL; GEO. H. BELL; shoes for GEO. when
going into service; tuition to PERROW for BOLLING BELL; suit mentioned:
BELL vs. SCRUGGS. ED. A. CABELL, JAS. HIGGINBOTHAM, PEYTON KEITH,
September 9, 1833.
Book 9, Page 133 -- Administrator's Account -- BENJ. P. WALKER, Ad-
ministrator's de bonis non Bond -- from October 4, 1834 -- legacy to
LUCY ANDREWS, MISS S. W. BELL, to WALKER as representative of G. H.
and P. B. BELL to A. TOLLE and ux, SOPHIA, formerly BELL, ALEX.
MUNDY, CHAS. M. CHRISTIAN.
Book 13, Page 235 -- Administrator's Bond -- STILLA W. BELL, HIRAM C.
KYLE, CHAS. M. WATTS, and WM. ROBERTS, September 19, 1853, for STILLA
BELL.

CALVIN F. BENNETT -- Book 8, Page 120 -- Refunding Bond -- CALVIN F.
BENNETT and JAS. BENNETT, to RO. TINSLEY, August 16, 1831, administrator of GEO. M. TINSLEY. CALVIN BENNETT has married LUCY TINSLEY,
legatee of GEO. M. TINSLEY, and has received legacy.

JAMES BENNETT -- Book 12, Page 568 -- August 17, 1852, written;
September 20, 1852, probated. Witnesses: ROY R. SCOTT, THOS. W.
SEAY, THOS. C. BLANKS and proved by them. CALVIN F. BENNETT qualified.
Bondsman: CHRISTOPHER McIVOR. Advanced in years. Son, CALVIN F.,
to administer. Grandchildren and any heirs: SARAH E., CHARLOTTE ANN,
GEO M. T. (?), and JAMES M. BENNETT. Ux, ELIZ.
Book 13, Page 34 -- Inventory, October term, 1852 - $8,520.75.
CALVIN F. BENNETT, administrator. November 27, 1852. THOS. W. SEAY,
ALEX. TINSLEY, and THOS. C. BLANKS.

TAYLOR BERRY -- Book 17, Page 6 -- Salt Agent's report, November 24,
1864. To county court on order - no disbursements for purchases of
soldiers' families for salt is difficult to get. Lynchburg has been
behind on 3 issues but not consecutively. Has secured order from
MAJOR R. C. SAUNDERS for 5,000 bushels tithe corn and confident that
families can't be fed without it. Account to COMMISSIONER BROWN here-
with. Next salt quota is ready, but bags are lacking and more are
required than before. Notes are due January 20, 1865, but gentlemen
on notes should be notified before sums are raised. They are: RO. A.
COGHILL, S. RICHESON, HENRY LOVING, N. C. TALIAFERRO, A. W. WILLIAMS,
and TAYLOR BERRY. Total due: $29,152.45.
(Note: TAYLOR BERRY was long active here and prominent in many ways.
He shows in many deed items.)

JOEL BETHEL -- Book 11, Page 107 -- Refunding Bond -- JOEL BETHEL and
ALEX. M. CAMPBELL to LEWIS S. CAMPBELL, December 21, 1842, administrator of WILEY CAMPBELL. WILEY CAMPBELL directed in will that division
to be made at end of year of his death. Done for all heirs except
THOS. S. CAMPBELL and BETHEL has received slaves valued at $719.92 in
right of his ux.
Book 12, Page 352 -- January 23, 1851, written; codicil, March --,
1851; August 18, 1854, probated. Witnesses to will and codicil: RO.
WINGFIELD and WM. W. THOMPSON and proved by them. Ux, MILDRED --
house and tract; lines of PIERCE; the bridge; DR. RO. WINGFIELD; half
of the orchard to my children who may occupy south side of tract.
Slave girl, Frances, when 14 is to be given to children of my first
marriage. My children by both marriages: HUDSON M. BETHEL, AMANDA C.
BETHEL, MARY B. BETHEL, JOSHUA S. BETHEL, WM. J., ROBT. M., THOS.
HOWARD BETHEL. Son, WM. J., is by my first marriage and is to remain
with my ux and be educated. Executor: JESSE MUNDY. Codicil: infant
daughter, JANE BETHEL, has been born since will was written. If
infants choose brother, HUDSON M. BETHEL, as guardian, he is to act
without security.
Book 12, Page 541 -- Inventory, February 26, 1852. $11,519.75.
JNO. P. WILSON, THOS. A. MILES, RO. WINGFIELD.

ROBERT BETHEL -- Book 12, Page 500 -- Guardian Bond, MILDRED BETHEL, LEWIS S. CAMPBELL, RO. R. KYLE, and JNO. S. TUCKER, March 15, 1852, for MILDRED BETHEL as guardian of ROBT., THOS. H. and CORNELIA BETHEL, orphans of JOEL BETHEL.

WILLIAM BETHEL -- Book 12, Page 501 -- Guardian Bond -- RO. R. KYLE and SAML. M. GARLAND, March 15, 1852, for RO. KYLE as guardian of WILLIAM BETHEL, infant son of JOEL BETHEL.

(Note: These marriages were copied while helping a man from West Virginia check on the family: Page 292, CHAS. BEVERLY and MARY JOHNS, March 29, 1827. Sureties: JAS. JOHNS and E. WATSON. Page 301, JAMES BEVERLY and SARAH ANN TAYLOR, January 6, 1829. Parent or guardian of wife, RICHERSON TAILOR (sic). Sureties: SAML. BEVERLY, ISABELLAR (sic) TAILOR, MARBELL E. STINNETT. Page 255, SAML. BEVERLY and RHODA TERRY, March 12, 1819. Sureties: WM. TERRY. Page 358, October 4, 1839, MATTERSON BEVLEY and ELIZ. BEVLEY. Parent or guardian of wife: SAML. BEVLEY. Surety and witnesses: JEFFERSON ROSE, PAULUS POWELL, POLLY CHRISTIAN.

ELIZABETH L. BIBB -- Book 13, Page 469 -- January 12, 1855, written; Monday, May 21, 1855, probated. Witnesses: WM. S. THORNTON and ROBERT BENNETT BIBB and proved by them. R. C. BIBB qualified. Formerly ELIZ. L. BURFORD - estate of my father, JOHN L. BURFORD; my husband, RO. C. BIBB, is to administer. Estate of my mother, SARAH BURFORD. Administrator's Bond on Page 469 of Book 13. Book 14, Page 157 -- Inventory -- $4,103.00, May 22, 1856. WIATT GATEWOOD, HARTWELL T. PRYOR, THOMAS B. GATEWOOD.

HARRIET E. BIBB (Indexed for MARY E. & C.) -- Book 11, Page 519 -- Guardian Bond -- MARTIN T. BIBB and R. C. BIBB, April 19, 1847, for MARTIN T. BIBB as guardian of MARY ELLEN, LUCY JANE, MARGARET, and HARRIET E. BIBB, infants of MARTIN T. BIBB.

JOHN BIBB -- Book 3, Page 97 -- July 27, 1781, written; April 7, 1789, probated. Witnesses: JNO. GREGORY, MARYAN BICKNELL, RICH. McCARY, JNO. STAPLES. Ux, ELIZ. -- 382 acres where I live; Son (sic): THOMAS, JOHN, JAMES; daughter, PEGGY BIBB and her grandfather, JOHN MARR - slave which he willed to her; my daughters: SALLY and ELIZ. BIBB; my father, THOS. BIBB, deceased. My three sons and daughters. Executors: my brother, WILLIAM BIBB and my ux.
Book 3, Page 99 -- Administrator's Bond -- ELIZ. BIBB, WM. BIBB, CLOUGH SHELTON, and JNO. STAPLES, on probate date for ELIZ. and WM. BIBB.
Book 3, Page 119 -- Inventory -- L 270-11-3. CHAS. STATHAM, WM. CRISP, JNO. STAPLES. (STATHAM is spelled STATHATHAM.)

MARTIN BIBB -- Book 6, Page 413 -- Administrator's Bond -- JOSEPH R. CARTER and ABRAM CARTER, November 18, 1823, for JOSEPH R. CARTER.
Book 6, Page 447 -- Guardian Bond -- CHAS. BIBB, ZEDEKIAH SHOEMAKER, and JNO. RUSSELL, March 15, 1824, for CHAS. BIBB as guardian of NANCY; WM. and MARTIN BIBB, orphans of MARTIN BIBB.
Book 6, Page 463 -- Inventory -- December 10, 1823 - $633.87. GIDEON C. GOODRICH, JNO. RUSSELL, WM. PRYOR.
Book 6, Page 753 -- Administrator's Account -- JOSEPH R. CARTER, from December 12, 1823. To RO. C., BENJ. B., NANCY C., and CHAS. BIBB - $646.42. WILL JOPLING, JNO. PRYOR, PETER P. THORNTON, March 20, 1827 (last item in this book). (This is the hardest book to decipher in all of the books, for the writing is terrible in most places.)

MARTIN J. BIBB -- Book 11, Page 217 -- Minister's Bond -- Methodist -- February 20, 1842. Bondsmen: WM. D. THURMOND, CHAS. MASSIE.
(Note: These bonds qualified a minister to perform marriages according to laws of his church and Virginia. Most of them mention denomination.)

NANCY BIBB -- Book 12, Page 475 -- August 13, 1830, written; December 17, 1849, probated. Witnesses: JNO. RUSSELL, WM. PRYOR, WIATT GATEWOOD. My two youngest sons, WM. H. and MARTIN T. BIBB.

(Note: In the BIBB genealogy, this woman is called NANCY CASH BIBB
and the will is cited as being on Page 447 of Book 12. This is an
error for there is no BIBB data on Page 447.)
Book 12, Page 476 -- Administrator's Bond -- WM. H. BIBB and WIATT
GATEWOOD, December 17, 1849, for WM. H. BIBB.

PERMELIA F. BIBB -- Book 16, Page 412 -- Guardian Bond -- R. W. SNEAD
and RO. A. COGHILL, November 16, 1863, for R. W. SNEAD as guardian of
PERMELIA F. BIBB. No parent set forth.

ROBERT C. BIBB -- Book 8, Page 412 -- Guardian's Account -- RO. J.
(I.) DUNCAN, guardian., April 26, 1834. JOS. R. CARTER, GEORGE W.
STAPLES.
Book 16, Page 404 -- Administrator's Bond -- W. C. BIBB, RO. W.
SNEAD, and FRANCIS A. SIMPSON, October 19, 1863, for W. C. BIBB.
Book 16, Page 406 (Indexed in Master as 466) -- Sales returned Decem-
ber 21, 1863. BIBB buyers: LUCY JANE, WM. C., JOSHUA; amount paid
to RO. C. BIBB.
Book 16, Page 414 -- Inventory -- W. C. BIBB, administrator, Novem-
ber 11, 1863. $702.00.
Book 17, Page 126 -- Administrator's Accounts -- Covers months of
November and December, 1863, and January - October, 1864. WM. C. BIBB,
administrator. J. BIBB, appraiser.
Book 17, Page 196 -- Division: September 14, 1866, by RO. H. CARTER
and CHAS. JONES and they state that the late WIATT GATEWOOD acted
with them. Lots to CYRUS T. BIBB - 44 acres; WM. C. BIBB - 48 acres;
JAMES M. - 60 acres; RO. B. BIBB - 45 acres; BAXTER H. BIBB - 44
acres; CHAS. M. BIBB, PERLINA F. BIBB, and each is to have right of
way to public road and free access to and from family graveyard.

SARAH BIBB -- Book 3, Page 299 -- Administrator's Bond -- MARTIN BIBB
and ZACH. TALIAFERRO, June 16, 1794, for MARTIN BIBB.
Book 9, Page 289 -- Estate Commitment to Sheriff, March, 1837. Motion
of JAS. WHITEHEAD. JNO. COLEMAN, Sheriff.

THOMAS BIBB -- Book 2, Page 29 -- January 29, 1781, written; Decem-
ber 3, 1781, probated. Witnesses: HENRY HARPER, SR., JAS. BIBB,
SALLY PATTERSON. Daughter, TEMPERANCE; ux, SARAH; equal parts to
WM., JOHN, HENRY, JAMES, MARTIN BIBB, MARY GRAY, FRANCES HARPER,
TEMPERANCE BIBB. My four oldest daughters: ELIZ. NICOLAS, ANNE KEY,
RACHEL ALAS, BARBARA COBB. Executors: WM. and JOHN BIBB. They
qualified on probate date; bondsmen: LUCAS POWELL, JAS. STEVENS.
Book 2, Page 79 -- Inventory on order of January 7, 1782. Done Jan-
uary 12, 1782. L 262-14-6. LUCAS POWELL, JAS. WILLS, MATT.
NIGHTINGALE.
Book 3, Page 312 -- Administrator's Account -- WM. BIBB - from Novem-
ber 10, 1784. To JNO. BIBB, for JNO. LOVING, to JAS. BIBB, to
mother - moving her from CHAS. IRVING's to WM. KNIGHT's and boarding
her. October 25, 1789. JAS. BIBB paid as overseer. Recorded
October 20, 1794. HENRY MARTIN, WM. WARWICK, W. M. LOVING.

WILLIAM BIBB -- Book 4, Page 392 -- Guardian Bond -- THOS. BIBB and
PARMENAS BRYANT, October 15, 1804, for THOS. BIBB as guardian of
WM. BIBB, orphan of JOHN BIBB.

WILLIAM BICKNALL -- Book 2, Page 10 -- July 13, 1780, written; May 7,
1781, probated. Witnesses: JNO. BIBB, JNO. GREGORY, AGATHA STAPLES,
JOSIAS WOOD. SAML., WM., JR., THOS., and JOHN BICKNALL have had
distributions and I now leave rest to my other children: RUTH, ANNA,
MARY ANN, and MICAJAH BICKNALL. MICAJAH is to administer. Times
are troublesome and he may be taken to the Wars. If so, my daughter,
MARY ANN BICKNALL is to act until he returns.
(Note: MICAJAH's name appears in list of Amherst Revolutionary
soldiers. A man named JAMES BICKNALL was killed in service.) MICAJAH
qualified on probate date; bondsman: ABRAHAM WARWICK.
Book 2, Page 19 -- Inventory, May 31, 1781. L 21-8-41(?). JNO. BIBB,
JNO. GRIGORY, JNO. STAPLES.

JOSEPH LINDSEY BLACK -- Book 8, Page 432 -- Minister's Bond --
Protestant Episcopal -- September 15, 1834. Bondsmen: EDMUND PENN,
CHAMPE CARTER, EHNRY L. DAVIES.

JOHN BLACKMORE (BLAKEMORE) -- Book 1, Page 142 -- Refunding Bond --
August 7, 1769 -- To secure HOWARD CASH who was security for LUCY
CARTER, executor of CHAS. CARTER. She has since married JOHN BLACK-
MORE. Bondsmen: GABL. PENN and THOS. REID. (Note: In marriage bond
here he is called JOHN BLAKEMORE - October 15, 1768. Bride was LUCY
CARTER, widow and relict of CHAS. CARTER, deceased. JOB CARTER was
bondsman and she gave her own consent.)

RACHEL BLAIN -- Book 1, Page 168 -- Administrator's Bond -- GEO. BLAIN,
RICH. McCARY, and AARON MOORE, May 8, 1770, for Guardian Bond.
Book 1, Page 177 -- Inventory, June 29, 1770. L 28-10-11. RICH.
ALLCOCK, AMBROSE JONES, HENRY BARNES.
Book 1, Page 82 -- Administrator's Bond -- GEO. BLAIN and JNO. MONT-
GOMERY, September 13, 1770, for Guardian Bond.

ALEXANDER F. BLAIR -- Book 8, Page 415 -- Guardian Bond -- JNO. S.
BLAIR and JAS. D. WATTS, June 16, 1834, for JNO. S. BLAIR, as guardian
of ALEX. F. BLAIR, orphan of WINSTON S. BLAIR.

ALLEN BLAIR -- Book 9, Page 72 -- December 26, 1834, written; May 18,
1835, probated. Witnesses: JNO. S. FRENCH, ABRAHAM EWERS, RICH.
JOHNSON, JESSE WOODS, and JAS. D. WATTS. Proved by WATTS, EWERS, and
WOODS. Ux, MARY ANN; daughter, POLLY; son, JAMES, now at a distance;
my grandson, FRANCIS ALLEN BLAIR, is to be kept by my daughter, POLLY;
one-fourth to heirs of PEGGY WILLIAMS; heirs of my daughter, BETSY
LAVENDER; children of ALEX. C. BLAIR; three children of WINSTON BLAIR,
deceased; my son, GEO. A. BLAIR; my son, JOHN S. BLAIR; slave loaned
to son, WILLIAM, and now in possession of his ux in Kentucky. Executors: JAS. D. WATTS and WM. WRIGHT. Slave to WILLIAM to raise for
FRANCIS A. BLAIR. (Note: ALLEN BLAIR, bachelor, and MARY ANN STAPLES,
spinster, got license, December 14, 1778. JNO. STAPLES, bondsman;
consent of SARAH STAPLES. ALLEN BLAIR's Revolutionary service is given
in data on soldiers in Amherst.) The two executors named declined
to serve and July 20, 1835, POLLY BLAIR qualified; bondsmen: JNO. S.
BLAIR, MOSES PHILLIPS & PEYTON KEITH.
Book 9, Page 91 -- Missing item indexed in Master.
Book 9, Page 93 -- Administrator's Bond -- See will data above.
Book 9, Page 128 -- Administrator's Account -- POLLY BLAIR - money
received on date of ALLEN BLAIR's death, April 23, 1835. Recorded
October 19, 1835.
Book 9, Page 270 -- Administrator's Account -- POLLY BLAIR from
July 21, 1835 - J. S. BLAIR for colt. Recorded November 21, 1836.
LINDSEY COLEMAN and HENRY L. DAVIES.
Book 11, Page 404 -- Administrator's Bond -- JAS. D. WATTS and DAVID
APPLING, March 16, 1846, for JAS. D. WATTS.
Book 11, Page 444 -- Inventory -- $1,912.00 Amherst and Lynchburg
slaves. JAS. W. KEITH, WM. S. TURNER, MOSES PHILLIPS. Bond payable
to MARY ANN BLAIR; slaves hired by J. S. BLAIR. JAS. D. WATTS, ad-
ministrator. November 16, 1846.
Book 12, Page 90 -- Administrator's Account -- JAS. D. WATTS from
March 25 -- F. BLAIR for groceries; credit to MARY A. BLAIR. RO. M.
BROWN, commissioner, December 18, 1848.

FRANCIS ALLEN BLAIR -- Book 9, Page 223 -- Guardian Bond -- MOSES
PHILLIPS and POLLY BLAIR, March 21, 1836, for MOSES PHILLIPS as
guardian of FRANCIS ALLEN BLAIR, son of WM. H. BLAIR.
Book 16, Page 111 -- Administrator's Bond -- EMILY F. BLAIR and JAS.
D. WATTS, July 20, 1862, for EMILY F. BLAIR.
Book 16, Page 126 -- Inventory, $5,992,50. JAS. KEITH, R. H. CARR,
JNO. A. SCRUGGS, DAVID APPLING.
Book 17, Page 217 -- Administrator's Bond -- WM. D. TURNER and LEWIS E.
TURNER, April 15, 1867, for WM. TURNER.

GILLA BLAIR -- Book 7, Page 9 -- Administrator's Bond -- WM. H. and
ALLEN BLAIR, June 18, 1827, for WM. H. BLAIR.

LYCURGUS BLAIR -- Book 14, Page 129 -- Constable -- June 16, 1856,
District 2; elected May 22, 1856. Bondsmen: J. D. PIERCE and M. C.
GOODWIN.

MARY ANN BLAIR -- Book 13, Page 237 -- Administrator's Bond -- FRANCIS
A. BLAIR and DAVID APPLING, September 19, 1853, for FRANCIS A. BLAIR.

NANCY BLAIR -- Deed Book X, Page 435. Deed of gift to my niece, ELIZ.
BRYANT, February 12, 1841. (Note: This is an item found in work for
a client and I am putting it herein.)

POLLY BLAIR -- Book 11, Page 345 -- August 16, 1845, written; Febru-
ary 16, 1846, probated. Witnesses: WM. L. WILLS, JAS. M. LOVING,
JAS. POWELL and proved by them. Nephew, ALEX. F. BLAIR; nephew,
FRANCIS A. BLAIR; interest in my father's estate bought by SAML.
LAVINDER.
Book 11, Page 400 -- Administrator's Bond -- JAS. W. KEITH and NICHL.
MAYS, February 16, 1846, for JAS. W. KEITH.
Book 11, Page 414 -- Inventory -- February, 1846, $199.25. March 24,
1846. JAS. D. WATTS, WM. S. WATTS, WM. S. TURNER.

SOPHRONIA BLAIR -- Book 8, Page 401 -- Guardian Bond -- NANCY BLAIR,
JAS. D. WATTS, RICH. A. TILLER, March 17, 1834, for NANCY BLAIR as
guardian of SOPHRONIA and LYCURGUS BLAIR, orphans of WINSTON S. BLAIR.

WILLIAM BLAIR -- Book 1, Page 394 -- Administrator's Bond -- ALLEN
BLAIR, NICHL. CABELL, and ROGER WILLIAMS, December 4, 1777, for
ALLEN BLAIR.
Book 1, Page 407 -- Inventory -- L 352-18-3, January 30, 1778. WM.
PERKINS, STEPHEN TURNER,and GROVES HARDING.

WILLIAM H. BLAIR -- Book 6, Page 594 -- Guardian Bond -- ALLEN BLAIR,
PEYTON KEITH, and STERLING CLAIBORNE, April 8, 1825, for ALLEN BLAIR
as guardian of his son, WM. H. BLAIR.

WINSTON S. BLAIR -- Book 8, Page 162 -- Administrator's Bond -- JAS. D.
WATTS, ALLEN BLAIR, and HAROLD B. SCOTT, December 19, 1831. for JAS. D.
WATTS.
Book 8, Page 231 -- Inventory -- June 20, 1832, JOS. STAPLES and E. B.
ESTES, and recorded July 16, 1832. Very interesting book list.
Book 9, Page 169 -- Administrator's Account -- JAS. D. WATTS, Novem-
ber 15, 1834, from December 30, 1831. Amounts to JNO. S. and NANCY
BLAIR. Commissioners: ED A. CABELL and WM. H. KNIGHT.
Book 9, Page 405 -- Administrator's Account -- JAS. D. WATTS from 1834.
Land bond of MICAJAH PENDLETON by WINSTON S. BLAIR. Certified in
Albemarle, February 15, 1837, and recorded in Amherst, March 20, 1838.
NATHL. BURLEY, RICH. WINGFIELD, JOSHUA JACKSON.
Book 11, Page 420 -- Administrator's Account -- JAS. D. WATTS, from
April 1846 -- Mention of ALEX. F. BLAIR and his mother, NANCY BLAIR,
and their being bonded as guardians of LUCINDA, LYCURGUS, and SOPHRONIA
BLAIR. Dates of April 22 and 27, 1846. Recorded July 20, 1846.
Commissioners: DAVID APPLING and JAS. W. KEITH.
Book 12, Page 374 -- Missing item, but indexed in Master.

VARIOUS DEED CLAIMS -- I did research on the family for a man several
years ago, but, unfortunately, I have lot his name and address. This
is not an exhaustive summary, but since I had them at hand, I thought
it wise to insert them herein. All references are to deed books.

Deed Book T, Page 444 -- September 19, 1831. ALLEN BLAIR of Amherst
sets up trust fund with CALVIN J. or I. HARDY and LITTLETON JOHNSON
of Hardiman County, Tennessee, for love borne his grandchildren by
his son, ALEX. BLAIR, of Hardiman County, Tennessee -- slaves to
support the present and any future children of ALEX. BLAIR; provisions
set forth at death of ALEX. BLAIR. I recall that the client identified
one of these men as a brother-in-law of ALEX. BLAIR, if memory serves
me correctly.

Deed Book O, Page 715 -- September 3, 1821, Deed of trust involving
GEO. A. BLAIR and JNO. PRYOR and JNO. MYERS.

Deed Book Y, Page 177 -- April 15, 1842. JNO. S. BLAIR and ux, ANN S.,
of Lynchburg, to JNO. G. WEEM of same place. Mention of ALLEN BLAIR's
will and land.

Deed Book B, Page 201 -- August 3, 1766, JAMES COLBARD BLAIR intends
shortly to go to province of South Carolina - to move there - and
gives power-of-attorney to BENJ. HIGGINBOTHAM to convey land on Pedlar
to ALEX. BAGGES of Augusta.

Deed Book B, Page 250 -- September 12, 1767, JOSEPH BLAIR of Amherst
to WM. BLAIR, a mare.

Deed Book A, Page 225 -- February, 1764, and recorded June 4, 1764.
WM. BLAIR and ux, MARY, of Albemarle and St. Anne's Parish to EDWARD
BOURMAR(?) - 150 acres bought by BLAIR from NICHL. THOMAS of Rockfish.

Deed Book E, Page 620; Deed Book F, Page 519; Deed Book H, Page 163,
etc. -- ALLEN BLAIR and ux, MARY ANN; JOHN MERRYMAN GRIFFIN and ux,
ELIZ.; THOS. GRIFFIN and ux, MILDRED are in deeds. See Sweeny's
Amherst in Revolution, Page 102, for data on ALLEN BLAIR and widow for
pension application by latter. She was MARY ANN STAPLES. They were
married in Amherst, December 22, 1778. Son, JNO. S. BLAIR, in Lynchburg in 1838.

WILLIAM F. BLAND -- Book 14, Page 590 -- Refunding Bond -- WM. F.
BLAND and RO. BLAND, Jan. 13, 1858, to JNO. SCHOOLFIELD, administrator
of FRANCES B. SHACKLEFORD. Administrator had paid WM. F. BLAND,
administrator of JAS. T. BOYD, bequest to BOYD under will of F. B.
SHACKLEFORD and recorded in Amherst.

NOEL BLANKENSHIP -- Book 3, Page 314 -- August 24, 1794, written;
October 20, 1794, probated. Witnesses: THOS. ANDERSON; NICHL.
CROSS, JAS. HILL and MICHL. STONEHOCKER. Son, ABELL -- 100 acres
next to where he lives. Ux, MARY. Son, NOEL; all of my sons and
daughters. Executors: ABELL BLANKENSHIP and REASON WRIGHT.
Book 3, Page 321 -- Administrator's Bond -- ABELL BLANKENSHIP, MICHL.
STONEHOCKER and THOS. ANDERSON on probate date for ABELL BLANKENSHIP.
Book 3, Page 333 -- Inventory -- total: none -- DAVID WOODROOF,
BENJ. and ISAAC RUCKER on February 16, 1795.
Book 3, Page 592 -- November 14, 1800, Committee consisting of DAVID
WOODROOF, JAMES HILL and JAS. LIVELY report that all personal property
has been sold and each legatee got L 8-14-0. Total: L 60-18-6.

GEORGE D. BLANKS -- Book 12, Page 507 -- Guardian Bond -- THOS. C.
BLANKS and CALVIN F. BENNETT, April 19, 1852, for THOS. C. BLANKS as
guardian of GEO. D., JAMES A., CAROLINE M., DYSON C., MARY, PARTHENIA,
SALLY, MARGARET, and SILAS BLANKS - no parent set forth.
Book 18, Page 152 -- Guardian's Account -- THOS. C. BLANKS, guardian,
October 11, 1871, and November 10, 1871, item states that JOHN P.
BLANKS was of age. Wards are named as above, Book 12, Page 507.
Account from April 29, 1852. Mention of chancery suit of BLANKS vs.
BLANKS, recorded December 18, 1871.

THOMAS C. BLANKS -- Book 7, Page 322 -- Guardian Bond -- DANL. L.
BURFORD and RICH. WHITTEN, January 18, 1830, for DANL. BURFORD as
guardian of THOS. C. BLANKS, orphan of JNO. BLANKS.

MICHAEL BLESSING -- Book 16, Page 76f -- July 9, 1858, written;
May 20, 1861, probated. Witnesses: SAML. M. GARLAND, A. C. HARRISON
and proved by them. Grandson, FREDERICK C. OTT to administer. Debt
due me from V. McGINNIA and RO. A. COGHILL from 1858. Granddaughter,
EMMA C. LAWRENCE, to be educated when 21; debts due from JNO. LAYMAN
and DANL. SHAW; grandchildren by daughters, REBECCA LAYMAN and ELIZ.
SHAW; daughter, LIDIA A. OTT, deceased; son-in-law, FREDERICK OTT,
deceased. FREDERICK C. OTT qualified on probate date. Bondsman:
CHAS. D. DAVIES.
Book 16, Page 282 -- Administrator's Account -- FREDERICK C. OTT from
July 6, 1861 - payments by DANL. J. SHAW and JNO. LAYMAN; children
of REBECCA LAYMAN; ELIZ. SHAW; LYDIA OTT. Layman heirs: HENRIETTA

and E. NAOMI LAYMAN; SHAW heirs: EZELLA M., R. R., and B. D. SHAW; OTT heirs: F. C., WM. J., and HENRIETTA DAVIES. Recorded January 20, 1862.

EDWARD BOLLING (Also see BOWLING) -- Book 1, Page 184 -- July 13, 1769, written; October 1, 1770, probated. Witnesses: ARCHELUS MITCHELL, HANNAH MITCHELL. Of Chesterfield County, Virginia; brothers: THOS. and JNO. - plantation called Falling River; brother, ROBT. - Buffalo Lick plantation on north side of James River; brother, ARCHIBALD, plantation called Old Town and warehouse at Pochahuntas (sic) and lots at Bermuda Hundred; sisters: MARY BLAND and SARAH TAZEWELL (?); sister, ANN BOLLING; Friend, RICH. KIDMEADE; my cousin, BOLLING ELDRIDGE.
Book 1, Page 187 -- Administrator's Bond -- RO. BOLLING, JR., WM. CABELL, EDMUND WILCOX, November 5, 1770, for RO. BOLLING, JR.
Book 1, Page 193 -- Inventory -- Shown to us at different times by ARCHALEUS MITCHELL - L 2061-7-6. BATTALIE HARRIS, JOS. CREWS, ABRAHAM NORTH.

JAMES BOLLING (BOWLING in some items) -- Book 9, Page 290 -- Administrator's Bond -- WM. M. BOWLING, ISAAC R. REYNOLDS, ZACH. D. TINSLEY, March 20, 1837, for WM. M. BOWLING. Will: September 21, 1833, written; June 28, 1835, probated; codicil: November 21, 1836. Witnesses to will: JNO. M. OTEY, JNO. M. WILLIAMS, RO. H. WIATT. Witnesses to codicil: SOLOMON TANNER and THORNTON RHOADES. Ux, LETTY; children and grandchildren; children of my deceased daughter, ELIZ. REYNOLDS. Sons: WM., LEWIS, JAMES; daughters: SALLY COX, PAMELIA JOHNSON, REBECCA HILL - present and future children of my daughter, SUSANNAH HUDSON. Executors: Son, LEWIS and friends, JESSE MUNDY and CHISWELL DABNEY. Codicil: slaves not to be sold publicly for would probably fall into hands of slave traders; to be divided among children. Proved by WIATT and codicil witnesses and by JNO. M. WILLIAMS on March 20, 1837.
Book 9, Page 311 -- Inventory -- April 4, 1837, $9,020.00; nine slaves; BENJ. B. TALIAFERRO, THOS. LEE, NATHAN GLENN.
Book 12, Page 409 -- Slave division - writing is quite fancy and hard to decipher. Lots to LEWIS BOWLING, MRS. HILL, MRS. HUDSON, JAMES BOWLING, WM. M. BOWLING, MRS. JANE (or SARAH?) WINGFIELD; two of the children took money in lieu of slaves. WM. KENT, THOS. W. JONES, THOS. LEE, JESSE MUNDY, May 19, 1851.
Book 12, Page 535 -- Administrator's Account -- WM. M. BOWLING from February 15, 1847. Also administrator of L. BOWLING; expenses in matters of estates of LEWIS and JAMES BOWLING as witnesses. Recorded June 21, 1852.

JOHN D. BOLLING -- Book 8, Page 190 -- Guardian's Account -- January 16, 1832. JNO. D. BOLLING as guardian of RO. ALLEN's children. GARLAND as attorney for wards takes exceptions. Reference to F. BROWN as late administrator of RO. ALLEN.

JOHN R. BOLLING -- Book 12, Page 489 -- December 14, 1840, written; February 16, 1852, probated. Witnesses: PATRICK H. RANDOLPH, WM. S. THORNTON, JNO. ROBERTS, SR., and SAML. B. MEGGINSON. Proved by JNO. ROBERTS, SR., and SAML. MEGGINSON. Of Buckingham, but late of Powhatan. Nephew, ARCHIBALD B. MEGGINSON of Buckingham gets slaves and property and is to administer.

WILLIAM BONES -- Book 3, Page 309 -- Administrator's Bond -- JNO. BONES, JOS. ROBERTS, and JAS. EDMONDS, September 15, 1794, for JNO. BONES.
Book 3, Page 318 -- Inventory -- L 191-16-5-1/2, Dec. 15, 1794. ALEX. McALEXANDER, ANDREW WRIGHT, JNO. LOVING.

WALTER B. BOSWELL -- Book B, Page 113 -- Estate Commitment to Sheriff, September 5, 1840; EDMD. PENN, Sheriff.
Book 11, Page 65 -- Estate Commitment to Sheriff, September, 1841. Motion of HENRY L. DAVIES and DABNEY P. GOOCH. NELSON CRAWFORD, Sheriff.

JESSE BOULWARE -- Book 1, Page 375 -- December 1, 1776 (?), written; July 7, 1777, probated. Witnesses: RICH. TALIAFERRO, JNO. CARR. Ux, ELIZABETH; daughter, SALLY; granddaughter, RHODA RIAN (sic) and her mother, RHACHL (sic) RYAN (sic); my won, WILLIAM, is to be left in hands of JOHN BARNETT to learn a trade and money for him is to be handled by COL. JOHN ROSE until of age. COL. ROSE is to administer and take son, if BARNETT does not do so.
Book 1, Page 376 -- Administrator's Bond -- JNO. ROSE and EDMUND WILCOX, September 1, 1777, for JNO. ROSE.
Book 1, Page 424 -- Inventory -- L 106-4-6, October 23, 1777. MATT. NIGHTINGALE, ROBT. BARNETT, BENJ. WRIGHT.
Book 1, Page 425 -- Division to widow and son, WILLIAM -- L 30-8-2, by same committed as inventory, December 29, 1777. (Note: It would appear that ELIZ. later married WM. HORRALL, but I find no record here. On August 3, 1782, SARAH BOWLER and CHAS. EADS got license to marry and were bachelor and spinster. WM. and ELIZ. HORRALL, "Parents-in-law" of SARAH gave consent; SARAH also consented. There is an old BOULWARE or BOWLER WHARF on the Rappahannock. I am interested in the family because it constitutes one of my wife's lines. WM. TAYLOR came into Fayette County, Kentucky, and was said to have been a resident of Essex and Revolutionary soldier. His name appears on the list of soldiers at Lexington, Kentucky, courthouse. His wife is reputed to have been ELIZ GUILHAM or GILLIAM and her father, WILLIAM, lived in Fayette and later moved to Illinois with his daughter. WILLIAM TAYLOR had died in Kentucky. Tradition has it that ELIZ.'s mother was ELIZ. BOULWARE or BOWLER. Three men show up in Fayette and one of them, STARK TAYLOR, is known to have been of this same TAYLOR line. The other two men were named STARK BOULWARE and STARK GUILHAM or GILLIAM. It is enough to drive one "STARK" mad, but I have never been able to untangle the BOULWARE, GUILHAM, and TAYLOR lineage for pre-Revolutionary days. I feel sure that there is a connection with the STARK family because of the use of the name by all three families.)

CHARITY BOURNE -- Book 11, Page 424 -- Estate Commitment to Sheriff, August, 1846, on motion of JAS. H. CASHWELL. Sheriff: WM. M. WALLER. Book 11, Page 489 -- December 21, ----, written; August 17, 1848, probated. Witnesses: JNO. PRYOR, NICHL. HICKS, JACOB PHILLIPS. Proved by PRYOR and PHILLIPS. Property to "pass as disposed of ...." Book 11, Page 549 -- Slave inventory; suit pending in Circuit Court between ELIJAH FLETCHER and C. BOURNE as to title of slaves. Valued at $3,175.00; JNO. WHITEHEAD for sheriff; WM. WALLER, NICHL. HICKS, WM. P. MORRIS, September 12, 1846.
Book 12, Page 143 -- Administrator's Account -- WM. M. WALLER, sheriff and administrator, from January 1, 1847. JUDITH HANSARD and JNO. PHILLIPS surrendered slaves under decree of court. Recorded December 20, 1849.

HENRY BOURNE (BOURN) -- Book 5, Page 232 -- February 20, 1813, written; July 19, 1813, probated. Witnesses: PETER CASHWELL, JAS. S. HIGGINBOTHAM, GUSTAVUS A. EDWARDS, NELSON C. CRAWFORD, LEONARD HENLEY. Proved by CASHWELL and HIGGINBOTHAM. JNO. & WM. BOURN qualified; bondsmen: CHAS. MUNDY & PETER CASHWELL. Ux, CHARITY, property received by her; son, CHANDLER; daughter, CATH. CLASBY; sons: JOHN, WM., HENRY, JEREMIAH; daughter, ELIZABETH BOURN; daughter, PHEBE BOURN; estate to be kept intact for two years; if any legatee marries; land where I live. Son, CHANDLER, is dead and has two sons: BENJ. H. and JNO. C. BOURN - when of age. Executors: Sons: JOHN and WM.;

JOHN H. McDANIEL and REV. WM. DUNCAN. Administrator's Bond is on Page 236 of Book 5.
Book 5, Page 373 -- Inventory, $6,287.67. THOS. HOLLOWAY, JNO. CASHWELL, GIDEON RUCKER.
Book 6, Page 184 -- Administrator's Account -- WM. BOURN from July 19, 1813 - paling graveyard; HENRY and JOHN BOURNE; LINDSEY SANDIDGE, administrator of JOHN BOURN; BENJ. BOURN; legacy to THOS. CLASBY; legacy to DANL. RUCKER; HENRY BOURN, JR.; JOSEPH B. CARTER, administrator of JEREMIAH BOURNE; heirs of CHANDLER BOURNE, when of age. September 23, 1819. JNO. WARWICK, RICH. HARRISON, WM. DUNCAN.

21

JEREMIAH BOURNE -- Book 5, Page 519 -- Guardian Bond -- WM. BOURNE, REUBEN COLEMAND and LINDSEY SANDIDGE, July 17, 1815, for WM. BOURNE as guardian of JEREMIAH BOURNE, orphan of HENRY BOURNE.
Book 5, Page 557 -- Administrator's Bond -- WM. BOURNE and WM. DUNCAN, January 1816, for WM. BOURNE; no testator named, but indexed in Master for JER. BOURNE.
Book 5, Page 566 -- Inventory -- JNO. McDANIEL, REUBEN COLEMAN, PETER COLEMAN, and PHILIP LIVELY, January 25, 1816 - $925.00; three slaves and furniture.
Book 6, Page 706 -- Guardian's Account -- WM. BOURNE, guardian, 1815 account as guardian of JEREMIAH BOURNE, deceased. Receipt of HENRY BOURNE; NANCY BOURNE, legacy for infants of JOHN BOURNE; THOS. CLASBY for legacy from estate of HENRY BOURNE; JOSEPH R. CARTER's receipt for legacy; paid to PETER CASHWELL, attorney-in-fact for guardian of infants of CHANDLER BOURNE, deceased and "living in Kentucky." Recorded November 20, 1826.

JOHN BOURNE -- Book 5, Page 540 -- Inventory -- "Say of that part at the Buffalo Springs," December 18, 1815. BENJ. TALIAFERRO, WM. SANDIDGE, CORNL. SALE.
Book A, Page 34 -- Administrator's Account -- LINDSEY SANDIDGE - from September 29, 1815 -- for conveying "corps" to burying place -- $4.00; accounts of WM. BOURNE; bond of ANN and JOHN BOURNE; JAMES M. BOURNE; WM. H. BOURNE; NANCY BOURNE - $6,841.38. NELSON CRAWFORD, BENJ. TALIAFERRO, CORNL. SALE. September 23, 1823.
Book A, Page 112 -- Administrator's Account -- LINDSEY SANDIDGE from November 1, 1823. Cash paid to MRS. NANCY BOURNE, guardian as per her acknowledgement; schooling of children.

MARY ANN BOURNE -- Book 5, Page 534 -- Guardian's Bond -- NANCY BOURNE, BENJ. and LINDSEY SANDIDGE, November 20, 1815, for NANCY BOURNE as guardian of MARY ANN; JELINZAY; ELIZ.; WM. HENRY; and BENJ. J. (I.) BOURNE, children of JOHN BOURNE, deceased.

PHEBE BOURNE -- Book 5, Page 533 -- Guardian's Bond -- WM. BOURNE & RICH. HARRISON, November 20, 1815, for WM. BOURNE as guardian of PHEBE BOURNE, orphan of HENRY BOURNE (indexed as BROWN, PHEBE).

WILLIAM BOURNE -- Book 12, Page 531 -- December 30, 1850; Nelson County, Virginia; probated February 28, 1851; recorded in Amherst, July 19, 1852. Witnesses: STERLING CLAIBORNE and W. H. ROSE and proved by them. CYRUS T. (F.) BOURNE qualified on probate date and bedroom were SAML. PETIT, GEO. JONES, WM. H. ROBERTS, WM. H. MANTIPLY and WM. H. OGDEN. Of Nelson County, Virginia - land to be sold; grandson, WM. H. MANTIPLY, son of my daughter, REBECCA, deceased. Son, CYRUS T. (F.?); daughter, ELIZ. CAROLINE, ux of ROBT. H. MANTIPLY; daughter, SUSAN MILDRED, ux of WM. H. OGDEN; daughter, HENRY ANN, ux, of WM. H. ROBERTS - they have had sums. Some doubt has been cast as to my grandson's being excluded from will of his grandfather, BENJ. TALIAFERRO - he is to be equal in division with my children. Daughters' parts to be in trust of husbands. CYRUS is to be guardian of my grandson and executor.

SALLY L. BOWCOCK -- Book 4, Page 530 -- Guardian Bond -- LEWIS and NELSON C. DAWSON, September 19, 1805, for LEWIS DAWSON as guardian of SALLY L. BOWCOCK, child of ELIJAH BOWCOCK, now a non-resident of Virginia.

BELINDA BOWLES -- Book 6, Page 440 -- Guardian Bond -- JOEL BOWLES and GEO. FEAGANS, February 16, 1824, for JOEL BOWLES as guardian of BELINDA BOWLES, orphan of CHARLES BOWLES, deceased.

CHARLES BOWLES -- Book 5, Page 599 -- Administrator's Bond -- CHARLES, STEPHEN and JOHN BOWLES, and WM. STAPLES, August 19, 1816, for STEPHEN BOWLES. No testator named, but indexed for CHAS. BOWLES.

DAVIS BOWLES -- Book 1, Page 395f -- Administrator's Bond -- WM. COOK WEAKLAND, RICH. BALDOCK, and WM. HORSLEY, December 3, 1777, for WM. WEAKLAND.

Book 1, Page 406 -- Inventory -- December 5, 1777 -- L 58-8-6. RO.,
DRURY, and JAS. CHRISTIAN.
Book 5, Page 609 -- Guardian Bond -- JAS. TARDY (TANDY?) and WM. LEE,
November 19, 1810, for JAS. TARDY as guardian of DAVID BOWLES, orphan
of CHARLES BOWLES.

ELIZA BOWLES -- Book 7, Page 315 -- Guardian Bond -- CHRISTOPHER
CHENAULT and LEWIS MAYS, December 21, 1829, for CHRISTOPHER CHENAULT
as guardian of ELIZA BOWLES, orphan of MARY BOWLES.

FANNY BOWLES -- Book 16, Page 116 -- February11, 1862, written;
March 18, 1862, probated. Witnesses: RO. L. COLEMAN and DAVID
BOWLES and proved by them. Sister, JANE E. JONES, ux of THOS. H.
JONES. Deed of trust for my benefit; DAVEY (?) BOWLES from THOS. H.
JONES. Book 16, Page 120 is missing and indexed as inventory.

JOEL BOWLES -- Book 6, Page 318 -- Guardian Bond -- LUCAS P. THOMPSON
and SAML. MANTIPLY, August 19, 1822, for LUCAS THOMPSON as guardian of
JOEL BOWLES, orphan of CHARLES BOWLES.

NAPOLEON D. BOWLES (B. in one item) -- Book 12, Page 394 -- Administra-
tor's Bond -- WM. STAPLES and ROBT. COGHILL, June 16, 1851, for WM.
STAPLES and NAPOLEON D. BOWLES here.
Book 13, Page 480 (Indexed as Book 12, Page 480) -- Administrator's
Account -- WM. STAPLES, SR., from July 12, 1851 -- L. D. LYONS,
trustee; G. M. TINSLEY, trustee; account of JAMES BOWLES, but no
legatees named as such. Called NAPOLEON D. BOWLES here. Recorded
June 18, 1855. P. C. BOWLES and P. BOWLES, trustees mentioned.

STEPHEN BOWLES -- Book 12, Page 271 -- Inventory -- $3,419.20 plus
slaves or $5,709.20 in all. May 20, 1850. HENRY FRANKLIN, JULIUS
SIMPSON, WM. P. MORRIS.
Book 12, Page 278 -- December 31, 1829, written; May 20, 1850, probated. Witnesses: JNO. PRYOR, JAS. Y.(?) FEAGANS, HENRY C. WILLIAMS,
RO. BOWLES. Ux, SALLY; sons: PAUL C., NAPOLEON B., and JOSEPH to
be supported; daughter, CAROLINE LYON, ux of LORENZO D. LYON; daughter,
CYNTHIA HADEN, ux of ABNER HAYDEN (two spellings noted); daughter,
ELIZ. RYAN, and children - former husband, JOHN RYAN, deceased; daugh-
ter, ELLIN TINSLEY, ux of GEO. Mc. D. TINSLEY and children. Execu-
tors: sons, PAUL and NAPOLEON BOWLES. Codicil: Date? ELIZ. RYAN
and children to be supported and to live with her mother.
Book 12, Page 281 -- Administrator's Bond -- PAUL C. BOWLES, probate
date. Bondsmen: DABNEY SANDIDGE, WM. STAPLES.
Book 12, Page 340 -- Sale: PAUL BOWLES, executor, December 9, 1850;
buyers not listed.
Book 12, Page 346 -- Slave division, November 1850. Lots to MRS.
MARGARET C. LYON and children; MRS. CYNTHIA HAYDON; PAUL C. BOWLES;
MRS. ELIZ. S. RYAN and children; NAPOLEON B. BOWLES; MRS. ELEANOR
TINSLEY and children; JOSEPH BOWLES. Commissioners: JULIUS SIMPSON,
WM. STAPLES, EDWIN S. RUCKER, February 20, 1851.
Book 12, Page 347 -- Administrator's Account -- PAUL C. BOWLES, from
February 19, 1850. To JOSEPH BOWLES and N. B. BOWLES. Commissioners:
RO. A. COGHILL, WM. STAPLES, RO. L. COLEMAN, January 20, 1851.
Book 13, Page 367 -- Administrator's de bonis non Bond -- WM. STAPLES,
RO. A. COGHILL, and SAML. M. GARLAND, September 18, 1854, for WM.
STAPLES.
Book 13, Page 478 -- Administrator's Account -- PAUL C. BOWLES from
December 16, 1850 -- enclosing graveyard. BOWLES and A-----?, WM.
STAPLES, Administrator de bonis non; recorded June 18, 1855.

GRACEY BOWLING -- Book 10, Page 214 -- Administrator's Bond -- JNO. D.
BOWLING and MAURICE H. GARLAND, April 20, 1840, for JNO. BOWLING.

JOHN BOWLING -- Book 7, Page 11 -- Administrator's Bond -- WM. BOWLING
and JAS. PETIT, June 18, 1827, for WM. BOWLING.
Book 7, Page 78 -- Inventory -- $563.38 -- WM. R. ROANE, RO. RIDGWARY,
and JAS. MYERS, November 29, 1827.
Book 8, Page 234 -- Estate Commitment to Sheriff -- Motion of JAS.
PETIT, July court, 1832, and unadministered by WM. BOWLING. NELSON
DAWSON, sheriff.

LETTY M. BOWLING -- Book 12, Page 296 -- Administrator's Bond -- WM. M.
BOWLING and JNO. R. McDANIEL, August 19, 1850, for WM. M. BOWLING.
Book 12, Page 535 (Same account is on Page 540, too) -- Administrator's
Account -- WM. M. BOWLING, February 27, 1851, as joint administer of
LETTA and JAMES BOWLING -- C. DABNEY, counsel, and WIATT PETTYJOHN,
agent for some of the legatees with MOSBY and SPEED, counsel. Continued March 17, 1851. April 24, JESSE MONDAY (sic), agent for
legatees; continued May 19th; continued May 31st in office of CHISWELL
DABNEY in Lynchburg; continued to June 4th. WM. M. BOWLING bonded as
administrator of JAS. BOWLING (see BOLLING), March 20, 1837, and for
LETTY M. BOWLING on August 19, 1850. Her estate was sold November 20,
1850, and so was that of JAS. BOWLING. WM. and JAS. BOWLING were
buyers. JAMES BOWLING died in November, 1836, and his widow, LETTA,
in fall of 1850. She enjoyed life estate and many slaves were born
and this old lady with growing family of slaves could not have been
supported on the poor place where she lived without a manager. Her
son, WM. M., had his own farm and home and kept no account of business.
Cash mentioned on account of pension money, April 13, 1850. To
ALFRED TAYLOR for enclosing graveyard and repair of house. Account
of JAS. BOWLING; runs to Page 548. Recorded June 21, 1852.

MARTHA JANE BOWLING -- Book 10, Page 366 -- Guardian Bond -- JOHN D.
BOWLING, THOS. BOWLING, and JNO. W. WHITTEN, July 19, 1841, for
JOHN D. BOWLING as guardian of MARTHA JANE BOWLING, orphan of GRACEY
ANN BOWLING, deceased.

NANCY JANE BOWLING -- Book 14, Page 85 -- Guardian Bond -- EGBERT T.
BOWLING, March 17, 1856, as guardian of NANCY J. BOWLING, orphan of
-----.
Book 14, Page 390 -- Guardian Bond -- EGBERT T. BOWLING and RO. L.
COLEMAN, July 20, 1857, for EGBERT T. BOWLING as guardian of
NANCY JANE BOWLING as orphan of SHELTON JONES, deceased.

SALLY BOWLING -- Book 10, Page 88 -- Administrator's Bond -- WASH.
WHITTON (signed JNO. W. WHITTON) and JNO. WATTS, January 21, 1839,
for JNO. W. WHITTON.
Book 10, Page 223 -- Administrator's Account -- JNO. WHITTEN, from
December, 1838 - to board for herself and entertaining visitors;
waiting on her in last illness until she died at my home - 8 days -
$12.00. January, 1839 - shroud, coffin, and digging grave - $3.50;
$7.00; $5.00 - which included conveyance of deceased to grave. Property removed from Campbell County - $3.00. RICH. CRAWFORD, RICH.
SMITH. Recorded May 18, 1840.

THOMAS H. BOWLING -- Book 9, Page 431 -- Trustee bond. (This is really
an item on RHODA BOWLING, but indexed for THOS. H.) THOS. H. BOWLING
and WM. and AMBROSE BURFORD, March 19, 1838, for THOS. H. BOWLING as
trustee of RHODA BOWLING and children.

WILLIAM L. BOWLING -- Book 8, Page 319 -- Estate Commitment to
Sheriff -- June 1833; Sheriff: EDMUND WINSTON.

GEORGE BOYD -- Book 9, Page 91 -- Administrator's Bond -- DAVID H.
BOYD and JNO. H. BOYD, July 20, 1835, for DAVID H. BOYD.

JONATHAN BRIDGWATER -- Book 4, Page 182 -- October 30, 1797, written;
July 15, 1805, probated. Witnesses: THOS. FITZPATRICK, MOTE RAPIER,
WM. FITZPATRICK. Proved by the FITZPATRICKS. SAML., JONATHAN and
WM. BRIDGWATER qualified; bonedsmen: THOS. FITZPATRICK and WM. LEE
HARRIS. Sons: SAML., NATHANIEL, and WILLIAM. Names daughters
by births - "oldest, next oldest, etc." -- SALLY MOORE; LUCY CLARK;
MARY HARDY; BETSY MOORE; and SALLY MOORE. Land where I live to sons,
SAML., WM., JONATHAN, and NATHANIEL. Executors: Sons, SAML., WM.,
JONATHAN and ROBT. HARDY. Administrator's Bond is on Book 4,
Page 408 - see above.
Book 4, Page 212 -- Inventory -- L 515-6. MICH. WOODS, THOS. FITZ-
PATRICK, MATT. HARRIS, February 17, 1805.
Book 4, Page 529 -- Division - all legatees of age and received shares,
January 23, 1807. Not named. HUDSON MARTIN, JOS. SHELTON, THOS.
FITZPATRICK. Recorded September 19, 1808.

FLORENCE BROCKMAN (Indexed for F. D. BROCKMAN, but no "D." in data) --
Book 16, Page 413 -- Guardian Bond -- W. A. and SIMS BROCKMAN, PATRICK
DRUMMOND, and HENRY LOVING, December 21, 1863, for W. A. BROCKMAN as
guardian of FLOUENCE (sic) BROCKMAN; no parent set forth.

JOHN BROCKMAN -- Book 3, Page 344 -- Administrator's Bond -- ELIZABETH
BROCKMAN and JNO. CRAWFORD, July 20, 1795, for ELIZABETH BROCKMAN.
Book 3, Page 465 -- Inventory -- L 576-12-2 -- JNO. DUNCAN, JNO. SMITH,
JOEL FRANKLIN, April 16, 1798.

MARGARET BROCKMAN -- Book 4, Page 307 -- Guardian Bond -- JASPER
FRANKLIN and ELIJAH BROCKMAN, October 21, 1799, for JASPER FRANKLIN as
guardian of MARGARET BROCKMAN, orphan of JOHN BROCKMAN.

WILLIAM BROCKMAN -- Book 4, Page 306 -- Guardian Bond -- ELIJAH BROCK-
MAN and JOEL FRANKLIN, October 21, 1799, for ELIJAH BROCKMAN as
guardian of WM., ELIZ., FRANCES, and MATILDA BROCKMAN, orphans of
JOHN BROCKMAN.

JAMES BROOKS -- Book 4, Page 267 -- December 6, 1806, written;
December 15, 1806, probated. Witnesses: CHAS. BURKS, MICHL. McKEELY,
JACOB RUDACILL, JOHN N. COORBENE (?), ANDREW SCRIVER and proved by
them. On July 20, 1807, ROBT. BROOKS qualified; bondsmen: WM. and
RICH. WOODS. Daughter, MARGARET; two married daughters; daughter,
MARIA, to be educated. Daughters: ELIZ. HUMPHREY, LYDA BABER and
children, JANE, CHARLES, and SUSANNA BABER. Amherst land where JNO.
HOUSRIGHT lives; land in Albemarle bought of WM. CARY. If LYDA moves
to Kentucky, land to be sold and money goes to her. My ux, ELIZABETH.
My three sons: ROBT., JAMES, and RICH. WOODS. THOS. STOCKTON is
to stay one year where he lives. Executors: JAMES WOODS, BENJ.
HARRIS and ROBER (sic) BROOKS. (WOODS and BROOKS differences noted.)
Book 4, Page 449 -- Administrator's Bond (See will above).
Book 4, Page 497 -- Inventory -- $3,701.92 -- February 12, 1808;
recorded February 15, 1808. JAS. and JNO. HAYS and CHAS. MARTIN.
Inventory of BOTETOURT property. September 2, 1807, JNO. and HUGH
ALLEN and WM. DODD.

ABRAM B. BROWN -- Book 12, Page 25 -- Minister's Bond -- Baptist --
October 18, 1847. Bondsmen: SAML. M. GARLAND and JOHN H. WATTS.

BENJAMIN BROWN, JR. -- Book 11, Page 415 -- Coroner, July 20, 1846.
Bondsman: RO. M. BROWN.
Book 13, Page 521 -- Administrator's Bond -- ROBERSON C. PIERCE,
GEO. D. DAVIES, JR.(?), E. WHITEHEAD, attorney, W. E. COLEMAN, WM. M.
PIERCE, RO. M. BROWN, and J. D. PIERCE, June 18, 1855, for ROBERSON C.
PIERCE.
Book 14, Page 96 -- Inventory -- December 5, 1855 -- $5,461.45 --
JNO. T. ELLIS, PETER G. JOINER, LEONARD DANIEL, JR. Recorded March 25,
1856.
Book 15, Page 107 -- Administrator's Account -- ROBINSON C. PIERCE from
September 20, 1856. To RO. M. BROWN; to MARY E. BROWN; settled by
RO. TINSLEY; due estate by C. PIERCE and children; mention of property
at Amherst Courthouse. Recorded July 15, 1858.
Book 15, Page 131 -- Administrator's Account -- ROBINSON C. PIERCE
from September 20, 1857 -- to MARY E. BROWN; recorded March 21, 1859.
Book 15, Page 546 -- Administrator's Account -- ROBINSON C. PIERCE
from September 20, 1858 - to M. E. BROWN; BENJ. BROWN, JR., for Lynch-
burg trip; to MARY J. WINN for tuition; SCOTT tract sold. Recorded
June 18, 1860.
Book 16, Page 292 -- Administrator's Account -- ROBINSON C. PIERCE
from September 20, 1859. To MOLLY BROWN; M. J. WINN for tuition; to
GEORGE D. DAVIS in full; M. E. BROWN; MARY BROWN's interest in SCOTT
tract and sale. Recorded April 20, 1863.

CHARLES WARREN BROWN -- Book 16, Page 188 -- April 24, 1861, written;
December 15, 1862, probated. Witnesses: J. POWELL, JR., A. R. SHRA-
DER, E. L. GILBERT. Money devised to me by my brother, JOHN MAT.
BROWN, deceased. Brothers: HENRY L. BROWN and JNO. T. BROWN; my
mother - what comes to my father by her; SALLY C. BROWN, ux of HENRY L.
BROWN; if HENRY L. is without issue. Executor: brother, JOHN T.
BROWN.

FIELDING T. BROWN -- Book 12, Page 401 -- Commissioner of Revenue --
April 21, 1851. Bondsman: JOSEPH BROWN.
Book 16, Page 464 -- Administrator's Bond -- JOSEPH BROWN and SAML.
GARLAND, April 18, 1864, for JOSEPH BROWN.
Book 16, Page 471 -- Inventory, $2,582.50, April 28, 1864. GEO. W.
DAVIES, HENRY T. WRIGHT, A. C. HARRISON.
Book 16, Page 473 -- Sale -- JOSEPH BROWN, administrator, April 28,
1864. He was the only family name buyer. Tobacco at $26.00 per hun-
dred. Recorded May 16, 1864.

HOWELL L. BROWN -- Book 10, Page 59 -- County surveyor for 7 years,
November 19, 1832. Bondsmen: SAML. M. GARLAND and JOS. K. IRVING.
Book 11, Page 346 -- Surveyor, November 17, 1845. Bondsman: JOS. K.
IRVING.
Book 15, Page 257 -- January 10, 1860, written; February 20, 1860,
probated. Witnesses: JAS. D. HALL, HENRY W. WILLS, RO. C. WILSHER.
My four sons: CHARLES W., JOHN M., HENRY L., and JNO. T. BROWN - if
without issue. Montpelier tract to CHAS. W. and portion of mill lot -
I bought it from him two years ago. Three small tracts in Augusta -
70 odd acres and two in Nelson of 43 and 35-1/2 acres - to be sold
to educate my two youngest sons, HENRY and THOMPSON BROWN. I own
scholarship at Hamden-Sidney (sic) College which I purchased some
years ago. My sister, SUSAN. THOS. WHITEHEAD is to be guardian of
my children.
Book 15, Page 274 -- Administrator's Bond -- THOS. WHITEHEAD, SAML.
GARLAND, RO. WHITEHEAD, and HENRY W. WILLS, February 20, 1860, for
THOS. WHITEHEAD.
Book 15, Page 577 -- Inventory -- no total; March 14, 1860. JNO. V.
WHEELER and H. W. WILLS. (Note: MRS. WARNER E. UNGER, nee BROWN, is
a member of my church and I performed her wedding ceremony. She is a
descendant of HOWELL BROWN's and has a portrait of him over the fire-
place. She does not know who painted it, but states that tradition
has it that "some friend who wa sa Kentuckian" did it.)

JACOB BROWN -- Book 3, Page 108 -- March 16, 1789, written; July 6,
1789, probated. Witnesses: BENJ. COLEMAN, THOS. TUCKER, JNO. BROWN,
SR. -- JNO. BROWN, son, qualified on probate date. Bondsmen: PETER
CARTER and JOSEPH ROBERTS. Thewidow also qualified with her son. Ux,
SUSANNA; sons: CHARLES and JAMES; daughter, BETSY - when all three
are of age; "They are to be raised as the rest of my children was."
My children: SARAH, JOHN, JACOB, HENRY, MAURICE, MILLY, JANE, ALLETT
(?), SUSANNAH, and BETSY. Executors: son, JOHN, and my ux.
Book 3, Page 125 -- Inventory -- July 31, 1789 -- L 103-18-5. JAS.
GOODRICH, THOS. TUCKER, JNO. BROWN, SR.

JAMES BROWN -- Book 4, Page 37 -- Inventory -- L 6-18-0, June 21, 1802.
WM. WARE, CHAS. TALIAFERRO, THOS. N. EUBANK.
Book 4, Page 329 -- Administrator's Bond -- HENRY BROWN and NELSON
CRAWFORD, April 20, 1801, for HENRY BROWN.
Book 5, Page 398 -- Administrator's Account -- HENRY BROWN, August 15,
1801; recorded November 15, 1813. JAS. BURFORD, NELSON CRAWFORD,
P. P. THORNTON, GODFREY TOLER.

JAMES M. BROWN, DOCTOR -- Book 6, Page 318 -- Sheriff's Bond --
August 19, 1822. Bondsmen: BENJ. TALIAFERRO, LEONDARD HENLEY, WM.
DUNCAN, A. ROBERTSON, RO. L. COLEMAN, SAML. M. GARLAND, WILL JOPLING,
CORNL. SALE, ABRAM CARTER.
Book 6, Page 323 -- Sheriff -- August 20, 1822, as to various duties;
bondsmen, same as above.
Book 6, Page 370 -- Sheriff -- July 21, 1823. Bondsmen: LEONARD
HENLEY, BENJ. TALIAFERRO, ABRAM CARTER, A. ROBERTSON, JNO. COLEMAN,
SAML. GARLAND. Three bonds.
Book 6, Page 460 -- October --, 1823, written; June 21, 1824, probated.
Witnesses: VAN TRUMP CRAWFORD, JAS. POWELL, MATT W. WEBBER. Proved
by POWELL, June 23, 1824, and by WEBBER on next day. ARCHIBALD ROBERT-
SON qualified. Bondsmen: NATHL. J. MANSON and SAML. M. GARLAND.
Grnadson, JAMES MURRAY ROBERTSON, and my ux, RHODA - my children.
Executors: ARCHIBALD ROBERTSON of Lynchburg and my son, JAMES MURRAY
BROWN.

Book 6, Page 522 -- Inventory -- $6,842.25. PEACHY FRANKLIN, JNO.
DILLARD, CORNL. POWELL, October 18, 1824.
Book 6, Page 641 -- Administrator's Account -- A. ROBERTSON from
May 21, 1824 -- bill of JNO. P. BROWN; CRAWFORD's executors; ALEX.
BROWN; J. P. BROWN of Liverpool; Bedford and Campbell County taxes;
MRS. (?) BROWN; cash of HENRY BROWN and NANCY HIGGINBOTHAM; Lynchburg
property now occupied by family of DR. BROWN. January 16, 1826. JNO.
D. MURRELL and GEO. W. TURNER.
Book 7, Page 100 -- Administrator's Account -- A. ROBERTSON from
July 31, 1825 -- Bedford taxes; cash of FIELDING BROWN; MARY BROWN;
MRS. THOMPSON in Scotland. July 31, 1827. SAML. CLAYTON, commissioner.
Book 9, Page 217f -- Inventory of Charlotte County slaves, January 27,
1836. ARCHIBALD VAUGHAN, WM. SMITH, JNO. BOOKER. Another list of
January 7, 1836 - no total - JAS. BULLOCK, R. B. NORVELL, GEO. T.
WILLIAMS.
Book 9, Page 146 -- Administrator's Bond -- JAS. MURRAY BROWN, HENRY
J. ROSE, CHAS. B. CLAIBORNE, JOS. K. IRVING, December 21, 1835, for
JAS. MURRAY BROWN.
Book 10, Page 65 -- Slave inventory, $2,400.00, November 20, 1838,
PAUL C. BOWLES, GEO. CALLOWAY, WM. H. KNIGHT.

JEREMIAH BROWN -- Book 11, Page 453 -- Administrator's Bond -- JOSEPH
BROWN and DABNEY SANDIDGE, November 16, 1846, for JOSEPH BROWN.
Book 11, Page 484 -- Inventory - no total - February 15, 1847. WIATT
TUCKER, JULIUS SIMPSON, JOEL F. SMITH.
Book 12, Page 365 -- Administrator's Account -- JOSEPH BROWN - "Board
for one year for him and horse." April 21, 1851. JULIUS SIMPSON
and HENRY FRANKLIN.
Book 12, Page 478 -- Refunding Bond -- FIELDING BROWN and RO. WING-
FIELD, April 21, 1851, to JOSEPH BROWN, administrator of JEREMIAH
BROWN. FIELDING BROWN has received $70.00 since JOSEPH W. WISE, grand-
son of JEREMIAH BROWN has not been heard from for more than seven
years.

JESSE BROWN -- Book 5, Page 211 -- May 30, 1812, written; April 19,
1813, probated. Witnesses: PETER and MILLY WATERFIELD and PETER
CARTER. Brother, JOHN BROWN, is to administer. My sister, RUTH BROWN.
JNO. BROWN qualified. Bondsman: GEO. M. BROWN.
Book 5, Page 427 -- Inventory - $170.37. ABRAM and PETER CARTER and
RICH. HATTEN, August 21, 1813.

JOHN BROWN -- Book 2, Page 261 -- Administrator's Bond -- RACHEL BROWN,
WM. LAIN, wagoner, and RICH. ALLCOCK, February 6, 1786, for RACHEL
BROWN.
Book 3, Page 8 -- Inventory -- L 201-3-9, June 26, 1786. LAWRENCE
CAMPBELL, JNO. HIGGINBOTHAM, JOELL CAMPBELL.

JOHN M. BROWN -- Book 15, Page 464 -- Adminsitrator's Bond -- THOS.
WHITEHEAD and SAML. M. GARLAND, July 16, 1860, for THOS. WHITEHEAD.

JOHN W. BROWN -- Book 16, Page 533 -- Administrator's Bond -- RO. M.
BROWN and JNO. THOMPSON, JR., August 15, 1864, for RO. M. BROWN.

JOSEPH S. BROWN -- Book 16, Page 400 -- Minister's Bond -- no denomi-
nation set forth -- September 21, 1863. Bondsman: RO. W. SNEAD.
Book 17, Page 153 -- Minister's Bond -- August 20, 1866. Bondsmen:
WILLIS WHITE, JNO. W. JENNINGS, H. E. SMITH.

MARTIN BROWN -- Book 16, Page 494 -- Administrator's Bond -- THOS. A.
BROWN and JOSEPH BROWN, June 20, 1864, for THOS. A. BROWN.

PHEBE BROWN -- Book 5, Page 533 -- Error in index; see PHEBE BOURNE.

SARAH P. BROWN -- Book 16, Page 468 -- Guardian Bond -- JNO. THOMPSON,
JR., and M. H. WHARTON, May 16, 1864, for JNO. THOMPSON, JR., as
guardian of SARAH P. BROWN. No parent set forth.

STARK BROWN -- Book 1, Page 243 -- Guardian Bond -- JAMES GATEWOOD,
JOHN and GABL. PENN, April 5, 1773, for JAMES GATEWOOD as guardian of
STARK BROWN, orphan of WILLIAM BROWN.

Book 4, Page 16 -- July 4, 1800, written; March 16, 1801, probated.
Witnesses: D. PATTESON (?), HECTOR CABELL, JOSEPH CABELL. Probed
by HECTOR CABELL on probate date and by JOSEPH CABELL on August 17,
1801. JAS. MURPHY and WM. H. CABELL qualified. Bondsmen: JNO. LOVING
and HECTOR CABELL. Has been in partnership with JAS. P. COKE (COCKE
in some items) from January 1, 1798. Contract runs for 10 years and
agreement "about July 1, 1800" is cited. Longer liver may buy out
from heirs of other and BROWN now owns one-fourth of business in land,
slaves, and equipment. My brother, JAMES BROWN; brother-in-law, CALEB
SAIL, near Winchester, Virginia; ABSALOM BEADD, Washington County,
Pennsylvania; to ALCEY BETHEL, daughter of JOHN BEHTEL, Amherst County,
and her daughter. Executors: JAS. MURPHY and WM. A. CABELL. MURPHY
qualified.
Book 4, Page 32 -- Inventory -- L 15-1-3, October 30, 1801. WILL
LOVING, DAVID TRAIL, PAREMENAS BRYANT. Book 4, Page 333 is Administrator's Bond - see above.
Book 4, Page 587 -- Administrator's Account -- L 17-7-3, JAS. MURPHY
from February 1810. JAMES P. COCKE paid for interest and profits to
date. JAMES HALL for making black walnut coffin -- L 4-10. Account
of DR. JAMES M. BROWN. Total: L 545-3-3, June 3, 1809. CHAS. YANCY,
NELSON ANDERSON, S. (L.) CROSTHWAIT.

THOMAS A. BROWN -- Book 13, Page 366 -- Commissionerof Revenue --
July 17, 1854. Bondsman: CHAS. H. MASSIE.
Book 14, Page 593 -- Commissioner of Revenue -- July 20, 1858.
Bondsman: GEO. H. DAMERON.
Book 16, Page 533 -- Commissioner of Revenue -- July 18, 1864.
Bondsman: RO. A. PENDLETON.

THOMAS R. BROWN -- Book 15, Page 251 -- Administrator's Bond --
September 19, 1859, JOHN R. (B.) ROBERTSON and A. F. ROBERTSON for
JOHN ROBERTSON. (Two pages bear the same number.)

WILLIS BROWN -- Book 6, Page 90 -- Administrator's Bond -- THOS. BROWN
and THOS. ALDRIDGE,September 20, 1819, for THOS. BROWN.
Book 6, Page 493 -- Administrator's Bond -- JOSEPH and FIELDING BROWN,
November 16, 1824, for JOSEPH BROWN.
Book 6, Page 537 -- Administrator's Bond -- Same men and data as
Page 493, January 17, 1825, for JOSEPH BROWN.
Book 6, Page 656 -- Inventory -- slave girl at $250.00, March 14, 1826.
ALLEN BLAIR, MOSES PHILLIPS, PEYTON KEITH.
Book 11, Page 201 -- Administrator's Account -- November 15, 1843,
JOSEPH BROWN - $59.82. JNO. H. FUQUA, CHAS. MASSIE; recorded Decem-
ber 18, 1843.

WILLIAM H. BROWNING -- Book 24, Page 192 -- May 20, 1873, written;
November 12, 1915, probated, Culpeper County, Virginia; recorded in
Amherst, November 19, 1915. Culpeper clerk, W. E. COONS, certified
that it is in Will Book W, Page 471. Witnesses signed June 16, 1873.
They were R. R. DUNCAN and J. S. EGGBORN. Executors are to carry out
pre-nuptial agreement between present ux and myself. Brother, JAMES
A. BROWNING; have advanced large sums to estate of CHAS. SMITH; my
sister, MILDRED SMITH and children; part of Boston estate on east of
road from Boston to Mt. Olivet; three daughters of MILDRED J. SMITH -
she is executress of CHAS. SMITH; HARRY GRIMSLEY, son of ELIZA A.
GRIMSLEY, who is now ux of KENNDOLPH CORDER of West Virginia; housekeeper, MRS. SARAH GUARD. Six parts to children of deceased sister,
ELIZ. TELLENS, or heirs of any dead; one-fourth to LUCY A. FINKS, who
was LUCY A. McQUEEN; sister, MILDRED J. SMITH or children, if dead;
sister, ANN KINSEY, or heirs; one-half to ELIZA A. SMITH, who was
ELIZA A. KINSEY, or heirs; one-half to the other children; brother,
JAS. A. BROWNING, or children, if dead; children of my deceased sister,
TABITHA SMITH. If I have children by present ux. COTTON FARRAR, of
color. Executors: CORNL. SMITH and also to be guardian of my child
or children, and JAS. A. BROWNING and SAML. A. GRIMSLEY.

SARAH JANE BRYAN -- Book 14, Page 213 -- Administrator's Bond -- WM. M.
BRYAN, November 17, 1856.

28

Book 14, Page 221 -- July 13, 1856, written; Monday, September 15, 1856, probated. Witnesses: JNO. V. PATTERSON, RO.(?) H. TREVEY, M. L. BERRY; proved by TRAVEY and Monday, November 17, 1856, by BERRY. WM. M. BRYAN qualified. My two children: JOHN LETCHER BRYAN, and VIRGINIA PITZER BRYAN - my Amherst County land - when they are 21. Executor: my husband, WM. M. BRYAN.

ANDERSON BRYANT -- Book 3, Page 569 -- Inventory -- L 4-10-10-1/2. JNO. THOMPSON, SAML. EDMUNDS, JOSEPH LOVING,October 21, 1799. Book 4, Page 3 -- Administrator's Account -- LANDON CABELL and JAS. MONTGOMERY fromOctober, 1799 -- L 3-1-0. MARTIN DAWSON, deputy of WM. CABELL, late sheriff. Balance of L 1-14-8 to legal representatives of BRYANT, February 16, 1801.

ANN PAKISS ROOKING BRYANT (BRYAN in some items) -- Book 1, Page 482 -- Guardian Bond -- JAMES WATSON and HENRY CHRISTIAN, July 5, 1779, for JAMES WATSON as guardian of ANN PAKISS (?) ROOKINGS BRYAN and orphan of BENJ. BRYAN. Book 1, Page 528 -- Guardian's Account -- JAS. WATSON, September 4, 1780, for his wards, ANN ROOKING BRYAN, and her brother, WM. BRYANT. From November 8, 1779. Book 2, Page 137 -- Guardian's Account by WATSON, February, 1779.

PAMELIA BRYANT (Indexed as PARMELIA and incorrectly as, Book 4, Page 118) -- Book 6, Page 118 -- Guardian's Bond -- MICAJAH NOEL and JNO. D. CRAWFORD, June 17, 1820, for MICAJAH NOEL as guardian of PAMELIA BRYANT, orphan of -----.

PARMENAS BRYANT -- Book 3, Page 513 -- Tobacco Inspector -- Tye River Warehouse, October 16, 1797. Bondsman: LANDON CABELL. Book 4, Page 243 -- Indexed as Tobacco Inspector, but not there. Book 4, Page 251 -- Tobacco Inspector -- September 20, 1802, Tye River. Bondsman: DAVIS S. GARLAND.

WILLIAM BRYANT (BRYAN) -- Book 1, Page 483 -- Guardian Bond -- JAS. WATSON and HENRY CHRISTIAN, July 5, 1779, for JAS. WATSON as guardian of WM. BRYAN, orphan of BENJ. BRYAN. Book 1, Page 528 -- Guardian's Account by JAS. WATSON, November 8, 1779. Book 2, Page 22 -- Guardian's Account by JAS. WATSON, September 3, 1781. Book 2, Page 73 -- Guardian's Account by JAS. WATSON, August 5, 1783. Book 2, Page 135 -- Guardian's Account by JAS. WATSON -- Amount received from WM. BLUNT. February --, 1783.

DAVID BUCHANAN -- Book 8, Page 373 -- Estate Commitment to Sheriff -- November 20, 1833. EDMD. WINSTON, Sheriff.

WILLIAM L. BUCKLEY (Indexed as PURSLEY) -- Book 4, Page 409 -- Administrator's Bond -- WM. PURSLEY and JOSEPH ANDERSON, July 15, 1805, for WM. PURSLEY. Book 4, Page 222 -- Inventory -- L 119-16-6, February25, 1806. JAC. TYREE, MOSES PHILLIPS, THOS. CLASBY.

SHEROD BUGG -- Book 4, Page 453 -- Constable -- June 20, 1803. Bondsmen: P. MARTIN, LEWIS DAVIS.

Book 4, Page 456 -- Constable -- June 18, 1805. Bondsman: WIATT POWELL. Book 4, Page 465 -- Constable -- June 15, 1807. Bondsman: WM. EVANS. Book 4, Page 489 -- Constable -- June 19, 1809. Bondsman: WM. HOWARD.

ALFRED BURFORD -- Book 13, Page 181 -- Administrator's Bond -- JACKSON L. (S.) BURFORD and GEO. PATTESON, May 16, 1853, for JACKSON BURFORD.

AMANDA G. BURFORD -- Book 8, Page 342 -- Guardian Bond -- GEO. OLD and WILLIS M. REYNOLDS, August 19, 1833, for GEO. OLD as guardian of AMANDA G.; ANN M., MARY E., and HUGH A. BURFORD, orphans of JOHN BURFORD.

Book 8, Page 414 -- Guardian Bond -- RICH. BURFORD and ELIJAH FLETCHER, June 16, 1834, for RICH. BURFORD as guardian of same orphans as above (Book 8, Page 342).
Book 9, Page 139 -- Guardian Bond -- SYLVESTER BURFORD and WILLIS M. REYNOLDS, January 18, 1836, for SYLVESTER BURFORD as guardian of AMANDA BURFORD (no G employed here), orphan of AMBROSE BURFORD.

AMBROSE BURFORD -- Book 9, Page 135 -- Administrator's Bond -- NANCY BURFORD, WM. TUCKER, and WILLIS M. REYNOLDS, November 16, 1835, for NANCY BURFORD.
Book 9, Page 213 -- Inventory -- $4,445.52 -- at late dwelling, December 3, 1835. WIATT PETTYJOHN, RO. RIDGWAY, GEO. W. PETTYJOHN.
Book 9, Page 252ff. Division: NANCY BURFORD, widow; lots to SILVESTER and GUSTAVUS BURFORD; BENJ. McCARY in right of ux, CATHERINE; MARTHA and AMANDA BURFORD; MICAJAH CLARK in right of ux, DELILAH; JAMES C. BURFORD; THEMUTHIS (?) BURFORD; infant children of MATILDA TINSLEY, deceased; ARCHELUS COX in right of ux, JULIANN. November 21, 1836. Also Administrator's Account -- NANCY BURFORD - from November 21, 1835. Recorded November 21, 1836. WIATT PETTYJOHN, ISAAC R. REYNOLDS, RO. RIDGWAY.
Book 18, Page 376f -- March 23, 1860, written; October 20, 1873, probated. Witnesses: RO. L. COLEMAN, PAULUS POWELL. MATILDA BURFORD qualified November 18, 1873. Bondsmen: THOS. H. BURFORD, DANL. F. M. BURFORD. Ux, MATILDA; SEATON STINNETT, who married my daughter, LUCY, and children; WM. STINNET, who married my daughter, ANN, and her children; HIRAM McGINNIS, who married my daughter, EMOLINE, and her children; A. DABNEY WHITTEN, who married my daughter, SALLIE, and her children; son, JAMES N. BURFORD, and his children; my unfortunate son, AMBROSE BURFORD.
Book 18, Page 407 -- Inventory -- March 16, 1874 - $195.25. J. BURLEY, JNO. S. LAVENDER, JNO. W. WHITTEN.

CAROLINE BURFORD -- Book 4, Page 496 -- Guardian Bond -- AMBROSE BURFORD and NELSON C. DAWSON, January 18, 1808, for Administrator's Bond as guardian of CAROLINE and POWHATAN BURFORD, orphans of ARCHS. BURFORD, deceased.

CATHERINE BURFORD -- Book 11, Page 87 -- Guardian Bond -- JAS. DOUD and CHAS. WINGFIELD, October 17, 1842, for JAS. DOUD as guardian of CATHERINE BURFORD, orphan of JAMES BURFORD, deceased.

DANIEL BURFORD -- Book 3, Page 48f -- May 1, 1787, written; July 2, 1787, probated. Witnesses: JNO. CREWS, ABEL and NOEL BLANKENSHIP. JNO. STEWART qualified on probate date. Bondsman: JOHN CABELL. Aged and infirm; daughter, VIRGINIA TAYLOR - 250 acres - her natural son, FLOYD BURFORD, and all of her children; granddaughter, MOURNING BURFORD STEWART; sons: JOHN and DANIEL BURFORD; daughter, MILLY CREWS; daughter, FRANCES GOODWIN; daughter, ELIZ. GOODWIN. Executors: Sons, JOHN and DANIEL and JOHN STEWART.
Book 3, Page 53 -- Inventory -- L 431-13-9 -- September 1, 1787. DAVID WOODROOF, JAS. LIVELY, JAS. CREWS.
Book 5, Page 75 -- Administrator's Bond -- ELIAS WILLS, NICHL. HARRISON, WILLIAM SHELTON, WM. BURFORD, and SPENCER NORVELL, August 11, 1811, for ELIAS WILLS.
Book 5, Page 104 -- Inventory -- $4,555.13, September --, 1811; recorded June 15, 1812. NELSON C. DAWSON, PLEASANT DAWSON, EDWD. TINSLEY.
Book 8, Page 342 -- Estate Commitment to Sheriff -- August term, 1833; EDMD. WINSTON, Sheriff.

ELIZA ANN BURFORD -- Book 6, Page 479 -- Guardian Bond -- JAS. WRIGHT, CHAS. MAYS, and WM. DAY, August 16, 1824, for JAS. WRIGHT as guardian of ELIZA ANN BURFORD, orphan of JOHN L. BURFORD.

GEORGE H. BURFORD -- Book 4, Page 485 -- Guardian Bond -- AMBROSE RUCKER and WM. WARE, December 21, 1807, for AMBROSE RUCKER as guardian of GEO. H. BURFORD, orphan of PHILIP BURFORD, deceased.
Book 12, Page 204 -- Administrator's Bond -- RO. M. BROWN and JNO. THOMPSON, JR., August 20, 1849, for RO. BROWN.

Book 12, Page 573 -- Administrator's Account -- RO. M. BROWN from August 20, 1849. Suit: McDANIEL vs. DAWSON and QUARLES. Recorded February 7, 1852.
Book B, Page 12 -- Estate Commitment to Sheriff -- Wednesday, September 5, 1838. Motion of GEO. McDANIEL; JNO. COLEMAN, Sheriff.

JAMES BURFORD -- Book 5, Page 33 -- October 14, 1790, written; October 21, 1811, probated. Witnesses: THOS. RIDGWAY, Q. SIMMOND, JAS. TAYLOR, JNO. MERRIT. Proved by TAYLOR and MERRIT. WM. BURFORD renounced administrator. JAS. WARE qualified. Bondsmen: HENRY BALLENGER and REUBEN PENDLETON. My ux and children; executor: my brother, WILLIAM BURGORD. Administrator's Bond is on Page 83.
Book 5, Page 85 -- Guardian Bond (Indexed in Master for POLLY BURFORD, but an incomplete item. In front of book it is indexed for heirs of JAMES BURFORD.) It is a Guardian Bond on October 21, 1811, wherein JAMES WARE and RICH. BURKS are bonded for JAMES WARE as guardian of -----.
Book 5, Page 97 -- Inventory -- $2,068.99 -- WM. SHELTON, DAVID TINSLEY, and NELSON C. DAWSON; but dates do not jibe for it is reported as being of November 5, 1812, and recorded March 16, 1812.
Book 6, Page 78 -- Administrator's Account -- JAMES WARE from April 8, 1811. MRS. MARY (POLLY) BURFORD, widow, was chief buyer at sale and "most of legatees" were on her bond. Division by consent. NELSON C. DAWSON, AMBROSE RUCKER, WM. SHELTON, June 21, 1819.
Book 6, Page 80 -- Division: MARY BURFORD, widow; seven legatees mentioned, but more named: JAMES, REUBEN, ROBT. McCALPHIN for ux, WILLIAM, AMBROSE R., JOSEPH McCARY for ux, SOPHIA, GABRIEL GORNEY (?) for ux, WINNEY. These did not share because of previous dividends: DANIEL L., JAMES SMITH and ux, NANCY, JAMES BENNETT and ux, BETSY. Amount due estate from estate of COL. AMBROSE RUCKER, June 21, 1819. Commissioner same as above in Book 6, Page 78. Seven legatees have loaned mother money.

JAMES C. BURFORD -- Book 10, Page 33 -- Inventory -- December 30, 1837. ZACH. TINSLEY, administrator - $103.06. GEO. TINSLEY, JAS. BENNETT, THOS. C. BLANKS. Recorded July 16, 1838.

JAMES S. BURFORD -- Book 15, Page 49 -- Administrator's Bond -- R. B. TUCKER, W. C. BURFORD, and V. T. BURFORD, December 20, 1858, for R. TUCKER.

JOHN BURFORD -- Book 4, Page 482f -- November 1, 1807, written; December 21, 1807, probated. Witnesses: PLEASANT DAWSON and HARRISON HUGHES and proved by them. AMBROSE BURFORD qualified. Bondsmen: DAVID and GEO. TINSLEY, PLEASANT DAWSON, and HARRISON HUGHES. Sons: DANIEL and AMBROSE - 212 acres between them where I live; granddaughter, MATILDA NORVEL; late sons: JOHN and ARCHIBALD; ARCHIBALD's children: CAROLINE and POWHATAN BURFORD. Property by deed of trust, PHILIP BURFORD trustee, and bought by me. Daughter, MARTHA CREWS; children of deceased daughter, MOURNING HAM: YANCY, MICAH, and SALLY HAM. Children of deceased son, PHILIP: CYNTHA ANN HEADLEY, GEORGE, and PHILLIP. Executors: Friends: THOS. MOORE, NELSON C. DAWSON, and AMBROSE BURFORD.
Book 4, Page 493 -- Inventory -- 55-3-6. Recorded January 18, 1808. PLEASANT DAWSON, JAS. LEE, WM. HUGHES.
Book 6, Page 160 -- Administrator's Bond -- August 22, 1820, EDITHA BURFORD, REUBEN NORVELL, and NELSON C. DAWSON for EDITHA BURFORD and REUBEN NORVELL. (Note: This is probably for the JNO. L. below, but indexed for JOHN BURFORD.)

JOHN L. BURFORD -- Book 6, Page 89 -- Administrator's Bond -- SALLY BURFORD and WM. TURNER, September 20, 1819, for SALLY BURFORD.
Book 6, Page 96 -- Inventory $1,461.80-1/2, October 18, 1819. JESSE BECK, HENRY TURNER, WM. DAY.

MARTHA ANN BURFORD -- Book 9, Page 193 -- Guardian Bond -- JNO. FREEMAN and SYLVESTER BURFORD, January 18, 1836, for JNO. FREEMAN as guardian of MARTHA ANN BURFORD, orphan of AMBROSE BURFORD.

MARY BURFORD -- Book 8, Page 326 -- Administrator's Bond -- LINDSEY and WM. McDANIEL, June 20, 1833, for LINDSEY McDANIEL.
Book 8, Page 343 -- Inventory -- August 7, 1833. $53.37-1/2.
EDMD. PENN, HENRY L. DAVIES, JOSEPH EWERS.

MARY E. BURFORD -- Book 8, Page 342 -- Guardian Bond -- See AMANDA G. BURFORD.
Book 8, Page 414 -- Guardian Bond -- See AMANDA G. BURFORD.

NANCY BURFORD -- Book 12, Page 286 -- Administrator's Bond -- GARLAND H. FREEMAN and SYLVESTER S. BURFORD, September 16, 1850, for GARLAND H. FREEMAN.

PHILIP BURFORD -- Book 4, Page 483 -- Administrator's Bond -- ELIZ. BURFORD, DAVID TINSLEY, GEO. TINSLEY, and AMBROSE BURFORD, December 21, 1807, for ELIZ. BURFORD.
Book 4, Page 484 -- Guardian Bond -- ELIZ. BURFORD, DAVID TINSLEY, and AMBROSE BURFORD, December 21, 1807, for ELIZ. BURFORD as guardian of PHILIP BURFORD, orphan of PHILIP BURFORD.
Book 14, Page 87 -- Administrator's Bond -- RO. TINSLEY and ZACH. TINSLEY, April 21, 1856, for RO. TINSLEY.
Book 14, Page 533 -- Administrator's Account -- RO. TINSLEY; recorded April 20, 1858. (Note: These two items are indexed for POLLY BURFORD, but her name does not appear therein.)

REUBEN BURFORD -- Book 5, Page 198 -- Guardian Bond -- JOSEPH McCRAY, DANL. BURFORD, and ISAAC RUCKER, January 18, 1813, for JOSEPH McCRAY as guardian of REUBEN BURFORD, orphan of JAMES BURFORD. (See JAS. EWERS - Book 9, Page 255, for data on ux of REUBEN BURFORD and granddaughter of JNO. EWERS.)

RUTHY BURFORD -- Book 6, Page 655 -- Guardian Bond -- CHAS. MAYS and WM. DAY, March 20, 1826, for CHAS. MAYS as guardian of RUTHY BURFORD, orphan of JNO. L. BURFORD.

SARAH BURFORD -- Book 13, Page 352 -- Administrator's Bond -- WM. BURFORD, JOEL F. SMITH, and RO. C. BIBB, April 17, 1853, for WM. BURFORD.
Book 13, Page 397 -- Inventory - 172 acres; slaves, etc. - $3,576.63. WM. KENT, JNO. T. RODES, RO. C. MARTIN, June 10, 1854.
Book 13, Page 399 -- Sale -- W. A. BURFORD, administrator, July 21, 1854. BURFORD buyers: JACKSON L. and WM. BURFORD. No total.

SYNTHY H. BURFORD -- Book 4, Page 484 -- Guardian Bond -- WM. WARE and AMBROSE RUCKER, December 21, 1807, for WM. WARE as guardian of SYNTHY H. BURFORD, orphan of PHILIP BURFORD.

VINCENT F. BURFORD -- Book 17, Page 9 -- Administrator's Bond -- WM. C. BURFORD, SAML. M. GARLAND, and THOS. WHITEHEAD, January 16, 1865, for WM. C. BURFORD.
Book 17, Page 33 -- Slave inventory -- two -- WM. A. RICHESON and SHEFFY MILLER, January 20, 1865.

WILLIAM BURFORD -- Book 8, Page 327 -- October 1, 1830, written; June 17, 1833, probated. Witnesses: LAWSON G. WILSHER, SAML. MAYS, GEO. HUDSON, GEO. E. DEMASTER, ANDERSON J. MAYS. Proved by WILSHER, and on July 15, 1833, by MAYS. DANL. DAY qualified; bondsmen: JNO. DILLARD, LEWIS and CHAS. MAYS. Ux, SUSAN - 100 acres - other lines of adjacent owners: MUNDY, the spring; JESSE BECK, the mill - also 18 acres bought of WM. TURNER, SR. Daughters: MATILDA and heirs of FRANCES MAYS. SARAH BURFORD, widow of my son, JNO. L.; daughter, SARAH THACKER; daughter, POLLY PALMORE. Here he seems to be confirming gifts to deceased children: son, JOHN L.; daughter, SUSAN BEDDOW; son, WM. J.; CHAS. MAYS for services. Executors: friend, DANL. DAY, JAS. DAVIS, and JESSE BECK.
Book 8, Page 336 -- Inventory -- August 12, 1833 - $2,968.08 - WILEY CAMPBELL, JNO. SEAY, JESSE MUNDY.
Book 8, Page 340 -- Plat and division on order of July, 1833, court. JNO. PRYOR, surveyor. Borders of Stovall Creek, east side Glade Road;

6 miles from Lynchburg. Lines of JESSE BECK; CHAS. MAYS; JESSE
MUNDY; LINNAEUS BOLLING; JAS. COFFLAND; LEWIS MAYS; BENJ. WATTS. DANL.
DAY, executor. Commissioners: JNO. SEAY; LEWIS MAYS; WILEY CAMPBELL.
Tract of 372 acres with mansion. Lots to MATILDA MAYS, ux of LEWIS
MAYS; SARAH BURFORD and heirs; mill and house to MRS. SUSAN BURFORD,
as dower. Consent of heirs of FRANCES MAYS who was us of CHAS. MAYS.
Book 15, Page 52 -- Administrator's Bond -- W. C. and VINCENT BURFORD;
SAML. GARLAND; THOS. WHITEHEAD; RO. B. TUCKER, December 20, 1858, for
W. C. BURFORD.
Book 17, Page 14 -- Slave division -- December 20, 1858, to widow
and legatees. Met at home of MRS. ELIZ. BURFORD. WM. C. BURFORD,
administrator. Twenty-two slaves divided to ELIZ. TUCKER, ux of
RO. B. TUCKER; JOSEPHINE BURFORD; N. JACKSON BURFORD; P. D. (Called
P. BENJ. in one place) BURFORD; V. F. BURFORD with his administrator;
WM. C. BURFORD; Commissioners: RO. A. PENDLETON; WM. E. COLEMAN;
TAYLOR BERRY.

ADALINE BURKS -- Book 14, Page 84 -- Administrator's Bond -- CHAS. M.
BURKS, JNO. P. J. CARTER, A. C. FLOOD, and ED. P. DAVIS, March 17,
1856, for CHAS. M. BURKS.

C. M. BURKS -- Book 14, Page 131 -- Constable -- June 16, 1856.
Bondsmen: RO. W. SNEAD, S. G. CASH.
Book 14, Page 588 -- Constable -- June 21, 1858. Bondsmen: RO. A.
COGHILL and R. W. SNEAD.
Book 15, Page 308 -- Administrator's Bond -- ABRAHAM F. BURKS, JOSIAH
C. BURKS, NANCY C. BURKS, and M. B. SANDIDGE, June 18, 1860, for
ABRAHAM F. and JOSIAH C. BURKS.

CHARLES BURKS -- Book 5, Page 410 -- Slave description by CHAS.
BURKS - son of DAVID, January 2, 1814.
Book 6, Page 65 -- September 7, 1795, written; May 19, 1819, probated. Witnesses: JNO. GOODRICH, DAVID BURKS, RICH. BURKS, WM.
WILSON and proved by DAVID and RICH. BURKS. CHAS. and SAML. BURKS
qualified. Bondsmen: JNO. DAVIS and GEO. BURKS. Ux, MARY - 500 acres
and mansion house; three sons: CHAS., SAML., and RICHARD. My five
girls: ELIZ., MILISENT, LEVINSIA (?), MARY, and JANE. My children
are to be educated. MILISENT PARKS is to be credited with sums advanced. (Note: She married WM. PARKS in 1791.) When my youngest
son, RICHARD, is 16. Executors: friends, JOSIAH ELLIS and DAVID
BURKS. Administrator's Bond is Book 6, Page 76.
Book 6, Page 286f -- Administrator's Account -- CHAS. M. BURKS from
1819 -- Rockbridge taxes; WM. B. WALKER, $10.00 for making coffin;
J. (?) P. BURKS for harvesting; accounts of SAML. and R. H. BURKS,
March 1821. THOS. N. EUBANK, JNO. ELLIS, JAS. WOOD. Slave division -
very poor scribe in most of Book 6 and hard to decipher. Lots to
WM. PARKS. LINDSEY BURKS, LAVINIA WRIGHT, SAML. BURKS, RANSOM GATE-
WOOD, RICH. H. BURKS, CHAS. M. BURKS, SAML. BURKS (son to DAVID?).
Recorded July 17, 1822. THOS. N. EUBANK, JNO. ELLIS, MARTIN PARKS.
Book 6, Page 300 -- Inventory -- October 8, 1819 - $8,123.50 -
THOS. N. EUBANK, JNO. ELLIS, MARTIN PARKS.

CHARLES M. BURKS -- Book 6, Page 410 -- Administrator's Bond -- RICH.
N. EUBANK and R. S. ELLIS, November 18, 1823, for RICH. EUBANK.
Book 6, Page 413 -- Administrator's Bond -- NANCY BURKS and RICH. N.
EUBANK and MANSFIELD WARE, November 19, 1823, for NANCY BURKS.

DAVID BURKS, SR. -- Book 7, Page 153 -- August 17, 1822, written;
May 19, 1828, probated. Witnesses: MARTIN PARKS, NANCY PARKS, MARY C.
PARKS and SAML. G. PARKS. Proved by MARTIN PARKS and SAML. G. PARKS.
DAVID BURKS, JR., qualified. Bondsmen: JAS. DAVIS and MARTIN PARKS.
Sons: RICH. and DAVID, JR. - land bought of JNO. F. P. LEWIS and
where they live - except 7 acres around the mill. JAS. DAVIS' Spring
branch. Land on Piney Mountain bought of HENRY PEYTON. Sons: JOHN
and SAML. - the church tract; son, GEORGE - where I live and small
tract on other side of Pedlar next to where I live. Tract on Tobacco
Row Mountain called Tuggle's Place. Son, CHAS., land bought of
FRAZURE on head of Pedlar - 154 acres. Mill to my six sons: RICH.,
DAVID, JNO., SAML., GEORGE, and CHAS. Daughters: ELIZ., OBEDIENCE,
PHEBE. PHEBE had slave, but I bought it for $150.00 when she and her

husband were financially embarrassed. Heirs of PHEBE as long as she lives. Executors: sons, GEO. and DAVID. Administrator's Bond is Book 7, Page 155.
Book 7, Page 279 -- Inventory -- $799.76, June 12, 1828. CHAS. L. BARRET, WM. H. McCULLOCH, JOSIAH ELLIS.

EDWARD A. C. BURKS -- Book 12, Page 492 -- Guardian Bond -- DAVID and ZACH. D. TINSLEY, February 16, 1852, for DAVID TINSLEY as guardian of EDWARD A. C. BURKS, orphan of NANCY M. BURKS.

GEORGE BURKS -- Book 13, Page 352 -- Trustee Bond -- GEO. A. BURKS qualified in room of WM. MORRIS who declined to serve as trustee in deed of trust made by GEO. BURKS, May 14, 1830. Done on April 17, 1854. JNO. T. DAVIS was bondsman; by attorney-in-fact, SAML. M. GARLAND.

GEORGE G. BURKS -- Book 16, Page 105 -- Guardian Bond -- V. McGINNIS and RO. A. COGHILL, December 16, 1861, for V. McGINNIS COGHILL as guardian of GEO. G. BURKS; no parent set forth.

HENRY BURKS -- Book 4, Page 422 -- Guardian Bond -- WM. BURKS and ANDREW MORGAN, December 16, 1805, for WM. BURKS as guardian of his children: HENRY, ELIZABETH CABELL, NANCY ROBERTS, and WILLIS BURKS. Book 5, Page 70 -- Guardian Bond -- RICH. BURKS and WM. HARRISON, March 18, 1811, for RICH. BURKS as guardian of HENRY BURKS, orphan of WM. BURKS.

JANE BURKS -- Book 17, Page 39 -- Administrator's Bond -- RO. W. SNEAD and RO. A. PENDLETON, December 18, 1865, for RO. W. SNEAD.
Book 17, Page 63f -- Inventory - no total - CHAS. L. ELLIS, RO. N. ELLIS, Z. DAMERON, December 29, 1865. Sale, December 29, 1865. R. M. BURKS was only family name buyer. $182.35. R. W. SNEAD, administrator.

JOHN BURKS -- Book 14, Page 477 -- October 8, 1857, written; January 18, 1858, probated. Witnesses: JAS. L. RICHESON and M. B. SANDIDGE and proved by them. CHAS. Z. BURKS qualified. Bondsman: J. M. MILLNER. Daughters: NANCY, PALPATINE, MARY DAVENPORT, widow, and EMILY BURKS. Mansion house and 80 acres. Son, JAMES M. - 200 acres; sons, JOHN or JACK, RICH., GEORGE, WILLIAM, CHARLES Z., ANDREW J., DAVID and ALEXANDER BURKS and daughters, PHEEBY DAVIDSON and ELIZA ANN CAMDEN, have received shares so get $1.00 each. Executor: son, JAMES M.

LINDSEY BURKS -- Book 3, Page 66 -- Guardian Bond -- GEO. BURKS, CHAS. BURKS, KILLIS WRIGHT, WM. HORSLEY, and JNO. BURKS, February 4, 1788, for GEO. and CHAS. BURKS as guardians of LINDSEY, SARAH and ELIZ. BURKS, orphans of SAML. BURKS.
Book B, Page 73 -- Estate Commitment to Sheriff -- April 2, 1859, on motion of BOY MILLER (?). M. C. GOODWIN, Sheriff.

MARCUS (MARCEL in some items) A. C. BURKS -- Book 14, Page 443 -- Administrator's Bond -- CAROLINE M. BURKS and THOS. C. BLANKS, September 21, 1857, for CAROLINE M. BURKS.
Book 15, Page 123 -- Administrator's Account -- CAROLINE M. BURKS from April 29, 1857; cash to A. B. BURKS - two infant children - administrators as widow; EDWARD M. TINSLEY, present administrator, and RO. TINSLEY as attorney for administrator. ROWLAND BURKS, deceased - amount collected. Recorded March 21, 1859.
Book 15, Page 32 -- Administrator's de bonis non Bond -- EDWARD M. TINSLEY and THOS. C. BLANKS, September 20, 1858, for EDWARD TINSLEY (indexed as Book 16, Page 32).
Book 16, Page 268 -- Administrator's Account -- EDWD. M. TINSLEY, administrator de bonis non, from September 19, 1860; CAROLINE M. TINSLEY, widow, and in her own right. Children are of tender years. Recorded April 20, 1863.
Book 19, Page 308 -- Administrator's Account -- EDWD M. TINSLEY, administrator, from September 19, 1861. To board of BURKS' two children for one year. SARAH JANE and M.A.C. BURKS are names of children. Recorded December 18, 1877.

MARGARET JANE BURKS -- Book 14, Page 388 -- Guardian Bond -- June 15, 1857, WM. L. BROWN and BOB H. THORNTON for WM. L. BROWN as guardian of MARGARET JANE BURKS and MARSHALL BURKS, orphans of MINERVA JANE BURKS, deceased.

MARY BURKS -- Book 14, Page 522 -- Inventory -- February 19, 1858 -- $519.50. JAS. M. MILLNER, WM. MILLNER, WM. TOLER. Sale on same date - no total - BURKS buyers: PALPATINE, CHAS. L., JAMES and CHARLES F. Book 15, Page 173 -- Administrator's Account -- CHAS. Z. BURKS, administrator of JOHN and MARY BURKS - from 1858, but taxes paid in 1856. Legatees: JAMES, PALPATINE and NANCY G. BURKS. MARY was widow of JOHN BURKS. Recorded June 20, 1859. (Note: Another MARY BURKS is under Cash, MARY F. BURKS - Book 24, Page 170.) MARY of this 15 item is indexed as POLLY below when Administrator's Bond made.

NATHANIEL D. BURKS -- Book 9, Page 145 -- Administrator's Bond -- WM. L. BURKS and ELLIOTT WORTHAM, December 21, 1835, for WM. BURKS.

POLLY BURKS -- Book 14, Page 517 -- Administrator's Bond -- CHAS. Z. BURKS and J. M. MILLNER, January 18, 1858, for CHAS. BURKS.

RACHEL BURKS -- Book 10, Page 384 -- Estate Commitment to Sheriff -- JNO. D. DAVIS, administrator of GEO. MORRIS, deceased, made motion at November court, 1840, to commit estates of RACHEL BURKS, PEGGY DAWSON and BETSY MORRIS to sheriff.

RICHARD BURKS -- Book 3, Page 65 -- Guardian Bond -- GEO. BURKS, KILLIS WRIGHT, and WM. HORSLEY, February 4, 1788, for Guardian Bond as guardian of WM. and RICH. BURKS, orphans of SAML. BURKS.

ROLAND (ROWLAND) BURKS -- Book 9, Page 361 -- Guardian Bond -- ZACH. and DAVID TINSLEY, December 18, 1837, for ZACH. TINSLEY as guardian of SUSANNAH, J. D., SARAH ANN, ELIZ. B., GEORGE, CICERO, EDWARD, and ROLAND BURKS, orphans of ROLAND P. BURKS.
Book 12, Page 508 -- Guardian Bond -- EDWIN S. RUCKER and GEO. HYLTON, April 19, 1852, for EDWIN RUCKER as guardian of ROWLAND BURKS, orphan of NANCY BURKS.

SAMUEL BURKS -- Book 2, Page 163 -- Administrator's Bond -- GEO. BURKS, KILLIS WRIGHT, and JAS. EDMONDS, April 5, 1784, for Guardian Bond.
Book 2, Page 187 -- Inventory -- L 632-18-9. JOSIAH ELLIS, JNO. BURKS, CHAS. BURKS, August 2, 1784.
Book 3, Page 332 -- Administrator's Account -- GEO. BURKS from August 3, 1784. SAML. BURKS - part of crop in 1791 - amounts to CHAS., JNO., and DAVID BURKS, February 16, 1795. RODERICK McCULLOCH, JOSIAH ELLIS, WM. WARE.
Book 4, Page 66 -- Dower in estate of SAML. BURKS to HUGH McCABE and ux, ELIZABETH (widow of SAML. BURKS). Mentioned, but not named are heirs of age and guardians of others, January 17, 1803. RODERICK McCULLOCH, JOSIAH ELLIS, WM. WARE.
Book 4, Page 402 -- Tobacco Inspector, Amherst County Warehouse, November 18, 1799. Bondsman: ISAAC TINSLEY.
Book 5, Page 402 -- Same, October 18, 1813. Bondsmen: GIDEON RUCKER and MARTIN PARKS.
Book 5, Page 456 -- Tobacco Inspector -- Same warehouse -- September 19, 1814. Bondsman: MARTIN PARKS.
Book 6, Page 489 -- June 17, 1824, written; October 18, 1824, probated. Witnesses: RO. C. SCOTT, HENRY FARNSWORTH, JNO. P. (F.) SHELTON. Proved by HENRY FARNSWORTH and RO. C. SCOTT. BURKS qualified. Bondsmen: JAS. PETIT, MARTIN PARKS, and MARTIN P. BURKS.
Ux, MARGARET and children living at my death. Grandchildren: THOS. G. TUCKER, SAML. B. RUCKER, AMBROSE P. RUCKER, RO. H. RUCKER, MARY T. RUCKER, and MARTIN P. RUCKER. My daughter, NANCY, got sums during her life and they are to be deducted from RUCKER childrens' parts. Son, WM. L. BURKS; son, MARTIN P.; daughter, MARY D., ux of RUSSELL DAWSON; daughter, SALLY, ux, of GARLAND RUCKER; son, ROBT. H. BURKS; daughters: MARGARET and JANE BURKS. Executors: WM. L., SAML., and MARTIN P. BURKS.
Book 6, Page 491 -- Administrator's Bond. See will.

Book 6, Page 652 -- Guardian Bond -- NELSON TINSLEY and SAML. GAR-LAND, February 20, 1826, for NELSON TINSLEY as guardian of SAML. BURKS, orphan of WM. BURKS.
Book 7, Page 230 -- Administrator's Account -- WM. L. BURKS from October 25, 1824 -- to SAML. BURKS, JR., JNO. P. BURKS, SAML. C. BURKS, MARTIN P. BURKS' bond. Commissioners: NELSON C. DAWSON, JNO. R. IRVINE, and AMBROSE RUCKER, May 18, 1829. (Note: SAML. BURKS, bachelor, and PEGGY PARKS, spinster, got marriage license, December 21, 1789. WM. TINSLEY, surety. Consent of her mother, MARY PARKS, con-sent of ZACH. DAWSON, guardian.)
Book B, Page 73 -- Administrator's Bond -- SAML C. BURKS and J. DUDLEY DAVIS, March 29, 1859, for SAML. C. BURKS. Also motion of SAML. C. BURKS to appoint appraisers: LANCELOT MINOR, HAZEEL WILLIAMS, and R. W. SWAN, May 29, 1858.
Book B, Page 85 -- Administrator's Bond -- SAML. C. BURKS and JNO. A. HUNT, September 3, 1860, for SAML. C. BURKS.

SARAH JANE BURKS -- Book 14, Page 451 -- Guardian Bond -- CAROLINE M. BURKS and THOS. C. BLANKS, September 21, 1857, for CAROLINE M. BURKS as guardian of SARAH JANE and MARCUS A. BURKS, orphans of MARCUS A. C. BURKS, deceased.

JOHN B. BURRESS -- Book 2, Page 148 -- August 22, 1783, written; November 3, 1783, probated. Witnesses: THOS. BUCKNALL, REBEKAH MONTGOMERY, JANE TUGGLE. Sister, SUSANNAH NASH; nephew, THOMAS NASH -- 100 acres on Dutch Creek, until of age. Eldest son of JAMES MONT-GOMERY. Exeuctor: JAMES MONTGOMERY.
Book 2, Page 149 -- Inventory -- no total -- November 24, 1783. JAS. TURNER, ZACH. PHILLIPS, HENRY L. SORROW.
Book 3, Page 16 -- Administrator's Account -- JAMES MONTGOMERY - to SUSANNAH NASH, legatee; returned July 3, 1786.

CHARLES BURRUS, CAPTAIN -- Book 3, Page 407 -- May 1, 1795, written; January 16, 1797, probated. Witnesses: GEO. DILLARD, JAMES DILLARD, WIATT SMITH, MARTIN BIBB. Son, JOSEPH - land where he lives - over 400 acres and formerly land of PHIL and WM. BURTON. 1,200 acres in Cantucke (sic) and the right to be made by ISAAC DAVIS, the Elder, Albemarle; slaves; children of deceased daughter, FANNY PENN; daughter, MOLLY ANN CRAWFORD, and children if any. My four children: JOSEPH, ELIZ. PICKETT, PAMELIA BURRUS, and heirs of FANNY PENN. My grandson, CHAS. BURRUS PICKETT; daughter, LUCY CAMDEN, if any. He then refers to children again, but spelling is different in some cases: JOSEPH, ELIZ. PICKETT, PERMELIA BURRUS, and CAROLUS BURRUS or heirs. Son, CAROLUS, gets land where I live and also that bought of CORNL. SALE and JOHNSON, of Goochland - all joins mansion tract - 100 acres and 800 in Cantucke which is balance of 2,000 acres mentioned goes to JOSEPH. If JOSEPH died without marrying . . . ux to get genteel maintenance and to live with my son, CHARLES. Executors: son, JOSEPH, CAROLUS, and friend, PHILIP JOHNSON. (Note: I am of opinion that CHAS. and CAROLUS are two spellings for same son. I have done all BURRUS deeds for Mrs. Eugene Dickson of Los Angeles, and find nothing on CAROLUS. In Deed Book H, Page 193, June 19, 1795, SALLY BURRUS, widow of CHARLES, renounced will and claimed dower. Witnesses: W. S. CRAWFORD, JNO. CAMM. There is no marriage here of record for CHAS. and SALLY BURRUS. In Deed Book L, Page 53, October 22, 1807, CHAS. BURRUS, Amherst County, to POLLY H. and ST. GEORGE TUCKER, heirs of DANL. TUCKER, deceased. CHARLES seeks to carry out contract as an interested person and also as legatee of CHARLES BURRUS. CHAS. BURRUS in his lifetime executed bond of L 100, June 13, 1792, to heirs and administrator of DANL. TUCKER, deceased, to make good title to land on Buffalo - 100 acres - part of where he lived. It is that part east of Mobley's Mountain - 82 acres involved. Lines: top of the Mountain; CHAS. BURRUS; WM. CAMDEN; and DANL. TUCKER, deceased. CHAS. BURRUS, as legatee, conveys all interest for L 100. Witnesses: DAVID S. GARLAND, ROBT. COLEMAN, JNO. EUBANK, JR., ALLEN BUGG, and CHAS. A. JACOBS. In Deed Book C, Page 25, in 1769, CHAS. BURRUS, Albemarle, bought 433 acres on Bever branch of Buffalo from LEONARD TARRANT, JR. Tarrant derived title from WM. CABELL, JR.)
Book 3, Page 410 -- Administrator's Bond -- JOSEPH and CHAS. BURRUS, January 16, 1797, for both to administer. Bondsmen: RO. WALKER and THOS. MOORE.

Book 3, Page 432 -- Inventory of CAPT. CHAS. BURRUS, June 19, 1797 -
long, but no total. JOS. and CHAS. BURRUS, executors; and DAVID GAR-
LAND and RICH. OGLESBY.

PARMELIA BURRUS -- Book 4, Page 118 -- Guardian Bond -- Indexed as
such, but nothing on her on this page.
Book 4, Page 314 -- Guardian Bond -- JOSEPH BURRUS and RO. HOLLOWAY,
September 17, 1798, for JOSEPH BURRUS as guardian of PARMELIA BURRUS,
orphan of CHARLES BURRUS.

SALLEY BURRUS (SARAH) -- Book 3, Page 479 -- Allotment of SARAH
BURRUS, widow of CHAS. BURRUS, to dower, November 9, 1799. DAVID
GARLAND,RO. WALKER, LEONARD HENLEY.
Book 3, Page 399 -- Administrator's Bond -- HENRY and MICAJAH CAMDEN,
November 15, 1813, for HENRY CAMDEN.
Book 5, Page 402 -- October 8, 1813, written; November 15, 1813,
probated. Witnesses: WASLEY L. DUNCAN, POLLY J. (I.) DUNCAN, NANCY
DUNCAN. Daughter, LUCY CAMDEN; bill of HENRY CAMDEN is erased;
grandchildren when of age. Granddaughter, SALLY WOODFORKS CAMDEN -
slaves loaned to her mother, LUCY, and same for POLLY CRAWFORD CAMDEN.
Grandson, HENRY L. W. CAMDEN. These "four grandchildren" are again
named and also WM. and HENRY CAMDEN. Administrators: HENRY and
MICAJEH CAMDEN.
Book 7, Page 335 -- Administrator's Bond -- WESLEY L. DUNCAN, WM.
DAVIDSON, HENRY L. W. CAMDEN, and WM. DUNCAN, March 16, 1830, for
WESLEY L. DUNCAN.

BETSY BURTON, MISS -- Book 9, Page 31 -- December 2, 1834, written;
December 15, 1834, probated. Witnesses: SAML. M. GARLAND, CHAS. H.
PAGE. My cousin, ANN MARIA MORGAN, at my request sold a slave some
years ago to DAVID WALKER. The slave is named PAULINA and to pre-
vent any confusion as to title, I now deed her to him. My brother,
GUSTAVUS BURTON; children of my brother, JESSE BURTON, and future
ones - until JESSE is 18. My brother, NEWTON BURTON; my sister,
ANGLINA PRICE, ux of LEWIS PRICE, and children - until youngest is
18. My cousin, CLEMENTOMIS IRVINE. Executor: DAVID R. EDLEY.
He qualified on probate date. Bondsman: ELIJAH FLETCHER. It is
indexed as being on Book 9, Page 38, but is not there. This data is
in will summary.
Book 9, Page 264 -- Administrator's Account -- DAVID R. EDLEY, from
January, 1835; certified in Lynchburg, July 2, 1836.
Book 10, Page 110 -- Administrator's Account -- DAVID R. EDLEY from
January, 1835; recorded May 20, 1839.

JAMES ALLEY BURTON -- Book 2, Page 115 -- Administrator's Bond --
HENRY ALLEY BURTON, CHAS. ROSE, and JAS. HOPKINS, August 4, 1783, for
HENRY ALLEY BURTON, but is signed HELEN HALLE BURTON.
Book 2, Page195 -- Indexed as inventory, but not there.

JAMES H. BURTON -- Book 4, Page 463 -- Constable -- June 15, 1807.
Bondsman: MATT. HARRIS.

NANCY BURTON -- Book 4, Page 168 -- ALEX. and ROBT. BURTON refuse to
serve as administrator of PHILLIP BURTON, February 14, 1805; JESSE
WOODROOF was a witness. NANCY BURTON, now NANCY DAWSON, stated that
under will of PHILLIP BURTON, now NANCY DAWSON, stated that under will
of PHILLIP BURTON, November 2, 1801, she was given certain slaves and
land privileges. Land on Harris Creek and in Bedford. She renounced
will and demands rights, February 16, 1805. Witnesses: JESSE WOOD-
ROOF and DANL. NORCUTT. (Note: Was she NANCY ANN JONES? In Order
Book, 1782-84, is minister's return by CHAS. CLAY. Therein PHILIP
BURTON, bachelor, and ANN JONES, spinster, were married by him on
October 30, 1783. NANCY was evidently bitter about her husband's
will because she was only given life estate in land and slaves. He
had a natural son, PATRICK CLAYTON, and leaves NANCY's share to him
at her death. She is called NANCY SIMPSON in will.)

PHILLIP BURTON -- Book 4, Page 164 -- November 2, 1891, written; December 17, 1804, probated. Witnesses: THOS. MOORMAN, JESSE JONES, REUBEN CRAWFORD, HEN. HOLLOWAY, WM. B. BANKS, GEO. CABELL, THOS. HIGGINBOTHAM, and HENRY RIVES. Ux, NANCY SIMPSON BURTON - life estate in slaves and land in Bedford and on Harris Creek in Amherst. At her death her interest goes to my natural son, PATRICK CLAYTON, son of NANCY CLAYTON. All other land goes to PATRICK CLAYTON. Executors: friends, ALEX. and ROBT. BURTON and we learn from Book 4, Page 168, that they declined to serve. May court, 1805, administrator granted to NELSON C. DAWSON.
Book 4, Page 185 -- Inventory -- May 28, 1805 - L 1719-19-10 (?) -- WM. SHELTON, RICH. POWELL, JAMES LEE. Pages are numbered wrong here - 185 on one side and 187 on the other.
Book 4, Page 402 -- Administrator's Bond -- NELSON C. DAWSON, PLEASANT DAWSON, HENRY TURNER, REUBEN RUCKER, ISAAC RUCKER, and JNO. McDANIEL, May 20, 1805, for NELSON C. DAWSON to administrator. On same page is Guardian Bond, May 20, 1805, for JNO. W. CLAYTON, WM. WARE, DANL. TUCKER, GEO. DOUGLAS, GEO. DILLARD, and LEONARD HENLEY for JNO. W. CLAYTON as guardian of PATRICK CLAYTON, natural son of PHILLIP BURTON, deceased, by NANCY CLAYTON.
Book 4, Page 420 -- Guardian Bond -- JOSHUA SHELTON, WM. WARE, DAVID TINSLEY, NELSON DAWSON, ISAAC and ANTHONY RUCKER, November 18, 1805, for JOSHUA SHELTON as guardian of PATRICK CLAYTON.
Book 4, Page 500 -- February 15, 1808, JOSHUA SHELTON gave counter security on above bond. Bondsmen: PETER P. THORNTON, JNO. SHELTON, and NICHL. HARRISON.

WILLIAM BURTON -- Book 1, Page 524 (Indexed as Book 1, Page 522) -- Guardian Bond, March 6, 1780, GEO. PENN, DAVID SHEPHERD, and GEO. COLEMAN for GEO. PENN as guardian of WM. BURTON, orphan of WM. BURTON. (Note: WM. BURTON, bachelor, and FRANCES PENN, spinster, got license March 6, 1790. Security: EDM. WILCOX.

PAULINA BUSBY -- Book 8, Page 64 -- Guardian Bond -- MATTHEW BUSBY, ISAAC RUCKER, SR. and WM. McDANIEL, December 11, 1829, for MATTHEW BUSBY as guardian and attorney-in-fact for PAULINA, NANCY, MATILDA, and EDWARD BUSBY -- guardian for them and attorney-in-fact for MILTON, TILFORD, and DAVID T. BUSBY. Receipt for $617.50 from EDWARD and ROBT. TINSLEY, administrators of DAVID TINSLEY. There is also mention of fact that MATILDA and WESLEY BUSBY are TINSLEY legatees.

LARKIN BYAS -- Book 10, Page387 -- Administrator's Bond -- JAMES BYAS and JNO. D. DAVIS, September 20, 1841, for JAMES BYAS.
Book 10, Page 399 -- Inventory, $1,708.92 -- JAS. B. DAVIS, LINDSEY DAVIS, ARCHIBALD REYNOLDS. Recorded November 15, 1841.
Book 11, Page 273 -- Administrator's Account -- JAMES BIAS, administrator, November 1, 1841. Sale and family buyers: JOEL, JAMES, REUBEN, ROLAND - $290.27. E. WOODSON MORRIS, clerk of sale.
Book 11, Page 289 -- Administrator's Account -- JAMES BIAS - to CORNELIUS BIAS - account and slave hire; debt of JOEL BIAS. Returned January 17, 1845. JAS. DAVIS, HAZEAL WILLIAMS, ELDRED W. MORRIS.

LINDSEY BYAS -- Book 10, Page 171 -- Administrator's Bond -- MATILDA BYAS, RODERICK WAUGH, and JAMES BYAS, November 18, 1839, for MATILDA BYAS.
Book 10, Page 255 -- Inventory, $799.00 -- PETER P. THORNTON, ARCHIBALD REYNOLDS, JAS. DAVIS. December 20, 1839.

PALENTINE BYAS -- Book 16, Page 104 -- Administrator's Bond -- R. N. ELLIS and SAML. M. GARLAND and December 16, 1861, for R. ELLIS.

MARGARET BYRNE -- Book 23, Page 434 -- February 13, 1897, written; March 15, 1897, probated. Witnesses: JNO. A. DAVIS, M. D. and RICH. GORMAN. Daughter, MRS. HARRIET MEEHAN (MECHAN?) and BRIDGET BYRNE. Executor: N. C. MANSON. He qualified on probate date.

-C-

ALICE WINSTON CABELL -- Book 14, Page 579 -- May 21, 1857, written;
April 5, 1858, probated. Witnesses: M. A. JAXE and L. F. GARLAND.
Of Tuscaloosa, Alabama - expectancy from my grandmother's estate; my
father, GEO. K. CABELL; my brother, BRECKENRIDGE CABELL; my cousin,
ALICE VIRGINIA GARLAND, daughter of LANDON C. GARLAND and LOUISA F.
GARLAND. Executor: WM. M. CABELL.
Book 14, Page 581 -- Administrator's Bond -- WM. M. CABELL and RO. A.
COGHILL, June 21, 1858, for WM. CABELL.

HECTOR CABELL -- Book 4, Page 442 -- Administrator's Bond -- RO. RIVES,
WILL and LANDON CABELL, February 16, 1807, for RO. RIVES.
Book 4, Page 446 -- Inventory -- $699.00; JAS. WILLS; WILL LOVING;
W. H. DIGGS, February 26, 1807.
Book 4, Page 523 -- Administrator's Account -- by administrator,
DR. JNO. CABELL; PAULINA CABELL; WM. CABELL - payments on negroes;
DR. GEO. CABELL; NICHL. CABELL; JNO. CABELL; FREDERICK CABELL; SAML. J.
CABELL; LANDON CABELL. May 17, 1808. WM. LOVING; WM. H. DIGGS;
S. CROSTHWAIT. This family is well treated in Brown's The Cabells
and Their Kin. There is much data in Nelson County, Virginia, too.
One is also cited to Perrin, Battle, and Kniffin and 4th edition of
their History of Kentucky, Page 809, for sketch of FREDERICK CABELL
who removed to my native Kentucky. If a reader lives outside of
Kentucky, and finds that your library has a second or fifth edition
of these Perrin, et. al., volumes -- or some other edition other
than 4th -- do not think that you are handling a revision. These works
are numbered editions, but I have never seen a revision. Each edition
deals with a different geographic section of the state and the 4th
covers Nelson, Washington, Mercer, Garrard, Marion and other counties.
They are regarded as the best source of Kentucky genealogy by many
authorities and I have my personal indexes of many editions. I have
released the one for the Sixth edition on Shelby, Spencer, Trimble,
and other counties.

JUDITH SCOTT CABELL -- Book 9, Page 243 -- Refunding Bond -- March 30,
1835, by JUDITH SCOTT CABELL and G. A. ROSE to CHISWELL DABNEY,
executor of LANDON CABELL. JUDITH has received legacy.

L. B. CABELL -- Book 16, Page 424 -- Slave Division -- owned by L. B.
CABELL and SAML. M. GARLAND, trustees for CAROLINE E. GARLAND,
January 18, 1864. THOS. WHITEHEAD, TAYLOR BERRY, W. E. COLEMAN.
Book 18, Page 99 -- Clerk of Courthouse District, June 20, 1871.
THOS. WHITEHEAD and EDGAR WHITEHEAD, bondsman.
Book 18, Page 203 -- Same type of bond, June 17, 1872; same bondsman.

LANDON CABELL -- Book 8, Page 388 -- Administrator's Bond -- CHISWELL
DABNEY, GUSTAVUS A. ROSE, JNO. M. OTEY, and JNO. ALEXANDER -- RO.
TINSLEY as attorney-in-fact for last two, January 20, 1834, for
CHISWELL DABNEY.
Book 8, Page 390 -- January 8, 1834; codicil on same day, written;
January 20, 1824, probated. Witnesses: SP. GARLAND, G. A. ROSE -
proved by them. My ux, JUDITH SCOTT CABELL -- many slves; Harris Creek
land bought of RO. H. ROSE, deceased. Three parts: to son, LANDON R.;
ROBT. HENRY; CHISWELL DABNEY, trustee for my daughter, ELIZ. PRESTON,
ux of WM. PRESTON, Botetourt County, and her children. If any of
them should marry before death of their mother. Executor: CHISWELL
DABNEY. Book 9, Page 12 is indexed for him, but nothing thereon
for CABELL.
Book 9, Page 113 -- Inventory -- long and interesting -- $18,685.99-1/4;
RO. RIDGWAY; JAS. LEE; JNO. M. WILLIAM. Books to two sons and receipt
returned. Widow's receipt for tobacco. Land on both sides of Harris
Creek. C. DABNEY, executor. August 17, 1835.
Book 9, Page 119 -- Sales, February 7, 1834 - $587.03-1/2, and
recorded August 17, 1835. Page 122, slave sale, March 1, 1834.
Family buyers: LANDON R., ROBT. H., and JUDITH CABELL. Certified to
Lynchburg -- JNO. R. D. PAYNE by JNO. M. OTEY, of lawful age,
May 28, 1834. Total: $8,994.00; plus others in separate list. Total
of both sales: $9,859.00.

Book 9, Page 243 -- Refunding Bond -- March 31, 1835. LANDON R. CA-
BELL and RO. H. CABELL to CHISWELL DABNEY, executor of LANDON CABELL.
LANDON R. has received legacy.
Book 11, Page 360 -- Administrator's Account by DABNEY from May 26,
1835. Trust fund for MRS. PRESTON and children. RO. H. CABELL, 1835 -
his folio; paid L. R. CABELL; JUDITH S. CABELL; ELIZ. PRESTON and
children - RO. H. CABELL, trustee; ABIDIAH F. REYNOLDS bought 544
acres from estate; ISAAC R. REYNOLDS in same account. Accounts with
different legatees: Pages 368-372. Certified: AMMON HANCOCK,
July 3, 1834. Recorded August 18, 1845.

NICHOLAS CABELL -- Book 4, Page 136 -- July 10, 1799, writte; codicil,
February 3, 1802; November 21, 1803, probated. Witnesses to will:
JAS. LOVING, JNO. JOHNSON, JESSE HIGGINBOTHAM, JAS. P. COAKE, JR.
Witnesses to codicil: D. R. PATTESON and LANDON CABELL. Son, WM. H. -
land bought of WM. RAY and patented land on Mill Creek; branch of
Mayo's Creek and land on Fluvanna where I live. Son, GEORGE; my ux,
HANNAH; son, NICHOLAS -- lots in Warminster; land where JNO. SCRUGGS
lives; son, JOS. C. - Albemarle land; WM. B. HARE and ux, ELIZABETH --
land next to NATHL. HILL and JNO. ROSE -- 4 houses and lot where they
live in Warminster; daughter, MARY ANN CABELL -- land in Albemarle
County and Augusta at Clair's Meadows; land on Pedlar taken in partnership with NELSON CRAWFORD; lots in Beverly near Wetham; slaves bought
of NATHL. W. PRICE to son, GEO. CABELL; My 4 sons and 2 daughters.
Executors: sons, WM. and GEO. and son-in-law, WM. B. HARE. MARY ANN
must have mother's consent to marry. WM. H. CABELL and WM. B. HARE
qualified on probate date. Bondsmen: GEO. and NICHL. CABELL, JR.
Note: NICHOLAS CABELL seems to have great dreams of Warminster and
its becoming a big town. My wife and I drove down the road which
borders the James River to see Warminster. There is a store operated
by a man named MOON and that is all that remains of the town. We
passed a few old homes as we drove towards the site and some more on
beyond as we drove towards Scottsville.

PAUL C. CABELL -- Book 20, Page 189 -- Supervisor, Amerst Courthouse,
June 21, 1881. Bondsman: EDGAR WHITEHEAD. Book 20, Pages 263 and
441 so indexed, but no CABELL data thereon.
Book 21, Page 162 -- Supervisor, as above, June 16, 1885. Bondsman:
JNO. L. LEE.
Book 24, Page 137 -- March 3, 1909, written; November 14, 1911,
probated. Witnesses: CARRIE M. GREGORY and S. V. KEMP and proved by
them. LOUISE CABELL, sole legatee, made motion for E. F. WALSH to
qualify. Bondsman: National Surety Co. by C. L. SCOTT. All to my
daughter, LOUISE CABELL.
        An earlier PAUL CABELL shows in Will Book B of old Circuit
wills; Page 7, May 5, 1836; September 5, 1836 -- written and probated,
respectively. Witnesses: WARNER JONES, ED. A. CABELL - proved by
them. MARY B. CABELL qualified on Friday, September 9, 1836. My ux,
MARY - land devised to me by my father, WM. CABELL, and small tract
bought of WM. SPENCER. My children. Ux to administer.

ROBT. H. CABELL -- Book 9, Page 242 -- Refunding Bond -- May 20,
1835. RO. H. CABELL and LANDON R. CABELL, to CHISWELL DABNEY, executor of LANDON CABELL. ROBT. has received legacy.

W. J. CABELL -- Book 14, Page 26 -- Administrator's Bond -- EDGAR
WHITEHEAD and RO. J. DAVIS, October 15, 1855, for EDGAR WHITEHEAD.
This is indexed for W. J., but WM. J. CABELL in data. I have pre-
pared index cards and this is really out of place, but would mean
changing a great many cards for the next item.

WILLIAM CABELL -- Book 1, Page 262 -- January 3, 1769, written;
June 6, 1774, probated. Witnesses: SAML. BURKS, RO. HENLEY, JNO.
HORSLEY, JNO. SAVAGE. Son, NICHOLAS, gets all of estate and to
administer.
Book L, Page 263 -- Administrator's Bond -- NICHL. CABELL, JNO. CABELL,
WM. SPENCER. THOS. MILLER on probate date for NICHL. CABELL.
Book 3, Page 466 -- October 7, 1795, written; June 18, 1798, pro-
bated. Witnesses: JAS. M. BROWN, JOEL THOMAS, DANL. CONNER, HENRY

READ. Eldest son, SAML. JORDAN CABELL -- land on north side of
Fluvanna - 1,640 acres, Shirley's Creek; Stephen's Creek, Haw Branch;
Ray's Old Path; NICHL. CABELL's line; bought of WM. RAY by N. CABELL.
Island of 9 acres - largest of the Swift Islands. Also 1,979 acres
on Rucker's Run; branch of Tye and formerly that of WALTER KING of
Great Britain. Son, WM. - land next to SAML. J. -- 1,605 acres;
lines of JAS. NEVIL; WM. HANSBROUGH's orphans; Fendley Creek. Buck-
ingham land on both sides of Shirley Creek and bought of FRANCIS
BAKER. 431 acres bought of SMYTH TANDY on north branch of Buffalo
and where Cabellsburg is -- to pay rent on tavern to my ux, MARGARET.
Son, LANDON - land on Fluvanna near dwelling of MRS. KEZIAH HANSBROUGH
and known as School House Ridge and Old Church Road - where there
was formerly a schoolhouse near head of the Pounding Mill Creek.
Woods' Island fishery and land on Piney, north branch, and includes
Crab Tree bottom. Top of Priest Mountain land; Buckingham land near
Seven Islands and later property of SAML. JORDAN, deceased. Son,
HECTOR CABELL - land in trust and to any issue. Sons named get my
sixth part of Albemarle Iron Works. Daughter, ELIZ., ux of WM. CABELL
-- land bought of the Commonwealth and was that of JNO. HAMNER of
Great Britain; Mayo Creek land bought of FRANCIS WEST and WM. AARON.
Daughter, MARGARET RIVES; daughter, PAULINE READ, my books. Execu-
tors: Sons: WM. and LANDON.
Book 4, Page 299 -- Administrator's Bond -- WM., LANDON, SAML. J.
CABELL, WM. B. HARE, and RO. RIVES, June 17, 1798, for WM. and LANDON
CABELL.
Book 13, Page 179 -- Administrator's de bonis non Bond -- April 18,
1853. N. FRANK CABELL and MAYO CABELL for N. CABELL.
Book 16, Page 380 and Page 390 indexed as Administrator's Account,
but not there.

DAVID CALDWELL -- Book 10, Page 367 -- Minister's Bond -- July 19,
1841. Protestant Episcopal. Bondsmen: HENRY L. DAVIES and BENJ. B.
TALIAFERRO.

DUDLEY CALLAWAY -- Book 11, Page 248 -- Administrator's Bond -- JAS. M.
CALLAWAY and JNO. MAHONE, October 20, 1844, for JAS. CALLAWAY.

GEO. CALLOWAY -- Book 10, Page 89 -- Administrator's Bond -- MAYO
CABELL and FREDERICK G. (?) PETERS, March 18, 1839, for MAYO CABELL.
Book 11, Page 80 -- Administrator's Account by CABELL from March 20,
1839. To PAUL C. CALLAWAY (so spelled) -- on-fourth of GEORGE's
interest in concern of PETER WILLS and Co. To ELIZA CALLAWAY -
guardian of SARAH C. and ELVIRA CALLAWAY. Account of MARY B. CABELL
in full. To WILLIS H. WILLS - one-fourth interest in concern of
PETER WILLS & Co. Recorded: July 18, 1842. Gold, silver, and notes
found in trunk of GEORGE - $1,055.87. Philadelphia trip; collected
by DR. CALLAWAY; borrowed money in Philadelphia on your way to the
south; To ELIZA CALLAWAY - your interest in estate of FAYETTE CALLAWAY.

JAS. CALLOWAY -- Book 3, Page 352 -- July 6, 1787, written; October 20,
1795, probated. Witnesses: JOS. DAVENPORT, JNO. LAMONT, GEO. COLE-
MAN, BENAMMI STONE. Ux, BETSY - lands, etc. Executor: Friend,
WM. S. CRAWFORD. He refused to qualify and ELIZ. CALLAWAY did so
and he was her bondsman by attorney, JAS. PENN. Administrator's Bond
is on Page 350.

BENJ. CAMDEN -- Book 13, Page 238 -- Administrator's Bond -- ALBERT
GANNAWAY, CHAS. L. JONE, CALVIN R. CAMDEN, & M. C. GOODWIN, October 17,
1853, for ALBERT GANNAWAY.
Book 13, Page 330 -- Inventory -- at home, November 25, 1853. Some
at Berr Planes (sic) Plantation: $1,167.00. CHAS. H. MASSIE, JAS. F.
TALIAFERRO, JNO. C. WHITEHEAD.
Book 13, Page 335 -- Sale, November 29, 1853 -- Family buyers: JNO. M.,
CAL. R., JNO. S., MRS. E. J. - $3,746.11 - someone has added the
figures with indelible pencil. Held November 29 and 30, 1853. Dis-
tributee list of divided articles and not sold publicly, but agreed
upon by them: JNO. M. CAMDEN, A. G. GANNAWAY, C. L. JONES, C. L. (D.)
CAMDEN, C. R. CAMDEN.
Book 14, Page 256 -- Administrator's Account by ALBERT GANNAWAY from
May 30, 1854. Decree of RHODA CAMDEN & CALVIN R.; JNO. M.; and,

41

JNO. F. CAMDEN - sale bonds; JNO. S. CAMDEN; widow's claims. One-fourth each to JNO. M., CALVIN R. CAMDEN, CHAS. L. JONES and ux; ALBERT GANNAWAY and ux. Recorded: Tuesday, December 16, 1856.
Book 18, Page 125 -- Administrator's Account by GANNAWAY from October 20, 1856. JNO. T. JENNINGS, legatee. May 1, 1871.
Book 21, Page 59 -- Administrator's Account by same administrator from April 1, 1882. To CHAS. JONES and JNO. M. CAMDEN and administrator. To each: $107.22. February 23, 1884; recorded, June 16, 1884.
Book 21, Page 147 -- Administrator's Account by same administrator, from February 25, 1885; recorded April 21, 1885.
Book 22, Page 440 -- Administrator's Account by same administrator, from June 15, 1884. Legatees: CHAS. L. JONES, JNO. M. CAMDEN, ALBERT GANNAWAY. Recorded August 22, 1890.
Book 22, Page 459 -- Administrator's de bonis non Bond -- C. J. CAMPBELL and CHAS. L. JONES, October 20, 1890, for C. CAMPBELL.
Book 23, Page 90 -- Administrator's Account by CAMPBELL, from October 31, 1890. Recorded: July 20, 1891.
Book 23, Page 114 -- Administrator's de bonis non Bond -- October 19, 1891. T. B. JONES and JAS. CANFIELD, for T. JONES.

BURFORD CAMDEN (BLUFORD in some data) -- Book 17, Page 38 -- Administrator's Bond -- THOS. WHITEHEAD, EDGAR WHITEHEAD, and RO. M. BROWN, October 16, 1865, for T. WHITEHEAD.
Book 17, Page 114 -- Inventory -- November 1, 1865, at residence. No total. WM. C. BURFORD, JNO. T. JENNINGS, LUCAS P. TYREE.
Book 19, Page 177 -- Administrator's Account -- THOS. WHITEHEAD, January 27, 1876. Tuition of children; M. C. CAMDEN for horse to work; widow; exemptions under Poor Man's Law; mutual guardian of her children. Farm. Recorded: July 17, 1876.

CALVIN R. CAMDEN -- Book 14, Page 392 -- Administrator's Bond -- JNO. M. CAMDEN, JNO. S. TUCKER, R. A. COGHILL, JAS. P. COLEMAN, August 17, 1857, for JNO. CAMDEN.
Book 15, Page 42 -- Sale -- November 24, 1857. Family buyers: JNO. M. and CALVIN R. CAMDEN: $4,741.22. JAS. P. COLEMAN, clerk of sale.
Book 15, Page 58 -- Inventory -- November 24, 1857; no total. HENRY LOVING, JAS. M. GANNAWAY, G. H. PAGE.

G. C. CAMDEN -- Book 16, Page 149 -- Administrator's Bond -- JANE CAMDEN and WM. B. TOLLER, August 18, 1862, for JANE CAMDEN.
Book 23, Page 191 -- Administrator's Account -- November 16, 1892; MRS. C. J. CAMDEN from July 20, 1862. PETER G. TOLER for burial expenses - $60.00 Account of BLUFORD CAMDEN; 1863 Confederate money appraised. Recorded: March 21, 1892. Note: The use of MRS. C. J. instead of MRS. G. C. CAMDEN seems puzzling, but when I release marriage data for CAMDENS from 1801 to 1854, it will be seen that he was GREENSVILLE C. CAMDEN and she was CHARITY JANE TOLER.

HENRY L. CAMDEN -- Book 21, Page 179 -- Power of attorney to WESLEY L. DUNCAN to receive from WM. A. RICHESON, administrator of THOS. TUCKER, deceased - slaves received in action by Court of Appeals confirming judgment of Circuit Court (Superior) in Amherst County in Wesley DUNCAN vs. HENRY L. CAMDEN et. al.; also, any sum due from Amherst County sheriff. Also, anything due from Plaintiff in suits vs. AUSTIN WRIGHT, administrator of HARTWELL T. PRYOR. June 14, 1849. Witnesses: ANDREW J. TAYLOR.

JNO. CAMDEN -- Book 5, Page 559 -- September 25, 1808, written; February 19, 1816, probated. Witnesses: WIATT DUNCAN, ELIZ. DUNCAN, BENJ. NOEL. WM. DUNCAN qualified; Bondsman: WM. BOURNE. My 4 daughters: ELIZ. GOODE, BARBARA KNOWEL, SALLY DUNCAN, EASTER CAMDEN -- these being part of my children -- land on both sides of Pedlar -- 270 acres. Panter Fall tract to be sold by WM. DUNCAN, executor. These have received shares: Sons, WM., BENJ., JNO. CAMDEN and AMERILER JONES.

JNO. C. CAMDEN -- Book 19, Page 357 -- Administrator's Bond -- JAS. M. MILLNER and HENRY E. SMITH, August 19, 1878, for JAS. MILLNER.
Book 19, Page 479 -- Inventory -- September 7, 1878 -- $89.00. W. L. VAUGHAN, G. C. LAYNE, WM. L. MILLNER. Sale, same date: $99.50.

Book 20, Page 155 -- Administrator's Account by administrator --
October 12, 1880, from July 30, 1878. Recorded February 21, 1881.

JNO. M. CAMDEN -- Book 17, Page 242 -- Trustee, RO. A. PENDLETON,
under deed of trust made by JNO. M. CAMDEN to secure creditors,
February 18, 1861 - slaves and delivery with sale account on that date.
Returned July 2, 1867; Recorded July 15, 1867.

JNO. S. CAMDEN -- Book 17, Page 509 -- Guardian Bond -- JNO. S. TUCKER
and ALFRED G. PETTITT, October 18, 1869, for JNO. TUCKER as guardian
of JNO. S. CAMDEN, orphan of RO. M. CAMDEN, deceased.
Book B, Page 62 -- April 12, 1855, written; March 23, 1857, probated.
Witnesses: N. N. MANTIPLY, RICH. H. VENABLE, HENRY LOVING and proved
by MANTIPLY and LOVING. SUSAN A. CAMDEN qualified. Ux, SUSAN A.,
to administer.
Book B, Page 64 -- Inventory -- August 1, 1857 - $481.00. DILLARD H.
PAGE, C. C. DILLARD, JNO. J. WHITEHEAD.

LEROY CAMDEN -- Book 6, Page 451 -- Administrator's Bond -- PETER G.
CAMDEN and SAML. P. DAVIES, April 19, 1824, for PETER CAMDEN.
ADA PROFFITT; ZELMA FULCHER; J. V. WARE, trustee for my husband,
JNO. M. CAMDEN, and at husband's death to GEO. TULLY FULCHER and
MATTIE GARDIE HITE. E. S. WARE qualified on probate date.

MARBLE CAMDEN -- Book 4, Page 259 -- Inventory -- L 2610-7-8 --
September 16, 1806. JAS. FRANKLIN and RO. WELCH.
Book 4, Page 418 -- Administrator's Bond -- November 18, 1805. WM.
CAMDEN. Bondsmen: WM. SLEDD and HENRY CAMDEN. Book 4, Page 521,
Administrator's Account from January 6, 1806. DAVIS S. GARLAND:
JAS. FRANKLIN; RO. WALKER. Recorded July 17, 1807. "Sallery" of
LEROY CAMDEN for assisting in books.
Book 4, Page 534 -- Administrator's Account by same administrator
and committee from 1808. Recorded October 17, 1808. Book 4, Page 627,
"Orphants" of MARBEL CAMDEN in account with WM. CAMDEN - tavern rent
for part of 1806. SARAH COURTS (?), guardian; lumber house rented
to LEROY CAMDEN. October 15, 1810; JAS. FRANKLIN; RO. WALKER; WIATT
POWELL.

MARY ELIZA CAMDEN -- Book 16, Page 375 -- Guardian Bond -- WM. L.
CAMDEN and H. E. SMITH, September 21, 1863, for WM. CAMDEN as guardian
of MARY ELIZA CAMDEN and PAULUS CAMDEN; no parents set forth.

MARY W. CAMDEN -- Book 7, Page 252 -- Guardian's Account -- JNO. WARE,
guardian from 1811; MAJOR WM. JOPLING for board; JNO. PRYOR for
tuition; MADISON WARE for tuition; chancery suit fee vs. MICAJAH
CAMDEN; executor made trips to Pedlar Mills and Amherst Courthouse;
division of WM. CAMDEN's estate and DABNEY WARE's name appears
several times. Amounts to ward in Lunchburg and Lexington at various
times. Amount paid to PETER CAMDEN; Children of the abbey; MICAJAH
CAMDEN as executor of WM. CAMDEN. Recorded June 15, 1829. ADDISON
and CHAS. P. TALIAFERRO. A long account and excellent data for
anyone interested in finery for woman of this time.

MICAJAH CAMDEN -- Book 5, Page 14 -- This is another illustration of
errors in the index. This is a HUDSON item and shows in H's in
proper place. CAMDEN was made guardian of LUCY HUDSON. 1810 item.

PETER G. CAMDEN -- Book 4, Page 428 -- Guardian Bond -- MICAJAH CAMDEN
and SPOTSWOOD GARLAND, May 21, 1806, for MICAJAH CAMDEN as guardian of
PETER G. and POLLY W. CAMDEN, orphans of WM. CAMDEN, deceased.

POLLY W. CAMDEN (Indexed COLEMAN) -- Book 4, Page 566 -- Guardian
Bond -- JNO. and WM. WARE, December 19, 1808, for JNO. WARE as
guardian of POLLY W. CAMDEN, under 14; orphan of WM. CAMDEN.
Book 5, Page 65 -- Guardian Bond -- JNO. WARE; CHAS. TALIAFERRO; and
DAVID TINSLEY, August 23, 1810, for JNO. WARE as guardian of POLLY W.
CAMDEN, orphan of WM. CAMDEN.

SALLY CAMDEN -- Book 4, Page 203 -- States that death of husband,
MARBELL CAMDEN, requires that administrator of perishable goods be

appointed. Not disposed to do it and asks that WM. CAMDEN, who is next of "kind" and most favored to favor interests of the Family be appointed. November 18, 1805. Witnesses: MICAJAH and CHRY (?) CAMDEN.

WM. CAMDEN -- Book 4, Page 257 -- Tobacco Inspector -- CAMDEN's Warehouse, October 17, 1803. Bondsman: DAVID S. GARLAND. Indexed for WM. CABELL.
Book 5, Page 214 -- May 14 or 18, 1813, written; June 21, 1813, probated. Witnesses: RO. L. COBBS; LUCY CAMDEN; SALLY DUNCAN. Proved by COBBS and DUNCAN. MICAJAH and LEROY CAMDEN made separate bonds: MICAJAH CAMDEN with bondsmen: JAS. GARLAND, JNO. CAMDEN. LEROY with bondsmen: WM. DUNCAN, JABEZ CAMDEN, WM. STINNET. Son, HENRY; grandson, WM. H. CAMDEN; son, JABEZ; grandson, JORDAN P. CAMDEN. Old Cove tract; son, MICAJAH CAMDEN; son, LEROY; my ux, SYBELL. Nine living children; granddaughter, NANCY D. GOODWIN; my five daughters: NANCY WHITEHEAD, PENEY (?) WHITEHEAD, SALLEY LEE DENT, ESTHER GOODWIN, SUSAN H. DUCAN. Land where I live to son, LEROY. To PETER GALETEEN (?) CAMDEN and POLLY WARE CAMDEN - Poplar Grove tract which was intended for their father; my Greenway tract; grandson, JNO. BELL CAMDEN, when 21; then to divide to NANCY T.; JNO. B.; and MARBELE CAMDEN. Grandson, JNO. WHITEHEAD; also FLOYED LEE WHITEHEAD; also JAS. WHITEHEAD, son of RICH. WHITEHEAD. My daughter-in-law, SALLY T. CAMDEN, widow of MARBELE CAMDEN, until her son, JNO. BELL CAMDEN, is 21 and then to NANCY T.; JNO. B.; MARBELE CAMDEN. Executors: MICAJAH, LEROY CAMDEN, and JNO. WHITEHEAD. Book 5, Page 225, Administrator's Bond - see will.
Book 5, Page 377 -- Inventory of WM. CAMDEN, The Elder; no total. September 17, 1813; DAVID S. GARLAND, RO. WALKER, JNO. SMITH.

WILLIAM CAMDEN, JR. -- Book 4, Page 251 -- Indexed as Inspector's Bond, but not there or in book index.
Book 4, Page 219 -- Inventory -- L 1027-12-3 -- June 16, 1806. WM. WARE, GEO. DILLARD, ROB. WATKINS.
Book 4, Page 404 -- Administrator's Bond -- MICAJAH CAMDEN, DAVID S. GARLAND, ISAAC RUCKER, June 17, 1805, for MICAJAH CAMDEN.
Book 5, Page 545 -- Slave division -- to POLLY W. CAMDEN and in possession of her guardian, CAPT. JNO. WARE. To PETER G. CAMDEN and his guardian, MICAJAH CAMDEN, June 20, 1811. HILL CARTER, RO. WALKER, BENJ. TALIAFERRO. Administrator's Account by MICAJAH CAMDEN from June 17, 1805. Cash -- not named as legatees - to JNO. W. and MARBEL CAMDEN; WM. CAMDEN; WM. COLEMAN for schooling; PETER G. CAMDEN; received of JABEZ CAMDEN; to LUCY CAMDEN; HENRY CAMDEN; JNO. WARE, guardian of POLLY W. CAMDEN. December 29, 1810. RO. WALKER; CHAS. and BENJ. TALIAFERRO.
Book 6, Page 681 -- Administrator's Account by same administrator, from 1813. Received of JABEZ CAMDEN; to SALLY T. CAMDEN; to LEROY CAMDEN; to HENRY CAMDEN -- by BURCHER and RICH. WHITEHEAD; by WARNER GOODWIN. April 26, 1826. BENJ. TALIAFERRO; ST. GEO. TUCKER; CHAS. L. BARRET.
Book 12, Page 108 -- Estate Commitment to Sheriff -- June term, 1849. Motion of WM. RICHESON, administrator of THOS. TUCKER; LINDSEY COLEMAN, sheriff. Note: One branch of the CAMDEN family settled in Woodford County, Kentucky, but I am unable to identify them. I am told by members of the family here that they think that this line went first to West Virginia and then into Kentucky. One became a state senator in Kentucky and the CAMDEN estate is just west of Versailles on U.S. 60.

DUNCAN CAMERON (CAMRON) -- Book 3, Page 322 -- Administrator's Bond -- HENRYETTA CAMRON; DAVID HUNTER; DUNKIN CAMRON (signed, but not named in bond), October 20, 1794, for HENRYETTA CAMRON.
Book 3, Page 323 -- Inventory -- L 89-7-4 -- December 15, 1794. GEO. GILLESPIE, GEO. CAMPBELL, BENJ. WRIGHT.

NANCY CAMERON -- Book 4, Page 375 -- Guardian Bond -- DAVID HUNTER and WM. KNIGHT, Setpember 19, 1803, for DAVID HUNTER as guardian of NANCY CAMERON, orphan of POLLY CAMERON.

POLLY CAMERON -- Book 4, Page 47 -- Nuncupative Will -- Testimony of
PLEASANT MARTIN, September 7, 1802 - She called him and observed that
she had some money coming from her father's estate. It should be
given to her child, NANCY CAMERON. SALLY COATS also heard her say
this. It happened on September 3rd. JOS. BURRUS, J.P., stated that
MARTIN swore to this before him, September 7, 1802. Admitted on
September 20, 1802. DAVID HUNTER became NANCY's guardian as noted in
her data. He married MARGARET CAMERON. REV. BENJ. COLEMAN officiated
January 8, 1784.

ELIZ. CAMM -- Book 6, Page 525 -- Guardian Bond -- BEN A. DONALD and
WM. L. SANDERS (?), December 20, 1824, for BEN DONALD as guardian
of ELIZ. CAMM, orphan of JNO. CAMM, deceased.
EMMA CAMM -- Book 6, Page 525 -- Guardian Bond -- WM. L. SAUNDERS and
BENJ. A. DONALD, December 20, 1824, for WM. SAUNDERS as guardian of
EMMA CAMM, orphan of JNO. CAMM.

JNO. CAMM -- Book 6, Page 27 -- Administrator's Bond -- JNO. WARWICK;
NICHL. HARRISON; HILL CARTER, August 17, 1818; no testator or ad-
ministrator named, but indexed for JNO. CAMM. A later item shows
that WARWICK was the administrator.
Book 6, Page 241 -- Guardian Bond -- ELIZ. CAMM; JNO. WARWICK; HILL
CARTER, and THOS. N. EUBANK, August 21, 1821, for ELIZ. CAMM as
guardian of ROBT.; MARY; SALLY; JNO.; EMILA CAMM - orphans of JNO.
CAMM.
Book 6, Page 510 -- Administrator's Account by JNO. WARWICK, from
November 27, 1817. Names of MRS. (?) CAMM, E. CAMM, M. or MRS. CAMM.
Land claimed by REUBEN NORVELL and reference to controversy between
NORVELL, MRS. CAMM, and administrator. September 4, 1824, committee
met at home of JNO. FRANKLIN at Amherst Courthouse and word ad-
ministrator is after his name. SAML. GARLAND for defendants: JNO.
ANDERSON; RO. CAMM; WM. L. SAUNDERS and BENJ. A. DONALD, adult repre-
sentatives of JNO. CAMM, deceased. Committee: BENJ. BROWN; EDMD.
WINSTON; WILL M. WALLER.
Book 8, Page 316 -- Division -- land on Salt, John, and Graham Creeks -
tributaries of James; intersected by Shelton's Road to Bethel; Trent
ferry road; road from Watts' Gap to Dawson's Mill. Lines of DAVID S.
GARLAND; GEORGE POWELL (Note: JNO. CAMM married BETSY POWELL in
1801); EDWD. TINSLEY; RICH. S. ELLIS; NELSON CRAWFORD; BENNETT A.
CRAWFORD; BENNETT tract; WM. I. (J.) ISBELL; SAML. BURKS' heirs;
WM. and JNO. SHELTON; JACOB HAAS (formerly NELSON C. DAWSON) and LEWIS
DAWSON. Tract where JNO. CAMM formerly lived and died. Order of
July, 1825, to THOS. N. EUBANK; WM. SHELTON; AMBROSE RUCKER; DABNEY T.
PHILLIPS; and PROSSER POWELL to divide land. Plat on Page 316. Di-
vided to his children and heirs. Lot of 25 acres for heirs of SAML.
BURKS, deceased -- sold to BURKS in lifetime by CAMM; 443 acres to
ELIZ. CAMM, widow; 236 acres surveyed by Lynchburg Chancery Order
in suit of JNO. ANDERSON and ux, ANNE, formerly CAMM, vs. THOMAS
LAINE. 182 acres on Salt Creek to ELIZ. CAMM, infant; Bethel Road
tract, 184 acres, to BENJ. A. DONALD and ux, SARAH, formerly CAMM;
210 acres to ROBT. CAMM. WOODROOF tract of 226 acres - to WM. L.
SAUNDERS and ux, MARY, formerly CAMM. York Road tract of 231 acres
to EMMA CAMM, infant. POWELL's tract of 190 acres to JNO. CAMM, JR.,
deceased, estate. 1,927 acres surveyed on July --, 1825, by JNO.
PRYOR. Recorded July 15, 1833.

ROBT. CAMM -- Book 6, Page 280 -- Guardian Bond -- ARTHUR B. DAVIES
and ELIJAH FLETCHER, March 18, 1822, for ARTHUR DAVIES as guardian
of RO. CAMM, orphan of JNO. CAMM.
Book 11, Page 97 -- Administrator's Bond -- JAS. M. COBBS and JNO. D.
ALEXANDER, December 19, 1842, for JAS. COBBS.
Book 11, Page 108 -- Inventory -- December 20, 1842, at late resi-
dence - $3,058.50. ISAAC R. REYNOLDS, WM. J. SHELTON, W. O. HARDIN,
WILLIS M. REYNOLDS.

BARTHOLOMEW CAMPBELL -- Book 7, Page 73 -- Administrator's Bond --
SAML. W. CHRISTIAN and LUCAS P. THOMPSON, November 21, 1827, for
SAML. CHRISTIAN.

BENJ. CAMPBELL -- Book 9, Page 431 -- Trustee bond, March 19, 1838, for LEVIESY CAMPBELL and CHILDREN. Bondsmen: WM. M. CAMPBELL, JNO. H. (?) CAMPBELL, WILL H. KNIGHT, JOEL CAMPBELL, LAWSON CAMPBELL.

DANIEL CAMPBELL -- Book 14, Page 437 -- Administrator's Bond -- WM. CAMPBELL and ABRAHAM MARTIN, October 19, 1857, for WM. CAMPBELL. Book 14, Page 584, Inventory, January 23, 1858 - $539.00. S. C. WATTS, WILKERSON WARE, C. C. DILLARD.

ELIZ. M. CAMPBELL -- Book 11, Page 103 -- ELIZ. M. CAMPBELL and ALEX. M. CAMPBELL to LEWIS S. CAMPBELL, administrator of WILEY CAMPBELL, December 21, 1842 - ELIZ. has received $719.92 as legacy. Recorded January 16, 1843.

F. N. CAMPBELL -- Book 16, Page 458 -- Administrator's Bond -- ELIZ. CAMPBELL and ROBT. L. COLEMAN, March 21, 1864. for ELIZ. CAMPBELL.

MRS. FRANCES CAMPELL -- Book 11, Page 89 -- Administrator's Bond -- JAS. CAMPBELL and GEO. W. CAMPBELL, October 17, 1842, for JAS. CAMP-BELL. Inventory of slaves and personal estate of MRS. FRANCES CAMP-BELL and helf (sic) for her life under will of late husband, JNO. CAMPBELL, deceased. Taken possession of by JAS. and GEO. W. CAMPBELL, executors of JNO. CAMPBELL -- $7,436.70, October 17, 1842. JNO. C. WHITEHEAD, WM. KNIGHT, J. B. HARDING.

FRANCES CAMPBELL -- Book 4, Page 352 -- Guardian Bond -- JNO. and GEO. CAMPBELL, July 19, 1802, for JNO. CAMPBELL as guardian of FRANCES CAMPBELL, orphan of JNO. CAMPBELL, waggoner.

FRANCIS JANE CAMPBELL (so indexed) -- Book 10, Page 49 -- Guardian Bond -- JAS. CAMPBELL, JNO. W. BROADDUS, and GEO. W. CAMPBELL, September 17, 1838, for JAS. CAMPBELL as guardian of FRANCIS JANE CAMPBELL, MARTHA, and RHODA P. CAMPBELL, orphans of JESSE CAMPBELL, deceased.

GEO. CAMPBELL -- Book 1, Page 334 -- November 1, 1776, written; May 5, 1777, probated. Witnesses: THOS. PANNELL, CHAS. PATRICK. Ux, MARGARET - where I live; daughter, CATHERINE; son, JNO.; Rest of my children: ELIZ., ARCHABALD, GEORGE, EDLEY, THOMAS, MARGARET and RUTH CAMPBELL as of age or married. If they abscond or entirely go off - Executors: ux and CHAS. PATRICK.
Book 1, Page 335 -- Administrator's Bond -- MARGARET CAMPBELL; JNO. HENDERSON; and ALEX. REID, JR., May 5, 1777, for MARGARET CAMPBELL.
Book 1, Page 362 -- Inventory -- no total, August 4, 1777. CHAS. RODES, THOMAS SHANNON, MICHL. CRAFT.
Book 3, Page 169 -- Probated February 7, 1791; no date when written. Witnesses: JNO. MASSEY; EDWD. CAMPBELL; JOS. DAVIS -- calls himself SENIOR. Daughters: SARAH, MARY, and CATY CAMPBELL (youngest) and she must "Weight" until mother's death for saddle. Sons, AMBROSE and JOEL when of age. My ux --. Executors: Son, GEO. and JNO. CAMPBELL.
Book 3, Page 170 -- Administrator's Bond -- GEO. and JNO. CAMPBELL, February 7, 1791, for both to administrator. Bondsmen: DANL. McDONALD and DAVID HUNTER.
Book 3, Page 176 -- Inventory -- March 29, 1791; GEO. GILLESPIE, JNO. MASSEY, BENJ. WRIGHT. No total.
Book 3, Page 575 -- Inventory -- L 378-9-0 -- April 21, 1800. JNO. HILL, JNO. CAMPBELL, BARTLETT CASH.
Book 4, Page 319 (indexed Book 3, Page 319) -- Administrator's Bond -- ELIZ. CAMPBELL, JNO. MASTERS, JAS. and GEO. CAMPBELL and JNO. CAMP-BELL, February 17, 1800, for ELIZ. CAMPBELL.
Book 4, Page 141 -- December 19, 1803. JOEL FRANKLIN, BARTLETT CASH, and NICHL. MORAN report that ELIZ. CAMPBELL failed to exhibit papers.

GEO. S. CAMPBELL -- Book 8, Page 286 -- Estate Commitment to Sheriff -- November court, 1832. Motion of SAML. GARLAND. Sheriff: NELSON DAWSON.

GEO. STANLEY CAMPBELL -- Book 24, Page 207 -- September 16, 1914, written; Wednesday, April 12, 1916, probated. Witnesses: W. E.

SANDIDGE and RO. H. DRUMMOND. Ux, MARY A., and my children. Ux
to administer. Produced by ux and attested by the witnesses. She
qualified.

GEO. T. CAMPBELL -- Book 14, Page 143 -- Administrator's Bond --
EADY CAMPBELL, S. H. WRIGHT, and A. J. WRIGHT, June 16, 1856, for
Estate Commitment.
Book 20, Page 229 -- Bowling & Co. vs. GEO. T. CAMPBELL's widow,
October term, 1881. Commissioners: HENRY LOVING, SR.; JNO. S. TUCKER;
SAML. M. WALLER; GEO. W. CAMPBELL. Lot 1 to EDDY B. CAMPBELL; lots
to H. H.; BENJ. M. and ux, JULIA CAMPBELL; A. M. BOWLING and ux, SARAH
J.; EDDY, widow, got 40 acres and house. Indian Creek land. Note
difference in spelling of her name.

HENRY CAMPBELL -- Book 1, Page 234 -- March 10, 1772, written;
December 7, 1772, probated. Witnesses: GABL. PENN, JAMES GATEWOOD,
ANDREW BROWN. Ux, CHARITY - where I live; son, JNO., one shilling;
son, AMBROSE - 100 acres next to GLEBE and where he lives; son,
AARON - 100 acres next to AMBROSE; son, JOELL - 100 acres where I
live; grandson, HENRY CASHWELL. Administrators: ux, LAWRENCE CAMP-
BELL, AARON CAMPBELL. CHARITY qualified with LAWRENCE CAMPBELL.
Bondsmen: JOS. CABELL and JAS. HIGGINBOTHAM.
Book 1, Page 240 -- Inventory -- December 22, 1772 -- GEO. PENN,
DUDLEY and JAS. GATEWOOD -- L 109-5-13.

JAS. CAMPBELL -- Book 13, Page 239 -- Administrator's Bond -- NANCY,
JNO. P. and RO. P. CAMPBELL and SHELTON H. WRIGHT and
EDWIN S. CAMPBELL, October 17, 1853, for NANCY CAMPBELL.
Book 13, Page 245 -- Senior here: September 8, 1853, written;
September 19, 1853, probated. Witnesses: WM. WRIGHT, BENJ. TALIA-
FERRO. Son, JAMES, who died in Kentucky--his three children: MAR-
CELLUS, NATHANIEL, and PERLINA MELVINA CAMPBELL - all infants. My ux,
NANCY; all of my children.
Book 16, Page 511 -- Inventory -- $1,717.00 -- HENRY LOVING, JAS. M.
GANNAWAY, JAS. F. TALIAFERRO, August 20, 1853.

JANE CAMPBELL -- Book 11, Page 19 -- Guardian Bond -- ANDREW FAUBER
and JNO. MYERS, April 18, 1842, for JNO. MYERS as guardian of JANE
CAMPBELL, orphan of ALONZO CAMPBELL.

JOEL CAMPBELL, SR. -- Book 8, Page 206 -- April 7, 1832, written;
May 21, 1832, probated. Witnesses: RO. and THOS. WINGFIELD; JOEL
CAMPBELL, JR. To NANCY MILLS - $100 per year, and may choose home
with one of my children. Son, WILEY; daughter-in-law, SUSANNAH, ux of
LEWIS CAMPBELL, and her children; daughter-in-law, NANCY, ux of
CATLETT CAMPBELL, and family; deceased son, CORNELIUS; deceased daugh-
ter, LUCY LIVELY, and their children when 21 or married. Daughter,
MILLY DINWIDDIE, and children, but nothing for her husband; daughter,
STILLY ALLCOCK. Executors: Son, WILEY, and friend, JNO. WARWICK.
WILEY CAMPBELL qualified. Bondsmen: CORNL. SALE and EATON CARPENTER.
Book 8, Page 224 -- Inventory -- May 25, 1832 -- $5,430.25 and $217.00.
WILEY CAMPBELL, executor; RO. WINGFIELD; JONAS PIERCE; THOS. WING-
FIELD.
Book 8, Page 237 -- Division of land on both sides of Rocky Creek and
lines of WILEY CAMPBELL; CHAS. WILSON: JNO. WARWICK; TERISHA TURNER;
heirs of NATHAN WINGFIELD. Owned by JOEL CAMPBELL, deceased. Sur-
veyed and divided on order of July court, 1832. Suit of WILEY CAMP-
BELL vs. CATLETT CAMPBELL, et. al. 464 acres. Commissioners: JONAS
PIERCE, RO. and THOS. WINGFIELD. To NANCY CAMPBELL, ux of CATLETT
CAMPBELL - and her children - 190 acres. To SUSANNAH CAMPBELL, ux of
LEWIS CAMPBELL - and children - 174 acres. July 28, 1832. JNO. PRYOR,
surveyor.
Book 9, Page 160 -- Administrator's Account by WILEY CAMPBELL from
November 15, 1833. N. CAMPBELL hired slaves; cash of L. and C.
CAMPBELL; cash to MILLEY DINWIDDIE for board of ANNA MILLS; JONAS
PIERCE; RO. WINGFIELD; J. PETTYJOHN, December 21, 1835.
Book 9, Page 363 -- Administrator's Account by same executor from
October 30, 1835. Many slaves hired out: MILLY DINWIDDIE for board
of NANNY (ANNA elsewhere) MILLS; to ELIJAH FLETCHER for CATLETT CAMP-
BELL's legacy; Cash to LEWIS S. CAMPBELL; to JAS. and JNO. DINWIDDIE.

Recorded December 18, 1837. Approved by J. PETTYJOHN.
Book 9, Page 392 -- Refunding Bond -- JOEL CAMPBELL and WM. LIVELY to
WILEY CAMPBELL, executor of JOEL CAMPBELL, SR., January 16, 1838--
under will clause: "I devise to be equally divided among all of my
children as follows -- the part of my deceased daughter LUCY LIVELY,
in trust for benefit of her children as they are of age or married,"
January 15, 1838, order of Amherst County court and comissioners
divided estate - 3 slaves to children of CORNL. CAMPBELL and JOEL
CAMPBELL, acting for himself, stated that CORNL. left 5 children:
JOEL, JAS., MARY, ELIZ., and NANCY, but he does not represent JAMES.
All are of ageand JAS. has received his share; so have others.
Book 9, Page 393 -- Refunding Bond of WM. LIVELY and JOEL CAMPBELL to
WILEY CAMPBELL as above, February 19, 1838. Portion of LUCY LIVELY,
deceased, daughter of JOEL CAMPBELL has been paid. JOEL represents
JAS. CAMPBELL, son of CORNL., who was brother of LUCY. JAS. is of age.
Book 11, Page 180 -- Administrator's de bonis non Bond -- January 15,
1844 -- LEWIS S. CAMPBELL and JESSE MUNDY for LEWIS CAMPBELL.
Book 11, Page 443 -- Inventory -- November 5, 1846, no total -- ELIZ.
CAMPBELL, administratrix; JOS. KYLE; JOEL BETHEL; PETER F. CHRISTIAN.
Book 11, Page 450 -- Administrator's Bond -- ELIZABETH CAMPBELL; HENRY
G. FULCHER; WM. P. WOODROOF, October 19, 1846, for ELIZABETH CAMPBELL.
Note: These are all indexed for JOEL SR., but I feel that the last
one is for JR. He married an ELIZ. FULCHER and I note a FULCHER on
her bond.

JNO. CAMPBELL -- Book 1, Page 341 -- Guardian Bond -- THOS. PANNELL
and CHAS. PATRICK, May 5, 1777, for THOS. PANNELL as guardian of JNO.
CAMPBELL, orphan of GEO. CAMPBELL, deceased.
Book 4, Page 46 -- Inventory -- July 24, 1802 -- L 202-4-10. DANL.
McDONALD; DAVID CLARKSON; THOS. JONES; CHAS. JONES.
Book 4, Page 351 -- Administrator's Bond -- JAS. MONTGOMERY and WM.
HARRIS, July 19, 1802, for JAS. MONTGOMERY as administrator of JNO.
CAMPBELL, wagoner.
Book 9, Page 379 -- May 16, 1837, written; February 19, 1838, probated.
Witnesses: JAS. MILLER, WM. WRIGHT, ELLIS WRIGHT and proved by them.
JAS. and GEO. CAMPBELL qualified. Bondsmen: WM. M. WALLER, JNO. F.
CAMDEN, GEO. G. WRIGHT, VALERIUS McGINNIS. Ux, FRANCES - where we
live; oldest son, JAS.; GEO. and JAS., sons and trustees for daughter,
LEVISY CAMPBELL, ux of BENJ. CAMPBELL, and children. Son, WIATE;
children of son, JESSE. Sons above to be trustees of daughter, SALLY
MASSIE, ux of JNO. MASSIE, and children; daughter, MEALISA MASSIE, ux
of JESSE MASSIE, and children; daughter, RODY BOWLING, ux of THOS.
BOWLING; children of daughters: BETSY MADDOX and NANCY WRIGHT. Note:
If I recall correctly, this estate is also shown in the Nelson County
records. Administrator's Bond is Book 9, Page 382 - See will.
Book 9, Page 428 -- Inventory -- March 1, 1838. Someproperty found at
home of THOS. H. BOLLING in Nelson County and rest at the mansion
house in Amherst County. Total: $6,584.25. February 1, 1838. JAS.
MILLER; WM. BOURNE; JNO. M. BROADDUS. Book 10, Page 167 is indexed as
Administrator's Bond, but not there.

JNO. S. CAMPBELL -- Book 11, Page 103 -- JNO. S. and GUSTAVUS CAMPBELL,
December 21, 1842, to LEWIS CAMPBELL, administrator of WILEY CAMPBELL --
testator directed that slave division take place at end of year of his
death; all have agreed except THOS. S. CAMPBELL. JNO. S. has received
$15.67. Note: For more on JNO. S. CAMPBELL, see PERRIN, BATTLE, and
KNIFFIN, op. cit., 3rd edition and Warren County, Kentucky, sketches.
LIVELY family also moved to Warren and data here in deeds on this
branch (LIVELY) of CAMPBELL family. I have not been able to find any
trace of a connection between the CAMPBELL clan here and my own ancestor, JNO. PRESTON CAMPBELL, of Nicholas County, Kentucky. He married
two daughters of GOV. THOS. "STONEHAMMER" METCALFE, and I descend from
first ux, JANE LEE METCALFE. I have many old CAMPBELL papers, but
they tell me nothing of his ancestors. I suspect that he belongs
somewhere in the Augusta and Botetourt CAMPBELL lines.

LAWRENCE CAMPBELL -- Book 5, Page 535 -- January 8, 1813, written;
October 17, 1814, probated. Witnesses: DAVID S. GARLAND; JER. FRANKLIN;
HENRY FRANKLIN. Ux, HENRIETTA (AMERILLA?) daughter, NANCY MALONY;
widow of my son, JAS.; sons: LAWRENCE and CATLETT; daughter, MARY ANN

48

BURK - paid to JOS. BURK; daughter, JUDITH MAGINNIS (?); daughter, SALLY TURNER, ux of JAS. L. TURNER; daughter, PAMILIA WAUGH; grand-daughter, ELIZA WAUGH. Proved by FRANKLIN; December 18, 1815, by GARLAND and HENRY FRANKLIN. FRANCIS L. CAMPBELL qualified. Bonds-man: DAVID S. GARLAND. Administrator's Account is indexed for Book 6, Page 234, but is not there.

LAWSON CAMPBELL -- Book 14, Page 131 -- Constable, elected May 22, 1856, District 4. Bondsmen: E. P. TUCKER, JAS. M. GANNAWAY, RO. W. SNEAD. June 16, 1856.
Book 17, Page 450 -- Inventory -- December 31, 1868. No total. WM. SANDIDGE, LEWIS S. CAMPBELL, JAS. M. GANNAWAY.
Book 18, Page 162 -- August 9, 1868, written; September 21, 1868, probated. Witnesses: JAS. M. GANNAWAY, LEWIS S. CAMPBELL, WM. JOS. JONES. Proved by CAMPBELL and JONES. Of advanced age; son, JOSIAH; son-in-law, SAML. LAURMAN (LAURMON (?)). Where I live -- 146 acres bought of G. H. PAGE and 58 acres bought of SHELTON H. WRIGHT; Ux and self; grandson, JOSIAH CAMPBELL; my ux, FRANCES - all of my children. Executors: Son, JOSIAH; and SAML. LAURMAN.

LUCINDA CAMPBELL (middle initial is C.) -- Book 10, Page 48 -- Guardian Bond -- JAS. CAMPBELL, JNO. W. BROADDUS, GEO. CAMPBELL, September 17, 1838, for JAS. CAMPBELL as guardian of LUCINDA C.; JAMES D.(?); and SOPHIA E. CAMPBELL, orphans of JESSE CAMPBELL. Note: See FRANCIS JANE CAMPBELL formore orphans.

NEILL CAMPBELL -- Book 1, Page 329 -- December 3, 1776, written; March 3, 1777, probated. Witnesses: EDMD. WILCOX and LAWRENCE CAMP-BELL. To TABITHY BALLOW(E), daughter of LEONARD BALLOE, formerly of Albemarle, but now living on New River - land bought of JAS. SMITH, furniture, etc. Plank ready to finish house. My sister, CATHERINE BROUGH -- her children of East Mill near Perth, North Britain -- the boys, eldest expected, and girls. My natural daughter, ELIZ. CAMPBELL, alias BALLOW(E), by TABITHA BALLOW--slaves and Amherst County land--when 18. To JNO. ROSE - my pistols; to CHAS. ROSE - my smooth gun; to CHAS. IRVING, my rifle gun. If ELIZ. dies single before 18.
Book 1, Page 332 -- Administrator's Bond -- JNO. and CHAS. ROSE; CHAS. IRVING; EDMD. WILCOX; NICHL. CABELL; PATRICK ROSE; GABL. PENN, probate date, for both ROSE men and CHAS. IRVING to administer.
Book 1, Page 342 -- Inventory -- several slaves - over 20 - no total. RODERICK McCULLOCH; BENJ. HIGGINBOTHAM; CHAS. TALIAFERRO, May 5, 1777. Note: TABITHA BALLOE(W) later married JOSEPH BALLINGER, widower, April 4, 1782. BENJ. COLEMAN made a return. In Deed Book I, Page 419, April 26, 1802, is relinquishment by ACHILLES, RICH., and JAS. BALLINGER as legatees of JOS. BALLINGER, on any claims against estates of BALLINGER and NEILL CAMPBELL as far as TABITHA is concerned.

PEGGY CAMPBELL -- Book 4, Page 424 -- Guardian Bond -- JNO. & GEO. CAMPBELL, January 20, 1806, for JNO. CAMPBELL as guardian of PEGGY CAMPBELL, orphan of JNO. CAMPBELL, deceased.

PETER CAMPBELL -- Book 4, Page 462 -- Constable -- June 15, 1807, Bondsman: LEWIS WHITE; 4th. Hundred.

ROBT. P. CAMPBELL -- Book 16, Page 304 -- Administrator's Bond -- JNO. P. CAMPBELL; ARCHIBALD BEARD (BAIRD) and CHAS. E. BEARD, April 20, 1863, for JNO. CAMPBELL.
Book 16, Page 330 -- Inventory, order of April court, 1863 - $640.00. HENRY LOVING; ALBERT GANNAWAY; WM. H. FULCHER. May 18, 1863.

WILEY CAMPBELL -- Book 11, Page 12 -- July 20, 1841, written; March 21, 1842, probated. Witnesses: THOS. WINGFIELD; MARMADUKE B. SISSON; RO. WINGFIELD. Proved by witnesses. LEWIS S. CAMPBELL qualified. Ux, ELIZ. M. - land; son, JOEL - 344 acres where he lives; 2 tracts - one bought from PETER BURRUS and one from JNO. WILSON. Division to be held at end of year of my death. My children: Sons: JNO. S.; JOEL; GUSTAVUS; daughter, ELIZA ANNE WOODROOF; son, THOS. S.; son, ALEX. M.; son, LEWIS S.; daughters, MILDRED BETHEL and ELIZ. M. CAMP-BELL -- nine in number. They are to "bring into hatch pot" advanced sums. Executor, son, LEWIS S., is to care for mother and younger

brothers and sisters while under parental roof. Administrator's
Bond is Book 11, Page 17.
Book 11, Page 22 -- Inventory -- $8,761.25; JESSE MUNDY; RO. WING-
FIELD; THOMAS WINGFIELD, April 18, 1842.
Book 11, Page 201 -- Slave division -- all legatees are of age.
Lots to JNO. S. CAMPBELL, who is a resident of Kentucky - (See 3rd
edition of Perrin et. al. History of Kentucky, Warren County
sketches--); JOEL CAMPBELL; JNO. TUCKER; ALEX. CAMPBELL; JOEL BETHEL;
THOS. S. CAMPBELL. Brother, LEWIS S. CAMPBELL, is executor. Land
inventory - 316 acres - widow's part. Total: $3,162.50. WM. KENT;

JESSE MUNDY; J. PETTYJOHN, December 12, 1843.
Book 11, Page 208 -- Administrator's Account -- LEWIS S. CAMPBELL
from March 11, 1842. Tobacco receipt of JOEL CAMPBELL; my part of
tobacco; ALEX. M. and ELIZ. CAMPBELL. JESSE MUNDY, commission.
Recorded: December 16, 1844.
Book 12, Page 513 -- Administrator's Account by same administrator
from June 11, 1851. October 20, 1851, to JNO. S.; JOEL; GUSTAVUS
CAMPBELL; WM. P. WOODROOF and ux, ELIZA; THOS. S.; ALEX. M. and
LEWIS S. CAMPBELL; JOEL BETHEL and ux, MILDRED; JNO. S. TUCKER and
ux, ELIZ. RO. M. BROWN, commissioner, April 19, 1852.

WM. CAMPBELL, SR. -- Book 3, Page 5 -- Administrator's Bond -- JNO.
CAMPBELL; GEO. GALASPIE; RICH. FULCHER, March 6, 1786, for JNO.
CAMPBELL.
Book 3, Page 31 -- Inventory -- L 25-4-0 -- April 2, 1787. JNO.
BARNETT; JNO. JONES; JAS. MASTERS.

WM. CAMPBELL, JR. -- Book 7, Page 161 -- Administrator's Bond -- WILL
and LAWSON CAMPBELL, May 19, 1828, for WILL CAMPBELL.

WM. H. CAMPBELL -- Book 16, Page 359 -- Administrator's Bond -- SOPHIA
P. CAMPBELL and ABRAM MARTIN, August 17, 1863, for SOPHIA CAMPBELL.
Book 24, Page 64 -- December 27, 1901, written; June 19, 1906, probated. Witnesses: W. E. SANDIDGE and R. H. DRUMMOND. Produced in
court by MARY E. CAMPBELL and proved by witnesses. Ux, ELIZABETH;
my single children or those becoming widows or widowers by death or
desertion. My property at death of ux; to be home of any single
children.

ROBT. CAMRON -- Book 5, Page 227 -- Lunatic bond, June 22, 1813. WM.
DUNCAN and GEO. M. BROWN for WM. DUNCAN as committee.

DAVID CANNON -- This involves more members of the PETIT or PETTITT
family than CANNONS, but is indexed for the above man. July 26, 1849,
power of attorney to JAMES PETTIT. State of Alabama, Madison County:
DAVID and LUCINDA CANNON grant powers. LUCINDA was widow of HUGH
PETIT, late of Franklin County, Alabama. HUGH was son of JAS. PETIT,
late of Amherst County, Virginia. HUGH died and left three children:
JAS., Memphis, Tennessee; PHILLIP, Madison County, Alabama; and CHAS.
PETIT, Franklin. Grandfather PETIT died and left land and by will
and law contains interest for the three grandchildren and their mother,
LUCINDA. LUCINDA is entitled to life interest. Land has been sold
and proceeds are now ready for distribution. DAVID CANNON and ux have
sold their interest to JAS. PETIT, Memphis, Tennessee, and grant him
powers to transact business of estate. JAS. IRVING, JR., acting
Justice of the Peace, Madison County, Alamaba, August 2, 1849, certified that CANNON and ux appeared before him. JNO. W. OTEY, Clerk of
Court, Madison County, certified as to IRVINE. EDWD. C. BITTS
(BETTS ?), Judge of County Court, certified as to OTEY, August 2,
1849. Recorded in Amherst County, November 19, 1849. Margin: Original delivered to SAML. E. (C.) PETTIT. Note the various spellings
of PETTITT.

ARCHY CAREY (CARY) -- Book 11, Pages 129 and 247 -- Estate Commitment
to Sheriff, June court, 1842; Sheriff: NELSON CRAWFORD. Same data.

AUSTIN CARPENTER -- Book 9, Page 346 -- Refunding Bond -- September 19,
1837, AUSTIN and EATON CARPENTER and CHAS. C. ROGERS to CORNL. SALE
and EATON CARPENTER, executors of BENJ. CARPENTER. Slaves have been

divided and AUSTIN has received his share -- $1,275.00. Witnesses:
SAML. M. GARLAND, G. W. STAPLES, JAS. F. TALIAFERRO, CHAS. TUCKER,
ABSALOM HIGGINBOTHAM.
Book 14, Page 383 -- April 29, 1857, written; June 15, 1857, probated.
Witnesses: HENRY LOVING, JAS. R. PRIBBLE, MOSES A. JOHNSON and proved
by them. JAS. M. GANNAWAY qualified. Bondsman: M. C. GOODWIN.
JAS. M. GANNAWAY to administer. My ux, CATH. J.; all of my children;
my son, BENJ.; ux may sell land, if she wises to remove.
Book 15, Page 121 -- Administrator's Account by GANNAWAY, January 14,
1858. Widow may elect to pay debts. Recorded March 21, 1859.

BENJ. CARPENTER -- Book 8, Page 208 -- June 24, 1825, written; May 21,
1832, probated. Witnesses: GEO. W. and ABSALOM HIGGINBOTHAM; STEPHEN
P. and LEWELLEN T. (?) CASH. Proved by ABSALOM HIGGINBOTHAM and L.
CASH. EATON CARPENTER and CORNL. SALE qualified. Bondsmen: DABNEY
SANDIDGE and WILEY CAMPBELL. Ux, MARY; son, AUSTIN -- Piney Mountain
tract; son, EATON. My 4 children: JAS., HENSLEY, AUSTIN, and MARY
ROGERS, ux of WM. ROGERS. Executors: CORNL. SALE and my son, EATON
CARPENTER.
Book 8, Page 226 -- Inventory -- June 2, 1832. GEO. W. HIGGINBOTHAM,
ABSALOM HIGGINBOTHAM, CHAS. and WM. TUCKER. Total: $2,381.75.

EATON CARPENTER -- Book 12, Page 65 -- April 1, 1848, written; September 1, 1848. Witnesses: J. POWELL, CHAS. TUCKER, CORNL. SALE and
proved by them. Slaves to be freed and estate sold to pay expenses to
some free state and division among them. Executor: friend, EDMD. P.
TUCKER. Administrator's Bond is on Page 134 for TUCKER.
Book 12, Page 195 -- Inventory -- September 26, 1848 -- $2,430 --
1,215 acres CORNL. SALE; ABSALOM HIGGINBOTHAM; DABNEY SANDIDGE; GEO. W.
HIGGINBOTHAM.
Book 12, Page 298 -- Administrator's Account by TUCKER, September 29,
1848. Recorded: June 1, 1850. Total: $431.88.
Book 13, Page 14 -- Administrator's Account by TUCKER from August 5,
1850. Total: $1,920.00. Recorded: September 20, 1852.

HENSLEY CARPENTER -- Book 9, Page 347 -- Refunding Bond, September 17,
1837 - same parties as for Book 9, Page 346 (No. 107). HENSLEY CARPEN-
TER is "of State of Tennessee." EATON CARPENTER was his attorney-in-
fact.

JAS. CARPENTER -- Book 3, Page 348 -- JAS., EATON, AUSTIN CARPENTER;
CHAS. ROGERS to CORNL. SALE and EATON CARPENTER, executors of BENJ.
CARPENTER, September 19, 1837. JAS. CARPENTER is "of state of Alabama." He has received $1,200.00 as his share of BENJ. CARPENTER's
estate. Witnesses: SAML. M. GARLAND, G. W. STAPLES, JAS. F. TALIA-
FERRO, CHAS. TUCKER, ABSALOM HIGGINBOTHAM. EATON CARPENTER was
attorney-in-fact.

RICH. CARPENTER -- Book 6, Page 256 -- Admini-trator's Bond -- EATON
CARPENTER and BENJ. TALIAFERRO, October 15, 1821, for EATON CARPENTER.
Book 9, Page 3 -- Administrator's Account by EATON CARPENTER from 1821.
To THOS. BOX, guardian of CLAIBORNE, DANGERFIELD, MICHL, and RICHARD
CARPENTER. Cash paid to BOX - legacy in full and sent by BOX to JNO.
WILSFORD -- Giles County, Tennessee, September 7, 1831. BENJ. TALIA-
FERRO, CORNL. SALE, WM. TUCKER, March 9, 1833.

JAS. CARR -- Book 16, Page 456 -- Administrator's Bond -- VIRGINIA F.,
H. S., ELIZ. P., and JNO. M. CARR, March 21, 1864, for VIRGINIA CARR.
Book 16, Page 466 -- Inventory -- April 2, 1864 - $4,305.00. JEFF
MAYES, A. L. FOGUS, DAVID APPLING. Recorded April 18, 1864.
Book 17, Page 377 -- Sales, VA. F. CARR, administratrix, February 5,
1867. W. D. TURNER, clerk of sale - $3,304.18. Recorded September 21,
1868. Family buyers: VA. F.; JAS. M. and R. H. CARR.

MARY A. E. CARRINGTON (N. CABELL) -- Book 24, Page 235 -- May 25,
1849, written; Monday, June 24, 1850, probated. Fluvanna County.
Codicil witnesses: JOS. C. CABELL, WM. P. HALL, RO. W. ELSOM. Proved
by MAYO B. CARRINGTON, but not named as witnesses. Witnesses to will:
MARY B. CARRINGTON, THOS. P. SHIELDS, WM. H. MAYO. Codicil written
on January 15, 1850. Proved also by WM. H. MAYO, DANL. C. HARTSOOK

qualified. To DANL. J. HARTSOOK; son, JAS. L. -- property bought
from Shepherd and Co. Dead son of JAS. L. - spoons with his initials.
ANN M. CARRINGTON, ux of JAS. L.; living children and grandchildren.
Children of JOS. N. CARRINGTON. Son, GEO. B. CARRINGTON and any
children. Granddaughter, MARY ANN CARRINGTON. To WM. CORNELIUS
CARRINGTON; to children of JAS. L. and GILBERT P. CARRINGTON. Executor: DANL. J. HARTSOOK. Codicil: To DANL. J. HARTSOOK - interest
in Pedlar River land which belonged to my father, NICHL. CABELL -- in
trust for my son, JAS. LAWRENCE CARRINGTON, and ux, ANN M. She refers
to her father as NICHL. CABELL, SR., and mentions "my brother, JOS. C.
CABELL." DANL. HARTSOOK is given middle initials of "J." and "C."
in places. Recorded Amherst County, October 17, 1917. ABRA. SHEPHERD,
Fluvanna clerk. Copy attested by WM. SCLATER, clerk; M. W. PERKINS,
deputy.

ABRAM CARTER -- Book 4, Page 453 -- Constable -- June 20, 1803. Bonds-
men: HENRY and GEO. M. BROWN.
Book 4, Page 462 -- Same, June 15, 1807. Bondsman: JOS. ROBERTS.
Book 4, Page 585 -- Same, July 19, 1809. Bondsman: JOS. CHILDRESS.

CAROLINE CARTER -- Book 6, Page 698 -- Guardian Bond -- MARY A. CARTER;
BARTLETT and WM. CASH, and HOWARD SALE, November 20, 1820, for MARY
CARTER as guardian of CAROLINE; Lawler(?) (Book 6 is hardest book to
decipher in the whole list of books); JULIA; JNO. and WALKER STANLEY
CARTER, orphans of EDWD. CARTER.

CHAS. CARTER -- Book 1, Page 83 -- June 21, 1766, written; December 1,
1766, probated. Witnesses: THOS. PARKS, BENJ. NORTH(?), BENJ.
STINET. Son, DALE; daughters: SUSANAH and ELIZ.; son, CHAS.; son,
JNO.; slaves, Sary and Rachell. If any child is without lawful issue.
My five children. Ux, LUCY, to administer. Administrator's Bond
on Page 84 for LUCY. Bondsmen: JOB CARTER, JNO. LOVING, HOWARD CASH.
Book 1, Page 103 -- Inventory -- L 764-12-8. March 3, 1767. CHAS.
TALIAFERRO, DAVID CRAWFORD, THOS. PARKS.
Book 2, Page 201 -- Guardian Bond -- JNO. BECKLEY, November 1, 1784,
guardian of CHAS., MIRTILDA, and JOS. CARTER, orphans of DALE CARTER.
Bondsman: DAVID CRAWFORD.

CHARLIE CARTER -- Book 24, Page 137 -- May 5, 1911, written; Decem-
ber 4, 1911, probated. Witnesses: C. J. CAMPBELL and J. B. RICHESON.
Proved by RICHESON. Of color; my living children. Friend, PATRICK
FLETCHER, is to administer and be guardian.

EDWARD CARTER, CAPT. (in some items, but there are several men by the
same name) -- Book 3, Page 569 -- EDWD. CARTER, by order of court, no
date - his lot -- slave, Nelson, valued at L 47; white horse and sad-
dle; feather bed with one sheet; blanket cover; pied cow. Total:
L 75. CHAS. TALIAFERRO, NELSON CRAWFORD. Returned: September 16,
1799.
Book 6, Page 648 -- Administrator's Bond -- January 16, 1826. WM. R.
McCULLOCH and RO. H. CARTER. Bondsmen: CORNL. SALE, LINDSEY COLEMAN,
ST. GEO. TUCKER, NICHL. WAUGH.
Book 6, Page 657 -- Inventory, no total; many slaves; called "CAPT."
herein. March 20, 1826. WM. M. WALLER, HILL CARTER, WM. DUNCAN.
Book 6, Page716 -- Slave division, December 28, 1826. Commissioners:
JNO. B. DUNCAN, WM. MANTIPLY, WM. SALE. Recorded January 15, 1827.
Widow, MARY A. CARTER - dower. There is a sum written and above is
name of LAURA CARTER. Could this be LANDON CARTER? Eleven lots:
Widow, LANDON, WALKER, WM., CAROLINE, WASHINGTON, JNO., JULIA, EDWD. C.,
CHAMPE, and PETER. It is noted that EDWD. C. has received two horses
and slave, but still has claim vs. estate.
Book 7, Page 139 -- Land division - order of February, 1827 - to
MARY A. CARTER, widow -- 86-1/2 acres with house; to EDWD., CHAMP, and
PETER CARTER -- 335 acres laid off in a body by consent; to GEO. WASH.;
WM.; CAROLINE; LAURA; JULIA; JNO. and WALKER STANLEY CARTER -- all save
GEO. are infant heirs. Commissioners: JNO. B. DUNCAN, WM. SALE,
WM. MANTIPLY. Infants got 618 acres next to dower tract. March 17,
1828.
Book 8, Page 313 -- Division of land of CAPT. EDWD. CARTER - plat on

Page 314; part of tract on road from Amherst Courthouse to Waugh's ferry; Southeast side of south boundary of Carter's Mill Creek. Adjoins JNO. BROCKMAN; NANCY FRANKLIN's berry Plain tract. Mention of suit of Farmers' Bank of Virginia vs. CARTER heirs. 335 acres divided to EDWD., CHAMPE, and PETER CARTER and divided into 3 tracts for them. JNO. PRYOR, surveyor. Commissioners: DNAL. L. COLEMAN, SAML. MANTIPLY. Recorded: July 15, 1833. Order to divide, November, 1830. Don, June 26, 1833.
Book 8, Page 281 -- Administrator's Account from August, 1826. Administrators: WM. H. McCULLOCH and RO. W. CARTER. Returned, February 18, 1831. Recorded: November 21, 1832. Commissioners: J. D. DAVIS, THOS. N. EUBANK, JOSIAH ELLIS. Shoes for CHAMPE CARTER - $2.50; board for C. W. CARTER; paid R. W. CARTER; paid H. I. ROSE; CHAS. CARTER's bond account; WM. H.; GEO. W.; MARY A.; RO. W. CARTER. Someone has used ink to make one item read, "MARY H."; to PETER J. CARTER.
Book 8, Page 219 -- August 23, 1831, written; May 21, 1832, probated. Witnesses: JNO. PRYOR; JOS. R.; RO. H., and ABRAM CARTER and RICH. EUBANK. Advanced in years; my grandchildren; GARRET and GRANVILLE LAYNE; ANN CASHWELL, ux of JAS. A. CASHWELL; MARY, THOS., POWHATAN and FRANCES LAYNE -- if any dies before 21 or without issue. My daughter, ELIZ., and my grandchildren. Estate is not liable for debts of THOMAS LAYNE, deceased. Executors: BENJ. TALIAFERRO and WM. AKERS.
Book 8, Page 223 -- Administrator's Bond -- June 18, 1832; WM. AKERS. Bondsmen: WILLIS M. REYNOLDS, BENJ. NORVELL, GARRET LAYNE, GRANVILLE LAYNE, JAS. H. CASHWELL.
Book 8, Page 235 -- Inventory -- July 6, 1832 - $4,766.50. RO. H. CARTER, LEE MILLNER, RICH. EUBANK.
Book 8, Page 426 -- Administrator's Account -- Returned July 17, 1834. WM. AKERS, administrator from 1832 and recorded December 15, 1834. To RO. H. CARTER; ferriage from Bethel for GARRET C. LAYNE - 25 cents. 4 lbs. of brown sugar at Amherst Courthouse - 50 cents. To PETER RUCKER on account; M. PENDLETON's execution. CARTER vs. RUSSELL shop account; ALFRED C. BURKS' schooling account - $5.00. GARRET C. LAYNE - overseer. Seven days attendance at Pedlar Mills, Lynchburg, and Amherst Courthouse.
It is obvious that we are no longer dealing with CAPT. CARTER after the will of Book 8, Page 219. This testator lived in Pedlar area.
Book 9, Page 261 -- Administrator's Account by AKERS from July 17, 1834 - to GARRET C. LAYNE; medicine for sick horse in Lynchburg - 31 cents. To RO. H. CARTER; CARTER and TAYLOR; JOS. R. CARTER as a commissioner. Returned May 27, 1836; Recorded November 21, 1836. Commissioners: JOS. R. CARTER and PETER RUCKER.
Book 9, Page 417 -- Administrator's Account by AKERS from March 28, 1836. G. C. LAYNE for P. (?) WOODROOF; THOS.; ELIZ.; GRANVILLE and GARRETT LAYNE; JAS. H. CASHWELL's bond. Commissioners: PETER RUCKER, JNO. R. IRVINE, RO. H. CARTER. Returned August 16, 1837; recorded April 16, 1838.
Book 10, Page 174 -- Administrator's Account by AKERS from October 16, 1839. To JAS. H. CASHWELL - his interest in estate of EDWD. CARTER, deceased. Ferriage for self and THOS. LAIN; to JOS. R. CARTER; schooling for 2 children - $3.00, October 16, 1839. Paid to E. LAIN by discount on bond of WM. FRANKLIN. Returned October 16, 1837. JNO. P. IRVINE; PITT WOODROOF. Recorded November 18, 1839.
Book 11, Page 1 -- Administrator's Account by AKERS from January 1, 1840. THOS. LAIN for his ferriage - 10 cents. To ELIZ.; GRANVILLE, and GARRETT LAIN; WM. FRANKLIN's bond; bond of JAS. H. CASHWELL. Returned September 26, 1841; recorded December 20, 1841. PITT WOODROOF and RO. H. CARTER.
Book 11, Page 5 -- Administrator's de bonis non Bond -- ELIZ. LAYNE, December 20, 1841. Bondsmen: GARRET C. LAYNE, WM. M. WARE, RICH. H. ANDERSON, GRANVILLE LAIN, WM. H. FRANKLIN, THOS. LAIN.
Book 11, Page 10 -- Inventory, January 3, 1842, ELIZ. LAYNE, administratrix. Order of December court, 1842. (So recorded). Total: $6,219.50. Returned January 3, 1842. JNO. PRYOR, PETER RUCKER, HENRY FRANKLIN. It is evident that a clerk made an error in order date.
Book 12, Page 493 -- Divided estate by commissioners, December 30, 1851, and undersigned legatees of EDWD. CARTER, deceased, and his

53

daughter, ELIZ. LAYNE, deceased, agreed to abide by the decision of
the commissioners: RO. H. CARTER, JNO. PRYOR, CHAS. H. RUCKER,
BLUFORD MORRIS, GEO. W. STAPLES. It is understood that JAS. H. CASH-
WELL and ux, NANCY, are not to be parties to division of slaves and
personal property since they elected to take share in real estate.
Interesting slave list -- Sylvia, an old woman, valued at nothing.
Bond of GRANVILLE LAYNE; GARRET C. LAYNE as trustee for ux and
children; POWHATAN LAYNE and THOS. LAYNE to pay other legatees to
balance sums. EDWD. RHODES and WM. M. FRANKLIN also to pay or be
paid by other legatees. THOS. LAYNE agrees to take old woman, Sylvia,
and to support her during lifetime. Returned February 16, 1852.

EDWD. CARTER, JR. -- Book 6, Page 579 -- Administrator's Bond --
March 22, 1825. THOS. LAINE. Bondsman: RICH. N. EUBANK.

ELISHA CARTER -- Book 3, Page 87 -- Guardian Bond -- ABRAHAM CARTER
and JOS. ROBERTS, October 7, 1788, for Amherst County as guardian of
ELISHA CARTER, orphan of SOLOMON CARTER.

GEO. WASHINGTON CARTER -- Book 7, Page 38 -- Guardian Bond -- RO. M.
and CHAMPE CARTER, September 17, 1827, for RO. CARTER as guardian of
GEO. WASHINGTON CARTER, orphan of EDWARD CARTER, deceased. (Indexed
as CUSTER)

HILL CARTER -- Book 6, Pages 720 and 727 -- Sheriff Bonds, February 19,
1827. Bondsmen: DAVID S. GARLAND, AJAX J. WALKER, EDWD. A. CABELL,
JNO. PENN, JESSE RICHESON.
Book 7, Page 144 -- Sheriff, March 17, 1828. Bondsmen: WILL M.
WALLER, RICH. S. ELLIS, WM. ROACH, WM. H. McCULLOCH, JAS. DAVIS.
Book 8, Page 106 -- Inventory -- July 18, 1831. No total. RO. L.
COLEMAN, RO. A. COGHILL.

JACOB CARTER -- Book 10, Page 340 -- Administrator's Bond -- CREASY
CARTER and SHADRICK CARTER, April 19, 1841, for CREASY CARTER.

JAS. CARTER -- Book 3, Page 570 -- Slave received, September 16, 1799.
Commissioners: CHAS. TALIAFERRO, NELSON CRAWFORD. No data as to
whose legatee he was in getting slave.

JAS. M. CARTER -- Book 16, Page 97 -- Administrator's Bond -- October 21, 1861. RO. L. COLEMAN and RO. A. COGHILL for COLEMAN.

JESSE CARTER -- Book 3, Page 203 -- July 15, 1791, received slave as
legatee of PETER CARTER. Commissioners: NELSON CRAWFORD, CHAS.
TALIAFERRO, CHAS. CRAWFORD.

JOB CARTER -- Book 2, Page 88 -- November --, 1779, written; Dec-
ember 2, 1782, probated. Witnesses: WM. WARE, LANDON CARTER, PATTA
WARE. Eldest son, SOLOMON; sons: PETER, JOB, and DALE CARTER.
Daughter, ELIZ. DAWSON; daughter, NANCY VAUGHAN; Son, WILLIAM, to
administer, and he qualified. Bondsmen: WM. WARE and WM. EDWARDS.
Book 2, Page 104 -- Inventory -- Someone who knew nothing of English
money has meddled with official records and put this total to
column: L 63-95-27. June 2, 1783. ISAAC WRIGHT; JOS. EDMONDS;
JOS. MILSTEAD.
Book 7, Page 66 -- Administrator's Bond -- November 20, 1827; ABRAM
CARTER, JAS. FLOOD for JAS. FLOOD.
Book 7, Page 151 -- Inventory -- February 4, 1828 - $240.75. FLOOD
is called JNO. here instead of JAS.; PETER RUCKER; WM. SHEPHERD;
GODFREY TOLER.

JNO. CARTER -- Book 2, Page 202 -- Guardian Bond -- November 1, 1784;
JNO. BECKLEY and DAVID CRAWFORD for JNO. BECKLEY as guardian of JNO.
CARTER, orphan of DALE CARTER.
Book 4, Page 314 -- Guardian Bond -- September 17, 1798; JNO. CLARKSON;
JNO. MASSIE; JAS. CLARKSON for JNO. CLARKSON as guardian of JNO. CARTER,
orphan of HENRY CARTER.
Book 9, Page 389 -- This item should come after will below, but is
put here to show multiplicity of JNO. CARTERS. Guardian Bond --
February 19, 1838; JNO. MASSIE and JAS. CLARKSON; GEO. W. CARTER; WM.

M. WALLER for GEO. W. CARTER as guardian of JNO. and WALKER S. CARTER, orphans of EDWD. CARTER, deceased. These three Guardian Bonds show three different JOHN CARTERS and there are others as well. The following will is for yet another one.
Book 8, Page 332 -- January 7, 1833, written; July 15, 1833, probated. Witnesses: JAS. D. WATTS, SPOTTSWOOD BRYANT, NELSON SEAY. Ux, CREASY, until youngest child living is 21 or married. My thirteen children: MARY N., MARTHA, JACOB D., SHEDRACK, WM. D., ELIZ. A., NANCY A., LUCY F., SARAH ANN, PETER D., VERJANE, JAS. R., CAROLINE M. CARTER. My oldest son, JOSEPH W. CARTER, gets nothing because of improper conduct. Executor: friend, RICH. W. TILLER.
Book 18, Page 236 -- Inventory -- November 22, 1871 - $77.75; GEO. W. SEAY, G. T. WOOD, MARTIN WIDDERFIELD.
Book 18, Page 465 -- Administrator's Account -- JNO. T. EDWARDS, late sheriff. July 20, 1874. One-sixth to MARY CARTER; RO. VIA and ux, MARTHA; GEO. SMOOT and ux, LUCY; SARAH CARTER; CAROLINE CARTER; GEO. W. SNEAD and ux, VIRGINIA -- one-sixth to each. September, 1874, bond for RO. VIA as security for WM. CARTER and purchase at sale. It is seen that these are some of the heirs of the JOHN with will above. VERJANE is VIRGINIA.

A word of caution needs to be uttered to those working on JOHN CARTER data in Amherst. Several years ago a client engaged me to work on this JOHN with ux, CREASY. She knew of the will and stated that the son, WM., married a NEWMAN in Orange. She was preparing a book on the line and cited a previous work wherein JOHN, ux, CREASY, is shown to be the son of PETER CARTER. It was my sad task to upset the applecart, but she was a good sport and competent genealogist. I cited a deed in Deed Book L, Page 9, wherein heirs of PETER CARTER were selling land. On June 13, 1807, Lincoln County, Kentucky, Justice of the Peace certified that JOHN, son of PETER, and ux, JEMIMA, were in that county of my native state. It was plain that the CARTER writer had picked out the wrong JOHN. It could have happened that the JOHN in Kentucky moved back here with a new wife for there is no marriage for a JOHN to a CREASY -- here. I found that the Kentucky JOHN went on to Missouri so we had to eliminate him.

This is not a Nelson County treatise, but I shall state that I found the answer in that county in the will of SHADRICK or SHADRACK CARTER. The mere fact that he named a son, JOHN -- 1827 -- and his share to his children -- was not conclusive. I did know that JOHN named a son, SHADRICK, in his will and that was strong evidence. The clincher was found in Nelson Deed Book 10, Page 442, December 26, 1834, when CREASY CARTER joined as widow of JOHN with other heirs of SHADRICK CARTER in a conveyance. CREASY also made bond in Nelson as guardian of her children. CREASY did not carry on the feud between JOHN and his son, JOSEPH. In Deed Book W, Page 41, Amherst County, March 2, 1837, CREASY, for love borne my son, JOS., and $1.00, conveys furniture, etc., to JOSEPH and his children until of age.

JNO. S. CARTER -- Book 8, Page 89 -- Inventory by BENJ. TALIAFERRO, Sheriff, and administrator de bonis non, December 31, 1830 -- $2,053.75. JNO. PRYOR, ORMUND WARE, BENJ. B. TALIAFERRO. Some slaves deeded for benefit of THOS. N. EUBANK and DABNEY SANDIDGE.
Book 8, Page 249 -- Administrator's Account -- BENJ. TALIAFERRO from November 27, 1830. CHAMPE CARTER, commissioner. Recorded August 23, 1832.
Book 14, Page 255 -- Administrator's de bonis non Bond -- February 17, 1857. ELISHA CARTER. Bondsman: RO. N. ELLIS.

JULIAN CARTER -- Book 9, Page 351 -- Guardian Bond -- BEVERLY DAVIES and ADDISON TALIAFERRO, November 20, 1837, for BEVERLY DAVIES as guardian of JULIAN CARTER, orphan of EDWARD CARTER. (Indexed as JULIA ANN)

LAURA CARTER (D., middle initial in data) -- Book 9, Page 143 -- December 21, 1835, CHAMPE and GEO. W. CARTER for CHAMPE CARTER as guardian of LAURA D. CARTER, orphan of EDWD. CARTER.

LUCY C. CARTER -- Book 24, Page 266 -- This is a peculiar type of will, but it is a joint will by LUCY C. and MARY E. CARTER. October 8, 1904, written; December 8, 1919, probated. Witnesses: J. W. JEN-

NINGS, W. L. KNIGHT. Niece, LUCY M. HIGGINBOTHAM, has cared for me for last 18 years. Our land known as estate of late PETER FLOOD and bequeathed to us in his lifetime. At LUCY's death, to her children. Executor: Nephew--HIGGINBOTHAM. Proved by JENNINGS. This is indexed for both testators, so it is impossible to tell which one died first since there is no other data.

LUNSFORD CARTER -- Book 6, Page 577 -- Administrator's Bond -- December 20, 1824. THOS. LAINE, ISAAC RUCKER, and CHAS. C. CARTER for THOS. LAINE.

MARTHA ANN CARTER -- Book 9, Page 339 -- Guardian Bond -- October 16, 1837, PETER FLOOD as guardian of MARTHA ANN CARTER, orphan of JOAB (sic) CARTER, deceased. Bondsmen: CHAS. C. BURKS, WM. ANTHONY RICHESON.

MARY CARTER -- Book 14, Page 22 -- May 21, 1844, written; October 15, 1855, probated; codicil of May 29, 1844. Ux of ABRAM CARTER, Amherst County; kinswoman, SALLY ROBERTS, has lived with me for 30 years. My four children: JOS. R., ROBT. H., ELIZ. GOODRICH (this is evidently clerical error, for she appears as GOODWIN in all other data. There is no bond here for an ELIZ. to a man by either of the names.) CREED C. CARTER. Son, JOS., and family. Executor: RO. H. CARTER. Codicil: My deceased son, WILLIAM -- widow nor anyone else to have his portion. Witnesses: JNO. PRYOR, E. B. GILBERT, JNO. DAVIS, WM. H. SALE.
Book 14, Page 26 -- Administrator's Bond -- ROBT. H. CARTER, probate date; Bondsmen: HENRY W. QUARLES, JAS. W. PHILLIPS.
Book 14, Page 103 -- Sale, October 21, 1855, "or till August 1, 1856" - $339.47-1/2. Buyers: RO. H. CARTER. Recorded, Monday, May 19, 1856.
Book 14, Page 105 -- Division: Special legacy for SALLY ROBERTS; JAS. M. TALIAFERRO - medical bill; slaves sold for $1,092.00. Lots to RO. H., JOS. R., and CREED C. CARTER; and ELIZ. GOODWIN. Recorded December 22, 1855. Page 8 contains interesting slave list and ages - 14 slaves valued at $5,190.17-1/2. JNO. PRYOR, CHAS. L. BROWN, JAS. H. CASHWELL, RO. H. THORNTON, RO. H. CARTER, executor.

MARY E. CARTER -- See joint will treated under LUCY C. CARTER.

NANCY E. CARTER -- Book 4, Page 541 -- Guardian Bond -- ELIZ. CARTER, NICHL. VANSTAVERN, STEPHEN CARTER, NELSON CARTER, WM. SLEDD, November 21, 1808, for ELIZABETH CARTER, as guardian of NANCY E., ELIZ. P., JOS., and WM. CARTER, orphans of WM. CARTER.
STAFFORD CARTER, to administer.

PETER CARTER -- Book 3, Page 59 -- Guardian Bond -- JNO. SANDIDGE and LARKIN SANDIDGE, September 3, 1787, for JNO. SANDIDGE as guardian of PETER CARTER, orphan of SOLOMON CARTER.
Book 3, Page 160 -- September 6, 1790, written; February 7, 1791, probated. Witnesses: JNO. HARRISON, JANE ELLIS, SALLY P. HARRISON, ISAAC WRIGHT, WM. HAYNES. Son, CHARLES; son, JESSE; son, PETER, when of age or married; daughter, SUSANNA, when of age or married; son, SOLOMON - when of age or married; same for daughters, MILLY and ELIZ., and son, JOHN. Ux, MARY. Executors: JOSIAH ELLIS and WM. CRAWFORD. They qualified, Page 162. Bondsmen: GABL. PENN and JNO. HARRISON.
Book 3, Page 187 -- Inventory -- L 849-1-6, June 7, 1791. JNO. BROWN, CHAS. TALIAFERRO, SAML. HIGGINBOTHAM. Page 466 of Book 3 is indexed as Administrator's Account, but not there. It is Book 4, Page 466, September 17, 1807. Legatees have received satisfaction. THOS. N. EUBANK, PETER P. THORNTON, MARTIN PARKS.
Book 24, Page 144 -- March 24, 1915, date of probate only. Witnesses: O. L. EVANS, ELLA F. ROSE. Ux, MARGARET; daughter, ANNIE CARTER PAYNE; Amherst Courthouse lot and reference to lot 18 and plat with deed - Deed Book 00, Page 264ff. Stepson, HENRY CARTER; daughter, PAULINA BUTLER, of Washington, D.C. Ux to administer, and she qualified. I might note that the deed book reference is not a clerical error on my part. The books begin with A and run through Z, and then they double with AA through ZZ. I realize that it is an impossible task to abstract all of them, but I have done some early ones: A through F. They began to number after ZZ, so we have a huge collection of deed books in the office.

PETER J. CARTER -- Book 6, Page 668 -- Guardian Bond -- WM. H. McCUL-
LOCH, RO. W. and CHAMPE CARTER,September 18, 1826, for WM. McCULLOCH as
guardian of PETER J. CARTER, orphan of EDWD. CARTER, deceased.

R. W. CARTER -- Book 11, Page 432 -- Administrator's de bonis non Bond,
July 20, 1846. RO. M. BROWN. Bondsman: BENJ. J. BROWN, JR.
Book 12, Page 95 -- Inventory, August 20, 1849: $2,430.00. CORNL.
SALE, ABSALOM HIGGINBOTHAM, DABNEY SANDIDGE, GEO. W. HIGGINBOTHAM.

RO. H. CARTER -- Book 6, Page 361 -- Constable, June 16, 1823. Bondsmen: WILL JOPLING, PETER P. THORNTON.

SOLOMON CARTER -- Book 3, Page 23 -- February 7, 1784, written;
October 2, 1786, probated. Witnesses: WM. TUCKER, DAVID CRAWFORD.
Son, WM. - Buffalo land; son, ABRAHAM - Buffalo and Lick Mt. Land;
daughter, MILLA DAVIS; son, PETER; son, ELISHA - one year of schooling;
daughter, SALLA CARTER; daughter, PATTEY CARTER; daughter, NANCY CARTER.
Three youngest to be educated. Ux, MARY ANN - 1 shilling as she has
left me and co-habitates with another man. One shilling to any children born to her. Executors: brother, PETER CARTER and my son,
ABRAHAM. Administrator's Bond -- Book 3, Page 25 for them. Bondsmen:
WM. TUCKER and JNO. CRAWFORD.
Book 3, Page 61 -- Inventory -- October 1, 1787; no total and no committee. Administrator's Account is Book 3, Page 486 by ABRAM CARTER
from 1787. Bond of WM. CARTER for the estate; GEO. DILLARD for
schooling P.; PETER, JR.; LANDON and EDWD. CARTER. Name of PETER, SR.,
appears. ELISHA, PATTEY, and NANCY CARTER are the three youngest
children. Hat for M. CARTER; board for NANCY for two years. Returned June 18, 1798. Name of JOSIAH ELLIS as executor of PETER
CARTER. Report of August 25, 1797. C. W. TALIAFERRO, JR.; WM.WARE;
HENRY BROWN.

WM. CARTER -- Book 4, Page 296 -- Administrator's Bond -- ELIZ. CARTER;
CHAS. TALIAFERRO; ABRAM CARTER, June 17, 1798, for ELIZ. CARTER.
Book 8, Page 155 -- Administrator's Bond -- WILLIS E. DICKERSON and
WM. M. WALLER, October 17, 1831, for WILLIS DICKERSON.
Book 8, Page 166 -- March 8, 1831, written; October 17, 1831, pro-
bated. Witnesses: BARTLETT CASH, WM. P. CASH, WILLIS E. DICKERSON.
Proved by DICKERSON. WALLER refused to qualify. Brother, JOHN; bro-
ther, GEO. WASHINGTON CARTER; my interest in estate of parents to GEO.
WASHINGTON CARTER, CAROLINE M., LAURA, JULIA, and WALKER S. CARTER.
Executor: WM. M. WALLER for benefit of my brothers and sisters.
Book 9, Page 224 -- Methodist Minister's Bond -- April 15, 1835.
Bondsmen: JNO. S. KYLE, GEO. MARKHAM.

WM. HENRY CARTER -- Book 7, Page 38 -- Guardian Bond -- RO. W. and
CHAMPE CARTER, September 17, 1827, for RO. CARTER as guardian of WM.
HENRY CARTER, Orphan of EDMUND CARTER.

W. STANLEY CARTER -- Book 24, Page 16 -- July 11, 1902, written;
Saturday, August 23, 1902, probated. Witnesses: R. B. WARE, W. T.
ROYSTER, C. L. ROYSTER. To ANGILINE FRANKLIN, colored woman who
waits on me -- 2/3 of a farm; Turkey Mountain - her house and that of
PAUL BROWN of color; to JIM FRANKLIN, of color; to SOPHRONIA CARTER,
of color, and her son, FRANKLIN CARTER. Executors: S. M. WALLER
and R. B. WARE.

JOS. W. CARVER -- Book 8, Page 338 -- Administrator's Bond -- ZA.
DRUMMOND and SAML. M. GARLAND, August 19, 1833, for ZA. DRUMMOND.
Book 8, Page 356 -- Inventory, no total, October 21, 1833. Z. DRUM-
MOND, administrator.

REUBEN CARVER -- Book 12, Page 184 -- Power-of-attorney by REUBEN
CARVER and ux, NANCY B., to WM. KENT, Amherst County, January 16,
1845. FRANCIS WATTS and JNO. JUTT, Pike County, Missouri, Justices
of the Peace; AYLETT H. BUCKNER, Pike County Clerk; HIRAM G. EDWARDS,
Pike County Judge. Bowling Green, Missouri; recorded Amherst County,
February 17, 1845. KENT to sell Amherst County land.

EDWARD CASEY -- Book 6, Page 649 -- Administrator's Bond -- AMBROSE
PLUNKET and DAVID STAPLES, January 16, 1826, for AMBROSE PLUNKET
Book 6, Page 672 -- Inventory -- $15.01-1/2 -- July 17, 1826. GEO.
EDWARD (?); REUBEN CARVER; THOS. JEWELL.
Book 8, Page 259 -- Administrator's Account by PLUNKET from 1826.
Recorded June 21, 1832. JAS. and GEO. STAPLES; REUBEN CARVER.

BARNET CASH -- Book 13, Page 355 -- Administrator's Bond -- SAML. D.
CASH, June 19, 1854. Bondsmen: M. C. GOODWIN, JAS. M. GANNAWAY,
JNO. W. CASH.
Book 13, Page 378 -- Inventory -- September 10, 1854. Recorded
September 18, 1854; no total. CHAS. H. MASSIE, WM. SANDIDGE, RO. W.
SNEAD; B. PATTESON, J.P.; SAML. M. GARLAND, Clerk.
Book 13, Page 420 -- Administrator's Account -- November 1, 1854;
recorded December 18, 1854. SAML. G. CASH, administrator. At sale:
family buyers: P. W., G. G., SAML. G., J. W., N. A., JNO. W., C. T.,
G. W., CHAS. T., and MRS. E. CASH.
Book 14, Page 403 -- Administrator's Account by SAML. G. CASH; report
on February 17, last and recorded April 7, 1857. Sales: $872.38.
Amounts paid to JNO. W., CHAS. T.; SAML. G. HENRY, commissioner -
September, 1857, report and recorded May 18, 1857. MARBLE C. GOODWIN
was paid an amount, and records show that he married a CASH. JAS. M.
GANNAWAY was assignee of NATHAN A. CASH who rendered "one year of
service in 1853-54.

BARTLETT CASH -- Book 9, Page 77 -- July 11, 1826, written; June 15,
1835, probated. Handwriting attested by JNO. PRYOR and CHAS. RUCKER.
RANDOLPH CASH renounced administration. Ux, ELIZ. - 320 acres where
I now live and at her death to our children. Son, JOEL - 1/6; son,
WILLIS - 1/6; daughter, MARY A. DICKERSON - 1/6; grandsons, WM. MOORE
and BARTLETT MOORE - 1/6 when of age; son, WILLIAM P. CASH; my sister,
KEZIAH CASH, has generally lived with me since my mother's death.
Executors: my brother, RANDOLPH CASH, and friend, WM. M. WALLER.
Book 9, Page 134 -- Inventory -- Nov. 4, 1835 -- $3,788.50. CORNL.
SALE, ABSALOM HIGGINBOTHAM, EATON CARPENTER.
Book 9, Page 126 -- Estate Commitment to Sheriff on motion of ELIZ.
CASH, September 21, 1835. Sheriff: THOS. N. EUBANK.
Book 10, Page 186 -- Administrator's Account by EUBANK, late sheriff -
from November 16, 1835, with will annexed. MATT. KNIGHT - rent; cash
from MRS. CASH. Balance of $792.07. Report received September 28,
1839. JNO. W. BROADDUS and JAS. F. TALIAFERRO.

BENJ. CASH -- Book 1, Page 325 -- June 5, 1776, written; February 3,
1777, probated. Witnesses: HENDRICK ARNOLD, FRANCIS SATTERWHITE,
NANCY and CALEB HIGGINBOTHAM. Ux, NANCY - where I live - 400 acres.
Children when of age; my boys - slaves (2) left me by my father. Ex-
ecutors: ux and RICH. BALLENGER and ROBT. CASH.
Book 1, Page 326 -- Administrator's Bond -- February 3, 1777. RICH.
BALLENGER and ROBT. CASH. Bondsmen: JOS. DILLARD and JNO. MARR.
NANCY, widow, renounced administrator or benefit of legacy.
Book 1, Page 347 -- Inventory -- May 5, 1777 - L 263-8-6; no committee
named.

CALPHUNEA CASH (S. middle initial) -- Book 12, Page 485 -- Guardian
Bond -- LEWELLIN T. CASH, MARBEL C. GOODWIN, and JAS. M. GANNAWAY,
November 17, 1851, for LEWELLIN CASH as guardian of CALPHUNEA S.,
SARAH H., CORDELIA A., MARGARET CASH. No parents set forth.

CARY J. CASH -- Book 12, Page 528 -- Constable, June 21, 1852. Bonds-
men: SHELTON H. WRIGHT, JOSHUA CAMPBELL, ARCHIBALD BEARD, M. C.
GOODWIN. District 3 election on May 27, 1852, for 2 years from
July 1, 1852.
Book 13, Page 356 -- Same, June 19, 1854. Bondsmen: M. C. GOODWIN,
E. P. TUCKER. Same district; electtion of May 25, 1854.
Book 14, Page 132 -- Same, June 16, 1856. Bondsmen: HENRY LOVING,
SIDNEY FLETCHER, W. H. ROSE. Same district.
Book 14, Page 572 -- Same, June 21, 1858. Bondsmen: J. S. PENDLETON,
ARCHER BEARD, THOS. WHITEHEAD, JAS. W. HENLEY, R. A. PENDLETON.
Book 15, Page 333 -- Same, June 18, 1860. Bondsmen: M. C. GOODWIN,
JAS. W. HENLEY, LOUIS CAMPBELL, W. S. CLAIBORNE.

Book 17, Page 106 -- Same, June 18, 1866. Bondsmen: RO. A. PENDLE-
TON, SAML. H. GARLAND.

CHAS. T. CASH -- Book 16, Page 494 -- Constable -- June 20, 1864.
Bondsmen: M. C. GOODWIN, J. W. CLARK. District 4.

HOWARD CASH -- Book 1, Page 228 -- February 28, 1772, written; October 6, 1772, probated. Witnesses: RODERICK McCULLOCH and DAVID
CRAWFORD. Ux, RUTH - land for life where I live; son, JOELL - 110
acres adjoining where he lives, and slaves; grandson, HOWARD CASH,
son of my son, JOELL CASH; daughter, MARY LIVELY, son, BENJ. CASH -
400 acres next to CAPT. AARON HIGGINBOTHAM; negro bought of THOS.
MITHCELL. Daughter, ROSANNA, and at her death to my grandson, MICAJAH.
Daughter, ANN POWELL - if without issue, to children of ROSANNA.
Son, ROBT. CASH - 240 acres between my land and that of STEPHEN CASH.
Daughter, MARY ANN CASH, if she or RUTH, my daughter, should die
single - daughter, ELIZ. NUCKLES; son, STEPHEN CASH; daughter, SARAH
MAUZE (This is hard to decipher. If it is MAUZE. I know that the
MAUZEY family is in Fauquier region. My wife is descended from JNO.
MAUZEY (sometimes pronounced as MOZEE) from Fauquier and ux, NEE
KAHOE, who married in that Virginia county and went to Madison County,
Kentucky. Executors: ux, and sons, JOEL, BENJ., and ROBT. CASH.
Book 2, Page 160 -- Guardian Bond -- March 1, 1784, RICH. OGLESBY as
guardian of HOWARD CASH, orphan of JOELL CASH, deceased. Bondsman:
RICH. BALLINGER.
Book 2, Page 164 -- Division, but no details; order of March court,
1784. Recorded April 5, 1784. DAVID CRAWFORD, RODERICK McCULLOCH,
SAML. HIGGINBOTHAM.

JAS. T. CASH -- Book 13, Page 26 -- Constable -- October 18, 1852.
Bondsmen: RO. A. PENDLETON, M. C. GOODWIN. This is indexed as
Administrator's Bond item.
Book 13, Page 256 -- Constable -- June 19, 1854. Bondsmen: SAML.
SCOTT, THOS. WHITEHEAD, M. C. GOODWIN. District 3.

JESSE CASH -- Book 14, Page 172 -- Administrator's Bond -- September 15,
1856. CARY J. CASH. Bondsman: EDMUND P. TUCKER.
Book 14, Page 284 -- Inventory -- October 4, 1854, but recorded
May 18, 1857. This seems to be clerical error for C. J. CASH is
listed as administrator, and he did not qualify until 1856. Total:
$27.96-3/4. RO. L. COLEMAN, T. L. TAYLOR.
Book 14, Page 285 -- Sales, October 4, 1856. Family buyers: OTIS,
C. J., J. T., LEED, CHAS., CHAP., and JAS. CASH. Administrator:
C. J. CASH.

JOEL CASH -- Book 1, Page 252 -- Administrator's Bond -- October 4,
1773, TABITHA CASH. Bondsman: JNO. MARR.
Book 3, Page 115 -- Refunding Bond -- July 6, 1789. TABITHA and BART-
LETT CASH and BENJ. ROGERS gave bond to protect JNO. MARR from any
loss on bond with TABITHA.
Book 14, Page 86 -- Administrator's Bond -- GEO. W. CARTER and WALKER
S. CARTER, March 17, 1856, for GEO. CARTER.

JOS. CASH -- Book 5, Page 63 -- Administrator's Bond -- January 21,
1811. JAS. MURPHY. Bondsman: JNO. WARWICK.

L. S. CASH -- Book 12, Page 22 (indexed as Page 15) -- Guardian Bond --
August 17, 1847. WM. M. CASH as guardian of L. S., S. M., and M. P.
CASH, orphans of REUBEN CASH, deceased. Bondsman: EPHINSTONE A. CASH.
This is indexed in "L.'s" of "C.'s" as given, but it does not jibe
with deed book data. This name of ELPHISTONE is spelled in several
different ways and it would appear that there were at least two such
persons. The deed cited shows that one was still a minor in 1847,
but one was old enough to be bondsman on this guardian item. There
are several items on REUBEN CASH in marriage as I shall show. In
Deed Book AA, Page 571, September 16, 1847, BASHEMIA CASH, widow of
REUBEN CASH, deceased; WILL M. CASH; HENRY CASH; JNO. E. JENKINS and
ux, ROSA (formerly CASH); CARY J. CASH and ux, MARTHA (formerly CASH);
ELPHENSTRON CASH; STANLEY M. CASH; and MARION CASH -- last three infants under 21 by guardian, WM. M. CASH to HENRY CAMPBELL under Amherst

County decree for REUBEN CASH estate division -- 214 acres. In light of the bond for WM. M. CASH just a month prior to this deed, it would appear that we can account for two of the wards under 21; M. P. seems to be MARION; S. M. seems to be STANLEY M.; but the one indexed as L. S. would seem to be ELPPENSTRON CASH and NOT L. S. CASH as indexed. Is BASHEMIA the BETHEMIA WRIGHT who married REUBEN CASH in Amherst County? Bond was made December 18, 1816. Parent or guardian of husband: JEMIMA CASH, JAS. and WM. CASH, guardians of REUBEN. Parent or guardian of bride: MOSES WRIGHT. Securities or witnesses: HOWARD CASH, STEPHEN CASH, JESSE WRIGHT, A. B. DAVIES. Another REUBEN CASH marriage shows on October 30, 1821, when he married MILLY LOGAN. Security: DAVID LOGAN and BEVERLY DAVIES.

LEWELLEN T. CASH -- Book 12, Page 492 -- Inventory -- February 4, 1852: $866.00. CHAS. H. MASSIE, ALEX. H. BURKS, CHAS. MASSIE.
Book 12, Page 525 -- Administrator's Bond -- January 19, 1852. MARBLE C. GOODWIN. Bondsman: BENJ. T. HENLEY.
Book 14, Page 487 -- Administrator's Account -- November 19, 1857, by GOODWIN from June 31, 1855. Amount paid to D. W. TAPSCOTT.

MAYO CASH -- Book 16, Page 97 -- Administrator's Bond -- October 21, 1861. RO. L. COLEMAN. Bondsman: RO. A. COGHILL.

PARMELIA CASH (Late HUDSON) -- Book 14, Page 254 -- Administrator's Bond -- January 19, 1857. CHAPMAN CASH. Bondsman: RO. L. COLEMAN. It is set forth that decedent is PARMELIA or PERMELIA CASH; late HUDSON.

RANDOLPH CASH -- Book 10, Page 132 -- April 2, 1838, written; June 17, 1839, probated. Codicil of July 13, 1838. Witnesses to will: CORNL. SALE, THOS. V. GOODRICH, JNO. H. CHRISTIAN; same for codicil - plus WM. M. WALLER. Granddaughter, SARAH E. HIGGINBOTHAM (formerly HARGROVE); grandson, HEZEKIAH HARGROVE ("B." and "R." used for initial in various placed); grandson, JOS. M. HARGROVE; grandson, WM. J. (I.) MITCHELL; granddaughter, LUCINDA MITCHELL; granddaughters: STELLEY and MARIA MITCHELL; grandson, ISHAM HARMER (Note: This name is spelled in many ways in data. In Deed Book AA, Page 40, when CASH heirs sell land, it is indexed and spelled ITHAMAN HARMON, and he was resident of Rockbridge.) -- when he is 21; MISS SEANSEY MITCHELL has lived with me for 4 years and gets $100 for attention to my household business. My land - if grandchildren of daughter HARGROVE are without issue; same as to daughter MITCHELL's children. Executors: CORNL. SALE, THOS. V. GOODRICH, JNO. H. CHRISTIAN. Codicil: Title to slaves to grandchildren: SARAH E. HIGGINBOTHAM, HEZ. R. HARGROVE, JAS. B. HARGROVE, JOS. M. HARGROVE, LUCINDA MITCHELL, MARTHA S. MITCHELL, and ITHAMA HARMER -- title may be contested. If so, executors are to retain Nead, devised to grandson, WM. J. MITCHELL, and hire him annually until title is determined. Page 133, ROBT. MITCHELL qualified, June 17, 1839. Bondsmen: EDWD. A. CABELL and CORNL. SALE. Page 137, RUFUS HIGGINBOTHAM qualified on same date. Bondsmen: ABSALOM HIGGINBOTHAM and CORNL. SALE.
Book 10, Page 147 -- Inventory -- no total, July 13, 1839. ABSALOM HIGGINBOTHAM, CORNL. SALE, ADDISON TALIAFERRO.
Book 10, Page 273 -- Administrator's Account from February 16, 1839, by RO. MITCHELL - paid to F. G. POWELL for walling in graveyard. Recorded September 21, 1840.
Book 10, Page 275 -- Administrator's Account by RUFUS HIGGINBOTHAM from June 17, 1839. Approved by JNO. WHITEHEAD and L. S. EMETT. Report of August 1, 1840; recorded September 21, 1840.
Book 11, Page 62 -- Administrator's Account by RO. MITCHELL from September 5, 1840. Suit vs. SANDIDGE, BROWN, and HARGROVE; paid in full to C. (?) MITCHELL for legacy in full. Recorded April 18, 1842.
Book 11, Page 58 (indexed Page 58) -- Administrator's Account by RUFUS HIGGINBOTHAM. Recorded April 18, 1842.
Book 11, Page 506 -- Administrator's Account by both administrators; recorded March 24, 1847. $169.27 to each legatee: WM. J. MITCHELL, RUFUS HIGGINBOTHAM, JOS. M. HARGROVE, JAS. B. HARGROVE, LUCINDA MITCHELL, ELSELLA (?) MITCHELL, ANN M. and MARTHA MITCHELL, ITHAMAN HARMAN, HEZEKIAH HARGROVE; A. L. FOGUS' receipt for share of my ux.
Book 11, Page 585 -- Administrator's Account -- ROBT. MITCHELL from

November 27, 1841; recorded December 20, 1847. To RUFUS HIGGINBOTHAM
for ELIZ. HIGGINBOTHAM's share; HEZEKIAH B. and JAS. B. HARGROVE;
LUCINDA MITCHELL; STILLEY MITCHELL; ANN M. MITCHELL; MARTHA MITCHELL;
ITHANER HARMAN - part returned; P., M., and SEATON MITCHELL; MARY and
C. MITCHELL - $1,214.47 divided by them.
Book 12, Page 1 -- Administrator's Account -- RUFUS HIGGINBOTHAM
from November 30, 1842. Recorded December 20, 1847. To witnesses:
MARY and P. MITCHELL. Paid to P. SEATON MITCHELL; P. and M. MITCHELL.

ROBT. CASH -- Book 2, Page 58 -- November 6, 1781, written; May 6,
1782, probated. Witnesses: CALEB HIGGINBOTHAM, THOS. POWELL (FA),
CHAS. BURRUS, MARYAN HIGGINBOTHAM. Ux, TAMSEY - 200 acres where I
live; my 2 sons, SAML. and BARNETT CASH; all of my children: PAMELA,
SOPHIA, FRANCES, SAML., BARNETT - 2 years of schooling; if any is
without issue. Executors: SAML. HIGGINBOTHAM; HENDRICK ARNOLD; ux,
TAMSEY.
Book 2, Page 59 -- Administrator's Bond -- May 6, 1782 -- TAMSEY CASH,
HENDRICK ARNOLD, SAML. HIGGINBOTHAM. Bondsmen: JAS. WARE and THOS.
POWELL.
Book 2, Page 66 -- Inventory -- July 1, 1782: L 317-1-10. JACOB
SMITH, NOELL JOHNSON, RICH. OGLESBY.

RUTH CASH -- Book 2, Page 159 -- Administrator's Bond -- March 1, 1784.
HENDRICK ARNOLD. Bondsman: CALEB HIGGINBOTHAM.

SAML. CASH -- Book 4, Page 468 -- Constable -- June 15, 1807. Bonds-
man: WM. SALE. Appointed for 4 years in 4th Hundred.
Book 5, Page 580 -- Minister's Bond, Methodist, May 20, 1816. To
GOV. WILSON C. NICHOLAS. Bondsman: RO. RIVERS.

SAML. G. CASH -- Book 15, Page 66 -- Administrator's Bond -- February 21, 1859. M. C. GOODWIN. Bondsman: DABNEY SANDIDGE.
Book 16, Page 20 -- Administrator's Account by GOODWIN from February 21,
1859. Recorded December 17, 1860. No details.
Book 17, Page 90 -- Administrator's Account -- Recorded April 18, 1866.
Amount paid to CHAS. T. CASH. Mention of suspension of business "con-
sequent upon the war" -- all sums paid in Confederate money and
scaled to their specie value. Paid to SANDY (F. C.) and administrator
of JAS. W. STAPLES.

STEPHEN CASH -- Book 3, Page 550 -- December 18, 1798, written;
June 17, 1799, probated. Witnesses: JNO. MASSIE, CHAS. TUCKER, JNO.
SMITH. Sons, WM. and JAS. - 295 acres where I live; my ux; rest of
my children.
Book 4, Page 4 -- Inventory -- February 16, 1801; no total. WM. S.
LANDRIDGE (?), CHAS. TUCKER, JNO. SMITH.
Book 4, Page 327 -- Administrator's Bond -- December 15, 1800. PETER
CASH. Bondsmen: WM.CASH and DANL. TYLER (TILER).
Book 5, Page 6 -- Administrator's Account -- PETER CASH from Febru-
ary 4, 1801. Land tax for 1801 and 1803. To RANDOLPH CASH; CHAS.
IRVINE's estate for beef; Amounts paid to LYDDA COTTRAL; HOWARD CASH;
JNO. CASH; SALLY TYLOR; JEREMIAH CASH; THOS. CASH. Cash received
from WM. and JAS. CASH. Recorded July 14, 1809.

SUSAN CASH -- Book 12, Page 486 -- Guardian Bond -- February 16, 1852.
MARBLE C. GOODWIN. Bondsman: AAML. G. CASH. Wards: SUSAN, SARAH,
CORDELIA, and SOPHIA CASH, orphans of LEWELLIN T. CASH, deceased.

    I wish that space permitted an excursus into order and deed
items on the CASH family, but this is out of the question. I have
hopes of continuing my deed works at a later date, and I would also
like to do some order books. Time is the question which faces me,
so I can only hope.

ELIZ. CASHWELL -- Book 5, Page 530 -- Administrator's Bond -- PETER
CASHWELL and CHAS. MUNDY, December 18, 1815, for PETER CASHWELL.
Book 5, Page 558 -- Inventory -- December 30, 1815 - $770.00. REUBEN
NORVELL, THOS. CREWS, JNO. WARWICK.

MILDRED CASHWELL -- Book 8, Page 399 -- August 5, 1826, written; March 17, 1834, probated. Witnesses: EDMD. WINSTON, ASA ADCOCK, RO. GRANT, DANL. F. CHRISTIAN. Proved by WINSTON and CHRISTIAN. PETER CASHWELL renounced administratorship, and ELIJAH FLETCHER qualified. Bondsman: WM. S. CRAWFORD. Brother, PETER CASHWELL -- 8 slaves and estate never divided; PETER to administer.
Book 8, Page 423 -- Inventory -- August 15, 1834 - $3,160.00. ZACH. D. TINSLEY, HENRY S. PENDLETON, RALPH C. SHELTON.

PETER CASHWELL, JR., and SR. -- Book 4, Page 150 -- no date when written; probated, June 18, 1804. Witnesses: RICH. WILSON, ANDREW MONROE, HENRY BROWN, CHANDLER BROWN, JNO. BROWN. Proved by WILSON, MONROE, and HENRY BROWN. JNO. and PETER CASHWELL qualified. Bonds-men: HENRY BROWN and JOS. DILLARD. Ux, CATHERINE; sons, HENRY, WM.; daughter, MILLY CASHWELL; daughters: BETSY, CHARITY, JUDITH, RACHELL; sons, JNO. and PETER - my land - 200 acres and house; son, JNO. - 50 acres bought of CHAPPELS and part of where I live. Still to JNO. and PETER. Executors: JNO. and PETER. Administrator's Bond on Page 382. This is Sr.
Book 11, Page 303 -- March 27, 1826, written; February 17, 1845, probated -- JR. -- Witnesses: F. F. BOWEN, JNO. T. MASON, ALEX. BRIDGLAND. BRIDGLAND is dead and the other two witnesses are out of Virginia. Their handwriting attested by C. DABNEY and NATHAN SCHOOLFIELD. STEPHEN BOWLES attested as to testator's handwriting. March 18, 1845, ELIJAH FLETCHER qualified. Bondsman: TIMOTHY FLET-CHER. Nephew, PETER C. HANSARD -- if without issue; to SIDNEY FLETCHER; sister, MILLY CASHWELL -- slave and to be freed at her death, if possible. Another slave at MILLY's death to LUCCAN FLETCHER. SIDNEY and LUCCAN FLETCHER, sons of E. FLETCHER of Lynchburg. Executor: ELIJAH FLETCHER. Administrator's Bond on Page 310. Note: This is one of the few references to LUCIAN FLETCHER in data. See F data for discussion of ELIJAH FLETCHER who owned Sweet Briar Plantation, and it was to become site of the famous college. INDIANA FLETCHER, daughter, of ELIJAH, inherited it and became ux of a WILLIAMS from New York. ELIJAH and INDIANA ignored LUCIAN in their wills and his heirs took steps to get a share of the Sweet Briar estate. There is an enormous box of papers in the courthouse about the settlement made upon them for $30,000.00 by Sweet Briar officials. The data is not too flattering and I have no intention of airing it to the public.

POWHATAN C. CASHWELL -- Book 16, Page 150 -- Administrator's Bond -- RO. N. ELLIS and RO. W. SNEAD, August 18, 1862, for RO. ELLIS.

WILLIAM CASHWELL -- Book 11, Page 536 -- Administrator's Bond -- JAS. H. CASHWELL and THOS. A. EUBANK, July 19, 1847, for JAS. H. CASHWELL.

ANTONETTA CAWTHORNE -- Book 6, Page 347 -- Guardian Bond -- ISAAC RUCKER, JNO. W. SMITH, and WM. DUNCAN, February 17, 1823, for ISAAC RUCKER as guardian of ANTONETTA and LULINA (?) CAWTHORNE, orphans of ROBT. CAWTHORNE, deceased; also spelled without final "e." Margin: Bill of administrator sent to clerk of General Court, April 3, 1823.

JANE CAWTHORN(E) -- Book 8, Page 309 -- Guardian Bond -- THOS. W. GLASS, WM. ARMISTEAD, PETER RUCKER, and BENJ. NORVELL, March 18, 1833, for THOS. GLASS as guardian of JANE CAWTHORNE, orphan of ROBT. CAW-THORNE, deceased.

ROBT. CAWTHORNE -- Book 6, Page 310 -- July 20, 1822, written; September 16, 1822, probated. Witnesses: ISAAC RUCKER, AARON HIGGIN-BOTHAM, JOS. MILSTEAD, JNO. or JOS. (blurred), H. CLEMENTS. Proved by RUCKER, HIGGINBOTHAM, and CLEMENTS. Ux, MARY - my lands; youngest daughter, JANE, when married or 21; whenever my children marry; Daughters: SARAH STONE and children; LUCINDA GLASS; GILEMENA; MARY ANN; ANTONETTA; LOUISA; and JANE CAWTHORNE; son, ROBT. - one share to each. If any are without heirs.
Book 6, Page 348 -- Inventory -- $2,869.00. WM. CARTER, WM. HAISLEP, AARON HIGGINBOTHAM, March 17, 1823. ISAAC RUCKER, administrator.
Book 10, Page 37 -- Estate Commitment to Sheriff, August, 1838. Motion of DABNEY SANDIDGE; JNO. COLEMAN, Sheriff.

PATSY CHASKEY (Also SHASTAN) -- Book 5, Page 66 -- Guardian Bond --
JAS. CHASKEY (signed SHASTEN); RO. CHAPAN; ABNER PADGETT, August 19,
1811, for JAS. CHASKEY as guardian of PATSEY CHASKEY. The bond is
also signed by POLLY SHASTAN and name of CHAPAN is not signed.

MINERVA CHEATHAM (COLEMAN) -- Book 24, Page 90 -- August 16, 1805,
written; Tuesday, December 17, 1907, probated. This is botched in
that date is given as 1805, but clerical error by clerk. Her name is
spelled MENERVA and MANERVA in places and one other error will be
cited. Of Amherst County - my son, EDWD. COLEMAN - house derived
from my son, SILAS COLEMAN, son of my first husband, WILLIAM COLEMAN.
Executors: son, WM. ED COLEMAN. Error seems to be clerical in naming
of witnesses: In on place they are given as THOS. WHITEHEAD, JR.,
and SILAS COLEMAN, but in summary, SILAS is called SILAS CHEATHAM.

ANNE ELIZ. CHEATWOOD -- Book 6, Page 39 -- Guardian Bond -- JESSE
SPINNER, JACOB and JONAH PIERCE,October 19, 1818, for JESSE SPINNER
as guardian of ANNE ELIZ. CEATWOOD, orphan of DANL. CHEATWOOD,
deceased.

DANIEL CHEATWOOD -- Book 6, Page 8 -- Ordinary Bond at house in county,
June 15, 1818. Bondsman: LAWSON WILTSHIRE.
Book 6, Page 31 -- Administrator's Bond -- FRANCES CHEATWOOD, STEVEN
WATTS, and BENJAMIN HARRISON, September 21, 1818, for FRANCES
CHEATWOOD.
Book 6, Page 35 -- Inventory -- order of September, 1818. November 12,
1818. Old negro, Chas., not appraised and reference to deed concern-
ing him; forbidden to do so by JESSE SPINNER and JONAH PIERCE.
Commissioners: THOS. WINGFIELD, JOS. KYLE, WILEY CAMPBELL.
Book 6, Page 128 -- Division -- To JONAS PIERCE in right of ux, SALLY,
late CHEATWOOD; to ANNE E.; HYRUM; LEVINA CHEATWOOD - 4 lots. Febru-
ary 21, 1820. CHAS. MONDAY; JNO. WARWICK; JAS. S. DILLARD.

HIRAM CHEATWOOD -- Book 6, Page 29 -- Guardian Bond -- JONAS and JACOB
PIERCE and WM. ARMISTEAD, September 21, 1818, for JONAS PIERCE as
guardian of HIRAM, orphan of DANL. CHEATWOOD.

LOUIVINIA CHEATWOOD (so indexed, but LEVINA above) -- Book 6, Page 40 --
Guardian Bond -- JESSE SPINNER, JACOB and JONAS PIERCE, October 19,
1818, for JESSE SPINNER as guardian of LEVISA (sic) CHEATWOOD, orphan
of DANL. CHEATWOOD.

MARY FRANCES CHEATWOOD -- Book 6, Page 40 -- Guardian Bond -- FRANCES
CHEATWOOD and WM. WOODROOF, October 19, 1818, for FRANCES CHEATWOOD
as guardian of MARY FRANCES CHEATWOOD, orphan of DANL. CHEATWOOD.
Note: She does not show in division of 1821 under DANL. CHEATWOOD.
Another ward also is named along with her: DANL. CHEATWOOD, and
he does not show in division either.

ANN CHENAULT -- Book 4, Page 615 -- Guardian Bond -- CHRISTOPHER ISBELL
and WM. ISBELL, January 15, 1810, for CHRISTOPHER ISBELL as guardian
of ANN CHENAULT, orphan of THOMAS CHENAULT.

BENJ. CHILDRESS -- Book 1, Page 293 -- January 18, 1775, written;
October 2, 1775, probated. Witnesses: JNO. VIGUST; THOS. J. JOP-
LING, JR.; JOSIAH JOPLING; DAVID SHELTON. My land; children until 21;
youngest son, ROYAL; my other sons; ux and daughters. Executors:
friends, THOS. JOPLING, SR., and JR.; JOSIAH and RALPH JOPLING.
Book 1, Page 295 -- Administrator's Bond -- THOS. JOPLING, SR.; JOSIAH
JOPLING; RALPH JOPLING, probate date. Bondsmen: JAS. NEVIL, JAS.
WARE, EDMD. WILCOX.
Book 1, Page 316 -- Inventory -- July 1, 1776 - L 185-11-4. JNO.
DIGGES; WM. HARRIS, JR.; ALEX. REID, JR.

JOSEPH CHILDRESS -- Book 5, Page 32 -- February 8, 1811, written;
October 21, 1811, probated. Witnesses: WM. DUNCAN, HUDSON DAWSON,
EDWD. TAYLOR and proved by them. LEONARD HENLEY qualified. Bondsman:
JNO. SMITH. Son, HENRY F.B.; my ux, POLLY; son, LEONARD H. is

without issue. 140 acres where JNO. CLEMENTS lives; my two sons pre-
viously named. Executors: three friends, LEONARD HENLEY, BENJ.
SANDIDGE, BENJ. TALIAFERRO. Administrator's Bond - Page 84.
Book 5, Page 391 -- Inventory -- L 553-2-6 -- October 18, 1813. EDMD.
T. COLEMAN, WM. DUNCAN, WM. SANDIDGE.

LEONARD H. CHILDRESS -- Book 7, Page 172 -- Guardian Bond -- RICHESON
HENLEY, JAS. F. TALIAFERRO, and BENJ. TALIAFERRO, August 18, 1828,
for RICHESON HENLEY as guardian of LEONARD H. CHILDRESS, orphan of
JOS. CHILDRESS, deceased.
Book 11, Page 150 -- Estate Commitment to Sheriff, June 21, 1843.
Motion of JNO. G. (Y.?) MEEM. JAS. POWELL, sheriff.

LUCY CHILDRESS -- Book 3, Page 366 -- January 26, 1792, written;
September, 1795, probated. Witnesses: GIDEON CREWS, J. N. POWELL,
NICHL. WEST. Son, JAMES THOMAS; daughter, BETHENIAH HILTON; daughter,
MARTHA HOPSON; daughter, JUDITH MITCHELL; grandson, JAS. TURNER;
granddaughter, SYLTHY TURNER; grandson, JESSE ALLEN; to ELIZ. DANIELL(?)
and granddaughters, MARTHA and BETHENIAH ALLEN, daughters of SAML.
ALLEN; grandsons, NORBOURN and NEIL THOMAS. Executors: Brother,
MICHL. THOMAS and friend, COL. WM. CABELL, JR., and HUDSON MARTIN.
Book 4, Page 298 -- Administrator's Bond -- LEWIS NEVIL and CORNL.
THOMAS. Bondsmen: NORBOURN THOMAS and GEO. HYLTON, February 16, 1796.

THOS. CHILDRESS -- Book 4, Page 460 -- Constable -- January 21, 1806.
Bondsman: RO. WRIGHT.

AGNES CHRISTIAN -- Book 17, Page 22 -- January 3, 1865, written;
February 20, 1865, probated. Witnesses: JOS. PETTYJOHN, THOS. A.
BROWN; GEO. M. CHRISTIAN qualified; Bondsman: JNO. H. WATTS, Brother,
GEO. H. CHRISTIAN to administer. Slaves held by EDGAR WHITEHEAD to
be sold by him and proceeds to HELEN CHRISTIAN and MARION GADDIS,
children of my deceased brother, CHAS. W. CHRISTIAN, Lynchburg.
Nieces, BETTY and EDMONIA CHRISTIAN, children of my brother, EDMOND
CHRISTIAN; money in Citizens' Savings Bank, Lynchburg. My sister,
ELIZA A. CHRISTIAN.

ALEX. CHRISTIAN -- Book 19, Page 316 -- Minister's Bond, February 18,
1878; no denomination.

BETSY CHRISTIAN -- Book 3, Page 284 -- Guardian Bond -- JAS. DILLARD
and STEPHEN WATTS, October 21, 1793, for JAS. DILLARD as guardian of
BETSY CHRISTIAN, orphan of GEO. CHRISTIAN.
Book 3, Page 310 -- Guardian Bond -- STEPHEN WATTS and HENRY BELL,
September 15, 1794, for STEPHEN WATTS as guardian of BETSY CHRISTIAN,
orphan of GEO. CHRISTIAN.

CHAS. CHRISTIAN -- Book 5, Page 208 -- Administrator's Bond -- WALTER
D. CHRISTIAN and ISAAC RUCKER, April 19, 1813, for WALTER CHRISTIAN.
Book 5, Page 227 -- Inventory -- $83.80. HENRY PIERCE, WILEY CAMP-
BELL, THOS. WINGFIELD, June 21, 1813.

CHARLES BURKS CHRISTIAN (Some are indexed for CHAS. B.) -- Book 12,
Page 501 -- Guardian Bond -- FRANCES A. CHRISTIAN and BENJ. P. WALKDER,
March 15, 1852, for FRANCES CHRISTIAN as guardian of CHAS. B.,

CHAS. H. CHRISTIAN -- Book 12, Page 205 -- Administrator's Bond --
JAS. H. JOINER and JAS. DILLARD, August 20, 1849, for JAMES JOINER.
Book 13, Page 88 -- Administrator's Account by JOINER from October,
1849; recorded November 17, 1852.

CHAS. L. CHRISTIAN -- Book B, Page 21 -- Estate Commitment to Sheriff --
Monday, April 3, 1843. Motion of ELIJAH L. CHRISTIAN; Sheriff:
JAS. POWELL.

CHAS. M. CHRISTIAN -- Book 11, Page 311 -- September 14, 1844, writ-
ten; March 17, 1845, probated. Witnesses: WM. DILLARD, JOS. J.
BURKS, IVERSON L. TWYMAN. Proved by BURKS and DILLARD. May 19, 1845,
FRANCES CHRISTIAN qulaified; Bondsmen: B. P. WALKER, JOS. J. BURKS,
THOS. FITCH. No division to be made until January 1, 1852, unless ux,

FRANCES ANN, remarries - then to be done immediately thereafter.
Three youngest children to be educated until January 1, 1852 --
$1,000.00 for each one to be educated. If daughter, MARY SUSAN, mar-
ries before January 1, 1852, or if any die without or with issue.
Administrator's Bond - p. 313.
Book 12, Page 15 -- Administrator's Account by administratrix from
March 25, 1845. WM. DILLARD and S. W. CHRISTIAN. December 20, 1847.
Book 12, Page 237 -- Administrator's Account from December 29, 1847.
Paid S. W. CHRISTIAN; WM. DILLARD, commissioner. November 19, 1849.
Book 12, Page 260 -- Inventory, January 26, 1850 -- $10,008.91. WM.
DILLARD, ALEX. MUNDY, STEPHEN W. CHRISTIAN.
Book 13, Page 36 -- Division, January 1, 1853. MRS. FRANCES A.
CHRISTIAN, widow--slaves. Lots to MARY SUSAN, VA. LEE, CHAS. B.,
SARAH ELIZ. CHRISTIAN. Commissioners: WM. DILLARD, JNO. DILLARD,
STEPHEN W. CHRISTIAN.

CHAS. EDWARD CHRISTIAN -- Book 8, Page 444 -- Guardian Bond -- WESLEY
E. CHRISTIAN and JNO. RUSSELL, November 18, 1834, for WESLEY CHRIS-
TIAN as guardian of CHAS. RICH.; JAS. THOMAS; MARY JANE; MARTHA ANN;
EMILY FRANCES; JNO. WESLEY; and WESLEY E. CHRISTIAN, infant children
of WESLEY E. CHRISTIAN.

DRURY CHRISTIAN -- Book 2, Page 137 -- March 18 (10?), 1783, written;
October 6, 1783, probated. Witnesses: JAS. PAMPLIN, JNO. CHRISTIAN,
RO. ROGERS. Presented by ELIZ. UPSHAW and she qualified. Bondsmen:
JAS. DILLARD and JAS. PAMPLIN. Of Lexington Parish; beloved com-
panion, ELIZ. UPSHAW - plantation; brother, JNO. CHRISTIAN; son, JNO.
CHRISTIAN UPSHAW, land at mother's death. My four children: JNO.
CHRISTIAN UPSHAW; ELIZ. CHRISTIAN UPSHAW; LUCY CHRISTIAN UPSHAW;
SALLY CHRISTIAN UPSHAW - when of age or married. Administrator's Bond
is Page 139.
Book 2, Page 164 -- Inventory, November 17, 1783 - L 645-11-6. LAR-
KIN GATEWOOD, HENRY BELL, DANL. PERROW.
Book 5, Page 488 -- Guardian Bond -- ELIZ. CHRISTIAN and THOS. CREWS,
March 20, 1815, for ELIZ. CHRISTIAN as guardian of DRURY, MARY, and
SALLY CHRISTIAN, orphans of JOHN CHRISTIAN.
Book 5, Page 592 -- Guardian Bond -- This is seemingly a mixed-up
item. JNO. DILLARD - August 19, 1816, as guardian of DRURY, MARY,
and SALLY DILLARD, orphans of JNO. DILLARD, deceased. Bondsmen:
SAML. TURNER, JOS. DILLARD, HENRY H. WATTS. It will be noted that
the names of wards are the same as those for Book 5, Page 488 above.
The item here is indexed for DRURY CHRISTIAN and that is why it is
included herein. I am inclined to think that it is a CHRISTIAN item
and that there is a clerical error naming them as DILLARD orphans.
Book 5, Page 506 -- Administrator's Bond -- MOURNING CHRISTIAN,
CHAS. L. CHRISTIAN, ABNER CHRISTIAN, June 19, 1815, for MOURNING
CHRISTIAN as administratrix.
Book 5, Page 544 -- Inventory, November 7, 1815 -- $5,591.65. CHAS.
BRIGHTWELL, HENRY H. WATTS, MICAJAH PENDLETON.
Book 8, Page 223 -- Constable, June 18, 1832. Bondsmen: JAS. G.
CHRISTIAN, PETER F. CHRISTIAN.
Book 8, Page 319 -- Same, June 17, 1833. Bondsmen: same.
Book 9, Page 78 -- Same, June 15, 1835. Bondsmen: JAS. G. CHRISTIAN
and LEWIS HARRISON.

ELIJAH L. CHRISTIAN -- Book 11, Page 115 -- Administrator's Bond --
ELIJAH L. CHRISTIAN, JAS. G. CHRISTIAN, JAS. McDANIEL, JNO. H. CHRIS-
TIAN, March 21, 1843, for ELIJAH CHRISTIAN.
Book 11, Page 175 -- Inventory, one mule colt-$60.00, shown to us by
administrator, October 5, 1843. JAS. F. SATTERWHITE, JNO. COLEMAN,
REUBEN COLEMAN.
Book 12, Page 32 -- Estate Commitment to Sheriff. January term,
1848. Motion of GEO. MARTIN. JAS. L. LAMKIN, Sheriff.

ELIJAH S. (L?) CHRISTIAN -- Book B, Page 28 -- Estate Commitment to
Sheriff., Wednesday, August 26, 1846. Motion of JNO. F.(?) CHRISTIAN.
WM. M. WALLER, Sheriff.

ELIZ. ANN MURRAY CHRISTIAN -- Book 7, Page 296 -- Guardian Bond --
NICHL. P. TAYLOR and JNO. RUSSELL, December 21, 1829, for NICHL. TAY-

LOR as guardian of ELIZ. ANN MURRAY CHRISTIAN, orphan of WALTER L. CHRISTIAN, JR.

ELIZ. H. CHRISTIAN -- Book 12, Page 576 -- August 25, 1852, written; September 20, 1852, probated. Witnesses: J. L. TWYMAN; JNO. ROBERTS, JR.; DAVID KYLE. Children of sisters, SOPHIA N. KYLE and LUCY CHRISTIAN, ux of STEPHEN W. CHRISTIAN. Grandniece, ELIZ. HARVEY CHRISTIAN, daughter of JAS. B. and LUCY J. CHRISTIAN--slave several years ago--when ELIZ. is 21. Executor: friend, STEPHEN W. CHRISTIAN. Proved by TWYMAN and ROBERTS. STEPHEN CHRISTIAN qualified. Bondsman: WM. DILLARD.
Book 13, Page 33 -- Inventory -- $1,000.00; three slaves. ALEX. MUNDY, JNO. J. DILLARD, T. W. DILLARD. December 8, 1852.

GEO. CHRISTIAN -- Book 2, Page 218 -- Administrator's Bond -- MARTHA CHRISTIAN; JAS. DILLARD, the Elder; JNO. CHRISTIAN; HENRY BELL, March 7, 1785, for MARTHA CHRISTIAN.
Book 2, Page 238 -- Inventory, no total, August 1, 1785. RO. CHRISTIAN, JAS. LONDON, JAS. GRAHAM.

HENRY CHRISTIAN -- Book 4, Page 174 -- December 14, 1804, written; June 17, 1805, probated. Witnesses: DRURY BELL, DRURY CHRISTIAN, JAS. DILLARD, CHAS. CHRISTIAN. Produced by ISAAC RUCKER and proved by BELL; DILLARD and CHAS. CHRISTIAN. ISAAC RUCKER qualified. Bondsman: DRURY BELL. Ux, MARTHA; daughters: SUSANNAH B., FRANCES C., and MARTHA P. CHRISTIAN. All of my children, too. Executor: WM. B. CHRISTIAN of Hanover County and ISAAC RUCKER.
Book 4, Page 194 -- Inventory -- $1,162.83, October 18, 1805. DRURY and CHAS. CHRISTIAN; JAS. DILLARD. Administrator's Bond is Book 4, Page 406.

JAS. CHRISTIAN -- Book 1, Page 66 -- Administrator's Bond -- WM. CABELL - not administered by WM. DUIGUID, deceased. Bondsmen: JNO. HARVEY and PETERFIELD TRENT, August 6, 1765.
Book 2, Page 16 -- October 20, 1772, written; June 4, 1781, probated. Witnesses: JNO. CHRISTIAN, MAR CHRISTIAN, JNO. EVANS. Brother, JNO. CHRISTIAN; Hooker's creekland next to HENRY BELL and WM. DUVALL. Brother, GEO. CHRISTIAN--where I live; slaves named. Executors: Brothers, JNO. and GEO. CHRISTIAN. Page 17, Admiminstrator's Bond by GEO. CHRISTIAN. Bondsman: HENRY CHRISTIAN, June 4, 1781. JNO. made bond on probate date. Bondsman: HENRY CHRISTIAN.
Book 2, Page 45 -- Inventory, L 624-13-1, February 21, 1782. RO.; HENRY; JNO.; and DRURY CHRISTIAN. Book 2, Page 18 -- Adminsitrators Bond, JNO. CHRISTIAN. Bondsmen: JAS. PAMPLIN, CHAS. PATTESON, September 3, 1781.

JAS. G. CHRISTIAN -- Book 12, Page 32 -- Estate Commitment to Sheriff, December term, 1847. Motion of A. C. HARRISON. JAS. L. LAMKIN, Sheriff.

CAPT. JNO. CHRISTIAN -- Book 4, Page 499 -- Administrator's Bond -- ELIZ. CHRISTIAN; JAS. DILLARD, JR.; DRURY CHRISTIAN; STEPHEN and JAS. DILLARD, February 15, 1808, for ELIZ. CHRISTIAN; JAS. DILLARD, JR. and DRURY CHRISTIAN.
Book 4, Page 631 -- Inventory of CAPT. JNO. CHRISTIAN -- L 1209-15-3. GEO. PENN, ABNER CHRISTIAN; August 21, 1810.
Book 5, Page 494 -- Administrator's Account by JAS. DILLARD from July 4, 1809. To ELIZ. UPSHAW; wool hat for DRURY; MR. HENDERSON for schooling SALLY; due DRURY CHRISTIAN. January 20, 1815. Due ELIZ. CHRISTIAN. Total: L 978-0-9. January 20, 1815. R. NORVELL; GEO. PENN; JNO. HORSLEY, JR.
Book 8, Page 410 -- Estate Commitment to Sheriff, May, 1834, with will annexed. EDMD. WINSTON, Sheriff. I find no will here and this may be JNO. CHRISTIAN, B. of next item.

JNO. CHRISTIAN, B -- I have explained the use of this B in deed data. I was puzzled until I ran across a deed item showing B as Buffalo. This means that this particular man lived on Buffalo.
Book 6, Page 416 -- April 26, 1823, written; November 17, 1823, probated. Handwriting attested by HUDSON M. GARLAND, CHAS. H. CHRISTIAN,

and CATLETT CAMPBELL. JUDITH CHRISTIAN and PETER F. CHRISTIAN
qualified. Bondsmen: SAMUEL D. CHRISTIAN and WM. J. (I.) ISBELL.
Ux, JUDITH--land, etc. Children "that is living." Son, SAML., and
son that he left. Daughter, MARY DAVENPORT, and her brothers, WM. and
PETER, to serve as her trustees for her and children. Executors: ux,
and sons, CHAS. L., JNO., ELIJAH, and PETER CHRISTIAN. My children:
POLLY DAVENPORT, CHAS., JNO., WM. L., ELIJAH, WALTER, PETE, ELISHA,
DANL., DRURY, and JAS. (GRISHAM in parenthesis for him), JUDITH and
SAMUEL son(sic). Ux to administer. Administrator's Bond -- Book 6,
Page 407.
Book 6, Page 422 -- Inventory -- JNO. CHRISTIAN, Buffalo -- $4,897.75.
JOS. KYLE; THOS. APPLIN, SR.; SAML. D. CHRISTIAN, December 12, 1823.
Book 8, Page 410 -- Estate Commitment to Sheriff -- See same item
in JNO. of 234.
Book 9, Page 86 -- (indexed Page 80) -- Administrator's Account by
JUDITH CHRISTIAN and PETER F. CHRISTIAN from November, 1823. To
D. CHRISTIAN; BRIDGE and CHRISTIAN; to J. G. CHRISTIAN; D. F.
CHRISTIAN; bond of WM. L. CHRISTIAN; DRURY CHRISTIAN's shop account;
bond of CHAS. H. CHRISTIAN. Recorded June 17, 1835. WILEY CAMPBELL;
THOS. WINGFIELD; JOEL CAMPBELL, JR.
Book 10, Page 381 -- Slave list -- $7,075.00. Legatees paid: MARY
DAVENPORT, JNO. CHRISTIAN, ELIJAH L. CHRISTIAN, WALTER L. CHRISTIAN,
DANL. F. CHRISTIAN, SAML. CHRISTIAN, PETER F. CHRISTIAN,
WM. L. CHRISTIAN, CHAS. L. CHRISTIAN, PETER F. CHRISTIAN, son of
SAML. CHRISTIAN, DRURY CHRISTIAN, JUDITH CHRISTIAN, JAS. G. CHRISTIAN.
July 19, 1841. D. P. GOOCH, JONAS PIERCE, WILEY CAMPBELL.

JNO. F. CHRISTIAN -- Book 11, Page 88 -- Guardian Bond -- RO. H.
BROWN and WM. HIX, October 17, 1842, for WM. HIX as guardian of
JNO. F. CHRISTIAN, orphan of SAML. C. CHRISTIAN, deceased.

JNO. J. CHRISTIAN -- Book 8, Page 54 -- Guardian Bond -- DRURY CHRIS-
TIAN, JAS. G. and PETER F. CHRISTIAN, November 16, 1830, for DRURY
CHRISTIAN as guardian of JNO. J. CHRISTIAN, orphan of SAML. L. CHRIS-
TIAN, deceased.
Book 12, Page 125 -- Guardian Bond -- DRURY CHRISTIAN and JUDITH F.
WOODSON, March 21, 1848, for DRURY CHRISTIAN as guardian of JNO. J.,
WALTER M., CHAS. M., PETER P., ROBT. W., MARY E., and ANDREW J.
CHRISTIAN, orphans of JAS. G. CHRISTIAN, deceased.

JNO. L. CHRISTIAN -- Book 12, Page 108 -- Estate Commitment to Sheriff,
August, 1849. LINDSEY COLEMAN, Sheriff.
Book 13, Page 56 -- Administrator's Account by COLEMAN, Sheriff, and
administered from July, 1859. To EDMD. WINSTON, administrator of JNO.
CHRISTIAN, B. To JUDITH F. WOODSON, assignee of PETER F. CHRISTIAN,
executor of JNO. CHRISTIAN. Recorded August 13, 1852.

JUDITH L. CHRISTIAN -- Book 10, Page 285 -- Guardian Bond -- October 19, 1840. ASA W. CHRISTIAN and PETER F. CHRISTIAN for ASA CHRIS-
TIAN as guardian of JUDITH L. CHRISTIAN, orphan of CHAS. L. CHRISTIAN,
deceased.

MARTHA CHRISTIAN -- Book 12, Page 248 -- Administrator's Bond --
THOS. C. CHRISTIAN, NICHL. P. TAYLOR, WM. H. BURKS, and WM. L. CHRIS-
TIAN, September 17, 1849, for THOS. CHRISTIAN.
Book 12, Page 285 -- Administrator's Account -- JAS. L. LAMKIN,
Sheriff, and administer from April, 1848, Deed of Trust by JAS. G.
CHRISTIAN to GEO. W. TYREE, trustee. MARSHALL HARRIS examined ac-
counts, September 17, 1849. Returned September 16, 1850.

MARY CHRISTIAN -- Book 17, Page 206 -- October 25, 1863, written;
November 21, 1864, probated. Witnesses: JOS. PETTYJOHN and WM. W.
WALLER. Proved by PETTYJOHN, but he refused to administer; GEO. H.
CHRISTIAN qualified. Bondsmen: DAVID TINSLEY and JNO. H. WATTS.
TINSLEY was appointed curator, September 18, 1865, and will then
proved by WALLER. Daughter, AGNESS; son, PAUL; son, GEO. H. (appears
to be GEO. W. in some places), is in the arm; Administrator: JOS.
PETTYJOHN.

MOURNING CHRISTIAN -- Book 9, Page 327 -- January 28, 1837, written;

August 21, 1837, probated. Witnesses: WINGFIELD EUBANK; CHAS. L. CHRISTIAN; DAVID KYLE; proved by EUBANK and KYLE. WM. DILLARD renounced administrator, September 18, 1837; STEPHEN W. CHRISTIAN qualified; Bondsmen: WM. DILLARD and ALEX. MUNDY. My four daughters: SOPHIA KYLE, LUCY CHRISTIAN, ELIZ. CHRISTIAN, MARY BURKS and children: son, CHAS. M.; reference to deed of trust in Amherst County. Executor: friend, WM. DILLARD. Administrator's Bond is Book 9, Page 337 and inventory is Book 9, Page 343 -- $847.87, October 16, 1837. STEPHEN W. CHRISTIAN, administrator; JNO. DILLARD, SR.(?); SILAS DAVIDSON; JNO. DILLARD.
Book 9, Page 403 -- Sale, November 21, 1837; buyers: BETSY, STEPHEN, JAS. B. and WM. R. CHRISTIAN -- $1,278.33. MADISON LOVING, clerk of sale.
Book 9, Page 416 -- Dower division held for estate of DRURY CHRISTIAN. To SAML. BURKS and ux, MARY (formerly CHRISTIAN); and represented by CHAS. M. CHRISTIAN; to STEPHEN W. CHRISTIAN who married LUCY CHRISTIAN; to SOPHIA KYLE, formerly CHRISTIAN; to ELIZ. CHRISTIAN. November 28, 1837. Commissioners: WM. and JNO. DILLARD; GILES DAVIDSON.
Book 10, Page 50 -- Administrator's Account from 1837. Wheat sold on May 16 --. Names of JAS., W. R., ELIZ., STEPHEN W., JAS. B., and CHAS. M. CHRISTIAN. Total: $1,573.75, October 1, 1838. BENJ. P. WALKER and ISAAC W. WALKER.

NANCY L. CHRISTIAN -- Book 8, Page 388 -- Guardian Bond -- JAS. G. and DRURY CHRISTIAN, January 20, 1834, for JAS. CHRISTIAN as guardian of NANCY L. (S.?) and WM. LaFAYETTE CHRISTIAN, orphans of RO. W. CHRISTIAN.

PATSY CHRISTIAN -- Book 12, Page 32 -- Estate Commitment to Sheriff, January term, 1848. Motion of THOS. CHRISTIAN and J. P. TAYLOR. Sheriff: JAS. S. LAMKIN.

PAUL CHRISTIAN -- Book 16, Page 538 -- September 7, 1863, written; November 21, 1864, probated. Handwriting attested by THOS. A. BWORN and SAML. M. GARLAND. To MARIA LOUISA LEE; she lives in Amherst County and near Smyrna Church and HICKS' grocery. She is daughter of THOS. LEE.

PAULUS P. CHRISTIAN -- Book 24, Page 260 -- October 11, 1916, written; May 2, 1919, probated. Witnesses: CURTIS and JAS. A. STORY and proved by them. ATWELL B. STORY qualified. Appraisers: JAS. A. STORY, J. S. WORTHAM, R. W. CASEY, SCOTT CHRIST, SAML. CHRIST. To PINK CHILDRESS, my niece; my sister, SARAH E. ROBINSON. Proper tombstone; Executor: ATWELL B. STORY.

ROBT. CHRISTIAN -- Book 3, Page 206 -- June 8, 1785, written; October 3, 1791, probated. Witnesses: WM. BRADLEY, ANNE SPEARS, WM. SPEARS, JNO. UPSHAW. Ux, where I live. She is to school children till they have learning suitable to my estate--when of age or married--one horse, etc. Son, DRURY--land whereon THOS. RIDGWAY lived; until my son, ROBT., is of age. Daughter, LUCY BRADLEY. Sons: ROBT., SAML., and ABNER. Daughters: MARY, MARTHA, and SOPHIA. Daughter, SALLY--any future children. Executors: ux and my brother, JOHN CHRISTIAN. MARY and JNO. CHRISTIAN qualified. Bondsmen: HENRY BELL; JAS., ROBT., and JNO. CHRISTIAN, B.
Book 3, Page 265 -- Inventory -- L 878-13-0, June 17, 1793. HENRY BELL. JAS. CHRISTIAN, STEPHEN WATTS.
Book 7, Page 152 -- Administrator's Bond -- COURTNEY CHRISTIAN and GEO. HOWARD, April 21, 1828, for COURTNEY CHRISTIAN.

SALLY CHRISTIAN -- Book 3, Page 276 -- Guardian Bond -- REUBEN NORVEL; STEPHEN WATTS; DANL. WHITE; and LEWIS NEVIL, September 16, 1793, for REUBEN NORVEL as guardian of JAMES, CHAS., and SALLY CHRISTIAN, orphans of GEO. CHRISTIAN.

SAML. CHRISTIAN -- Book 3, Page 554 -- April 16, 1797, written; September --, 1799, probated. Witnessed by JNO. CHRISTIAN. My mother during her lifetime. He then calls her M. CHRISTIAN and she is to administer.

SARAH CHRISTIAN -- Book 6, Page 358 -- Administrator's Bond -- WM. C.
CHRISTIAN and CHAS. H. CHRISTIAN, June 16, 1833, for WM. CHRISTIAN.
Book 6, Page 394 -- Inventory -- October 20, 1823: $118.25. JONAS
PIERCE; ABSALOM HOWL; THOS. MILES.

SARAH E. CHRISTIAN -- Book 12, Page 502 -- Guardian Bond -- FRANCES A.
CHRISTIAN and BENJ. P. WALKER, March 15, 1852, for FRANCES CHRISTIAN
as guardian of SARAH E. CHRISTIAN, orphan of CHAS. M. CHRISTIAN,
deceased.

VICTORIA CHRISTIAN -- Book 16, Page 367 -- Guardian Bond -- DAVID D.
HARRISON and SHEFFY MILLER, September 21, 1863, for DAVIS HARRISON
as guardian of VICTORIA CHRISTIAN; no parent set forth.

WALTER M. CHRISTIAN -- Book 7, Page 333 -- Inventory, December 14,
1829 -- $250.17. DUDLEY SANDIDGE; PETER RUCKER; JNO. FLOOD.
Book 8, Page 153 -- Administrator's Account -- LYNE S. TALIAFERRO,
deputy sheriff, for BENJ. TALIAFERRO, sheriff, of Amherst County and
administrator from January 18, 1830; recorded October 17, 1831.
JNO. PRYOR; THOS. N. EUBANK.
Book 8, Page 351 -- Curator bond, September 16, 1833: JAS. G. and
DRURY CHRISTIAN, for JAS. CHRISTIAN.
Book 9, Page 10 -- Administrator's Account -- BENJ. TALIAFERRO,
sheriff and curator from 1831. To JAS. G. CHRISTIAN for spirits at
sale; WESLEY E. CHRISTIAN as witness in a suit; Sale, October 6, 1831.
LINDSEY COLEMAN, November 21, 1833.
Book 9, Page 76 -- Inventory -- $800.00; May 18, 1835. JOS. KYLE,
LEWIS HARRISON, DAVID APPLING.
Book 9, Page 277 -- Curator, JAS. G. CHRISTIAN, from 1833: many
tavern bills and trip to Kanawha River after negroes. PETER F.
CHRISTIAN also took the trip. November 17, 1836. RO. WINGFIELD and
JOS. KYLE, commissioners.
Book 16, Page 109 -- Administrator's Bond -- PETER F. CHRISTIAN and
CHAS. M. CHRISTIAN, January 20, 1862, for PETER CHRISTIAN.
Book 16, Page 118 -- Inventory -- $1,900.00, March 1, 1826. ZACH.
BOWLES, B. P. MORRIS, DAVID APPLING. MORRIS as Justice of the
Pieace; OWEN SMITH.
Book 17, Page 16 -- Slave list, December 29, 1864, of MARY CHRISTIAN,
deceased, widow. Seven legatees: MISS ANN ELIZA CHRISTIAN; SAML. W.
CHRISTIAN; GEO. W. CHRISTIAN; MISS AGNES CHRISTIAN; PAUL, JR.; EDMUND;
and CHAS. W. CHRISTIAN. Commissioners: A. C. HARRISON, JR.; JO.
PETTYJOHN; HENRY LOVING; EDGAR WHITEHEAD; M. C. GOODWIN.
Book 17, Page 411 -- Plat and land division: At request of JNO. B.
GADDIS, who married one of the daughters of CHAS. W. CHRISTIAN, we
attached interest of heirs of CHAS. W. to land given GEO. W. CHRIS-
TIAN. Right-of-way to public road through lands of GEO. W. and heirs
of CHAS. W. CHRISTIAN; WM. E. COLEMAN; HENRY LOVING; and JESSE E.
ADAMS. South side of Buffalo and both sides of Tribulation; east
side of Main road from Amherst County Courthouse to Buffalo Springs.
Lines of JNO. C. HARRISON; HEISKELL; WM. THOMPSON and surveyed in
1853 by JNO. PRYOR; again in 1867 by E. P. TUCKER for JNO. W. BROAD-
DUS, Amherst County syrveyor. 185 acres to GEO. W. CHRISTIAN;
77 acres to heirs of CHAS. W. CHRISTIAN, deceased. 127 acres to
A. COX and ux, ELIZA; GEO. W. CHRISTIAN owned four shares and two
were for ELIZA COX (formerly CHRISTIAN). September 1867.

WESLEY E. CHRISTIAN -- Book 9, Page 68 -- March 17, 1835. My father,
WALTER CHRISTIAN, SR., died in 1829. His will is in Amherst County
Clerk's office and unrecorded and not proved. He devised to me all
bounty lands due him as a Revolutionary soldier. I doubt that this
was his will and want my brothers and sisters and the children of my
deceased brother, ROBT. CHRISTIAN, to share. He renounced will and
claimed only his "just proportion." Witness: HENRY T. PENDLETON.

WM. CHRISTIAN (Really WM. LaFAYETTE, but middle name found after
numbers were set up) -- Book 9, Page 62 -- Guardian Bond -- JAS. G.
and DRURY CHRISTIAN, March 18, 1835, for JAS. CHRISTIAN as guardian
of WM. LaFAYETTE CHRISTIAN and NANCY LANDRUM CHRISTIAN, orphans of
ROBT. CHRISTIAN, deceased.

WM. A. CHRISTIAN -- Book 13, Page 321 -- Guardian Bond -- RO. H.
CARTER and LEONARD DANIEL, January 16, 1854, for RO. CARTER as guardian of WM. A. CHRISTIAN, orphan of ANTHONY CHRISTIAN.

WM. BROWN CHRISTIAN -- Book 1, Page 453 -- Guardian Bond -- HENRY
CHRISTIAN, AMBROSE RUCKER, and JNO. PENN, December 7, 1778, for
HENRY CHRISTIAN as guardian of WM. BROWN CHRISTIAN, orphan of JNO.
CHRISTIAN, deceased.
Book 1, Page 493 -- Guardian's Account -- Schooling and board --
L 12-0-0 and L 56-2-9-1/2, August 2, 1779.
Book 4, Page 483 -- Constable, February 20, 1809. Bondsman: JNO.
CHRISTIAN.
Book 4, Page 590 -- Same, July 17, 1809. Bondsman: Same. WM. is
called WM. L.

WM. C. CHRISTIAN -- Book 10, Page 188 -- Refunding Bond, October 21,
1839 -- WM. C. CHRISTIAN and RO. TINSLEY to J. PETTYJOHN, administra-
tor of CHAS. WILSON, deceased. RICH. WILSON, father of CHAS. WILSON,
has since died and an heir. Estate Commitment to Sheriff.
Book 10, Page 242 -- so indexed, but it is Book 11, Page 242 --
Administrator's Bond -- RO. M. BROWN; JNO. THOMPSON, JR.; CHAS. L. and
BENJ. BROWN, October 20, 1845, for RO. BROWN.
Book 10, Page 347 -- so indexed, but it is Book 11, Page 347 --
Inventory -- November 14, 1845: $6,340.49. LINDSEY COLEMAN, WM. A.
RICHESON, JNO. M. PRICE, CHAS. H. MASSIE.
Book 10, Page 408 -- so indexed, but no such number. It is Book 11,
Page 408 -- Sale -- December 23, 1845. Family buyers: MARY, GEO. W.,
ANN ELIZA, AGNES, PAUL, SAML. W., EDMUND CHRISTIAN: $1,123.90 and
$15.00 for gun, etc. GEO. W. CHRISTIAN, clerk of sale. RO. M.
BROWN, administrator.
Book 11, Page 556 -- Administrator's Account from October 1, 1845.
PAUL and EDMUND D. CHRISTIAN were buyers. Distributees: MARY, GEO.
W., ANN E., AGNES, PAUL, EDMUND D., SAML. W., CHAS. W., PATRICK H.
MARY--widow; very long and names repeated several times--to Page 571.
Recorded: September 20, 1847. Another Administrator's Account on
Book 12, Page 215, from December 30, 1846. Recorded August 20, 1849.

WM. R. CHRISTIAN -- Book 17, Page 33 -- Administrator's Bond -- JNO. A.
SCRUGGS, JAS. W. KEITH, and NICHL. MAYS, February 20, 1865, for
JNO. SCRUGGS.

WM. W. CHRISTIAN, DR. (Indexed for WM. R., but someone has tampered
with middle initial and it appears to be "W.") -- Book 10, Page 152 --
Administrator's Bond -- JAS. SPILLER and ALEX. MUNDY, August 19,
1839, for JAS. SPILLER.
Book 10, Page 157 -- Inventory -- interesting list of medical and
other books, September 16, 1839. J. POWELL, WM. DILLARD, CHAS.
CHRISTIAN.
Book 10, Page 159 -- Depositions by WM. C. and GEO. W. CHRISTIAN--both
of age. Present on day of his death and few hours prior to death,
he called and said that he wanted all papers in trunk and press
burned; private letters and not to be read. JAS. M. SPILLER to select
enough accounts to pay him and debts to be put in a collector's
hands. Owed brother, GEO., $45.00; balance to GEO. and my two sis-
ters. My instruments and medicine to my brother, PATRICK. August 19,
1839.

WILSON CHRISTIAN -- Book 6, Page 237 -- Constable, June 21, 1819.
Bondsman: DAVID S. GARLAND; to GOV. JAS. P. PRESTON.

ELIZ. CHRISTIE -- Book 6, Page 279 -- Guardian Bond -- WM. D. HILL
and JNO. HORNER, January 21, 1822, for WM. HILL as guardian of ELIZ.
CHRISTIE, orphan of HUGH CHRISTIE, deceased.

BULLER CLAIBORNE -- Book 8, Page 371 -- Administrator's Bond --
STERLING CLAIBORNE and CHAS. S. MOSLEY, November 19, 1833, for STER-
LING CLAIBORNE.
Book 11, Page 128 -- Administrator's Account -- Petersburg decree;
Chancery Superior Court; BACPRAN(?) vs. PEGRAM et. al. Agents. Sum
for U.S. $1,700 with interest from December 31, 1834. Commissioner:

SAML. M. GARLAND. Recorded: May 15, 1843.

JANE M. CLAIBORNE -- Book 18, Page 103 -- February 23, 1858, written;
Monday, October 16, 1871, probated. Witnesses: GEO. JONES and C. G.
FULKS. Proved by JONES, but FULKS deceased. of Nelson County;
granddaughters: MILLY ROSE COLEMAN and MARTHA JANE IRVING--free
from any husband present or future. No demands on any of my children
or grandchildren. Executors: MILLY ROSE COLEMAN and husband,
RO. C. T. COLEMAN and MARTHA JANE IRVING.

BENJ. CLARK (Clerk in some places) -- Book 1, Page 358 -- March 5,
1776, written; July 7, 1777, probated. Witnesses: JNO. JOHNSON and
WM. JOHNSON. Yeoman; estate in hands of CHAS. ERWIN, merchant, and
crop of tobacco in hands of WILLIAM MARTIN--distinguished by name
of "Dutch Creek Martin." Cattle in hands of my father and to go to
my mother. My brothers and sisters; my uncle, NATHANIEL CLERK, of
Henrico; my father, WM. CLERK, to administer and also JOS. ROBERTS.
Produced by executors who qualified. Bondsmen: ALEX. REID, JR.,
and RO. LASBY (LASTLY?).

BENJ. CLARK, JR. -- Book 2, Page 74 -- October 10, 1781, written;
June 3, 1782, probated. Witnesses: ALEX. McALEXANDER; DAVID CLARK;
WM. CLARK. Sons: ZACHARIAH and SAML.; ux, SUSANNAH; daughter,
JUDITH CLARK. Executors: friends, NATHL. CLARK; ALEX. McALEXANDER,
and DAVID CLARK. Administrator's Bond is on Page 75: NATHL. CLARK,
September 2, 1782. Bondsman: JNO. WITT, JR.

FANNY CLARK -- Book 14, Page 213 (two pages so numbered) -- Guardian
Bond -- WILEY CLARK and MICAJAH CLARK, November 17, 1856, for WILEY
CLARK as guardian of FANNY; FLOYD; WESLEY; ROBT.; ELVIRA and GEO.
CLARK, orphans of WOODSON CLARK, deceased.
Book 15, Page 171 -- Guardian's Account -- D. R. CLARK for board;
FANNY, FLOYD, WESLEY, ROBT., ELVIRA, and GEORGIA (GEO. above),
children of WOODSON CLARK, deceased. February 20, 1859.

JOS. S. CLARK -- Book 16, Page 134 -- Administrator's Bond -- ELIZ. A.
CLARK, June 16, 1862. Bondsman: GEO. W. OLD.
Book 16, Page 508 -- Inventory -- August 8, 1862: $221.50. JNO. D.
L. RUCKER, A. COX, S. R. WORTHAM, GEO. H. DAWSON.
Book 18, Page 30 -- Indexer's error; division of JOS. R. CARTER.

KEZIAH CLARK -- Book 13, Page 2 -- Administrator's Bond -- ARTHUR B.
CLARK and ROBT. H. GRAY, October 18, 1852, for ARTHUR CLARK.

NATHANIEL CLARK -- Book 3, Page 349 -- Administrator's Bond -- SAML.
BRIDGWATER and RO. DINWIDDIE, October 19, 1795, for SAML. BRIDGWATER.
Book 3, Page 387 -- Inventory, no total, June 22, 1796. ALEX.
McCLURE, WM. MOORE, JOS. MONTGOMERY.

WOODSON CLARK -- Book 14, Page 84 -- Administrator's Bond -- DOROTHY
R. CLARK, WILEY CLARK, and PUBLUS CLARK, March 17, 1856, for DOROTHY
CLARK.
Book 14, Page 156 -- BEDFORD inventory, March 31, 1856: $31.42.
WM. P. SCOTT, RALPH C. SHELTON, GEO. W. OLD.
Book 14, Page 339 -- Administrator's Account from January 1, 1856.
WM. CLARK for wagon; Bedford taxes; PUBLUS CLARK; Charlotte County
taxes; land rented in Charlotte. Recorded February 28, 1857.

WILLIAM CLARKE -- Book 6, Page 259 -- Administrator's Bond -- GEO.,
HENRY, and JAS. CLARKE, and ISAAC RUCKER, October 15, 1821, for the
three CLARK men to administer. June 21, 1821, written; October 15,
1821, probated. Witnesses: ISAAC RUCKER, NOTLEY M. CAMM, LEROY(?)
BIBB, JOSHUA MAYSE. Proved by RUCKER, BIBB, and MAYSE. My sons:
GEO., HENRY, and JAS. CLARK (note two spellings), Amherst County and
Rockbridge land; daughter, REBECCA CLARK. My three daughters: MARY
HARTLESS, JANE HARTLESS, NELLY PAINTER. Executors: Sons, GEO.,
HENRY, and JAS.
Book 6, Page 273 -- Inventory, on order of October, 1821: $58.92-1/2.
ANDERSON WARE, THOS. JOURDAN, WM. HASLEP, JNO. H. CLEMENTS, ANGUS
McCLOUD appointed and done by WARE, JOURDAN and HASLEP. Recorded
December 19, 1821.

ANSELM CLARKSON -- Book 5, Page 512 -- Constable, June 19, 1815.
Bondsmen: WM. JOPLING, PHILIP SMITH.

DAVID CLARKSON -- Book 4, Page 159 -- Inventory -- October 12, 1804,
L 1182-9-10; NICHL MORAN, WM. JACOBS, DANL. McDONALD, CHAS. JONES.
Book 4, Page 389 -- Administrator's Bond -- DAVID and JAS. CLARKSON,
September 17, 1804. Bondsmen: JAS. MONTGOMERY, JAS. CLARKSON.

ELIZ. CLARKSON -- Book 4, Page 162 -- "Burthen" to great to administer
estate of deceased. Husband, DAVID CLARKSON. September 17, 1804.
Witnesses: JAS. MONTGOMERY, NATHAN BARNETT.
Book 4, Page 208 -- Dower in Piney River tract - Tavern tract; mill
and tract; upper tract where he lived and mansion house; One third
each to WM. B. JACOBS; RO. SHIELDS; JNO. JACOBS, JR. October 21,
1805. See will of JNO. JACOBS, SR., in Nelson for BETSY CLARKSON
as his daughter.

WM. CLARKSON -- Book 11, Page 215 -- Administrator's Bond -- JAS.
SMILETY and WM. M. FRANKLIN, February 19, 1844, for JAS. SMILETY.

WM. CLASBY -- Book 4, Page 280 -- Tobacco Inspector, Tyle River
Warehouse, November 18, 1805. Bondsman: JNO. CLASBY.
Book 4, Page 282 -- Same, September 15, 1806; Bondsman: THOS. CLASBY.
Book 4, Page 512 -- Same, September 21, 1807. Bondsman: J. P.
GARLAND.

PATSEY CLASKEY--no numbered assigned, but so indexed. See PATSEY
CHASKEY.

MILLEY (EY)(?) CLAYBROOKES -- Book 3, Page 262 -- August 16, 1792,
written; June 17, 1793, probated. Witnesses: ALEX. McALEXANDER;
JENNIE DAWSON; MOLLY BURNETT...My part of my father's estate to my
sister, ELIZ. BURNETT.

JNO. P. B. CLAYTON -- Book 5, Page 177 -- Guardian Bond -- JAS. MAR-
TIN, CHAS. TALIAFERRO, HENRY and WM. TURNER, August 19, 1812, for JAS.
MARTIN as guardian of JNO. P. B. CLAYTON, orphan of PHILIP BURTON.
Note: This is natural son of BURTON, so see his will in my B work.

POLLY J. CLEMENS -- Book 6, Page 437 -- Guardian Bond -- BARTLETT
CLEMENS and ISAAC RUCKER, January 19, 1824, for BARTLETT CLEMENS
as guardian of POLLY J.; JOICE T.(?) and NANCY B. CLEMENS, infants
of BARTLETT CLEMENS.

JEREMIAH CLEMENTS -- Book 5, Page 430 -- Administrator's Bond -- JNO.
CREWS and CHRISTOPHER FLETCHER, May 16, 1814, for JNO. CREWS.

WM. RIGHT CLEMENTS -- Book 4, Page 110 -- March 26, 1803, written;
June 20, 1803, probated. Witnesses: AMBROSE RUCKER; TINSLEY
RUCKER; RANDOLPH CASH. Proved by witnesses. My daughter, JOICY--
100 acres, house, and furniture. Daughter, MARY TOMBLEN; sons,
JAS. and FRANCIS; my ux, MARY; my children: STEVEN, WM., JAS.,
JESSEY, JNO., FRANCIS, MARY TOMBLEN, JOICE CLEMENTS, and children of
my deceased daughter, ELIZ. ROBERTS. Executors: ux, MARY; and son,
JAS. and JESSE CLEMENTS.

FRANCES COALTER (COULTER) -- Book 4, Page 80 -- Inventory; no total;
February 21, 1803. JNO. WINGFIELD; WM.TRUNER (TURNER?); JESSE BECK.
Book 4, Page 356 -- Administrator's Bond -- PHILIP JOHNSON and JOS.
BURRUS, October 18, 1802, for PHILIP JOHNSON.

JAS. N. B. COBBS -- Book 12, Page 437 -- Constable, June 16, 1845.
Bondsmen: JNO. THOMPSON, JR.; SAML. SCOTT; RO. A. PENDLETON.

MARTHA A. COBBS -- Book 15, Page 81 -- Administrator's Bond -- WM.
KENT, WM. S. CLAIBORNE, December 19, 1859, for WM. KENT.
Book 15, Page 569 -- Administrator's Account from May 24, 1858.
GEO. M. OTT for coffin; V. McGINNIS for shroud; Chancery suit: HART-
SOCK vs. PARROTT; in account with WM. G. THOMAS. Recorded August 20,
1860.

WM. COCKRAN -- Book 3, Page 17 -- JNO. WIATT, factor for IRVING GALT & Co., September 4, 1786, for JNO. WIATT. Bondsman: WM. LOVING.
Book 3, Page 21 -- Inventory -- January 1, 1787, L 12-14-10-1/2: JOS. CREWS; DAVID WOODROOF; BENJ. RUCKER.

HENRY COFFEY -- Book 12, Page 344 -- Administrator's Bond -- HENRY COFFEY, ADDISON TALIAFERRO, and WM. H. OGDEN, January 20, 1851, for HENRY COFFEY. HENRY COFFEY acting trustee for ELIZ. COFFEE(sic) and children. Deed of trust from WM. McDANIEL, June 15, 1829--chancery suit involving part of property. Witness: HENRY W. QUARLES.
Book 18, Page 108 -- Administrator's Bond -- HENRY E. SMITH and ADDISON C. RUCKER, August 21, 1871, for HENRY SMITH.

P. J. COFFEY (Probably PETER J. of next item) -- Book 15, Page 204 -- Guardian Bond -- HENRY COFFEY and HENRY E. SMITH, June 20, 1859, for HENRY COFFEY as guardian of P. J.; AVERILLA; H. L.; and MARY F. COFFEY, infant children of ELIZ. COFFEY.

ELIZ. COFLIN (This family has many variations in spelling: CAWFLAN, COFFLIN, ETC. I have found an error and noted it for one man.) -- Book 5, Page 529 -- September 14, 1815, written; November 20, 1815, probated. Witnesses: JESSE BECK, JNO. L. BURFORD, EZEK. DAY, DANL. ROSELY. Proved by BECK, DAY, and ROSELY. JNO. LONDON qualified. Bondsman: JESSE BECK. My son, MAJOR J. B. COFLIN; daughter, ANN COFLIN; daughter, KEZIAH WRIGHT (she got $1.00 and large iron pot); debt due from JNO. LONDON and he is administrator. Administrator's Bond is Book 5, Page 534.
Book 5, Page 554 -- Inventory -- November 25, 1815: $186.46. WM. TURNER, HENRY TURNER, JAS. MARR. Note: She was ux of BENJ. CAWFLIN (sic) who is away out of sequence because of error in Master Index and not found until I had begun to check the CRAWFORD data.)

M.J.B. COFFLIN, MAJOR (Shown to be JAS. BENJ. in BENJ. CAWFLIN.) -- Book 13, Page 62 -- -----, written; March 23, 1849, probated. Witness: RICH H.(?) ANDERSON. Ux. ELIZ.--land surveyed by Amherst County surveyors under COL PRYOR and reference to plats. My four children: JNO. BENJ., HARRIET ANN, WM. JOSEPH, and ANDREW JACKSON COFFLIN. Executor: LEWIS MAYS.

Book 14, Page 14 -- Guardian Bond -- GEO. PATTERSON and JACKSON L. BURFORD, August 20, 1855, for GEO. PATTERSON as guardian of WM. JOS. and LOUIS B. COFLIN, orphans of JAS. B. COFLIN, deceased.

JAMES LINDSEY COGHILL (Indexed as JAS. L. and LINDSEY) -- Book 15, Page 275 -- Constable, February 20, 1860. Bondsman: R. B. TUCKER.
Book 15, Page 323 -- Same, District 5, June 18, 1860. Bondsman: RO. B. TUCKER.
Book 16, Page 141 -- Administrator's Bond -- MARY J. COGHILL and RO. W. SNEAD, July 21, 1862, for MARY COGHILL.
Book 16, Page 229 -- Inventory and called JAS. L., February 27, 1863-- $3,508.50. RO. N. ELLIS, STEPHEN WATTS, R. WM. SWANN.

ROBT. A. COGHILL -- Book 6, Page 597 -- Guardian Bond -- JANE AL-DRIDGE, JNO. and JOS. PENN, June 21, 1825, for JANE ALDRIDGE as guardian of RO. COGHILL, orphan of RICH. COGHILL.
Book 6, Page 680 -- Guardian's Account from June, 1824 -- amount in hands of JNO. BELFIELD, administrator, January 1, 1826. Recorded August 23, 1826.
Book 7, Page 51 -- Guardian's Account from 1826 -- paid for bringing from Richmond home; paid BENNET--expenses to SPRINGS; MR. (?) LITTLE-FORD for schooling; cash received for house and lot in Berkley, September 17, 1827. JAS. ROSE and WM. H. GARLAND.
Book 8, Page 253 -- Guardian's Account from June, 1829 -- Ward is called infant of RICH. and NANCY COGHILL herein.
Book 9, Page 18 -- Guardian's Account from November, 1831 -- Tuition; tax on lot; received of C. PENDLETON's children. Total of sums handled is $13,372.24. November 19, 1834. WM. H. KNIGHT; EDWD. M. PENN.
Book 22, Page 218 -- February 25, 1888; codicil, February 25, 1888; March 8, 1889. Produced by TAYLOR BERRY who made bond of $100,000.00. Handwriting attested by JNO. P. BROWN and STEPHEN ADAMS. Appraisers:

RO. A. PENDLETON; STEPHEN ADAMS; J. T. THOMPSON BROWN; ALLEN W. TALLEY;
C. L. SCOTT; BENJ. BROWN; GREEN H. NOWLING. To be buried by aunt,
JANE ALDRIDGE, and cousin, ADDISON GLASSCOCK, with whom I was reared--
they were to me as mother and brother. Slab to be placed stating
date of birth and death. Cousin, FANNIE B. GORDON, ux of W. W. GOR-
DON, Richmond City; cousin, MRS. LOUISA B. ROBERTSON and widowed
sister of MRS. GORDON. Cousin, B. B. HAILE; to HARRIET NORVELL, ux
of WM. NORVELL; my house and lot bought of W. S. CLAIBORNE; small
tract occupied by SAWNEY HILL--life estate to he--I bought it of
KITTY HARVEY and DAVID TINSLEY--for her sole support and free from
husband. She has been faithful servant. To EDWD. and DELIA E.
STAPLES who have lived with me--son and daughter of AMANDA STAPLES--
DELIA free from any husband she may have. The other children of
AMANDA STAPLES: ALICE, ux of HUGH WRIGHT; FANNIE, widow of CHAS.
WHITLOCK; FAITHY, ux of THOS. PAINE; MARIA, ux of HENRY MINOR; and
JO STAPLES. Their mother was my faithful and attached nurse. To
ADELAIDE PENDLETON; to RO. A. PENDLETON for ux and 3 children--my
DAVID APPLING tract; debt vs. W. M. PRICE; to MRS. D. E. JOHNSON; to
MRS. JANE E. ROSE--house and lot on Diamond Hill, Lynchburg, and
occupied by her--got by decree sale in Corporation Court in case of
MITCHELL vs. ALLEN and ROSE; to MRS. LUCY A. PENDLETON, widow of
JAS. S. PENDLETON--in full for any claims vs. house and lot known as
DAVID S. GARLAND Mansion, which I sold. My cousin, MARY E. WHITSON,
Pine Plains, South Carolina, and MARY E. BOOKER before marriage; to
JANE DAWSON of Mississippi--amount bequeathed to me by aunt--for her
life and remainder to me; friend, TAYLOR BERRY--law and miscellaneour
library; remainder to JANE E. ROSE; LUCY A. PENDLETON, and FANNIE B.
GORDON, LOUISA B. ROBERTSON, and RO. A. PENDLETON. Executor:
TAYLOR BERRY. Codicil: No depreciations expected, but executor to
pro rate, if needed. Codicil two: Debt of B. B. MINOR is erased;
amount due me from HUGH WRIGHT for dwelling house bought by me at sale
as commissioner, DAVIS vs. MEADE & C., I give to THOS. L. TAYLOR.
Debt due from WRIGHT for land bought of JAS. T. CASH and assigned to
me by V. McGINNIS, SR., is to be collected.
Administrator's Bond is Book 22, Page 220 -- March 18, 1889.
Book 22, Page 337 -- Inventory by BERRY--securities in vault of First
National Bank, Lynchburg, March 20, 1889; order of March, 1889, of
Amherst County court. Appraisers: RO. A. PENDLETON, C. L. SCOTT,
G. H. NOWLIN, A. W. TALLEY, B. BROWN. Railroad stocks in main;
Page 338--261 acres next to A. L. FOGUS--$34,292.98; New Glasgow
depot--337 acres next to C. B. CLAIBORNE near New Glasgow; storehouse
occupied by B. B. HAILE at New Glasgow; 50 acres next to JEFF MAYS
near the depot; 98 acres on Big Piney; 225 acres on Blue Ridge near
White's Gap; one lot next to HARRIET NORVEL and MRS. GOODE's estate.
$9,958.00. Page 339--debts due--$16,816.40. Recorded November 9,
1889.

BERRY COLEMAN (Probably LITTLEBERRY) -- Book 3, Page 297 -- Guardian
Bond -- AMBROSE RUCKER, JR.; WM. TUCKER; JESSE CARTER, April 22,
1794, for AMBROSE RUCKER as guardian of BERRY COLEMAN, orphan of
JNO. D. COLEMAN.

BETSY ANN COLEMAN -- Book 12, Page 206 -- Administrator's Bond --
JAMES P. COLEMAN and CHAS. A. PENN, September 17, 1849, for JAMES
COLEMAN.
Book 12, Page 221 -- August 13, 1849, written; September 17, 1849,
probated. Handwriting attested by C. A. PENN and JNO. COLEMAN. SAML.
M. GARLAND has promised to be guardian of my son, THOS. TAYLOR DANIEL
COLEMAN until 21; want no one to serve who is so closely related as
to be interested in his death--this excludes his uncles by blood or
marriage. He is to be placed at CAPT. JNO. COLEMAN's, Amherst
County, so as to live with his sister, BETTY FLOYD COLEMAN. SARAH
W. COLEMAND and my husband, JAS. P. COLEMAN, will be in charge until
eight. Then my husband is to take him to Hanover and place him with
DR. GEO. FLEMING and ux, MARY P. FLEMING, and pray that they will be
guardians. I object to his being educated at Concord for I don't
wish my brothers to control him. He is a delicate child and I hope
that DR. FLEMING (also FLEMMING) will send him to the Springs or some
watering place. When not in school, I hope that my children can be
together and that they may love one another. If DR. FLEMMING dies,

I want EDWARD MORRIS and ux, MATILDA E.--she is my niece--to be
guardians. I want the girl, Harry Ann, to attend to him as she is a
trustworthy servant. She then refers to estate of her son's grandmother and divisions and trusts that GARLAND will attend to same.
RO. TINSLEY, Amherst Courthouse, is to act as trustee for the children. Speaks of "child or children" by the last marriage and if
children are without heirs. LEWIS ALDERSON, GREEN BRIAR, is my
husband's brother-in-law and is to be trustee for husband. My son,
THOS., gets nothing for he is wealthy and my last child or children
are poor. Executors: JAS. P. COLEMAN and RO. TINSLEY.

CAROLINE CHAPMAN -- Book 6, Page 292 -- Guardian Bond -- LINDSEY
COLEMAN and Bondsmen, ST. GEO. TUCKER and RICHESON HENLEY, May 20,
1822, for LINDSEY COLEMAN as guardian of CAROLINE COLEMAN, orphan
of REUBEN COLEMAN, deceased. Note: I have another item indexed for
her, but it is for CAROLINE COLEMAN.

DANIEL L. COLEMAN -- Book 6, Page 112 -- Guardian Bond -- JNO. B.
and WM. DUNCAN, MICAJAH CAMDEN and WM. BOURNE, December 20, 1819,
for JNO. DUNCAN as guardian of DANL. and MARY C. COLEMAN, orphans of
EDMUND T. COLEMAN.
Book 6, Page 568 -- Guardian Bond -- HILL CARTER, WM. DUNCAN, and
JNO. COLEMAN, February 21, 1825, for HILL CARTER as guardian of the
same orphans as in Book 6, Page 112.
Book 6, Page 728 -- Plat of 310 acres -- north of Buffalo and west
of Carter's Mill creek--land of EDMD. T. COLEMAN, deceased. Lines
of ST. GEO. TUCKER; WM. MANTIPLY; BROCKMAN; DUKE(?), and DANL. COLE-
MAN (infant heir of EDMUND T. COLEMAN). Allotted to JNO. B. DUNCAN
and ux, MILDRED (widow of EDMUND T. COLEMAN).
Guardian's Account of JNO. B. DUNCAN is on Page 729 as guardian of
MARY COLEMAN from 1821; tuition to 1825; DANL's account, too, begins
on Page 730--same guardian and date. DUNCAN qualified in 1819;
reference to portion of his ux; MISS COLEMAN "advanced in life and
tuition was advanced"; children were sent to "the best schools or
tutored at DUNCAN's home." February 17, 1827: DABNEY SANDIDGE;
CORNL. SALE; ADDISON TALIAFERRO.
Book 8, Page 61 -- Guardian's Account by HILL CARTER from May 21,
1825; slave hired to JNO. COLEMAN; accounts paid to WM. and RO.
COLEMAN; CARTER also administrator of J. B. DUNCAN, former guardian.
November 18, 1830. JAS. POWELL and CHAMPE CARTER.
Book 11, Page 339 -- Administrator's Bond -- BETTY ANN COLEMAN and
JAS. D. COLEMAN, August 19, 1845, for BETTY COLEMAN.
Book 11, Page 343 -- Inventory -- October 14, 1845, slaves appraised
in lifetime of MILDRED COLEMAN DUNCAN--her life interest in estate
of DANL. COLEMAN; plus other slaves with no total. October 20,
1845. LINDSEY COLEMAN; RICH. P. SMITH; J. PETTYJOHN.
Book 11, Page 540 -- Administrator's Account by BETTY COLEMAN from
1845. DUIGUID for funeral expenses - $3.00 (Note: It may be of
interest to know that this firm is still in operation in Lynchburg
and has a branch in Amherst. No member of the family is now connected
with the business, but the name has been retained.) Amounts paid
to DAVID CAULWELL and SAML. B. RICE; amounts from JAS. D. and CAPT.
LINDSEY COLEMAN; CHAS. A. PENN and ux under her father's will. Debts
of RO. L. and J. P. COLEMAN. September 20, 1847: LINDSEY COLEMAN;
WM. M. WALLER.
Book 12, Page 130 -- Administrator's Bond -- June 20, 1848, JAS. P.
COLEMAN. Bondsmen: C. A. PENN and PAULUS POWELL.
Book 12, Page 155 -- Inventory -- March 19, 1849 -- SAML C. GIBSON;
M. C. GOODWIN; WM. M. WALLER.
Book 12, Page 160 -- Dower of BETTY ANN COLEMAN; many slaves and
same commissioners as above plus RO. M. BROWN. 325 acres surveyed
by JNO. PRYOR. Plat space is vacant. North side of Buffalo and
west side of Carter's Mill Creek and next to DANL. COLEMAN, deceased;
LINDSEY COLEMAN; WM. MANTIPLY; JNO. BROCKMAN; DUDLEY SANDIDGE and
included mansion house for the widow.
Book 12, Page 162 -- Survey by JNO. PRYOR, November 8, 1848; plat
attached.

EDMUND T. COLEMAN -- Book 5, Page 648 -- April 9, 1817, written;
May 20, 1817, probated. Witnesses: WM. DUNCAN; JACOB SMITH; GEO. L.

COLEMAN and proved by them. HILL CARTER and JNO. COLEMAN qualified.
Bondsmen: STERLING CLAIBORNE and THOS. ALDRIDGE. Ux, Mildred--
where I live. Son, DANL. L.--land bought of HENRY CAMDEN--BROCK's
fence to Buffalo and Mill path--when DANL. is of age. Daughter, MARY
COLEMAN--land bought of HENRY CAMDEN and JAS. HIX. Brother, JNO.
COLEMAN--stud horse, Ajax. JNO. SMITH has promised to supintend
estate for three years. My ux and two children. Executors: Bro-
thers, JNO. and RO. L. COLEMAN; HILL CARTER and THOS. P. COLEMAN,
CAROLINE CO. (middle initial seems to be "B." when THOS. qualified.)
Book 5, Page 689 -- Administrator's Bond -- THOS. B. COLEMAN,
July 17, 1817. Bondsmen: WM. DUNCAN and WM. H. DIGGES.
Book 6, Page 14 -- Inventory, July 20, 1818. Total: $8,748.75.
JNO. SMITH and WM. DUNCAN.

ELIZ. COLEMAN (Some data is for JNO. COLEMAN, too.) -- Book 6,
Page 82 -- Administrator's Bond -- THOS. COLEMAN, August 16, 1819.
Bondsmen: AMBROSE RUCKER and RICH. HARRISON.
Book 6, Page 102 -- Division of estate of ELIZ. and JNO. COLEMAN and
recorded November 15, 1819. Commissioners: REUBEN NORVELL; EDMD.
WINSTON; AMON TINSLEY. 102-1/2 acres with mansion house to THOS.
COLEMAN; 166 acres to SAML. COLEMAN; 300 acres to JAS. COLEMAN; JAS.
gets lot next to THOS. COLEMAN; 186 acres Mountain tract to POLLY
COLEMAN and 120 acres balance next to THOMAS COLEMAN. 216 acres to
children of RICH. HARDWICK who married a daughter of the testator--
rest of Mountain tract and divided to JAS. HARDWICK--52 acres; 52
acres to LINDSEY HARDWICK; 40 acres to JNO. HARDWICK; 36 acres to
ELIZ. HARDWICK; 36 acres to ROBT. HARDWICK. This was JOHN's land
and that of ELIZ. has been divided as follows: 45 acres of upper end
of BENNETT tract to JAS. COLEMAN; 95 acres--lower end to SAML. COLE-
MAN; 44 acres near fork of CRAWFORD and WARE's roads and east side
of Harris Creek to POLLY COLEMAN; 86-3/4 acres including residence
of WM. WATTS to THOS. COLEMAN. HARDWICKS are set forth as above;
slaves of both put together for division.

FRANCES R. COLEMAN -- Book B, Page 17 -- Administrator's Bond --
WM. T. HIGGINBOTHAM and JNO. C. CARTER, April 1, 1841, for WM.
HIGGINBOTHAM.

GEO. COLEMAN -- Book 3, Page 67 -- July 6, 1787, written;
February 4, 1788, probated. Witnesses: JOS. DAVENPORT, PHILIP
ROOTES, JNO. LAMONT, BANAMMI STONE. Ux, JUDITH--where I live; my
four children when of age. Executors: Brother, LINDSEY COLEMAN,
and friends, JAS. FRANKLIN and JAS. CALLAWAY. My son or sons.
Executors named made bond. Bondsmen: JOS. PENN and JNO. CRAWFORD.
Book 3, Page 74 -- Inventory -- March 31, 1788; no total;
JAS. DAVENPORT, BENAMMI STONE, JNO. PENN.
Book 3, Page 313 -- Administrator's Account by LINDSEY COLEMAN from
April 27, 1788. To JAS. VIGUST for schooling--1790; ANTHONY DIBRELL
for same in 1791; WM. TANDY for same; also CAPT. CALLAWAY; CAPT.
DANL. TUCKER; JNO. COONEY for same, December 24, 1792. Recorded
September 9, 1794. A later report recorded October 20, 1794.
Book 3, Page 334 -- Administrator's Account by CALLAWAY from 1788,
by LIN COLEMAN, executor. October 20, 1794. DAVID S. GARLAND;
GEO. DILLARD; JAS. BALLINGER.
Book 3, Page 492 -- Administrator's Account -- LINDSEY COLEMAN from
September 9, 1794. Cuberland County Clerk for tickets; RO. HOLLOWAY
for teaching WM. COLEMAN at the Dancing School and board while there;
to JAS. DILLARD; amount for division of estate of ROBT. COLEMAN,
deceased. Received of JOSHUA HUDSON on account of WM. GILLESPIE,
June 18, 1798. DAVID S. GARLAND, GEO. DILLARD, JOS. BURRUS.
Book 5, Page 693 -- Guardian's Bond -- JNO. COLEMAN, HILL CARTER,
STERLING CLAIBORNE, November 18, 1815, for JNO. COLEMAN as guardina
of GEO. COLEMAN, orphan of LINDSEY COLEMAN, deceased.

GEO. L. COLEMAN -- Book 8, Page 317 -- Estate Commitment to Sheriff --
June, 1833. EDMD. WINSTON, Sheriff.

HENRY LANDON COLEMAN -- Book 6, Page 300 -- Guardian Bond -- LINDSEY
COLEMAN, GEO. TUCKER, and RICHARDSON (signed RICHESON) HENLEY,
May 20, 1822, for LINDSEY COLEMAN as guardian of HENRY LANDON COLEMAN,
orphan of REUBEN COLEMAN, deceased.

JAS. P. COLEMAN -- Book 17, Page 144 -- July 4, 1861, written;
October 16, 1865, probated. Witnesses: CHAS. B. CHRISTIAN, W. B.
HENLEY and proved by them. RO. L. COLEMAN qualified. Bondsmen:
M. C. GOODWIN and RO. A. PENDLETON, November 20, 1865. Deed to
secure debt made to my children: BETTY F. and JNO. R. COLEMAN.
My sister, LUCY STOUT, is to have control of and educate my children.
Book 17, Page 349 -- Inventory -- law books - 84 volumes at $150.00,
June 16, 1868. RO. A. PENDLETON, B. J. RUCKER, V. McGINNIS.
Book 20, Page 77 -- October 2, 1878 -- To JUDGE G. A. WINGFIELD,
circuit judge--SAML. H. HENRY, administrator--two children: J. R.
COLEMAN's share; BETTY F. HITE's share. LUCY STOUT, guardian.
Recorded June 19, 1880.

JANETTA E. COLEMAN -- Book 11, Page 396 -- Guardian's Bond -- LINDSEY
COLEMAN and CHAS. T. COLEMAN, January 19, 1846, for LINDSEY COLEMAN
as guardian of JANNETTA E. COLEMAN, orphan of MARY E. COLEMAN,
deceased.

JNO. DANIEL COLEMAN -- Book 2, Page 207 -- September 17, 1784, writ-
ten; December 6, 1784, probated. Witnesses: THOS. LUCAS; THOS.
COLEMAN; JNO. CHRISTIAN, JR. Ux, MILLION--250 acres where I live;
sons: JAS, JESSE, DANL., LITTLEBERRY, WM., and SPILSBY COLEMAN.
Daughters: ELIZ., NANCY, SALLY, MILLION, and LUCY COLEMAN. Execu-
tors: JNO. CHRISTIAN, son of ROBT. CHRISTIAN; WM. OGLESBY, son of
JACOB OGLESBY.
Book 2, Page 208 -- Administrator's Bond -- JNO. CHRISTIAN, Decem-
ber 6, 1784. Bondsmen: THOS. PENN, CHAS. CHRISTIAN.
Book 2, Page 240 -- Inventory -- no total, August 1, 1785. WM. WARE,
ISAAC TINSLEY, JOS. CHILDRESS.
Book 3, Page 383 (Indexed for 583) -- Administrator's Account by
CHRISTIAN--WM. OGLESBY as partner; due JNO. COLEMAN from father's
estate; schooling for children for one year. October 19, 1795.
AMBROSE RUCKER, DAVID WOODROOF, ISAAC TINSLEY, JNO. TALIAFERRO.

LINDSEY COLEMAN -- Book 4, Page 593 -- June --, 1808, written; May 16,
1809, probated. Proved by JNO., ROBT., and EDMUND T. COLEMAN, and
they qualified. Bondsmen: DAVID S. GARLAND, SPOTSWOOD GARLAND,
BENJ. TALIAFERRO. Ux, LUCY--where I live; son, JNO.--570 acres where
he lives; sons, ROBT. and EDMD. T. COLEMAN. ROBT. gets 729 acres
bought of NICHOLAS under Buffalo Ridge and another where he lives;
various Buffalo River tracts; land bought of P. SLAUGHTER--763 acres.
Daughter, LUCY COLEMAN; daughter, P.(?) C. COLEMAN--in proportion
with my first children, but not mentioned in my will; Lynchburg
property; son, GEO. L.--where I live on north side of Buffalo and
bought of MAG BURKS; S--(?) and JOHN's--; GEO. L.--when of age; my
five other children. Note: It is hard to decipher the daughter's
name for P., but it could be "C." instead of "P." and middle initial
of M.
Administrator's Bond is Book 4, Page 596 -- Inventory is Book 4,
Page 608, November 20, 1809 - $9,831.77. DAVID S. GARLAND, JEREMIAH
FRANKLIN, JNO. SMITH.
Book 12, Page 15 -- Sheriff's Bond -- February 19, 1849. Bondsmen:
RO. TINSLEY, SAML. M. GARLAND, RO. M. BROWN, CHAS. MASSIE, W. A.
RICHESON, HENRY L. DAVIES. Two bonds, various duties. Another
Sheriff's Bond is Page 263, February 18, 1850. Bondsmen: CHAS.
MASSIE; RO. M. BROWN; A. TALIAFERRO; S. M. GARLAND; HENRY L. DAVIES;
RO. TINSLEY; W. A. RICHESON; B. BROWN, JR.
Book 19, Page 170 -- Curator's Bond -- June 19, 1876. RO. M. BROWN.
Bondsmen: ALVIN P. ROBERTS and RO. WHITEHEAD.
Book 19, Page 198 -- November 15, 1865, written; codicil of April 13,
1870; June 19, 1876, probated. Witnesses to will: LEO DANIEL, JR.;
ROBT. M. BROWN and also to codicil. Motion to admit by ALVIN PRINCE
ROBERTS; A. B. STRATTON and ux, ALICE V.; CHAS. T. and JANETTA
COLEMAN. Contestants: CHAS. H. MASSIE and ux, MARY. Continued and
RO. M. BROWN appointed curator by consent of parties. My ux--where
I live on Buffalo River and next to JAS. W. HENLEY--Long or Thorough-
fare branch--"to which I bought of JNO. PENN's estate"; old road to
Mt. Moriah Church; new road; where my son, JOS. lives--eastern foot
of Mobley's Mountain; son, CHAS. T.; daughter, LUCY ELLEN SMITH;
grandson, ALVIN PRINCE ROBERTS; land north side of Buffalo and next

to THOS. COLEMAN and WM. H. WRIGHT; DAVID S. MILLER; JNO. PENN's
estate; new road; and land where son, JOS. lives. JOS. adjoins
DANL. S. MILLER; WM. BURFORD; POWHATAN JENNINGS; Mobley's Mountain
and to top of it. Granddaughter, JANNETTA E. COLEMAN--five shares
of Orange and Alexandria Railroad. My six children: WM. E., CHAS. T.,
JOS., MARY MASSIE, LUCY ELLEN SMITH, and RICH. M. COLEMAN. My two
grandchildren: ALICE V. STRATTON and ALVIN PRINCE ROBERTS. Executors: WM. E. and CHAS. T. COLEMAN. Codicil: Recent death of my
son, JOS.--his land to LUCY ELLEN ROYSTER (formerly SMITH) and her
husband, THOS. B. ROYSTER. My son, CHAS. T., trustee for LUCY ELLEN.
Grandson, ALVIN PRINCE ROBERTS and granddaughter, ALICE V. STRATTON,
free from her husband, ALEX. B. STRATTON, but he is to be her trustee.

LUCY COLEMAN -- Book 4, Page 134 -- August 4, 1803, written;
October 17, 1803, probated. Witnesses: SAML. COLEMAN, RICH. HARD-
WICK, BLANFORD HIX. Proved by HARDWICK and HIX. On January 16,
1804, THOS. COLEMAN qualified. Bondsman: JESSE CLEMENTS. Sister,
NANCY; brother, JESSE; money in hands of CAPT. AMBROSE RUCKER, JR.
My brothers and sisters: JAS., JESSE, DANL., WM., SPILSBY, JESSE
CLEMENTS, SALLY COLEMAN, LITTLEBERRY COLEMAN. My bed in Campbell
County when I came over last; estate of my mother. Executor: THOS.
COLEMAN.
Book 4, Page 184 -- Guardian's Account of JESSE COLEMAN as guardian
of LUCY COLEMAN, deceased. July 15, 1805. EDMD. WINSTON, ISAAC
TINSLEY, RICH. HARRISON.
Book 4, Page 315 -- Guardian's Bond -- JESSE COLEMAN and AMBROSE
RUCKER, JR., June 17, 1798, for JESSE COLEMAN as guardian of
LUCY COLEMAN, orphan of JNO. COLEMAN, deceased.
Book 4, Page 381 -- Administrator's Bond -- THOS. COLEMAN as shown
above.
Book 5, Page 675 -- Administrator's Bond -- JNO. COLEMAN and STERLING
CLAIBORNE, September 15, 1817, for JNO. COLEMAN.

MARGARET H. R. COLEMAN -- Book 6, Page 285 -- Guardian Bond --
FRANCES COLEMAN, JNO. LONDON, and JOS. DILLARD, May 23, 1822, for
FRANCES COLEMAN as guardian of MARGARET H. R. and MARY F. COLEMAN,
orphans of REUBEN COLEMAN.

MARY C. COLEMAN -- Book 8, Page 51 -- Guardian Bond -- DANL. L.
COLEMAN and S. CLAIBORNE, November 15, 1830, for DANL. COLEMAN as
guardian of MARY COLEMAN, orphan of EDMUND T. COLEMAN.
Book 8, Page 59 -- Guardian's Account by HILL CARTER, guardian of
MARY C. COLEMAN from 1825. Received from J. B. DUNCAN, former
guardian. CARTER's account, presented by his administrator, THOS. N.
EUBANK. DANL. L. COLEMAN is present guardian November 18, 1830.
CHAMPE CHARTER and JAS. POWELL. Slave hired to J.(?) COLEMAN;
accounts of WM., RO. L., D., and JNO. COLEMAN.

MILLEY COLEMAN -- Book 3, Page 552 -- -----, 1779, written; June 24,
1799, probated -- (blurred, but 1779 written above). Witnesses:
JAS. MARR; AMBROSE RUCKER, JR. Son, DANL.; sons: WM., SPILSBY,
JAS., JESSE, DANL., BERRY; daughters: ELIZ., NANCY, SALLY, and LUCY.
Deceased daughter, MILLEY. Executor: son, JESSE. He qualified.
Bondsman: AMBROSE RUCKER, JR., Page 306 of Book 4 on September 16,
1799.

REUBEN COLEMAN -- Book 4, Page 369 -- Guardian Bond -- DANL. TUCKER,
JNO. CHRISTIAN, WM. and RO. H. COLEMAN for DANL. TUCKER as guardian
of REUBEN and LINDSEY COLEMAN, orphans of GEO. COLEMAN, deceased.
There isn't any date, but items hereon are for June 1803. The
summary provides no date, either.
Book 6, Page 285 -- Administrator's Bond -- FRANCES R. COLEMAN,
April 15, 1822. Bondsmen: JNO. LONDON and JOS. HIGGINBOTHAM. On
same page FRANCES qualified as guardian of MARGARET R. H. and MARY F.
COLEMAN, May 23, 1822. They were orphans of REUBEN COLEMAN. Bonds-
men: JNO. LONDON and JOS. DILLARD. MARY F. appears as MARY T.
in later data.
Book 6, Page 294 -- Inventory -- $8,314.50. June 17, 1822. THOS.
CREWS, CHAS. P. TALIAFERRO, WM. BOURNE.
Book 6, Page 445 -- Administrator's Account fromApril22, 1822. Seed

potatoes (Irish); WM. JORDAN for coffin - $12.00; WM. S. READ for
funeral sermon - $10.00. Amounts from LINDSEY and WM. COLEMAN,
March 17, 1824. JNO. McDANIEL, THOS. CREWS, THOS. S. HOLLOWAY.
Book 6, Page 475 -- Sales -- September 17, 1822 - $705.66. F. R. and
LINDSEY COLEMAN were buyers. Recorded March 17, 1824.
Book 6, Page 647 -- Division: to widow; to RO. LANDON COLEMAN;
MARY T.; MARGARET R.; and to LUCY C. PENN (others are COLEMANS);
January 3, 1826. THOS. CREWS, BENJ. BROWN, P. POWELL.
Book 8, Page 188 -- Administrator's Account -- from November 1, 1829.
WM. COLEMAN's executor vs. the estate and defense costs. L. P.
THOMPSON, attorney, vs. SIMMONS; damages by location of Lynchburg
and Charlottesville Road; JNO. J. LONDON's horse fed when at New
Glasgow and attending warrant vs. SIMMONS; jury for new road and
appeal from County to Superior Court; repair of porch; plantation
rent; Portions due LUCY C. PENN; RO. L. COLEMAN; MARGARET and MARY F.
COLEMAN. October 4, 1831. WILKINS WATSON, JAS. OGDON, BENJ. BROWN.
Book 8, Page 273 -- Land division -- 450 acres -- 180 acres next to
MRS. FRANCES COLEMAN, widow; WM. H. HARRIS who married CAROLINE COLE-
MAN, daughter of REUBEN COLEMAN--Lynch Road; 80 acres to MARY FRANCES
COLEMAN on Lower creek; 95 acres to MARGARET COLEMAN--Upper creek;
to RO. L. COLEMAN--all children of REUBEN COLEMAN. September 14,
1832. JNO. PRYOR, surveyor; JAS. POWELL; JNO. PENN; A. B. DAVIES.
Plat on Page 274--between Lynch's Road and Rutledge Creek and on
both sides of new road from Amherst Courthouse to Lynchburg. Land
joins: A. B. DAVIES, BENJ. BROWN, THOS. HIGGINBOTHAM, JAS. HIGGIN-
BOTHAM, and heirs of BENAMMI STONE. Survey by order of August, 1832,
directed to JAS. POWELL, et. al.--Crooked Run. Recorded September 17,
1832. It is noted that CAROLINE and RO. LANDON COLEMAN are of full
age.
Book 8, Page 382 -- Administrator's Account from October 14, 1831.
Amounts to MARGARET R. COLEMAN, MARY F., and RO. L. COLEMAN, and
LUCY C. PENN. September 15, 1832. BENJ. BROWN, WILKINS WATSON,
A. B. DAVIES.

SALLY COLEMAN -- Book 4, Page 143 -- August 21, 1803, written;
January 16, 1804, probated. Witnesses: FRANK CLEMENTS, BERRY COLE-
MAN, FANY CLEMENTS, THOS. COLEMAN. Proved by all save FANY CLEMENTS.
JESSE CLEMENTS qualified. Bondsman: THOS. COLEMAN. My "two only
children"--JUDY COLEMAN and BENJ. COLEMAN when they are of age. My
brother, SPILSBY COLEMAN; my father's estate in hands of SPILSBY.
Executor: JESSE CLEMENTS.
Administrator's Bond is on Page 380.

SALLY W. COLEMAN -- Book 12, Page 556 -- February 19, 1851, written;
codicil of April 15, 1851; July 19, 1852, probated. Witnesses:
CHAS. A. PENN and DAVID LOGAN and they also witnessed codicil. PENN
was dead at probate time, but proved by LOGAN. RO. L. COLEMAN
qualified along with JAS. P. COLEMAN. Husband, JNO. COLEMAN, con-
sents to my will; my children get slaves, but share of JAS. P. COLE-
MAN goes to his children. Son, RO. L. COLEMAN; daughter, SARAH A. W.
COLEMAN; daughter, MILLIE and children; daughter, ELIZA and children.
The children of JAS. P. COLEMAN are BETTIE FLOYD and JNO. R. COLEMAN.
My single daughters and orphan grandchildren--if husband of CORNELIA
P. COLEMAN dies, she and children are to live on land on same terms
as others. CORNELIA P. and ELIZA ALDERSON are to have no slaves until
after 12 years, unless CORNELIA's husband dies. If married daughters
are without issue, but speaks of children of CORNELIA P. and ELIZA
ALDERSON. If SARAH, LUCY, and MILLIE remain single. If son, ROBT.,
has no children living at my death, he is to remain on land and to
be paid for caring for the family. Executors: son, RO. L. and
JAS. P. COLEMAN. Codicil: Children alone are to determine the time
of division.
Administrator's Bond is on Page 558.

SPILSBY COLEMAN -- Book 3, Page 320 -- Guardian Bond -- ISAAC TINSLEY
and AMBROSE RUCKER, October 20, 1794, for ISAAC TINSLEY as guardian
of SPILSBY COLEMAN, orphan of JNO. DANL. COLEMAN.
Book 4, Page 12 -- Guardian's Account -- June 15, 1801 -- delivered
to ward and he is satisfied. Bond of MILIAN COLEMAN on June 1,
1796. Names of JESSE, SAML., and THOS. COLEMAN appear herein.

Book 10, Page 71 -- Administrator's Bond -- JNO. COLEMAN, December 17, 1838. Bondsmen: JACOB PHILIPS, REUBEN COLEMAN, and BLUFORD HIX. Inventory, December 18, 1838 - $616.43. PETER RUCKER, BLANDFORD HICKS, PETER CASHWELL, RANDOLPH MORRIS.
Book 10, Page 83 -- Sale -- December 27, 1838; JNO. and REUBEN COLEMAN were among buyers. Two old negroes put out and cried to lowest bidder. JNO. COLEMAN bought them for $70.00 and obligated himself to care for them during their lives. House and lot rented to JACOB PHILIPS; WM. COLEMAN listed as buyer; grocery mentioned; where REUBEN and JNO. COLEMAN lived. Recorded March 18, 1838.
Book 11, Page 331 -- Guardian Bond -- BETTY ANN, JAS. D. COLEMAN, and CHAS. A. PENN, August 19, 1845, for BETTY COLEMAN as guardian of THOS. COLEMAN, orphan of DANL. L. COLEMAN.

THOS. D. COLEMAN -- Book 12, Page 244 -- Guardian Bond -- SAML. M. GARLAND, R. A. PENDLETON, RO. A. COGHILL, and M. C. GOODWIN, and SAML. CASH, December 17, 1849, for SAML. GARLAND as guardian of THOS. D. COLEMAN, orphan of DANL. L. COLEMAN.

COLONEL WM. COLEMAN -- Book 3, Page 306 -- Guardian Bond -- AMBROSE RUCKER, JR., and GEO. McDANIEL, September 15, 1794, for AMBROSE RUCKER as guardian of WM. COLEMAN, orphan of JNO. DANL. COLEMAN.
Book 9, Page 376 -- Administrator's Bond -- LINDSEY COLEMAN and HENRY L. DAVIES, January 15, 1838, for LINDSEY COLEMAN.
Book 9, Page 383 -- Inventory -- January 31, 1838 - $1,219.75. RO. H. CARTER, LEE MILLNER, WM. B. SHEPHERD.
Book 10, Page 233 -- Administrator's Account from February 8, 1838. L. DAWSON for funeral sermon - $10.00, January 13, 1840--J. POWELL and H. L. BROWN.
Book 10, Page 390 -- Land division and plat. Commissioners: RO. H. CARTER, WM. B. RUCKER, PITT WOODROOF. Order of September court, 1840. JNO. DAVIS and SAML. C. GIBSON also named on commission. Land on both sides of Pedlar and adjoins WM. PRYOR; JNO. DAVIS; AMOS BRYANT--594-1/2 acres. Surveyed November 6, 1840. Lots to RICHARD S. ELLIS and others as heirs of COL. WM. COLEMAN. Other heirs are not named herein. This is indexed for RO. L. COLEMAN and R. S. ELLIS-- land division.
Book 13, Page 380 -- Administrator's Account from January 1, 1839. Division of land expenses. Recorded September 18, 1854.

WM. A. COLEMAN -- Book 20, Page 440 -- Constable, Pedlar District, June 18, 1883. Bondsmen: THOS. J. M. GOODWIN, WM. COLEMAN, JNO. H. PARR.

WM. E. COLEMAN -- Book 14, Page 99 -- Assessor, May 19, 1856. Bondsmen: LINDSEY COLEMAN and SAML. M. GARLAND.

CHARLOTTE COOPER -- Book 1, Page 500 -- Guardian Bond -- LUCAS DOWELL and WM. LOVING, September 6, 1779, for LUCAS DOWELL as guardian of CHARLOTTE COOPER, orphan of PHILLIP COOPER.
Book 2, Page 70 -- Guardian's Account from January 1, 1779. MR. RHODES for one month of schooling; MATT. NIGH(T)INGALE for same; to WM. POWELL for difference in slaves, August 5, 1782. Part of land sold.
Book 3, Page 80 -- Guardian's Account from November 1, 1782. C. KINEY for schooling; MR. LEWIS for dancing. Commissioner: CHAS. ROSE, July 7, 1788.

MISS COURTNEY COOPER -- Book 1, Page 499 -- Guardian Bond -- Same data as above on Book 1, Page 500 for CHARLOTTE.
Book 2, Page 71 -- Guardian's Account -- Her part of bond for schoolmaster; MATT. NIGHTINGALE for same; WM. POWELL for difference in slaves. Part of land sold. August 5, 1782.
Book 3, Page 82 -- Guardian's Account from November 1, 1782. CHESLEY KINNEY for schooling. Commissioner: CHAS. ROSE, July 7, 1788.

JANE COOPER -- Book 2, Page 147 -- WM. POWELL and NATHL. POWELL for WM. POWELL as guardian of JANE COOPER, orphan of PHILLIP COOPER, November 3, 1783.

NATHAN COOPER -- Book 9, Page 313 -- Estate Commitment to Sheriff --
June, 1837. Motion of JESSE RICHESON. JNO. COLEMAN, Sheriff.

ROBT. COOPER -- Book 1, Page 498 -- Guardian Bond -- LUCAS POWELL and
WM. LOVING, September 6, 1779, for LUCAS POWELL as guardian of ROBT.
COOPER, orphan of PHILLIP COOPER.
Book 2, Page 72 -- Guardian's Account from April 15, 1779. To
CHARLOTTE COOPER, August 5, 1782.
Book 3, Page 83 -- Guardian's Account from November 10, 1782. Board
and schooling for several years. Commissioner: CHAS. ROSE, July 7,
1788.

CHAS. COPPIDGE (also COPPEDGE) -- Book 6, Page 221 -- Administrator's
Bond -- THOS. COPPIDGE, JR.; SAML. WATTS; GEO. CORNELIUS; GEO. W.
HUDSON; and JNO. GLASS, February 19, 1821, for THOS. COPPIDGE, JR.

NANCY COPPIDGE -- Book 6, Page 708 -- Guardian Bond -- THOS. COPPEDGE,
JR.; SAML. WATTS; and JNO. GLASS, November 21, 1826, for THOS.
COPPEDGE, JR., as guardian of NANCY COPPEDGE, orphan of CHAS.
COPPEDGE.

THOS. COPPIDGE -- Book 11, Page 173 -- Administrator's Bond -- ABRAHAM
MARTIN and JNO. WHITEHEAD, October 16, 1843, for ABRAHAM MARTIN.

GEO. CORNELIUS -- Book 7, Page 90 -- June 9, 1827, written; December 17, 1827, probated. Witnesses: WM. JOPLING, E. B. GILBERT,
and CREED C. CARTER. Proved by GILBERT and CARTER. ELIZ. and GEO.
CORNELIUS qualified. Bondsman: BENJ. B. TALIAFERRO. Ux, ELIZ.;
daughters: LUCY and ELVIRA when of age or married. ELVIRA is to
have six months of school, if she desires. Sons: THOS. and GEO.
WASHINGTON CORNELIUS--same period of school; son, EDWIN(?)--two years
of schooling. Executors: ux and WM. CORNELIUS. It will be noted that
there are differences in names for WM. and GEO.
Book 6, Page 137 -- Inventory -- March 17, 1828. Here they are called
ELIZ. and WM. CORNELIUS; several slaves - $1,910.00. JNO. WARE; JNO.
PRYOR; CREED C. CARTER. An item is indexed for Book 6, Page 445,
but nothing shown.

THOS. COTTRELL -- Book 1, Page 21 -- -----, 1762, written; May 2,
1763, probated. Witnesses: JOEL CASH, JNO. CREWS, WM. BRYANT. Son,
THOMAS; son, GILBERT; son, WM.--700 acres where I live to my five
sons. Executors: ux, SUSANNA, and friend, HOWARD CASH.
Book 1, Page 30 -- Inventory -- June 15, 1763. L 78-14-9. RICH.
POWELL, JACOB SMITH, AARON HIGGINBOTHAM.

ARCHELAUS COX -- Book 3, Page 106 -- February 15, 1789, written;
July 6, 1789, probated. Witnesses: JNO. MORRETT, JESSE BECK, JACOB
PETTYJOHN. Children when of age; ux, MARY ANN; executors: WM. HUGHES
and VALENTINE COX.
Book 3, Page 107 -- Administrator's Bond -- WM. HUGHES and VALENTINE
COX. Bondsmen: DAVID WOODROOF, JAS. LIVELY. Probate date.
Book 3, Page 137 -- Inventory -- no total; JAS. CREWS, JOS. DAWSON,
CHAS. REYNOLDS, SHELLING JOHNSON. June 7, 1790.
Book 3, Page 517 -- Administrator's Account -- land division post-
poned; 7 equal parts--two parts to MILNER COX; WM. PENDLETON and ux,
PATSEY. December 26, 1795. Both administrators.
Book 4, Page 5 -- Administrator's Account by HUGHES, October 28,
1799. JNO. WHITE, THOS. MOORE, GEO. McDANIEL. Recorded April 20,
1801. No estate is named and also indexed for Page 4--not there.
Book 4, Page 344 -- Guardian Bond -- JNO. COX and JAS. BOWLING,
April 19, 1802, for JNO. COX as guardian of ARCHELAUS COX and WM.
COX, orphans of ARCHELAUS COX.

CAROLINE COX -- Book 11, Page 96 -- Guardian Bond -- ARCHELAUS COX,
SPOTSWOOD H. COX, and WM. R. COX, December 19, 1842, for ARCHELAUS
COX as guardian of CAROLINE COX, orphan of REUBEN COX, deceased.

EDWARD COX -- Book 1, Page 533 -- May 28, 1780, written; October 2,
1780, probated. Witnesses: WM. OGLESBY, JR.; BENJ. COX; JNO. LIVELY;
SARAH PARSONS. Ux, MARGARET; daughter, CLARY COX--200 acres on

Rockfish to be sold; nephew, JNO. BARD--one horse; if no accident happens in a suit depending upon my estate. CLARY is to have good education. Executors: RICH. OGLESBY and HENDRICK ARNOLD.
Book 1, Page 536 -- Administrator's Bond -- MARGARET COX and SAML. HIGGINBOTHAM, October 7, 1780, for MARGARET COX.
Book 2, Page 3 -- Inventory -- L 35191-0-0; JNO. HILL, EDMD. POWELL, CHAS. TALIAFERRO. February 5, 1781.

EDWARD L. COX -- Book 16, Page 148 -- Administrator's Bond -- SAML. F. WORTHAM and GEO. H. DAMERON, August 18, 1862, for SAML. WORTHAM.

ELIZ. COX -- Book 1, Page 260 -- Guardian Bond -- THOS. JOPLING and JAS. NEVIL, April 4, 1774, for THOS. JOPLING as guardian of ELIZ. COX, orphan of JNO. COX, deceased.
Book 1, Page 265 -- Guardian's Account from May, 1774. Recorded October 3, 1774.
Book 1, Page 436 -- Guardian's Account from 1774 -- L 52-10-6. Recorded September 7, 1778.

JNO. COX -- Book 4, Page 317 -- Guardian Bond -- REUBEN PENDLETON, MOSES RUCKER, RICH. HARRISON, June 17, 1798, for REUBEN PENDLETON as guardian of JNO. COX, orphan of ARCHELAUS COX, deceased.
Book 12, Page 525 -- Administrator's Bond -- WM. COX, WYATT COX (by SAML. M. GARLAND), June 21, 1852, for WM. COX.
Book 13, Page 25 -- Inventory -- August 7, 1852; shop; lot of unfinished work; timber; spokes; tools - $334.50, August 7, 1852. JNO. A. MOSELY; B. J. SCHOOLFIELD; RO. B. EVANS.
Book 15, Page 72 -- Administrator's Account by WM. COX--placed accounts before THOS. WHITEHEAD who resigned; some shop accounts have no vouchers; assigned items to widow; from July 10, 1852. Accounts paid to WM. P. COX; paling of graveyard. Recorded March 21, 1859.

MARTHA COX -- Book 7, Page 330 -- So indexed, but not in Books 6 through 14.
Book 11, Page 97 -- Guardian Bond -- SPOTSWOOD H. COX, ARCHELAUS COX and WM. R. COX, December 19, 1842, for SPOTSWOOD COX as guardian of MARTHA COX, orphan of REUBEN COX, deceased. The same bond appears in Book 11, Page 149.

MARY E. COX -- Book 23, Page 438 -- April 5, 1894, written; June 3, 1895, probated. Witnesses: WM. M. MAUZY, D. M. DABNEY, ALEX. THURMAN. Proved by DABNEY and THURMAN. Recorded Amherst County, November 2, 1897. Of Amherst County--sisters: FANNIE THURMAN COFFEE, MARTHA THURMAN WIGHTMAN, LELIA THURMAN BOYD. Brothers: ALEXANDER, CHAS., and EDWIN R. THURMAN. My husband, WM. FLETCHER COX--to live in our home at Amherst Courthouse--business buildings, and shops. My brother, SAML. THURMAN, and children. Nephews: CHAS. HAMILTON BOYD, HARRY FULLETON BOYD; my sister, ANNIE G. SHULTZ; brother, WALTER D. THURMAN; sister-in-law, MRS. ROSA V. CHRISTIAN; undertaker's stock; children of sister, LELIA BOYD. Executor: brother, EDWIN R. THURMAN; if dead, brother, CHAS. THURMAN. Probated in Lynchburg.

MILLNER COX -- Book 6, Page 138 -- Ordinary at house in county, May 15, 1820. Bondsman: REUBEN NORVELL.
Book 6, Page 386 -- Same -- August 18, 1823. Bondsman: WALKER (WALTER(?)) TERRY.
Book 7, Page 209 -- Administrator's Bond -- SARAH COX, February 16, 1829. Bondsmen: WIATT PETTYJOHN, JAS. L. LAMKIN, LEWIS L. BOLLING.
Book 7, Page 224 -- Inventory at dwelling house, February 26, 1829. Many slaves; personal property valued at $8,179.46-1/2. JESSE BECK, JAS. PETTIT, CHAS. WINGFIELD; SARAH COX, administratrix. Debts due estate; REUBEN COX; very long list of names--$2,239.45-1/2--due at death of my husband.
Book 8, Page 120 -- Administrator's Account from January 15, 1829; coffin - $20.00; MISTRESS CAMERON for bonnets; to and from Courthouse - $4.25; for hand to shore from RICH. in place of sick - $1.00; GEO. and BEN, watermen; JNO. J. PADGETT for paling in grave - $5.00; WIATT PETTYJOHN for his part of $1,000.00 divided among legatees; Cash laid out by NANCY, MARTHA, and REUBEN COX--for bran; trunk for NANCY; ISAAC REYNOLDS for his wife's part of legacy; FLETCHER for

ad; my part of legacy--one third; MARTHA COX's share--when she chooses guardian. ROBT. TINSLEY for smith's work for GEO. M. TINSLEY estate.
Book 8, Page 12 -- Division -- delivered $1,289.75 to distributees after settlements, December 8, 1829. WM. WARWICK, CHAS. WINGFIELD, WM. BOURNE were on commission. Widow's dower; WIATT PETTYJOHN; WM. PETTYJOHN as guardian of his late ux, deceased; ISAAC R. REYNOLDS; MARTHA ANN COX. Returned December 8, 1829.

P. G. (C.?) COX -- Book 16, Page 148 -- Administrator's Bond -- SAML. R. WORTHAM and GEO. H. DAMERON, August 18, 1862, for SAML. WORTHAM.

PATSY COX -- Book 13, Page 50 -- Administrator's Bond -- RO. A. COGHILL and WM. M. CABELL, March 22, 1853, for RO. COGHILL.

REUBEN COX -- Book 11, Page 8 -- January 4, 1842, written; codicil of same date; January 17, 1842, probated. Witnesses: RO. RIDGWAY, LUDWELL L. DAWSON, WM. TUCKER and to codicil. Proved by DAWSON and RIDGWAY. ARCHELAUS COX and SYLVESTER L. BURFORD qualified. Bondsmen: ISAAC R. REYNOLDS and L. L. DAWSON. My children by ux, MARTHA: ARCHELAUS, SUSAN J. BURFORD, NANCY CAWTHORN, SPOTSWOOD, WIATT, ELIZ. COX, RADFORD, MARTHA, and CAROLINE COX. Executors: ARCHELAUS COX and SYLVESTER L. BURFORD.
Book 11, Page 97 -- Guardian Bond -- SPOTSWOOD H. COX, ARCHELAUS COX, and WM. R. COX, December 19, 1842, for SPOTSWOOD COX as guardian of MARTHA COX, orphan of REUBEN COX, deceased.
Book 11, Page 258 -- Inventory -- December 16, 1844. Many slaves. Sale at which ARCHELAUS and SPOTSWOOD were buyers. Inventory: $6,888.25; sale: $1,009.88.

ROBT. W. COX -- Book 16, Page 147 -- Administrator's Bond -- S. R. WORTHAM and GEO. H. DAMERON, August 18, 1862, for S. WORTHAM.

SAML. P. COX -- Book 17, Page 46 -- Constable -- District 1; elected August 3, 1865. Bondsmen: J. A. BLANKS, SAML. R. IRVINE, RO. K. HARGROVE, CHAS. J. MAYS, ISAAC R. REYNOLDS.

WM. and ACHILLIS COX -- Book 4, Page 68 -- Guardian's Account -- JNO. COX, guardian of WM. COX, from 1799; part in the division; also as guardian of ACHILLIS COX; account with HARRISON HUGHES, administrator of WM. HUGHES, January 17, 1803. NELSON C. and PLEASANT DAWSON; JAS. LEE
Book 4, Page 344 -- Guardian's Bond -- JNO. COX and JAS. BOWLING, April 19, 1802, for JNO. COX as guardian of WM. and ACHILLIS COX, orphans of ACHS. COX, deceased.

WM. RADFORD COX -- Book 12, Page 138 -- Administrator's Bond -- JNO. L. TURNER and SAML. HEISKELL, November 20, 1848, for J. TURNER.
Book 12, Page 218 -- Inventory -- slaves; recorded September 17, 1849. CHAS. WINGFIELD, WM. PETTYJOHN, WM. M. BORG.

REBECCA A. and WM. CRAFT -- Book 17, Page 29 -- Guardian Bond -- JNO. S. McDANIEL and NELSON SEAY, March 20, 1865, for J. McDANIEL as guardian of WM. and REBECCA CRAFT; "A" her middle initial; no parents set forth.

ALEX. P. CRAWFORD -- Book 5, Page 591 -- Guardian's Bond -- SOPHIA CRAWFORD, CHAS. CRAWFORD, NELSON CRAWFORD, ARTHUR B. DAVIES, ALBIN B. SPOONER, July 15, 1816, for SOPHIA CRAWFORD as guardian of WM. S., ALEX. P., GABRIELLA S., and JULIA ANN CRAWFORD, orphans of WM. S. CRAWFORD, deceased.

ANNE CRAWFORD -- Book 4, Page 130 -- August 28, 1802, written; July 18, 1803, probated. Witnesses: HUDSON MARTIN, WM. EWERS.
Codicil of November 11, 1802, with same witnesses. Grandson, PETER CRAWFORD, son of JNO.; grandson, JNO. SMITH; daughter, SALLY JACOBS, ux of JNO. JACOBS; debt of my deceased husband to THOS. CRAWFORD of South Carolina; annuity for faithful slave, Tye; four great-grand-

children: BENNETT and FRANCES CRAWFORD, children of JOEL CRAWFORD of
Georgia; JOEL is dead - ANDERSON SMITH - son of my grandson, JNO.
SMITH; ANNE ANDERSON, daughterof my grandson, JNO. JACOBS. Executors:
Son, NATHAN CRAWFORD, and grandson, JNO. SMITH. Codicil: grandson,
JNO. SMITH, has bought slave at my request; L 100 to be put aside
for slave, Tye, and at her death to JNO. SMITH.
Book 4, Page 292 -- Administrator's Bond -- JNO. SMITH and JAS. WOODS,
September 19, 1803, for JNO. SMITH.
Book 4, Page 377 -- Inventory by NATHAN CRAWFORD who is called one
of the administrators. He is to make true inventory, but it appears
to be Administrator's Bond. Bondsman: NELSON ANDERSON, October 18,
1803.

BENJ. CAWFLIN -- (This is an error noted in proper places and caught
as I came to the CRAWFORD items. I have had it corrected in Master
Index. It is indexed for BENJ. CRAWFORD, but it is for Benj. Cawflin.)
This is also found as COFFLIN.
Book 3, Page 524 -- August 19, 1789, written; October 16, 1797,
probated. Witnesses: NATHL. GUTTRY, MARY JOHNS, BARTLET JOHNS, JNO.
JOHNS. Held for more proof and not told as to outcome. No Administrator's Bond. Son, MAJOR JAS. BENJ. CAWFLIN -- 306 acres joins
COL. JOS. CREWS and STEPHEN HAM. Daughter, KEZIAH CAWFLIN -- next
to where I live in Porage; son gets his on Stoval Creek. Porage
trace is next to CAPT. JAS. DILLARD and RICH. PETERS. Ux, ELIZ - my
son and daughter; my ux and two children. ROBT. CHRISTIAN is to be
trustee for them. Bond of SAML. BALEY.

DAVID CRAWFORD (Sr. and JR. items) -- Book 1, Page 6 -- December 1,
1761, written; September 6, 1762, probated. Witnesses: ANDREW REID,
DAVID DOACK, DANL. GOON, NICHL. N. BALDEN. Ux - where I live and
280 acres; son, DAVID; daughter MARTIN's children; son, JOHN's
children; daughter RODES' children; daughter, JUDITH TERRY and husband, JOS. TERRY and their four children: LUCY, DAVID, CHAMPNESS,
and ELIZ. - LUCY is eldest - if any die, then to daughter TERRY's
children who may be younger. If son-in-law, JOS. TERRY, can prove
any "write" to my negro wench, Amelsy(?) given to my son, DAVID, in
Hanover County. My son, JOHN, deceased; daughter MARTIN deceased.
Granddaughter, SUSANAH BARNET, WM. CRAWFORD, son of DAVID. Execu-
tors: son, DAVID, and son-in-law, JNO. RODES.
Book 1, Page 10 -- Administrator's Bond -- DAVID CRAWFORD, WM. CABELL,
and JNO. HARVIE, September 6, 1762, for DAVID CRAWFORD.
Book 1, Page 34 -- Inventory -- No total, but long, October 6, 1783.
FRANS MERIWETHER, ANDREW REID, EZEKIEL INMON.
Book 1, Page 76 -- DAVID CRAWFORD, SR., June 21, 1766, written;
August 4, 1766, probated. Witnesses: JNO. MORRISON, RO. DINWIDDY,
STEPHEN MARTIN. My ux -- son JOHN's son, PETER; son, DAVID; daughter
SMITH's children; son, JOEL; son, NATHAN -- 400 acres bought of JNO.
DAVIES and 74 acres bought from RO. DINWIDDIE; son, CHAS.; son, WM.;
daughter, SUSANNAH; daughter, SARAH; daughter, ANNE--after my mother's
death - slave, Robin, under will of my father. Daughter, MARY; ux
to make her three youngest children who are now single, equal to my
elder children. He then names SUSANNAH, JOEL, CHAS., SARAH, MARY,
NATHAN, WM., and ANNE CRAWFORD. If NATHAN, WM.; SARAH or ANNE are
without issue - then to NATHAN, WM., and ANNE (sic). Executors:
sons, JNO., DAVID, JOEL CRAWFORD.
Book 1, Page 78 -- Administrator's Bond -- JNO, DAVID, JOEL CRAWFORD,
CORNL. THOMAS and FRANS. MERIWETHER and JNO. MORRISON, August 4, 1766,
for CRAWFORDS.
Book 1, Page 99 -- Inventory -- March 2, 1767 -- L 649-2-6 and other
totals for some other property. DAVID MERIWETHER and JNO. MORRISON.
Book 1, Page 391 -- Administrator's Account of SR. and JR. in hands
of JOELL CRAWFORD - to WM. T. (?) LEWIS; JNO. MARTIN; JUDITH TERRY;
OBEDIAH MARTIN; JAS. MARTIN, JR.; THOS. ANTHONY; DAVID MARTIN; THOS.
CRAWFORD; AZARIAH MARTIN; DAVID CRAWFORD, JR.; JNO. RODES; WM. MAR-
TIN; cash from DAVID JR.'s executors. JOEL CRAWFORD, executor
of SR.; cash from SAML. SHANNOR, executor to D. CRAWFORD, JR.
Settlement of the two estates, December 1, 1777. FRANCIS MERIWETHER;
JNO. GILMORE; ALEX REID, JR.
Book 4, Page 49 -- December 14, 1801, written; September 20, 1802,
probated. Witnesses: WM. and JNO. PRYOR; STILLA SULLIVAN. Son,

DAVID -- land on Herod Creek in Kentucky. (Note: As a Kentuckian, I know that Harrod is proper spelling.); son, REUBEN - land on same creek; son, NATHAN, land in Shelby County, Kentucky, on Barsher (Brashear is proper spelling here and this is county where I was reared. B.D.) -- 1,500 acres and where he lives; daughter, SALLY COCKE; daughters, ELIZ. DAVIS; NANCY JONES; son, CHAS. - land bought of RICH. TALIAFERRO - Tobacco Row to ELIAS WILLS' line. Sons: NELSON; JNO., and WM. S. CRAWFORD - Buffalo Ridge land of May 27, 1789, patent. My ux - land bought of RO. JOHNSTON and some bought of WM.HAYNES. My children: JNO., WM. S., NELSON, CHAS., REUBEN, DAVID, ELIZ. DAVIS, NANCY JONES, SALLY COCKE. Salves to be kept, if family can divide agreeably. Son, NATHAN, gets L5 in addition for being deprived of assistance and support in setting out in life in a remote and distant country. He has son JOHN's bond to make me a fee simple title to lands located by him on the western waters in Kentucky. He has sold some lands to THOS. LUCAS. If any children are without heirs. Executors: Sons, JNO., WM. S., NELSON, and CHAS. CRAWFORD. Codicil: Land to son, WM. to be sold, and divided among other legatees; son, JNO., to manage plantation; sons, DAVID and REUBEN to be furnished with all those necessaries equal to my other children "that has gon" off. March 14, 1802. Negroes left to my ux are to be divided and he names them. Proved by WM. and JNO. PRYOR. JNO., WM. S., NELSON, and CHAS. CRAWFORD qualified. Bondsmen: CHARLES TALIAFERRO, DANL. WARWICK, NELSON ANDERSON, W. PRYOR. CHAS. is called Reverend in bond.
Book 4, Page 146 -- Inventory -- February 1, 1804 -- L 1455-14-9. WM. WARE, JNO. EUBANK, WM. PETER. Administrator's Bond is on Page 355 of Book 4.
Book 5, Page 613 -- Administrator's Account by CHAS. CRAWFORD from June 1, 1799. NA CRAWFORD - legacy; three annual payments due N. C. DAVIES; RO. JONES; T. N. EUBANK for D. (?) CRAWFORD and paid to THOW. W. COCKE; ROWLAND JONES in account with estate (I have a man so named who is a deacon in my church); bond assigned to WILLIAM S. CRAWFORD by CHAS. CRAWFORD, JNO. CRAWFORD for negro boy. Seven legatees owe estate: NICHL. DAVIES in account; to NELSON CRAWFORD; to B. (?) A. CRAWFORD on order. Legatees received L 2676-5-8 in equal share: JNO., WM. S., NELSON, NATHAN, CHAS., DAVID, REUBEN, NICHL. DAVIES, ROWLAND JONES, THOS W. COCKE. December 16, 1816. CHAS. TALIAFERRO, BENJ. TALIAFERRO, JNO. PRYOR.

HANNAH H. CRAWFORD (N. HARE) -- Book 6, Page 414 -- Administrator's Bond -- BENNETT A. CRAWFORD, RICH. CRAWFORD, and WM. McDANIEL, November 21, 1823, for B. CRAWFORD to administrator estate of HANNAH H. CRAWFORD,formerly HANNAH H. HARE; daughter and devisee of WM. B. HARE, deceased.

JAMES CRAWFORD -- Book 10, Page74 -- Estate Commitment to Sheriff -- February, 1839. Motion of CARUTHERS and CO. JNO. COLEMAN, Sheriff.

JNO. CRAWFORD, CAPT. -- Book A, Page 21 -- April 21, 1818, written; April 29, 1818, probated. Witnesses: PETER P. THORNTON, JAS. M. BROWN, ABRAM CARTER and proved by first two witnesses. ABRAM CARTER, WM. JOPLING, JOS. R. CARTER qualified. Bondsmen: AMBROSE RUCKER, NELSON CRAWFORD. To ELIZ. CARTER, ux of JNO. CARTER, JNO. ELLIOTT, son of ELIZ. CARTER - when he is of age. He is to be educated. Slaves to JNO. C. BURRUS, son of CHAS. BURRUS. Executors: ABRAM CARTER, WM. JOPLING and JOS. R. CARTER. Administrator's Bond is on Page 25.
Book A, Page 28 -- Inventory -- $12,272.00, April 13, 1821. JNO. PRYOR, JAS. WARE, RICH. JONES.
Administrator's Account is on Book A, Page 70, by three executors from 1818. Taxes for 1817. JNO. S. CARTER for boarding PERMELIA BURRESS, CHAS. BURRESS as her trustee; Lynchburg suit - HENRY CAMDEN, executor of SARAH BURRESS, deceased versus JNO. CRAWFORD's estate (his executors). February 17, 1825. PETER P. THORNTON, CHAS. L. BARRET, JNO. PRYOR.
Book A, Page 123 -- Administrator's Bond -- ABRAM CARTER, September 25, 1828. Bondsmen: JOS. R. CARTER, BENNETT A. CRAWFORD, THOS. E. PLEASANTS.
Book A, Page 133 -- Administrator's Bond -- LYNN S. TALIAFERRO and

85

BENJ. TALIAFERRO, May 30, 1831, for LYNN TALIAFERRO to administer
unadministered estate.

JNO. D. CRAWFORD -- Book 10, Page 53 -- Administrator's Bond -- BENJ.
J. RUCKER and ZACH. DRUMMOND, October 15, 1838, for BENJ. RUCKER.
Book 10, Page 68 -- Inventory -- November 5, 1838, ALFRED TINSLEY,
ZACH. OGDEN, RO. W. WATTS.
Book 10, Page 351 -- Administrator's Account from November, 1836.
COFFIN (1836 date); May 6, 1837 - to MARGARET CRAWFORD - one-third
of corn on plantation. Same to ELIZ. CRAWFORD. Recorded May 17,
1841.

LUCY CRAWFORD -- Book 11, Page 161 -- November --, 1838, written;
August 21, 1843, probated. Witnesses: HENRY L. DAVIES, WARNER JONES.
My husband, NELSON CRAWFORD - deeds to me for separate estate of
March 11, 1830, and May 20, 1831; recorded in Amherst County.
Son-in-law, BENJ. B. TALIAFERRO; my father, NATHAN CRAWFORD - late
of Nelson County and will recorded there. My sons: EDMUND and RICH.
CRAWFORD; daughters, ELIZ. and NANCY CRAWFORD. If my husband
outlives me; my children: BENNETT A., HUGH NELSON, JUDITH TALIAFERRO.
Executors: son, RICH. CRAWFORD, and BENJ. B. TALIAFERRO. Proved
by witnesses. No Administrator's Bond found.

NATHAN CRAWFORD -- Book 4, Page 551 -- Sheriff -- November 17, 1800.
Bondsmen: NELSON CRAWFORD, JOS. SMITH, JAS. MONTGOMERY, HUDSON
MARTIN, NELSON ANDERSON.

NELSON CRAWFORD -- Book 4, Page 526 -- Coroner -- July 18, 1808.
Bondsmen: ABRAM CARTER, WM. S. CRAWFORD.
Book 4, Page 628 -- Sheriff -- July 16, 1810. Bondsmen: THOS. MOORE,
WM. S. CRAWFORD, ABRAM CARTER, CHAS. TALIAFERRO, JAS. P. GARLAND.
Book 5, Page 79 -- Sheriff -- July 19, 1811. Same bondsmen as above.
Book 10, Page 331 -- Sheriff -- March 15, 1841. Bondsmen: E.
FLETCHER, A. B. DAVIES, HENRY L. DAVIES, RICH. CRAWFORD, DABNEY
SANDIDGE, WM. M. WALLER.
Book 11, Page 14 -- Sheriff -- March 21, 1842. Bondsmen: E. FLETCHER,
BENJ. TALIAFERRO, RICH. CRAWFORD, WM. M. WALLER, HENRY L. DAVIES,
DABNEY SANDIDGE.
Book 11, Page 174 -- So indexed, but not there.
Book 11, Page 471 -- Estate Commitment to Sheriff -- March 10, 1847.
Motion of THOMPSON A. WRIGHT. Sheriff: JAS. L. LAMKIN.

VANSTROUP CRAWFORD -- Book 5, Page 592 -- Guardian Bond -- ALBIN B.
SPOONER, ELIJAH FLETCHER, CHAS. and NELSON CRAWFORD, A. B. DAVIES,
July 15, 1816, for ALBIN SPOONER as guardian of VANSTROUP CRAWFORD,
orphan of WM. S. CRAWFORD, deceased.

WILLIAM SID CRAWFORD -- Book A, Page 14 -- Inventory -- $10,477.00,
September 26, 1815. JNO. SMITH, LEONARD HENLEY, EDMUND T. COLEMAN,
E. FLETCHER, SOPHIA CRAWFORD - Tye River plantation.
Book A, Page 37 -- Administrator's Bond -- SOPHIA CRAWFORD and ELIJAH
FLETCHER, April 25, 1815. Bondsmen: THOS. CREWS, EDMD. PENN,
NELSON CRAWFORD, CHAS. CRAWFORD. A verylong Administrator's Account
by ELIJAH FLETCHER from February 20, 1815. Indian Creek land;
Buffalo River land; MRS. CRAWFORD for coffee; MRS. E. CRAWFORD for
yearly stipend in 1816; A. B. SPOONER, guardian of V. TROUP; my share
and MR. VANNERSON's; SPOONER received his testator's before testator's
death and refuses to give Refunding Bond; suits pending on accounts.
September 28, 1821. JOS. DILLARD, THOS. ALDRIDGE, PEACHY FRANKLIN.
This goes to Page 55.
Book 5, Page 641 -- Division: to legatees: SARAH PATTEN; MARIAH
A. C. FLETCHER; HENRIETTA VANNERSON; ELIZ. H. SPOONER; widow. Nine
heirs: JNO. PATTEN and ux, SARAH; ELIJAH FLETCHER and ux, MARIA
A. C. (See my F will work for his very interesting data); WM. VANNER-
SON and ux, HENRIETTA; ABELON B. SPOONER and ux, ELIZ. H. (note
variation in his name); VANSTROUP CRAWFORD; WM. CRAWFORD; ALEX P.
CRAWFORD; GABRIELLA S. CRAWFORD; JULIAN CRAWFORD.
Book 6, Page 266 -- Division of Indian Creek land by HILL CARTER;
EDWD. CARTER; WM. MOORE. Lots to VANSTROUP CRAWFORD; WM. S.; ALEX.;
GABRIELLA and JULIANNA CRAWFORD--children of WM. on order of August,

1821. Margin: Recorded in deed book; surveyed by REUBEN NORVELL, ACS; VANTRUMP's (sic) part exceeds by 39 acres and others get 225 acres each, but nature and situation of case and land was considered. December 17, 1821, and reference to plat.

CHAS. CREASY -- Book 4, Page 164 -- SALLY JOHNSON declined to serve as administratrix, November 2, 1804. Witne-s: JNO. BIBB. Book 4, Page 166 -- Inventory -- L 54-15-6; ELISHA ESTIS; WM. BREED-LOVE; THOS. BIBB, December 20, 1804. Book 4, Page 395 -- Administrator's Bond -- WM. C. JOHNSON and LANDON CABELL, November 21, 1804, for WM. JOHNSON.

GIDEON CREWS -- Book 3, Page 474 -- Inventory -- October 3, 1797 -- L 1025-2-3. DAVID WOODROOF, RO. WALKER, B. STONE. Book 4, Page 294 -- Administrator's Bond -- JOS. CREWS, JR.; JAS. FRANKLIN; (by W. S. CRAWFORD) September 19, 1797, for JOS. CREWS, JR.

JOSEPH CREWS -- Book 4, Page 56 -- November 29, 1798, written; codicil of December 14, 1801; October 18, 1802. Witnesses to will: PROSSER POWELL, JNO. CREWS, JAS. PENDLETON. Witnesses to codicil: PROSSER POWELL, THOS. WOODROOF, FRANCIS HILL. Proved by FRANKLIN, PENDLETON and THOS. WOODROOF. THOS. CREWS qualified. Bondsman: JAS. FRANKLIN; son, THOS. - 486 acres on each side of Lynch road; daughter, ELIZ. POWELL; daughter, NANCY FRANKLIN; daughter, MARY CREWS; daughter, SARAH CREWS; son, JOSEPH. Executors: sons, THOS. and JOS. Codicil: Reason to believe that son, JOS., is dead; his share to my daughter, NANCY FRANKLIN. Book 4, Page 69 -- Inventory -- November 26, 1802 -- L 1862-16-6; DAVID WOODROOF, JAS. PENDLETON, GEO. DILLARD. Administrator's Bond is Page 360 of Book 4. Book 5, Page 68 -- Administrator's Bond -- THOS. CREWS and JAS. FRANKLIN, February 18, 1811, for THOS. CREWS. Book 5, Page 699 -- Administrator's Bond -- THOS. CREWS and BENJ. BROWN, January 19, 1818, for THOS. CREWS. Note: Sweet Briar House is said to be old CREWS home. Was JOS. CREWS one of the family by that name in early Madison County, Kentucky, and, if so, was he killed by Indians? At least one WOODROOF is buried in the Sweet Briar cemetery.

SALLY CREWS -- Book 9, Page 132 -- (Index Book 8) -- May 12, 1835, written; October 19, 1835, probated. Witnesses: CHAS. H. PAGE and LINDSEY COLEMAN and proved by them, December 19, 1835. HENRY L. DAVIES qualified. Bondsman: HOWELL L. BROWN. BROWN also qualified and DAVIES was his bondsman. Niece, SALLY LEE, daughter of JAS. LEE; grandchildren of my sister, NANCY FRANKLIN. Administrator's Bond is on Page 276 of Book 9. They are children of ANN C. DAVIES; SALLY W. DAVIES; and ELIZ. H. BROWN. Also any born hereafter and as they are of age or married. Executors: HENRY L. DAVIES and ux, ANN C.; SALLY W. DAVIES; HOWELL L. BROWN, and ux, ELIZ. H. Book 9, Page 276 -- Administrator's Bond -- HOWELL L. BROWN, December 19, 1836, for HOWELL BROWN.

WM. CRISP -- Book 4, Page 271 -- Inventory -- many slaves -- L 895-14-6, February 14, 1807. WM. JOHNSON, GEO. VAUGHAN, WILL LOVING. Book 4, Page 439 -- Administrator's Bond -- LUCY CRISP, JAS. MURPHY, JNO. LOVING, January 19, 1807, for LUCY CRISP.

SARAH CROUCHER (Indexed as CROUCH) -- Note variations -- Book 1, Page 241 -- Guardian Bond -- PHILIP and GEO. PENN, March 1, 1773, for PHILIP PENN as guardian of THOS., SARAH, and MARY CROUCHER, orphans of WM. CROUCHER, deceased. Book 1, Page 288 -- Guardian's Account by PENN by order of August Court, 1775; Returned September 1775. Same orphans as above. Book 1, Page 435 -- Guardian's Account and returned September 2, 1778. To NATHANIEL MANTIPLY who married SALLY CROUTCHER (legal representatives of THOS. CROUTCHER, deceased) to MOLLY CROUTCHER - her portion of the estate of THOS. CROUTCHER, deceased.

WM. CROUCHER -- Book 1, Page 287 -- Administrator's Account by JOS.
CABELL, HUGH ROSE, and GABL. PENN, September 4, 1775. Division and
sale; expenses to Caroline County office. To THOS. DICKERSON for
his wife's part and paid to SAML. and WM. CROUCHER; to PHILLIP PENN
for wife's part and as guardian of SARAH, THOS., and MOLLY CROUCHER --
L 196-11-0.

NANCY CROXTON -- Book 1, Page 285 -- Guardian Bond -- MORDECAI BROWN,
GEO. and HENRY GILBERT, July 3, 1775, for MORDECAI BROWN as guardian
of NANCY and JOSHUA CROXTON, orphans of SAML. CROXTON, deceased.

MARTHA CRUMP -- Book 6, Page 488 -- July 31, 1824, written; Octo-
ber 18, 1824, probated. Witnesses: JNO. TALBOT, LINDSEY COLEMAN,
NANCY J. THORNTON, and SALLY CREWS. Proved by TALBOT and female
witnesses. Sister, ANN M. HOLLOWAY and at her death to her children:
GUS (LUS?); THOS. HOLLOWAY. Executor: HENRY L. DAVIES. He qualified. Bondsman: A. B. DAVIES.
Book 6, Page 638 -- Inventory -- $1,102.25. THOS. CREWS, LINDSEY
COLEMAN, WM. WATSON, December 11, 1825.
Book 7, Page 162 -- Administrator's Account -- November, 1824,
written; recorded May 19, 1828. WILKINS WATSON; LINDSEY COLEMAN;
JAS. POWELL. Note; I am interested in CRUMP data. My great-grand-
mother was MARTHA JANE CRUMP, and I have old marriage date from BYRD
family Bible. She married JESSE BYRD and tradition has it that they
were married in Sumner County, Tennessee, but I have only the Bible
data and can find nothing in this Tennessee area. I did find CRUMP
data, though. The family spoke of CRUMP relatives in Texas and
Tennessee data refers to Texas names. JESSE BYRD had JNO. MATHIS
BYRD who married LUCY ANN WILLIAMS in Graves County, Kentucky, and
they were my great-grandparents. WM. CRUMP was traditional name of
older BYRD clan used to identify MARTHA JANE's father. They also
insisted that they were "red-haired CRUMPS."

CHAS. CURRY -- Book 11, Page 98 -- Administrator's Bond -- ZA.
DRUMMOND and SAML. M. GARLAND, January 16, 1843, for ZA. DRUMMOND.
Book 11, Page 125 -- Inventory -- February 3, 1843 - $319.62. W.
ANTHONY RICHESON, THOS. ALLEN, A. DANDIDE (sic).
Book 11, Page 326 -- Administrator's Account from 1843. JNO. PRYOR,
T. C. GOODWIN. March 18, 1845.
Book 11, Page 573 -- Administrator's Account from1845 - land sold to
JESSE RICHESON; ELIZ. CURRY named. Commissioner: JNO. PRYOR,
March 5, 1847.
Book 13, Page 300 -- Administrator's Account from December 14, 1850.
Legatees: WM., JAS., SARAH, and LUCY CURRY. December 19, 1853.
Book 14, Page 481 -- Administrator's Account from November 22, 1853.
Surveyor's fee. ELIZ. CURRY, widow - life share; JAS. ROWSEY(ZEE)
and ux; WM., JAS. and SARAH CURRY. January 18, 1858. Note: JAS.
ROSEY married LUCY A. CURRY, July 26, 1852.

JAS. T. CURRY -- Book 13, Page 258 -- Guardian's Account by ELIZ.
CURRY, guardian, from June 1, 1853. Expense of raising since 1848
and same accounts as guardian (same page) of SARAH and LUCY CURRY;
called her children. Commissioner: ZACH. DRUMMOND; Recorded
November 25,1853.
Book 14, Page 226 -- Guardian Bond -- February 17, 1857. CHAS. M.
BURKS and RO. W. SNEED; CHAS. BURKS as guardian of JAS. T. CURRY,
orphan of C. CURRY, deceased.

LUCY CURRY -- Book 11, Page 309 -- Guardian Bond -- ELIZ. CURRY,
ZA. DRUMMOND, RO. WATTS, JAS. POWELL, March 17, 1845, for ELIZ. CURRY
as guardian of LUCY, JAMES, and SARAH CURRY, orphans of CHAS. CURRY,
deceased.

CALEB CUSHING -- Book 20, Page 298 -- March 2, 1876, written;
March 10, 1879, probated. New York City -- OS-1 - Book 134; Page 129.
Petition of JNO. N. CUSHING, Newburrport, to admit and to qualify
without bond. GEO. F. CHOATE, Probate Jude; JER. T. MAHONEY, Register of Essex Co., Massachusetts; Recorded Amherst County, June 19,
1882. Witnesses: A. AUGUSTUS ADIE, March 2, 1876. Secretary of
U. S. Legation at Madrid, Spain, but of New York City. Written at

Legation of U.S.A. at Madrid. Of Salisbury, Massachusetts, and
Minister of U. S. in Spain. Brother, JNO. N. CUSHING, Newburrport,
Massachusetts -- to his children and children of deceased brother,
WM. CUSHING. JNO. N. CUSHING to administer. Witnesses: EDWARD
BELKNAP and CHAS. D. TYNG.

-D-

MARY JANE DABNEY -- Book 9, Page 283 -- Guardian Bond -- CHISWELL
DABNEY and JNO. M. OTEY, February20, 1837, for CHISWELL DABNEY as
guardian of his infant daughter, MARY JANE DABNEY. On same page
OTEY of Lynchburg gives power of attorney to RO. TINSLEY, Amherst
County Clerk, to sign for him, February 18, 1837. Witness: CHAS. S.
MOSBY.

CHAS. DAIRY -- Book A, Page 125 -- Power of attorney to JAS. POWELL
to collect rents of WILLIS GILLESPIE,tenant on lands next to CORNL.
SALE, ABSALOM HIGGINBOTHAM, etc. September 22, 1828.

CHAS. DAMERON -- Items indexed for Book 11, Pages 45, 66, 310 are
not there.
Book 12, Page 159 -- Sale: GEO. H. HUCKSTEP, administrator -- $303.01.
March 19, 1849.
Book 12, Page 189 -- Administrator's Account from 1841. Dower of MARY
E. DAMERON. March 10, 1849. GEO. POWELL, EDWD. TINSLEY, JNO. D. L.
STEWART.
Book 12, Page 339 is not in Book 12 index.

DUNMORE DAMERON -- Book 11, Page 69 -- Administrator's Bond -- DAVID
PATTESON and RO. CAMM, July 18, 1842, for DAVID PATTESON.
Book 11, Page 334 -- Administrator's Account -- from July 16, 1842:
THOS. CAMPBELL for tuition; board for DUNMORE to MRS. M. E. DAMERON.
Recorded May 5, 1845.

GEO. H. DAMERON -- Book 12, Page 175 -- Constable -- June 18, 1849.
Bondsmen: PETER G. JOINER and JNO. CARDEN.
Book 12, Page 416 -- Same -- June 16, 1851. Bondsmen: GEO. HYLTON
and PETER G. JOINER.
Book 12, Page 529 -- Same -- District 1, June 21, 1852. Bondsmen:
DISON C. BLANKS, BEVERLY P. MORRISS, SYLVESTER L. BURFORD.
Book 13, Page 358 -- (Indexed for Book 12, Page 358) -- Same, June 19,
1854. Bondsmen: GEO. HYLTON, THOS. W. JONES, N. B. MAGRUDER.
Book 14, Page 229 -- Same -- June 16, 1856. Bondsmen: N. B. MAGRU-
DER, B. P. MORRISS, S. L. BURFORD.
Book 14, Page 574 -- Same -- June 21, 1858. Bondsmen: M. DAMERON
and SAML. R. WORTHAM.

MALACHI DAMERON -- Book 10, Page 334 -- Guardian Bond -- RICH.
SHELTON and WILLIS M. REYNOLDS, March 15, 1841, for RICH. SHELTON
as guardian of MALACHI DAMERON, orphan of CHAS. DAMERON.

MARY E. DAMERON -- Book 16, Page 356 -- Administrator's Bond --
MALACHI DAMERON and GEO. H. DAMERON,July 20, 1863, for MALACHI DAMERON.
Book 17, Page 108f -- Inventory -- September 26, 1863, $512.50.
S. R. WORTHAM, A. COX, J. S. PERROW. Sale on same date. GEO. H.
DAMERON and M. DAMERON were buvers: $1,624.80. Recorded July 16,
1866.
Book 17, Page 112 -- Administrator's Account on same date as above --
accounts of GEO. H. and CHAS. D. DAMERON; GEO. H. as guardian of
FANNIE and JENNIE HUCKSTEP. Legatees: CHAS. D. and L. DAMERON;
HENRY A. WHITE as guardian of his children; J. B. OGLESBY for ux;
ANDREW M. KYLE for ux; administrator's legacy; M. DAMERON as guardian
of WM. NORVELL. JOSHUA OGLESBY is shown to be J. B. OGLESBY later
and CATHERINE and SALLY MARGARET WHITE are children of HENRY A. WHITE.

PHOEBE E. DAMERON -- Book 11, Page 210 -- Guardian Bond -- RALPH C.
SHELTON, RICH. F. RUCKER, and JNO. D. F. RUCKER, February 19, 1844,
for RALPH SHELTON as guardian of PHOEBE E., CHAS. D., SARAH F.,
and SUSAN P. DAMERON, orphans of CHAS. DAMERON, deceased.

ROBT. DAMERON -- Book 11, Page 68 -- Administrator's Bond -- DAVID
PATTESON and RO. CAMM, July 18, 1842, for DAVID PATTESON.
Book 11, Page 335 -- Administrator's Account from July 1842. J. M.
DANIEL for board: $12.00. Recorded July 21, 1845.

SUSAN P. DAMERON -- Book 14, Page 452 -- Guardian Bond -- GEO. H.
DAMERON and LEO DANIEL, JR., November 17, 1857, for GEO. DAMERON as
guardian of SUSAN P. DAMERON, orphan of CHAS. DAMERON.

WM. DAMERSON -- Book 4, Page 164 -- Inventory by WM. WARE, Sheriff.
Slaves hired to JAS. WARD; BENJ. WATTS; horse in hands of PLEASANT
DAWSON, October 21, 1804. Recorded November 19, 1804.
Book 4, Page 172 -- Inventory by WARE of L 258-12-0.
Book 4, Page 389 -- so indexed, but nothing there.

ZACHARIAH DAMERON -- Book 11, Page 9 -- Guardian Bond -- RALPH C.
SHELTON and EDWIN L. SHELTON, January 17, 1842, for RALPH SHELTON as
guardian of ZACH. DAMERON, orphan of CHAS. DAMERON, deceased.
Book 23, Page 406 -- April 10, 1891, written; April 16, 1894, probated.
Witnesses: RICH. A. HUGHES, JAS. E. JENNINGS, and R. NEWMAN ELLIS.
Proved by JENNINGS who proved presence of HUGHES. Widow, MARGARET W.
DAMERON, qualified. Bondsmen: H. D. and C. W. DAMERON. Ux, as
long as she does not remarry, to care for my two boys until 21;
GERTRUDE - my youngest daughter. First and last children; charges
in memo book.

JAS. M. DANIEL, JR. -- Book 9, Page 323 -- Constable -- June 20, 1837.
Bondsmen: THOS. N. EUBANK and WM. M. WALLER.
Book 10, Page 135 -- Same -- June 18, 1839. Bondsmen: JAS. M. DANIEL,
SR.; WM. M. WALLER.
Book 10, Page 357 -- Same -- June 21, 1841. Bondsmen: Same.
Book 11, Page 153 -- Same -- June 19, 1843. Bondsmen: PETER RUCKER,
JNO. D. L. RUCKER, JNO. L. EUBANK, JO. R. ELLIS.
Book 11, Page 318 -- Same -- June 16, 1845. Bondsmen: JAS. M.
DANIEL, SR., and JNO. D. L. RUCKER.
Book 11, Page 526 -- Same -- June 21, 1847. Bondsmen: JAS. M. DANIEL,
SR.; SAML. WATTS; RO. N. ELLIS.
Book 12, Page 32 -- Estate Commitment to Sheriff -- July, 1848.
Motion of M. C. GOODWIN. Sheriff: JNO. L. LANKIN.

LEONARD DANIEL, JR. -- Book 12, Page 539 -- Circuit Clerk, July 5,
1852; elected for six years. Bondsman: W. A. RICHESON; LUCAS P.
THOMPSON, judge.
Book 16, Page 510 -- County clerk, May 26, 1864; elected for six
years. Bond of June 20, 1864. Bondsmen: M. C. GOODWIN and W. A.
RICHESON.
Book B, Page 90 -- County Clerk , September 18, 1865; elected for
six years. Bondsmen: R. A. PENDLETON and TAYLOR BERRY. Note: This
man was removed from office by GEN. STONEHAM during Reconstruction
days. I have data in the L section showing that one LUCAS was put
in his place. In some old DAMERON papers in my hands is a statement
that LUCAS was a "northern man." STONEHAM also deposed PENDLETON
at the same time and replaced him with WILLIAMS. WILLIAMS was also
a northern man and married INDIANA FLETCHER. They were the parents
of DAISY WILLIAMS for whom Sweet Briar was to be a memorial. I did
not meet the man, but the clerk told me that a man came here from
Mississippi and he was a descendant of DANIEL. It seems that DANIEL
left here for that state.

ACHILLES DAVENPORT -- Book 9, Page 306 -- Administrator's Bond --
WM. DAVENPORT and JONATHAN A. STOUT, April 17, 1837, for WM.
DAVENPORT.

JOS. DAVENPORT -- Book 3, Page 289 -- Tobacco Inspector, Tye River
Warehouse, November 18, 1793. Bondsman: AMBROSE RUCKER.
Book 3, Page 514 -- Same -- Camden's Warehouse, November 20, 1797.
Bondsman: CHAS. CHRISTIAN.

POLLY DAVENPORT -- Book 16, Page 198 -- Administrator's Bond -- JOS.
DAVENPORT and GEO. ABBETT(ITT) and JNO. P. HUGHES, January 19,
1863, for JOS. DAVENPORT.

SARAH DAVENPORT -- Book 11, Page 101 -- April 9, 1841, written;
January 16, 1843, probated. Witnesses: JESSE T. WOOD, MAHALA ALL-
COCK, RICH. H. ALLCOCK. Proved by WOOD and RICH. ALLCOCK. MARY
DAVENPORT qualified, February 20, 1843. Bondsman: DAVID APPLING.
All to my sister, MARY DAVENPORT. Executor: friend, DAVID APPLING.
Administrator's Bond is Book 11, Page 126.
Book 11, Page 157 -- Inventory -- May 24, 1843. Several slaves --
$1,816.00. MOSES PHILLIPS, G. H. CRANK, WM. S. TURNER.

WILLIS DAVENPORT -- Book 9, Page 305 -- Administrator's Bond -- WM.
DAVENPORT and JONATHAN A. STOUT, April 17, 1837, for WM. DAVENPORT.

WILSON T. DAVENPORT -- Book 14, Page 187 -- Administrator's Bond --
ALEX. R. BURKS and CHAS. Z. BURKS, April 21, 1856, for ALEX BURKS.

GILES DAVIDSON -- Book 12, Page 34 -- January 5, 1848, written;
October 16, 1848, probated. Witnesses: JAS. M. HARRIS, CHAS. D.
MUNDY, THOS. T. EMMET. Proved by HARRIS and by MUNDY on November 20,
1848. JAS. B. DAVIDSON qualified. Bondsman: ALEX. MUNDY. Son,
EDWARD; daughter, FRANCES; son, BENJAMIN; son, MICAJAH and family;
son, MICHAEL; son, JOSEPH; daughter, LOUISANA LANDRUM; child of my
granddaughter, MARTHA MASSIE (formerly DAVIDSON) - her husband is
THOS. MASSIE; granddaughter, CAROLINE MASSIE (formerly DAVIDSON) (I
have been told that she married RO. MASSIE, but have not checked on
it.) Executors: sons, BENJ. and MICHL.
Administrator's Bond is Book 12, Page 138.
Book 12, Page 194 -- Division: to daughter, FRANKEY WINGFIELD - trustee, JAS. M. HARRIS; daughter, LOUISANA LANDRUM; to JAS. B. DAVIDSON;
trsutee of MICAJAH DAVIDSON; MICHL. DAVIDSON; JOS. P. DAVIDSON.
August 20, 1849. WM. DILLARD, A. B. MDGGINSON, STEPHEN W. CHRISTIAN.

JAS. B. DAVIDSON -- Book 13, Page 98 -- Report of sale in DAVIDSON vs.
DAVIDSON, March 12, 1853. JNO. J. DILLARD bought land at $3.00 per
acre; FRANCIS A. BLAIR bought a slave, Sarah, at $700.00 and Isaac
at $408.75. TO. A. COGHILL; F. (T.) W. DILLARD: bond of JNO. J.
DILLARD with WM. DILLARD, bondsman, for JAS. B. DILLARD, March 12,
1853. Also bond of FRANCIS A. BLAIR with W. C. JORDAN as bondsman.
Suit styled J. B. DAVIDSON vs. M. E. DAVIDSON. March 21, 1853.

STEPHEN DAVIDSON -- Book 12, Page 31 -- August 2, 1847, written;
February 21, 1848, probated. Witnesses: W. DILLARD, S. W. CHRISTIAN,
B. T. HAWKINS. Proved by DILLARD and CHRISTIAN. JAMES M. HARRIS
qualified. Sister, FRANCES DAVIDSON - 195 acres where my father,
GILES DAVIDSON, lives on Elk Island Creek and small island in James
near Appomattox shore - one acre - upper part of Horsley's or Allen's
Island. Sister, LOUISIANA LANDRUM; brother, MICAJAH DAVIDSON;
nephew, STEPHEN LANDRUM. Executor: JAS. M. HARRIS.
Book 12, Page 43 -- Inventory -- March 17, 1848 - $635.75-1/2. WM.
DILLARD, STEPHEN W. CHRISTIAN, W. C. JORDAN. Administrator's Bond
is Book 12, Page 125. It is to be noted that he refers to LOUISIAN
and LOUISA LANDRUM in two different places and calls each one "my
sister."

THOS. D. DAVIDSON (Indexed for MARY JANE DAVIDSON) -- Book 12,
Page 507 -- Guardian Bond -- F. A. BLAIR and RO. A. COGHILL, April 19,
1852, for F. BLAIR as guardian of THOS. D. DAVIDSON, orphan of
MICAJAH DAVIDSON.
Book 16, Page 352 -- Guardian's Account by FRANCIS A. BLAIR from
September 1, 1852. Recorded: June 17, 1863 (?).

ADDISON L. DAVIES (Indexed A. L. DAVIS) -- Book 9, Page 340 --
Guardian Bond -- MARTIN D. TINSLEY and ARTHUR B. DAVIES, October 16,
1837, for MARTIN TINSLEY as guardian of ADDISON L. DAVIES, orphan
of FRANCIS A. K. DAVIES, deceased.

ARTHUR B. DAVIES (Indexed for A. B. DAVIS) -- Book 6, Page 255 --
not there.
Book 6, Page 324 -- Clerk of court; various duties. August 20, 1822.
Bondsman: ELIJAH FLETCHER.
Book 6, Page 384 -- Same -- August 22, 1823. Bondsman: WM. DILLARD.

Book 6, Page 474 -- Same -- February 21, 1821. Bondsman: WM.
ARMISTEAD.
Book 6, Page 619 -- Same -- September 19, 1825. Bondsman:
SAML. R. DAVIES.
Book 6, Page 689 -- Same -- February 21, 1821. Bondsman: WM.
ARMISTEAD.
Book 7, Page 65 -- Same -- February 21, 1821. Bondsman: WM.
ARMISTEAD.
Book 7, Page 174 -- Same -- August 19, 1828. Bondsman: RO. TINSLEY.
Book 7, Page 280 -- So indexed, but not there.
Book A, Page 56 -- Same -- February 21, 1821. Bondsman: ELIJAH
FLETCHER.
Book A, Page 66 -- Same -- September 30, 1824. Bondsman: BENJ. BROWN.
Book A, Page 122 -- Same -- September 18, 1827. Bondsman: ALEX.
MUNDY.
Book A, Page 129 -- Same -- October 3, 1829. Bondsman: RO. TINSLEY.
Book 13, Page 51 -- January 13, 1853, written; March 21, 1853, pro-
bated. Witnesses: RO. M. BROWN and M. W. PETTICOLAS. Ux, SUSAN M.;
fifteen slaves named and they are to be freed and to be removed to a
free state or to Liberia. If they don't want freedom, they are to
choose masters. Debt due from CHAS. L. (S.) BROWN. Has been guardian
for niece, LAURA B. DAVIES; debt of WM. E. COLEMAN; brothers: HENRY
L. and WHITING DAVIES; sister, EDITHA DAVIES; children of deceased
brother, FRANCIS A. K. DAVIES: MARY F. CUNNINGHAM, SARAH A. WARE,
and CHAS. DAVIES. Executors: HENRY L. and WHITING DAVIES.
Book 13, Page 52 -- Administrator's Bond -- HENRY L. DAVIES, probate
date. Bondsmen: WHITING DAVIES, GEO. HYLTON, W. DILLARD.
Book 13, Page 256 -- Inventory -- September 1, 1853. RO. H. CARTER,
STEPHEN TURNER, TANDY JONES.
Book 13, Page 318 -- Land division, June 3, 1853. JNO. PRYOR, sur-
veyor -- 638 acres plus on both sides of Horsley and about two
miles from Pedlar Mills. Plat on Page 419 - Windsor Tract - widow,
SUSAN M., gets her part and so do "rest of devisees." TANDY JONES,
LANCELOT MINOR, BENJ. B. WINN.

BEVERLY DAVIES -- Book 5, Page 458 -- Guardian Bond -- FRANCIS A. K.
DAVIES, September 19, 1813, as guardian of BEVERLY DAVIES, orphan
of NICHL. C. DAVIES.
Book 10, Page 82 -- Slave division to widow and his infant child,
LAURA BEVERLY DAVIES. Committee met at his late residence and men-
tion made of guardian of LAURA. Recorded March 19, 1839. NELSON C.
DAWSON, JAS. DAVIS, J. L. WINGFIELD.
Book B, Page 10 -- Administrator's Bond -- ARTHUR B. DAVIES and HENRY
L. DAVIES, April 12, 1838, for ARTHUR DAVIES.
Book B, Page 11 -- Inventory -- September 3, 1838 - $4,097.75. MARTIN
D. TINSLEY, J. L. WINGFIELD, NELSON C. DAWSON.
Book B, Page 14 -- Administrator's Account from 1838 -- to widow;
living on estate and caring for infant child; Rev. sale for funeral -
$15.00; references to executor of ANTHONY RUCKER, WHITING DAVIES
for D. PATTESON's account on N. DAVIES; due HENRY L. DAVIES on deed
of trust; BEV. DAVIES as one of heirs of his brother, NICHL. DAVIES -
land sold for distribution after B. DAVIES' death and his share was
$300.00. A. B. DAVIES as administrator and guardian of the infant
child. SAML. M. GARLAND, commissioner. April 2, 1840.
Book B, Page 24 -- Administrator's Account from March 16, 1840. Mention of administrator of ANTHONY RUCKER; debt of HENRY L. DAVIES;
widow and child RO. M. BROWN, commissioner. Recorded August 25,
1845.

CATHERINE M. DAVIES (Indexed DAVIS) -- Book 12, Page 126 -- Guardian
Bond -- HENRY L. DAVIES and WHITING DAVIES, March 21, 1848, for HENRY
DAVIES as guardian of his infant children: CATHERINE M., SARAH B.,
and CHAS. P. DAVIES.

CHAS. C. DAVIES (Indexed DAVIS) -- Book 9, Page 349 -- Guardian Bond --
MARTIN and ZACH. D. TINSLEY, November 20, 1837, for MARTIN TINSLEY as
guardian of CHAS. C. DAVIES, orphan of FRANCIS A. K. DAVIES.
Book 11, Page 520 -- Refunding bond by CHAS. C. and ADDISON DAVIES
to MARTIN D. TINSLEY. Ward is now of age. TINSLEY has given bond to

administrator of FRANCIS A. DAVIES--A. B. DAVIES. Bond bears date of May 17, 1847.

EDITHA DAVIES -- Book 6, Page 193 -- Guardian Bond -- FRANCIS A. K. DAVIES and ARTHUR B. DAVIES, December 18, 1820, for FRANCIS DAVIES as guardian of EDITHA DAVIES, orphan of NICHOLAS C. DAVIES.

ELIZ. DAVIES -- Book 5, Page 404 -- November --, 1813. ELIZ. takes slaves in right of dower in estate of late husband, NICHOLAS C. DAVIES. WM. S. CRAWFORD, clerk. Note: Page 52 of marriage register, October 13, 1789, MICHL. CLAYTON DAVIES, JUNIOR, bachelor, and ELIZ. CRAWFORD, spinster, secured bond. His father, HENRY L. DAVIES, gave his consent. Her father, CAPT. DAVID CRAWFORD, consented and she was not of age. Published data does not show that he was called Junior and gives only one bondsman: NATHAN CRAWFORD, JR. Others were: JNO. and NELSON CRAWFORD and ARTHUR L. DAVIES.
Book 6, Page 133 -- Administrator's Bond -- FRANCIS A. K. DAVIES; ARTHUR B. DAVIES and JOHN McDANIEL, April 17, 1820, for FRANCIS DAVIES.
Book 6, Page 188 -- Division by MARTIN PARKS, MERIT W. WHITE and J. L. WINGFIELD, July 24, 1820. Heirs of NICHL. C. DAVIES--ELIZ. DAVIES, widow. Lots to SAML. R. DAVIES; FRANCIS A. K. DAVIES; ARTHUR B. DAVIES; JNO. DAVIES; BEVERLY DAVIES; MAYO DAVIES; WHITING DAVIES; HENRY ANNE DAVIES; HENRY L. DAVIES; EDITHA DAVIES; and NICHL. DAVIES.
Book 6, Page 532 -- Administrator's Account by administrator from July 15, 1820. Accounts of F. K. and HENRY DAVIES; mention of A. B. DAVIES; H. L.; MAYO DAVIES; September 15, 1824. MARTIN PARKS; J. L. WINGFIELD; WM. ARMISTEAD.

ELIZ. M. DAVIES -- Book 11, Page 521 -- Refunding Bond -- May 17, 1847, by DAVID TINSLEY to MARTIN D. TINSLEY. MARTIN has been guardian of ELIZ. M. DAVIES, daughter of FRANCIS A. K. DAVIES, deceased, and she has married DAVID TINSLEY. ARTHUR B. DAVIES was admr. of FRANCIS DAVIES. All claims due ELIZ. M. have been paid.

FRANCIS A. K. DAVIES -- Book 8, Page 205 -- Administrator's Bond -- ARTHUR B. DAVIES; ADDISON TALIAFERRO, and BEVERLY DAVIES, May 21, 1832, for ARTHUR DAVIES.
Book 8, Page 241 -- Inventory -- August 20, 1832 - very long and interesting - $7,087.13. JNO. PRYOR; RANDOLPH MORRIS; WM. HAYNES.
Book 9, Page 82 -- Administrator's Account from June 18, 1832. Various members of DAVIES family are named: A. B., S. R., H. L., JNO. N., MRS. E. DAVIES. June 16, 1835. LINDSEY COLEMAN, J. PETTY-JOHN, EDMD. PENN.
Book 9, Page 299 -- Administrator's Account from 1835. Names of S. R. and WM. B. DAVIES on court decree. BEVERLY DAVIES named. Sale by W. B. DAVIES of Persimmon Isle to M. TINSLEY. JNO. N. DAVIES; reference to deed of trust. Recorded March 22, 1837.
Book 10, Page 258 -- Administrator's Account from 1837. Mention of WM. B. DAVIES and ux. August 18, 1840.
These items were indexed as DAVIS:
Book 9, Page 423 -- Division of slaves and land - river tract - met at the home of MRS. DAVIS (sic) -- Mansion House tract which is known as CRAWFORD's Old Tract - 343 acres. MARTIN D. TINSLEY owns five shares bought from these legatees: JNO. N., WM. M., and CHAS. C. DAVIES, and WM. P. PARKS and share by his marriage. Three children are under age; dower to ELIZ. DAVIS (sic), widow. Five younger children; ARTHUR B. DAVIES is administrator. Consent of grown children. Ten tickets were drawn by legatees: JNO. N. DAVIES; EMILY TINSLEY; WM. M. DAVIES; CHAS. C. DAVIES; PERLINA PARKS; ADDISON L. DAVIES; ELIZ. M. DAVIES; SARAH ANN DAVIES; ARTHUR B. DAVIES, JR.; MARY F. DAVIES. October 16, 1837. JAS. DAVIS and AMBROSE RUCKER, commissioners. On Page 425 are the plats -- met at MRS. DAVIS' home, April 13, 1838 - for younger children: ADDISON L. DAVIES and ELIZ. MARGARET - next to AMBROSE LUCAS. Three youngest children: SARAH ANN; ARTHUR B., JR.; and MARY FRANCES DAVIES. Same commissioners as above. Land on west side of Tobacco Row and both sides of road from Crawford's Gap to Horsley Creek--next to GEO. T. PLEASANTS; AMBROSE LUCAS; WM. TERRY's heris; E. M.; ADDISON L. DAVIES; RICH.

JONES' heirs. Surveyed by WM. PRYOR, assistant to JNO. PRYOR,
April 13, 1838. Recorded April 16, 1838. Page 426 - 190 acres on
north side of JAMES and next to EDWD. TINSLEY; WHITING DAVIES;
MARTIN D. TINSLEY; part of testator's land to infants; MARY F.;
ARTHUR B., JR.; SARAH A. DAVIES; also land west of Tobacco Row to
infants: ADDISON L. and ELIZ. MARGARET - 117-1/4 acres. - 289 acres
on north side of FLUVANNA and next to WHITING and MARY F. DAVIES;
lot to MARTIN D. TINSLEY who married EMILY DAVIES (daughter of
testator), and she owns by purchase of husband lots of JNO. N.,
WM. M., CHAS. DAVIES and WELDON B. PARKS. Recorded April 15, 1838.

HARRIAN DAVIES (Indexed for HARRISON DAVIS) -- Book 5, Page 457 --
Guardian Bond -- ELIZ. DAVIES, WM. M. McDANIEL, and FRANCIS A. K.
DAVIES, September 19, 1814, for ELIZ. DAVIES as guardian of HARRIAN;
NICHOLAS; EDITHA; and WHITING DAVIES, orphans of NICHOLAS C. DAVIES,
deceased. Note: In Guardian Bond for HENRY and C. there is comma
between HENRY and ANN, and NICHL. and WHITON (sic) are named. In
division of NICHOLAS' land, she is called HARRY ANN. Bedford land was
given to "her" as her share of father's land. August 23, 1961,
MRS. ROBT. NAPIER (RACHEL BAKER NAPIER), 21 Huguenot Drive, Larchmont,
New York, wrote to DAR, Blue Ridge Chapter, Lynchburg, and Dr. Cornelius called me and then sent me the letter. Therein was qury
about one HENRI ANN DAVIES and it was stated that she was born (probably) in Lynchburg in 1817 since 1860 census of New London Township,
Iowa, shows her age as 43. She married in Campbell County, Virginia,
December 3, 1837, CHAS. B. WALL. Mrs. Napier thought that she was
grandchild of HENRY LANDON DAVIES, Amherst, who had 7 children by
first ux, ANN CLAYTON, and two by second ux, LUCY WHITING CLAYTON
MANSON. He married his second ux, LUCY WHITING MANSON, widow, here
on August 15, 1786. CHAS. TALIAFERRO was bondsman. Some of the
children are shown here: NICHL. CLAYTON DAVIES married ELIZ. CRAW-
FORD; ARTHUR LANDON DAVIES--she cited Tyler's Quarterly, Vol. X,
Page 287, and Bible record therein; SAML. BOYLE DAVIES and ux, ELIZ.
McCULLOCH - 1802; ADDISON DAVIES, son of LUCY; DR. HOWELL DAVIES
had daughter, HARRIET JUNE, who married DR. RO. EARLY, Lynchburg.
She mentioned RUTH HAIRSTON EARLY who wrote Campbell County
Chronicles and Early Genealogy as possible informant.

HENRY DAVIES -- Book 6, Page 257 -- Guardian Bond -- This has been
cited under HARRIAN DAVIES as to punctuation. October 15, 1821,
ARTHUR B. DAVIS (sic) and WM. ARMISTEAD for ARTHUR DAVIS as guardian
of HENRY ANN, NICHL., and WHITON (sic) DAVIES, orphans of NICHL. C.
DAVIES.

JNO. DAVIES (Indexed as DAVIS in Book 4, Page 395, but it is DAVIES) --
Book 5, Page 395 -- Guardian Bond -- October 18, 1813, NATHANIEL
MANSON, guardian of JNO. DAVIES, orphan of NICHL. C. DAVIES. Bonds-
man: NELSON CRAWFORD.

JNO. HUGHES DAVIES -- Book 14, Page 27 -- Guardian Bond -- October 15,
1855, HENRY L. DAVIES as guardian of JNO. HUGHES DAVIES, orphan of
JNO. DAVIES, deceased. Bondsman: SAML. SCOTT.

LANDON DAVIES (Not indexed in Master) -- Book 5, Page 375 -- Guardian
Bond -- ARTHUR B. DAVIES and JNO. PENN, September 20, 1813, for
ARTHUR DAVIES as guardian of LANDON DAVIES, orphan of N. C. DAVIES.

LAURA B. DAVIES -- Book 10, Page 53 -- so indexed as Guardian Bond,
but it is Book 10, Page 65 -- Guardian Bond -- ARTHUR B. DAVIES;
WHITING DAVIES; and MARTIN D. TINSLEY, November 19, 1838, for ARTHUR
DAVIES as guardian of LAURA B. DAVIES, orphan of BEVERLY DAVIES. She
is called LAURA BEVERLY DAVIES in other items.
Book 11, Page 461 -- Guardian's Account by guardian; Commissioner:
RO. M. BROWN. Slave list for her estate share from 1839. Carrying
you to school in Lynchburg and detained overnight; tolls on turnpike
and bridge - 1843. Trip to Cumberland; WHITING DAVIES for slave
hired in 1843; June 1845 - pocket money - 25 cents. Recorded:
December 21, 1846.
Book 11, Page 467 -- Guardian's Account from April 21, 1845. Postage

for three letters - 35 cents; pocket money - 25 cents; E. H. CHAPLIN
for tuition. Dancing - $10.00. Bond of WHITING DAVIES. Recorded
December 21, 1846.
Book 14, Page 7 -- Guardian's Account by RO. M. BROWN from Septem-
ber 30, 1854. By letter to Staunton; Virginia Female Institute for
tuition; store account of JNO. Y. DAVIES. Recorded August 20, 1855.
Book 14, Page 209 -- Guardian's Account by BROWN from June 30, 1855.
To SUSAN M. DAVIS for board; Virginia Female Institute for 1856.
Recorded May 21, 1855.
Book 14, Page 248 -- Guardian's Account as above from March Court,
1853. Paid by me at Christmas - $1.00; expenses to Richmond; flowers
for bonnett - 75 cents; school at Staunton - $150.00; from H. L.
DAVIES, executor of A. B. DAVIES; WHITING DAVIES for hire of slave;
from JNO. H. DAVIES. Recorded May 19, 1855.
Book 14, Page 453 -- Guardian's Account from June 1, 1856; store
account of JNO. F. DAVIES. Recorded July 11, 1857.

NICHOLAS C. DAVIES -- Book 5, Page 71 -- Administrator's Bond --
ELIZ. DAVIES; WM. S. CRAWFORD; JNO. and CHAS. CRAWFORD, June 17, 1811,
for ELIZ. DAVIES. On Page 72, NELSON CRAWFORD also qualified on same
date. Bondsmen: BENJ. TALIAFERRO and ABRAM CARTER.
Book 5, Page 404 -- Relinquish of Dowry by ELIZ. DAVIES, Nov. 11,
1813, under General Assembly Act of January, 1805.
Book 6, Page 199 -- Administrator's Account by NELSON CRAWFORD from
September, 1811. Cash to ELIZ. CRAWFORD; FLETCHER for tuition; MAYO
DAVIES tuition and board; amounts to HENRY and JAS. DAVIES on accounts;
estate of DAVID CRAWFORD, deceased. Recorded November 21, 1820.
JAS. DAVIS, GARRET GILLIAM, NATHAN (?) MANSON.
Book 7, Page 94 -- Division of real estate -- HARRY ANN DAVIES -
Bedford tract next to Trent's Ferry - 215-1/2 acres for her share of
her father's estate; dower of mother is excepted; reference to former
court order to divide; land to MAYO DAVIES between HARRY ANN and
EDITHA DAVIES; EDITHA DAVIES - next to DR. JNO. CABELL and MAYO
DAVIES; NICHOLAS DAVIES - 369 acres on both sides of Pedlar, north-
side of JAMES, and mouth of Pedlar; RODERICK DAVIES - Buck branch;
WHITING DAVIES; JNO. DAVIES; HENRY L. DAVIES - Fishing Island, etc.;
BEVERLY DAVIES - where town of Bethel stands; widow, ELIZ. DAVIES,
gets 800 acres and Mansion House - next to ARTHUR L. DAVIES; also
adjoins CALEB WATTS; JNO. WINGFIELD; MARY MONTGOMERY; JAS. DAVIES
and others. Land to FRANCIS A. K. DAVIES - on JAMES at Holcomb Rock
and Posimmon (sic) Island; to ARTHUR B. DAVIES--Bedford land on
Hunting Creek. Land on Piny Mt. is to be divided. It is stated
that each DAVIES - save widow - gets his or her part of father's
land. Commissioners: MARTIN PARKS, JAS. DAVIES, JARRATT GILLIAM.
December 17, 1827.

Book 9, Page 229 -- So indexed, but nothing thereon for DAVIES.
Book 9, Page 246 -- Lunatic Bond -- October 17, 1836. BEVERLY and
ARTHUR B. DAVIES; ADDISON TALIAFERRO; MARTIN D. TINSLEY for BEVERLY
DAVIES to administer estate of NICHL. DAVIES of unsound mind.
Book 9, Page 418 -- Administrator's Bond -- WHITING DAVIES, April 16,
1838. Bondsmen: HENRY L. and WM. B. DAVIES.

REBECCA E. P. DAVIES -- Book 19, Page 87 (Indexed for R.E.P. DAVIS) --
She renounces the will of her late husband, H. L. DAVIES, deceased, as
in her best interests, but claims dower rights. Witnesses: F. F.
VOORHIES and J. F. DAVIES.

RODERICK DAVIES (Indexed DAVIS) -- Book 5, Page 459 -- Guardian Bond --
A. B. DAVIES and FRANCIS A. K. DAVIES, September 19, 1814, for
A. DAVIES as guardian of RODERICK DAVIES, orphan of NICHL. C. DAVIES.

SAML. R. DAVIES -- Book 8, Page 229 -- Administrator's Bond --
July 16, 1832. SARAH W. (M.) DAVIES. Bondsmen: A. B.: HENRY L.
and BEVERLY DAVIES.
Book 13, Page 465 -- Slave division -- December 28, 1854, by GEO. W.
CHRISTIAN, D. H. TAPSCOTT, and SAML. HEISKELL. Recorded February 19,
1855. Lots drawn by MRS. SARAH M. (W.) DAVIES, MISS SALLIE R. DAVIES,
and JNO. H. (?) DAVIES. Note: See my F will work and NANCY FRANKLIN
for more on SARAH DAVIES.

SARAH ANN DAVIES (SARAH W. DAVIES--see 84 A) -- Book 9, Page 340 --
Guardian Bond -- ARTHUR B. DAVIES and MARTIN D. TINSLEY, October 16,
1837, for ARTHUR DAVIES as guardian of ARTHUR B. DAVIES, JR.; SARAH
ANN DAVIES; and MARY F. DAVIES, orphans of FRANCIS A. K. DAVIES.

SUSAN M. DAVIES -- Book 17, Page 34 -- May 8, 1861, written; April 17,
1865, probated. Witnesses: M. R. VAUGHAN and THOS. L. BROWN.
Niece, SALLIE B. TUCKER, and child or children - ux of G.A.R. TUCKER.
My brother, RO. M. BROWN; my nephew, ARTHUR DAVIES BROWN, son of
RO. M. BROWN; my niece, JANE RANDOLPH PETTICOLAS; my little niece,
LIZER MEREDITH TUCKER; my sister, MILDRED W. PETTICOLAS. Executor:
Brother, RO. M. BROWN.
Book 17, Page 35 (Indexed for 38) -- Administrator's Bond -- RO. M.
BROWN; THOS. WHITEHEAD, SAML. M. GARLAND on probate date for
RO. BROWN.
Book 17, Page 46 -- Inventory -- November 15, 1865 - $608.50, SAML. M.
GARLAND; LEO DANIEL, JR.
Book 19, Page 59 -- Administrator's Account -- July 19, 1875 - from
April 17, 1865 - $2,022.99 for the son of administrator, ARTHUR
DAVIES BROWN; to JANE R. PETTICOLAS; G.A.R. TUCKER and ux. Bond of
April , 1865, of W. W. and ADOLPHUS and PHILIP A. PETTICOLAS. Con-
federate bond of $500.00. W. FARIS for enclosing grave. Another bond
by the PETTICOLAS men in 1873. R-corded September 20, 1875.

WHITING DAVIES -- Book 6, Page 268 -- Guardian Bond -- FRANCIS A.K.
DAVIES and SAML. BURKS, December 17, 1821, for FRANCIS DAVIES as
guardian of WHITING DAVIES, orphan of NICHL. C. DAVIES.
Book 11, Page 381 -- Commissioner of Revenue -- April 20, 1846.
Bondsman: H. L. DAVIES. In room of JNO. H. ROBERTS, deceased.
Book 11, Page 447 -- Same -- September 21, 1846. Bondsman: MARTIN D.
TINSLEY.
Book 12, Page 25 -- Commissioner of Revenue -- September 20, 1847.
Bondsman: HENRY L. DAVIES.

Book 12, Page 134 -- Same -- September 18, 1849. Bondsman: Same.
Book 12, Page 228 -- Same -- September 17, 1849. Bondsman: ADDISON
TALIAFERRO.
Book 12, Page 296 -- Same -- October 21, 1850. Bondsman: HENRY L.
DAVIES.

WM. B. DAVIES, DR. (Indexed for JNO. D. DAVIS) -- Book 16, Page 306 --
Administrator's Bond -- RO. M. BROWN, April 20, 1863. Bondsman: JNO.
THOMPSON, JR.
Book 16, Page 331 -- Inventory -- June 1, 1863; medical library -
"say 40 vols." - no total. RO. L. COLEMAN; WM. S. CLAIBORNE; J. O.
STANFIELD. At sale EDITHA DAVIES was a buyer. Recorded June 18,
1863.
Book 17, Page 132 -- Administrator's Account from April 20, 1863.
EDITHA DAVIES named. Recorded June 2, 1866.

CHAS. DAVIS -- Book 5, Page 484 -- Administrator's Bond -- JAS.
DAVIS, THOS. N. EUBANK; DAVID J. BURKS and LEWIS DAVIS, January 16,
1815, for JAS. DAVIS.
Book 7, Page 74 -- Inventory -- January 20, 1815 -- L 1207-12-6.
JAS. WARE and MARTIN PARKS.

CHAS. LEWIS DAVIS -- Book 12, Page 223 -- July 17, 1840, written;
October 15, 1849, probated. Witnesses: BARNETT C. RAY, ANDREW
HANNAH, THOS. G. McCLINTOCK, JNO. D. DAVIS, JNO. PRYOR. Ux, NANCY--
where I live; children by present ux: SAML.; THOS. MORRISS; GEO.;
WM. LUDWELL; HENRIETTA NANCY (not sure as to one or two children
here because of lack of any punctuation); SUSAN FRANCES and CAROLINE
LEWIS. Children by first marriage: DABNEY WHITE; OVATON LEWIS;
ELIZ. ANNE and JANE AMANDA. First set to have $300.00 more for each
one to make them equal because of legacies devised to them by their
late grandfather, CAPT. JACOB WHITE, Bedford, and thus put them on
equal footing -- here is a confusing statement since he ends with
"thereby to put them on equal footing with my four children by first
ux." It would appear that first set must have been WHITE descendants since the name is employed, but the sentence is garbled. Land

on Coal River, devised to me by my father, has not been sold--
Kanawaha County land. Executors: Son, THOS. and SAML. and ux.
Codicil, July 22, 1849, names his son, WM. LUDWELL, as an executor.
Witnesses: JNO. PRYOR, JAS. BYASS, JNO. D. DAVIS.
Book 12, Page 250 -- Administrator's Bond -- NANCY and WILL L. DAVIS,
November 19, 1849, for both.
Book 12, Page 252 -- Inventory -- November 29, 1849. ARCHIBALD
REYNOLDS, RODERICK L. WATTS, RODERICK WAUGH.
Book 12, Page 455 -- Administrator's Account by WM. L. DAVIS from
November 19, 1849--to administer and store account of JNO. D. DAVIS.
Recorded October 20, 1851. There is a listing in Master for Admin-
istrator's Account on Page 127, but it is not there. 12 index does
not have it listed.

EDWARD J. DAVIS (Indexed for EDWD. P. DAVIES) -- Book 22, Page 122 --
Adminsitrator's Bond -- WM. W. DAVIS and JNO. R. WRIGHT, July 16, 1888,
for WM. DAVIS. Inventory is Page 303 of same book, September 10,
1888. CHAS. E. COFFEY; DANL. R. COFFEY; JNO. R. WRIGHT - $54.03.
Sale is Page 304 of the same book and is same amount as inventory -
September 25, 1888. JNO. M. and JNO. E. DAVIS were buyers; latter
was clerk.

ELIZA ANN DAVIS -- Book 8, Page 303 -- Administrator's Bond -- CHAS. L.
DAVIS and bondsmen: WM. H. McCULLOCH and ELLIOTT WORTHAM, February 18,
1833.

ELIZ. DAVIS -- Book 6, Page 675 -- Administrator's Bond -- ISHAM
DAVIS and WM. FLANAGAN, August 22, 1826, for ISHAM DAVIS.
She was widow of NATHANIEL (see will.) Published data says that she
was nee ATKINS.

ISRAEL DAVIS -- Book 3, Page 418 -- December 14, 1796, written;
July 18, 1797, probated. Witnesses: PEACHY FRANKLIN, SAML. McGEHEHEE,
GIDEON CREWS. Daughter, SARAH SMALL; son, JNO.; son, LEWIS; my four
children: ISRAEL, JOSHUA, MARY DAVIS, RICHARD DAVIS. My ux, MARY.
Executors: Ux and WILLIAM SANDIDGE.
Book 3, Page 442 -- Inventory -- July 31, 1797 -- L 245-9-6. JOEL
FRANKLIN, BARTLETT CASH, RICH. OGLESBY.
Book 4, Page 287 -- Administrator's Bond -- MARY DAVIS, JOS. ROBERTS,
and JAS. CARPENTER, July 17, 1797, for MARY DAVIS.

JAMES DAVIS (CAPT. in some data) -- Book 3, Page 125 -- Guardian
Bond -- WM. and JNO. WARE, October 5, 1789, for WM. WARE as guardian
of JAS. DAVIS, orphan of NATHANIEL DAVIS, deceased.
Book 6, Page 333 -- Tobacco Inspector -- Amherst Warehouse, October 21,
1822. Bondsman: WM. ARMISTEAD.
Book 6, Page 338 -- Same type of bond; not there.
Book 6, Page 475 -- Same -- September 20, 1824. Bondsman: WM. ARMI-
STEAD, Amherst County Warehouse.
Book 6, Page 624 -- Same -- September 19, 1825. Bondsman: CHAS. L.
DAVIS.
Book 6, Page 688 -- Same -- September 18, 1826. Bondsman: WM. ARMI-
STEAD.
Book 7, Page 33 -- Same -- September 17, 1827. Bondsman: Same.
Book 7, Page 195 -- Same -- December 15, 1828. Bondsman: GEO. BURKS.
Book 8, Page 51 -- Same -- Amherst Warehouse in town of Bethel.
Bondsman: JNO. DUDLEY DAVIS.
Book 11, Page 230 -- February 24, 1844, written; August 19, 1844,
probated. Witnesses: CATH. WATTS, DANL. DAY, JESSE F. HUTCHESON,
STEPHEN WATTS, THOS. HUTCHERSON, J. T. RODES. Proved by DAY, JESSE
HUTCHESON, S. WATTS. JESSE MUNDY qualified. Bondsman: LEWIS CAMPBELL
("S." middle initial). Ux, MILDRED - land, etc. - named slaves to be
sold - my horses excepted. Children and children of deceased chil-
dren - except son, SAML.; viz.: my grandchildren inherit their deceased parents' portions - grandchildren: MILDRED and SALLY OGDEN -
at grandmother's death. They are children of my deceased daughter,
SALLY OGDEN -- if they die before age of 21. My daughter, CATH.
HENLEY; daughter, PEGGY BOWLING; son, SAML., gets $10.00 at mother's
death for he has had considerable sums. Sons, JNO. and JAMES; daughter, ELIZ. STEVENS - her children -- and free from control of her

husband. If children are without heirs. Executor: friend, JESSE
MUNDY.
Administrator's Bond is Book 11, Page 253, and inventory is Page 255 -
$5,320.50, December 16, 1844 - THOS. HUTCHESON, NATHAN GUTHRIE, WM.
BECK.
Book 11, Page 448 -- Administrator's Bond -- October 19, 1846. JNO.
D. DAVIS. Bondsmen: NELSON TINSLEY, JAMES GILLIAM, GEO. T. PLEASANTS.
Book 12, Page 385 -- Administrator's Account from December 16, 1850 --
heirs of SAML. DAVIS - special legacy at death of widow - "say
September 18, 1848"; advances by testator in lifetime -- MILDRED and
SALLY OGDEN, children of SALLY OGDEN, deceased; to WM. HENLEY and ux;
JAS. BOWLING and ux; JAS. DAVIS, JR.; ELIZ. STEPHENS; JNO. DAVIS.
HENRY M. OGDEN as guardian of children and buyer of JAS. DAVIS, JR.'s
share; CATH. HENLY, ux of WM. HENLEY; PEGGY BOWLING, ux of JAMES
BOWLING. Under OGDEN record of payments - JAS. MASSON (or MAJORS)
and ux, MILDRED; JNO. DAVIS, deceased - item of December 31, 1850;
name of H. S. (?) DAVIS, SAML. DAVIS, legatee - May 18, 1829 - Amount
attached in hands of executors of LODERWICK D. SIMPSON - administrators of LEWIS P. SIMPSON -- 2 suits; JNO. DAVIS, deceased - legacy.
Recorded April 21, 1851.

Book 12, Page 427 -- Administrator's Account from December 31,
1850 - same legatees and many references to estate of JNO. DAVIS,
deceased. Interest in estate of MILDRED DAVIS; SALLY OGDEN's children
have taken their shares. RO. M. BROWN, commissioner. June 16, 1851.
Book 13, Page 342 -- Order of November, 1845 -- suit of JNO. D. DAVIS
vs. SALLY DAVIS, et.al. JNO. PRYOR, surveyor - 844 acres - including
10 acres given by CAPT. JAS. DAVIS to MICAJAH PENDLETON. 190 acres
to MRS. SALLY DAVIS, widow of CAPT. JAS. DAVIS. Lot to JNO. D. DAVIS;
lot to children of LOUISA J. PENDLETON: EDMUND, ANNE G., JAS. D.,
SUSAN F., and SARAH D. PENDLETON. To SARAH J. PARKS,formerly WORTHAM;
to JAS. D.; MARY LOUISA; SAML. R.; CHAS. E.; FRANCES D.; and RICH.
BEVERLY WORTHAM - children of NANCY B. WORTHAM, deceased. Care
taken to protect heirs for JAMES had laid off portions and they had
built houses and planted orchards. December 9, 1846. JNO. PRYOR,
RO. H. CARTER, A. C. JOHNSON, JO. R. ELLIS.

JNO. DAVIS -- Book 1, Page 521 -- September 7, 1779 (probate date
only here) - Ux, ELIZ. - 100 acres. Daughter, HANNAH; sons, PHILLIP
and WM. - 374 acres to divide; PHILLIP gets tract where WM. MURRAY
lives, and WM. gets tract where BENJ. LANDRUM formerly lived; also
100 acres on south side of Gilmer's Mountain. Sons: BENJ. and JESSE -
Shoe Creek land. Executor: brother, DAVID DAVIS. Witnesses: DANL.
McDONALD, GILBERT HAY, JAS. MURRAY. Proved by McDONALD and HAY, and
HAY qualified. Bondsmen: JNO. JACOBS and JNO. THOMPSON.
Administrator's Bond is on Page 523.
Book 4, Page 454 -- Indexed for JNO. C. DAVIS, but no "C," only JOHN.
Constable Bond -- June 20, 1803. Bondsmen: NATHL. BRIDGWATER and
ALEX. ROBERTS.
Book 5, Page 99 -- Indexed JNO. B. but no initial here: Baptist
minister's bond, March 16, 1812. THOS. HOLLOWAY.
Book 6, Page 204 -- Administrator's Bond -- January 15, 1821. WM.
DAVIS. Bondsman: WM. ARMISTEAD.
Book 6, Page 225 -- Inventory -- May 20, 1821; no total. THOS.
MORRIS; LEWIS DAVIS; GEO. MORRIS, JR.
Book 12, Page 495 -- September 6, 1842, written; March 15, 1852, pro-
bated. Witnesses: JOS. R. CARTER, SAML. C. GIBSON, WM. D. DAVIS.
Proved by CARTER and DAVIS. Recorded on motion of S. C. GIBSON and
he qualified. Bondsmen: WM. D. DAVIS and JAS. W. HENLEY. Ux, MARY,
and her children: SOPRONA BARKER, JAS. L. DAVIS, JANE A. GIBSON,
LUTHER R. DAVIS, WM. DANIEL DAVIS, THOS. DAVIS, MARY ELIZ. DAVIS, and
FIELDING DAVIS. Sons by first ux: MADISON and JNO. DAVIS have
received estate which came by her, and get $1.00 each. Executors:
son, JAMES L. DAVIS and SAML. C. GIBSON.
Administrator's Bond is Page 499.
Book 13, Page 223 -- Inventory -- September 18, 1852. RO. H. CARTER,
JOS. R. CARTER, CHAS. L. BROWN - $210.25.
        DAVIS Excursus:
        The family of DAVIS is a very difficult one because all of us
love to use JNO., DAVID, ISAAC, and JAMES for our children. I am the

son of JNO. FULTON DAVIS of Bourbon County, Kentucky. My father
had an uncle named JOHN LUCKEY DAVIS (LUCKEY for our LUCKEY ancestor)
and also a great-uncle named JOHN. My father's grandfather, ABRAM
HENSON DAVIS, was the son of JAMES DAVIS and JAMES was a son of JOHN.
This JOHN was a Revolutionary soldier and from Prince William County,
Virginia. My father's father was THOS. ISAAC DAVIS, and one brother
of my father is named DAVID DAVIS. I named my oldest son, JOHN FULTON
DAVIS, and he is now a captain in the U. S. Army. He has a son
named JOHN FULTON DAVIS, and all of this illustrates the usage of the
names cited above.
     I have established no connection with the Amherst clan, but one
will note the use of the names of JOHN, JAMES, DAVID DAVIS herein.
I have a member in my Amherst Baptist Church named J. BIGBY DAVIS,
and he turned over several old Bibles for me to copy. (Note: BIGBY
DAVIS died at 5:45 Wednesday afternoon, 14 January 1970. I held
funeral at Amherst Baptist Church 16 January 1970, assisted by
JNO. MOORE, former pastor, Lexington, Virginia, and PAUL CARTER,
Methodist, of Louisiana.) I had done work for a descendant of this
JOHN DAVIS and he was quite indignant when I sent him the will data
above showing a former marriage. He KNEW that his ancestor had only
one ux and refused to believe that the will was proof positive. I
accept the data as authentic for Amherst data clearly shows the whole
story. I cite my G work for the grandfather of the two children by
the first marriage. Their grandfather GILLIAM names them in his will
and their mother was JUDITH GILLIAM. JOHN DAVIS married JUDITH
GILLIAM here in 1804 and I am in possession of the data.
     The Bible data furnished therein through the courtesy of J.
BIGBY DAVIS; it will be noted that JOHN DAVIS was one of the active
and prominent Baptist ministers in Amherst County. ADDIE E. DAVIS is
a descendant of his, and it is eminently fitting that this data should
be included. She is the daughter of JOHN LUTHER DAVIS and WILLE
ENTSMINGER. JNO. LUTHER DAVIS was the son of JNO. DAVIS and HETTIE
OGDEN. J. BIGBY DAVIS is a son of JAS. L. DAVIS and EUGENIA SANDIDGE,
and JAS. L. and JNO. LUTHER DAVIS were brothers.
     The second ux was MARY LIVELY and he married her in 1811. The
Bibles were those of the DAVIS and LIVELY families. The latter is the
oldest one handled by me in copying data, but it will not be included
herein. It will appear, Deo volente, in L will data. The DAVIS
Bible was in my hands for copying and I cite data from it. It was
printed at the Clarendon Press by WM. JACKSON and WM. DAWSON, Printers
to the University, and sold at the Oxford Bible Warehouse in Pater-
noster Row, London, 1795 - Cum Privilegio. Some of the writing is
dim, but we have left out no data. Two columns were used to put down
family data. First column - no attempt is made to change writing:
     JOHN DAVIS and MAREY LIVELY was married December 19, 1811.
               (Note: Bond bears date of December 18th;
               Page 229 of Register).
     JOHN DAVIS was born Ano March the 8th, 1782.
     MARY LIVELY was Born Ano May 17, 1787.
     SOPHRONIA (C or A above line) DAVIS was born Ano
               October the 19th, 1812.
     JAMES L. DAVIS Ano January the 12th 18--. There is
               a hole to one side and someone has tried to
               correct with pencil, but only 181- is legible.
     ANN DAVIS -- was -- Ano January 31, 1816. There
               may have been a middle name, but if so, it is
               not legible.
     LUTHER R. DAVIS was Born February the 20th, 1818.
     WM. D. DAVIS was born Ano May the 11th, 1820.

Second column:
     CLAUDIA DAVIS was born Ano February 9, 1822.
     MARY DAVIS was born December 19, 1823.
     FIELDING DAVIS was born June the 9th, 1825.

     GEO. BRAXTON TAYLOR speaks of "the venerable JOHN DAVIS" when
he baptized 31 candidates in Buffalo River, August, 1833. Fourth
Series; Page 118: Virginia Baptist Ministers. He was then pastor
of Mt. Moriah Baptist Church which is no longer active, but has merged
with Central Church.

JNO. DUDLEY DAVIS -- Book 12, Page 343 -- Sheriff -- February 17,
1851. Bondsmen: RO. M. BROWN, SAML. M. GARLAND, THOS. WHITEHEAD (by
JNO. WHITEHEAD), JNO. WHITEHEAD (by THOS. WHITEHEAD), GEO. D. DAVIS,
PLEASANT PRESTON (by GEO. D. DAVIS), S. C. HURT, JNO. T. DAVIS,
MICAJAH DAVIS, EDGAR WHITEHEAD, RO. A. COGHILL, RO. WHITEHEAD.
Book 18, Page 101 -- Administrator's Bond -- JNO. E. WILLIAMS and
GEO. R. WILLIAMS, July 17, 1871, for JNO. WILLIAMS. GEO. gives power
of attorney to his son, JOHN, to sign bond, July 14, 1871; both of
Amherst County. SAML. R. WORTHAM, Justice of the Peace.

JNO. T. DAVIS -- Book 13, Page 354 -- Power of attorney to SAML. M.
GARLAND, clerk of Amherst County, to sign for him on bond of GEO. A.
BURKS as trustee and administrator of his father, GEO. BURKS, deceased.
April 15, 1854.

MILDRED (MILLIE) DAVIS -- Book 12, Page 135 -- Administrator's Bond --
JESSE MUNDY and LEWIS S. CAMPBELL, September 18, 1848, for JESSE
MUNDY. Inventory is Book 12, Page 154- March 19, 1849 - $211.50.
DANL. DAY; EPHRAIM HULVER; JAS. HUTCHESON.
Administrator's Account is Book 12, Page 328 -- September 17, 1850;
sales on October 30, 1848 - $234.38. Burial expenses of October 13,
1848. Account paid HENRY L. DAVIES.
Another Administrator's Account -- Book 12, Page 395 -- from Decem-
ber 16, 1850. One sixth to these legatees: SAML. DAVIS; JAS. BOWLING
and ux; ELIZ. STEPHENS; JAS. DAVIS; and one half of one sixth to
JAS. MAJORS and ux, Mildred; WM.HENLEY and ux. Reference to suit of
LODEWICK D. SIMPSON, administrator of LEWIS P. SIMPSON. Names of
these distributees: SALLY OGDEN; WM. HENLEY and ux, CATH.; JAS.
BOWLING and ux, PEGGY. Recorded February 17, 1851.

NANCY DAVIS -- Book 16, Page 178 -- Administrator's Bond -- W. L.
DAVIS and J. DUDLEY DAVIS, October 20, 1862, for W. DAVIS.
Book 16, Page 193 -- Inventory -- October, 1862, order and done on
November 1, 1862. Cedar Creek land, etc. - $2,777.00. Tenant in
Confederal service. Commissioners: JAS. H. WAUGH and DANL. E.
BAILEY, December 15, 1862.

NATHANIEL DAVIS -- Book 1, Page 513 -- Administrator's Bond -- ELIZ.
DAVIS; CHAS. DAVIS; RODERICK McCULLOCH; THOS. WAUGH, November 1, 1779,
for ELIZ. and CHAS. DAVIS.
Book 2, Page 83 -- May 10, 1778, written; November 1, 1779, probated.
Witnesses: RO. DAVIS, JNO. DUNCAN, JAS. TULEY, JNO. BANKS. Son,
CHAS. - Thomas Mill Creek land; Sons: ROBT., ISHAM, and JAS. DAVIS -
Maple Creek land and where I live; son, NATHL. - Tobacco Row Mountain
land; daughter, ELIZ. DAVIS; daughters: SARAH, THEDOSHA, and MITILDE
DAVIS; daughter, NANCY, at husband's death; ux, ELIZ. - when youngest
child is 18. If children are without heirs.
Book 3, Page 243 -- Guardian Bond -- JOSIAH ELLIS and CHAS. DAVIS,
October 15, 1792, for JOSIAH ELLIS as guardian of NATHL. DAVIS, orphan
of NATHL. DAVIS. This is indexed for ELLIS, and I found it when
working on E's.
Book 3, Page 255 -- Division of L 98-6-8; slaves, etc. Lots to
CHAS. DAVIS; ISHAM DAVIS; JAS. DAVIS; NATHL. DAVIS; ELIZ. BURKS - a
daughter of deceased; amount due from estate of JNO. BURKS; daughter,
NANCY LEWIS; and amount due from JNO. LEWIS; SARAH DAVIS; THEODOCIA
DAVIS; MATILDA DAVIS. December 17, 1792. Commissioners: RODERICK
McCULLOCH, DAVID CRAWFORD, ASHCRAFT ROACH.
Book 4, Page 123 -- Guardian's Account by JOSIAH ELLIS from August 3,
1793. To CHAS. DAVIS for land. Commissioners: D. WARWICK, HENRY
BROWN, JNO. EUBANK. July 18, 1803.

NELSON DAVIS -- Book 6, Page 632 -- Constable -- November 21, 1825.
Bondsmen: THOS. N. EUBANK and WM. ARMISTEAD.
Book 7, Page 13 -- Same, June 19, 1827, for Second Hundred. Same
bondsmen.

PHILLIP DAVIS -- Book 3, Page 62 -- March 2, 1787, written; October 1,
1787, probated. Witnesses: DANL. McDONALD and WM. TAYLOR. Pre-
setned by HANNAH DAVIS, executrix, and DAVID DAVIS. Proved by witnesses. HANNAH and DAVID qualified. Bondsmen: DANL. McDONALD and

GEO. CAMPBELL. Ux, HANNAH - 200 acres; two sons: WM. and JABEZ
DAVIS; ELIZ. DAVIS, widow of my son, JNO. - where she lives for life
and then to her son, DAVID DAVIS. My son, DAVID; my grandson, GEORGE
DAVIS - 150 acres between them; my sons: BENJ. and PHILIP - 20 shillings each. 99 acres on the north branch of Piney and tract on head
branches of Cattle Creek -- 84 acres to be sold and proceeds to
daughters: MARGARET, WINIFRED, and JEAN DAVIS. Executors: ux and
sons, WM. and DAVID.
Book 3, Page 158 -- Inventory -- October 4, 1790 - L 43-4-6. DAVID
McDONALD; JNO. and BENJ. CAMDEN; JNO. HIGHT.

ROBT. DAVIS -- Book 2, Page 33 -- Administrator's Bond -- THOS. and
JOSIAH JOPLING, March 4, 1782, for THOS. JOPLING.
Book 2, Page 40 -- Inventory -- March 1782, order; April 1, 1782.
No total. NEAL M. CAMM; CHAS. and JNO. BURKS.

SARAH W. DAVIS (DAVIES) -- I have found this name spelled both DAVIS
and DAVIES, but majority of spellings are DAVIES. It is plain that
this item is a DAVIES item, but despite all of my care in separating
them, I have erred here. Proper note has been made under DAVIES.
Book 14, Page 152 -- Administrator's Bond -- RO. and ZACH D. TINSLEY,
August 18, 1856, for RO. TINSLEY.
Book 14, Page 529 -- Administrator's Account from August 18, 1856.
REV. M. NOWLIN for funeral sermon: $20.00. JNO. H. DAVIS, waggoner
bill.
Book 15, Page 69 -- Administrator's Account from August 17, 1857 - To
JNO. H. DAVIS - one half and to L. J. FRITH and ux, SALLY - one half.
Nelson court decree.
Book 15, Page 330 -- Refunding Bond by JNO. H. DAVIS to TINSLEY to
protect him for legacy paid. August 17, 1859. Bondsman: L. J. FRITH.
Book 15, Page 335 -- Administrator's Account from August 20, 1858. To
same legatees, but SALLY is called SALLY R. FRITH. FRITH is called
LILBORN J. FRITH.
Book 16, Page 140 -- Administrator's de bonis non Bond -- July 21,
1862. L. J. FRITH. Bondsman: A. C. HARRISON.
Book 16, Page 264 -- Administrator's Account from October 10, 1859 -
legatees as above. Recorded April 20, 1863.

SALLY DAVIS - (Widow of JAMES and nee RAGLAND) -- Book 13, Page 49 --
Administrator's Bond -- J. DUDLEY DAVIS, CHAS. L. ELLIS, and MILTON M.
PRAKS, February 21, 1853, for J. DAVIS.

SAML. DAVIS -- Book 7, Page 13 -- Constable -- June 18, 1827. Bondsmen: JAS. DAVIS and LEWIS P. SIMPSON.

STAGE DAVIS -- Book 6, Page 637 -- Administrator's Bond -- THOS.
STRANGE and JAS. OGDEN, December 19, 1825, for THOS. STRANGE.
Book 6, Page 650 -- Inventory -- December 22, 1825 - $97.75. WM.
BOURNE, ALLISON OGDEN, PROSSER POWELL.

SUSANNAH DAVIS -- Book 11, Page 571 -- February 24, 1847, written;
November 15, 1845, probated. Witnesses: JNO. PRYOR, GEO. W. RAY,
DANL. SHRADER and proved by them. JNO. D. DAVIS qualified. Advanced
in years; two tracts - Amherst County and Kanawaha - agreement re-
corded in Amherst County with heirs of late husband, CHAS. DAVIS.
EDMUND PENDLETON, son of my niece, LOUISA J. PENDLETON, deceased;
SAML. M. GARLAND, trustee for my nephew, JNO. D. DAVIS; JAS. D.;
CHAS., and SAML. R. WORTHAM, sons of my niece, NANCY B. WORTHAM,
deceased -- if they die before 21 - if so, to brothers and sisters
who are children of NANCY B. My sister, SALLY DAVIS -- named slaves
and executor to manage them for benefit of EDMUND PENDLETON; ANNE G.;
JAS. DUDLEY; SUSAN F. and SALLY D. R. PENDLETON who are children
of my niece, LOUISA J. PENDLETON -- if they die before 21. SARAH
JANE PARKS, ux of MILTON M. PARKS; JAS. D.; MARY LOUISA; FRANCIS
DUDLEY and RICH. BEVERLY WORTHAM - children of my niece, NANCY B.
WORTHAM, deceased -- if dead before 21. Deceased nieces, MRS. PEN-
DLETON and MRS. WORTHAM. Executor: nephew, JNO. D. DAVIS.
Administrator's Bond is Book 12, Page 27, and inventory is Book 12,
Page 37 - $4,567.00, January 1, 1848. JO. R. and JNO. E. ELLIS,
and NICHL. WAUGH.

WM. DAVIS -- Book 6, Page 609 -- Administrator's Bond -- So indexed,
but not there.
Book 6, Page 656 -- Inventory -- March 20, 1826; no total, but small.
HENRY TURNER, CHAS. PALMORE, WM. DAY.

WM. DANIEL DAVIS, DR. -- Book 14, Page 586 -- May 24, 1858, written;
June 21, 1858, probated. Witnesses: G. W. THORNHILL, D. P. ROBERTSON,
D. S. EVANS, CHRISTOPHER MOORE. Proved by EVANS and MOORE. Execu-
tors: PAULUS POWELL and RO. A. COGHILL; house and lot in New Glasgow
to be sold. My ux, VIRGINIA.
Book 14, Page 595 -- Inventory -- August 5, 1858; dental instruments
mentioned - $300.21. Signed by VA. M. DAVIS on condition that certain
articles are to be sold for her and credit for sale purchases for her.
Book 15, Page 32 -- Administrator's Bond -- RO. A. COGHILL, September 21, 1858. Bondsman: R. A. PENDLETON.
Book 15, Page 50 -- Inventory -- blank date in 1858 - $301.80. PAUL C.
CABELL; J. L. (S.) PENDLETON; W. H. ROSE.
Book 15, Page 293 -- Commissioner's office -- September 17, 1859.
COGHILL made report, 18 July last -- estate lacked enough to pay
debts. MRS. VA. DAVIS was a buyer. Accounts of creditors amounted
to $298.41. Recorded July 16, 1860.

WM. H. DAVIS -- Book 11, Page 306 -- Administrator's Bond -- LINDSEY
DAVIS and JAS. B. DAVIS, February 17, 1845, for LINDSEY DAVIS.
Inventory is Book 11, Page 324 -- February, 1845, and recorded
March 24, 1845. One slave, Caesar, at $425.00; trunk at $1.00;
sorrel horse at $20.00. ARCHIBALD REYNOLDS; CHAS. DAVIS; JNO. BARKER.
Book 11, Page 472 -- Administrator's Account -- debts due estate.
Signed by administrator and CHAS. DAVIS. Recorded January 18, 1847.

ADALINE DAWSON -- Book 6, Page 317 -- Guardian Bond -- LUCAS P.
THOMPSON and SAML. MANTIPLY, August 19, 1822, for LUCAS THOMPSON as
guardian of ADALINE THOMPSON, orphan of ----- DAWSON, deceased.

BEN R. DAWSON -- Book 9, Page 67 -- Methodist Episcopal minister's
bond, March 16, 1835. Bondsmen: CHAMP CARTER and ZACH D. TINSLEY.
Book 9, Page 101 -- Refunding Bond -- April 9, 1834, by BEN R. DAWSON
and MARTIN N. DAWSON, bondsman, to LINDSEY McDANIEL, executor of
JESSE WOODROOF. Executor has paid legacies to children of BEN DAWSON
as WOODROOF heirs. Children named: JANE, LUCY ANN, WM., FRANCES
CAROLINE, and SUSAN. Witnesses: JAS. H. HIGGINBOTHAM and WILSON J.
MITCHELL. There is a separate item for same reference for FRANCIS
DAWSON -- is this FRANCES CAROLINE or FRANCIS and CAROLINE? It reads
as given above. It reads FANNY CAROLINE in JANE DAWSON item to be
given in proper place.

CHURCHWELL P. DAWSON -- Book 9, Page 196 -- June 24, 1835, written;
August 17, 1835, probated. Witnesses: RO. G. JINNINGS, WM. I. (J.)
ISBELL, and LUDWELL S. DAWSON. Proved by DAWSON on probate date and
by JINNINGS on January 18, 1836. WILLIS M. REYNOLDS qualified.
Bondsmen: WM. KENT and JESSE J. SALMONS. My ux, LUCY, and son,
ALEX. LEWIS DAWSON.

ELIZA JANE DAWSON -- Book 10, Page 385 -- Guardian Bond -- BENJ. B.
HALE and JAS. P. COLEMAN, August 17, 1841, for BENJ. HALE as guardian
of ELIZA JANE, WM. P., and CATH. DAWSON, orphans of SAML. J. DAWSON,
deceased.

JANE DAWSON -- Book 8, Page 387 -- Guardian Bond -- BENJ. R. DAWSON
and MARTIN M. DAWSON, January 20, 1834, for BENJ. DAWSON as guardian
of JANE, ANN, WM., FANNY CAROLINE, and SUSAN DAWSON, infant children
of BEN R. DAWSON.

JNO. DAWSON -- Book 3, Page 94 -- Administrator's Bond -- CHARITY
DAWSON, JOS. NICHOLS, JNO. STEWART, JAS. FOWLER, and JER. WADE,
December 1, 1788, for CHARITY DAWSON.
Book 3, Page 110 -- Inventory, L 194-5-6, July 6, 1789. RICH. SHELTON,
MARTIN DAWSON, and JOS. DAWSON.
Book 4, Page 357 -- Administrator's Bond -- JAS. and PLEASANT DAWSON,
October 18, 1802, for JAS. DAWSON.

Book 4, Page 386 -- Administrator's Bond -- JNO. S. DAWSON, RO. RIVES, and PLEASANT DAWSON, July 16, 1804, for JNO. S. DAWSON.
Book 4, Page 559 -- Sheriff, November 17, 1794 -- Bondsmen: PETER LYON, JNO. S. DAWSON, WM. TURNER, ZACH. DAWSON, NELSON DAWSON, PLEASANT DAWSON, HENRY TURNER, PLEASANT MARTIN, DANL. McDANIEL, THOS. MOORE, RICH. PERKINS, RO. RIVES, WM. HARRIS.
Book 4, Page 561 -- Sheriff -- two bonds for various duties - same men and date as above.
Book 5, Page 28 -- Inventory, L 1929-9-3, October 24, 1804 -- PETER LYON, SR.; ZACH. ROBERTS; ALEX. ROBERTS.
Book 5, Page 31 -- Credits and additional inventory by same men and report on June 1, 1810. Widow SORREL had life estate. JNO. S. DAW-SON, administrator.

JONATHAN DAWSON -- Book 4, Page 414 -- Guardian Bond -- REUBEN RUCKER, NELSON C. DAWSON, and DAVID TINSLEY, September 16, 1805, for REUBEN RUCKER as guardian of JONATHAN DAWSON, orphan of ZACH. DAWSON.

JOSEPH DAWSON -- Book 6, Page 330 -- Administrator's Bond -- NELSON C. DAWSON, JR.; BENJ. R. DAWSON; JNO. WINGFIELD; and LINDSEY McDANIEL, September 16, 1822, for NELSON DAWSON, JR.
Book 8, Page 248 -- Estate Commitment to Sheriff -- August Court, 1832; NELSON C. DAWSON, JR., administrator, has been dead more than three months. Motion of BENJ. R. DAWSON. Estate unadministered. Sheriff: NELSON C. DAWSON.

LEWIS DAWSON -- Book 7, Page 93 -- Administrator's Bond -- JNO. H. PATTESON and WILLIS M. REYNOLDS, December 17, 1827; Bondsmen: ISAAC R. REYNOLDS and LUDWELL DAWSON.
Book 7, Page 111 -- Inventory, January 21, 1828: $2,591.62-1/2; NELSON C. DAWSON, JAS. L. LAMKIN, WIATT PETTYJOHN.
Book 8, Page 272 -- Division -- WILLIS REYNOLDS for ux has received two slaves during testator's lifetime; other slaves at $2,020. REYNOLDS is administrator and legatee; other legatees: BETSY DAWSON; CHURCHWELL DAWSON; MARY PATTERSON (late DAWSON); LUCY, CHAS., SAML. K., and LUDWELL DAWSON. Eight are mentioned.
Book 8, Page 278 -- Administrator's Account by WILLIS REYNOLDS - 1826 and '7; share in plantation and mill; LUDWELL DAWSON; CORNL. CROW - whiskey at sale; Tutor fees for CHAS. and BETSY DAWSON; LEWIS DAWSON's board; CHISWELL DABNEY, attorney for C. CROW and LEWIS DAW-SON was on bond; account of NELSON C. DAWSON; tuition to SAML. IR-VINE for SAML. K.; ELIZ. and LUCY DAWSON; JAS. LAMKIN - tuition for S. K. DAWSON during testator's lifetime; WILLIS REYNOLDS for board and clothes for MARY; ELIZ.; SAML. K.; CHAS.; and LUCY DAWSON and furnishing wedding clothes for MARY DAWSON. These accounts bear date of December 10, 1829. LUDWELL DAWSON as overseer; plank for coffin and date of report is January 21, 1830; recorded September 17, 1832. JAS. L. LAMKIN, JACOB HAAS, J. PETTYJOHN.
Book 9, Page 22 -- Administrator's Account by REYNOLDS, November 19, 1834. LAMKIN and PETTYJOHN as above were commissioners.

LUDWELL L. DAWSON -- Book 11, Page 154 -- Administrator's Bond -- WILLIS M. REYNOLDS and ISAAC R. REYNOLDS, June 19, 1843, for WILLIS REYNOLDS.
Book 11, Page 218 -- Methodist Episcopal minister's bond, December 19, 1842; Bondsmen: WILLIS M. REYNOLDS and BURWELL H. TUCKER.
Book 11, Page 245 -- Inventory -- July 22, 1843 -- $2,092.25. FAYETTE H. NORVELL; SYLVESTER L. BURFORD; ARCHELAUS COX. GEO. W. PETTYJOHN, Notary Public.
Book 11, Page 329 -- Administrator's Account -- Tuition to MRS. HEN-RIQUE; WILLIS P. BOCOCK, administrator of JAS. WATTS -- debt due; board of self and children. April 24, 1845. F. H. NORVELL and SYLVESTER L. BURFORD.

MARTIN DAWSON -- Book 5, Page 94 -- September 1, 1808, written; March 16, 1812, probated. Witnesses: THOS. MOORE, B. WILSON, J. L. WINGFIELD. Proved by MOORE and WINGFIELD. NELSON C. DAWSON qualified. Bondsman: R. PENDLETON. Sons and daughters by first ux PRISCILLA DAWSON: JOHN, NANCY COX, THOMAS, MILDRED HANCOCK, MARTIN, MARY BURKS (Someone has partially erased BURKS and inserted PARKS), MARGARET

FRANKLIN, WM. DAWSON. My son, NELSON C. Children by my last ux,
ELIZ.: NELSON CARTER DAWSON - 356 acres where I live; JESSE; grand-
daughter, MAHALA REED (ead); daughter, MILLY READ; to ELIZ. RUCKER;
daughter, SUSANNAH TINSLEY; children of my son, ZACH., deceased.
Children above mentioned. Executors: ANTHONY RUCKER; DAVID TINSLEY;
and NELSON C. DAWSON.
Administrator's Bond is Page 96 of Book 5.
Book 5, Page 106 -- Inventory, L 184-14-0, April 2, 1812 -- SPENCER
NORVELL, SR.; REUBEN PENDLETON; THOS. MOORE; JAS. WARE.
Book 5, Page 380 -- Division -- NELSON C. DAWSON, administrator.
Legatees: NANCY COX; THOS. DAWSON's legatees; MILDRED HANCOCK's
legatees; MARTIN DAWSON; MARY PARKS; MILLY REED; MARGARET FRANKLIN;
WM. DAWSON; JESSE DAWSON; MAHALA REED; ZACH. DAWSON's legatees; ELIZ.
RUCKER; SUSANNA TINSLEY. September 3, 1813. SPENCER NORVELL, SR.;
REUBEN NORVELL; DAVID TINSLEY.

MARTIN N. DAWSON -- Book 14, Page 575 -- Constable -- elected May 27,
1858. Bondsmen: JNO. D. and WM. L. DAVIS.

MARY JANE DAWSON -- Book 11, Page 52 -- Guardian Bond -- SAML. R.
CAMPBELL and JNO. D. DAVIS, May 17, 1847, for SAML. CAMPBELL as
guardian of MARY J. (no JANE here, but so indexed) DAWSON, orphan of
ELIJAH DAWSON, deceased.

MILDRED DAWSON -- Book 13, Page 227 -- Administrator's Bond -- CADDIS
B. DAWSON, SIDNEY M. DAWSON, and ARCHIBALD REYNOLDS, August 15,
1853, for CADDIS DAWSON.

NANCY BURTON DAWSON -- Ux of PHILIP BURTON and she later married
NELSON DAWSON. See PHILIP BURTON.

NELSON C. DAWSON, SR. -- Book 8, Page 77 -- Sheriff, February 21,
1831. Bondsmen: MARTIN PARKS, JNO. L. LAMKIN, A. B. DAVIES, WILLIS M.
REYNOLDS, LINDSEY McDANIEL, WM. McDANIEL, ADDISON TALIAFERRO, BEVERLY
DAVIES, GEO. TINSLEY, LINDSEY COLEMAN, FRANCES M. DAVIES.
Book 8, Page 167 -- Same -- February 20, 1832. Same bondsmen with
exception of name of SAML. G. PARKS for WM. McDANIEL.
Book 11, Page 117 -- Administrator's Bond -- JAS. L. LAMKIN and RO.
TINSLEY, March 20, 1843, for J. L.
Book 11, Page 120 -- Inventory, April 17, 1843 -- Two sums: $1,264.87-
1/2 and $1,000.00 in bonds. WHITING DAVIES, WM. P. PARKS, E. WOODSON
MORRIS, CHAMPE CARTER.

NELSON C. DAWSON, JR. -- Book 8, Page 222 -- Administrator's Bond --
BENJ. R. DAWSON and MARTIN N. DAWSON, June 18, 1832, for BENJ. DAWSON.
Book 8, Page 311 -- Inventory: $89.37-1/2. MARTIN PARKS,
HENRY OGDEN, WM. WATTS.
Book 14, Page 173 -- Administrator's Bond -- JAS. N. LAMKIN and
SAML. H. LAMKIN, September 15, 1856, for JAS. LAMKIN.

PEGGY DAWSON -- Book 10, Page 384 -- Estate Commitment to Sheriff --
November, 1840, on motion of JNO. D. DAVIS, administrator of GEO.
MORRIS - along with estate of RACHEL BURKS and BETSY MORRIS.

PLEASANT DAWSON -- Book 5, Page 400 -- Tobacco Inspector -- Amherst
Warehouse, November 15, 1813. Bondsman: JOS. KENNERLY.
Book 5, Page 456 -- Same -- September 19, 1814. Bondsman: NELSON C.
DAWSON.

SAML. G. DAWSON -- Book 11, Page 614 -- Estate Commitment to Sheriff,
November, 1847. Sheriff: JAS. L. LAMKIN.

SAML. J. DAWSON -- Book 11, Page 177 -- Administrator's Bond -- BENJ.
B. HAILE and JANE ALDRIDGE, October 16, 1843, for BENJ. HAILE.

SAML. K. DAWSON -- Book 7, Page 320 -- Guardian Bond -- WILLIS REY-
NOLDS and ISAAC R. REYNOLDS, December 21, 1829, for WILLIS RENOLDS
as guardian of SAML. K., CHAS., ELIZ., and LUCY DAWSON, orphans of
LEWIS DAWSON, deceased.
Book 9, Page 53 -- Administrator's Bond -- CHURCHWELL P. DAWSON and

WILLIS M. REYNOLDS, Mary 16, 1835, for CHURCHWELL DAWSON. This page is very faded.
Book 9, Page 66 -- Inventory -- April 18, 1835 -- $287.50. EDWD. TINSLEY, WM. TUCKER, BEVERLY DAVIES.

SIDNEY M. DAWSON -- Book 18, Page 383 -- Overseer of the Poor, December 15, 1873. Bondsmen: RO. A. PENDLETON, JAS. M. MILLNER, WM. H. KENT.
Book 19, Page 29 -- Same -- June 30, 1875, and same bondsman.
Book 19, Page 320 -- Superintendent of Poor, March 19, 1878. Bondsman: JESSE E. ADAMS.
Book 19, Page 373 -- Bond to support and clothe paupers at Poor Farm -- October 1, 1878. ADAMS was bondsman.
Book 19, Page 448 -- Same -- June 25, 1879. Bondsman: same.
    Note: I cannot forget my experience as a minister in going to this old farm. It is now owned by a Mr. Bailey who is in the sawmill business. It is located northwest of Amherst. I was asked to officiate at the burial of a Kentuckian whose body was found in a ditch near the Village of Amherst. I had been contacted by the town officials and we managed to locate his people, but they made no attempt to have his body returned to them. It was a deeply tragic feeling to walk between rows of field stones which marked the graves of these poor folk who died at the one-time Poor Farm. The entire place is now grown up in trees and some had to be cut down for the grave site of the Kentuckian who found his last resting place in Amherst County.

THOS. DAWSON -- Book 1, Page 188 -- December 10, 1767, written; November 5, 1770, probated. Witnesses: WM. CABELL and RICH. MURROW. Of Johnson County, North Carolina; ux, MARY; my six children by former ux; my brother, WM. DAWSON, and my brother-in-law, JNO. CARTER.
Book 1, Page 190 -- Administrator's Bond -- JNO. and JOSIAH CARTER and EDMD. WINSTON, November 5, 1770, for JNO. CARTER.
Book 1, Page 202 -- Inventory on order of court; recorded October 7, 1771, and done on November 14, 1770, in Pittsylvania County. ARCHELAUS or ARCHIBALD GRYMES; WM. SWANSON; RO. HILL. Order of Amherst County Court.

WM. B. DAWSON -- Book 4, Page 398 -- Guardian Bond -- PLEASANT and NELSON C. DAWSON, February 18, 1805, for PLEASANT DAWSON as guardian of WM. B. DAWSON, orphan of WM. O. DAWSON.

ZACH. DAWSON -- Book 4, Page 573 -- Administrator's Account -- JNO. McDANIEL, administrator, from August, 1801. To WM. STEEL for MRS. DAWSON; cash to NELSON C. DAWSON; clothing for JONATHAN; NELSON; MARTIN; BENJ.; and BETSY DAWSON from July 16, 1801, until January 1, 1803; schooling for MARTIN; JNO. COONEY for schooling NELSON; to JNO. DAWSON; board and clothing for Hackett (slave?) and expenses to Cumberland and removal from there. Suit of LONG and ux vs. CAPT. B. RUCKER, January 3, 1809. JAS. FRANKLIN, NELSON C. DAWSON, JNO. WARWICK, and PHILLIP JOHNSON. Division on order from suit of JONATHAN R. DAWSON vs. JNO. McDANIEL et al. Lots to BETSY DAWSON, BENJ., MARTIN, and NELSON C. HACKETT is shown to be a slave here. Recorded January 16, 1809.

DANL. DAY -- Book 16, Page 137 -- December 8, 1855, written; July 21, 1862, probated. Witnesses: RO. J. DAVIES, JOSEPH COLEMAN, C. DABNEY. Proved by DAVIS (sic); and DABNEY. RO. C. MARTIN, SAML. J.(H.) TURNER and LEWIS S. CAMPBELL qualified. Advanced in years; cousin, ELIZA H. HURT; housekeeper, ELIZ. E. DICKEY; SUSAN STORY and sisters-daughters of PLEASANT STORY, deceased; to NICHL. HICKS; to NANCY HICKS, ux of BLUFORD HICKS; to NANCY L. MARTIN, daughter of RO. C. MARTIN; brother, SAML. DAY, deceased - his children; deceased sister, SALLY CARTER - her children; brother, JNO. DAY, deceased - his children; sister, POLLY HILL, deceased - her children; same for children of his deceased brothers, SOLOMON and WM. DAY; children of, and brother, EZEKIEL DAY. Slaves to be sent to Liberia when 21, if they desire, and also their children. Executors: friends and neighbors, RO. C. MARTIN, SAML. H. TURNER, and LEWIS S. CAMPBELL. Administrator's Bond is on Page 140 of same book.
Book 16, Page 179 -- Inventory -- 277-3/4 acres; September 22, 1862 --

$52,498.17. WM. KENT, ISAAC R. REYNOLDS, JAS. HIGGINBOTHAM. Recorded October 20, 1862.

REBECCA DAY -- Book 11, Page 227 -- Administrator's Bond -- DANL. DAY and WM. PETTYJOHN, July 15, 1844, for DANL. DAY.

SAMUEL DAY -- Book 4, Page 370 -- Minister's bond, Christian Church, June 20, 1803. Bondsman: NICHL. MORAN.

WILLIAM A. DEARING -- Book 16, Page 227 -- March 23, 1861, written; February 16, 1863, probated. Witnesses: S. R. WORTHAM and EDWD. L. COX. Proved by WORTHAM; COX is dead. Ux, JANE E.; my children are to be educated; when of age; interest in estate of my mother. Ux to administrator. She qualified on April 20, 1863; Page 305 of same book.

WM. DEMPSEY -- Book 9, Page 228 -- Administrator's Bond -- WILSON DEMPSEY and PETER RUCKER, June 20, 1836, for WILSON DEMPSEY.
Book 9, Page 315 -- Inventory: $88.32, May 15, 1837. LEE MILLNER; WM. B. SHEPHERD; WM. B. TOLER.
Book 10, Page 368 -- Administrator's Account from 1828; accounts of WILSON M. and WESTLEY G. DEMPSEY - for the family in 1835. July 19, 1841: W. L. SAUNDERS and PITT WOODROOF.
Book 11, Page 82 -- Administrator's Account -- WILLIAM M. DEMPSEY account -- WILSON M. in others - business trip to King William; land rent by WILSON M. DEMPSEY; same for WESTLEY G. and SEATON Y. DEMPSEY. Administrator is called WM. M. at end in summary. July 18, 1842.

SARAH O. DIBRELL -- Book 12, Page 563 -- Trustee account by RO. M. BROWN and commissioner from January 23, 1850 - letters to Richmond; clothing at asylum. Recorded February 7, 1852. Another account - Book 13, Page 504 -- from August 1, 1851. Reference to trust fund and life estate therein. Recorded May 19, 1855. Another account - Book 14, Page 377 -- from May 30, 1855. Recorded June 26, 1856. Another - Book 15, Page 114 -- from July 17, 1856. Recorded March 21, 1859 - reference to asylum account. Another account - Book 15, Page 145 -- and recorded April 19, 1859.
Book 17, Page 387 -- Administrator's Account by BROWN from January 27, 1859 - at her death and deate of August 21, 1868 (death date?) - one gold watch and State stock in name of S. MARR. Recorded October 19, 1868.

ELIZ. H. DICKEY -- Book 16, Page 397 -- No date when written; November 16, 1863, probated. Handwriting attested by WM. C. MARTIN and CATH. DICKEY. RO. C. MARTIN qualified; bondsman: WM. A. WOOD. My three sisters: NANCY MARTIN, JANE DICKEY, and MARTH WOOD, and MARTH is youngest.
Administrator's Bond is Book 16, Page 405.

JNO. DIGGES (DIGGS) -- Book 4, Page 124 -- April 3, 1803, written; July 18, 1803, probated. Witnesses: JNO. HARRIS, WM. B. HARRIS, JAS. JOPLING. Proved by JOPLING and WM. B. HARRIS. WM. H. and JNO. DIGGS qualified. Bondsmen: JAS. MURPHY, JOSEPH MONTGOMERY, WM. LEE and MATT. HARRIS. Ux, ELIZ. - where I live and slaves; daughter, ELIZ. DARNEILLE and children - in trust of JNO. HARRIS of Albemarle - 400 acres on Hatt; if either of her children die before lawful age. All of my children; I am security for ISAAC DARNEILLE in suit between him and THOS. BARNETT in Virginia Court of Appeals. My daughter, DORATHA DURRETT and children; my daughter, NANCY; my son, WM. HARRIS; daughter, CHARLOTTE MOON and children; daughter, KITTY HARRIS; son, JNO., where I live; daughter, LUCY; grandson, BENJ. HARRIS. Children are listed again and WM.HARRIS is evidently WM. H. DIGGS -- Executors: sons, WM. H. and JNO. DIGGES and friend, HAWES COLEMAN.
Book 4, Page 144 -- Inventory -- MATT. HARRIS, JNO. HARRIS, ZACH. ROBERTS, and WM. HARRIS, January 16, 1804: $8,962.00. Administrator's Bond is Book 4, Page 371.
Book 4, Page 577 -- Administrator's Account by both administrators, from July, 1803. To MARSHALL DURRETT; to Pedlar for mother; to JNO. DARNEILLE; G. W. VARNUM for teaching J. DARNEILLE; JOPLING's executor per statement; JAS. DURRETT for spices and managing plantation from

May, 1803, to fall of 1806.   February 20, 1809. NATHL. CRAWFORD;
HUDSON MARTIN; LANDON CABELL.

ELIZA DILLARD -- Book 5, Page 99 -- Guardian Bond -- JOS. and JAS.
DILLARD of NELSON and JNO. COLEMAN, March 16, 1812, for JOS. DILLARD
as guardian of ELIZA DILLARD, by her choice - orphan of GEO. DILLARD,
deceased.

GEO. DILLARD -- Book 4, Page 477 -- Administrator's Bond -- JOS. and
JAS. DILLARD and CHAS. WATTS, November 16, 1807, for JOS. DILLARD.
Book 4, Page 529 -- Inventory -- December 7, 1807, L 1633-0-0; JAS.
FRANKLIN, RO. WALKER, THOS. CREWS. Recorded September 19, 1808.
Book 5, Page 338 -- Administrator's Account from August, 1808. To
J. HUCHESON for keeping negroes, GEO. and ux, in confinement two
nights to present "them from running away when I was about to start
with them for purpose of selling them in Tennessee." To NANCY SHIELDS
for decedent's bond of September 29, 1807; interesting and long;
tuition at New Glasgow Academy to JNO. HENRY for JNO. JAS. DILLARD;
tuition at Ann Smith Academy; business trip to Madison; JNO. JAS.
DILLARD's expenses for visit to his sister at Lexington, July 23,
1808. JNO. JAS. DILLARD's expenses for tea party given by the students of New Glasgow Academy at close of session in April last (1808
items). JNO. NICHOLS of Nashville bought Geo. and Bett; bond of
THOS. DILLARD; horses received of JNO. AVERITT of Kentucky; claim for
arms lost after delivery to decedent as captain of militia for his
company, May 22, 1811 item. Money for ELIZ. DILLARD to see the
Elephant and Wax Works. Expenses to Buffalo Springs for JNO. JAS.
and ELIZ. DILLARD; wedding dress for ELIZ. (ELIZA) - March 13, 1812
and "hatt" for JNO. JAS.; paling of graveyard for December. Sale,
December 11 and 12, 1807. JAS. DILLARD hired slaves; mention of
435 acres; tenants' accounts carried to Page 412 from 368 -- long
and interesting account; JNO. HILL, son of JAS., debtor; CAPT. JNO.
HILL, etc. Remarks on debtors: JNO. BENNETT went to Tennessee;
MADISON HILL went to the western country; NOTLEY W. MADDOX removed
to Georgia; JAS. NICHOLAS is insolvent and lives in Kentucky; ELISHA
SORRELL removed to Greenbrier; JNO. STATTON, JR. is insolvent and in
Kentucky; SAML. STEWART is insolvent and to Georgia; WIATT SMITH has
gone to Kentucky; ZACH TUCKER has gone to Kentucky; DANDRIDGE TUCKER
has gone to western country; JACOB WOOD - to western country,
January 16, 1813. EDMD. PENN; WM. G. PENDLETON; THOS. ALDRIDGE.
Page 417 - exceptions by HENRY H. WATTS and ux, ELIZA, orphan of GEO.
DILLARD.
Book 5, Page 418 -- Administrator's Account from January 15, 1813,
and recorded July 19, 1813. RO. WALKER, JNO. WARWICK, THOS. CREWS.

JAS. DILLARD -- Book 3, Page 319 -- Administrator's Bond -- JAS. and
JNO. DILLARD, and STEPHEN WATTS, October 20, 1794, for JAS. DILLARD.
Book 3, Page 371 -- Inventory -- no total, February 15, 1796; no
committee.
Book 3, Page 379 -- Inventory -- L 387-6-11, December 19, 1794. DANL.
MAYO; JAS. LONDON; HENRY BELL.
Book 6, Page 19 -- Sheriff -- July 20, 1818. Bondsmen: SAML. TURNER;
JNO. DILLARD; CHAS. MUNDY.
Book 6, Page 93 -- Sheriff, September 20, 1819. Bondsmen: CHAS.
MONDY and JAS. S. DILLARD.
Book 6, Page 99 -- Sheriff -- December 20, 1819 - various duties and
same bondsmen.
Book 6, Page 156 -- Sheriff -- June 20, 1820. Bondsmen: THOS. CREWS
and JAS. S. DILLARD.
Book 6, Page 164 -- Sheriff -- September 18, 1820. Bondsmen: JAS. S.
DILLARD, CHAS. MUNDY, JNO. DILLARD.
Book 8, Page 197 -- January 21, 1831, written; codicil of April 15,
1831; April 16, 1832, probated. Witnesses to will: JAS. M. BRANHAM,
WM. H. CASEY, HENRY L. DAVIES; witnesses to codicil: CHAS. MUNDY,
JAM. M. BRANHAM, JAS. L. MAYS. Proved by CASEY, DAVIES, BRANHAM,
and MAYS. WM. and JOS. L. or S. DILLARD qualified. Bondsmen: JNO.
DILLARD and ALEX. MUNDY.
     Son, JOS. S. -- where he lives during lifetime of his mother;
my ux, JANE - except four slaves at JAS. P. ANDERSON's; daughter,
FRANCES H. HARDWICK and her four children: JNO. J., BENJ. D.,

ELIZ. J. and MORTIMER HARDWICK. My son, JAS. S. - one dollar and
no more. Codicil: JOS. and WM. are to manage plantation for ux -
one slave to ELIZABETH ANDERSON. Sons: JOS. S., JNO. and WM., JOS. S.
DILLARD and STEPHEN TURNER are to be trustees for lawful children of
my son, JAS. S., and his ux. Mention of Buffalo Island tract; other
tracts - except Indian Creek land. Land advanced to my son, JOS. S.
in Buckingham. Grandson, JAS. D. WATTS; my daughter, MARY A. H.
WATTS and children; daughter, NANNY W. PHILLIPS (also called NANCY);
daughter, JANE C. CUNNINGHAM and children -- she is ux of REES CUNNING-
HAM; daughter, ELIZ. ANDERSON and children; daughter, SARAH WALTHAL.
Executors: my 4 sons: JOS. S., JAS. S., JNO., and WM. DILLARD.
Administrator's Bond is Book 8, Page 199, April 16, 1832.
Book 8, Page 202 -- Administrator's Bond by same men, May 21, 1832.
Book 8, Page 220 -- Inventory -- May 3, 1832. GEO. STAPLES, CHAS. M.
CHRISTIAN, THOS. WINGFIELD: $4,445.87.
Book 8, Page 375 -- Administrator's Account by JOS. S. DILLARD from
1832 - coffin - DUIGUID - $35.00; JANE DILLARD for funeral expenses -
$30.00; received of GEO. D. PHILLIPS; JOS. P.(?) DILLARD; JAS. D.
WATTS, trustee of MARY WATTS; JNO. DILLARD, trustee of ELIZ. ANDERSON;
WM. DILLARD, trustee of JANE C. CUNNINGHAM; WM. DILLARD has received
and disbursed amounts August 15, 1833. CHAS. MUNDY; STEPHEN B. TURNER;
JESSE MUNDY.
Book 11, Page 205 -- Real estate inventory, October, 1843, order.
Three - exclusive of canal - Plat A - Mansion house on Buffalo
Island - 214-3/4 acres; Plat B - Isham Mountain tract - 676 acres;
Plat C - River Hill - 433 acres. Buckingham land advanced to
JOS. S. DILLARD - 500 acres - divided under will. Buffalo, Sycamore,
Isham Islands; Dry Channel Island below canal; river and banks above
canal; high land. To JOS. S. DILLARD and STEPHEN TURNER as trustees
for children of JAS. DILLARD; to JNO. and WM. DILLARD; COL. JNO.
PRYOR, Amherst County surveyor, December 7, 1843. JAS. L. LAMKIN;
WM. KENT; JNO. W. STRATTON. Mansion house on Porridge Creek; Isham
Mountain and adjoins CHAS. MUNDY; JAS. CHRISTIAN's heirs; PLEASANT
STORY's heirs. Mention of Iron Mine or River Hill tract - to WM.;
JOS. S.; JNO. DILLARD and children of JAS. S. DILLARD. Recorded
December 18, 1843.
Book 11, Page 490 -- Administrator's Account by WM. DILLARD from 1833.
To JNO. DILLARD; to JONATHAN P. HARDWICK and children; account of
JAS. P. CASH; estate of JANE DILLARD - WM. DILLARD, agent; bond of
JOS. S. DILLARD; LAWSON CAMPBELL bought land; Page 500 JAS. DILLARD's
estate and Page 502 JAS. and JANE DILLARD estate. Recorded January 18,
1847.
Book 12, Page 63 -- Plat and division of Christian's Mill and con-
tiguous to James River and Kanawaha Canal -- lines of H. H. WATTS'
heirs; CHAS. MUNDY's heirs; bought by JAMES DILLARD of JAS. CHRISTIAN's
trustees under Nelson County chancery decree. One-fourth to children
of JAS. CHRISTIAN; 243 acres left to divide among heirs of JAS. DIL-
LARD; order of Amherst County Court, 1847. Lots to JNO., WM., JOS. S.
DILLARD, JAS. S. DILLARD's children - JOS. S. DILLARD and STEPHEN
TURNER, trustees. April 17, 1848. WM. KENT, JAS. L. LAMKIN, J. L.
TWYMAN.
Book 14, Page 517 -- Inventory -- January 30, 1858; no total. PETER G.
JOINER, Administrator. JNO. L. TURNER; ZACH. BOWLES; JNO. S. CHRIS-
TIAN.
Administrator's Bond for JOINER is on same page, January 18, 1858.
Bondsman: THOS. WHITEHEAD.

JAS. J. DILLARD, JR. -- Book 7, Page 249 -- Constable -- June 15,
1829. Bondsmen: JAS. DILLARD, SR., and JNO. DILLARD.

MRS. JANE DILLARD -- Book 11, Page 174 -- Administrator's Bond --
WM. and JNO. DILLARD, October 16, 1843, for WM. DILLARD.
Book 11, Page 228 -- Inventory; no total, November 22, 1843. Recorded
July 15, 1844. STEPHEN W., CHAS. M., and JAS. B. CHRISTIAN.
Book 11, Page 492 -- Agent's account by WM. DILLARD -- this follows
his account for JAS. DILLARD, December 31, 1833. Indian Creek land
rent paid to you. Recorded January 18, 1847. Then follows his ac-
count for her estate from October 14, 1843. To JNO. DILLARD; MARY
STORY; amount of pension mentioned, December 29, 1843. Recorded
January 18, 1847.

JNO. DILLARD -- Book 6, Page 147 -- Ordinary bond at house in county,
June 19, 1820. Bondsman: THOS. ALDRIDGE.
Book 11, Page 392 -- June 19, 1836, written; February 16, 1846,
probated. Witnesses: DAVID C. JONES, RICH. SHEPHERD, MICHL. F.
DAVIDSON, and STEPHEN DAVIDSON. Proved by SHEPHERD and STEPHEN
DAVIDSON. JAS. M. and PETER H. DILLARD qualified. Bondsman: ALEX.
MUNDY. Administrators named refused to qualify. Ux, ELIZ; my two
sons, JAS. M. and PETER H. are sons of my last marriage to ELIZ. --
Amherst County and Nelson land; Amherst County land bought of DABNEY P.
GOOCH and where I now live and some bought of LEWIS L. JEFFERSON; Tye
River land is in Nelson. Daughter, ELIZ.; son, JNO.; son, FRANCIS;
daughters, MARTHA and LUCY; son, GEO. Reference to deed of trust for
them to JNO. PENN. Executors: ALEX. MUNDY and WM. DILLARD.
Administrator's Bond is Book 11, Page 399.
Book 15, Page 251 -- Administrator's Bond -- STEPHEN T. DILLARD,
September 19, 1859. Bondsmen: WILLIS H., JNO. A., SAML. T., T. W.,
JNO. JAS., and NANCY F. DILLARD.
Book 15, Page 305 -- Inventory -- River Hill farm -- $32,969.21.
CHAS. PETTYJOHN, JNO. R. MABEN, STEPHEN W. CHRISTIAN,
STEPHEN T. DILLARD, administrator. Recorded December 22, 1859.
Book 15, Page 318 -- Sale, December 30 and 31, 1859. River Hill
farm. DILLARD buyers: NANCY F., SAML. F., JNO. Q. A., JAS. W.,
WILLIS H., JNO. J., T. W. DILLARD. Copper mine farm sold: $2,951.43.
STEPHEN DILLARD, administrator.

JNO. J. DILLARD -- Book B, Page 47 -- Administrator's Bond -- SAML. M.
GARLAND and STERLING CLAIBORNE, August 22, 1853, for SAML. GARLAND.
Book 18, Page 205 -- Supervisor in Amherst Courthouse district,
May 23, 1872; Bondsman: WM. DILLARD. This is indexed for JNO. D.
DAVIS.

JOSEPH DILLARD -- Book 3, Page 142 -- April 29, 1790, written;
June 7, 1790, probated. Witnesses: JAS. DILLARD, AMBROSE CAMPBELL,
CHAS. WATTS. Tye River land; ux, MARY; son, JNO.; Piney River land
bought of HAYS family; Indian Creek land; my three daughters: FANNY
MADDOX, SUSANNAH CANDY (Note: it is actually KENNEDY and she married
JESSE KENNEDY in 1780). EDMD. WILCOX was surety for this marriage,
and JOSEPH DILLARD, father, gave his consent -- JEAN STONEHAM (third
daughter). Executors: son, JNO., and REUBEN THORNTON and WM. SID
CRAWFORD.
Administrator's Bond is Page 144. REUBEN THORNTON and JNO. DILLARD
qualified on probate date. Bondsmen: STEPHEN WATTS, CHAS. WATTS,
and AMBROSE CAMPBELL.
Book 3, Page 147 -- Inventory -- L 450-13-6, July 5, 1790. N. SPENCER;
SAML. EDMONDS; JAS. DILLARD.
Book 8, Page 422 -- Estate Commitment to Sheriff, June, 1834. Motion
of ELIJAH FLETCHER. EDMD. WINSTON, sheriff.

TERISHA W. DILLARD, GENERAL -- Book 16, Page 366 -- Administrator's
Bond -- MARY E. DILLARD and WM. DILLARD, September 21, 1863, for
MARY DILLARD. Inventory for late GENERAL T. W. DILLARD, Book 16,
Page 462, October 22, 1863; $39,207.00. C. PETTYJOHN; STEPHEN W.
CHRISTIAN; J. R. MABIN; SILAS B. LILLARD.

WM. DILLARD -- Book 6, Page 193 -- Administrator's Bond -- JNO.
TYLER; CHAS. H. CHRISTIAN; and JONAH PIERCE, December 18, 1820, for
JNO. TYLER as curator.
Book 7, Page 32 -- So indexed as division, but not there. I am
saving space just in case that I can find this item. However, I
feel that available data reveals the family picture.
Book 8, Page 346 -- Administrator's Account by JONAS PIERCE, administrator from January 15, 1825. Estate suit -- to LARKIN LONDON and
ux - 1/7th; bond of MILDRED J.(?) ENNIS; JAS. DILLARD - 1/7th; JNO.
TYLER's interest paid by WM. DILLARD in lifetime -- to ELIZ. TYLER
since death of her husband up to January 1. 1832; ONEY GARNER's
interest; Amherst County deed shows that JONAS PIERCE bought interest
of ISAAC SCOTT and ux, PATSY, and BEVERLY DAVIES, trustee of SCOTT,
in another deed: JONAS PIERCE has also paid THOS.; WM. and ROBERT
WARREN; JNO. HAGGARD and ux, RACHEL (formerly WARREN); ELEANOR
WILLIAMS (formerly WARREN) - children of SALLY WARREN, deceased

(formerly DILLARD); LARKIN LONDON and ux, MARY; MILDRED ENNIS (formerly DILLARD). July 27, 1833. RO. WINGFIELD; WILEY CAMPBELL; JOS. KYLE.
Book A, Page 28 -- JONAS PIERCE and JAS. S. DILLARD, April 27, 1821, for JONAS PIERCE.
Book A, Page 35 -- Inventory -- May 19, 1821 - $1,488.75, WILEY CAMPBELL; THOMAS WINGFIELD; JOS. KYLE.

WM. DINSMORE (Indexed for DISMORE) -- Book 4, Page 321, Administrator's Bond -- ELIZ. DINSMORE, DANL. McDANIEL, and WM. FORBUS, June 16, 1800, for ELIZ. DINSMORE.

JAS. DINWIDDIE (Indexed for DUNWOODY) -- Book 2, Page 129 -- May 27, 1783, written; September 1, 1783, probated. Witnesses: NATHAN CRAWFORD, JNO. M. KNIGHT, WM. M. KNIGHT. ANN DINWIDDIE qualified. Bondsmen: KNIGHTS just mentioned. Ux, ANNE - 316 acres where I live; five children of brother, ROBERT; JNO. DINWIDDIE - six yards of cloth and summer suit that I've made up. To WM.; ROBT. JR. DINWIDDIE; MARGARET SIMPSON, ux of DAVID; SARAH HENDERSON, ux of ALEXANDER; written bargain to be made good with THOS., TOMS. BROTHER ROBERT'S sons above mentioned (evidently WM. and RO. JR., above). Executors: NATHAN CRAWFORD and my ux, ANNE. Administrator's Bond is Book 2, Page 130 -- Invoice is Book 2, Page 162; no total; April 5, 1784. NATHAN CRAWFORD; THOS. MORRISON; SIMON RAMSEY.

JNO. DINWIDDIE --Book 9, Page 435 -- Trustee Bond, April 6, 1838, for JOHN DINWIDDIE as trustee of MILDRED DINWIDDIE and children. Bondsman: LEWIS CAMPBELL - to WILDEY CAMPBELL, executor of JOEL CAMPBELL, SR., deceased. Joel bequeathed to his daughter, MILDRED, apart from her husband, JNO DINWIDDIE, and by court decree of Circuit Superior Court, April 5, 1838. JNO. has been substituted as trustee in room of Wiley CAMPBELL. Division was made on January, last, and MILDRED got two slaves valued at $1,250.00. Witnesses: PAULUS POWELL and SAML. M. GARLAND.

ROBT. DINWIDDIE -- Book 3, Page 280 -- September 16, 1786, written; January 20, 1791, probated. Witnesses: DAVID SIMPSON, ALEX. HENDERSON, NATHAN BARNETT, WM. BARNETT, HENRY TOMS, JAS. MORRISON. Sons: JNO. and WM.; daughter, ELIZ; ux, ELIZ. -- plantation where I live. Son, ROBT. when of age. Executors: ux and JAS. REID.
Administrator's Bond is Book 3, Page 303, and is garbled item. July 21, 1794, RO. DINWIDDIE qualified. Bondsmen: JAS. CARPENTER, WM. HARRIS, ALEX. McALEXANDER, JOS. MONTGOMERY. Bond with the name of ROBT. at start and signed ROBT., but name of THOS. DINWIDDIE in body of document.
Invoice is Book 3, Page 346 -- July 20, 1795 - L 119-16-5. RO. DINWIDDIE, administrator; NATHAN CRAWFORD; HUDSON MARTIN; HAWS COLEMAN.

SAML. DINWIDDIE -- Book 3, Page 345 -- Administrator's Bond -- JAS. HENLEY & JOS. MONTGOMERY, July 21, 1795, for JAS. HENLEY.
Inventory is Book 3, Page 377, February 15, 1796. Debt of his ux during her widowhood. No total. THOS. and JAS. MORRISON; RO. DINWIDDIE.

ARDELA DODD -- Book 7, Page 212 -- Guardian Bond, JORDAN CREASY & NICHL. GUTHRIE, February 16, 1829, for JORDAN CREASY as guardian of ARDELA DODD, orphan of THOS. DODD, deceased.

BETSY DODD -- Book 12, Page 418 -- Administrator's Bond -- JAS. & WM. DODD, June 16, 1851, for JAS. DODD.

JOSEPH DODD -- Book 6, Page 218 -- Administrator's Bond -- LUCY DODD and CHAS. MASSIE; JOEL F. SMITH; JNO. M. YOUNG & JAS. DODD, March 19, 1821, for LUCY DODD and CHAS. MASSIE. (Note: CHARLES MASSIE was son-in-law of testator for he married FRANCES DODD IN 1813. JOS. DODD was her parent.
Book 6, Page 248 -- Inventory, March 31, 1821 - $1,120.01. PULLIAM and LINDSEY SANDIDGE.
Book 6 Page 530 -- Administrator's Account by MASSIE from June 6, 1821. To JOS. C. DODD for tobacco; cash paid to CHAS. P. TALIAFERRO and JAS. F. TALIAFERRO: amounts to JAS.; SUSANNAH and JOS. C. DODD (his 1/4th

of tobacco) -- crop made in 1821, amount from JAS. TANDY'S executor, JAS. W. SMITH; CATH. DODD executor -- JAS. F. TALIAFERRO. Recorded in December, 1824 - day not given. BENJ. & BENJ. B. TALIAFERRO; CORNL. SALE.
Book 6, Page 699 -- Administrator's Account by MASSIE from May 16, 1825. CHAS. P. TALIAFERRO; RICH. SMITH, JR.; BENJ. B. TALIAFERRO.
Book 8, Page 146 -- Administrator's Account from November 18, 1825, by MASSIE. Recorded November 22, 1831. ADDISON & BENJ. B. TALIAFERRO; RICH. SMITH, JR.
Book 9, Page 17 -- Administrator's Account by MASSIE from December 30, 1830. ADDISON TALIAFERRO & RICH. SMITH, JR., January 17, 1833.
Another Administrator's Account -- Book 9, Page 250, from February 17, 1834, JOS. BROWN & ADDISON TALIAFERRO, November 21, 1836.
Book 9, Page 413 -- Administrator's Account from February 9, 1832. Bond of LUCY DODD and MASSIE mentioned, January 16, 1837. Recorded February 18, 1838. JOS. BROWN and JNO. R. IRVINE.
Another Administrator's Account -- Book 10, Page 212 by MASSIE from 1837. Recorded: March 17, 1840, JOS BROWN and ADDISON TALIAFERRO.
Another is Book 11, Page 423 -- from December 12, 1845. JNO. H. FUQUA, commissioner.
Book 11, Page 574 -- Administrator's Account by MASSIE from 1846. Bonds mentioned for LUCY DODD; SUSANNAH DODD; JOEL SMITH; ELIZ. C. DODD; CATH. DODD. $116.90 to each of these legatees: JNO.; JAS.; ELIZ. C.; SUSANNAH, and CATH. DODD. JOEL F. SMITH; CHAS. MASSIE. Recorded December 20, 1847. JNO. PRYOR, commissioner.

ROBT. DOUGLAS -- Book 6, Page 114 -- Inventory: November 27, 1819 - $1,871.83. WM.TURNER; HENRY TURNER; CHAS. WINGFIELD.
Book 6, Page 216 -- Administrator's Bond -- SUSANNAH DOUGLAS & JNO. LONDON, July 19, 1819, for SUSANNAH DOUGLAS.

HUGH DOYLE -- Book 11, Page 183 -- Administrator's Bond -- RO. and ZACH. D. TINSLEY, January 15, 1844, for RO. TINSLEY. No testator named, but indexed for HUGH DOYLE.

MARY DOYLE -- Book 11, Page 181 -- Administrator's Bond -- RO. and ZACH. D. TINSLEY, January 15, 1844, for RO. TINSLEY.

SUSAN DOYLE --Book 11, Page 182 -- Administrator's Bond -- Same men and date as above in 166.

WM. DOYLE -- Book 11, Page 184 -- Administrator's Bond -- Same men and date as above in 166. One wonders if a cholera epidemic wiped out this entire family.

JACOB DRUMHELLER -- Book 16, Page 215 -- Administrator's Bond -- SUSAN J. DRUMHELLER & JNO. A. DRUMHELLER, June 17, 1862, for SUSAN DRUMHELLER.

ANN DRUMMOND -- Book 11, Page 185 -- Guardian Bond -- ZACH. DRUMMOND & DABNEY SANDIDGE, December 18, 1843, for ZACH DRUMMOND as guardian of ANN, EDWARD, HENLEY, JNO., and ZACHARIAS DRUMMOND, JR., children of ZACH DRUMMOND.

EDWARD DRUMMOND -- Book 11, Page 348 -- Constable, October 20, 1845. Bondsman: ZA. DRUMMOND.
Book 11, Page 525 -- Same -- June 21, 1847. Bondsmen: ZA. DRUMMOND & CORNL. SALE.
Book 12, Page 177 -- Same -- June 18, 1849. Bondsmen: P. DRUMMOND & DABNEY SANDIDGE.
Book 12, Page 415 -- Same -- June 16, 1851. Bondsmen: ZA. DRUMMOND.
Book 12, Page 529 -- Same -- June 21, 1852. Bondsmen: T. C. GOODWIN & N. DRUMMOND.
Book 13, Page 358 -- Same -- District 4; elected May 25, 1854. Bondsmen: ZA. and P. DRUMMOND.

HENLEY DRUMMOND - Book 3, Page 515 -- Tobacco Inspector -- Camden's Warehouse, November 20, 1797. Bondsmen: GEO. HYLTON, RICH. TALIAFERRO.
Book 3, Page 520 -- Same -- September 17, 1798. Bondsman: MICAJAH CAMDEN.
Book 4, Page 134 -- Inventory -- September 1, 1803: L 1219-9-0.

Recorded October 18, 1803.   JNO. HORSLEY; SAML. FRANKLIN; WM. HORSLEY:
Book 4, Page 239 -- Tobacco Inspector -- Camden's Warehouse, September
16, 1799. Bondsman: JESSE JOPLING.
Book 4, Page 367 -- Administrator's Bond -- MARY B. DRUMMOND; CHAS.
TALIAFERRO (son of ZACHARIAS) and JNO. TALIAFERRO. May 17, 1803.

NEWTON DRUMMOND -- Book 16, Page 128 -- Administrator's Bond -- JANE A.
DRUMMOND; HENLEY DRUMMOND; and T. C. GOODWIN, June 16, 1862, for JANE
DRUMMOND.
Book 17, Page 416 -- Inventory -- October 15, 1864, and sale. Inventory:
$1,027.75. Sale buyers: JANE A.; and NEWTON DRUMMOND --$17,834.75.
CHAS. L. ELLIS, clerk.
Book 17, Page 431 -- Administrator's Account -- by JANE ANN DRUMMOND
from May 22, 1862; cash of H. DRUMMOND; amounts distributed to JANE A. -
one-third; and to CHAS. O.: NEWTON; FANNY J.; ELIZ. D.; EDWARD; JULIA,
infant died and share to MRS. DRUMMOND and children. Recorded December
21, 1868.

RHODA DRUMMOND -- Book 16, Page 73 -- Administrator's Bond -- BENJ. S.
TALIAFERRO and JESSE T. WOOD, April 16, 1861, for BENJ. TALIAFERRO.

RICHARDSON DRUMMOND -- Book 21, Page 74 -- Not in 21 index and indexed
in Master as Commissioner of Revenue.
Book 21, Page 97 -- Sheriff -- September 15, 1884. Bondsmen: HENLEY &
EDWD. DRUMMOND, WM. H. SMITH, WM. A. RICHESON.
Book 21, Page 108 -- Sheriff -- October 21, 1884; same Bondsmen.
Book 21, Page 432 -- Commissioner of Revenue, District 1, June 20, 1887.
Bondsmen: HENLEY; EDWD. and R. DRUMMOND.

ZACHARIAH DRUMMOND -- Book 12, Page 36 -- School Superintendant --
February 22, 1848. Bondsman: WM. A. RICHESON.
Book 12, Page 141 -- Same -- November 21, 1848. Bondsman: RO.H. CARTER.
Book 12, Page 224 -- Same -- November 20, 1849. Same Bondsman as above.
Book 12, Page 327 -- Same -- November 28, 1850. Bondsman: same as above.
Book 15, Page 264 -- March 7, 1859, written; April 16, 1860, probated.
Proved by SAML. M. GARLAND & H. E. SMITH. Sons: PATRICK and HENLEY;
ux, RHODA P. -- sons to be her trustees -- Cold Mountain Lands; my
children at death of ux: MARY; NEWTON; JANE; PATRICK; EDWD.: HENLEY;
ANN; JNO.; ZACHARIAS. JANE is ux of WILLIS WHITE.
Book 15, Page 446 -- Administrator's Bond -- P. H. & HENLEY DRUMMOND;
SAML. M. GARLAND; JAS. M. GANNAWAY; CARY J. CASH; JAS. F. TALIAFERRO,
August 20, 1860, for P. DRUMMOND.
Book 16, Page 246 -- Trustee account by P. H. and H. DRUMMOND from
March 25, 1860. To MRS. R. P. DRUMMOND; WILLIS WHITE -- $1,529.99.
Recorded November 12, 1860.
Book 16, Page 420 -- Administrator's Account by PAT H. DRUMMOND from
September 15, 1860; cash of H. DRUMMOND; RHODA P. DRUMMOND - legatee.
Recorded October 19, 1863.

ANN DUDLEY (PENN) -- Book 3,Page 302 -- May 6, 1794, written; July 21,
1794, probated. Witnesses: DAVID S. GARLAND and GEO. DILLARD.
Daughter, FRANCES TUCKER; sons, GEO.; PHILLIP; GABL., and ABRAHAM PENN.
Executors: Son, GEO. PENN & friend, JAS. CALLOWAY.
Administrator's Bond is Book 3, Page 304 -- GEO. PENN & JAS. CALLOWAY:
probate date. Bondsman: LINDSEY COLEMAN.

JNO. F. DUFF -- Book 9, Page 354 -- In account with PEYTON KEITH,
administrator of ROBT. ALLEN -- 1836 share in estate. Recorded:
November 22, 1837. W. S. CRAWFORD; WM. H. KNIGHT; GEO. CALLOWAY.

DAVID DUNCAN -- Book 1, Page 337 -- Administrator's Bond -- JNO.
DUNCAN & CHAS. ROSE, May 5, 1777, for JNO. DUNCAN.
Book 1, Page 339 -- Inventory, June 22, 1777 - L 48-11-8. JNO. SALE;
GILBERT HAY; NICHL. WREN; JAS. MARTIN.

EDITHA S. DUNCAN -- Book 8, Page 100 -- Guardian Bond -- JNO. RUSSELL
& JOS. R. CARTER, June 20, 1831, for JNO. RUSSELL as guardian of EDITHA
DUNCAN, orphan of FLEMING DUNCAN (H middle initial), deceased.
Book 9, Page 19 -- Guardian Bond -- From February 20, 1832. WIATT
GATEWOOD for six months of schooling; two pairs of coarse shoes

furnished and made by me - $3.50; Lynchburg business; one pair of fine
shoes - $2.00; your part of your father's estate -- one-eleventh; rest
of legatees (not named). August 23, 1834; JNO. PRYOR; RO. F. CARTER.
Book 9, Page 239 -- Release of former guardian, JNO. RUSSELL: March 7,
1836. Witness: JOS. R. CARTER.

FLEMING H. DUNCAN -- Book 6, Page 712 -- Administrator's Bond -- PETER
P. THORNTON; GIDEON C. GOODRICH; JNO. RUSSELL; EZEKIEL B. GILBERT; and
CREED C. CARTER, January 15, 1827, for PETER THORNTON and GIDEON
GOODRICH.
Book 6, Page 715 -- December 19, 1826, written; January 15, 1827,
probated. Witnesses: RICH. M. THORNTON; P. P. THORNTON, JR., and E. B.
GILBERT and proved by "two" witnesses. Ux, Sarah; three youngest
children, ROBT.: Editha S.; and SAML. H. - three years of education;
son, JNO. R. Executors: friends, P. P. THORNTON; GIDEON C. GOODRICH;
and JOS. R. CARTER.
Book 6, Page 736 -- Inventory -- February 18, 1827 - $1,959.50. ABRAM
CARTER; RO. H. CARTER; JNO. TERRY (?).
Book 8, Page 18 -- Administrator's Bond -- JNO RUSSELL and PETER RUCKER,
August 16, 1839, for JNO. RUSSELL and indexed for him.
Book 8, Page 52 -- Inventory -- October 19, 1830 - $1,677.40. RO. H.
CARTER: JOS. R. CARTER; JNO. PRYOR.
Book 8, Page 254 -- Administrator's Account -- from August 25, 1829 by
PETER P. THORNTON; sugar & salt for family. September 17, 1832, WM.
SHELTON.
Book 9, Page 11 -- Administrator's Account -- by RUSSELL from October
17, 1830. Account of ELIZ. MORRIS; ROSEMARY GUE; JNO. R. DUNCAN's bond;
account of NANCY BIBB; SARAH DUNCAN for weaving; F. H. DUNCAN --various
accounts; A. A. BROWN - legatee; MARTIN BIBB - legatee; GEO. W. DUNCAN,
legatee; PHILLIP THURMOND, agent; names of SAML. P. RUSSELL and BENJ.
B. BIBB, but not clear that they are legatees. February 8, 1833. JNO.
PRYOR; RO. H. and JOS. R. CARTER.

JNO. DUNCAN -- Book 4, Page 434 -- Administrator's Bond -- SALLY & WM.
DUNCAN; WM. and JNO. CAMDEN, September 15, 1806, for Sally and WM.
DUNCAN.
Book 4, Page 448 -- Guardian Bond -- WM. DUNCAN & LEONARD HENLEY, June
15, 1807, for WM. DUNCAN as guardian of POLLY; JNO.; SPICEY; PATSEY;
WILLIS; and WESLEY DUNCAN, orphans of JNO. DUNCAN. This item is indexed
for JNO. P. DUNCAN, but I find no such initial for him. There is also
a JNO. B. DUNCAN in RO. HAMBLETON data: See my H will work.

MARTHA A. DUNCAN -- Book 8, Page 10 -- Guardian Bond -- SAML. P.
RUSSELL & JNO. RUSSELL, August 16, 1830, for SAML. RUSSELL as guardian
of MARTHA A. DUNCAN, orphan of FLEMING H. DUNCAN when "he" is of age.
Clerk has underlined to denote the clerical error.

MARY DUNCAN - Book 9, Page 433 -- Administrator's Bond -- JNO. B.
DUNCAN & JOS. K. IRVING, May 21, 1838, for JNO. DUNCAN.

MILDREN DUNCAN -- Book 7, Page 728 -- Plat and division - north
Buffalo and west of Carter's Mill Creek; eastern end of larger tract of
EDMUND T. COLEMAN, deceased, and next to SAINT GEO. TUCKER; WM. MANTIPLY:
BROCKMAN; DUKE and DANL. COLEMAN - allotted to JNO. B. DUNCAN and ux,
MILDREN (formerly widow of EDMD. COLEMAN) and her dower -- 310 acres,
February 18, 1824. CORNL. SALE; ADDISON TALIAFERRO; and DABNEY SANDIDGE.
JNO. PRYOR, assistant surveyor for REUBEN NORVELL.

MILDREN C. DUNCAN - Book 14, Page 584 -- April 19, 1858, RO. L. and
JAS. P. COLEMAN for Ro. Coleman as committee for MILDRED C. DUNCAN.

ROBT. DUNCAN -- Book 8, Page 81 -- Guardian Bond -- RO. C. BIBB; JNO.
RUSSELL; BENJ. B. BIBB; and FLEMING H. DUNCAN, February 21, 1831, for
RUSSELL BIBB as guardian of RO. DUNCAN, orphan of FLEMING H. DUNCAN.

SAML. H. DUNCAN -- Book 8, Page 353 -- Guardian Bond -- PETER P.
THORNTON & PETER RUCKER, September 16, 1833, for PETER THORNTON as
guardian of SAML. H. DUNCAN, orphan of FLEMING DUNCAN.

SARAH DUNCAN -- Book 6, Page 726 -- Administrator's Bond -- WM. DUNCAN; AMBROSE McDANIEL; JAS. WOOD, February 19, 1827, for WM. DUNCAN..
Book 7, Page 4 -- Non-cupative will - court of March 1827; motion of WIAT DUNCAN and oaths of SPICEY DUNCAN & POLLY CAMDEN; January 11th, last, during last illness of SARAH DUNCAN, at usual habitation where she died, she told of her wishes - items to WESLEY L. DUNCAN; her children: NANCY, WIAT, BETSY, POLLY, SPICEY, JNO. B. DUNCAN & LEVINIA SALE (SULE?)
Book 7, Page 61 -- Inventory, no total; February 21, 1827; DABNEY SANDIDGE: RICHARDSON HENLEY; MICAJAH CAMDEN.

W. R. DUNCAN -- Book 14, Page 153 -- Administrator's Bond -- RO. H. THORNTON & JAS. F. THORNTON, August 18, 1856, for RO. THORNTON.

WESLEY L. DUNCAN -- Book 7, Page 244 -- Constable, June 15, 1829.
Bondsmen: WM. DUNCAN & A. J. WALKER.
Book 8, Page 102 -- Same -- June 20, 1831. Bondsmen: JNO. PENN & JNO. MORGAN.
Book 13, Page 29 --Baptist minister's bond -- November 15, 1852.
Bondsmen: ZACH DRUMMOND and JNO. C. WHITEHEAD.
Book 22, Page 216 -- (This will was not indexed and clerk entered it.)
January 27, 1886, written; February 22, 1886, probated. Bedford County, Virginia; recorded Amherst County, March 1, 1889. Witnesses: A. S. THOMASON & W. J. LANKFORD and proved by them. WM. E. DUNCAN qualified, but DANL. L. DUNCAN declined. Of Bedford; ux, SUSAN; sons, DANL. and ROBT. DUNCAN; Amherst County land in lieu of bond of DANL. DUNCAN of September 9, 1872. Sons: WM. E.; CHAS. B.; and daughter: LUCY A. LOWRY; granddaughter, SARAH E. HOLLAND (?). Executors: son, WM. E., for Amherst County lane and son, DANL. for Bedford lane.

WM. R. DUNCAN -- Book 6, Page 725 -- Administrator's Bond -- PETER P. THORNTON & GIDEON C. GOOCH, February 19, 1827, for PETER THORNTON.

WYATT DUNCAN -- Book 6, Page 199 -- Ordinary Bond, December 18, 1820.
Bondsman: JNO. PRYOR; at house in country.

WM. DUPRIEST (DEPRIEST) -- Book 2, Page 155 -- Administrator's Bond -- ANN DEPRIEST; WM. ELLIOTT; & JNO. DEPRIEST, March 1, 1784, for ANN DEPRIEST.
Book 2, Page 196 -- Inventory, no total; October 4, 1784. AZARIAH MARTIN; NATHL. HARLOE; THOS. BIBB.

AMANDA DUPUY -- Book 18, Page 251 -- Administrator's Bond -- JAS. L. DUPUY & JNO. B. ROBERTSON, April 16, 1877, for JAS. DUPUY to administer estate of deceased ux.

MARGARET DYER -- Book 9, Page 138 -- Guardian Bond -- GEO. A. NICHOLSON; ROBT. DYER; and HEROD B. SCOTT, November 17, 1835, for GEO. NICHOLSON as guardian of MARGARET & ALEX DYER, infant children of WM. H. DYER.

- E-

BARTLETT EADS -- Book 4, Page 460 -- Constable's Bond -- May 18, 1806.
Bondsman: REUBEN RUCKER. To GOVERNOR WM. H. CABELL.

CARLTON EADS -- This is not an indexed item, but was found in a page by page check. Book 1, Page 238 -- Guardian's Account -- by WM. MARTIN - Guardian's Account from 1772. Cash of McCARY; CHAS. STATHAM, and SAML. STAPLES, December 7, 1772. In Order Book, 1776-69, Page 389 - September 5, 1768, court - WM. MARTIN was called up - on to give account as guardian of CARLTON EADES. No parent set forth.

REBECCA B. EADES (Indexed Edes) -- Book 6, Page 242 -- Guardian Bond -- on August 20, 1821. Guardian: AMBROSE RUCKER. Bondsman: NELSON C. DAWSON. Orphan of BARTLETT EADES, deceased.

THOS. EADES, JR., (in one item) -- Book 1, Page 82 -- September 1, 1765.
Guardian: JACOB EADES. Bondsman: JNO. SNYDER. Orphan of THOMAS EADES, deceased.
Book 1, Page 158 -- Guardian's Account by JACOB from December 9, 1769.

Recorded March 5, 1770 -- "since THOMAS came of age." Commissioners: JAS. NEVIL; HENRY KEY; CORNL. THOMAS.

WILLIAM EADS -- Book 4, Page 316 -- Guardian Bond -- July 16, 1798. Guardian: JNO. STAPLES. Bondsman: THOS. MORRISON. Orphan of JNO. EADES, deceased.
Book 6, Page 440 -- Administrator's Bond -- February 16, 1824 for NANCY SHIELDS. Bondsman: STERLING CLAIBORNE.
Book 6, Page 524 -- Inventory -- April 19, 1824, NANCY SHIELDS, administrator -- $725.00. Commissioners: T. S. HOLLOWAY; JAS. PETIT; WM. TURNER. Certified by RICH. HARRISON, April 19, 1824. Recorded December 20, 1824.

EZEKIEL A. EAST -- Book 7, Page 85 -- Administrator's Bond -- November 19, 1827, by JNO. MELTON. Bondsman: ALEX. BROWN.
Book 7. Page 222 - Administrator's de bonis non -- March 18, 1829, by by WM. COLEMAN. Bondsman: LINDSEY COLEMAN.

Book 7, Page 122 -- Inventory -- November 22, 1827 - $717.70-3/4. LINDSEY COLEMAN; WILKINS WATSON; SAML. R. DAVIES.
Book 7, Page 263 -- Administrator's Account from November 21, 1827. Administrator: JNO. MELTON. Many names, but not as legatees in most cases. Grandson, MOSELY. Amounts to A. STRATTON for S. J. CRUMP and JABEZ PARKER. Payment to Buckingham Constable, DANL. GUERRANT. Received June 16, 1829; recorded July 20, 1829: JAS. POWELL; SAML. R. DAVIESS; A. B. DAVIESS.
Book 10, Page 37 -- Estate Commitment to Sheriff -- estate put in hands of Sheriff. June Court, 1838. SAML. M. GARLAND, Clerk.

JNO. EDMONDS -- Book 2, Page 92 -- September 24, 1782, written; March 3, 1783, probated. Witnesses: JAS. PAMPLIN, GEO. HILTON, EDMONDS, son of SAML., when of age.
Book 2, Page 93 -- Administrator's Bond on probate date by GEO. HILTON. Bondsman: SAML. EDMONDS.
Book 2, Page 103 -- Inventory -- May 2, 1783 -- L 223-13-6. JAS. PAMPLIN, SAML., SAML. ALLEN, DANL. PERROW.
Book 2, Page 181 -- December 30, 1782, written; June 1784, probated. Witnesses: J.(?) RAINES, RICHARD BATTERSWORTH, ALEX. EDMONDS. Executors named refused to qualify and JAS. EDMONDS qualified on probate date. Bondsmen: AMBROSE CAMPBELL. Ux, MARY; son, JAS.; my children: SAML., ELIZ. BELEW, SARAH WOODRUGH. Executors: MOSES and AMBROSE CAMPBELL.
Book 2, Page 197 -- Inventory -- L 61-0-3. ARCHELAUS WRIGHT, MOSES CAMPBELL, AMBROSE CAMPBELL. Recorded October 4, 1784.
Book 2, Page 223 -- Administrator's Bond -- March 7, 1785. MARY EDMONDS. Bondsman: JAS. EDMONDS.

CHARLES EDMUNDS -- All items are incorrectly indexed for Book 3.
Book 4, Page 236 -- Tobacco Inspector, Tye River Warehouse, January 21, 1799. Bondsman: LEWIS NEVIL.
Book 4, Page 275 -- Same, September 21, 1804. Bondsman: SAML. EDMUNDS.
Book 4, Page 279 -- Same, September 10, 1805. Bondsman: ROWLAND EDMONDS.
Book 4, Page 282 -- Same, September 15, 1806. Bondsman: WM. PAMPLIN.

POLLY ANN EDMUNDS, MRS. -- Book 5, Page 460 -- Guardian's Account -- September 19, 1814 -- formerly POLLY ANN PENN; JNO. PENN, SR., guardian. Settlement of WM. EDMUNDS who married POLLY ANN. JNO. PENN, JR. mentioned. Recorded September 19, 1814. RO. WALKER, WM. ARMSTEAD, DAVID S. GARLAND.

JAS. B. EDWARDS -- Book 12, Page 23 -- Administrator's Bond -- September 20, 1847. CAROLINE JANE EDWARDS. Bondsman: JAS. C. BECK.

JOHN EDWARDS -- Book 1, Page 24 -- Administrator's Bond -- May 2, 1763. GEO. HOPPER and ux, ELIZ. HOPPER. Bondsman: HENRY KEY.
Book 1, Page 31 -- Inventory -- July 4, 1763 -- L 27-12-2. W. HANSBROUGH, AUGUSTINE SHEPHERD, GEO. MURRILL.
Book 1, Page 129 -- Administrator's Account -- November 7, 1768 by administrators above. 4 barrels of corn for support of children. They

are named in Order Book, 1766-69, Page 417, when GEO. HOPPER qualified
as guardian of JUDITH, SARAH, and MARY ANN EDWARDS, orphans of JNO.
EDWARDS. Bondsmen: JNO. RYAN and W. HANSBROUGH. November 7, 1768.
This bond should be indexed in wills, but it is not there. I don't
know just how many cases of this sort will be found whenever I get to
study the orders.

JNO. M. EDWARDS -- Book 11, Page 310 -- Administrator's Bond -- MARCH 18,
1845 -- F. W. and W. I. ISBELL. This is indexed for JAS. M. EDWARDS.

NANCY EDWARDS -- Book 11, Page 419 -- Administrator's Bond -- June 15,
1846 -- GUSTAVUS A. EDWARDS. Bondsmen: PAULUS POWELL and EDMD. J.
(I.) HILL.
Book 11, Page 589 -- Administrator's Account by administrator above
from July 8, 1837. $613.76 - reference to Superior Court decree.
LEWIS HARRISON, GEO. W. HOWL, ALLISON OGDEN.

THOS. A. EDWARDS -- Book 16, Page195 -- Administrator's Bond --
December 15, 1862 -- JNO. T. EDWARDS and PETER A. SHEARER. Bondsmen:
ELIZA M. EDWARDS and JAS. B. L. WILLIAMS.
Book 16, Page 215 -- Inventory -- December 19, 1862 - $18,305.00.
ISAAC R. REYNOLDS, WM. KENT, WM. HIX.
Book 16, Page 217 -- Slave Division, January 19, 1863. Widow's share;
To JOHN; to WESLEY -- when of age; MRS. SHEARER - not clear that she
is legatee, but note a SHEARER was an administrator. ISAAC R. REY-
NOLDS, WM. KENT, WM. HIX.

WESLEY P. EDWARDS -- Book 16, Page191 (indexed for 196) -- Guardian
Bond -- December 15, 1862. Guardian: JNO. T. EDWARDS. Bondsman:
PETER A. SHEARER. No parent set forth.

WM. W. EDWARDS -- Book 7, Page 193 -- Guardian Bond -- GUSTAVUS A.
EDWARDS, guardian. Bondsmen: THOS. EDWARDS and JNO. L. HIGGIN-
BOTHAM. Ward as above and orphan of VINCENT EDWARDS. Dated: Decem-
ber 15, 1828.

JNO. ELLIOT -- Book 1, Page 118 -- October 27, 1764, written; March 7,
1768, probated. Witnesses: JAS. and AMBROSE JONES. To JAS. ELLIOT
of Baltimore County, Maryland - land called ELLIOT's Rirsque. My ux,
ANN. To MARGARET DAVIS, daughter of PHILIP DAVIS. To SAML. SNOWDON;
to JAS. MURY; To PHILIP DAVIS - MERKAME's house ferrier at the "Wid-
dow Reid's" and SENECA's "Morralls" and the "Sceratory Guids"; also
DR. HALL's works. Administrator: PHILIP DAVIS. He qualified on
probate date. Bondsmen: GEO. MONROE and AMBROSE PORTER. Decedent
had no land so no appraisers.
Book 1, Page 121 -- Inventory -- March 7, 1768 - L 75-7-0. WM. RYAN,
JAS. JONES, JAS. MURRAH.
Book 1, Page 132 -- Administrator's Account by DAVIS from July 8,
1768. Legacy of JAS. MURRY, SAML. SNOWDEN. Tools were left to them.
Legacy of MARGARET DAVIS, PHILIP DAVIS. Accounts of RO. HAYS and WM.
GREGGS not given for they have moved out of country. Contra: MRS.
ELLIOT for AARON MOORE. Recorded April 3, 1769.
Book 1, Page 132 -- Refunding Bond by RO. CAMPBELL and ANNE CAMPBELL,
late consort of JNO. ELLIOT, deceased. Witnesses: EDMD. WILCOX and
JNO. ROSE. March 13, 1769; recorded April 3, 1769.

JNO. C. ELLIOT -- Book A, Page 114 -- Guardian Bond -- Superior
Court, April 28, 1827. Guardian: THOS. N. EUBANK. Bondsmen: JNO.
S. CARTER and RICH. N. EUBANK. Ward above was infant of ELIZ., ux of
JNO. S. CARTER.

BETHEMIAH ELLIS, et. al. -- Order Book, 1766-1769, Page 317 -- JOSIAH
ELLIS, guardian of BETHEMIAH, ELIZ., and ROSANNAH ELLIS, orphans of
CHAS. ELLIS, deceased. This is another illustration of data in orders, but not in wills. Page 322, May 6, 1768; name of SARAH appears
with these others.

CHARLES ELLIS -- Book 8, Page 369 -- June 14, 1828, written; August 5,
1828, probated. Witnesses: D.B.S. (L.?) WORTHINGTON and ANDREW H.
TUCKER. Summary is different for therein they are called SAML. D.B.S.

WORTHINGTON and HENRY TUCKER, JR. Certified by JAS. H. NORFOLK,
Clerk Pro Tem of Perry County, Missouri; FREDERICK C. HASE, Clerk.
DAVID BURRUS, President and Presiding Justice of Perry County,
Missouri. Recorded in Amherst County November 20, 1833. SAML. M.
GARLAND appointed administrator and bond is Book 8, Page 372 with
MAURICE and JAS. GARLAND as bondsmen, November 20, 1833. Of Perry
County, Missouri; daughter, LUCREATIA MARTIN, ux of ROBT. MARTIN;
ELIZ. TUCKER, deceased - her heirs; to LUNSFORD ELLIS; to SUSANNAH
TUCKER, deceased, ux of JOSEPHUS TUCKER - her heirs; my son, JOSIAH
ELLIS; to CHAS. ELLIS, JR., deceased - his heirs; daughter, JULIA, and
husband, ROWLAND BOYD; to MATILDA TUCKER, daughter of ELIZ. and HENRY
TUCKER. These legacies to be paid out of sums due me in Amherst Coun-
ty from Estate of my mother, SUSANNAH BECKLEY, deceased...Money in
hands of JNO. ELLIS and other administrator; WILLIS ELLIS and ux,
POLLY, get balance of my estate. Codicil: Son, WILLIS and ux, POLLY,
have first claim on estate to repay them for trouble and expense of
my last illness and other legacies from any residue.
Book 9, Page 316 -- Administrator's Account by SAML. GARLAND from
September 12, 1834; recorded May 15, 1837. To Amherst and Lynchburg
clerks; A. TALIAFERRO, coroner, on execution vs. ELLIS et. al.; execu-
tion in name of G. HURT's administrator. AMMON HANCOCK, Lynchburg
alderman, certifies as to account, February 18, 1837.
Book 20, Page 121 -- June 17, 1880, RO. M. BROWN, JR., certifies that
POWHATAN ELLIS appeared to settle accounts as trustee of heirs of
CHAS. ELLIS, deceased. Paid CHAS. ELLIS, administrator of CHAS. ELLIS,
deceased. CHAS. MUNDY attorney for judgment vs. H. WILLIAMS. CHAS. L.
ELLIS, clerk of Amherst County Court, August 18, 1880.
Book 22, Page 229f -- Administrator's Account -- POWHATAN ELLIS, trus-
tee from January 7, 1887 - to taxes on Missouri land. To CHAS. ELLIS,
administrator of CHAS. ELLIS; to clerk of Rankin County, Mississippi -
payment of R. L. WILSON, buyer of Rankin County land and to W. L.
BARROW, another buyer. Recorded August 21, 1888. Also recorded of
January 21, 1889, of 400 acres in Rankin County, Mississippi, to
A. D. McKAY. Recorded March 19, '89.

EMILY H. ELLIS -- Book 12, Page 473 -- Administrator's Bond -- Decem-
ber 15, 1851, for D. H. TAPSCOTT. Bondsman: SAML. M. GARLAND.
Book 16, Page 422 -- Administrator's Bond -- December 21, 1863. RO. M.
BROWN. Bondsman: JNO. THOMPSON.
Book 17, Page 128 -- Administrator's Account by BROWN from December 21,
1863; Chancery suit of ELLIS vs. ELLIS. Deposit in Citizens Savings
Bank of Lynchburg. July 14, 1866.

JNO. ELLIS -- Book 6, Page 42 -- Indexed as division, but not there.
This is probably the item on Page 42 of Book 10.
Book 6, Page 691 -- Administrator's Bond -- September 18, 1826. RICH.
T. ELLIS and THOS. N. EUBANK. Bondsmen: WM. ARMSTEAD and HILL CARTER.
Book 10, Page 42 -- Division on order of December Court, 1836, JNO.
PRYOR, surveyor. 684 acres to NANCY ELLIS, widow - A on plat -
Mansion House - both sides of Maple Creek. Lines: NICHL. SHUMAKER;
JAS. and MARY GILLIAM; THO. N. EUBANK; RICH. S.(?) ELLIS; MICAJAH PEN-
DLETON; ELIOT WORTHAM; JARRAT GILLIAM; ARCHELAUS GILLIAMS; heirs.
Tract on both sides of Pedlar - 1248 acres and 95 acres on Burford's
old road. Pedlar tract - B on Plat. Lines: RICH. S. ELLIS; ALFRED T.
DILLARD; THORNTON; JNO. TERRY; R. C. BIBB; JOS. R. CARTER; E. B. GIL-
BERT. Summary speaks of lines of A as having JAS. DAVIS et. al. ad-
joining. C - on Burford Road - lines of THOS. WAUGH's heirs; NICHL.
WAUGH; CHAS. L. DAVIES; THOS. A. MORRIS; LUKE RAY's heirs. B and C
division - 708 acres to CHA. L. ELLIS, son of JNO. and BURFORD tract;
540 acres to JOSIAH R. ELLIS, son of JNO., April 15, 1837. JOS. R.
CARTER and WM. L. WATTS.
Book 13, Page 176 -- Division of land - plat attached, April 15, 1850.
Both sides of Maple Creek - south side of road from Pedlar Mills to
Waugh's Ferry - about 2-1/2 miles from former and four from latter.
Lines: JAS. DAVIS' heirs; RICH. S. or L. ELLIS heris; N. SHUMAKER.
Mansion house tract of COL. JNO. ELLIS, deceased - 68-9/12 to widow.
JOSIAH R. ELLIS, son and heir - 297-3/4 acres and CHAS. L. ELLIS, son
and heir - 391-3/4 Surveyed April 12, and 13 - no year. Committee
appointed at February term of court: RO. H. CARTER, JNO. D. DAVIS,
ARMISTEAD OGDEN. JNO. PRYOR, surveyor.

Book 14, Page 39 -- Salve division - to JOSIAH R. ELLIS, CHAS. L. ELLIS, January 17, 1855. Commissioners: J. DUDLEY DAVIS, RO. N. ELLIS, MILTON M. PARKS. JNO. D. DAVIS appointed to divide slaves at December Court, 1854. Final report, September 17, 1855.

JNO. E. ELLIS, et. al. -- Book 8, Page 387 -- Guardian Bond -- January 20, 1834. JOSIAH ELLIS, guardian. Bondsmen: RICH. S. ELLIS, RICH. N. EUBANK, WM. H. GARLAND. Wards: JOHN E., JOSHUA S., and POWHATAN ELLIS, orphans of JOSHUA S. ELLIS, deceased.

JNO. T. ELLIS -- Book 12, Page 479 -- Commissioner of Revenue -- September 15, 1857. Bondsman: RO. N. ELLIS.
Book 16, Page 519 -- Administrator's Bond -- December 21, 1863. SAML. M. GARLAND. Bondsman: RO. N. PENDLETON.

JOSIAH ELLIS -- Book 3, Page 243 -- Guardian Bond -- a DAVIS item and he was guardian; should have been indexed for DAVIS.
Book 4, Page 554 -- Sheriff's Bond -- November 19, 1798. Appointed by Governor, August 25th last. Bondsmen: WM. WARE, NELSON CRAWFORD, JNO. TALIAFERRO, CHAS. DAVIS, HARDIN HAYNES, REUBEN NORVELL, CHAS. TALIA-FERRO, JNO. CAMM, D.E.
Book 4, Page 55f -- same men and bonds as to various duties of sheriff.
Book 5, Page 62 -- Administrator's Bond -- December 17, 1810 -- CHAS., JOSIAH, and JNO. ELLIS. Bondsmen: WM. and JNO. WARE; NELSON DAWSON; CHAS. TALIAFERRO; JAS. WAUGH; THOS. MOORE; JNO. CAMM.
Book 5, Page 382 -- Inventory -- March 1, 1811 - long and interesting as to books, etc. 36 slaves. BEN SHACKELFORD, EDMD. GOODRICH, MARTIN PARKS.
Book 11, Page 267 -- Land division -- someone has made note with pencil that this is for JUNIOR. Order of September Court, 1842, on motion of RICH. S. ELLIS - 103 acres - 45 to RICH. S. ELLIS, JR.; 58 acres to heirs of JOSIAH ELLIS. JNO. PRYOR; LEONARD DANIELS, JR.; CHAS. C. DAVIES. Plat.

JOSIAH C. ELLIS -- Book 12, Page 33 -- June term, 1848 - motion of GEO. T. PLEASANTS to put in hands of sheriff. JAS. S. LAMKIN.

JOSIAH R. ELLIS, et. al. -- Book 9, Page 277 -- Guardian Bond -- December 19, 1836. JNO. D. DAVIS, guardian. Bondsmen: ELLIOT WOR-THAM, R. N. EUBANK, JAS. GILLIAM. Wards: JOSIAH R. and CHARLES S. (L.?) ELLIS, orphans of JNO. ELLIS, deceased.

JOSHUA S. ELLIS -- Book 6, Page 634 -- Administrator's Bond -- November 22, 1825 -- RICH. S. ELLIS. Bondsman: THOS. N. EUBANK.
Book 8, Page 397 -- Inventory -- February 6, 1834 - $3,912.25. J. D. DAVIS, WM. HAYNES, JAS. DAVIS. Recorded February 17, 1834.
Book 8, Page 406ff -- Land division -- plats - order of January term, 1834, JNO. PRYOR, surveyor. Mansion house tract of 467 acres. Lot A, 182 acres to widow, MARGARET ELLIS. Lot 1, 58 acres to RO. N. ELLIS. Lot 2, 58 acres to JNO. E. ELLIS. Lot 3, 89 acres to POWHATAN ELLIS. Lot 4, 80 acres to JOSHUA S. ELLIS. Lot 5, Dancing Creek tract of 470 to JOSIAH C. ELLIS. "All children and heirs." Commissioners: JOS. R. CARTER, JNO. PRYOR, WM. HAYNES, WM. SHELTON. Pedlar River tract divided to widow and first four heirs on west side of Pedlar and both sides Waugh Ferry Road -- was mansion house of the decedent. Other tract was known as his Dancing Creek tract - 937 acres in all. In final summary the clerk has named JOSHUA S. and JOSHUA C. ELLIS. Recorded March 18, 1834. Plats show adjoining owners to Mansion tract as CHAS. DAMRON, FRANCIS E. QUARLES, RICH. ELLIS; adjoining Dancing Creek tract was LARKIN BIAS.
Book 10, Page 169 -- July 16, 1839, written; November 20, 1839, probated. Witnesses: RODERICK M. THORNTON and BALLARD E. GIBSON. My mother, MARGARET ELLIS. Executors: friends, JNO. D. DAVIS; EDWIN L. SHELTON; WM. SHELTON.
Book 13, Page 239 -- Administrator's Bond -- October 17, 1853. RO. N. ELLIS; bondsman: JNO. DUDLEY DAVIS.
Book 14, Page 250 -- Division on order of March term, 1856; motion of R. N. ELLIS. Lands to divide of JOSHUA S. ELLIS, deceased; JNO. E. ELLIS, deceased; MARGARET ELLIS, deceased. Committee: JNO. PRYOR,

J. DUDLEY DAVIS, RO. H. CARTER. Page 251 - reference to Mansion house division of February, 1834. Herein are listed: JNO. E. ELLIS; MARGARET ELLIS; POWHATAN ELLIS, JOSHUA S. ELLIS, JR., and all are termed as deceased. New division: (1) RO. N. ELLIS; (2) WILIE ELLIS, infant son of POWHATAN ELLIS, deceased -- only heirs of JOSHUA ELLIS. Balance belongs to R. N. and E.R.N. ELLIS. Recorded November 22, 1856.
Book 16, Page 109 -- Slaves divided by committee of JOSHUA S. ELLIS, JAS. D. HALL, JAS. HIGGINBOTHAM. Signed by CHAS. L. ELLIS, but name not in committee list. He stated: "I met RO. N. ELLIS and JNO. THOMPSON, JR., attorney for BENJ. H. PEYTON, guardian of W. M. ELLIS at Amherst Courthouse on July 6, 1862. The other committeemen did not appear and parties desired me to proceed. Divided five slaves with value of $2,250. Lots fell to RO. N. and WM. M. ELLIS. An old slave, Sylvia, mother of all five and since she is old and blind, she is not in division. RO. N. ELLIS allowed sum for caring for her - food and clothing.

MARGARET ELLIS -- Book 13, Page 240 -- Administrator's Bond -- October 17, 1853. RO. N. ELLIS. Bondsman: JNO. DUDLEY DAVIS.

NANCY ELLIS -- Book 12, Page 265 -- Administrator's Bond -- February 19, 1850. CHAS. L. ELLIS. Bondsmen: RO. N. ELLIS and JOSIAH R. ELLIS.

NANCY N. ELLIS (probably same as above, but so indexed) -- Book B, Page 42 -- Administrator's Bond -- April 2, 1850. CHAS. L. ELLIS. Bondsman: JNO. D. DAVIS.

RICHARD S. ELLIS -- Book 10, Page 390 -- Land division recorded September 20, 1841. At September court, 1840, motion of LINDSEY COLEMAN, administrator of WM. COLEMAN, deceased, to divide land owned jointly by RICH. S. ELLIS and WM. COLEMAN. Commissioners: RO. H. CARTER, WM. B. RUCKER, PITT WOODROOF, JNO. DAVIS, SAML. C. GIBSON. Plat: both sides of Pedlar. Lines of WM. PRYOR, JNO. DAVIS, AMOS BRYANT, et al. 594 1/2 acres surveyed by agreement on November 6, 1840, for division between RICH. S. ELLIS and legatees of COL. WM. COLEMAN, deceased. 266 1/2 acres to COLEMAN heirs and 328 to RICH. S. ELLIS. Book 2, Page 234 -- Tobacco stemmer bond, May 21, 1821. Bondsmen: JNO. ELLIS and THOS. N. EUBANK. No tobacco to be exported until stemmed. Bond for 12 months.
Book 11, Page 513 -- Estate commitment to sheriff, July court, 1846. Motion of creditors of RICH. S. ELLIS, dead more than three months; N. N. and JOS. R. ELLIS creditors. WM. M. WALLER, Sheriff.
Book 11, Page 527 -- Sales account at Mountain Bower, November 20, 1846, of estate -- $184.30 WM. M. WALLER, Sheriff, by M. C. GOODWIN. Recorded June 22, 1847.
Book 12, Page 95 -- Administrator's Account by WALLER as sheriff and administrator from May 18, 1846. RO. M. BROWN, commissioner. Certified by WM. S. CLAIBORNE, Justice of the Peace, December 20, 1847. Recorded December 18, 1848. SAML. M. GARLAND, clerk.
Book 12, Page 232 -- Estate commitment to sheriff, February term, 1850. Motion of CHAS. ELLIS. Sheriff: LINDSEY COLEMAN.
Book 12, Page 420 -- Sales by D. H. TAPSCOTT, agent for CHAMPE CARTER, trustee in deed of trust by RICH. S. ELLIS to secure CHAS. ELLIS, deceased - Pedlar Mills. Tavern lot bought by WM. TUCKER. November 14, 1850. Lot No. 1 by DAVIS and ELLIS. Lots by heirs of CHAS. ELLIS, deceased -- Mill lot; Water Power lot; Bower tract; Maple Creek; MRS. McCABE's lot; SAML. HOG's lot; HARTLESS lot; Nelson County lot; Blue Ridge tract. EDWIN RUCKER bought lots and store house in Bethel. Recorded June 16, 1851.

ROBT. N. ELLIS -- Book 8, Page 392 -- Guardian's Bond -- January 20, 1834. Guardian: JOSIAH ELLIS. Parent, JOSHUA S. ELLIS. Bondsmen: RICH. S. ELLIS, R. N. EUBANK, WM. H. GARLAND.
Book 9, Page 288 -- Guardian's Bond -- March 20, 1837. Guardian: EDWIN S. (L.) SHELTON. Parent: JOSHUA S. ELLIS. Bondsmen: RALPH C. SHELTON, BENJ. SHELTON.

SALLIE JANE ELLIS -- This is incorrect for no ELLIS data shows herein.

It is for SALLIE JANE DAVIS. Trustee's Report account from September 12, 1863, and put under DAVIS data.

WILLIE M. ELLIS -- Book 14, Page 490 -- Guardian's Bond -- January 18, 1858. Guardian: RO. N. ELLIS. Parent: POWHATAN L. (S.) ELLIS.

LUTHER EMERSON -- Book 10, Page 392 -- Minister's Bond -- September 20, 1841. Presbyterian. Bondsman: RO. M. BROWN

JNO. ENGLAND -- Book 11, Page 20 -- Administrator's receipt. April 18, 1842. Margin: OD to CHAS. TUCKER, May 16, 1842. Signed by JNO. WHITEHEAD, administrator of ENGLAND and GUARD; payment by CHAS. TUCKER of $155.54 in full for all claims of JNO. ENGLAND in right of ux, NANCY PARSONS, and of WM. GUARD, in right of his ux, PATSEY PARSONS -- their wives respectively. Shares of wives for consideration money for land sold to CHAS. TUCKER "in his lifetime."
Book 11, Page 21 -- Administrator's Bond -- April 18, 1842. JNO. WHITEHEAD. Bondsman: RO. M. BROWN.

DAVID ENOCK (ENIX;ENOX) -- Book 3, Page 553 -- Apri 19, 1799, written; June 17, 1799, probated. Witnesses: NATHL. WADE, JNO. SNIDER, CARSEY (?) TRAIL. Ux, SARAH, and sons, SHADRACK and MESHACK.
Book 3, Page 559 -- Inventory October 17, 1799. L 46-12-6. ENOX here. WM. BALL, EDWD. HARDING, NORBORNE THOMAS.
Book 4, Page 1 (indexed 2) -- Administrator's Account from June 20, 1800, M. DAWSON, Deputy. Sheriff for JOSIAH ELLIS, Sheriff. Payments to MESHACK ENIX, SARAH ENIX, DAVID ENIX, and C., ELIZ. ENIX and C. Other payments to various persons, but not of family names.

ANN E. EUBANK -- Book 16, Page 145 -- December 24, 1858, written; September 18, 1862, probated. Witnesses: WM. B. and SALLIE J. DAVIES. Ux of THOS. N. EUBANK; marriage contract of record May 25, 1842. Suits and decrees to me in SALE vs. EUBANK and Washington College vs. EUBANK. Husband to be provided for; my grandchildren alive at his death. Child or children of my son, WM. D. NELSON, and my deceased son, DR. NELSON. My slaves are to be hired out to support my husband. SAML. M. GARLAND to administer THOS. N. EUBANK signed statement agreeing to this or any will made by his ux, December 24, 1858.
Book 16, Page 146 -- is evidently clerical error in one place for Administrator's Bond bears two dates in spots: August 18, 1862, and September 18, 1862. SAML. M. GARLAND qualified. Bondsman: WM. E. COLEMAN.
Book 16, Page 513 -- Inventory, January 8, 1863; no total. SAML. M. GARLAND.
Book 16, Page 516 -- Sale, January 9, 1863; recorded February --, 1863. E. N. EUBANK bought a bed.
Book 17, Page 395 -- Administrator's Account -- September 2, 1868, by SAML. M. GARLAND -- from August 18, 1862 - $10.00 to servant who went for coffin and to inform the family of MRS. EUBANK's DEATH. $300.00 Confederate taxes, February 25, 1865. Expenses of REBECCA and child for 1863 and '64, "up to their pardon" - 2 years and six months: $933.00. Suite: EUBANK vs. WILSON. Recorded September 29, 1868.

MRS. CATHERINE EUBANK -- Book 17, Page 3 -- Administrator's Bond -- December 19, 1864 - RO. W. SNEAD. Bondsman: RO. N. ELLIS.
Book 17, Page 11 -- Inventory, December 30, 1864. No total. S. L. (?) MINOR, CHAS. S. ELLIS, B. MORRIS.
Book 17, Page 12 -- Slave division on decree of December 1864 court. Lots to GEO. R. WILLIAMS and ux, MARGARET E.; PAT. R. EUBANK; MRS. MARTHA A. NACE; RICH. B. EUBANK and ux, SUSAN; RO. N. ELLIS and ux, MARY LOUISA; JNO. NICHOLAS EUBANK: JAMES NOFTSINGER and ux, SALLY C.; RO. H. EUBANK. Estate to pay RICH. B. EUBANK and ux, SUSAN, for caring for old woman, BETSY; GEO R. WILLIAMS and ux, MARGARET C., for caring for old woman, SUKEY. Recorded January 16, 1865. L. MINOR; CHAS. L. ELLIS; BLUFORD MORRIS.

GEORGE EUBANK -- Book 6, Page 749 -- Administrator's Bond -- March 19, 1827. THOS. A. EUBANK. Bondsman: THOS. N. EUBANK.
Book 7, Page 328 -- Inventory, February 11, 1830 - $1,299.50, THOS. A. EUBANK, administrator. JNO. PRYOR; JNO. WARE; WILL JOPLING.

GEORGE A. EUBANK -- Book 12, Page 230 -- Administrator's Bond --
November 19, 1849. WM. P. EUBANK. Bondsman: THOS. A. EUBANK.
Book 12, Page 256 (indexed as 236) -- Inventory, January 14, 1850.
$75.00. RO. H. CARTER; BLUFORD MORRIS; JOS. R. CARTER.
Book 12, Page 365 -- Sales recorded January 26, 1851 - WM. P. EUBANK,
administrator, Pedlar Mills. Family names among buyers: WM. P.; JAS.
N.; JNO. PRYOR as trustee for his children; RUTH B. EUBANK; MARGARET L.
EUBANK. JNO. PRYOR, auctioneer.

JAMES EUBANK -- Book 6, Page 232 -- Constable, June 18, 1821.
Appointed 2 years in 1st Hundred. Bondsman: THOS. N. EUBANK.
Book 6, Page 362 -- Same men, June 16, 1823. 2 years in 2nd Hundred.

JNO. EUBANK -- Book 6, Page 164 -- Administrator's Bond -- October 16,
1820. THOS. N. EUBANK. Bondsman: JESSE RICHERSON.
Book 7, Page 82 -- Inventory -- discrepancies in dates: JAS. DAVIS,
JAS. WARE, and CHAS. R. CARTER swore before THOS. N. EUBANK, Justice of
the Peace in November 1829 and WARE and DAVIS are also recorded as
doing this in November, 1820. Recorded November 19, 1827.
Book 11, Page 223 -- Estate Commitment to Sheriff, November court, 1843.
Motion of President and directors of Washington College. Sheriff:
JAS. POWELL.

THOMAS N. EUBANK -- Book 16, Page 193 -- Administrator's de bonis non
Bond, December 15, 1862. CHAS. L. ELLIS. Bondsman: RO. N. ELLIS.
Book 16, Page 515 -- Inventory, January 8, 1863 - $438.00. Interesting
book list. SAML. M. GARLAND, clerk.
Book 16, Page 517 -- Sale, January 9, 1863, CHAS. L. ELLIS,
administrator. E. N. EUBANK was a buyer, recorded, February, 1863.
    I have put these estate items first, but he was a very active
man in county affairs for many years.
Book 6, Page 522 -- Treasurer of School Commission, November 19, 1824.
Bondsman: HILL CARTER.
Book 6, Page 708 -- Same men and bond, November 21, 1826.
Book 7, Page 92 --Same for School Board Treasurer, December 17, 1827.
Book 7, Page 216 -- Same men and bond, November 17, 1828; recorded,
March 17, 1829.
Book 7, Page 290 -- Same men and bond on November 19, 1829.
Book 8, Page 63 -- Same bond with EDMD. WINSTON, bondsman on November
18, 1830.
Book 8, Page 159 -- Same bond, November 23, 1831. Bondsman: WILL M.
WALLER.
Book 8, Page 283 -- Same men and bond, November 21, 1832.
Book 8, Page 373 -- Same bond, November 19, 1833. Bondsman: CORNL.
SALE.
Book 8, Page 449 -- Same bond, November 19, 1834. Bondsman: CORNL.
SALE.
Book 9, Page 34 -- Sheriff, January 19, 1835. Bondsmen: WM. ARMSTEAD;
RICH. S. ELLIS; ZA. DRUMMOND; WM. M. WALLER; CORNL. SALE.
Book 9, Page 139 -- School Bond Treasurer, November 17, 1835. Bondsman:
CORNL. SALE.
Book 9, Page 215 -- Same men and bond, February 15, 1836.
Book 9, Page 218 -- Sheriff, March 21, 1836. Bondsmen: CORNL. SALE;
RICH. S. ELLIS; ZA. DRUMMOND; WM. M. WALLER; WM. ARMISTEAD.
Book 9, Page 269 -- School Bond Treasurer, November 23, 1836. Bondsman:
CORNL. SALE; DAVID PATTESON.
Book 9, Page 350 -- Same Bond, November 21, 1837. Bondsman: CORNL.
SALE.
Book 9, Page 377 -- School Bond Treasurer, January 21, 1838. Bondsman:
CORNL. SALE.
Book 10, Page 59 -- Same, November 20, 1838. Bondsman: ZA. DRUMMOND.
Book 10, Page 166 -- Same, November 19, 1839. Bondsman: WM. M. WALLER.
Book 10, Page 287 -- Same, November 17, 1840. Bondsman: ZA. DRUMMOND.
    This amusing story really belongs under CAPT. EUBANK, No. 62,
but is worth recording. It is told that a "Dandy" decided to unseat
him in one campaign. The old campaigner, CAPT. EUBANK, would mount his
white horse and ride all over the county and stay with residents each
night. It is assumed that his rival employed like tactics. One
morning found the captain out in the Blue Ridge in the western part of
Amherst County. He knew that a certain old woman was the matriarch of

a large clan and started up the path to her home. His rival had beaten
him to the draw for they met halfway up the path. The "Dandy" jocularly
informed him that he had just called upon the old woman and that she
had promised to see to it that her influence would be thrown to him.
The captain thanked him, but continued his climb. He found the
matriarch out in the yard making up a big batch of soap. The captain
greeted her and then walked over to a pot and lifted the paddle out and
smelled it. He then said, "Why this soap does not smell bad at all."
The old lady was aroused by this comment and asked just why he made it.
He replied, "I met -- on the way up here and he told me that you were
making up the WORST SMELLING SOAP that he had ever smelled." The
result was that she promised CAPT. EUBANK to see to it that her
influence would be exerted in his behalf. The record does not show
just what offices the old captain held, but this is the story which
old timers tell.

WILLIAM EUBANK -- Book 8, Page 97 -- Administrator's Bond -- May 16,
1831. JAS. F. MARTIN. Bondsman: THOS. A. EUBANK.

WM. E. J. EUBANK -- Book 9, Page 85 -- Constable Bond, June 18, 1835.
Bondsmen: THOS. N. & R. N. EUBANK, ELLIOT WORTHAM.
Book 12, Page 528 -- Constable Bond - elected District 5, May 27, 1852.
Bondsman on June 21, 1852: RO. N. ELLIS.
Book 13, Page 364 -- Constable Bond, same district - elected May 25,
1854. Bondsmen on July 17, 1854: JO. R. and RO. N. ELLIS.
Book 14, Page 130 -- Constable Bond, same district - elected May 22,
1856. Bondsmen; June 16, 1856: JO. R. ELLIS and R. H. EUBANK.

FANNY EVANS -- indexed for JOHNS and found when checking JOHNS data.
Book 9, Page 192 -- Guardian Bond -- January 18, 1836: JOSHUA JOHNS,
guardian. Bondsman: WM. B. JOHNS. Orphan of JNO. EVANS, deceased.

JAMES EVANS -- Book 11, Page 215 -- Administrator's Bond -- February
19, 1844. WM. GOING. Bondsman: JOS. KYLE.

MILLIE EVANS -- Book 8, Page 416 -- Administrator's Bond -- June 17,
1834: WM. GOWING (GOWIN). Bondsmen: RO. WINGFIELD; GEO. GOWING.
Book 8, Page 589 -- Administrator's Account -- so indexed, but not
there and not in 9 or 10 on these pages.

RICHARD EVANS -- Book 6, Page 673 -- Administrator's Bond -- July 17,
1826. MOLLY EVANS. Bondsman: WM. JOHNS.

SAML. EVANS -- Book 14, Page 388 -- Administrator's Bond -- July 21,
1857. JNO. DUDLEY DAVIS. Bondsman: SAML. M. GARLAND.
Book 14, Page 393 -- April 23, 1857, written; July 20, 1857, probated.
Witnesses: WM. B. DAVIES; PLEASANT LANGFORD; JORDON M. KENNEY. Names
ten slaves and their children. All future children are also to be
treated under same terms. He wants them all emancipated, but has little
or no property, so they are to be freed as their hires build up. They
are to be sent to some free state or country.
Book 17, Page 204 -- Administrator's Account -- so indexed, but not
there.

THOMAS EVANS -- Book 1, Page 264 -- June 28, 1774, written; September
5, 1774, probated. The spelling is very poor. Witnesses: MARGARET
GATEWOOD; ANN GATEWOOD; WM. GATEWOOD, SR.; Son, BENGMAN (BENJ.?);
"Darters," MAREY and HANEH; "Grandsone," THOMAS -- as long as he abides
with daughters above. My "sones," CHARLES, THOMAS, WILLIAM; STANUP.
My "darter," NELEY.

SAML. J. EVERETT -- Book 15, Page 255 -- Administrator's Bond --
November 23, 1859. A. J. EVERETT; Bondsman: JAS. M. MILLNER.

ABRAHAM EWERS -- Book 15, Page 254 -- February 12, 1855, written;
Monday, September 19, 1859, probated. Witnesses: FRANCIS A. BLAIR;
JESSE T. WOOD. Ux, ANNA; sister, JUDITH WOOD - to be supported from
my land. Nephew, DANL. C. WOOD, son to JESSE T. WOOD, who is to
administer. JESSE T. WOOD qualified on probate date. Bondsman: F. A.
BLAIR -- Book 15, Page 253.

JOHN EWERS -- Book 8, Page 421 -- December 19, 1832, written; July 21, 1834, probated. Witnesses: WM. S. CRAWFORD; R. W. P. CARTER; ALLEN BLAIR. Ux, BETSY. My children: BETSY HALL, now of Kentucky; son, ABRAM (some items ham): Sons, THOMAS and JOSEPH. Daughter, JUDY WOOD. Son, STEPHEN and his children: EVALINA, BETSY, FRANKY, NANCY, JANE, MARTHA, and JOHN. If ABRAM is without lawful issue. Granddaughter, SALLE EWERS. Administrators: Sons, THOS. and ABRAHAM.
Book 8, Page 422 -- Administrator's Bond -- by THOS. EWERS. Bondsman: JOS. and ABRAHAM EWERS.
Book 8, Page 437 -- Inventory, August 2, 1834, on order of July Court, 1834. Total: $1,806.00. JNO. ALLCOCK; JAS. D. WATTS; MOSES PHILLIPS.
Book 9, Page 191 -- Administrator's Account -- THOS. EWERS from July, 1834. MOSES PHILLIPS; JAS. D. WATTS; NELSON C. DAWSON, Notary Public. Recorded December 21, 1835.
Book 9, Page 272 -- Administrator's Account -- by administrator from August, 1835. Tavern bill while attending to business of estate. Amounts to STEPHEN and JOS. EWERS. Amount due A. WOODS' estate by JNO. EWERS, administrator. Legacy of SALLY EWERS; E. EWERS, widow, $1,554. 85 to be divided into six parts. February 20, 1826. MOSES PHILLIPS; DAVID APPLING; PEYTON KEITH.
Book 9, Page 255 -- REUBEN and WM. BURFORD --Refunding Bond to THOS. EWERS, administrator of JNO. EWERS, November 15, 1836. To indemnify administrator who has paid legacy to BETSY BURFORD, ux of REUBEN BURFORD. She is granddaughter of JNO. EWERS and legatee.
Book 9, Page 345 -- Refunding Bond by FRANCIS HALL, ELIZ. HALL, and LEWIS COLEMAN to THOS. EWERS as above, October 28, 1837. FRANCIS HALL and ux, ELIZ., have received tehir share of estate of JNO EWERS. Witness: PAULUS POWELL.

JOSEPH EWERS -- Book 9, Page 306 -- Refunding Bond -- to THOS. EWERS, administrator of JNO. EWERS. Widow of JNO. had life estate, but agreement has been reached as to division. It is reported that sale has been made. Witness: W. S. CRAWFORD: Recorded May 15, 1837.
Book 9, Page 308 -- SARAH EWERS and JUDITH WOOD to THOS EWERS, December 30, 1835. JUDITH has received one sixth - subject to widow's life estate -- and under covenant to divide.
Book 9, Page 309 -- Memo of agreement between ELIZ. EWERS, widow of JNO. EWERS, October 9, 1834, and THOS., ABRAHAM, JOSEPH and STEPHEN EWERS and JUDITH WOOD -- all of Amherst County and FRANCIS HALL and ux, ELIZ., formerly EWERS, "somewhere in Kentucky." Widow is protected and bond is to protect administrator in case HALLS appear and object. October 28, 1837, JAS. COLEMAN signs as attorney in fact for HALLS and they agree to document.

-F-

MARY FANGLEPOLES -- Book 10, Page 394 -- (Indexed 794) Guardian Bond, November 15, 1841. JNO. BREEN, guardian. Bondsman: PATRICK QUIN. Parent: HENRY FANGLEPOLES.

ALEXANDER FARMER -- Book 16, Page 156 -- Administrator's Bond -- September 15, 1862. RO. N. ELLIS. Bondsman: RO. W. SNEAD.

FLEMING FARRAR -- Book 4, Page 271 -- Inventory of FLEMING FARRAR, December 20, 1806; recorded January 19, 1807. WM. SMITH; THOS. ROBERTSON; WM. B. HARRIS.
Book 4, Page 436 -- Administrator's Bond -- October 20, 1806. ANNA FARRA (sic). Bondsman: JNO. BETHEL.

JNO. FARRAR -- Book 4, Page 451 -- Constable Bond -- June 20, 1803. Bondsmen: WM. HARRIS, SAML. BAILEY.

MARY D. FARRAR and children -- Book 4, Page 475 -- Guardian Bond -- October 19, 1807. ANNE FARRAR, guardian. Bondsman: JNO. BETHEL. Wards: MARY D., JNO. S., SALLY, LUCY, and JOSEPH FARRAR. Parent: FLEMING FARRAR, deceased.

PERRIN FARRAR -- Book 3, Page 226 -- Administrator's Bond -- June 18, 1792. RICH. FARRER (sic). Bondsman: WM. SPENCER.

THOS. FARRAR -- Book 6, Page 222 -- Estate Commitment to Sheriff --
This has "error" written by it and I can find no other data.

A. M. FAULKNER (indexed FALCONER) -- Book 15, Page 55 -- Ordinary
Bond -- December 20, 1858, to be kept at Amherst Courthouse. W. H.
SHRADER was jointly licensed. Bondsmen: JNO. J. SHRADER, PETER G.
JOINER.

ANDREW FENDLEY -- Book 3, Page 33 -- Administrator's Bond -- April 2,
1787. SARAH FENDLEY. Bondsmen: BENNETT NALLEY and JOS. SMITH.
Book 3, Page 88 -- Inventory -- October 6, 1788, L 23-10-0 -- PETER
LYON, BENJ. MOOR, BENNETT NALLEY.

STAUNTON FIELD -- Book 11, Page 218 -- Minister's Bond -- Methodist,
February 20, 1843. Bondsmen: ED S. RUCKER, WM. A. BURFORD.
Book 17, Page 161 -- Administrator's Bond -- August 20, 1866, MARY
JANE FIELD. Bondsman: ALFRED W. WILLIAMS.
Book 17, Page 208 -- Inventory -- November 30, 1866. M. J. FIELDS
(sic), administratrix. WM. G. RUCKER, THOS. M. COX, JNO. T. EDWARDS.

MARY E. FIELDS -- Book 24, Page 4 -- September 6, 1901, written;
Monday, November 18, 1901, probated. Witnesses: I. P. WHITEHEAD,
H. C. DAWSON. Of Madison, Amherst County - debt due law firm of
Whitehead and Whitehead - special charge vs. property where I live.
Husband, LEWIS FIELDS. My two children: LEANNA and NANNIE PEARL
FIELDS.

WILLIAM L. FIGGAT -- Book 16, Page 102 -- Trustee Account -- June 1,
1859, by HENRY W. QUARLES -- to JNO. E. FIGGAT, deed of trust to
QUARLES to secure creditors of January 16th last -- 195 acres and one
slave. Recorded December 16, 1861.

DAVID FISH -- Book 10, Page 248 -- Administrator's Bond -- August 19,
1840, DAVID S. GARLAND. Bondsman: SAML. M. GARLAND.

PATRICK FISHER -- Book 3, Page 365 -- Administrator's Bond -- December 21, 1795. ANN FISHER; Bondsmen: DANL. McCOY (signed COY),
HENRY REID.

FITZGERALD -- Book 16, Page 183 -- So indexed as Guardian Bond, but
not there. Indexed thus in Master and in front of book. On Page 72
of same book is item of April 15, 1861, wherein JAS. M. MILLNER,
bondsman: RO. P. TALIAFERRO, made bond as commissioner to sell lands
in suit pending in county styled FITZGERALD vs. FITZGERALD.

JAS. FITZGERALD -- Book 16, Page 28 -- Administrator's Bond -- JAS. M.
MILLNER, February 18, 1861. Bondsman: WM. H. BARNES.
Book 16, Page 398 -- so indexed, but nothing on him on page.

MARY FITZGERALD -- Book 5, Page 702 -- Slave description, February 16,
1818, and certified by JAS. MURRAY BROWN. Two slaves brought into
state by MARY FITZGERALD, late HARPER, who married SAMUEL FITZGERALD.
SAML. swore that they were brought into Virginia about 1807, but not
to sell.

NANCY FLANNARY -- Book B, Page 45 -- Administrator's Bond -- March 23,
1853, JAS. PENDLETON. Bondsmen: MANSON MEHONE and WM. G. PENDLETON.

NANCY FLEMING -- Book 10, Page 384 -- Estate Commitment to Sheriff --
April Court, 1841. Motion of JNO. CROUSE; Sheriff: NELSON DAWSON.

ELIJAH FLETCHER -- Book 14, Page 527 -- Written at Sweet Briar Plantation, July 30, 1852; April 19, 1858, probated. Witnesses: LEO
DANIEL, JR.; R. A. COGHILL; SAML. M. GARLAND. SIDNEY FLETCHER qualified on probate date and bond was $150,000. Mentions "my ux" and
property with dwelling house in Lynchburg. Daughters, INDIANA and
ELIZABETH - my Sweet Briar Plantation and tracts adjoining which con-
sists of land deeded by THOS. A. HOLCOMB, Marshall; JAS. McDANIEL,
adjoining; WOODROOF heirs; one by WM. H. BOURNE; one by JNO. CROUSE;
JNO. BOURNE's interest in his mother's estate; tract where MRS. SMITH

lives and called ----- MRS. MITCHELL and MRS. KELLUS also live thereon.
Stock and utensils at the plantation. INDIANA gets the harp and ELIZ.
gets the piano. My son, SIDNEY FLETCHER. Very long list of slaves
given to the daughters and Lynchburg property to them at mother's
death. No division is to be made for 20 years and the executor,
SIDNEY FLETCHER,is to invest in good stocks. The Administrator's
Bond is on Page 538.
Book 16, Page 52 -- Administrator's Account from February 16, 1858,
by SIDNEY FLETCHER. To MISS INDIANA FLETCHER; 6-1/2 acres bought by
testator and given to said daughters; payment to THOS. A. MILLER; P.
FLETCHER for tearing down building; $10.00 to DANL. for fidelity to
his master. Very long and interesting account. W. H. MOSBY and ux,
ELIZ.; INDIANA FLETCHER; and SIDNEY FLETCHER as legatees. Returned
January 25, 1861; recorded March 18, 1861.
Book 16, Page 376 -- Administrator's Account by same administrator
from April 20, 1860; recorded September 23, 1863.
Another on Page 380 from May 4, 1861; recorded September 21, 1863.
Book 17, Page 130 -- Administrator's Account by same administrator
to RO. M. BROWN, Commissioner. Dates of September 19, 1864, and
November 2, 1865. Recorded July 18, 1866. Others on
Book 17, Page 319 -- March 23, 1868, and
Book 18, Page 141 -- from April 18, 1865. This one returned September
28, 1871; recorded November 20. 1871.
       These land divisions appear in previous books.
Book 16, Page 524 -- January 19, 1860: SAML. M. GARLAND and RO. TIN-
SLEY, commissioners. Three lots and values set by HENRY LOVING.
Lot 1 to INDIANA FLETCHER - seven tracts - Buffalo Ridge, Holiday,
Bean Mountain, and other areas. Lot 2 - six tracts to WM. H. MOSBY
and ux, ELIZ. - Pendleton tract; Harris Creek; Long Mountain; Watts
tract. Lot 3 to SIDNEY FLETCHER - 5 tracts on Cold Mountain, part
of Tan Yard, etc. Recorded June 20, 1864.
Book 16, Page 525 is slave division, January 4, 1860. Slaves arranged
in families. Very long list divided to the three heirs: WM. H. MOSBY
for ux, ELIZ.; SIDNEY FLETCHER; and MISS INDIANA FLETCHER. Recorded
June 20, 1864.
       It should be noted that this man came here to teach in the
Academy at New Glasgow and was graduate of University of Vermont. He
married MARIA ANTONIETTA CRAWFORD who was daughter of WM. SID. CRAW-
FORD. Her name appears with variations in data. Tusculum is the
seat of the CRAWFORD family and stands north of the Village of Amherst.
It is now owned by FLETCHER descendants, MR. TIM WILLIAMS and his ux.
They are gracious in showing the historic home to their friends and
other interested parties. ELIJAH FLETCHER was one of the most fasci-
nating characters of Amherst County. He published a paper in Lynchburg and made a fortune in this and his land ventures. He is treated
in great detail in the book, The Sweet Briar Story, published in
1957 by MARTHA LOU LEMMON STOHLMAN. MISS MARTHA VON BRIESON, Director
of Public Relations as Sweet Briar College, is working on a contemplat-
ed work on the CRAWFORD and FLETCHER families.
       The plantation called "Sweet Briar" became the property of
INDIANA FLETCHER and she later married a man from New York named
JAMES HENRY WILLIAMS. His story and that of his ux belong in the
"W" section of wills. It will suffice to say that both left wills in
Amherst. INDIANA changed the bequest which he mentioned for he set
forth that it was not obligatory. Sweet Briar College is a memorial
to their daughter, DAISY WILLIAMS.
       ELIJAH FLETCHER had another son named LUCIEN, and I have found
an order book item showing that he was admitted to the bar here in
Amherst. ELIZABETH MOSBY, his sister, mentions him in her will, but
INDIANA does not refer to him. His story is not too pleasant in many
particulars and is set forth in detail in a suit brought by his children. Perhaps I should say that it was a settlement rather than a
suit by them. The box regarding the settlement by Sweet Briar offi-
cials is a huge one and reposes in the office of the Circuit Clerk
of the county. I have examined some of the papers and it seems best
to "let sleeping dogs lie."

ELIZABETH FLETCHER -- Book 15, Page 325 -- Refunding Bond -- This
is really a MOSBY item, but is indexed as above. January 6, 1860,
WM. H. MOSBY made a bond to protect SIDNEY FLETCHER from claims against

the estate of ELIJAH FLETCHER. He acted as trustee for his ux.
SIDNEY has paid her $40,225.00 plus household furniture. Bondsmen:
SAML. M. GARLAND and CHAS. L. MOXBY. Estimate of payment by committee
of GARLAND, RO. TINSLEY, and WM. E. COLEMAN. I am not conversant
with the story of this man and his ux, but I believe that it is set
forth in the book on Sweet Briar. There is a long trustee account
under ELIZ. MOSBY wherein WM. HAMILTON MOXBY refers to the fact that a
house in northern Virginia has been done over to suit "her elegant
and refined tastes."

INDIANA FLETCHER -- Book 15, Page 310 -- Refunding bond by INDIANA
FLETCHER to protect her brother in payments made as administrator of
ELIJAH FLETCHER, January 6, 1860.

JOHN FLOOD -- Book 11, Page 99 -- October 14, 1842, written; January 16,
1843, probated. Witnesses: PITT WOODROOF, LINDSEY SANDIDGE, CARTER
IRVING, SAML. C. GIBSON, J. POWELL. Ux, MARTHA -- where I live;
sons: PETER and NELSON D. FLOOD - part of tract to them. Daughter,
ADALINE BURKS; son, DANL. FLOOD. My 5 children: ADALINE BURKS,
PETER FLOOD, NANCY C. BURKS, NELSON D. FLOOD, MARY HILL - have re-
ceived $200.00 each. My 2 children: ABRAM C. and JNO. C. FLOOD.
Cold Mountain land. The children of DANL. FLOOD are mentioned, but
not named. PETER gets Long Mountain land - lines of JAS. GRAHAM and
JNO. HARTLESS. NELSON D. gets land next to JAS. MARTIN and HENRY
HARTLESS. My seven children and those of DANIEL FLOOD. Administra-
tors: PETER and NELSON D. FLOOD.
Page 124 -- PETER FLOOD qualified, May 15, 1843. Bondsmen: CHAS. M.
BURKS and NELSON D. FLOOD.
Book 11, Page 163 -- Inventory -- July 1, 1843 - $2,393.87 -- T. C.
GOODWIN; PITT WOODROOF; WILLIS WHITE; ZA. DRUMMOND, J.P. July 3,
1843.
Book 12, Page 57 -- Administrator's Account -- November term, 1847 --
PETER FLOOD, administrator. Motion to appoint commission of ZA. DRUM-
MOND, PITT WOODROOF, JNO. H. FEAGANS. Sums to N. D. and M. FLOOD.
JNO. H. FUQUA certified as to account. April 14, 1848.
Book 12, Page 317 -- Administrator's Account by administrator from
April 14, 1848. To N. D. FLOOD for E. HARDING. Recorded February
term, 1850. JNO. D. DAVIS, CHAS. L. ELLIS, THOS. N. EUBANK.
Book 13, Page 90 -- Administrator's Account -- August 25, 1851. D. H.
TAPSCOTT, Commissioner. June 16, 1852.
Book 15, Page 135 -- Administrator's Account by PETER FLOOD from
July 1, 1850. Legatees are WM. S. FLOOD, A. C. FLOOD, MARTHA FLOOD
for schooling and in full; CHAS. F. FLOOD, JNO. R. FLOOD. Amounts
collected by A. D. FLOOD and CHAS. M. BURKS. Legatees not yet paid -
1 of 4 children of DANL. FLOOD - name of JNO. FLOOD and then JNO. C.
FLOOD. Reference to February 18, 1856, and bond of PETER FLOOD to
administer. Bondsmen: JAS. P. COLEMAN, HENRY W. QUARLES, CHAS. M.
BURKS.
Book 15, Page 161 -- Administrator's Account and recorded April 19,
1859. Property hired and rented at home of JNO. FLOOD. Mention of
MARTHA FLOOD, deceased. Sales on April 1, 1859.
Book 16, Page 2 -- Administrator's Account from November 30, 1858.
JNO. FLOOD, son of DANL. FLOOD, is still due $50.00. Here again we
have JNO. and then JNO. C. FLOOD. Sale of perishable estate after
widow's death - October 9, 1859. Chancery suit of BURKS vs. FLOOD is
still pending. Recorded December 17, 1860.

MARTHA FLOOD (indexed M. FLOOD) -- Book 15, Page 104 -- Administra-
tor's Bond -- March 31, 1859. PETER FLOOD. Bondsman: CHAS. M. BURKS.
Book 15, Page 164 -- Inventory -- April 1, 1859; no total. HENRY E.
SMITH, JAS. S. RICHESON, JNO. M. BROWN.

NELSON D. FLOOD (indexed N. D. FLOOD) -- Book 14, Page 83 -- Adminis-
trator's Bond -- February 18, 1856. PETER FLOOD. Bondsmen: JAS. P.
COLEMAN, HENRY W. QUARLES, CHAS. M. BURKS.
Book 14, Page 220 -- Inventory -- February 29, 1856 -- February Order -
not summarized. HENRY E. SMITH, WM. B. TOLER, WM. MILLNER, THOS. H.
RUCKER, but he did not serve.
Book 15, Page 139 -- Administrator's Account from February 29, 1856 --
recorded March 21, 1859. Paid to A. C. FLOOD, Henson's Institute.

Returned February 14, 1859.

CALLAHILL FLOYD -- Book 16, Page 175 -- Guardian Bond -- October 20, 1842. ELIZA A. FLOYD, guardian. No parent set forth.

ANGUS FORBUSH (also see FURBUSH) -- Book 2, Page 133 -- Inventory -- August 21, 1783. MARY FORBUSH, administratrix - no total - CHAS. STATHAM; ANDREW WRIGHT; DAVID MONTGOMERY; JAS. STEPHENS, J.P. She qualified - Book 2, Page 116, August 4, 1783. Bondsmen: ROBT. MAYO and JAS. CONNER. FARBUSH also employed in spelling.

BENJAMIN FORTUNE -- Book 2, Page 204 -- Administrator's Bond -- SARAH FORTUNE, November 1, 1784. Bondsman: HEZEKIAH HARTGROVE. Book 2, Page 210 -- Inventory -- FORTAIN here -- January --, 1785. L 86-1-4-1/2. Recorded February 7, 1785. WM. POWELL, RO. THOMPSON, THOS. FORTUNE.

THOMAS FORTUNE -- Book 4, Page 160 -- -----, written; October 15, 1804, probated. Ux, ELIZ. - mansion house. He numbers sons after first naming them: (1) ZACHARIAH; (2) JNO.; (3) JESSE; (4) EDDY; (5) THOS. EUBANK. Eldest daughter, ELIZ. LOVING, and children; second daughter, FRANKEY SEAY, and children; third daughter, LUCY HENDERSON, and children. Land on Davies Creek and other tracts.
Book 4, Page 165 -- Slave inventory -- November 22, 1804, and various articles - L 1,384-3-3. JAS. WILLS, SAML. SPENCER, JAS. STEVENS.
Book 4, Page 391 -- Administrator's Bond -- ZACH. and THOS. FORTUNE. Bondsmen: JAS. STEVENS, JR.; ABRAHAM SEAY, JR., October 15, 1804.

JAS. FOSTER -- Book 16, Page 75 -- Inventory -- April 12, 1861 - no total - JAS. M. STINNETT; WM. STINNETT; JNO. M. WARE; A. C. HARRISON, sheriff and administrator.

JOSHUA FOWLER -- Book 1, Page 249 -- Administrator's Bond -- ELIZ. FOWLER, September 6, 1773. Bondsmen: THOS. LUMPKIN, JNO. HARDWICK, WM. FOWLER.
Book 1, Page 254 -- Inventory -- September 7, 1773 - L 80-5-7. RICH. SHELTON, HENRY TRENT, RICH. POWELL.

ELIZ. H. FRANKLIN -- Book 5, Page 235 -- Guardian Bond -- July 19, 1813. THOS. CREWS, guardian. Bondsman: BENJ. BROWN. Orphan of JAS. FRANKLIN, deceased.

HENRY FRANKLIN, JR. and SR. -- Book 2, Page 60 -- Administrator's Bond MARY ANN FRANKLIN, June 3, 1782. Bondsmen: RICH. BALLENGER, JNO. FRANKLIN.
Book 3, Page 68 -- Inventory -- August 3, 1782 - L 234-11-9. EDMD. POWELL, RICH. OGLESBY, JOS. HIGGINBOTHAM.
Book 2, Page 205 -- Administrator's Bond -- MARY ANN ARNOLD, November 2, 1784. Bondsmen: SAML. HIGGINBOTHAM, HENDRICK ARNOLD.
        This second HENRY is not father of one above called JR., but his son, called HENRY in will, is seen to have been HENRY TARLTON FRANKLIN.
Book 3, Page 233 -- April 10, 1792, written; September 17, 1792, probated. Witnesses: PHILIP SMITH, AARON FRANKLIN, ANDREW HARRISON, JOEL FRANKLIN. Son-in-law, JOS. BALLENGER; son, JOHN FRANKLIN; daughter, ELIZ. BALLENGER; son, HENRY FRANKLIN; son, JAS. FRANKLIN; daughter, PEGGY HARRISON; daughter, PHEBE FRANKLIN; son, JOEL FRANKLIN; son, SAML. FRANKLIN - land at mother's death. Daughter, PHILADELPHIA SMITH; Ux, MARGARET; daughter, JUDITH FRANKLIN. Executors: Sons, JOEL and SAML. FRANKLIN.
Book 3, Page 239 -- Administrator's Bond -- JOEL and SAML. FRANKLIN, September 17, 1792, for both.
Book 3, Page 252 -- Inventory -- October Court Order, 1792. SAML. FRANKLIN, an administrator. RICH. OGLESBY; JNO. SALE; JNO. BROCKMAN; LEONARD HENLEY. WM. SIDNEY CRAWFORD, Clerk.

HENRY TARLTON FRANKLIN -- Book 3, Page 247 -- Guardian Bond -- October 15, 1792. REUBIN FRANKLIN, guardian. Bondsman: SAML. FRANKLIN. Ward: orphan of HENRY FRANKLIN, deceased.

MAJOR JAMES FRANKLIN -- Book 5, Page 235 -- Administrator's Bond --
July 17, 1813. THOS. CREWS. Bondsmen: BENJ. BROWN, EDMD. WINSTON,
JNO. McDANIEL, HENRY TURNER.
Book 5, Page 370 (Note: Page 369 is blank.) -- Top of 370 begins:
Memo: my plantation on south side of Rutledge with mansion house -
to NANCY C. FRANKLIN (she is called ux later in document. She was
NANCY CREWS - December 15, 1796, JAS. FRANKLIN, bachelor, and NANCY
CREWS, spinster. REUBEN CRAWFORD, surety. Marriage rite by REV. WM.
CRAWFORD.). Daughter, SALLY W. FRANKLIN gets land on Turkey Mountain
where JEREMIAH FRANKLIN lives. He then employs initials only and says
"JRF" - tract called B Plain and bought from P. SLAUGHTER. Daughter,
BETSY H. FRANKLIN, at death of my ux, NANCY FRANKLIN. Daughter, SALLY
WILSON FRANKLIN. Administrator N.F.T. CREWS. March 11, 1813, written;
August 16, 1813, probated. Handwriting attested by JNO. CAMM, JAS. P.
GARLAND, BENJ. BROWN.
Book 5, Page 370 -- Administrator's Bond -- THOS. CREWS, August 16,
1813. Bondsmen: BENJ. BROWN, HENRY TURNER, JNO. CAMM.
Book 5, Page 520 -- Inventory -- very long and many slaves, August 22,
1815. T. S. HOLLOWAY, B. STONE, GIDEON RUCKER.
Book 6, Page 623 -- Division of estate of MAJOR JAS. FRANKLIN as of
December --, 1820; recorded September 19, 1825. Committee: JAS.
POWELL, JNO. McDANIEL; Lot 1: MISS SALLY W. FRANKLIN. Lot 2: JNO. R.
FRANKLIN. Lot 3: ELIZ. H. FRANKLIN. Lot 4: MRS. ANN C. DAVIS.
Mention of MRS. NANCY FRANKLIN.

JASPER FRANKLIN -- Book 3, Page 245 -- Guardian Bond -- October 15,
1792. REUBEN FRANKLIN, guardian. Bondsmen: JOHN and WM. SMITH.
Ward: orphan of HENRY FRANKLIN.

JEREMIAH FRANKLIN -- Book 6, Page 214 -- Administrator's Bond -- HENRY
FRANKLIN, June 21, 1819. Bondsmen: WM. STAPLES, CHAS. MOORE (?),
JNO. MOUNTCASTLE.

JOEL FRANKLIN -- Book 4, Page 473 -- December 16, 1806, written;
October 19, 1807, probated. Witnesses: RO. RIVES, BARTLETT CASH,
THOS. PENN, JAS. FRANKLIN. Ux, SUSANNAH - 842 acres where I live. My
five daughters and child that ux is to deliver. Land on Big Maple Run,
Indian Creek Road, Church field, and main road. If any child dies
before marriage or lawful age. Administrators: ux, JAS. and JER.
FRANKLIN.
Book 4, Page 474 -- Administrator's Bond -- October 19, 1807: SUSANNAH,
JAS. and JER. FRANKLIN. Bondsmen: THOS. CREWS, BENJ. BROWN, SPOTS-
WOOD GARLAND.
Book 4, Page 492 -- Inventory -- no total, January 18, 1808. HILL
CARTER, BARTLETT CASH, JNO. SMITH.
Book 6, Page 304 -- Inventory of September 1, 1820, for purpose of
assigning property to one heir, POLLY FRANKLIN, who married RO. W.
CARTER. To widow, MRS. FRANKLIN. POLLY gets one-fifth. Total:
$4,741.41. JNO. SMITH, HILL CARTER, WM. M. WALLER, DAVID S. GARLAND.
SUSANNAH FRANKLIN, administratrix. June 17, 1822, recorded.
Book 6, Page 383 -- Sale at late residence of MRS. FRANKLIN, August 28,
1823, recorded. HILL CARTER and WM. M. WALLER.

JNO. FRANKLIN -- Book 3, Page 394 -- Indexed as Guardian Bond, but not
there or in 4 or 5 on 394.
Book 6, Page 180 -- Indexed as 181 - Ordinary Bond -- November 21,
1820, at house in county. Bondsman: THOS. ALDRIDGE.
Book 6, Page 386 -- Ordinary Bond -- August 18, 1823, at house in
county. Bondsman: SAML. R. DAVIES.
Book 7, Page 285 -- Administrator's Bond -- November 20, 1829. POLLY
FRANKLIN. Bondsman: POWHATAN D. FRANKLIN.

JOHN R. FRANKLIN -- Book 6, Page 268 -- Guardian Bond -- December 17,
1821. HENRY L. DAVIES, guardian. Bondsmen: ARTHUR B. DAVIES, THOS.
CREWS. Ward: orphan of JAMES FRANKLIN.
Book 6, Page 665 -- Guardian's Account by HENRY L. DAVIES. Very in-
teresting: races, whiskey, springs, many clothes. $1,330.87-1/2.
LINDSEY COLEMAN, WILKINS WATSON, S. HEISKELL. Recorded May 15, 1826.
Book 6, Page 744 -- Inventory -- March 23, 1827. $3,080.00. THOS.
CREWS, WILKINS WATSON, LINDSEY COLEMAN.

JUDITH FRANKLIN -- Book 5, Page 38 -- May 12, 1810, written; November 18, 1811. Witnesses: JAS. FRANKLIN, JR., ABNER FRANKLIN, WILLIS FRANKLIN. Sister, PHEBE, and nephews: HENRY and BENJ. FRANKLIN. Book 5, Page 86 -- Administrator's Bond -- November 18, 1811. HENRY FRANKLIN. Bondsman: JER. FRANKLIN.

NANCY FRANKLIN -- Book 11, Page 314 -- June 30, 1842, written; May 19, 1845, probated. Witnesses: EDMD. PENN, JNO. H. ROBERTS. One-third to children of my deceased sister, ANN C. DAVIES; one-third to SALLY W. DAVIES and her children; my deceased daughter, ELIZ. H. BROWN - her children or issue. Administrator: HENRY L. DAVIES; HOWELL D. BROWN, and SALLY W. DAVIES. Codicil: my granddaughter, ANN E. SCOTT, ux of DR. SAML. SCOTT - surviving issue; rest of my grandchildren - ANN SCOTT's brothers and sisters. March 15, 1843. Book 11, Page 378 -- Administrator's Bond -- SARAH W. DAVIES, December 15, 1845. Bondsmen: HENRY L. DAVIES, HOWELL D. BROWN. Book 12, Page 46 -- Inventory -- January --, 1847. $2,275.00. SAML. M. GARLAND, MARSHALL S. HARRIS, ALBERT C. HARRISON. Book 12, Page 47 -- Division -- June 19, 1848. (1) HOWELL BROWN, guardian of four children of deceased ux, ELIZ. BROWN. SARAH W. DAVIES - lifetime interest with remainder to her children. Children of ANN C. DAVIES, deceased. SAML. M. GARLAND and MARSHALL HARRIS, commissioners. Book 12, Page 81 -- Administrator's Account by SARAH W. DAVIES. To H. L. BROWN as guardian of his children. To DR. DAVIES' grandchildren. H. L. DAVIES - amount due from him to MRS. FRANKLIN. From December 15, 1845. Recorded December 18, 1848. Mention of accounts "doubtful if not worse." Book 13, Page 166 -- Administrator's Account by same administratrix from May 9, 1848. Postage to Petersburg and Botetourt. To SARAH W. DAVIES and children - 1/3; Children of ELIZ. H. BROWN - 1/3; and same to children of ANN C. DAVIES. Recorded May 16, 1853.

NANCY C. FRANKLIN and children -- Book 5, Page 234 -- Guardian Bond -- THOS. CREWS, guardian. Bondsmen: EDMD. WINSTON, JNO. McDANIEL, HENRY TURNER, July 19, 1813. Wards: NANCY C., SALLY, and JNO. R. FRANKLIN, orphans of JAMES FRANKLIN. Another Guardian Bond for Book 6, Page 261, but not there.

PEACHY FRANKLIN -- Book 3, Page 242 -- Guardian Bond -- JEREMIAH FRANKLIN, October 15, 1792, guardian of PEACHY FRANKLIN, orphan of HENRY FRANKLIN. Bondsman: NELSON CRAWFORD. Book 4, Page 464 -- Constable Bond -- June 15, 1807, 3rd Hundred. Bondsmen: GEORGE DILLARD and THOS. PAGE. There is an ordinary bond indexed as Book 6, Page 78, but it is not there.

PEGGY FRANKLIN -- Book A, Page 10 -- Guardian Bond -- April 27, 1812. BENJ. FRANKLIN, guardian of PEGGY FRANKLIN, orphan of JOEL FRANKLIN, deceased. Bondsman: BENJ. BROWN. It should be noted that the 26 will books covered in the index from 1761 to 1919 include A and B of old circuit wills, too. This explains the use of A and B for some items.

PHOEBE FRANKLIN -- Book 11, Page 66 -- July 27, 1841, written; June 20, 1842, probated. Witnesses: JNO. PRYOR, JULIUS SIMPSON, THOS. LAIN. PHEBE is also employed. Sons, HENRY, BENJ., and WILLIS FRANKLIN; daughter, JANE B. MOSS, ux of ANDERSON MOSS; children of deceased daughter, LUCINDA, ux of WM. CLARKSON; land in Virginia, North Carolina and Alabama. Daughter-in-law, JANE C. FRANKLIN, ux of my son, HENRY FRANKLIN, and her children. HENRY is to administer. Page 67 is his bond on probate date.

SAMUEL FRANKLIN -- Book 4, Page 249 -- Tobacco Inspector at Camden's Warehouse, December 21, 1801. Bondsman: JOEL FRANKLIN. Book 4, Page 252 -- Same -- September 20, 1802. Bondsman: MICAJAH CAMDEN. Book 4, Page 278 -- Same -- October 15, 1804. Bondsman: JOEL FRANKLIN. Book 4, Page 283 -- Same -- September 15, 1806. Bondsman: LEWIS TINDAL. Book 4, Page 513 -- Same -- September 21, 1807. Bondsman: ANDERSON MOSS.

JAMES FRAZIER (FRAZER also in data) -- Book 3, Page 547 -- Inventory --
September 16, 1799 - L 72-3-0. HUGH CAMPBELL, JOS. BALLENGER, THOS.
GRAYHAM(?).
Book 4, Page 307 -- Administrator's Bond -- MARGARET FRAZER; WALTER
FRAZER; JNO. FRAZER; WM. CAMDEN; PHILIP SMITH, April 15, 1799, for
MARGARET and WALTER FRAZER to administer.

JAMES A. FRAZIER -- Book 16, Page 146 -- Administrator's Bond --
August 18, 1862. C. S. FRAZIER and RO. L. COLEMAN for C. S. FRAZIER.

JAMES FREELAND -- Book 1, Page 163 -- March 14, 1770, written; May 7,
1770, probated. Witnesses: STEPHEN PERROW, MACE FREELAND, FLETCHER
GREGORY. Ux, MARY, and her son, ROBT. WILLIAMS and his heirs. Land
where I live; also 200 acres on Elk Island Creek; 200 acres on Cold
Mobeley's Creek; 480 acres on David Creek in Buckingham and called
"The Meadow"; 350 acres on Buffalo. Executor: RO. WILLIAMS.
Book 1, Page 165 -- Administrator's Bond -- RO. WILLIAMS, 7th day of
-----, 1770. Bondsmen: JOS. CABELL, MACE FREELAND, WM. HORSLEY.

SILAS C. FREEMAN (Indexed for SIDNEY C. FREEMAN) -- Book 6, Page 372 --
Minister's Bond -- July 21, 1823. To GOV. THOS. RANDOLPH. Bondsmen:
RICH. S. ELLIS, A. B. DAVIES, Clerk. No denomination.

ASAHEL FRENCH -- Book 9, Page 242 -- Administrator's Bond -- JNO. S.
FRENCH. Bondsman: JOS. KYLE, September 19, 1836.

ELIZ. FULCHER -- Book 6, Page 309 -- June 8, 1821, written; August 19,
1822, probated. Witnesses: JAS. MILLER; CHAS. B. HILL; JNO. HUDSON,
JR. Daughter, ELIZ. FULCHER; son, WM. H. FULCHER; son, JNO. J. (?)
FULCHER; land from my father and my mother's third. Daughter, JANE L.
CHRISTIAN. My five children: HENRY G. FULCHER, JANE L. CHRISTIAN,
JNO. J. (?) FULCHER, ELIZ. FULCHER, and WM. H. FULCHER. Administra-
tors: DABNEY HILL and WM. MOORE.
Book 6, Page 317 -- Administrator's Bond -- August 19, 1822, DABNEY
HILL. Bondsmen: BARTHOLOMEW WHITEHEAD, JNO. TUCKER, MICAJAH CAMDEN,
CHAS. TUCKER.
Book 6, Page 331 -- Guardian Bond -- September 16, 1822. SAML. D.
CHRISTIAN, guardian. Bondsmen: CHAS. H. and HENRY FULCHER. Ward:
orphan of JNO. FULCHER.
Book 6, Page 334 -- Inventory -- November 18, 1822; slaves; recorded
November 19, 1822. A. B. DAVIES, Clerk. Committee: THOS. ALDRIDGE,
J. P., HILL CARTER, JNO. CAMPBELL, WM. M. WALLER.

HENRY G. FULCHER -- Book 12, Page 171 -- March 9, 1849, written;
July 10, 1849, probated. Witnesses: WM. M. WALLER, CURTIS GILL. Ux,
DELILAH; my single children; all of my children: MAHALAH WHITEHEAD;
OSCAR F. FULCHER; ELIZA; MARCELLUS ANDREW and SARAH ANN FULCHER. Any
grandchildren to share with parents. Ux and son, OSCAR F., to
administer.
Book 12, Page 174 -- Administrator's Bond -- DELILAH and OSCAR F.
FULCHER, July 10, 1849.
Book 12, Page 224 -- Inventory -- October 15, 1849; no total; done
September 28, 1849. DILLARD H. PAGE, JNO. S. TUCKER, SAML. D.
CHRISTIAN.

HEZEKIAH S. FULCHER -- Book 6, Page 492 -- Constable -- October 18,
1824. Bondsman: JAS. FULCHER.
Book 6, Page 598 -- Same -- June 20, 1825; Second Hundred. Bondsmen:
WM. ANGUS and WM. H. KNIGHT.
Book 7, Page 28 -- Same -- June 16, 1827. Bondsmen: WM. ANGUS and
JAS. FULCHER.
Book 7, Page 248 -- To GOV. WM. B. GILES, June 15, 1829. Bondsmen:
ISAAC RUCKER and WM. ANGUS.

JAMES FULCHER -- Book 5, Page 230 -- Constable Bond -- June 21, 1813.
Bondsman: JNO. ROSE (N. middle initial).
Book 5, Page 514 -- Same men and bond, June 19, 1815. GOV. WILSON C.
NICHOLAS.
Book 5, Page 697 -- Same bond -- June 17, 1817. Bondsman: PETER P.
THORNTON.
Book 6, Page 78 -- Same bond -- June 21, 1819. GOV. JAS. P. PRESTON.

Bondsman: STERLING CLAIBORNE.
Book 6, Page 231 -- Same men -- June 18, 1821. in Second Hundred.
Book 6, Page 360 -- Same bond to GOV. JAS. PLEASANTS, June 16, 1823.
Bondsman: MANSFIELD WARE.

JOHN FULCHER -- Book 5, Page 59 -- Administrator's Bond -- BETSY
FULCHER, June 18, 1810. Bondsmen: SAML. HUCKSTEP, MICAJAH CAMDEN,
JAS. FULCHER. No decedent named herein, but indexed for JNO. FULCHER.
Book 6, Page 241 -- Guardian Bond -- August 20, 1821. DABNEY HILL,
guardian of JNO. FULCHER, orphan of JNO. FULCHER. Bondsman: PHILIP
THURMOND.
Book 6, Page 322 -- Administrator's Bond -- HENRY FULCHER, August 20,
1822. Bondsmen: CHAS. CHRISTIAN, JAS. FULCHER, STERLING CLAIBORNE.
Book 6, Page 330 -- Guardian Bond -- HENRY FULCHER, September 16, 1822,
as guardian of JNO. FULCHER, orphan of -----. Bondsmen: CHAS. H.
CHRISTIAN, JAS. FULCHER.
Book 6, Page 418 -- Inventory -- November 16, 1822 - $1,808.59.
BARTLETT CASH, WM. MOORE, HILL CARTER. Certified by WM. M. WALLER;
A. B. DAVIES, Clerk.
Book 6, Page 659 -- Real estate division -- February 25, 1826. CHAS.
L. CHRISTIAN, BARTLETT CASH, JNO. F. CAMDEN. South side of Little
Piney. Lines of PIERCE MAYS, deceased; DAVID S. GARLAND; JAS. FULCHER;
JNO. F. CAMDEN; CRAWFORD; DABNEY HILL. Lot 1 to heirs of PIERCE MAYS.
Lot 2 to HENRY FULCHER - all contain 36 acres. Lot 3 to WM. FULCHER.
Lot 4 to JOEL CAMPBELL. Lot 5 to JNO. FULCHER.
Book 7, Page 147 -- Administrator's Bond -- ELIZ. FULCHER, March 17,
1828. Bondsmen: JESSE BECK (JR.?); WM. TURNER.
Book 10, Page 79 -- Administrator's Account -- HENRY FULCHER, admin-
istrator from 1822. Seven legatees: HENRY G. and WM. FULCHER; SAML. D.
CHRISTIAN; JNO. FULCHER; JOEL CAMPBELL; JESSE CAMPBELL; five children
of PIERCE MAYS: JNO. J., RO. MAYS, MARIA SMITH, EDWIN MAYS, EDILY
PADGET. JESSE MAYS is guardian of MARIAH MAYS, ux of THOS. SMITH.
RO. WINGFIELD is guardian of PIERCE MAYS' children. October 23, 1838.
JNO. C. WHITEHEAD and JOEL BETHEL. SAML. M. GARLAND, Clerk.

SARAH FULCHER -- Book 15, Page 287 -- Administrator's Bond -- JAS.
FULCHER, January 16, 1860. Bondsmen: JOS. and L. D. FULCHER.

WILLIAM FULCHER -- Book 6, Page 322 -- Guardian Bond -- HENRY FULCHER,
CHAS. H. CHRISTIAN, JNO. FULCHER, SAML. D. CHRISTIAN, and S. CLAIBORNE,
August 20, 1822, for HENRY FULCHER as guardian of WM. FULCHER, orphan
of JNO. FULCHER.

WILLIAM FURBUSH (also see FORBUSH) -- Book 2, Page 37 -- June 15,
1781, written; April 1, 1782, probated. Witnesses: WM. FITZPATRICK,
THOS. EADES, JOSIAH WOOD. Ux, SALLY FURBUSH - 199 acres; Son, WILLIAM;
daughter, MOLLY FURBUSH; my brother, JOHN FURBUSH "which I was gargain
for"; remainder to raise and school my children. Equal division at
death of my ux to WM. and MOLLY FURBUSH. Administrators: my brother-
in-law, JNO. M. HADEN (?) and my father-in-law, CHAS. STATHAM and my
brother, ROBERT FURBUSH.
Book 2, Page 39 -- Administrator's Bond -- CHAS. STATHAM and ROBT. FUR-
BUSH, April 1, 1782. Bondsmen: JNO. LOVING, JR.; JNO. BIBB.
Book 2, Page 47 -- Inventory -- L 397-12-0, May 6, 1782. JNO.
DEPRIEST; JNO. STAPLES; WM. CRISP.
Book 4, Page 304 -- Administrator's Bond -- CHAS. STATHAM and JAS.
STEPHENS, June 17, 1799, for STATHAM to administer.
Book 3, Page 55 -- Guardian Bond -- CHAS. STATHAM and JAS. WRIGHT,
September 3, 1787, for CHAS. STATHAM as guardian of WM. and POLLY
FURBUSH, orphans of WM. FURBUSH, deceased, "when of age."

SALLIE FURLONG and children -- Book 4, Page 422 -- Guardian Bond --
ZACHARIAH ISBELL and CHRISTOPHER ISBELL, December 17, 1805, for
ZACHARIAH ISBELL as guardian of SALLY and LUCY FURLONG, orphans of
ROBERT FURLONG, deceased.

THOMAS GAILEY (GOLEY or GOALEY in places) -- Book 1, Page 111 --
April 24, 1767, written; September 7, 1767, probated. Witnesses:
PETER LYON, JNO. LYON, JNO. BAILEY. My brother, ABRAHAM NALLEY; my
mother; my sister, SARAH CRAWFORD's children.
Book 1, Page 112 -- Administrator's Bond -- JNO. LYON. Bondsman:
WM. MARTIN, JNO. DEPRIEST. It is followed by inventory of L 5-0-0 and
both bear date of October 5, 1767.

JAMES GAMBLE -- Book 1, Page 144 -- Administrator's Bond -- SAML.
WOODS, September 4, 1769. Bondsmen: LANGDON DEPRIEST, ROBT. STEPHEN-
SON.
Book 1, Page 153 -- Inventory -- L 9-6-6; taken September 4(?), 1769,
and returned February 5, 1770. JOEL CRAWFORD, RO. DUNWODY, WM.
SIMPSON.

BRECKENRIDGE GARLAND -- Book 13, Page 282 -- Guardian Bond -- MARTHA M.
PENDLETON and JNO. L. TURNER, December 19, 1853, for MARTHA PENDLETON
as guardian of above; orphan of LETITIA GARLAND.

CAROLINE E. GARLAND -- Book 16, Page 424 -- Slave division -- owned
jointly by L. R. CABELL and SAML. M. GARLAND, trustee for CAROLINE E. -
$14,550.00 for six slaves. January 7, 1864. THOS. WHITEHEAD, TAYLOR
BERRY, WM. E. COLEMAN.

DAVID S. GARLAND -- Book 3, Page 52 -- Guardian Bond -- EDWD. and THOS.
GARLAND, September 3, 1787, for EDWD. GARLAND as guardian of DAVID and
JAS. GARLAND, orphans of WM. GARLAND, deceased.
Book 3, Page 384f -- Guardian Bond -- indexed for DAVID, but belong
under PENN. He was guardian of SALLY and LUCY PENN, orphans of GEO.
PENN.
Book 5, Page 585 -- Sheriff Bond -- July 15, 1816 - also same men and
bonds for duties on 586f. Bondsmen: REUBEN PENDLETON, EDMD. WINSTON,
THOS. N. EUBANK.
Book 7, Page 337 -- This is really a WOODROOF item and indexed for
GARLAND as an official. JESSE WOODROOF - Refunding Bond by LINDSEY
McDANIEL as executor of WOODROOF, April 19, 1830. Bondsmen: JAS.
OGDON, WM. McDANIEL; SAML. WATTS bonded to GARLAND for a report.
Book 7, Page 339 -- Refunding Bond -- November 15, 1827, by DAVID S.
and WM. GARLAND to HILL CARTER, administrator of WM. MOORE, deceased -
DAVID S. has received assignment from GEO. W. TRIBBLE and ux, POLLY,
of their interest in estate of MOORE. Creditors have notified CARTER
to make no delivery until bond is made. Slaves involved.
Book 10, Page 394 -- Administrator's Bond -- WM. M. WALLER, SAML. M.
GARLAND, JOS. K. IRVING, and ZACH. DRUMMOND, November 15, 1841, for
WM. WALLER and SAML. GARLAND.
        This man was DAVID SHEPHERD GARLAND and I am told that he was
known as "King David" because of the large land holdings which he
built up in (his) lifetime. I believe that I am safe in stating that
there are more deed items for him than for any other person in Amherst
County.

JAMES GARLAND -- Book 5, Page 568 -- April 9, 1815, written; March 18,
1816, probated. Witnesses: WM. CRUTCHER; JACOB SCOTT; JNO. P. COBBS;
DANL. CHEATWOOD; WILLIS CRUTCHER. My brother, DAVID S. GARLAND - my
share in partnership with him, JAS. GARLAND, and DANL. HIGGINBOTHAM.
My natural son, PRESTON H. GARLAND - otherwise PRESTON HARRISON, son
to FRANCES HARRISON, daughter to JAS. HARRISON. He is to have comfortable support and schooling for seven years. REUBEN PENDLETON and
children by my sister, FRANCES PENDLETON. Administrators: DAVID S.
GARLAND and friend and relation, JAS. P. GARLAND, who is to be guardian
of my son, PRESTON, and is to administer his third, slaves, schooling
and all of my lands. My mother has several of my slaves.
        Slaves are to remain with my mother for her lifetime. My
sister, POLLY CAMDEN, has no children and no prospects, but assistance
shall be given to her, if needed.

Book 5, Page 700 -- Administrator's Bond -- DAVID S. GARLAND, JAS. P.
GARLAND, THOS. N. EUBANK, WM. TURNER, and JAS. PENDLETON, March 18,
1816, for both GARLANDS.
Book 1, Page 90 -- Administrator's Account -- DAVID S. GARLAND from
February, 1816 - articles for MRS. CAMDEN and MRS. HARPER; book for
PRESTON; $1,451.94 due JAS. GARLAND at time of death; grave stones;
REUBEN PENDLETON and children; many items for PRESTON GARLAND - Greek
testament, etc. Horse for JAS. S. PENDLETON. Very long account to
Page 102. Returned September 29, 1825; HILL CARTER; PEACHY FRANKLIN;
JNO. DILLARD. Page 102 -- Administrator's Account -- JAS. P. GARLAND
administrator from March 24, 1816 - to PRESTON H. GARLAND; JAS. GAR-
LAND, JR.; amount of WM. BAILEY's sale; Nelson County trip; WM. G.
PENDLETON for repairing watch. Returned July 4, 1825. Committed as
above in DAVID GARLAND's account.
Book 6, Page 150 -- Inventory -- indexed for JAS. P. GARLAND - many
slaves; one named RACHEL TYE RIVER has died. Total: L 3,357-4-9.
September, 1816. JNO. LONDON; B. STONE; RO. WALKER.
Book 6, Page 152 -- Division -- indexed for JAS. P. GARLAND - between
DAVID S. GARLAND; REUBEN PENDLETON and children by his deceased ux,
FRANCES; PRESTON H. GARLAND - JAS. P. GARLAND his guardian and admin-
istrator of JAS. GARLAND with DAVID S. GARLAND. November --, 1816.
Committee as above.

JANE GARLAND -- Book 23, Page 304 -- Administrator's de bonis non
Bond -- September 20, 1892, for M. J. GARLAND; Bondsman: P. P. GARLAND.

JANE H. GARLAND -- Book 14, Page 54 -- May 5, 1853, written; December 17, 1855, probated. Witnesses: WARNER JONES, H. M. GARLAND,
HENRY L. DAVIES, and DAVIES and JONES as to codicil of June 22, 1855.
Daughter, JANE M. COBBS; son, SAML. GARLAND; daughter, ANN S. ROSE;
daughter, SARA A. WALLER; daughter, MARY R. CABELL; Virginia Bible
Society and Domestic Missions. Their father wished to do equal jus-
tice to all of his children. Daughter, LOUISA and granddaughter,
ALICE W. CABELL; granddaughter, JANE M. THWING (THIVING?); grand-
daughter, JANE M. PHILLIPS; granddaughters JANE N. WALLER; JANE M.
CABELL; JANE M. GARLAND (daughter of my son, SAML.), and JANE M. GAR-
LAND (daughter of my daughter, LOUISA). Rest of estate to be divided
into six parts: to LANDON C. GARLAND in trust for my daughter,
LOUISA, and children, for my son-in-law, L. C. GARLAND, has my confidence as a husband and father; son, SAML. C. - son, WM. H. and children; son, PATRICK H. and children. Stones for husband and daughter,
E. V. CABELL, and son, D.L.G. CABELL at Winston graveyard. Grandchildren: ALICE W. and GEO. K. CABELL, brother and sister, until
ALICE is married and GEO. is 21. Daughter, CAROLINE E. GARLAND and
grandson, L. B. CABELL--if CAROLINE has issue. Codicil: Slave has
been given son, WM., and sum to son, P. H. GARLAND; legacy to daughter
WALLER to her children since her death. L. B. CABELL is to receive
education. Administrators in main body: sons, SAML. M. and W. H.
GARLAND.
Book 14, Page 59 -- Administrator's Bond -- SAML. M. GARLAND, Decem-
ber 17, 1856. Bondsmen: RO. A. PENDLETON, R. A. COGHILL, H. L.
BROWN.
Book 14, Page 148 -- Inventory -- December 31, 1855 - $6,000.00.
J. POWELL, RO. M. BROWN, W. E. COLEMAN. Recorded March 17, 1856.
Book 15, Book 176 -- Slave division -- long list and ages and names
of various children of slaves. Tom, 70, and Minerva, 53, are
"Together." One sixth to SAML. M. GARLAND; LANDON C. GARLAND, trustee
for ux and children; WM. H. and PATRICK H. GARLAND as trustees for
children; SAML. M. as trustee for CAROLINE E. GARLAND and L. B. CABELL;
LANDON C. as trustee for ALICE and G. K. CABELL; WM. H. as trustee
for ALICE W. and GEO. M. CABELL; PATRICK H. as trustee for C. E.
GARLAND and L. B. CABELL. L. C. or S. C. and SAML. M. GARLAND,
trustees. October ter, 1858.

JNO. GARLAND -- Book 7, Page 185 -- April 9, 1828, written; November
Court, 1828, probated. Witnesses: STITH MEAD, W. WARWICK, FANNY T.
MARKHAM, LORENZO D. LYON. Wants it understood in plain and obvious
meaning--no technical nor law terms - my dear mother, NANCY MOORE--
legacy delivered by January 1, 1829. Ux, CHRISTIAN B. GARLAND; my
two children to be educated: JNO. RICHARD and PANTHEA ANN GARLAND.

Ux to administer. When children are of age or married. She qualified
on November 17, 1828 -- Book 7, Page 186.
Book 7, Page 196 -- Inventory -- December 11, 1828 - $2,674.97 - JESSE
BECK, GEO. MARKHAM, JNO. WILLIAMS.

JNO. R. GARLAND -- Book 23, Page 453 -- November 4, 1864, written;
January 13, 1879, probated. Witnesses: RALPH W. NEWTON; DAVID CRAW-
FORD, JR.; ALGERNON S. SULLIVAN; EZEK. C. KING, JR., testified
to handwriting -- resident of New York. Ux MARY; son, JNO. R.; my
father, sisters, and children. My brothers, HUDSON S. and WM. P.
GARLAND. SULLIVAN testified that he had known GARLAND for 15 years
and that he was upwards of 21 and of sound mind. NEWTON and CRAWFORD
are dead.
Produced in Amherst County by MAURICE H. GARLAND and handwriting
attested by JNO. B. ROBERTSON and P. P. GARLAND. MAURICE GARLAND
qualified. Appraisers: H. M. SACKETT, JNO. H. CRISTIAN, J. S. DIGGS,
J. W. HARVEY. Resident of Davidson County, Tennessee - farm in
Amherst County, Virginia, managed by my son, MAURICE H. GARLAND. I
presume that he kept account, but I am in a distant state. Plantat-
tion in Coahoma County, Mississippi - possessed by late SAML. M.
GARLAND, SR. - one fourth devised to GEN. SAML. GARLAND, JR. and one
half of one fourth to his mother, MRS. C. M. GARLAND, and she gave
me this interest by deed of gift - recorded in Lynchburg. Lands in
Phillips and Monroe Counties, Arkansas - possessed by GEN. SAML.
GARLAND, JR. - one half to my mother and deed of gift as above. One
is very valuable and lies along Railroad - Helena to Clarendon - about
1,200 acres, and other about 1,600 or 1,800 acres. Second bottom
land of White River. Money in Nashville Bank and insurance policy
with Mutual Life Insurance Company of New York. My library - sons-
in-law to select books; some valuable scientific books and offers
quoted, but most are trash. Grandchildren: WILLIE and CARRIE THOMP-
SON, children of my deceased daughter, CAROLINE. I sold MRS. R. G.
LEWIS one acre at Blount Springs, Alabama, and she is to give receipt
for it. It will be $300.00 of her legacy. Like sale and terms to
DR. E. A. SMITH. My sister, MRS. C. M. or E. M. - someone has used
corrective fluid and blurred this name. My legatees are MRS. R. G.
LEWIS; MRS. E. A. SMITH; MRS. ANNIE R. FULTON; MRS. LOUISE F. HUM-
PHREYS; MRS. MAURICE H. GARLAND and children of MRS. CAROLINE M.
THOMPSON (sic), deceased. Executors: son, MAURICE H. GARLAND and
friend, WILLS WILLIAMS - the former of Virginia and latter of
Tennessee. Codicil: money invested for sister, MRS. E. M. GARLAND.

MARY GARLAND -- Book 3, Page 112 -- Guardian Bond -- July 6, 1789 -
EDWD. GARLAND and bondsmen: WM. TUCKER and THOS. GARLAND. Ward:
orphan of WM. GARLAND, deceased.

PRESTON H. GARLAND -- Book 5, Page 573 -- Guardian Bond -- JAS. P.
GARLAND, B. STONE, and JNO. N. ROSE (ROSS?) and WM. ARMISTEAD,
March --, 1816, for JAS. P. GARLAND as guardian of PRESTON H. GARLAND,
orphan of JAS. GARLAND.
Book 8, Page 4 -- Inventory -- April 9, 1830 - $3,261.75 - WM. DUNCAN,
DABNEY SANDIDGE, WM. HENLY.
Book 8, Page 91 -- Administrator's Account -- BENJ. TALIAFERRO, ad-
minister from April, 1830. To WM. H. GARLAND for articles furnished
for funeral - $16.32. SAML. M. GARLAND per receipt. Property
bought by SAML. M. GARLAND and afterwards taken by FRANCES HARRISON,
October 1, 1830. Judgment of RO. GARLAND. Cash furnished MISS
FRANCES HARRISON. Purchase of D. S. GARLAND. JAS. P. GARLAND for
redemption of negro boy, BILLY. Returned April, 1831.
Book 8, Page 232 -- Administrator's Account -- same administrator
from June 18, 1832. Paid to WM. H. GARLAND balance due estate in
full. Slaves to WM. H. GARLAND and RICH. N. EUBANK and certified by
them, July 18, 1832 -- agreed to by interested parties. RO. TINSLEY,
Clerk. Order drawn upon my account by FRANCES HARRISON and son. Suit
and name of JAS. P. GARLAND and RO. STANNARD, attorney, August 9,
1831, and later termed RICHMOND suit. JAS. P. GARLAND vs. F. HARRISON
and SONS and myself. JNO. THOMPSON - expenses to Milton, North
Carolina, to take evidence in suit in Lynchburg. Sums expended for
us of FRANCES HARRISON and children in certain controversies relative

to estate of PRESTON H. GARLAND and rights still undetermined.
July 17, 1832. WM. S. CRAWFORD and CHAMPE CARTER. Note: It would
seem that PRESTON H. GARLAND was not only child of JAMES by FRANCES
HARRISON, natural mother, but I find no indicaton of others being
named here in Amherst County. It could be that the Lynchburg suit
reveals more data.

ROBT. GARLAND -- One item indexed as Book 3, Page 244 for him is a
LUCAS Guardian Bond and has been placed in proper place in "L's."
Book 8, Page 119 -- Coroner, August 17, 1831. Bondsmen: WM. and
LINDSEY McDANIEL.
Book 8, Page 244 -- Coroner, August 20, 1832. Bondsmen: SAML. MAN-
TIPLY and JNO. MEHONE.
Book 8, Page 319 -- Coroner, June 17, 1833. Bondsmen: SOLOMON DAY
and RO. WINGFIELD.
Book 8, Page 434 -- February 20, 1834, written; October 20, 1834,
probated. Witnesses: LINDSEY COLEMAN and WM. D. MILES and to codi-
cil of February 20, 1834. My ux, NANCY; --- HART -$200.00 to estate of
NATHL. GARLAND, deceased; to BERRY HARDIN; to MISS ----- HALL; sum to
ALEX. McALEXANDER; to GEO. M. WOODS - to be paid to them, if living,
at death of ux. Codicil: No interest to be paid on sums of these.
Memo by me endeavoring to give some information as to how the persons
named may be found. HART gave me directions in 1800 or 1801 to ne-
gotiate the business with FRANCES PRESTON of Washington County on
arranging business in partnership with MR. PRESTON. I gave him up
the papers and at this time have lost recollection of nearly all the
business. MR. HART then lived in North Caroline and think that he
told me that he was not entitled to the money -- acting for some
friend. Order by PRESTON on COL. SAML. MEREDITH, then of Amherst
County, so by applying to MR. PRESTON and executors of SAML. MEREDITH
matter may be traced. No one authorized has ever applied for the
money. The case of BERRY HARDIN -- he is now dead. BEN HARDIN once
pretended to have benefit of the money, but never produced evidence.
Nor do I recall of either of them applying for it. BEN lives in
Nelson County. Miss ----- HALL has been paid by JNO. PILSON a part
of the money and perhaps by applying to him - he lives in Albemarle -
he can give some information on the subject. She is the granddaughter
of old MR. DAVID HUMPHREY, formerly of Albemarle. MR. McALEXANDER
lives in Nelson. These sums are rather above than below (range from
$40.00 to $200.00 in will) what the parties are entitled to, but had
rather be over than under. GEO. M. WOODS lives in Albemarle. The
claims are long out of date, but I wish them settled.

SAML. GARLAND (Some have "M" as initial) -- Book 9, Page 344f --
County Clerk, October 16, 1837. Bondsmen: HOWELL D. BROWN, ED. A.
CABELL, WM. M. WALLER. Several bonds for duties.
Book 10, Page 343 -- County Clerk, April 19, 1841. Bondsman: PAULUS
POWELL.
Book 11, Page 305 -- County Clerk, April 21, 1844. Bondsman: WM. M.
WALLER and H. D. BROWN.
Book 12, Page 440 -- County Clerk, October 20, 1851. Bondsmen:
RO. A. PENDLETON and D. H. TAPSCOTT.
Book 14, Page 577 -- County Clerk, June 21, 1858. Bondsmen: H. L.
BROWN and J. DUDLEY DAVIS.
WM. GARLAND -- Book 1, Page 393 -- Administrator's Bond -- DAVID
SHEPHERD, December 1, 1777. Bondsman: EDMD. WILCOX.
Book 1, Page 403 -- Inventory -- January 3, 1778; no total. JAS.
COFFEY, NICHL. MORAN, JNO. JACOBS.
Book 3, Page 100 -- Administrator's Bond -- EDWD. GARLAND, April 7,
1789. Bondsman: JNO. CLARKSON.
Book 3, Page 133 -- Administrator's Account -- DAVID SHEPHERD, deceased,
and account approved by committee of SAML. MEREDITH, JAS. FRANKLIN,
and JNO. PENN, May 24, 1790. Account from 1777.

WM. H. GARLAND -- This is really a TOMLINSON item.
Book 8, Page 8 -- Administrator's Bond -- June 21, 1830. WM. H.
GARLAND - administrator of a TOMLINSON.

JNO. C. GARLICK -- Book 10, Page 342 -- Minister's Bond -- April 19,
1841. Bondsmen: DANL. DAY and LEWIS S. EMMET. To acting Governor,

JNO. RUTHERFORD. Methodist Episcopal.

JOSEPH M. GARNER -- Book 9, Page 34 -- Refunding Bond -- January 19, 1835. GARNER has received of PETER RUTHERFORD, administrator of SARAH WILCHER, deceased, and guardian of my ux, formerly SARAH A. WILCHER, a negro boy from estate.

ONEY GARNER -- Book 10, Page 218 -- August 30, 1837, written; April 20, 1840, probated. Witnesses: ED. A. CABELL and JNO. SEAY. About 49 acres near Rockey Creek Mill. Children of my first husband, JNO. ALEX. JOHNS: WM. C., LEWIS H., and JAS. D. JOHNS; S. JOHNS and NANCY TYLER. My four children by second husband, JOS. GARNER; CAROLINE and MARY, infant children of my daughter, MARY HANSFORD; ELIZ. TAYLOR, PENCY SCOTT, and JOS. M. GARNER. SAML. M. GARLAND trustee for CAROLINE and MARY and their father is to have no control or interest. My daughter, ELIZ. TAYLOR, and her husband, JAS. TAYLOR, is to have no control or interest. Executor: SAML. M. GARLAND.
Book 10, Page 219 -- Administrator's Bond -- SAML. M. GARLAND, May 18, 1840. Bondsman: JOS. K. IRVING.
Book 10, Page 282 -- Inventory -- $135.00. JOS. KYLE; ALEX. GOOCH; DRURY CHRISTIAN, May 30, 1840. Land on Rockey Creek and next to HENRY HAGGARD - 39 acres.

BENJ. F. GARVIN (Indexed as GARNER) -- Book 16, Page 152 -- May 2, 1862, written; July 21, 1862, probated. Witnesses: SAML. J. TURNER; J. C. MUNDY; J. H. BALDOCK. JESSE MUNDY was named as administrator, but he refused to serve. My aged mother; my sister, PERLINE GARVIN; my sister, ANN E. BANTON and children; children of my brother, JAS. M. GARVIN, by his present ux. My nephews and nieces. Executor: friend, JESSE MUNDY.
Book 16, Page 154 -- Administrator's Bond -- NANCY GARVIN, September 15, 1862. Bondsman: THOS. J. GARVIN.

THOS. GATEWOOD -- Book 15, Page 34 -- Minister's Bond -- September 21, 1858. Bondsman: THOS. WHITEHEAD. No denomination.

WM. GATEWOOD -- Book 3, Page 104 -- January 3, 1789, written; June 1, 1789, probated. Witnesses: JNO. CHRISTIAN (B); EDMD. ROWSEY; NOTLEY WARREN MADDOX; FANNY MADDOX. Sons: REUBEN and WILLIAM - land up Buffalo where I formerly lived. My two other sons, EDMUN (sic) and FOSTER - all other land down Buffalo. Ux, SARAH. Daughters: NANCY, DOLLEY, JUDITH. If my boys "marrys" or goes off to housekeeping - to get cow and calf "apeace." Proved by CHRISTIAN and ROWSEY.
Page 105 -- SARAH GATEWOOD qualified on probate date. Bondsmen: JNO. and CHAS. CHRISTIAN.
Book 3, Page 120 -- Inventory -- June 26, 1789. L 188-15-0. SAML. MIGGINSON, WM. PHILLIPS, NOTLEY MADDOX, WM. DILLARD.
Book 3, Page 576 -- Division -- Committee: STEPHEN WATTS, JNO. CHRISTIAN, JAS. FLOYD, WIATT SMITH,January 23, 1800. Widow got slave and child; SAML. WRIGHT who married NANCY GATEWOOD - slave; WM. LAYNE who married JUDITH GATEWOOD - slave and stock.
       There is a good bit of GATEWOOD data in deeds and in Kentucky books in my library. AMEY GATEWOOD married here as spinster, March 5, 1776, JNO. UPSHAW. JAS. PAMPLIN, surety. Many of the family went to Georgia and then some came into my native Kentucky. I knew a family of them in one town where I served and they were Methodists. I have a long sketch on them in a Kentucky book and an older member of the family brought it up to date for me.

ROBT. GEORGE -- Book 4, Page 302 -- Guardian Bond -- WM. GARRETT and JAS. LIVELY, nOvember 18, 1799, for WM. GARRETT as guardian of RO. and LANDERICK (?) GEORGE, orphans of LANDERICK (?) GEORGE, deceased.

SARAH GEORGE -- Book 4, Page 44 -- Inventory -- August 19, 1802 - $756.43: JAS. LIVELY, JAS. MARR, JAS. HILL, WM. KNIGHT.
Book 4, Page 141 -- Administrator's Account -- December 2, 1803, ISAAC RUCKER, administrator. No details. Returned January 16, 1804. Committee: DAVID WOODROOF, REUBEN RUCKER, REUBEN NORVELL. Reference to "several legatees."

Book 4, Page 350 -- Administrator's Bond -- ISAAC RUCKER, June 21, 1802. Bondsmen: WM. GARRETT and GEO. DILLARD.

ISAAC GIBSON -- Book 3, Page 111 -- Administrator's Bond -- July 6, 1789. JACOB GIBSON. Bondsmen: FRANK LEE and WM. WARE.
Book 3, Page 120 -- Inventory -- L 147-5-9, August 14, 1789. JAS. HIGGINBOTHAM, JNO. PHILLIPS, JACOB TYREE, FRANK LEE.

MARTHA W. GIBSON -- Book 9, Page 58 -- Guardian Bond -- EZEK. B. GILBERT, MARTIN N. DAWSON, and JAS. A. GIBSON, March 17, 1835, for EZEK. GILBERT as guardian of MARTHA W. and JNO. GIBSON, orphans of WM. H. GIBSON.

WM. H. GIBSON -- Book 6, Page 405 -- April 5, 1823, written; November 17, (19?), 1823, probated. Witnesses: JOS. R. CARTER, ABRAM CARTER, GIDEON C. GOODRICH. Tract bought for my sister, MARY CHILDRES, and her children "agreeabley" to my father's will and to be conveyed to them. My ux is to have land for life and then to my children. Executors: friends: JNO. GARTH and EZEK. GILBERT.
Book 6, Page 450 -- Administrator's Bond -- ELVIRA GIBSON, April 19, 1824. Bondsmen: WILKINS WATSON, ISAAC RUCKER, EZEK. GILBERT.
Book 6, Page 570 -- Inventory -- order of May 10, 1824 - $1,602.20. JOS. R. CARTER, GIDEON C. GOODRICH, ABRAM CARTER. March --, 1825.
Book 8, Page 433 -- Administrator's de bonis non Bond -- October 20, 1834 -- RICHARD S. ELLIS. Bondsmen: THOS. N. EUBANK, WM. HAYNES, THOS. TUCKER.
Book 9, Page 45 -- Inventory -- RICH. S. ELLIS, administrator -- November 7, 1834. $1,850.52. JOS. R. CARTER, RO. H. CARTER, JNO. PRYOR.

Book 10, Page 235 -- Administrator's Account -- RICH. S. ELLIS from November 22, 1834 - to schooling S. C. GIBSON; THURMOND trustees. JAS. A. GIBSON; MRS. GIBSON; W. B. GIBSON - interest as legatees in personal estate W. W. GIBSON (probably clerical error for "H." as initial). BALLARD E. GIBSON for interest in estate of what appears to be M. H. GIBSON. The writing is hard to decipher. JAS. A. GIBSON - interest in estate of M. H. GIBSON (This could be MARTHA W. above). Same interest for LOUISA A. R. TURNER, formerly GIBSON; same for EDWD. and MARTHA W. GIBSON and she received remaining half of EDWD's interest; same for JNO. E. GIBSON.
Book 10, Page 236 -- Slave list - one legged slave, Dick, priced at $101.00. Jackson, a boy, at $600.00. Others in interesting list. February 6, 1840. JOS. R. CARTER; RO. H. CARTER; PETER C. THORNTON.

ED. B. GIBSON signed for following legatees: JAS. A. GIBSON, LOUISA A. R. TURNER, ED. B. GIBSON, MARTHA W. GIBSON, JNO. G. GIBSON (appears to be JNO. E. in one place); B. E. GIBSON. Recorded June 15, 1840.

ANN W. GILBERT -- Book 12, Page 433 -- Guardian Bond -- MARTHA R. GILBERT and THOS. N. EUBANK, July 21, 1851, for MARTHA GILBERT as guardian of ANN W. and MARTHA R. GILBERT, orphans of E. B. GILBERT, deceased.
Book 12, Page 490 -- Division on order of August, 1851, to divide slaves of BENJ. E. SCRUGGS and MARTHA R. GILBERT, guardian of her two daughters, ANN W. and MARTHA R. GILBERT. Done November 20, 1851, by JNO. PRYOR, RO. H. CARTER, and JOS. R. CARTER. Returned February 16, 1852. Reported as division of slaves formerly those of F. W. and ----- GILBERT.

ELIZ. GILBERT -- Book 16, Page 144 -- Guardian Bond -- MARY J. P. GILBERT, August 18, 1862, for guardian of ELIZ. and SOPHIA H. GILBERT, orphans of -----. Bondsman: WM. E. COLEMAN.

EZEKIEL GILBERT (Some are indexed for EZEKIAH) -- Book 6, Page 359 -- Administrator's Bond -- EZEK. B. GILBERT, May 20, 1823. Bondsmen: WILKINS WATSON and BENJ. BROWN.
Book 6, Page 463 -- Inventory of DR. EZEK. GILBERT, December 13, 1823. $56.00. GIDEON C. GOODRICH; JO. CARTER; ABRAM CARTER.
Book 13, Page 223 -- Guardian Bond -- WM. ROGERS and RO. H. CARTER, June 20, 1853, for WM. ROGERS as guardian of EZEK. GILBERT, orphan of

EZEK. GILBERT.

EZEK. B. GILBERT, DR. -- Book 12, Page 325 -- Administrator's Bond --
GEO. W. STAPLES, November 18, 1850. Bondsmen: THOS. A. EUBANK,
M. C. GOODWIN.
Book 12, Page 407 -- Inventory -- November 27, 1850 -- Doctor's books;
no total. JNO. PRYOR, RO. H. CARTER, CHAS. L. BROWN.
Book 12, Page 424 -- Sale -- December 20, 1850. Recorded June 16,
1851. MARTHA P. GILBERT was a buyer.

EZEK. L. GILBERT -- Book 16, Page 470 -- Administrator's Bond --
May 16, 1864. MARY J. GILBERT. Bondsman: BENJ. RUCKER.

CAPT. HENRY GILBERT -- Book 1, Page 418 -- February 23, 1778, written;
May 4, 1778, probated. Witnesses: DANL. GAINES; JNO. STEWART, SR.;
MARY BROWN; DAVID SHEPHERD; JOEL FRANKLIN -- Plantation where I live -
450 acres to ux, MARY. Sons: THOS. and RICH. - my children when of
age. Son, HENRY, where he lives - 360 acres and to pay amount to
CARTER BRAXTON. Note: Each son is to pay BRAXTON for deeds show
that HENRY bought his land from him and evidently still owes.
   Deeds show that GILBERT bought two tracts from CARTER BRAXTON.
One was Round Top Plantation on Tribulation and there is still a small
mountain by that name in the area. The other was on Rutledge. The
first tract took in what is now a part of the Village of Amherst on
the southwestern side. The VOORHEIS hom and Allen Tavern lot are
thereon. The other tract has an hold home on it and early deeds refer
to the place as Hunting Tower. It is now owned by MADISON SETTLE and
is not far from the Central High School. GILBERT names son, GEORGE -
360 acres and slave in Hanover in hands of JNO. WIATT; son, JNO.
WIATT GILBERT - 360 acres; son, EZEKIEL - 360 acres; son, JOSIAS -
tract called The Poison Field; son, MAURICE - land on Cabin Branch
and Braxton Ridge; son, THOS.; son, RICHARD; daughter, ANNE GILBERT;
daughter, MARY GAINES. Mares named Lady Legs and Sally. Executors:
GABL. PENN and DANL. GAINES. Son, HENRY, gets razor case and sword.
Executors qualified as named, Book 1, Page 422, probate date. Bondsmen: CHAS. ROSE, JNO. PENN, AMBROSE RUCKER.
Inventory is on Book 1, Page 511 - L 5,700-1-4, May 2, 1778. DAVID
SHEPHERD, JNO. STEWART, JNO. RICHESON.
Book 3, Page 37 -- Administrator's Account by GAINES from March,
1778 -- RICH. TALIAFERRO for schooling ye boys - L 6, September 7,
1778. Estate's portion for enlisting a soldier; District soldier;
EZEK. GILBERT bought slave; trip to Hanover to settle accounts and
also to Richmond - executors of BLAIR and HAWKINS. GEO. GILBERT's
half of L 80 to WM. COLEMAN for putting roof on prison. Returned
February 5, 1787. JNO. WIATT, BENJ. RUCKER, JAS. DILLARD.
Book 3, Page 156 -- Administrator's Account by GABL. PENN of CAPT.
HENRY GILBERT's estate. From May, 1778. JOSIAH GILBERT named;
DR. EZEK. GILBERT on order of MARY GILBERT. Same committee as above.
THOS. GILBERT also named.
Book 6, Page 240 -- Administrator's Bond -- CHAS. L. BARRET; STERLING
CLAIBORNE, August 23, 1821, for CHAS. BARRET.
Book 6, Page 302 -- Estate schedule and inventory, April 15, 1822:
$1,108.46. JOS. R. CARTER, GIDEON E. GOODRICH, JNO. RUSSEL.
Book 6, Page 578 -- Administrator's Account by BARRET from 1822.
Returned January 31, 1825. JAS. S. PENDLETON, JAS. ROSE, JOS. STAPLES.

HENRY C. GILBERT -- Book 13, Page 326 -- Administrator's Bond --
POWHATAN M. GILBERT and JNO. D. GILBERT, February 24, 1854, for
POWHATAN GILBERT.
Book 14, Page 511 (indexed as Book 13, Page 511) -- Administrator's
Account -- POWHATAN GILBERT from February 3, 1854. Paid SALLY TAYLOR;
amounts to WM. and J. D. GILBERT. POWHATAN resigned and accounts
finished by STERLING CLAIBORNE. Recorded May 20, 1857. On Page 513,
DR. HENRY GILBERT and J. D. GILBERT named.
Book 13, Page 511 -- Administrator's Account by GEO. B. THURMAN of
estate of DR. HENRY GILBERT. May 21, 1857.

JNO. D. GILBERT -- Book 23, Page 159 -- November 9, 1891, written;
January 18, 1892, probated. Witnesses: JNO. THOMPSON, M.D.; C. J.
HIGGINBOTHAM. Sister, FANNIE C. GILBERT and daughter MAUDE C. GILBERT,

my niece. FANNIE C. is to administer.
Book 23, Page 200 -- Inventory -- $188.90 -- April 13, 1892. POWHATAN
PADGETT, CHESTER HIGGINBOTHAM, E. T. WARE.
Book 23, Page 227 -- Administrator's Bond -- FANNIE C. GILBERT,
March 21, 1892.

JNO. WIATT GILBERT -- Book 2, Page 24 -- February 12, 1781, written;
September 3, 1781, probated. Witnesses: GEO. GILBERT, JNO. HORSLEY,
WM. CHAPPELL, EZEK. GILBERT. Ux, SALLY - 400 acres - until ELIZ.
GILBERT is of age or married. Various items - such as sermond books.
Daughter, MARY WYATT GILBERT - until of age or married; daughter,
ANN STARK GILBERT. Son, GEO. GILBERT. Executors are to make title
to JERRY TAYLOR and he is to make title to my land known as Megann's
Ordinary. Executors: DANL. GAINES, GEO. GILBERT, JNO. HORSLEY.
Book 2, Page 26 -- Administrator's Bond -- GEO. GILBERT, September 3,
1781. Bondsmen: HUGH ROSE, DANL. GAINES.
Book 2, Page 65 -- Inventory -- March 30, 1782. EDWARD WATSON, JNO.
STEWART, WM. CHAPPELL.

JUDITH GILBERT -- Book 6, Page 250 -- Indexed for her, but really JNO.
GUE item.
Book 9, Page 304 -- Estate Commitment to Sheriff -- June Court,
1837. JNO. COLEMAN, Sheriff.

MARTHA C. GILBERT -- Book 10, Page 260 -- August 20, 1840, written;
September 21, 1840, probated. Witnesses: RO. H. CARTER, WM. B.
GIBSON, N. D. SMILEY (?) -- Sister, FRANCES W. GILBERT; infant children
of my brother, DR. E. B. GILBERT: ANNE, WILMOUTH, and MARTHA R. GIL-
BERT. Bookcase to CHAS. ANTHONY GILBERT. Executors: sister, FRANCES
W. GILBERT.

POWHATAN M. GILBERT -- Book 16, Page 153 -- June 28, 1861, written;
September 15, 1862, probated. Handwriting attested by W. E. COLEMAN
and JAS. HIGGINBOTHAM. If I should not survive the present - administer, J. D. GILBERT - his business and mine. Keep estate together, especially MARIAH and family - unless FANNY gets married. Some
of MARIAH's children are to have some of estate. J. D. GILBERT is
to get one fourth. My brothers and sisters. J. D. and F. C. to
choose "thares in MARIAH and AMERLY so as to keep them in family."
Refers to half-brothers and sisters.

RICHARD GILBERT -- Book 1, Page 504 -- Guardian Bond -- DANL. GAINES,
JOS. CABELL, and AMBROSE RUCKER, October 4, 1779, for DANL. GAINES as
guardian of RICH. GILBERT, orphan of HENRY GILBERT.
Book 2, Page 189 -- Guardian's Account by GAINES, Returned August 2,
1784. MAURICE GILBERT mentioned and MARY GILBERT has slaves.

SOHPIA GILBERT -- Book 16, Page 144 -- Guardian Bond -- MARY J. P.
GILBERT, August 18, 1862, as guardian of SOPHIA and ELIZ. GILBERT.
SOPHIA's initial was "H." No parent set forth. Bondsman: WM. E.
COLEMAN.

THOMAS GILBERT -- Book 1, Page 505 -- Guardian Bond -- DANL. GAINES,
JOS. CABELL, and AMBROSE RUCKER, October 4, 1779, for DANL. GAINES
as guardian of THOS. GILBERT, orphan of HENRY GILBERT, deceased.

W. W. GILBERT, JR. -- Book 21, Page 482 -- Constable, September 21,
1887. Bondsmen: THOS. A. BARBOUR, J. P. BEARD, W. S. OGDEN.
Book 22, Page 286 -- Constable -- June 17, 1889. Bondsmen: BARBOUR
and W. S. OGDEN as above.

WM. GILBERT -- Book 16, Page 114 -- Administrator's Bond -- JNO. D.
GILBERT, February 17, 1862. Bondsmen: THOS. WHITEHEAD and SAML. M.
GARLAND.
Book 16, Page 129 -- Inventory -- March 7, 1862. WM. KNIGHT, BENJ. J.
RUCKER, VINCENT F. BURFORD.
Book 16, Page 131 -- Sale, March 11, 1862. Family name buyers: MRS.
GILBERT, JAS.; LUDLOW (Cash in one place); JNO. D., CLIFTON L. GIL-
BERT. Returned June 17, 1862.

Book 16, Page 368 -- Administrator's Account by JNO. D. GILBERT from March 1, 1862. Widow: MRS. MARY J. P. GILBERT, P. M. GILBERT and then mention of 13 distributees, but it does not seem to come out of 13 distributees, but it does not seem to come out that way: JNO. D.; WM. W.; CLIFTON L.; JAS. M. OGDON and ux, MARY A.; LEWELLEN J. (I.) COPPEDGE and ux, MARTHA A.; JNO. D. GILBERT as executor of POWHATAN GILBERT, deceased; JAS. C. - another place it seems to be JAS. L. or S. - FRANCES C. GILBERT; E. L. (S.) GILBERT; RO. N. GILBERT; JUDITH C., SOPHIA A.(?), and OLIVIA E. GILBERT. Returned July 1, 1863.

WILMOUTH GILBERT -- Book 10, Page 393 (indexed 390) -- Guardian Bond -- EZEK. B. GILBERT, October 18, 1841, as guardian of his infant children: WILMOUTH, ANN, and MARTHA ROOKINS GILBERT. Bondsman: THOS. A. EUBANK.

ROWLET GILL -- Book 16, Page 365 -- January 25, 1863, written; June 15, 1863, probated. Witnesses: M. B. WOODSON and SAML. D. CHRISTIAN. Brother, CURTIS GILL to administer. Sister, HANNAH GILL. Proved by WOODSON and Monday, September 21, 1863, by CHRISTIAN. CURTIS GILL qualified. Bondsman: ABRAHAM MARTIN. Administrator's Bond is on Page 16, Page 401.

THOS. GILLENWATER -- Book 1, Page 519 -- August 11, 1779, written; March 6, 1780, probated. Witnesses: THOS. WRIGHT, SNELLING JOHNSON, JNO. MERRITT. Sons, ELIJAH and JOELL - Duck Bill land - if JOELL stays another year and works on his place as usual. My ux, MARTHA, to raise my children. Son, THOS. Executors: ux and ELIJAH GILLEN-WATERS.
Book 1, Page 520 -- Administrator's Bond on probate date for MARTHA GILLENWATERS ("s" is added in some items). Bondsmen: BENJ. RUCKER and JNO. MERRITT.
Book 5, Page 433 -- March 21, 1814 -- lunatic Bond. ELISHA GILLEN-WATER to be committee. Bondsmen: JAS. GILLENWATER and NELSON DAWSON. Found insane by PHILLIP JOHNSON, CHAS. MUNDY, and NELSON DAWSON.

GEORGE GILLESPIE -- This man is an ancestor of my wife's. She was MILDRED MILLER. The name appears here with variations of GALASPY, GALASPIN and perhaps others. GEO. had a son, WILLIAM, who married in Amherst in 1777 to ANN HUDSON.
    ANN was daughter of JOSHUA HUDSON and is named in his will. In Madison County, Kentucky, her name sometimes shows as NANCY and she died testate there. WM. moved to Madison County, Kentucky, and carried the mail between Kentucky and Charlottesville. There is a power-of-attorney in Lincoln County to him from the Kentucky Postmaster to sell a slave when next in Virginia. WM. was killed in a duel with THOS. KENNEDY in 1794 and one is referred to WINSTON COLEMAN's work on Famous Kentucky Duels. This duel took place in Garrard County in the yard of the home known today as site of Uncle Tom's Cabin story.
    I have been able to trace the HUDSON family of JOSHUA HUDSON and ux, MARY TERRELL, or Orange, but I am stymied on lineage of GEO. GILLESPIE. The line from GEO. to present is easy through daughter, MARY, daughter of WM., who married HENDERSON THURMAN in Madison. GEO. and first wife, MARY, appear in a deed in Albemarle and I feel sure that she was a MOORE. Two of their children bear the name of MOORE and one was CAPT. SHEROD MOORE GILLESPIE of Amherst.
    GEO. married a second time to a widow, MARY FARIS, in Louisa, December 26, 1785. Two of his children were to marry FARIS children in Amherst later. GEO. and ux moved to Amherst and deeds show a good deal on them. He lived in Roseland area until he made a trade with one of the ROSE men for land on Piney River. Deeds show that he operated a mill there. I had a difficult time locating his grave site. I had names of all heirs in Amherst from a deed and quizzed every WRIGHT, CASH, JONES, and GILLESPIE family. He did state, though, that they had saved a huge collection of old papers found in saddle bags of his grandfather, DR. WRIGHT. He also recalled that there was a plat of a graveyard in the collection and remembered that his mother was much disturbed when a man named WOODS bought the site and plowed it up for crops. I made a trip to examine the papers and my heart sank because there were so many of them. I was quite for-

tunate in thumbing through them and located a copy of the deed which
had puzzled me for some time. The Amherst heirs of GEO. had sold
400 acres on south side of Piney to DAVID S. GARLAND and therein reserved the graveyard "where our father, GEO., is buried." There are
so many deeds involving DAVID S. GARLAND that I despaired of ever
finding the site. The Kentucky heirs made a deed, too, but did not
refer to the graveyard. HENDERSON THURMAN acted therein for his ux
who was granddaughter of GEO.
        The copy of the old deed had a surveyor's plat showing the
location of the graveyard. MR. WRIGHT knew exactlywhere it was since
his mother had asserted that "many of our people are buried there."
It is at the end of a lane between his property and that of a MR.
CAMPBELL. Little Friar Mountain is in the background. MR. WRIGHT
pointed out a chimney which still stands on a level spot on the moun-
tain side, but he did not know just whose home it formerly was. He
was a GILLESPIE descendant and living on part of theoriginal tract,
but, like so many folk, had never traced his lineage.
Book 4, Page 84 -- Inventory -- February 26, 1803 - L 980-16-9. JNO.
CAMDEN, JNO. CAMPBELL, WM. MOORE. 12 slaves and other property.
Book 4, Page 364 -- Administrator's Bond -- CHAS. JONES, JAS. MURPHY,
JAS. MONTGOMERY, SHELTON CROSTHWAIT. February 21, 1893, for CHAS.
JONES and JAS. MURPHY.
Book 5, Page 41 -- Administrator's Account -- CHAS. JONES from 1803 --
JNO. MORRAN for one sixth of tobacco: LEWIS GILLESPIE - 1/2 crops;
ALEX. GILLESPIE - MARY MASTERS per receipt. MARY GILLESPIE - relin-
quishment of dower. SAML. McGEEHE for making coffin - L 2-2. FRANCIS
CLARK's judgment in Fluvanna, DABNEY CARR, attorney clerk at Charlottes-
ville; division to 12 children of heirs: L 66-9 to each with interest
from November 30, 1804. Sale of November 30, 1803. Reference to
papers with accounts. Committee of DANL. McDONALD, WM. B. JACOBS, and
JAS. MONTGOMERY. Report of December 7, 1811. Many bonds due estate
and among them were those of SHERROD M.; MARY, ALEX., GEO. and LEWIS
GILLESPIE. Legatees: SHEROD M. GILLESPIE; LUCY HUDSON; JAS. BOLLING
and ux, LETTIE; children of WM. GILLESPIE; CHAS. JONES and ux, BETSY;
AMBROSE CAMPBELL and ux, NANCY; HOWARD CASH and ux, SALLY; JESSE
WRIGHT and ux, DICEY; ALEX. GILLESPIE; LEWIS GILLESPIE; JESSE CART-
WRIGHT and ux, FANNY; GEO. GILLESPIE, the Younger. Committee of
December 16, 1811: PHILIP THURMOND, JAS. CAMDEN, and JAS. CARTWRIGHT.
        I might note that there is a good bit of data on the Kentucky
GILLESPIE line in Madison and Perrin work, 4th edition, Page 793 --
JOS. S. BOGGS. The BOGGS sketch is garbled for it states that PHILIP
GILISBIE was the mail carrier who was killed in duel with THOS.
CANNADY (sic). ANN HUDSON GILLESPIE is called NANCY in Madison County,
Kentucky, will - see Will Book F, Page 422. Therein she only names
two children: MARY THURMAN, who was ux of HENDERSON THURMAN, and
LEWIS GILLESPIE. LEWIS GILLESPIE also left a will in Madison and in
it he gives a good picture of his brothers, sisters, and nieces and
nephews.
        Deeds here show that WM. was in Kentucky prior to removal with
family. I am trying to establish that he was the WM.GILLESPIE who
was confidant of BENJ. LOGAN. LOGAN left a WM. GILESPIE in charge of
St. Asaph at an early day and WM. GILESPIE planted an early crop there.
WM. GILLESPIE is listed as a Revolutionary soldier from Amherst. The
problem is a hard one to solve, though, for I have found the GILLESPIE
family in Orange, Botetourt, Albemarle, Louisa, and Prince Edward as
well. Perrin's third edition carries a GILLESPIE sketch in Simpson
County, Kentucky, data. The family is said to stem from a MATTHEW
GILLESPIE of "Orange County, New York," but I am inclined to believe
that they meant Orange County, Virginia, for a MATT. GILLESPIE proved
his importation there quite early.
        The MOORE name shows in the Albemarle deed wherein GEO. GILLES-
PIE and first ux, MARY, are involved. It will be noted that a WM.
MOORE shows in the data here on a committee for GEORGE's estate.
Correspondence is invited with anyone who has unscrambled these differ-
ent GILLESPIE and MOORE lines.

ARCHELAUS GILLIAM -- Book 12, Page 70 -- August 30, 1845, written;
October 16, 1848, probated. Witnesses: JOS. HARMER; JAS. BYAS -
"of LARKIN BYAS" - ALFORD BYAS; WM. BYAS. Proved by HARMER and ALFORD
and WM. BYAS. Ux, ELIZ. J. D. - 200 acres where I live; my 5 chil-

dren: JAS. F.; JNO. D.Q.S.N.; THOS. E.; MILDRED MARY ELIZ. and
JUDITH ANNA DAWSON GILLIAM - my half interest in Pedlar land next to
GEO. MORRIS - 300 acres. Ux to administer.
Book 13, Page 13 -- Administrator's de bonis non Bond -- October 18,
1852. JAS. GILLIAM. Bondsman: JAS. B. DAVIS.

ARCHELAUS GILLIAM, SR. -- Book 9, Page 267 -- Administrator's Bond --
JAS. GILLIAM, November 21, 1836. Bondsmen: THOS. N. EUBANK and
LINDSEY DAVIS.
Book 9, Page 275 -- Inventory on order of November last, December 17,
1836. CAPT. JAS. DAVIS; WM. ROACH; JNO. D. DAVIS. Total: $3,057.00.

ELIZ. GILLIAM -- Book 6, Page 448 -- Guardian Bond -- WM. H. GILLIAM,
WILL JOPLING, and R. N. EUBANK on March 15, 1824, for WM. GILLIAM as
guardian of ELIZ. GILLIAM, orphan of JNO. GILLIAM, deceased.

JAS. GILLIAM -- Book 14, Page 389 -- Administrator's Bond -- JAS. H.
WAUGH, July 20, 1857. Bondsman: DANL. E. BAILEY.
Book 14, Page 395 -- June 12, 1857, written; Monday, July 20, 1857,
probated. Witnesses: DANL. SHRADER, JAS. T. FEAGANS, MARTIN E.
FEAGANS and proved by them. JAS. WAUGH qualified. CAPT. DANL. E.
VAILEY who married JUDITH F., daughter of my sister, MARY J. WAUGH -
may buy my 2 tracts: (1) 135 acres where I live; (2) 160 acres bought
of JNO. P. and WM. A. GILLIAM. Executors may sell, if he declines.
Sisters: MARY J. WAUGH and ELIX. SLAUGHTER, widow of RO. L. SLAUGHTER
of Missouri. Children of deceased sister, JUDITH DAWSON of Missouri.
Children of deceased brother, ARCHELAUS GILLIAM: JNO, THOS, ELIZ.,
and JUDITH GILLIAM. Executor: nephew: JAS. H. WAUGH.
Book 14, Page 446 -- Inventory -- September 14, 1857 -- $5,586.88.
JO. R. ELLIS, CHAS. L. ELLIS, PETER FLOOD.
Book 14, Page 591 -- Sale -- November 25, 1857 -- D. E. BAILEY and
JNO. GILLIAM were buyers. Monday, July 19, 1858. GEO. O. PHILLIPS
and JAS. WAUGH.
Book 15, Page 97 -- Sale, $5,586.83. JNO. L. (S.) GILLIAM and D. E.
BAILEY were buyers. Recorded March 21, 1859.

JAS. R. GILLIAM -- Book 16, Page 108 -- Guardian Bond -- A. S. GILLIAM,
January 20, 1862, as guardian of JAS. R. GILLIAM; no parent set forth.
Bondsman: MARY E. BECK.

JARRATT GILLIAM -- Book 8, Page 322 -- December 24, 1832, written;
June 17, 1833, probated. Witnesses: WM. A. GILLIAM, JAS. GILLIAM,
RODERICK WAUGH. Proved by GILLIAM witnesses. WM. W. GILLIAM quali-
fied. Bondsmen: THOS. N. EUBANK; RICH. S. ELLIS; WM. HAYNES.
Daughter, MARY TALOR BURKS; my four youngest children: WM. WHITING
GILLIAM; RO. JARRATT GILLIAM; ELIZA DAVIS GILLIAM; CHAS. DAVIS
GILLIAM. Executors: WM. W. and RO. J. GILLIAM.
Book 9, Page 148 -- Land division by JOSIAH ELLIS, JAS. DAVIS, and
GEO. BURKS, November 6, 1834. JNO. PRYOR, surveyor - 235-1/2 acres.
To his children (1) Mansion house - 36 acres to WM. H. (?) GILLIAM;
(2) Barn lot - 74 acres - to CHAS. D. GILLIAM; (3) 62-3/4 acres to
RO. J. GILLIAM; (4) BUCK BRANCH - 62-3/4 acres to ELIZA D. GILLIAM,
ux of WM. A. GILLIAM. Plat on Page 149 - waters of Buck Creek and
Lewis Spring branch; tributary of Pedlar. Lines: heirs of JNO.
ELLIS; JAS. DAVIS; THOS. H. MORRIS; GEO. P. (S.) BURKS; THOS. N.
EUBANK; ELVIRA JANE ROACH, and 1-1/2 miles from James River. Re-
corded December 21, 1835.
Book 9, Page 265 -- Administrator's Account -- WM. W. GILLIAM from
June 5, 1835. BEVERLY DAVIES, GEO. T. PLEASANTS, NELSON C. DAWSON.
Recorded November 21, 1836.

JNO. GILLIAM -- Book 6, Page 225f -- Administrator's Bond -- JNO. P.
and WM. A. GILLIAM, May 21, 1821. Bondsmen: JNO. ELLIS and EZEK. B.
GILBERT. Will: March 1, 1821, written; May 21, 1821, probated.
Witnesses: EZEK. B. GILBERT, JAS. GILLIAM, FLEMING H. DUNCAN. Ux,
MARY - mansion house; daughter ANNE's orphan sons: SAML. and ALFRED
BURKS - until of age. To get 2 years of education. Daughter, JUDITH's
two orphan sons: MADISON and JOHN DAVIS. Daughter: MARY JANET
GILLIAM; daughter, ELIZ. PORTER GILLIAM. My four living children:
JNO. PATTERSON GILLIAM; WM. ANDERSON GILLIAM; MARY JANET and ELIZ.

PORTER GILLIAM - if without issue. Executors: Ux, MARY; sons, JNO.
PATTERSON and WM. ANDERSON GILLIAM, and friend, CAPT. JAS. DAVIS.
Book 6, Page 283 -- Inventory -- October 8, 1821 - $2,281.13 - THOS. N.
EUBANK, WM. H. McCULLOCH; JAS. WAUGH.
Book 6, Page 307 -- Division - heirs of NANCY BURKS (called ANNE in
will) - formerly NANCY GILLIAM; heirs of JUDITH DAVIS - MADISON and
JNO. DAVIS; JNO. P., WM. A.; POLLY and ELIZ. GILLIAM; widow, MARY.
March 19, 1822. THOS. N. EUBANK; JARRATT GILLIAM; JAS. WAUGH.
     DAVIS excursus: REV. JNO. DAVIS, Baptist minister, married
JUDITH GILLIAM and marriage is of record here. This DAVIS family
data was sent to a man who was a descendant of JNO. DAVIS and second
ux, MARY LIVELY. He was highly indignant because I named the two
sons, MADISON and JOHN, for he "knew that his grandfather, JOHN, was
never married but once." We broke off correspondence and dealings
and this is one of the few such episodes in my long and pleasant
work with folk who are interested in Amherst data. It was indeed unfortunate for him since I was loaned the old DAVID and LIVELY family
Bibles to copy just after this exchange of correspondence and end
thereof. The LIVELY Bible is the oldest one which I have ever seen
in a private collection. It was printed by a Swiss Society in 1776
and contains very old LIVELY data.

MARY GILLIAM -- Book 11, Page 450 -- Administrator's Bond -- WM. and
JAS. GILLIAM, October 19, 1840, for WM. GILLIAM.

SARAH GILLIAM -- Book 8, Page 302 -- Guardian Bond -- SARAH ROACH,
February 18, 1833, for SARAH ROACH as guardian of SARAH GILLIAM,
infant of ARCHELAUS GILLIAM. Bondsmen: GEO. S. PLEASANTS, NICHL.
SHUMAKER, WM. H. McCULLOCH.

     I have often wondered about the GILLIAM family in this area.
My wife descends from a WM. GILLIAM who is said to have gone to Kentucky (Fayette County), from Essex area. His daughter, HANNAH,
became ux of WILLIAM TAYLOR and after TAYLOR's death in Fayette, she
and her father moved to Illinois. I am unable to find any Illinois
data on them. WM. GILLIAM is said to have married in Virginia, ELIZ.
BOULWARE. I am stymied on BOULWARE and GILLIAM (GUILHAM, etc.) data.
I often state that it all drives me "Stark" mad for there is a STARK
connection somewhere in BOULWARE or GILLIAM lines. WM. TAYLOR's
daughter married HUGH PEEL in Fayette and STARK TAYLOR, brother, was
a bondsman. Early Fayette data shows these men as residents: STARK
TAYLOR; STARK BOULWARE; and STARK GILLIAM.

ELEANER GILLILAND -- Book 1, Page 266 -- Administrator's Bond --
JNO. and HUGH GILLILAND and JAS. MENEES, JR., October 3, 1774, for
JNO. GILLILAND.

SUSANNAH GILLILAND -- Book 4, Page 510f -- October 15, 1807, written;
February 15, 1808, probated. Witnesses: STEPHEN REES, PASEY REES,
BETSY REES, REBECCA RUCKER. Proved by BETSY and STEPHEN REES. REUBEN
NORVELL qualified. Bondsmen: ANTHONY RUCKER and NICHL. HARRISON.
Daughter, ELIZ. THURMOND - land bought of JAS. WILMORE. Daughter,
JUDITH LYON - land bought of RICH. PADGETT for 9 years "on condition
that she has no intercourse with her husband, ALEX. LYON, and no
more children." Granddaughter, SUSANNA LYON and granddaughter, SU-
SANNAH HILL (daughter of my son, MADERSON). Executors: freinds:
REUBEN NORVELL and JAS. MARR.

ADDISON GLASSCOCK -- Book 8, Page 157 -- Guardian Bond -- WM. M.
WALLER and CORNL. SALE - November 23, 1831, for WM. WALLER as
guardian of ADDISON GLASSCOCK, orphan of ISRAEL GLASSCOCK.
Book 8, Page 194 -- and 256 -- so indexed, but they are in Book 9.
Book 9, Page 194 -- Guardian Bond -- by WALLER from 1833 -- Trip to
Fredericksburg, Tappahannock, Fauquier, Frederick and Essex - to JANE
ALDRIDGE; to THOS. GLASSCOCK. AUSTIN BROKENBROUGH, administrator, of
B. BLAKE; DAVID O. GLASSCOCK's administrator. WARD is young man,
fully grown, with comfortable estate and should not be limited to
necessities; mingles in society circles. Estate of PETER GLASSCOCK
and claim vs. ISRAEL GLASSCOCK, father of ward. JAS. S. PENDLETON
made trips and was allowed fees. Recorded December 21, 1835. FRANK-

LIN THWING, WM. H. KNIGHT, WM. M. WALLER.
Book 9, Page 246 -- Administrator's Bond -- JANE ALDRIDGE, October 17, 1836.
Book 9, Page 230 -- March 23, 1836, written; June 20, 1836, probated.
Witnesses: WARNER JONES; JNO. THOMPSON, JR.; JAS. S. PENDLETON;
LEROY GOODWIN. Proved by JONES, THOMPSON, and PENDLETON. Under 21 -
owes accounts in New Glasgow to WM. H. TYLER; WM. H. KNIGHT; MR.
ROYSTER; EMMET and GIBBS and WHITEHEAD and ESTES in Lynchburg. My
guardian, WM. M. WALLER; Hiram, a slave, taken to Mississippi by me.
My aunt, JANE ALDRIDGE, is to administer.
Book 9, Page 256 -- Guardian's Account by WALLER -- slaves hired -
from December, 1833. Recorded March 12, 1836, and committee same as
in first Guardian's Account above.

CHAS. GLENN -- Book 3, Page 578 -- Inventory -- L 75-9-1, May 21,
1800. NELSON ANDERSON; JAS. HANSBROUGH; NORBORNE THOMAS.
Book 4, Page 320 -- Administrator's Bond -- JNO. GLENN and WADDY
THOMPSON, May 20, 1800, for JNO. GLENN.

NATHAN GLENN -- Book 8, Page 238 -- Refunding Bond -- December 11,
1829, to EDWD. and RO. TINSLEY, administrators of DAVID TINSLEY.
NATHAN acts as attorney-in-fact as to claims under purchase from WILLIS
DAVIDSON and ux, NANCY. Share of $133.75 is due NANCY as devisee
under will of DAVID TINSLEY.

JNO. GOFF -- Book 1, Page 25 -- November 30, 1762, written; March 7,
1763, probated. Note: At beginning he put November 30, 1763, but
later it is 62. Witnesses: THOMAS GILLENWATERS; ELIJAH MORAN; JOS.
GOFF. Ux, ANNE; son, JOSEPH. Estate to be divided between JOS.;
JNO.; AMBROSE; and ELIZ. GOFF. Land on Stovall and Bowling to them,
but AMBROSE is to take plantation at death of his mother. Son,
LEONARD, gets 100 acres that he had bond for. Grants Power of attorney
to sons, LEONARD and JOS.
Book 1, Page 32 -- Inventory -- May 2, 1763 - before DANL. BURFORD,
Justice of the Peace, for L 267-12-0. Returned September 5, 1763.
RICH. SHELTON; BENJ. RUCKER.
Book 1, Page 125 -- Administrator's Account -- AMBROSE RUCKER,
administrator, in 1764 - To WM. CHEEK for schooling; board at school
for AMBROSE GOFF; cash for ANN GOFF; bond of CAPT. DANL. BURFORD.
September 5, 1768. DANL. BURFORD; GEO. STOVALL, JR.; DANL. GAINES.

ALBERT J. GOOCH -- Book 9, Page 372 -- Refunding Bond -- December 23,
1837, to LAWSON G. WILSHER, administrator of GIDEON GOOCH. ALBERT J.
has received slaves as his part of estate.

ALEXANDER GOOCH -- Book 9, Page 86 -- Constable -- June 17, 1835.
Bondsmen: LAWSON G. WILSHER and JONATHAN STOUT.
Book 9, Page 324 -- Same, June 20, 1837. Bondsmen: JAS. G. CHRISTIAN
and LAWSON G. WILSHER.
Book 9, Page 371 -- Refunding Bond-- December 23, 1837. Bondsman:
ALBERT GOOCH. To LAWSON G. WILSHER, administrator of GIDEON GOOCH.
ALEX. has received slaves as legatee of GIDEON GOOCH.
Book 10, Page 136 -- Constable -- June 19, 1839. Bondsmen: JAS. G.
CHRISTIAN; DRURY CHRISTIAN; ALBERT GOOCH.
Book 16, Page 89 -- Notary Public Bond -- June 17, 1861. Bondsman:
SAML. M. GARLAND.
Book 19, Page 172 -- Administrator's Bond -- JAS. M. MILLNER,
June 19, 1876. Bondsman: JESSE L. MILLNER.

CLAIBORNE GOOCH -- Book 4, Page 442 -- Guardian Bond -- SPOTSWOOD
GARLAND, January 19, 1807, for SPOTSWOOD GARLAND as guardian of
CLAIBORNE GOOCH, orphan of PHILIP GOOCH, deceased. Bondsman: HUDSON
MARTIN.

ELIZ. H. GOOCH -- Book 4, Page 439 -- Guardian Bond -- WM. B. GOOCH,
DRURY BELL, and HUDSON M. GARLAND on January 19, 1807, for WM. GOOCH
as guardian of ELIZ. GOOCH, orphan of PHILIP GOOCH, deceased. Justices of Amherst at this time were JOS. BURRUS, NELSON CRAWFORD, WM.
LOVING, and PHILIP JOHNSON. I did work for a MR. ROBT. MILLER of

St. Louis some years ago and was never able to locate places around
Richmond for him. There is more about this in PHILIP GOOCH data.
Her grave is marked in St. Louis and she married FERGUS FERGUSON,
but her name is on back of bond only. C. W. GOOCH was surety. A
deed here shows them in Prince Edward. Her stone has birth date and
she was child of second marriage.

FRANCES GOOCH -- Book 4, Page 264 -- July 4, 1806, FRANCES renounces
will of husband, PHILIP GOOCH, and asks for dower. Witnesses: HUD-
SON M. GARLAND; SAML. GARLAND. She was FRANCES PHILLIPS, daughter of
WM. PHILLIPS. She was a spinster and GOOCH was widower.

GIDEON GOOCH -- Book 9, Page 329 -- Administrator's Bond -- LAWSON G.
WILSHER, SAML. M. GARLAND, and JOSEPH K. IRVING. August 21(?), 1837,
for LAWSON WILSHER.
Book 9, Page 334 -- Inventory -- Order of December, 1837. 10 slaves,
etc., to LAWSON G. WILCHER (sic) who married PERMELIA GOOCH, daughter
of GIDEON GOOCH. Each slave valued at $458.33. Lots to JNO. NORVELL
and ux, LUCY; another lot to them -- that of JNO. M. GOOCH; lot to
ALEX G. GOOCH; another lot to NORVELL and ux -- that of MARY GOOCH.
Returned December 23, 1837. JONAS PIERCE; JOS. KYLE; PEYTON KEITH.
Book 10, Page 46 -- Administrator's Account -- by WILSHER from
May 28, 1837. To PARSON WRIGHT, minister - $5.00; bond of A. GOOCH;
A. G. GOOCH named. Returned August 14, 1838. DANL. L. COLEMAN and
RO. WINGFIELD.
Book 10, Page 161 -- Administrator's Account by same administrator
from 1838. Note of LUCRETIA CARTER; bonds of A. and A. G. GOOCH;
JNO. M. GOOCH; POLLEY GOOCH; LUCY NORVELL; JNO. M. GOOCH; ALBERT C.
GOOCH; ALEX. GOOCH; LAWSON G. WILSHER. R. HENLEY and DANL. L. COLE-
MAN, August 19, 1839.

JNO. M. GOOCH -- Book 9, Page 371 -- Refunding Bond -- JNO. M. and
ALBERT G. GOOCH to LAWSON G. WILSHER, administrator of GIDEON GOOCH,
December 23, 1837. JOHN has received slaves from administrator.
Book B, Page 9 -- Inventory -- small - DANL. SHRADER; GEO. S. FEA-
GANS; RO. N. ELLIS, May 18, 1866. Sale by RO. W. SNEAD, sheriff,
and administrator. Friday, May 18, 1866.
Book 16, Page 228 -- December 25, 1862, written; February 16, 1863,
probated. Witnesses: M. L. BENG, GEO. FEAGANS, MALINDA FEAGANS.
Proved by BENG and GEORGE FEAGANS (FULEGUM here). Estate left to
HARRIET ANN EVANS and AMELIA CARTER.

PHILIP GOOCH -- Book 4, Page 193 -- July 13, 1804, written; October 21,
1805, probated. Witnesses: JNO. PHILLIPS; HUDSON M. GARLAND. MOSES
PHILLIPS to codicil of May 26, 1805. Ux - half of personal estate
for life and life estate in my land called The Folly - 426 acres.
Children by present ux - 200 acres of Folly at her death - southern
part. Money that I got for their mother's part of her father's estate.
If negro Jim is alive at my death, children by first ux are to confirm
sale of him to WM. WARE. Labor of their negroes has been applied to
their education. WATSON tract and 407-1/2 acres of that called
LOCKEY's - 162 acres to be sold. Debt on land to be paid JAS. LYLE.
Executors: ux and RO. WALKER and son, WM. B. GOOCH - even though
he may be under 21. WALKER need not trouble himself unless the 2
others disagree. Then his vote is final. Codicil: ux gets one half
moiety in land bought of JNO. THOMPSON and his brother - 180 acres.
Book 4, Page 210 -- Inventory -- January 20, 1806. Interesting list of
books. JNO. CHRISTIAN; DRURY CHRISTIAN; JAS. DILLARD; JNO. CHRISTIAN
(B) - $1,1117.75.
Book 4, Page 418 -- Administrator's Bond -- WM. B. GOOCH, JNO. CHRIS-
TIAN (B), and JESSE SPINNER, October 21, 1805, for WM. GOOCH.
Book 4, Page 602 -- Administrator's Account -- RO. WALKER and WM. B.
GOOCH, administrators - several suits - one in Albemarle; trip to
Richmond; ABNER CHRISTIAN - wife's part for sums PHILIP GOOCH received
from estate of JINNEY BERNARD as guardian of LUCY GOOCH. DABNEY
GOOCH named. Subscription to New Glasgow Academy; claim vs. WM. B.
GOOCH to be paid by PHILIP GOOCH. SWANSON's executors vs. GOOCH
executors. ABNER CHRISTIAN - part for negro boy which belonged to his
ux and W. B. GOOCH and sold to COL. WARE by PHILIP GOOCH. To CHAS. L.
CHRISTIAN for laying off dower lot. LUCY GOOCH's note paid by D. C.

GOOCH. Note of MOSES PHILIPS. PHILIP GOOCH's bond to MAYS' execu-
tors. Mention of Powhatan County. PHILIP's bond at division of MRS.
BERNARD's slaves. Recorded August 11, 1809, and very long - to Page
608. Mention of sale of JENNY BERNARD of Goochland and she was guardian of LUCY F. and WM. B. GOOCH. Slaves of MARY BERNARD. Returned
August 21, 1809.
Book A, Page 36 -- CLAIBORNE W. GOOCH and DANL. CHEATWOOD to ARCHI-
BALD STEWART, Judge of Superior Court, Amherst County, September 25,
1816, for CLAIBORNE W. GOOCH to administer.
Book 5, Page 34 -- Administrator's Account -- July, 1809, WM. B.
GOOCH, acting executor. To Staunton, Albermarle, Nelson, Henrico,
and other areas on business. PHILIPS vs. GOOCH, executors. Cash
from DABNEY GOOCH. October 22, 1811. JAS. FRANKLIN; DRURY CHRISTIAN;
WM. ARMISTEAD.
        PHILIP GOOCH is not in Brown's list of Revolutionary soldiers,
but Mrs. Sweeny has included him. It is seen by the slave sale that
LUCY F. and WM. B. are by his first ux and CLAIBORNE W. and ELIZ. H.
are by second ux, FRANCES PHILLIPS.
        The Folly is located in the area of the Amherst Wayside Park
on U.S. Highway 60 East on Richmond road. ALFRED PERCY tells me that
it was quite a spot in its day and races and gambling took place there.
He says that there was a cabin which had no windows and all grudge
fights were held in it. The combatants entered and went at it -
tooth and nail - with no holds barred. The one who managed to emerge
was the winner. ALFRED PERCY says that the site is just east of the
park on the right of the road to Richmond.
        MR. ROBT. L. MILLER, 4441 Westminster Place, St. Louis 8,
Missouri, says that there is a good treatment of PHILIP GOOCH FERGU-
SON, son of ELIZ. H. GOOCH and FERGUS FERGUSON, in Bieber's book
entitled, The Southwest Historical Series, Vol. IV, "Marching with
the Army of the West." The original data is in the hands of the
St. Louis Historical Society. MR. MILLER is interested in locating
Airfield which is near Richmond. FERGUSON tells of a visit there in
1852 and refers to AUNT MARIA, ARTHUR FLEMMING, MA and ZELIE. He
also mentions Brook Church. MR. MILLER says that PHILIP GOOCH FERGU-
SON "was a prominent man in the newspaper field in and around
St. Louis," and cites Bieber's work, Pages 22f and 68f. I have not
seen this work, but it sounds quite interesting and should be studied
by GOOCH seekers.

POLLY GOOCH -- Book 9, Page 372 -- Lunatic Bond -- December 18, 1837.
LAWSON G. WILSHER and ALBERT G. GOOCH for LAWSON G. WILSHER as
committee.

WM. B. GOOCH -- Book 5, Page 602 -- Administrator's Bond -- ABNER
CHRISTIAN, JOS. KENNEDY, and CHAS. M. CHRISTIAN, September 16, 1816,
for Amherst County.
Book 5, Page 663 -- Inventory -- November 19, 1817 - $1,963.75.
DANL. CHEATWOOD, JNO. COLEMAN, JNO. CHRISTIAN (B).

DANIEL GOODE (Not indexed, but found) -- Book 3, Page 298 -- Adminis-
trator's Bond -- PHEBE GOODE, JNO. SMITH, and JNO. CAMDEN, June 16,
1794, for PHEBE GOODE.
Book 3, Page 323 -- Inventory -- December 16, 1794 - L 74-8-6. GEO.
GILLESPIE, GEO. CAMPBELL, JNO. CAMPBELL. I am inclined to think that
Bedford may have more GOODE data than Amherst. JOSHUA GOAD and SALLY
TOLER, December 9, 1799. STEPHEN TOLER, surety - are Bedford couple.
This is another one from that county: EDMD. GOODE and SALLY BRANCH,
November 19, 1791. JAS. BRANCH, surety. Consent of SUSANNAH BRANCH,
mother of SALLY.

MARTHA W. GOODE -- Book 20, Page 396 -- September 13, 1850, written;
July 19, 1869, probated. Witnesses: RO. A. COGHILL, WARNER JONES,
WM. S. CLAIBORNE. Codicil witnessed by JONES and CLAIBORNE, March 5,
1851. My daughter, MARY VA. McGINNIS and children living or to be
born. House and lot in New Glasgow bought by me of EDWIN S. RUCKER -
The Parsonage - when children are 21. Their father is VALERIUS
McGINNIS - my daughter's husband - all brothers and sisters. Slave,
whom I named Wm., saved the life of my grandson, EDWARD BEVERLY
McGINNIS, and goes to EDWARD at mother's death. Executor: VALERIUS

McGINNIS. Codicil: Slaves to my daughter, MARY McGINNIS, and my grandsons: EDWD. B. and VALERIUS McGINNIS, JR. The marriage of VALERIUS McGINNIS and MARY GOOD (sic) took place in Lynchburg. It is a minister's return on Page 121 of register and bears date of March 16, 1837. REV. WM. S. REID.

EDMOND GOODRICH -- Book 6, Page 551 -- Administrator's Account -- WIATT DUNCAN, THOS. GOODRICH, and GIDEON C. GOODRICH, administrators, from January 1, 1820. To SALLY GOODRICH; bond of EDMOND GOODRICH and THOS. GOODRICH. Names of GIDEON C. GOODRICH, ABIGAIL GOODRICH, JNO. B. GOODRICH - $64,446.69-1/2. JNO. PRYOR, CHAS. S. BARRET, THOS. N. EUBANK. February 22, 1825.
Book A, Page 23 -- Administrator's Bond -- GIDEON C. GOODRICH and ABRAM CARTER, September 27, 1819, for GIDEON C. GOODRICH.
Book A, Page 24 -- Administrator's Bond -- WIATT DUNCAN and WM. BOURNE, September 27, 1819, for WIATT DUNCAN.

JNO. GOODRICH -- Book 4, Page 158 -- September 3, 1803, written; February 20, 1804, probated. Witnesses: ABRAM CARTER, WM. BURKS, GEO. GILLESPIE. Proved by CARTER and BURKS. October 15, 1804, EDMOND GOODRICH qualified. Bondsman: ABRAM CARTER. Daughter, NANCY HAYNES; daughter, SALLY GOODRICH; son, JOHN; daughter, LUCY TUB(?); granddaughter, KITTY HOGG, daughter of RANDOLPH HOGG. Ux, MARY; my daughter, PATTY, until married; daughter, MARY HOGG. If RANDOLPH HOGG needs a place - 1/2 of that part on southside of path from road to my house. Executors: Ux; EDMUND GOODRICH and RANDOLPH HOGG.
Book 4, Page 171 -- Inventory - L 360-5-10, February 18, 1805. JNO. EUBANK; THOS. MORRIS; GEO. MORRIS.
Administrator's Bond on Book 4, Page 392 - see will.

JNO. B. GOODRICH -- Book 8, Page 425 -- Estate Commitment to Sheriff. August, 1834. Motion of D. and D. HIGGINBOTHAM. EDMD. WINSTON, Sheriff. Indexed for JNO. B. GOOCH.

MARY ANN GOODRICH -- Book 4, Page 152 -- Renounces will of deceased husband, JNO. GOODRICH, March 31, 1804. Witnesses: WM. BURKS, ABRAM CARTER. Proved by CARTER, July 16, 1804.

THOS. V. GOODRICH -- Book 11, Page 522 -- Administrator's Bond -- S. CLAIBORNE and C. SALE, May 17, 1847, for S. CLAIBORNE.

THOS. GOODRUM -- Book 1, Page 452 -- April 1, 1778, written; December 7, 1778, probated. Witnesses: JNO. DAWSON, JNO. MORRISON, JESSE MORRIS. Ancient and infirm - "ballance" between JAS. DOUGLASS and myself to him. To JOS. MORRIS. I have heirs at law, but have seen fit to cut them off according to law. Executor: JOS. MORRIS. Proved by JESSE MORRIS and JNO. MORRISON.

EDWD. GOODWIN -- Book 11, Page 480 -- Guardian Bond -- January 18, 1847. JNO. S. GOODWIN and JAS. LEE for JNO. GOODWIN as guardian of EDWD., SAML., MARY and EMILY GOODWIN, orphans of POLLY GOODWIN, deceased.

GEO. GOODWIN -- Book 4, Page 536 -- Administrator's Bond -- SARAH GOODWIN, NELSON C. DAWSON, RICH. WHITEHEAD, October 17, 1808, for SARAH GOODWIN.
Book 4, Page 567 -- Inventory - L 412-1-9, November 3, 1808. JNO. LEE, GEO. M. TINSLEY, WM. PETTYJOHN.

JNO. H. GOODWIN -- Book 11, Page 452 -- Administrator's Bond -- ISAAC R. REYNOLDS and WIATT PETTYJOHN, November 16, 1846, for ISAAC REYNOLDS.
Book 11, Page 474 -- Inventory - many slaves and interesting price list - $19,051.64. December 28, 1846. WM. KENT, JNO. A. MOSELY, CHAS. WINGFIELD.
Book 11, Page 477 -- Division at late residence, December 31, 1846 - 35 slaves - (1) To children of POLLY GOODWIN; (2) To ROBT. GOODWIN or representatives; (3) To NANCY RALEIGH or representatives; (4) HEZEKIAH JONES in right of his ux, VIRGINIA; (5) GREENSVILLE R. W. REYNOLDS in right of ux, FRANCES; (6) SUSAN MINTON -- 6 legatees mentioned.

Committee as above in inventory.
Book 12, Page 92 -- Administrator's Account by ISAAC REYNOLDS from November 16, 1846. JNO. L. GOODWIN for wheat and enclosing graveyard, October 12, 1848. WM. KENT and JNO. A. MOSELEY. Campbell County certificate by JNO. CARLY, Justice of the Peace, October 21, 1848.

JNO. L. GOODWIN -- Book 14, Page 227 -- Administrator's Bond -- RO. A. COGHILL and SAML. M. GARLAND, February 16, 1857, for RO. COGHILL.
Book 14, Page 371 -- Inventory -- $5,527.75, February 23, 1857. N. B. MAGRUDER, ISAAC R. REYNOLDS, WM. KENT.
Book 14, Page 379 -- Sale, Wednesday, February 25, 1857. JAS. GOOD-WIN, buyer. "Family of trustees desired to remain on land." R. A. COGHILL, administrator.

MARBLE C. GOODWIN -- Book 11, Page 425 -- Ind. Bond -- February 19, 1844 -- M. C. GOODWIN, JNO. WHITEHEAD, and RO. M. BROWN to MARSHALL M. HARRIS -- HARRIS and many bondsmen for JAS. POWELL, sheriff - lately of Amherst County - NATHAN A. CASH, deputy, in default. GOODWIN will indemnify HARRIS. Recorded August 24, 1846.
Book 14, Page 132 -- Sheriff's Bond -- June 16, 1856. Bondsmen: E. P. TUCKER, RO. W. SNEAD, RO. M. GANNAWAY, L. G. CASH, JAS. G. DAVIES, RO. A. COGHILL, GEO. T. PLEASANTS, A. TALIAFERRO.
Book 14, Page 376 -- Sheriff's Bond -- June 21, 1858. Bondsmen: S. M. GARLAND, WM. S. CLAIBORNE, J. S. PENDLETON, JAS. M. GANNAWAY, A. TALIAFERRO, RO. A. COGHILL, A. C. HARRISON, RO. W. SNEAD.
Book 18, Page 54 -- Inventory -- December 7, 1868 - $808.55. HENLEY DRUMMOND, CARY J. CASH, WM. TUCKER. On Page 56, Poor Law claimed by the widow - $83.60. Inventory and sale, December 10, 1868. MRS. GOODWIN was buyer - $365.16 total. Page 75, Commissioner's Report - RO. N. ELLIS, sheriff, from November, 1868. Sold to MRS. E. D. GOODWIN under Poor Law; counsel, T. WHITEHEAD. Most of debts contracted prior to February 20, 1867, when exemptions were smaller. Due from estate of S. G. CASH; judgment in name of JNO. S. SANDIDGE who sues for benefit of SAML. R. IRVINE vs. REBECCA R. CASH and JNO. W. CASH, assignees of intestate, M. C. GOODWIN, April 21, 1866.

MICAJAH GOODWIN -- Book 6, Page 10 -- Administrator's Bond -- JNO. GOODWIN and AMBROSE RUCKER, June 15, 1818, for JNO. GOODWIN.
Book 6, Page 631 -- Administrator's Bond -- CORNL. and JNO. GOODWIN and WM. I. (J.) ISBELL, November 21, 1825, for CORNL. GOODWIN.

POLLY GOODWIN -- Book 11, Page 478 -- Slave division, January 27, 1847, to her children: GUSTAVUS GOODWIN, JAS. GOODWIN, EDWD. GOODWIN, SAMUEL GOODWIN, MARY GOODWIN, EMILY GOODWIN. Two legatees are of age. Committee: JNO. A. MOSELY and WM. KENT.

SALLY GOODWIN -- Book 6, Page 163 -- Administrator's Bond -- JESSE BECK and NELSON C. DAWSON, September 18, 1820, for JESSE BECK.
Book 6, Page 270 -- Sale, recorded November --, 1821. $409.60. SPICEY GOODWIN was a buyer. JESSE BECK, administrator.

SPICEY GOODWIN -- Book 4, Page 537 -- Guardian Bond -- JNO. BURFORD and ABSALOM RUCKER, October 17, 1808, for JNO. BURFORD as guardian of SPICEY and EDITHA GOODWIN, orphans of GEO. GOODWIN.

THOS. C. GOODWIN -- Book 16, Page 415 -- June 20, 1860, written; January 18, 1864, probated. Witnesses: HENRY E. SMITH, JAS. M. MILLNER, JAS. E. JENNINGS. Proved by SMITH and JENNINGS. Ux, LUCINDA-BURKS and FARRIS tracts on Maple Creek - at her death to JANE ANN DRUMMOND with NEWTON DRUMMOND as trustee. To ELIZ. D. RAINE and her heirs; my son, THOS. J. M. GOODWIN - where I live on Buffalo. HAAS tract to be sold and money to JANE ANN DRUMMOND and ELIZ. D. RAINE. ELIZ. has no son and is to select trustee. Grandson, CHAS. DRUMMOND, trustee for JANE ANN DRUMMOND. Trustee for my son, THOS. J. M. - so that my children will be free of my old debts. Son-in-law, NEWTON DRUMMOND. Executors: son, THOS. J. M. GOODWIN and my grandson, CHAS. DRUMMOND.
Book 16, Page 443 -- Administrator's Bond -- H. E. SMITH and W. A. RUCKER, February 5, 1864, for H. SMITH.

ALEXANDER GOOLSBY -- Book 14, Page 521 -- Administrator's Bond --
THOS. WHITEHEAD and EDGAR WHITEHEAD, March 15, 1858, for THOS. WHITE-
HEAD.
Book 15, Page 599 -- Inventory and sale - MRS. MARY GOOLSBY, widow,
was a buyer. Administrator's Account from March 15, 1858 -- graveyard
enclosed. Legatees: WM., JOSHUA, PAUL, LIDIA ANN GOOLSBY. ELIJAH B.
MAYS, guardian. Recorded March 19, 1860. Note: There are several
ALEX. GOOLSBY marriages and one was son of SAML. and bride was EFFIE
MARR. Her name is spelled in several ways.

EFFIA GOOLSBY -- Book 10, Page 367 -- Administrator's Bond -- JAS. M.
GOOLSBY, V. McGINNIS, July 19, 1841, for JAS. GOOLSBY. Also spelled
EPHPHEY in data.
Book 11, Page 71 -- Inventory - EFFY here - $81.75 - ABSALOM HIGGIN-
BOTHAM, WM. TUCKER, WILLIS WHITE. WM. M. WALLER, Justice of the
Peace. Date of July 18, 1842.

JAMES GOOLSBY -- Book 5, Page 701 -- Guardian Bond -- DAVID S. GARLAND
and STERLING CLAIBORNE, January 19, 1818. DAVID GARLAND as guardian
of JAS. GOOLSBY, orphan of SAML. GOOLSBY.
Book 6, Page 9 -- Guardian Bond -- JAS. W. SMITH and DAVID S. GARLAND,
June 15, 1818, for JAS. SMITH as guardian of JAS. GOOLSBY, orphan of
SAML. GOOLSBY.

JAS. M. GOOLSBY -- Book 16, Page 98 -- Administrator's Bond -- RO. L.
COLEMAN and RO. A. COGHILL, October 21, 1861, for RO. COLEMAN.

JOSHUA GOOLSBY -- Book 17, Page 184 -- Administrator's Bond -- WM. E.
GOOLSBY, CHAS. J. MAYS, and JNO. M. BRADSHAW, September 17, 1866, for
WM. E. GOOLSBY.

LIDIA ANN GOOLSBY -- Book 15, Page 53 -- Guardian Bond -- E. B. MAYS
and JNO. L. TURNER, January 17, 1859, for E. MAYS as guardian of
LIDIA A. GOOLSBY, orphan of ALEX. GOOLSBY, deceased.

PAULUS A. GOOLSBY -- Book 15, Page 54 -- Guardian Bond -- E. B. MAYS,
and JNO. L. TURNER, and CHAS. J. MAYS, December 20, 1858, for E. MAYS
as guardian of PAULUS A., JOSHUA W., and WM. E. GOOLSBY, orphans
of ALEX. GOOLSBY, deceased.

STEPHEN GOOLSBY -- Book 2, Page 31 -- Administrator's Bond -- MARTHA
GOOLSBY, JOSIAH ELLIS, and NEAL McCANN, March 4, 1782, for MARTHA
GOOLSBY.
Book 2, Page 64 -- Inventory -- L 87-3-0, June 3, 1782. JNO. and
CHAS. BURKS and NEAL McCANN.

WM. GOOLSBY -- Book 15, Page 65 -- Guardian Bond -- E. B. MAYS and
SAM. J. TURNER, February 21, 1859, for E. MAYS as guardian of WM.
GOOLSBY, orphan of ALEX. GOOLSBY, deceased.

EDWARD GRADY -- Book 1, Page 215 -- Administrator's Bond -- July 6,
1772, DAVID SHEPHERD and EDMD. WILCOX, for DAVID SHEPHERD.

ELIAS GRANDY -- Book 4, Page 179 -- Inventory -- L 101-12-0, April 14,
1804. SHELTON CROSTHWAIT; JNO. ALFORD; JAS. BIBB, SR.
Book 4, Page 379 -- Administrator's Bond -- CHAS. EDMUNDS, THOS. BIBB,
ROWLAND EDMUNDS, December of 1803 for CHAS. EDMUNDS.

MARY B. GRANT -- Book 16, Page 313 -- Guardian Bond -- SARAH A. GRANT,
DAVID OGLESBY, and GEO. H. KEITH, May 18, 1863, for SARAH GRANT as
guardian of MARY B. GRANT; no parent set forth.

ROBT. GRANT, SR. -- Book 10, Page 60 -- May 26, 1835, written; November 19, 1838, probated. Witnesses: PHILIP THURMOND, SR.(?); WM. I.
ISBELL; PETER CASHWELL, and proved by the last two. December 17,
1838, PETER RUCKER qualified. Bondsman: WM. A. RICHESON. Daughter,
MARY GRANT; ux, SUSANNAH, and her son, JAMES GRANT, is to manage for
her; one or more of her other sons. My son, LITTLEBERRY, when of age
is to get 12 more months of school. Son, PRESTON J. is to get 6 more
months of school; my single children - if any leave children. Chil-

dren by first ux are: ELIZ. BURLEY; WM. GRANT; RHODA SIMPSON; and
SAML. GRANT. Children by 2nd ux are: NANCY COLEMAN, ROBT. D., JAS.,
POLLY, PATRICK H., SUSAN, PRESTON J., and LITTLEBERRY GRANT. Execu-
tors: Sons, JAS. and ROBT. D. GRANT.
Book 10, Page 149 -- Inventory -- PETER RUCKER, administrator, Decem-
ber 29, 1838 - $2,382.48. JOS. R. and RO. H. CARTER, PETER FLOOD.
Sale, January 2, 1839 - family buyers: SUSAN, BERRY, and PRESTON
GRANT - $284.97. JOS. R. CARTER, clerk.
Book 11, Page 26 -- Administrator's de bonis non Bond -- PETER RUCKER,
from 1838; in accounts are names of LITTLEBERRY, SUSAN, and PRESTON
GRANT. April 18, 1842. JNO. PRYOR and RO. H. CARTER.
Book 11, Page 243 -- Administrator's Account by same administrator
from 1842. Botetourt ticket; April 25, 1844. PITT WOODROOF, JOS. R.
CARTER, PETER FLOOD.
Book 11, Page 423 -- Estate Commitment to Sheriff -- September, 1846.
Motion of SUSAN GRANT. JAS. POWELL, Sheriff.
Book 11, Page 545 -- Administrator's Account by PETER RUCKER,
Administrator's de bonis non from 1846. JNO. WHITEHEAD, attorney-in-
fact for ELIZ. BURLEY. Recorded December 21, 1846. JOS. R. CARTER,
JNO. PRYOR, RO. H. CARTER.

MARTHA GREEN -- Book 1, Page 180 -- Guardian Bond -- WM. TRICE and
CHAS. RICE, September 3, 1770, for WM. TRICE as guardian of MARTHA
and MARY GREEN, orphans of FORRISTER GREEN.

ANN GREGORY -- Book 8, Page 170 -- Guradian Bond -- JNO. J. MAYS and
HENRY T. GREGORY, January 16, 1832, for JNO. MAYS as guardian of ANN
GREGORY, orphan of WM. GREGORY.

CLEMENTINE GREGORY -- Book 11, Page 553 -- Guardian Bond -- WM. LAW-
HORNE and GEO. SHRADER, August 16, 1847, for WM. LAWHORNE as guardian
of CLEMENTINE GREGORY; no parent set forth.

HARRIET GREGORY -- Book 7, Page 117 -- Guardian Bond -- JAS. LONDON
and JESSE MUNDY, February 21, 1828, for JAS. LONDON as guardian of
HARRIET GREGORY, orphan of LEWIS GREGORY, deceased.

HENRY GREGORY -- Book 6, Page 633 -- Guardian Bond -- JAS. LONDON,
JR., and RICH. W. LOND, November 21, 1825, for JAS. LONDON, JR.,
as guardian of HENRY ANN GREGORY, orphan of LEWIS GREGORY, deceased.

JAS. GREGORY -- Book 4, Page 452 -- Constable's Bond -- June 20,
1803. Bondsmen: SAML. SPENCER and JNO. ALFORD. To Governor JNO.
PAGE.
Book 4, Page 457 -- Constable's Bond -- June 18, 1805. Bondsman:
ZACH. WHITE.

JNO. GREGORY -- Book 3, Page 538 -- Inventory -- L 53-14-6, December 24,
1798. WM. BREEDLOVE, ALEX. BLAIN, CHAS. WATTS. WM. GREGORY, administrator.
Book 4, Page 309 -- Administrator's Bond -- WM. GREGORY and THOS.
GREGORY, December 17, 1798, for WM. GREGORY.

WM. GREGORY -- Book 7, Page 295 -- December 3, 1829, written; Decem-
ber 21, 1829, probated. Witnesses: LAWSON TURNER, ELLIS P. OMOHUNDRO,
DANL. DAY and proved by them. HENRY T. GREGORY refused to qualify
and March 15, 1830, MARTHA GREGORY qualified; Bondsmen: STEPHEN B.
TURNER and HENRY T. GREGORY. Ux, MARTHA, and children: WM. S.,
RUTH A., JACKSON, WASHINGTON, MARTHA F., AMANDA S., and JAS. H.
GREGORY - until youngest is 21. My 12 children: SARAH T. BREEDLOVE,
MARY MAYS, CATH. P. GREGORY, HENRY T., and ELIZ. L. STOREY and others
previously named above. My son, HENRY T., is to administer.
Book 8, Page 281 -- Administrator's de bonis non Bond -- October 15,
1832. STEPHEN B. TURNER and LAWSON TURNER for STEPHEN TURNER.
Book 8, Page 284 -- Inventory -- November 15, 1832 - $416.00. JONAS
PIERCE, WILEY CAMPBELL, JOS. KYLE.
Book 9, Page 26 -- Administrator's de bonis non Bond -- WINSTON PUR-
VIS and JAS. GARLAND, December 15, 1834, for WINSTON PURVIS.

JNO. GREINER -- Book 13, Page 283 -- Guardian Bond -- ISAAC O. STAN-

FIELD and RO. A. COGHILL, December 19, 1853, for ISAAC STANFIELD as guardian of JNO. GREINER, orphan of JNO. E. GREINER, deceased.

JNO. E. GREINER -- Book 13, Page 243 -- Administrator's Bond -- ANN F. GREINER, RO. A. COGHILL, and HENRY Y.(?) GREINER and ISAAC STANFIELD, November 21, 1853, for ANN GREINER.

REUBEN GRIFFIN -- Book 1, Page 380 -- March 1, 1776, written; September 1, 1777, probated. Witnesses: BENJ. TALIAFERRO, THOS. HAWKINS, THOS. GRIFFIN, WILL POWELL. Have engaged in service of my country. Brother, JNO. GRIFFIN, and his son, THOS., until of age. Bonds are due from HENRY LONG and SAML. STAPLES. Executors: WM. MARTIN and ABRAHAM WARWICK. Codicil: This will is of no effect, if I return. Same witnesses, but no date. Proved by HAWKINS, GRIFFIN, and POWELL.

CHAS. GRISSOM -- Book 5, Page 56 -- Inventory -- L 108-6-0, December 26, 1811. WM. JOPLING, TINSLEY RUCKER, MOZA PETERS. Book 5, Page 80 -- Administrator's Bond -- THOS. GRISSOM and THOS. COLEMAN, September 14(?), 1811, for THOS. GRISSOM. Book 5, Page 196 -- Administrator's Account by administrator from September 26, 1811. Recorded February 18, 1813.

LUCINDA GRISSOM -- Book 5, Page 204 -- Guardian Bond -- BENJ. CARTER and JNO. RICHESON, February 15, 1813, for BENJ. CARTER as guardian of LUCINDA GRISSOM, orphan of ROBT. GRISSOM.

POLLY GRISSOM (Most of these are indexed for GRISSON) -- Book 4, Page 284 -- Relinquishes right to administer estate of deceased husband, THOS. GRISSOM, and asks that her father, WM. SLEDD, be appointed. March 14, 1807. Witnesses: N. VANSTAVERN, WM. WARE, CARROLINE SLEDD.

ROBT. GRISSOM -- Book 4, Page 444 -- Administrator's Bond -- WM. SLEDD, WM. CAMDEN, and NICHL. VANSTAVERN, March 16, 1807, for WM. SLEDD. Book 4, Page 566 -- Inventory -- no total. JOS. PERKINS, JR.; JA.(?) TINSLEY; RICH. (PRICHARD?) PENDLETON, December 19, 1808. Book 5, Page 646 -- Administrator's Account by SLEDD from 1803. Cash to SALLY, THOS., and WM. GRISSOM, March 1, 1817. THOS. N. EUBANK, BENJ. TALIAFERRO, WM. JOPLING, JNO. WARE.

THOS. GRISSOM -- Book 4, Page 612 -- March 14, 1808, written; December 18, 1809, probated. Witnesses: RODERICH McCULLOCH, SAML. BURKS, WM. WARE, TINSLEY RUCKER, MADISON WARE. Reference to codicil, but not there, January 15, 1810. Proved by RUCKER. CHAS. GRISSOM qualified. Bondsmen: WM. WILMORE, THOS. GRISSOM, SALLY GRISSOM, TINSLEY RUCKER. Sons: JNO., THOS., and CHAS.; daughter, SALLY GRISSOM; daughter, SUSANNA WILLMORE; granddaughter, LUNDY(?) GRISSOM, orphan daughter of my son, ROBERT, deceased. Either of my single children - where I live and other land on Harris Creek. Ux, SUSANNA; LUCINDA, daughter of deceased son, ROBERT - in one place it seems to be LUNDY and in another it appears to be LUCIDA, but here it is LUCINDA. Executors: Sons, THOS. and CHAS. and friend, AMBROSE RUCKER, JR. Book 5, Page 77 -- Administrator's Bond -- THOS. GRISSOM, BENJ. RUCKER, RICH. BURKS, and TINSLEY RUCKER, August 19, 1811, for THOS. GRISSOM. Book 5, Page 201 -- Inventory -- L 590-10-9, February 15, 1813. WM. JOPLING, EDMD. GOODRICH, WM. PETER. Book 6, Page 203 -- Administrator's Bond -- THOS. GRISSOM, JAM (TOM?) COLEMAN, and CHAS. MOORE, January 13, 1821, for THOS. GRISSOM. Book 6, Page 227 -- Administrator's Account by THOS. GRISSOM from June 4, 1811 - to EDMD. GOODRICH for sums borrowed before marriage; DR. JENNINGS' deed from Kentucky; deed to R. BURKS; account of CHAS. GRISSOM; land sold to WM. WILMORE. June 18, 1821. R. NORVELL; ELIAS WILLS, N. C. DAWSON.

WM. GRISSOM -- Book 4, Page 275 -- Inventory -- L 33-9-4 -- ISAAC or JA.(?) TINSLEY; RICH. PENDLETON; WM. PETER, February 16, 1807. Book 4, Page 441 -- Administrator's Bond -- THOS. GRISSOM and WM. WARE, January 19, 1807, for THOS. GRISSOM.

WM. GUARD -- Book 11, Page 20 -- Administrator's Bond -- JNO. WHITE-

HEAD and RO. M. BROWN, April 18, 1842, for JNO. WHITEHEAD. On margin:
May 16, 1842, original delivered to CHAS. TUCKER. Beneath Administrator's Bond is item about estate. April 18, 1842. Received of CHAS.
TUCKER, one of administrators of CHAS. TUCKER, deceased - $155.54 in
full of all claims and demands of JNO. ENGLAND in right of his ux,
NANCY PARSONS, and of WM. GUARD in right of his ux, PATSEY PARSONS --
their wives respective shares of consideration money for land sold to
CHAS. TUCKER in his lifetime. JNO. WHITEHEAD, administrator of England
and Guard.

JNO. GUE (Indexed for JUDITH GILBERT) -- Book 6, Page 250 -- Adminis-
istrator's Bond -- ROSEMARY GUE and MARTIN PARKS, September 17, 1821,
for ROSEMARY GUE. I might point out that ROSEMARY is not a woman in
this case.

ELIZ. GUTHRIE -- Book 7, Page 189 -- Administrator's Bond -- CAMPBELL
FRANKLIN, THOS. FRANKLIN, JNO. and NICHL. GUTHRIE, November 17, 1828,
for CAMPBELL FRANKLIN.
Book 7, Page 202 -- Inventory -- $648.06-1/2, January 19, 1828.
JESSE BECK, JAS. DAVIS, WILLIS REYNOLDS.
Book 7, Page 188 -- Guardian Bond -- CAMPBELL FRANKLIN, and others as
in Book 7, Page 189 - same date - for CAMPBELL FRANKLIN as guardian
of NATHAN, SUSAN, SARAH, OLIVER P. and ELIZ. GUTHRIE, orphans of
WM. GUTHRIE.
        Some scribe has put "P" above LAWRENCE and must have done so
after consulting a later item herein.

LUCY GUTHRIE -- Book 7, Page 145 -- Guardian Bond -- ELIZ. GUTHRIE,
WM. TURNER, JAS. PETIT, WM. M. BOLLING, and WILLIS M. REYNOLDS,
March 17, 1828, for ELIZ. GUTHRIE as guardian of LUCY, NATHAN, SUSAN,
SARAH, LAURENCE, OLIVER and ELIZ. GUTHRIE, orphans of WM. GUTHRIE,
deceased.

NATHAN GUTHRIE -- Book 14, Page 585 -- October 23, 1849, written;
July 19, 1858, probated. Witnesses: RO. C. MARTIN, WM. M. BOWLING.
Sisters: SUSAN STOCKTON and SARAH GUTHRIE. Executrix: SUSAN STOCK-
TON.

NICHOLAS GUTHRIE -- Book 6, Page 619 -- Guardian Bond -- ELIZ. GUTHRIE,
JAS. S. LAMKIN, WM. TURNER, DANL. DAY, September 19, 1825, for ELIZ.
GUTHRIE as guardian of NICHL., LUCY, NATHAN, and SUSAN GUTHRIE, or-
phans of WM. GUTHRIE.
Book 8, Page 187 -- Guardian Bond -- NICHL. GUTHRIE, THOS. WINGFIELD,
and NATHAN GUTHRIE, March 21, 1832, for NICHL. GUTHRIE as guardian
of SALLY, LAURENCE P., OLIVER, and ELIZ. GUTHRIE, orphans of WM.
GUTHRIE.

WM. GUTHRIE -- Book 6, Page 454 -- Administrator's Bond -- ELIZ.
GUTHRIE, HENRY TURNER, JESSE BECK, JAS. DAVIES, and WM. DAY, May 17,
1824, for ELIZ. GUTHRIE.
Book 6, Page 602 -- Inventory -- $7,381.78, September 1, 1824. WM.
TURNER, ELIAS WILLS, CHAS. PALMORE.
Book 6, Page 644 -- Sale, January 2, 1826. Buyers: ELIZ. and JNO.
GUTHRIE.
Book 7, Page 187 -- Administrator's Bond -- CAMPBELL FRANKLIN, THOS.
FRANKLIN, JNO. and NICHL. GUTHRIE, November 17, 1828, for estate to
be administered by CAMPBELL FRANKLIN; unadministered by ELIZ. GUTHRIE.
Book 8, Page 7 -- Administrator's Account -- ELIZ. GUTHRIE, May 17,
1830 -- probably submitted by committee after her death. Necessaries
for family in 1825 and taxes in 1824. Committee of CHAS. MUNDY and
GEO. STAPLES.

                              -H-

HENRY HAGGARD -- Book 9, Page 237 -- Guardian Bond -- NELSON J. LONDON
and JAS. G. CHRISTIAN, July 18, 1836, for NELSON LONDON as guardian of
HENRY HAGGARD, orphan of JNO. HAGGARD, deceased.

EDNA HALEY -- Book 13, Page 17 -- Guardian Bond -- TANDY JONES and
S. M. GARLAND, September 20, 1852, for TANDY JONES as guardian of
EDNA HALEY, orphan of GEO. W. HALEY.

FRANCIS HALL -- Book 9, Page 345 -- Refunding Bond -- October 28,
1837, FRANCIS and ELIZ. HALL, and LEWIS COLEMAN to THOS. EWERS, executor of JNO. EWERS, deceased. HALLS have received $297.42 as share
of estate of JNO. EWERS.

JNO. HALL -- Book 12, Page 325 -- Administrator's Bond -- RO. H. CAR-
TER and ZACH. DRUMMOND, November 18, 1850, for RO. CARTER.
Book 12, Page 350 -- Inventory -- December 12, 1850 - no total. HART-
WELL T. PRYOR, WM. H. BARNES, PITT WOODROOF.
Book 12, Page 471 -- Sale, December 23, 1850. CHAS. L. B., DAVID N.,
R. H. CARTER, administrator. CHAS. L. and DAVID were HALL buyers.
Total: $41.36.
Book 13, Page 96 -- Administrator's Account -- RO. H. CARTER from
November 18, 1850. Recorded November 17, 1852.

MOSES HALL -- Book 5, Page 492 -- Administrator's Bond -- THOS. N.
EUBANK and JAS. WARE, March 20, 1815, for THOS. EUBANK.
Book 5, Page 531 -- Inventory -- November 20, 1815 - $633.02. NELSON
CRAWFORD, GEO. M. BROWN, ABRAM CARTER.

SALLY HALL -- Book 5, Page 599 -- Guardian Bond -- HANNAH HALL,
PHILLIP THURMOND, and JNO. MEHONE, August 19, 1816, for HANNAH HALL
as guardian of SALLY and ELVIRA HALL, orphans of MOSES HALL.

WILLIAM HALL -- Book 6, Page 354 -- May 8, 1817, written; May 19,
1823, probated. Witnesses: JNO. S. BLAIR, JACOB HAY, GEO. MAYS. Of
New Glasgow, Amherst County - adopted daughter, SEPHONIA HALL. Executors: friends: JNO. P. COBBS and THOMAS ALDRIDGE. JNO. FRY, husband
of SEMPHRONIA (sic) HALL, qualified. Bondsmen: HENRY KNIGHT,
HEZEKIAH FULCHER on probate date; Page 356.

        I am putting no numbers for HALLOWAY for all data is spelled
HOLLOWAY and shows thus.

ANDREW HAMBLETON -- Book 4, Page 461 -- Constable's Bond -- June 16,
1806. Bondsman: JOSEPH MILSTEAD.
Book 5, Page181 -- Admini-trator's Bond -- ELIZ. HAMBLETON, September 21, 1812. Bondsmen: JNO. MAYS and JNO. CRAWFORD.

FRANCES HAMBLETON (Indexed FRANCIS HAMILTON) -- Book 5, Page 395 --
Guardian Bond -- October 18, 1813. ZACH. LANGSDON and MERRIT M. WHITE
for ZACH. LANGSDON as guardian of FRANCES HAMBLETON, orphan of ANDREW
HAMBLETON.

JAMES PRESTON HAMBLETON (Indexed for JNO. P.) -- Book 10, Page 386 --
Guardian Bond -- JNO. P. HAMBLETON, NELSON COFFEE, and WM. HAMBLETON,
August 16, 1841, for JNO. HAMBLETON as guardian of JAS. PRESTON
HAMBLETON,orphan of ROBT. HAMBLETON, deceased.

LUKE HAMBLETON -- Book 3, Page 26 -- Administrator's Bond -- SUSANNAH
HAMBLETON, JAS. HAMBLETON, and RICHARD LITTRELL, February 5, 1787,
for SUSANNAH HAMBLETON.

ROBT. HAMBLETON -- Book 10, Page 342 -- Administrator's Bond -- JNO. B.
DUNCAN, JNO. W. BROADDUS, and EDMD. C. MOORE, April 19, 1841, for
JNO. DUNCAN.
Book 10, Page 354 -- Inventory -- someone has added total and put it
in with pencil - CORNL. SALE, ABSALOM HIGGINBOTHAM, WM. TUCKER,
CHAS. TUCKER. Memo: Horses improperly appraised because he had given
them out in lifetime to make portions of the three to whom given equal
to rest in distribution. Admitted by all distributees--they being
of full age. JNO. B. DUNCAN, administrator, May 17, 1841.

ROBT. LEWIS HAMBLETON -- Book 10, Page 386 -- Guardian Bond -- NELSON
COFFEE, JNO. P. HAMBLETON, and WILLIAM HAMBLETON, August 16, 1841,
for NELSON COFFEE as guardian of RO. LEWIS HAMBLETON, orphan of
ROBT. HAMBLETON.

ARCHER HAMLET -- Book 3, Page 378 -- September 29, 1795, written; February 15, 1796, probated. Witnesses: WM. FITZPATRICK, GEO. MARTIN, WM. JOHNSON. Ux, SUSANNAH; heirs of my body; NANCY; FANNY; WILLIAM; THOMAS; LUCY; JOHN; and SUSANNA HAMLET. Executors: ux, HENRY MARTIN, and RO. RIVES.
Book 3, Page 415 -- Administrator's Bond -- SUSANNAH HAMLET, BARTLETT EADES,and RO. RIVES, February 15, 1796, for SUSANNAH HAMLET.
Book 3, Page 449 -- Inventory -- October 14, 1797 -- L 312-2-6. HENRY MARTIN, SR.; JNO. ENNIS; WM. JOHNSON.
Book 4, Page 298 -- Administrator's Bond -- SUSANNAH HAMLET, BARTLETT EADES, and RO. RIVES, February 15, 1796, for SUSANNAH HAMLET.

JAS. HAMM -- Book 5, Page 67 -- Indexed as Guardian Bond, but it is incomplete. There are gaps for names on blank day of October, 1810. Signed by JAS. HAM and WM. TURNER.

STEPHEN HAMM -- Book 5, Page 57 -- September 1, 1810, written; February 17, 1812, probated. Witnesses: JNO. LONDON and WM. TURNER. Ux, MILLY; son, JOHN; four grandchildren - children of my deceased daughter, FRANCES PLUNKETT: JONATHAN, WILLIS, WILLIAM, and MILLY RUCKER PLUNKETT. My sons, JAS. and AMBROSE HAMM; daughter, LUCY TURNER; daughter, ELIZABETH KNIGHT; son, WILLIAM; son, SAMUEL; daughter, SUSANNA DOUGLAS - sum loaned to ROBT. DOUGLAS, to her. Daughter, POLLY DOUGLAS; son, BARTLETT HAMM; daughter, SALLY TURNER. Executors: Ux and friends, JESSE BECK and CHAS. MUNDY.
Book 5, Page 91 -- Administrator's Bond -- CHAS. MUNDY, HENRY and WM. TURNER, July 17, 1812, for CHAS. MUNDY.
Book 5, Page 98 -- Administrator's Bond -- JESSE BECK, ELIAS WILLS, March 16, 1812, for JESSE BECK.
Book 5, Page 101 -- Inventory -- May 2, 1812 -- $4,584.94, JNO. LONDON; HENRY TURNER; WM. CLINKSCALES.
Book 6, Page 573 -- Administrator's Account -- JESSE BECK and CHAS. MUNDY - mention of Campbell County sheriff; CAPT. TURNER for services; JESSE BECK "for pailing in graveyard"; legacy of JAS. HAMM; SAML. HAMM; ELIZ. KNIGHT; DAVID DOUGHLAS; RICH. TURNER; SUSANNA DOUGLAS and legatees of BENJ. PLUNKETT. Total: $11,437.50. JNO. GARTH; JNO. WARWICK; GEO. STAPLES.
Book 7, Page 3 -- Administrator's Account by same administrators. To WM. HAMM; ELIZ. KNIGHT; JAMES HAMM; R. TURNER - $1,159.75. Recorded April 15, 1829.

STEPHEN HAMMOND -- Book 3, Page 194 -- Guardian Bond -- JACOB GIBSON and JACOB TYREE, August 4, 1791, for JACOB GIBSON as guardian of STEPHEN, SAML., and HARMOND HAMMOND, orphans of JANE HAMMOND.

JNO. HAMNER, SR. -- Book 14, Page 450 -- Administrator's Bond -- WM. A. HAMNER, GEO. W. FOSTER, and JAS. S. HAMNER,September 21, 1857, for WM. HAMNER.
Book 15, Page 256 -- Inventory -- November 21, 1859: CHAS. L. BROWN, HENRY WHITE, RO. H. THORNTON.

WM. HANNAH -- Book 24, Page 213 -- May 3, 1837; Botetourt County and recorded in Amherst County on September 18, 1916. Attested by TURNER McDOWELL, Clerk of Circuit Court of Botetourt. Ux, JANE C. - one-fourth of three-fourths to my three children: PRESSLY T., WM. S., and ANN ELIZ. -- at marriage or when 21. Witnesses: JACOB FEAZEL; WM. NACE. I have not checked, but suspect that some THORNTON estate may have been involved. In the unrecorded marriages here is one of August 21, 1820, for WM. HANNAH and JANE C. THORNTON. Bondsman: PETER P. THORNTON.

CAROLINE HANSARD -- Book 5, Page 508 -- Administrator's Bond -- June 19, 1815, for JNO. HANSARD to administer. Bondsman: WM. McDANIEL.
Book 8, Page 430 -- Administrator's Bond -- September 15, 1834, for HENRY W. QUARLES. Bondsman: LINDSEY McDANIEL. Another unrecorded marriage here is for CAROLINE HANSARD to PHILIP BURFORD, October 23, 1821. Her father, JNO. HANSARD, gave consent. SAML. HEISKELL was surety and he and GEO. H. BURFORD were witnesses. The CAROLINE who died in 1815 was a RUCKER and first ux of JNO. HANSARD. A study of

JOHN HANSARD's will does not show a first set of children for he merely names all of them. There is a very long suit in order book for 1821 ff period which sets out the whole family picture as to first ux and second.

ISAAC HANSARD -- Book 6, Page 744 -- Guardian Bond -- THOS. STRANGE and LINDSEY McDANIEL, March 19, 1827, for THOS. STRANGE as guardian of ISAAC HANSARD, orphan of JOHN HANSARD, deceased.

ISAAC R. HANSARD -- Book 17, Page 252 -- Administrator's Account -- RO. W. SNEAD, sheriff, and administrator from December 31, 1860, to December 31, 1864.

JNO. HANSARD -- Book 5, Page 7 -- Guardian's Account -- JNO. PALMORE, guardian -- to STEPHEN ROBERSON to carry you to Cumberland; to WM. HANSARD; to THOS. JOHNSON's part of land. THOS. S. McCALALAND(?); JNO. CAMM, November 21, 1810.
Book 6, Page 710 -- Administrator's Bond -- December 18, 1826: WM. McDANIEL, JNO. TALBOTT, H. L. DAVIES for WM. McDANIEL.
Book 6, Page 717 -- Inventory -- January 15, 1817 - $4,228.22. Harris Creek land. D. STRANGE, LINDSEY McDANIEL, SAML. WATTS.
Book A, Page 125 -- March 10, 1825, written; April term, 1827, probated. Witnesses: PETER CASHWELL, LINDSEY COGHILL, THOS. STRANGE. February 19, 1827, ANSON TINSLEY and ELIJAH DAVIS, appellees - court refused to admit to probate. I have found a very long account of the contest over the will in orders, but have never had the chance to read every page of some data which is faded. I have read enough of it, though, to be positive as to some points: JOHN HANSARD was much the worse for his love of the flowing bowl; his first wife was a RUCKER - her brother testified to this - all of his children were by first ux, save PETER C. HANSARD. PETER was by second ux, JUDITH CASHWELL; there was "common" education for first set and one, not named, became a doctor. The marriage to JUDITH CASHWELL is not of record here. His His first marriage to CAROLINE RUCKER took place in 1793 -- see Amherst marriages to 1801 by Sweeny. In deed data here JUDITH refers to PETER C. as "my only child." JOHN made a deed of trust for two of his girls, and one was in Alabama. The suit refers to fact that first set of children were in poor circumstances. It would take pages to abstract this interesting suit. The will was admitted. Therein he refers to ux, JUDY - 260 acres on Linch Road; slaves; son, PETER C.; son, ISAAC - land adjoining TINSLEY, WM. McDANIEL, and ANTHONY RUCKER. My children: JOHN, AMBROSE, ARCHY, SOPIA, POLEY, PERMELY, and CAROLINE. (Mother was CAROLINE RUCKER, daughter of AMROSE RUCKER.)
Book A, Page 132 -- Inventory -- RICHARDSON HENLEY, deputy sheriff and administrator: $3,168.50. JAS. S. LAMKIN, WM. BOURNE, JNO. WILLIAMS. ("M." middle initial), February 19, 1830.
Book B, Page 6 -- Inventory at residence of PETER CASHWELL, December 31, 1835. Many slaves and ages. BLANSFORD HICKS; JAS. McDANIEL; WM. J. SHELTON.
Book B, Page 6 -- Administrator's Bond -- RICHARDSON HENLEY, BENJ. TALIAFERRO, and JNO. W. BROADDUS, September 4, 1834, for RICHARDSON HENLEY.
Book 11, Page 254 -- Administrator's Bond -- WM. McDANIEL and SAML. WATTS, January 30, 1845, for WM. McDANIEL with will annexed.
Book 13, Page 479 -- Administrator's Account -- JAS. S. LAMKIN, late sheriff from September 20, 1849. Recorded July 31, 1854.

JUDITH HANSARD (N. CASHWELL) -- Book 12, Page 266 -- January 30, 1850, written; February 18, 1850, probated. Witnesses: NELSON and NICHL. HICKS. Old and infirm and incapable of handling affairs. Appoints DR. JAS. POWELL to act for her. In one deed book item, she states that her son, PETER C. -- "my only child" - is "an easy prey" and she takes affairs out of his hands. PETER C. signed the document.
Book 12, Page 273 -- April --, 1849, written; July 15, 1850, probated. Witnesses: STEPHEN BOWLES, NICHL. HICKS, WM. P. MORRIS. To JAS. POWELL, SR.; my niece, POLLY ALLEN and POWELL as trustee "during her widowhood." Children of POLLY: JAS. M. and ANN ALLEN; to JAS. M. CASHWELL; my niece, FANNY CASHWELL; sister of POLLY ALLEN. Faithful servant, Oney - house and two acres. Executors: friends: SAML. M. GARLAND and PAULUS POWELL.

JAMES HANSBROUGH -- Book 3, Page 512 -- October 16, 1797, Tye River
Warehouse Tobacco Inspector. Bondsman: JNO. LOVING, JR.
Book 3, Page 512 -- September 17, 1798. Inspector at Swan Creek
Warehouse. Bondsmen: JNO. BAGBY and JOS. SHELTON.
Book 4, Page 188 -- February 7, 1805, written; September 16, 1805,
probated. Signed HANSBERRY, but indexed HANSBROUGH. Witnesses:
NELSON ANDERSON, EDWIN H. WAIDE. Ux, MARTHA - land devised to me by
my father, WM. HANSBERRY. Brother, SAML. - land bought from him. My
4 children: MARY HICKMAN; ELIZ., HENRIETA, and PETER - until of age
or married. Executors may see fit to buy more of my father's land.
Executors: Brother, SAML., and JAS. MURPHY of town of Warminster.
Book 4, Page 221 -- Inventory -- November 29, 1805. L 100-5-0.
JNO. HIGGINBOTHAM, AUSTIN WRIGHT, S. CROSTHWAIT. Recorded June 16,
1806.
        These various bonds were not recorded until later:
Book 4, Page 256 -- Tobacco Inspector -- Tye River Warehouse,
September 19, 1803. Bondsman: JNO. LOVING.
Book 4, Page 237 -- Same -- September 16, 1799. Bondsman: JNO.
LOVING.Book 4, Page 241 -- Same -- October 16, 1798. Bondsman: JNO.
LOVING, JR.
Book 4, Page 243 -- Same -- September 15, 1800. Bondsman: JNO.
LOVING.
Book 4, Page 246 -- Same -- September --, 1801. Bondsman: JNO.
LOVING.
Book 4, Page 250 -- Same -- September 20, 1802. Same bondsman.
Book 4, Page 411 -- Administrator's Bond -- SAML. HANSBROUGH, JAS.
MURPHY, NELSON ANDERSON, and WM. LEE HARRIS, September 16, 1805, for
SAML. HANSBROUGH and JAS. MURPHY.
Book 6, Book 6 444 -- December 18, 1823, written; March 15, 1824, pro-
bated. Witnesses: JNO. W. YOUNG, CHAS. L. BARRET, ELIJAH BARNES.
Of county of Monroe, but presently in Amherst County. Sisters:
MARY H. BOWLES, Monroe County; ELIZ. SMITH, Nelson County; aunt,
SALLY HANSBROUGH, Amherst County. Executors: friends: MORDIQUE
BOWLES, Monroe County; and NELSON SMITH, Nelson County.

SAML. HANSBROUGH -- Book 3, Page 391 -- Tobacco Inspector -- Warmin-
ster Warehouse, September 19, 1796. Bondsmen: CHAS. STATHAM and
JESSE WILLS.
Book 3, Page 511 -- Tobacco Inspector -- Swan Creek Warehouse,
September 18, 1797. Bondsman: WM. B. HARE.
Book 4, Page 238 -- Tobacco Inspector -- Swan Creek Warehouse,
September 16, 1799. Bondsman: GEO. LOVING.
Book 4, Page 244 -- Tobacco Inspector -- Swan Creek Warehouse,
September 15, 1800. Bondsman: BENJ. CHILDRESS.
Book 4, Page 253 -- Same -- September 20, 1802. Bondsman: JNO.
THOMPSON.
Book 4, Page 259 -- So indexed, but nothing there on him.

WILLIAM HANSBROUGH -- Book 1, Page 494 -- September 30, 1778, written;
September 6, 1779, probated. Witnesses: JNO. PETER, ELIZ. BALL,
EZEKIAH BAILEY, GEO. HAY, REBECCA BAILEY. Son, CALEB; daughter, ELIZ.
BALL; daughter, RACHEL KEY; son, WILLIAM - land next to WM. CABELL;
JULIAN NEAL and JAS. NEVIL. Daughters, SARAH and CHARLOTTE, when
married; mention of non-patented land on Glade and Cabell's Mill
Creek. Son, JNO., when 21; sons, JAS., SAML., and PETER, when 21.
Ux, KEZIAH. Sons are to be bound out to learn trades when 17.
Executors: ux, KEZIAH; son, WILLIAM; and friends, WM. and JNO.
LOVING, and WM. CABELL, JR.
Book 1, Page 497 -- Administrator's Bond -- KEZIAH HANSBROUGH; JNO.
LOVING, JR.; EZEKIAH BAILEY; and JNO. PENN, September 6, 1779, for
KEZIAH HANSBROUGH and JNO. LOVING, JR.
Book 2, Page 4 -- Inventory -- L 2,152-10-0, February 5, 1781. RICH.
MURROW, JAMES MATTHEWS, ABRAM WARWICK.
Book 3, Page 580 -- Administrator's Account by executors above from
1781. Recorded August 18, 1800. WM. JOHNSON; JAS. STEWART, JR.;
JNO. WARWICK.
Book 6, Page 221 -- Administrator's Bond -- JAS. MURPHY, SAML. HANS-
BROUGH, and HENRY H. WATTS, February 19, 1821, for JAS. MURPHY.
        These two items are indexed under JAS. HANSBROUGH:
Book 6, Page 263 -- Administrator's Account -- SAML. HANSBROUGH from

March 15, 1805. Bond of KEZIAH HANSBROUGH; estate of WM. HANSBROUGH -
1/2 of land proceeds. JESSE JOPLING, ZACH. NEVIL, WILLIS H.(?) WILLS.
Book 6, Page 264 -- Administrator's Account -- SAML. HANSBROUGH -
from October 1, 1821 - land sold agreeable to will of WM. HANSBROUGH.
Same committee.
     Note: This family was in Nelson cut-off and there is more on
them in Nelson. I recall one will wherein a mother refers to a son
as being in Shelby County, Kentucky. I was reared there and there are
members of the HANSBROUGH family there. Data in my Kentucky books
seems to show at least two branches in Shelby, but may be connected.

JNO. HARDIN and Children -- Book 7, Page 336 -- Guardian Bond --
April 19, 1830. ZACH. DRUMMOND and WM. DILLARD for ZACH. DRUMMOND as
guardian of JNO., CHAS., and JANE HARDIN, infant children of JNO.
HARDIN.

GROVES HARDING -- Book 2, Page 41 -- July 20, 1781, written; April 2,
1782, probated. Witnesses: THOS. FARRAR; SAML. WARD; SUSANNAH WARD;
JAS. NEVIL, JR. Son, EDWARD - ROBERT's tract where he lives. Son,
JOHN - 410 acres where I live - when JNO. is of age. Daughters:
BETSY, SALLY, and LUCY. 4 youngest - BETSY, SALLY, JNO., and LUCY -
when of age; or married. Executors: friends, JAS. NEVIL, NICHL.
CABELL, STEPHEN TURNER. They qualified on same date - probate.
Book 2, Page 48 -- Inventory -- April 22, 1782. JAS. MATTHEWS, THOS.
JOPLING, WM. JOHNSON - done on Monday.

PHOEBE HARDING -- Book B, Page 44 -- ZACH. DRUMMOND and CHAS. MASSIE,
August 24, 1852, for ZACH. DRUMMOND; no parent set forth. ZACH.
DRUMMOND to be guardian.

WM. HARDING -- Book 6, Page 389 -- Administrator's Bond -- September 15, 1823, RO. J. KINCAID. Bondsmen: JAS. GARLAND and JAS. M.
BROWN for RO. KINCAID.

JAS. HARDWICK -- Book 6, Page 435 -- Guardian Bond -- SAML. GARLAND
and JACOB HAAS, January 19, 1823, for SAML. GARLAND as guardian of
JAS. HARDWICK, orphan of RICH. HARDWICK.

JNO. HARDWICK -- Book 3, Page 5 -- March 6, 1786. JNO. HARDWICK and
EDMD. WINSTON to secure BALLINGER WADE et. al. on bond to executors
of PIERCE WADE.

LINDSEY HARDWICK (Indexed as HENDRICK) -- Book 6, Page 396 -- Guardian
Bond -- SAML. and DAVID S. GARLAND, October 20, 1823, for SAML. GAR-
LAND as guardian of LINDSEY HARDWICK, orphan of RICHARD HARDWICK.

ROBT. C. HARDWICK -- Book 6, Page 280 -- Guardian Bond -- SAML. M.
GARLAND and THOS. COLEMAN, March 19, 1822, for SAML. GARLAND as guardian of RO. C. HARDWICK, orphan of RICHARD HARDWICK. RICH. HARDWICK
got bond to marry NANCY COLEMAN, October 20, 1794. Bachelor and
spinster. JAS. MARR was surety. ELIZ. COLEMAN, mother of NANCY, gave
consent.

NATHANIEL HARLOW -- Book 4, Page 503 -- Constable's Bond -- February 15, 1808. Bondsmen: JAS. H. BURTON and MATT. HARRIS.

HENRY MEAD HARRIS -- Book 12, Page 141 -- Guardian Bond -- MARSHALL L.
HARRIS, JNO. THOMPSON, and SAML. M. GARLAND, December 18, 1848, for
MARSHALL HARRIS as guardian of his infant son, HENRY MEAD HARRIS.

JNO. HARRIS -- Book 3, Page 411 -- Inventory -- L 280-11-8, Novem-
ber 13, 1795. RICH. SHELTON, P. BURTON, RICH. POWELL.
Book 3, Page 565 -- Inventory -- November 30, 1799. MATT. HARRIS,
ALEX. McALEXANDER, BENJ. CHILDRESS. Indexed for HARRISON.
Book 4, Page 308 -- Administrator's Bond -- ELIZ. HARRIS, April 15,
1799. Bondsman: WM. HARRIS.

JOSHUA HARRIS -- Book 4, Page 285 -- Guardian Bond -- SARAH HARRIS,
JNO. BUCK, and REUBIN HARRIS, October 21, 1799, for SARAH HARRIS
as guardian of JOSHUA, JNO., and BETSY HARRIS, orphans of SAML.

HARRIS, deceased.

LEE HARRIS -- Book 3, Page 220 -- January 14, 1792, written; April 16, 1792, probated. Witnesses: PLEASANT MARTIN, BENJ. CHILDRESS, JOS. SHELTON. Sons, MATT. and WM. LEE HARRIS - land where they live - CHILDRESS line; across the cree; Mountain to CLOUGH SHELTON which he bought of ROBERTSON. My 4 youngest sons: JNO, JESSE, EDWD., and NATHAN. My six youngest: JNO., JESSE, EDWD., NATHAN, POLLY and SALLY - if no issue. Ux, WINNEY; daughter, ELIZ. MONTGOMERY, deceased. Executors: friends: WM. HARRIS and JOS. SHELTON.
Book 3, Page 228 -- Administrator's Bond -- WM. HARRIS and JOS. SHELTON, June 18, 1792, for both to administer. Bondsmen: NATHAN CRAWFORD and WM. LEE HARRIS.
Book 3, Page 254 -- Inventory -- L 1,168-12-6; many slaves - PLEASANT MARTIN, JOSIAH JOPLING, WM. LYON. December 17, 1792.

MARY HARRIS -- Book 3, Page 320 -- Guardian Bond -- JNO. HARRIS, PLEASANT MARTIN, and LEWIS NEVIL, October 20, 1794, for JNO. HARRIS as guardian of MARY and SALLY HARRIS, orphans of LEE HARRIS, deceased.

MATT. HARRIS -- Book 4, Page 417 -- (Indexed for MARTHA HARRIS) -- Inventory, June 16, 1805. L 3,240-6-0. HAWES COLEMAN, SAML. BRIDGWATER, THOS. FITZPATRICK.

SAML. HARRIS -- Book 3, Page 567 -- Inventory -- December 2, 1799; no total. MATT. HARRIS, JOSEPH ROBERTS, A. McALEXANDER.
Book 4, Page 285 -- (Indexed as 255) -- Administrator's Bond -- SARAH HARRIS, JNO. BUCK, REUBIN HARRIS, October 21, 1799, for SARAH HARRIS.
Book 4, Page 503 -- Administrator's Account -- December 5, 1807, order of October, 1806. STEVEN HENDERSON and ux, SALLY, late HARRIS, administratrix. L 83-13-11-1/2. JAS. WILLS, JR.; JAMES STEVENS, JR.; THOS. E. FORTUNE.

WM. HARRIS -- Book 4, Page 545 -- Sheriff's Bond -- November 19, 1804. Bondsmen: RO. RIVES, WM. H. CABELL, NATHAN CRAWFORD.

WINNEY HARRIS -- Book 5, Page 397 -- Administrator's Bond -- RICH. and SAML. BURKS, November 15, 1813, for RICH. BURKS.

ALBERT HARRISON -- Book 10, Page 136 -- Constable -- June 17, 1839. Bondsmen: LEWIS HARRISON and JAS. S. HIGGINBOTHAM.
Book 15, Page 333 -- Sheriff - elected May 24, 1860. Bond of July 16, 1860. Bondsmen: THOS. WHITEHEAD; JNO. THOMPSON, JR.; TAYLOR BERRY; RO. W. SNEAD; CHAS. MASSIE; A. L. FOGUS; M. C. GOODWIN; R. MABEN; JNO. R. HARRISON; RO. A. PENDLETON; RO. A. COGHILL; JAS. B. DAVIS; B. L. TALIAFERRO; ALFRED W. WILLIAMS; DAVID APPLING.
Book 17, Page 466 -- Guardian's Account -- Indexed for him, but his name is not there. See JNO. R. HARRISON.

BATTAILE HARRISON -- Book 1, Page 317 -- December 3, 1775, written; October 7, 1776, probated. Witnesses: AMBROSE TOMLINSON, WM. WHITTEN, JAS. HARRISON, RICH. SHELTON. Ux, FRANCES - where I live; daughter, FRANKEY HARRISON; daughter, BETTY TINSLEY; son, REUBEN - when he married; son, JOHN, when he married; son, RICHARD, when he married. My 7 children - youngest: JAS., WM., and FRANKEY.
Book 1, Page 318 -- Administrator's Bond -- REUBEN HARRISON, RICH. BALLINGER, GEO. McDANIEL, October 7, 1776, for REUBEN HARRISON.
Book 1, Page 385 -- Inventory -- L 536-19-8-1/2. RICH. SHELTON, BENJ. RUCKER, ANTHONY RUCKER. October 6, 1777.
Book 3, Page 101 -- Division, but no details. April 7, 1789. RODERICK McCULLOCH and DAVID WOODROOF.

CAROLINE HARRISON -- Book 11, Page 75 -- Division report: ZACH. D. TINSLEY, JNO. H. ROBERTS, RO. ISBELL, December 29, 1841, divided estate for PAUL E. HARRISON, CAROLINE HARRISON; BENJ. B. TALIAFERRO, guardian of RICH. and SOPHIA HARRISON - slaves to them. PAUL is called PAULUS in summary. Nothing is said here of parents.

FRANCIS HARRISON -- Book 3, Page 96 -- Administrator's Bond -- RICH. HARRISON, JNO. HARRISON, GEO. LEE, and CHAS. BURKS, April 7, 1789,

for both HARRISONS to administer.
Book 3, Page 137 -- Inventory -- L 53-19-0, June 7, 1790. DAVID and JNO. TINSLEY and GEO. McDANIEL.

JNO. HARRISON -- Book 3, Page 411 -- Inventory -- L 280-11-8, RICH. SHELTON, P. BURTON, RICH. POWELL. November 13, 1795.

JNO. C. HARRISON -- Book 13, Page 363 -- July 3, 1854, written; July 21, 1854, probated. Witnesses: A. C. HARRISON, PAUL CABELL and proved by them. SAML. M. GARLAND qualified. Bondsmen: WM. M. WALLER and EDGAR WHITEHEAD. My three sons: JNO. R., DAVIS D., and LEWIS HARRISON. Daughter, FRANCES JANE MYERS. Executor: SAML. M. GARLAND. Book 13, Page 510 -- is trustee account. Indexed for LEWIS HARRISON - SAML. M. GARLAND, trustee from October 16, 1854. Deed of trust to secure L. and D. D. HARRISON. Recorded May 21, 1853.

JOHN R. HARRISON -- Book 16, Page 186 -- March 26, 1862, written; December 15, 1862, probated. Witnesses: RO. A. PENDLETON, A. C. HARRISON and proved by them. SARAH M. HARRISON qualified. Ux, SARAH M.; my five children to be educated - when of age or married. Desires happiness of my children and earnestly advises against any of their marrying any member of the family of ISAAC D. TINSLEY. If any child marries into that family, all estate rights are forfeited. Sons, JAMES H. and GEORGE L. HARRISON. Ux is to administer. Administrator's Bond is Book 16, Page 191 for SARAH M. Book 17, Page 353 -- Sale -- November 23, 1865. SARAH M. and JAS. H. HARRISON were buyers. Total: $1,691.78.
     I have friends here who are members of both of the HARRISON and TINSLEY clans and have teased the latter a great deal about this will. I am unable to substantiate the story told me that both men were ardent Confederates and that TINSLEY was a soldier. He is said to have been at home on furlough and told JNO. HARRISON that the Federals would win and he would lose all of his slaves. This infuriated HARRISON and caused him to insert this clause since he had a son who was courting TINSLEY's daughter. This story was related to me by my good friend, BLEDSO TINSLEY, who is a grandson of ISAAC D. TINSLEY. Love triumphed and ROBT. HARRISON, son of JNO. R., married ANNIE E. TINSLEY, daughter of ISAAC, in 1874. The heirs waived the clause and ROBT. received his share. Another TINSLEY is one of my deacons and he laughingly said, "The land sure was not much that they got."

LEWIS HARRISON -- Book 13, Page 362 -- August 4, 1852, written; August 21, 1854, probated. Witnesses: PAULUS POWELL and GEO. HUDSON and proved by them. A. C. HARRISON qualified. Son, WILLIAM, is now living in Florida; daughter, HARRIET JANE BERRY; my other children. Daughter, MARY E. RYAN, in trust of my son, ALBERT C. HARRISON - her husband, CHAS. RYAN, and children. My ux, NANCY. Executor: son, ALBERT C. HARRISON.
Book 13, Page 442 -- Inventory -- no total. ALLISON OGDEN, JACOB SMITH, T. R. OGDEN, December 28, 1854.
Book 14, Page 25 -- Administrator's Bond -- ALBERT C. HARRISON, August 21, 1854; no bondsman.
Book 14, Page 111 -- Administrator's Account by administrator from February 9, 1854 - account of JNO. L. HARRISON, MRS. HARRISON, JNO. R. HARRISON, amount to administrator of BENNETT HUDSON. Recorded May 19, 1856.
Book 14, Page 289 -- Sale by administrator. November 10, 1856. $639.34. JNO. R. and A. C. HARRISON were buyers. Recorded May 18, 1857.Book 15, Page 12 -- Administrator's Account by administrator from November 30, 1855 - legacy of HARRIET J. BERRY. Recorded Monday, August 16, 1858.
Book 15, Page 47f - December 14, 1858. Legatees by consent of widow of LEWIS HARRISON - slaves sold before her death and each legatee to bid: Legatees: WM. M. HARRISON; JNO. GIBBS for his mother, HARRIET J. BERRY; A. C. HARRISON, guardian of MARY RYAN and children of JNO. L. (S.) HARRISON. A. C. HARRISON, administrator.

MARY B. HARRISON -- Book 17, Page 38 -- Guardian Bond -- SAML. H. HENRY and ALBERT C. HARRISON, November 20, 1865, for SAML. HENRY as

guardian of MARY B., GEO. L., and ROBT. L. HARRISON, orphans of
JNO. R. HARRISON.

PAULUS HARRISON -- Book 10, Page 298 -- Guardian Bond -- BENJ. B.
TALIAFERRO and RO. TINSLEY, December 21, 1840, for BENJ. TALIAFERRO
as guardian of PAULUS, CAROLINE T., RICH. P., and SOPHIA L. HARRISON,
orphans of RICH. HARRISON, deceased.

RICHARD HARRISON -- Book 4, Page 464 -- Constable - 3rd Hundred,
June 15, 1807. Bondsman: NICHL. HARRISON.
Book 10, Page 384 -- Estate Commitment to Sheriff -- March, 1841.
Motion of C. J. MITCHELL. NELSON CRAWFORD, Sheriff.
Book 11, Page 88 -- Guardian Bond -- RICH. F. RUCKER, PAULUS E. HARRI-
SON, and JNO. D. L. RUCKER, October 17, 1842, for RICH. RUCKER as
guardian of RICH. HARRISON, orphan of RICH. HARRISON, deceased.

ROBT. L. HARRISON -- Book 17, Page 465 -- Guardian's Account -- SAML.
H. HENRY, March 2, 1868 - bond of November 20, 1865; bondsman: A. C.
HARRISON. Paid MRS. S. M. HARRISON; account of SARAH M. HARRISON,
executrix of JNO. R. HARRISON - wards' interest in estate. HARRISON
vs. HARRISON suit mentioned. From November 20, 1865.

WILLIAM L. HARRISON -- Book 4, Page 584 -- Constable -- June 19, 1809.
Bondsmen: RICH. HARRISON and HENRY CAMDEN. This is also indexed for
WM. as above, but it is clearly WM. L. herein.

HENRY HARTLESS -- Book 4, Page 140 -- Inventory -- L 777-7-2, Decem-
ber 19, 1803. J. WARE, BENJ. HIGGINBOTHAM, PETER WATERFIELD.
Book 4, Page 292 -- Administrator's Bond -- HENRY, JAS., WM. and
RICH. HARTLESS, September 19, 1803. Bondsmen: WM. SLEDD, HUGH
CAMPBELL, NICHL. VANSTAVERN.
Book 5, Page 64 -- Guardian Bond -- WM. HARTLESS and WM. SLEDD, Feb-
ruary 19, 1810, for WM. HARTLESS as guardian of HENRY HARTLESS, orphan
of JAS. HARTLESS.

JAMES HARTLESS -- Book 4, Page 190 -- Inventory -- L 71-6-8, Septem-
ber 16, 1805. SAML. PAXTON, REUBEN TINSLEY, SAML. McCLAIN.
Book 6, Page 223 -- Administrator's Account -- WM. SLEDD, administrator from 1805 but some 1804 items. Schooling, 1 year for RICH.
HARTLESS; bonds of HENRY and JAS. HARTLESS in 1804; Sale, June 1,
1806. Legacy of JOS. JARVIS - March 1, 1817. THOS. N. EUBANK, BENJ.
TALIAFERRO, WM. JOPLING.
Book 6, Page 306 -- Administrator's Account -- WM. SLEDD from 1805.
Board and schooling for 1 year for RICH. HARTLESS; to HENRY HARTLESS;
interest on bond of JAS. HARTLESS. CAPT. WARE's settlement. March 1,
1817. Same committee as above.

PETER HARTLESS -- Book 9, Page 124 -- March 16, 1828, written; September 17, 1835, probated. Witnesses: CHAS. TYLER; CHAPMAN SIMS;
JNO. D. CRAWFORD, JR. Proved by TYLER and CRAWFORD, September 21,
1835. Ux, JANE; NANCY MAXON, daughter of LARSONS MASON; PETER H.
MASON - land joins Pedlar and to top of Pine Ridge. If NANCY MASON
is without issue and same for PETER H. MASON.
Book 9, Page 398 -- Estate Commitment to Sheriff -- January, 1838.
Motion of GIBBS and EMMETT. JNO. COLEMAN, Sheriff. This man is shown
to have been a Revolutionary soldier in order book items. I have
found a number of additional names not previously shown in published
data.

POLLY HARTLESS (MARY) -- Book 10, Page 34 -- Administrator's Bond --
JAS. F. TALIAFERRO and JNO. W. BROADDUS, July 16, 1838, for JAS.
TALIAFERRO.
Book 10, Page 83 -- Inventory -- small, August 4, 1838 - MARY here,
JAS. F. TALIAFERRO, administrator. J. D. TURPIN; REUBEN RHOAD; AUSTIN
M. DAVIS.
Book 10, Page 116 -- Administrator's Account from September, 1838 --
amounts to NANCY and LINDSEY HARTLESS; expense of removal of coffin
and remains from Lexington to Amherst and digging grave. Sale of
her father's real estate and legacy from him. HIRAM McGINNIS; JNO. C.

WHITEHEAD; JOEL BETHEL. May 20, 1839.

SARAH ELIZ. HARTLESS -- Book 14, Page 153 -- Guardian Bond -- WM.
TYREE and JORDAN PROFFITT, August 18, 1856, for WM. TYREE as guardian
of SARAH ELIZ. HARTLESS, orphan of NANCY HARTLESS.

WILLIAM HARTLESS -- Book 9, Page 204 -- December 27, 1835, written;
January 18, 1836, probated. Witnesses: J. D. TURPIN, REUBEN ROADS,
JACK RHOADES. Proved by both RHOADES, and MARCH 21, 1836, JAS. F.
TALIAFERRO qualified; bondsmen: RICHARDSON HENLEY and JNO. W. BROAD-
DUS. Daughters: NANCY, BETSY, POLLY -- all of my children. Ad-
ministrator: BENJ. TALIAFERRO.
Administrator's Bond is on Book 9, Page 223.
Book 9, Page 232 -- Inventory -- March 21, 1836. $172.12-1/2. JNO. R.
IRVINE, THOS. A. EUBANK, AUSTIN M. DAVIES.
Book 10, Page 114 -- Administrator's Account -- JAS. F. TALIAFERRO
from August 15, 1836. Legacies of NANCY, BENJ.(?), POLLY, HENRY
and LINDSEY HARTLESS. April 1, 1837. LEONARD H. CHILDRESS, HIRAM
McGINNIS, JNO. C. WHITEHEAD.

RICHARD HARVIE -- Book 4, Page 31 -- Inventory -- January 18, 1802.
JAS. WILLS, JNO. THOMPSON, BURWELL SNEED - L 1,405-6-0.
Book 4, Page 341 -- MARY ANN HARVEY (sic), JAS. HARVEY, JNO. NEWTON,
December 21, 1801, for MARY ANN HARVEY.

THOS. HAWKINS -- Book 1, Page 191f -- Guardian Bond -- LUCAS POWELL
and EDMD. WILCOX, March 4, 1771, for LUCAS POWELL as guardian of
THOS. HAWKINS, orphan of YOUNG HAWKINS.

GILBERT HAY -- Book 2, Page 144 -- January 8, 1777. written;
November 3, 1783, probated. Witnesses: THOS. DICKERSON, SR.; CHAS.
TYLER, SR.; FRANCIS SATTERWHITE. Ux, DINAH - where I live; son,
CHARLES - where he lives; "Hole" of my children. Executors: CHAS.
HAY, HUGH ROSE, CHAS. ROSE, WM. HAY.
Book 2, Page 146 -- Administrator's Bond -- WM. HAY, CHAS. HAY, HEN-
DRICK ARNOLD, NATHL. HILL, November 3, 1783, for WM. and CHAS. HAY.
Book 2, Page 154 -- Inventory -- L 155-0-0, March 1, 1784. JNO. and
NATHL. HILL; HENDRICK ARNOLD.

ELIZ. H. HAYDEN (HAYDON) -- Book 14, Page 60 -- Guardian Bond -- ABNER
HAYDON and RICH. HADEN, December 17, 1855, for ABNER HAYDON as guar-
dian of ELIZ. H., WM. J., ALEX., and MARGARET HAYDON, orphans of
JARVIS HAYDON, deceased.

FRANCES A. HAYES (HAYS) -- Book 17, Page 29 -- Guardian Bond --
LUCINDA R. WILLIAMS and JNO. S. McDANIEL, March 20, 1865, for LUCINDA
WILLIAMS as guardian of FRANCES A. HAYS; no parent set forth.

THOS. C. HAYES (HAYS) -- Book 15, Page 35 -- Administrator's Bond --
JULIANNA HAYS, GEO. W. CARTER, THOS. WHITEHEAD, October 18, 1858,
for JULIANNA HAYS.
Book 15, Page 67 -- Inventory -- December 13, 1858; no total. THOS.
WHITEHEAD; SAML. H. HENRY; LEO DANIEL, JR. Recorded February 21,
1859.
Book 15, Page 561 -- Note: this book jumps from 342 to 443 and this is
indexed in master for 361. Administrator's Account by JULIANNA HAYS
from November 1, 1858 - to widow, JULIANNA HAYS; distributees: THOS.
G., WM. C., and JULIANA J. (I.) HAYS. Recorded September 17, 1860.

CHAS. HAYNES (Indexed HAYES) -- Book 5, Page 81 -- Guardian Bond --
EDY HAYNES and ELIAS WILLS, September 16, 1811, for EDY HAYNES as
guardian of CHAS. HAYNES, orphan of HARDIN HAYNES.
Book 15, Page 34 -- Administrator's de bonis non for C. HAYNES,
November 16, 1858. RO. and ZACH. D. TINSLEY for ZACH. D. TINSLEY.
Book 15, Page 291 -- Administrator's Account -- from November 16, 1858;
cash of WM. HAYNES' administrator; decree in HAYNES vs. RUCKER,
September, 1859. Recorded April 16, 1860.

ELIZ. HAYNES -- Book 15, Page 20 -- Administrator's Account -- CHAS. H.
RUCKER, administrator from 1857 - amount out of fund; legatees' parts -

in hands of administrator - $1,075.60 - $268.90 to each legatee:
PETER RUCKER and ux; HARDEN P. HAYNES, JR.; CHAS. HAYNES; HENRY E.
HAYNES, SR. Summary of January 15, 1858 - CHAS. H. RUCKER, administrator of ELIZ. CHILES and HARDEN HAYNES, deceased, and then name of
CHAS. HAYNES, deceased, added. RO. TINSLEY, attorney for estate of
WM. HAYNES - debts vs. estate of CHAS. HAYNES. RUCKER's ux for share
of PHILIPI debt; WM. HAYNES' attorney states that CHAS. HAYNES moved
to Kentucky and was insolvent. WM.'s inventory of December 19, 1821,
for $120.24. Much time has elapsed and proof needed of insolvency
of CHARLES. Estate liable for any interest or part to CHAS. from
estate of WM. HAYNES. Reference to RUCKER and ux, vs. HAYNES - 1857.
To THOS. M. NEWMAN and ux, NANCY; BAIRD STERRITT(?) and ux, ELIZ.;
appears later to be STENNETT. Recorded -----, --, 1858.

HARDIN HAYNES -- Book 4, Page 145 -- Inventory -- $1,590.18. EDMD.
GOODRICH; JNO. EUBANK; JNO. TALIAFERRO. February 20, 1804. Also
Administrator's Bond, EDY HAYNES and LEONARD HENLEY, November 21,
1803, for EDY HAYNES.
Book 5, Page 50 -- Division -- EADY HAYNES, widow; PETER RUCKER and
ux, JINNEY; HENRY HAYNES - 189 acres - CHAS. HAYNES, WM. HAYNES,
BETSY PERKINS HAYNES, HARDIN HAYNES. December 14, 1811. RO. N.
EUBANK, EDMD. GOODRICH, WM. JOPLING.

HENRY HAYNES -- Book 4, Page 408 -- Guardian Bond -- LEONARD HENLEY
and PETER P. THORNTON, July 15, 1805, for LEONARD HENLEY as guardian
of HENRY HAYNES, orphan of HARDIN HAYNES.

JESSE HAYNES -- Book 4, Page 445 -- Administrator's Bond -- MILLEY
HAYNES, RICH. BURKS, and HARRISON HUGHES, April 20, 1807, for MILLEY
HAYNES.
Book 4, Page 476 -- Inventory -- not summarized, October 6, 1807.
NICHL. HARRISON, JOS. PERKINS, SAML. BURKS.

WM. HAYNES -- Book 5, Page 82 -- Guardian Bond -- THOS. N. EUBANK
and JNO. ELLIS, September 16, 1811, for THOS. EUBANK, as guardian of
WILLIAM HAYNES, orphan of HARDIN HAYNES.
Book 6, Page 197 -- Guardian Bond -- RICH. H. BURKS, RICH. BURKS,
and RICH. HARRISON, December 18, 1820, for RICH. H. BURKS as guardian
of WM., EDITH, HANNAH, and SALLY HAYNES, orphans of JESSE HAYNES,
deceased.
Book 9, Page 225 -- Administrator's Bond -- HENRY E. HAYNES and PETER
RUCKER, May 16, 1836, for HENRY HAYNES.
Book 9, Page 240 -- Inventory -- June 17, 1836 -- $4,416.55 -- JOS. R.
CARTER, GEO. T. PLEASANTS, THOS. TUCKER, TANDY JONES.

ELIZ. HEALEY -- Book 12, Page 33 -- Estate Commitment to Sheriff,
June term, 1848. Motion of VIRGINIA HEALEY. Sheriff: JAS. L. LAMKIN.

JUDITH HEISKILL -- Book 11, Page 232 -- May 22, 1844, written;
August 19, 1844, probated. Witnesses: CARTER H. IRVING; JNO. R.
McDANIEL and proved by them. ANN BASS qualified, September 16, 1844.
Ux of SAML. HEISKILL; daughter, NANCY BASS - one third of all con-
veyed to me by my husband, March 16, 1841. Interest in estate of
my brother, LINDSEY McDANIEL, deceased. My other children. Daughter,
NANCY, to administer.
Administrator's Bond is on Book 11, Page 239.

AMBROSE HENDERSON -- Book 12, Page 33 -- Estate Commitment to Sheriff,
April term, 1849. Motion of RICH. HENDERSON. LINDSEY COLEMAN, Sheriff.
Book 12, Page 244 -- Inventory -- April term, 1849. THOS. A. EUBANK,
JNO. IRVINE, WINSTON MANTIPLY, ISAAC IRVINE HITE. Negro in possession
of ROBT. HENDERSON - given to his children.

AMBROSE R. HENDERSON -- Book 16, Page 147 -- Administrator's Bond --
August 18, 1862. RO. B. HENDERSON and RO. N. ELLIS for RO. HENDERSON.

JNO. HENDERSON -- Book 3, Page 576 -- January 5, 1800, written;
June 16, 1800, probated. Witnesses: HUDSON MARTIN, THOS. BRUMHALL,
NELSON MARTIN. Son, ROBT. - 215 acres patent to me - he is to pay
L 20 in 2 years to my daughter, EASTER McLANE, ux of HENRY McLANE -

appears to be Mc. - my daughter, MARY SMALL, ux of WM. SMALL. My daughters and heirs. Son, JAMES - 2 bonds of MICHL. McMULLIN. My ux, MARGARET - where I live. Sons, JOS. and JNO. - land warrant for 937-3/4 acres in possession of JAS. ANDERSON - to locate on vacant land. Daughter, SARAH DINWIDDIE, ux of JNO. DINWIDDIE. Heirs of deceased daughter, AGNES ALEXAN(D)ER. Executors: Ux and son, ROBT. Administrator's Bond on Book 4, Page 321, June 16, 1800, for them. Bondsman: HUDSON MARTIN.

WM. HENDERSON -- Book 2, Page 183 -- October 22, 1783, written; June 7, 1784, probated. Witnesses: JAS. VIGUST. Ux, REBECKAH; sons, JOEL PONTON(?) and STEVEN HENDERSON. If STEVEN is without heirs - his part to all of my children, JOEL PONTON excepted. Executors: CAPT. JNO. LOVING and WM. WATTS.
Administrator's Bond on Book 2, Page 184 -- WM. WALTON and JNO. LOVING, JR., June 7, 1784, for WM. WALTON.
Book 2, Page 186 -- Inventory -- L 94-3-0, June 15, 1784. ABRAHAM SEAY, THOS. FORTUNE, EDWD. HORCHENS(?).

LINDSEY HENDERICK - incorrect and in proper place as HARDWICK.

BENJ. T. HENLEY -- Book 16, Page 143 -- Administrator's Bond -- RO. L. HENLEY and HENLEY DRUMMOND, WM. SANDIDGE. SAML. M. GARLAND, JNO. W. WHITTLE, July 21, 1862, for RO. HENLEY and HENLEY DRUMMOND.
Book 16, Page 361 -- Inventory -- order of July, 1862. HENRY LOVING: M. C. GOODWIN; C. J. CASH.

CAROLINE C. HENLEY -- Book 13, Page 114 -- Guardian's Account -- MARY A. M. HENLEY, guardian from December 20, 1848; store account of JAS. W. HENLEY; E. J. DRUMMOND, tuition fee; HENLEY and PETTITT store account; received of B. T. HENLEY, December 18, 1849; administrator of R. HENLEY - share of slave hires; RO. L. HENLEY - tuition fee for February 9, 1850; due MARY C. HENLEY; due R. HENLEY. There are various guardian accounts by same guardian for wards: Page 110, for MILDRED T. HENLEY from September 10, 1849; Page 112, WOODFORD B. HENLEY from January 31, 1849; Page 116, MARY C. HENLEY from December 31, 1848; Page 118, RICH. HENLEY from December 31, 1848; Page 120, ISABELLA M. HENLEY from December 31, 1848.

ELIZ. O. HENLEY -- Book 12, Page 135 -- Guardian Bond -- MARY A. M. HENLEY, DABNEY SANDIDGE, and JNO. C. WHITEHEAD, December 18, 1848, for MARY HENLEY as guardian of ELIZ. O.; MILDRED T.; CAROLINE C. HENLEY, orphans of RICHESON HENLEY (spelled RICHARDSON, too.)

ISABELLA M. HENLEY -- Book 13, Page 120 -- Guardian's Account -- MARY A. M. HENLEY, guardian, from December 31, 1848.

JAS. W. HENLEY -- Book 11, Page 531 -- Guardian Bond -- BENJ. T. HENLEY, JAS. F. TALIAFERRO, and DABNEY SANDIDGE, June 22, 1847, for BENJ. HENLEY as guardian of JAS. W., ELIZ. O., MILDRED T., and CAROLINE C. HENLEY, orphans of RICHESON HENLEY.
Book 12, Page 426 -- August 18, 1851 -- JAS. W. HENLEY and GEO. W. HENLEY and EDMD. P. TUCKER to Commonwealth of Virginia for HENLEY men to sell and divide land - order of July 21, 1851.
Book 12, Page 484 -- Refunding Bond -- December 30, 1850 - JAS. W. HENLEY to BENJ. T. HENLEY, administrator of RICHARDSON HENLEY. JAS. W. has received legacy. Bondsmen: RO. L. and G. W. HENLEY.
Book 18, Page 386 -- JAS. W. HENLEY grants power of attorney, August 11, 1873, for signature as bondsman of RO. L. HENLEY as administrator of BENJ. T. HENLEY.

MARY A. M. HENLEY -- Book 12, Page 483 -- Guardian's Account -- MARY A. M. HENLEY, guardian of MILDRED T.; CAROLINE C.; WOODFORD B.; MARY C.; RICHARDSON, and ISABELLA HENLEY - her children, and RO. L.; JAS. W. HENLEY and HENLEY DRUMMOND to BENJ. T. HENLEY, administrator of RICHARDSON HENLEY, deceased. December 30, 1850. MARY has received $1,151.34 as share of wards in estate of their father.
Book 18, Page 108 -- Administrator's Bond -- WM. SANDIDGE, HENLEY

DRUMMOND, and JAS. W. HENLEY, August 21, 1871, for WM. SANDIDGE.
Book 18, Page 110 -- July 28, 1871, written; August 21, 1871, pro-
bated. Witnesses: W. B.; R.; and S. C. HENLEY and MARY E. DAVIS.
Proved by W. B. and RICHARDSON HENLEY. Granddaughter, BELLE HENLEY
HARBOLD when 21 - interest in estate of my deceased son, BENJ. T.
HENLEY. Executor is MAYO DAVIES. All of my children and descendants.
Son, RICHARDSON HENLEY, is to be guardian of BELLE HENLEY HARBOLD.

MARY C. HENLEY -- Book 13, Page 116 -- Guardian's Account by MARY A. M.
HENLEY from December 31, 1848. It is simply noted that these accounts
follow same pattern and same names of wards as one given so it would
be more repetition to insert all data time after time for each ward.

MILDRED T. HENLEY -- She shows in same accounts with her brothers
and sisters which I have cited.
Book 17, Page 509 -- Administrator's Bond -- WOODFORD B. HENLEY and
HENLEY DRUMMON, October 18, 1849, for WOODFORD HENLEY.

RICHESON HENLEY -- Book 11, Page 177 -- Guardian Bond -- BENJ. TALIA-
FERRO, WM. BOURNE, ADDISON TALIAFERRO, and JAS. F. TALIAFERRO,
November 20, 1843, for BENJ. TALIAFERRO as guardian of RO. T., BENJ.
T., JAS. W., ELIZ. O., MILDRED T., CAROLINE C., WOODFORD B., MARY C.,
RICHESON, and ISABELL M. HENLEY, orphans of RICHESON HENLEY, deceased.
Book 11, Page 189 -- Inventory -- no total; many slaves. TANDY
RUTHERFORD, DANL. L. COLEMAN, CHAS. A. PENN. December 18, 1843.
Book 11, Page 264 -- Administrator's Account -- BENJ. TALIAFERRO from
September 30, 1843. HANSARD estate case and name of JNO. M. OTEY -
his portion; DABNEY vs. HANSARD; PERMELIA WILSHER, executrix of
LAWSON G. WILSHER; PHILLIP WEBBER bought cow and calf; SHARP vs.
HANSARD. Amount of $5,005.69. Reported October 2, 1844; Recorded
December 16th.
Book 11, Page 445 -- Administrator's de bonis non -- August 17, 1846.
BENJ. T. HENLEY. Bondsmen: JAS. F. TALIAFERRO, JNO. C. WHITEHEAD,
RO. L. HENLEY.
Book 11, Page 439 -- Inventory -- October 17, 1846 - $2,351.50. C. A.
PENN, W. L. DUNCAN, JOS. SMITH.
Book 11, Page 504 -- Administrator's Account -- BENJ. TALIAFERRO
from October 1, 1844. RO. L. HENLEY for his part of tobacco; MISS E.
BROCKMAN for tuition - 4 months for CAROLINE - $8.00; coffin for
old MRS. HENLEY and paid to DABNEY SANDIDGE - $6.66. Administrators
of CAPT. BENJ. TALIAFERRO; MAYO DAVIES; WM. BOURNE; DABNEY SANDIDGE;
ABSALOM HIGGINBOTHAM; HENRY LOVING, March 15, 1847, and additional
account recorded September 21, 1847.
December 12, Page 356 -- Slave Division -- HENLEY vs. HENLEY admin-
istrators et. al. December 30, 1850. To widow. M. C. GOODWIN;
TANDY RUTHERFORD; JNO. W. BROADDUS. Slaves sold at home of MRS.
M.A.M. HENLEY and divided to 10 legatees. Sold to R. L.; J. W.; and
M.A.M. HENLEY.
Book 12, Page 375 -- Sale -- BENJ. T. HENLEY, administrator, April 21,
1851. Buyers: MARY HENLEY, M. HENLEY, B. T. HENLEY. Sale was on
December 1, 1848, but not recorded until 1851.
Book 13, Page 172 -- Administrator's Account -- B. T. HENLEY, admin-
istrator from July 10 -- store account of J. W. HENLEY; executors of
BENJ. TALIAFERRO; DR. S. C. GIBSON; to M. A. HENLEY; RO. L. HENLEY;
M. A. HENLEY as guardian of infant children. D.R.C. HARRIS; JAS. R.
RICE bought land; trust money for MARY CHILDRESS; LEONARD DANIEL
bought land. DABNEY SANDIDGE; M. C. GOODWIN; J. W. BROADDUS, March 14,
1850.
Book 13, Page 188 -- Administrator's Account -- BENJ. T. HENLEY from
March 14, 1850. HENLEY vs. TALIAFERRO. Recorded November 8, 1851.

RO. L. HENLEY -- Book 11, Page 179 -- Guardian Bond -- BENJ. TALIA-
FERRO, WM. BOURNE, ADDISON TALIAFERRO, JAS. F. TALIAFERRO, Novem-
ber 20, 1843, for BENJ. TALIAFERRO as guardian of RO. L., BENJ. T.,
JAS. W., ELIZ. O., MILDRED T., CAROLINE C., WOODFORD B., MARY C.,
RICHESON, and ISABELLA M. HENLEY, orphans of RICHESON HENLEY, deceased.
Book 12, Page 191 -- Guardian's Account by BENJ. HENLEY, guardian
from September 2, 1847 - heirs of R. HENLEY, deceased; Tuition to E. J.
BROCKMAN for MILDRED T.; CAROLINE C.; WOODFORD B. HENLEY - one third
rent to MARY A. M. HENLEY. JAS. W. HENLEY for store account. RO. L.;

MARY C.; RICHESON; ISABELLA M. and ELIZ. O. HENLEY - MARY A. M. HEN-
LEY, guardian of CAROLINE C., MILDRED T., ELIZ. O., WOODFORD B.,
RICHARDSON, MARY E., and ISABELLA M. HENLEY. January 6, 1849. J. W.
BROADDUS; DABNEY SANDIDGE.
Book 12, Page 484 -- Refunding Bond -- December 30, 1850, RO. L. HEN-
LEY, to BENJ. T. HENLEY, administrator of RICHESON HENLEY - RO. L.
has received legacy. Bondsmen: JAS. W. and G. W. HENLEY.
Book 18, Page 439 -- Administrator's Bond -- W. B. HENLEY, JAS. W.
HENLEY, RICHESON HENLEY, HENLEY DRUMMOND, and WM. SANDIDGE. August 17,
1874, for W. B. HENLEY.
Book 18, Page 448 -- June 24, 1874, written; July 20, 1874, probated.
Witnesses: R. HENLEY, JAS. M. TALIAFERRO. Mother's dower land which
I bought and land bought of my sister, MOLLIE C. HENLEY - RUTHERFORD
tract. Land bought of my brother, R. HENLEY. To infant children of
MOLLIE MITCHELL: WALKER and SAML. MITCHELL. To infant children of
CAROLINE MITCHELL: WM. and EDWD. MITCHELL and RO. CHRISTIAN when
youngest is of age. MOLLIE and CAROLINE MITCHELL to live on land and
RO. CHRISTIAN is to manage. Executor: brother, W. B. HENLEY.

SARAH C. HENLEY (Indexed HENDLEY) -- Book 12, Page 280 -- Guardian
Bond -- G. W. HENLEY; J. W. HENLEY; R. HENLEY; B. T. HENLEY, May 20,
1850, for G. W. HENLEY as guardian of SARAH C. HENLEY, orphan of
WM. HENLEY, deceased.
Book 14, Page 50 -- Guardian Bond -- JAS. W. HENLEY and B. T. HEN-
LEY, November 20, 1855, for JAS. W. HENLEY as guardian of SARAH C.
HENLEY, orphan of WM. HENLEY.

MAJOR WILLIAM HENLEY -- Book 9, Page 381 -- October 20, 1837, written;
February 19, 1838, probated. Witnesses: LAWSON G. WILSHER; LEONARD H.
CHILDRESS; JNO. E. MARTIN and proved by them. RICHESON HENLEY quali-
fied. Bondsmen: LEONARD H. CHILDRESS, ZA. DRUMMOND, JNO. W. BROADDUS.
Ux, ELIZ. A.; my children: GEO. W., THOS. H., BETSY L., SARAH C.
HENLEY - until youngest is eighteen. Executor: Brother, RICHARDSON
HENLEY.
Administrator's Bond is Book 9, Page 382.
Book 11, Page 172 -- Administrator's Bond -- CHAS. H. MASSIE, Septem-
ber 18, 1843. Bondsman: WILKINS WATSON.
Book 11, Page 176 -- Inventory of MAJOR WM. HENLEY, November 21, 1843 -
$1,946.50. DANL. COLEMAN, CHAS. A. PENN, RICH. P. SMITH. Also same
inventory on Page 178.
Book 11, Page 199 -- Sale -- November 25, 1843. CHAS. H. MASSIE,
administrator. $251.82. WM. HENLEY was a buyer.
Book 11, Page 376 -- Administrator's Account by MASSIE from Novem-
ber 25, 1845 - tuition for G. and T. HENLEY to A.(?) B. BROWN; MARY
HENLEY - tuition of E. and S. HENLEY to SARAH M. DAVIES; coffin made
by JAS. W. HENLEY - $2.50. Board of WM. HENLEY; DR. SAML. C. GIBSON's
bill. Recorded December 15, 1845.
Book 11, Page 470 -- Inventory -- January 2, 1847 - slaves. DABNEY
SANDIDGE; C. A. PENN; SAML. C. GIBSON.
Book 11, Page 516 -- Administrator's de bonis non Bond -- December 21,
1846. MOSES SNEAD. Bondsman: WILKINS WATSON.
Book 11, Page 579 -- Administrator's Account by MASSIE from May 18,
1845 - to JAS. W. HENLEY for THOS.; SARAH; and BENJ. HENLEY; R. HEN-
LEY's administrator and recorded December 20, 1847. WM. W. THOMPSON;
H. L. BROWN; SAML. M. GARLAND.
Book 12, Page 283 -- Administrator's Account by MOSES SNEAD from
December 18, 1846. Shoes for THOS. HENLEY; clothes for BETTIE HENLEY;
school trip to -- for S. HENLEY; cash to G. W. HENLEY; MRS. MARY
CHILDRESS for children; J. W. HENLEY's receipt. September 16, 1850:
DABNEY SANDIDGE and J. W. BROADDUS.
Book 13, Page 306 -- Administrator's Account -- by Snead - note two
spellings - from February, 1850. J. W. HENLEY's store account.
JORDAN S. QUINN - shoemaker; THOS. C. GOODWIN - tailor; JAS. W. HEN-
LEY for ux, legatee, vs. SNEAD to account. GEO. W. HENLEY appeared
with JAS. W. HENLEY - will recorded February 19, 1838. Clause in
will: "if wife remarried" - his four children: GEO. W., THOS. H.,
BETSY L., and SARAH C. HENLEY. Ux remarried about March 21, 1843,
to WILKINS WATSON. Youngest child is married, but not 21. Recorded
June 17, 1852.

WOODFORD B. HENLEY -- Book 11, Page 532 -- Guardian Bond -- BENJ. T. HENLEY, JAS. F. TALIAFERRO, and DABNEY SANDIDGE, June 22, 1847, for BENJ. HENLEY as guardian of WOODFORD B., MARY C., RICHESON, and ISABELLA ANN HENLEY (she is called ISABELLA M. in all other items), orphans of RICHESON HENLEY, deceased.
Book 12, Page 145 -- Guardian Bond -- MARY A. M. HENLEY, DABNEY SANDIDGE, and JNO. C. WHITEHEAD, December 18, 1848, for same orphans as above for MARY A. HENLEY as guardian.
Book 13, Page 112 -- Guardian's Account by MARY HENLEY from January 31, 1849. Tuition to J. DRUMMOND for RO. L. HENLEY; HENLEY and PETTITT store account; JAS. W. HENLEY store account. Received of B. T. HENLEY, administrator of R. HENLEY. Also accounts for CAROLINE C., MARY C., RICHARDSON and ISABELLA M. HENLEY. Recorded November 8, 1851.

ELVIRA ANN HENRY -- Book 4, Page 401 -- Guardian Bond -- ELVIRA A. HENRY, WM. CABELL, THOS. S. McCLELLAND, LANDON CABELL, and W. H. CABELL, May 20, 1805, for ELVIRA HENRY as guardian of ELVIRA ANN HENRY, orphans of PATRICK HENRY.

SARAH HENRY -- Book 2, Page 229 -- March 12, 1784, written; May 2, 1785, probated. Witnesses: JAS. FRANKLIN, JAS. HIGGINBOTHAM, JOS. BARNETT. Presented by EDMOND WINSTON and attested by witnesses. Widow, A. C.; son, JNO. SYME; son, WM. HENRY; son, PATRICK - each got mourning ring. One of these is still preserved at Winston estate in Fayette County, Kentucky. ELIZ. HENRY, daughter of son, PATRICK. Son-in-law, WM. RUSSELL, and my daughter, ELIZ. RUSSELL; son-in-law, SAML. MEREDITH, and my daughter, JANE HENRY MEREDITH. Daughter, LUCY WOOD; daughter, ANNE CHRISTIAN, and her daughter, SARAH WINSTON CHRISTIAN; my daughter, SUSANNA MADDISON, and her son, JNO. HENRY MADDISON, and her daughter, SARAH MADDISON; my grandson, CHAS. HENRY CAMPBELL; If ELIZ. RUSSELL is without issue; my deceased husband, JNO. HENRY; my granddaughter, SARAH BUCHANAN CAMPBELL; land in Amherst County sold to PETER RIPPTOE - proceeds to grandchildren until of age; to JNO. LANCASTER for land improvements to be paid by son-in-law, SAML. MEREDITH; Clothes to daughters. Executors: Son-in-law, SAML. MEREDITH; son, PATRICK; son-in-law, WM. CHRISTIAN; son-in-law, THOS. MADDISON, and my worthy friend, EDMOND WINSTON.
Administrator's Bond is on Page 232 of Book 2. EDMOND WINSTON quali-fied, May 2, 1785. Bondsman: SAML. MEREDITH. The PATRICK HENRY mentioned in her will is the famed Virginia. She is buried at Winston Estate and the DARs of this region hold a meeting at Clifford, the village adjoining, each spring. A roadside marker tells that her grave is nearby. Justices when the administrator made bond were WM. CABELL, JAS. DILLARD, RODERICK McCULLOCH, and JAS. HOPKINS.

ALEX. HENSON -- Book 16, Page 105 -- Administrator's Bond -- ELLUTE HENSON and PETER C. SHEPHERD, January 20, 1862, for ELLUTE HENSON.

GEO. B. HENSON -- Book 16, Page 192 -- Administrator's Bond -- MAHALA F. HENSON and CHAS. A. STINNETT, December 15, 1862, for MAHALA HENSON.

MURRAY HENSON -- Book 12, Page 498 -- July 24, 1848, written; March 15, 1852, probated. Witnesses: P. H. ROWSEY and RO. H. HENDERSON and proved by them. Son, ELLJOT HENSON and grandson, RODERICK HENSON.

CATH. HICKEY -- Book 1, Page 426 -- Administrator's Bond -- JOS. ROBERTS and JNO. JACOBS, May 4, 1778, for JOS. ROBERTS.
Book 1, Page 431 -- Inventory -- August 1, 1778 - L 22-3-0. MICHL. McNEELY, JOELL CRAWFORD, SAML. DAVIS. Recorded August 3, 1778.

EBENEZER HICKOK -- Book 11, Page 119 -- June 18, 1842, written; April 17, 1843, probated. Witnesses: JNO. B. DUNCAN; JNO. H.(?) PAMPLIN, THOS. L. TAYLOR. Proved by DUNCAN and TAYLOR, May 15, 1843, PATRICK H. HICKOK qualified; Bondsmen: CHAS. A. PENN and STERLING CLAIBORNE. One sixth to each of these: Son, PATRICK H.; son, MOSES; daughter, POLLY LANDRUM; son, SAML.; daughter, SALLY STAPLES; children of CATH. HILL, deceased - my daughter. All have received furniture etc. Son, JOHN, and daughter NANCY's children have received their shares. Executors: son, PATRICK H. and RICH. LANDRUM.

Administrator's Bond on Book 11, Page 124 -- see above.
Book 11, Page 164 -- Inventory -- May 26, 1843 -- 52 acres - all that
he had: $543.01. WM. STAPLES, STEPHEN J. JONES, SEATON LANDRUM.
Book 11, Page 167 -- Sale by administrator, May 26, 1843. RICH. and
SEATON LANDRUM; P. H. HICKOK; WM. STAPLES, SR., and JR. were buyers.
Total: $467.04-1/2. JNO. H. PAMPLIN, Clerk of Sale.
Book 11, Page 382 -- Administrator's Account by administrator. From
May 15, 1843. To MISS STAPLES; JNO. WHITEHEAD on account of pension.
Recorded: July 21, 1845.

BLANSFORD HICKS -- Book 11, Page 301 -- September 13, 1844, written;
February 17, 1845, probated. Witnesses: JNO. PRYOR, STEPHEN BOWLES,
LEWIS E. EMMETT, GEO. HAYDON. Proved by BOWLES and PRYOR. NICHL.
HICKS and WM. P. MORRIS qualified; Bondsmen: BLUFORD HICKS; PRESTON,
NELSON, and MADISON HICKS. Ux, POLLY; my single children to get
same when they marry, as those previously married. Son, LEROY;
daughter, ELIZ. - money given to her when she removed to the west;
my minor children. Executors: Son, NICHL., and WM. P. MORRIS.
Book 11, Page 307 -- Administrator's Bond -- see above.

NELSON HICKS -- Book 11, Page 321 -- Constable Bond -- June 16, 1845.
Bondsmen: NICHL HICKS and STEPHEN BOWLES.
Book 11, Page 527 -- Same -- June 21, 1847. Bondsmen: STEPHEN BOWLES
and EDWIN M. WARE.
Book 12, Page 177 -- Same -- June 18, 1849. Bondsmen: STEPHEN BOWLES
and NICHL. SHOEMAKER.
Book 14, Page 130 -- Same -- June 16, 1856. Bondsmen: NICHL. HICKS
and JAS. P. McDANIEL.
Book 14, Page 573 -- Same -- June 21, 1858. Bondsmen: JNO. W. WHITTEN
or JNO. M. and JAS. P. McDANIEL.
Book 15, Page 463 -- Same -- June 18, 1860. Bondsman: CHRISTOPHER
McIVER.

AARON HIGGINBOTHAM (Early items indexed for CAPT.) -- Book 2, Page 254,
September 19, 1778, written; October 3, 1785, probated. Witnesses:
CHAS. BURRUS, RICH. OGLESBY, RICH. WHITEHALL. Son, SAML. - 262 acres
where I live and land next to PHILIP WATHERS; carpenter and cooper
tools; daughter, FRANCES and children; daughter, MARY ANN and children;
daughter, TAMSIN, and children; son, AARON, at death of my ux - where
I live and where daughter, MARY ANN, lives - called The Cove; also
tract between Cove and GILES; daughter, MARGARET, and children; ux,
CLARA; if children are without heirs. Executors: brother, JAMES,
and sons, SAML. and AARON.
        (Also see RO. HIGGINBOTHAM.)
Book 2, Page 256 -- Administrator's Bond -- JAS., SAML., and AARON
HIGGINBOTHAM, November 7, 1785. Bondsmen: SAML. MEREDITH and JOS.
PENN.
Book 2, Page 259 -- Inventory -- November 25, 1785. L 1,236-10-1.
RICH. OGLESBY, HENRY FRANKLIN, JACOB SMITH, February 6, 1786.
Book 3, Page 326 -- Administrator's Bond -- NANCY HIGGINBOTHAM, WM.
SANDIDGE, JNO. SMITH, JNO. TALIAFERRO, WM. WARE, December 15, 1794, for
NANCY HIGGINBOTHAM and WM. SANDIDGE.
Book 3, Page 335 -- Inventory of CAPT. here -- April 20, 1795(?,
blurred); CHAS. TALIAFERRO; RICH. OGLESBY; CHAS. TALIAFERRO, JR.
Book 3, Page 375 -- Division: to JOS. H. MORRISON; legatees of HENRY
FRANKLIN, JR.; to HENRY FRANKLIN; to WM. SANDIDGE; to THOS. MORRISON.
February 15, 1796. Committee: NELSON CRAWFORD, CHAS. TALIAFERRO,
JNO. TALIAFERRO.
Book 3, Page 470 -- Division of slaves -- To JOS. H. MORRISON who
married FRANCES HIGGINBOTHAM; to HENRY FRANKLIN's legatees who are
children of MARY ANN, daughter of AARON HIGGINBOTHAM; to WM. SANDIDGE,
who married TAMSIN, daughter of AARON HIGGINBOTHAM; to THOS. MORRISON
who married PEGGY, daughter of AARON HIGGINBOTHAM. June 19, 1798.
Same committee, but "JR." after CHAS. TALIAFERRO.
Book 12, Page 500 -- Administrator's Bond -- WM. A., ALEX. B., ABSALOM
HIGGINBOTHAM and RO. L. HENLEY, March 15, 1852, for W. A. and ALEX. B.
HIGGINBOTHAM.
Book 12, Page 311 -- Inventory -- March 25, 1852. $3,633.00. RUFUS A.
HIGGINBOTHAM; WILLIS WHITE; ENOCH P. JEFFRIES.
Book 12, Page 521 -- Sale, March 26, 1852. Buyers: WM. A., RUFUS A.,

JNO. J., JOS., ALEX. B., BENJ. J. HIGGINBOTHAM - $846.95. Certified by JAS. A. HIGGINBOTHAM.
Book 13, Page 268 -- Administrator's Account -- WM. A.HIGGINBOTHAM from March 15, 1852. Bond of A. HIGGINBOTHAM, JR.; MRS. HIGGINBOTHAM; paid JAS. A. HIGGINBOTHAM; share of WM. A. HIGGINBOTHAM; LEANN J. and BETTIE - beds to be put in guardian account; ROBT. H.; AARON; LEANA J. - W. A. HIBBINBOTHAM, guardian; WM. C. - WM. A. HIGGINBOTHAM, guardian. Paid to RUFUS HIGGINBOTHAM; ALEX. B. HIGGINBOTHAM as administrator. Recorded July 16, 1853.
Book 13, Page 498 -- Commissioner account -- WM. A. HIGGINBOTHAM from June 30, 1853; also A. B. and WM. A. as commissioners. March 17, 1855; to sell land of testator. Recorded April 16, 1855. Accounts with AARON, JNO. J., BENJ. W., ROBT. W.

ABSALOM HIGGINBOTHAM -- Book 17, Page 150 -- August 11, 1860, written; July 16, 1866, probated. Witnesses: LEWIS S. CAMPBELL; JOS. A. HIGGINBOTHAM; THOS. H. CAMPBELL and proved by them. JAS. HIGGIN-BOTHAM qualified. Bondsmen: JNO. THOMPSON, JR.; SAML. M. GARLAND; HENRY L. DAVIES; LEWIS S. CAMPBELL; JNO. J. SHRADER. Ux, MARY C.; 7 children - sums advanced to them. Daughter, NANCY C.; sons: JAS., RUFUS A., BENJ. S., ABSALOM, ARON (sic), PAUL, NANCY C. and children trustee for them. JAS. and RUFUS A. HIGGINBOTHAM to serve as trustees for NANCY C., BENJ. S., and ux, MARGARET A., and their children; ABSALOM and ux, ELIZ.; ARON L. and children; PAUL and family - as long as single. Executors: JAS. and RUFUS A. HIGGINBOTHAM.
Administrator's Bond on Book 17, Page 152.
Book 17, Page 158 -- Inventory -- August 7, 1866; no total. JAS. HIG-GINBOTHAM, only acting executor: WM. SANDIDGE; C. T. HILL; WM. R. HILL.

BENJ. HIGGINBOTHAM -- Book 8, Page 435 -- Estate Commitment to Sheriff, August Court, 1834. Motion of JOHN ALLCOCK and JNO. L. (S.) DAVEN-PORT. EDMD. WINSTON, sheriff.

BETTIE ANN (BETSY ANN) HIGGINBOTHAM -- Book 12, Page 526 -- Guardian Bond -- WM. A., A. B. HIGGINBOTHAM, and JAS. W. HENLEY, June 21, 1852, for WM. HIGGINBOTHAM as guardian of LEANNA J., BETSY ANN, and WM. C. HIGGINBOTHAM, orphans of AARON HIGGINBOTHAM, deceased.
Book 15, Page 93 -- Guardian's Account by guardian from June 22, 1852; AARON HIGGINBOTHAM's estate; bond retained from January 14, 1853. Account has been presented to D. H. TAPSCOTT, but he died before final settlement. Guardian altered accounts subsequently to 1853 to complete report - $488.29. Recorded February 21, 1859.
Book 17, Page 287 -- Guardian's Account by WM. A. HIGGINBOTHAM, January 7, 1867. Bond by guardian. Ward is of age, December, 1855. Recorded January 20, 1868.

CATHERINE E. HIGGINBOTHAM -- Book 15, Page 468 -- Guardian Bond -- JOSEPH A. HIGGINBOTHAM and M. C. GOODWIN September 17, 1860, for JOSEPH HIGGINBOTHAM as guardian of CATH. E. HIGGINBOTHAM, daughter of JOS. HIGGINBOTHAM.

CHARLES HIGGINBOTHAM -- Book 5, Page 493 -- Administrator's Bond -- JOS. and WM. HIGGINBOTHAM, March 20, 1815, for JOS. HIGGINBOTHAM.
Book 5, Page 503 -- Inventory -- first column is blank; second - 1-6. JACOB PEARCE; JACOB SCOTT; CHAS. H. CHRISTIAN, May 15, 1815.

CYRUS W. HIGGINBOTHAM -- Book 15, Page 165 -- Guardian's Account -- WM. A. HIGGINBOTHAM from September, 1852. To JOS. HIGGINBOTHAM; your trip to Kentucky; ROBT. HIGGINBOTHAM; portion of AARON HIGGINBOTHAM's estate; to A. B. HIGGINBOTHAM. Recorded March 12, 1858.
Book 18, Page 498 -- Guardian's Account by same guardian from 1858, June 15. Recorded April 20, 1875.

DANIEL HIGGINBOTHAM -- Book 16, Page 150 -- Administrator's Bond -- WM. A. HIGGINBOTHAM, GEO. H. DAMERON, RO. A. PENDLETON, August 18, 1862, for WM. HIGGINBOTHAM.
Book 16, Page 181 -- Inventory -- July term, 1862. No total. RO. L. HENLEY, M. C. GOODWIN, WM. SANDIDGE. September 26, 1862.
Book 16, Page 182 -- Sale -- September 2, 1862. Buyers: JAS. A.

and R. A. HIGGINBOTHAM.
Book 16, Page 188 -- Sale -- November 6, 1862. MAJOR TALIAFERRO was
buyer. $429.40. Also sale for MARY F. and WM. R. HILL - one third
belonged to DANL. HIGGINBOTHAM. WM. A. HIGGINBOTHAM was a buyer
and administrator - $391.90. Recorded November 17, 1862.
Book 16, Page 512 -- Division -- paid February 13 and 20, 1863, to
WM. A. HIGGINBOTHAM; JOS. A. HIGGINBOTHAM; MARY F. HIGGINBOTHAM;
WM. R. HILL. Half shares to JAS. H. H. HIGGINBOTHAM; O. D. DILLARD;
GEO. W. HIGGINBOTHAM. Commissioner: WM. A. HIGGINBOTHAM. Slave
division and sale, February 13, 1863. WM. A. and JOS. A. HIGGINBOTHAM
were buyers.
Book 17, Page 284 -- Administrator's Account by WM. A. HIGGINBOTHAM
from February 6, 1861. To WM. A. - loan. Account of JAS. H. HIGGIN-
BOTHAM. Legatees: JAMES H., GEO. W. HIGGINBOTHAM, O. D. DILLARD
and ux, ELIZ. - now dead; WM. A.; JOS. A.; MARY F. HIGGINBOTHAM;
WM. R. HILL and ux, ANN J. Recorded January 7, 1867.

EUGENE HIGGINBOTHAM -- Book 13, Page 39 -- Administrator's Bond --
JNO. J. LONDON and S. CLAIBORNE, January 17, 1853, for JNO. LONDON.
Book 14, Page 212 -- Administrator' Bond -- JAS. HIGGINBOTHAM and
DANL. H. LONDON (by RO. TINSLEY*, December 15, 1856, for JAS. HIGGIN-
BOTHAM.
Book 14, Page 254 -- Inventory -- December 29, 1856; two slaves:
$400.00. THOS. N. EUBANK, WM. E. COLEMAN, JNO. T. ELLIS.

JAMES HIGGINBOTHAM -- Book 6, Page 298 -- Constable -- First Hundred,
June 17, 1822. Bondsman: GEO. W. HIGGINBOTHAM.
Book 6, Page 360 -- Same -- June 16, 1823. Bondsman: JOS. DILLARD.
Book 13, Page 181 -- Administrator's Bond -- WM. A. HIGGINBOTHAM and
CHAS. W. STATHAM, May 16, 1853, for WM. HIGGINBOTHAM.
Book 18, Page 472 -- Administrator's Bond -- JAS. HIGGINBOTHAM died
intestate and widow, ANN ELIZA, qualified. Her children were securi-
ties and appointed their brother, CHESTER HIGGINBOTHAM, to sign
for them. Bondsmen: ALICE (signed ALLIE) HIGGINBOTHAM; FLORENCE
HIGGINBOTHAM; ROSA A. HIGGINBOTHAM; L. T. RUCKER; CHESTER J. HIGGIN-
BOTHAM. Recorded October 19, 1874.

JAMES S. HIGGINBOTHAM -- Book 17, Page 182 -- July 16, 1864, written;
September 17, 1866, probated. Witnesses: JNO. THOMPSON, JR., and
NEWTON S. BOWIE and proved by them. JAS. HIGGINBOTHAM appointed, but
refused to qualify. WM. M. WARE made both to administer; bondsman:
JNO. M. WARE. "Attained great age" - will of father, JOS. HIGGIN-
BOTHAM - land where I live. Son, THOS.; my sister, McDANIEL; THOS.
is, if not an idiot - his estate will go to McDANIEL cousins. Slave
went to Pennsylvania with freed ux and slaves sold because of bad
habits. 162 and 39 acres bought of MILES and ROGERS. My daughter-
in-law, LAURA A. HIGGINBOTHAM; great niece, FANNY WARE; niece, MARY
WARE, ux of WM. M. WARE - their children. THOS. - when 21; my sister
WARE's children. There are 4 of them. Sister McDANIEL's children.
My neighbor and kinsman, JAS. HIGGINBOTHAM, to administer. WM. M.
WARE to care for THOS.
Book 17, Page 190 -- Inventory -- October 13, 1866 - $658.75. JAS.
HIGGINBOTHAM; JOEL H. CAMPBELL; M. H. WHORTON.

JESSE A. HIGGINBOTHAM -- Book B, Page 32 -- September 30, 1848,
written; April 5, 1849, probated. At Amherst Courthouse. Witnesses:
PAULUS POWELL and LEO McDANIEL and proved by them. JNO. THOMPSON,
JR., and SAML. M. GARLAND qualified. Tennessee debts and property
there. To CAPT. JNO. THOMPSON, JR. - brother-in-law, WM. WIRT HENRY -
law library; his brother, THOS. S. HENRY - flute and music. Friend,
SAML. M. GARLAND. $2,000.00 to GARLAND and JNO. THOMPSON, JR., to
erect within sight of my house a basement for Academy and above for
Clinton Masonic Lodge to which I belong. Ux, ELVIRA M. - estate of
my uncle, DANL. HIGGINBOTHAM, deceased. About to go to Cuba; if ux
is without issue. MAYO CABELL, Nelson County, trustee for father
and mother-in-law, MR. and MRS. JNO. HENRY, and children. THOMPSON
and GARLAND to administer and theyqualified. More due from DANL.
HIGGINBOTHAM estate. JNO. J. LONDON to pay estate more, if due.
227 acres near Nashville, Tennessee - to my half-uncle, HIRAM VAUGHAN,

of Tennessee. My interest in dower of step-grandmother. Note: HIGGINBOTHAM Academy is house now known as the WEBSTER Home on South Main. I have seen plat in early 1830's and it was then home of JNO. THOMPSON, JR. It was called Edgewood.

JOANNA C. HIGGINBOTHAM, MRS. -- Book 16, Page 24 -- Administrator's Bond -- WM. A. and JOS. A. HIGGINBOTHAM, January 22, 1861, for WM. HIGGINBOTHAM.
Book 16, Page 30 -- Salve Division on order of January, 1861. To WM. A., JOS. A., DANL., MARY and ANNA J. HIGGINBOTHAM, February 7, 1861. M. C. GOODWIN, JAS. W. HENLEY, WM. SANDIDGE.
Book 16, Page 182 -- Sale -- DANL. HIGGINBOTHAM sale is on same page - and inventory, September 26, 1862. Buyers: JOS., JAS., J., WM., JAS. A., A., WM. A., GEO. and R. HIGGINBOTHAM - $859.83. Recorded October 20, 1862.
Book 17, Page 277 -- Administrator's Account -- September 21, 1863. WM. A. HIGGINBOTHAM. Sums paid during her lifetime to MARY F. HIGGIN-BOTHAM; ANNA J. HILL; DANL. HIGGINBOTHAM; WM. A. HIGGINBOTHAM. Legatees: WM. A., JOS. A., MARY F., DANL. HIGGINBOTHAM, WM. R. HILL and ux, ANNA J.

JNO. HIGGINBOTHAM -- Book 5, Page 451 -- June 22, 1813, written; September 19, 1814, probated. Witnesses: WM. S. CRAWFORD; JAS. HIG-GINBOTHAM; JAS. H. DILLARD; YOUNG HAWKINS and provied by them. October 17, 1814, JNO. and THOS. HIGGINBOTHAM qualified. Bondsmen: WM. S. CRAWFORD, JAS. MURPHY, ELIAS WILLS. My ux, RACHEL; son, JNO.; daughter, FRANCES R. HIGGINBOTHAM, while single; daughter, NANCY HIGGINBOTHAM; son, JAMES; daughter, TIRZA LONDON and children; after death of my ux - 8 parts. Sons: THOS., DAVID, JNO., JESSE, DANL., REUBEN; daughter, FRANCES R. HIGGINBOTHAM; sons, THOS. and DAVID - trustees for son, EUGENE. Exeuctors: sons, JNO. and THOS.
Book 5, Page 465 -- Administrator's Bond -- see above.
Book 5, Page 476 -- Inventory -- $9,452.50, December 19, 1814. JNO. McDANIEL; GIDEON RUCKER; B. STONE.
Book 6, Page 271 -- Administrator's Account -- October 10, 1821. $12,936.95. THOS. ALDRIDGE, CORNL. POWELL, JNO. DILLARD. From July 31, 1814. THOS. HIGGINBOTHAM, JNO. HIGGINBOTHAM, JAS. M. BROWN, WHITEHEAD and HIGGINBOTHAM; MRS. THURMOND; JESSE HIGGINBOTHAM's bond; JNO. LONDON; JOS. HIGGINBOTHAM; DANL.; WM.; and DAVID HIGGINBOTHAM.

JOSEPH HIGGINBOTHAM -- Book 4, Page 178 -- October 23, 1802, written; June 17, 1805, probated. Witnesses: HENRY BALLINGER; BENJ. SANDIDGE; JACOB PHILIPS, SR. Sons, JOS. and BENJ. - 150 acres where I live and 99 acres adjoining; 80 acres part of 300 acres joining; also 20 and 5-1/2 acres joining 150 acres where I live. 70 acres on middle fork of Pedlar; 290 acres next to it; daughter, SUSANNA - 200 acres on both sides RUTLEDGE and next to PETER CASHWELL and HENRY BOURNE; daughter, RACHEL HIGGINBOTHAM - 39 acres on Buffalo and next to JAS. HIGGINBOTHAM, N. B. (sic); FRANCES MORRISON and HANNAH BALLOW. My daughter (sic) have received their legacies. My children: FRANCES MORRISON; JOS.; WM.; JACOB HIGGINBOTHAM; HANNAH BELOW; BENJ. HIGGIN-BOTHAM. Sons and daughter: JOS.; BENJ.; SUSANNA HIGGINBOTHAM. Executors: Sons: JOS. and BENJ. Presented by JOS. and BENJ. who qualified. Bondsmen: WM. and BENJ. SANDIDGE. JNO. CLARKSON; HENRY BALLINGER.
Book 4, Page 203 -- Inventory -- L 801-0-4, December 16, 1805. BENJ. SANDIDGE, HENRY BALLINGER, BENJ. TALIAFERRO.
Book 4, Page 403 -- Administrator's Bond -- JOS. HIGGINBOTHAM, son of JOS. - bond to administrator.
Book 6, Page 353 -- Administrator's Bond -- May 19, 1823, CORNL. SALE, ZA. DRUMMOND, DUDLEY SANDIDGE, bondsmen for DABNEY SANDIDGE to administer.
Book 6, Page 354 -- February 27, 1818, written; May 19, 1823, probated. Witnesses: PHILIP SMITH, DUDLEY SANDIDGE, JNO. W. YOUNG. Proved by SANDIDGE and YOUNG. DABNEY SANDIDGE qualified as above. Brother, BENJ. HIGGINBOTHAM; newphew, JAS. HIGGINBOTHAM, son of JOSEPH HIGGIN-BOTHAM, and of this county. If JAMES will support his sister, SUSANNAH SMITH, ux of JAS. SMITH. If JAS. HIGGINBOTHAM is without heirs. Brother, JACOB HIGGINBOTHAM. Children of my sister, FRANCES MORRISON. Exeuctors: friends, WM. DUNAN and DABNEY SANDIDGE and BENJ.

TALIAFERRO.
Book 6, Page 391 -- Inventory -- $8,292.00. Recorded September 15, 1823. ABSALOM HIGGINBOTHAM, JACOB SMITH, WM. DUNCAN.
Book 6, Page 734 -- Administrator's Account -- DABNEY SANDIDGE from November 2, 1823. Appraisers' dinners for 3 at Springs; claim of D.H.D. HIGGINBOTHAM vs. estate; funeral expenses - $10.00; bond of ABSALOM HIGGINBOTHAM; bond of GEO. W. HIGGINBOTHAM. Sale, December 6, 1823. Recorded May 7, 1825. PEACHY FRANKLIN, ED. A. CABELL, JOS. STAPLES. Additional account received on February 19, 1829. JOSEPH STAPLES; JNO. DILLARD, SR.; JAS. ROSE. DABNEY SANDIDGE, administrator.
Book 7, Page 34 -- November 11, 1826, written; codicil, September 6(?), 1827; September 17, 1827, probated. Witnesses: JESSE and EUGENE HIGGINBOTHAM and SAML. CHRISTIAN. Witnesses to codicil: JESSE and EUGENE HIGGINBOTHAM and ALLISON OGDON. Proved by will witnesses. JAS. L. HIGGINBOTHAM (middle initial could be "S"). Bondsmen: THOS. HIGGINBOTHAM and JNO. PENN. Son, JAS. L. or S. - land - except that of my right to that of my brother, CHAS., deceased. If JAS. has issue. Children of my daughter, FRANCES McDANIEL: JOS., PRESTON, and MARY McDANIEL. Babtist (sic) meeting house and lot - building to be erected next to McDANIEL. Executors: THOS. HIGGINBOTHAM; my brother, WM.; and son, JAS.
Book 7, Page 36 -- Administrator's Bond -- JAS. S. HIGGINBOTHAM, THOS. HIGGINBOTHAM, and JNO. PENN, September 17, 1827, for JAS. HIGGINBOTHAM.
Book 7, Page 68 -- Inventory -- September 29, 1827 - $6,423.88. JAS. P. GARLAND; JAS. OGDON; WM. BOURNE; B. BROWN.
Book 7, Page 91 -- Division -- slaves, tools, crops - to JAS. S., JOS. H. McDANIEL; JNO. JAS. McDANIEL; PRESTON GREEN McDANIEL and MARY JANE McDANIEL, infants of FRANCES McDANIEL, deceased - late HIGGINBOTHAM. GEO. McDANIEL, guardian of four children. December 12, 1827. WM. BOURNE, JAS. OGDON, JAS. P. GARLAND.
Book 8, Page 32 -- Administrator's Account from August 20, 1827. Bond of MOSES HIGGINBOTHAM; blacksmith accounts due. November 13, 1829. JAS. P. GARLAND, BENJ. BROWN, JAS. OGDON.
Book 8, Page 154 -- Administrator's Account -- DABNEY SANDIDGE, administrator, from February 28, 1828. D. and D. HIGGINBOTHAM accounts. Mention of several suits. JOS. STAPLES, WM. H. GARLAND, WM. H. KNIGHT and recorded November 22, 1831.

JOSEPH D. HIGGINBOTHAM -- Book 16, Page 99 -- May 17, 1861, written; November 18, 1861, probated. Handwriting attested by HORACE WILSON and WM. T. SIMPSON. JAS. HIGGINBOTHAM qualified. Bonds: RUFUS HIGGINBOTHAM. My interest in estate of my father, JAS. S. HIGGIN-BOTHAM; my ux, LAURA F., if I should not return. In Marriage Register, No. 2, Page 45, JOS. D. HIGGINBOTHAM and LAURA F. HIGGINBOTHAM, April 4, 1860 - no other date.

LEANNA J. HIGGINBOTHAM -- Book 12, Page 526 -- Guardian Bond -- WM. A. and A. B. HIGGINBOTHAM and JAS. W. HENLEY, June 21, 1852, for WM. HIGGINBOTHAM as guardian of LEANNA J., BETSY ANN, and WM. C. HIGGIN-BOTHAM, orphans of AARON HIGGINBOTHAM.
Book 15, Page 156 -- Guardian's Account -- WM. A. HIGGINBOTHAM before D. H. TAPSCOTT, Commissioner - now deceased. Advertised by commissioner, August court, 1853. Ward is now of age, February 26, 1858.

MICHA (MICHIE) HIGGINBOTHAM, MRS. -- Book B, Page 89 -- December 9, 1863, written; codicil, March 24, 1864; August 29, 1864, probated. Witnesses: JAS. HIGGINBOTHAM, SAML. M. GARLAND; to codicil: JAS. HIGGINBOTHAM and NEWTON S. BOWIE(?). Proved by witnesses; JAS. FRANK-LIN failed to qualify within 3 months, and DAVID KYLE made motion for sheriff to administer. Estate apart from my husband. Son, THOS., and husband to be supported. To MARY WARE - MILES (MILLS?) tract bought of RODGERS - at her death, to her heirs. To FANNY WARE. My niece, LAURA ANN KYLE; niece, BETTIE WALKER KYLE; to MARY R. CHICKS - after death of my son, THOS. My niece, MARY JANE BROWN, apart from her husband. My daughter-in-law, LAURA F. HIGGINBOTHAM. Children of my brothers, DAVID and WM. (shown later to be KYLE). My sisters, POCHAHUNTAS (sic) TURNER and SARAH HUDSON and heirs of any children. Executor: JAS. FRANKLIN. Codicil: Niece, BETTY W. KYLE - a slave to her; a clock to MARY R. CHICK, but to remain in the house until

death of my husband. A sugar chest to MARY JANE BROWN; also cow and calf. $1,000.00 to my brother, DAVID KYLE.
Book 18, Page 477 -- Administrator's Account -- RO. W. SNEAD, late sheriff, July 20, 1874. Continued to August 17, 1874; Recorded December 21, 1874.

MOSES HIGGINBOTHAM -- Book 3, Page 165 -- September 29, 1790, written; February 7, 1791, probated. Witnesses: JNO., JAS., and RACHEL HIGGINBOTHAM. Administrator's Bond on Page 166. JOS. HIGGINBOTHAM, son of MOSES, and FRANCES, JAS. and CHAS. HIGGINBOTHAM. Ux, FRANCES; son, JOS. - land on both sides of RUTLEDGE; Sons: ROBT., MOSES, WM. Daughter, RACHEL HIGGINBOTHAM (A deed here shows that she became ux of DANL. NORCUTT, but no marriage is here). - 200 acres on Harris Creek. Son, CHAS.; daughter, FRANCES HIGGINBOTHAM; Blacksmith tools to sons, JOS., WM., and CHAS. Administrators: Ux; Sons, JOS. and WM.
Book 3, Page 174 -- Inventory -- April 2, 1791 -- L 1,546-19-10. JAS. MEREDITH, GABL. PENN, JAS. FRANKLIN.

ROBT. HIGGINBOTHAM -- Really belongs to estate of AARON HIGGINBOTHAM. Book 15, Page 615 -- Commissioner's report and sale by WM. A. HIGGIN-BOTHAM, October 2, 1854. ALEX. B.; AARON; ROBT. H. - one ninth of land sold. One ninth to these: A. B., AARON, JNO. J., BENJ. W. HIGGINBOTHAM. Sale of AARON HIGGINBOTHAM, deceased. Land bought by OSMUND TOMLINSON. Recorded August 13, 1860.

SHANNON HIGGINBOTHAM -- Book 14, Page 13 -- October 20, 1854, written; August 20, 1855, probated. Proved by G. H. CABELL and F. A. MILES. SAML. D. STAPLES qualified - Page 15 - Bondsman: RO. A. COGHILL. Sister, SARAH K. HIGGINBOTHAM, if single, when I die. Niece, LILBON PENN STAPLES, daughter of S. D. STAPLES is to receive a good educa-tion. If SARAH marries; all to LILBON STAPLES. Executors: SAML. D. STAPLES and F. A. MILES.

SOLON HIGGINBOTHAM -- Book 12, Page 150 -- Administrator's Bond -- WM. B. ROANE and J. ROYAL HOLCOMBE, January 15, 1849, for WM. ROANE. Book 15, Page 54 -- Administrator's Bond -- WM. D. MILES and SAML. M. GARLAND, December 20, 1858, for WM. MILES.

THOMAS HIGGINBOTHAM -- Book 9, Page 47 -- February 12, 1834, written; February 16, 1835, probated. Handwriting attested by STERLING CLAI-BORNE and JNO. G. LAYNE. DANL. HIGGINBOTHAM also qualified on probate date. Bondsmen: JOS. K. IRVING, CHAS. B. CLAIBORNE, BENJ. BROWN. JAS. S. HIGGINBOTHAM, ARTHUR B. DAVIES, ALEX. MUNDY, and PEYTON KEITH. Sister, TIRZAH LONDON - where I live - 200 acres and 40 acres next to it; bought of GEO. McDANIEL. TIRZAH's two youngest children: MARY BANK and WM. AUGUSTUS. To JNO. J. LONDON - land bought of WM. BOURNE. To DANL. H. LONDON - land bought of CHAS. P. TALIAFERRO; FRANCES WOODROOF and children - land called Camden's and bought of D. and D. HIGGINBOTHAM. Sister, ANN STANTON HIGGINBO-THAM, late of Georgia - and her children - Farmer's Bank stock. Chil-dren of my brother, JAS. - late of Kentucky - bank stock. Bank stock to ANN E. LONDON. Brother, DANL.; my sister, FRANCES R. COLEMAN; to WESLEY; JANE's children; ux, ARCHY CAREY. Brother, DANL. - trustee for JESSE, EUGENE; my brother MEEKA HIGGINBOTHAM, ux of JAS. S. HIG-GINBOTHAM. These slaves to be freed: Nancy, my cook woman; Maria, my house woman; Tom - Carey Maria's son; Jno. Walter, Maria's son. They may leave Virginia or choose one of my brothers or sisters. Children of my late brother, JAS. Children of my sister, ANN HIGGIN-BOTHAM: DAVID, DANL., and WM. S. HIGGINBOTHAM. Sons of my brother, REUBEN; JESSE and EUGENE in trust. Sister, FRANCES R. COLEMAN; sister, TIRZAH LONDON. Executor: my brother, DANL. HIGGINBOTHAM.
Book 11, Page 433 -- Administrator's de bonis non Bond -- JNO. J. LON-DON and STERLING CLAIBORNE, July 20, 1846, for JNO. LONDON.
Book 12, Page 41 -- Administrator's Account by LONDON from July 25, 1846. For marbe tombstone by M. LYON - $36,00 (sic). HENRICO suit vs. ISAAC WHITE; redemption of land sold for taxes during controversy with RIVES; J. HIGGINBOTHAM for putting up stone; account of D and D HIGGINBOTHAM & Co.; suit in Nelson in favor of THOS. HIGGINBOTHAM as executor of RO. RIVES; Richmond, Virginia, certificate; CHAS. C.

HUDSON and JAS. EVANS, Richmond. Recorded in Amherst County March 21,
1848.
Book 18, Page 307 -- Administrator's de bonis non Bond -- JAS. HIGGIN-
BOTHAM and DANL. H. LONDON, March 16, 1857, for J. HIGGINBOTHAM. RO.
TINSLEY, attorney for LONDON.

THOMAS R. HIGGINBOTHAM -- Book 15, Page 46 -- Guardian Bond -- DAVID
KYLE, D. PATTESON, and PAULUS POWELL, November 15, 1858, for DAVID
KYLE as guardian of THOS. R., JOS. D. HIGGINBOTHAM - infants of
JAMES S. and MICA HIGGINBOTHAM.

WM. HIGGINBOTHAM -- Book 8, Page 166 -- Administrator's Bond -- ROBT.
and JAS. S. HIGGINBOTHAM and WM. H. KNIGHT, February 20, 1832, for
ROBT. HIGGINBOTHAM.
Book 8, Page 173 -- January 2, 1832, written; February 20, 1832, probated. Witnesses: H. M. GARLAND and WM. H. KNIGHT and proved by
them. Stricken in years; son, ROBT., to care for MARY - my ux and his
mother, if she outlives me. 204 acres where I live; lot in New Glasgow; 13 slaves; ROBERT's children; my former grocery at New Glasgow.
My grandchildren: SHANON T. WATTS, STERLING F. WATTS, RO. WM. WATTS,
and JAS. M. WATTS, children of my deceased daughter, JANE S. WATTS;
11 slaves to them - until children are of age or married. Land of my
deceased brother, CHARLES, on Buffalo; ROBERT's children when of age.
Executors: Son, ROBT., and son-in-law, JAMES D. WATTS.
Book 8, Page 176 -- Administrator's Bond -- JAS. D. WATTS and GEO. T.
PLEASANTS, March 19, 1832, for JAS. WATTS.
Book 8, Page 292 -- Inventory -- February, 1832, order; January 19,
1833 - $6,335.00. JOS. STAPLES, HENRY J. ROSE, ED. A. CABELL.
Book 11, Page 127 -- Slave Division - in hands of JAS. D. WATTS. Lots
to JAS. M. WATTS, SHANNON T. WATTS, STERLING F. WATTS, ROBT. W. WATTS.
December 28, 1842. D. R. GOODMAN, RICH. WINGFIELD, N. BURLEY.

WILLIAM S. HIGGINBOTHAM -- Book 9, Page 196 -- Guardian Bond -- JAS. A.
HIGGINBOTHAM and DAVID APPLING, January 18, 1836, for JAS. HIGGIN-
BOTHAM as guardian of WM. S. HIGGINBOTHAM, infant son of JAS. HIGGIN-
BOTHAM.

AJAX G. A. HILL -- Book 14, Page 82 -- indexed for Book 13, Page 82 --
Committee bond, February 18, 1856, for EDMD. HILL as committee for
AJAX A. G. HILL. Bondsman: L. E. WARE.

BETSY ANN HILL -- Book 7, Page 217 -- Guardian Bond -- WM. McCAUL,
April --, 1827, guardian of BETSY ANN, JANE CATH., SALLY and FRANCIS
HILL, orphans of SAML. HILL. Recorded March 17, 1829.

EDMUND J. HILL -- Book 8, Page 158 -- Guardian Bond -- LEWIS E. WIL-
LIAMS, REUBEN D. HILL, and RICH. J. HILL, November 21, 1831, for
LEWIS WILLIAMS as guardian of EDMD. J.; ELVIRA   B. M.; AJAX G. A.;
AMANDA; WM. N. F. and CAMILLA HILL, orphans of WM. D. HILL.

ELIZ. HILL -- Book 4, Page 340 -- Guardian Bond -- BEVERLY WILLIAMSON,
December 21, 1801, as guardian -- ELIZ. HILL, orphan of JNO. HILL.
Book 6, Page 590 -- Guardian Bond -- WM. McCALL and LINDSEY SANDIDGE,
March 24, 1825, for WM. McCALL as guardian of ELIZ. HILL, orphan of
SAML. HILL, deceased.

FRANCES HILL -- Book 9, Page 105 -- Guardian Bond -- DILLARD H. PAGE
and WM. H. GARLAND, August 17, 1835, for DILLARD PAGE as guardian
of FRANCES HILL, orphan of SAML. HILL, deceased.

GEO. HILL -- Book 5, Page 462 -- Administrator's Bond -- THOS. AL-
DRIDGE and MICAJAH CAMDEN, October 17, 1814, for THOS. ALDRIDGE.
Book 5, Page 468 -- August 11, 1812, written; October 17, 1814, pro-
bated. Witnesses: JNO. WHITEHEAD, JNO. MYERS, JAS. S. PENDLETON.
I conveyed to THOS. ALDRIDGE certain real and personal property. I
am ordered to active service. If I should die - brother, NATHL. HILL
and sister, POLLY BIBB, to share. Debt - from deceased father,
NATHL. HILL.

JACOB HILL -- Book 17, Page 258 -- Administrator's Account -- RO. W.

SNEAD, administrator from June 1863. Expenses to Tennessee to collect funds on estate business. Received of J. C. SHIELDS in Tennessee - June 30, 1863. Recorded March 10, 1866.

JAMES HILL, SR. -- Book 8, Page 117 -- Administrator's Bond -- AMBROSE PLUNKET, JAS. S. HIGGINBOTHAM, LEWIS P. SIMPSON, and WM. McDANIEL, August 15, 1831, for AMBROSE PLUNKET.
Book 8, Page 128 -- January 1, 1818, written; codicil of February 18, 1830; June 18, 1831, probated. Witnesses: H. WILSON, JESSE SPINNER, PHILIP LIVELY, LINDSEY McDANIEL; Witnesses to codicil: DANL. B. DALY, JAS. R. LIVELY, JAS. OGDON, WASH. M. NORVELL. Held for more proof and on August 15, 1831, proved by WILSON, McDANIEL, OGDON, LIVELY, and NORVELL. Son, THOS. D.; granddaughter, ELIZ. ROBINSON; my ux, ANNE. Amounts have been given to deceased son, JOHN. My children: POLLY WATTS; NANCY CREWS (formerly ROBINSON); PERMELIA BOBBITT; JEPTHA PLUNKETT; ELIZ. ANDERSON; SUSANNA NORVELL; JAS., JR.; SAML. HILL; FRANCES COX; SALLY GARRETT and children; NANCY MANURVIA - name of LUCY GARVIN is last, but it is not clear that she is a child. Daughter, NANCY, has been married twice and has children by each husband. First four are by ROBT. ROBINSON and last ones are by ARCHELAUS CREWS. Daughter, SALLY, has died and left NANCY and MANURVIA. Executors: Son, THOS. D. HILL; SPENCER NORVELL; and JNO. McDANIEL. Codicil: Granddaughter, ELIZ. ROBERTSON (ROBINSON above) has received bed and furniture; grandson, JNO. H. WATTS; daughter-in-law, SUSAN B. HILL, for attention to me in my crippled condition for last six years. Her husband is THOS. D. HILL. Slave in hands of my son, JAMES HILL.
Book 8, Page 182 -- Sale -- October 19, 1831. A. PLUNKET, administrator. SUSAN B. HILL was a buyer; all items came to $2,542.91. JAS. HILL also was a buyer. Recorded March 19, 1832. RO. TINSLEY, Clerk.
Book 8, Page 204 -- Inventory -- 309 acres - several slaves - $2,300.81-1/2. Girl, Delia, not listed as part of estate at $300 - this is POLLY DILLY and given to daughter-in-law. RICH. HARRISON; PROSSER POWELL; BENJ. NORVELL, April 21, 1890.

JNO. HILL -- Book 4, Page 121 -- Administrator's Account -- EZEKIEL HILL from June, 1802. Rockbridge sheriff paid. Cash from ELIZ. HILL, December 1802. Recorded June 21, 1803. D. S. GARLAND, NELSON C. DAWSON, DAVID TINSLEY, REUBEN PENDLETON.
Book 4, Page 215 -- Inventory -- L 108-7-10, March 15, 1806. MARTIN PARKS; CHAS. BURKS, SR.; DAVID BURKS, SR.
Book 4, Page 336 -- Administrator's Bond -- EZEK. HILL, SAML. HILL, JNO. THOMPSON, September 21, 1801, for EZEK. HILL.
Book 4, Page 510 -- Administrator's Account -- JANE HILL, administratrix from March 1, 1806. Judgment of SAML. HILL and SAML. HILL, JR. THOS. MOORE and PETER P. THORNTON, April 16, 1808. I find no Administrator's Bond for her.

JNO. TALIAFERRO HILL -- Book 4, Page 376 -- Guardian Bond -- NICHL. HARRISON and WM. WOODROOF, September 19, 1803, for NICHL. HARRISON as guardian of JNO. TALIAFERRO HILL, orphan of TALIAFERRO HILL.

MARY F. HILL -- Book 15, Page 105 -- Trustee, November 13, 1858. Trustee: WILKERSON D. TUCKER.

NANCY HILL -- Book 14, Page 80 -- Administrator's Bond -- LEWIS E. WILLIAMS and EDMUND HILL, February 18, 1856, for LEWIS WILLIAMS.
Book 14, Page 394 -- Inventory -- $506.50. RO. K. HARGROVE, ANSON BURFORD, WM. PARR. March 1, 1856.
Book 14, Page 491 -- Administrator's Account and sale -- July 24, 1857. Buyers: E. J. and EDMUND J. HILL. Recorded August 17, 1857 - $519.86.
Book 14, Page 401 -- Sale -- March 1, 1856 - E. J. HILL was buyer and amount as above.

NATHANIEL HILL -- Book 4, Page 478 -- Administrator's Bond -- JNO. JACOBS, JR.; JAS. MURPHY; JAS. MONTGOMERY, November 16, 1807, for JNO. JACOBS, JR.
Book 4, Page 487 -- Inventory -- L 2,056-15-6. D. McDANIEL; THOS. MASSIE; RO. SHIELDS, December 9, 1807.

ROBT. E. (A.) HILL -- Book B, Page 88 -- Guardian Bond -- R. W. SNEAD, A. C. HARRISON, WIATT TUCKER, BENJ. L. TALIAFERRO, THOS. WHITEHEAD, JAS. P. COLEMAN, RO. A. PENDLETON, and J. DUDLEY DAVIS, March 29, 1861, for R. W. SNEAD as guardian of RO. E. (A.?) HILL, orphan of ----- HILL.

SAMUEL HILL -- Book 5, Page 692 -- Administrator's Bond -- POLLY HILL and JAS. FULCHER, August 18, 1817, for POLLY HILL.
Book 8, Page 160 -- Administrator's Bond -- JACOB COFFMAN and WM. H. KNIGHT, December 19, 1831, for JACOB COFFMAN - unadministered by former administrator.
Book 9, Page 99 -- Administrator's de bonis non Bond -- JACOB COFFMAN - account from 1830. ED. A. CABELL and PAUL C. BOWLES, July 20, 1835.

SUSANNAH HILL -- Book 4, Page 341 -- Guardian Bond -- WASHINGTON HILL and MARK LIVELY, December 21, 1801, for WASHINGTON HILL as guardian of SUSANNAH HILL, orphan of JNO. HILL, deceased.

TALIAFERRO HILL -- Book 4, Page 340 -- Administrator's Bond -- NICHL. HARRISON, RICH. BURKS, and DAVID WOODROOF, November 16, 1801, for NICHL. HARRISON.

THOMAS HILL -- Book 3, Page 95 -- Administrator's Bond -- ELIZ. HILL, RICH. FULCHER, and JNO. HALEY, February 2, 1789, for ELIZ. HILL.

THOS. D. HILL -- Book 5, Page 512 -- Constable's Bond -- June 19, 1815. Bondsmen: RICH. HARRISON, GEO. W. TAYLOR.
Book 5, Page 654 -- Constable -- First Hundred, June 17, 1817. Bondsman: RICH. POWELL.
Book 6, Page 232 -- Constable -- June 18, 1821. Bondsmen: JAS. G. HIGGINBOTHAM, MATT. LIVELY.
Book 6, Page 362 -- Constable -- First Hundred, June 16, 1823. Bondsmen: WM. KNIGHT, WM. J. (I.) ISBELL, WM. D. HILL.
Book 6, Page 599 -- Constable -- June 20, 1825. Bondsmen: THOS. HUTCHESON, ELIAS WILLS.
Book 14, Page 520 -- Administrator's Bond -- March 15, 1858. WM. R. and JOS. HILL for WM. HILL.

WILLIAM D. HILL -- Book 7, Page 286 -- Administrator's Bond -- REUBEN D. HILL, WM. Y. WINSTON, RICH. J. HILL, and LEWIS E. WILLIAMS, November 16, 1829, for REUBEN D. HILL. Will: October 8, 1829, written; November 16, 1829, probated. Witnesses: WM. Y. WINSTON; JNO. H. GOODWIN, SR. and JR., and proved by WINSTON and JR. Ux, NANCY - 2 small tracts. One on Lynch Road and 4-1/2 miles from Lynchburg and one bought of trustees of MICAJAH CLARK, deceased. These constitute one of the two small tracts. The other - under sale made by CAPT. REUBEN NORVELL, trustee of deed made by WM. C. MUSE to NORVELL to secure debt to MILNOR COX. My mother, ELIZ. EDWARDS, has slaves. Saddle to ELVIRIA B. M. HILL and one for JULIET AMANDA HILL. Son, EDMUND J. HILL, may raise stock with his mother. My children: REUBEN D.; ELIZA W. CREASY and children; RICH. J. HILL; EDMUND J. HILL; ELVIRIA B. M. HILL; AJAX C. A. HILL; WM. N. F. HILL, and NANCY CAMILLA HILL. EDMUND is to help care for younger brothers and sisters. Executors: Ux, REUBEN D. and RICH. J. HILL.
Book 7, Page 310 -- Inventory -- $1,457.90, November 17, 1829. JNO. H. GOODWIN, CHAS. WINGFIELD, MICAJAH L. CLARK.
Book 8, Page 80 -- Inventory -- $149.83, December 31, 1829. Deed of trust to C. DABNEY. Sold by L. E. WILLIAMS as agent of executor.
Book 8, Page 180 -- Administrator's Bond -- NANCY HILL - unadministered estate, March 19, 1832. Bondsman: W. R. ROANE.
Book 8, Page 196 -- Administrator's Account -- REUBEN D. HILL from November 16, 1829. Four trips to Augusta - REUBEN lived in that county. Bond of NANCY HILL. Recorded March 22, 1832. At sale she bought everything.
Book 14, Page 80 -- Administrator's de bonis non Bond -- February 18, 1856. LEWIS E. WILLIAMS and EDMD. HILL for LEWIS WILLIAMS.

JAMES HIX -- Book 6, Page 179 -- Ordinary at house in county, October 16, 1820. Bondsman: JNO. RICHESON.

175

JNO. F. HIX -- Book 12, Page 277 -- Ordinary at Dillard's Store, July 15, 1850. Bondsman: W. HIX.

LUCY HOBSON -- Book 11, Page 471 -- Estate Commitment to Sheriff -- March, 1847. Motion of SAML. C. GIBSON. Sheriff: JAS. L. LAMKIN. Book 12, Page 297 -- Inventory -- July 23, 1847. LAMKIN as administrator. Sale: $16.87, same date. CHAS. MASSIE, JOEL F. SMITH, L. T. CASH.
Book 12, Page 566 -- Administrator's Account by LAMKIN, June 15, 1850. SAML. C. GIBSON, Commissioner.

MATILDA HODY -- Book 11, Page 614 -- Estate Commitment to Sheriff -- November term, 1847. JAS. LAMKIN, Sheriff.

RICH. HOG -- Book 5, Page 505 -- Lunatic Bond -- May 16, 1815. SAML. HOG, ROSEMARY GUE, RODERICK NOEL, for SAML. HOG.

JNO. HOGG -- Book 5, Page 409 -- Administrator's Bond -- HEZEKIAH SHOEMAKER and JNO. FLOOD, January 17, 1814, for HEZEKIAH SHOEMAKER. Book 5, Page 442 -- Inventory -- June 20, 1814 -- L 45-13-0. THOS. MORRIS; GEO. MORRIS; NICHL. WEST; JAS. DAVIES.

NANCY HOGG -- Book 8, Page 86 -- March 29, 1814, written; March 21, 1831, probated. Witnesses: ROWLAND P. BURKS; GEO. MORRIS, JR.; THOS. MORRIS. Nephew, JOHNSON GUE, son of ROSE MARY GUE, when 21 - and to administer.
Book 8, Page 134 -- Administrator's Bond -- JOHNSON GUE and SAML. BURKS, September 19, 1831, for JOHNSON GUE.

ELIZ. HOLLOWAY -- Book 5, Page 65 -- Guardian Bond -- THOS. T. HOLLOWAY, ROBT. COLEMAN, and DANIEL HIGGINBOTHAM, June 19, 1810, for THOS. HOLLOWAY as guardian of GEORGE G., and ELIZ. HOLLOWAY, orphans of ROBT. HOLLOWAY.
Book 6, Page 498 -- Guardian Bond -- ANN M. HOLLOWAY and HENRY L. DAVIES, November 16, 1826, for ANN HOLLOWAY as guardian of ELIZ. HOLLOWAY, orphan of THOMAS S. HOLLOWAY (also called ELIZA). LUCAS P. THOMPSON signed, but name is not at head of bond. Note: GEORGE G. is a mistake by clerk; data later shows that he was GEO. SEATON and not GEO. G.

GEORGE SEATON HOLLOWAY -- Book 5, Page 65 -- Guardian Bond -- see first item above on ELIZ. HOLLOWAY. He is indexed as GEO. G. therein. Book 5, Page 193 -- Guardian Bond -- CHAS. B. PENN, ROBT. COLEMAN, NICHL. HARRISON, and THOS. ALDRIDGE, January 18, 1813, for CHAS. PENN as guardian of GEO. S. HOLLOWAY, one of devisees of HENRY HOLLOWAY, and orphan of ROBT. HOLLOWAY.

CAPT. HENRY HOLLOWAY -- Book 4, Page 624 -- Saturday, August 5, 1808, written; June 18, 1810, probated. Handwriting attested by JAS. P. GARLAND and JAS. ALLEN. THOS. S. HOLLOWAY qualified. Bondsmen: DAVID S. GARLAND and REUBEN NORVELL. Desired Masonic funeral; sister, SALLY SLAUGHTER and husband, F. SLAUGHTER; sister YANCY is very poor. Debt of DRURY BELL to go to support his ux and then to her daughter, SALLY, or all of her children. Debt of CHAS. H. SLAUGHTER and hope that he will care for his brother, HENRY. GEO. S. (SEATON written above in different ink) and his sister - son and daughter of RO. HOLLOWAY, deceased. Executors: friends, THOS. S. HOLLOWAY, STEPHEN WATTS, and JAS. FRANKLIN. When GEO. S. and sister are of age. Freedom desired for faithful servant, Glaster, ux, Nancy, and daughter, but Virginia law forbids it. Executors may give them $100 to send them away.
Book 5, Page 55 -- Inventory -- August 22, 1810 - L 1,162-16-0. THOS. CREWS, ROBT. COLEMAN, JAS. PENDLETON.
Administrator's Bond is Book 5, Page 61 -- see will.
Book 6, Page 18 -- Division consented to by NICHL. KINNEY who married ELIZ. HOLLOWAY and GEO. S. HOLLOWAY, by guardian, CHAS. B. PENN. Committee: MICAJAH CAMDEN, DR. JAS. POWELL, THOS. S. HOLLOWAY. Division on December 30, 1817, to the heirs of. CAPT. HOLLOWAY.
Book 6, Page 22 -- Administrator's Account by THOS. S. HOLLOWAY from July 14, 1810. Legacy of MRS. B. YANCEY; JINNINGS vs. HOLLOWAY;

account of ROBT. HOLLOWAY as guardian of his ux; legacy of SARAH
SLAUGHTER; DOCTOR GILBERT for pulling LUCY's tooth - 3 shillings;
guardian of G. S. HOLLOWAY, C. B. PENN; C. B. PENN - for trip to
Staunton with E. HOLLOWAY; FRANCIS SLAUGHTER; coffin for LUCY - 18
shillings; C. B. PENN as guardian of G. S. and ELIZ. HOLLOWAY - 1817
accounts. JNO. DILLARD's bonds due estate; sale to DR. POWELL; account
of WIATT POWELL due estate of ROBT. HOLLOWAY. Total: L 3,509-12-5.
May 11, 1818. Committee: JAS. POWELL, EDMD. WINSTON, RO. WALKER.
Book 8, Page 410 -- Estate Commitment to Sheriff -- April term, 1834.
THOS. S. HOLLOWAY, administrator, dead more than three months.
Sheriff: EDMD. WINSTON.

ROBERT HOLLOWAY -- Book 4, Page 48 -- August 16, 1802, written;
September 20, 1802, probated. Witnesses: JAS. FRANKLIN, DRURY BELL,
SEATON M. PENN.
Administrator's Bond is on Page 353, same date: HENRY HOLLOWAY quali-
fied. Bondsmen: DRURY BELL and JNO. DILLARD. Brother, HENRY HOLLO-
WAY, is to administer. My ux, SALLY, is with child. My children:
GEO. SEATON HOLLOWAY; BETSY CATHERINE SLAUGHTER; PENN HOLLOWAY - when
of age or married. Note: ROBT. HOLLOWAY got bond to marry SARAH
PENN, spinster, November 18, 1797. GEO. DILLARD was surety. REV.
CHAS. CRAWFORD made a return.
Book 4, Page 60 -- Inventory -- L 1,155-17-0, October 20, 1802.
STEPHEN WATTS, DRURY BELL, DAVID S. GARLAND.
Book 5, Page 1 -- Administrator's Account -- HENRY HOLLOWAY - from
December 10, 1800 (sic) - to MISS BETSY PENN - Callimes shoes; slippers
bought in Culpeper, August 5, 1801(?), by your brother, SEATON when at
B. Springs - and dancing school. Order of May Court, 1805. JOS. BUR-
RUS, DAVID S. GARLAND, GEO. DILLARD, LEONARD HENLEY, BENJ. TALIAFERRO -
to settle accounts of HENRY HOLLOWAY, executor of ROBT. HOLLOWAY, de-
ceased, who was guardian of BETSY PENN, infant orphan of JOS. PENN.

THOMAS S. HOLLOWAY, CAPT. -- Book 5, Page 100 -- Coroner -- April 20,
1812. Bondsman: HENRY BOURNE.
Book 6, Page 459 -- Same -- May 17, 1824. Bondsmen: JAS. POWELL, AR-
THUR B. DAVIES, HENRY L. DAVIES.
Book 6, Page 478 -- Administrator's Bond -- August 16, 1824. HENRY L.
DAVIES qualified. Bondsman: A. B. DAVIES.
Book 6, Page 580 -- Inventory of CAPT. THOS. S. HOLLOWAY, deceased.
September of 1824. Recorded March 22, 1825. HENRY L. DAVIES, adminis-
trator: $6,057.54-1/2. THOS. CREWS, JNO. TALBOT.
Book 6, Page 737 -- Administrator's Account by DAVIES from October 5,
1824. G. S. HOLLOWAY's land tax; to GEO. HOLLOWAY; MRS. ANN M. HOLLO-
WAY. April 25, 1826. JAS. P. GARLAND, WILKINS WATSON, LINDSEY COLEMAN.

FRANKLIN HOOD -- Book 14, Page 57 -- Administrator's Bond -- RO. A.
COGHILL and SAML. M. GARLAND, January 21, 1856, for RO. COGHILL.
Book 14, Page 77 -- Inventory -- January 22, 1856 - $51.09. RO. A.
PENDLETON; THOS. L. TAYLOR; WM. H. ROSE. Sale, January 26, 1856 -
$82.93.
Book 14, Page 335 -- Administrator's Account by COGHILL from Janu-
ary 21, 1856 - digging grave - $5.00; V. T. SETTLE for funeral sermon -
$5.00. Total: $2,162.70. Recorded Monday, March 16, 1857.

EDWARD T. P. HOPKINS -- Book 13, Page 394 -- June 27, 1854, written;
December 18, 1854, probated. Witnesses: GALLATIN M. BIBB, BENJ. S.
HIGGINBOTHAM and proved by them. HIRAM CHEATWOOD qualified - bond
on Page 397. My ux; either of my children - as of age or married. He
then speaks of either or all of my children. Executor: HIRAM CHEAT-
WOOD.
Book 14, Page 65 -- Inventory -- December 19, 1855 - $11,289.25.
WHITING DAVIES; CHAS. L. ELLIS; MARTIN D. TINSLEY.
Book 14, Page 187 -- Administrator's Account by CHEATWOOD from Decem-
ber 6, 1854. To MRS. LUCY E. HOPKINS for family. Recorded Monday,
October 20, 1856.
Book 15, Page 8 -- Administrator's Account by same administrator
from March 17, 1856. To Amherst Courthouse on business (Note: old-
timers still use this term in speaking of the Village of Amherst.)
He charged 88 cents for this trip. MRS. HOPKINS for family. Recorded
December 18, 1854.

Book 15, Page 181 -- Administrator's Account by same administrator
from August 26, 1857. To MRS. HOPKINS for tuition fees. Recorded
June 20, 1859.
Book 16, Page 236 -- Administrator's Account by same administrator
from December 31, 1858. Tuition fees. Recorded March 30, 1861.
Book 16, Page 336 -- Administrator's Account by same administrator
from July 30, 1860. Tuition to C. MANSON for SUSAN, HARRIET, and R. P.
HOPKINS. B. CHAPLAIN bought 300 acres; widow's dower. Expenses at
Virginia Military Institute for R. P. HOPKINS. Recorded October 20,
1862.

JAMES HOPKINS, DOCTOR -- I wish to state that this is one of the most
interesting wills in Amherst County between 1761 and 1919. I have
cited some others as well, but I feel sure that every reader will be
fascinated by this one. It is also one of the longest and most com-
plicated documents in the books for the cited period. I am unable to
say just what action, if any, was taken on his elaborate plan for
hospital farms. It may be that they are mentioned in some of the
works on the history of medical practices in Virginia, but I have not
consulted them. It will be noted that he baited a grandson to change
his name from POLLARD to HOPKINS and I have found that this was done
from order book items not treated herein.
Book 4, Page 86 -- October 31, 1802, written; May 16, 1803, probated.
Witnesses: LEONARD PHILLIPS; LITTLEPAGE DAMERON; EDWARD THOMPSON;
TOMS (sic); PLEASANT GRIFFIN. Proved by PHILLIPS and GRIFFIN. RICH.
C. POLLARD qualified on November 21, 1804. Bondsmen: AMBROSE and
ROBT. CAMP. Wished to be buried by parents in Albemarle; family grave-
yard and to be kept in repair. Father's land, but now that of SAML.
DYER. Friend, DR. GEO. GILMER, deceased, Albemarle - his heirs; to
COL. WILSON MILES CAREY, formerly of Fluvanna; to EDMUND BIBEY (car-
penter), formerly of Amherst, but now of Bedford or Pittsylvania; to
WM. ALLEN STONE, mason, formerly of Amherst, but, now--I think--of
Kentucky. Several slaves are to be freed. The cook of my ux, ANNE
SPARKS HOPKINS, is to be supported. Instructions to executors as to
emancipation. My head waterman, Jacob, bought of MR. (?) CARTER.
Have engaged single man for some years as overseer, but might be well
to exchange him for some prudent man with a family. If not, must
lodge in some other house and have only his diet and washing done in
the Mansion House. Rachel is hired to THOS. NASH until Xmas (sic)
next; Lydia is at MR. TOM's; my daughter, POLLARD; three water-men to
run boats; Cato is to be carpenter and prepare stocks of planks of
poplar, etc., and weatherboard our house this Fall and shingles next
Spring; to build servants' houses and overseer in Cherry orchard and
Cove - where one lately burned there. Cato may be hired to some white
man. My boys, SQUIRE and ROBT., may work as carpenters and not run
river in rigorous season. In November, 1803, my 866 acres to be
divided into two equal parts - north and south line. Eastern will have
Mansion for ux and Eastern which I here call Athivistor(?) and former
is called Annadale. In October, 1803, Amherst court is to appoint
committee to divide other property. Slave, Phebe, at that time may
return to Pittsylvania where she lately lived with my sister, LUCY
ROBINSON. Her younger children will also be there, and I understand
that she also has a husband there. Phebe's children are loaned to my
sister, LUCY and they are Mary, Jenny, Betty, and Darius. Darius has
been loaned to doctor in Albemarle. My sister, LUCY, and her children.
Male slaves are to be freed at age of 44 and females at age 40. PLEA-
SANT GRIFFIN and J. WESLEY GREEN are to improve Cato in carpenter
trade and JAS. and ROBT. in winter months. My Athiviston (hard to
decipher) -- interesting instructions here and classification of
slaves: plantation, carpenters, watermen. Jacob, though black, illi-
terate - has established his character and executors may rely upon him.
Cato, after freedom, to have priority in employment on boats, etc.
Boat receipts are to build up to L 300 and then L 200 to be used to
buy farm and dwelling. A doctor with satisfactory credentials is to
be placed thereon. He will be employed on annual basis by executors.
He shall receive at least three consumptives per year in his hospital -
other ailments of 2 years standing, such as kidney stones, etc. Cures
are to be certified to court. One more patient is to be added. If no
cures, then meeting to be held to discuss keeping doctor. Due publici-
ty to be given and $10.00 bounty for each cure. Fund to be used to set

up - after purchases - sites in upper end of Buckingham, Bedford, or Campbell counties for same purposes. Hydrophobia is to be treated; effort to be made to discover American plants or raising foreign ones or transplanting from foreign counties. Trustees of hospitals are to be: WM. CARY NICHOLAS, ALBEMARLE; WM. LEWIS, son-in-law of my sister, MARY CABELL, of Buckingham; WM. CALLOWAY, son-in-law of my sister, E. SMITH, near New London; and SAML. CALLALAND, also son-in-law of my sister, E. SMITH. Hospital and farms not to be more than 12 or 15 miles from James River and from Town of New London. Trustees are to keep books on patients and disorders; vacancies on board to be filled by rest of members and recorded in courts where hospitals are built. Instructions as to porch on house - about 16 by 12 feet. Where my road leads into Loving's Gap - and JOS. PHILLIPS onto Main Road. Land may be bought of MR. JNO. GRIFFIN or MR. HARVIE for Preaching House - 2 acres -- to REV. JNO. SHEPHERD, TANDY KEY, and RICHARD BREEDLOVE of Methodist Society -- to be called Christ Church and open to other preachers as well.

My brother, WILLIAM HOPKINS, TANDY KEY, and SKYLER HARRIS, Albemarle, to erect meeting house on 2 acres of my Waterford tract in Fluvanna - where my freed man, SQUIRE JACKSON, lives - off from the river - to be called Waterford Preaching House -- perpetual fund to be set up for both churches. Mentions land in Albemarle and Fluvanna. Son-in-law, RICH. C. POLLARD, and nephew, JAMES HOPKINS, son of my brother, ARTHUR HOPKINS, late of Pittsylvania. Plantation fund to educate 2 youths of near relation to me -- my grandson, ARTHUR, eldest and at present only son of my surviving child, ELIZ. BOUSH POLLARD, and ARTHUR, eldest son of my nephew, JAS. HOPKINS, Pittsylvania. Private school to be established nearest convenient academy - able and pious teachers to be obtained; parents of named youths to be consulted and trustees selected. They are to have grammar, Latin, Greek, and then to some college or seminary, say, Williamsburg. Hopes that one will become M.D. and other a preacher or will serve fellow men. Does not put restraint upon their choices. At end of 7 years, trustees and parents to discuss further steps -- both should study until 21. Hopes that grandson, ARTHUR POLLARD, will not be prevented from securing education by perverse nature of his father, RICH. C. POLLARD. Eldest son of my nephew, WM. HOPKINS, son of my brother, WM. HOPKINS - of name of JACOB - to take grandson's place, if his father refused education for his son. ARTHUR, eldest son of my nephew, JAMES. Daughter, ELIZ. POLLARD, and her children -- unfortunate conduct of her husband, RICH. C. POLLARD. Chest and other furniture to her; Annadale plantation. Grandson, ARTHUR, born in February, 1794; my daughter and her younger children; when eldest, save ARTHUR, are married. My books - many religious. Surviving brothers and sisters. To REV. JNO. SHEPHERD - one lent to HENRY SMITH; medical books to brother-in-law, DR. WM. MARTIN. Limestone tract bought of my brother, WM. HOPKINS - my father's will - to be called Limerick. Books to friends: HENRY and TANDY KEY; DR. EDWD. T. TOMS (in hands of DR. E. WILLIAMS) - DR. TOMS is to act as librarian. My nephew, JAS. HOPKINS DAVIS, son of my sister, AMELIA; children of my sister, FRANCES DAVIS, deceased. Children of my sister, ISABELLA TOWNS; JOHN DAVIS, son of my sister, JANE DAVIS, deceased. Brother-in-law, MR. (?) BAXTER DAVIS, Mecklinburg County; my nephew, JOSEPH CABELL; niece, MRS. MARY HOPKINS BRECKENRIDGE and nephew, GENERAL SAML. HOPKINS -- to last named of Kentucky. RICH. C. POLLARD bought slave, Daniel, from estate of my father-in-law and I was security. I took mortgage and of record in Amherst County - mention of June, 1801. If, by grace of God, POLLARD becomes reformed from former immoral conduct, and becomes a kind, prudent, and affectionate husband and father - then executors to wait some years for money due. Reference to deed of 1799 to RICH. C. POLLARD for ux and children. Wants grandson, ARTHUR POLLARD, when 21 to drop POLLARD name and use HOPKINS instead and to record change in Amherst County. If he does so, he gets entire estate--real and personal in Amherst County - Albemarle and Fluvanna. He has a year to decide after maturity. If he does not comply, then to be divided to ARTHUR HOPKINS, eldest son of my nephew, JAMES; son of my brother, ARTHUR; JACOB HOPKINS, son of my nephew, WM. HOPKINS, Albemarle; and grandson of my brother, WILLIAM. My daughter, ELIZ. POLLARD, and future issue. Executors: Brother, WM. HOPKINS, and friends: HENRY FRY, Culpaper; EDWD. GARLAND; TANDY KEY; SAML. MURRELL of Albemarle;

179

WM. H. CABELL, Amherst County. Hospital trustees: W. C. NICHOLAS,
Albemarle; W. LEWIS of -----; W. CALLAWAY of Bedford; SAML. CALLAND of
Pittsylvania.
Book 4, Page 269 -- Inventory -- Many slaves; no total. RICH. C.
POLLARD, administrator. January 19, 1807. JOS. SHELTON; WM. HARRIS;
MATT. HARRIS.
Book 4, Page 273 -- Dower to ANN SPARKS HOPKINS, widow. Plats - not
herein - county surveyor and deputies. Mansion house part of tract;
slaves; conditional bequest to grandson, ARTHUR POLLARD. ZACH. PHIL-
LIPS, neighbor and oversee, and ELIJAH CHRISTIAN, to divide items into
2 lots. November 1, 1804. HUDSON MARTIN; WM. HARRIS; HAWES COLEMAN;
NATHAN CRAWFORD.
Book 4, Page 393 -- Administrator's Bond -- RICH. C. POLLARD; AMBROSE
CAMP and ROBT. CAMP, bondsmen (both bondsmen of Culpeper), November 21,
1804, for RICH. POLLARD.

JOHN HORSLEY -- Book 4, Page 531 -- October 22, 1804, written; September 19, 1808, probated. Witnesses: WM.; R. and SAML. HORSLEY. JNO.
and HECTOR HORSLEY qualified. Bondsmen: MICAJAH PENDLETON and WM.
HORSLEY. Son, JOHN - where I live - 200 acres. Son, HECTOR, land in
Buckingham - 160 acres. One half of land JNO. MILLER and I contended
for and I recovered of him. 100 acres in Amherst County on James to
HECTOR HORSLEY and given to me by will of my brother, ROBT., at death
of his widow. Daughter, JANE ROBERTS; daughter, ELIZ. HORSLEY;
slaves from estate of brother, ROBT. - at his widow's death.

MARTHA HORSLEY -- Book 4, Page 427 -- Administrator's Bond -- MICAJAH
PENDLETON, GEO. PENN, and JOSEPH HORSLEY, April 21, 1806, for
R. P. (sic).

NICHOLAS HORSLEY -- Book 4, Page 435 -- Guardian Bond -- MICAJAH PEN-
DLETON and GEO. PENN, September 15, 1806, for MICAJAH PENDLETON as
guardian of NICHL. HORSLEY, orphan of WILLIAM HORSLEY.

ROBERT HORSLEY -- I found that this will was incomplete and wrote to
Virginia State Library to see about the film made by Mormons some
years ago. Their copy of this book also showed missing pages were
gone when film was made. The clerk found the original and made a film
of the original and placed it in the book.
Book 3, Page 12f -- March 9, 1786, written; July 3, 1786, probated.
Witnesses: JAMES PAMPLIN; MARY BOAZE; ISBELL VIA. Ux, JUDAH - where
I live; 6 slaves; my two brothers, WM. and JNO. HORSLEY. Ux and
brothers to administer. The brothers qualified. Bondsman: GEO.
HILTON.

WILLIAM HORSLEY -- Book 3, Page 200 -- April 15, 1791, written; Septem-
ber 5, 1791, probated. Witnesses: EZEKIAL GILBERT; JAS. PAMPLIN; BAR-
RETT STEPHENS; ANN and FRANCES TALIAFERRO. MARTHA HORSLEY, JNO. HORS-
LEY, and RODERICK McCULLOCH qualified. Bondsmen: SAML. MEGGINSON and
DAVID WOODROOF. Ux, MARTHA - 200 acres where I live; my children as
of age. My six sons: WM., JOS., ROBT., SAML., JOHN, and NICHOLAS.
Executors: ux and friends, SAML. MEGGINSON, RODERICH McCULLOCH; JNO.
HORSLEY and ZACH. TALIAFERRO.
Book 3, Page 234 -- Inventory -- L 838-10-1, September 20, 1791. JAS.
PAMPLIN, GEO. HILTON, DANL. PERROW.

WILLIAM ANDREW HORSLEY -- Book 7, Page 333 -- Guardian Bond -- JNO. and
ROBT. HORSLEY, March 15, 1830, for JNO. HORSLEY as guardian of WM.
ANDREW HORSLEY, infant son of JNO. HORSLEY.

ANNE HOWARD -- Book 4, Page 206 -- October 17, 1805, written; December 17, 1805, probated. Witnesses: NANCY TAYLOR, JNO. A. SMITH,
and MARY SMITH. Proved by SMITHS. Husband, WM. HOWARD - 140 acres
where I live and left to me by my first husband, THOS. POWEL.

JOHN HOWARD -- Book 4, Page 438 -- Administrator's Bond -- REUBEN B.
PATTERSON and JAS. MURPHY, December 15, 1806, for REUBEN PATTERSON.
JOHN's name has been underlined, but I do not know whether it denotes
clerical error or just marking (illegal) by some researcher. It
could be an official error since there is an Administrator's Account

indexed for him as Book 4, Page 585, and it is not there.

SUSAN L. HOWARD -- Book 13, Page 403 -- November 25, 1854, written;
codicil on same date; January 15, 1855, probated. Witnesses to will
and codicil: B. C. MEGGINSON; JNO. ROBERTS, SR.; J. G. MEGGINSON;
SAML. J. WALKER. Resident of Harisburg, Pennsylvania, but now in
Amherst County. $200.00 to MRS. CAROLINE ROBERTS, Harisburg, Pennsyl-
vania, because of my love and esteem for her. Same amount to vestry
of St. Stephen's Church in same city. Same to ALEX. RAY, Washington,
D.C., in trust for my sister, MARTHA ANN ROSS; interest to be used
for her and at her death to Protestant Episcopal Bishop of Pennsylvania
and orphanage (Episcopal) at Lancester, Pennsylvania, and for foreign
missions. Executors: ALEX. RAY, Washington, D.C.; and RO. J. ROSS,
Harisburg, Pennsylvania. Codicil: Sum to my friend, DR. B. C. MEG-
GINSON.

ABSALOM HOWL -- Book 10, Page 263 -- Administrator's Bond -- ELIZ.
HOWL; BENJ.; GEO.; and ABSALOM HOWL; WM. JOYNER, and JNO. CHRISTIAN,
September 21, 1840, for ELIZ. HOWL.
Book 10, Page 283 -- Inventory -- October 9, 1840 -- $3,556.50. JAS. S.
HIGGINBOTHAM; JOS. KYLE; JNO. P. WILSON.
Book 10, Page 300 -- Sale, November 13, 1840 -- Family buyers: AB-
SALOM, GEO., ELIZ., BENJ., and CATHERINE HOWL. $749.54.
Book 11, Page 194 -- Administrator's Account -- ELIZ. HOWL - to ABSA-
LOM HOWL and GEO. HOWL. December 18, 1843. JNO. P. WILSON and JAS. S.
HIGGINBOTHAM.
Book 13, Page 190 -- Administrator's Account by ELIZ. HOWL from Au-
gust 15, 1842. To ELIZ. HOWL, widow; GEO.; BENJ.; MICHAEL C.; and
CATH. HOWL; JNO. H. CHRISTIAN and ux; JAS. A. KEYTON (also spelled
KEATON in some places) and ux; WM. JOINER and ux; JNO. HOWL; REBECCA
HOWL; JANE HOWL as administrator of ABSALOM HOWL, JR.; GEO. HOWL as
guardian of CATH. and MICHL. C. HOWL; JANE HOWL as assignee of WM.
JOINER, distributee, and ux; ELIZ. HOWL as guardian of JNO. and REBEC-
CA HOWL. Recorded November --, 1852.

ABSALOM J. HOWL -- Book 11, Page 70 -- Administrator's Bond -- JANE
HOWL, RO. PATRICK; GEO. W. HOWL; JNO. H. CHRISTIAN, and BENJ. F. HOWL,
July 18, 1842, for JANE HOWL.
Book 11, Page 84 -- Inventory -- no total, September 19, 1842. JANE W.
HOWL, JAS. L. HIGGINBOTHAM, THOS. A. MILES, JNO. P. WILSON.

CATHERINE HOWL -- Book 10, Page 278 -- Guardian Bond -- GEO. W. HOWL,
JAS. S. HIGGINBOTHAM, ROBT. PATRICK, October 19, 1840, for GEO. HOWL,
as guardian of CATH. HOWL, orphan of ABSALOM HOWL, deceased.
Book 13, Page 216 -- Guardian's Account -- by guardian from 1842.
December 31 - your expenses to Staunton; paid ELIZ. HOWL, 1846; suit
HOWL vs. HOWL; ELIZ. HOWL's account as administratrix of ABSALOM HOWL,
deceased. RO. M. BROWN, Commissioner. Recorded November 15, 1852.
Book 13, Page 474 -- Guardian's Account -- GEO. W. HOWL, guardian from
December 31, 1842. Expenses to Staunton; ELIZ. HOWL for board; settle-
ment of ELIZ. HOWL's account as administratrix of ABSALOM HOWL.
March 4, 1852; recorded August 15, 1852.

GEO. W. HOWL -- Book 12, Page 355 -- Inventory -- January 4, 1851,
DAVID PATTESON, LEWIS S. CAMPBELL, and W. KENT. 163-3/4 acres.
Reference to will of RICH. TURNER, father of MRS. GEO. W. HOWL; slaves
are property of MRS. HOWL and children, and GEO. W. HOWL had only
life estate. Recorded January 20, 1851.

JNO. JAS. HOWL -- Book 10, Page 277 -- Guardian Bond -- ELIZ. HOWL;
ABSALOM HOWL; and JAS. A. KEATON, October 19, 1840, for ELIZ. HOWL as
guardian of JOHN JAMES HOWL, orphan of ABSALOM HOWL.
Book 12, Page 373 -- Guardian Bond -- ELIZ.; MICHAEL; and BENJ. HOWL,
April 21, 1851, for ELIZ. HOWL as guardian of JNO. JAS. HOWL, orphan
of ABSALOM HOWL.

MICHAEL HOWL (so indexed, but really MICH. C. as will be seen by
next entry) -- Book 10, Page 278 -- Guardian Bond -- GEO. W. HOWL,
ROBT. PATRICK, and JAS. S. HIGGINBOTHAM, October 19, 1840, for GEO.
HOWL as guardian of MICHL. HOWL, orphan of ABSALOM HOWL. Patrick is

called JAS. in bond, but it is signed as ROBT.
Book 12, Page 287 -- Guardian's Account -- by guardian from May 6,
1841. Various tuition fees--HOWL vs. HOWL. September 17, 1850. RO.
WINGFIELD, LEWIS S. CAMPBELL, DAVID PATTESON.

MICHAEL C. HOWL -- Book 15, Page 63 -- December 15, 1858, written;
February 21, 1859, probated. Witnesses: WM. B. DAVIES and JAS. P.
COLEMAN. Sister, CATHERINE B. HOWL; nephew, DANL. W. KEITEN; mother,
ELIZABETH--where she lives. Executor: brother, JNO. J. HOWL - may
sell my land. Proved by witnesses. JNO. J. HOWL qualified. Bonds-
men: R. A. COGHILL and J. P. COLEMAN.

REBECCA HOWL (also HOWLE) -- Book 10, Page 277 -- Guardian Bond --
ELIZ. HOWL, ABSALOM J. HOWL, and JAS. A. KEETON, October 19, 1840,
for ELIZ. HOWL as guardian of REBECCA HOWL, orphan of ABSALOM HOWL,
deceased.
Book 12, Page 401 -- Guardian Bond -- ELIZ. HOWL, MICHL. C., and BENJ.
F. HOWL, April 21, 1851, for ELIZ. HOWL as guardian of REBECCA HOWL,
orphan of ABSALOM HOWL, deceased.

ANNA HUCKSTEP -- Book 5, Page 520 -- Slave allotment as widow of SAML.
HUCKSTEP, April --, 1815; recorded July 17, 1815. No committee
names.
Book 6, Page 59 -- June 4, 1817, written; March 18, 1819, probated.
Witnesses: JAS. and JOS. HIGGINBOTHAM. Cousin, GEO. W. SCOTT; bro-
ther, BENJ. MILES to administer. He qualified. Bondsman: JOS. HIG-
GINBOTHAM.

F. A. HUCKSTEP -- Book 13, Page 29 -- Guardian Bond -- GEO. H. DAMERON
and WM. P. SCOTT, November 15, 1852, for GEO. DAMERON as guardian of
F. A. and VIRGINIA HUCKSTEP, orphans of GEO. C. HUCKSTEP, deceased.
Book 15, Page 147 -- Guardian's Account by guardian, from January 1,
1857. Also as administrator of LUCY T. and GEO. C. HUCKSTEP. January 17, 1859.

GEO. C. HUCKSTEP -- Book 9, Page 251 -- Guardian Bond -- JAS. S. HIG-
GINBOTHAM, HENRY J. ROSE, JOS. KYLE, and ROBT. HIGGINBOTHAM, Novem-
ber 21, 1836, for J. HIGGINBOTHAM as guardian of GEO. C. HUCKSTEP,
orphan of RICHARD HUCKSTEP, deceased.
Book 11, Page 401 -- Administrator's Bond -- LUCY T. HUCKSTEP, PETER G.
JOINER, and GEO. H. DAMERON, February 16, 1846, for LUCH T. HUCKSTEP.
Book 11, Page 406 -- Inventory -- March 9, 1846 - $1,616.12. EDWIN L.
SHELTON, EDWD. TINSLEY, WM. RUCKER.
Book 12, Page 187 -- Administrator's Account by LUCY T. HUCKSTEP FROM
January 1, 1846. Two infant children - board. Recorded March 10,
1849. GEO. POWELL, EDWD. TINSLEY, JNO. D. L. RUCKER.
Book 13, Page 28 -- Administrator's Bond -- GEO. H. DAMERON and WM. P.
SCOTT, November 15, 1853, for GEO. DAMERON.
Book 14, Page 115 -- Administrator's Account -- LUCY T. HUCKSTEP from
March 20, 1846. To GEO. H. DAMERON for his portion arising from e-
state of CHAS. DAMERON (GEO. C. HUCKSTEP was administrator of CHAS.
DAMERON); Bedford ticket; board for two infant children. Recorded
November 2, 1855. Note: This was evidently filed by DAMERON in 1855
for it will be seen that LUCY died in 1852.
Book 14, Page 310 -- Administrator's Account -- GEO. H. DAMERON from
January 1, 1853. Tuition of two children. December 12, 1856. Note:
The two children are never named, but shown in data under F. A.
HUCKSTEP above.

GEO. H. HUCKSTEP -- Indexed as Constable's Bond, Book 12, Page 416,
but not there.

LUCY T. HUCKSTEP -- Book 13, Page 28 -- Administrator's Bond -- GEO.
H. DAMERON and WM. P. SCOTT, November 15, 1852, for GEO. DAMERON.
Book 13, Page 44 -- Inventory -- July 11, 1853 - $91.50. PETER G.
JOINER, THOS. R. TERRY, WALKER TERRY or TENY. Sale, January 11, 1852.
No buyers named - $88.52. DAMERON, administrator.
Book 14, Page 244 -- Administrator's Account by DAMERON -- Septem-
ber 13, 1856. Two lists and one with total above of $88.52 and other
of $91.50 so probably inventory above. Same committee as Book 13,

Page 44, but TERRY, and not questionable as to TENY. January 17, 1853. Recorded November 22, 1856.

RICHARD C. HUCKSTEP -- Book 8, Page 9 -- January 16, 1830, written; July 19, 1830, probated. Witnesses: JNO. L. TYLER, SR. and JR.; JONAS PIERCE; JAS. S. HIGGINBOTHAM. Proved by TYLER, JR., and PIERCE and HIGGINBOTHAM. ONEY D. HUCKSTEP qualified. Bondsmen: JAS. S. HIGGINBOTHAM and WM. H. TYLER. Ux, ONEY D. to administer; my two children: GEORGE C. and ELIZA ANN when 21.
Book 8, Page 82 -- Inventory -- December 24, 1830 - $4,596.75-1/2. CHAS. WILSON, JONAS PIERCE, JAS. OGDON.

SAMUEL HUCKSTEP -- Book 5, Page 489 -- Administrator's Bond -- ANNA HUCKSTEP, BENJ. MILES, SAML. ARRINGTON, CHRISTOPHER ISBELL, March 20, 1815, for ANNA HUCKSTEP.
Book 5, Page 509 -- Inventory -- L 195-1-2. Administratrix named; no committee; June 19, 1815.
Book 6, Page 87 -- Administrator's de bonis non Bond -- August 16, 1819. CHAS. F. CHRISTIAN and S. CLAIBORNE for CHAS. CHRISTIAN.

We now enter the HUDSON data. If you come to Amherst and meet someone, but you are not real sure that you caught the name, just call the person MR. CAMPBELL, JR. HUDSON, or MR. WRIGHT and your chances of being right are fine. Many families treated in my will encyclopedia have disappeared from Amherst, but these families remain here in force. There are many others who remain, but these three suffice as illustrations of present Amherst countians.

BENNETT HUDSON -- Book 4, Page 338 -- Guardian Bond -- LUCY HUDSON, GEO. CLASBY (really GILLESPIE) and BARTLETT CASH, October 19, 1801, for LUCY HUDSON as guardian of BENNETT, EDMUND, and PAMELIA HUDSON, orphans of ROBT. HUDSON, deceased. Note: The GILLESPIE and HUDSON lines cross in several instances. GEO. GILLESPIE was the ancestor of my wife, MILDRED MILLER. He had a son, WILLIAM, who married ANN HUDSON here in 1777. She was a sister of ROBT. HUDSON and it will be seen that they were children of JOSHUA HUDSON and ux, MARY TERRELL, who came here from Orange County and settled on Turkey Mountain. One HUDSON attends my church and still owns land on Turkey Mountain. We attend the family picnic each year and HUDSON clansmen attend in droves. This is only ONE branch and I would not even attempt to estimate how many would assemble for a picnic of ALL branches stemming from JOSHUA HUDSON.
Book 12, Page 72 -- Indexed as Book 5, Page 74 -- Inventory -- December 14, 1848 - $2,039.75. JNO. COLEMAN, WM. MANTIPLY, WM. M. WALLER, JAS. P. COLEMAN.
Page 74 has sale, December 15, 1848. SAML. GARLAND, administrator. Family buyers: W. W. and MICAJAH HUDSON. BENNETT was almost of age when guardian was appointed for all are said to be "over 14." BENNETT HUDSON married SALLY GILLESPIE (GILLASPIE), March 19, 1804 - bond date. LUCY HUDSON is shown as parent or guardian in the bond. Surety or witness: SHEROD MOORE GILLESPIE (another son of GEORGE GILLESPIE); SAML. GARLAND; HENRY BROWN.

DAVID HUDSON -- Book 5, Page 87 -- Guardian Bond -- PEYTON KEITH and WM. KNIGHT, November 18, 1811, for PEYTON KEITH as guardian of DAVID HUDSON, orphan of REUBEN HUDSON.

FRANCES HUDSON -- Book 6, Page 281 -- Guardian Bond -- LUCY HUDSON and JNO. COLEMAN, March 23, 1822, for LUCH HUDSON as guardian of FRANCES HUDSON, orphan of REUBEN HUDSON, deceased.

Book 9, Page 376 -- Administrator's Bond -- GEO. HUDSON and HENRY J. ROSE, January 15, 1838, for GEO. HUDSON.

GEO. HUDSON -- Book 6, Page 387 -- Guardian Bond -- DAVID S. GARLAND and EDMD. A. CABELL, August 19, 1823, for DAVID GARLAND as guardian of GEO. HUDSON, orphan of REUBEN HUDSON, deceased.

JOSHUA HUDSON -- This man is an ancestor of MILDRED MILLER DAVIS, my

wife. He married MARY TERRELL, but I have not found the record. She is mentioned in the will of her father, ROBT. TERRELL, in Orange, and so is her son, RUSH HUDSON (called grandson by TERRELL). JOSHUA is styled as being of Orange when he bought land here in 1769 on Turkey Mountain. GILLESPIE data gives material on ANN HUDSON who married WM. GILLESPIE here in 1777 and they moved to Madison County, Kentucky. WM. was son of GEO. GILLESPIE and WM. had daughter, MARY, who married HENDERSON THURMAN in Madison. The site of old HUDSON graveyard is no longer in hands of any HUDSON and many markers are merely fieldstones. Book 4, Page 6 -- January 5, 1799, written; April 20, 1801, probated. Witnesses: SHEROD BUGG; RUSH HUDSON, JR.; JNO. HUDSON. Daughter, SARAH WRIGHT had share; son, RUSH, 8 acres on end of Turkey Mountain-- my old peach orchard. Daughter, MARY DAWSON - REUBEN HUDSON to be her trustee; daughter, ELIZ. DENNIS; HORATIO and NANCY HUDSON, children of my deceased son, JOSHUA; (HORATIO went to Kentucky and a descendant, MISS MARIE KLOOZ, has done a wonderful piece of work on this line. She is a Sweet Briar graduate and Quaker lawyer in D.C.) My land is to be sold and money to sons, REUBEN and GEORGE; daughter, FRANCES TATE; heirs of ROBT. HUDSON, deceased; daughter, ANN GILLESPIE - 4 shares as she has received negro girl; daughter, LUCY SANDIDGE - to PULLEM SANDIDGE and her children as of age; daughter, PEGGY CHILDRESS; daughter, MOLLY BALENGER; daughter, RACHEL MILES; representatives of daughter, PATSEY RUCKER; granddaughter, RACHEL HUDSON MILLS; granddaughter, MILLY DAWSON; grandson, FLEMING DAWSON; land to be sold and money to REUBEN and heirs of ROBT. HUDSON, deceased. Executors: PULLEM SANDIDGE and my son, REUBEN. Codicil: misconduct of FLEMING DAWSON caused me to withdraw his legacy; it goes to RUSH HUDSON instead. Second codicil: children of JOSHUA JR. have received legacies. Witnesses to first codicil: RUSH HUDSON, JR., and D. S. GARLAND. To second codicil: ISAAC RUCKER, BENNETT HUDSON, GEO. WILLIS. (Note: JOSHUA was son of RUSH HUDSON and ux, WILLIS, so I wonder as to identity of GEO. WILLIS. JOSHUA's mother was later married to a TUBERVILLE.)
Book 4, Page 19 -- Inventory -- September 15, 1801 - 7 slaves; shoemaker's tools; much stock; 5 books and dictionary - L 587-17-9. Returned September 21, 1801. LINDSEY COLEMAN, CHAS. BOALS, NATHL. MANTIPLY.
Book 4, Page 332 -- Administrator's Bond -- July 20, 1801 -- PULLIAM SANDIDGE, SHARAD BUGG, GEO. HUDSON, WALLER SANDIDGE, REUBEN HUDSON for PULLIAM SANDIDGE and REUBEN HUDSON.
Book 4, Page 232 -- Administrator's Account -- Indexed for JOSEPH HUDSON, but patently an error. PULLIAM SANDIDGE, one of executors - L 47-1-3; land tax of JOSHUA HUDSON; also of GEO. HUDSON; RUSH HUDSON, legatee; MILLY DAWSON, legatee; date of July 21, 1806. Tax on 315 acres; JOSHUA's land tax for 1802. RUSH HUDSON, witness and legatee; GEO. HUDSON as witness; JESSE MILLS, legatee; RUSH and REUBEN HUDSON, legatees; legacy of my ux, LUCY SANDIDGE and heirs of her body; LUCY HUDSON, legatee; RACHEL HUDSON MILLS, legatee; children of ROBT. HUDSON, legatees.
Page 234 -- Administrator's Account of REUBEN HUDSON and received as joint account of executors. Orphans of ROBT. and REUBEN HUDSON. Committee: DAVID S. GARLAND, LINDSEY COLEMAN, JER. FRANKLIN. REUBEN's account from April 16, 1806. To GEO. HUDSON as witness against JESSE MILLS. Guardian of ROBT. HUDSON. Recorded May 13, 1806.

JOSHUA HUDSON, JR. -- Book 3, Page 277 -- Administrator's Bond -- JOSHUA HUDSON, SR., and REUBEN HUDSON, September 16, 1793, for JOSHUA HUDSON, SR.
Book 3, Page 296 -- Inventory -- L 52-9-0, September 26, 1793. JER. FRANKLIN, NATHL. MANTIPLY, SHEROD BUGG.
Book 3, Page 590 -- Administrator's Account from October 18, 1793. Small hat for HORATIO HUDSON - 3 shares and his board and washing for 3 years; Total of L 6; board and washing for NANCY HUDSON for 5 years - L 15. Returned October 22, 1800. DAVID S. GARLAND, JER. FRANKLIN, JOS. BURRUS.

LEWIS D. HUDSON -- Book 16, Page 178 -- Administrator's Bond -- MICAJAH HUDSON and JAS. P. COLEMAN, October 20, 1862, for MICAJAH HUDSON.

LUCY HUDSON -- Book 5, Page 14 -- Guardian Bond -- MICAJAH CAMDEN and

JAS. P. GARLAND, May 22, 1810, for MICAJAH CAMDEN as guardian of LUCY
HUDSON, orphan of REUBEN HUDSON, deceased.
Book 6, Page 469 -- Guardian's Account -- by CAMDEN, up to time she
ceased to get support from guardian. Question as to his claim
contested and confirmed, March --, 1824.

MARTHA HUDSON, MRS. -- Book 2, Page 179 -- January 30, 1784, written;
June 7, 1784, probated. Witnesses: JAS. GOODRICH; LANDON and MARY
CARTER. Daughter, NANCY CARTER, ux of GRIFFIN CARTER; daughter,
MARTHA HUDSON. Executors: MARTHA HUDSON, WM. WARE, EDMD. GOODRICH.
Book 2, Page 180 -- (indexed for 150) -- Administrator's Bond -- WM.
WARE and JNO. DUNCAN, June 7, 1784, for WM. WARE.
Book 2, Page 199 -- Inventory of MRS. MARTHA HUDSON - L 15-0-0.
November 1, 1784. JAS. GOODRICH, ROBT. CARTER, ISAAC WRIGHT.
Book 3, Page 145 -- May 1, 1787, written; June 7, 1790, probated.
Witnesses: WM. WARE, JAS. GOODRICH, ABM. CARTER, HENRY BROWN. To
LANDON CARTER - 78 acres where he lives and his son, JAMES CARTER, when
21. To EDWD. CARTER - one bed. Executors: WM. WARE and EDMD. GOOD-
RICH.
Book 3, Page 146 -- Administrator's Bond -- LANDON CARTER and WM. WARE,
July 5, 1790, for LANDON CARTER.
Book 3, Page172 -- Inventory -- L 17-4-2. CHAS. TALIAFERRO, MOSES
DAVIES, WM. PRYOR. February 17, 1791. Note: I am unable to tie this
group of HUDSONS in with the family of JOSHUA HUDSON at this time.
It could be that there is a connection to be found in Orange or some
other county in that area.

PAULUS HUDSON -- Book 15, Page 276 -- Guardian Bond -- WM. S. CLAI-
BORNE and W. KENT, December 19, 1859, for WM. CLAIBORNE as guardian
of PAULUS HUDSON, orphan of JNO. P. HUDSON, deceased.

REUBEN HUDSON -- Book 4, Page 582 -- Administrator's Bond -- SARAH
HUDSON, SHAROD BUGG, JNO. HUDSON, and JAS. HUDSON, February 20, 1809,
for SARAH HUDSON.
Book 4, Page 592 -- Inventory - $1,234.06, September 18, 1809. JER.
FRANKLIN, NATHL. MANTIPLY, THOS. LANDRUM.
Book 5, Page 53 -- Administrator's Account by SARAH HUDSON from 1809.
Accounts vs. JNO. and JAS. HUDSON; bond of RUSH HUDSON. January 20,
1812. DAVID S. GARLAND, EDMD. PENN, JOS. SWANSON.

ROBT. HUDSON -- Book 3, Page 221 -- March 27, 1791, written; April 16,
1792, probated. Witnesses: JOSHUA HUDSON, SR.; ELISHA DENNIS; ALEX.
HUDSON. 100 acres of my land next to EDWD. CARTER and ELISHA DENNIS.
Ux, LUCY; my three children; BENNETT; EDMUND; and PAMELIA when of
age. Executors: GEO. GILLESPIE; RUSH HUDSON; ux, LUCY. ROBT. HUDSON
also married into the GILLESPIE family. October 25, 1779, he got
bond to marry LUCY GALASPIE, spinster, daughter of GEO. GALASPIE.
SHERRED MOORE GALASPIE was surety. Her father gave his consent. There
is no Administrator's Bond, but it merely states that executors named
produced the will.

RUSH HUDSON, SR. -- Book 5, Page 90 -- Guardian Bond -- SARAH HUDSON
and THOS. ALDRIDGE, January 20, 1812, for SARAH HUDSON as guardian
of RUSH, FRANCES, and GEO. HUDSON, orphans of REUBEN HUDSON, deceased.
Book 5, Page 206 -- Guardian Bond -- THOS. ALDRIDGE and RICH. HARRI-
SON, February 15, 1812, for THOS. ALDRIDGE as guardian of same orphans
as above.
Book 6, Page 122 -- Inventory -- August 24, 1819, $921.19. Recorded
February 21, 1820. PEACHY FRANKLIN, JAS. S. PENDLETON, JNO. DILLARD.
Book 7, Page 201 -- Administrator's Account -- JAS. DILLARD, sheriff
and administrator from September 3, 1820. Names ofBENNETT HUDSON;
R. HUDSON; bond of LUCY MOUNTCASTLE; JNO. HUDSON; BETSY HUDSON; M.
HUDSON. Commissioner: HENRY H. WATTS. March 20, 1828.
Book 12, Page 337 -- Administrator's Bond -- PERMELIA HUDSON, JNO. C.
HARRISON, SHELTON HUDSON, and DANL. SHAW, December 16, 1850, for
PERMELIA HUDSON.
Book 12, Page 349 -- Inventory -- December 27, 1850 - $5,038.50. RO.
L. COLEMAN, CHAS. A. PENN, LINDSEY COLEMAN.
Book 12, Page 533 -- August 21, 1841, written; codicil of July 20,
1849; no probate date set forth, but widow qualified on December 16,

1850. Witnesses to will: H. M. GARLAND, JR.; JNO. H. PAMPLIN; DAVID
S. GARLAND. Witnesses to codicil: GEO. T. and RICH. M. COLEMAN. "The
Elder" - ux, PERMELIA - where I live - 100 acres. Sons, EDMUND and
SHELTON HUDSON - land at mother's death. This for caring for and
remaining with me. My other children; children of my son, ROBT.
JEFFERSON HUDSON. Daughter, SOPHIA, who married JNO. HUDSON - his
treatment of me is such that he deserves nothing. Children of daugh-
ter, SUSAN, who married REUBEN HUDSON, but he has no care nor industry
and gets nothing. Daughter, JANE FRASHUR, and children. Executors:
Friend, DANL. COLEMAN. Codicil: DANL. L. COLEMAN has died and
SAML. M. GARLAND is to administer. Daughter, JANE FRAZIER - note
spelling change for her - her part in trust and at death to her children. Son, EDMOND, lives on my land and by permission; no rent due.
Slave to my son, SHELTON, at death of my ux.

SALLIE HUDSON -- Book 16, Page 398 -- October 7, 1850, written;
September 21, 1863, probated. Witnesses: RO. L. COLEMAN and THOS. H.
RUCKER and proved by them, October 19, 1863. Widow of BENNET HUDSON;
children and ux of my son, WM. W. HUDSON. Congressional bounty lands,
if any, as widow of BENNET HUDSON - in War of 1812.
Book 16, Page 479 -- So indexed, but no HUDSON data thereon.

SAML. HUDSON -- Book 15, Page 273 -- Guardian Bond -- JNO. L. TURNER
and WM. KENT, April 16, 1860, for JNO. TURNER as guardian of JNO.,
SAML., and GEO. HUDSON, orphans of JNO. P. HUDSON, deceased.

D.S.G. HUGHES -- Book 5, Page 394 -- Guardian Bond -- JESSE BECK and
WM. PENDLETON, October 18, 1813, for JESSE BECK as guardian of D.S.G.
HUGHES, and L. H. HUGHES, orphans of WM. HUGHES.

FANNY HUGHES -- Book 24, Page 104 -- July 15, 1908, written; July 24,
1908, probated. Witnesses: HENRY NICHOLAS and F. H. DANIEL. Daughter, AVERY AMANDA HUGHES; son, MATTHEW NICHOLAS RAMIREZ; grandson,
RAYMOND RAMIREZ; and C. C. RAMIREZ.

MARIA W. HUGHES -- Book 14, Page 438 -- January 15, 1857, written;
September 21, 1857, probated. Witnesses: THOS. WHITEHEAD, WM. PARR.
Brother, JNO. W. SMITH, Baltimore, and children; my cousin, WM. M.
WALLER, deceased--his children, late of Amherst County. Executor:
THOS. WHITEHEAD.
Book 14, Page 444 -- Administrator's Bond -- THOS. WHITEHEAD; SAML.
GARLAND; and WM. M. WALLER, October 19, 1857, for THOS. WHITEHEAD.
Book 14, Page 524 -- (indexed as 324) -- Inventory - October 27, 1857 -
$1,700.00. RO. RIDGWAY, E. P. HILL, N. B. MAGRUDER.
Book 14, Page 525 -- Sale -- November 6, 1857, December 31, 1857, and
January 6, 1858. No family buyers named. Total: $8,191.18.
Book 15, Page 232 -- Administrator's Account -- July 8, 1859. THOS.
WHITEHEAD. Total: $8,192.08.

ORLANDER HUGHES -- Book 5, Page 433 -- Lunatic, March 21, 1814.
Committee: PLEASANT and NELSON DAWSON. Found insane by J. P.; NELSON
DAWSON; CHAS. MUNDY; P. JOHNSON. Indexed for OLEANDER HUGHES.

SCHUYLER HUGHES -- Book 21, Page 451 -- Administrator's Bond -- P. H.
WOOD and L. P. PLEASANTS, July 18, 1887, for P. WOOD.

WILLIAM HUGHES -- Book 4, Page 36 -- September 20, 1800, written;
June 21, 1802, probated. Witnesses: JAS. STEWART, JNO. RICE,
RODERICK TALIAFERRO. Son, HARRISON HUGHES - 92 acres next to land I
bought of JOS. and JNO. CREWS. Son, WM. - mansion house - 190 acres.
My ux; my 6 daughters; son, ORLENDER - land next to NORCUT on Fawn
Creek - if without issue. Executors: Sons, WM. and HARRISON HUGHES.
Book 4, Page 67 -- Slave Inventory -- L 438-17-0. NELSON C. DAWSON,
PLEASANT DAWSON, ARCHELAUS WRIGHT, January 8, 1803.
Book 4, Page 81 -- Inventory -- same committee - L 1-14-0, after
taking off what is due his ux, February21, 1803.
Book 4, Page 348 -- Administrator's Bond -- HARRISON HUGHES, PLEA-
SANT DAWSON, AMBROSE and PHILIP BURFORD,June 21, 1802, for HARRISON
HUGHES.
Book 5, Page 372 -- Administrator's Bond -- JESSE BECK, CHAS. MUNDY,

and WM. TURNER, September 20, 1813, for JESSE BECK.
Book 5, Page 393 -- Inventory - $1,308.69, October 2, 1813. PLEASANT
DAWSON, ARCHELAUS REYNOLDS, NELSON C. DAWSON.

OTIS HUGHSON -- Book 22, Page 243 -- Baptist minister's bond, April 15,
1889. Indexed as THOS. B. HOUGHTON. I am unable to find either name
in my three volumes of Geo. Braxton Taylor's Virginia Baptist
Ministers.

BENNETT ANN MAHALA HUNT -- Book 9, Page 43 -- JNO. S.(?) HUNT, JNO.
VICOR, and BENJ. T.(?) HUNT, January 19, 1835, for JOHN HUNT.

ISAAC HUNTER -- Book 12, Page 27 -- Guardian Bond -- December 20, 1847.
JAS. W. KEITH and STERLING CLAIBORNE -- JAS. KEITH as guardian of
ISAAC; ROBT.; and MARIA LOUISA HUNTER, infant children of DAVID HUNTER.

WM. HUNTER -- All items in 13 are indexed for HUNTON.
Book 13, Page 12 -- Administrator's Bond -- CATH. HUNTER and RO. A.
COGHILL, October 18, 1852, for CATH. HUNTER.
Book 13, Page 27 -- Inventory -- October 21, 1852 - $649.00. V.
McGINNIS, JAS. T. CASH. CATH. HUNTER, administratrix. Received
November 15, 1852.
Book 19, Page 324 -- Plat and Division -- one mile south of New Glas-
gow and next to J. J. HITE and heirs of E. MATTHEWS(?). Committee:
VALERIUS McGINNIS, W. S. CLAIBORNE; on plat: ELIZ. HUDSON; GEO. HUN-
TER; MARGARET HUNTER; WM. HUNTER, JR.; MRS. D. MAYS; MRS. ROBT. PARKS.

WM. J. HUNTER -- Book 16, Page 125 -- Minister's Bond -- May 19, 1862.
Bondsman: JAS. M. MILLNER. No denomination set forth.

SAMUEL HUSKILL -- Book 17, Page 172 -- April 18, 1860, written;
May 19, 1860, codicil; July 16, 1866, probated. Witnesses to will:
R. A. COGHILL, JAS. P. COLEMAN, D. MANTIPLY. Witnesses to codicil:
DANDRIDGE MANTIPLY and JOS. H. STAPLES. My ux, ELIZABETH - where I
live; my brothers: WM., FREDERICK S., DANIEL; and my sisters: SOPHIA
and SALLY - now living - and their children. Executors: ux and R. A.
COGHILL. Codicil: ux may elect to take slave. Proved by COGHILL and
JAS. P. COLEMAN. MANTIPLY is dead, but COGHILL attested to his sig-
nature. Codicil proved on September 17, 1866. STAPLES did not appear,
but COLEMAN attested as to signature. ELIZ. HUSKILL qualified. Bonds-
man: R. A. COGHILL.
Administrator's Bond is Book 17, Page 174.
Book 17, Page 189 -- Inventory -- September 19, 1866 - $1,192.00.
LEO DANIEL, JR.; WM. E. COLEMAN; G.H.R. TUCKER.

ANN HUTCHERSON -- Book 7, Page 322 -- Guardian Bond -- WM. TURNER,
JNO. PENN, JAS. POWELL, JNO. MEHONE, January 18, 1830, for WM. TURNER
as guardian of ANN, ELEANOR, PERMELY, JNO., ELIZ., JOSHUA, and LUCINDA
HUTCHERSON, orphans of JNO. HUTCHINSON (sic). This is another illustration of index system whereby only one name of many wards of same
family will appear in index. Also note variation in spelling of last
name.

ELEANOR HUTCHERSON -- Book 9, Page 44 -- Guardian Bond -- WILLIS M.
REYNOLDS, JNO. MEHONE, and CHURCHWELL DAWSON, January 19, 1835, for
WILLIS REYNOLDS as guardian of ELEANOR, PERMELIA, ELIZ. and LUCY
HUTCHERSON, orphans of JNO. HUTCHERSON, deceased.

JNO. HUTCHERSON (HUTCHINSON in some items) -- Book 3, Page 539 -- In-
ventory, February18(?), 1799; no total. NATHAN WINGFIELD; JOS. DAVEN-
PORT; CHAS. CHRISTIAN.
Book 4, Page 43 -- Administrator's Account -- THOS. EDWARDS,
administrator - land and slaves, etc., sold and each legatee got
L 91-19-5. REUBEN NORVELL, JNO. CHRISTIAN, JOS. DAVENPORT. Febru-
ary 26, 1802; returned July 19, 1802.
Book 4, Page287 -- Administrator's Bond -- ELLENDER HUTCHESON (sic);
THOS. EDWARDS, January 21, 1799, for ELLENDER HUTCHESON.
Book 4, Page 337 -- Administrator's Bond -- THOS. EDWARDS and ABNER
PADGETT, July 20, 1801, for THOS. EDWARDS.

Book 6, Page 675 -- May 25, 1826, written; August 21, 1826, probated.
Witnesses: GUST. A. EDWARDS, WM. DAY, and THOS. HUTCHESON. Proved
by EDWARDS and DAY. Ux, LUCINDA; son, JNO. and JOSHUA, when of age
or married. Ux is with child. Children when of age or married and
it is hard to separate names as written: SARAH ANN ELINDA PERMELIA
and ELIZ. Child expected is to share withsisters. Executors:
friends, JAS. DAVIS, JAS. PETTIT, and THOS. CLEMENTS and DANL. DAY.
Book 6, Page 713 -- Administrator's Bond -- LUCINDA HUTCHERSON, CHAS.
MUNDY, and GEO. M. TINSLEY, January 15, 1827, for LUCINDA HUTCHERSON.
Book 6, Page 739 -- Inventory -- $37,301.42-1/2, February 19, 1827.
JAS. PETTITT, JAS. DAVIS, THOS. HUTCHERSON, WM. DAY.
Book 7, Page 174 -- August 22, 1828, Administrator's Bond -- WM. R.
ROANE, JNO. MEHONE, JAS. PETTITT for WM. R. ROANE - unadministered
estate by HILL CARTER, Sheriff.
Book 7, Page 207 -- Division to widow - now LUCINDA MAHONE - slaves --
guardians should be appointed for the children, January 5, 1829.
THOS. STRANGE, JAS. OGDON, JESSE MUNDY - order of December, 1827.
168 acre tract and dwelling house -- 72 acres - lines of THOS. WILCOX
estate; THOS. EDWARDS. JOSHUA HUTCHINSON, youngest son of JOHN, de-
ceased, entitled under father's will to other half. Bought of THOS.
EDWARDS by testator. No guardians and great timber waste. Mother
objected to the will.
Book 7, Page213 -- Sale, HILL CARTER, Sheriff, January 1, 1829.
Received October Court, 1828. JAS. P. GARLAND, THOS. STRANGE, JAS.
OGDON, WM. BOURNE.
Book 7, Page 232 -- Administrator's Account -- LUCINDA MEHONE, now
ux of JNO. MEHONE and formerly HUTCHINSON from September 9, 1826.
Returned January 15, 1829. MEHONE made use of corn, bacon, and to-
bacco when he married.
Book 8, Page 182 -- Slave division to MANSON MEHONE and ux; to ELEANOR;
PERMELIA; ELIZ.; and LUCY. March 19, 1832 - WM. L. BOWLING and CAMP-
BELL FRANKLIN. HUTCHINS here.
Book 9, Page 247 -- Estate Commitment to Sheriff -- Setpember, 1836.
Motion of THOMAS HUTCHINSON. Sheriff: THOS. N. EUBANK.
Book 10, Page 94 -- Guardian's Account -- WM. TURNER, guardian from
1830. WM. KENT, executor of TURNER - from WM. R. ROANE, former execu-
tor of WM. WARE, ELEANOR, oldest daughter; PERMELIA; ELIZ. and LUCY -
board from 1829. JNO. MEHONE - board for seven children - 1831-1834.
MEHONE, step-father, agreed to board and educate them from estate.
February 10, 1838. JESSE MUNDY and DANL. DAY.
Book 10, Page93 -- Guardian's Account -- WILLIS REYNOLDS ("M." middle
initial) - guardian of heirs of JNO. HUTCHINSON, deceased - 1835.
ELEANOR - about 15; PERMELIA - 14; ELIZ. - about 12; LUCY - about 9.
JNO. MEHONE for board and clothing, 1835-37. JESSE MUNDY and DANL.
DAY, March 21, 1839.
Book 14, Page 215 -- Guardian's Account -- WM. KENT and DAVID PATTE-
SON, November 17, 1856, for WM. KENT as guardian of JNO., SAML.,
and ANN HUTCHESON, orphans of THOMAS HUTCHESON.

CHAS. HUTCHESON -- Book 5, Page 540 -- Administrator's Bond -- JNO.
HUTCHESON and WM. CLINKSCALES, August 15, 1814, for JNO. HUTCHESON.

JNO. HUTCHESON -- Book 14, Page 215 -- Guardian Bond -- WM. KENT and
DAVID PATTESON, November 17, 1856, for WM. KENT as guardian of JNO.;
SAML. and ANN HUTCHESON, orphans of THOS. HUTCHESON, deceased.

THOMAS HUTCHESON -- Book 12, Page 487 -- June 14, 1850, written;
February 16, 1852, probated. Witnesses: RO. C. MARTIN, DANL. DAY.
Codicil: February --, 1852. Ux, PELINA - 333-1/3 acres where I live
and 48 acres called Griffy's Tract or Sugar Hill. Sons, SAML. and
JNO., when of age. Sons: JESSE, JAS., WM.; daughters: ELIZ. OMO-
HUNDRO; LUCY; ANN; FRANCES TURNER, deceased - her representatives;
daughter, SUSAN PLUNKETT; daughter, MARY CERRELIA PLUNKETT. Land
bought of JNO. J. LONDON. Sum to educate my three children: JNO.,
SAML., and ANN. Executor: friend, WM. KENT. Codicil: Slave in
trust for CATHERINE HUTCHESON, ux of my son, JAMES. Proved by
witnesses.
Book 12, Page 491 -- Administrator's Bond -- WM. KENT and ISAAC R.
REYNOLDS, February 16, 1852, for WM. KENT.
Book 12, Page 540 -- Sale, March 5, 1852. MRS. HUTCHESON and JNO. H.

were buyers. Total: $248.08.
Book 13, Page 35 -- Land and slave sale -- 225 acres bought by SAML. J.
TURNER - Total: $1,854.85. WM. KENT, administrator.
Book 13, Page 416 -- Administrator's Account -- WM. KENT from February 20, 1852. Books for the children. SILVESTER L. BURFORD for
burial - $14.00. To MRS. HUTCHESON; to account of JAS. A. HUTCHESON;
to JNO. J. HUTCHESON. Recorded: March 10, 1854.

WILLIAM HUTCHESON -- Book 4, Page 335 -- Guardian Bond -- THOS. ED-
WARDS, NATHAN WINGFIELD, and JNO. HUTCHESON, September 21, 1801, for
THOS. EDWARDS as guardian of WM. and CHAS. HUTCHESON, orphans of
JNO. HUTCHESON, deceased.
Book 5, Page 450 -- Administrator's Bond -- JNO. HUTCHESON and WM.
CLINKSCALES, August 15, 1814, for JNO. HUTCHESON.

GEO. HYLTON -- Book 8, Page 21 -- Guardian Bond -- WM. DILLARD, JNO.
DILLARD, and ZACH. DRUMMOND, September 20, 1830, for WM. DILLARD as
guardian of GEO., LUCY, JANE, and JAS. D. HYLTON, orphans of VALENTINE
HYLTON, deceased. Note: LUCY JANE may be one name, but difficult to
decipher.

JAMES D. HYLTON -- Book B, Page 5 -- Administrator's Bond -- EDWIN S.
RUCKER and PITT WOODROOF, April 11, 1834, for EDWIN RUCKER.

                              -I-

WM. INGRAM -- Order Book, 1766-69, Page 519 -- August 7, 1869,
Church wardens to bind him out -- "an orphan boy."

ANN M. IRVINE and Children -- Book 14, Page 391 -- July 20, 1857,
Guardian Bond -- L. D. ISBELL, JNO. H. FLOOD and H. F. BOCOCK for
L. D. ISBELL as guardian of ANN M., SAML. W., FRANCIS E., HUGH R.,
HAMPDIN P., AMANDA V., MARY E. S., and JAMES I. IRVINE, orphans of
SAMUEL R. IRVINE, deceased.

ELIZABETH IRVINE -- Book 10, Page 44 -- October 14, 1834, written;
September 17, 1838, probated. Witnesses: DABNEY CARR and MARY ANN
SANGSTER. Of Albemarle County. Son, DAVID IRVINE, of territory of
Michigan; my deceased son, JNO. IRVINE; my granddaughter, MARGARET
SANGSTER. Administrator: friend, J. W. GARETT.

JOHN R. IRVINE -- Book 16, Page390 -- Trustee account from December 27,
1861. SAML. R. IRVINE and NATHL. N. MANTIPLY are called legatees, but
these appear: LANDON C. IRVINE; SAML. R. IRVINE along with MANTIPLY.
To September 21, 1863.

SAML. R. IRVINE -- Book 14, Page389 -- Administrator's Bond -- L. D.
ISBELL, JNO. H. FLOOD, and H. F. BOCOCK, July 20, 1857, for L. D.
ISBELL.

PAULUS A. E. IRVING -- Book 8, Page 161 -- Indexed as Guardian Bond,
but it is an Administraotr's Bond on December 19, 1831, for JAS. POWELL
and STERLING CLAIBORNE for JAS. POWELL to administer.

CHRISTOPHER ISBELL -- Book 8, Page 419 -- July 23, 1833, written;
July 21, 1834, probated. Witnesses: JNO. RICHESON, HENRY WILLIAMSON,
and GEO. W. DAWSON. Ux, ELIZ.; daughter, SALLY WOOD and children by
first marriage to JOHN WOODSON: JNO.; ELIZ.; LINEUS; and BETSY ANN
WOODSON. My son, WM. I. ISBELL. If daughter, SALLY, has more children, they are to share. Administrator: WM. I. ISBELL.
Book 8, Page 425 -- Administrator's Bond -- MARUICE H. GARLAND and
SAML. GARLAND, August 18, 1834, for MAURICE H. GARLAND.
Book 9, Page 56 -- Inventory -- October 18, 1834 - tract of 100 acres
adjoining JNO. RICHESON near Lynchburg; Conyer's tract of about
200 acres; 237 acres near Bethel; white house on Scuffle Town lot
(this is now known as Madison Heights); 500 acres in Bedford County
near Peaks of Otter; tract near Mead's Chapel; lots in Madison; un-
divided interest in tract formerly that of ZACHARIAH ISBELL; many

slaves. Total: $9,208.00. JNO. RICHESON, RO. M. WARWICK, HENRY
WILLIAMSON.
Book 9, Page 129 -- Administrator's Account from August, 1834 - list
of initials which are impossible to decipher and accounts versus
them. WM. I. ISBELL - money sent to widow; mention of MURRELL assignee
vs. ISBELL. JNO. R. BABB, executor of RICH. BABB - bond - intestate;
several suits mentioned; Mention of ROBT. ISBELL. Recorded
October 19, 1835. GEO. W. TURNER and CHAS. W. WILLIAMS.
Book 9, Page 284 -- Sales by MAURICE GARLAND and account from January
1836. ROBT. and WM. I. ISBELL were buyers. House in Madison was
occupied by widow until her death, but no new tenant could be found
until end of year. Rents reported for 1835 and up to December 31,
1836.
Book 10, Page 97; 200ff -- Administrator's Account -- by MAURICE
GARLAND. These are very interesting. One is styled list of slave
hires and rents. From January, 1838, and one item shows fifty cents
paid to a constable for whipping Moses on order from magistrate. On
200ff are many pathetic items: report of public hiring at MRS.
TAYLOR's and ROBT. and WM. I. ISBELL hired a number of slaves.
Biolet and child, Allen, hired for $34.00. Jenny and 3 children are
named; John, a boy, Essex, diseased; Clem, deranged; Squire Beverly,
very old; Sal Island, an old woman; Simeon or Daybreak - several
references to his being a chronic run-away; One MORGAN hired Clem and
refused to pay fee when he learned that he was deranged. A committed
adjudged that he owed no fee. It was set forth that Clem, ux, Nelly,
and child were "miserably clothed at the hiring." There are several
references to the Bedford tract and one THOS. DOYLE lived thereon.
He was "so miserable poor" that he was unable to pay the annual rent
of $5.00, but administrator stated that DOYLE only used a small portion
of the land and lived in a "hut so miserable that no one else would
live in it." It would be "cruelty" to eject him. Old Squire Beverly
is old and of no use so he was sold that he might have "a finall
home." Maria is "effected with something like a cancer" and in all
probability will never be worth anything. Essex "being diseased and
generally laid up" -- thought best to sell him since his doctor's bill
almost consumed his hire. February 16, 1839: T. S. MOSBY, WM. I.
ISBELL, CHAS. W. CHRISTIAN.
Book 10, Page 290 -- This is indexed for CHARLES ISBELL, but it is an
item for CHRISTOPHER. It is an Administrator's Bond, November 16,
1840, for SAML. GARLAND and JNO. F. HAWKINS for SAML. GARLAND to
administer.

FLORENTINE L. D. ISBELL -- Book 6, Page235 -- Guardian Bond -- WM.
PENDLETON, BLANFORD HIX, and WM.PETER, July 16, 1821, for WM. PENDLE-
TON as guardian of above named orphan of ZACHARIAH ISBELL.

GEORGE ISBELL and Children -- Book 12, Page 231 -- WM. I. ISBELL
intends to apply as administrator of estates of GEO. ISBELL, THOS. D.
ISBELL: SALLY SLADON and ZACHARIAH ISBELL and undersigned are willing
to unite on his bond and grant power of attorney to SAML. M. GARLAND
to sign for us: ROBT. and FREDERICK W. ISBELL, November 19, 1849.
Book 12, Page 249 -- Bond made by WM. I. ISBELL with the above bondsmen
to administer estate of GEO. ISBELL on November 19, 1849.

SALLY ISBELL and Children -- Book 6, Page 395 -- Guardian Bond --
SALLY and CHRISTOPHER ISBELL, October 20, 1823, for SALLY ISBELL as
guardian of SALLY, ZACHARIAH, ANDREW, BETSY, and PARCEMIA ISBELL, orphans of ZACHARIAH ISBELL. On next page is separate bond as guardian
of ELIZA ISBELL, orphan of ZACHARIAH.

THOS. D. ISBELL -- Book 12, Page 231 -- WM. I. ISBELL, ROBT. and
FREDERICK W. ISBELL, November 19, 1849, for WM. I. ISBELL as
administrator.

WILLIAM I. ISBELL -- Book 5, Page 13 -- Constable in First Hundred,
April 17, 1810. Bondsman: WM. TURNER. To Governor JNO. TYLER.
Book 13, Page 221 -- Administrator's Bond -- ROBT., FREDERICK W.,
and JNO. W. ISBELL, June 20, 1853, for ROBT. ISBELL to administer.

ZACHARIAH ISBELL -- Book 6, Page 217 -- Administrator's Bond -- SALLY

ISBELL, CHRISTOPHER ISBELL, DANL. CHRISTIAN, PHILLIP THURMOND, SAML.
COLEMAN, JAS. COLEMAN, THOS. WOODSON, and WM. I. ISBELL, March 19,
1821, for SALLY and CHRISTOPHER ISBELL to administer.
Book 6, Page 333 -- Inventory -- No total, April 12, 1821.   AMBROSE
RUCKER; BLANSFORD HIX, and WM.PETER.   Indexed for Book 6, Page 233.

JAMES ISON (ISOM) -- Book 1, Page 57 -- Administrator's Bond --
DARKESS ISON and JOS. BALLENGER, July 1, 1765, for DARKESS ISON.
Book 1, Page 61 -- Inventory -- July 20, 1765 - L 46-11-10.   AARON
HIGGINBOTHAM, SAML. AYRES, THOS. PARKS.
Book 1, Page 95 -- Administrator's Account -- JOS. BALLENGER from
August 4, 1766.   Cash from DARCUS KING by JOSEPH KING - L 41-5-10.
THOS. PARKS, GABL. PENN, August 5, 1766.   In order book, 1766-1769,
Page 6, reference is made to DORCAS ISAM, now KING.

-J-

JAMES RIVER REPORT -- Book 6, Page 308 -- Returned August 18, 1822.
THOS. LAINE and DAVID STAPLES appointed by James River Company under
Section 3 of Act of February 28, 1821, for improving navigation of
James River and for uniting eastern and western waters by James and
Kanawaha Rivers.   Duties assigned for Amherst County and reported
under oath.   Average prices from residence at Amherst Mills and
freight to and from Bethel; German Mills, and Amherst Mills for three
years from January 1, 1820.   Sample: Bethel to Richmond on one hundred pounds of tobacco - 56 cents; flour per bbl. - $1.12; other
articles per hundred pounds - 56 cents.

THOMAS JAMESON -- Book 1, Page 20 -- Administrator's Bond -- MARTHA
JAMESON, May 2, 1763.   Bondsman: JNO. SMALL and WM. ROBERTSON.
Book 1, Page 41 -- Inventory -- June 23, 1763 - various accounts.
Recorded March 5, 1764.   THOS. and DAVID MONTGOMERY and JNO. WAIDE.

RICHARD JANNEY -- Book 6, Page 83 -- Administrator's Bond -- August 16,
1819.   WM. HALL and bondsman, WM. KNIGHT.

JOHN JARVIS, SR. -- Book 3, Page 551 -- March 24, 1799, written;
June 17, 1799, probated.   Witnesses: HENRY HARTLESS, JNO. FRASER,
EDWD. VICKERS.   Eldest son, THOS. JARVIS; my daughter, MARGARY STATON,
diseasst (sic); daughter, SARAH STATON; youngest daughter, BETSY
JARVIS; my ux, SARAH - 99 acres where I live; son, JNO.; son, JOSEPH;
JOS. STATION, son of BARTHOLOMEW and MARGARY STATON, to get three
years of schooling.   Executors: SARAH, JNO., and JOS. JARVIS.   First
two bonded: Bondsmen: WM. HALL and WM. STINNETT.
Book 3, Page 570 -- Inventory -- August 7, 1799; recorded October 21,
1799 - L 124-8-5; THOS. GRAYHAM, JNO. McCLAIN, HENRY HARTLESS.
Book 16, Page 28 -- Administrator's Bond for SARAH JARVIS.   Bondsman:
WM. JARVIS - probate date.   Witnesses: WO. W. SNEAD.

JOS. JARVIS (JARVIES) -- Book 15, Page 514 -- June 5, 1858, written;
January 21, 1861, probated.   Witnesses: ANDERSON SANDIDGE; SAML.
LAWMAN; JNO. D. WHEELER.   Everything to ux, SALLY JARVIES.

JEMIMA JENKINS -- Book 7, Page290 -- December 21, 1829; JOS. PETTY-
JOHN qualified.   Bondsman: GEO. W. PETTYJOHN.
Book 7, Page 323 -- Inventory -- January 4, 1830 - $1,788.70, but
subtract two insolvent bonds of WM. MITCHELL for total of $1,598.70.
JAS. L. LAMKIN, Justice of the Peace.   Committee: ARCHELAUS REYNOLDS,
BEVERLY WADE, JAS. LEE.   Returned January 18, 1830.   ARTHUR B. DAVIES,
Clerk.
Book 7, Page 329 -- Administrator's Account from January 4, 1830;
distributees: WM. JENKINS, CORNL. MAYS, DICEY JENKINS, SUSAN BUR-
NETT; suit vs. WM. D. HILL's executors mentioned.   CORNL. MAYS for
ux, SALLY (nee JENKINS); JNO. JENKINS for ux, BETSY (nee JENKINS);
THOS. CEENAULT for ux, MOLLY (nee JENKINS); SUSAN BURNETT (nee JEN-
KINS); WM. and DICEY JENKINS.   Returned January 16, 1830.   REYNOLDS
and LEE, as above.

JNO. JENKINS (JINKINS and JINKENS) -- Book 4, Page 444 -- Administra-

191

tor's Bond -- February 16, 1807. WM.TURNER. Bondsman: JAS. LIVELY.
Book 4, Page 468 -- Inventory -- L 123-12-5. Returned October 19,
1807. JESSE BECK, STEPHEN HAM, CHAS. MUNDY. WM. S. CRAWFORD, Clerk.

POWHATAN JENNINGS -- Book 15, Page 31 -- August 18, 1858, written;
September 20, 1858, probated. Witnesses: A. C. HARRISON, HIRAM C.
KYLE, TALIAFERRO STINNETT, URIAH BURLEY. One of my sons to super-
intend estate until youngest child is 21 - my older children. Ux,
ELIZ. P. - if all can't live in peace and harmony, ux gets office
standing in the yard and Springfield as now enclosed - also slave boy,
furniture, and utensils for comfort. Executor: friend, SAML. M.
GARLAND.
Book 15, Page 159 -- Administrator's Bond -- April 18, 1859. JNO. W.
JENNINGS. Bondsman: DANL. W. JENNINGS.
Book 15, Page 205 -- Inventory -- $5,495.75, April 15, 1859. W. A.
RICHESON, JNO. H. WATTS, JNO. W. WHITTEN.
Book 15, Page 607 -- Administrator's Account from March 1, 1859 - To
JNO. T. JENNINGS for family use; to W. JENNINGS - clothes, slate,
and paper for children; 30 cents to CAROLINE JENNINGS. Recorded
November 19, 1860.
Book 16, Page 382 -- Administrator's Account from April 17, 1860.
To JNO. T., ANN W., JNO. W., WM. H., and ELIZ. P. JENNINGS. Recorded
September 21, 1863.
Book 17, Page 50 -- Administrator's Account from April 17, 1863 -
to ELIZ. P., WM. H. JENNINGS; soldier's tax to TURNER, December 12.
1864; sale of cider and apples. September 1, 1864. Total: $225.00.
Recorded December 18, 1865.
Book 17, Page 103 -- Sale -- Commissioner - P. P. JENNINGS, November 2,
1865. Land rental; family buyers: JNO. T. and CHAS. E. JENNINGS.
Recorded May 15, 1866.
Book 17, Page 134 -- Administrator's Account from October 11, 1865;
wheat sold to ELIZ. JENNINGS. Recorded June 2, 1866.

WILLIE ANN JENNINGS -- Indexed for Book 16, Page 404, but has line
through it and nothing is on the page. See POWHATAN P. JENNINGS.

ALEX. JEWELL -- Book 11, Page 307 -- Estate Commitment to Sheriff --
Motion of JESSE MUNDY. Sheriff: JAS. PWELL - February Court, 1845.
        These next items are all indexed for ALLISON JEWELL, but are
all for ALEX. JEWELL.
Book 12, Page 229 -- Administrator's Bond -- November 19, 1849 --
POWHATAN P. JENNINGS. Bondsman: URIAH BURLEY.
Book 12, Page 259 -- Inventory -- November 30, 1849 - $40.84. JNO. L.
TURNER, PLEASANT STORY, JNO. T. RODES.
Book 12, Page 565 -- Administrator's Account -- No family data set
forth and another is indexed for Book 15, Page 307, but nothing is
thereon.

CATH. JEWELL -- Book 8, Page 355 -- Guardian Bond -- October 21,
1833. JESSE JEWELL, JAS. JEWELL, and TERISHA JEWELL for JESSE as
guardian of CATH. JEWELL, orphan of THOS. JEWELL, deceased.

LAVINA (VINEY) JEWELL -- Book 12, Page 532 -- June 3, 1852, written;
June 21, 1852, probated. Witnesses: HIRAM C. KYLE, FRED. W. ISBELL,
LUCRETIA RHODES. Son, JAS.; son, GEO. JEW(E)LL - all future rights
and inheritance. Executor: POWHATAN P. JENNINGS.
Book 12, Page 567 -- Administrator's Bond -- August 18, 1852. RO. M.
BROWN. Bondsman: THOS. WHITEHEAD.
Book 13, Page 24 -- Inventory and Sale -- September 22, 1852 -
$41.27. L. D. SIMPSON, POWHATAN P. JENNINGS, PLEASANT STORY. Sale
amount was same total. GEO. JEWELL was a buyer. Recorded October 18,
1852.
Book 13, Page 496 -- Administrator's Account from July 6, 1852. To
GEO. JEWELL; interest in estate of ALEX. JEWELL, deceased. Mention
of suit: JENNINGS vs. HIGGINBOTHAM.

THOS. JEWELL -- Book 8, Page 354 -- Administrator's Bond -- September 16, 1833. JESSE MUNDY. Bondsman: CHAS. MUNDY.
Book 8, Page 364 -- Inventory -- Farmer - $3,607.76. September 30,

1833. WM. KENT; LAWSON TURNER; REUBEN CARVER.
Book 9, Page 22 -- Division to legatees: JESSE JEWELL, WM. WOODSON,
JAS. JEWELL, CATH. JEWELL, URIAH BURLEY, TERISHA JEWELL. October 30,
1833. JNO. DILLARD: WM. KENT, D. STAPLES.

EDITH JOHNS -- Book 16, Page 242 -- Trustee account by NELSON HICKS
from January 1, 1858, for EDITH and children. To WM. JOHNS, SR.;
land tax; distributees: EDITH, WILLIAM, CHRISTIANNA, MARTHA JANE,
SARAH, ARIANNA, and LOUISA A. JOHNS. Recorded September 30, 1857.
Book 16, Page 244 -- Another account from March 3, 1860; same names
as above.

JNO. A. JOHNS -- Book 4, Page 342 -- Administrator's Bond -- December 21, 1801. ONEY JOHNS and WM. STINNETT and JNO. TYLER for ONEY
JOHNS.

JOSHUA JOHNS -- This is another of those index errors. I have included
it in proper place under EVANS data. It is Book 9, Page 192 --
Guardian Bond -- January 18, 1836 -- JOSHUA and WM. B. JOHNS as
guardian of FANNEY EVANS, infant orphan of JNO. EVANS, deceased.

RO. JOHNS -- Book 1, Page 456 -- Administrator's Bond -- MARY JOHNS;
DANL. GAINES and AMBROSE RUCKER, March 1, 1779, for MARY JOHNS.
Book 1, Page 481 -- Inventory -- large estate -- slaves alone total
L 4,026-7-0. Additional inventory brings it to L 4,493-7-4. ISAAC
RUCKER; ELIJAH and GEO. CHRISTIAN. July 5, 1779.

TARLTON JOHNS -- Book 16, Page 412 -- June 29, 1863, written; Au-
gust 17, 1863, probated. Witnesses: WM. ADCOCK, FIELDING BROWN,
WM. W. THOMPSON. Ux and children when latter are of age. Executor:
SAML. M. GARLAND.

WM. JOHNS -- Book 1, Page 323 -- Administrator's Bond -- THOS. JOHNS,
DUDLEY GATEWOOD, JNO. PENN, January 6, 1777, for THOS. JOHNS.
Book 1, Page 340 -- Inventory -- May 5, 1777 - L 523-0-0. HENRY
GILBERT, DAVID SHEPHERD, JNO. STEWART.
Book 16, Page 307 -- February 7, 1861, written; April 20, 1863, pro-
bated. Witnesses: NELSON HICKA(?); ALEX. N. WARE; JNO. M. WARE.
Granddaughter, JUDITH BRANHAM. Executor: my friend, EDMUND BRANHAM.
Book 16, Page 356 -- Administrator's Bond -- EDMUND BRANHAM and G. W.
SMOOT, June 17, 1863, for EDMUND BRANHAM.

WM. C. JOHNS -- Book 12, Page 129 -- Power of attorney, April 3, 1848,
by WM. C. JOHNS, Tazewell County, Tennessee, to ANDREW J. JOHNS to act
for him as to will of ONEY JOHNS in Amherst County; also money due
him as heir of JNO. ALEX. JOHNS, deceased of Amherst County. WM. B.
PARKER, Notary Public, of Tazewell, Tennessee.

    It should be pointed out that there is semmingly no connection
between the early JOHNS Family - prior to 1800 - and the ones in
latter data. The history of these latter ones is shrouded in mystery
for there is mostly only legend and little, if any, court data. I
recognize so many of these names as being used for the JOHNS Family in
present Amherst. The modern group lives mostly in the area where the
folk known as "indian-mixed" are congregated. My wife has taught at
the St. Paul Mission where so many of them have attended. Tradition
has it that they are descendants of Indians who were enroute to Washington to protest the impending move to the west. These Indians
camped near Buena Vista and white residents drove them at gun point
into the mountains because they said that some of them had smallpox.
This is merely legend, but these people do have strong Indian charac-
teristics: straight black hair, copper skin, and high cheek bones.
Some of the men are quite handsome and many of the girls and younger
women are exotic in appearance. The Episcopal Church has maintained
a mission at St. Paul's, but the school is operated on church property
at county expense.

ANN JOHNSON, MRS. -- Book 4, Page 618 -- February 11, 1804, written;
April 16, 1810, probated. WM. HOWARD, JNO. PIGG, SUKEY SNEAD. BUR-

WELL SNEAD, JNO. SWANSON, NANCY FINCH(?), MARY GRIFF(?), JNO. D. HART,
and JNO. TANKERSLEY. (Note: She must have had a big party for the
ceremony. BFD.) Son, PHILIP JOHNSON; daughter, MARY GOODWIN and
children; estate of daughter, FANNY COALTER; granddaughter, ANNE B.
RALEY; granddaughter, FANNY GOODWIN; grandson, RO. GOODWIN; grand-
daughter, MARY BUSTER - her children; granddaughter, ANNE BUSTER.
Executors: son, PHILIP JOHNSON; and son-in-law, JNO. H. GOODWIN;
nephew, JOS. BURRUS. JOHNSON qualified. Bondsmen: NELSON C. DAWSON
and NICHL. HARRISON.
Book 5, Page 4 -- Inventory -- October 17, 1810 -- $2,463.82. ELIAS
WILLS, WM. TURNER, JOS. KENNERLEY.
Book 5, Page 194 -- Administrator's Account -- December 10, 1812.
PHILIP JOHNSON, administrator -- my legacy in FANNY COALTER's estate -
WM. BROWN & Co. - amounts charged to me from 1793 to 1799. Legacies
to RO. GOODWIN; JNO. A. GOODWIN; WM. and CLAUDIUS BUSTER; slaves from
estate of JONATHAN JOHNSON are included. WM. BUSTER is not entitled
to ANN JOHNSON's estate, but to his children and JONATHAN JOHNSON.

BENJ. JOHNSON -- Book 3, Page 128 -- Administrator's Bond -- KNIGHT
BOWLS. Bondsmen: REUBIN HARRISON and THOS. COLEMAN, December 7,
1789.
Book 3, Page 131 -- Inventory -- Hanover County, December 29, 1789.
DAVID ROYSTER, JOSIAH and HENRY ATTKISSON.
Book 6, Page 385 -- Administrator's de bonis non Bond -- August 18,
1823. JAS. W. FANNIGAN. Bondsman: WM. FLANNIGAN - probably both
are FLANNIGANS.

CHAS. JOHNSON -- Book A, Page 4 -- Independent Bond -- January 4,
1787. CHAS. JOHNSON, Goochland County, to CHAS. BURRUS, Amherst County, to make deed to Bever Creek land next to RICHARD OGLESBY and CHAS.
BURRUS -- formerly land of RICH. BALLENGER -- 232 acres. Witnesses:
JOS. BURRUS and MARTIN BIBB.

CHAS. T. JOHNSON -- Book 10, Page 282 -- Refunding Bond -- April 13,
1838; JAS. JONES; bondsmen: JNO. THOMAS and WM. M. COATES -- to
BENJ. TALIAFERRO, administrator of JNO. T. JOHNSON. JONES as guardian
of CHAS. T. JOHNSON, infant son of CHAS. T. JOHNSON, deceased, has
received $20.00 under will of JNO. T. JOHNSON.

FRANCIS JOHNSON -- Book 1, Page 351 -- Guardian Bond -- May 5, 1777.
CHAS. BURRUS and THOS. MOFFITT for CHAS. BURRUS as guardian of
FRANCIS JOHNSON, orphan of JONATHAN JOHNSON.

JNO. JOHNSON -- Book 3, Page 213 -- Administrator's Bond -- Decem-
ber 5, 1791. JNO. BALDING. Bondsman: WM. WRIGHT, JR.
Book 3, Page 391 -- Tobacco Inspector -- September 19, 1795. Bonds-
man: JAS. WILLS.
Book 3, Page 520 -- Same -- Swan Creek Warehouse in Amherst County,
September 17, 1798. Bondsman: same.
Book 4, Page 276 -- Same -- September 17, 1804. Bondsman: JNO.
LOVING.
Book 10, Page 282 -- Refunding Bond -- April 13, 1838. JAS. JONES
(indexed under ALEX. JONES). See CHAS. T. JOHNSON, above. This
data also pertains to JNO. THOS. JOHNSON, below.

JNO. THOS. JOHNSON -- Book 9, Page 436 -- October 28, 1837 -- Refund-
ing Bond by JNO. THOS. JOHNSON. Bondsman: TANDY K. KIDD - to BENJ.
TALIAFERRO -- same facts as for CHAS. T. JOHNSON, above. JNO. THOMAS
JOHNSON is one of the children of CHAS. T. JOHNSON. Witnesses:
C. DABNEY. Recorded May 21, 1838.

JNO. Y. JOHNSON (JOHNSTON in data, but so indexed) -- Book 7,
Page 288 -- August 12, 1828, written; July 6, 1829, probated. Louisville, Kentucky; Jefferson County; Witnesses: WM. H. BROADDUS, WM.
PICKETT, MICHL. J. O'CALLAGHAN. My brother, WM. JOHNSTON, executor--
to children of my brother, CHAS. Y. JOHNSTON "that is living"; my
sister, MILDRED Y. PICKETT's children. WORDEN POPE, Jefferson County
Clerk; JNO. BELL, Judge. September 23, 1829. Recorded in Amherst
County, November 18, 1829. Administrator did not appear to qualify
and handed to sheriff to administer. Note: In my native state of

Kentucky, we still employ the office of County Clerk in all such
matters. Virginia now uses the Circuit Clerk system to store wills,
deeds, and other such data.
Book 10, Page 269 -- Administrator's Account -- BENJ. TALIAFERRO,
late sheriff -- will annexed -- to JNO. T. JOHNSON (so employed
here -- legacy in full; also paid in full to A. W. WIMBUSH; MRS.
BOOKER; MRS. JONES; MRS. OMOHUNDRO; and to JAS. JONES, guardian of
CHAS. Y. JOHNSON. From CHAS. DABNEY - in full costs collected by him
of HARRIS executors from estate of THOS. JOHNSON -- OMOHUNDRO and ux.
Returned August 11, 1840.

JONATHAN JOHNSON (JOHNSTON) -- Book 1, Page 277 -- Administrator's
Bond -- March 6, 1775. ANN JOHNSON, CHAS. BURRUS, THOS. LUMPKIN for
ANN JOHNSON.
Book 1, Page 411 -- Inventory -- several slaves; April 6, 1778.

RICH. BENNETT, ABRAHAM NORTH, JNO. MERRITT.
Book 2, Page 113 -- Administrator's Account -- JOHNSTON here -- from
March, 1777 - L 114-17-10-1/2. Each child will get L 52-14-3-1/2.
DANL. GAINES; JNO. MERRITT; no names of children are given herein.

MARY JOHNSON -- Book 1, Page 350 -- Guardian Bond -- May 5, 1777.
THOS. MOFFITT and CHAS. BURRUS for THOS. MOFFITT as guardian of MARY
JOHNSON, orphan of JONATHAN JOHNSON.
Book 2, Page 21 -- Administrator's Bond -- August 6, 1781. UNITY
EVANS. Bondsman: ALEX. REID, JR.

PHILIP JOHNSON -- Book 1, Page 349 -- Guardian Bond -- May 5, 1777.
CHAS. BURRUS and JNO. PENN for CHAS. BURRUS as guardian of SNELLING
and PHILLIP JOHNSON, orphans of JONATHAN JOHNSON. I have previously
pointed out that many Guardian Bonds are indexed for only one ward,
but several names are often found in many items.
Book 5, Page 610 -- Administrator's Bond -- November 20, 1816 --
JNO. H. GOODWIN. Bondsman: REUBEN NORVELL, SPENCER NORVELL, JNO. M.
DANIELS, and WM. I. (J.) ISBELL.
Book 6, Page 137 -- Administrator's Account -- June 12, 1819 -- all
legatees are of age and have been paid (no names). NELSON C. DAWSON;
CHAS. WINGFIELD; THOS. JOHNSON.

PHOEBA JOHNSON -- Book 6, Page 267 -- Guardian Bond -- November 21,
1821. PHOEBA JOHNSON; LEWIS LAINE and THOS. CARTER for PHOEBA JOHN-
SON as guardian of THOS. JOHNSON, orphan of THOS. JOHNSON. This is
an example of a wrong index for it should have been set up in the
name of the ward.

SALLY JOHNSON -- Book 4, Page 164 -- Certificate -- November 21, 1804,
that SALLY JOHNSON relinquished right to administer estate of CHAS.
CREASY, deceased. Witness: JNO. BIBB.

SNELLING JOHNSON -- Book 3, Page 152 -- Administrator's Bond -- Octo-
ber 4, 1779 -- PHILIP JOHNSON, JOS. BURRUS, and ZACH. DAWSON for
PHILIP JOHNSON.
Book 3, Page 173 -- Inventory -- May 2, 1791 - L 347-1-2. JNO. Q.
PERRATT, GEO. McDANIEL, THOS. JOHNSON.

STEPHEN JOHNSON -- Book 3, Page 263 -- Administrator's Bond -- June 17,
1793. WM. JOHNSON and NORBORN THOMAS for WM. JOHNSON.
Book 4, Page 196 -- December 30, 1791, written; October 21, 1805,
probated. Witnesses: DIV(?) DONALD; WM. and MARGARET JACOBS. Ux,
SUSANNAH - lands and slaves for life and then to my living children.
She is to administer.
Book 4, Page 208 -- Inventory -- October 16, 1805 -- $2,895.68. Re-
turned November 15, 1805. JOS. BARGER, CHAS. JONES, JNO. HUGHS.
Book 4, Page 415 -- Administrator's Bond -- October 21, 1805 --
DANL. McDONALD and DAVID S. GARLAND for DANL. McDONALD.
Book 14, Page 165 -- March 3, 1856, written; August 18, 1856, probated.
Witnesses: GEO. W. HIGGINBOTHAM, SAML. R. IRVINE, JOS. A. HIGGINBO-
THAM. Daughter-in-law, ANNE JOHNSON - 50 acres - lower end of plan-
tation and next to ROWLAND TUCKER and SAML. R. IRVINE; lawful heirs of

MOSES JOHNSON - 50 acres next to ANNE; rest of 127 acres to be sold and divided, but proceeds of 27 acres to son, MOSES; rest of my children: STEPHEN, GEO. R., LAWSON M. JOHNSON, SOPHIA TUCKER; grandchildren: STEPHEN T. DODD and ELIZ. C. HIGGINBOTHAM. Executors: HENRY LOVING and JAS. GANNAWAY. Produced two times: Monday, August 18, 1856, and Monday, September 15, 1856. HENRY LOVING refused to administer and sheriff, E. P. TUCKER, appointed. Appraisers: CHAS. TUCKER, ABSALOM HIGGINBOTHAM, SAML. R. IRVINE, ROWLAND TUCKER, H. LOVING.
Book 14, Page 563 -- So indexed; nothing there.
Book 22, Page 474 -- March 31, 1888, written; November 17, 1890, probated. Witnesses: SIDNEY FLETCHER and ANDREW EDWARDS. Ux, MINERVA - land for life and then to her two children: FANNY and EDDIE, who labored and assisted me in my old age. Ux to administer. Appraisers: S. B. CLAIBORNE, SIDNEY FLETCHER, R. S. FOGUS.
Book 22, Page 488 -- Ux qualified on probate date.

THOS. JOHNSON -- Book 6, Page 251 -- Administrator's Bond -- JNO. Y. JOHNSON, WM. JOHNSON, and WM. TURNER, September 17, 1821, for JNO. Y. JOHNSON. This is probably the item indexed for Book 6, Page 246, and not there.
Book 6, Page 260 -- Inventory -- October 15, 1821 - $5,354.62-1/2. JAS. L. LAMKIN, JESSE BECK, THOS. JURRIL.
Book 6, Page 425 -- Guardian Bond -- JNO. ALCOCK and LEWIS LAINE, December 15, 1823, for LEWIS LAINE as guardian of THOS. JOHNSON, orphan of THOS. JOHNSON.
Book 7, Page 59 -- Administrator's Account from 1825 and return, September 17, 1827. Administrator is called JNO. T. and JNO. Y. herein.
Book 10, Page 270 -- Administrator's Account -- BENJ. TALIAFERRO, late sheriff - guardian of JAS. JONES - "four sheares"; CHAS. Y. JOHNSON's heirs; legacy of IRA ALLCOCK; CHAS. DABNEY in full - OMO-HUNDRO's order to A. W. WIMBUSH, August 11, 1840. DANL. COLEMAN.

THOS. C. JOHNSON -- Book 7, Page 73 -- Guardian Bond -- November 19, 1827. JAS. D. WATTS and JNO. DILLARD for JAS. WATTS as guardian of THOS. C. JOHNSON, orphan of THOS. JOHNSON.
Book 9, Page 167 -- Guardian's Account from January 1, 1831 - cloth for slave, Nealy; clerk of Campbell County; to SHADRICK CARTER's executor - share in slave; amount from L. LAYNE's estate and interest on it from January 1, 1829, to November 15, 1834. ED. A. CABELL and WM. H. KNIGHT. December 21, 1835.
Book 9, Page 170 -- Guardian's Account from January, 1828 - suit vs. I. ALLCOCK; to IRA ALLCOCK for 3 years board at $25.00 per year; from L. LAYNE's estate, January 2, 1829. SHADRICK CARTER's estate; to L. LAYNE for benefit of THOS. C. JOHNSON. ED. A. CABELL, JAS. ROSE, JOS. STAPLES. July 21, 1830.
Book 9, Page 406 -- Guardian's Account from January, 1835 - to JNO. S. BLAIR (just before this is item of WATTS as administrator of WINSTON BLAIR), March 20, 1838. N. BURNLEY, RICH. WINGFIELD, JOSHUA JACKSON.
Book 10, Page 87 -- Guardian's Account from May, 1837 - college expenses - $200.00; hire of slave, Nealy; same committee as above. Albemarle certificate before JAS. D. WATTS, Justice of the Pieace, January 17, 1839.

WALTER B. JOHNSON -- Book 7, Page 8 -- Guardian Bond -- MILDRED HALKDRSTONE and WALTER B. BOSWELL, June 19, 1827, for MILDRED HALK-DRSTONE as guardian of WALTER B. JOHNSON, orphan of ANDREW JOHNSON.

WM. JOHNSON -- Book 1, Page 442 -- June 8, 1776, written; November 5, 1778, probated. Witnesses: WM. GUTTRY, PEARCE WADE, AARON HIGGIN-BOTHAM, THOS. DAWSON, CALEB RALLS. Mother, ANN JOHNSON - slave, Comer, for lifetime; my brothers: SNELLING and PHILLIP JOHNSON; my sisters, MARY and FRANCES; MARY MAFFITT, daughter of THOMAS MAFFITT; land next to SAML. BAUGHAN, deceased, to PHILLIP; land bought by my father of SAML. BAUGHAN - to SNELLING JOHNSON; also entry on Fawn Creek; sisters above named get entry on branch of Bowling Creek; if sisters and MARY MAFFITT are without issue. Executors: my friends, RICH. BENNETT, CHAS. BURRUS, and JNO. MERRITT.
Book 1, Page 491 -- Administrator's Bond -- August 2, 1779. JNO. MERRITT; Bondsman: CHAS. BURRUS.

ALEX. S. JONES -- Book 6, Page 690 -- So indexed, but not there.
Book 9, Page 342 -- Refunding Bond -- October 15, 1837 -- MARTHA
JONES; ALEX. S. JONES; and WILEY CAMPBELL to CORNL. SALE. SALE has
delivered 2 slaves to MARTHA and ALEX. S. JONES at $1,874.00 to go to
children of JNO. C. JONES, deceased, under will of THOS. JONES, deceased, of Nelson County. SALE as attorney-in-fact and guardian of
children. MARTHA, et al. are to pay over to the other children.

DAVID W. JONES -- Book 12, Page 491 -- Administrator's Bond -- WM. E.
SHEPHERD and RICHMOND C. TERRELL (attorney: BENJ. H. JONES) Febru-
ary 16, 1852, for WM. SHEPHERD.
Book 12, Page 502 -- Inventory -- February 17, 1852 -- $121.00.
THOS. A. EDWARDS, JNO. REYNOLDS, SAML. K. MEAD.
Book 13, Page 225 -- Sale, February 17, 1852 -- THOS. W. JONES was
buyer; sale also of February 22, 1853.

FRANCES J. JONES -- Book 10, Page 173 -- Guardian Bond -- RICH. P.
JONES and RANDOLPH MORRIS, November 18, 1839, for RICH. JONES as
guardian of FRANCES J. JONES, orphan of RICH. JONES, deceased. It is
difficult to distinguish male or female spelling of FRANCIS or ES
here since it is spelled both ways in data.

JAS. L. JONES -- Book 12, Page 133 -- Guardian Bond -- August 21, 1848,
CLAIBORNE G. FULKS and TANDY JONES; STERLING CLAIBORNE; and SAML.
PETTIT for CLAIBORNE FULKS as guardian of JAS. L. JONES, orphan of
STEPHEN J. JONES.

JAS. R. JONES -- Book 11, Page 535 -- Administrator's Bond -- July 19,
1847. JNO. & WM. DILLARD for JNO. DILLARD.
Book 12, Page 60 -- Inventory -- concluded on February 8, 1848.
D. STAPLES, HIRAM C. KYLE, PLEASANT N. STORY.
Book 15, Page 282 -- Administrator's Bond -- J. D. TURNER and JNO.
Q. A. DILLARD, April 16, 1860, for J. TURNER.

JANE JONES (Different persons: one is MRS.) -- Book 7, Page 85 --
Guardian Bond -- EDWD. A. CABELL and PLEASANT MITCHELL, November 20,
1827, for EDWD. CABELL as guardian of JANE JONES, orphan of JESSE
JONES.

JESSE JONES -- Book 3, Page 228 -- Guardian Bond -- June 18, 1792.
DAVID JONES; AMBROSE RUCKER and REUBEN PENDLETON for DAVID JONES as
guardian of JESSE JONES, orphan of RICH. JONES, deceased. Indexed
for DAVID JONES.

JNO. C. JONES -- Book B, Page 85 -- Guardian Bond -- CHAS. L. JONES
and JNO. S. TUCKER, September 5, 1860, for CHAS. JONES as guardian of
JNO. C.; JULIA F.; and REYNOLDSON R. JONES, orphans of ELIZ. A. JONES,
deceased.

JNO. J. JONES -- Book 15, Page 249 -- Guardian Bond -- JEFF. D. TURNER
and RO. A. PENDLETON, October 17, 1859, for JEFF. TURNER as guardian
of JNO. J. and EMILY M. JONES, orphans of JAS. R. JONES, deceased.

JNO. M. JONES -- Book 10, Page 53 -- Guardian Bond -- RICH. P. JONES
and TANDY JONES, October 15, 1838, for RICH. JONES as guardian of
JNO. M. JONES, orphan of RICH. JONES, deceased.

JNO. W. JONES -- Book 19, Page 86 -- Administrator's Bond -- October 18, 1875. JNO. THOMPSON, JR. Bondsman: J. THOMPSON BROWN.

LUCY A. JONES -- Book 14, Page 213 -- Administrator's Bond --
April 20, 1857. RICH. P. JONES and BLUFORD MORRIS for RICH. JONES.

MARY JONES -- Book 6, Page 436 -- Guardian Bond -- ALEX. N. JONES and
bondsmen: JNO. McDANIEL and THOS. STRANGE, January 19, 1824, for
ALEX. JONES as guardian of MARY and ELIZ. JONES, orphans of RICH.
JONES.

RICH. JONES -- Book 6, Page 412 -- Administrator's Bond -- November 18,

1823. JNO. McDANIEL; MARY and ALEX. N. JONES; WM. and LINDSEY
McDANIEL and SAML. HEISKELL for JNO. McDANIEL; MARY and ALEX. JONES.
Book 6, Page 430 -- Inventory -- January 19, 1824 - $3,057.70.
CHAS. C. CARTER, WILL JOPLING, and ABRAM CARTER.
Book 7, Page 180 -- Dower of MARY JONES, widow of RICH. JONES,
September 22, 1828. THOS. N. EUBANK; CHAS. L. BARRETT; JNO. PRYOR -
plat on Page 181 - under west side of Tobacco Row Mountain - branch
of South Fork of Horsley Creek; east side of road from Crawford's
Gap to Pedlar Mills; about 3 miles from Pedlar. Lines of WM. JONES,
deceased, south west corner bought by JNO. McDANIEL and RICH. JONES
from heirs of W. S. CRAWFORD - 124 acres; surveyed for widow, September 22, 1828, by JNO. PRYOR, assistant to REUBEN NORVELL, Amherst
County surveyor.
Book 11, Page 222 -- Estate Commitment to Sheriff -- November Court,
1843 -- Motion of WILL McDANIEL; JAS. POWELL, Sheriff.

RICH. M. JONES -- Book 14, Page 211 -- Guardian Bond -- October 20,
1856. RICH. P. JONES and BLUFORD MORRIS for RICH. JONES as guardian
of his own children: RICH. M.; JNO. W., and THOS. G. JONES.

RICH. P. JONES -- Book 8, Page 248 -- Guardian Bond -- September 17,
1832. THOS. TUCKER, RICH. S. ELLIS for THOS. TUCKER as guardian of
RICH. P., LINDSEY, JNO., and FRANCES JONES, orphans of RICH. JONES,
deceased.

SARAH JONES -- Book 17, Page 250 -- Dower, February, 1862 -- widow
of TANDY JONES - 102 acres, 92 acres of it around mansion house,
10 acres detached timber land and right of way to other owners.
Order - 1862; returned January 15, 1863. MARTIN D. TINSLEY; BLUFORD
MORRIS; STEPHEN WATTS; GEO. T. PLEASANTS - adjoining owners.
Book 22, Page 471 -- This is widow of BEVERLY JONES, October, 1887,
decree of Circuit Court, JONES vs. JONES' Widow. Committee: A. F.
WILLS, E. S. WARE, JAS. B. STAPLES, EDWD. SLAUGHTER, B. V. CASH.
Land and dwelling.

STEPHEN J. JONES -- Book 12, Page 66 -- Inventory -- $3,729.99-1/2;
September 6, 1848. WM. STAPLES; RICH. LANDRUM; BURTON LANDRUM.
Book 12, Page 132 -- Administrator's Bond -- CLAIBORNE G. FULKS,
TANDY JONES, STERLING CLAIBORNE, SAML. PETIT. August 21, 1848, for
CLAIBORNE FULKS.
Book 12, Page 377 -- Administrator's Account -- CHAS. JONES' bond
to TANDY JONES; SARAH JONES; tuition for JAS. L. JONES; to JNO. L.(?)
JONES; GEO. JONES in part; JNO. J. LANDRUM's part; slaves held by
grandmother of JAS. JONES and his part of estate of uncle, JNO.
JONES - his guardian. Certified by JAS. L. JONES; returned Febru-
ary 17, 1851.
Book 12, Page 380 -- Sale -- buyers: GEO. T.; WARNER; BEV. JONES.
Returned February 17, 1851. Sale on September 6, 1848.
Book 13, Page 122 -- Administrator's Account from September 1, 1850.
To SAML. PETTIT for board of JAS. L. JONES; tuition for BEVERLY JONES;
JAS. L. is named as only distributee. June 20, 1853.
Book 13, Page 304 -- Administrator's Account from September 20, 1852 -
to JAS. L. JONES for father's estate. Receipt by administrator and
guardian: FULKS.

TANDY JONES -- Book 15, Page 251 -- Administrator's Bond -- OLIVER P.
and CHAS. JONES, September 19, 1859, for OLIVER JONES.
Book 15, Page 276 -- Administrator's Bond -- February 20, 1860, for
same men.
Book 16, Page 31 -- Sales, November 30, 1860. Buyers: M. T.; MISS
PAULINA; CHAS. L.; WM.; L. W.; MISS SARAH; OLIVER P. and LUWELLYN W.
JONES - $2,103.95.
Book 16, Page 318 -- Administrator's Account from November 8, 1859.
Paid to SALLIE F. and PAULINA P. JONES. Recorded May, 1863.
Book 16, Page 434 -- Administrator's Account from January 26, 1860.
CHAS. JONES forwheat. O. P. JONES for corn; SARAH W. JONES for
wheat. Recorded October 19, 1863.
Book 17, Page 202 -- So indexed, but not there.

WARNER JONES, DR. -- Book 16, Page 135 -- Administrator's Bond --

ELIZ. M. JONES; W. M. HITE; W. S. CLAIBORNE, June 16, 1862, for
ELIZ. JONES.
Book 16, Page 194 -- Inventory of late DR. WARNER JONES - $1,209.60.
V. McGINNIS, W. S. CRAWFORD, V. T. SETTLE.

WM. JONES -- Book 3, Page 227 -- Guardian Bond -- RICH. JONES, AMBROSE
RUCKER, REUBEN PENDLETON, June 18, 1792, for RICH. JONES as guardian
of WM. JONES, orphan of RICH. JONES.

BENNETT JOPLING -- Book 4, Page 350 -- Guardian Bond -- June 21,
1802. JAS. JOPLING, JR.; WM. JOPLING; JESSE JOPLING for JAS. JOPLING,
JR., as guardian of BENNETT JOPLING, orphan of JOSIAH JOPLING, deceased.

ELIZ. JOPLING -- Book 4, Page 308 -- Guardian Bond -- April 15, 1799.
SUSANNAH JOPLING; WM. LEE HARRIS; WM. H. DIGGES and SAML. BRIDGWATER
for SUSANNAH JOPLING as guardian of ELIZ. and SALLY JOPLING, orphans
of JOSIAH JOPLING, deceased.

GEO. JOPLING -- Book 6, Page 698 -- Constable -- Second Hundred,
October 15, 1826. Bondsmen: WM. HAYNES, RO. H. CARTER.
Book 7, Page 25 -- Same -- June 18, 1827. Bondsmen: WM. HAYNES and
GIDEON C. GOODRICH.
Book 9, Page 398 -- Estate Commitment to Sheriff, February Court,
1838. Motion of PHILIP THURMOND. JNO. COLEMAN, Sheriff.

JOSIAH JOPLING -- Book 3, Page 463 -- November 16, 1797, written;
April 16, 1798, probated. Witnesses: SAML. BRIDGWATER, BENJ. CHIL-
DREE, PLEASANT GRIFFIN, EDWD. THOMPSON TOMS. My ux; my surviving
children and heirs; daughter, HANNAH BRIDGWATER, and at death to
JNO. WOOD JOPLING; ELIZ. WARE WOOD and JOSIAH BRIDGWATER JOPLING;
son, JAMES - Kentucky land; son, WM. - land on Cedar Creek - 325
acres; son, EDWARD WARE JOPLING - Kanawaha land; son, THOS. - one
half of where I live and where son, JAS., lives; son, HOLEMAN JOP-
LING - Kanawaha land. Son, BENNETT; daughter, ELIZ. BRIDGWATER
JOPLING; daughter, SARAH JOPLING; if sons are without heirs. Execu-
tors: Sons, JAS. and WM. JOPLING.
Book 3, Page 535 -- Inventory -- $3,401.50, December 13, 1798. THOS.
SHELTON; JAS. WOODS; THOS. EWERS; ZACH. ROBERTS.
Page 463 -- September 17, 1798, SUDANNAH JOPLING renounced the will.
Book 4, Page 310 -- Administrator's Bond -- same date; JAS. JOPLING
qualified. Bondsmen: JNO. SMITH, PLEASANT MARTIN, WM. WARE, SAML.
BRIDGWATER, WM. JOPLING.

RALPH JOPLING -- Book 3, Page 195 -- June 23, 1791, written; Septem-
ber 5, 1791, probated. Witnesses: SHEROD GRIFFIN, JNO. SNIDER, JAS.
ENIX, JAS. TRAIL. Land in Buckingham County, North Caroline, to sons,
RALPH and JAS.; daughter, SARAH JOPLING; daughter, ANN JOPLING; sons,
THOS.; WM.; DANL.; JNO.; BEN; daughter, CATH. THURMOND; daughter,
MARTHA THOMAS; children of deceased daughter, MARY THOMAS; MICHL.;
RALPH, and BETSY at marriage or of age. "If either" of my children
are without issue. Executors: ux, CATH.; and sons, JAS. and THOS.;
and RICH. FARRAR.
Book 3, Page 197 -- Administrator's Bond -- RICH. FARRAR and WM.
SPENCER, probate date, for RICH. FARRAR.
Book 3, Page 211 -- Inventory -- L 423-13-4, September 15, 1791;
HENRY MARTIN, HENRY ROBARDS, WM. JOHNSON.

THOS. JOPLING -- Book 3, Page 116 -- August 10, 1789, written;
September 7, 1789, probated. Witnesses: HENRY MARTIN, JOS. THOMAS,
THOS. FARRAR, JNO. JOPLING. Executors: sons, JAS. and JOS. and
friend, HENRY MARTIN. Ux, HANNAH - Gladys Creek land; grandson,
JESSE JOPLING - if without heirs; sons, JOSIAH and JAS. - Piney
Mountain land bought of JESSE MARTIN; son, THOS.; JNO. GRIFFIN who
married my daughter, MARTHA; my daughters: ANN CHILDERS, JANE DAVIS,
LUCY POWELL, REBECCA MARTIN, HANNAH ALLEN.
Book 2 (3?), Page 126 -- Inventory -- December 1, 1789 - L 534-17-6.

HENRY MARTIN, WM. JOHNSON, HENRY ROBERTS.
Book 4, Page 351 -- Guardian Bond -- June 21, 1802. JAS.; WM. and
JESSE JOPLING for JAS. JOPLING as guardian of THOS. JOPLING, orphan
of JOSIAH JOPLING.

It is interesting to note the enormous changes in the families
represented in these will items. I have looked at the 'phone direc-
tory for the Village of Amherst and many of these families are no
longer in the area. The majority of J's are of the JENNINGS and
JONES families. I know that some of these are not of families mentioned in these will items.

There is much JONES data in the records of Nelson County, Virginia. The vast majority of it pertains to the same families found
in Amherst. I have just had an experience in working on the THOS.
JONES family for Revolutionary line. I began with only fragmentary
data for the person seeking information only knew the names of her
grandparents, FITZGERALD and HARVIE. I got off to a bad start for
this marriage bond was for a FITZGERALD and HARRIS, but a look at
original bond showed that she was a HARVIE. The copy did not help
for the last names of the parents were not given. I was able to work
back through the HARVIE line and a marriage to a SAUNDERS. This
connected with the SHELTON C. JONES line and those who have studied
it know that he was a son of THOS. JONES who was a Revolutionary
soldier - captain and wounded. Mrs. Sweeny had done a fine piece of
work on this THOS. JONES and had found a Bible record attached to
his pension data.

As is well known, a great many families moved to Kentucky and
other points. Deed books show many references to the heirs who have
gone elsewhere and sell land back in Amherst. I often think that
deed books show more genealogical data than is to be found in wills,
but this is merely my "horseback" opinion and many will disagree
with me.

I think of such a family as that of BREEDLOVE as a case in
point. I am acquainted with the group which went from Nelson County,
Virginia, to Warren and Simpson in Kentucky. There is nothing here
in wills to help us with them, but I am working on Deed Book G at
present and know of two men by BREEDLOVE name who bought land which
is of record in this particular book.

ABSTRACTS FROM HARDESTY AND BROCK

(1) GEN. JACKSON -- Page 437 - War of 1812; AUSTIN CARPENTER
served under him. CARPENTER formerly of King and Queen to Amherst
County; ux, CATH. (SCOTT).

GEN. JACKSON, Confederate: JAS. E. JARVIES served under him -
Page 440. JARVIES was a private.

(2) JARVIES FAMILY -- Page 440f. JAS. E. JARVIES, subject;
son of WM. and ELIZA ANN (LAWMAN) JARVIES and JAS. E. JARVIES born
in Rockbridge, April 22, 1843. Father was born February 11, 1816,
and his mother was born January 22, 1813. They came to Amherst County
when JAS. E. JARVIES was 3 and still live here. WM. was son of JOS.
and NANCY JARVIES - early to Amherst County. JOS. was born May 21,
1779; and NANCY was born October 6, 1781. Of English stock. LAWMANs
are German stock. JAS. E. grew up in Amherst County; June, 1861,
enlisted in Rockbridge Artillery Company; CAPT. MILLER; JACKSON's
Division; private; 1864 promoted gunner under CAPT. McDONALD; twice
wounded; captured and escaped in fighting around Petersburg and stam-
pede at its evacuation. JAS. E. JARVIES married near Oronoco,
May 31, 1877, ANN MARIA HEARTLESS (spelled HARTLESS in Amherst County
data). Number of children: CHAS. EDWARD - born March 6, 1879;
ROBERTA MAUDE - born January 16, 1881; SARAH ELIZA - born March 7,
1883. Ux of JAS. E. JARVIES, nee HARTLESS, born in Amherst County
November 1, 1852; daughter of PRESTON H. and SARAH ANN (HARVIE)
HARLESS and granddaughter of JNO. HARTLESS of Amherst County. Parents
now in Rockbridge. JAS. E. JARVIES owns and manages saw and grist
mill in Pedlar District. Post Office: Oronoco, Virginia, in Amherst
County.

(3) VIRGINIA A. JEFFRIES (JENNINGS) -- Page 441 - first ux of
MATT W. JENNINGS and she died July 29, 1876; left 3 children (see
MATT. W. JENNINGS).

(4) GEN. JENKINS - Confederate -- Page 443 -- EDWD. A. PENN
was his special courier: Confederate.

(5) CHAS. E. JENNINGS Sketch -- Page 441 -- CHAS. E. JENNINGS was born in Amherst County, September 23, 1843; and spent four years in Kentucky and Arkansas; farmer; half-owner; Temperance District; carpenter and wheelwright. Before he was 18, March 2, 1861, enlisted Company H, 19th Virginia Infantry, for duration. In Battles of Williamsburg and Seven Pines; detached service for time and rejoined his regiment just before Appomattox. Son of POWHATAN P. and CATH. B. (JEWELL) JENNINGS. Father was born in Appomattox and mater in Amherst County; both died in Amherst County. December 23, 1873, CHAS. E. JENNINGS married NANNIE J. JOHNSTON who was born in Amherst County, June 12, 1856; daughter of WM. M. and MARTHA A. (JENNINGS) JOHNSTON. Her pater born Bedford, March 24, 1822; mater born in Buckingham, August 28, 1832. Pater from Bedford to Amherst County in 1826 and still in County of Amherst. CHAS. E. JENNINGS and ux have 4 children: WM. P. - born May 18, 1875; DAN M. - born September 15, 1877; CHAS. A. - born June 27, 1879; VIOLA LOVING - born December 5, 1881. Post Office: Clifford, Amherst County, Virginia.

(6) MATTHEW W. JENNINGS Sketch -- Page 441 -- Son of JNO. W. and ELIZA (VERNON) JENNINGS - residents of Amherst County. MATTHEW born in Amherst County July 19, 1846; grandfather, JNO. JENNINGS from eastern shore to Amherst County. First ux of MATTHEW W. was VIRGINIA A. JEFFRIES; died July 29, 1876, and left: LUCY J. - born November 24, 1867; LESLIE L. - born January 28, 1870; WALTER R. - born January 14, 1873. May 13, 1877, MATTHEW W. married WILLIE R. PARR - born in Amherst County, February 12, 1847; died July 4th next was date of their first child, WILSON V. - born January 13, 1879. Next child was PERCY L. - born August 31, 1880; ASHBY P. - born August 1, 1882. WM. and MARTHA A. (BLUNT) PARR were parents of WILLIE R. PARR; pater died August --, 1870; mater still living.
In 18th year, MATTHEW W. enlisted in MOSBY's Command - served for duration. His brother, PETER, was in Company I, 19th Virginia Infantry; wounded 5 times; his brother, J. E., was in Company E, 2nd Virginia Cavalry. MATTHEW's ux had 4 brothers in Confederate Army: JNO. H., JAS. HYTER, GEO. F., and THOS. W. PARR. Another brother of MATTHEW W.'s, ABNER JENNINGS, died in service, and GEO. F. PARR was killed. MATTHEW W. is farmer at Pedlar Mills, Amherst County.

(7) JENNINGS found in other Amherst County sketches of H and B; some repeats -- Page 442 -- ANNA M. JENNINGS, born February 20, 1850; married ALEX. MILLER, October 22, 1868. 8 children -- will list under MILLER for ALEX. is subject of sketch. ANNA M. was daughter of DANL. W. and MARTHA ANN (STAPLES) JENNINGS; her pater born Amherst County and mater in Appomattox County.
Page 443 -- JAS. JENNINGS married MARGARET E. PARR (WM. PARR sketch) and resides in Amherst County. WILLIE R. PARR is shown herein to be ux of M. W. JENNINGS - repetition of MATT. W. data (6).
Page 441 -- MARTHA A. JENNINGS married WM. M. JOHNSON in Amherst County, November 6, 1851. Eleven children (see WM. JOHNSTON herein). MARTHA A. was born Buckingham County, August 28, 1832; daughter of JNO. W. and ELIZA E. (VERNON) JENNINGS. Pater born Buckingham - 1805; mater born Charlotte County, 1814; they came to Amherst County from Buckingham about 1845.

(8) ANNA JOHNSON (CHILDRESS) -- Page 437 -- She married BENJ. CHILDRESS and was mater of BENJ. W. CHILDRESS (subject). She died in 1843; husband, BENJ. CHILDRESS, died in 1852. CHILDRESS family of Albemarle.

(9) Page 443 -- GEN. BRADLEY JOHNSON, Confederate -- EDWD. A. PENN (subject) served under him.

(10) Page 440 -- GEN. JOHNSON - Confederate -- JNO. HODGE (subject) served 1 year in western Virginia under him.

(11) Page 445 -- SARAH W. JOHNSON married JAS. H. HIGGINBOTHAM and was mater of ELIZ. HIGGINBOTHAM who married ROLAND TUCKER (subject). ELIZ. was born July 8, 1846, in Amherst County. Her mater died when ELIZ. was 2; pater still in Amherst County.

(12) Page 441 -- ABNER DEWITT JOHNSTON - son of WM. M. and MARTHA A. JENNINGS was born June 26, 1872; died January 27, 1875.

(13) Page 436 -- BUSHROD JOHNSTON - Confederate -- WM. A. BAL-LOWE (subject) served under him and was standard bearer; WISE's Brigade.

(14) Page 441 -- WM. M. JOHNSTON Sketch. WM. M. married MARTHA A. JENNINGS. ELIZA SUSAN - born October 15, 1863, to WM. M. and ux. ELIZ. JOHNSTON (nee TRIBLE) - mater of WM. M. JOHNSTON. She married pater of WM. M. - RICH. JOHNSTON - and from Bedford to Am-herst County in 1826. FANNY CALVIN JOHNSTON - born August 9, 1870; daughter of WM. M. and ux. JAS. HENRY JOHNSTON - born July 16, 1854; son of WM. M. and ux. JNO. WM. JOHNSTON - born March 18, 1858; son of WM. M. and ux. LUCY ANN JOHNSTON - born May 10, 1861; daughter of WM. M. and ux. MARTHA A. JOHNSTON (nee JENNINGS) - (5) and above in (7). MARTHA ELLEN JOHNSTON - born March 19, 1868; daughter of WM. M. and ux. MARY ELIZ. JOHNSTON - born September 14, 1852; daughter of WM. M. and ux. NANCY JANE JOHNSTON - born June 12, 1856; daughter of WM. M. and ux. NANNIE B. JOHNSTON (nee JENNINGS) - see CHAS. E. JENNINGS. OLIVER BELL JOHNSTON - born October 8, 1874; son of WM. M. and ux. RICH. LEE JOHNSTON - born February 28, 1866; son of WM. M. and ux. WM. M. JOHNSTON was son of RICH. & ELIZ. (TRIBLE) JOHNSTON - to Amherst County from Bedford in 1826 when WM. M. was about 4. WM. M. - born Bedford, March 24, 1822. RICH. JOHNSTON - born Spotsylvania County, January 4, 1777; died April 21, 1851. ELIZ. - ux of RICH. - born Spotsylvania; died November 27, 1840. WM. M. married November 6, 1851, MARTHA A. JENNINGS - children are listed herein. WM. M. served at start of Civil War; put in substitute who died; re-enlisted Company A, 52nd Virginia Infantry, wagoner for duration. Owns 154 acres near Buffalo River. Post Office: Clifford.

(15) Page 441 -- Sketches of THOS. J. and WM. R. JONES -- ANN J. JONES - born March 28, 1862; daughter of THOS. J. and ux, FRANCES E. (nee NORTH) - stated that 12 of 13 children live in Nelson with or near parents - 13th child dead. THOS. J. served in JONES' Battalion, Confederate; MARMADUKE's Battery of Artillery; unharmed and enlisted April 1, 1862. BETTIE W. (nee BURKS) JONES, ux of WM. R. JONES - married January 28, 1874; born in Rockbridge, July 20, 1849. Daughter of ALEX. H. and ELLEN T. (BROADUS) BURKS. Pater lives in Rockbridge and mater died in Amherst County. ALEX BURKS was captain of a Rock-bridge Company and captured. Her grandparents were SAML. C. BURKS and JNO. W. BROADUS - both capitains in War of 1812; her great-grandfather, BENJ. TALIAFERRO, was captain in Revolution. CAMILLA P. JONES - born March 25, 1868; daughter of THOS. J. JONES and ux. CATH. J. JONES - born May 9, 1856; daughter of THOS. J. JONES and ux. CHAS. JONES - pater of WM. R. JONES - married LUCY A. JONES (nee JONES). CHAS. died in Amherst County, but widow still here; made home in Amherst County in 1859. CHAS. B. JONES - born June 9, 1877; son of WM. R. JONES and ux. FRANCES E. (nee NORTH) JONES, ux of THOS. J. JONES; married March 22, 1852, in Frederick City, Maryland; born Appomattox, July 10, 1835; daughter of JAS. O. and DOROTHY P. NORTH. FRANCES E. JONES - born March 21, 1870; daughter of THOS. J. JONES and ux. JAS. F. JONES - born April 9, 1876; son of WM. R. JONES and ux. JAS. S. JONES - born July 14, 1848; son of THOS. J. JONES and ux. LEWIS JONES - paternal grandfather of WM. R. JONES (son of CHAS. and LUCY A. JONES) - lived in Cumberland County, Virginia. LUCY A. JONES was ux of CHAS. JONES; she was daughter of TANDY JONES - War of 1812, and resident of Amherst County. MONA (nee HITE) JONES - ux of SHELTON C. JONES and mater of THOS. J. JONES who was born in Nelson County.
Page 444 -- NANCY R. JONES (ARTHUR) - mater of SARAH D. ARTHUR who married DR. JAS. M. TALIAFERRO, October 4, 1860, in Bedford. NANCY R. JONES was ux of LEWIS C. ARTHUR. SARAH D. was born in Bed-ford in 1841; parents died in Bedford. NANNIE E. JONES - born November 15, 1872; daughter of THOS. J. JONES and ux. R. W. JONES - born June 12, 1866; son of THOS. J. JONES and ux. ROBT. A. JONES - born December 22, 1874; son of WM. R. JONES and ux. ROBT. M. JONES - born March 25, 1860; son of THOS. J. JONES and ux. SAML. J. JONES - born December 2, 1878; son of WM. R. JONES and ux. SHELTON C. JONES -

pater of THOS. J. JONES. SHELTON C. JONES married MONA HITE. TANDY
JONES - grandfather of WM. R. JONES - maternal grandfather; daughter,
LUCY A. THOS. H. JONES - born October 19, 1854; son of THOS. J.
JONES and ux. THOS. J. JONES - son of SHELTON C. JONES and MONA
(HITE) JONES - born Nelson, June 12, 1830; married FRANCES E. NORTH;
enlisted April 1, 1862; JONES Battalion. Owns 210 acres on Tye and
part in Temperance District. Post Office: Tye River. WALTER M.
JONES - born March 5, 1880; son of WM. R. JONES and ux. WM. C.
JONES - born April 7, 1853; son of THOS. J. JONES and ux.
        Page 443 -- GEN. WM. E. JONES - Confederate -- EDWD. A. PENN
was courier under him. WM. H. JONES - brother of THOS. J. JONES;
served as Confederate for duration. WM. R. JONES - subject - born
Nelson, August 15, 1845; son of CHAS. and LUCY A. JONES - married
BETTIE W. BURKS in Amherst County, January 28, 1874; children all born
at farm, Pedlar District, Amherst County; served last year of Civil
War in Company G, 19th Virginia Infantry - Farmer. Post Office: Sandidges, Amherst County -- I have pointed out elsewhere that this
hamlet still exists and is still known as "Sandidges."

        (16) Page 441 -- JOYNER sketch of HOUSTON C. JOYNER - farmer -
Courthouse District; born and married Amherst County - born
November 20, 1830; married CAROLINE M. COX, November 20, 1859; Con-
federate and in first Manassas; Williamsburg, Seven Pines; Gaines
Mills; 2nd Manassas; Gettysburg; Cold Harbor; Hatcher's Run; and
Sailor's Creek; Wounded Cold Harbor in left arm by ball; Deputy
Treasurer, Amherst County, 1875-78; July, 1879, became sheriff, and
still in office until July, 1887. Post Office: Amherst County
Courthouse. Son of JAS. H. JOYNER and SOPHIA B. (TILLER) - early to
Amherst County; JAS. H. died August 11, 1854; SOPHIA still lives in
Amherst County.

                                -K-

PEYTON KEITH -- Book 11, Page 85 -- October 7, 1842, written;
October 17, 1842, probated. Witnesses: J. POWELL, WM. L. WATTS,
WARNER JONES (to codicil) - WARWICK JONES, SAML. M. GARLAND. Codicil
of October 10, 1842. My ux; daughter, LUCY, ux of LANDON PROFFITT -
children at her death - first marriage as well and others that she
may have; my son, JAMES W. KEITH and heirs; memo of sums advanced to
each; estate advanced to LUCY charged with annual payments to my two
grandsons, PEYTON and GEO. WATTS until 21 - no interest thereon, but
age changed to 25. Executors: sons, MARSHALL M. and JAS. W. KEITH.
Codicil: change as to slave for LUCY - goes to two WATTS grandsons
above named and then to her. Here PEYTON WATTS is called WM. P. KEITH.
Book 11, Page 87 -- Administrator's Bond -- October 17, 1842. JAS. W.
KEITH. Bondsman: ELIJAH FLETCHER.
Book 11, Page 241 -- Administrator's Account from 1842 - $51.00 each
to DRS. POWELL and JONES for bills; WM. P. WATTS for making shoes
for negroes; ROBT. ARNOLD's blacksmith account. Committee: J. PIERCE,
D. APPLING, WM. S. TURNER. Recorded December 23, 1843.
Book 11, Page 400 -- Administrator's Account from November 9, 1843.
Amount held by widow: $460.55. Total of $2,207.01.
Book 11, Page 170 -- Inventory on April order of Court, 1842 --
Recorded September 18, 1843. Total: $5,159.00. DAVID APPLING,
J. M. LOVING, WM. S. TURNER.

SARAH KEITH -- Book 11, Page 249 -- Guardian Bond -- JAS. W. KEITH
and STERLING CLAIBORNE, October 21, 1844, for JAS. KEITH as guardian
of SARAH, JNO. ALFRED, and THOS. KEITH, orphans of SARAH KEITH.

CYNTHA KENNEDY -- Book 4, Page 356 -- Guardian Bond -- October 18,
1802. CHAS. WATTS and JONATHAN BOLLING for CHAS. WATTS as guardian
of CYNTHA KENNEDY, orphan of JESSE KENNEDY, deceased.

JESSE KENNEDY -- Book 4, Page 30 -- Inventory -- December 18, 1801.
STEPHEN WATTS, JAS. DILLARD and GEO. DILLARD.
Book 4, Page 330 -- Administrator's Bond -- SUSANNA KENNEDY and JNO.
DILLARD, June 15, 1801, for SUSANNA KENNEDY.
Book 6, Page 679 -- Administrator's Bond -- JAS. POWELL, HUDSON M.

GARLAND, JNO. COLEMAN, and PETER G. CAMDEN, August 23, 1826, for
POWELL and GARLAND to administer.
Book 6, Page 673 -- February 11, 1826, written; July 17, 1826, pro-
bated. Handwriting attested by MICAJAH CAMDEN, RODERICK DAVIES,
WIATT DUNCAN, SAML. SIMMONS. Brother, NICHOLAS KENNEDY - all interest
in my father's estate; brother, JOSEPH KENNEDY - interest from his
will; sister-in-law, ELIZ. KENNEDY - all land conveyed to me by my
brother, JOS. KENNEDY (will recorded in Amherst County); nephew,
JESSE POINDEXTER; interest in my mother's dower; my two nephews:
JESSE WRIGHT and JESSE KELLY. Executors: friends, BENNETT A. CRAW-
FORD and HENRY L. DAVIES.

JOSEPH KENNEDY -- Book 6, Page 546 -- Administrator's Bond -- JONAS
PIERCE, WM. DILLARD, and LEWIS LAYNE, February 21, 1825, for JONAS
PIERCE.
Book 6, Page 597 -- Administrator's Bond -- Same date -- WM. WRIGHT,
JAS..D. WATTS, and JNO. ALCOCK for WM. WRIGHT.
Book 6, Page 540 -- March 9, 1824, written; February 21, 1825, pro-
bated. Witnesses: JAS. G. APPLING, DAVID APPLING, WM. O. BRYANT.
Ux, ELIZ. - dower land to me from my mother, SUSANNAH ALFRED, late
KENNEDY; slaves to ux which are property of heirs of JESSE KENNEDY,
deceased, at death of my mother; brother, JESSE, gets tract where I
live and bought of DAVID S. GARLAND; brother, NICHOLAS, gets land
bought of JACOB PIERCE - 20 acres; my sister, NANCY KELLY; sister,
JANE DORNIN - land that I got from JOS. DILLARD and JNO. LONDON;
mother gets a slave. Executors: JONAH PIERCE and WILLIAM WRIGHT.
Book 6, Page 614 -- Inventory -- August 15, 1825: $2,529.19. ALLEN
BLAIR, ABRAM EVINS, THOS. APPLING.
Book 8, Page 184 -- Administrator's Account by JONAS PIERCE from
December 1, 1828; recorded on Friday, January 21, 1831. A. B. and
SAML. R. DAVIES; and LINDSEY COLEMAN. Cash to MRS. KENNEDY for
necessaries for self and family - March 27, 1827 - $20.00. WM.
KELLY, trustee - $2.12. Recorded March 21, 1832.
Book 8, Page 251 -- indexed as Page 351 -- Administrator's Account
by WRIGHT from May, 1825. To ELIZ. KENNEDY; KENNEDY and KELLY; DRS.
APPLING and DAVIES; MRS. ALFRED; JESSE and JOS. KENNEDY - SUSANNAH
ALFRED for rent. September 12, 1828. A. B. DAVIES; JAS. POWELL;
SAML. R. DAVIES. Recorded September 17, 1832.

MARY KENNEDY -- Book 5, Page 180 -- Guardian Bond -- DAVID S. GARLAND
and JNO. LONDON, September 21, 1812, for DAVID GARLAND as guardian
of MARY KENNEDY - above 14 years of age, orphan of JESSE KENNEDY.

SUSAN KENNEDY -- Book 5, Page 578 -- Guardian Bond -- May 20, 1816;
JOS. and JESSE KENNEDY for JOS. as guardian of SUSAN KENNEDY, orphan
of JESSE KENNEDY.

JNO. T. KENT -- Book 17, Page 39 -- Administrator's Bond -- MARY C.
KENT, WM. A. RICHESON, and SAML. M. GARLAND, December 18, 1865, for
MARY KENT as administratrix.
Book 17, Page 60 -- Inventory -- $741.50. W. A. RICHESON, H. DRUM-
MOND, JNO. H. WATTS. December 21, 1865. Sale on same day: $804.87.

SALLY ANN KENT -- Book 8, Page 3 -- Administrator's Bond -- WM. KENT
and WM. TURNER and JAS. C. LAMKIN, June 21, 1830, for WM. KENT.

WM. KENT -- Book 14, Page 27 -- School Superintendent as appointed
by Board of Amherst County for year beginning January 1, 1856.
Bondsman: TERRY W. DILLARD. School Commissioners: M. C. GOODWIN
and J. O. STANFIELD.
Book 14, Page 253 -- Same on November 17, 1856 - for one year from
January 1, 1857. Bondsman: WM. DILLARD. Commissioners: HARTWELL
PRYOR and RO. WINGFIELD.
Book 14, Page 483 -- Same from January 1, 1858. Bondsman: W. DILLARD.
Commissioners: J. O. STANFIELD, EDWIN S. RUCKER, JNO. CASH.
Book 15, Page 60 -- Same -- December 3, 1858 from next January. Ap-
pointed November 15, 1859. Bondsman: W. DILLARD. Commissioners:
W. SANDIDGE, M. C. GOODWIN, RO. WINGFIELD.
Book 15, Page 443 -- Same by appointed move of November 20, 1859 -
from January, 1860. Bondsman: F. W. DILLARD. Commissioners: JAS.

HIGGINBOTHAM, J. O. STANFIELD, M. C. GOODWIN.

JNO. J. KIDD -- Book 10, Page 287 -- Guardian Bond -- RO. I. (J.)
KIDD and WM.H. DIGGS, November 16, 1840, for RO. KIDD as guardian
of JNO. J., CAROLINE M., AMANDA M., WM. C., and ANNA H. KIDD, orphans
of -----, deceased.

JNO. NORMAN KIDD -- Book 3, Page 339 -- February 9, 1795, written;
July 20, 1795, probated. Witnesses: TILMAN WALTON, MARY MILLS,
OBEDIENCE KIDD. Ux, JINIAH; my children; my two daughters, AMY and
RUTH KIDD; ux and my brother, WM. KIDD, to administer.
Book 3, Page 340 -- Administrator's Bond -- JURIAH (appears to be
JINIAH in will) KIDD and JOHN NEWMAN and WM. WOOD on probate date
for JURIAH KIDD.

WM. KIPPERS (Indexed for KEPPUS) -- Book 1, Page 148 -- April 22,
1769, written; November 6, 1769, probated. Witnesses: WM. PETER,
STEPHEN GOLDSBY, JNO. HOGG. My ux - horses, land; son, JNO., until
18 - gets land; SARAH CLARK (relationship not stated) - when 18.
Administrators: DAVID CRAWFORD and ABRAHAM PENN.
Page 150 -- PENN qualified. Bondsmen: EDMD. WILCOX and WM. HORSLEY.

WM. KIRKWOOD -- Book 6, Page 343 -- Administrator's Bond -- November 19, 1822. JNO. FRANKLIN. Bondsman: WILKINS WATSON.

BETSY ANN KNIGHT -- Book 10, Page 389 -- Guardian Bond -- SOPHIA W.
KNIGHT and EDMUND HILL, September 20, 1841, for SOPHIA KNIGHT as
guardian of CHAS. M., BETSY ANN, MARY J., SIGNORA F., and EDNA F.
KNIGHT, orphans of MATTHEW KNIGHT. (Note: "F." is middle initial
of last two wards.)

ELIZ. KNIGHT -- Book 11, Page 181 -- Administrator's Bond -- WM.
KNIGHT and JNO. WHITEHEAD, January 15, 1844, for WM. KNIGHT.
Book 11, Page 193 -- Inventory -- February 8, 1844; no total; CHAS.
TUCKER; C. A. PENN; WM. TUCKER.

MATTHEW KNIGHT -- Book 10, Page 146 -- Administrator's Bond -- SOPHIA
W. KNIGHT, EDMD. HILL, THOS. G. HILL and JNO. BROADDUS, June 17,
1839, for SOPHIA KNIGHT.
Book 10, Page 166 -- Inventory -- October 11, 1839 - $1,379.50. WM.
TUCKER, CHAS. TUCKER, JNO. W. BROADDUS.

WM. KNIGHT -- Book 6, Page 139 -- Ordinary Bond -- May 16, 1820, at
his house in county - to GOV. JAS. P. PRESTON. He will permit no
unlawful gaming and shall keep good, wholesome, and "cleanly Diet"
and lodging for travellers and stableage for their horses - "nor shall
he permit on the Sabbath day any person to drink more than is
necessary." Bondsman: JNO. MOUNTCASTLE.
Book 18, Page 166 -- Administrator's Bond -- SUSAN B. KNIGHT, STEPHEN
H. KNIGHT, E. P. SMILEY, March 18, 1872, for SUSAN KNIGHT to administer
estate of deceased husband, WM. KNIGHT.
Book A, Page 67 -- March 19, 1824, written; April 30, 1824, probated.
Of town of New Glasgow, Amherst County; my ux and family; son, WM.
HENRY KNIGHT and GEO. W. KNIGHT to get my tools - saddler - and my
patent right for manufacture of spring saddles; to WM. until GEO. is
21 and then to divide equally. WM. is to have all leather and other
items pertaining to tools. My daughter, KNIGHT; my daughter, JANE
FULCHER; my ux, MARGARET; and my single children. My sons, WM. HENRY
and GEO. W. KNIGHT - house and lot where I live; daughter, FLORA
HIGGINBOTHAM; daughters: LUCINDA KNIGHT, JANE FULCHER, MARY KNIGHT -
my "four daughters." WM. HENRY is to be guardian of GEO. W. KNIGHT
and MARY KNIGHT until of age. Administrators: son, WM., and my ux,
MARGARET. On probate date, Page 69, WM. KNIGHT qualified. Bondsmen:
JNO. COLEMAN, HEZEKIAH S. FULCHER, and ROBT. HIGGINBOTHAM.
Book A, Page 83 -- Administrator's Account -- May 1, 1824 - several
reports. Committee: JOS. STAPLES, JNO. DILLARD, ROBT. TINSLEY.
Recorded September 18, 1824. Interesting because of the many accounts.
Another Administrator's Account on Page 116, and many more accounts.
Recorded September 21, 1827. Committee: JOS. STAPLES, JAS. ROSE,
SAML. M. WOLFE.

GEO. W. KYLE -- Book 10, Page 355 -- Constable Bond to LT. GOV. JNO.
RUTHERFORD, June 21, 1847. Bondsmen: JOS. KYLE and JAS. HIGGIN-
BOTHAM.
Book 11, Page 151 -- Same men and bond to GOV. JAS. McDOWELL,
June 19, 1843.
Book 11, Page 523 -- Same men and bond, June 21, 1847.

JAMES C. KYLE -- Book 17, Page 28 -- Administrator's Bond -- DAVID
KYLE and DAVID APPLING, March 20, 1865, for DAVID KYLE.

JOSEPH KYLE, SR., and JR. -- Book 12, Page 498 -- Administrator's
Bond -- March 15, 1852: LEGUS M. KYLE; GEO. W. KYLE; ROBT. R. KYLE;
JOS. KYLE, JR.; DAVID KYLE; SAML. M. GARLAND; and WM. W. THOMPSON
for LEGUS M. KYLE as administrator of JOSEPH KYLE, SR.
Book 12, Page 570 -- Inventory -- JOS. SR. - $5,588.37, September 11,
1852. L. W. CHRISTIAN, WM. P. WOODROOF, WM. M. PIERCE, and T. W.
DILLARD.

MATTHEW KYLE -- Book 9, Page 216 -- Administrator's Bond -- JNO. S.
KYLE and LEWIS S. EMMIT, February 15, 1836, for JNO. KYLE.

ROWLAND KYLE -- Book 6, Page 397 -- Administrator's Bond -- CHAS. M.
CHRISTIAN, JONAS PIERCE, DABNEY P. GOOCH, and WM. DILLARD, October 20,
1823, for CHAS. CHRISTIAN.
Book 6, Page 417 -- Inventory, November 8, 1823 - $955.93. THOS.
WINGFIELD, ROBT. WINGFIELD, GILES DAVIDSON.
Book 9, Page 258 -- Administrator's Account from April 26, 1824; sale
on November 8, 1823 - to March 18, 1834. WHITE, KYLE & CO. and
DAVID KYLE, SR., buyers.

ABSTRACTS FROM HARDESTY AND BROCK

Page 437 -- Wife of WM. H. CAMPBELL was BETSY LAWLER and they
married September 28, 1854. BETSY was daughter of THOS. and MARY
(KELLEY) LAWLER.

Page 440 -- KEMPER's Brigade is mentioned.

Page 439 -- CAPT. KENT's Company of Bedford Volunteers mentioned.

Page 441 -- Sketch of WILLIAM H. KENT -- Courthouse District
farmer - born and married in Amherst. Born 20 November 1830; married
CAROLINE M. COX, 20 November 1859. CAROLINE M. was daughter of
REUBEN N. COX and she was born in Amherst County in 1842. Parents are
dead. WM. H. and ux had six children: oldest daughter married and
in Nelson, and others are at home: ELIZ. R., GORDON, JAS. R., MARY A.,
WM. H., and DONALD. WM. H. is son of WM. H. and ELIZ. L. (TURNER)
KENT. WM. H. died in 1879 and ELIZ. L. in 1882. ELIZ. L. TURNER was
daughter of WM. TURNER - early to Amherst County and of Irish lineage.
Subject was in Company G, 11th Virginia Infantry, Confederacy.
Wounded at Seven Pines by minnie ball. Post Office: Amherst County
Courthouse, Virginia.

Page 443 -- EDWIN LEWIS RICHESON married May 15, 1879, SALLIE
RHUEHAMMER KENT. She was born in Amherst County 12 July 1859, and
was daughter of JNO. T. and MARY C. KENT who were formerly of Fluvanna County. JNO. T. KENT died in 1864.

KIRKPATRICK's Brigade - Confederacy -- Pages 436, 438, 440, 445.

Page 441 -- CHAS. M. KNIGHT - sketch - born June 11, 1832, in
Amherst County; married on December 22, 1874, VIRGINIA HILL - born
in Nelson County, Virginia, January 2, 1837. Children: WM. M. -
born October 13, 1876; BESSIE M. - born February 23, 1878; NELLIE T. -
born January 4, 1880. CHAS. M. KNIGHT was son of MATTHEW L. and
SOPHIA W. (HILL) KNIGHT; mother still living; father died December 10,
1835. SOPHIA HILL was daughter of EDMUND and ELIZ. (HARGROVE) HILL.
EDMD. HILL was born in County of Amherst and mother was born in
Nelson. EDMD. died May 12, 1872; mother "is now also deceased."
MATTHEW L. KNIGHT was in War of 1812 and his widow draws a pension.

CHAS. M. KNIGHT enlisted March 15, 1862, in Company D, 19th Virginia Battalion, and served until end of war. He was never wounded nor captured. Farmer since war ended and owns 100 acres of well-situated land in Temperance District. Post Office: Sandidges, Virginia. (Note: This place is a small hamlet and is still known as Sandidges. B.F.D.).

Page 439 -- PATRICK H. DRUMMOND married on January 11, 1866, to FANNIE E. KNIGHT (DRUMMOND's second ux). She was born in Amherst County on October 6, 1837, and was daughter of MATTHEW KNIGHT and SOPHIA (HILL) KNIGHT. There were children by his first ux, but I am only naming the six by his 2nd ux here: PEARL - born May 6, 1867; PATRICK H. - born July 24, 1868; THOMAS H. - born February, 1870; PERRY W. - born July 25, 1873; BIRDIE - born October 12, 1875; and LINNIE - born August 19, 1878.

-L-

JNO. LACKEY -- Book 2, Page 101 -- March 5, 1772, written; March 3, 1783, probated. Witnesses: ALEX. REID, JNO. BARNETT, ROBERT STEPHEN-SON, ANDREW REID. Ux, HANNAH - house and plantation; my sons, SAML., JAMES, ADAN, JOHN, ANDREW; my daughter, HANNAH ALEXANDER. Executors: sons, JNO. and SAML. and son-in-law, FRANCIS ALEXANDER.
Page 102f -- May 5, 1783 - Administrator's Bond for SAML. LACKEY. Bondsman: ALEX. REID.
Book 2, Page 153 -- Inventory - L 17-11-0; recorded March 1, 1784; done, August 10, 1783. WM. BARNETT, ABNER WITT, JOS. ROBARDS.

WM. LACKEY -- Book 1, Page 211 -- September 2, 1771, written; July 6, 1772, probated. Witnesses: JOS. and JAS. HIGGINBOTHAM; JAS. LEACKEY (sic); ANDREW LEACKEY (sic); SAML. LACKEY. Ux, EVE - house and plan-tation; son, JNO., when of age; ux is with child. Executors: ux; ANDREW LACKEY; SAML. LACKEY; and JAS. HIGGINBOTHAM. EVE qualified on probate date. Bondsmen: SAML. WOODS, JOS. CABELL - Page 214.
Inventory is Book 1, Pages 219 -- L 223-12-8, July 23, 1772. BENJ. RUCKER, ISAAC RUCKER, GEORGE McDANIEL.

GRANVILLE LAINE (also see variations of spelling of name) -- Book 11, Page 55 -- June 20, 1842; refunding bond to JESSE MUNDY, executor of JESSE BECK, deceased -- GRANVILLE LAIN who married LUCY ANDERSON; JNO. RHOADS who married MARY ANDERSON; RICH. ANDERSON and MARVILLE L. BERRY - all have received their shares in BECK's estate from executor.

MARY LAIN (Indexed for MARGARET) -- Book 9, Page 146 -- Guardian Bond -- JAS. H. CASHWELL and WM. FRANKLIN, December 21, 1834, for JAS. CASH-WELL as guardian of MARY LAIN, orphan of THOS. LAIN, deceased.

THOS. LAIN -- Book 7, Page 28 -- Inventory of $1,707.07 on December 8, 1826. MAURICE H. GARLAND for SAML. GARLAND, administrator. EDMD.(?) CRAWFORD, EDMOND TINSLEY, MERIT M. WHITE.

JAS. LAINE -- Book 6, Page 105 -- Administratorr's Bond -- SALLY LAINE and WILEY CAMPBELL, November 17, 1819, for SALLY LAINE.
Book 6, Page 115 -- Inventory -- November 20, 1819: $482.65. JACOB and JONAS PIERCE, THOS. WINGFIELD.
Book 6, Page 118 is indexed as ordinary bond, but it is not there.

JNO. LAINE -- Book 1, Page 430 -- Administrator's Bond -- WM. LAINE and WM. LAINE, waggoner, August 3, 1778, for WM. LAINE.
Book 1, Page 441 -- Inventory -- October 5, 1778: L 13-10-6. MINOS WRIGHT, WM. ALFORD, ARCHILLES WRIGHT.

WM. LAINE (LANE) -- Book 3, Page 241 -- August 26, 1791, written; October 15, 1793, probated. Witnesses: PETER and JESSE HENDRICKS; JNO. COUNEY. Ux, HANNAH; grandson, MIDDLETON LANE; Friend, ALEX. CHISNEL to administer.

RICH. LAMASTER -- Book 1, Page 311 -- November 15, 1774, written; June 3, 1776, probated. Witnesses: WM. SCOTT, DAVID LONDON, WM.

JOHNS. Brother, ABRAHAM LAMASTER; my mother, ANN LAMASTER - my pay
that is coming to me; my brother, RALPH LAMASTER.

JAMES L. LAMKIN -- Book 11, Page 482 -- Sheriff -- appointed by
Governor on January 18th last; February 15, 1847. Bondsmen: JOS.
and WIATT PETTYJOHN, GEO. T. PLEASANTS, JNO. DILLARD, WILKINS WATSON.
For one year.
Book 12, Page 55 -- Same -- March 20, 1848. Bondsmen: JOS., WIATT,
GEO. W. PETTYJOHN; ROBT. TINSLEY; WM. DILLARD; ZACH. D. TINSLEY.
Book 14, Page 25 -- Administrator's Bond -- September 17, 1855.
ANN G. LAMKIN. Bondsmen: JESSE E. ADAMS, JAS. N. LAMKIN, and SAML.
ROBT. LAMKIN.

MARY LANCASTER -- Book 3, Page 30 -- Guardian Bond -- April 2, 1787.
DAVID SIMPSON and THOS. WILLIAMSON for DAVID SIMPSON as guardian of
MARY LANCASTER, orphan of WM. LANKESTER (sic), deceased.

ADELAIDE E. LANDRUM -- Book 13, Page 16 -- Guardian Bond -- September 20, 1852, LOUISIANA A. WILSON; JAS. B. DAVIDSON, bondsman;
LOUISIANA WILSON as guardian of ADELAIDE E. and STEPHEN J. S. LANDRUM,
orphans of SEATON LANDRUM, deceased.

FELICIANNA LANDRUM -- Book 12, Page 128 -- Guardian Bond -- LOUISIANA
LANDRUM and ALEX. MUNDY, April 17, 1848, for LOUISIANA LANDRUM as
guardian of FELICIANNA LANDRUM, orphan of SEATON LANDRUM, deceased.

FLETCHER C. LANDRUM -- Book 22, Page 408 -- Guardian Bond -- April 21,
1890, BETTIE S. LANDRUM, R. S. FOGUS, and H. C. JOYNER, for BETTIE
LANDRUM as guardian of FLETCHER C. LANDRUM.

JAMES LANDRUM -- Book B, Page 43 -- Estate Commitment to Sheriff --
March 21, 1851; dead more than three months - motion of JAS. H.
COPPEDGE and JAS. H. JOINER. Sheriff: JNO. D. DAVIS.

PATSY LANDRUM -- Book 4, Page 305 -- Guardian Bond -- GEO. WRIGHT and
THOS. SPENCER, August 21, 1797, for GEO. WRIGHT as guardian of PATSY
LANDRUM, orphan of JAS. LANDRUM, deceased.

RICHARD LANDRUM -- Book 14, Page 478 -- October 27, 1857, written;
March 15, 1858, probated. Witnesses: JAS. B. STAPLES; THOS. WHITE-
HEAD; Ux, POLLY; son-in-law, FREDERICK J. MAYS, husband of my daugh-
ter, SARAH JANE - 1/12th; son, PATRICK H.; son, JNO. H.; son, RICH. D.;
children of deceased daughter, MARY C., who married JNO. J. LANDRUM;
son-in-law, FAYETTE KNIGHT; son-in-law, WM. STANFIELD; son, BENJ. W.
LANDRUM; son-in-law, JOSEPH HILL; son, PAUL C. LANDRUM; son, SILAS
LANDRUM; son, JAS. B. LANDRUM; son, JOSEPH W. LANDRUM. Division at
death of ux to SARAH J. MAYS; P. H. LANDRUM; JNO. N. (seems to be
H. above); RICH. D. LANDRUM; children of MARY C. LANDRUM; ELIZ.
KNIGHT; ANNE(?) M. STANFIELD; BENJ. W. LANDRUM; SERENA L. HILL;
PAUL C. LANDRUM; SILAS LANDRUM; and JAS. B. LANDRUM. Executors:
JOS. HILL and JNO. N. LANDRUM and friend, THOS. WHITEHEAD is to
counsel with them and to be guardian of underaged children.
Book 14, Page 518 -- Administrator's Bond -- JOS. HILL, JNO. N. LAN-
DRUM, RO. A. COGHILL, and SAML. M. GARLAND, probate date, for HILL
and LANDRUM to administer.
Book 14, Page 561 -- Inventory -- April 21, 1858; quite long. CHAS.
B. CLAIBORNE; RO. A. PENDLETON; SAML. PETIT.
Book 14, Page 567 -- Sale -- April 22, 1858 and recorded May 17,
1858. P. H.; BENJ.; PATRICK H.; JOS.; DANIEL; J. H.; JNO. J. and
MRS. LANDRUM were buyers.
Book 15, Page 277 -- Administrator's Account by administrators from
March 22, 1858 - wages to R. D. and JAS. E. LANDRUM; MRS. MARY LAN-
DRUM for garden. Recorded October 18, 1859.
Book 16, Page 160 -- Administrator's Account by administrators from
February 22, 1859. Tuition; church subscription; P. H. LANDRUM for
paling graveyard; board for J. J. LANDRUM; legacy for widow, MARY
LANDRUM; bonds of P. H. and R. D. LANDRUM; JNO. H. N. LANDRUM assignee
for B. W. LANDRUM; bond for P. C. LANDRUM.
Page 164ff -- legatees: FREDERICK J. MAYS and ux; PATRICK H. LAN-
DRUM; JNO. H. LANDRUM; RICH. D. LANDRUM; children of MARY C. LANDRUM;

WM. L. KNIGHT; WM. STANFIELD; BENJ. W. LANDRUM; JOS. HILL; PAUL C. LANDRUM; SILAS LANDRUM; JAS. E. LANDRUM; MARY LANDRUM, widow; BENJ. W. LANDRUM as guardian of SILAS LANDRUM. Recorded February 18, 1861.

SEATON LANDRUM -- Book 11, Page 512 -- Inventory and Sale -- April 1, 1847. WM. STAPLES; STEPHEN J. JONES; A. G. CHEWNING. Family buyers: BURTON LANDRUM and ux; MRS. JNO. JAS. LANDRUM; RICH. LANDRUM; MRS. BURTON LANDRUM and by it: "charged to JNO. JAS. LANDRUM."
Book 11, Page 517 -- Administrator's Bond -- BURTON LANDRUM and S. CLAIBORNE, March 16, 1847, for BURTON LANDRUM.
Book 12, Page 193 -- Administrator's Account for muster fine - 75¢; sale receipts and amounts for JNO. J.; RICH. and widow LANDRUM. April 14, 1849. FRANS. V. SUTTON, SR., and JR.
Book 14, Page 40 -- Independent Bond for BURTON LANDRUM -- Administrator's Account from April 16, 1849. To LOUISIANA LANDRUM; WM. LANDRUM for slave hire; due S. LANDRUM estate from administrator; balance due L. LANDRUM by WM. L. (J.) LANDRUM; distributees: WM. A. THACKER; L. (S.) P. LANDRUM; LOUISIANA LANDRUM; widow is 50 years of age. STEPHEN P. LANDRUM; S. CLAIBORNE agent for WM. A. THACKER; L. LANDRUM, widow. Signed by WM. J. and STEPHEN P. LANDRUM and CLAIBORNE for WM. THACKER. May 21, 1855.

SILAS W. LANDRUM -- Book 15, Page 218 -- Guardian Bond -- BENJ. W. LANDRUM; J. H. HILL; R. A. COGHILL, June 20, 1859, for BENJ. LANDRUM as guardian of SILAS W. and JAS. E. LANDRUM, orphans of RICH. LANDRUM, deceased.
Book 16, Page 310 -- Guardian's Account from Jun 17, 1858 -- expenses of R. LANDRUM, executors; reference to bond of June 20, 1859. Recorded October 8, 1862.

STEPHEN J. LANDRUM -- Book 16, Page 90 -- Administrator's Bond -- MARY J. LANDRUM and JNO. R. MABEN, July 15, 1861, for MARY LANDRUM. Inventory by her and WM. DILLARD; ALEX. MUNDY; STEPHEN W. CHRISTIAN: $493.00. September 16, 1861.
Book 17, Page 192 -- Guardian Bond -- THOS. B. DAVIDSON and AMBROSE R. BURFORD, October 15, 1866, for THOS. DAVIDSON as guardian of STEPHEN J. LANDRUM - no parent set forth.

THOMAS LANDRUM -- Book 10, Page 209 -- January 9, 1831, written; March 16, 1840, probated. Witnesses: JOS. STAPLES, PAUL C. CABELL, WM. STAPLES, RICH. and BURTON LANDRUM (names written above word "Witnesses"). Codicil of December 28, 1837. Witnesses: WM. STAPLES, SR., and JR.; and JNO. ALLCOCK. Ux, DORATHY; my nine children; FRANCES; JAME (sic, but JAMES later); NELSON; JNO. J.; SOPHIA; RICH.; BURTON; WM. and NANCY. Lot at Amherst Courthouse - if Nelson is without issue; Sons, RICH. and BURTON, trustees for my daughter FRANCES CHRISTIAN and her three daughters. Son, SEATON LANDRUM. Codicil: Son, NELSON, is now in Kentucky.
Book 10, Page 211 -- Administrator's Bond -- RICH. and BURTON LANDRUM, probate date. Bondsmen: LEWIS S. EMMETT; JOEL BOWLES; STEPHEN JONES. Book 10, Page 237 -- Inventory -- March 21, 1840 - $9,340.19. WM. STAPLES; RICH. NORTH; SPOSTSWOOD G. LOVING.

WM. H. LANDRUM -- Book 15, Page 160 -- Guardian Bond -- JNO. J. and JNO. H. N. LANDRUM, April 19, 1859, for JNO. J. LANDRUM as guardian of WM. H., THOS. R., and R. L. (S.) LANDRUM, infants of JNO. J. LANDRUM.

W. J. LANDRUM -- Book 16, Page 534 -- Administrator's Bond -- FELECEANNA LANDRUM and JNO. R. MABEN, August 15, 1864, for FELECEANNA LANDRUM.

ELISHA LANGLEY -- Book 10, Page 244 -- Administrator's Bond -- August 19, 1840. DAVID S. and SAML. M. GARLAND for DAVID GARLAND.

BERRY LANHAM -- Book 4, Page 363 -- Administrator's Bond -- CATH. LANHAM and JAS. BIBB, February 21, 1803, for CATH. LANHAM.

MARY A. LANKFORD -- Book 13, Page 237 -- Guardian Bond -- JEFFERSON CASH, September 19, 1853, for JEFFERSON CASH as guardian of MARY A.

LANGFORD (sic), orphan of JNO. LANKFORD, deceased.

ALLEN LAVINDER (LAVENDER) -- Book 3, Page 503 -- October 27, 1797,
written; June 18, 1798, probated. Witnesses: JNO. COONEY; ROWLAND
EDMONDS; JNO. ALFORD. My ux and children until youngest is 21. Execu-
tor: my brother, CHAS. LAVENDER.
Inventory is Book 3, Page 541, April 15, 1799: L 185-8-4. JNO.
ALFORD, ACHILLES WRIGHT, JAS. EDMONDS.
Administrator's Bond is Book 4, Page 313, CHAS. LAVENDER and ALEX.
CHISNALL on probate date for CHAS. LAVENDER.

ANTHONY LAVINDER -- Book 4, Page 333 -- Administrator's Bond --
July 20, 1801: GEO. and JOS. DILLARD for GEO. DILLARD.

CHAS. LAVINDER -- Book 4, Page 132 -- Inventory -- July 23, 1803:
L 148-5-6. ALLEN BLAIR; JOS. STAPLES; BENJ. WATTS.
Administrator's Bond is Book 4, Page 372 -- July 18, 1803. JAS. MUR-
PHY and JNO. LOVING for JAS. MURPHY.

GEO. W. LAVINDER -- Book 16, Page 364 -- Administrator's Bond --
September 21, 1863: WM. H. LAVENDER and JAS. N. BURFORD for WM.
LAVENDER.

JNO. LAVINDER -- Book 1, Page 311 -- Administrator's Bond -- WM.
LAINE and JNO. STRATTON, July 1, 1776, for WM. LAINE.
Book 1, Page 369 -- Inventory -- October 1, 1776; no total; JNO.
WARREN; CHAS. WARREN; JNO. CHRISTIAN: "Prasers."

WM. LAVINDER -- Book 1, Page 297 -- Administrator's Bond -- MILLY
LAVENDER, GEO. CLASBEY; EDMD. WILCOX, February 5, 1776, for
MILLY LAVENDER. Note: CLASBEY signed with mark of "GG" which was
used by GEO. GILLESPIE - Clerk signed it "GILLESPIE."
Book 1, Page 432 -- Inventory -- March 15, 1776: L 183-8-1, WM.
POLLARD, LUCAS POWELL, RICH. TANKERSLY(EY). I am not including order
book items, but note to see Page 509 for 1793, for more data. I
hope to do these some day.
Book 17, Page 273 -- Plat of division - 100 acres on branch of Huff
Creek - both sides of road from Sardis Church to Hicks' grocery. To
widow; JNO. S. (L.) LAVINDER; WM. H. LAVENDER; CHAS. and WM. H.
NORTH, infants of FRANCIS NORTH, deceased shares bought from JAS. D.;
PITT E.; and PAULUS P. LAVINDER by JNO. P. HAMBLETON; 3 bought of
WM. T. BURLEY and ux and one of C. M. LAVINDER. E. P. TUCKER,
assistant surveyor for JNO. W. BROADDUS, Amherst County surveyor.
December 16, 1867.

JAS. W. LAWLESS -- Book 14, Page 86 -- Guardian Bond -- HUGH NELSON
COLEMAN, April 21, 1856, as guardian of JAS. W. LAWLESS, orphan of
BENNETT LAWLESS.

ELIZ. LAYNE (Also see LAIN and LAINE (nee CARTER)) -- Book 12,
Page 363 -- Administrator's Bond -- RO. H. CARTER; THOS. LAYNE;
GARRETT C. LAYNE; trustees; GRANVILLE LAINE; WM. M. FRANKLIN, and
POWHATAN LAIN, March 17, 1851, for RO. H. CARTER as administrator.
EDWD. RHOADES also signed, but name is not in list above.
Book 12, Page 431 -- Inventory -- March 24, 1851; many slaves -
$7,075.48. CHAS. H. RUCKER, JOS. BROWN, THOS. A. EUBANK.
Book 12, Page 493 -- Heirs of EDWD. CARTER, deceased, and his daughter,
ELIZ. LAYNE, deceased, bind themselves to abide my divisions of
commissioner: ROBT. H. CARTER, JNO. PRYOR, CHAS. H. RUCKER, BLUFORD
MORRIS, and GEO. W. STAPLES. It is understood that JAS. H. CASHWELL
and ux, NANCY, are not to be in slave division since they elected to
take real estate. December 30, 1851. Signed: WM. M. FRANKLIN;
THOS. LAINE; POWHATAN LAIN; GARET C. LAYNE for ux and child as trus-
tee; EDWD. RHOADS; GRANVILLE LAIN; JAS. H. CASHWELL.
Book 13, Page 46 -- Administrator's Account -- RO. H. CARTER from
April 19, 1851. Bond of POWHATAN LAYNE; THOS. LAYNE - for six lega-
tees. Recorded December 29, 1852. JOS. R. CARTER and JNO. PRYOR.
Signed by legatees: EDWD. RHOADES; WM. M. FRANKLIN; GRANVILLE LAIN;
GARRET C. LAYNE (trustee for children); POWHATAN LAIYNE; THOS. LAIN.
Book 18, Page 17 -- RO. H. CARTER; JAS. W. MILLARD; H. E. SMITH -

appointed August term, 1870, in case of LAYNE vs. MORGAN and under
decree - make report: 248 acres in bill to divide into six equal
parts for legatees: JNO. T. LAYNE, HENRY D. LAYNE, PETER G. TOLER
and ux, MARGARET - 2 shares for TOLER has bought share of MARION
NORVELL and ux, SARAH; JOS. FRANKLIN and ux, MARY; heirs of ANN MARIA
MORGAN (formerly LAYNE) -- Pryor's Vale Road; Buffalo Springs; Lynchburg Turnpike and near residence of WM. FARIS on Horsley Creek.
Plat on Page 18

GEO. W. LAYNE -- Book 16, Page 222 -- September 23, 1858, written;
February 16, 1863, probated. Witnesses: RO. TINSLEY, JNO. T. ELLIS.
My ux; son, NAPOLEON B. and children to live with his mother; daugh-
ter, ELVIRA M. CHRISTIAN and at her death to her youngest children:
CORDELIA W. and VICTORIA E. CHRISTIAN; oldest son of JNO. C. LAYNE -
GEO. S. LAYNE, and youngest (I do not recall his name); to DISON C.
BLANKS as trustee for his ux and my daughter, SARAH R. BLANKS; Cedar
Creek tract bought from E. W. and B. P. MORRIS; SARAH's children -
title to slave, Viney, which title is now in court and the contestant
is MORRIS; JAS. CUREY in trust for his ux and my daughter, MARTHA;
SHEFFEY MILLER in trust for my daughter, JANE W. RICHARDSON (RICHESON
elsewhere); ROWLAND N. RICHARDSON (also RICHESON) in trust for my
daughter, LUCY A., his ux. Executor: son, NAPOLEON B. LAYNE. He
qualified, Page 224, on probate date.
Inventory on Page 411 -- December 8, 1863. RO. L. COLEMAN; RO. A.
PENDLETON; GEO. W. CHRISTIAN.
Book 17, Page 44 -- Administrator's Account and sale, November 17,
1865. Family buyers: N. P. and SARAH LAYNE. Recorded December 18,
1865.

LEWIS LAYNE -- Book 7, Page 71 -- October 30, 1827, written; Novem-
ber 19, 1827, probated. Witnesses: JNO. CARTER, GEO. HYLTON, EDMUND
D. ALLCOCK, RICH. TILLER. JAS. D. WATTS and NANCY LAYNE qualified.
Bondsman for WATTS: JNO. DILLARD. Ux, NANCY; children of brother,
SAML. LAYNE - one third to him for their education; sister, MILDRED
STRATTON's children; my sister, NANCY JOHNS' children. Executors: ux
and JAS. D. WATTS.
Page 86 is Administrator's Bond.
Book 8, Page 256 -- Administrator's Account by WATTS - WATTS as guar-
dian of THOS. C. JOHNSON. Committee: JOS. STAPLES and JAS. ROSE.
September 17, 1832. Suit of LAYNE vs. ALLCOCK mentioned. NANCY gave
account on Page 258 from January 1, 1828. Recorded September 17, 1832.
Book 9, Page 158 -- Administrator's Account by WATTS from November,
1827; amount for benefit of THOS. C. JOHNSON; to R. HENLEY for benefit
of NANCY FRANKLIN's exeuctor vs. L. LAYNE estate. July 21, 1830:
JOS. STAPLES; JAS. ROSE; ED. A. CABELL.
Book 9, Page 169 -- Administrator's Account by NANCY from April 18,
1829; Nelson County Sheriff item; WM. H. BLAIR for attendance at
court; ALLCOCK vs. LAYNE's executors. To J. and W. BLAIR for ux - con-
tracted before marriage; midwife fee; cash from WM. CARTER, executor
of SHADRACK CARTER. December 21, 1835. ED. A. CABELL; JAS. ROSE;
JOS. STAPLES.
Book 9, Page 166 -- Administrator's Account by WATTS from July 20,
1830; guardian of S. C. JOHNSON. L. LAYNE's bond to MILDRED EVANS.
December 21, 1835, recorded.
Another on Book 9, Page 410 from February 14, 1835 -- to NANCY BLAIR,
executrix of MILDRED EVANS. To widow BLAIR. Albemarle certificate,
February 15, 1839. N. BURNLEY, RICH. WINGFIELD, JOSHUA JACKSON.
JAS. D. WATTS, administrator.
Book 10, Page 91 -- Another Administrator's Account by WATTS. The
three men who seemed to be of Albemarle now sign from Amherst County,
but WATTS, Justice of the Peace, of Albemarle. March 19, 1839.
Another account by WATTS - Book 12, Page 78 -- from November 14, 1842.
To Nelson County Clerk. To NANCY BLAIR, formerly NANCY LAYNE; cash
to W. L. LAYNE - children of SAML. LAYNE, but not named. December 18,
1848. JAS. W. KEITH and DAVID APPLING.

NANCY LAYNE -- Book 8, Page 75 -- Guardian Bond -- December 20, 1830.
GARRET LAINE and RICH. CRAWFORD for GARRET LAINE as guardian of NANCY
LAINE, orphan of THOS. LAINE (sic).

211

SALLY M. LAYNE (Indexed for S. M. LYNN) -- Book 15, Page 462 --
Administrator's Bond -- NAPOLEON B. LAYNE and GEO. LAYNE, by SAML.
GARLAND, October 15, 1860, for NAPOLEON LAYNE.

SARAH E. LAYNE -- Book B, Page 66 -- Guardian Bond -- GARRETT C.
LAYNE and GRANVILLE LAYNE, August 27, 1857, for GARRETT C. LAYNE as
guardian of his infant child, over 14, SARAH E. LAYNE.

THOS. A. LAYNE (Indexed LAINE) -- Book 13, Page 238 -- Administrator's
Bond -- ANN LAYNE and WILSON M. DEMPSEY, October 17, 1853, for ANN
LAYNE.
Book 13, Page 247 -- Inventory of $846.50, October 20, 1853: THOS. A.
EUBANK, JAS. M. MILLNER, HENRY FRANKLIN.
Book 13, Page 248 -- Sale -- October 31, 1853, and ANN LAYNE, ad-
ministratrix, was only family buyer.
Book 14, Page 183 -- Administrator's Account and Inventory --
October 31, 1854; spelled LAIN here.

ALFRED L. (S.) LEE -- Book 9, Page 360 -- Guardian Bond -- THOS. LEE;
RO. RIDGWAY; NATHAN GLENN, and ALBERT G. GOOCH, December 18, 1837,
for THOS. LEE as guardian of ALFRED L. (S.) LEE, over 14; orphan
of LODOWICK LEE, deceased.
Book 9, Page 389 -- Guardian's Account -- January 3, 1838; several
slaves.
Book 10, Page 295 -- Guardian's Account from January 3, 1838. To
ALBERT G. GOOCH - due him in slave transportation and division;
slaves brought from Prince George to Lynchburg. January 12, 1838.
WM. N.(?) BOWLING, ALBERT G. GOOCH. Recorded August 21, 1840.

AMBROSE LEE -- Book 1, Page 44 -- October 23, 1764, written; November 5, 1764, probated. Proved by GABL. PENN and WM. LEE. Will was
not signed, but approved. 1,074 acres on north side of Buffalo;
400 acres belongs to GEO. PENN where he has plantation. WM. CABELL,
JR., is to divide land. GLEAB (sic) line; Poplar Thickett Place;
my ux and intended dwelling house. Sons: FRANK, AMBROSE, GEO.,
RICH. LEE; my 4 daughters: ELIZ., JEANE, SUCKEY, and NANCY - when
20 or married. My sons when 21. Executors: Ux, GEO. PENN, WM. LEE,
and GABL. PENN.
Book 1, Page 47 -- Administrator's Bond -- GEO. PENN, DANL. BURFORD,
GABL. PENN, and WM. LEE, probate date, for GEO. PENN.
Book 1, Page 62 -- Inventory -- L 700-3-3, August 5, 1765. AMBROSE
RUCKER, JAS. HIGGINBOTHAM, GEO. McDANIEL.
Book 4, Page 181 -- Administrator's Account -- GEO. PENN, executor:
RICH. and FRANK LEE and WM. TUCKER. To SAML. CAMP for schooling
RICH. LEE; account of DRURY TUCKER; for NANCY LEE; ARCHLAUS MITCHELL
for repair of house where he lives; to ISAAC TINSLEY and SAML. CROUCH
for part of child's debt and same to RICH. HARRISON; bond of GEO. LEE
(one GEO. LEE of Amherst is on Page 915 of Perrin, Battle, and
Kiffin - 4th edition - of History of Kentucky), June 23, 1792. SAML.
MEREDITH, JAS. FRANKLIN, AMBROSE RUCKER, DAVID WOODROOF.
Book 4, Page 616 is another Administrator's Account from November,
1764: to WM. LEE, F. LEE, FRANCES LEE; tuition for children; estate
of GEO. PENN, deceased; DRURY TUCKER on a division; part of a debt
to ISAAC TINSLEY and SAML. CRUTCHER. October, 1809. HUGH ROSE,
DANL. GAINES, THOS. WIATT.

FANNY LEE (WATTS) -- Book 3, Page 591 -- Guardian's Account --
October 30, 1800. JAMES LEE, guardian, to FANNY WATTS, late LEE, who
married BENJ. WATTS. Committee: NELSON C. DAWSON, THOS. MOORE, JNO.
LOVING.

FRANCES LEE (FRANK in some items) -- Book 1, Page 448 -- Guardian
Bond -- GEO. PENN, CHAS. BURRUS, and JAS. FRANKLIN, November 2, 1778,
for GEO. PENN as guardian of FRANCIS LEE, orphan of AMBROSE LEE,
deceased.
Book 1, Page 494 -- Guardian's Account for FRANK LEE by GEO. PENN,
September 6, 1779. Debt of GEO. LEE.
Book 2, Page 28 -- Guardian Account from 1779. Bond of GEO. LEE due.
Recorded December 3, 1781.
Book 3, Page 209 -- January 8, 1791, written; October 3, 1791, pro-

bated. Witnesses: RICH. LEE, WM. PAMPLIN, ELIZ. SHIP. Ux, NANCY;
daughter, SOPHIA; son, WM.; land bought of my brother, GEO. LEE; when
children are of age or married; guardians for SOPHIA and WM. - CAPT.
LINDSEY COLEMAN; CAPT. RICH. HARRISON; CAPT. JAS. CALLAWAY; also to
be executors.
Book 3, Page 210 -- CALLAWAY and HARRISON qualified on probate date.
Bondsmen: JOS. BURRUS and ZACH. DAWSON.
Book 3, Page 375 -- Inventory -- December 10, 179?; recorded June 18,
1798. No total: B. STONE, DAVID WOODROOF, JAS. LIVELY.
Administrator's Account is Book 3, Page 478ff, by JAS. CALLAWAY
from 1795. To COL. MEREDITY; MORAN vs. FRANK LEE estate; MRS. LEE.
March 3, 1798. JAS. HIGGINBOTHAM; DAVID S. GARLAND; ROBT. WALKER.
Administrator's Account by RICH. HARRISON is Book 3, Page 482 --
shoes for MRS. LEE - 7 shillings 6 pence; selling your father's estate
to WIATT POWELL; to RICH. LEE; to GEO. PENN, executor of AMBROSE LEE.
Same committee as report just above. Recorded June 16, 1798.

GEO. LEE -- Book 1, Page 203 -- Guardian Bond -- GEO. PENN and
ABRAHAM PENN, November 4, 1771, for GEO. PENN as guardian of GEO. LEE,
orphan of AMBROSE LEE, deceased.

JAS. LEE -- Book 8, Page 115 -- Indexed as report in Master and book,
but it is not there.
Book 13, Page 228 -- July 11, 1853, written; August 15, 1853, probated.
Witnesses: T. H. NELSON, WIATT PETTYJOHN, JNO. A. MOSELY. Codicil
of July 12, 1853. Witnesses: PETTYJOHN and JNO. S. GOODWIN. Children
of my first marriage and of my deceased daughters, LUCY PHELPS and
ANN SAMMONS. Son, CHAS. P. LEE; daughters, FRANCES MOORMAN, and SUSAN
LEE; daughter-in-law, MARY JANE LEE, ux of my son, CHAS. P. LEE; my
son, JAS. MADISON LEE; land bought of WM. and GARLAND ANDERSON.
Children by both marriages. Executor: friend, CHISWELL DABNEY,
Lynchburg. Codicil: my daughters: MARY F. RUCKER, CATH. A. VENABLE,
MARTHA J. SUTPHAN (sic) - really SUTPHIN and she moved to Kentucky.
JOE J. BOWMAN, pastor of College Hill Baptist Church, Lynchburg, is
descendant. See Hart County, Kentucky, sketches of PERRIN, et al.
(op. cit.) in 3rd edition. If son, JAS. M. LEE, is without issue.
DABNEY declined to serve. JESSE SALMONS qualified, Page 230,
September 19, 1853. Bondsmen: JAS. W. MOORMAN, JAS. LEE, and
JAS. H. PHELPS.
Book 13, Page 241 -- Inventory -- October 17, 1853: $2,755.00. CHAS.
WINGFIELD, SIMON M. NOELL, JNO. L. GORDON.
Book 14, Page 304 -- Administrator's Account from July 14, 1853.
CHAS. P. LEE - legatee; Recorded May 18, 1857.

JAS. C. LEE -- Book 10, Page 358 -- Administrator's Bond -- SAML.
SIMMONS and JNO. THOMPSON, June 21, 1841, for SAML. SIMMONS.

MARY F. LEE and Children -- Book 11, Page 145 -- Order of January
Court, 1842 -- Motion of WM. G. RUCKER and ux, MARY F. (late LEE) -
to divide slaves of DAVID ANDERSON, deceased, late of Prince Edward
County, Virginia - grandfather of MARY F., CATH. A., and MARTHA J.
LEE. May 15, 1843. WM. KENT, RO. RIDGWAY, CHAS. WINGFIELD.

NANCY LEE -- Book 3, Page 386 -- Guardian Bond -- NANCY LEE, GEO.
DILLARD, and NOTLEY MADDOX, July 18, 1796, for NANCY LEE as guardian
of WM. and SOPHIA LEE, orphans of FRANCIS LEE, deceased.
Book 3, Page 477 -- Dower, March 3, 1798; widow of FRANK LEE.
Interesting list. JAS. HIGGINBOTHAM, RO. WALKER, DAVID S. GARLAND.

RICH. LEE -- Book 1, Page 447 -- Guardian Bond -- November 2, 1778.
GEO. LEE and DANL. GAINES for GEO. LEE as guardian of RICH. LEE,
orphan of AMBROSE LEE, deceased.
Book 1, Page 498 -- Guardian's Account -- November 18, 1778 - two
slaves.

SOPHIA LEE -- Book 4, Page 167 -- Guardian's Account by NANCY LEE
(called SHIELDS at close of report) as guardian of SOPHIA and WM. LEE,
orphans of FRANCIS LEE. February 26, 1803. DAVID S. GARLAND, JOS.

BURRUS, RO. WALKER.
Book 4, Page 361 -- Guardian Bond -- JNO. and GEO. DILLARD, December 20, 1802, for JNO. DILLARD as guardian of SOPHIA LEE, orphan of FRANCIS LEE, deceased.

THOS. LEE -- Book 16, Page 459 -- February 1, 1861, written; May 16, 1864, probated. Witnesses: WM. H. WARE; ux, SALLY; five daughters: ELLEN L. BARBOUR; MARY E. SANDIDGE; SARAH ANN LEE; REBECCA JANE LEE; MARIA LOUISA LEE; Money in Lynchburg Citizens Savings Bank.
Book 16, Page 469 -- Administrator's Bond -- ALFRED S. LEE, probate date. Bondsman: JOS. PETTYJOHN.
Book 17, Page 4 -- Inventory -- May term, 1864; reference to currency fluctuation. July 23, 1864. Z. D. TINSLEY, WM. P. MORRIS, BLUFORD HICKS.

WM. LEE -- Book 2, Page 235 -- March 4, 1785, written; August 1, 1785, probated. Witnesses: RICH. HARRISON, CORNL. SALE, ROBT. DAWSON; Sons, JAS. and WM. LEE; ux may be with child; "whole of my children when he or she is 21." Each of my daughters when married or age of 19. Ux, SUSANNAH. Executors: JOS. DAWSON, JNO. WIATT, GEO. LEE. Executors qualified on probate date - Page 236. Bondsmen: GABL. and GEO. PENN.
Book 2, Page 249 -- Inventory -- L 995-9-6; November 7, 1785. AMBROSE RUCKER, RICH. SHELTON, THOS. POWELL.
Book 3, Page 279 -- Guardian Bond -- JAS. LEE, ZACH. DAWSON, December 16, 1793, for JAS. LEE as guardian of WM. and FANNY LEE, orphans of WM. LEE.
Book 4, Page 352 -- Guardian Bond -- JNO. DILLARD, HENRY HOLLOWAY, RO. COLEMAN, September 20, 1802, for JNO. DILLARD as guardian of WM. LEE, orphan of FRANCIS LEE, deceased.

NANCY LEEBRICK (TINSLEY) -- Book 16, Page 159 -- January 14, 185?, written; Monday, October 20, 1862, probated. Witnesses: JNO. R. HARRISON, JOS. BROWN. Attested by BROWN, but HARRISON was dead. HARRISON's handwriting attested by A. C. HARRISON. Sons, ISAAC D. and JAS. TINSLEY - land bought of JACOB SHULTZ. Has lived during last widowhood with son, ISAAC TINSLEY, who has been kind and affectionate and he is to administer.
Book 16, Page 181 -- Administrator's Bond by TINSLEY on probate date. Bondsman: RO. A. PENDLETON.

WM. LEIGH -- Book 3, Page 310 -- September 2, 1788, written; September 15, 1794, probated. Witnesses: JAS. BROOKS, JNO. MARTIN, THOS. MOORE, MOLLIE GOLDEN. 100 acres to be bought with sale of one third of my negroes. Ux, ANN; son, JNO. LEIGH, and BETSY KINGSOLVING - one part to each; my younger children: WM., HENRY, GEO. WARE, FERDINAND, PATSEY MOORE, MARU (MARY?) JANE ANN PENDLETON. "To be divided amongst THOMAS." Sons, GEO. WARE and FERDINAND to be educated. Executors: son, GEORGE and ux, ANN.
Book 3, Page 327 -- Administrator's Bond -- ANN LEIGHT, WM. H. LEIGH, and SAML. REID, December 15, 1794, for ANN LEIGHT(?).
Book 3, Page 331 -- Inventory -- February 16, 1795; no total: SAML. HILL, ELIJAH MORAN, PATRICK ROSE.
Book 3, Page 415 -- Guardian Bond -- blank date in 1796 - CHAS. TUCKER and BENJ. ROGERS for CHAS. TUCKER as guardian of FURDNAN (sic) LEIGH, orphan of WM. LEIGH, deceased. (Indexed for TUCKER)
Book 8, Page 285 -- Administrator's Bond -- GEO. W. KINGSOLVING, JAS. GARLAND, WM. H. KNIGHT, December 17, 1832 - will annexed - for CK (GEO. KINGSOLVING?).
Book 9, Page 155 -- Administrator's Account by administrator from January 4, 1835 - 164 acres sold; old negro, Ben, in dispute with JOEL YANCEY; cash for coffin. Suit in Chancer vs. HART. Recorded December 21, 1835.

THOS. LENOX -- Book 4, Page 323 -- Administrator's Bond -- DAVID TYRALL and JNO. HIGGINBOTHAM, September 15, 1800, for DAVID TYRALL.

BENJ. H. LEWIS -- Book 14, Page 39 -- Power of attorney and of

Lynchburg to SAML. M. GARLAND to sign bond for his as security of
JNO. W. SCHOOLFIELD as executor of FRANCES B. SCHOOLFIELD, deceased.
September 12, 1855. JNO. THOS. SMITH, Notary in Lynchburg.

CHAS. LEWIS -- Book 3, Page 446 -- October 16, 1797. Division to
CHAS. LEWIS and ux, SALLY, of estate of JAS. NEVIL, deceased.

SETH LIGGIN -- Book 4, Page 440 -- Guardian Bond -- January 19, 1807.
NELSON CRAWFORD, JR., and SR.; for JR. as guardian of SETH and LITS
LIGGIN, orphans of JOS. LIGGIN, deceased.

JNO. W. LIGHTFOOT -- Book 6, Page 278 -- Administrator's Bond --
PEGGY LIGHTFOOT and RO. W. CARTER, January 21, 1822, for PEGGY LIGHT-
FOOT.

ROBT. LINDSEY (LINSEY) HARDWICK (Indexed as LINSEY) -- Book 6,
Page 104 -- Guardian Bond -- RICH. HARDWICK, JAS. and SAML. COLEMAN,
November 15, 1819, for RICH. HARDWICK as guardian of ROBT. LINDSEY
and JAS. HARDWICK, orphans of RICH. HARDWICK, deceased.
Book 6, Page 198 -- Guardian Bond -- JAS. & SAML. COLEMAN, and DANL.
CHRISTIAN, December 18, 1820, for JAS. COLEMAN as guardian of same
orphans. Note: I have put this here since it was not found until
H's were completed. There is HARDWICK data in numbers 43f, of his,
but indexer messed up names and thus caused this confusion. It will
be noted in 43 of H's that LINDSEY HARDWICK was indexed as HENDRICK.
These two items were indexed incorrectly so appear under L's.

THOS. LINTHCUM -- Book 6, Page 243 -- Administrator's Bond -- SALLY
LINTHCUM, SAML. SMITHSON, and JNO. T. LINTHCUM, August 20, 1821, for
SALLY LINTHCUM.
Book 6, Page 253 -- Inventory -- total blurred; September 17, 1821.
WM. TURNER; JESSE BECK, SR.; CHAS. PALMER.
Book 7, Page 119 -- Administrator's Account from July 13, 1821; black
stuff and shoes for MARY JANE and some books. Boot teas (sic) for
THOS. and shoes for MARY JANE. Buckingham taxes; to HENRY LINTHCUM,
November 25, 1823 - evidently in account. Bond of EDWD. LINTHCUM;
suit of LINEAS BOLING. Recorded July 14, 1825. J. T. BOCOCK, GEO.
CHRISTIAN, WM. STEPHENS.

MARGARET H. LIPSCOMB -- Book 15, Page 275 -- Guardian Bond -- W. L.
(S.) DAVIS; RO. H. COX; and ROLAND G. TURPIN, December 19, 1859, for
W. DAVIS as guardian of MARGARET H. and CLEMENT J. LIPSCOMB, orphans
of HENRY LIPSCOMB, deceased.

JAS. LIVELY -- Book 5, Page 425 -- January 14, 1814, written;
March 21, 1814, probated. Witnesses: ALLISON OGDON, WM. KNIGHT, JNO.
McDANIEL. Ux, JANE - slaves and land; three sons: MATTHEW, PHILIP,
and JAS. LIVELY - land. My 4 daughters: ELIZ. HILL, ANN CAMPBELL,
MARY DAVIS, and LUCY. Executors: sons, MATT. and PHILIP. They
qualified - Page 426. Bondsmen: JNO. McDANIEL and WM. KNIGHT.
Book 5, Page 435 -- Inventory -- April 2, 1814: $7,058.50. WM. TUR-
NER, RICH. JONES, JAS. MARR.
Book 5, Page 504 -- Division of Slaves -- to daughters: ELIZ. HILL,
ux of JAS. HILL; ANNE CAMPBELL, ux of CORNL. CAMPBELL; MARY DAVIS, ux
of JNO. DAVIS; LUCY OGDEN, ux of ALLISON OGDEN. May 15, 1815. CHAS.
MUNDY, JAS. MARR, WM. TURNER. These items are for JAMES R. LIVELY:
Book 6, Page 361 -- Constable -- June 16, 1823. First Hundred.
Bondsman: JAS. POWELL.
Book 8, Page 367 -- Curator's Bond -- November 18, 1833. Bondsmen:
ZACH. DRUMMOND and BENJ. TALIAFERRO.
Book 9, Page 224 -- Curator's Account. May 16, 1836. Names of
JAS. R. LIVELY, JNO. DAVIS, ALLISON OGDEN. Committee: W. L. SAUNDERS
and WILLIS WHITE.

JANE LIVELY -- Book 8, Page 305 -- September 28, 1832, written;
February 18, 1833, probated. Witnesses: HENRY L. DAVIES, JAS. DAVIS.
Sons: MATT., PHILIP, and JAS. LIVELY. Slave, Amey, bought of MATT.
LIVELY - to trustee, JAS. POWELL, for son, JAS. LIVELY; my four
daughters: ELIZ. HILL, MARY DAVIS, LUCY ODGEN, and ANN CAMPBELL -
apart from husbands. Executors: friends: WM. BOURNE and -----;

granddaughter, JANE DAVIS.
Page 304 is Administrator's Bond on probate date: WM. BOURNE; bonds-
man, ALLISON ODGEN.
Book 8, Page 366 -- Inventory -- February 19, 1833: $444.00. WM.
KNIGHT, PROSSER POWELL, WM. GILBERT.

JOS. LIVELY -- Book 3, Page 282 -- Administrator's Bond -- MARK
LIVELY, JNO. HILL, and WM. HILL, October 22, 1793, for MARK LIVELY.
Book 3, Page 293 -- Inventory -- December 16, 1793. L 240-14-6.
LUCAS POWELL, JAS. STEVENS, and WIATT LOVING.
Book 3, Page 450 -- Administrator's Account -- two sales for total
of L 240-9-0. Memo as to wagon bought by JNO. CHESTNUT who went
"of" without giving a bond. He later sold it and only got L 5-13-9,
but paid L 10 for it. Amount to JOS. LIVELY. August 19, 1797.
JOEL FRANKLIN, JAS. DILLARD, JNO. HILL.

WM. LIVELY -- also family Bible is affixed herein -- Book 3,
Page 393 -- Refunding Bond -- January 16, 1838, to WILEY CAMPBELL,
executor of JOEL CAMPBELL, deceased, by WM.LIVELY and JOEL CAMPBELL.
Will of JOEL CAMPBELL had stipulation as to estate "among my children"
and among them were CORNL. CAMPBELL and LUCY LIVELY - both deceased -
and trusteeship for their children until 21 or married. Order of
January 15, 1838, for committee to divide. CORNL. left five children
and JAS. CAMPBELL gave power-of-attorney to WM. CAMPBELL. JAS. CAMP-
BELL is now 21 and gets one fifth. JOEL CAMPBELL, brother of JAS.,
represents his three sisters: MARY, ELIZ., and NANCY CAMPBELL.
LIVELY has received slaves. R-corded February 19, 1838. RO. M.
BROWN, L. G. WILSHER.
Book 9, Page 397 -- Same men and type of bond as above and recorded
February 19, 1838. WM. LIVELY is acting for his brothers: GEO. and
JAS., and sister, MARTHA, and for JAS. WALTON (This is difficult and
seems to be WALLER or WATERS in places) and ux, NANCY (nee LIVELY).
Five shares of LUCY LIVELY and 7 children are alive; five are above
full age; JOEL and PATRICK LIVELY are infants. Same witnesses as
above. In Deed Book ZZ, Page 241, is an item from Warren County,
Kentucky, May 10, 1844. WM., GEO., JAS., JOEL C., and HENRY LIVELY
and NANCY WALTERS (WATERS?) all of Warren County to ALLISON OGDEN,
Amherst County, for $1.50 per acreage of 48-part of land of JAS.
LIVELY, SR., which descended to MATT. LIVELY, deceased.

        I have given the data from the Bible of REV. JNO. DAVIS in
the D section of wills. The second wife of JNO. DAVIS was MARY or
POLLY LIVELY. One DAVIS descendant in another state was highly
indignant when I sent the will of JOHN showing children by a previous
ux. I have identified her in the D data. I borrowed both Bibles
from descendants of JOHN DAVIS and copied them. This LIVELY Bible was
printed in Edinburgh by WM. DARLING. It was sold at his shop in
Bridge Street and by all booksellers in Great Britain and Ireland and
bears date of 1776. It is not a King James version: "The New Testa-
ment of our Lord and Saviour Jesus Christ with Arguments to the
Different Books and Moral and Theological Observations Illustrating
Each Chapter and Shewing the Use and Improvement to be Made of It.
Composed by The Reverend MR. OSTERVALD, Professor of Divinity and
One of the Ministers of the Church at Newfchatel in Swifferland (sic).
Translated at the Desire of and Recommended by the Honorable Society
for Propagating Christian Knowledge. Edinburgh, etc., as above."
As a minister, I would like to know the text used for translation.
Here are the entries (No attempt made to change any data).

JAMES LIVELY was Born November the 25th, 1740 (?, not clear).
JEAN LIVELY wife of JAS. LIVELY was born November the 20th Anno
        Domine 1752.
JAMES LIVELY and JEAN his wife was married April 27th, 1774.
MATTHEW LIVELY Son of JAMES LIVELY and JEAN his wife was Born Janry 20,
        1782.
ELIZABETH LIVELY daughter of JAMES LIVELY and JEAN his wife was Born
        October 19, 1783.
ANN LIVELY daughter of JAMES LIVELY and JEAN his wife was Born Feby 15,
        1785 (dim and could be July).
MARY LIVELY daughter of JAMES LIVELY and JEAN his wife was Born

May 17, 1787.
JANE LIVELY a wife to JAMES LIVELY departed this life the 13th day of
February in the year of our Lord 1833. Below someone has
subtracted 1792 from 1847 and put 55.
PHILIP LIVELY son of JAMES and JEAN LIVELY was born December 31st,
1788.
WINIFRED LIVELY daughter of JAMES and JEAN LIVELY was born August 31,
1790.
JEAN LIVELY was born August 31, 1790, and departed this life July 31,
1798. (Evidently she was a twin.)
JAMES RICHESON - LIVELY son of JAMES and JEAN LIVELY was born
14th of October, 1792. (The ink is different here.)
LUCY LITHGO (SITHGO?) LIVELY daughter of JAMES and JEAN LIVELY was
born July 29, 1796.
JAMES LIVELY died February 8, 1814 and then same entry where he
is called SENIOR.

I am unable to declare just who JEAN or JANE LIVELY was before
her marriage to JAMES LIVLEY, but examination of data will show that
both left wills here in the years mentioned for their death dates.
I have not checked that wonderful standby on early Amherst names:
Register of Parson Douglas. I note that a distant kinsman of my
wife's, DR. MALCOLM HARRIS, gives a JOS. LIVELY in Louisa in 1777.

BUTLER LOCKHART -- Book 3, Page 202 -- Administrator's Bond --
PHILIPA LOCKHART and JOSEPH PENN, September 5, 1791, for PHILIPA
LOCKHART.

WM. LOCKHART(D) -- Book 11, Page 173 -- Administrator's Bond --
WINSTON LOCKHART and JNO. WHITEHEAD, October 16, 1843, for WINSTON
LOCKHART. I note various spellings of the name: PHILIP is also
spelled "ART" and WINSTON is spelled "ARD," but the men are indexed
as LOCKHART.

DAVID LOGAN -- Book 14, Page 133 -- Administrator's Bond -- CARY J.
CASH and SAML. M. GARLAND, June 17, 1856, for CARY CASH.
Book 14, Page 192 -- Inventory -- $180.00; October 20, 1856. "Us
Commrs" - no names. SAML. M. GARLAND, Clerk.
Book 14, Page 338 -- Sale -- July 8, 1856; NANCY LOGAN, buyer; plantation and wheelwright tools.
Book 15, Page 14 -- Administrator's Account from December 21, 1857;
recorded August 16, 1858. Note: DAVID LOGAN's marriage is one of
those which I have copied for the clerk since they were never recorded:
50 plus marriages. November 18, 1820, bond to marry NANCY CASH.
REUBEN CASH was bondsman. PETER CASH consented for marriage of "my
daughter, NANCY WHITSON CASH, December 18, 1820." Attest: REUBEN
and THOS. CASH. The discrepancies in dates are noted. We are not
sure that this is THOS. CASH since the page is torn; it could be
some other last name.

FRANCES M. LOGAN -- Book 14, Page 597 -- Administrator's Bond -- WM.
LOGAN, JNO. M. BROWN, POWHATAN PADGETT(?, smeared) and J. P. COLEMAN,
August 16, 1858, for WM. LOGAN.

JAS. LOGAN -- Book 6, Page 325 -- Administrator's Bond -- WM. NEVILL
and JNO. PENN, August 21, 1822, for WM. NEVILL.

WM. LOGAN and Children -- Book 9, Page 354 -- WM. LOGAN and ux; to
share in estate of MARTHA JANE ALLEN. December 24, 1836. See my
A will work on ROBT. ALLEN for clarification.

FRANCES LONDON -- Book 7, Page 41 -- Guardian Bond - indexed for
JAS. LONDON, October 15, 1827. FRANCES R. COLEMAN and JAS. HIGGIN-
BOTHAM for FRANCES COLEMAN as guardian of FRANCES LONDON, orphan of
JNO. LONDON.

IRVING L. LONDON -- Book 13, Page 231 -- August 16, 1853, written;
September 19, 1853, probated. Witnesses: LEWIS S. CAMPBELL, B. W.
CHILDRESS, JNO. H. CHRISTIAN. Ux, SALLY; daughter, AMANDA J. (I.)
LONDON. Executor: friend, JESSE MUNDY.

Book 13, Page 242 -- Administrator's Bond -- November 21, 1853.
SALLY LONDON. Bondsman: AMANDA J. LONDON.
Book 13, Page 322 -- Inventory -- November 24, 1853. Blacksmith
tools, etc.; $5,623.25. D. PATTESON, JESSE MUNDY, LEWIS S. CAMPBELL.
November 24, 1853.

JAMES LONDON (There seem to be several JAS. LONDONs herein) --
Book 7, Page 53 -- June 15, 1820, written; October 15, 1827, probated.
Witnesses: HENRY TURNER; WM. TURNER, JR.; STEPHEN B. TURNER; NANCY B.
TURNER. Heirs of my son, WM. LONDON, in lifetime received certain
sums - part on July 3, 1806; my son, JOHN, at death of his mother is
to receive certain bequests; son, JAMES - land bought of CHAS. CHRIS-
TIAN; son, MARTIN; daughter, SUSANNAH HENDERSON; daughter, SALLEY
LONDON; daughter, POLLY GREGORY; daughter, ELIZ. WHITTINGTON, daugh-
ter, NANCY GRIGORY (sic); daughter, LUCINDA KNIGHT; my five daughters:
names all save NANCY again. Executors: friends: CHAS. MUNDY; COL.
JAS. DILLARD; and son, JAS. LONDON. Codicil: my two granddaughters,
HARRIOT and HARRIAN GREGORY, daughters of my daughter, NANCY, will
get bequests at death of their grandmother, June 17, 1820, and same
witnesses as to will.
Book 7, Page 87 -- Administrator's Bond -- November 20, 1827, for
JAS. LONDON. Bondsmen: CHAS. MUNDY and THOS. HUCHESON.
Book 7, Page 113 -- Inventory -- $2,411.87-1/2, December 24, 1827.
JESSE MUNDY, WM. DAY, JACOB WOODSON, E. P. OMOHUNDRO.
Book 7, Page 312 -- Administrator's Account - account of R. H. LON-
DON; IRVINE L. LONDON; Amherst and Bedford taxes; trips "on the
river"; November 16, 1829. Same committee as for above inventory.
Book 8, Page 275 -- Administrator's Account from January 1, 1830,
WIATT LONDON for whiskey; LEWIS P. SIMPSON for wife's legacy; same
to WM. W. CLEMENTS; N. I. LONDON for wool; LARKIN LONDON for same.
November 19, 1831. Committee same as above with exception of
ELIJAH L. CHRISTIAN for Omohundro.
Book 8, Page 425 -- Estate Commitment to Sheriff, August Court, 1834;
unadministered with will annexed. Sheriff: EDMD. WINSTON.
Book 9, Page 29 -- Administrator's Account by JAS. LONDON from Decem-
ber, 1831. Taxes in Amherst County and Bedford; R. H. LONDON;
J. LONDON; PLEASANT STOREY and NANCY STOREY (not named as legatees).
Recorded November 13, 1833. WM. KENT, RO. WINGFIELD, WILEY CAMPBELL.
Book 9, Page 74 -- Inventory of JAS. LONDON, SR.; May 18, 1835.
JESSE MUNDY, WM. KENT, LAWSON TURNER.
Book 9, Page 200 -- August 15, 1835, written; Monday, November 11,
1835, probated. Witnesses: GUSTAVUS A. EDWARDS; JNO. J. PADGETT;
NELSON J. LONDON. To MATILDA LONDON; brother, MARTIN LONDON; nephews,
JAS. S. or L. WHITTINGTON and LEWIS GREGORY - land known as Park
Field; reference to bond for TIRZAH LONDON, administratrix of JNO.
LONDON, deceased; bond or letter from THOS. HIGGINBOTHAM is in my
papers. Executors: JAS. L. (S.) WHITTINGTON and LEWIS GREGORY.
Produced by named executors. OBADIAH HENDERSON for ux, SUSANNAH,
in court as one of lawful heirs and contested. Depositions and
letters produced on January 9, 1836, and admitted to record. Defen-
dants to pay costs; administrators bonded with bondsmen: RO. WING-
FIELD, GUSTAVUS A. EDWARDS, JAS. C. BECK: Book 9, Page 212.
Book 9, Page 229 -- Inventory -- February 6, 1836 - $2,526.87. WM.
KENT, REUBEN CARVER, THOS. HUTCHERSON.
Book 10, Page106 -- Inventory of SR. at Mansion House, January 3,
1839 - $2,748.75. WILEY CAMPBELL, ALEX. JEWELL, WM. KENT, JNO. DIL-
LARD, administrator, with will annexed.
Book 10, Page 142 -- Administrator's Account by EDMD. WINSTON,
Sheriff - to MRS. LONDON. Recorded June 19, 1839.
Book 10, Page 293 -- Administrator's Account -- JNO. DILLARD,
Administrator's de bonis non, with will annexed. To NATHAN P. BREED-
LOVE for services; receipt to EDMUND WINSTON for settlement of his
accounts. Recorded December 21, 1840.

JNO. LONDON -- Book 6, Page 357 -- Administrator's Bond -- TIRZA
LONDON, JAS. PETTIT, and JAS. LONDON, May 19, 1823, for TIRZA LONDON.
Book 6, Page 364 -- Inventory - $4,689.37-1/2; June 16, 1823. JNO.
McDANIEL, JAS. BOWLING, WM. DAY.
Book 7, Page 140 -- Administrator's Account from May 19, 1823.
Several suits; Campbell Co. tickets; Feb. 9, 1828. BENJ. BROWN; WM.

BOURNE; JAS. OGDON.
Book 8, Page 312 -- Adminsitrator's Account from February 8, 1828.
Several suits; one in Lynchburg; BENJ. BROWN and WILKINS WATSON.
March 29, 1833.

LARKIN LONDON -- Book 8, Page 344 -- Division; July 1833, Court
Order; JONAS PIERCE vs. LARKIN LONDON and ux, MARY ANNE; ELIZ. TYLER;
MILDRED INNIS; ONEY GARNER; ISAAC SCOTT and his ux, MARTHA; JAS.
DILLARD; JNO. HAGGARD and ux, SUSAN; and THOS.; ELEANOR; ROBT., and
WM. WARREN. JNO. PRYOR, surveyor - 292 acres. Lots to LARKIN LONDON
and ux, MARY ANNE; MILDRED INNIS; ONEY GARNER; SALLY WARREN's heirs;
ELIZ. TYLER; JAS. DILLARD and JONAS PIERCE who bought interest of
ISAAC SCOTT and ux, MARTHA.
Page 345 -- Plat - both sides of Rocky Creek and west side of Glad
Road to Folly. Lines of CLAIBORNE GOOCH ("W." initial); DANL. CHEAT-
WOOD's heirs; JNO. TYLER's heirs; JACOB PIERCE; ROWLAND VIA; WM. S.
and CHAS. B. CLAIBORNE and which WM. DILLARD died seized of -
292 acres. Division is among heirs of WM. DILLARD by RO. WINGFIELD;
JOS. KYLE; and WILEY CAMPBELL at instance of JONAS PIERCE who bought
SCOTT interest and JAS. DILLARD and others; MARY ANNE ux of LARKIN
LONDON et al. Surveyed: August 9, 1833.
Book 9, Page 241 -- Administrator's Bond -- WIATT LONDON, IRVING S.
LONDON, NELSON J. LONDON, September 19, 1836, for WIATT LONDON.
Book 9, Page 263 -- Inventory -- November 21, 1836: $1,059.37.
ROBT. and THOS. WINGFIELD; WILEY CAMPBELL.

LAVINDER LONDON -- Book 4, Page 281 -- Tobacco Inspector -- Tye
River Warehouse: November 18, 1805; Bondsman: AUSTIN WRIGHT.

MOLLY LONDON -- Book 10, Page 294 -- Administrator's Bond -- OBADIAH
HENDERSON, December 21, 1840.
Book 10, Page 299 -- November 16, 1839, written; November 16, 1840,
probated. Witnesses: JACOB WOODSON, PLEASANT STORY, WIATT LONDON.
JAS. F. DILLARD as trustee for my daughter, SUSANNAH HENDERSON; my
4 granddaughters: (by my daughter, ELIZ. WHITTINGTON); granddaughter,
SALLY, daughter of SALLY; daughter, SALLY; granddaughter, MARY F.
SIMPSON, and my daughter, NANCY SIMPSON. Suit vs. me by JNO. DILLARD
and REUBEN CARVER and my son-in-law, OBADIAH HENDERSON, has employed
at my request T. W. and J. T. DILLARD to represent me; fee to CHAS.
L.(?) MOSBY; executor: OBADIAH HENDERSON.

MOSES LONDON -- Book 1, Page 368 -- Administrator's Bond -- ALEX.
CHISNAL (CHAZNALL); JOS. CABELL; EDMD. WILCOX, August 4, 1777, for
Amherst County. Inventory is Page 379, September 1, 1777: L 28-8-1.
CHAS. LAVENDER; KILLIS WRIGHT; JAS. EDMONDS.

NELSON O. LONDON -- Book 13, Page 244 -- Administrator's Bond --
WIATT LONDON and RICH. H. LONDON, November 23, 1853, for WIATT LONDON.

RICH. H. LONDON -- Book 14, Page 60 -- Administrator's Bond -- WIATT
LONDON and CHAS. M. WATTS, December 17, 1855, for WIATT LONDON.
Book 14, Page 90 -- Inventory -- April 16, 1856: $66.95-1/2. B. W.
CHILDRESS, W. HOLLINGSWORTH, CHAS. M. WATTS.

TIRZAH LONDON (nee HIGGINBOTHAM) -- Book B, Page 18 -- July 6, 1839,
written; Saturday, August 28, 1841, probated. Witnesses: HENRY L.
DAVIES, NELSON BURCH and also to codicil of July 28, 1841. Education
for the following granddaughters: MARY ANN WOODROFF, TIRZAH ELIZ.
HIGGINBOTHAM, VA. DANIEL WOODROOF. To JNO. J. and DANL. H. LONDON,
slave in trust for my daughter, FRANCES J.(?) WOODROOF and children;
lands bought for me and formerly that of my deceased husband, JNO.
LONDON; 6 parts for my children: JNO. J., DANL. H., FRANCES J. WOOD-
ROOF and children; ANN ELIZA HIGGINBOTHAM and heirs; MARY BANKS LON-
DON - if any children; son, WM. AUGUSTUS LONDON. Executors: my
brother, DANL. HIGGINBOTHAM, and my sons, JNO. J. and DANL. H. LONDON.
Codicil: If sons have no legal heirs. Codicil: Granddaughters:
FRANCES L. WOODROOF, MARY A. HIGGINBOTHAM; land bought of JAS. L. (S.)
HIGGINBOTHAM; to MARY B. and W. A. LONDON.
Book B, Page 20 -- Administrator's Bond - probate date: JNO. J. LON-
DON. Bondsmen: WINSTON WOODROOF and JAS. HIGGINBOTHAM.

Book B, Page 62 -- Administrator's de bonis non Bond -- March 23, 1857. JAS. HIGGINBOTHAM. Bondsman: DANL. H. LONDON by RO. TINSLEY.

W. AUGUSTUS LONDON -- Book 11, Page 18 -- Guardian Bond -- JAS. HIG-GINBOTHAM, WM. C. CHRISTIAN, JAS. S. HIGGINBOTHAM, March 21, 1842, for JAS. HIGGINBOTHAM as guardian of WM. A. LONDON, orphan of JNO. LONDON. Indexed W. AUGUSTUS LONDON.

WYATT LONDON -- Book 5, Page 513 -- Constable -- July 19, 1815. Bondsmen: WM. HARRISON and LAWSON G. TYLER.
Book 5, Page 653 -- Same -- June 17, 1871. Bondsman: REUBEN COLEMAN. First Hundred.
Book 6, Page 239 -- Same -- September 20, 1819. Bondsman: RO. GRANT
Book 6, Page 338 -- So indexed, but nothing there.

BETSY LONG (nee PENN) -- Book 9, Page 38 -- October 9, 1834, written; January 19, 1835, probated. Witnesses: LINDSEY COLEMAN, HENRY L. DAVIES. Nephew, ALEX. B. DYER, son of WM. H. and PEGGY DYER, of Missouri; niece, ANN DYER, of Missouri; niece, MARGARET DYER, daughter of WM. H. and ux as above; rest of negroes in trust for me by WILLIAM CRAWFORD (reference to Amherst County deeds by THOS. CREWS, ELIZ. BRYDIE and others); they are to be divided among my nieces: PEGGY DYER, of Missouri; ELIZ. SHARP, ux of RO. SHARP, Richmond, Virginia; and ELIZ. NASH of Missouri. Nieces: SARAH PENN; JANE PENN; and CATH. PENN - reference to deed of October 9, 1834, in Amherst County. Nephews: JNO. G. McCREDIA and GEO. McCREDIA. Nieces: ANN CRAWFORD and BETSY NASH, SARAH PENN, and CHRISTIAN WATSON. Slave families to be kept intact, if possible. My beloved husband, WM. LONG; brother, EDMD. PENN; and nephew, JNO. G. McCREDIE are to administer. WM. S. CRAWFORD qualified.
Book 9, Page 59 -- Inventory -- January 25, 1835: $5,291.25. LINDSEY COLEMAN, H. L. (S.) DAVIES, SAML. HEISKELL.
Book 9, Page 367 -- Slave division by LINDSEY COLEMAN; ----- PETTYJOHN; HOWELL L. BROWN - valued at $5,291.25 - 13 named "plus children" - to PEGGY H. DYER, ux of WM. H. DYER; ELIZ. SHARP, ux of RO. SHARP; ELIZ. F. NASH; GEO. M. PAINE had attorney power for MRS. DYER and SHARP was present for ux. Reference to a previous distribution under will, June 17, 1837.
Page 368 -- WM. H. DYER, of Missouri, and GEO. M. PAYNE, Buckingham County - refunding bond to WM. S. CRAWFORD, administrator, January 17, 1837. Administrator has delivered slaves to PEGGY DYER under suit of W. S. CRAWFORD vs. WM. H. DYER and ux, et al.

WM. LONG -- Book 9, Page 202 -- Estate Commitment to Sheriff -- September 21, 1835. Motion of WM. CRAWFORD, administrator of BETSY LONG. Sheriff: THOS. N. EUBANK.

JAS. LOVING -- Book 4, Page 302 -- Guardian Bond -- November 18, 1799. RICH. C. POLLARD and JAS. STEVENS, JR., for RICH. POLLARD as guardian of JAS. LOVING, orphan of WM. LOVING, deceased.

JNO. LOVING -- Book 3, Page 1 -- Administrator's Bond -- WM. LOVING and JAS. REID, March 7, 1786, for WM. LOVING.
Book 3, Page 14 -- Inventory -- This page is missing in book, but clerk has inserted copy from original on film. July 3, 1796 - L 25-13-11. RO. WRIGHT, THOS. HAWKINS, JNO. MONTGOMERY. Part of will of RO. HORSLEY was also gone and copy has been made.

JNO. LOVING, SR. -- Book 4, Page 155 -- No date when written; probated September 17, 1804. Witnesses: RICH. C. POLLARD, GEO. PURVIS. Ux, AMY (or ANNY); my children: GEO.; JNO.; JAS.; WM.; LUNSFORD; NANCY, ux of JAS. LOVING, JR.; SCYNTHY FORTUNE; LUCINDA LOVING; SALLY TEAS; MOLLY WOODS; ELIZ. VAUGHAN. JAS. and JNO. have not been furnished horses; SALLY TEAS' part to her children at her death: JNO. STEWART and ELINOR TEAS. ELIZ. VAUGHAN's at her death to RODERICK TALIAFERRO; if any daughters are not with heirs. MOLLY WOODY (appears to be WOODS above) at death, to her heirs. Executors: ux and sons, GEO., JAS., and JNO.
Book 4, Page 162 -- Inventory -- L 969-13-9, September 29, 1804.

JOS. SHELTON, JAS. WRIGHT, JNO. MILTON.
Book 4, Page 388 -- Administrator's Bond -- JAS. LOVING, September 17,
1804. Bondsmen: LANDON CABELL and WM. LOVING.
Book 6, Page 91 -- Administraotr's Bond -- LUNSFORD LOVING, September 20, 1819. Bondsman: CHAS. PERROW.

JOSEPH LOVING -- Book 4, Page 275 -- Tobacco Inspector -- Tye River
Warehouse. Bondsman: JNO. LOVING.

NANCY LOVING -- Book 4, Page 322 -- Guardian Bond -- August 21, 1800,
CHAS. TALIAFERRO; JNO. and JOS. LOVING for CHAS. TALIAFERRO as
guardian of NANCY LOVING, orphan of WM. LOVING, deceased.

PEGGY LOVING -- Book 4, Page 323 -- Guardian Bond -- JNO. TALIAFERRO,
JNO. and JOS. LOVING, August 21, 1800, for CT (JNO. TALIAFERRO?) as
guardian of SAML. and PEGGY LOVING, orphans of WM. LOVING, deceased.
Two bonds.

SAML. LOVING -- See bond above. CHAS. TALIAFERRO was guardian and
same bondsmen.

SPOTSWOOD G. LOVING -- Book 10, Page 229 - Constable -- June 15,
1840. Bondsmen: LEWIS S. EMMETT and JNO. D. DUNCAN.
Book 10, Page 36 -- Same -- June 21, 1841. Bondsmen: WM. H. TYLER
and WM. T. HARGROVE.
Book 11, Page 395 -- Administrator's Bond -- STERLING CLAIBORNE and
WM. S. CLAIBORNE, January 19, 1846, for STERLING CLAIBORNE.
Book 11, Page 437 -- Inventory -- January 29, 1846; no total; WM.
STAPLES, SEATON LANDRUM, BURTON LANDRUM. Recorded October 19, 1846.
Book 11, Page 609 -- Administrator's Account from January 30, 1846;
to widow; mention of suit in Nelson County; report of sale and
WINSTON LOVING was a buyer. JNO. M. WHITEHEAD, commissioner. Recorded February Term, 1847.
Book 12, Page 190 -- Administrator's Account from 1847; linsey for
2 girls; Grandmother for girls. RO. M. BROWN, commissioner.
August 20, 1849.
Book 12, Page 463 -- Administrator's Account from September 1, 1849.
To CHAS. N. PATTESON - proper part for enclosing graveyard; to NANCY
RINE, the widow; to children: CLEOPHAS, JAS. EWELL, ARMANIA and
ENDORA LOVING; to AUSTIN B. RINE - slave hire; same by NANCY LOVING;
to AUSTIN B. RINE and NANCY LOVING - board of children and books.
RO. M. BROWN, commissioner. Recorded October 20, 1851, Monday.
Book 14, Page 444 -- Administrator's de bonis non Bond -- October 19,
1857; JAS. P. COLEMAN. Bondsman: RO. A. COGHILL.
Book 14, Page 465 -- Administrator's Account by STERLING CLAIBORNE -
MRS. NANCY LOVING hired a slave. To NANCY RINE, widow; to children:
same list as above, but EWELL is givin initial of "A." To AUSTIN B.
RINE (RENE in one place) and ux, NANCY; tuition for the girls. Recorded September 21, 1857.

WM. LOVING, CAPT. -- Book 3, Page 215 -- June --, 1791, written;
February 20, 1792, probated. Presented by WM. and JNO. LOVING,
two of named executors. Son, WM. - land bought of DABNEY MINOR; son,
JNO. - land bought of WM. BIBB; son, JOSEPH - land bought of MARBLE
STONE in Fluvanna; son, SAML. - land bought of CHAS. STEWART and JNO.
DEPRIEST; son, JAS. - where I live; Ux, BETTY - land next to JAS.
THOMPSON and TILMAN WALTON; daughter, MILLY LOVING; daughters: LUCY
TALIAFERRO and BETSY TALIAFERRO - sum due me from RICH. TALIAFERRO;
JNO. TALIAFERRO, husband of daughter, BETSY; daughter, MOLLY, ux of
JOS. STAPLES; daughter, SUKEY; daughter, SALLY, when of age; same
as to daughters, PEGGY and NANCY. Sons, JAS. and SAML. when of age
or married. Run-away slave, Abraham; if sons are without issue;
eldest son, WM.; if MILLEY, SUKEY, SALLY, PEGYY, and NANCY don't
marry. Executors: Sons, WM. and JNO. and ux.
Book 3, Page 218 -- Administrator's Bond -- WM. and JNO. LOVING,
February 20, 1792. Bondsmen: JAS. CALLAWAY and PLEASANT MARTIN.
Book 3, Page 222 -- Inventory -- called CAPT. herein - L 2,133-4-5.
March 14, 1792. HENRY MARTIN; HEZ. HARGROVE; JNO. STAPLES; WM.
LOVING - acting executor - trips to Buckingham.
Book 4, Page 225 -- Administrator's Account by WM. LOVING, acting

executor from February 28, 1792. To New Glasgow "when the clerk
office was examined." To Buckingham; to JNO. and WM. LOVING; to
CHAS. TALIAFERRO - Legacy; JNO. LOVING, JR. November, 1792. It is
interesting to study names of sheriffs and deputies of many Virginia
counties in this long report. CHAS. TALIAFERRO is called JR. Trip
to Hanover and Richmond about slave, Abraham. Various suits mentioned.
Recorded July 21, 1806. RO. RIVES, L. CABELL, S. CROSTHWAIT.

ALFRED W. LUCAS -- Book 17, Page 467 -- April 19, 1869. TAYLOR BERRY,
bondsman, for him to become clerk of Amherst County. Took place of
LEONARD DANIEL by order of BREVET MAJOR GEN. GEORGE STONEHAM, Comman-
der of Military District 1, March 20, 1869.
Book 18, Page 20 -- Same men -- March 5, 1870, for Virginia legislature required renewed bonds. I believe that in DAMERON papers
in my possession is data showing that LUCAS' widow was allowed sum
to return his body "up north." He and WILLIAMS, husband of INDIANA
FLETCHER, both came in during Reconstruction days, it appears, and
STONEHAM put both of them in offices of Amherst men. LUCAS did not
hold office too long for WILL F. ROSE took over, April 18, 1870.
LEO DANIEL was his bondsman.

JNO. LUCAS -- Book 16, Page 134 -- Guardian Bond -- HUGH N. COLEMAN
and SEATON COLEMAN, June 16, 1862, for HUGH COLEMAN as guardian of
JNO. LUCAS - no parent set forth.

RICH. LUCAS -- Book 10, Page 37 -- Estate Commitment to Sheriff,
August, 1838. Motion of ROBINSON and ELLIOTT.
Book 10, Page 54 -- Inventpry -- September, 1838 - $18.00. RO. L.
COLEMAN, Deputy Sheriff. PETER RUCKER; BLANSFORD HICKS; NICHL. HICKS.

THOS. LUCAS -- Book 3, Page 129 -- Administrator's Bond -- AMBROSE
RUCKER, JR.; EDWD. GARLAND; RICH. FULCHER; and REUBEN HARRISON,
January 4, 1790, for AMBROSE RUCKER, JR. I am deviating from policy
not to wander off into Orders here, but tried to help an old woman
in the county on this family. In Orders, 1790-94, Page 619, October
Court, 1793 - Motion of AMBROSE RUCKER to certify and court satisfied
that MARY HAMNER; ELIZ. RUCKER; FRANCES CARTER; and NANCY LUCAS are
co-heirs and representatives of THOS. LUCAS. This item is indexed
for RO. GARLAND -- Book 3, Page 244 -- Guardian Bond -- October 5,
1792 - RO. GARLAND qualified as guardian of FRANCES and NANCY LUCAS,
orphans of THOS. LUCAS.

SARAH MILDRED LYNN -- Book 15, Page 557 -- Administrator's Account --
JOS. S. BROWN, trustee - from November 24, 1858 - To Hollins Insti-
tute; gives account as administrator of MARY ALLEN (see her will
under A's). Recorded July 16, 1860.
Book 16, Page 350 -- Account by BROWN as trustee - legatee of MARY
ALLEN. Recorded June 17, 1863.

GEO. P. LUCK(E) -- Book 6, Page 7 -- Ordinary Bond -- May 18, 1818;
house in county. Bondsman: JAS. WARE.
Book 8, Page 373 -- Estate Commitment to Sheriff -- November 20, 1833.
EDMD. WINSTON, Sheriff.
Book 9, Page 337 -- April 26, 1833, written; August 21, 1837, probated.
Held for further proof and September 18, 1837, oaths of JNO. TANKERS-
LEY and RO. C. BIBB; RO. C. REDD and RO. H. PRYOR - admitted to probate. Debts are to be paid and then estate goes to my slaves: Delia,
Jane, Edney, Oliver, and Overton. Some are in possession of my
nephew, ALFRED T. DILLARD. They are to be sent to Ohio and freed. If
debts are too much, then oldest males are to be cared for first since
I want to be just and abide by law of the land where I live. Does not
believe that DILLARD "has power to thwart me," but the question is
now in court. However, because of "blood red" between us, I call upon
him not to block my wishes. He knows the reason for my anxiety upon
this subject. Executors: CAPT. THOS. N. EUBANK, BEVERLY DAVIES,
COL. WM. ARMISTEAD. There is no record of Administrator's Bond.

CHAS. H. LYNCH -- Book 16, Page 149 -- Power-of-attorney to SAML. M.
GARLAND to sign for him in bond of CHISWELL DABNEY as administrator
of EDWIN S. RUCKER - Administrator's de bonis non - June 10, 1862.
Done at Lynchburg.

JNO. LYON, JR. (so indexed) -- Book 1, Page 58 -- September 6, 1763, written; July 1, 1765, probated. Witnesses: JNO. and JAS. LYON and MARTIN KEY. Parish of St. Ann, Albemarle - ux, RACHEL and at death to my son, RICH. TANULTY (sic) LYON. Executors: ux, JNO. LYON and RICH. TANKETY (sic).
Page 60 -- Administrator's Bond -- RACHEL LYON; RICH. TANKERSLEY; LEONARD TARRANT, JR.; and WM. SPENCER - probate date - for RICH. TANKERSLEY and RACHEL LYON.
Book 1, Page 64 -- Inventory -- L 33-0-8, August 5, 1765. BENJ. TARRANT; AMBRAS JONES.
Book 1, Page 178 -- Guardian Bond -- RICH. TANKERSLEY, JNO. LYON, and JAS. STEVENS, July 2, 1770, for RICH. TANKERSLEY and JNO. LYON as guardians of RICH. TANKERSLEY LYON and SALLY LYON, orphans of JNO. LYON, deceased.
Book 1, Page 201 -- Guardian's Account -- August 28, 1771 - suit by BLAIN.
Book 1, Page 217 -- Guardian's Account and recorded August Court, 1772.
Book 1, Page 220 -- Guardian Bond -- RICH. TANKERSLEY; RICH. ALLCOCK; and RICH. TANKERSLEY, JR., August 3, 1772, for RICH. TANKERSLEY as guardian of RICH. TANKERSLEY LYON, orphan of JNO. LYON.
Book 1, Page 506 -- Guardian Bond for SAML. ANDERSON and ALEX. REID, October 7, 1779, for SAML. ANDERSON as guardian of RICH. TANKERSLEY LYON, orphan of JNO. LYON.

The following L's are treated in Hardesty and Brock - see K section for discussion of this work - Amherst sketches.

(1) BENJ. W. LANDRUM - subject - born Amherst County December 11, 1833; ux, BETTIE S. FOGUS - born Amherst County, September 2, 1849; married April 10, 1872. Two sons and two daughters: ERNEST L. - born December 8, 1874; CLINTON F. - born January 7, 1878; ETHEL PEARL - born July 24, 1879; BETTIE WATSON - April 27, 1881. BENJ. W. LANDRUM was son of RICH. LANDRUM - died February 11, 1858, and MARY (HICOK) LANDRUM - died February 4, 1884. BETTIE S. FOGUS was daughter of ANDREW L. and STELLA E. (MITCHELL) FOGUS. Her parents now live in Amherst County. June 3, 1861, BENJ. W. entered Confederate Army, Company E, 2nd Virginia Cavalry; New Year's day, 1862, detailed as courier for GEN. LONGSTREET and served until May, 1863. Wounded at Beaver Dam; recovered; served for duration. Had 3 brothers in same company; one lost arm at Malvern Hill and another killed at Gettysburg. BENJ. W. owns fine farm and is owner and manager of a saw mill; merchant and man of influence in New Glasgow; Post Master for past three years and still in office.

(2) LANE, Page 440 -- H. D. LANE married LILLIAN H. HUDSON - daughter of R. J. HUDSON - subject of sketch - she was born January 3, 1854.
    Page 443 -- JANE LANE, ux of PAGE BLUNT (WM. PARR sketch).
    Page 444 -- MARY F. LANE was mother of ALEX. SALE (subject) and ux of BENJ. SALE who died in Amherst County about 1857. MARY F. still lives in Amherst County. BENJ. F. SALE was in War of 1812.

(3) Law Index -- "To the Amendments to the Code of Virginia"; 1883, by ABRAM WARWICK SAUNDERS, JR. (subject).

(4) Page 437 -- BETSY LAWLER (CAMPBELL) -- MARY LAWLER (nee KELLEY): THOS. LAWLER. See K Wills; 1761-1919; Hardesty and Brock Supplement data.

(5) Page 440 -- ELIZA ANN LAWMAN (JARVIES) - mother of JAS. E. JARVIES (subject) and ux of WM. JARVIES. JAS. E. JARVIES born Rock-bridge; mother born January 22, 1813 - to Amherst County with husband when JAS. E. was 3; still in Amherst County. LAWMANs of German descent.

(6) Page 442 -- JANE W. LAYNE (MILLER) - ux of DANL. SHEFFY MILLER who was born Nelson County, Virginia, 1816; JANE W., born in Nelson in 1816. Parents of ALEX. MILLER (subject). To Amherst County from Nelson in 1845; still in Amherst County.

(7) LEDBETTER -- Page 436 -- JAS. EDWD. CAMDEN (subject) - native of Botetourt and born September 11, 1857. Son of WM. C. and MARTHA J. (CLEMENS) CAMDEN. JAS. EDWD. CAMDEN married ROSA MAY LEDBETTER, daughter of RICH. T. and MAHALY ALLEN (TUCKER) LEDBETTER. ROSA born in Cabell County (now West Virginia) April 23, 1857, and married in Lynchburg, November 1, 1882.

(8) LEE -- Page 437 -- FITZ LEE's Confederate Division mentioned.
Page 443 -- COL. H. C. LEE - Union Army - mentioned - 27th Massachusetts Infantry - captured at Drury's Bluff with men and 4 standards of colors by JOS. H. PARR, et al. (Confederates).
Page 442 -- JNO. LYNCH LEE (subject), born New Orleans, Louisiana, July 6, 1861; son of JNO. LYNCH LEE and JULIA G. (CASH) LEE. Father - Confederate, and he and ux are deceased. Since 1877 subject has lived in Amherst County at Amherst Courthouse. April 26, 1882, married to ROSE CABELL; She was born in Amherst County, 1863; daughter of PAUL CARRINGTON CABELL and NANNIE (ROSE) CABELL. Both parents natives of Amherst County and deceased. Reference to CABELL lineage "elsewhere in these pages." Subject is lawyer at Amherst County Courthouse.

(9) Lehigh University - CABELL and RO. LEE WHITEHEAD students there. CABELL was born October 6, 1863, and RO. L. was born April 11, 1865.

(10) Page 445 -- Libby Prison -- WM. M. VIA (subject) served as guard there.

(11) Page 444 -- R. D. LILLY's Battalion - Confederate - DANL. TAYLOR SWISHER (subject) served in it.

(12) Page 436 -- GEN. LONG - Confederate - JAS. D. BALLOWE was on his staff.

(13) Page 440 -- LONGSTREET's Corps - THOS. JOS. MONTGOMERY GOODWIN (subject) served therein.

Please remember that this book was published in 1884. As stated, see K will supplement for full discussion of work. These are all L's and connected families in sketches. ("Subject" means that this person is subject of a sketch.) I have gone through all of the sketches and have given data on each name of L's.

(14) LOVING -- all of Page 442 -- HON. HENRY LOVING, SR. - subject - born Nelson County, May 11, 1811; resident of Amherst County since December, 1842. Son of LUNSFORD and MARGARET (HAWKINS) LOVING of Nelson. HENRY married SARAH A. LUCK, daughter of NATHAN P. and CORINA ANN (MAUPIN) LUCK. NATHAN was born Caroline County; died July 28, 1861. CORINA ANN MAUPIN, born Fluvanna; died April 14, 1851. SARAH A., born Botetourt County, June 11, 1824; married there to HENRY LOVING, 24 February 1842. Issue: ALMA SIDNEY, December 9, 1843 - lives in Botetourt; NATHAN PHILIP - September 21, 1845; died April 10, 1846; HENRY MARSHALL - born March 4, 1847, and lives in Amherst County; EDWIN LUNSFORD - born February 25, 1849; died April 12, 1882; CORINNA ANN - February 15, 1851; died same day; JNO. THOMPSON - born January 27, 1852; ALBERT GALLATIN - born May 2, 1854 - lives in Amherst County; SALLIE WALLER - born November 2, 1856, and lives in Richmond; WM. GOVAN - born December 22, 1858; JAS. MARION - born May 8, 1862; FANNY O. - born August 6, 1864; MARGARET LOUISA - born February 9, 1868; "these at home"; LUCAS POWELL - born October 28, 1870; died February 26, 1872. HENRY LOVING has estate in Temperance District; supervisor for number of years; in 2nd term as Amherst County representative. Post Office: Lowesville, Virginia, Amherst County.

(15) LUCAS -- Page 438 -- ELIZA (GRANT) - PATRICK H. GRANT and ux, ELIZA (LUCAS) GRANT were parents of ELIZ. GRANT who married WM. COLEMAN (subject). ELIZA is deceased, and PATRICK lives in Amherst County.

(16)   LUCK -- See No. 14 above.

(17)   Lynchburg Home Guards -- Page 436 -- DR. THOS. H. BALLOWE
served in this outfit.

The names in these sketches are shown by number of above items;
such as RICH. LANDRUM - (1) appears in that numbered section.

-M-

ELIZ. MADDOX -- Book 1, Page 243 -- 3 November 1772, written; April
Court, 1772, probated. Witnesses: ANTHONY STREET, JNO. and JAS.
OWNBY. This is poorly written and hard to read. To JAMES MADDOX;
to young BEN HANCOCK (sic); to ELIZ. HANCOCK; my grandn (sic),
NANCY MACCRAW; JOBSAM MACCRAW; WM. MACCRAW; to USLEY MACCRAW - to buy
another cow. Produced by the two OWNBY witnesses.

MERITT MAGAN -- Book 1, Page 365 -- Administrator's Bond -- JOS.
MAGANN, GABL. PENN, EDMD. WILCOX and CHAS. ROSE, 4 August 1777
for JOS. MAGANN to administer.

PERRY MAHANNAN -- This is not a will book item, but one picked up in
an unindexed order book, 1766-69. Church wardens to bind out a poor
orphan boy by this name. Page 482, May Court, 1769.

DANDRIDGE MANTIPLY -- Book 16, Page 112 -- Administrator's Bond --
RO. A. COGHILL, SAML. R. IRVINE, and WINSTON C. MANTIPLY, 20 January
1861, for RO. A. COGHILL.
Book 16, Page 510 -- Inventory -- $5,040.00; recorded 21 March 1864:
NATHL. N. and WINSTON C. MANTIPLY.
Book 17, Page 301 -- Administrator's Account by COGHILL, 13 December
1867. MANTIPLY's administrator vs. HARRIS; judgment of S. S. HARRIS;
cash of W. and N. N. MANTIPLY - $88.33 and $39.62 of it Confederate
money and reduced to national currency at $20.00 per $195, which
made $48.71 added and $50.66 debt due SAML. H. MANTIPLY.

ELIZ. CAROLINE MANTIPLY, MRS. -- Some are indexed for MRS. CAROLINE
MANTIPLY.
Book 13, Page 37 -- Inventory of trustee estate by NATHL. N. MANTIPLY,
22 September 1852 - no tota; several slaves; sale of estate of RO.
MANTIPLY on Page 38 - see RO. MANTIPLY.
Book 13, Page 325 -- Sales by trustee above, 24 November 1853 -
$406.26-1/2.
Book 13, Page 414 -- Trustee account by same trustee from 1 November
1852. To BLANKS and MANTIPLY; to JAS. G. MANTIPLY; to S. MANTIPLY.
THOS. WHITEHEAD, commissioners. 20 November 1854.
Book 14, Page 373 -- Trustee account from 14 January 1854. Account
of MANTIPLY and ROSE F. M. BARKER for benevolent purposes; MRS. JULIA
WOOLRIDGE for tuition for F. and J. Mountain land rented to WM.
MANTIPLY; SAML. MANTIPLY hired a slave; administrator of R. H. MANTI-
PLY; executor of WM. BOURNE, deceased. I think that I am right in
stating that BOURNE left will - of Nelson, but of record in Amherst
County - and ELIZ. CAROLINE is named as his daughter. Your dower
in slaves; tuition of FANNY and JAMES(?). Recorded April 30, 1857.
Book 15, Page 16 -- Trustee account from 9 May 1856. Subscription
to Religious Herald; to SAML. W. MANTIPLY; to WM. MANTIPLY; WM. H.
MANTIPLY for expense of trip to Lexington; WINSTON C. MANTIPLY; subscription to Mt. Moriah - $5.00. Recorded Monday, 16 August 1858.
The Religious Herald is our Virginia Baptist paper. Mt. Moriah was
one of the oldest Baptist churches in Amherst County and it is a
shame that when they merged with Central at Lowesville that the name
of Mt. Moriah was not used. The old building still stands. I have
a MRS. ROBT. MANTIPLY and her daughter, MRS. THOS. HOWELL, who are
members of Amherst Baptist Church. MR. MANTIPLY is a vestryman of the
Episcopal Church at Clifford. Members of the MANTIPLY family are
still quite active in Central Church at Lowesville and one of them is
a graduate of my alma mater, Southern Baptist Theological Seminary,
and is a Baptist minister. One of the wives of one of the Lowesville
group teaches at Amelone with my wife.

MARTHA J. MANTIPLY -- Book 16, Page 113 -- Guardian receipt by N. MANTIPLY - wards: MARTHA J., WILLIAM S., CYRUS T., and CAROLINE R. MANTIPLY, orphans of ROBERT MANTIPLY, deceased, 1 January 1861. Book 16, Page 443 -- Guardian Bond -- NATHL. N. MANTIPLY and SAML. R. IRVINE, 15 February 1864, for NATHL. N. MANTIPLY as guardian of above named children.

NATHANIEL MANTIPLY -- Book 5, Page 674 -- Administrator's Bond -- HILL CARTER, NELSON MANTIPLY, EDWD. CARTER, JNO. CAMM, WM. MANTIPLY, and SAML. MANTIPLY, 21 July 1817, for HILL CARTER - very faded page. Book 6, Page 161 -- Inventory -- (?) August 1820 - $12,751.66. JNO. SMITH, DABNEY HILL, JNO. W. LIGHTFOOT. NATHL. MANTIPLY was the first of the family to appear in Amherst County.

NELSON MANTIPLY -- Book 8, Page 85 -- Administrator's Bond -- SAML. and WM. MANTIPLY, 21 March 1831, for SAML. MANTIPLY. Book 8, Page 145 -- Inventory -- 27 April 1831 -- $6,042.00 -- WILLIS E. DICKINSON, BENNETT HUDSON, JOEL BETHEL.

ROBT. MANTIPLY -- Book 11, Page 526 -- Constable -- 21 June 1847. Bondsmen: WARNER JONES and NATHL. MANTIPLY. Book 12, Page 176 -- Constable -- 18 June 1849. Bondsmen: NATHL. and WINSTON C. MANTIPLY. Book 12, Page 490 -- Administrator's Bond -- 16 February 1852, for NATHL. N. MANTIPLY to administer. Bondsman: S. CLAIBORNE. Book 12, Page 505 -- Inventory -- 4 March 1852 - $1,294.75. SIMS BROCKMAN, LEROY MITCHELL, MICAJAH HUDSON. Book 13, Page 38 -- Sale by administrator -- 8 December 1852. Family buyers: MRS. CAROLINE E., NATHL. N., and SAML. MANTIPLY, administrator, bought "sword and rigging" - Total of sale $212.40. Book 13, Page 109 -- Indexed as sale, but not there. Book 13, Page 249 -- Inventory and Sale by Administrator -- family buyers: CAROLINE, SAML., N. N., WM., PAUL, WM. E., W. C., widow; mention of BLANKS and MANTIPLY. Recorded August 8, 1853. Book 15, Page 250 -- Indexed as sale, but not there -- not in 15 index (found in Master Index); not in 16 or 17.

SAML. MANTIPLY -- Book 15, Page307 -- Administrator's Bond -- WINSTON C., NATHL. N., WM., JAS. G. MANTIPLY; and RO. A. COGHILL, 21 May 1860, for WINSTON C. and NATHL. N. MANTIPLY. Book 15, Page 312 -- Inventory -- $76,327.89, 14 July 1860. ALBERT GANNAWAY, HENRY LOVING, WM. S. CLAIBORNE. This is a case of getting the cart before the horse for the will is not of record until Page 327 of Book 15: 16 August 1858, written; 22 December 1858, codicil with no witnesses. Probated, Monday, 21 May 1860. Witnesses: JAS. F. TALIAFERRO and WALKER L. (S.) CARTER. Produced by NATHL. and WINSTON C. MANTIPLY and WM. MANTIPLY and continued by counsel. Agreed to admit and to ignore codicil. NATHL. N. rejected codicil. Proved by witnesses. Lands to be sold; newphew, NATHL. N., son of my bro- ther, WM. MANTIPLY, and his children; WM. H. MANTIPLY, son of NATHL. N., if without issue; children of RO. H. MANTIPLY, deceased; negroes to be loaned to CHAS. L. BROWN; SAML. R. IRVINE; WINSTON C. MANTIPLY, NATHL. N. MANTIPLY and my brother, WM. MANTIPLY. The children of brother, WM., if without issue. Share of estate received by ELIZ. V. IRVINE and in trust to her husband, SAML. B. IRVINE, for her and her children; same for SARAH A. BROWN, ux of CHAS. L. BROWN; NATHL. N. is to be guardian of children of R. H. MANTIPLY, deceased. Adminis- trators: NATHL. N. and WINSTON C. MANTIPLY. Codicil: to prevent difficulties and increase the share of NATHL. N. -- WM. H. has died and his slave to his father, NATHL. N. - any loss to my brother, WM., to be made good by NATHL. N. Book 15, Page 460 -- Sale -- 1 August 1860; buyers with family names: JAS. G., NATHL. N., WESLEY, WM., WINSTON C. - $4,291.11. Recorded 17 October 1860. Book 16, Page 42 -- Sale -- 16 November 1860; family buyers: SAML. W., NATHL. N., JAS. MANTIPLY. Total: $249.83. Book 16, Page 340 -- Administrator's Account by both administrators from 18 June 1860. ROSE and MANTIPLY; bond of JAS. G. MANTIPLY; amount paid to executor of WARREN JONES; amount from DANDRIDGE MANTI- PLY; amount to SAML. W. MANTIPLY. Recorded June, 1863.

Book 16, Page 478 -- Administrator's Account by WINSTON C. MANTIPLY:
SAML. R. IRVINE, commissioner, from 4 October 1862. To WM. for clothing slave. Returned 17 September 1863.
Book 16, Page 480 -- Administrator's Account by both administrators
from 27 December 1860. Paid orphans; board of PERMELIA and clothing
for one year to NATHL. N. MANTIPLY; account of JAS. G. MANTIPLY; hire
of WM. Returned 12 May 1863. Recorded ----- 1864.
Book 17, Page 70 -- Commissioner account by WINSTON C. MANTIPLY and
SAML. R. IRVINE from 28 July 1863. Account of N. MANTIPLY; Confederate State Agents -- several taxes -- 2/3 of estate of WM. MANTIPLY
taxes.
Book 18, Page 250 -- Administrator's Account by NATHL. N. and WINSTON
C. MANTIPLY from 21 September 1863; May 15, 1871, support of PAMELIA;
to DANDRIDGE MANTIPLY; RO. A. COGHILL, administrator of DAN MANTIPLY -
1864; Confederate land and soldier tax; SAML. W. MANTIPLY for rent
of land; Nelson County tickets; SAML. R. IRVINE as trustee of ux and
children; one ninth each to EDWD., MARY L. - both have died without
issue; JAS. G.; NATHL. N.; SAML. W.; NATHL. N. as guardian of RO.
MANTIPLY's children; CHAS. L. BROWN as trustee of ux and children;
WINSTON C. MANTIPLY; seven living legatees. Recorded 17 March 1873.

WM. MANTIPLY -- Book 16, Page 419 -- August 8, 1860, written;
January 18, 1864, probated. Witnesses: V. McGINNIS; J. S. PENDLETON;
RO. A. COGHILL. Proved by first and last witnesses. WINSTON C.
MANTIPLY qualified. Bondsmen: SAML. R. IRVINE, C. L. BROWN, and
R. A. COGHILL. Ux, MARY - mansion house; brother, SAML., has recently died; unusual occurences - some children unusually successful so
all must adjust - SAML. gave my son, NATHL. N., much larger portion
than any of my other children; loves NATHL., but wants to be fair to
others; daughter, ELIZ. V., ux of SAML. R. IRVINE; daughter, MARY J.;
son, WINSTON C.; son, JAS. G.; son, DANDRIDGE; son, SAML. W.; son,
WM. E.; son, CYRUS; daughters, ROSE and JENNIE - if any are without
issue. My grandchildren - son, NATHL. N., is guardian of ROBERT's
children. Administrators: WINSTON C. and DANDRIDGE MANTIPLY.
Page 423 -- Administrator's Bond.
Book 16, Page 426 -- Inventory -- 815 acres - to amounts for totals:
$70,656.50 and $1,355.00. HENRY LOVING and SIMS BROCKMAN. February 15, 1864.
Book 16, Page 428 -- Division under wills of WM. and SAML. MANTIPLY -
two tracts - SAML. MANTIPLY - 452-3/4 acres next to SAML. MILLER,
deceased, and DR. DUPUY; WM. MANTIPLY - 817-3/8 acres next to MICAJAH
HUDSON, THOS. COLEMAN and SIMS BROCKMAN. To MARY, widow of WM. MANTI-
PLY; to SAML. R. IRVINE and ux, SUSAN (nee MANTIPLY); to WINSTON C.,
JAS. G.; heirs of RO. MANTIPLY; CHAS. L. BROWN and ux, SARAH (nee
MANTIPLY); SAML. W. MANTIPLY. Heirs of SAML. are the same - widow
excepted and NATHL. N. added. Right of way paid to A. G. LONG, SAML.
MANTIPLY is not entitled to land of WM. No date, but one item just
before bears date of November, 1871. RO. L. COLEMAN, E. P. TUCKER,
A. GANNAWAY.
Book 18, Page 236 -- Inventory of WM. and MARY MANTIPLY - $113.00.
18 December 1871. GEO. H. DAMERON, JOEL H. CAMPBELL, THOS. B. ROYSTER.

WM. H. MANTIPLY -- Book 15, Page 35 -- Administrator's Bond -- NATHL.
N. MANTIPLY and RO. A. COGHILL, 18 October 1858, for NATHL. MANTIPLY.
Book 15, Page 41 -- Inventory -- 27 November 1858 - $2,902.00.
JNO. C. WHITEHEAD, JAS. F. TALIAFERRO, WALKER S. CARTER. Recorded
3 December 1858.
Book 15, Page 51 -- Sales -- 27 November 1858 - $74.75.
Book 15, Page 567 -- Administrator's Account by NATHL. N. MANTIPLY
from 15 October 1858. To SAML. MANTIPLY; ROSE and MATNIPLY - active
interest in blacksmith shop. Recorded 20 August 1860.
Book 18, Page 440 -- Administrator's Bond -- 20 July 1874, for NATHL.
N. MANTIPLY; Bondsman: RO. A. COGHILL.

WM. S. MANTIPLY -- Book 15, Page 496 -- Guardian Bond -- NATHL. N.
MANTIPLY and RO. A. COGHILL, 19 November 1860, for NATHL. MANTIPLY as
guardian of WM. S.; CYRUS T.; JANE B. and CATH. B. MANTIPLY, orphans
of R. H. MANTIPLY, deceased.
Book 17, Page 296 -- Indexed for Book 16 - names do not jibe here
for wards in NATHL's account, are called WM. S., C. R., M. J. - paid

amount to WINSTON C. MANTIPLY; amount deposited in Confederate
States Depository - Confederacy collapsed and money perished - $1,200
and $1,136.50. Recorded February 17, 1868.

ELMIRA TAYLOR MARKHAM -- Book 8, Page 419 -- Guardian Bond -- BENJ. F.
HESSER and NORBORNE B. SPOTSWOOD, 19 June 1834, for BENJ. HESSER as
guardian of ELMIRA TAYLOR MARKHAM, orphan of JAS. L. (S.) MARKHAM.

SETH MAROMBER -- Book 4, Page 427 -- Administrator's Bond -- LUMAN
BISHOP and JNO. RUCKER, 17 February 1806, for LUMAN BISHOP.

ALEX. MARR -- Book 9, Page 247 -- Estate Commitment to Sheriff,
September, 1836; motion of JNO. NORVELL. THOS. N. EUBANK, Sheriff.

HENRY S. (L.) MARR -- Book 6, Page 725 -- Administrator's Bond --
CHAS. L. DAVIS, WM. ARMISTEAD, and MARTIN PARKS, 19 February 1827,
for CHAS. DAVIS.

JNO. MARR -- Book 4, Page 33 -- June 27, 1797, written; April 19,
1802, probated. Witnesses: BARTLETT CASH, THOS. POWELL, WM. BACON.
Proved by CASH and BACON. ALEX. MARR qualified; bondsmen: JOEL
FRANKLIN, HENRY BALLINGER, BARTLETT CASH. Ux, MARGARET; daughter,
ELIZ. BIBB; son, JNO.; grandson, JNO., now in Georgia; son, ALEX,
trustee for my daughter, EFFIA GOOLSBY, and children. Administrators:
ALEX. MARR and my ux.
Page 346 -- Administrator's Bond.
    I found THOS., THOS. H., and WM. D. MARR in index, but they are
all MORRIS items. They were in Book 6, and anything goes in it.

SARAH J. MARSTON -- Book 12, Page 509 -- Administrator's Bond --
HENRY W. QUARLES and SAML. H. HENRY, April 19, 1852, for HENRY QUARLES.
Here are other errors: in 15 and 16 are names indexed MARSTON and
all are MARTINS. I feel that this one is, too.

ABRAHAM MARTIN -- Book 10, Page 242 -- July 13, 1840, written; codicil,
July 14, 1840; August 17, 1840, probated. Witnesses to will: JNO. H.
CHRISTIAN, MADISON BLACK, CHRISTIAN as to codicil. Proved by them.
JAS. POWELL qualified; bondsmen: JNO. W. BROADDUS, SAML. M. GARLAND,
JOS. K. IRVING. Daughter, POLLY CLEMENTS, ux of JESSE CLEMENTS, and
children - land where I live and bought of my father. Granddaughter,
FRANCES CLEMENTS; my son, ABRAHAM and his daughter, ELIZ. MARTIN; my
sons, BLUFORD and FENDALL MARTIN - land where JESSE CLEMENTS and son,
BLUFORD, live. Grandson, DILLARD MARTIN; my son, LEWIS, and my four
single daughters. Daughter of my daughter, KEZIAH; my little boy,
JAS. POWELL, to be set free at 18, but to remain with my son, ABRAHAM,
until then. Administrator's: friend, JAS. POWELL. Codicil: slave,
JAS. POWELL, to remain with the other twin children and with my
daughter, POLLY CLEMENTS, until 18.
Book 10, Page 244 -- Administrator's Bond.
Book 10, Page 262 -- Inventory -- several slaves; no total. Septem-
ber 12, 1840. RICH. SMITH, CHAS. TUCKER, ABSALOM HIGGINBOTHAM.

ABRAM MARTIN -- some are indexed ABRAHAM -- Book 17, Page 198 --
August 13, 1864, written; November 19, 1866, probated. Witnesses:
EDWIN S. WARE, CHAS. H. CHRISTIAN, CHAS. H. TUCKER; proved by WARE
and TUCKER. HENRY LOVING qualified; bondsman: N. C. TALIAFERRO.
Ux, FRANCES; my children; my daughters; children of my deceased sons,
JAS. and CHAS., until of age; Administrator: HENRY LOVING; daughters,
MARY ANN TUCKER and SOPHIA P. CAMPBELL.

CHAS. A. MARTIN -- Book 16, Page 401 -- Administrator's Bond -- LUCY A.
MARTIN and HENRY CAMPBELL, 19 October 1863, for LUCY MARTIN.

CYNTHIA MARTIN -- Book 6, Page 594 -- Guardian Bond -- THOS. TAYLOR
and ISAAC RUCKER, 18 April 1825, for THOS. TAYLOR as guardian of
CYNTHIA MARTIN - no parent set forth.

DAVID MARTIN -- Book 1, Page 96 -- November 6, 1766, written; March 2,
1767, probated. Witnesses: JNO. JOHNSON and ANN CROW. Blacksmith;
my natural mother, JENNET MARTIN, and heirs living in county of Down -

228

Carreagh and Parish of Cardonnal. Friend, WILLIAM SIMPSON. Proved
by witnesses and SIMPSON qualified; bondsmen: SAML. WOODS and ALEX.
PATTON.
Book 1, Page 109 -- Inventory -- 6 July 1767 -- L 14-16-0. JAS. DIN-
WIDDIE, SAML. SHANNON, THOS. SHANNON.

HENRY MARTIN, SR., CAPT. -- Book 3, Page 500 -- 22 September 1797,
written; 18 June 1798, probated. Witnesses: WM. FURBUSH, DANL. MOS-
BY. HUDSON, JAS., and SPARKS MARTIN qualified. Bondsmen: WM. HARRIS,
LANDON CABELL, JOS. ROBERTS. Son, GEO., where he lives and bought of
JNO. STAPLES - 265 acres; son, JAS. - at line of JOSHUA WILLOUGHBY and
RICH. C. POLLARD - place DR. HOPKINS bought of JOS. PAGE; my ux,
JUDITH - mill tract - children that she has with her. Son, SPARKS
MARTIN - 1/2 acre behind garden for cemetery; son, RICH. - my mill;
negro, BRISTOL, to choose master. My children: HENRY, WM., JOHN,
HUDSON, MARY HOPKINS, ANN SPARKS HOPKINS, ABIGAIL GREEN, SALLY H.
MARTIN; children of my daughter, JUDITH TANDY, who died in Kentucky;
children of my daughter, ELIZ. WARWICK; chancery suit pending vs. my
nephew, HENRY MARTIN, Great Britain; Administrators: son-in-law,
DR. JAS. HOPKINS, and sons, HUDSON, SPARKS, and JAS. MARTIN.
Book 4, Page 295 -- Administrator's Bond.

J. J. MARTIN -- Book 8, Page 49 -- October 12, 1830, written; November 15, 1830, probated. Witnesses: WM. TUCKER, JAS. ROBERTS, AMBR.
TOMLINSON. Son, JAS., when married; daughter, ROSANNA, when married;
daughter, NANCY PATTERSON; daughter, REBECCA LANGHORNE, gets nothing
for reasons known to myself; same as to daughter, LUCINDY LANGHORNE;
same as to son, MOSES (someone has tampered with this MOSES item and
has erased it, but still legible); daughter, SALLY LANGHORNE, while
single, but at marriage her part to JAS., ROSANNA, and SUSANNA RO-
BERTS. Administrator: WM. TUCKER.

J. W. MARTIN -- Book 16, Page 530 -- Administrator's Bond -- MARY C.
MARTIN and WM. FALLS, July 18, 1864, for MARY MARTIN.

JAS. MARTIN -- Book 1, Page 279 -- September 25, 1771, written;
March 6, 1775, probated. Witnesses: FRANS. MERIWETHER, WM. DEPRIEST,
SAML. COLWELL. Son, AZARIAH - 360 acres on north branch Rockfish
where I live; sons, JNO., WM., JAS., DAVID MARTIN; son-in-law, WM.
TERIL LEWIS; son-in-law, THOS. ANTHONY; my son, OBADIAH MARTIN.
Administrators: sons, WM., JAMES, and AZARIAH MARTIN.
Book 1, Page 282 -- Administrator's Bond -- Administrators named
qualified on probate date. Bondsmen: CHAS. RODES, WM. LOVING, JNO.
THURMOND.
Book 1, Page 284 -- Inventory -- April 3, 1775; no total; JNO. GILMER;
FRANS. MERIWETHER; DAVID MERIWETHER.
Book 6, Page 404 -- September 27, 1823, written; November 17, 1823,
probated. Witnesses: WM. GATEWOOD, VARLAND RICHESON, JNO. RICHESON.
JESSE RICHESON qualified; bondsman: ABRAM CARTER. Ux, NANCY; daugh-
ter, JUDAH MARTIN - 77 acres bearing date of March 17, 1762; son,
CHAS. - balance of survey not deeded to JAS. MARTIN. One ninth to
each of these: REUBEN, CHAS., JAS. T., JUDAH MARTIN, THOS. SANDS
(LANDS?), AMBROSE TOMLINSON, GEO. HARRISON; children of ELIZ. NEW -
2 children of ELIZ. crossed out and name of JUDAH above; BELINDA and
MATILDA MARTIN. Son, OBADIAH, has received his part and his children
have no claim; CLAIBORNE HOWARD and ux, SALLY, are to receive no part
for reasons best known to myself; same as to my son, PETER MARTIN.
Administrators: Son, JAS. T. MARTIN, and JESSE RICHESON.
Book 6, Page 406 -- Administrator's Bond.
Book 6, Page 434 -- Inventory -- no total. JNO. WARE, JNO. D. CRAW-
FORD, ABRAM CARTER, January 19, 1824.
Book 6, Page 626 -- Administrator's Account by RICHESON from Janu-
ary 22, 1824 - to MRS. NANCY MARTIN; Shoemaker's note transferred.
Commissioner: CHAS. BARRET; October 17, 1825.
Book 6, Page 747 -- Administrator's Bond -- JACOB PHILLIPS and SAML.
GARLAND, March 20, 1827, for JACOB PHILLIPS.

JAS. M. MARTIN -- Book 16, Page 363 -- Inventory exhibited by family, March 15, 1860: $701.00, JAS. S. RICHESON; J. R. BROWN; RUFUS COLE- MAN. Sale by RO. W. SNEAD, Sheriff and administrator, August 13, 1863. Family buyers: JAS. M. MARTIN, JR., and NANCY MARTIN - $721.00.

JNO. MARTIN -- Book 2, Page 194 -- Administrator's Bond -- SARAH MARTIN, JNO. HENDERSON, LANGSDON DEPRIEST, October 4, 1784, for SARAH MARTIN.
Book 2, Page 216 -- Inventory -- March 7, 1785; no total; WM. SIMPSON; JNO. McCLURE; LANGDSON DEPRIEST.
Book 5, Page 490 -- Administrator's Bond -- ABRAHAM MARTIN and JOSIAH MARTIN, March 20, 1815, for ABRAHAM MARTIN.
Book 5, Page 499 -- Inventory -- $25.96, March 29, 1815, by EATON and ENOCH CARPENTER.
Book 8, Page 239 -- Guardian Bond -- EDWD. W. G. WINGFIELD; ROVINA L. MARTIN; and JOSEPH F. WINGFIELD, August 20, 1832, for EDWD. WINGFIELD as guardian of JNO., WM., and NANCY MARTIN, orphans of JAS. MARTIN.

JNO. J. MARTIN -- Book 11, Page 65 -- Estate Commitment to Sheriff, November, 1841; motion of JNO. PRYOR; Sheriff: NELSON CRAWFORD.

SHEROD MARTIN -- Book 4, Page 147 -- May 3, 1803, written; June 18, 1804, probated. Witnesses: ELIJAH L. WILLIAMS, CHAS. SMITH, WM. FOX. Son, SHEROD; son, GEO., and his oldest son, JOS. MARTIN, and his son, THOS., when they are of age; my gun, commonly called "Jeoffrey"; my son, JOS., and his two oldest sons, SHEROD and JAS. - land near Irving's Road and Rockfish Gap Road to widow HENDERSON's. Grandson, MARSHALL INNIS, son of WM. INNIS - mountain plantation next to RICH. RICHARDSON and where my son, SHEROD, and WM. INNIS built a warehouse last year - line of CHAS. SMITH; granddaughter, DECCA INNIS - slaves to stay with her parents as long as either of them lives; grandson, JEOFFREY MARTIN, son of MOLLY MARTIN; daughter, SALLY, where she lives and at her death to grandson, JEOFFREY MARTIN. My ux, MARY - land to where JAS. SHIELDS lives from top of Stoney Hill. Our son, ELISHA's, child or children. Mare bought of THOS. D'PRIEST. Grandson, REUBEN MARTIN, son of ELISHA MARTIN; my four grandchildren: JOS., GEO., ELISHA, and SHEROD MARTIN. Executors: friends, CAPT. AZARIAH MARTIN and HUDSON MARTIN and my sons, SHEROD and GEO. MARTIN.
Book 4, Page 174 -- Inventory -- June 14, 1805; CHAS. SMITH, CHAS. BRIDGWATER, RO. HENDERSON.
Book 4, Page 396 -- Administrator's Bond -- GEO. and HUDSON MARTIN and THRUSTON DICKERSON, December 17, 1804, for GEO. MARTIN. This is indexed for THOS. MARTIN, but in document it appears to be SHD. MARTIN.

STEVEN MARTIN -- Book 1, Page 399 -- December 15, 1768, written; August 7, 1769, probated. Witnesses: FRANS MERIWETHER, JAS. MARTIN, WM. HENDERSON. Son, JNO.; my ux, ANNE; son, GIDEON - land by BEN CRAWFORD; SIMPSON's branch; JNO. MARTIN; GIDEON's plantation. Son, STEPHEN; my daughter, ANN SMITH; daughter, ELIZ. GRAGG; daughter, MARY MARTIN; my son, SHEROD MARTIN. Administrator: WM. MARTIN.
Book 1, Page 140 -- Administrator's Bond -- WM. MARTIN, HENRY KEY, JNO. JACOBS, August 7, 1769, for WM. MARTIN.
Book 1, Page 152 -- Inventory -- no total; November 6, 1769. ALEX. PATTON, JNO. MARTIN, SHEROD MARTIN.
Book 1, Page 198 -- Administrator's Account by administrator - lega- tees: WM. GRAGG, DAVID MARTIN, SHEROD MARTIN, RO. McWHORTER, GIDEON MARTIN, STEPHEN MARTIN, ANN SMITH, JNO. MARTIN. Committee: FRANCIS MERIWETHER; ALEX. REID, JR.; July 1, 1771.
Book 4, Page 392 -- Administrator's Bond -- STEPHEN MARTIN and JAS. BROOKS, February 18, 1805, for STEPHEN MARTIN.

T.F.A. MARTIN -- Book 13, Page 30 -- Minister's Bond -- October 18, 1852; Protestant Episcopal Church. Bondsman: HENRY L. DAVIES.

WM. MARTIN, SR. -- Book 8, Page 209 -- March 8, 1832, written; May 21, 1832, probated. Witnesses: WILLIS GILLESPIE, CHAS. TUCKER, ANDREW HAMBLETON. August 20, 1832, administrators named refused to qualify and EDWD. W. G. WINGFIELD qualified. Bondsmen: ROBINA L. MARTIN and JOS. F. WINGFIELD. Ux and children of my son, JAS. H.

MARTIN: ROBINA L.; SOPHIA HAMBLETON; WM.; NANCY; JNO. and SUSAN
MARTIN - ux and five children of JAS. H. MARTIN. Free from his debts
or control. To be divided to all save ux and children - of WM. as
he received share during my life. Administrators: friends: JAS. F.
THORNTON and JAS. HAMBLETON.
Book 8, Page 239 -- Administrator's Bond -- ROVINA here.
Book 8, Page 389 -- Sale -- October 18, 1832 - buyers: JNO. H.;
MRS. ROBINA; MONTRIVILLE HAMBLETON; ANDREW HAMBLETON - $209.71-1/2.
January 20, 1834.
Book 9, Page 27 -- Administrator's Account from December 18, 1832,
ANDREW HAMBLETON for coffin - $3.00; to ROBINA MARTIN, November 23,
1833. DABNEY SANDIDGE; RICH. SMITH, JR.; CORL. SALE.

WM. MARTIN, JR. -- Book 7, Page 218 -- Administrator's Bond -- JNO.
LANGHORNE, JR., and WM. MARTIN, March 17, 1829, for JNO. LANGHORNE.
Book 7, Page 240 -- Inventory -- March 26, 1829 - $113.25. ABSALOM
HIGGINBOTHAM, CHAS. TUCKER, CORNL. SALE.

WM. W. MARTIN -- Book 15, Page 331 -- Constable -- District 4,
Jun 18, 1860. Bondsmen: PETER G. JOINER and GEO. H. DAMERON.
Book 15, Page 451 -- Same -- August 20, 1860; same bondsmen.
Book 16, Page 229 -- Constable -- March 16, 1863. Bondsmen: HOWARD
MARTIN, JAS. D. MARTIN, and two bondsmen above.

ANN MASON -- Book 12, Page 132 -- Administrator's Bond -- JNO. MASON
and HOLEMAN JOPLING, August 21, 1848, for JNO. MASON.

JAS. H. MASON -- Book 17, Page 27 -- Administrator's Bond -- SAML. W.
MASON and EDWD. TURNER, March 29, 1865, for SAML. MASON.

SAML. W. MASON -- Book 14, Page 55 -- Notary Public -- so indexed,
but not there. It is Book 15, Page 55, W. H. QUINN, bondsman, December 20, 1858.

CHAS. W. MASSIE -- Book 13, Page 49 -- Guardian Bond -- JNO., EDMUND,
and ELI MASSIE, February 21, 1853, for JNO. MASSIE as guardian of
CHAS. MASSIE, orphan of SALLY MASSIE, deceased.
Book 13, Page 226 -- Guardian Bond -- JNO. F. CAMDEN and W. A. RICHE-
SON, July 18, 1853, for JNO. CAMDEN as guardian of CHAS. W. MASSIE,
orphan of SALLY MASSIE, deceased.

JESSE MASSIE or JESSIE -- Book 9, Page 431 -- Trustee bond for
JESSE MASSIE with bondsman, JNO. W. BROADDUS -- JESSE MASSIE as trustee of PAMELA MASSIE and children.

JNO. MASSIE -- Book 4, Page 5 -- Inventory -- April 6, 1801 -
L 41-3-6. WM. MOSS; (LANDRUM ?); THOS. MAYS.
Book 4, Page 328 -- Administrator's Bond -- SUSANNA MASSIE(EY); JNO.
CAMDEN; HENRY CAMPBELL, January 16, 1801, for SUSANNA MASSIE.
Book 4, Page 623 -- Inventory -- Various debts owed; money in hands
of administratrix. WM. MOORE, JAS. CAMDEN, JNO. CAMDEN, WM. EVANS.
Book 9, Page 432 -- JNO. MASSIE, SR., and JR.; CHAS. CAMPBELL and
CHAS. MASSIE and as trustee for JNO. MASSIE, SR., of SALLY MASSIE
and children, March 20, 1838.

JNO. MATLOCK -- Book 1, Page 91 -- Administrator's Bond -- NEILL
CAMPBELL and HUGH ROSE, February 2, 1767, for NEILL CAMPBELL.
Book 1, Page 102 -- Inventory -- L 110-16-7-1/2. WM. WALTON, W. HANS-
BROUGH, DAVID PROPHET. Don February 5, 1767; recorded March 3, 1767.

JNO. MATTHEWS -- Book 4, Pag- 316 -- Guardian Bond -- THOS. NASH and
LANDON CABELL, July 16, 1798, for THOS. NASH as guardian of JNO.
MATTHEWS, orphan of WM. MATTHEWS.

LUCY MATTHEWS -- Book 4, Page 319 -- Guardian Bond -- JNO. FOX and
GEO. OZBOURN, February 17, 1800, for JNO. FOX as guardian of LUCY
MATTHEWS, orphan of -----.

THOS. MATTHEWS -- Book 2, Page 233 -- August 16, 1783, written;

June 6, 1785, probated. Witnesses: JAS. and JNO. TURNER and
STEPHEN TURNER. Daughter, SARAH MATTHEWS; daughter, ELIZ. MATTHEWS;
Ux, ELIZ. Sons, JNO. and THOS. - rest of land. Ux to administer.
Page 234 -- Administrator's Bond -- for ELIZ.; bondsman: JAS. TURNER.
Book 2, Page 245 -- Inventory -- September 9, 1785 - JAS. TURNER,
MATT. NIGHTINGALE, MATT. PHILLIPS.

ALFRED A. MAYS -- Book 8, Page 343 -- Guardian Bond -- CHAS. MAYS;
bondsmen: LEWIS MAYS and WILLIS M. REYNOLDS, August 20, 1833, for
CHAS. MAYS as guardian of ALFRED A., LEWIS S., MATILDA JANE, SUSAN ANN
and OLIVER J. MAYS, infants of CHAS. MAYS.

CHAS. MAYS -- Book 12, Page 136 -- Administrator's Bond -- CHAS.
MAYS and JAS. W. KEITH, October 16, 1848, for CHAS. MAYS.
Book 12, Page 154 -- Administrator's Bond -- JESSE T. DUIGUID and
WM. L. (S.) DUIGUID; S. DUIGUID and GEO. S. DUIGUID, March 18, 1849,
for JESSE DUIGUID.
Book 12, Page 156 -- Guardian Bond -- JESSE T. DUIGUID, WM. S.,
SAMSON, and GEO. S. DUIGUID, March 19, 1849, for JESSE T. DUIGUID
as guardian of CHAS. J. MAYS, orphan of CHAS. MAYS.
Book 12, Page 164 -- February 8, 1849, written; March 19, 1849, pro-
bated. Witnesses: D. STAPLES; JAS. W. MAYS; JNO. W. MAYS; RICH. H.
ANDERSON. JESSE T. DUIGUID qualified; bondsmen: W. S., SAMSON, and
GEO. S. DUIGUID. Ux, SARAH, 334 acres where I live and slaves;
youngest son, CHAS. JOS. - mill and tract of 161-1/2 acres to my
eight children - when youngest is of age. My five children: ALFRED
A.; LEWIS L.; MATILDA JANE DUIGUID; SUSAN ANN MAYS; and OLIVER J.
MAYS. My three youngest: ELIJAH B.; SARAH ANN ELIZ. MAYS and CHAS.
JOS. MAYS. Land left to me by ELIJAH MAYS, Nelson County. Adminis-
trators: Son, LEWIS L.; and son-in-law, JESSE T. DUIGUID.
Book 12, Page 172 -- Inventory -- March 21, 1849; slaves at $5,950;
furniture at $6,108.50. WM. KENT, CHAS. P. LEE, JNO. M. WILLIAMS,
D. STAPLES. Recorded July 16, 1849.
Book 12, Page 217 -- Division -- Children by first marriage are all
of age - residue to ALFRED A. MAYS, LEWIS L. MAYS, JESSE DUIGUID,
SUSAN A. MAYS, OLIVER J. MAYS, ELIZ. D. MAYS - note discrepancies
in initials of some heirs - SARAH B. and A; OLIVER A. and OLIVER J.
Same committee, August 20, 1849.
Book 12, Page 543 -- Inventory and Sale and legacies to ELIJAH MAYS;
LEWIS L. MAYS; OLIVER J. MAYS; JESSE T. DUIGUID; MADISON MAYS; ALFRED
A. MAYS; BENJ. F. HOWL, JR.; and ux, SARAH A. E., and guardian of
CHAS. J. MAYS. Very long. Recorded July 19, 1852.

ELIZ. MAYS -- Book 4, Page 65 -- Report of land sale, May or June,
1818. JOS. B. MAYS bought it for $415.00. Sold by WM. DUNCAN, JAS.
W. TRIBBLE, and ABSALOM HIGGINBOTHAM for infant children.

GEO. S. MAYS -- Book 17, Page 30 -- July 12, 1858, written; codicil
of November 26, 1864; February 20, 1865, probated. Witnesses to
will: GEO. VAUGHAN, JAS. POWELL, SAML. M. GARLAND. Witnesses to
codicil: RO. A. COGHILL, BETTY WHITE, SAML. SCOTT, G.A.R. TUCKER.
JAS. W. KEITH and NICHL. MAYS qualified., Ux, ELIZ. L. - my lands -
CRAWFORD tract and where my house is located. Son, NICHL.; daughter,
CARY ANN KEITH and children; son-in-law, JAS. W. KEITH - two grandchildren - children of NICHL. MAYS - are living with me. Executors:
son and son-in-law. Codicil: slaves to my ux; children of my son,
NICHL.: GEO. W. and BETTIE SUSAN MAYS. Other children of NICHL.

HARRISON H. MAYS -- Book 16, Page 459 -- Pages 457 and 458 are missing
in book, but probably mistake in numbering by some clerk as no note
is made of missing pages. Administrator's Bond -- HENRY T. GREGORGY(?)
and SAML. J. TURNER, March 21, 1864, for HENRY GREGORGY.

JAS. W. MAYS -- Book 16, Page 532 -- Constable -- July 18, 1864;
elected District 2 on May 26, 1864. Bondsmen: WILSON B. MAYS and
RO. A. PENDLETON.

JNO. MAYS -- Book 6, Page 142 -- September 20, 1815, written; May 16,
1820, probated. Witnesses: ABRAM, WM., and CREED C. CARTER and

ANDREW YOUNG. JOS. CARTER qualified. Bondsmen: WM. BOURNE and
ABRAM CARTER. Ux, FRANCES; ten of my children: JOS., GEO., SAML.,
LARKIN, JOSHUA, BETSY HAMBLETON, RACHEL RUSEL, LUCY DEAN, POLLY DEAN,
FRANCES TULY - one shilling to JNO. MAYS and MILLY HAMBLETON. Ad-
ministrators: JOS. R. CARTER, GIDEON C. GOODRICH, RO. H. CARTER.
Page 143 -- Administrator's Bond.
Book 6, Page 144 -- Inventory of $1,889.29-1/2: PETER P. THORNTON,
NELSON CRAWFORD, WM. COLEMAN, June 19, 1820.
Book 6, Page 554 -- Administrator's Account from 1820 - to GEO. MAYS;
JNO. RUSSELL; suit of DONALD vs. MAYS; CHAS. TULEY, JOSHUA MAYS;
SAML. P. MAYS. It is stated that 10 legatees got $268.45 each.
February 15, 1825. JNO. PRYOR, GIDEON C. GOODRICH, WM. COLEMAN.
Book 6, Page 753 -- Administrator's Account from 1824: PETER P.
THORNTON, WILL JOPLING, JNO. PRYOR, committee. Recorded March 16,
1827.

JNO. D. MAYS -- Book 22, Page 30 -- Constable -- Elon District,
January 30, 1888. Bondsmen: J. P. MAYS, WM. N. PROFFITT, J. W. MAYS.

JNO. F. MAYS -- Book 15, Page 250 -- Indexed as Book 14, Page 250 --
Administrator's Bond -- WM. A. MAYS and JAS. L. MAYS, September 19,
1859, for WM. MAYS.

JNO. J. MAYS -- Book 8, Page 51 -- Guardian Bond -- ROBT. and THOS.
WINGFIELD, November 15, 1830, for ROBT. WINGFIELD as guardian of
JNO. J.; ROBT. H.; EDITHA and EDWIN MAYS, orphans of PIERCE W. MAYS,
deceased.
Book 8, Pages 65 and 69 are indexed for him, but these are for JNO.
MOUNTCASTLE and no MAYS data thereon.

JOS. MAYS, SR. -- Book 3, Page 498 -- January 7, 1797, written;
June 18, 1798, probated. Witnesses: JNO. COONEY; JAS. EDMONDS, JR.;
PETER CAMPBELL. Son, JNO.; son, JAS.; daughter, LYDIA MAYS, ux of
JAS. WALTERS; sons, JOS. and ELIJAH - Juniper Creek land; daughter,
JEMIMA HOLLINGSWORTH; son, JESSE; son, CHAS. - Tye River land. Son,
ELIJAH; son, ROBT.; son, MOSES; son, LEWIS. My ux, SARAH - where I
live - my mill. Administrators: friends: JAS. EDMUNDS, JNO. DIL-
LARD and CHAS. WATTS. They qualified. Bondsmen: SAML. EDMUNDS and
MOSES MAYS.
Book 3, Page 530 -- Inventory -- December 15, 1798 - L 217-15-9: JOS.
LOVING, JNO. THOMPSON, SAML. EDMUNDS.
Book 4, Page 151 -- Administrator's Account -- JAS. EDMUNDS from
July 16, 1798. WARE's suit; "2 or 3 years attendance at court";
JESSE MAYS' bond; Clerk notes at close that it is account of STEPHEN
WATTS, one of administrators. Recorded July 15, 1804.
Book 4, Page 299 -- Administrator's Bond -- JAS. EDMUNDS, JNO. DIL-
LARD, CHAS. WATTS, SAML. EDMUNDS and MOSES MAYS, June 17, 1798, for
first three to administer.
Book 10, Page 58 -- Estate Commitment to Sheriff -- October term,
1838; motion of BLUFORD CAMDEN; JNO. COLEMAN, Sheriff.

MARIA MAYS -- Book 2, Page 341 -- so indexed, but found in Book 6,
Page 341 -- Guardian Bond -- JESSE MAYS and JNO. FULCHER, December 16,
1822, for JESSE MAYS as guardian of MARIA MAYS, orphan of PIERCE W.
MAYS, deceased.

MARTHA ANN MAYS -- Book 11, Page 335 -- Guardian Bond -- WM. M. WALLER
and SAML. M. GARLAND, August 19, 1845, for WM. WALLER as guardian of
MARTHA ANN MAYS and RUFUS ANDERSON MAYS, orphans of WILLIS MAYS.

NANCY MAYS -- Book 6, Page 697 -- Guardian Bond -- JOS. B. MAYS and
JAS. FULCHER, October 15, 1826, for JOS. MAYS as guardian of NANCY W.;
BEVERLY W.; TALIAFERRO W. and RO. B. MAYS, orphans of JOS. B. MAYS.
Book 6, Page 692 -- Guardian's Account -- JOS. B. MAYS as guardian of
infants of ELIZ. MAYS, deceased: NANCY W., etc., as above - SAML.
MILLER for tuition for NANCY W.; tuition to WM. WAUGH for BEVERLY,
September 18, 1826. WM.DUNCAN and WM. TUCKER, committee.

ROBT. MAYS -- Book 4, Page 519 -- June 3, 1806, written; July 18,
1808, probated. Witnesses: CHAS. and PETER TALIAFERRO; JAS.

233

CLEMENTS. CHAS. TUCKER, JNO. SMITH. and PEARCE MAYS qualified;
bondsmen: JNO. CRAWFORD and JNO. FULCHER. Son, JESSE - 100 acres
bought of WM. TUCKER and where JESSE has built; son, PEARCE MAYS;
ux, SUSANNAH MAYS - where I live; sons, JOS. B. and BALLENGER MAYS;
daughter, POLLY MAYS. Administrators as in Administrator's Bond
above - Page 520.
Book 4, Page 531 -- Inventory -- L 551-19-10, BARTLETT CASH, WM.
SANDIDGE, JNO. BALL.
Book 7, Page 10 -- Administrator's de bonis Bond -- June 18, 1827:
WM. M. WALLER and JNO. FULCHER for WM. WALLER.

SAML. H. MAYS -- Book 12, Page 227 -- Guardian Bond -- ANDERSON MAYS
and WM. JAS. WILLS,October 15, 1849, for ANDERSON MAYS as guardian
of SAML. H.; CORNELIUS; WM.; JNO. L. (S.) and MORRISON MAYS, orphans
of SAML. MAYS, deceased.

ELIZ. H. McBRIDE -- Book 5, Page 703 -- Guardian Bond -- ELIZ.
McBRIDE, REUBEN NORVELL and JAMES DILLARD, 16 March 1818, for ELIZ.
McBRIDE as guardian of ELIZ. H. McBRIDE, orphan of JOHN McBRIDE.

JNO. McBRIDE -- Book 5, Page 459 -- Administrator's Bond -- JAS. S.
DILLARD and JAS. DILLARD, September 19, 1814, for JAS. S. DILLARD.
Book 5, Page 477 -- Inventory -- $825.13, October 22, 1814. DAVID
TINSLEY, NELSON C. and PLEASANT DAWSON.
Book 7, Page 131 -- Administrator's Account by JAS. S. DILLARD from
January 1, 1815 - to widow for the family; Lynchburg and Amherst
County fees; to SARAH PIERCE; suits mentioned: Appeal by HENRY H.
WATTS. January 18, 1828. Held over and recorded May 19, 1828.

HUGH McCABE -- Book 1, Page 433 -- Administrator's Bond -- SARAH
McCABE, JOS. HIGGINBOTHAM, RICH. BALLINGER and JNO. SANDIDGE, Au-
gust 3, 1778, for SARAH McCABE.
Book 1, Page 445 -- Inventory -- L 216-4-6, October 30, 1778. CHAS.
ISON, WM. HIGGINBOTHAM, WALTER POWER.

WM. McCALL -- Book 7, Page 272 -- Division of estate of WM. MOORE,
December 15, 1827, by committee - not named. WM. McCALL got 2
slaves; RO. PAGE got 3; ROYAL McCALL got 2 - all in right of wives.
Independent Bond to HILL CARTER, administrator of WM. MOORE. Witnesses: S. CLAIBORNE. Recorded August 19, 1829.

ANGUS McCLOUD (McCLOUT) -- Book 4, Page 535 -- Administrator's Bond --
ANGUS McCLOUD and JNO. H. CLEMENTS, October 17, 1808. Bondsmen:
JAS. SANDIDGE and WM. TOMLINSON. Indexed McCLOUD, but spelled McCLOUT.

JAS. McCLURE -- Book 2, Page 244 -- Administrator's Bond -- ISAAC
McCLURE, JNO. MONTGOMERY, AUGUSTUS SMITH, October 3, 1785, for
ISAAC McCLURE.
Book 2, Page 251 -- Administrator's Bond -- JNO. McCLURE and JNO.
HENDERSON, November 7, 1785, for JNO. McCLURE.

EDWD. McCORMICK -- Book 18, Page 413 -- May 11, 1861, written; July 12,
1870, probated. Proved by PROVENCE McCORMICK and SAML. J. C. MOORE
and on next day by MRS. E. L. McCORMICK who qualified - both at
special meetings of court. Of Clermond County, Virginia - ux, ELLEN
L.; my children; ux to administer and be guardian of children.

RODERICK McCULLOCH -- Book 6, Page 701 -- Administrator's Bond --
WM. H. McCULLOCH, RICH. L. ELLIS, and MARTIN PARKS, November 20, 1826,
for WM. McCULLOCH.
Book 6, Page 703 -- October 17, 1826, written; November 20, 1826,
probated. Witnesses: GEO. L. SHRADER, JAS. P. (T.) REYNOLDS, CHAS. L.
DAVIS. Stricken in years; son, RODERICK H. (This has been scratched
and ROBT. appears above, but I find no ROBT. in data and think it is
RODERICK); daughter, FRANCES SHACKELFORD; my 4 daughters: MARY THORN-
TON, ELIZ. DAVIS, ISABELLA WAUGH, NANCY E. GLASGOW - small tract of
400 acres, patent burned. Grandson, RODERICK H. McCULLOCH; son,
WM. H. to administer.
Book 6, Page 742 -- Inventory -- no total; many slaves, December 1,
1826. JAS. DAVIS, CHAS. L. DAVIS, GEO. MORRIS.

Book 8, Page 55 -- Administrator's Account from November, 1826, to CARTER and WAUGH. Recorded June 21, 1830. THOS. N. EUBANK, JAS. DAVIS, CHAS. L. BARRET.

WM. H. McCULLOCH -- Book 5, Page 82 -- Commissioner of Revenue, September 16, 1811. Bondsmen: PETER P. THORNTON and BENJ. SHACKELFORD.

AMBROSE McDANIEL -- Book 15, Page 253 -- Administrator's Bond -- RO. and ZACH. D. TINSLEY, November 21, 1859, for RO. TINSLEY.
Book 15, Page 259 -- March 13, 1857; probated Barren County, Kentucky, November 21, 1858. Witnesses: R. C. SNODDY and G. B. ELLIS; handwriting of SNODDY by JAS. H. LEWIS. Certified by TRAVIS COCKRILL, Clerk of Court, April 22, 1859; W. R. FERREN, County Judge; recorded Amherst County, Monday, November 21, 1859. RO. TINSLEY qualified as above. Ux, MARY; M.; sons, GIDEON, DABNEY, and LINDSEY D.; my children: LUCINDA WILLIAMS; WM. H.; JNO. T.; TAMSEY J. HAZLETT. Administrator: JNO. G. ROGERS.
Book 16, Page 270 -- Administrator's Account by TINSLEY from November 21, 1859; decree in DANL. vs. McDANIEL. From L. McDANIEL under the suit. Recorded April 20, 1863.

ANN McDANIEL -- Book 12, Page 470 -- Administrator's Bond -- JNO. S. McDANIEL and PAULUS POWELL, 17 November 1851, for JNO. McDANIEL.

BENJ. McDANIEL -- Book 17, Page 29 -- Guardian Bond -- JNO. S. McDANIEL and NELSON SEAY, 20 March 1865, for JNO. McDANIEL as guardian of BENJ. McDANIEL; no parent set forth.

CHAS. L. McDANIEL -- Book 17, Page 145 -- Constable Bond -- District 4; elected 24 May 1866. Bondsmen: WM. H. McDANIEL and THOS. J. M. GOODWIN.

FRANCIS McDANIEL -- Book 11, Page 451 -- Guardian Bond -- JNO. S. McDANIEL and ANTHONY R. OGDEN, November 16, 1846, for JNO. McDANIEL as guardian of FRANCIS; JNO.; NANCY; MARY; and BENJ. McDANIEL, orphans of REBECCA ANN McDANIEL, deceased.

GEORGE McDANIEL, JR. -- Various Tobacco Inspector Bonds -- Book 3, Page 258 -- December 17, 1792; bondsman: JNO. McDANIEL - Amherst Warehouse.
Book 3, Page 406 -- September 19, 1796; bondsman: ZACH. DAWSON.
Book 3, Page 513 -- October 16, 1797; bondsman: AMBR. RUCKER.
Book 3, Page 518 -- September; bondsman: WM. WARE.

GEO. McDANIEL, SR. -- Book 6, Page 267 -- Administrator's Bond -- DABNEY WARE, NELSON C. DAWSON, SPENCER NORVELL, JNO. WARE, and AMBR. RUCKER, December 17, 1821, for DABNEY WARE and NELSON C. DAWSON.
Book 6, Page 270 -- May 28, 1818, written; December 17, 1821, probated. Witnesses: WILLIS BURKS, CHAS. P. LEE, THOS. EUBANK, DABNEY WARE. Confirms all previous gifts of slaves and money to children and grandchildren. Tried last fall to distribute L 8,000, but not in my power to make it out on proportinate (sic) basis. Have receipts to date. Daughter, NANCY TINSLEY; my ----- GEO. McDANIEL; 8 shares for children and grandchildren; heirs of deceased daughter, MARGARET BURFORD; son, JNO. McDANIEL; son, GEO.; heirs of deceased daughter, LUCY TINSLEY - stock in former Bank of Virginia reserved for my afflicted negro woman. AMBR. RUCKER to get dividends for attending to this. Administrators: friends: DABNEY WARE, JAS. WARE, NELSON C. DAWSON.
Book 8, Page 329 -- Administrator's de bonis non Bond -- July 15, 1833. HENRY QUARLES, WM. and LINDSEY McDANIEL for HENRY QUARLES.
Book 9, Page 340 -- Same bond and men on October 16, 1837.
Book B, Page 70 -- Administrator's de bonis non Bond -- JNO. B. ROBERTSON and SAML. M. GARLAND, September 3, 1858, for JNO. ROBERTSON.
Book B, Page 91 -- Administrator's Account by ROBERTSON from November 5, 1859; McDANIEL vs. McDANIEL. Recorded March, 1866.

JNO. McDANIEL -- Book 7, Page 42 -- Guardian Bond -- GEO. McDANIEL, ABROSE McDANIEL, and THOS. STRANGE, 15 October 1827, for GEO. McDANIEL as guardian of JOS., JNO., PRESTON, and MARY McDANIEL, infants of

GEO. McDANIEL.
Book 10, Page 77 -- Administrator's Bond -- LINDSEY McDANIEL, SAML.
WATTS, WINSTON WOODROOF, and HENRY W. QUARLES, 18 February 1839, for
LINDSEY McDANIEL. Will of June 3, 1835, written; February 18, 1839,
probated. Proved by JAS. POWELL and RO. TINSLEY. Greatly advanced in
years; my six children: AMBROSE, LINDSEY, GIDEON, BETSY DAVIS, PEGGY
WARE, SOPHIA STRANGE. My four children: WM., GEO., MARY JONES, and
JUDITH HEISKELL had their shares thirty odd years ago. Administrator:
son, LINDSEY McDANIEL.
Book 10, Page 154 -- Inventory -- no total; March 12, 1839. J. R.
McDANIEL, NATHAN D. RUCKER, BENJ. OGDEN.
Book 10, Page 204 -- Administrator's Bond -- WM. McDANIEL, SAML.
WATTS, HENRY W. QUARLES, and WM. McDANIEL (Note 2), February 17, 1840,
for WM. McDANIEL.
Book 14, Page 480 -- Guardian Bond -- H. E. SMITH and PETER FLOOD,
December 21, 1857, for H. SMITH as guardian of JNO., ROBT., FANNIE,
MARY, FIELDING, EDWD. McDANIEL, children of WM. McDANIEL.

LINDSEY McDANIEL -- Book 9, Page 350 -- Guardian Bond -- DABNEY SAN-
DIDGE, RANDOLPH CASH, November 21, 1837, for DABNEY SANDIDGE as
guardian of LINDSEY D., GEO., and GIDEON McDANIEL, orphans of OLIVE
McDANIEL.
Book 10, Page 192 -- Administrator's Bond -- JNO. R. McDANIEL, WM.
McDANIEL, JAS. P. McDANIEL and SAML. WATTS, January 20, 1840, for
JNO. R. McDANIEL.
Book 10, Page 193 -- July 13, 1836, written; January 20, 1840, pro-
bated. Handwriting by RO. TINSLEY, HENRY W. QUARLES, and ELIJAH
FLETCHER. Aged father, JNO. McDANIEL, is to be supported; slaves
named and to be freed and sent from Virginia with $1,000.00 from land
sale. My brothers, WM., GEO., AMBROSE, GIDEON and my sisters, MARY
JONES, JUDY HEISKELL, BETSY DAVIES, PEGGY WARE, and SOPHIA STRANGE.
Administrator: nephew, JNO. R. McDANIEL. Codicil of October 3,
1836 - administrator to have ten 10%.
Book 10, Page 213 -- Inventory of $8,100.75, April 20, 1840. PROSSER
POWELL, WILKINS WATSON, NATHAN D. RUCKER, BENJ. OGDEN.
Book 13, Page 69 -- Guardian's Account -- WM. McDANIEL from Septem-
ber 16, 1838 - account of PHILIP McDANIEL is also with it. From
JNO. R. McDANIEL your interest in sales of real estate of JAS. PENDLE-
TON; also account of SOPHIA McDANIEL.
Page 74 -- JNO. R. McDANIEL, administrator of WM. McDANIEL, deceased,
who was guardian of LINDSEY; PHILIP B. and SOPHIA B. McDANIEL --
SOPHIA B. by husband, H. A. TURNER. LINDSEY in person. Guardian
gave bond, September 17, 1838. Bondsmen: JAS. P., JNO. R., and
WM. McDANIEL and NATHAN GLENN and HENRY W. QUARLES.

PHILIP McDANIEL -- Book 10, Page 50 -- Guardian Bond -- WM.; LINDSEY
McDANIEL and HENRY W. QUARLES, 17 September 1838, for WM. McDANIEL
as guardian of PHILIP and SOPHIA McDANIEL, orphans of ELIZ. McDANIEL,
deceased. On same page and parties for WM. as guardian of LINDSEY,
JR., and MARY ANN McDANIEL, orphans of ELIZ.

PRESTON McDANIEL -- Book 8, Page 444 -- Guardian Bond -- JAS. S.
HIGGINBOTHAM and JNO. PENN, November 18, 1834, for JAS. HIGGINBOTHAM
as guardian of PRESTON G. McDANIEL, son of GEO. McDANIEL.
Book 9, Page 61 -- Order of Court to divide slaves between PRESTON G.
and WILLIAM WARE who married MARY JANE McDANIEL, 17 March 1835.
CORNL. SALE, R. HENLEY, TANDY RUTHERFORD - quite faded page.

REBECCA ANN McDANIEL -- Book 11, Page 452 -- Administrator's Bond --
JNO. S. McDANIEL and ANTHONY R. OGDEN, November 16, 1846, for
JNO. McDANIEL.

SARAH McDANIEL -- Book B, Page 71 -- This is hard to decipher: HENRY
E. SMITH and GEO. HYLTON to CHAS. L. McDANIEL; SALLIE McDANIEL; WM.
McDANIEL; and WILLIAM ALLEN to Commonwealth of Virginia, August 27,
1858. Circuit Court decree of 23 August 1858, in Tucker's executors
vs. STOREY and Children. CHAS. McDANIEL was appointed trustee of
SARAH McDANIEL and children.

TAMSEY JANE McDANIEL -- Book 8, Page 50 -- Guardian Bond -- AMBROSE

McDANIEL and DABNEY SANDIDGE, 15 November 1830, for AMBROSE McDANIEL as guardian of TAMSEY JANE, JNO., DABNEY, LINDSEY, GEORGE, and GIDEON McDANIEL, infants of AMBROSE McDANIEL.

W. H. McDANIEL -- Book 19, Page 188 -- Administrator's Bond -- SALLIE McDANIEL, widow, and WM. A. McDANIEL, 21 August 1876, for SALLIE McDANIEL.
Book 19, Page 207 -- Inventory -- October 13, 1876 - $236.30. JOS. A. HIGGINBOTHAM, WM. R. HILL, and JNO. A. WARE.

WM. McDANIEL -- Book 12, Page 434 -- June 5, 1851, written; July 21, 1851, probated. Witnesses: JAS. POWELL, WILKINS WATSON, CHAS. C. DAVIS. JNO. R. McDANIEL qualified. Bondsmen: WM. M. BOWLING, LINDSEY McDANIEL, JAS. P. McDANIEL. Son, LINDSEY, where I live; many slaves named. L. LAMBERT and children to be cared for for ten years and then to be divided to my children: JAS., LINDSEY, PHILIP, WM., SOPHIA, and CATH. Administrators: JAS. and JNO. McDANIEL - sums advanced to LINDSEY, WM., and CATH.
Book 13, Page 76 -- Inventory and Administrator's Account by LINDSEY and JNO. R. McDANIEL - this is wrong indexing for it really is estate of WM. WRIGHT, November 17, 1862.
Book 13, Page 412 -- Administrator's Account by JNO. R. McDANIEL from July 31, 1852 - LINDSEY McDANIEL, manager of Huff Creek Farm. Recorded November 20, 1854.
Book 17, Page 385 -- August 21, 1841, written; January 17, 1867, probated - Placer County, California - Witnesses: THOS. H. DEARMON, RO. C. and LEAH B. THURMOND. Produced by MARY E. McDANIEL -- all heirs in Placer County -- H. H. FELLOW, attorney for minors. MARY E. qualified as resident of Osage County, Missouri, and named in will to administer.

ANDREW McDOWAL -- Book 3, Page 381 -- March 14, 1796, written; April 18, 1796, probated. Witnesses: EDWD. WILLS, DAVID RIDDLE, WM. B. HARE. To friend, GIDEON CREWS; friend, JAS. LOVING - violin and case; musuc books; pistols. Friend, WILLIS WILLS - gold Masonic medal, etc. My uncle, PATRICK McWILLIAMS, brother of my mother, who lives in Great Britain - a stone mason or cutter. Administrators: friends, ALEX. BRYDIE and WILLIS WILLS. They qualified; bondsmen: WM. B. HARE and W. S. CRAWFORD. I wish that space permitted the copy of entire will and inventory. He must have been the music master and his inventory shows that he was an elegant dresser.
Book 3, Page 438 -- Inventory -- L 85-2-6, September 18, 1797. RO. RIVES, WM. B. HARE, N. CABELL - books, etc.

LAFAYETTE McFALL -- Book 14, Page 155 -- Guardian Bond -- HENRY McFALL and W.E.P. EUBANK, July 21, 1856, for HENRY McFALL as guardian of LAFAYETTE McFALL, orphan of SAMPSON McFALL, deceased.

HIRAM McGINNIS -- Book 14, Page 575 -- Constable -- June 21, 1858. Bondsmen: RO. A. COGHILL, RO. A. PENDLETON, JNO. D. DAVIS.
Book 15, Page 446 -- Same -- June 18, 1860; Bondsmen: RO. A. PENDLETON, RO. A. COGHILL, THOS. WHITEHEAD.

W. D. McIVER -- Book 15, Page 464 -- Constable -- Elected, May 24, 1860; District 1; bond of June 18, 1860. Bondsman: CHRISTOPHER McIVER. The family uses McIVOR in spelling, too. There is a place known as McIVOR's Station. My wife has a little second grader at Amelon and his name is BOBBY McIVOR.

JORDAN McKINNEY -- Book 17, Page 8 -- August 22, 1864, written; January 16, 1865, probated. Witnesses: JAS. POWELL and JANNA DEMPSEY. Debt due RO. SNEAD; proceeds of suit vs. RO. WADE to go to BUTLER E. KNIGHT and MARY J. DAVENPORT.

RICH. McLAIN -- Book 1, Page 389 -- Administrator's Bond -- SAML. WOODS and EDMD. WILCOX, October 6, 1777, for SAML. WOODS.

POLLY McMANAWAY -- Book 8, Page 334 -- Administrator's Bond -- AMBROSE PLUNKETT; WM. and LINDSEY McDANIEL, July 15, 1833, for AMBROSE PLUNKETT.

ALEX. McPHERSON -- Book 1, Page 105 -- March 6, 1765, written; December 1, 1776, probated. Witnesses: HUGH and CHAS. ROSS and CHAS. McPHERSON. Codicil of March 6, 1765, and same witnesses. Produced by HUGH ROSE and held for more proof until May 4, 1767, when CHAS. ROSE attested. Recorded May 5, 1767. DANL. BURFORD, Sheriff, qualified as no administrator appeared. Church rites; granddaughter, ELIZ. ALLEN, at death of her grandmother; Ux, SUSANNAH; children of SARAH ALLEN when of age or married. Administrators: JNO. and PATRICK ROSE. Codicil: To grandson, DANL. ALLEN; to ELIZ. PATTERSON or PATTESON.
Book 1, Page 123 -- Inventory -- L 15-0-0 -- HUGH ROSE, AMBR. JONES, BARTHOLOMEW RAMSEY. September 5, 1768.

JAS. McWHORTER -- Administrator's Bond -- RO. McWHORTER and DAVID MARTIN, THOS. SHANNON, 7 March 1763, for RO. McWHORTER.

STITH MEAD -- Book 10, Page 36 -- Administrator's Bond -- WM. I. ISBELL and RO. ISBELL, August 21, 1838, for WM. ISBELL. Deed books show much on this famous Methodist minister; also consult ALFRED PERCY's work on Piedmont.

JANE MEGANN (nee WATTS) -- Book 9, Page 301 -- Refunding Bond -- February 13, 1837, by JANE MEGANN, JOS. WRIGHT, LEWIS WRIGHT, ARCHELAUS REYNOLDS, and MOSES H. MEGANN to SAML. WATTS, curator of CALEB WATTS, deceased. CALEB WATTS was father of JANE and by will of December 14, 1825, gave JANE full share after deducting for advance of horse and cow. She has received legacy. Witnesses: CHAMPE CARTER as to JANE; MERIT M. WHITE as to MOSES H. MEGANN.

JOS. CABELL MEGGINSON - also MIGGINSON -- Book 1, Page 434 -- Guardian Bond -- JS. CABELL and SAML. WOODS, August 3, 1778, for JS. CABELL as guardian of JOS. CABELL MEGGINSON, orphan of WM. MIGGINSON.

DANL. MEHONE -- Book B, Page 45 -- Administrator's Bond -- JNO. PENDLETON, WM. G. PENDLETON, and JNO. J. HUCHINSON, 23 March 1853, for MANSON MEHONE to administer.

RO. MEHONE -- Book B, Page 45 -- Same parties and date as above.

WM. MEHONE -- Book B, Page 46 -- Same parties and dates as above.

SARAH MENIFEE -- Book 8, Page 169 -- Guardian Bond -- WARNER M. YATES, WM. M. WALLER, and JAS. S. PENDLETON, February 20, 1832, for WARNER M. YATES as guardian of SARAH and ELIZ. MENIFEE, orphans of JNO. MENIFEE.

JANE MEREDITH -- Book 6, Page 85 -- June 21, 1819, written; August 16, 1819, probated. Witnesses: G. ROSE and CORNL. POWELL. DAVID S. GARLAND refused to qualify and was bondsman for JNO. P. COBBS who qualified. To be buried in family cemetery at Winton by husband. Mourning rings to daughters and granddaughters. Grandsons, WM. HENRY GARLAND and PATRICK HENRY GARLAND; granddaughters, JANE MEREDITH COBBS.

RICE MEREDITH -- Book 1, Page 502 -- Administrator's Bond -- MARGARET MEREDITH, HUGH ROSE, and JAMES HIGGINBOTHAM, 4 October 1779, for MARGARET MEREDITH.
Book 1, Page 509 -- Inventory -- L 1,643-5-0, November 1, 1779; JNO. HIGGINBOTHAM; LAWRENCE and JOEL CAMPBELL.
Book 3, Page 64 -- October 1, 1787, written; November 1, 1779, probated. Witnesses: HENRY CASHWELL, JOEL CAMPBELL. Ux, to MEDIRAYARS(?) son BELOW(?) - his grandchildren; LEN BELOW son-in-law(?) and ux. Produced by EASTER BELLOW.

SAML. MEREDITH -- Book 3, Page 388 -- Coroner Bond -- July 18, 1796. Bondsman: PHILIP GOOCH.
Book 4, Page 569 -- Administrator's Bond -- DAVID S. GARLAND and WM. S. CRAWFORD and DANL. HIGGINBOTHAM. January 16, 1809, for DAVID S. GARLAND. Also WM. ARMISTEAD qualified on same date with bondsmen: EDMD. WINSTON, JR.; HILL CARTER; and EDMD. T. COLEMAN.

Book 4, Page 570 -- August 6, 1808, written; January 16, 1809, pro-
bated. Witnesses: JAS. WOODS, JAS. GARLAND, BARTLETT THOMPSON,
JNO. HENDRON. Codicil of November 30, 1808, and witness was JAS.
GARLAND. Codicil gives gold watch to son, SAML., JR. Son, SAML. -
Kentucky lands - power-of-attorney some years ago to him and JNO.
BRECKENRIDGE, deceased. Money to DAVID S. GARLAND for education of
my grandson, SAML. MEREDITH GARLAND. My ux, JANE; son, WM.; daughter,
MARY MAY; son, SAML., JR.; daughter, JANE H. GARLAND. To WM. B. HARE
in trust for my daughter, SARAH ARMISTEAD; debts due from estate of
DR. JNO. POWELL; also from estate of ROBT. WATKINS; my grandchildren;
SARAH ARMISTEAD - land deeded to WM. ARMISTEAD, 20 April 1801 - 4 or
5 acres - if she has heirs who become 21. Children of daughter,
JANE H. GARLAND; son-in-law, DAVID S. GARLAND and son-in-law, WM.
ARMISTEAD, to administer.
Book 4, Page 610 -- Inventory of $13,111.96. THOS. ALDRIDGE, JER.
FRANKLIN, JAS. WOODS.
Book 6, Page 500 -- Administrator's Account by DAVID S. GARLAND from
March, 1809 - blacksmith shop account for 1812; SAML. B. CHRISTIAN
for ELIZ. BRAXTON's dower claim in lands of JOS. HIGGINBOTHAM and
SAML. HUCKSTEP. Part allowed to MARY MAY, December 29, 1815 - THOS.
ALDRIDGE, PEACHY FRANKLIN, and EDMD. PENN. WM.MEREDITH has sold
interest to D.M.C. PAYNE and assigned to DAVID S. GARLAND. Division
to take place at death of widow -- heirs are named as in will. WM. B.
HARE is dead and JAS. S. PENDLETON is now trustee for heirs in
interest in 192-3/4 acres of land of their father. November 24,
1821. ROBT. TINSLEY, JNO. DILLARD, HILL CARTER.

SUSAN J. MERIT -- Book 12, Page 108 -- Estate Commitment to Sheriff,
June Term, 1849; LINDSEY COLEMAN, Sheriff.

JNO. MERRITT -- Book 12, Page 35 -- July 20, 1848, written; August 22,
1848, probated. Witnesses: WM. M. PAGE and W. PETTYJOHN. Daughter,
SUSAN J. MERRITT - where I live; daughter, MARTHA DAY; children of
deceased daughter, EDITHA DAWSON; sons, JAMES S. and JNO. L.; de-
ceased daughter, RHODA P. LAIN; deceased daughter, LUCINDA P. CREASY;
sons, CORNL. and THOS. P.; granddaughters, MARY F. CREASY and RHODA
N. J. LAIN. Bond on THOS. PADGETT. Administrator: friend, JESSE
MUNDY.
Book 12, Page 558 -- Administrator's Account by LINDSEY COLEMAN,
Sheriff; agent, GEO. D. DAVIS, May 19, 1851. COLEMAN bonded on
February 19, 1849. Bondsmen: RO. TINSLEY, SAML. M. GARLAND, RO. M.
BROWN, CHAS. MASSIE, WM. A.RICHESON, HENRY L. DAVIES. Sale of
June 15, 1849, and JNO. MERRITT was buyer. SYLVESTER L. BURFORD
bought land. Special legacies to CORNL. MERRITT and THOS. P. MERRITT;
legacy to MARY F. CREASY; debt of THOS. PADGETT; same for ROSA N. J.
LAIN; legacy to MARTHA DAY; to children of EDITHA DAWSON, deceased;
to JAS. S. and JNO. L. MERRITT; to children of RHODA P. LAIN, deceased; children of LUCINDA P. CREASY, deceased. Recorded July 19,
1852.
Book 13, Page 33 -- Estate Commitment to Sheriff - so indexed, but
not there and not in 13 index - only in Master.

THOS. MERRITT -- Book 4, Page 454 -- Constable -- June 20, 1803;
Bondsmen: CHRISTOPHER ISBELL and DANL. NORCUTT.

ARCHIBALD B. MIGGINSON (MEGGINSON) -- Book 12, Page 354 -- Administrator's Bond -- B. C. MEGGINSON, JOS. H. ROBERTS, W. A. ROBERTS
and S. B. MEGGINSON, February 17, 1851, for B. MEGGINSON.
Book 12, Page 421 -- Inventory -- March 20, 1851. STEPHEN W. CHRIS-
TIAN, JNO. L. TURNER, JOHN JAS. DILLARD - TERISHA DILLARD did not
serve.
Book 12, Page 423 -- Schedule of property jointly owned by ALEX. P.
CAMPBELL and to be sold; some doubt, but separate accounts to be
kept. June 16, 1851.

BENJ. MILES -- Book 6, Page 481 -- Administrator's Bond -- WM.
McDANIEL and BENNETT CRAWFORD, 19 August 1824, for WM. McDANIEL.
Book 6, Page 610 -- Inventory -- August 25, 1824 - $3,340.75. PROSSER
POWELL, BENJ. OGDEN, THOS. LAIN.

Book 9, Page 268 -- Administrator's Account -- NELSON C. DAWSON, administrator, from 1833 - to JNO. MYERS for children of decedent; tuition; SARAH MYERS' bond; $839.60. LINDSEY COLEMAN, HENRY J. ROSE, JNO. H. ROBERTS. Also see BENJAMIN J. MILES data below.

BENJ. B. MILES -- Book B, Page 22 -- July 29, 1843, written; August 25, 1843, probated. Witnesses: IVERSON L. TYMAN, WM. D. MILES, THOS. A. MILES, CHAS. L. BROWN, WM. L. CAMPBELL. ALFRED V. CRENSHAW qualified; bondsmen: JOS. MAYS, MANN S. VALENTINE, and CRENSHAW signed as attorney-in-fact for bondsmen. Now of Amherst County; ux, SARAH M., to select books from library; rest to my father and his family. Administrator: ALFRED V. CRENSHAW, Richmond, Virginia.
Book 11, Page 220 -- Inventory of Library - 128 Volumes - $100.00. January 16, 1844. JAS. P. GARLAND, JNO. P. WILSON, JNO. S. HIGGINBOTHAM.

BENJAMIN J. MILES -- Book 9, Page 145 -- Refunding Bond by SAML. M. GARLAND, WM. M. WALLER, and WM. H. KNIGHT, January 2, 1834, to NELSON C. DAWSON, administrator of BENJ. MILES, deceased. DAWSON has divided slaves of BENJ. to his two children: SARAH and BENJ. MILES. Widow has married JNO. MYERS. SAML. M. GARLAND is guardian of B. MILES and ward's slaves received.
Book 11, Page 342 -- BENJ. J. MILES releases all claims vs. late guardian. SAML. M. GARLAND, October 18, 1845.
Book 14, Page 85 -- Administrator's Bond -- RO. A. COGHILL and SAML. M. GARLAND, March 19, 1856, for RO. COGHILL. Note: These are indexed for BENJ. J., but first clearly belong with BENJ. MILES account above.

JAS. MILES -- Book 5, Page 228 -- Administrator's Bond -- PEGGY MILES, JNO. MEHONE, DABNEY PHILLIPS, 21 June 1813, for PEGGY MILES.
Book 5, Page 376 -- Inventory; no total. September 29, 1813; CHAS. MUNDY, WM. TURNER, JNO. CASHWELL.

SARAH ANN MILES -- Book 8, Page 326 -- SAML. M. GARLAND, WM. H. GARLAND, RICH. N. EUBANK, PHILLIP WEBBER, and JNO. MYERS. 20 June 1833, for SAML. GARLAND as guardian of SARAH ANN and BENJ. MILES, orphans of BENJ. MILES, deceased.
Book 13, Page 213 -- Guardian's Account by guardian from September 26, 1834 - to N. BREEDLOVE, to BENJ. MILES to make lot equal; suit in Lynchburg Court, Recorded August 20, 1835 - JNO. S. KYLE, Commissioner.

THOS. MILES -- Book 8, Page 16 -- Division and plat on east branch of Rutledge, August 16, 1830 - 265 acres. Lots to SARAH MYERS and lines of JAS. HIGGINBOTHAM, BENAMMI STONE. SARAH is relict of BENJ. MILES - 71-1/4 acres and 193-3/4 acres in possession of THOS. MILES. JNO. MYERS married SARAH, widow. JONAS PIERCE, WM. BOURNE, JAS. S. HIGGINBOTHAM.
Book 11, Page 427 -- THOS. MILES, SR., March 20, 1843, written; codicil of January 5, 1844; July 20, 1846, probated. Witnesses to will: C. H. CHRISTIAN, JNO. L. TYLER, H. L. BROWN. Witnesses to codicil: same, WM. D. and THOS. A. MILES qualified. Ux, PHEBE; son, THOS. A. - where I live - CLASBY tract; my seven children. Administrators: sons, BENJ. B., WM. D., and THOS. A. MILES; my four daughters. Codicil: daughters to be free from control of husbands. Trustees for them are my sons, WM. D. and THOS. A. MILES.

THOS. A. MILES -- Book 16, Page 419 -- September 18, 1863, written; January 18, 1864, probated. Witnesses: WM. W. THOMPSON, WM. M. WALLER, WM. D. MILES. Ux, MARTHA F., formerly HIGGINBOTHAM; nephew, WM. A. ROSE, until 21; nephew, EDMD. C. ROSE, if both are without

WM. MILES -- Book 4, Page 171 -- October 1, 1804, written; February 18, 1805, probated. Witnesses: JOS. B. WINGFIELD, WALTER CHRISTIAN, JOS. HIGGINBOTHAM. October 21, 1805, BENJ. and THUDDEUS MILES qualified; Bondsmen: HUDSON M. and DAVID S. GARLAND. To my mother - L 40; my sister, NANCY MILES; niece, PEGGY HENDERSON; to WALTER CHRISTIAN, SR.; brothers, sisters, "nese" and "nefes": GEO. SCOT, to witnesses; my brothers, BENJ., THOS., JAS., THADES, and AMEY HUCSTEPT,

SARAH STUART, NANCY MILES, SALLY WHITTEN, PEGGY HENDERSON - not to
part MARTIN and ux (probably slaves).
Book 4, Page 504 -- Administrator's Account by administrators.
L 727-18-10; bonds of POLLY STEWART; SAML. DAY; THOS. MILES - one
third of 200 acres, February 15, 1808. JNO. McDANIEL, ISAAC RUCKER,
JNO. COLEMAN.

WM. D. D. MILES -- Book 8, Page 161 -- Guardian Bond -- JNO. J.
MILES, JAS. S. HIGGINBOTHAM, THOS. MILES, December 19, 1831, for
JNO. MILES as guardian of WM. D. D.; and ELIZ. MILES, orphans of
THADDEUS MILES.

ALEX. MILLER -- Book 2, Page 54 -- July 21, 1781, written; May 6,
1782, probated. Witnesses: FRANS. MERIWETHER; ALEX. REID, JR.;
JAS. REID; JAS. DIGUST. Ux, MARTHA; my four children: ANDREW; MARY;
ALEX. and expected child - if any die before maturity. Treasury
warrant for 425 acres supposed to be on waters of the Kentucky to
NATHAN, ANDREW, and ALEX. Executors: ux; ALEX. REID, JR.; NATHAN
CRAWFORD; and JOS. HIGGINBOTHAM, May 6, 1782, for MARTHA MILLER;
WM. BARNETT; and ALEX. REID, JR.
Book 2, Page 78 -- Inventory -- L 147-2-10 -- MICHL. McNEALY, NATHAN
CRAWFORD, ALEX. REID, October 7, 1782.

BARSHEBA E. MILLER -- Book 6, Page 279 -- Guardian Bond -- March 18,
1822, SOLOMON DAY, JAS. L. DILLARD, WM. TURNER for SOLOMON DAY as
guardian of SALLY ANN and BARSHEBA E. MILLER, orphans of WM. E.
MILLER.
Book 8, Page 110 -- Guardian's Account by guardian from January 1,
1823 - expense to Bartee County, North Carolina, on estate business;
board and tuition - Bertie County, North Carolina, expenses in 1828;
1831; settlement of H. H. HENSLEY. Recorded June 21, 1831. JESSE
BECK, CHAS. MAYS, JAS. B. EDWARDS.

LEANNA E. MILLNER -- Book 11, Page 250 -- Guardian Bond -- JAS. M.
MILLNER and WM. L. MILLNER, November 18, 1844, for JAS. M. MILLNER
as guardian of LEANNA E. and MILDRED H. MILLNER, orphans of LEE MILL-
NER, deceased.
Book 12, Page 48 -- Guardian's Account by guardian from 1845; school
expenses to C. H. RUCKER, RO. H. CARTER. July 17, 1848.
Page 50 -- Guardian's Account for MILDRED H. and on Page 52 for
MARY J. - all of same date.
Book 13, Page 64 -- Guardian's Account from January 18, 1848, to
WM. L. MILLNER; account of MILLNER and RUCKER. Recorded June 5,
1852.
Book 13, Page 144 -- Guardian's Account on February 21, 1853.

LEE MILLNER -- Book 10, Page 281 -- Administrator's Bond -- MILDRED
MILLNER, WM. L. MILLNER, and ZACH DRUMMOND, October 19, 1840, for
MILDRED MILLNER and WM. MILLNER.
Book 10, Page 291 -- Inventory -- $3,936.00; RO. H. CARTER, PETER
FLOOD; WM. B. RUCKER, December 21, 1840.
Book 11, Page 603 -- Administrator's Account by both from 1840.
MILDRED's account up to July 1, 1844, "which was about time of her
death." Recorded March 10, 1847, PITT WOODROOF, RO. H. CARTER, JNO.
PRYOR. WM. L. MILLNER's account on Page 607. To JAS. M. MILLNER;
bond of SUSAN HARGROVE. Same committee and date.
Book 13, Page 406 -- Administrator's Account by WM. L. MILLNER from
1847 - amount from JAS. M. MILLNER; account of MARY JANE MILLNER;
bond of LITTLEBERRY GRANT; amount from MILDRED MILLNER, LEANNAH and
SARAH MILLNER named. Recorded November 20, 1854; JNO. PRYOR and
THOS. A. EUBANK.
     I am unable to give documentation on this data, but it was in
some papers loaned to me by Mrs. Mary Hesson Pettyjohn (Mrs. Thos.
Pettyjohn) who is the mother-in-law of my third son, THURMAN BLANTON
DAVIS, who married MARY GAYLE PETTYJOHN. MARTHA A. MILLNER married
ALBERT D. WATTS, March 11, 1844. She is shown to be the child or
ward of MILDRED MILLNER. MILDRED MILLNER was ux of LEE MILLNER and
the notes give her birth as April 1, 1782, in Buckingham and her
marriage on December 13, 1813. The notes say that she was the
daughter of a HARRIS and LEE and PENDLETON lines are in families -

PENN, too, but I have no documentation. MILDRED had brothers and one was the Baptist minister named HARRIS who lived in Bedford. I do not know just where LEE MILLNER married MILDRED HARRIS - Buckingham or Bedford.

MARY JANE MILLNER -- Book 11, Page 251 -- Guardian Bond -- JAS. M. and WM. L. MILLNER and PITT WOODROOF, November 18, 1844, for JAS. M. MILLNER as guardian of MARY JANE MILLNER, orphan of LEE MILLNER, deceased.
Book 12, Page 26 -- Guardian Bond -- WM. L. MILLNER and ZA. DRUMMOND, October 18, 1847, for WM. MILLER as guardian of same orphan.
Book 12, Page 52 -- Guardian Account by JAS. M. MILLNER, guardian of MARY HICKS, formerly MARY JANE MILLNER F. DAVIS for tuition; RO. H. CARTER. July 17, 1848.

SARAH E. MILLNER -- Book 11, Page 252 -- Guardian Bond -- PITT WOOD-ROOF, JAS. M. and WM. L. MILLNER, November 18, 1844, for PITT WOOD-ROOF as guardian of SARAH E. MILLNER, orphan of LEE MILLNER.

I have done very little on the MILLNER family data, but did pick this up in Bedford. Will Book 5, Page 233: WM. MILLNER, SR. - us, ELIZ. (family states that she was a LEE from Buckingham). Executor: WILLIAMSON MILLNER, Pittsylvania, and "ABSALOM of Lynch of Campbell" (sic). Reference to deed of gift to his children, 13 February 1819, written; 27 November 1820, executed. Witnesses: JAS. NOEL, NELSON A. THOMPSON, JESSE NOEL. Deed Book 16, Page 126: December 4, 1818, WM. MILLNER relinquished all rights to property which ux, ELIZ., had at time of marriage. Deed Book 15, Page 21: April 15, 1816, WM. MILLNER, SR., Bedford, makes deed of gift to his children: WILLIAMSON, JNO.; WM., JR.; RICH.; THOS.; ROBT.; LEE; OWEN; and NANCY (now NOELL) - 600 or 700 acres on Ivy and not lately surveyed; 179 acres on Sycamore and 280 acres where I live.

RACHEL H. MILLES (indexed MILES) -- Book 4, Page 356 -- Guardian Bond -- JESSE MILLS and THOMAS DICKERSON, 14 October 1802, for JESSE MILLS as guardian of RACHEL H. MILLS, child of JESSE MILLS, by his ux, RACHEL MILLS.

WM. MILLS -- Book 1, Page 73 -- September 6, 1755, written; August 4, 1766. Witnesses: JNO. STAPLES, ISHAM DAVIS, WM. FLOYD, CHAS. TULEY, RO. DAVIS. Of Albemarle (Amherst County was nor formed until 1761). Ux, MARY; son, AMBROSE, at death of his mother; son, WM.; my daughters, SARAH WATTS MILLS; ELIZ. LEARWOODS; ANNA MILLS; son, JESSE; daughter, MILLY MILLS; children of my son, THOS.; AMBROSE, JR.; and ELIZ. MILLS - son and daughter of my deceased son, THOS. Executors: ux and THOS. JOBLIN.
Book 1, Page 75 -- Administrator's Bond -- MARY MILLS, JESSE MILLS, WM. LAVINDER, August 4, 1766, for MARY MILLS.
Book 1, Page 104 -- Inventory -- L 265-4-9, February 27, 1767; HENRY KEY and WM. WELTON.

BETSY MILSTRED -- Book 4, Page 535 -- March 19, 1808, written; October 17, 1808, probated. Witnesses: WALLER SANDIDGE, BETSY ROWSEY, ABRAM CARTER. Codicil by NELSON CRAWFORD and ABRAM CARTER - no date - Son, PETER - heifer at JOSH MILSTRED's; daughter, ANNA KING. Executors: PETER MILSTRED and JNO. ROWSEY. Codicil: son, LINDSEY MILSTRED; daughter, BELINDA KEY - small amounts as shares have been given to them.

JOS. MILSTRED(STEAD) -- Book 4, Page 127 -- April 6, 1803, written; July 18, 1803, probated. Witnesses: RANDOL SNEAD, DANL. SHRADER, JNO. C. DAVASHER. BENJ. HIGGINBOTHAM and JOS. MILSTEAD qualified; bondsmen: HENRY BALLINGER and DANL. SHRADER. Ux, REBECCA; sons: JOS., WM. and ux, BETTY; to AARON MILSTEAD· son, ZEALOS MILSTEAD; my daughters, ELIZ. VEAL, BENEDICTOR DAVIS PATTY VEAL, MILLY BROWN. JINEY VEAL. Executors: friends: JOS. HIGGINBOTHAM, BENJ. HIGGIN-BOTHAM, JOS. MILSTEAD.
Book 4, Page 140 -- Inventory -- no total; CALEB RALLS, BENJ. TALIA-FERRO, JNO. CRAWFORD, December 19, 1803. Administrator's Bond on Page 374.

PETER MILSTRED -- Book 4, Page 516 -- Guardian Bond -- DANL. SHRADER,
JNO. CRAWFORD, ABRAM CARTER. June 21, 1808, for DANL. SHRADER as
guardian of PETER MILSTRED, orphan of JOS. MILSTRED.

FANNY C. MINOR -- Book 13, Page 282 -- Guardian Bond -- LANCELOT MI-
NOR and JOEL F. SMITH, December 19, 1853, for LANCELOT MINOR as guar-
dian of FANNY CO., ALICE W., and MARY A. MINOR, orphans of SARAH A.
MINOR, deceased.

GEO. A. MINOR -- Book 11, Page 71 -- Guardian Bond -- RAYMOND R.
MINOR and WM. HIX, July 18, 1842, for RAYMOND MINOR as guardian of
GEO. W. MINOR, son of R. R. MINOR.
Book 11, Page 149 -- Same bond.

LANCELOT MINOR -- Book 20, Page 380 -- Guardian Bond -- MARY A. MACLIN
and LANCELOT MINOR, October 16, 1882, for MARY MACLIN as guardian of
her infant sons, HENRY and LANCELOT MINOR.
Book 21, Page 406 -- September 15, 1884, written; May 16, 1887, pro-
bated. Produced by MARY A. MINOR. Handwriting by RO. W. SNEAD,
E. W. MITCHELL and CHAS. L. ELLIS. Ux, MARY ANNA - 100 acres at
Waugh's Ferry Road on south and DR. DABNEY on east; my daughter, MRS.
BERKLEY - FANNIE C. - has 67 acres given by me and 8 acres. 67 acres
to my daughter, MRS. SALLY WAUGH; ux, 80 acres; daughter, CARRY
RICHESON. My other children: KITTY T. (MRS. ROGERS); BETTY and
LUCY L. In latter part of 1854, I became guardian of first wife's
children: FANNY C., SALLY, and MARY A.; have received share from my
second ux - larger. JOHN B. MINOR, my brother and brother-in-law,
L.F.V. WINSTON. Ux to administer and also son-in-law, R. C. BERKELEY.
He qualified - Book 21, Page 417, June 20, 1887.
Book 22, Page 16 -- Inventory -- shown by widow, MARY ANN MINOR,
October 31, 1887 - $566.35 - J. R. BIBB, JAS. T. FEAGANS, M. W. JEN-
NINGS; also property of widow and single daughter, LUCY L. MINOR;
legal code cited.

JNO. MINTON -- Book 5, Page 612 -- Administrator's Bond -- ELIZ.
MINTON, RICH. PERKINS, and JNO. LONDON, December 16, 1816, for ELIZ.
MINTON.
Book 5, Page 637 -- Inventory -- $3,315.78. CHAS. MUNDY, JESSE BECK,
HENRY TURNER, February 17, 1817.
Book 6, Page 355 -- Administrator's de bonis non Bond -- WM. Y.
MINTON, REUBEN COX, WM. D. HILL, April 21, 1823, for WM. MINTON.
Book 6, Page 468 -- Inventory -- no total nor committee, July 9, 1824.
Book 10, Page 2 -- Administrator's Account by WM. Y. MINTON from 1823;
very long; through Page 29. Recorded June 18, 1838: JAS. L. LAMKIN,
JNO. WARWICK, D. STAPLES.

NANCY MINTON -- Book 6, Page 92 -- Guardian Bond -- MICAJAH STONE and
CHAS. MUNDY, September 20, 1819, for MICAJAH STONE as guardian of
NANCY, BETSY, SUSAN, and SELINA MINTON, orphans of JNO. MINTON, de-
ceased.

SALINE MINTON -- Book 6, Page 373 -- Guardian's Account for various
orphans of JNO. MINTON by MICAJAH STONE from 1819, recorded August 18,
1823. This list varies with one for wards above: SUSANNA MINTON,
JNO. P. MINTON, WM. Y. MINTON, ELIZ. MINTON, GEO. GUTHRIE for tuition
for SUSANNA and ELIZ. and PAMELIA MINTON and NANCY MINTON. From
October 30, 1819; recorded August 18, 1823.

WM. Y. MINTON -- Book 6, Page 356 -- Guardian Bond -- WM. Y. MINTON,
HENRY TURNER, MAJOR, and THOS. DELAWARE HILL, JAS. S. HIGGINBOTHAM,
JORDAN CREASY, WM. D. HILL, May 19, 1823, for WM. MINTON as guardian
of JNO., NANCY, BETSY, SUSAN and SALINE MINTON, orphans of JNO. MIN-
TON, deceased.

ARCHELAUS MITCHELL -- Book 3, Page 566 -- Inventory -- L 279-8-4,
September 12, 1799. DAVID TINSLEY, RICH. POWELL, NELSON C. DAWSON.
Book 4, Page 3 -- Allotment to HANNAH MITCHELL on third of estate of
ARCHELAUS MITCHELL, deceased. January 1, 1800. THOS. MOORE, RICH.
POWELL, DAVID TINSLEY.
Book 6, Page 277 -- Administrator's Bond -- RICH. N. EUBANK, DABNEY

WARE, January 21, 182?, for RICH. EUBANK.

JAS. MITCHELL -- Book 5, Page 475 -- Administrator's Bond -- JOS.
KENNEDY and AMBR. RUCKER, December 19, 1814, for JOS. KENNEDY.

NORBORNE A. MITCHELL -- Book 13, Page 294 -- Guardian's ACcount --
LANDON A. PROFFITT, guardian, from January 22, 1844. To MITCHELL
and ARRINGTON; Lovingston Academy, November 26, 1849 - $6.85. To
WM. M. CABELL, administrator of LANDON A. PROFFITT. Recorded July 21,
1853. CABELL presented accounts of PROFFITT from 1845 to 1853.
THOS. WHITEHEAD, commissioners, August 8, 1853.

PLEASANT MITCHELL -- Book 14, Page 226 -- Administrator's Bond -- EDWD.
W. MITCHELL, HENRY W. QUARLES, and J. DUDLEY DAVIS, February 18, 1857,
for EDWD. MITCHELL.
Book 14, Page 276 -- May 16, 1856, written; February 16, 1857, pro-
bated. Witnesses: JNO. PRYOR, CHAS. F. PENDLETON. Ux. MARY; two
youngest children: EDWD. and SARAH; to ROBT. HILL, son of JACOB HILL;
children by first ux: JNO. J.; WM. A.; MARY ANN, ux of CALVIN JOHN-
SON; JULIA ANN, ux of JNO. GLOVER; NORBORNE, son by second ux. If
EDWD. is without heirs and same for SARAH - then to RO. HILL. Execu-
tors: friends, RO. H. THORNTON and son, EDWD.
Book 14, Page 292 -- Inventory -- two slaves at $600.00. RO. W.
SWANN; THOS. D. WOODS; RO. N. ELLIS, March 13, 1857.

POWHATAN MITCHELL -- Book 17, Page 9 -- Administrator's Bond -- WM. P.
SCOTT and GEO. H. DAMERON, January 16, 1865, for WM. SCOTT.

STELLA MITCHELL -- Book 4, Page 318 -- Guardian Bond -- JNO. B. TRENT;
JER. TAYLOR, and SAML. HILL, January 20, 1800, for JNO. TRENT as
guardian of STELLA MITCHELL, orphan of ARCHELAUS MITCHELL.

STEPHEN T. MITCHELL -- Book 6, Page196 -- Guardian Bond -- THOS.
MITCHELL, NICHL. HARRISON, and STERLING CLAIBORNE and RICH. H. BURKS
for THOS. MITCHELL as guardian of STEPHEN T., RO. C., FREDERICK R.,
MARY JANE, MARTHA ANN and SARAH L. MITCHELL, orphans of WM. MITCHELL,
deceased.

THOS. MITCHELL -- Book 1, Page 113 -- -----, written; October 5, 1767,
probated. Witnesses: WM. CABELL, JR.; EDWD. TILMAN; WM. TRICE. Pro-
duced by JNO. STRANGE and HARDIN PERKINS who qualified. Daughters,
ELIZ. and NANCY MITCHELL when ELIZ. is 18; son, CHARLES when of age;
son, JOAB - children to be educated. Executors: JNO. STRANGE of
Albemarle and HARDIN PERKINS of Buckingham.
Book 1, Page 134 -- Inventory -- L 149-12-8. W. HANSBROUGH, WM.
WALTON, WM. TRICE, June 5, 1769 - not indexed.

WM. MITCHELL -- Book 6, Page 596 -- Order to turn estate over to
sheriff; went to residence and found nothing, June Court, 1825. He
took oath of insolvent before death. CHAS. MUNDY by Deputy, JOS.
PETTYJOHN.
Book 11, Page 233 -- Administrator's Bond -- JOHN CARDEN, WM. O.
HARDING, and JAS. F. SATTERWHITE, August 19, 1844, for JOHN CARDEN.
Book 11, Page 246 -- Inventory -- on order of August 23, 1844 -
$1,749.26. ARMSTEAD OGDEN, BENJ. B. BIBB, A. C. JOHNSON.

WM. W. MITCHELL -- Book 12, Page 131 -- Guardian Bond -- JNO. CARDEN
and DAVID H. TAPSCOTT, June 19, 1848, for JNO. CARDEN as guardian
of WM. W. MITCHELL, orphan of WM. MITCHELL, deceased.

ZACH. MITCHELL -- Book 18, Page 350 -- Administrator's Bond -- TAYLOR
BERRY and RO. A. COGHILL, October 20, 1873, for TAYLOR BERRY.

BENJ. MODERAS -- Book 4, Page 301 -- Guardian Bond -- JAS. WRIGHT
and W. LEE HARRIS, December 16, 1797, for JAS. WRIGHT as guardian of
BENJ. MODERAS, orphan of BENJ. MODERAS, deceased.

MARY MOFFITT -- Book 2, Page 161 -- Guardian Bond -- SNELLING JOHN-
STON; CHAS. BURRUS and JOS. PENN, March 1, 1784, for SNELLING JOHN-
STON as guardian of MARY and ANN MOFFITT, orphans of THOS. MOFFITT.

Book 3, Page 84 -- Guardian's Account -- December 17, 1787 - estate of THOS. MOFFITT by guardian. AMBR. RUCKER, Commissioner.
Book 3, Page 198 -- Guardian Bond -- PHILIP JOHNSON, JOS. PENN, and JNO. BARNETT, September 5, 1791, for PHILIP JOHNSON as guardian of MARY MOFFITT, orphan of THOS. MOFFITT - in account on Page 84 both orphans are named, but only MARY here.

NANCY MOFFITT -- Book 3, Page 199 -- PHILIP JOHNSON, et al. - as on Page 198 - September 5, 1791, for PHILIP JOHNSON as guardian of NANCY MOFFITT, orphan of THOS. MOFFITT. Was she NANCY ANN? Note that THOS. only names two daughters in will.

THOS. MOFFITT -- Book 1, Page 472 -- November 11, 1778, written; May 3, 1779, probated. Witnesses: FRANCES JOHNSON, CHAS. ELLIS, HENRY TRENT, JNO. MERRITT. Daughters, MARY and ANN to be educated. Ux, ELIZ. - mansion house. Executors: JAS. BARNETT, EDMD. WILCOX, JOS. CABELL, EDMD. WINSTON.
Book 1, Page 473 -- Administrator's Bond -- JAS. BARNETT, JR. and JNO. MONTGOMERY, 3 May 1779, for JAS. BARNETT, JR.
Book 1, Page 478 -- Inventory -- very long; no total; June 7, 1779. THOS. GILLENWATERS, THOS. WRIGHT, JNO. COTTRELL.

ANDREW MONROE -- Book 4, Page 518 -- Administrator's Bond -- JNO. MONROE, RICH. WILSON, REUBEN NORVELL, JNO. McDANIEL, JAS. MARR, July 18, 1808, for first two to administer.
Book 4, Page 517 -- April 10, 1808, written; July 18, 1808, probated. Witnesses: RICH. WILSON, JNO. MONROE, MARTIN WILSON, JER. and JNO. WILSON. Produced by last two. Ux, SARAH; nephew, ANDREW MONROE, son of JNO. MONROE - land above CARTER BRAXTON's old line where my house stands. Sister, MARY PEYTON; CHAS. WILSON, son of RICH. WILSON; brother, JNO. MONROE; niece, LUCY MONROE, daughter of WM. MONROE; nephew, JAS. PEYTON, son of WM. PEYTON; brothers, JNO. and WM. RIGHTS in Culpeper land to RICH. WILSON on Summer Duck Run. Executors: ux, JNO. MONROE and RICH. WILSON.

JAS. MONTGOMERY -- Book 1, Page 412 -- Administrator's Bond -- RO. WRIGHT, JAS. WRIGHT, GEO. BLAIN, April 7, 1778, for RO. WRIGHT.
Book 1, Page 454 -- Inventory -- L 1,040-19-0, DAVID SHELTON; JNO. LOVING, JR.; JNO. GRIFFIN, December 7, 1778.
Book 1, Page 464 -- Administrator's Account by WRIGHT; trustees of Rockfish congregation; account of DAVID MONTGOMERY; JNO. MONTGOMERY (SMITH); cash of JAS. MONTGOMERY, son of THOS.; DAVID MONTGOMERY, JR.
Book 4, Page 362 -- Surveyor and road bond: January 17, 1803. Bondsman: WM. LOVING, JNO. THOMPSON.
Book 10, Page 180 -- Administrator's Bond -- CHAMP CARTER and SAML. M. GARLAND, December 16, 1839, for CHAMP CARTER.

JNO. MONTGOMERY -- Book 2, Page 176 -- March 11, 1784, written; June 7, 1784, probated. Witnesses: JNO. DIGGS, WM. LYON, JOSIAH JOPLING. Son, ALEX., where he lives in Washington County; son, JOS. - 215 acres on Buck Creek; sons, WM.; JNO.; JAS.; NATHAN; daughter, ANNE; daughter, MARY - 600 acres in Kentucky; rest of Kentucky land to sons, JNO. JAS. & NATHAN.

Book 2, Page 178 -- Administrator's Bond -- JOS. and JNO. MONTGOMERY, June 7, 1784. Bondsman: JNO. DIGGS, WM. BARNETT.
Book 2, Page 209 -- Inventory -- no total. WM. HARRIS, JR.; JAS. WOODS; LEE HARRIS; JOSIAH JOPLING, December 6, 1784.

MARY W. ELLIS MONTGOMERY -- Book 8, Page 186 -- Guardian Bond -- RICH. L. ELLIS, THOS. N. EUBANK, WM. ARMISTEAD, RICH. N. EUBANK. March 21, 1832, for RICH. EUBANK as guardian of MARY W. ELLIS MONTGOMERY, orphan of THOS. MONTGOMERY.

MICHL. MONTGOMERY -- Book 1, Page 115 -- February 3, 1764, written; March 7, 1768, probated. Witnesses: ALEX. REID, SAML SHANNON, JAS. REID. Ux, MARGARET - where I live; sons, MICHL.; THOS. and JAS. Daughter, ABIGAIL MONTGOMERY; son, JNO.; daughter, ELIZ. MONTGOMERY; daughter, SARAH MONTGOMERY. Executors: ux and son, THOS. They made bond on probate date. Bondsmen: RO. BARNETT, JAS. McALEXANDER.

Book 1, Page 122 -- Inventory -- no total; March 27, 1768; no committee.
Recorded: July 4, 1768.

THOS. MONTGOMERY -- Book 10, Page 181 -- Administrators Bond -- CHAMP
CARTER and SAML. M. GARLAND, December 16, 1839.

JNO. W. MOODY -- Book 20, Page 141 -- Administrators Bond -- RO. B.
MOODY and SAML. C. KIRKPATRICK, April 18, 1881, for RO. B. MOODY.
W. is not used here, but so indexed.
Book 20, Page 234 -- W is used in inventory -- $131.00. P. C. CABELL;
POWHATAN PADGETT; J. E. SMITH, April 26, 1881 sale; R. W. MOODY,
buyer; property taken by widow.
Book 20, Page 254 -- Administrators Account from May 11, 1881;
digging grave--$1.50; coffin and burial--$20.00; widow's share under
Poor Man's Law. Recorded January 16, 1882.

RO. B. MOODY -- Book 24, Page 256 -- July 12, 1918; Monday, February 10,
1919. Witnesses: W. E. SANDIDGE; DAYTON L. WATTS. Produced by
PAUL MOODY who qualified. Sons: PAUL; SAML.; FRANK; and ERNERST
MOODY; daughters, CORA LEE MOODY and LAURA V. CROCKETT. Three acres
about a mile from courthouse on Clifford Pike and opposite Amherst
cemetery. Executor: son, PAUL MOODY.

WM. MOON -- Book 5, Page 443 -- May 24, 1814; June 20, 1914.
Witnesses: AMBR. RUCKER; ANDERSON WARE; GEO. MC DANIEL. Wife,
BETSY; two youngest children, WOOD and POLLY MOON; children by first
wife have shares. Executor: son, WIATT MOON.
Book 13, Page 463 -- Administrators Bond -- JAS. M. TALIAFERRO and
RO. J. SMITH, January 15, 1855, for JAS. M. TALIAFERRO.
Book 13, Page 467 -- Inventory -- shown by wife, January 18, 1855.
$127.00. RO. H. CARTER; JAS. W. PHILLIPS; JNO. PRYOR.
Book 14, Page 222 -- Administrators Account from August 1, 1855;
JNO. PRYOR, trustee. Recorded: Saturday, November 22, 1856.

BENJ. MOORE -- Book 3, Page 230 -- February 15, 1792; September 17,
1792. Witnesses: BENNETT NALLEY; BENJ. PAYNE; JOS. MARTIN; WM.
EUBAKS(BANTS). Wife, LETISHER--300 acres where I live; sons, JNO.
and WM. when of age; daughter, ELIZ. PERKINS; sons, THOS. and BENJ.
at marriage or November 1, 1792; son, OBADIAH, when 23 or November,
1795; daughter, MILLY PERKINS; daughter, SALLY MOORE, two years after
maturity; grandson, BENJ. PERKINS, when of age; JNO. and WM. to be
educated--equal to other sons. Executors: sons, THOS., BENJ. and
OBADIAH. They qualified. Bondsmen: WM. HARRIS; PLEASANT MARTIN;
BENNETT NALLY.
Book 3, Page 268 -- Inventory -- L1314-1-9 PLEASANT MARTIN; SAML.
MERRILL; PETER LYON, October 26, 1792.
Book 4, Page 71 -- Administrators Account -- by THOS. and BENJ. from
1792; dress for SALLY MOORE; estate total: L164-5-8. Through
February 16, 1796.

ELIZ. MOORE -- Book 11, Page 522 -- Administrators Bond -- DILLARD H.
PAGE and STERLING CLAIBORNE, May 17, 1847, for DILLARD H. PAGE.
Book 12, Page 61 -- Inventory -- July 14, 1847--$25.75. HENRY LOVING;
THOS. G. HILL, JAS. F. TALIAFERRO.
Book 12, Page 89 -- Administrators Account -- from 1847; WM. WRIGHT;
JNO. S. CAMDEN; M. C. GOODWIN. Recorded: December 18, 1848.

LETISHA MOORE -- Book 3, Page 389 -- Allotment to her of land devised
by BENJ. MOORE, June 20, 1796. SAML. MURRELL; JAS. WOODS; PETER
LYON. Lines of JNO. DAWSON; ridge between Cove and Hiclory Creeks--
300 acres; many other items and timber from land.
Book 4, Page 266 -- October 21, 1800; October 21, 1806. Witnesses:
BENNETT NALLEY; NANCY MASSUPLEURY(?); MARY NALLY. Daughter, ELIZ.
PERKINS--what was left me by commissioners and she names one above.
Executors: friends, CAPT. BENJ. HARRIS; MAHOR SAML. MURRELL; both
of Albemarle and BENJ. PERKINS, Bedford County.

MARY M. MOORE -- Book 11, Page 160 -- Administrators Bond -- EDMD. C.
MOORE and SAML. M. GARLAND, August 22, 1943, for EDMD. C. MOORE.

PETER MOORE -- Book 9, Page 95 -- Administrators Bond -- JONAS PIERCE
and DRURY CHRISTIAN, July 20, 1845, for JONAS PIERCE.

SUSAN MOORE -- Book 9, Page 94 -- Administrators Bond -- JONAS PIERCE
and DRURY CHRISTIAN, July 20, 1835, for JONAS PIERCE.

THOS. MOORE -- Book 4, Page 538 -- Sheriffs Bond -- November 25, 1808.
Bondsman: JNO. CAMM; NELSON CRAWFORD; NELSON DAWSON; REUBEN PENDLETON;
WM. TURNER. Two bonds are indexed Book 4, pages 549 and 543, but not
there.
Book 4, Page 628 -- Sheriffs Bond -- July 16, 1810. Bondsman:
NELSON and WM. S. CRAWFORD; JNO. CAMM; J. P. GARLAND.

WM. MOORE -- Book 1, Page 92 -- 1766; February 2, 1767. Witnesses:
HARRIS TONEY; JNO. JACOBS; ALEX. MOORE. "Sum," JOHN--one half of land
in "Hamherst"; son, JAS.; son, AARON; daughter, SARAH TONEY; wife,
MARY--rest of my children--married and "Dutifuls" children--I leave it
to her to give them as she "things" fit.
Book 1, Page 94 -- Administrators Bond -- MARY MOORE; RO. BARNETT;
ALEX. and AARON MOORE; date, for MARY MOORE.
Book 7, Page 67 -- Administrators Bond -- HILL CARTER; WM. and ROYALL
MC CALL; DILLARD and RO. PAGE, November 20, 1827, for HILL CARTER.
Book 7, Page 269 -- Administrators Account -- from December 11, 1827
ELIZ. MOORE was buyer at sale; bond of TANDY MOORE; GEO. W. TRIBBLE
and wife, August 19, 1829. JAS. ROSE; ED. A. and PAUL C. CABELL.

JOS. MORAN -- Book 5, Page 424 -- Administrators Bond -- CHAS. MUNDY;
JNO. MORAN; WM. TURNER, March 21, 1814, for CHAS. MUNDY.
Book 5, Page 431 -- Inventory -- April 4, 1814--$1017.72. JNO. LONDON;
HENRY TURNER; WM. CLINKSCALES.
Book 6, Page 571 -- Administrators Account -- from February 20, 1815--
Nelson coltickets; March 21, 1825. JNO. GARTH; GEO. STAPLES; JNO.
WARWICK. Also see MORRAN.

JNO. JAS. MORGAN -- Book 8, Page 298 -- Guardians Bond -- ZACH.
DRUMMOND; RICHESON HENLEY; CORNL. SALE, February 18, 1833, for
ZX as guardian of JNO. J. MORGAN, orphan of BENJ. MORGAN, deceased.
Book 8, Page 415 -- Guardians Bond -- JAS. TAYLOR and JNO. HAGAN,
June 16, 1834, for JAS. TAYLOR as guardian of JNO. JAS. MORGAN,
orphan of BENJ. MORGAN, deceased.
Book 9, Page 395 -- Guardians Account -- by TAYLOR--from June 9, 1834--
$997.41. Scattered estate of the business--WM. LUSK; RO. C. CAMPBELL;
THOS. S. MOORE.
Book 10, Page 307 -- Guardians Account -- from 1836. Recorded:
January 18, 1841. WM. LUSK; RO. REA; THOS. S. MOORE.

NICHL. MORRAN -- Book 4, Page 184 -- June 12, 1805; codicil not dated;
July 15, 1805. Witnesses: DANL. M. DONALD; CHAS. JONES; JOS. BURGHER.
To codicil: D. M. DONALD; and same others as above. Wife, WINNIFRED;
my children. Executors: JNO. MORRAN of Kentucky; ELIJAH MORRAN of
Amherst County; and JNO. MASTERS of Amherst County. Codicil: ELIJAH
MORRAN and JAS. CAPBELL (sic) to occupy same part of land as now and
rent free. Son, ELIJAH, may pay L15 and have my 16 acres entry right.
ELIJAH MORRAN and JNO. MASTERS qualified--Page 407.
Book 4, Page 195 -- Inventory -- $4654.14. DANL. M. DONALD; JOS.
BURGHER (also on bond for administrators); CHAS. JONES; JOHN JACOBS.
September 5, 1805.

   The following are for MORRIS and MORRISS, but some have both
spellings and so I have just arranged them in order as MORRIS items.

ALISON MORRISS -- Book 8, Page 423 -- Administrators Bond -- RANDOLPH
MORRIS, TANDY JONES; THOS. WALKER, and BLUFORD MORRIS, August 18, 1834,
for RANDOLPH MORRIS.
Book 9, Page 221 -- Inventory -- $3425.25; August 19, 1834. JNO.
PRYOR; GEO. L. SHRADER; PETER RUCKER.
Book 9, Page 248 -- land division: East side Tobacco Row and head
border of Harris Creek and both sides of Ware's Gap. Lines of BLANFORD
HICKS; ZACH ISBELL's heirs; JABEZ CAMDEN; --Mansion house tract of

100½ acres; two other tracts--1. 107 acres on headwaters of Maple
and Thomas Mill Creeks; lines: RICH. L. ELLIS; GEO. BURKS(B).
2. 100 acres or River tract. Lines: JARRET GILLIAM's heirs; PETER
RUCKER; WM. HAYNES; GEO. L. SHRADER; JNO. N. DAVIS; JNO. PRYOR. All
legatees of full age and shares to MRS. NANCY MORRIS; widow; WM. P.
MORRIS; BLUFORD MORRIS; RANDOLPH MORRIS; MRS. ANNE PETTIGREW (formerly
MORRIS), and wife of ELI PETTIGREW; MAURICE MORRIS; THOS. H. MORRIS.
Plats, March 21, 1836. Dower agreement for division--page 250.

BEVERLY PRESTON MORRIS -- Book 9, Page 361 -- Guardians Bond -- JNO. M.
PARKS, WELDON B. PARKS; WHITING DAVIES; ISAAC REYNOLDS, December 18,
1837, for JNO. M. PARKS as guardian of BEVERLY PRESTON MORRIS, orphan
of GEO. MORRIS, deceased.
Book 10, Page 183 -- Guardians Account -- JNO. M. PARKS from April 28,
1839: J. PHELPS for tuition; bond to E. W. MORRIS; copy of plat;
clothing for winter and summer--$3.50 and $1.00; one blanket at 75¢;
socks at 25¢. December 16, 1839, HAZAEL WILLIAMS; NICHL. WAUGH.
Book 10, Page 189 -- Guardians Bond -- ELDRED W. MORRIS; GEO. T.
PLEASANTS; NICHL. WAUGH; WM. P. MORRIS; JNO. M. PARKS, December 16,
1839, for ELDRED W. MORRIS as guardian of BEVERLY P. MORRIS, orphan
of GEO. MORRIS.
Book 10, Page 295 -- so indexed, but nothing there.
Book 11, Page 374 -- Guardians Account by PARKS from 183--last figure
erased. Summary for PARKS as guardian of BEVERLY P.; MARY JANE; and
GEO. L. MORRIS. Recorded: December 15, 1845.

ELIZ. MORRIS -- Book 11, Page 480 -- Guardians Bond -- JAS. POWELL and
WM. W. THOMPSON, January 18, 1847, for JAS. POWELL as guardian of
ELIZ. MORRIS, orphan of NATHAN G. MORRIS, deceased.
Book 14, Page 59 -- Committee of JAS. B. DAVIS; RICH. L. ELLIS;
M. C. GOODWIN, December 17, 1855, for JAS. B. DAVIS.
Book 14, Page 288 -- Inventory -- small; RO. H. THORNTON; NICHL.
WAUGH; TARLTON CHILDS; Monday, May 18, 1857.
Book 14, Page 396 -- Inventory -- by same men; March 17, 1857.
Book 15, Page 115 -- Administrators Account -- by M. C. GOODWIN,
sheriff from June 21, 1858. SUSAN MORRIS was buyer. Recorded March 21,
1859.

GEO. MORRIS--JR. in some items -- Book A, Page 115 -- Administrators
Bond -- BETSY E. MORRIS; JAS. DAVIS, and CHAS. L. DAVIES, September 24,
1827, for BETSY E. MORRIS.
Book 6, Page 704 -- Administrators Bond -- ELIZ. MORRIS; THOMAS
MORRIS; PETER P. THORNTON, November 20, 1826, for ELIZ. MORRIS.
Book 6, Page 745 -- Inventory -- December 5, 1826--$2814.71; no
committee named.
Book 7, Page 16 -- Division -- ELIZ. MORRIS, widow--76 acres and mansion
house; Lots to GEO. W.; NATHAN G.; WM. C. MORRISS; SALLY DAVIS, wife
of LINDSEY DAVIS (nee MORRISS); BELINDA MORRISS; MAURICE MORRISS;
infant; NANCY G. BURKS, nee MORRIS, wife of GEO. BURKS; POLLY MORRISS;
to estate of THOS. MORRISS (A middle initial); SUSAN MORRIS, infant--
all children of GEO. MORRISS--525 acres. JNO. PRYOR for REUBEN
NORVELL, surveyor. Slaves also divided; plat on page 164: Cedar and
Big Dancing Creek and both sides of road from Pedlar mill to CURTIS
WATTS. Adjoins WATTS; CHAS. L. DAVIES; heirs of GEO. MORRIS, JR.;
GEO. P. LUCK; FLEMING H. DUNCAN heirs; PETER P. THORNTON. Committee:
P. P. THORNTON; CURTIS WATTS; JOS. R. CARTER, February 13, 1828.
Book 9, Page 336 -- Administrators Bond -- JNO. D. DAVIS; THOS. N.
EUBANK; ANTHONY RICHESON, September 18, 1837, for JNO. D. DAVIS.
Book 10, Page 29 -- division to GEO. MORRIS, JR. went on lands,
March 22, 1838, JNO. PRYOR; assistant surveyor, WM. PRYOR. 194 acres
to MARY JANE MORRIS, infant; 194 acres to GEO. LEWIS MORRIS, infant;
both tracts on Cedar Creek. Mansion house tract of 435 acres: 87
acres to BEVERLY PRESTON MORRIS; Otter Creek--142 acres--to JNO. M.
PARKS; Brier Branch--206 acres to ELDRIDGE WOODSON MORRIS, of age.
March 23, 1838. JAS. DAVIS; ARCHIBALD REYNOLDS; CHAS. L. DAVIS.
Book 10, Page 69 -- December 18, 1837. Motion of JNO. D. DAVIS,
administrator to have RICH. L. ELLIS; JAS. DAVIS; ARCHIBALD REYNOLDS;
CHAS. L. DAVIS to divide personal estate. Slaves to five children,
December 27, 1837. Except one old man of no value and left with

administrator. To W. W. MORRIS; JNO. M. PARKS who married SUSAN
MORRIS; BEVERLY P. MORRIS; MARY JANE MORRIS; GEO. L. MORRIS.
November 20, 1838.

GEO. L. MORRIS -- Book 10, Page 184 -- JNO. M. HARKS as guardian of
GEO. L.; MARY JANE; E. W. MORRIS; BEVERLY P. MORRIS and all together,
from April 28, 1838.
Book 10, Page 185 -- Guardians Account -- by guardian for GEO. L.
MORRIS.
Book 10, Page 183 -- for BEVERLY P. MORRIS--account by guardian.
April 4, 1839. HAZAEL WILLIAMS; NICHL. WAUGH.
Book 11, Page 291 -- Guardians Account -- 1840 by E. W. MORRIS for
BEVERLY P. MORRIS; MARY JANE's account. February 17, 1845.
Book 11, Page 359 -- Guardians Account -- by PARKS from June 22, 1839.
Recorded: December 15, 1845.
Book 12, Page 64 -- Inventory -- July 10, 1848--$3016.30. J. D. DAVIS;
JNO. E. ELLIS; R. P. JONES.
Book 12, Page 122 -- Administrators Bond -- ELDRED W. MORRIS and
ALEX. C. JOHNSON, April 17, 1848, for ELDRED W. MORRIS and DAVID
PATTESON.
Book 12, Page 245 -- Administrators Account -- by ELIZ. MORRIS from
February 16, 1826; tuition to THOS. PAXTON, July 28, 1849. THOS. N.
EUBANK; JNO. PRYOR; RO. H. CARTER.
Book 13, Page 208 -- Administrators Account -- ELDRED W. MORRIS from
October 28, 1844--to H(?) M. MORRIS; G. L. MORRIS--share in estate
of GEO. MORRIS, JR. Bond of WM. and HENRY MORRIS; B. P. MORRIS'
account. Suit versus C. L. DAVIS; cash paid you at camp meeting and
other items. E. W. MORRIS, guardian for G. L. MORRIS, deceased.
Recorded: April 9, 1849.
Book 13, Page 212 -- division: to E. W. MORRIS; GAINES W. PARKS;
JNO. M. PARKS; BEVERLY P. MORRIS. December 26, 1848. JNO. D. DAVIS;
R. P. JONES; JNO. E. ELLIS.

HENRY T. (L) MORRIS -- Book 7, Page 148 -- Administrators Bond --
CHAS. L. DAVIES; WM. H. MC CULLOCH; CHAS. L. BARRETT; WM. ARMISTEAD,
March 18, 1828, for CHAS. L. DAVIES.
Book 8, Page 263 -- Administrators Account -- from March 19, 1827.
JNO. PRYOR and GEO. L. SHRADER. Recorded: January 15, 1829.

JNO. R. MORRIS -- Book 15, Page 215 -- Administrators Bond -- NELSON
HICKS; EDWIN B. WARE; BLUFORD MORRIS, July 18, 1859, for NELSON HICKS.
Book 15, Page 219 -- Inventory and sale -- $240.70, inventory:
JAS. M. ALLEN; BLUFORD HICKS; GEO. W. CASH. Sale, August 6, 1859.
Buyers: MRS. MORRIS; J. MORRIS--$252.96.
Book 16, Page 13 -- Inventory -- $238.03. JUDITH MORRIS; ALBERT D.
WATTS, assignee. Recorded: December 17, 1860.

MARY JANE MORRIS -- Book 10, Page 184 -- Guardians Account -- JNO. M.
PARKS from April 28, 1838. This and following pages contain account
for wards: MARY JANE and GEO. L. MORRIS; amount from BEVERLY P. MORRIS,
December 16, 1839. HAZAEL WILLIAMS; NICHL. WAUGH.
Book 10, Page 188 -- Guardians Bond -- ELDRED W. MORRIS; GEO. T.
PLEASANTS; NICHL. WAUGHT; WM. P. MORRIS; JNO. M. PARKS, December 16,
1839, for ELDRED W. MORRIS as guardian of MARY JANE and GEO. L.
MORRIS, orphans of GEO. MORRIS, deceased.
Book 11, Page 293 -- Guardians Account -- from 1840; BEVERLY P.
MORRIS named; ELIZ. MORRIS. February 7, 1845.
Book 11, Page 358 -- Guardians Account -- by PARKS from February 29,
1837. Recorded December 15, 1845.

MAURICE MORRIS -- Book 7, Page 116 -- Guardians Bond -- GEO. BURKS and
SAML. R. DAVIES, January 21, 1828, for Guardians Bond as guardian of
MAURICE MORRIS, orphan of GEO. MORRIS, deceased.

MRS. NANCY MORRIS -- Book 14, Page 452 -- Administrators Bond --
BLUFORD MORRIS and WM. P. MORRIS, November 17, 1857, for BLUFORD
MORRIS.
Book 14, Page 489 -- Inventory -- November 21, 1857, slaves, etc.
$3192.75. Bonds of MORRIS MORRIS; MARY ALLEN; JNO. R. and BLUFORD

MORRIS, administrator of R. MORRIS; January 18, 1858. JOS. R. CARTER;
ZACH. D. TINSLEY; EDWIN M. WARE; JNO. J. WARE; MARSHALL R. CUNNINGHAM.
WM. P. MORRIS was a buyer at sale.
Book 15, Page 123 -- Administrators Account -- from November 21, 1857
to JNO. R. MORRIS; bond of MARY ALLEN; MAURICE MORRIS; BLUFORD MORRIS;
JNO. B. MORRIS, administrator. January 18, 1858.

CAPT. NATHAN G. MORRIS -- Book 11, Page 349 -- Administrators Bond --
JAS. B. DAVIS and LINDSEY DAVIS, November 18, 1845, for JAS. B. DAVIS.
Book 11, Page 397 -- Inventory -- $262.11 and some small items.
February 16, 1846. JAS. RICHESON; CHAS. TYLER; PETTICUS RICHESON.
Book 11, Page 612 -- plat and division -- east side Blue Ridge and
both sides Robert's Creek--next to Pedlar River. Lines: CHAS. TYLER;
Washington College lands; WM. RAMSEY; 348 acres. Order of March, 1847.
Widow, MRS. ELIZ. MORRIS; son, GEO. W. MORRIS; infant daughter--
"MRS. ELIZABETH MORRIS" (sic), but in summary it is ELIZ. L. (S)
MORRIS, infant--only heirs. April 27, 1847. JAS. S. and JESSE
RICHESON; JAS. POWELL, guardian for ELIZ.
Book 12, Page 62 -- bonds and papers inventory -- from 1819. WM.
DAVIS, 1819. GEO. W. MORRIS; FITZGERALD and MORRIS rent, 1846;
amount from GEO. W. MORRIS and purchases by MRS. MORRIS; JNO. W.
PAINE's medical bill; July 15, 1848. JNO. PRYOR and WM. D. DAVIS.

RANDOLPH MORRIS -- Book 13, Page 366 -- Administrators Bond -- JNO. R.
MORRIS and WM. P. MORRIS, July 17, 1854, for JNO. R. MORRIS.
Book 13, Page 404 -- Inventory -- November 25, 1854. JNO. R. MORRIS,
administrator: $871.25. THOS. LEE; ABNER HAYDEN; BLUFORD HICKS.
Book 15, Page 249 -- Administrators Bond -- EDWIN M. WARE and BLUFORD
HICKS, October 17, 1859, for EDWIN M. WARE.
Book 15, Page 309 -- Inventory -- JNO. R. MORRIS, former administrator,
deceased. June, 1859. $563.00 October 29, 1859. ZACH. D. TINSLEY;
MARSHAL R. CUNNINGHAM; JAS. M. ALLEN; PRESTON HICKS.
Book 15, Page 613 -- Administrators Account -- of JNO. R. MORRIS from
July 20, 1858; administrator is dead. To BLUFORD MORRIS. JNO. T.
ELLIS, commissioner. November 19, 1860.

RHODA MORRIS -- Book 3, Page 193 -- Guardians Bond -- BEVERLY WILLIAM-
SON and CORNL. SALE, July 4, 1791, for BEVERLY WILLIAMSON as guardian
of RHODA MORRIS, orphan of JAS. MORRIS.

SUSAN A. MORRIS -- Book 9, Page 339 -- Guardians Bond -- JNO. D. DAVIS
and WM. H. GARLAND, October 16, 1837, for JNO. D. DAVIS as guardian of
SAM, orphan of GEO. MORRIS, JR. (?), deceased.

THOS. MORRISS -- Book 7, Page 140 -- Administrators Bond -- CHAS. L.
DAVIS; WM. H. MC CULLOCH; CHAS. L. BARRET and WM. ARMISTEAD, March 17,
1828, for CHAS. L. DAVIS.
Book 7, Page 265 -- Guardians Bond -- margin: October 20, 1829,
original delivery to BEVERLY B. BOSTON, New Albany, Floyd County,
Indiana--May 18, 1829, motion of Boston for REBECCA MORRISS, widow of
MAURICE MORRISS, deceased. REBECCA is guardian of THOS.--age 16;
GEO.--14; NATHANIEL--13; MAURICE--11; WM. DUNCAN--9--all infant heirs
of MAURICE MORRISS. Bondsman: BOSTON; BERRY WILCOXSON. HARVEY
SCRIBNER, Clerk of Circuit Court: JNO. ROSS, judge.
Book 8, Page 262 -- Account by LINDSEY DAVIS, administrator of THOS. A.
MORRISS--some data for THOS. seems to belong with THOS. A.
Book 8, Page 264 -- Administrators Account -- CHAS. L. DAVIS,
administrator from February 25, 1827--crossing James to Bedford on
business; to ELIZ. MORRIS, administratrix of GEO. MORRIS, deceased;
letter from Indiana--postage of 25¢; expense of land division; slave
account. March 21, 1829; JNO. PRYOR; GEO. L. SHRADER; JNO. W. YOUNG.

THOS. A. MORRISS -- Book 14, Page 535 -- Administrators Account --
LINDSEY DAVIS from September 9, 1825 and returned January 14, 1858.
JESSE RICHESON, bondsman, is dead.
Book 8, Page 13 -- LINDSEY DAVIS from December 9, 1826; bonds of
ELIJAH DAVIS; N. C. MORRIS; ROSEMARY GUE; CHAS. TYLER; A. NOEL.
November 15, 1828. JOS. R. CARTER; RO. H. CARTER.
Book 8, Page 262 -- Administrators Account -- by DAVIS from 1829.
Recorded: September 17, 1832.

THOS. G. MORRIS -- Book 6, Page 700 -- Administrators Bond -- LINDSEY
DAVIS and JESSE RICHESON, November 20, 1826--this seems to be same
item mentioned above; confusion as to index and middle initials has
been noted in this work.
Book 6, Page 743 -- Inventory -- no total; February 19, 1827; ELISHA
DAVIS; NATHL. G. MORRIS; WM. NOELL.
Book 6, Page 750 -- Inventory -- March 3, 1827: $601.75 and March 14th.
$5558.25 many slaves; THOS. N. EUBANK; WM. H. MC CULLOCH; JAS. DAVIS;
JNO. PRYOR.
Book 7, Page 1 -- division of Maple Creek land and Cedar Creek:
1640 acres: five lots to heirs of MAURICE MORRIS; GEO. BURKS who
married RACHEL MORRIS; MARTIN DAWSON who married PEGGY MORRIS; heirs
of GEO. MORRIS; CHAS. L. DAVIS who married NANCY MORRIS; Banks Mountain
tract and mansion house tract can't be divided equally and suggest
sale. JAS. DAVIS; THOS. N. EUBANK; JNO. PRYOR and WM. H. MC CULLOCH.
March 19, 1829.
Book 8, Page 268 -- Administrators Account -- by CHAS. L. DAVIS from
April 7, 1827; paid SALLY ROACH; paid estate of GEO. MORRIS, JR.,
deceased. On 269 is account by DAVIS as administrator of THOS. MORRIS.
Recorded September 17, 1832. JNO. PRYOR and GEO. L. SHRADER.

THOS. H. MORRIS -- Book 6, Page 724 -- Administrators Bond -- CHAS. L.
DAVIS and WM. ARMISTEAD, and MARTIN PARKS, February 19, 1827, for
CHAS. L. DAVIS.
Book 7, Page 143 -- Administrators Bond -- CHAS. L. DAVIS, WM. H.
MC CULLOCH, CHAS. L. BARRET and WM. ARMISTEAD, March 18, 1828, for
CHAS. L. DAVIS.

WM. MORRISS -- Book 14, Page 519 -- Guardians Bond -- JNO. R. MORRIS
and W. J. BETHEL, January 18, 1858, for MNO. R. MORRIS as guardian
of WM. LEANNA and JAS. MORRIS, orphans of RANDOLPH MORRIS, deceased.

WM. D. MORRIS -- Book 6, Page 723 -- Administrators Bond -- CHAS. L.
DAVIS, WM. ARMISTEAD, and MARRIN PARKS, February 19, 1827, for
CHAS. L. DAVIS.
Book 7, Page 149 -- Administrators Bond -- CHAS. L. DAVIES (sic),
WM. H. MC CULLOCH, and CHAS. BARRETT, March 18, 1828, for CHAS. L.
DAVIS.
Book 7, Page 250 -- so indexed, but it is Book 8, Page 250 -- Adminis-
trators Account -- by DAVIS from 1827; muster fine; JNO. PRYOR and
GEO. L. SHRADER, September 17, 1832.
Book 8, Page 258 -- so indexed, but not there.

ANNA MORRISON -- Book 4, Page 320 -- Guardians Bond -- SAML. BAILEY;
JNO. FARRAR, and THOS. PUGH, April 21, 1800, for SAML. BAILEY as
guardian of ANNA MORRISON, orphans of WM. MORRISON, deceased. Clerk
notes it as recorded on April 17, 1800.

JAS. MORRISON -- Book 1, Page 36 -- September 21, 1763; November 7,
1763. Witnesses: DAVID CRAWFORD; ANDREW REID; ALEX. PATTON. Wife,
with child--400 acres; my honored father and mother; my brother,
THOS.; executor: brother, JNO. MORRISON and my wife.
Book 1, Page 38 -- Administrators Bond -- REBECCA MORRISON; SAML.
WOODS, and THOS. WEST, November 7, 1763, for REBECCA MORRISON.
Book 1, Page 43 -- Inventory -- December 10, 1763; no total; JNO.
WOODS; FRANS. MOORE; JAS. LOCKEY.
Book 3, Page 163 -- October 20, 1790; February 7, 1791. Witnesses:
THOS. PROSSER; SAML. WINFREY; SAML. SPENCER; SAML. SPENCER, JR.;
NICHL. CABELL. Estate in Virginia and Great Britain--or may become
an heir; brother, JNO. MORRISON. Executors: friends, CHAS. IRVING
of Albemarle. He qualified, page 164; bondsman: JAS. FRANKLIN.

JNO. MORRISON -- Book 2, Page 246 -- April 10, 1785; October 3, 1785.
Witnesses: JNO. MORRIS; JNO. COLE; ZACH MORRIS; REBECCA COLE. Wife,
WINNEFORD, supposed to be with child; my brothers and sisters; my
brother, WM.--land next to ELIJAH STONE; my brother, MICHL. Executors:
JNO. DAWSON; ELIJAH STONE; EPHRAIM BLAINE; JNO. THOMAS. Executors
refused to serve.
Book 2, Page 248 -- CHAS IRVING and EDMD. WINSTON, November 8, 1785,
for CHAS. IRVING.

Book 3, Page 2 -- Inventory -- no total; JNO. S. DAWSON; BENJ. MOOR;
JNO. THOMAS, March 6, 1786.
Book 3, Page 341 -- March 10, 1795; July 20, 1795. Witnesses: JNO.
MORAN; THOS. PATTON; RO. DINWIDDIE. Sons: THOS.; JAS.; ROBT.;
daughters, JANE BLAINE; MARY MONTGOMERY; son, JNO.; daughter, REBECCA
BARNETT; my wife; granddaughter, MARY MORRISON, eldest daughter of my
son, JAS. Son, ROBT., to be completely educated.
Book 3, Page 343 -- Administrators Bond -- JAS. MORRISON; RO. MORRISON;
HUDSON MARTIN; JAS. WOODS, July 20, 1795, for first two.
Book 3, Page 372 -- Inventory -- no total; JOS. and JAS. MONTGOMERY;
HAWES COLEMAN.
Book 4, Page 330 -- Guardians Bond -- THOS. PUGH; AUGUSTINE SHEPHERD;
JAMES JOPLING, June 15, 1801, for THOS. PUGH as guardian of JNO.
MORRISON, orphan of JNO. MORRISON, deceased.

JOS. H. MORRISON -- Book 4, Page 348 -- Administrators Bond -- THOS.
STEWART and AMBROSE RUCKER, JR., June 21, 1802, for THOS. STEWART.

WM. MORRISON -- Book 3, Page 34 -- December 21, 1785; April 2, 1787.
Witnesses: JNO. MORRIS; FREDERICK PUGH; GEO. MORRIS. Wife, MARY
PERRIN MORRISON--plantation; daughter, ANN, when 18; slaves named;
my brothers and sisters: JNO. KING; RO. YOUNG; THOMAS MORRISON;
THOS. HENDERSON; MICHL. MORRISON--are these half and full all lumped
together?
Book 3, Page 86 -- Inventory -- L213-11-10, BENJ. MOOR; PETER LYON,
June 4, 1787.
Book 3, Page 42 -- Administrators Bond -- MARY MORRISON, JAMES TURNER;
JNO. MORRIS, June 4, 1787, for MARY MORRISON and JAMES TURNER.
Book 3, Page 104 -- Individual Bond -- by MARY PERRIN FARRAR; RICH.
FARRAR and JAS. DILLARD, June 1, 1789, to JNO. MORRIS for bond when
she qualified to administrate.
Book 3, Page 584 -- Compromise of estate by JNO. DIGGS; JNO. DAWSON,
and WM. HARRIS, commissioner, October 20, 1800--JNO. FARRAR married
executrix and SAML. BAILEY married only heiress at law. BAILEY pays
FARRAR L70 and FARRAR delivers estate to BAILEY.

ALEX. C. MOSELEY -- Book 16, Page 531 -- Guardians Bond -- RO. H.
THORNTON and JNO. A. MOSELEY, July 18, 1864, for RO. H. THORNTON as
guardian of ALEX. C. MOSELEY; no parent set forth.
Book 19, Page 434 -- Administrators Bond -- GRANDISON W. MOSELY and
SAML. B. RUCKER, May 19, 1879. The testator is not plain here, but
could be JNO. A.

JNO. N. MOSELEY -- Book 16, Page 531 -- Guardians Bond -- JNO. A.
MOSELEY and RO. H. THORNTON, July 18, 1864, for JNO. N. MOSELEY as
guardian of JNO. N.; WM. S. and MARY A. MOSELEY; no parent set forth.

JNO. MORTON (MORSTON and MORTON) -- Book 5, Page 422 -- Administrators
Bond -- GEO. and WM. MC DANIEL, February 21, 1814, for GEO. MC DANIEL.
Book 5, Page 428 -- Inventory -- no total; Harris Creek mill; JNO.
MC DANIEL; JNO. CASHWELL; JOS. HIGGINBOTHAM; GIDEON RUCKER.

NANCY MORTON -- Book 5, Page 463 -- Guardians Bond -- JOSHUA RUCKER
and WM. RUCKER, October 17, 1814, for JOSHUA RUCKER as guardian of
NANCY MORTON, orphan of JNO. MORTON.

MRS. ELIZ. F. MOSBY (N FLETCHER) -- Book 19, Page 399 -- Trustee
Account -- October 28, 1878--WM. HAMILTON MOSBY, trustee of wife,
ELIZ., under marriage settlement--from January 29, 1870. West
Virginia taxes; board and tuition of EDWD.; Campbell County taxes;
Baltimore trip to dentist; contribution to parsonage at Amherst
Court House; for prayer book; side walk expense on Clay Street
property in Lynchburg; Stanton tract rent of ALBERT BERRY; EDWARD
KERR's tuition; expense to Alexandria to see about turnout on H. H.
place; Hunset Hall rebuilt; BRINKHOLDER and BAILEY suit versus MOSBY;
Recorded March 17, 1789. Trip to Europe for health and rebuilding
Hunsted Hall to gratify elegant and refined tastes.
Book 22, Page 462 -- May 27, 1890; October 20, 1890. Produced by
SIDNEY FLETCHER and handwriting by CHAS. L. SCOTT and WM. R. CHASE.

SIDNEY FLETCHER qualified. Appraisers: J. J. AMBLER, E. B. AMBLER, WM. R. CHASE, S. B. CLAIBOREN, G. LANDON SCOTT. To ELIZ. AMBLER GISK of Lynchburg; to LAURA AMBLER RHODES; to INDIANA F. WILLIAMS--the engraving in parlor, The Parting Day; Russian marble mantle clock; other souveniers of my departed niece, DAISY WILLIAMS. To LUCIAN FLETCHER--$200.00 annuity. Cousin, L. R. PAGE; 100 acres to HAMILTON KERR; my brother, SIDNEY FLETCHER--where I live to Sisters of Charity of Holy Cross for use. Reversion to heirs of SIDNEY FLETCHER and he is to administrate. Administrators Bond on page 464.
Book 22, Page 475 -- Inventory -- November 13, 1890--$15,228.03 by appraisers above. This woman was sister of INDIANA FLETCHER WILLIAMS who established Sweet Briar Institute--now College--as a memorial to her daughter, DAISY WILLIAMS.

JNO. MOSBY -- Book 3, Page 287 -- Tobacco inspector, Swan Creek Warehouse, October 22, 1793. Bondsman: WM. HARRIS; WM. LEE HARRIS.

BETSY MOSS -- Book 6, Page 50 -- Guardians Bond -- WILLIS FRANKLIN and S. CLAIBORNE, December 21, 1818, for WILLIS FRANKLIN as guardian of BETSY (ELIZ.) MOSS, orphan of WM. MOSS.

COURTNEY MOSS -- Book 5, Page 488 -- Guardians Bond -- JNO. MOSS; THOS. ALDRIDGE; STERLING CLAIBORNE, March 120, 1815, for JNO. MOSS as guardian of COURTNEY MOSS, orphan of WM. MOSS.

POLLY MOSS -- Book 5, Page 234 -- JNO. MOSS; HENRY FRANKLIN, and HENRY H. WATTS, July 19, 1813, for JNO. MOSS as guardian of POLLY MOSS, orphan of WM. MOSS, deceased.

RO. MOSS -- Book 6, Page 56 -- Guardians Bond -- WILLIS FRANKLIN and WM. STAPLES, and HENRY FRANKLIN, February 15, 1819, for WILLIS FRANKLIN as guardian of RO. MOSS, orphan of WM. MOSS.

WM. MOSS -- Book 5, Page 15 -- Administrators Bond -- CHARLOTTE MOSS; JNO. THOMPSON (Meret--sic); CHAS. WATTS; and JNO. MARR, March 21, 1810, for CHARLOTTE MOSS.
Book 5, Page 23 -- Inventory -- $5170.06; JNO. N. ROSE and CHAS. MOORE, July 15, 1811.
Book 5, Page 594 -- Administrators Account -- from May 5, 1810--J. MOSS muster fines for 1809; use of the family in Spring after WILLIAM's death; Richmond and Lynchburg trips; New Glasgow house rented; mention of SAML. MEREDITH's estate--not clear. Recorded: July 15, 1816. THOS. ALDRIDGE; MARTIN WILSON; WM. KNIGHT.
Book 6, Page 234 -- Guardians Bond -- JNO. MOSS and CHAS. WATTS, July 16, 1821, for JNO. MOSS as guardian of WM. and CHARITY MOSS, orphans of WM. MOSS.

JNO. MOUNTCASTLE -- Book 8, Page 19 -- Administrators Bond -- August 18, 1830--by Lynchburg Marshall of Chancery at Amherst; October Court, 1830, to pay decree of EDMD. F. COFFEE versus PENDLETON and MOUNTCASTLE. MRS. JNO. MOUNTCASTLE was a buyer--$2.56 left after debt paid.
Book 8, Page 69 -- Inventory -- at dwelling on November 1, 1830; many listed as slaves and note on margin says that they are encumbered by Deed of Trust of Amherst County record. JNO. PENN; JNO. COOEMAN; ED. A. CABELL.

SOPHIA MOUNTCASTLE -- Book 8, Page 20 -- Guardians Bond -- DABNEY SANDIDGE and BARNET CASH, August 18, 1830, for DABNEY SANDIDGE as guardian of SOPHIA; REBECCA and JNO. MOUNTCASTLE, orphans of JNO. MOUNTCASTLE.

CHAS. MUNDY -- Book 6, Page 461 -- indexed as 61; Sheriff, June 21, 1824; Bondsman: JNO. WARWICK; THOS. N. EUBANK; HENRY H. WATTS; JOS. PETTYJOHN.
Book 6, Page 466 -- Sheriff, June 23, 1824. Bondsman: JNO. WARWICK; JOS. PETTYJOHN; A. B. DAVIES.
Book 6, Page 652 -- Sheriff. March 20, 1826. Bondsman: JAS. DILLARD; JESSE BECK; JOS. PETTYJOHN; HENRY H. WATTS; WM. BOURNE.
Book 11, Page 226 -- Administrators Bond -- MARY MUNDY; J. PETTYJOHN; ALEX. MUNDY, July 15, 1844, for MARY MUNDY.

Book 11, Page 234 -- Inventory -- July 23, 1844--$6247.75. JNO. and
WM. DILLARD; JAS. L. LAMKIN.
Book 11, Page 237 -- additional inventory -- July 23, 1844; bond of
JESSE MUNDY; MARY MUNDY. Recorded: August 19, 1844.
Book 11, Page 275 -- Sale of November 20, 1844, with consent of
legatees: ALEX; CATH. MUNDY WATTS; JOS. PETTYJOHN; JAS. S. DILLARD.
All present save JESSE MUNDY; MARY MUNDY, widow. They divided articles:
$500.75. Buyers: JESSE: MARY by JOS. PETTYJOHN. Recorded:
January 20, 1845.
Book 11, Page 285 -- Slave division: to widow and five legatees:
JESSE MUNDY, absent; put lots in hat--CAPT. JAS. M. DILLARD has consent
of JESSE; CATH. WATTS; JOS. PETTYJOHN. February 17, 1845. WM.
DILLARD: D. STAPLES; JAS. L. LAMKIN.
Book 11, Page 596 -- Administrators Account -- from July 23, 1844, by
MARY MUNDY; A. MUNDY; bond of JAS. D. WATTS; SAMPSON DUIGUID's
account of $25.00; MRS. C. WATTS and JOS. PETTYJOHN.
Book 11, Page 601 -- Debts due estate: ALEX; MARY MUNDY; CATH.
WATTS; JESSE MUNDY; JOS. PETTYJOHN; SILAS P. VAWTER, trustee--advanced
sums to legatees. Accounts of RO. ISBELL and DAVID STAPLES--not as
legatees.
Book 12, Page 275 -- Administrators Account -- from 1847; surveyor
fee; JNO. DILLARD, administrator of JAS. JONES for land rent.
Legatees: MARY, widow; JESSE MUNDY; JOS. PETTYJOHN and wife; ALEX.
MUNDY; JAS. M. DILLARD and wife; CATH. WATTS. Recorded: July 15,
1850.

JNO. MUNDY -- Book 6, Page 393 -- July 20, 1822; September 15, 1823.
Witnesses: HENRY BALLINGER; JNO. PATTEN; RO. ADAMS. CHAS. MUNDY
refused to serve; JAS. L. LAMKIN made bond and CHAS. MUNDY was
bondsman. Nephew, JAS. L. LAMKIN--344 acres where I live; to JAS.
DAVIS--slaves and one was given to him some years ago. My niece,
CATH. MONDY (sic); nieces NANCY and MARY MUNDY. Executor: friend
and brother, CHAS. MONDAY (sic). Administrators Bond is page 389.
Book 6, Page 432 -- Inventory -- $4491.50, January 19, 1824. JESSE
BECK; WM. TURNER; JAS. LEE.

SAML. MURPHY -- Book 1, Page 170 -- Administrators Bond -- THOS. REID
and RICH. ALCOCK, May 8, 1770, for THOS. REID.
Book 1, Page 196 -- Inventory -- December 10, 1770-L134-5-10½. JOS.
DILLARD; GABL. PENN. Recorded May 1771.

THOS. MURRELL -- Book 6, Page 337 -- Ordinance Bond at house in county,
December 16, 1822. Bondsman: JNO. Y. JOHNSON.

CORNL. MURRIL -- Book 4, Page 265 -- Inventory -- L114-16-3; JANE
MURRELL made mark; BENJ. PRYOR; THOS. NASH; JOS. MATTHEWS, September 15,
1806.
Book 4, Page 423 -- Administrators Bond -- JANE MURRELL (sic) HENRY
SMITH; THOS. STATHAM, December 16, 1805, for JANE MURRELL.

RICH. MURROW -- Book 3, Page 421 -- Inventory -- L60-17-0 LEWIS
NEVIL; RICH. BREEDLOVE; JAS. HANSBROUGH, January 31, 1797.
Book 4, Page 285 -- Administrators Bond -- RICH. MURROW; JOS. ROBERTS;
JNO. HAGER; GEO. BLAIN, December 19, 1796, for RICH. MURROW as
administrator of RICH. MURROW, JR.
Book 4, Page 486 -- Administrators Bond -- PARMENAS BRYANT and CHAS.
WATTS, December 21, 1807, for PARMENAS BRYANT; no JR. used here.

JAS. MUSE -- Book 8, Page 410 -- Guardians Bond -- WM. P. MUSE and
REUBEN COX, April 21, 1834, for WM. P. MUSE as guardian of his
children: JAS.; LOUISA; and FRANCES MUSE.
Book 9, Page 65 -- Guardians Bond for him for same orphans, April 20,
1835. Bondsman: GEO. ROYALTY; WM. D. D. MILES.

WM. MUSE, JR. -- Book 5, Page 405 -- Ordinary Bond at house in county,
December 20, 1813. Bondsman: GEO. W. TAYLOR.

JAS. S. MUTTER -- Book 7, Page 178 -- Administrators Bond -- WM. M.
WALLER, RO. TINSLEY; SAML. M. GARLAND, October 20, 1828, for WM. M.
WALLER.

JNO. MYERS -- Book 6, Page 603 -- Constables June 21, 1825. Bondsmen:
WM. MC DANIEL; JNO. MC DANIEL.
Book 7, Page 27 -- Same; June 19, 1827; Bondsmen: WM. and LINDSEY
MC DANIEL.
Book 10, Page 190 -- Refunding Bond -- November 19, 1839: JNO.
MYERS and WM. H. KNIGHT to JOS. PETTYJOHN, administrator of CHAS.
WILSON. RICH. WILSON, father of CHAS. WILSON, has since died and
Estate Committment to Sheriff, JNO. COLEMAN. Note: The office of
sheriff of Amherst is now held by my good friend, HENRY MYERS. I do
not know his genealogy. He has a brother who operates a store on
West U.S. 60 at Forks of Buffalo.

Abstracts from Hardesty and Brock

1766-1769 -- September 6, 1768, JAMESTOWN PATTERSON - page 405 - in
case versus WM. MOORE, "The Ugley." Dismissed by mutual consent. I
find several references to this WM. MOORE and evidently his looks did
not match those of some other WM. MOORE and it got him this cognomen.

1773-1782 -- August Court, 1780, motion of JAS. HENDERSON to bind out
bastard child, JNO. MORAN, of ANN MORAN. This seemed to be a habit
with poor ANN MORAN for on page 48, May Court, 1774, church wardens
were ordered to bind out another bastard child of hers by the name
of MARY MORAN.

-N-

MOSES NAPIER -- Book 8, Page 181 -- Administrators Bond -- JOS. H.
MC DANIEL; JAS. S. HIGGINBOTHAM, and WM. M. WARE, March 19, 1832, for
JOS. H. MC DANIEL.
Book 8, Page 201 -- Inventory -- Several slaves, etc.--$1478.75.
BENJ. TALIAFERRO; ORMUND WARE; JAS. F. TALIAFERRO.

ELIZ. NASH -- Book 9, Page 326 -- Refunding Bond -- ELIZ. F. NASH;
RO. KYLE to WM. KYLE, administrator with will annexed of BETSY LONG,
deceased--will of 1836 and recorded on August 21, 1837. Slaves
delivered to DAVID R. EDLEY, agent and attorney-in-fact for ELIZ. F.
NASH and allotment to her by decree of Superior Court of Chancery
in Amherst County: WM. S. CRAWFORD versus ELIZ. NASH, ALEX. B. DYER
et als. Signed by D. R. EDLEY for ELIZ. F. NASH.

ENOCH NASH -- Book 2, Page 9 -- Of "Culleny of Virginia"; daughter,
LUCRESIA DIXSON--100 "akers" and at her death to ELIZ. and ANN DIXSON,
daughters of WM. DIXSON--to be taken from tract I got of GERREMIAH
PATRICK. To my --son ?--JOS.; my son, ENOCH; daughter, MARY NASH;
my wife, SUSANNA; my son, THOS.; daughters, SARAH and ELIZ. NASH.
Administrator: JAS. NEVIL. March 12, 1772; March 5, 1781. Witnesses:
JAS. MATHIS; WM. DICKSON; LUCRETIA DICKSON--note differences in DIXSON
spelling.

CORNL. NEVIL -- Book 4, Page 303 -- Guardians Bond -- ABRAHAM WARWICK;
LEWIS NEVIL; ROWLAND EDMUNDS, October 21, 1799, for ABRAHAM WARWICK
as guardian of CORNL. NEVIL, orphan of JAS. NEVIL, deceased.

ESTHER NEFIL -- Book 4, Page 304 -- Guardians Bond -- ZACH. NEVIL and
ROWLAND EDMUNDS, October 21, 1799, for ZACH. NEVIL as guardian of
ESTHA (sic) NEVIL, orphan of JAS. NEVIL, deceased. Note: indexed
ESTHER, but spelled ESTHA.

JAS. NEVIL -- indexed COLONEL -- Book 2, Page 211 -- Wife, MARY, land
on south fork of Rockfish and Maple Branch--minor children and single
daughter; son, LEWIS--land next to CORNL. THOMAS, deceased--where DICK
made a conoe; top of a hill where CAPTAIN was killed; sons, JAS.;
ZACH.; CORNL.; daughter, ELIZ. NEVIL; daughter, MOLLY NEVIL; daughter,
EASTHER NEVIL; my share of dower of MRS. LUCY CHILDRESS. If any
children die without heirs or before maturity. Administrators:
friends: WM. CABELL, SR. and NICHL. CABELL. May 19, 1784; February 7,
1785. Witnesses: MATT. NIGHTINGALE; NORBORN THOMAS; JAS. MATTHEWS;

RICH. MURROW; JNO. PRICHARD; WM. DIKSON. Page 215 Administrators Bond by administrators named in will. Bondsmen: EDMD. WINSTON; SAML. MEREDITH on probate date.
Book 2, Page 224 -- Inventory -- of COL. JAS. NEVIL--many slaves-- L2344-6-3, March 19, 1785. ABRAHAM WARWICK; JAS. MATTHEWS; RICH. MURROW.
Book 3, Page 121 -- Administrators Account - by WM. CABELL from February, 1785--to REV. MR. PEASLEY for preaching his father's funeral and paid by LEWIS NEVIL--L2-16-0; coffin made by FRANCIS WEST--12-6. Militia and provision certificates are of record. September 7, 1789. Many interesting items.
Book 3, Page 20 -- Division, December 26, 1786, on order of October Court last: slaves to LEWIS and JAS. NEVIL by ARAHAM WARWICK; JAS. MATTHEWS; WM. CABELL, JR.
Book 4, Page 1 -- indexed as Book 4, Page 4 -- RO. RIVES; JAS. MURPHY; RICH. POWELL, February 16, 1801--slaves to ESTHER and CORNL. NEVIL under will of father, JAS. NEVIL.

WM. L. NEWCOME -- Book 12, Page 30 -- Wife, POLLY T.; two youngest children: RO. C. and MARTHA E. NEWCOME; all of my children: SUSANNAH B. LANKFORD; my first child: WM. P. NEWCOME; my second child: JNO. J.; my third: HENRY A.; my fourth: MARY J. (I) NEWCOME; my fifth: RO. C.; my sixth: and my seventh: MARTHA E. NEWCOME. Administrators: sons, JNO. J. and WM. P. November 4, 1847; January 17, 1848. Witnesses: GEO. FEAGANS; JAS. GILLIAM; NEWTON DRUMMOND.

SAML. NICELY -- Book 8, Page 436 -- Calls himself SR.; wife, HANNAH; my six children: BENJ.; JOHN (first in list); JONAS; REBECCA; SALLY; and SAML. March 23, 1834; October 20, 1834. Witnesses: RICH. BOWEN and RODERICK WAUGH. Administrators Bond on page 128 of book 9-- SAML. B. MITCHELL and GEO. BURKS, October 19, 1835, for SAML. NICELY.

ROBT. NIMMO -- Book 11, Page 79 -- Estate Commitment to Sheriff, December Court, 1841; motion of JAS. POWELL. Sheriff: NELSON CRAWFORD. The same item is repeated on Book 11, Page 129.

MATT. NIGHTINGALE is given no number since he is not a testator. He shows here and later went to Kentucky. See Douglas Register for his marriage and baptisms of children.

AMBERCILLA NOEL -- Book 6, Page 129 -- Guardians Bond -- JNO. D. CRAWFORD and MICAJAH NOEL, January 17, 1820, for JNO. D. CRAWFORD as guardian of AMBERILLA NOEL, orphan of JNO. NOEL, deceased.
Book 6, Page 32 -- Same bond and she is called AMBERCILLA here.

MARY G. NOEL -- Book 17, Page 195 -- August 2, 1860; codicil of August 21, 1865; October 16, 1865. To MARY FRANCES PENDLETON, daughter of HARRIET R. PENDLETON, deceased, all of my estate including that to which I am entitled under deed of marriage settlement encated in 1830 in contemplation of my marriage to JNO. SEAY. Administrator: GEO. H. DAMERON. Witnesses: H. C. PIERCE and RO. A. PENDLETON. Codicil: since writing my will, my sister, FRANCES STAPLES and her son, WM. STAPLES, have been reduced by causes that they could not control to state of great need and dependence--greatest love for them and desire home for them during lives. Land is not to be sold during their lives and wish them and my niece, MARY FRANCES PENDLETON, to live in harmony and love there. GEO. H. DAMERON, administrator, is to pay RO. A. COGHILL amount due from estate of my sister, HARRIET R. PENDLETON, as she has probably expended her estate in educating FRANCES--my niece.
Book 17, Page 196 -- Administrators Bond -- GEO. H. DAMERON; MALACHI DAMERON, and RO. A. COGHILL, November 19, 1866, for GEO. H. DAMERON.
Book 17, Page 216 -- Inventory -- February 22, 1867, for $640.00. CHAS. WINGFIELD; THOS. M. COX; ABNER HADEN.

SIMON M. NOEL -- Book 14, Page 280 -- March 29, 1857; Monday, May 18, 1857. Witnesses: C. DABNEY; N. B. MAGRUDER; P. H. GILMER. Infirm; Bedford County land on south side of Otter and in fork of it. Daughter, MARY S. NOEL, if she gets married; slaves named are to go to children:

JNO. G. NOEL; SALLY M. FUQUA; CHAS. G. NOEL; ROBT.; RICH. C. and
ERASMUS NOEL. My wife--any heirs who protest, lose shares. Administrators: WM. KENT, Amherst County, and JNO. GOODE, JR., Bedford.
Book 14, Page 347 -- Administrators Bond -- JNO. GOODE, JR. and SR.
and EDMUND GOODE, May 18, 1857, for JR. as administrator.
Book 14, Page 441 -- Inventory -- no total on 81 items, June 19,
1857. ISAAC REYNOLDS; THOS. A. EDWARDS; N. B. MAGRUDER. They
reported that MRS. MARY E. NOEL, widow, claims all slaves and listed
items in her hands.
Book 14, Page 445 -- Bedford County: BENJ. WILKES; MILTON LOWRY;
ALANNSON NOELL and three of Amherst County committee appeared before
JAS. S. WOOLFOLK, Justice of the Peace of Bedford and placed value of
$3000.00 on estate.
Book 15, Page 37 -- Sale in Bedford County, October 31, 1857; by
JNO. GOODE, JR. Family buyers: E. D.; LAFAYETTE NOEL or NOWELL;
J. C. NOELL; MISS MARY NOEL; CHAS. NOEL--land on Otter bought at
$11.59 per acre. Recorded Amherst County, September 20, 1858.
Amherst sale on page 39 and there MRS. NOWEL (sic) and J. E. NOWEL
were buyers.
Book 15, Page 521 -- Inventory -- MRS. MARY E. NOELL, and property
bequeathed to her; slaves to E. D. NOEL; MARY NOEL; cow and calf
bought by LAFAYETTE NOEL; J. C. NOEL was buyer of Bedford property.
Bedford sale: $5055.36, and Amherst County sale: $725.87. S. H.
HENRY, commissioner reports delay because of correspondence carried
on with executor as to details, June 21, 1859.
Book 15, Page 553 -- Administrators Account -- by GOODE--from
August 24, 1855; mention of suit; SEAY versus NOEL et al. $4573.81
and recorded: September 3, 1859.
Book 17, Page 523 -- Administrators Account -- by GOODE and suit
mentioned again; MRS. M. G. NOEL's bonds. Bedford Sheriff--interest
to date of MRS. SEAY's death and date of August 22, 1868. GEO. H.
DAMERON, administrator of MARY G. NOEL, on decree of Amherst County
Circuit Court in NOELL's executor versus NOELL. Recorded: December 20,
1869.

DANL. NORCUT -- Book 6, Page 14 -- Administrators Bond -- REUBEN
NORVELL and WM. ROBINSON, June 16, 1818, for REUBEN NORVELL--NORCUTT
here.
Book 6, Page 88 -- Inventory on May 16, 1818--$267.00: JNO. MERRITT;
CHAS. WINGFIELD; WM. MUSE, SR. I might add that DANL. married
RACHEL HIGGINBOTHAM, daughter of MOSES HIGGINBOTHAM. See No. 21 for
more on family.

JAS. NORCUTT -- Book 6, Page 90 -- Administrators Bond -- REUBEN
NORVELL and TINSLEY RUCKER, September 20, 1819, for REUBEN NORVELL.

MARTHA NORCUTT -- Book 9, Page 102 -- JNO. CRUMPECKER and WILLIS M.
REYNOLDS, August 17, 1835, for JNO. CRUMPECKER as guardian of MARTHA
NORCUTT, orphan of WM. NORCUTT, deceased.

NANCY H. NORCUTT -- Book 6, Page 215 -- Guardians Bond -- JAS. DUNN
and WM. WARE, July 17, 1819, for JAS. DUNN as guardian of NANCY,
orphan of DANL. NORCUTT, deceased.

RACHEL NORCUTT -- Book 8, Page 373 -- Daughters: MARTHA E. KING;
NANCY DUNN--"who was about moving to the western country"; son, JOS.
NORCUTT; children of daughter, PERMELIA MUSE, by her last husband,
WM. P. MUSE; children of my daughter, SOPHIA TINSLEY; daughter, POLLY
CARTER. My granddaughter, MARTHA NORCUTT, daughter of WM. NORCUTT;
children of PERMELIA; SOPHIA, and POLLY. February 10, 1833; Septem-
ber 16, 1833. Witnesses: REUBEN NORVELL; LUDWELL S. DAWSON; WASH. M.
NORVELL. Executors: friends, ARCHELAUS and WM. REYNOLDS.
Book 8, Page 374 -- WILLIS M. REYNOLDS and ISAAC R. REYNOLDS,
November 18, 1833, for WILLIS M. REYNOLDS.
Book 8, Page 409 -- Inventory -- Perishable property--$34.00; slaves--
$1985.00. LUDWELL S. DAWSON; JNO. H. GOODWIN; CHAS. WINGFIELD.
Note: POLLY married FREDERICK CARTER, but no marriage is found here.
This is also confirmed in a deed of FREDERICK CARTER's wherein it is
set forth that his wife, POLLY, was formerly a NORCUTT.

ELIZ. NORTH -- Book 15, Page 510 -- April 19, 1869 (1860?); codicil
of July 13, 1859; December 17, 1860. Witnesses: THOS. A. MILES;
JNO. M. WARE; WM. W. THOMPSON (who signed for her at her request);
to codicil: MILES and WARE. Daughters, ELIZA NORTH; SARAH and SUSAN
STINNETT; DOLLY NORTH; sons, ABRAM; WM. D.; PUTNAM; children of my
daughter, REBECCA COX: WM. HENRY and RICH. N. COX, when of age.
Granddaughter, MARY NORTH. Executor: SAML. M. GARLAND. Future
children of slaves to go with their mothers. Codicil: legacy of
MARY NORTH, granddaughter, revoked. Husbands of SARAH and SUSAN
STINNETT, are to be trustees for wives; if no children, then revert
to estate. Parts for my children: ELIZA; DOLLY; ABRAM and W. D.,
in trust, and to children, if any at deaths. WM. M. WALLER was also
a witness to codicil. Another codicil of February 4, 1860--slave,
MARTHA, has child, HENRIETTA, and to my daughter, ELIZA; SARAH gets
PAULUS, a boy, before devised to her and releases debt of $200.00
of her husband, URIAH D. STINNETT. Daughter, ELIZA, gets annuity of
$50.00 to use for my son, THOS. NORTH, but not for his debts or
contracts. She is to use it for him as she thinks best. WARE and
MILES witnessed this codicil.

JAS. O. NORTH -- Book 13, Page 240 -- JNO. H. and JAS. A. NORTH,
October 17, 1853, for JNO. H.

RICH. NORTH -- Book 12, Page 345 -- THOS. and JAS. NORTH, January 20,
1851, for THOS. NORTH.
Book 13, Page 320 -- Inventory -- August 22, 1853--$100.00. BENJ. T.
RUCKER; AMBR. R. BURFORD; URIAH BURLEY.

EMMA and SARAH NORVELL -- Book 15, Page 308 -- WM. S. CLAIBORNE and
SAML. M. GARLAND, December 19, 1859, for WM. S. CLAIBORNE as guardian
of EMMA and SARAH NORVELL, infants of MARY C. NORVELL, deceased.

EVERIT R. NORVELL -- Book 11, Page 226 -- Guardians Bond -- THOS. S.
NORVELL and JAS. R. BURFORD, July 15, 1844, for THOS. S. NORVELL as
guardian of EVERITT R. NORVELL, orphan of THOS. S. NORVELL, deceased.

HUGH NORVELL -- Book 5, Page 230 -- Constables, June 21, 1813.
Bondsman: SPENCER NORVELL--first hundred under Act of January 31,
1803.
Book 5, Page 513 -- Constables, June 19, 1815, for two years.
Bondsman: RICH. HARRISON and GEO. W. TAYLOR. Bond to GOV. WILSON C.
NICHOLAS.
Book 5, Page 698 -- Constables, June 17, 1817, for two years: first
hundred. Bondsman: RICH. POWELL.
Book 6, Page 237 -- Constables -- to GOV. PRESTON--for one year in
first hundred; June 21, 1819. Bondsman: CHAS. WINGFIELD.
Book 6, Page 182 -- Administrators Bond -- MATILDA NORVELL, REUBEN
NORVELL and SPENCER NORVELL, November 22, 1820, for MATILDA NORVELL
as executrix--small SR. appears by name of SPENCER NORVELL.
Book 6, Page 183 -- October 27, 1820; November 22, 1820. Witnesses:
S. S. ROSE; TINSLEY RUCKER; JAS. R. LIVELY. Wife, MATILDA; my
brothers and sisters; wife's sister, ELIZ. NORVELL; BENJ. CARY--a
young man raised by wife and me. Wife is to administrate.
Book 6, Page 633 -- Inventory -- $750.00, November 21, 1825--JAS.
PETIT; REUBEN COX; ALEX. TINSLEY.
Book 6, Page 449 -- Administrator's de bonis non Bond -- for BENJ.
NORVELL on April 19, 1823. Bondsman: REUBEN NORVELL.
Book 8, Page 96 -- Administrators Bond -- BENJ. NORVELL; LEWIS P.
SIMPSON, and HARMON GENTRY, May 16, 1831, for BENJ. NORVELL.
Book 8, Page 306 -- Administrators Account -- by BENJ. NORVELL;
bonds of HUGH and REUBEN NORVELL; account from November, 1818--
HOLCOMB's receipt for GARLAND's estate; Fluvanna and Goochland
mentioned; ELIAS and MATT. WILLS mentioned, but not as legatees.
Recorded: November 19, 1832. Note: There is some connection between
this NORVELL family and that of the SPENCER one, but I have not found
it. There is a NORVELL SPENCER and also a SPENCER NORVELL in data.

JNO. NORVELL -- Book 10, Page 73 -- JNO. NORVELL and SAML. DYER,
Refunding Bond to LAWSON Y. WILSHER, administrator of GIDEON GOOCH,

December 23, 1837. JNO. NORVELL has received slave, REUBEN, as his
one-sixth share of estate by court order. SAML. DYER appeared before
Albemarle Justices of the Peace, JNO. D. MOON, and GILLEY M. LEWIS,
January 24, 1839.
Book 11, Page 614 -- Estate Commitment to Sheriff -- JNO. THOMPSON, JR.
made motion. June term, 1847; JAS. L. LAMKIN, Sheriff.
Book 12, Page 180 -- JNO. L. LAMKIN, Deputy. Sheriff gave account
and reports that they found no estate "whatsoever."

JNO. P. NORVELL -- Book 9, Page 398 -- January court, 1838, motion
of RO. ISBELL to place estate in hands of Sheriff, JNO. COLEMAN.
Book 11, Page 183 -- Administrators Bond -- RO. TINSLEY and ZACH D.
TINSLEY, January 15, 1844, for RO. TINSLEY.
Book 16, Page 81 -- Administrators Account -- Sale on January last
and shown to commissioners and posted on courthouse door on February
last. Balance of $1225.80. Recorded: March 11, 1861.

MARGARET JONES NORVELL -- Book 11, Page 43 -- indexed as such but it
is on page 239. WASH. M. NORVELL and JAS. BURFORD, September 16,
1844, for WASH. M. NORVELL as guardian of MARGARET JONES NORVELL
and LUCINDA NORVELL, orphans of THOS. NORVELL, deceased.

MARTHA F. NORVELL -- Book 9, Page 419 -- BENJ. NORVELL and JAS. S.
HIGGINBOTHAM, April 16, 1838, for BENJ. NORVELL as guardian of
MARTHA F.: HUGH I.; MARY S. and BETTY ANN NORVELL, orphans of
PAT--page is tucked under, but on same page the same men made bond --
Administrators Bond -- as to PATSY NORVELL.

PATSY NORVELL -- Book 8, Page 187 -- March 23, 1832, Estate Commitment
to Sheriff, NELSON C. DAWSON.
Book 9, Page 419 -- Administrators Bond -- BENJ. NORVELL and JAS. S.
HIGGINBOTHAM, April 16, 1838, for BENJ. NORVELL.

REUBEN NORVELL -- Book 5, Page 171 -- Sheriffs Bond, July 3, 1812.
Bondsmen: SPENCER NORVELL; DAVID S. GARLAND; PHILIP JOHNSON; ELIAS
WILLS; WM. TURNER. Appointed on date above by GOV. JAS. BARBOUR;
bond of July 20, 1812.
Book 5, Page 400 -- Same men as before--appointed. August 9, 1813;
bond of November 17, 1813.
Book 5, Page 403 -- same men and dates as Book 5, Page 400.

SPENCER NORVELL and item on SPENCER H. NORVELL -- Book A, Page 126 --
First part is blurred, but enough can be deciphered to see that it
is usual terminology. Land where I live; children of my daughter,
PEACHY DOYLE; son, SPENCER D. NORVELL in trust; son, THOS.; children
of my deceased daughter, SUSANNAH SNEAD--sums advanced to her and
husband; son, JNO. P. NORVELL; son, LUDIMAN NORVELL; son, NATHL.
NORVELL; son, JAS. NORVELL; son, BENJ. NORVELL; children of son,
THOS. NORVELL; children of my daughter, FRANCES APPLEBERRY. If
SPENCER D. leaves heirs. Executors: CHISWELL DABNEY; JAS. POWELL,
and son, BENJ. NORVELL. June 26, 1829; September 29, 1829. Witnesses:
LEWIS CAMPBELL; JAS. POWELL; NATHAN GLENN.
Book A, Page 128 -- Administrators Bond -- BENJ. NORVELL, WM. TURNER,
and NATHAN GLENN, September 29, 1829, for BENJ. NORVELL. Bond made
to Judge ARCHIBALD STUART of Amherst Superior Court.
Book A, Page 130 -- Inventory -- land; slaves--$7562.40, April 29,
1830. JAS. PETIT; JAS. OGDEN; WM. MC DANIEL.
Book 16, Page 83 -- SPENCER H. NORVELL--May 20, 1861, RO. TINSLEY
gave account as administrator of JNO. P. NORVELL. It appears to
court--SPENCER H. NORVELL is son of JNO. P. and is entitled to one-
sixth of estate. TINSLEY is to pay him $204.30 with 6% interest
from June 30, 1860. SAML. M. GARLAND, Clerk.

THOS. NORVELL -- Book 10, Page 383 -- Estate Commitment to Sheriff --
motion of WM. L. WILLIS, October, 1839. Sheriff: EDMD. PENN.

THOS. S. NORVELL -- Book 11, Page 114 -- Guardians Bond -- JAS. R.
BURFORD and THOS. C. BLANKS, November 21, 1842, for JAS. R. BURFORD
as guardian of THOS. S. NORVELL, orphan of THOS. NORVELL.

WM. NORVELL -- Book 16, Page 357 -- Guardians Bond -- MALACHI and GEO. H. DAMERON, July 20, 1853, for MALACHI DAMERON as guardian of WM. NORVELL, orphan of THOS. M. NORVELL. This is indexed for NORVELL, but sometimes these names seem to be NOWELL.

-O-

Office of Clerk -- Book 12, Page 472 -- Everything is in good condition, with exception of old Executive books which begin in 1819, and run back to the beginning of the county. They need new bindings to preserve them for they contain valuable information pertaining to the history of suits. All papers have proper labels and are filed in a way that will preserve them. More room is needed and some addition for record space; necessary even now in this department. Fee books are in line, with few exceptions, and in these the clerks have charged less instead of too much. RO. M. BROWN and JAS. P. COLEMAN, December 15, 1852. This is all very interesting for in January of 1961 the clerk, WM. E. SANDIDGE, reported to Supervisors that more room was needed. They dragged their feet until the Circuit Judge ordered them to get busy. There is now a fine addition to the courthouse and the clerk now has a big room for the current records. I came here from Kentucky in 1957 and all data from 1761 to present was housed in two tiny rooms. Most of the books were in what is now the room for records from 1761 to 1900; some modern data is also therein. The building is also air-conditioned.

AGNES OGDEN -- Book 17, Page 7 -- Two sons, ANTHONY R. and JAS. M. OGDEN--slaves; to FRANCES I. (J) WOODY; MARY E. MC DANIEL; NANCY E. MC DANIEL and her two brothers and sister. Executor: son, ANTHONY R. September 6, 1858; January 16, 1865. Witnesses: SAML. SCOTT; THOS. H. OGDEN; JNO. D. GILBERT.
Book 17, Page 8 -- Administrators Bond -- ANTHONY R. and JAS. M. OGDEN, January 16, 1865, for ANTHONY R. OGDEN.
Book 17, Page 20 -- Administrators Account -- from January 25, 1865--funeral--$23..50; blacksmith account; for land division; leather for shoes for SOPHIA RYAN; F. I. WOODY--part of legacy; RO. A. PENDLETON, surveyor. Total: $12,259.00, January 31, 1865. JAS. M. OGDEN and RO. A. PENDLETON. Refunding bond to administrator for $5000.00.
LEO DANIELS, Clerk.

AGNES J. OGDEN -- Book 12, Page 440 -- Guardiand Bond -- LUCINDA R. WILLIAMS and JNO. S. MC DANIEL, November 17, 1851, for LUCINDA R. WILLIAMS as guardian of AGNES J. and BENJ. A. OGDEN, orphans of ALBERT OGDEN.

ALBERT OGDEN -- Book 10, Page 383 -- incorrectly indexed as Book 10, Page 286 -- JNO. THURMOND's motion, June Court, 1839; EDMD. PENN, Sheriff.

BENJ. OGDEN -- Book 11, Page 429 -- Inventory -- July 21, 1846; slaves; tools; etc.: $3325.75, WM. HIX; NATHAN D. RUCKER; JNO. R. MC DANIEL; ALLISON OGDEN, administrator; ZACH D. TINSLEY, Justice of the Peace.
Book 11, Page 431 -- Administrators Bond -- ALLISON and ANTHONY R. OGDEN, and WM. KNIGHT, July 20, 1846, for ANTHONY R. OGDEN.
Book 11, Page 458 -- Sale -- November 27, 1846. OGDEN buyers: AGNES; JAS. M.; ALLISON; A. R.; and J. M. OGDEN.
Book 12, Page 111 -- Administrators Account -- from July 21, 1846--A. R.; JAS. M.; AGNES; ANTHONY R.; THOS. R. OGDEN are named in items. Shop account; negroes to unnamed legatees. Widow got $473.40 and unnamed heirs got $946.81. WM. HIX; JAS. HIGGINBOTHAM; WINSTON WOODROOF. Recorded: December 18, 1848.

CAROLINE OGDEN -- Book B, Page 66 -- Guardians Bond -- JNO. JAS. OGDEN; WALKER R. OGDEN; CHAMPE OGDEN, and RO. W. SNEAD, August 24, 1857, for JNO. JAS. OGDEN as appointed guardian of WM.; CAROLINE; JNO. HENRY and JAS. OGDEN, infants of SARAH ANN OGDEN, deceased.

HENRY OGDEN -- OGDON is used in most of these items -- Book 10, Page
61 -- Daughter, POLLY WHITE and children; WM. WHITE is her husband;
Sons, ALLISON; AQUILLA; WM. OGDEN; daughter, MINTY RUCKER; daughter,
ANN SEAY; son, BENJ.; son, JNO.; son, ELIJAH; son, ZACHARIAH; son,
HENRY OGDON. Executor: Son, ALLISON OGDON. May 13, 1836; November 19,
1838. Witnesses: JNO. B. DUNCAN; JULIUS SIMPSON; DANL. L. COLEMAN.
Book 10, Page 64 -- Administrators Bond -- ALLISON OGDEN; DANL. L.
COLEMAN; BENJ. OGDEN; and JULIUS SIMPSON, November 19, 1838, for
ALLISON OGDEN.
Book 10, Page 80 -- Inventory -- December 27, 1838: $3571.80.
DANL. L. COLEMAN; RICH. P. SMITH; JAS. F. TALIAFERRO.
Book 10, Page 401 -- Sale and account by administrator, December 27,
1838. OGDEN buyers: A.; JNO.; BENJ. THOS.: ZA.; and HENRY OGDEN.
Book 11, Page 3AA -- from October, 1838--$382.11 on hand at testator's
death. OGDENS named: JNO.; Z.; BENJ.; HENRY; JOS. S. EFFINGER,
assignee of W. OGDEN, of Kentucky, to make his share equal with other
heirs; ELIJAH OGDEN; MRS. ANN SEAY (SAY); legatees portion: $669.50.
Total of estate: $5012.94. DANL. L. COLEMAN; CHAS. A. PENN; JNO. W.
BROADDUS. December 20, 1841. Note: An OGDEN went to Warren County,
Kentucky and started Ogden College--now part of Western State.

HENRY M. OGDEN -- Book 11, Page 405 -- He acts as guardian of MILDRED
ANN and SALLY OGDEN, infants of SALLY OGDEN, formerly DAVIS, and heirs
and grandchildren of JAS. DAVIS, deceased. ALLISON OGDEN is security
of JESSE MUNDY, administrator of JAS. DAVIS, and January 19, 1846,
MUNDY paid HENRY M. OGDEN $342.68 as part of DAVIS' estate. Bond is
to protect MUNDY. March 16, 1846.

JAS. OGDEN -- Book 9, Page 80 -- January 13, 1827; May 18, 1835.
Witnesses: WM. MC DANIEL; WM. BOURNE; SAML. WATTS. Executors:
trusty friends, THOS. STRANGE and LINDSEY MC DANIEL; land where I
live to my father, HENRY OGDEN, and my mother, NANCY OGDEN. Slaves
given and not to be parted during lives of my parents; slaves named
to be freed at that time. Legislature to be petitioned to permit
their leaving Virginia as free men; otherwise to be sent to Ohio or
next convenient state. My brothers and sisters: AQUILLA; WM.;
BENJ.; JNO.; ALLISON; HENRY; ELIJAH; ZACHARIAH; ANN SAY; MINTY RUCKER;
MARY WHITE. Some slaves are given to them and some are named to be
sold.
Book 9, Page 80 -- Administrators Bond -- June 13, 1835, LINDSEY
MC DANIEL; bondsman: WM. MC DANIEL; AMBROSE R. MC DANIEL; SAML.
WATTS.
Book 9, Page 244 -- Inventory -- July 25, 1835; six slaves named as
having been set free under will; horse claimed by HENRY OGDEN, SR.;
390 acres at $4.00 per acre; total: $5463.50. PROSSER POWELL;
WM. KNIGHT. December 2, 1835. Administrators Account.
Book 10, Page 224 -- Legacies to THOS. R. OGDEN; SUSAN and children;
A. OGDEN; BENJ. OGDEN; MARY WHITE; Commissioners: A. B. DAVIES;
JNO. H. ROBERTS; J. A. STOUT. Legacies paid to ANN SAY; AQUILLA
OGDEN; WM. OGDEN; MINTY RUCKER; ZACH. OGDEN; ALLISON and JNO. OGDEN
and POLLY WHITE; HENRY M. OGDEN; BENJ. OGDEN; ELIJAH OGDEN. Recorded:
May 18, 1840.

MARGARET OGDEN -- Book 11, Page 185 -- Guardians Bond -- JNO. R.
MC DANIEL and JAS. P. MC DANIEL, December 18, 1843, for JNO. R.
MC DANIEL as guardian of MARGARET OGDEN, orphan of ZACH. OGDEN.

MILDRED F. ANN OGDEN -- Book 11, Page 101 -- Guardians Bond -- JNO. S.
MC DANIEL and DABNEY SANDIDGE, January 16, 1845, for JNO. S. MC DANIEL
as guardian of MILDRED F. ANN OGDEN; AGNES J. and BENJ. A. OGDEN,
infants of ALBERT OGDEN, deceased.
Book 12, Page 151 -- Guardians Bond -- for JNO. S. MC DANIEL--Bondsman:
ANTHONY OGDEN, January 15, 1849, for same orphans.
Book 13, Page 105 -- Guardians Account -- by MC DANIEL as guardian of
MILDRED N. (sic); AGNES J.; and BENJ. A. OGDEN, March 5, 1852.
December 31, 1851, payments made to JNO. J. MAYSE; and wife, MILDRED;
and to AGNES J. and BENJ. A. OGDEN. He sets forth bond with ANTHONY
OGDEN as bondsman. Reference to interest in estate of BENJ. OGDEN,
deceased. Recorded: March 5, 1852.

ZACH. OGDEN -- Book 11, Page 222 -- Estate Commitment to Sheriff --
November Court, 1843; motion of JNO. J. MORGAN; JAS. POWELL, Sheriff.

ANNA P. OLD -- indexed ANDREW C. OLD -- Book 6, Page 178 -- Guardians
Bond -- THOS. EUBANKS and DABNEY WARE, October 16, 1820, for THOS.
EUBANKS as guardian of ANNA P. OLD, Orphan of JNO. OLD, deceased.

ELLIS P. OMOHUNDRO -- Book 12, Page 496 -- Son, SPOTSWOOD J.--services
to me prior to 1849 when he left me; my wife and daughter, LOUISA, and
younger children until of age. Administrator: son, SPOTSWOOD.
October 7, 1851; March 15, 1852. Witnesses: WM. KENT; D. STAPLES.
Book 12, Page 497 -- Administrators Bond -- March 15, 1852: SPOTSWOOD J.
OMOHUNDRO; no bondsman.
Book 12, Page 510 -- Inventory -- March 22, 1852--$4003.25 D. STAPLES;
GEO. H. TURNER; SAML. J. TURNER.
Book 13, Page 86 -- indexed Book 12, Page 86 -- sales, December 4,
1852, and recorded on March 21, 1853.
Book 13, Page 310 -- indexed for Book 12, Page 310 -- from March 15,
1852; account by administrator: 25¢ for mending MRS. OMOHUNDRO's
shoes; four pounds coffee at 50¢; six pounds sugar at same price;
DR. FLOOD for rent; ELLIS P. OMOHUNDRO--wages as overseer in 1852;
cash to widow; vest for THOMAS--$1.38; cash received of WM. (no last
name), but later WM. W. OMOHUNDRO; to ELLIS P. and WM. W. OMOHUNDRO
for log chain; crop at Island Place; December 19, 1853.
Book 14, Page 193 -- Administrators Account -- from January 2, 1853.
Paid to MARY D. OMOHUNDRO; ELLIS P. or B.(?) for cutting wheat; to
TIPTON T. OMOHUNDRO as overseer. Recorded: Monday, October 20, 1856.
Book 14, Page 199 -- Administrators Account -- to T. T. OMOHUNDRO;
hat for JNO. OMOHUNDRO--25¢; to LOUISA OMOHUNDRO for expense to go
see her sister--$5.20; WM. W. OMOHUNDRO for horse; S. P. OMOHUNDRO
for threshing wheat; T. T. OMOHUNDRO in full for 1853 wages as
overseer and same to S. J. OMOHUNDRO; W. W. OMOHUNDRO for boot in
horses; MARY D. OMOHUNDRO--cash freight on SISTER MARY's clothing.
Recorded: Monday, October 20, 1856.

Book 14, Page 455 -- Administrators Account -- from July 1, 1855--
amounts to T. T. and MARY D. OMOHUNDRO. Recorded: July 30, 1857.
Book 15, Page 183 -- quite long and takes up many pages--from
February 16, 1857--to T. T. and S. J. OMOHUNDRO--oats and wheat work.
Recorded: May 30, 1859.
Book 15, Page 453 -- Administrators Account -- from August 6, 1858 --
to W. W. OMOHUNDRO for two horses--$180.00. Page 458, November 29,
1859, to T. T. OMOHUNDRO for wagon--$34.00. Recorded September 17,
1860.
Book 15, Page 462 -- Sale: no buyers listed--$1241.39. Recorded:
May 21, 1860.

MILLIE J. OMOHUNDRO -- Book 15, Page 254 -- Guardians Bond -- S.J.
OMOHUNDRO and SAML. M. GARLAND, November 23, 1859, for S. J. OMOHUNDRO
as guardian of MILLIE J. and JNO. B. OMOHUNDRO, orphans of E. P.
OMOHUNDRO, deceased.

RO. M. OMOHUNDRO -- Book 10, Page 286 -- Refunding bond to BENJ.
TALIAFERRO, administrator of JNO. T. JOHNSON, deceased, will annexed
(not herein)--$20.00 paid by administrator to RO. M. OMOHUNDRO in
full for legacy of RO. M. OMOHUNDRO's wife. A. W. WIMBISH, bondsman:
Recorded: November 16, 1840.

ELIZ. ORENDORF -- an error by indexer -- Book 16, Page 350 -- RO. W.
SNEAD, June Court, 1865; this is really an error for SNEOD is reporting
as curator only. ELIZ. ORENDORF's estate. It is indexed as an
Administrators Bond for ELIZ. OMOHUNDRO.

JNO. M. OTEY -- Book 9, Page 283 -- Power of attorney by OTEY of
Lynchburg to RO. TINSLEY, Clerk of County Court, Amherst County, to
sign for him as security of CHISWELL DABNEY as guardian of his
infant daughter, MARY JANE DABNEY, February 18, 1837.

FREDERICK OTT -- Book 14, Page 23 -- My two sons, FREDERICK and WM.
OTT for care and industry in managing my business from time that they

became 21. My wife, LYDIA A.--money in hands of WASH. SNOAP (?) and
JONATHAN GALEDY, Augusta; wife gets land where I now live; my four
children: FREDERICK, GEO., WM. and HENRIETTA OTT. My two daughters
when last heard from in Ohio--ANN ELIZ. who married JOS. GIBSON and
ANNA BARBARA who married JACOB FLENNING--if living; if dead, to any
other of their children (if any)--HENRIETTA, if not 21 when I die,
to have guardian. Executors: wife and three sons. June 2, 1851;
September 17, 1855. Witnesses: RO. A. PENDLETON and JAS. T. (Y)
CASH. This reminds me of a queer thing which took place several
years ago. A woman in Lynchburg--from abroad--and living in a trailer
park wrote that she had a guest from Germany who was interested in
this OTT. They came to see me and we entertained the German woman
in our home for luncheon. She spoke broken English. She had old
papers showing that this man lived in Amherst, but said that others
had been lost. I traced down land and he lived on North side of
Buffalo and the old house is known as the Tucker house. The poor
soul had raked together money to come to America in hope of getting
a large sum as a distant relative. She was flabbergasted when she
learned that he was married and left heirs. I tried to explain that
statute of limitations would work against her claims in any case.
She went away with a puzzled look and I never heard from her again.
Someone had evidently sold her a bad bill of goods.

GEO. M. OTT -- Book 15, Page 281 -- Administrators Bond -- F. C. OTT
and J. O. STANFIELD, February 20, 1860, for F. C. OTT.
Book 16, Page 238 -- Administrators Account -- February 23, 1860--two
drafts on New York "which is supposed to have been destroyed by fire"
for $3059.40. Recorded: April 20, 1863.

BARNETT OWENS -- Book 6, Page 326 -- Administrators Bond -- GABL.
PAGE and JNO. WARWICK, August 21, 1822, for GABL. PAGE.
Book 6, Page 329 -- August 31, 1822; inventory: $104.46. JACOB
SCOTT, JACOB PIERCE, JONAS PIERCE. There was a DR. BARNETT OWENS
in Louisville when I was a high school boy. I recall that I injured
by neck in playing football and he examined me. He also operated
on my mother at one time.

-P-

BEVERLY PADGETT -- Book 5, Page 446 -- Administrators Bond -- POLLY
PADGETT, JAS. GARLAND, and WM. CRUTCHER, June 20, 1814, for POLLY
PADGETT.
Book 5, Page 467 -- Inventory -- September 24, 1814-L44-19-6. RO.
RIVERS, JER. FRANKLIN, JNO. SMITH.

HENRY G. PADGETT -- Book 5, Page 461 -- Guardians Bond -- JAS. FULCHER
and MICAJAH CAMDEN, 18 October 1814, for JAS. FULCHER as guardian of
HENRY G. and RHODA PADGETT, orphans of BEVERLY PADGETT, deceased.

REUBEN PADGETT -- Book 6, Page 130 -- Administrators Bond -- CATH. A.
PADGETT, CATLETT CAMPBELL, THOS. HUTCHERSON, February 21, 1820, for
CATH. A. PADGETT.
Book 6, Page 148 -- Inventory -- 4 March 1820--$1132.44: CHAS. MUNDY,
WILEY CAMPBELL, JACOB PIERCE.
Book 6, Page 392 -- Inventory -- September 12, 1823: $928.75. THOS.
WINGFIELD, JONAS PIERCE, JOS. KYLE.
Book 7, Page 87 -- wrongly indexed: Administrators Bond -- for
REUBEN PENDLETON.
Book 8, Page 191 -- Administrators Account -- by A. ROBERTSON from
January 17, 1825; bond of S. PADGETT, ANN PADGETT, December 15, 1830.
MAJOR ALBON MC DANIEL, Lynchburg Corporation Court; bond of D. G.
MURRELL. Recorded: Amherst County, 22 March 1832.

SOPHIA PADGETT -- Book 13, Page 63 -- Administrators Bond -- RO. M.
BROWN and RO. WHITEHEAD, March 21, 1853, for RO. M. BROWN.
Book 13, Page 484 -- Administrators Account -- from March 6, 1853;
postage for letter to REUBEN B. PADGETT; one-fifth to each of these
legatees: GEO. POWELL, JAMES NOWALL and wife, NANCY WARD, CATH.

PADGETT's children--seven in number, but not named; TINSLEY PADGETT
and wife. JNO. T. ELLIS, commissioner, Monday, July 16, 1855.

FRANCES PAGE -- Book 11, Page 548 -- January 18, 1847; September 20,
1847. Witnesses: JOS. and FIELDING T. BROWN. DILLARD H. PAGE
qualified; bondsman: WYATT TUCKER. Recorded 12:24. Four grand-
children--children of my son, HUGH PAGE: PAULUS, CLEOPHUS, DANDRIDGE D.
and TULLY HUGH PAGE; son, DILLARD H.; daughters: RACHEL PAGE; LUCY
SMITH; children of deceased daughter, BETSY TUCKER: DILLARD TUCKER
and FRANCIS HILL; executors: son, DILLARD H. PAGE, and son-in-law,
WYATT TUCKER.
Book 11, Page 552 -- Inventory -- September 23, 1847: $1099.50.
JOEL F. SMITH, JACOB SMITH, LEWILLIN T. CASH.

GABL. PAGE -- Book 8, Page 14 -- June 27, 1830; August 16, 1830.
Witnesses: GEO. W. HIGGINBOTHAM; WM. TUCKER; AMBR. R. MC DANIEL.
WIATT TUCKER qualified; bondsman: DILLARD H. PAGE and BARNETT CASH.
Wife, FRANCES, where I live; son, DILLARD H. PAGE; daughters, RACHEL
and LUCY C. PAGE; two grandchildren: MARY E. and WILKINSON TUCKER--
121 acres bought of CASH; tract bought of WILLIAMSON heirs--50 and
30 acres where I live at lower end and joins WM. TUCKER; AMBR.
MC DANIEL. Son, GABL. H. is not grown and to be educated; daughters,
RACHEL and LUCY, are to live with mother until married. Son-in-law,
WIATT TUCKER, is to act for my grandchildren. Executors: W. TUCKER
and DILLARD H. PAGE.
Book 8, Page 24 -- Inventory -- order of August, 1830--$2361.37.
GEO. W. HIGGINBOTHAM, CORNL. SALE, ABSALOM HIGGINBOTHAM. September 20,
1830.
Book 10, Page 267 -- Administrators Account -- by TUCKER, August 13,
1840. Certified by GEO. W. HIGGINBOTHAM. Amount paid to MRS.
FRANCES PAGE.

GABL. H. PAGE -- Book 14, Page 574 -- Constables Bond -- June 21,
1858. Bondsmen: JAS. P. COLEMAN, CHAS. M. WRIGHT, PAULUS POWELL.
Book 15, Page 465 -- Constables Bond -- August 4, 1860. Bondsmen:
JAS. P. COLEMAN, PAULUS POWELL, RO. A. PENDLETON, JACOB TYREE.

JAS. PAGE -- Book 12, Page 251 -- April 2, 1847; February 18, 1850.
Witnesses: SAML. HEISKELL, MARSHALL L. HARRIS, HENRY L. DAVIES.
RO. TINSLEY qualified; bondsman: LINDSEY COLEMAN. Nieces, NANCY
and MARY LAYNE have been kind to me for many years; if either is
without issue.
Book 12, Page 265 -- Administrators Bond.
Book 12, Page 305 -- Inventory -- March 2, 1850. D. H. TAPSCOTT,
WM. E. COLEMAN, LEO. DANIEL, JR.

FREDERICK PAINTER, SR. -- Book 6, Page 694 -- September 7, 1826;
October 15, 1826. Witnesses: MATT. P. STURDIVANT, ISAAC RUCKER, SR.,
JNO. CLARKSON, GEO. HESLEP. HENRY PAINTER qualified; bondsman:
E. WATSON. Land bought of THOS. JOURDAN to be sold; my wife is to
receive no part for reasons best known to myself; my five children:
FREDERICK, JR.; JNO.; SAML.; ELIZ.; and HENRY PAINTER. ELIZ.'s part
in trust and desire that she leave her mother and live with one of
her brothers.
Book 15, Page 255 -- Administrator's de bonis non Bond -- September 21,
1859, JAS. P. COLEMAN and SAML. W. HENRY for JAS. P. COLEMAN.

BENJ. PALMER -- some items are indexed PALMORE -- Book 4, Page 485 --
Administrators Bond -- WM. BURFORD, HARRISON HUGHES, HUGH NORVELL,
December 21, 1807, for WM. BURFORD.
Book 4, Page 491 -- Inventory -- L383-13-0 THOS. MOORE, PHIL JOHNSON,
REUBEN PENDLETON, DANL. MEHONE, January 18, 1808.
Book 5, Page 639 -- Administrators Account -- from 1806. POLLY
PALMORE, now SLED; S. R. PALMORE, infant, February 17, 1817. ELIAS
WILLS, JOS. BECK, WM. PETTYJOHN; this is indexed for BEVERLEY PADGETT.

DETHIA PALMER -- Book 4, Page 334 -- Guardians Bond -- JNO. HANSARD
and GEO. MC DANIEL, September 21, 1801, for JNO. HANSARD as guardian
of BETHIA PALMER, orphan of PLEDGE PALMER. This is a hard item to read.

JNO. PALMER -- Book 4, Page 335 -- Guardians Bond -- GEO. MC DANIEL
and JNO. HANSARD, September 21, 1801, for GEO. MC DANIEL as guardian
of JNO.; RHODA, and TINDAL PALMER, orphans of PELDGE PALMER, deceased.
Book 5, Page 7 -- Guardians Account -- by HANSARD: to carry you to
Cumberland; suit of M. WADE; ticket for guardian; tuition to WM.
HILL, THOS. MC CLELAND and JNO. CAMM, commissioners. November 21,
1810.

SALLY PALMER -- Book 5, Page 581 -- Guardians Bond -- JNO. L. BURFORD
and WM. BURFORD, May 21, 1816, for JNO. L. BURFORD as guardian of
SALLY PALMER, orphan of BENJ. PALMER, deceased.
Book 5, Page 608 -- Guardians Bond -- JNO. SLEDD and RICH. BURKS,
November 18, 1816, for JNO. SLEDD as guardian of SALLY PALMER, orphan
of BENJ. PALMER, deceased.

WM. PALMER -- Book 4, Page 382 -- Guardians Bond -- JNO. HANSARD and
ISAAC RUCKER, January 16, 1804, for JNO. HANSARD as guardian--WM.;
CHAS.; and JNO. PALMER, orphans of PLEDGE PALMER.

JNO. H. PAMPLIN -- Book 11, Page 67 -- Constables Bond -- June 20,
1842; Bondsman: THOS. L. TAYLOR and H. M. GARLAND.
Book 11, Page 152 -- Constables Bond -- June 2, 1843; Bondsman:
THOS. L. TAYLOR and RO. A. COGHILL.

MARGARET PAMPLIN -- Book 11, Page 17 -- February 14, 1842; March 22,
1842. Witnesses: WARNER JONES, SAML. GARLAND, JAS. P. COLEMAN.
Daughter, SARAH ANN TAYLOR, wife of THOS. TAYLOR--land joining in
Amherst County and Nelson Counties--where my son, ALEX., lives and
got by commissioners deed from SAML. M. GARLAND.

WM. PAMPLIN -- Book 4, Page 478 -- Tobacco Inspector, Camden's
Warehouse, November 16, 1807; bondsman: JAMES PAMPLIN.

ANN E. PARKS -- Book 16, Page 137 -- Guardians Bond -- JNO. R.
CUNNINGHAM and M. R. CUNNINGHAM, June 16, 1862, for JNO. R. CUNNINGHAM
as guardian of ANN E. PARKS; no parent set forth.
Book 17, Page 429 -- Guardians Account -- October 22, 1868; ward
was 21 on February 27, 1865; Conf. money from estate of RO. TINSLEY,
deceased.

ARTHUR WILSON PARKS -- Book 16, Page 136 -- Guardians Bond -- ARTHUR B.
DAVIES and JNO. CUNNINGHAM, June 16, 1862, for ARTHUR B. DAVIES as
guardian of ARTHUR W. PARKS; no parent set forth.
Book 17, Page 440 -- Guardians Account -- from June 16, 1865. Amount
from GRANVILLE P. PARKS; ward was 21 on July 16, 1868. Money lost
by Conf. collapse, but no charges made for clothing and board since
ward worked for him.

CHAS. M. PARKS -- Book 14, Page 171 -- Guardians Bond -- B. P. MORRIS,
WHITING DAVIES, E. W. MORRIS and GEO. HYLTON, September 15, 1856, for
B. P. MORRIS as guardian of CHAS. M., ELIZ. M., VA. A. and ELDRED B.
PARKS, orphans of GAINES W. PARKS, deceased.

Book 15, Page 585 -- Guardians Account -- by MORRIS from November 30,
1858, for all wards above; trip to Missouri to bring wards and slaves
of G. W. PARKS to Virginia--$300.00; Z. PARIS, undertaker; mountain
land sold. JNO. M. PAKRS, administrator of G. W. PARKS in Missouri;
RO. TINSLEY, administrator of MARTIN PARKS; amount due estate of
G. W. PARKS by B. P. MORRIS, administrator. Recorded: November 19,
1860.
Book 16, Page 266 -- Guardians Account -- by same guardian for same
wards as above from September 15, 1859; bond of CHARLEY, BETTY,
JINNIE and BEVERLY PARKS for one year--this work may be board instead
of bond. Recorded April 20, 1863.
Book 16, Page 354 -- Guardians Account -- from September 15, 1860.
ELDRED is called EDWD in one place. Recorded: June 17, 1863.
Book 16, Page 379 -- so indexed, but not here or in 16, 17, or 18.

ELIZ. PARKS -- Book 3, Page 58 -- Guardians Bond -- ZACH DAWSON and BENJ. RUCKER, September 3, 1787, for ZACH DAWSON as guardian of ELIS. PARKS, orphan of WM. PARKS.

GAINES W. PARKS -- Book 12, Page 142 -- Power of attorney by him in Lafayette County, Missouri, to WHITING DAVIES to recover from estate of GEO. L. MORRIS, Amherst County, in right of my wife, MARY JANE, formerly MORRIS, August 31, 1848. LEWIS W. SMALLWOOD, clerk of Lafayette County, Missouri.
Book 14, Page 299 -- Administrators Bond -- BEVERLY P. MORRIS and E. W. MORRIS, March 16, 1857, for E. W. MORRIS.
Book 15, Page 571 -- Administrators Account -- by administrator from December 20, 1858, as guardian of orphans--see No. 26.

JNO. PARKS -- Book 3, Page 7 -- Administrators Bond -- ELIZ. PARKS, PHILIP THURMOND, GEO. GILLESPIE, March 6, 1786, for ELIZ. PARKS.
Note: I have commented on fact that THURMOND and GILLESPIE familes are often seen together in Amherst. I have mentioned an enigma as to HENDERSON THURMAN who married MARY GILLESPIE in Madison County, Kentucky. We know that she was granddaughter of this GEO.--daughter of WM. GILLESPIE who married ANN HUDSON here in 1777 and to Kentucky-- but we have never been able to solve mystery of parentage of HENDERSON THURMAN.
Book 3, Page 10 -- Inventory -- September 4, 1786-L196-0-0; ISAAC WRIGHT; PETER CARTER; WM. HAYNES.
Book 3, Page 76 -- Administrators Account -- by ELIZ. from September, 1785. JNO. WIATT, JNO. PENN, DAVID WOODROOF April 19, 1788.

MARGARET PARKS -- Book 3, Page 56 -- Guardians Bond -- ZACH DAWSON and BENJ. RUCKER, September 3, 1787, for ZACH DAWSON as guardian of MARGARET PARKS, orphan of WM. PARKS.
Book 15, Page 286 -- Administrators Bond -- GRANVILLE T. PARKS and GEO. HYLTON, January 16, 1860, for GRANVILLE T. PARKS.
Book 15, Page 463 -- Inventory -- $2091.83--DANL. H. RUCKER, J. C. HENDRICK, May 21, 1860.
Book 16, Page 303 -- indexed as Administrators Account, but not there.

MARTIN PARKS -- Book 2, Page 250 -- Guardians Bond -- GABL. PENN and SAML. HIGGINBOTHAM, November 7, 1785, for GABL. PENN as guardian of MARTIN PARKS, orphan of WM. PARKS.
Book 2, Page 358 -- so indexed, but book does not go that far.
Probably Book 3, Page 58 -- Guardians Bond -- ZACH DAWSON and BENJ. RUCKER, September 3, 1787, for ZACH DAWSON as guardian of MARTIN PARKS, orphan of WM. PARKS.
There are many tobacco inspector bonds: All for Amherst Warehouse.
Book 5, Page 527 -- November 20, 1815; bondsman: SAML. BURKS.
Book 5, Page 606 -- September 16, 1816; bondsman: NELSON C. DAWSON.
Book 5, Page 679 -- September 15, 1817; bondsman: JESSE BECK.
Book 6, Page 33 -- not there.
Book 6, Page 174 -- September 18, 1820; bondsman: JAS. DAVIES.
Book 6, Page 252 -- September 17, 182 ; bondsman: WM. ARMISTEAD--who is also bondsman for these:
Book 6, Page 332 -- September 16, 1822.
Book 6, Page 388 -- September 15, 1823.
Book 6, Page 474 -- September 20, 1824.
Book 10, Page 230 -- February 28, 1840; May 18, 1840. Witnesses: JNO. D. DAVIS, CHAMPE CARTER. Proved by DAVIS on June 15, 1840, and by CARTER on probate date. NANCY PARKS qualified. Plantation to be sold; wife, NANCY; my children and grandchildren as of age or married. Sons: WM. H., WILDON B., JNO. M.--my daughter, SARAH ANNE, wife of WHITING DAVIES: my daughter, MARY C. PARKS; daughter, ELIZ. G. PARKS; daughter, LUCY A. PARKS; son, MILTON M.--he and three daughters just named have received no shares; others have and to deduct; son, GAINES M., has received nothing to date; same for daughter, CAROLINE T.; daughter, MARGARET N.; son, GRANVILLE P. Wife, NANCY, to administrate.
Book 13, Page 463 -- Administrators Bond -- WITTING DAVIES, GRANVILLE P. PARKS and GEO. HYLTON, March 19, 1855, for WITTING DAVIES.

SARAH F. PARKS -- Book 16, Page 136 -- Guardians Bond -- MARTIN D. TINSLEY and ZACH D. TINSLEY, June 16, 1862, for MARTIN D. TINSLEY as guardian of SARAH PARKS; no parent set forth. Book 17, Page 260 -- Guardians Account -- from July 15, 1862; she is called ELIZ. DAVIES in places; EDWIN M. WARE is present guardian, July 15, 1867; Recorded: September 16, 1867.

WALDEN B. PARKS -- Book 16, Page 90 -- Administrators Bond -- MARTIN D. TINSLEY and ZACH. D. TINSLEY, June 15, 1861, for MARTIN D. TINSLEY.

WM. PARKS -- Book 1, Page 451 -- Administrators Bond -- MARY PARKS, MARTIN DAWSON, and JOS. TUCKER, December 7, 1778, for MARY PARKS. Book 1, Page 475 -- September 27, 1769; December 7, 1778. Witnesses: MARTIN DAWSON, EDDY DAWSON, BENJ. BROMHEAD. Son, JNO., when of age-- he is by my first wife; TABITHA PAKRS--slave, NELL, which came to me by first wife; son, MARTIN, by second wife, MARY; wife, MARY; child next heir at law; daughter, SARAH PARKS; when youngest child is of age. Executors: BENJ. PARKS and WM. DAWSON. Book 1, Page 477 -- Inventory -- L384-12-0; recorded May 3, 1779. RICH. SHELTON, HENRY TRENT, DAN BURFORD, JR. Book 3, Page 57 -- Guardians Bond -- WM. TINSLEY, JR., RICH. FULCHER, JNO. MAYS, September 3, 1787, for WM. TINSLEY, JR. as guardian of WM. PARKS, orphan of WM. PARKS. Book 3, Page 188 -- Guardians Bond -- RICH. HARRISON and PHILIP BURTON, July 4, 1791, for RICH. HARRISON as guardian of same ward.

DAVID PARRICK -- Book 3, Page 582 -- April 1, 1800; October 20, 1800. Witnesses: ALEX. MARR, THOS. HARVEY, MILLEY MARR, WM. THOMPSON. Sons, HENRY and ZEPHANIE; wife, JOYCE--land etc. Wife and son, HENRY, to administrate. Administrators Bond is Book 4, Page 326 for her--also PARROCK; Bondsman: DAVID S. GARLAND on probate date.

ELIZ. PARSONS -- Book 5, Page 502 -- Administrators Bond -- JESSE CASH and WM. TUCKER, May 15, 1815, for JESSE CASH.

SALLY PARSONS -- Book 4, Page 33 -- Nuncupative will made at her residence during last illness on April 6, 1802 and put in writing within six days from that time. WM. ALLEN to take and bring up my son, JNO. JNO. PARSONS (sic); JNO. MATTHEWS to do same for her son, TANDY PARSON; WM. ALLEN to take property at her home and divide it among her children. Witnesses signed and stated that will was made a few hours before her death--LEWIS MC QUEEN, JNO. and SARAH MATTHEWS, LUCY NASH, April 19, 1802. ALLEN qualified and LANDON CABELL was bondsman: Book 4, Page 38 -- Inventory -- of L22-11-2, May 7, 1802. THOS. NASH, JOSHUA WILLOUGHBY, WM. BAILEY. Administrators Bond is Book 4, Page 346.

ELIZ. PATRICK -- Book 15, Page 217 -- Administrators Bond -- ROBT. PATRICK, PAULUS POWELL, and HENRY L. DAVIES, August 18, 1859, for ROBT. PATRICK.

WM. J. PATRICK -- Book 12, Page 175 -- Constables Bond -- June 18, 1849; Bondsman: R. PATRICK and L. D. SIMPSON.

CHAS. J. PATTESON -- Book 12, Page 23 -- Guardians Bond -- A. C. JOHNSON and W. O. HARDING, August 16, 1847, for A. C. JOHNSON as guardian of CHAS. P. PATTESON, orphan of CHAS. J. PATTESON.

SKYLOR PATTESON -- Book 12, Page 494 -- Guardians Bond -- March 15, 1852--GEO. PATTESON and RADFORD THOMAS for GEO. PATTESON as guardian of SKYLOR PATTESON, orphan of JNO. PATTESON.

VA. L. PATTESON (indexed PATTERSON) -- Book 12, Page 22 -- Guardians Bond -- SARAH A. PATTESON and A. C. JOHNSON and WM. O. HARDING, August 16, 1847, for SARAH A. PATTESON as guardian of VA. L. (S) ELIZ. A. and ELLA H. PATTESON, orphans of WM. N. PATTESON, deceased.

ALEX. PATTON -- Book 2, Page 171 -- Administrators Bond -- THOS. PATTON, ALEX. REID, JR. and NATHL. CLARKE, May 3, 1784, for THOS. PATTON.
Book 2, Page 173 -- Inventory -- L79-19-0 THOS. MORRISON, JR., JAS. and ALEX. HENDERSON, June 7, 1784.

JANE PATTON -- Book 2, Page 198 -- Dower as widow of ALEX. PATTON: L26-13-6, November 1, 1784. Commissioners as for inventory above in 50.

ANN MARIA PENDLETON -- Book 11, Page 156 -- Estate Commitment to Sheriff -- motion of WM. P. GARLAND, July, 1843; JAS. POWELL, Sheriff.

EDMUND PENDLETON -- Book 13, Page 55 -- Administrators Bond -- JNO. THOMPSON, JR. and RO. M. BROWN, March 21, 1853, for JNO. THOMPSON, JR.

FRANCIS A. PENDLETON -- Book 11, Page 113 -- Guardians Bond -- WM. M. WALLER and RO. A. COGHILL, November 22, 1842, for WM. M. WALLER as guardian of FRANCES A. (sic), JAS. S., and ELIZA J. PENDLETON, orphans of CATH. PENDLETON.

HARRIET PENDLETON -- Book 14, Page 538 -- Administrators Bond -- GEO. H. DAMERON and RO. A. COGHILL, April 19, 1858, for GEO. H. DAMERON. Book 15, Page 45 -- Inventory -- January 14, 1859; order of April, 1858; Recorded January 17, 1859: $2810.00. W. A. EDWARDS, CHAS. WINGFIELD, W. KENT.

JAS. PENDLETON -- some have SR. -- Book B, Page 1 -- May 9, 1828; September 14, 1832. Witnesses: JNO. T. HILL, JOS. SWANSON, HOWELL L. BROWN, RO. TINSLEY--WM. MC DANIEL versus JUDITH CHURCHWELL--appeal from order and judgement of court of August last--admitting will to probate. Deposition of JOS. SWANSON read and court of opinion that PENDLETON was under no undue influence; deposition of RO. TINSLEY; handwriting attested for JNO. T. HILL as he is out of commonwealth; HOWELL BROWN examined. Probate confirmed and appellee to recover versus appellant. WM. MC DANIEL in court and declined to qualify and intends to apply for supersede as to judgement. He does not give up the right to qualify, if will is finally established. LINDSEY MC DANIEL qualified; bondsman: WM. MC DANIEL--will states that JUDITH CHURCHWELL has lived with me for some years as housekeeper and manager--she is alias EVANS--she gets slaves; furniture, etc., and 30 acres on east side of creek and next to RO. WALKER, deceased. Executors: friends, RO. GARLAND and JAS. POWELL. My daughter, BETSY MC DANIEL, and children. Her husband, WM. MC DANIEL, is her trustee and also for children.
Book B, Page 2 -- Administrators Bond.
Book B, Page 3 -- Inventory -- October 13, 1832; many slaves; $7883.19. EDMD. PENN, SAML. WATTS, JOS. EWERS.
Book 10, Page 54 -- slave division at late residence, September 16, 1838. In possession of HENRY W. QUARLES; chancery decree pending in Amherst Court court in MC DANIEL versus MC DANIEL. In life PENDLETON gave slaves to CATH. GLENN and ELIZ. OGDEN; we allotted HENRY W. QUARLES a negro girl--in possession since his marriage and loaned to him by MRS. MC DANIEL who had life estate--seven lots: to JAS. MC DANIEL, JNO. MC DANIEL, WM. MC DANIEL, PHILIP MC DANIEL, MARY MC DANIEL, SOPHIA MC DANIEL, LINDSEY MC DANILE, WM. MC DANIEL. Note: seven lots are mentioned, but there are eight--all MC DANIELS could be under one lot--to NATHAN GLENN, ZACH OGDEN, HENRY W. QUARLES, WM. MC DANIEL inherited by death of infant distributee. October 15, 1838. A. B. and HENRY L. DAVIES and JAS. POWELL.
Book 10, Page 65 -- indexed as Estate Committment to Sheriff, but not there.
Book 12, Page 418 -- Administrators Bond -- RO. A. COGHILL and EDGAR WHITEHEAD, June 17, 1851, for RO. A. COGHILL.

JNO. PENDLETON -- Book 13, Page 54 -- Administrators Bond -- RO. TINSLEY and ZACH D. TINSLEY, March 21, 1853, for RO. TINSLEY. Book 13, Page 428 -- Administrators Account -- RO. TINSLEY from April 14, 1853--cash to JNO. PENDLETON's administrator in Lincoln County, Kentucky; LUCAS versus PENDLETON, December 18, 1854.

Book 13, Page 224 -- Inventory -- April 14, 1853; his interest in estate of WM. PENDLETON--RO. TINSLEY, administrator of RICH. and JNO. PENDLETON. JOHN's domicile in Kentucky.

MARTHA G. PENDLETON -- Book 6, Page 577 -- Guardians Bond -- ELIAS WILLS, CORNL. CROW, and WM. TURNER, March 21, 1825, for ELIAS WILLS-- guardian of MARTHA G. and HARRIET PENDLETON, orphans of REUBEN PENDLETON.
Book 6, Page 747 -- Guardians Bond -- CORNL. CROW, ELIAS WILLS, WM. I. ISBELL, SETH WOODROOF, and WM. W. SCHOT, March 19, 1827, for CORNL. CROW as guardian of same wards.

MARY E. PENDLETON -- Book 14, Page 49 -- Administrators Bond -- JAS. F. TALIAFERRO and CHAS. MASSIE, November 19, 1855, for JAS. F. TALIAFERRO. Book 14, Page 51 -- July 10, 1855; November 19, 1855. Witnesses: MARGARET ROSE, WM. WALLER, WM. H. MANTIPLY. Husband, RO. N. PENDLETON; daughter, JANE ROSE PENDLETON until 21; my brothers, PATRICK R., JAS. E. and JNO. N. TALIAFERRO; ALEX. and AMBROSE SHEPHERD, children of my deceased sister, MARY SHEPHERD--if no issue--family is dying so rapidly. Children of T. T. EMMETT--nieces and nephews of my husband. Executors: my father, JAS. F. TALIAFERRO, and friend, HENRY LOVING. Book 14, Page 81 -- Inventory -- $6820.61. N. N. MANTIPLY; WM. M. WALLER; JNO. S. TUCKER, January 21, 1856.
Book 14, Page 471 -- Inventory by same men. Bonds of BENJ. TALIAFERRO-- Bondsman: JAS. F. and ADDISON and N. C. TALIAFERRO. J. J. PENDLETON on a note as bondsman. Recorded: January 12, 1856.
Book 15, Page 127 -- Administrators Account -- from April 3, 1857-- tuition for J. R. PENDLETON to R. N. PENDLETON, August 15, 1858.
Book 15, Page 543 -- Administrators Account -- legacy of RO. N. PENDLETON; bond of JAS. S. PENDLETON; RO. N. from estate of wife, June 11, 1860.
Book 16, Page 482 -- Administrators Account -- from October 15, 1859-- legacy of RO. N. PENDLETON; board and tuition to HENRY R. CARTER and EMMA C. CARTER. Recorded: July 28, 1863.

MARY FRANCES PENDLETON -- Book 15, Page 452 -- Guardians Bond -- August 21, 1860 MAGY G. NOEL, RO. A. COGHILL, and R. A. PENDLETON, August 21, 1860, for MAGY G. NOEL as guardian of MARY FRANCES PENDLETON; no parent set forth.

PATSY PENDLETON -- Book 7, Page 170 -- Administrators Bond -- PATSY PENDLETON and REUBEN COX, July 21, 1828, for PATSY PENDLETON as executrix of WM. PENDLETON. This is just another of those queer index items.

REUBEN PENDLETON -- Book 7, Page 87 -- Administrators Bond -- JAS. S. and MICAJAH PENDLETON, November 21, 1827, for JAS. S. PENDLETON. Indexed for PADGETT.

RICH. PENDLETON -- Book 7, Page 244 -- April 3, 1828; June 15, 1829. Witnesses: WM. SHELTON, W. P. SISSON, JAS. MC DANIEL, JR., DANL. F. CHRISTIAN. HENRY T. PENDLETON qualified. Bondsmen: JAS. PENDLETON, ISAAC RUCKER, WM. L. BURKS, JAS. MC DANIEL, JR., CHAS. L. BARRET. Wife, MARY--600 acres where I live; slaves; debts to be paid from crops, if possible. Wife, MARY, 600 acres where I live; my unfortunate son, REUBEN; sons, HENRY T. and RICH., JR., if no issue; my children and grandchildren; daughter, ELIZ. LUCAS--ten equal parts--children of my son, WM. and future ones--for his life and under his control; ELIZ. LUCAS and children; daughter, PERMELIA ZEVELY, and children; daughter, SALLY JONES, and children (GEO. JONES' marriage bond is incomplete--page 242, March 16, 1816--GEO. JONES, 21 years of age-- bride--PENDLETON and ? mark. He is shown to be son of GEO. JONES); son, JAMES, and his children; daughter, POLLY HAYNES, and children; daughter, LUCY CHRISTIAN, and children; son, HENRY T., and any children or heirs; son, RICH., JR.; son, REUBEN--if any are without issue. Executors: sons, JAS. and HENRY T. and RO. TINSLEY. Administrators Bond is Book 7, Page 262.
Book 7, Page 291 -- Inventory -- 384 acres; many slaves. WM. TUCKER, BLANSFORD HICKS, W. P. SISSON, December 21, 1829--$4199.50.

Book 9, Page 8 (indexed as Book 8, Page 8) -- Administrators Account --
from 1829; WM. PENDLETON hired slave; H. T. PENDLETON, overseer; cash
to JAS. PENDLETON; PERMELIA ZEVELY; $5.00 for coffin. August 18, 1834,
AMBRO. RUCKER, JNO. PRYOR, WM. P. SISSON.
Book 9, Page 102 -- Committee: ZACH. D. TINSLEY, MARTIN TINSLEY,
August 17, 1835, for ZACH. D. TINSLEY as committee for RICH. PENDLETON
of unsound mind.
Book 9, Page 153 -- Administrators Account -- from August, 1834--MARY,
widow, has compromised with legatees and whole estate sold--$3782.55,
November 24, 1834. JNO. PRYOR, W. P. SISSON, JAS. W. DANIEL, JR.--
March 27, 1835.
Book 11, Page 100 -- Administrators Bond -- ZACH. D. TINSLEY and
MARTIN D. TINSLEY, January 16, 1843, for ZACH D. TINSLEY.
Book 11, Page 122 -- slave inventory -- one man at $400.00; JAS.
MC DANIEL, EDWIN S. RUCKER, JAS. F. SATTERWHITE.
Book 13, Page 54 -- Administrators Bond -- RO. and ZACH. D. TINSLEY,
March 25, 1853, for RO. TINSLEY.
Book 13, Page 224 -- Inventory -- April 14, 1853; sum received from
C. DABNEY and RO. A. COGHILL as commissioners in LUCAS versus
PENDLETON; decedent's interest in personal estate of WM. PENDLETON,
deceased; inventory of JNO. PENDLETON is just below; RO. TINSLEY,
administrator of JNO. and RICH. PENDLETON. July 18, 1853.
Book 13, Page 430 -- Administrators Account -- by RO. TINSLEY from
April 14, 1853--legacies paid to SILVERSTER L. BURFORD for two
shares of JAS. and H. T. PENDLETON; GEO. JONES and wife, SALLY;
WM. PENDLETON's children; LUCY CHRISTIAN's children; POLLY HAYNES'
children; PERMELIA ZEVELY and children; ELIZ. LUCAS and children;
Recorded: December 18, 1854.

RO. PENDLETON -- Book 6, Page 640 -- Guardians Bond -- JAS. S. PENDLETON
and HILL CARTER, December 19, 1825, for JAS. S. PENDLETON as guardian
of RO. PENDLETON, orphans of REUBEN PENDLETON and FRANCIS PENDLETON,
deceased.
Book 6, Page 745 -- Guardians Bond -- Same man and bondsman, MICAJAH
PENDLETON, March 19, 1827, for JAS. S. PENDLETON as guardian of RO.
PENDLETON, orphan of REUBEN PENDLETON.

RO. A. PENDLETON -- Book 14, Page 578 -- Circuit Clerk, June 30, 1858.
Bondsman: R. A. COGHILL.
Book 16, Page 529 -- Same, July 14, 1864; bondsman: SAML. M. GARLAND.
Book 17, Page 35 -- Same, August 24, 1865, bondsman: R. A. COGHILL.
Note: he was removed from office by GEN. STONEHAM in Reconstruction
days in 1869, but took office again.
Book 20, Page 186 -- Circuit Clerk, Juen 20, 1881; bondsman: H. E.
SMITH, JNO. R. CUNNINGHAM, JNO. B. ROBERTSON, JNO. J. SHRADER, THOS.
J. M. GOODWIN.
Book 21, Page 420 -- Circuit Clerk, June 20, 1887--bondsman: JNO. J.
SHRADER, JAS. T. JORDAN, JOEL H. CAMPBELL.
Book 23, Page 165 -- January 23, 1892; February 15, 1892. Witnesses:
HENRY W. WILLS, W. SANDIDGE. JACOB D. PENDLETON qualified; appraisers:
A. C. HARRISON, BENJ. BROWN, W. W. ALCOCK, ED. HEWITT, JR., A. D.
BEARD. Cousin, RO. A. COGHILL, by will devised to -- my second wife
and children 486 acres in Amherst County and I was their trustee; son,
JACOB, Lynchburg; daughter, NELLIE (S), Amherst Court House; daughter,
OLLIE, Lynchburg; son, ROBT., St. Louis; children of my daughters,
MILDRED, SALLIE, and ANN MARIA. Wife, dower; mansion house and land
between Mill road, Buffalo, and creek; daughter, BETTIE, when married;
daughter, LUCY; daughter, MARY, in Montgomery County. Executor:
son, JACOB D.

RO. N. PENDLETON -- Book 12, Page 147 -- Refunding Bond -- to HIRAM
CHEATWOOD, July 19, 1847; bondsman: RO. A. COGHILL; distribution to
LOUISA E., wife of RO. from estate of JONAS PIERCE by CHEATWOOD has
been received.

SAML. PENDLETON -- Book 6, Page 595 -- Guardians Bond -- JAS. S.
PENDLETON and RICH. N. EUBANK, April 18, 1825, for JAS. S. PENDLETON
as guardian of SAML. PENDLETON, infant of REUBEN PENDLETON.

WM. PENDLETON -- Book 1, Page 507 -- January 2, 1774; November 1,
1779. Witnesses: JNO. and ISAAC TINSELY, WM. WHITTEN, AMBR. RUCKER.
Planter; wife, ELIZ.--where I live; my children: BENJ., JAS., EDMUND,
RICH., MARY, JOHN, REUBEN, WM., SARAH, FRANKA, ISAAC, BETTA--BENJ.,
JAS., and EDMUND have partial shares and wife to give cow and calf
to each of others who have had nothing or as of age; to RICH. VERNAL
(?), Culpeper, land on Smith's run where I formerly lived; Executors:
wife, and sons, JAS. and EDMUND. They qualified--page 508--for JAS.
and ELIZ.; bondsman: AMBR. RUCKER, ISAAC TINSLEY.
Book 1, Page 537 -- Inventory -- L5062-12-6; September 30, 1780.
RICH. HARRISON, AMBRO. RUCKER, JNO. HARRISON, GEO. MC DANIEL.
Book 7, Page 127 -- WM. PENDLETON, SR. -- February 16, 1828; March 17,
1828. Witnesses: AMBR. RUCKER, THOS. CLEMENTS, GUSTAVUS CLEMENTS.
PATSY PENDLETON qualified July 21, 1828. Bondsman: REUBEN COX--
liberty for others to join--on margin. Wife, PATSY, and at death to
my connexions (sic) as law directs. Executors: Wife and JNO. COX.
Administrators Bond is Book 7, Page 171.
Book 7, Page 175 -- Inventory -- August 26, 1828; several slaves;
JAS. LEE; ARCHELAUS REYNOLDS; J. PETTYJOHN, September 15, 1828.
$2969.74.
Book 10, Page 51 -- Administrators Bond -- JAS. S. PENDLETON and
RO. A. PENDLETON, September 17, 1838, for JAS. S. PENDLETON as
guardian of WM.; ADELADE; JAS. S., JR., and ELIZA JANE PENDLETON,
orphans of CATH. PENDLETON, deceased.
Book 12, Page 393 -- Administrators Bond -- RO. A. COGHILL, JANE
ALDRIDGE, SAML. HEISKELL, May 19, 1851, for RO. A. COGHILL.

ALEX. S. PENN -- Book 5, Page 212 -- March 2, 1813; May 17, 1813.
Witnesses: ARTHUR B. DAVIES, THOMPSON NOEL, HENRY BALLENGER. Wife,
NANCY, now pregnant; my two children, EDWD. and CHAS., when of age;
whatever my father thinks proper to leave me--to my children.
Executors: brother, JNO. PENN, and COL. JNO. DILLARD.
Book 5, Page 398 -- Administrators Bond -- JNO. PENN and EDMD. T.
COLEMAN, November 15, 1813, for JNO. PENN.
Book 5, Page 688 -- Inventory -- November 24, 1813; $3737.78. THOS.
HOLLOWAY and LINDSEY COLEMAN.

BETSY PENN -- Book 4, Page 330 -- Guardians Bond -- RO. HOLLOWAY,
CHAS. WATT, JOEL FRANKLIN, June 15, 1801, for RO. HOLLOWAY as guardian
of BETSY PENN, orphan of JOS. PENN.
Book 4, Page 371 -- indexed as ELIS. -- Guardians Bond -- CHAS.
BURRUS and JOS. BURRUS, June 20, 1803, for CHAS. BURRUS as guardian
of same orphan.
Book 4, Page 632 -- Guardians Account -- by CAPT. CHAS. BURRUS with
MISS ELIZ. PENN from November 2, 1803--your ticket at suit of Floyd,
July 8, 1805; when starting for Carolina at the spring; horse you
brought from the mountain; singing master; when you and your sister,
HOLLOWAY, were going to Lynchburg; cash from HENRY HOLLOWAY; WM. LEE
who married BETSY PENN--May 2, 1810, item. Recorded: September 6,
1810. RO. HOLLOWAY, RO. WALKER, LEONARD HENLEY, BEN. TALIAFERRO.
Book 5, Page 1 -- Account of RO. HOLLOWAY from December 10, 1800--
slippers bought in Culpeper for you, August 5, 1800; cloth got by
your brother, SEATON, when estate was divided at death of RO.
HOLLOWAY; dancing school; HEN HOLLOWAY's draft; HENRY HOLLOWAY,
executor of ROBT. HOLLOWAY, who was guardian of BETSY PENN, orphan
of JOS. PENN. Order of May Court, 1805. JOS. BURRUS, DAVID S.
GARLAND, GEO. DILLARD, LEONARD HENLEY, BENJ. TALIAFERRO.

CATH. PENN -- Book 4, Page 302 -- Guardians Bond -- WM. LONG and
WM. S. CRAWFORD, December 16, 1799, for WM. LONG as guardian of
CATH. PENN, orphan of GABL. PENN, deceased.
Book 4, Page 527 -- Guardians Bond -- EDMD. PENN and WM. S. CRAWFORD,
July 19, 1808, for EDMD. PENN as guardian of same orphan.

CHAS. A. PENN -- Book 12, Page 517 -- Administrators Bond -- CHAS. H.
MASSIE, CHAS. MASSIE, SAML. H. GARLAND, HENRY LOVING, L. D. SIMPSON,
May 17, 1852, for CHAS. H. MASSIE.
Book 13, Page 11 -- Inventory -- September 11, 1852--$16,701.00--and
other items not in total; M. C. GOODWIN, LINDSEY COLEMAN, JAS. P.

CHAS. A. PENN (continued)   COLEMAN, WM. TUCKER, SR.
Book 13, Page 40 -- Sale, November 24, 1852 -- MARY C. and MRS. PENN
were buyers; no total.
Book 13, Page 512 -- Administrators Account -- from May 24, 1852.
Recorded: July 17, 1855.
Book 14, Page 125 -- Administrators Account -- from September 1,
1852; due PENN and MASSIE from MC DANIEL as trustees of ZACH. OGDEN's
children. February 18, 1856.
Book 14, Page 179 -- Administrators Account -- from June 8, 1853;
MISS M. W. PENN's bill at springs; also MISS MARIAH's. August 8,
1856.
Book 14, Page 601 -- Administrators Account -- from October 8, 1855;
tuition fees; MARIAH PENN; July 19, 1858.
Book 15, Page 503 -- Administrators Account -- from August 26, 1857;
tuition fees and money for children. May 21, 1860.
Book 16, Page 12, -- Guardians Bond -- RO. L. COLEMAN, MARY C. PENN
(by SAML. M. GARLAND), December 17, 1860, for RO. L. COLEMAN as
guardian of MARIA W., MILLIE A., BETTIE D., SUSAN M., and EDMD. C.
PENN, orphans of CHAS. A. PENN.
Book 16, Page 248 -- Administrators Account -- from January 1, 1859;
recorded: April 29, 1863.
Book 16, Page 425 -- slave division on order of December, 1863--to
his children: MARIA W., MILLIE A., BETTIE D., SUSAN S., EDMD. A.--I
have checked and discrepancies are as given January 18, 1864; JAS. P.
COLEMAN; HENRY LOVING; M. C. GOODWIN.

CHAS. B. PENN -- Book 4, Page 304 -- Guardians Bond -- RO. HOLLOWAY,
GEO. DILLARD, ELISHA ESTES, June 17, 1799, for RO. HOLLOWAY as
guardian of CHAS. B. PENN, orphan of JOS. PENN, deceased.
Book 4, Page 352 -- Guardians Bond -- HENRY HOLLOWAY, JNO. DILLARD,
DRURY BELL, September 20, 1802, for HENRY HOLLOWAY as guardian of
same ward.
Book 5, Page 12 -- The estate of HENRY HOLLOWAY in account with
CHAS. B. PENN from 1799; cash from JNO. PENN; land sold to BURKS.
October 10, 1800; RO. HOLLOWAY's account on October 10, 1802, as
guardian. October 17, 1810. JAS. FRANKLIN, RO. WALKER.

EDMD. PENN -- Book 10, Page 75 -- Sheriff, January 21, 1839. Bondsman:
HENRY L. DAVIES, JNO. THOMPSON, JR., R. HENLEY, DANL. L. COLEMAN,
LINDSEY COLEMAN, A. B. DAVIES, ADDISON TALIAFERRO, JNO. W. BROADDUS,
RICH. CRAWFORD.
Book 10, Page 195 -- Sheriffs Bond -- February 17, 1840. Bondsman:
RICH. CRAWFORD, WM. E. COLEMAN, DANL. L. COLEMAN, CHAS. L. BROWN,
R. HENLEY, A. B. DAVIES, HENRY L. DAVIES, BENJ. B. TALIAFERRO.

FRANCES ANN PENN -- Book 5, Page 66 -- Guardians Bond -- RICH. HARRISON,
NICHL. HARRISON, STERLING and WM. HARRISON, September 17, 1810, for
RICH. HARRISON as guardian of FRANCES and SEATON M. PENN, orphans of
SEATON M. PENN, deceased.
Book 6, Page 721 -- Guardians Bond -- RO. L. COLEMAN and JNO. PENN,
February 19, 1827, for RO. L. COLEMAN as guardian of FRANCES ANN PENN,
orphan of SEATON M. PENN.

GABL. PENN -- Book 3, Page 506 -- November 21, 1794; July 16, 1798.
Witnesses: GEO. DILLARD; REUBEN CRAWFORD; JAS. M. BROWN. Son,
JAS.--land warrant rights (military) of my brother, WM., deceased.
Daughter, BETSY CALLAWAY; debts due me by estate of DAVID SHEPHERD,
deceased; one bond paid by me to CARTER BRAXTON, February 16, 1775,
for lands bought by SHEPHERD from BRAXTON and one to EZEK. GILBERT
for land bought by D. SHEPHERD; daughters, SOPHIA CRAWFORD; PERMELIA
HASKINS; MATILDA NASH; FANNY WHITE; NANCY PENN, when 21 or married;
son, EDMD., at death of my wife--land survey of January 8, 1794, by
Amherst County surveyor, JAS. HIGGINBOTHAM--when EDMD. is 21 or
married. Daughters, SALLY and CATH. PENN, when 21 or married. Wife,
SARAH--HIGGINBOTHAM Mill tract; Freeland tract near Buffalo; Kentucky
lands; Jas. River Co. shares. JAS. PENN to be guardian of my son,
EDMD. THOS. HASKINS guardian for SALLY PENN; JAS. CALLAWAY for CATH.
PENN. Executors: son, JAMES; sons-in-law, WM. CRAWFORD and JAS.
CALLAWAY.

Book 4, Page 310 -- Administrators Bond -- JAS. PENN, PHILIP GOOCH, JOS. BURRUS, GEO. PENN, WM. PENN, THOS. PENN and W. S. CRAWFORD, July 16, 1798, for JAS. PENN.
Book 5, Page 92 -- Administrators Account -- JAS. PENN -- 1798--paid EDMD. PENN's tuition while at Academy; expense to Richmond to SALLY PENN; EDMD's expense at Princeton; expense of sale of Kentucky land; piano and Richmond trip for SALLY PENN. Recorded: January 11, 1813. JAS. STEPTOE, WM. CALLAWAY, JR., JNO. WATTS.
Book 6, Page 94 -- Administrators Bond -- THOS. CREWS and WM. MC DANIEL, October 18, 1819, for THOS. CREWS.
Book 6, Page 698 -- so indexed as inventory; not there; it is Book 6, Page 678 August 22, 1826; no total; J. L. PENDLETON; JAS. HIGGINBOTHAM; JNO. DILLARD.
Book 7, Page 30 -- Residue division to legatees; SOPHIA CRAWFORD; MATILDA NASH; SAML. WHITE; THOS. CREWS; EDMD. PENN; NANCY MC CREDIE; THOS. HASKINS--several items to divide later. Met at late residence, December 24th last, and divided slaves. Two legatees absent, JNO. HOLDER and JAS. PENN; three portions received from JAS. PENN's executor. WM. LONG was present and stated that he had received share. July 14, 1827, JNO. DILLARD, HILL CARTER, ED. A. CABELL.

GEO. PENN -- Book 3, Page 367 -- February 5, 1790; February 15, 1796. Witnesses: MATT. WALTON, JAS. M. BROWN, JAS. BALLENGER; daughter, FRANKEY BURTON; daughters, MOLLY HARRISON; NANCY SAVAGE; LUCY PENN; SALLY PENN; sons, WM.; GEO.; WILSON; THOS.; MOSES--my ten children-- five sons--land where I live to be sold. Executors: sons, WM., GEO., WILSON, and THOS. PENN; friend, DAVID S. GARLAND. Page 370, Administrators Bond: GEO., THOS. and WM. PENN and DAVID S. GARLAND. Bondsman: THOS. POWELL--probate date.
Book 3, Page 399 -- Inventory -- many slaves, L1257-12-6. March 2, 1796. RO. WALKER, BENAMMI STONE, JOEL FRANKLIN.
Book 3, Page 389 -- Administrators Account -- by GARLAND--to GEO. PENN, JR; saddle for MISS SALLY PENN; WM. PENN; JAS. SAVAGE--L140-16-9. ROB. WALKER; DAVID WOODROOF; GIDEON CREWS, June 18, 1798.
Book 4, Page 44 -- Administrators Account -- by GARLAND from February 25, 1797--To MOSES PENN; order of WM., GEO., and WILSON PENN. April 24, 1802. JNO. PENN, JOS. BURRUS, RO. WALKER.

JNO. PENN -- Book 11, Page 302 -- January 9, 1845; February 17, 1845. Witnesses: J. and CHAS. PETTYJOHN. March 17, 1845, DANL. L. COLEMAN and CHAS. A. PENN qualified; bondsman: STERLING CLAIBOREN; JAS. F. TALIAFERRO; DABNEY SANDIDGE. To EDWD. A. PENN, son of ALEX. PENN; CHAS. A. PENN; to DANL. COLEMAN, son of EDWD. J. COLEMAN; to POLLIE, CAROLINE, and RICH. HARRISON and SOPHIA RUCKER (spelling here is somewhat worse than poor); AMANDY LEE, daughter of WM. LEE, and her four children--three boys and one girl, when of age. To RO. and COLEMAN PENN--a "det" RO. PENN's estate owes me; to LUCY DILLARD who is LUSEY MICHEL (sic)--my land where I live and still house tract; old mill tract; negroes that I shall have at Whitehead to be sent to a free state, and lands provided there for them. Executors: CHAS. A. PENN and SANL. L. COLEMAN.
Book 11, Page 304 -- Administrators Bond -- see will.
Book 11, Page 337 -- Inventory -- June 28, 1845, many slaves; tracts: Mill; home; Still House; Whitehead; no total. August 19, 1845. HENRY L. DAVIES, J. PETTYJOHN, W. L. DUNCAN, WM. KNIGHT, CHAS. H. MASSIE.
Book 11, Page 394 -- slave division; to RICH. P.; PAULUS E. and CAROLINE HARRISON and RICH. RUCKER (F middle initial), January 10, 1846, by EDWIN L. and RALPH C. SHELTON.
Book 12, Page 13 -- Administrators Account -- by surviving executor, CHAS. A. PENN, from February, 1845--Duiguid for funeral and burial-- $42.00; legacies to EDWD. M. PENN; land bought by HARRISON; Still house tract bought by SAML. M. GARLAND. September 20, 1847--LINDSEY and JAS. P. COLEMAN.

JNO. PENN, SR. -- Book 6, Page 49 -- February 12, 1818; December 21, 1818. Witnesses: JNO. SMITH, LEROY CAMDEN, ST. GEO. TUCKER, CORNL. POWELL. JNO. PENN, JR. qualified, January 18, 1819. Wife, ELIZ.; son, JOHN--where he lives on north side Huff Creek--it divides from

GARLAND's land; old mill seat; main road; mill seat on south side
Huff and next to RO. WALKER; Indian Creek plantation; four daughters
and heirs: LUCY, NANCY, BETSY, and SALLY. Three children of my
son, ALEX. PANN; grandsons: JOS. and RO. ALEX. PENN; my sons, JNO.,
WM. and ALEXANDER. Daughter SALLY's heirs as married or of age; same
for ALEX's children; unsettled accounts between daughter, NANCY, and
me. Executors: son, JNO. and friends, RO. WALKER and JAMES POWELL.
Book 6, Page 54 -- Administrators Bond -- JNO. PENN, JR., January 18,
1819; bondsman: DAVID S. GARLAND.
Book 6, Page 555 (or 540?) -- Administrators Account -- from 1822--
surveys of Indian Creek and mansion house tracts--JNO. J. DILLARD's
legacy. Total: $4886.17. EDMD. PENN; CHAS. L. BARRET; P. L.
PENDLETON(?), February 22, 1825.

JOS. PENN -- Book 3, Page 246 -- Administrators Bond -- JOS. BURRUS,
FANNEY PENN, BENAMMI STONE, October 15, 1792, for first two.
Book 3, Page 427 -- Administrators Account -- by BURRUS from October 26,
1792. JNO. SWANSON for making coffin; REV. CHAS. CRAWFORD for sermon
at funeral; MR. (?) FRANKLIN's will in part; MRS. SUSANNAH MARTIN's
account; CAPT. NOWELL for seven gallons whiskey; JNO. PENN, guardian
for estate; MRS. FANNEY PENN. June 19, 1797, SAML. MEREDITH; GEO.
DILLARD; LINDSEY COLEMAN.
Book 4, Page 431 -- Guardians Bond -- JNO. PENN, JR., RO. COLEMAN,
and ALEX. PENN, July 21, 1806, for JNO. PENN, JR. as guardian of
JOS. PENN, orphan of JOS. PENN, deceased.
Book 10, Page 146 -- indexed as Administrators Account, but not there.
Book 10, Page 252 -- Administrators Bond -- JNO. PENN and DANL. L.
COLEMAN, August 18, 1840, for JNO. PENN.
Book 10, Page 391 -- Inventory -- no total; May 8, 1841. JNOATHAN A.
STOUT, J. PETTYJOHN, LEWIS HARRISON.
Book 11, Page 325 -- Administrators Account -- from January 1, 1842;
to CHAS. A. PENN; PENN and MASSIE. November 7, 1843. JNO. WHITEHEAD,
V. MC GINNIS, JNO. H. PAMPLIN.
Book 11, Page 375 -- Estate Commitment to Sheriff -- April, 1845.
Motion of CHAS. A. PENN and DANL. L. COLEMAN. WM. M. WALLER, Sheriff.
Book 11, Page 428 -- Inventory by WALLER, Sheriff -- several slaves;
no total; May 19, 1845. WM. C. CHRISTIAN, M. C. GOODWIN, JNO. M.
PRICE.
Book 12, Page 136 -- Administrators de bonis non Bond -- CHAS. B.
and CHAS. A. PENN, October 16, 1848, for CHAS. B. PENN.
Book 12, Page 229 -- Estate Commitment to Sheriff -- January, 1850;
LINDSEY COLEMAN, Sheriff.
Book 12, Page 339 -- Inventory and slave division by COLEMAN, Sheriff
and Administrators de bonis non Bond by GEO. D. DAVIS, deputy: to
WM. EDMUNDS and wife; to ELIZA WILL, SR., (WATSON or WILSON--very
hard to read); L. L. BOLLING; S. L. (B) PENN, executors of CHAS. B.
PENN, September 5, 1850.
Book 13, Page 184 -- Administrators Account -- by COLEMAN from
December, 1850--to EDWARDS as agent for E. LEE; executor of CHAS. B.
PENN; J. S. BOLLING for LEWIS L. BOLLING; N. C. KENNEY (?).
December 19, 1853.

LUCY PENN -- Book 3, Page 385 -- Guardians Bond-- JOEL FRANKLIN and
DAVID S. GARLAND, June 20, 1796, for JOEL FRANKLIN as guardian of
LUCY PENN, orphan of GEO. PENN. Note: her name is not in index and
this is indexed for J. FRANKLIN.

MARY PENN -- Book 1, Page 133 -- Guardians Bond -- LARKIN GATEWOOD
and GABL. PENN, May 2, 1769, for LARKIN GATEWOOD as guardian of MARY
PENN, orphan of JOS. PENN, deceased.
Book 2, Page 188 -- Guardians Account -- from 1769; your half of
tobacco; MRS. REID's store account. Called MOLLY here.

MARY C. PENN -- Book 13, Page 182 -- Dower assigned as widow of
CHAS. A. PENN--#13,585 and one-third to her, December 28, 1852.
ADAM M. SHULTZ, WM. WRIGHT, SIMS BROCKMAN, SAML. M. GARLAND, G. W.
HENLEY.

MOSES PENN, JR. -- Book 1, Page 268 -- August 3, 1774; October 3, 1774.
Witnesses: EDMD. WILCOX, JNO. LAMONT, DAVID SHEPHERD. Brother,
PHILIP; niece and godchild, PARMELIA PENN, daughter of my borther,
GABL. PENN; nephew and godson, GEO. PENN, son of my brother, GEO.;
my brother, WM.--slave loaned to him for his journey through some
of the southern states; my nephew, FRANK LEE; nephew, RICH. LEE;
godson, BEN PHILLIPS, son of WM. PHILLIPS; to JOHN CONNER for waiting
on me in my sickness; my niece, NANCY LEE, for maintenance and
education. Executors: brothers, GEO. and GABL. PENN. They qualified
on probate date, page 270; bondsman: DUDLEY GATEWOOD and MARTIN DAWSON.
Book 1, Page 382 -- Inventory -- L282-10-10, July 26, 1777; EDMD.
WILCOX, JOS. CABELL, JOSHUA HUDSON.
Book 2, Page 91 -- Administrators Account -- by GABL. PENN--JNO.
SWANSON for coffin--15 sh., December 1, 1774; legacy to WM. PENN;
account of JNO. PENN; GABL. PENN; cash from MOSES PENN, SR.: L 127-10-
0½, January 1, 1783.
Book 3, Page 274 -- Administrators Account -- JNO. SWANSON for coffin--
date here is August 31, 1774; legacy of WM. PENN; to WIATT POWELL,
administrator of RICH. POWELL; to WM. PHILLIP's son, BENJ., by amount
paid to father; PHILLIP PENN's account; WM. PENN; MOSES PENN, SR.
April 13, 1793. JAS. FRANKLIN; RO. WALKER; JAS. HIGGINBOTHAM.
Book 3, Page 479 -- Inventory -- L19-10-0, September 26, 1797.
Book 3, Page 510 -- Administrators Account -- by WM. PENN, SR.--to
EZEK. HILL for coffin, June 14, 1797. DAVID S. GARLAND, JOS. BURRUS,
W. WARWICK.
Book 4, Page 291 -- Administrators Bond -- WM. PENN, GEO. DILLARD,
and RICH. HARRISON (MAJOR), June 19, 1797, for WM. PENN. Note:
these last two items are probably for MOSES, SR., since another man
furnished the coffin.

POLLY ANN PENN -- Book 5, Page 460 -- Guardians Account -- POLLY ANN
EDMUNDS, formerly PENN, by her guardian, JNO. PENN, SR., from July 20,
1805; settlement by WM. EDMUNDS; account of JNO. PENN, JR. WM. EDMUNDS
is later called her husband. September 19, 1814. RO. WALKER, WM.
ARMISTEAD, DAVID S. GARLAND.

RO. A. PENN -- Book 7, Page 150 -- Administrators Bond -- JNO. PENN
and HENRY H. WATTS, March 17, 1828, for JNO. PENN.
Book 8, Page 310 -- Guardians Bond -- WM. D. HARRIS, BEN D. HARRIS,
JNO. S. HARRIS, and LINDSEY COLEMAN, May 20, 1833, for WM. D. HARRIS
as guardian of RO. A. and REUBEN COLEMAN PENN, orphans of RO. A.
PENN, deceased. BEN. D. by attorney in fact, WM. D.

SALLY PENN -- Book 3, Page 376 -- Guardians Bond -- JNO. PENN, W. S.
CRAWFORD, JAS. CALLAWAY, September 16, 1793, for JNO. PENN as guardian
of SALLY, SEATON, CHAS., BETSY, POLLY and JOS. PENN--orphans of JOS.
PENN, deceased.
Book 3, Page 384 -- Guardians Bond -- DAVID S. GARLAND, JOEL FRANKLIN,
June 20, 1796, for DAVID S. GARLAND as guardian of SALLY, orphan of
GEO. PENN, deceased.
Book 4, Page 365 -- not there.

SARAH PENN -- Book 6, Page 710 -- Administrators Bond -- DAVID S.
GARLAND, HUDSON M. GARLAND, December 18, 1826, for DAVID S. GARLAND.

SEATON M. PENN -- Book 4, Page 317 -- Guardians Bond -- JOS. BURRUS,
JNO. PENN, June 17, 1798, for JOS. BURRUS as guardian of SEATON M.
PENN, orphan of JOS. PENN.
Book 4, Page 526 -- Administrators Bond -- SOPHIA PENN, JNO. PENN, JR.,
NANCY SHIELDS, July 19, 1808, for SOPHIA PENN.
Book 4, Page 625 -- Inventory -- $3249.75 September 2, 1808; JAS. P.
GARLAND, WM. CASHWELL, RO. COLEMAN.
Book 6, Page 636 -- Guardians Bond -- WM. MC DANIEL and JNO. PENN,
November 23, 1825, for WM. MC DANIEL as guardian of SEATON M. PENN,
orphan of SEATON M. PENN.
Book 7, Page 273 -- Committee to manage, September 22, 1829: JNO. PENN,
and bondsman: WM. M. WALLER.
Book 10, Page 325 -- Report from 1830; support to 1840; PENN deceased
when filed January 18, 1841. JONATHAN A. STOUT, JNO. H. ROBERTS,
J. PETTYJOHM.

SEATON M. PENN (cont.) -- Book 10, Page 330 -- Division--slaves to
LEWIS BOWLING and wife, FRANCES; ANN seems to be her middle name;
PAULUS, CAROLINE, RICH. and SOPHIA HARRISON--half brothers and
sisters to SEATON M. PENN; land not yet divided--all have same
guardian: BENJ. B. TALIAFERRO. February 15, 1841.
Book 10, Page 371 -- not there.

THOMAS PENN -- Book 1, Page 182 -- Inventory filed by LARKIN GATEWOOD,
September 3, 1770; estate of THOS. and MARY PEN (sic)--slaves and
money "to each."

WM. PENN -- Book 1, Page 355 -- August 13, 1776; July 7, 1777.
Witnesses: EDMD. WILCOX, DAVID SHEPHERD, THOS. LANDRUM. Intends
to enlist in Armies of the United Colonies of America. Brothers,
GEO., PHILIP, GABL. and ABRAHAM to share equally, if he does not
return. GEO. and GABL. to administrate.
Book 1, Page 383 -- Inventory -- several slaves, October 6, 1777.
EDMD. WILCOX, JOS. CABELL, JNO. WIATT.
Book 5, Page 473 -- Administrators Bond -- JNO. PENN and RICH.
HARRISON, November 21, 1814, for JNO. PENN.
Book 5, Page 637 -- indexed for 652 -- Inventory -- no total,
December 29, 1814. REUBEN COLEMAN, RO. WALKER, WILKINS WATSON.

WILSON PENN -- Book 4, Page 235 -- Tobacco Inspector, Camden's
Warehouse, January 21, 1799. Bondsman: MICAJAH CAMDEN.

CHAS. PERROW -- Book 4, Page 334 -- Guardians Bond -- ANNE PERROW,
HENLEY DRUMMOND, GUERRANT PERROW, September 21, 1801 for ANNE PERROW
as guardian of CHAS. and DANL. PERROW, orphans of DANL. PERROW,
deceased.
Book 4, Page 387 -- Guardians Bond -- SPOTSWOOD GRALAND and JNO.
LOVING, September 17, 1804, for SPOTSWOOD GRALAND as guardian of
CHAS. PERROW, orphan of DANL. PERROW.

DANL. PERROW -- Book 4, Page 11 -- June 15, 1801. Proved by WM.
HORSLEY; SAML ALLEN; RO. WINGFIELD; MICAJAH PENDLETON. GUERRANT
PERROW qualified--bondsmen: HENLEY DRUMMOND; WILSON PENN; JAS.
PAMPLIN. Page 331 is Administrators Bond and more bondsmen: also
page 373: CHRISTOPHER ISBELL; REUBEN NORVELL; GEO. ALLEN; LEWIS
TINDALL; JESSE ALLEN; LEROY PAMPLIN, July 18, 1803--indexed for
GUERRANT PERROW. Wife and children; daughters; MAKEY PERROW and
LUCY PERROW; three sons, GUERRANT; DANL. and CHAS. Wife, ANNA, to
administrate along with CAPT. JNO. CHRISTIAN; GUERRANT PERROW;
JNO. HORSLEY.
Book 4, Page 14 -- Inventory -- L819-19-5½, July 20, 1801. MICAJAH
PENDLETON, WM. JORDAN, WM. PAMPLIN.
Book 4, Page 412 -- Guardians Bond -- SPOSTWOOD GARLAND and JNO.
LOVING, September 16, 1805, for SPOSTWOOD GARLAND as guardian of
DANL. PERROW, orphan of DANL. PERROW.
Book 4, Page 513 -- Administrators Bond -- SPOSTWOOD GARLAND and
JAS. P. GARLAND, March 22, 1805, for SPOSTWOOD GARLAND. GUERRANT
PERROW failed to give counter security.

WM. PETER -- Book 14, Page 101 -- March 10, 1856; Monday, May 19,
1856. Witnesses: WM. M. WARE, JNO. R. MORRISS, JNO. L. HARRIS.
Wife, where I live; my children; executor: WM. P. MORRISS.
Book 14, Page 133 -- Administrators Bond -- SUSAN, ELDRIDGE, SEATON
and WM. PETERS, June 16, 1856, for SUSAN PETERS. Note: indexed
PETER, but data is PETERS.
Book 14, Page 175 -- Inventory -- June 16, 1856, $203.00; JNO. R.
MORRISS, BLUFORD HICKS, NICHL. HICKS.

FRANCES PETERS -- Book B, Page 12 -- Estate Commitment to Sheriff --
September 6, 1839; Friday; EDMD. PENN, Sheriff.
Book 8, Page 369 -- Committee: BLANFORD HICKS; THOS. COLEMAN;
HENRY T. PENDLETON, November 18, 1833, for BLANFORD HICKS as committee
for FRANCES PETERS of unsound mind--to provide support while she is
in the hospital.

PLEASANT PETERS -- Book 6, Page 411 -- Administrators Bond -- JNO.
HAAS, MAT. DUNCAN, November 18, 1823, for JNO. HAAS.

SIMON PETERS -- Book 10, Page 153 -- Lunatic Bond -- August 19, 1839.
BLUFORD and BLANSFORD HICKS for BLUFORD HICKS.

WM. PETERS -- Book 5, Page 654 -- June 3, 1817; July 21, 1817.
Witnesses: MATT. TUCKER, RICH. DAVENPORT, THOS. COLEMAN, SAML.
COLEMAN, POLLY HARPER, NANCY HOG. MOZA PETER and BLANSFORD HICKS
qualified. Bondsmen: RICH. HARRISON, AMBRO. RUCKER, ALLISON MORRIS.
Son, JESSE; sons, JNO, MOZA, WM., CHAS., SIMON (his is to live with
mother--no board); JESSE, JOHN, and MOZA have received land.
Daughters: SUSANNA, NANCY, LUCY, POLLY, BETSY. Wife, FRANCES.
BARKSDALE SLEDD, husband of my daughter, LUCY. Executors: son,
MOZA, and BLANSFORD HICKS. Page 672 is Administrators Bond.
Book 6, Page 10 -- Inventory -- July 22, 1817--$2312.59. WM. MC DANIEL,
WM. JOPLING, RICH. PENDLETON, THOS. GRISSOM.
Book 9, Page 14 -- Administrators Account -- from 1817; cash of MOZA
PETER; SLEDD versus PETERS' executor; cash to FRANCES PETERS; LEROY
COLEMAN, overseer; certificate of WM. PETER and evidence of THOS.
COLEMAN; tobacco expenses; 8½ years for attendance at suit of
BARKSDALE SLEDD versus myself and MOSES PETERS at $1.00 per day--
$70.00. November 19, 1834. JNO. PRYOR; HENRY T. PENDLETON; ZACH. D.
TINSLEY.
Book 9, Page 165 -- Administrators Account -- by MOSES PETERS from
1817--commissioners as above, March 17, 1834.
Book 10, Page 108 -- Inventory -- $256.24½, May 20, 1839. PETER
RUCKER, ORMUND WARE, WM. M. DAVIES.

MISS NANCY L. PETROSS -- Book 12, Page 148 -- May 28, 1844; Monday,
January 15, 1849. Proved by MARTIN and NATHAN GUTHRIE. Witnesses:
OLIVER and NATHAN GUTHRIE; RO. C. MARTIN. My brother-in-law, DANL.
DAY, for kindness and protection of last twenty years--not to grant
any part of real estate to any of my relations. DAY is to is to
administrate; he qualified on probate date.
Book 12, Page 167 -- Inventory -- many slaves; $5825.00. NATHAN
GUTHRIE, WM. PETTYJOHN, MANSON MAHONE.

CHAS. PETTIT -- Book 12, Page 227 -- Guardians Bond -- SAML. PETTIT
and STERLING CLAIBORNE, November 19, 1849, for SAML. PETTIT as
guardian of CHAS. PETTIT, orphan of H. PETTIT.

SAML. PETTIT -- Book 16, Page 396 -- June 21, 1863; October 19, 1863.
Witnesses: C. G. FULKS, JNO. J. L. STEVENS. D. J. C. SLAUGHTER and
ALFRED PETTIT qualified; bondsman: WM. JORDAN, W. A. CROBKMAN, WM. H.
PETTIT, E. H. PETTIT, JAS. C. PETTIT. Wife, LUCINDA--Rose Mills
property; thirty acres of Piney Woods; one acre to MRS. HUDSON;
daughter, MARY F. SLAUGHTER; son, ALFRED G.; son, JAS. C.; granddaughter, FLORENCE A. BROCKMAN--daughter of WILLIS A. BROCKMAN and
he had cash; guardian may act--D. J. C. SLAUGHTER or WM. VENIBLE;
my son, EDWD. H.; son, WM. H.; daughter, SUSAN A. VANDESLIVE;
daughter, VA. VENIBLE; if children or grandchildren are without heirs.
Executors: D. J. C. SLAUGHTER, ALFRED G. PETTIT, JAS. C. PETTIT.
Book 16, Page 399 -- Administrators Bond
Book 16, Page 409 -- Inventory -- excepting wife's part, November 14,
1863; no total; D. R. MC ALEXANDER, H. N. FOX, R. M. WADDILL.
Book 17, Page 17 -- Division, order of October, 1863 -- to JAS. C.,
EDWD. H., ALFRED G., WM. H. PETTIT, GEO. C. VANDERSTICE (slice above),
WM. VENABLE, FLORENCE A. BROCKMAN. 525 acres--plat--PETTITS got
81¼ acres each and others got 66 2/3 acres in Nelson and Amherst
Counties--both sides Piney River. Commissioners: HENRY LOVING,
STERLING CLAIBORNE, G. FULCHER, GEO. JONES. Joins THOS. BOWLING,
deceased; HENRY WOODS; WM. THOMPSON, deceased. JESSE MASSIE; ARCH
BEARD; JOS. FULCHER; WM. FULCHER; JNO. H. HILL, Nelson County surveyor,
January 16, 1865.
Book 17, Page 47 -- Administrators Account -- by SLAUGHTER, November 21,
1864. Funeral expenses, August 1, 1863--$110.00. NONNETT (sic) for
MRS. PETTIT--$30.00--1863. 144 pounds of salt--$14.40. Recorded:
December 18, 1865.

WM. H. PETTIT -- Book 17, Page 37 -- Administrators Bond -- JAS. C.
PETTIT and D. J. C. SLAUGHTER, October 16, 1865, for JAS. C. PETTIT.
Book 18, Page 61 -- Administrators Account -- from December 1, 1863;
January 1, 1866--paid out in trying to recover remains of testator;
to ALFRED G. PETTIT for services of horse during War--$100.00.
Recorded: May 12, 1871. Note: For more data on the PETTIT family
see No. 105--Cannon--in my C will work--Alabama, etc.

The next series of items deals with the PETTYJOHN family. My
third son, THURMAN BLANTON DAVIS, married MARY GAYLE PETTYJOHN,
March 5, 1966, in Bethany Methodist Church, Amherst County. She
is the daughter of THOS. WATTS PETTYJOHN and MARY HESSON PETTYJOHN.
I shall include some data which was sent to me after I got up my
index so the material will not be indexed. MRS. FRED FUQUA of
Lynchburg sent it to me for study. MARY GAYLE's line is from WM.;
son, GEO. WASHINGTON; JNO. P., son of GEO. W.; OTEN, son of JNO. P.;
and THOS. WATTS, son of OTEN; (OTEN R.)

ELIZ. J. PETTYJOHN -- Book 8, Page 155 -- At request of JOS. PETTYJOHN
an inventory was made, April 29, 1831, at the house. Nothing has
come into hands of administrator. Commissioners: JAS. LEE; REUBEN
BALDOCK; ISAAC R. REYNOLDS. There was nothing for us to do since
administrator could show us no estate to administrator. He says
that he can do nothing until he can sustain debt claims due estate.
Note: This seems to be the widow of WM. who was first one of family
to show here. MRS. FUQUA thinks that she was ELIX. CREWS, but there
is no marriage bond in Amherst County. I have not checked elsewhere
for this marriage. WM. only refers to wife in his will, but accounts
and deeds show her to be ELIZ.

FRANCIS E. PETTYJOHN -- Book 7, Page 239 -- Guardians Bond -- WM.
PETTYJOHN and RO. RIDGWAY, May 18, 1829, for WM. PETTYJOHN as
guardian of FRANCIS E.; SARAH ANN; MARY JANE; ARCHELAUS B. (?) and
WM. M. PETTYJOHN, infants of WM. PETTYJOHN.

JOS. PETTYJOHN, SR. -- Book 17, Page 40 -- February 24, 1862; in
66th year of my age; December 18, 1865. Handwriting attested by
SAML. M. GARLAND and GEO. W. CHRISTIAN. JOS. and JESSE M. PETTYJOHN
qualified. Wife, NANCY--400 acres where I live and the house;
married daughters and children; sons, JOS. and JESSE--1239 3/4 acres
Pedlar road; daughter, CAROLINE, wife of WM. M. WALLER--Mt. place
next to COL. RICHESO; her children--Huff Creek on Pedlar road;
daughter, MARY ELIZ., wife of ALFRED S. LEE; daughter, CATH., wife
of GEO. M. RUCKER; daughter, MISSOURI, wife of JAS. V. WHEELER;
daughter, LOUISIANA, wife of GEO. W. DOUNAN; son, THAS. Executors:
wife, JOS., JESSE and CHAS. SCHEDULE of advances to heirs.
Book 17, Page 43 -- Administrators Bond

KATE R. PETTYJOHN -- Book 24, Page 264 -- December 2, 1918; September 5,
1919. Handwriting by JNO. P. and A. P. PETTYJOHN. Three single
sisters: SUSIE E., MAUDA D. and CARRIE W. PETTYJOHN; living brothers
and sisters.

PAULINA PETTYJOHN -- Book 16, Page 197 -- Administrators Bond --
W. H. CURLE and J. C. DEANE, January 19, 1863, for W. H. CURLE.

R. H. PETTYJOHN -- Book 15, Page 33 -- Guardians Bond -- PAULINA L.
PETTYJOHN and R. A. COGHILL, September 20, 1858, for PAULINA L.
PETTYJOHN as guardian of R. H. and infant daughter of WILL PETTYJOHN,
deceased.

WILLIAM PETTYJOHN -- Book 6, Page 288 -- August 1, 1821; May 26, 1822.
Witnesses: ARCHELAUS REYNOLDS, WM. PENDLETON, WM. TURNER. Proved by
them. JOS., WIATT, and GEO. W. PETTYJOHN qualified. Estate to be
intact until death of my wife or marriage or marriage of single
children. My children: WM., JOS., WIATT, GEO. WASHINGTON, POLLY
RIDGWAY, and ELIZ. WILLS. Grandson, SETH WOODROOF, son of my deceased
daughter, RHODA WOODROOF--where I live; if any child has no issue;
when SETH is 21. Have given POLLY RIDGWAY $4999.16; Wm.--$2415.26;

WILLIAM PETTYJOHN (cont.) -- ELIZ. WILLS--$2654.33; SETH WOODROOF--
$500.00. If dispute arises, reputable umpire to be used to save legal
expenses. Executors: Sons, WM., JOS., WIATT, and GEO. WASHINGTON.
At end is account: POLLY--slaves bought of BENJAMIN RUCKER; ELIS.
WILLS--slaves and cattle; deceased daughter, RHODA WOODROOF--$500.00;
WM., JR.--slaves; same witnesses.
Book 6, Page 311 -- Inventory -- about 48 slaves named; family bible;
very long; $14,542.61. WM. PENDLETON, JAS. LEE, ARCHILLES REYNOLDS,
JESSE BECK, WM. TURNER. JOS. returned an additional inventory and
says that GEO. W. claimed a black colt and red steer on verbal gift
and will not sign for them, but is willing to sign for the rest.
October 21, 1822.
Book 6, Page 340 and 342 -- WIATT and JOS. PETTYJOHN qualified,
November 18, 1822; no bondsman required.
Book 6, Page 377 -- not there.
Book 7, Page 14 -- Administrators Account -- WIATT PETTYJOHN from
December, 1822. To WM., JOS. PETTYJOHN, GEO. W. PETTYJOHN; account
of WM. THURMOND; JNO. D. WILLS, legatee and buyer; MRS. ELIZ.
PETTYJOHN--labor of her slaves in 1823; legatees: WIATT: JOS.;
GOE. W. PETTYJOHN; JNO. D. WILLS and wife and SETH WOODROOF; RO.
RIDGWAY was not present, but made exceptions.
Book 8, Page 86 -- Administrators Account -- J. PETTYJOHN from
July, 1827; March 2, 1831--same legatees.
Book 8, Page 256 -- slave division to the same heirs, March 2, 1831.
WM. BOURNE, CHAS. WINGFIELD, D. P. GOOCH.

    The next items deal with WM., JR., who married a CREWS--March 12,
1839--PAULINA L.--"without parents of guardian." I wonder if there
could be confusion as to identity of his father's wife with this
woman. As stated, I have done no research outside of Amherst on the
family.

PAULINA L. PETTYJOHN -- Book 14, Page 214 -- Administrators Bond --
November 17, 1856.
Book 14, Page 277 -- November 24, 1855; codicil of December 18, 1855;
Monday, November 17, 1856. Witnesses to will: C. DABNEY, WM. J.
WILLS, SYLVESTER M. BURFORD; to codicil: RICH. M. ANDERSON and
C. DABNEY. Objection W. C. FOWLER and wife; ARCHER C. PETTYJOHN;
CHAS. REYNOLDS and wife, SARAH ANN, by attornies. Infirm; slaves to
WM. CURLE; my daughter, FRANCES E. CURLE--child or children; my sons,
WM., ARCHY C.; daughters: SARAH ANN REYNOLDS, RHODA PETTYJOHN.
Son-in-law, CHAS. REYNOLDS. Wife, PAULINA, to administrate.
Book 14, Page 293 -- Inventory -- many slaves; $16,829.80, December 30,
1856. WM. KENT, WM. S. WILLS, WM. A. STAPLES. Lynchburg certificate
by administratrix, JNO. A. LEGGET, J. P.; recorded Amherst County,
February 16, 1857.
Book 16, Page 198 -- Administrators de bonis non Bond -- WM. H. CURLE,
WM. PETTYJOHN, J. C. DEANE, January 19, 1863, for first two.
Book 16, Page 232 -- Inventory -- January 22, 1863--$26,712.00
ISAAC R. REYNOLDS; S. L. BURFORD; WM. KENT.
Book 16, Page 455 -- Administrators Account -- by CURLE from January 22,
1862--land surveyed; Duiguid for burial--$40.00; MRS. PETTYJOHN's
account; WM. C. FOWLER and wife--legatees; Mill tract; ARCH PETTYJOHN--
legatee; WM. M. PETTYJOHN's account; MRS. RHODA H. DEANE, legatee;
WM. H. CURLE and wife, FRANCES, legatees. Commissioners: A. CHRISTIAN.
March 21, 1864.
Book 16, Page 449 -- Sale--buyers: WM. PETTYJOHN; CAPT. DEANE--Mill
tract sold--$6263.45. March 21, 1864.
Book 16, Page 453 -- slave division: to ARCHY PETTYJOHN; WM. FOWLER
and wife; WM. PETTYJOHN; MISS RHODA; WM. CURLE and wife. March 21,
1864.
Book 23, Page 269 -- Inventory -- J. P. BEARD, Sheriff and Administrator
de bonis non, $171.03. Received of E. S. BROWN. June 27, 1892.

    I am jumping the track here to give some of the data on the
PETTYJOHN family which has been given me by MRS. FRED FUQUA and MRS.
THOS. WATTS PETTYJOHN (Nee MARY HESSON) who is the mother-in-law of
my third son, THURMAN BLANTON DAVIS.

MRS. FUQUA says that tradition in family is that WM. and a brother, JACOB, were Huguenots and came to Virginia. JACOB went on to the southern part of the country. I have been told that there are many PETTYJOHN families in Alabama and it could be that these descend from JACOB.

GEO. WASHINGTON PETTYJOHN had a son, JOHN PATTERSON PETTYJOHN. He was born February 8, 1846; died, January 8, 19959. MRS. FUQUA lists his children as follows: WALKER married MISS RAINE of Danville, Virginia; OTEN R. married ANN WATTS of Amherst County; MAMIE married RO. WATSON of Warrenton, North Carolina; HENNIE married JNO. BURWELL; ALBERT M.; ARCHER married ELIZ. STEWART of Stuart, Alabama (she has Birmingham above this); MARTHA or MATTIE married FRED FUQUA of Lynchburg; RUTY married MAYNARD MONROE of Williamsburg, Virginia; ANNIE died young. MARY GAYLE's grandfather, OTEN REYNOLDS PETTYJOHN, was by his second wife, BELLE WATTS of Amherst County. BELLE WATTS was born 13 March 1859; died August 18, 1927, according to notes of MARY HESSON PETTYJOHN, MARY GAYLE's mother. She notes that JNO. P. PETTYJOHN was buried in Spring Hill, Lynchburg, January 10, 1939. OTEN R. PETTYJOHN married ANNIE WATTS in Bethany Methodist Church, Amherst County, November 25, 1896.

May 13, 1966, Ferrum Junior College, Ferrum, Virginia, celebrated Founders' Day--1913--1966. I have a copy of the program and JOHN P. PETTYJOHN was a member of the first board of trustees. Those Honored Today--JNO. P. PETTYJOHN--"The founder Ferrum College honors today was a leader in the Methodist Church and in education throughout Virginia. That his generous interest and concern reached out to the school that became Ferrum College is of importance to its growth. He was of Lynchburg, Virginia, and a member of the Conference Committee which believed the Methodist Church should have a school in Southwest Virginia; served on the Sites Committee which located the school in Ferrum; worked hard, gave generously, in the school's maiden and struggling years. DR. BENJ. MOORE BECKHAM, Ferrum's first president, said, 'But for him, Ferrum could not have survived.' He was born on the James River near Lynchburg in 1846; became a charter member of Court Street Methodist Church, Lynchburg; trustee and lay leader. For more than sixty years he attended the sessions of the Virginia Annual Conference; member of Virginia Conference and General Conference committees. President of Methodist Childrens' Home, Richmond; first president of Preachers' Aid Society which he established in 1882; started the Superannuate Home Association in 1885. In Lynchburg he established the oldest contracting firm in Virginia which built many colleges and schools; first president of Lynchburg's Chamber of Commerce; on the city council; director of old National Exchange Bank (now Fidelity National). He was a founder, trustee, and president of Board of Randolph-Macon System; made large contributions to these schools at Lynchburg and Ashland; president of Rivermont Realty Company when it gave 100 acres on which to establish the Woman's College. Has touched thousands of lives." His portrait was unveiled by his son, ARCHER P. PETTYJOHN.

WYATT or WIATT PETTYJOHN (also called JNO. W. in data) -- Book 14, Page 174 -- September 12, 1856, WIATT PETTYJOHN died intestate and left widow, JANE M., and children, EDWD. L. and JNO. W. PETTYJOHN, and many slaves. Had bought slaves at sale made by CHAS. B. REYNOLDS and EDWD. L. PETTYJOHN at a commissioners sale--this JNO. W. seems to be WIATT's son and not another name for WIATT--Undersigned legatees are of age and no administrator. They agree to divide slaves bought by the said JNO. W. PETTYJOHN. Signed by both sons and widow.

WM. PHAUP -- Book 12, Page 270 -- Administrators Bond -- ALLEN L. WILEY and JNO. M. WILLIAMS, June 17, 1850, for --. Book 12, Page 274 -- Inventory -- July 12, 1850: $10,485.00; CHAS. WINGFIELD; WIATT PETTYJOHN; JNO. A. MOSELY. Book 12, Page 357 -- Sale -- November 21, 1850. MRS. PHAUP was a buyer; also JNO. J. and certified by WM. R. PHAUP--or MRS. R. PHAUP-- not clear. I have not checked this man, but it is said that he owned the old brick house just south of intersection of U.S. 29 and Natural Bridge road.

Note: There are no wills for the PEYTON or PAYTON family, but the deed books contain much data showing genealogy--also ROACH family connection. I have about five pages of data and this shows Kentucky angles as well. If my deed books are available, I suggest a search of them. Begin with Book B, Pages 310-1768, PHILIP PEYTON, and continue through a number of books. The last item that I have is in Book O, Page 631 and is an interesting division to heirs: BURKS, ROACH, KELLY, and PEYTON--1815. I have jotted down this note: Overwharton Parish: September 15, 1748, PHILIP PEYTON and WINIFRED PEYTON (nee BURFORD?).

BENJ. PHILLIPS -- Book 4, Page 416 -- October 22, 1808--found insane by Justices of the Peace. MOSES PHILIPS bonded to care for estate. Bondsmen: REUBEN NORVELL, CHAS. WATTS, SATON M. PENN, JNO. LOVING. NORVELL and WATTS are to assist him.
Book 4, Page 443 -- Administrators Bond -- DAVID S. GARLAND and HUDSON M. GARLAND, February 16, 1807, for DAVID S. GARLAND--now dead.

DABNEY PHILLIPS -- Book 4, Page 370 -- Guardians Bond -- June 20, 1803. JNO. DILLARD and CHAS. WATTS for JNO. DILLARD as guardian of DABNEY PHILLIPS, orphan of WM. PHILLIPS, deceased.
Book 10, Page 383 -- Estate Commitment to Sheriff, March Court, 1841; motion of DAVID HIGGINBOTHAM.

GEO. PHILLIPS -- Book 4, Page 429 -- Guardians Bond -- June 16, 1806-- DAVID S. and SPOTSWOOD GARLAND for DAVID S. GARLAND as guardian of GEO. PHILLIPS, orphan of WM. PHILLIPS.

GEO. D. PHILLIPS -- indexed for GEO., but GEO. D. in data -- Book 14, Page 215 -- Constables Bond -- September 15, 1856; election District 6-2 years from July 1, 1856. RICH. H. EUBANK, bondsman.
Book 14, Page 587 -- June 21, 1858; Constables Bond; elected May 27, 1858--two years. Bondsman: JAS. W. PHILLIPS.

JNO. PHILLIPS -- Book 4, Page 455 -- Constables Bond -- June 20, 1803; two years. Bondsman: LEWIS TINDALL and JNO. LOVING.
Book 4, Page 458 -- June 17, 1805; constable two years. Bondsman: JACOB TYREE and RO. PAMPLIN.
Book 6, Page 352 -- January 7, 1823; April 21, 1823. Witnesses: RO. WARREN, JOS. BRYANT, JNO. CARTER. Daughter, ELIZ., wife of CALEB WOOD; wife, PENELOPEY; granddaughter, SOPHIAN PHILLIPS--daughter of my daughter, ELIZ., who since married CALEB WOOD--when of age. Executor: friend, HENRY H. WATTS. He qualified of probate date. Bondsman: JNO. COLEMAN.
Book 6, Page 383 -- Inventory -- May 2, 1823; no total; GILES DAVIDSON, LEWIS LAINE, CHAS. M. CHRISTIAN.

LEONARD PHILLIPS -- Book 3, Page 480 -- Inventory -- no total; February 14, 1798. Recorded: August 18, 1798. JAS. TURNER, WM. BREEDLOVE, WM. MARTIN.
Book 4, Page 289 -- Administrators Bond -- LUCY BAILEY, ZACH PHILLIPS, WM. LEE HARRIS, July 17, 1797, for LUCY BAILEY.

MARY PHILLIPS -- Book 11, Page 537 -- February 18, 1840; September 20, 1847. Witnesses: JNO. S. FRENCH, C. H. CRANK, JNO. L. DAVENPORT. Daughter: FRANCES CHEATWOOD; son, MOSES PHILLIPS; granddaughter, MARY JANE WOODROOF; granddaughter, SARAH S. PHILLIPS.

MARY M. PHILLIPS -- Book 23, Page 96 -- Administrators Bond -- C. J. CAMPBELL and JOS. O. HUNTLEY, July 20, 1891, for C. J. CAMPBELL.
Book 23, Page 231 -- Inventory -- September 17, 1891--$161.45. R. J. HUDSON, E. W. MITCHELL, JOS. O. HUNTLEY.
Book 23, Page 234 -- Sale -- November 19, 1892. Buyers: J. D. and CHAS. PHILLIPS.

MARY W. PHILLIPS -- Book 9, Page 233 -- Guardians Bond -- July 18, 1836; WM. P. SISSON; JNO. S. KYLE; LEWIS S. EMMITT for WM. P. SISSON as guardian of MARY W. PHILLIPS, orphan of DABNEY T. PHILLIPS. The DABNEY is plain, but initial of T is hard.

MATT. PHILLIPS -- Book 3, Page 177 -- Statement of January 18, 1791--
LEONARD PHILLIPS, SR. and JR. and MARY PHILLIPS, being pregnant--
called in as witnesses by MATT. before his death. Wife to get
maintenance or at remarriage, a child's part. DAVID PHILLIPS and wife,
ANN (MATT's wife) to manage estate. ANNE, widow, presented statement
and JNO. PHILLIPS, oldest son, consented to probate. ANNE's bondsmen:
MATT. HARRIS, DAVID and LEONARD PHILLIPS.
Book 3, Page 240 -- Inventory -- August 6, 1791: L286-13-0. JNO.
THOMAS, JNO. GRIFFIN, MATT. HARRIS.

NANCY PHILLIPS (indexed N. PHILLIPS) -- Book 14, Page 139 -- Trustee
account for her and children by LINDSEY COLEMAN, Sheriff and Trustee,
by his agent, GEO. D. (B?) PHILLIPS. Suit of MEEM (?) PHILLIPS versus
PHILLIPS, September 4, 1852.
Book 15, Page 203 -- Administrators Bond -- June 20, 1859; JAS. W.
PHILLIPS, TARLTON W. CHILDS and JAS. F. THORNTON, for JAS. W. PHILLIPS.
Book 15, Page 573 -- Inventory -- $194.92, and sale, Recorded July 21,
1860. $651.32. JAS. W., GEO. D. and JNO. D. PHILLIPS were buyers.
Book 17, Page 316 -- indexed for MARY PHILLIPS -- Administrators
Account -- by JAS. W. PHILLIPS from February 15, 1863. To GEO. D.
PHILLIPS. Recorded April 20, 1868.

SARAH PHILLIPS -- Book 6, Page 112 -- Administrators Bond -- December 20, 1819; JACOB PHILLIPS. Bondsman: THOS. COLEMAN.

ZACHARIAH PHILLIPS -- Book 4, Page 470 -- June 11, 1807; September 21,
1807. Witnesses: HENRY T. HARRIS, RICH. G. POLLARD, WM. L. HARRIS.
Wife, FRANCES; sons, JOHN, ZACH., LEONARD, THOS., JOS. Daughter,
ANN GRIFFIN--friends, HAWES COLEMAN, CAPT. JNO. HARRIS and ZACH.
ROBERTS--negroes got from THOS. GOODWIN and money in trust for my
daughter, JOAHANNAH RUCKER, and children. Sons, CONYERS and JOSHUA
PHILLIPS; daughter, FRANCES W. BAILEY. Executors: wife and sons,
ZACH. and JOS.
Book 4, Page 471 -- Administrators Bond -- JNO. and ZACH. PHILLIPS,
ISAAC WHITE, JAS. WHITE, WM. LEE HARRIS, October 19, 1807, for first
two to administrate.
Book 4, Page 489 -- Inventory -- December 21, 1807; no total;
RICH. C. POLLARD, MATT. HARRIS, ZACH. ROBERTS.
Book 5, Page 505 -- Administrators Bond -- JOS. PHILLIPS and MATT.
HARRIS, February 15, 1808, for JOS. PHILLIPS as one of administrators.

CORNL. PIERCE -- Book 6, Page 230 -- Constables Bond -- June 18, 1821;
bondsman: JONAS PIERCE.
Book 6, Page 359 -- ditto, first hundred, June 16, 1823; bondsman:
JACOB and JONAS PIERCE.
Book 6, Page 609 -- ditto, June 23, 1825; bondsman: same.
Book 9, Page 279 -- Trust fund for MRS. CORNL. PIERCE--PETER and
JNO. W. DUDLEY, trustees from October 22, 1835. WM. R. REID for
tuition for daughter, MARY, April 6, 1835; cash to MARY for Queen
of the May--50¢; veil for MARY--$1.00; for hat--$6.00; fine comb--
38¢; two pairs Prunell slippers--$2.50; boys' shoes--$1.25; chancery
suit in Amherst County; cash from JONAS PIERCE's executor November 22,
1836.
Book 9, Page 399 -- Trust account by same men from November 22, 1836--
cash paid to daughter, SUSAN; plantation rented to W. GRANT and PAGE;
slave hired to ASA BERRY. Recorded: March 20, 1838.
Book 15, Page 111 -- trustee account by ROBINSON C. PIERCE as
trustee--from December 31, 1856; one half tax of J. PIERCE estate.
March 21, 1859.
Book 15, Page 141 -- Trustee account by same man from January 15,
1858--CORNL. PIERCE and children; Recorded April 21, 1859.
Book 15, Page 537 -- Same from January 15, 1859--slaves hired by
C. PIERCE without consent of trustee. February 28, 1860.
Book 16, Page 290 -- Same from January 15, 1860. Recorded April 20,
1863.

DANL. PIERCE -- Book 5, Page 609 -- Guardians Bond -- JACOB PIERCE,
THOS. ALDRIDGE, WM. ARMISTEAD, November 18, 1816, for JACOB PIERCE
as guardian of DANL., THOS., PETER, NAN, CHAS. PIERCE, orphans of

282

DANL. PIERCE (cont.) -- PETER PIERCE, deceased, and WM. PIERCE, son
of JNO. PIERCE. This is just another good illustration of poor
indexing since only one of these wards is indexed.

HARRIET and HIRAM PIERCE et al. -- Book 12, Page 113fff -- Guardians
Account -- by WM. M. PIERCE as guardian of JACOB K., LAVINIA F.,
HARRIET, VA. and HIRAM PIERCE. HARRIET's follows usual pattern.
Book 12, Page 119 -- from February, 1846; school books; to SARAH
PIERCE; to RO. W. WATTS for tuition; HIRAM CHEATWOOD, administrator
of JONAS PIERCE. December 18, 1848.

JACOB PIERCE -- Book 9, Page 69 -- February 18, 1835; May 18, 1835.
Witnesses: BARNET O. PAGE, WILLIS M. PAGE, HENRY L. DAVIES. JONAS
PIERCE qualified; bondsmen: LINDSEY COLEMAN, WM. DILLARD. Grand-
daughters, MARY and SUSAN ANN PIERCE, daughters of CORNL. PIERCE;
son, CORNL. and family; granddaughter, ELIZ. PIERCE, daughter of
JONAS PIERCE; daughter, SARAH ANN--daughter of JONA PIERCE (sic);
grandson, JACBO DANIEL, son of JONAH PIERCE--CH property; sons,
CORNL. and JONAH--CH property--White House Tavern and two acres.
Five years to elapse and then to children of CORNL. JONAH (sic)
PIERCE; CORNL. is in financial straits and to children and to be
managed by SAML. M. GARLAND, RO. TINSLEY, and HENRY L. DAVIES. CORNL.
and wife are to be supported. Executor: son, JONAH PIERCE.
Administrators Bond is page 71.
Book 9, Page 96 -- Inventory -- May 23, 1835: $7090.12. WILEY
CAMPBELL, JOS. KYLE, RO. WINGFIELD.
Book 9, Page 150 -- plat of 293 5/8 acres Franklin Mill Creek; north
branch Buffaloe. Survey of August 28, 1835. Lot to JONAS PIERCE--
WM. HILL, Nelson County, surveyor; plat and summary 151f. 1079 south
side and next to Buffaloe. 658 acres to trustees of children of
CORNL. PIERCE and joins Braxton ridge; JONAS PIERCE; Wilcher's branch;
JNO. HORSLEY; VIA's house; DILLARD's heirs; Megginson road; Poor
House land; Poplar Meeting house; JOS. PETTYJOHN (formerly JACOB
SCOTT). 420 3/4 acres north edge Megginson road; a spring; widow
TYLER; WILEY CAMPBELL; Stovall's old road; another road; ABSALOM
HOWL; RO. PATRICK; JOS. PETTYJOHN; Poor House land; Wilcher's branch,
Poplar Meeting house. September 3, 1835. JOS. PETTYJOHN; WILEY
CAMPBELL; LINDSEY COLEMAN. Plat on 150 shows lines of RANDOLPH
CASH; EIFOR MOUNTCASTLE; THOS. V. GOODRICH, COL. CORNL. SALE,
DABNEY SANDIDGE.
Book 9, Page 279 -- Trust fund of MRS. CORNL. PIERCE from October 22,
1835. Daughter, MARY for Queen of the May; PETER and JNO. W. DUDLEY.
Book 9, Page 319 -- Administrators Account -- from May, 1835, deed
of gift to MARTHA WARD; CH property; repair of tavern; CAPT. THOMPSON--
part rent for tavern; Poor Farm items; P. S. PIERCE's estate, J.
OGDEN, administrator; CORNL. PIERCE's account on page 321 on order
of March, 1837. Recorded: April 21, 1837. LINDSEY COLEMAN and
J. PETTYJOHN.
Book 10, Page 362 -- Administrators Account -- from April 21, 1837.
Repair of tavern; blacksmith shop rental for 1836; rent of field
near Bowles; family of CORNL. PIERCE. Trustee account by J. PIERCE,
executor of JACOB PIERCE; to trustee, CAPT. DUDLEY. Recorded:
June 21, 1841. Same commissioners as above.
Book 11, Page 261 -- Administrators Account -- from June, 1841.
ZACH BOWLES for "pailing" graveyard; shed for tavern roof and rent.
May 17, 1844. Same commissioners.
Book 12, Page 266 -- Administrators Account -- from 1844. HIRAM
CHEATWOOD, administrator of JONAS PIERCE; order of February, 1849.
C. PIERCE's family. BENJ. BROWN, trustee. Page 270 has fund account
of C. PIERCE. Recorded February 18, 1850.

JACOB D. PIERCE -- Book 12, Page 115 -- Guardians Account -- WM. M.
PIERCE from January, 1846--while at school in Rockbridge and Appomattox.
WM. M. acts as guardian of heirs of JONAS PIERCE; HIRAM CHEATWOOD,
administrator of JONAS PIERCE; receipt of SARAH PIERCE; rent of SCOTT's
place. December 18, 1848.
Book 12, Page 145 -- Refunding Bond -- by guardian of hei-s--see
HARRIET and HIRAM PIERCE for complete list--infants and $5000.00
received for wards. Bond of MILDRED and WM. PIERCE--MILDRED has

JACOB D. PIERCE (cont.) -- received legacy; also bond for SARAH ANN
and WM. PIERCE for SARAH ANN who has received legacy. July 20, 1847.
Book 12, Page 147 -- Refunding Bond -- RO. A. PENDLETON and RO. A.
COGHILL, July 19, 1847, to HIRAM CHEATWOOD, administrator. PENDLETON
has received legacy in right of wife, LOUISA E. Same page, SALLY W.
and MILDRED W. PIERCE, to CHEATWOOD. SALLY has received legacy.
July 20, 1847.
Book 12, Page 148 -- Refunding Bond -- by WM. M. PIERCE and SARAH A.
PIERCE; same date; SARAH A. has received legacy.
Book 15, Page 585 -- Surveyor Bond -- June 21, 1858; Bondsman:
RO. A. PENDLETON.
Book 16, Page 532 -- Same, July 18, 1864; bondsman: RO. W. WATTS.

JACOB G. PIERCE -- Book 5, Page 581 -- Administrators Bond -- JACOB
PIERCE, DAVID S. GARLAND, WM ARMISTEAD, June 17, 1816, for JACOB
PIERCE.
Book 5, Page 606 -- Inventory -- July 30, 1816--$4767.50; JAS. T.
DILLARD; JNO. COLEMAN; DANL. CHEATWOOD.
Book 6, Page 41 -- Sale at residence -- November 27 and 28th--buyers:
JONAS, JACOB, CORNL., WM. and SALLY PIERCE--$1188.97.
Book 6, Page 44 -- Administrators Account -- from 1816. WM. PIERCE,
overseer; surveying land and laying off in two lots; total of estate:
$13,318.40½; Recorded: November 16, 1818. DAVID S. GARLAND,
JAS. S. PENDLETON, THOS. ALDRIDGE.

JAS. PIERCE--but appears to be PENN--indexed PIERCE -- Book 6, Page
480 -- Administrators Bond -- WM. I. ISBELL, CHRISTOPHER ISBELL,
August 18, 1824, for WM. I. ISBELL.

COL. JONAS PIERCE -- Book 8, Page 351 -- Agent for Board of Overseers
of Poor, September 16, 1833. Bondsman: JOS KYLE, RO. and THOS.
WINGFIELD, PHINEAS S. PIERCE.
Book 11, Page 312 -- Administrators Bond -- HIRAM CHEATWOOD, April 21,
1845. Bondsman: DANL. A. CHEATWOOD, WM. S. and JEFF D. TURNER,
WM. M. PIERCE.
Book 11, Page 384 -- Inventory -- November 11, 1845; slaves: $10,825;
other inventory at $11,728.66. JOS. KYLE, DAVID APPLING, JAS. W.
KEITH; Sale, November 18, 1845--buyers not listed--$410.59.
Book 11, Page 591 -- Land division, order of October, 1846; to widow,
SARAH W. PIERCE; to WM. and MILDRED PIERCE; Mill tract on east side
Braxton ridge; to HIRAM PIERCE--land on north side of Megginson road;
to Virginia; Jacob-Mt. tract; HARRIET PIERCE--CH property; SARAH and
LAVINIA PIERCE; ELIZ. PENDLETON; RO. A. PENDLETON et al. versus
SARAH W. PIERCE et al. December 21, 1846. H. L. BROWN, JAS. D.
WATTS, DAVID APPLING.
Book 12, Page 292 -- Administrators Account -- from May 17, 1847
Ferriage; to MILDRED PIERCE to equalize slave division; to SARAH A.
PIERCE; to RO. A. PENDLETON; PIERCE versus PIERCE; to WM. M. PIERCE;
to HIRAM and VA. PIERCE; to HARRIET PIERCE; WM. M. PIERCE, guardian
of JACOB and HARRIET PIERCE; C. PIERCE and family. September 16,
1850; HOWELL L. BROWN, commissioner.
Book 13, Page 408 -- Administrators Account -- from June 30, 1850;
recorded: July 26, 1854.

LAVINIA F. PIERCE -- Book 12, Page 117 -- Guardians Account -- WM. M.
PIERCE, guardian, from February, 1846; account of SARAH PIERCE in
1847; July 26; paid your boy, DAVID, 25¢; HIRAM CHEATWOOD, administrator
of JONAS PIERCE. Recorded: December 18, 1848.

MILDRED W. PIERCE -- Book 11, Page 392 -- Guardians Bond -- WM. M.
PIERCE, HIRAM CHEATWOOD, SAML. HEISKELL, and HOWELL L. BROWN,
January 19, 1846, for WM. M. PIERCE as guardian of MILDRED W.,
JACOB D. and LAVINIA F. PIERCE; no parent set forth.
Book 12, Page 146 -- Refunding Bond -- July 20, 1847, MILDRED and
WM. PIERCE to HIRAM CHEATWOOD, administrator of JONAH (sic) PIERCE;
MILDRED has received legacy.

NATHL. PIERCE -- Book 6, Page 333 -- Guardians Bond -- JAS. D. WATTS
and HENRY H. WATTS, October 21, 1822. JAS. D. WATTS as guardian of
NATHL. PIERCE, orphan of PETER PIERCE, deceased.

PETER W. PIERCE -- Book 6, Page 258 -- indexed as inventory, but it
is Guardians Bond -- WM. PIERCE, guardian of PETER W. PIERCE, orphan
of PETER PIERCE, October 15, 1821. Bondsman: JNO. HORSLEY, JR.

PHINEAS PIERCE (S initial) -- Book 8, Page 411 -- Inventory -- order
of February, 1834--$1277.12. WILEY CAMPBELL, JOS. KYLE, HENRY
CHRISTIAN.
Book 9, Page 71 -- Administrators de bonis non Bond -- May 18, 1835,
JONAS PIERCE, LINDSEY COLEMAN, WM. DILLARD for JONAS PIERCE.
Book 9, Page 319 -- Administrators Account -- from June 15, 1835--
transfer to account of JACOB PIERCE estate. November, 1830. On
same page is Administrators Account by same administrator of JACOB
PIERCE.

SALLY W. PIERCE -- Book 12, Page 147 -- Refunding Bond -- to HIRAM
CHEATWOOD, administrator of JONAS PIERCE; bondsman: MILDRED W. PIERCE.

SARAH ANN PIERCE -- Book 12, Page 146 -- Refunding Bond -- to above
administrator, July 20, 1847; bondsman: WM. PIERCE.

THOS. PIERCE -- Book 6, Page 204 -- Guardians Bond -- WM. PIERCE and
JNO. HORSLEY, January 15, 1821, for WM. PIERCE as guardian of THOS.
PIERCE, orphan of PETER PIERCE.

VA. PIERCE -- Book 12, Page 121 -- Guardians Account -- WM. M. PIERCE
from January 2, 1846.

WM. PIERCE -- Book 2, Page 94 -- Administrators Bond -- JESSE MORRIS,
JNO. DAWSON, WM. MORRISON, March 3, 1783, for JESSE MORRIS.
Book 2, Page 100 -- Inventory -- March 7, 1783--L44-13-8. TERISHA
TURNER, WM. TURNER, SAML. ANDERSON.
Book 2, Page 185 -- Sale -- July 5, 1784. Buyers: CHAS. and
OBEDIAH PIERCE L49-12-1.

WM. M. PIERCE -- Book 12, Page 149 -- Refunding Bond -- July 20, 1847,
to HIRAM CHEATWOOD, administrator of JONAS PIERCE. Bondsman: SARAH A.
PIERCE. WM. has received legacy.

THOS. E. PLEASANTS -- Book 7, Page 296 -- Administrators Bond --
GEO. T. PLEASANTS, JAS. D. WATTS, JNO. DILLARD, GEO. SHRADER, H. B.
SCOTT, December 21, 1829, for GEO. T. PLEASANTS.

JNO. PLUNKET -- Book 8, Page 335 -- Administrators Bond -- AMBROSE
PLUNKET, WM. MC DANIEL, LINDSEY MC DANIEL, July 15, 1833, for
AMBROSE PLUNKET.

GARLAND POINDEXTER -- Book 13, Page 434 -- SAML. POINDEXTER in Deed
of Trust of GARLAND POINDEXTER; also his account as trustee from
August 6, 1853; to WILLIS POINDEXTER--satchel for daughter, BETTY
WILMORE, SAML. P. POINDEXTER, overseer--is it JR. ? hard to decipher;
MRS. POINDEXTER; sum from JULIA POINDEXTER. Recorded: December 18,
1854.
Book 13, Page 438 -- Trustee account from January 2, 1854--to MRS.
POINDEXTER; to GARLAND POINDEXTER; tuition for son, GARLAND; city
tax on horse and wagon--$10.25; tuition for BETTIE. October 28, 1854.

WM. POLLARD -- Book 7, Page 261 -- Administrators Bond -- CHAS. H.
and SAML. D. CHRISTIAN, July 20, 1829, for CHAS. H. CHRISTIAN.

HENRY POOL -- Book 16, Page 423 -- Administrators Bond -- ANN E. POOL
and THOS. BARBOUR, January 18, 1864, for ANN E. POOL.

LEROY POPE -- Book 4, Page 147 -- November 15, 1803; February 21, 1804--
Inventory: L151-16-6. WM. JOPLING: JOO. EUBANK, WM. PRYOR.

LEROY POPE (cont.) -- Book 4, Page 293 -- Administrators Bond --
ELIZ. POPE, JNO. CRAWFORD, September 19, 1803, for ELIZ. POPE.

ELIZ. PORTER -- Book B, Page 44 -- Administrators Bond -- JNO.
PENDLETON, MANSON MEHONE, WM. G. PENDLETON, March 23, 1853, for
JNO. PENDLETON.

ELIZ. POWELL -- Book 9, Page 63 -- Division of estate of RICH. POWELL;
slaves held by widow, ELIZ--life estate. Prefers to hold some, but
will distribute others--lot to JAS. LEE in right of deceased wife; to
PROSSER POWELL and also as administrator of GEO. POWELL, deceased, and
administrator of RICH. POWELL, JR., deceased. February 21, 1835.
RICH. HARRISON, LINDSEY COLEMAN, LINDSEY MC DANIEL.
Book 10, Page 219 -- August 31, 1835; May 18, 1840. Witnesses:
WM. KNIGHT, WINSTON WOODROOF, WM. W. HARRISON. PROSSER POWELL
qualified, July 20, 1840; bondsman: JOS. K. IRVING. Son, PROSSER,
has been dutiful and affectionate and attentive in my old age--has
left his home and taken his property--to live with me. My other
children; slave bought at estate sale of my son, RICH. POWELL.
PROSSER is administrator of RICH. and to administrate my estate.
Administrators Bond is page 251.

FRANCES G. POWELL -- Book 9, Page 163 -- Guardians Account -- PROSSER
POWELL, guardian of MISS FRANCES G., ELIZ. C., and GEO. POWELL,
infants of GEO. POWELL, deceased. To W. PADGETT and wife--interest
in land; same to BEVERLY WADE and wife and JAS. NORVELL and wife.
Widow's part in lieu of dower. POWELL is guardian of NORVELL's
wife. December 15, 1835.

GEO. POWELL -- Book 6, Page 106 -- Administrators Bond -- PROSSER
POWELL and JAS. S. PENDLETON, November 16, 1817, for PROSSER POWELL.
Book 6, Page 141 -- Inventory -- November 27, 1819--$4474.17. EDWD.
TINSLEY, SAML. BURKS, WM. N. SCOTT, WM. PENDLETON.
Book 6, Page 420 -- Administrators Account -- from December 21, 1819;
boat sold coffin made--$2.50; $5.00 to WM. S. READ for personal
oration; SOPHIA POWELL--board and tuition of six children; widow's
share. December 15, 1823. NELSON C. DAWSON, AMRB. RUCKER, DABNEY
WARE.
Book 7, Page 147 -- Guardians Bond-- PROSSER POWELL and S. M.
GARLAND, March 17, 1828, for PROSSER POWELL as guardian of GEO.,
FRANCES G. and ELIZ. POWELL, orphans of GEORGE POWELL.
Book 13, Page 53 -- Administrators Bond -- WM. P. SCOTT and EDWD.
TINSLEY, March 21, 1853, for WM. P. SCOTT.
Book 19, Page 121 -- Administrators Account -- JAS. R. GILLIAM,
Deputy Sheriff for C. T. HILL, October 25, 1875. One-fourth each to
EM. E., GEO. F., JNO. T. POWELL and ELIZ. CASEY. February 23, 1876.

GEO. F. POWELL -- Book 16, Page 80 -- Guardians Bond -- JNO. B.
ROBERTSON and ARTHUS F. ROBERTSON, June 17, 1861, for JNO. B. ROBERTSON
as guardian of GEO. F., JANE E., JNO. T. and WM. E. POWELL, orphans
of GEO. POWELL, deceased.
Book 17, Page 68 -- Guardians Account -- from December 2, 1865 for
wards named above: $251.27. Recorded: March 19, 1866.
Book 17, Page 292 -- Guardians Account -- from November, 1865; wards
as above. February 17, 1868.

GIDEON POWELL -- Book 5, Page 407 -- Administrators Bond -- RICH.
POWELL and JAS. P. GARLAND, January 17, 1814, for RICH. POWELL.

DR. JAMES POWELL -- Book 1, Page 261 -- Guardians Bond -- MARTIN
DAWSON, JNO. SALE, DANL. GAINES, May 2, 1774, for MARTIN DAWSON as
guardian of JAS. POWELL, orphan of JNO. POWELL.
Book 11, Page 110 -- Sheriffs Bond -- March 20, 1843. Bondsman:
JNO. H. FUQUA, WIATT P. SMITH, WM. M. WALLER, W. A. RICHESON, DABNEY
SANDIDGE, BARNETT CASH, ZA DRUMMOND, SAML. G. CASH, J. S. MC DANILE,
JR., PAULUS POWELL, M. C. GOODWIN, CHAS. H. MASSIE, ABRAHAM MARTIN,
WILLIS M. REYNOLDS, R. A. PENDLETON, PHILLIP WEBBER, W. W. THOMPSON,
WARNER JONES, MARSHALL T. HARRIS, NATHAN A. CASH, JNO. M. PRICE,
DANL. L. COLEMAN.

Book 11, Page 272 -- Same, February 19, 1844. Bondsman: JOEL BETHEL,
RO. A. COGHILL, JNO. WHITEHEAD, ABRAHAM MARTIN, WILLIS M. REYNOLDS,
R. A. PENDLETON, PHILLIP WEBBER, W. W. THOMPSON, and others as above.

MILDRED POWELL (N IRVING) -- Book 8, Page 280 -- August 24, 1832;
October 15, 1832. Witnesses: THOS. J. WALKER, JNO. H. ROBERTS,
JAS. A. ROSE. My children, my husband, JAS. POWELL has given me
house and lot where I live and land known as the Brick Tavern; may
have to be sold, but executor to confer with my husband--for benefit
of my children. Executors: my brother, RO, IRVING and friend,
ARTHUR B. DAVIES and son-in-law, SAML. M. GARLAND.
Book 8, Page 372 -- Administrators Bond -- JAS. POWELL and STERLING
CLAIBORNE, November 20, 1833, for JAS. POWELL. The Brick Tavern
stood on west side of main street in the village and roughly across
from Amherst Publishing office.

NANCY POWELL -- Book 6, Page 159 -- Guardians Bond -- SOPHIA POWELL,
REUBEN PENDLETON, JAS. S. PENDLETON, September 18, 1820, for SOPHIA
POWELL as guardian of NANCY; CATH.; FRANCES; BETSY; JANE and GEO.
POWELL, orphans of G. POWELL, deceased.

PROSSER POWELL -- Book 6, Page 160 -- not there and ? by it in Master.
It may be Book 6, Page 106 which is PROSSER as administrator of GEO.
POWELL, November 16, 1819; bondsman: JAS. S. PENDLETON.
Book 14, Page 229 -- Administrators Bond -- WM. KENT, DAVID PATTESON,
SAML. GARLAND and HIRAM C. KYLE, February 16, 1857, for WM. KENT.
Book 14, Page 345 -- Inventory -- many slaves, April 20, 1857.
WM. A. STAPLES, WM. J. WILLS, RO. C. MARTIN, CHAS. B. PALMER.
Book 15, Page 189-2 (pages so numbered) -- Administrators Account --
from March 3, 1857; recorded: July 18, 1859.
Book 15, Page 507 -- Administrators Account -- from November 13,
1858; recorded: May 21, 1860.
Book 16, Page 260 -- Administrators Account -- from February 16, 1859;
recorded: April 20, 1863.

RICH. POWELL -- Book 1, Page 257 -- January 25, 1766; April 4, 1774.
Witnesses: THOS. POWELL, AMY POWELL, JACOB SMITH. Son, EDMUND--283
acres on Buffaloe where he lives; son, WYATT, 400 acres on Thresher--
where I formerly dwelt son, THOS.--245 acres near Lynch's ferry and
which I had of MICAJAH MORRMAN; wife, ELIZ.--217 acres where I now
dwell; son, RICH.; grandson, JAS. POWELL, son of JNO. POWELL--five
years schooling; daughter, WINNEFORD POWELL when married; daughter
RHODA, same; daughter, CLARY WOODROOF; RHODA gets horse and saddle
when 14. My children: WYATT, THOS., RICH., WINNEY, RHODA. Executors:
CORNL. THOMAS, RICH. SHELTON, and son, WYATT (WIATTE).
Book 1, Page 259 -- Administrators Bond -- WIATT POWELL, THOS.
POWELL, EDMD. POWELL, and JACOB SMITH, April 4, 1774, for WIATT POWELL.
Book 1, Page 275 -- Inventory -- L509-5-9, March court, 1775. GEO.
MC DANIEL, H. L. DAVIES, RICH. SHELTON.
Book 5, Page 477 -- November 16, 1814; December 19, 1814. Witnesses:
JNO. CAMM, JNO. WARWICK. Lf Lynchburg, but sick at brother JAS.
POWELL's place in Amherst County; debt of my father is wiped out;
same for brother, JAS.; money to STEPHEN TRAIL; slave, ROBIN, to
choose master among my borthers and brothers-in-law; has chosen JAS.,
but may take steps for complete freedom; brother, CORNL. and children;
land lately bought of NOEL; friend, DANL. WARWICK; my brothers and
sisters. Executors: brother, JAS., and RO. WALKER.
Book 5, Page 528 (so indexed), but Book 5, Page 538 -- November 11,
1815; December 18, 1815. Witnesses: JNO. MC DANIEL, JAS. WOODROOF,
PHILIP LIVELY. PROSSER POWELL, JAS. LEE, RICH. POWELL, JR., qualified;
bondsmen: THOS. CREWS and REUBEN PENDLETON. Wife, ELIZ.--where I
live and 201 acres; son, RICH., and heirs; my four other children:
PROSSER, THOS., GEO. POWELL, and NANCY LEE. 386 acres to be sold.
Executors: son, PROSSER and JAS. LEE. Administrators Bond is Book 5,
Page 539.
Book 5, Page 555 -- Inventory -- January 12, 1816; JNO. MC DNAIEL,
JAS. HILL, JAS. MARR, WILL WOODROOF, JAS. PETIT.
Book 5, Page 574 -- Inventory -- December 9, 1814; GEO. CABELL,
NATHL. RIVES, ROB. MORRIS.

RICH. POWELL (cont.) -- Book 5, Page 600 -- Administrators Account -- from November 1815, by JAS. POWELL, administrator; note to take up in name of RO. WALKER; Campbell County taxes; NATHL. RIVES; TRYALL's bill; STEPHEN TRYALL. August 20, 1816. R. NORVELL, THOS. CREWS, T. S. HOLLOWAY, August 20, 1816.
Book 5, Page 710 -- Administrators Account -- by JAS. POWELL from 1816.
Book 6, Page 52 -- Administrators Account -- by JAS. POWELL as from Book 5, Page 600; recorded: April 19, 1819.
Book 6, Page 189 -- Administrators Bond -- PROSSER POWELL, REUBEN PENDLETON, September 18, 1820, for PROSSER POWELL.
Book 6, Page 210 -- Inventory -- November 17, 1820--$1436.10. DABNEY WARE, SAML. BURKS, EDWD. TINSELY.
Book 6, Page 418 -- Administrators Account -- PROSSER POWELL, administrator, JAS. LEE, and RICH. POWELL, administrators from May 6, 1816; land sold on --ck.; legatees got $2806.40 each. Amounts to JAS. LEE, PROSSER, THOS., and GEO. POWELL. Page 420 is Administrators Account by PROSSER POWELL as administrator of GEO. POWELL, August 15, 1823. NELSON C. DAWSON, DABNEY WARE, AMBR. RUCKER.
Book 5, Page 526 -- Administrators Account -- PROSSER POWELL from January 2, 1821. Bond of ELIZ. POWELL, THOS. POWELL, GEO. POWELL's estate for plantation rent; DR. POWELL's medical bill. April 10, 1823. Same commissioners as above.

THOS. POWELL -- Book 2, Page 150 -- Administrators Bond -- AMEY POWELL, CHAS. TALIAFERRO, JAS. WARE, November 3, 1783, for AMEY POWELL.
Book 2, Page 153 -- Inventory -- March 1, 1784--L75-6-6. PETER CARTER, CHAS. TALIAFERRO, JAS. WARE.
Book 3, Page 93 -- Administrators Bond -- SALLY POWELL, WM. SID CRAWFORD, JOS. PENN for first two, January 26, 1789.
Book 3, Page 472 -- Administrators Account -- by CRAWFORD from same date--CHAS. CLAY for sermon; SALLY POWELL for beef sold; THOS. POWELL (taylor--sic) account of JNO. ROSE; orphans of THOS., June 18, 1798. JNO. WIATT, RODERICK MC CULLOCH, JNO. MC DANIEL.
Book 4, Page 28 -- Inventory -- L67-5-6; November 16, 1801. JNO. WIATT, RICH. SHELTON, BENJ. RUCKER.
Book B, Page 30 -- Administrators Bond -- RO. and ZACH. TINSLEY, August 26, 1847, for RO. TINSLEY.
Book B, Page 31 -- ISAAC D. POWELL and JOSHUA WHEELER to RO. TINSLEY, administrator of THOS. POWELL, November 13, 1848--TINSLEY has paid ESENTH POWELL, administrator of THOS. POWELL in Kentucky--place of domicile. Witness: WM. H. LAMBETH.

WM. POWELL -- Book 3, Page 444 -- Inventory -- September 12, 1797 L63-1-6. WM. MOSS, SAML. HILL, JNO. POOL (?).
Book 3, Page 531 -- Administrators Bond -- MARY POWELL, Administrators Account from August 21, 1798. PLEASANT MARTIN, PATRICK ROSE, SAML. HILL.
Book 4, Page 288 -- Administrators Bond -- MARY POWELL, THOS. HAWKINS, FRANCIS WEST, July 17, 1795, for MARY POWELL.

WYATT POWELL -- Book 6, Page 13 -- December 12, 1816; September 21, 1818. Witnesses: A. B. DAVIES, B. WALKER. JAS. and CORNL. POWELL qualified. Bondsmen: EDMD. WINSTON and JNO. PENN, JR. Wife, SALLY-- plantation and slaves; son, CORNL.; son, JAS.--and they are to administrate. Page 29 is Administrators Bond.

WALTER POWER -- Book 4, Page 37 -- February 9, 1798; June 21, 1802. Witnesses: ANDREW MOORE, THOS. JARVIS, JAS. FRAZIER. Wife, SUSAN-- one-third of land; JNO. FRAZIER, who lives with me--154 acres; WALTER FRAZIER, second son of my daughter, MARGARET FRAZIER--150 acres next to JOS. HIGGINBOTHAM; THOS. FRAZIER--99 acres held by me by grant to him; JAS. and WM. FRAZIER--380 acres. Executors: wife, THOS. GRAYHAM, BENJ. HIGGINBOTHAM.
Book 4, Page 359 -- Administrators Bond -- BENJ. HIGGINBOTHAM, HUGH CAMPBELL, HENRY BALLINGER, JNO. FRAZIER, NICHL. VANSTAVERN, October 18, 1802, for first two.

ELIZ. PRESTON -- Book 12, Page 297 -- Guardians Bond -- CHAS. R. SLAUGHTER, SAML. GRALAND, C. R. SLAUGHTER, attorney-in-fact, October 21, 1850, for CHAS. R. SLAUGHTER as guardian of ONACHETA (QUEHALA), ELIZ., ISADORE, THOS. and REBECCA PRESTON, orphans of WM. R. PRESTON, deceased.
Book 13, Page 488 -- Guardians Account -- from July 1, 1854; to MRS. PRESTON on SALLY's order. July 16, 1855.

HENRY PRESTON -- Book 13, Page 260 -- Guardians Account -- CHAS. R. SLAUGHTER--guardian of HENRY, ELIZA M., THOS. B., ISADORE, and REBECCA PRESTON--decree of RO. H. CABELL, trustee; to MRS. PRESTON, January 1, 1853.

ISADORE PRESTON -- Book 13, Page 487 -- Guardians Account by "her guardian" from September 1, 1854. To J. A.; SALLY or SALLEY--could be one word or name--hard to decipher. July 15, 1855.

REBECCA PRESTON -- Book 13, Page 494 -- Guardians Account -- from -- by SLAUGHTER. Recorded: Monday, July 15, 1855.

THOS. B. PRESTON -- Book 13, Page 490 -- Guardians Account -- by same guardian as above. July 16, 1855.

WM. PRICE -- Book 3, Page 284 -- Administrators Bond -- THOS. GREEN and JNO. SHELTON, October 22, 1793, for THOS. GREEN.

RICH. PRICHARD -- Book 2, Page 132 -- June 4, 1783; September 1, 1783. Witnesses: LEWIS NEVIL, RICH. MURROW, WM. BRADLES. Son, JNO.--after his mother's death; 50 acres where I live. Daughter-in-law, NANCY WATKINS--90 acres where she lives. Wife, MOLLY--mt. land to JNO. Executors: friends, WM. CABELL and wife, MOLLY.

DAVID PROFFITT -- Book 4, Page 117 -- Inventory -- L 262-6-9, May 6, 1803. SHELTON CROSTHWAIT, CHAS. EDMUNDS, ZACH. WHITE.
Book 4, Page 366 -- Administrators Bond -- JNO. and ROWLAND PROFFITT and JAS. MURPHY, April 19, 1803, for first two.
Book 4, Page 368 -- Guardians Bond -- BETSY PROFFITT, ARTHUR ROBERSON, BENJ. ROBERSON, June 20, 1803, for BETSY PROFFITT as guardian of DAVID and AUGUSTINE PROFFITT, orphans of AUGUSTINE PROFFITT.

LANDON A. PROFFITT -- Book 13, Page 177 -- Administrators Bond -- WM. M. CABELL and RO. L. BROWN, April 18, 1853, for WM. M. CABELL.
Book 13, Page 220 -- Inventory -- May 10, 1853--$775.00. JAS. E. GUADMAN (?), JNO. A. CLEMENT, THOS. M. WILKINSON. Lynchburg cett. before DAVID P. REES, Justice of the Peace.
Book 13, Page 410 -- Administrators Account -- from May 12, 1853. THOS. WHITEHEAD, commissioner. February 20, 1854.
Book 15, Page 119 -- Administrators Account -- from 1854; Nelson County clerk's ticket. March 21, 1859.
Book 19, Page 108 -- Administrators de bonis non Bond -- November 15, 1875, ALEX. W. BOXLEY; Bondsman: RO. A. COGHILL.

MOLLY (MILLY) ANN PROFFITT -- Book 6, Page 95 -- Guardians Bond -- October 18, 1819. EDWD. CASH; bondsman: JESSE WRIGHT for HOWARD CASH as guardian of MILLY ANN PROFFITT, orphan of RANDOLPH PROFFIT (PROFIT), deceased.

PATRICK H. PROFFITT -- Book 13, Page 179 -- Guardians Bond -- JAS. W. KEITH, STERLING CLAIBORNE, GEO. S. (L) MAYS, April 18, 1853, for JAS. W. KEITH as guardian of PATRICK PROFFITT, orphan of LANDON PROFFITT--A initial, deceased.
Book 15, Page 533 -- Guardians Account -- from September, 1853. Balance of principal, January 1, 1854, from administrator of LANDON A. PROFFITT. Executed on January 17, 1859, and recorded: May 18, 1860.

ROWLAND (ROWLING) PROFFITT -- Book 8, Page 435 -- Administrators Bond -- LANDON PROFFITT; JAS. and KEZIAH PROFFITT, October 20, 1834, for LANDON PROFFITT. September 25, 1834; October 20, 1834. Witnesses: ED. A. CABELL, PEYTON KEITH, DRURY BELL. Until youngest child is of

ROWLAND (ROWLING) PROFFITT (cont.) -- age; sons, LANDON and JAS. and
wife, KEZIAH, to manage and administrate. Grandson, NORBORNE A.
MITCHELL, son of my daughter, CATH. MITCHELL, deceased--when 21.
Book 9, Page 33 -- Inventory -- $5664.50; several slaves, December 10,
1834. PEYTON KEITH, JAS. HIGGINBOTHAM, ED. A. CABELL.
Book 21, Page 154 -- Administrators Bond -- JORDAN M. PROFFITT and
WM. G. LOVING, May 18, 1885, for JORDAN M. PROFFITT.

SALLY K. PROFFITT -- Book 12, Page 473 -- Guardians Bond -- LANDON A.
PROFFITT, RO. A. COGHILL, and SAML. M. GARLAND, December 15, 1851,
for LANDON A. PROFFITT as guardian of SALLY K., and PATRICK H.
PROFFITT, orphans of LUCY M. PROFFITT, deceased.

SARAH C. PROFFITT -- Book 13, Page 180 -- Guardians Bond -- JAS. W.
KEITH, GEO. S. MAYS, STERLING CLAIBORNE, April 18, 1853, for JAS. W.
KEITH as guardian of SARAH C. PROFFITT, orphan of LANDON A. PROFFITT,
deceased.
Book 13, Page 293 -- Plat and division--head branch Raven Creek--south
tributary Buffaloe. Lines: PEYTON KEITH heirs; MAYO CABELL; A. L.
FOGUS; ALLEN BLAIR heirs--401 acres. Property of LUCY PROFFITT's
heirs et al. Order of December, 1851: PROFFITT versus WATTS.
Division of February 18, and 19, 1852. Divided by JAS. D. WATTS,
MOSES PHILLIPS, DAVID APPLING, ANDREW L. FOGUS. Lot 1 to SALLY C.
PROFFITT, infant daughter of LUCY PROFFITT; deceased--107 acres;
lot 2 to PATRICK H. PROFFITT, infant son of LUCY 118 acres. Lot 3
to GEO. W. WATTS--100 acres. Lot 4 to LANDON A. PROFFITT--76 acres.
JNO. PRYOR, surveyor. L. A. PROFFITT and C. versus W. P. WATTS in
chancery. Recorded: April 19, 1852.
Book 16, Page 116 -- Guardians Bond -- A. W. BOXLEY and WM. S. CLAI-
BORNE, March 17, 1862, for A. W. BOXLEY as guardian of SALLY C.
PROFFITT; no parent set forth.

ELIZ. PRYOR -- Book 11, Page 572 -- Estate Commitment to Sheriff --
April, 1848; motion of SAML. R. CAMPBELL; JAS. L. LAMKIN, Sheriff.
Book 12, Page 33 -- Estate Commitment to Sheriff -- this is same bond
and date.

HARTWELL T. PRYOR -- Book 14, Page 228 -- Minister's Bond -- December 15, 1856; no denomination; Bondsman: THOS. WHITEHEAD.

JNO. PRYOR -- Book 8, Page 136 -- Surveyor Bond -- October 17, 1831.
Bondsman: JNO. DILLARD, BEVERLY DAVIES.
Book 12, Page 26 -- Same -- October 18, 1847; Bondsman: DABNEY
SANDIDGE, ZA DRUMMOND.
Book 12, Page 527 -- Same -- June 21, 1852; bondsman: DABNEY
SANDIDGE, WM. KENT.
Book 15, Page 332 -- Administrators Bond -- on June 18, 1860. JAS. N.
PRYOR; bondsman: JAS. W. PHILLIPS.
Book 16, Page 399 -- Administrators Bond -- MARY S. PRYOR, September 21,
1863; bondsman: WM. L. MILLNER.
Book 18, Page 105 -- Administrators Account -- JAS. N. PRYOR from
1861; JNO. PRYOR, JR.--decree in case--$483.06, October 19, 1863;
recorded March 1871.
Book 19, Page 310 -- Administrators Account -- by JAS. N. PRYOR from
September 16, 1863; $821.51. Recorded: June 25, 1875.

MADISON C. PRYOR -- Book 13, Page 16 -- Administrators Bond -- THOS. B.
GATEWOOD and THOS. D. WATTS, September 20, 1852, for THOS. B. GATEWOOD.
Book 13, Page 222 -- Inventory -- $54.00; RO. H. CARTER; RO. C. BIBB;
WM. C. TURPIN. June 20, 1853.
Book 13, Page 227 -- Sale -- October 7, 1852; $47.95. Bay mare and
saddle sold at $50.00. Recorded August 15, 1853.

N. M. PRYOR -- Book 14, Page 382 -- Guardians Bond -- HARTWELL T.
PRYOR and WIATT GATEWOOD, June 15, 1857, for HARTWELL T. PRYOR as
guardian of N. M. and H. A. PRYOR and JOSEPHINE and ARTHUR BIBB--
called orphans, but no parents set forth. No. 244 shows data.

ROBT. H. PRYOR -- Book 11, Page 175 -- nothing there.
Book 12, Page 75 -- Inventory -- August 10, 1848--$59.00 RO.N. ELLIS,
JNO. E. ELLIS, JNO. H. FUQUA.
Book 12, Page 76 -- Sale at Pedlar Mills, August 1, 1848. VA. PRYOR
was a buyer.
Book 12, Page 130 -- Administrators Bond -- DACID H. TAPSCOTT and
JNO. COLEMAN, June 19, 1848, for DACID H. TAPSCOTT.

WM. PRYOR -- Book 9, Page 40 -- November 16, 1833; January 19, 1835.
Witnesses: BARTLETT CASH, WESLEY E. CHRISTIAN, HENRY FRANKLIN,
JOS. R. CARTER. JNO. PRYOR qualified. Of PRYOR's Vale, Amherst
County--son, JNO.; son-in-law, RICH. EUBANK; wife, NANCY; daughter,
MARGARET L. EUBANK, wife of RICH. EUBANK; grandchildren; JNO.'s
children--living or to be born. Tract where I live and joins JNO. S.
CARTER's heirs; Horsley Creek; MADISON WARE's heirs; mill on Horsley
known as PRYOR's and CRAWFORD's Mill--2/3 interest in it. ·If JOHN's
children do not marry; if EUBANK children are without issue.
Executor: son, JNO. Administrators Bond is page 43.
Book 9, Page 54 -- Inventory -- $3943.13; JOS. R. CARTER, PETER RUCKER,
RO. H. CARTER. March 16, 1835.
Book 14, Page 229 -- Commissioners of February 17, 1857: RO. C.
BIBB; with bondsman: HARTWELL T. PRYOR and WIATT GATEWOOD.
Book 16, Page 220 -- nothing there.
Book 16, Page 274 -- Commissioners account from February, 1857. To
H. T. PRYOR--GEO. T. PLEASANTS versus R. C. BIBB, commissioner.
Book 16, Page 422 -- Commissioners November 16, 1863. HARTWELL T.
PRYOR; bondsman: RO. W. SNEAD.
Book 19, Page 385 -- February 16, 1856; August 20, 1866. Witnesses:
JNO. PRYOR, RO. H. THORNTON, M. L. BERRY. LOUISA JANE PRYOR versus
HARTWELL T. PRYOR in matter of the will. LOUISA acts for self and
children. Proved by RO. H. CARTEF and someone has put ? by his
name. Also proved by M. L. BERRY and JAS. W. PHILLIPS (not in list
above as witness). Agreement of November 21, 1863, between contestants:
WM. A. and SUSAN A. E. PRYOR, children of LOUISA J. PRYOR; HARTWELL T.
PRYOR, guardian of WM. H. BIBB's children; MADISON C. PRYOR's children;
children of WIATT GATEWOOD--all of Amherst County. Agreed to drop
suit. H. T. PRYOR agrees to take 50 acres--formerly that of NICHL.
PRYOR; it is known as the JESSE PRYOR place. LOUISA is to get
balance and both will pay costs. Witnesses: RO. H. CARTER and
JAS. W. PHILLIPS--this explains mystery of his name above. Will
then follows: son, HARTWELL T.--$1.00, for reasons best known to
myself; daughter, MELINDA, wife of WYATT GATEWOOD--$1.00; children
of daughter, JANE, deceased, who married WM. H. BIBB--$1.00; children
of MADISON C. PRYOR, deceased--$1.00. Wife, LOUISA JANE and her two
children, WM. and SUSAN, when of age.

WM. S. PRYOR -- Book 4, Page 453 -- indexed as Constables Bond, but
not there.

MARTHA M. PUGH -- Book 12, Page 226 -- Master has it for MARY PUGH
on page 229, but nothing there. Guardians Bond--STERLING CLAIBORNE
and CHISWELL DABNEY, November 19, 1849, for STERLING CLAIBORNE as
guardian of MARTHA M. PUGH, orphan of JAS. PUGH.

GEO. PURVIS -- Book 3, Page 324 -- August 11, 1794; December 15, 1794.
Witnesses: THOS. HAWKINS, JNO. STAPLES, JAS. STEVENS, JR. and WM.
JOHNSTON. Very sick and low; son, GEO.--100 acres where I live;
son, WM.--200 acres where he lives and next to Loving Lane; son,
CHAS.--100 acres where he lives; daughter, ELIZ. PURVIS; money due
me in hands of RO. RIVES. Daughter, ALIY (?) RIVES--not legible--
land where CHAS. EVANS lives.

-Q-

ANN E. QUARLES -- Book 20, Page 137 -- August 18, 1875; December 20,
1881. Witnesses: oaths of H. J. DOBBS and H. F. QUARLES. Nephew
HENRY F. QUARLES; nephew, GEO. W. QUARLES; nieces, VA. WEST, MARY
HENRY, and ELLA JANE QUARLES (all with last name of QUARLES); brother,

291

ANN E. QUARLES (cont.) -- GEO. BATHURST QUARLES; kind relative,
JUDGE S. H. HENRY, and his son, EDWD. REID HENRY. Executor: SAML. H.
HENRY.
Book 20, Page 138 -- Administrators Bond -- S. H. HENRY, on probate
date; bondsman: H. F. QUARLES. Also names niece, ANN DANGERFIELD
DOBBS.

HENRY Q. QUARLES -- Book 17, Page 513 -- April 3, 1863; August 16,
1869. Two sons, HENRY FRANCIS and GEO. WM. QUARLES--to be educated
and hopes that one will be a lawyer and puts him in care of my friend,
S. H. HENRY. Sisger?, ANNE E. QUARLES, to remain with my wife and
children. Executors: friend, PAULUS POWELL; SAML. H. HENRY; and my
wife.
Book 17, Page 498 -- Administrators Bond -- JANE QUARLES--also on
page 514.
Book 12, Page 509 -- Administrators Bond -- H. W. QUARLES and SAML. H.
HENRY, April 19, 1852, for H. W. QUARLES. This is an error in index
for it is Administrators Bond for QUARLES as administrator of SARAH J.
MARSTAIN. (MARSTON).

LUCY D. QUARLES -- Book 12, Page 502 -- HENRY W. QUARLES and SAML. H.
HENRY, April 19, 1852, for HENRY W. QUARLES.

JORDAN S. QUINN -- Book 12, Page 411 -- Receiver's Bond -- May 21,
1851. For QUINN with bondsman, RO. A. COGHILL in chancery suit of
QUINN versis BIAS.

-R-

MILES RAILEY (RILEY in some items) -- Book 1, Page 400 -- April 20,
1772; January 5, 1778. Witnesses: RICH. MC CARY, WM. MATTHEWS,
JOS. MATTHEWS, BENJ. LANHAM. Wife, SARAH, lands etc. Son, JAS.--
Cove Creek tract on north side Rockfish; son, JNO., land in same
area. My three daughters, ELIZ., MARY, and HANNAH. Wife to adminis-
trate.
Book 1, Page 402 -- Administrators Bond -- SARAH RAILEY, JNO. MARTIN,
CHAS. FITZPATRICK, probate date for SARAH RAILEY.
Book 1, Page 416 -- Inventory -- RILEY here, L120-0-9. BENJ. MOORE,
JNO. LYON, HENRY ROBERTS, May 4, 1778.

ALICE L. RAINE -- Book 13, Page 365 -- Guardians Bond -- RO. A. COGHILL
and WM. M. CABELL, July 17, 1754, for RO. A. COGHILL as guardian of
ALICE L.; CHAS. J.; and JNO. R. RAINE, orphans of G. W. A. RAINE.

FRANCIS H. RALEIGH -- Book 11, Page 313 -- Administrators Bond --
RO. TINSLEY and WM. C. CHRISTIAN, May 19, 1845, for RO. TINSLEY.

LEVIN W. RALEIGH -- Book 11, Page 515 -- Refunding Bond -- by LEVIN W.
RALEIGH and JAS. S. DALLAM to RO. TINSLEY, administrator of FRANCIS H.
RALEIGH, June 8, 1846. TINSLEY has paid LEVIN W. RALEIGH, administra-
tor--appointed by court of Livingston County, Kentucky. Recorded:
July 23, 1846.

CALEB RALLS -- Book 6, Page 423 -- May 23, 1821; December 15, 1823;
codicil of September 3, 1821; codicil of March 21, 1821--naming
executors: NELSON CRAWFORD and SAML. HANSBROUGH; no witnesses to
codicils. Witnesses to will: ANDERSON SANDIDGE, GEO. W. RAY.
Wife, POLLY--100 acres and mansion house; mare received from her
father; land to be sold; sons, GEO. and ROBERTSON and executors to
handle GEORGE's part; daughter, NANCY SEBILL; sons, CALEB, HECTOR,
JAS. Daughter, SUSANNAH CARPENTER. Codicil one gives slave to
sons, JAS. and HECTOR. Codicil proved by HUDSON M. GARLAND and WM.
DILLARD. NELSON CRAWFORD qualified; bondsman: HENRY L. DAVIES.
Book 6, Page 547 -- Inventory -- of January 22, 1825: $2693.86.
ISAAC RUCKER, ABRAM CARTER, LINDSEY SANDIDGE.
Book 6, Page 630 -- Administrators Account -- from January 3, 1824--
to GEO. RALLS, Campbell County land; ROBINSON RALL; ELIZ. RALL or

CALEB RALLS (cont.) -- BALL (?) Amherst County Sheriff and account of
M. PENDLETON estate, November 19, 1825. PETER P. THORNTON, WILL
JOPLING, JOS. R. CARTER.
Book 7, Page 330 -- Administrators Account -- from November, 1825;
to ROBERTSON RALLS, SALLY RALLS, widow of HECTOR RALLS. November 11,
1829. THORNTON and CARTER as above.
Book 10, Page 140 -- Administrators Account -- from May 27, 1830.
Campbell County tickets and Amherst County tickets; CHAS. F.
TALIAFERRO, administrator of POLLY RALLS and guardian of MAHALA
RALLS, infant; POLLY's legacy in cash; ROBINSON RALLS in own right
and guardian of GEO. RALLS--took exceptions; CRAWFORD has not accounted
for large sums; WM. CARPENTER in right of wife, SUSANNAH, late RALLS,
also took exceptions; overruled. June 18, 1839.
Book 11, Page 196 -- Administrators Account -- from June 1, 1832.
ROBERTSON RALLS bought slave--much diseased. No exceptions.
December 18, 1843.

MAHALA RALLS -- Book 6, Page 436 -- Guardian Bond -- PULLIAM SANDIDGE,
DABNEY SANDIDGE, JACK CARTER, January 19, 1824, for PULLIAM SANDIDGE
as guardian of MAHALA RALLS, orphan of CALEB RALLS.
Book 7, Page 179 -- indexed MARTHA RALLS--CHAS. P. and LYNE S.
TALIAFERRO, October 20, 1828, for CHAS. P. TALIAFERRO as guardian
of MAHALA RALLS, orphan of CALEB RALLS.

MRS. POLLY RALLS -- Book 6, Page 437 -- Administrators Bond -- PULLIAM
SANDIDGE, JACK CARTER, DABNEY SANDIDGE, January 19, 1824, for PULLIAM
SANDIDGE.
Book 6, Page 593 -- Administrators Bond -- CHAS. P. TALIAFERRO and
DABNEY SANDIDGE, April 18, 1825, for CHAS. P. TALIAFERRO.
Book 6, Page 618 -- Inventory -- slave at $320.00, August 15, 1825.
JNO. FLOOD, LINZA BURKS, WM. HAYSLEY, CHAS. P. TALIAFERRO, administra-
tor.

JNO. RAY -- Book 1, Page 49 -- August 15, 1764; November 5, 1764.
Witnesses: RICH. WHITEHALL, PHILIP DAVIS, CHAS. TYLER. Sons, JAS.
and WM.--Pedlar River tract next to JAS. SMITH--125 acres and 100
acres next to it--when JAS. is 21. Wife is with child; brother,
WM.--tract on Stoney Run and entered by my father, FERGUS RAY.
Executors: brother, WM., and JAS. BUNTING.
Book 1, Page 51 -- Administrators Bond -- WM. RAY, JAS. BROWN,
FRANCIS MOORE, probate date for WM. RAY.
Book 1, Page 53 -- Inventory -- L53-17-9, November 12, 1764. PHILIP
DAVIS, JAS. JONES, JAS. MURRY.
Book 3, Page 374 -- Minister's Bond -- February 15, 1796; Protestant
Episcopal Church. Bondsman: JNO. HORSELEY, CHAS. STATHAM.

LUKE RAY -- Book 7, Page 11 -- Administrators Bond -- DABNEY G. RAY,
BARNETT C. RAY, AMBROSE R. MC DANILE, DABNEY SANDIDGE, June 18, 1827,
for first two.
Book 7, Page 48 -- Inventory -- September 20, 1827--$3151.59. WM. H.
MC CULLOCH, CHAS. L. DAVIS, WM. ROACH, MARTIN DAWSON, DABNEY C. and
B. C. RAY.
Book 7, Page 198 -- Real estate division -- 323 acres and Mansion
house--98 acres to widow, PAMELIA RAY. 1. DILLARD's Schoolshouse
lot of 45 acres to BENNET C. (BARNETT above)--could be BARNETT here;
2. Lower Wilderness lot of 45 acres to DABNEY G. RAY. 3. RALL's
Spring lot to SAML. H. RAY--54 acres. 4. BURFORD's old road--50
acres to WM. RAY; rest of Mansion house tract to GEO. W. RAY and
30 acres on Thomas Mill Creek--part of tract known--as SLEDD's to
TAMSEY RAY, wife of PLEASANT WHITE--97 acres. 6. SLEDD tract of
101 acres to SCHUYLER G. RAY. March 17, 1823. Plat on 199. WM. H.
MC CULLOCH, MARTIN N. DAWSON, WM. ROACH. Mansion house tract on both
sides of road to WAUGH's ferry and joins heirs of MAURICE MORRIS;
heirs of JNO. RLLIS, THOS. WAUGH, WM. H. MC CULLOCH; JAS. GILLIAM--
headwaters of Wilderness Creek--323 acres and SLEDD tract adjoins,
but not contiguous--Thomas Mill Creek next to JNO. ELLIS' heirs;
ALLISON MORRIS, SAML. NICELEY, JAS. BIAS and heirs of THOS. WAUGH--
228 acres to widow and children. JNO. PRYOR, surveyor; R. NORVELL,
assistant.

MADGE M. RAY -- Book 22, Page 73 -- data as for No. 19.

MOSES RAY -- Book 1, Page 123 -- May 22, 1766; September 5, 1768.
Witnesses: AUGUSTINE SHEPHERD, SARAH SHEPHERD. Prod. by WM. CABELL,
JR. who qualified. Bondsman: WM. CABELL, SR. Son, WM. GILBERT's
creek tract and next to MAYO--345 acres. Son, MOSES--400 acres
where I live and Island; son, THOS.--400 acres in Buckingham--Rock
Island Creek; Money to educate children. When MOSES is of age; sons,
when of age; Executors: COL. WM. CABELL, JAS. NEVIL, JOS. CABELL
(CAVEL).
Book 1, Page 130 -- Inventory -- no total, May 1, 1769. WM. WALTON,
WM. HANSBROUGH, DAVID REYNOLDS.
Book 2, Page 2 -- Administrators Account -- L84 and one penny due
THOS. RAY, October 19, 1780; JAS. NEVIL and YOUNG LANDRUM.

PERMELIA RAY -- Book 8, Page 17 -- December 13, 1829; August 16,
1830. Proved by SCHYLER G. and DABNEY G. RAY. Granddaughter,
ALMYRA E. A. M. RAY; my last son, SCHUYLER G. RAY, to manage for her
until of age; Page 18 both RAYS above qualified for SCHUYLER G. RAY.
Book 8, Page 20 -- Inventory -- PAMELY here, September 17, 1830--
$31.12½. WM. H. MC CULLOCH, MARTIN N. DAWSON, CHAS. L. DAVIS.

SCHUYLER G. RAY -- Book 8, Page 18 -- Administrators Bond -- as above
for PERMELIA RAY.

FARGUS REA -- Book 1, Page 14 -- Administrators Bond -- ELIZ. RHEA,
AMBROSE JONES, GILBERT HAYS, March 7, 1763, for ELIZ. RHEA. Note:
he is called RAY in will by a son in a previous item.
Book 1, Page 18 -- Inventory -- April 22, 1763. PHILIP DAVIS, JAS.
JONES, HENRY FRANKLIN. L79-9-10. RAY here.
Book 1, Page 55 -- Inventory -- could not be had when rest appraised--
same men, and very small inventory. November 6, 1764.

ADOLPHUS D. READ (REID) -- Book 6, Page 686 -- Guardians Bond --
WM. WARWICK and CHISWELL DABNEY, April 21, 1826, for WM. WARWICK as
guardian of ADOLPHUS D. READ, orphan of NATHL. READ.

JANE READ (Nee POWELL) -- Book 18, Page 87 -- October 29, 1845;
January 17, 1871. Witnesses: WIATT POWELL, J. POWELL, JR., JAS.
POWELL. JAS. swore to signature of WIATT POWELL, deceased. My
three children: NANCY P., EDMD. and WILLIE READ--until youngest is
21; my brother, PAULUS POWELL; my sisters, MILLY GARLAND and ELIZ.
POWELL; my deceased mother, MILDRED POWELL--my father, JAS. POWELL.
He is not liable for my part of my mother's estate. Executors:
SAML. M. GARLAND and PAULUS POWELL.

WM. P. READ -- Book 11, Page 129 -- Estate Commitment to Sheriff --
June, 1842; motion of R. L. COLEMAN; Sheriff: NELSON CRAWFORD.

JNO. REDCROSS -- Book 4, Page 13 -- Inventory -- July 20, 1801--$6.95.
HENRY WOOD, ANDREW MORGAN, H. M. ENGLAND.
Book 4, Page 327 -- Administrators Bond -- DAVID S. GARLAND and
DANL. MC DANIEL, Feburary 16, 1800, for DAVID S. GARLAND.

JANE REDMAN -- Book 5, Page 229 -- Administrators Bond -- BARKSDALE
SLEDD, JABEZ CAMDEN, WM. STINNETT, June 21, 1813, for BARKSDALE
SLEDD.
Book 5, Page 408 -- Administrators Bond -- SLEDD and WM. I. ISBELL,
January 18, 1814, for BARKSDALE SLEDD.
Book 5, Page 664 -- Inventory -- $15.00; TINSLEY RUCKER, CHAS.
COPPEDGE, BLANSFORD HICKS, August 18, 1817.

ALEX. REID (indexed REED, but plainly REID) -- Book 4, Page 152 --
March 21, 1804; July 16, 1804. Witnesses: NATHAN CRAWFORD, HANNAH
OWINGS, RO. SHIELDS. SAML. REID qualified; bondsman: JESSE JOPLING,
RO. SHIELDS, NELSON ANDERSON, HUDSON M. GARLAND. On November 19,
1804, HUDSON MARTIN and JAS. WOODS qualified; bondsman: NATHAN
CRAWFORD, JAS. MONTGOMERY. Son, SAML.--136 acres patent and next
to MOSES HUGHES AND 250 acres in Lincoln County, Kentucky. Son-in-law,

ALEX. REID (cont.) -- JAS. REID; heirs of my son, JNO. FINLEY, deceased--one half of 1200 in Kentucky and part of survey of 3556½ acres by patent. Son-in-law, JAS. DAVIS; daughter, MARY SHANNON-- 300 acres in Kentucky and part of 4620 acres surveyed and allotted to me. Amherst County land to be sold. Grandsons--ALEX.; JNO. and JAS. REID, sons of my son, JNO. NATHAN REID, deceased, and their sisters, SUSANNA; JANE and ANN REID in Kentucky land for them-- part of 4620 acres; if they die before age or marriage--same for brothers just named. Two grandsons--sons of son-in-law, JAS. REID-- ALEX. and JNO. REID--Kentucky land. Executors: son, SAML. and friends, JAS. WOODS and HUDSON MARTIN.
Book 4, Page 207 -- Administrators Account -- SAML. REID from May 21, 1804; cash in hands of CAPT. JOS. MONTGOMERY. December 16, 1805: HUDSON MARTIN, JR.; HAWES COLEMAN; JAMES HUGHS.
Book 4, Page 266 -- Guardians Account -- October 21, 1806; WM. WOODS as guardian of ALEX. REID; items bought by WM. WHITE--cloth, nuttons, etc.
Book 4, Page 384 -- Administrators Bond -- SAML. REID, JESSE JOPLING, RO. SHIELDS, NELSON ANDERSON, HUDSON M. GARLAND, July 16, 1804, for SAML. REID.
Book 4, Page 393 -- Guardians Bond -- WM. WOODS (B.C. sic), JAS. BROOKS, JAS. MONTGOMERY, October 15, 1804, for WM. WOODS as guardian of ALEX. REID, orphan of JONATHAN REID, deceased.
Book 4, Page 394 -- Administrators Bond -- JAS. WOODS, HUDSON MARTIN, JAS. MONTGOMERY, NATHAN CRAWFORD, November 19, 1804, for first two.

ANDREW REID (indexed REED) -- Book 1, Page 67 -- September 20, 1765; October 7, 1765. Witnesses: JAS. and JNO. REID, JNO. BARNETT. Of Rockfish; my six children: MARTHA, AGNES, FLORENCE, SARAH, ANDREW and ESHER (sic)--until ANDREW is 21. If any daughter married or dead before 18. Executors: friends, THOS. STUART and RO. WEIR. Page 69 is Administrators Bond and both qualified; bondsman: WM. SIMPSON, SAML. WOODS, ALEX. REID, JR., THOS. WEST.
Book 1, Page 80 -- Inventory -- December 5, 1765; recorded August 4, 1766; ROBT. BARNETT, JNO. MORRISON, JNO. MONTGOMERY.

JNO. N. (JONATHAN) REID -- Book 3, Page 556 -- May 28, 1799; October 21, 1799. Witnesses: JOS. MONTGOMERY, JOS. WEAVER, ISHAM READY, JOS. STRICKLAN--Gent of Amherst County; 48 acres near Rockfish Gap; 19 acres next to WM. MOORE and JAS. WOODS; Kentucky land; my wife and children and what my father will give them; I gave wife a child's part during life--real and personal; when youngest child is of age or married; son, ALEX.; surveying instruments; land in partnership with JOS. STRICKLAN (LIN); Executors: brother, SAML. REID, and MICHL. WOODS.
Book 4, Page 204 -- Administrators Account -- of JONATHAN REID's estate by SAML. REID from October, 1799; cash to JOS. STRICKLAND. October 2, 1805. HUDSON MARTIN, JAS. HUGHES, HAWES COLEMAN.
Book 4, Page 286 -- Administrators Bond -- SAML. RIED, JOS. ROBERTS, ALEX. MC ALEXANDER, October 21, 1799, for SAML. RIED and MICHL. WOODS--WOODS is not named at first of bond.

JNO. W. REID (indexed READ) -- Book 4, Page 475 -- Guardians Bond -- MICHL. WOODS, ALEX. MC ALEXANDER, JAS. HUGHES, October 19, 1807, for MICHL. WOODS as guardian of JNO. W. REID, orphan of JONATHAN N. REID.

ABSALOM REYNOLDS -- Book 2, Page 156 -- Administrators Bond -- THOS. POWELL (TAYLOR--sic) and THOS. HAWKINS, March 1, 1784, for THOS. POWELL.
Book 2, Page 173 -- Inventory -- May 3, 1784, L22-19-0. WM. BIBB, G. GLASBY, and LUCAS POWELL.

CHAS. REYNOLDS -- Book 6, Page 274 -- Administrators Bond -- ARCHELAUS REYNOLDS, JAS. LEE, ELIAS WILLS, January 21, 1822, for ARCHELAUS REYNOLDS. (Note: ARCHELAUS REYNOLDS is another ancestor of my daughter-in-law, MARY GAYLE PETTYJOHN, who married my son, THURMAN BLANTON DAVIS. ARCHELAUS married ELIZ. RUCKER).
Book 6, Page 275 -- June 11, 1821; January 21, 1822. Witnesses: WM. W. CLEMENTS, JAS. LEE. Codicil: "This being a true copy of the

CHAS. REYNOLDS (cont.) -- original will made in July, 1813, with the
exceptions of some items altered by the direction of the testator."
Wife, ANNE--where I live; sons, JNO.; OBADIAH--Bedford land on Otto
(sic--probably Otter) river where he lives; two sons of OBADIAH:
JAS. and WM. REYNOLDS; my son, ARCHELAUS--where I live--lines on
south of JAS. LEE; my half of mill; grandson, ISAAC REYNOLDS; grand-
daughter, PERMELIA TINSLEY (late REYNOLDS); grandson, WILLIS M.
REYNOLDS. Executors: JNO., OBADIAH, and ARCHELAUS REYNOLDS. Codicil:
ARCHELAUS is to be trustee for JAS. and WM. REYNOLDS, sons of OBADIAH
REYNOLDS, until they are 21. Proved by the witnesses.
Book 6, Page 284 -- Inventory -- March 18, 1822; several slaves--
$4458.00. WM. W. SCOTT, WM. PENDLETON, THOS. CLEMENTS.

WILLIS M. REYNOLDS -- Book 5, Page 472 -- Guardians Bond -- ARCHELAUS
REYNOLDS, PLEASANT DAWSON, HUGH NORVEL, November 21, 1814, for
ARCHELAUS REYNOLDS as guardian of WILLIS M., ISAAC R., CHAS. B.,
OBADIAH F. and NANCY T. (?) REYNOLDS, children of ARCHELAUS REYNOLDS.
Note: The T. is correct and used when NANCY T. married GEO. WASHINGTON
PETTYJOHN in 1825.

ARCHIBALD RHEA -- Book 4, Page 161 -- September 25, 1803; October 15,
1804. Witnesses: JAS. CAMPBELL, THOS. FULTON, JANE FULTON. JEAN
and ARCHIBALD RHEA qualified; bondsman: JAS. CAMPBELL. Wife, JEAN;
daughter, MARY; five sons: ARCHIBALD, WM., JNO., ROBT., and ANDREW;
my four daughters: ANN, JEAN, MARTHA, and REBECCA. Daughter,
ISABELLA's children--Executors: son, ARCHIBALD and my brother,
ANDREW MC CAUSLIN (MC CASLIN?)--sic--and guardians of minor children.
Book 4, Page 173 -- Inventory -- no total: June 17, 1805. WM.
FORBES: JAS. DURHAM, EDMD. COFFEY, JNO. CAMPBELL. Administrators
Bond is page 390.

REUBEN RHODES -- Book 11, Page 229 -- April 6, 1844; August 19, 1844.
Witnesses: FRED J. TINSLEY, JAS. F. EUBANK, THOS. LAIN. October 21,
1844, JNO. RHOADS (sic) qualified; bondsman: EDWD. RHOADS, WM.
BECK, JOS. RHOADS, PASKILL RHOADS, and RUBIN RHODES. Wife, TABITHA--
where I live--164 acres; all of my children; son, REUBEN, JR.;
daughter, EVELINA DEMPSEY; children of my daughter, ISABELLA RUTLEDGE;
daughter, ANN ROADS--note variations in spelling--; sons, JNO.,
EDWD., JOS., and PASCAL--land has been deeded to them. Executors:
sons, JNO. and EDWD. and friend, CAPT. THOS. A EUBANK. Administrators
Bond is page 249.
Book 11, Page 426 -- Inventory -- November 15, 1844. $2868.75.
JNO. PRYOR, THOS. A. EUBANK, HENRY FRANKLIN.
Book 11, Page 455 -- Administrators Account from 1844; PASCAL RHODES'
part. December 21, 1846. JNO. PRYOR, RO. H. CARTER, PETER RUCKER.

SARAH C. RHODES -- Book 11, Page 481 -- Guardians Bond -- JNO. C.
HARRISON and JNO. N. LINTHICUM, February 15, 1847, for JNO. C.
HARRISON as guardian of SARAH C. and WM. RHODES, infants of JNO. and
LUCRETIA RHODES.

SUSAN RHODES -- Book 11, Page 481 -- Same men and date for JNO. C.
HARRISON as guardian of SUSAN and ELIZ. RHOADES, infants of same
parents.

TABITHA RHODES -- Book 14, Page 49 -- Administrators Bond -- REUBEN
ROADS and EDWD. ROADS, November 19, 1855, for REUBEN ROADS.
Book 14, Page 61 -- Inventory -- November 1855; sale--REUBEN and
EDWD. were buyers; also PASCAL RHODES. JNO. PRYOR, auctioneer--
$278.34½. Recorded: January 21, 1856. Inventory of $389.66½.
JNO. PRYOR, JAS. M. MILLNER, THOS. N. EUBANK.
Book 14, Page 353 -- Administrators Account -- from November, 1855.
To JNO., R. and LEROY RHODES. Recorded: April 20, 1857.

WM. RICE -- Book 4, Page 315 -- Guardians Bond -- JAS. BROOKS and
MARTIN DAWSON, November 20, 1798, for JAS. BROOKS as guardian of
WM. RICE, orphan of WM. RICE.

JESSE RICHESON -- Book 11, Page 159 -- Administrators Bond -- WM. A.
RICHESON and JAS. RICHESON, August 21, 1843, for WM. A. RICHESON.
Book 13, Page 465 -- May 2, 1855; Monday, May 21, 1855. Witnesses:
JAS. A. HIGGINBOTHAM, POWHATAN LAYNE, THOS. D. WATTS, THOS. H.
RUCKER, ARTHUR WHITE. JAS. RICHESON and CHAS. H. RUCKER qualified;
bondsman: PETTICUS and SAMUEL RICHESON, R. A. COGHILL. Son,
WM. A.--Rockey Row tract; son, JNO.--where he lives; daughters:
AMELIA GRAVES and MARY T. JONES; heirs of deceased daughter,
REBECCA J. TUCKER--same for NANCY R. COGHILL and VARELLA SOMERVILLE.
Someone has erased in part data after SOMERVILLE, but still legible.
Son, VARLAND, deceased, and any heirs; my six remaining children:
JAS., THOS. PETTICUS, SAML., JOSEPHINE MILLNER, LUCY RUCKER. Executors:
JAS. RICHESON and CHAS. H. RUCKER. Administrators Bond is page 468.
Book 14, Page 16 -- Inventory -- June 15, 1855; bond of JAS. RICHESON.
Total: $28,379.03.
Book 14, Page 67 -- Sale, September 4, 1855. TYLER trace, WRIGHT or
TOMLINSON tract, Brown Mt. tract, HOWARD or NEW's tract. SANDIDGE
or LONG Mt. tract, COOPER or TLIAFERRO tract, IRISH or P. MARTIN
tract, HIX or JUDITH MARTIN tract. CURRY, WARE and Mansion House
tracts. Buyers: JAS. L., P. L. RICHESON. Sale took two days.
SAM RICHESON was buyer, too. $1670.80--P. L. RICHESON, Clerk of Sale.
Began at 10:00. Recorded: December 17, 1855.
Book 14, Page 71 -- Sale -- December 19, 1855. DR. P. L. RICHESON,
JAS. L. RICHESON, SAML. RICHESON--buyers. $24,779.32. Recorded:
April 21, 1856.
Book 14, Page 167 -- Refunding Bond -- by JAS. M. MILLNER--bondsman:
SAML. and P. L. RICHESON--MILLNER gives bond to JAS. L. RICHESON and
CHAS. H. RUCKER, administrators--he has received legacy for wife,
JOSEPHINE, from her father's estate. Page 168 same type of bond to
same men by THOS. RICHESON--bondsman: PETTICUS and SAML. RICHESON--
and by attorney-in-fact, P. L. RICHESON. THOS. has received legacy.
Same date.
Book 14, Page 170 -- SAML. RICHESON makes same type of bond to same
administrators--SAML. has received share from father's estate.
Book 14, Page 169 -- PETTICUS L. RICHESON makes same type of bond
for his legacy. Page 170 CHAS. H. RUCKER makes same type of bond
for wife, LUCY. Bondsman: PETER RUCKER, P. L. and SAML. RICHESON.
Book 14, Page 232 -- Administrators Account -- by both administrators--
accounts of P. L. and JAS. L. RICHESON; SAML. RICHESON for support of
slaves. Legatees: JAS. L., THOS., PETTICUS L., SAML. RICHESON,
JOSEPHINE MILLNER, LUCY RUCKER. Recorded: Monday, December 15, 1856.

JNO. RICHESON -- Book 5, Page 192 -- Administrators Bond -- JESSE and
JNO. RICHESON, December 21, 1812, for JNO. RICHESON.
Book 3, Page 572 -- Inventory -- L1956-15-4. June 20, 1799, THOS.
MORRIS, JOSIAH ELLIS, NELSON CRAWFORD.
Book 4, Page 297 -- Administrators Bond -- MARY RICHESON, JNO. CRAWFORD,
JNO. EUBANK, EDWD. SANDERSON, June 17, 1798, for MARY RICHESON.
Book 4, Page 324 -- Guardians Bond -- MARY RICHESON, JESSE RICHESON,
ARMSTEAD RUCKER, NELSON CRAWFORD, September 15, 1800, for MARY
RICHESON as guardian of JNO., BETSY, PATSY, and THOS. RICHESON,
orphans of JNO. RICHESON, deceased.
Book B, Page 43 -- Estate Committment to Sheriff -- April 1, 1851.
JNO. D. DAVIS, Sheriff.
Book 9, Page 220 -- Estate Commitment to Sheriff -- March 21, 1836;
motion of MAURICE H. GARLAND, administrator de bonis non of CHRISTOPHER
ISBALL; THOS. N. EUBANK, Sheriff.

MARY RICHESON -- Book 5, Page 174 -- Administrators Bond -- JESSE and
JNO. RICHESON, WM. SHELTON, JAS. WARE, ARMSTEAD RUCKER, July 20, 1812,
for J. R.
Book 5, Page 221 -- Inventory -- L1294-3-0, June 21, 1813, WM.
JOPLING, EDMD. GOODRICH, MARTIN PARKS.

DR. PETTICUS L. RICHESON -- Book 11, Page 319 -- Constables Bond --
June 16, 1845. Bondsman: JNO. and W. A. RICHESON.
Book 16, Page 158 -- Minister's Bond -- March 17, 1862. Bondsman:
JAS. M. MILLNER; no denomination.
Book 18, Page 44 -- Inventory -- December 27, 1870--$3568.80. CHAS. H.
RUCKER, JAS. M. MILLNER, WM. L. MILLNER. Debt of JAS. S(L) RICHESON.

DR. PETTICUS L. RICHESON (cont.) -- Book 18, Page 434 -- December 16,
1861; October 17, 1870. Handwriting by WM. A. RICHESON. VA. E.
RICHESON qualified. Bondsmen: C. H. RUCKER, W. A. RICHESON, JAS. M.
MILLNER. Appraisers: bondsman named and H. E. SMITH. To wife,
VA. E., and any issue.
Book 19, Page 476 -- Administrators de bonis non Bond -- August 18,
1879--J. M. MATTHEWS, JNO. M. WRIGHT; J. McH. PETERS for J. M.
MATTHEWS.
Book 19, Page 493 -- Inventory -- $4841.22. Liberty, Virginia.
August 26, 1879. CHAS. H. RUCKER, J. E. NILMS, JNO. R. STEPTOE.

THOS. RICHESON -- Book 5, Page 173 -- Guardians Bond -- THOS. N.
EUBANK and HILL CARTER, July 20, 1812, for THOS. N. EUBANK as guardian
of THOS. RICHESON, orphan of JNO. RICHESON.

JANE RICKETTS -- Book 4, Page 421 -- Administrators Bond -- WM.
TURNER and PLEASANT STORY, December 16, 1805, for WM. TURNER.

THOS. RICKETTS -- Book 4, Page 374 -- Administrators Bond -- MATT.
RICKETTS, WM. EVANS, MADISON HILL, October 18, 1803, for MATT.
RICKETTS.
Book 4, Page 417 -- Administrators Bond -- counter-security, October 21,
1805; JESSE BECK, bondsman for WM. TURNER. This is indexed for THOS.,
but note that TURNER was administrator for JANE RICKETTS.

ROBT. RIDGWAY -- Book 16, Page 77 -- December 20, 1848; August 19,
1861. Witnesses: THOS. LEE and WM. M. BOWLING. BOWLING dead and
handwriting by JNO. L. MC DANIEL. Proved by LEE, September 16, 1861.
Wife, MARY; if single children marry before her death. Son, WM.--
$15.00, but had received large sums. Daughters: ELIZ. C., RHOAD A.,
HARRIET and SALLY J. RIDGWAY. Son, ROBT.; granddaughter, MARIA L.
HYLTON. If they are without heirs. Executors: friends, WYATT
PETTYJOHN and SETH WOODROOF.
Book 17, Page 318 -- Provisions of will set forth: SALLY J. and
MARIA L. are dead--no issue; three daughters and mother are left;
division to widow by JESSE E. ADAMS; SYLVESTER L. BURFORD; RO. C.
MARTIN--in "hatch pot" and amount credited to RO. RIDGWAY. Signed
by legatees--three daughters and RO. on April 28, 1868. Land and
50 acres on northeast side State road and some on south side of State
road. Lines: NELSON GREGORY; 40 acres to RO. RIDGWAY and lines of
WM. PETTYJOHN, WM. C. ALLEN, and WINSTON. South side joins S. L.
BURFORD, NELSON GREGORY and to RHODA A. and HARRIET (next to MRS.
TYREE); land on northeast to ELIZ.
Book 18, Page 53 -- Administrators Bond -- JESSE E. ADAMS, TAYLOR
BERRY, CHAS. MUNDY, November 21, 1870, for JESSE E. ADAMS, but this
is to administrate estate of RO., JR. Appraisers: page 51--S. L.
BURFORD, R. B. WORTHAM, CALVIN F. BENNETT.
Book 18, Page 52 -- Inventory for SR. -- $415.50--November 20, 1870.
Book 18, Page 63 -- Administrators de bonis non Bond -- January 16,
1871, for JESSE E. ADAMS; bondsman: as on page 53--no SR. or JR.
used, January 16, 1871.
Book 18, Page 87 -- so indexed, but not in 18 or 19.

ROBT. RIVERS (RIVES?) -- Book 8, Page 297 -- Administrators Bond --
JAS. POWELL and S. M. GARLAND, January 21, 1833, for JAS. POWELL.
Book 10, Page 383 -- Estate Commitment to Sheriff -- June court,
1840--along with estates of LUCY A. SPENCER and FRANCIS SLAUGHTER;
motion of SPOTSWOOD G. LOVING; will of CHAS. SPENCER; Sheriff: EDMD.
PENN.

AMY ROACH -- Book 5, Page 563 -- Guardians Bond -- WM. ROACH and JAS.
WARE, February 19, 1816, for WM. ROACH as guardian of AMY ROACH,
orphan of -- ROACH. Someone has tampered with this record and put
in pencil notation: "JNO. ROACH."

ASHCRAFT ROACH -- Book 5, Page 479 -- Administrators Bond -- HENRY and
WM. ROACH, JAS. DAVIES, T. N. EUBANK, January 16, 1815, for HENRY and
WM. ROACH.

ASHCRAFT ROACH (cont.) -- Book 5, Page 628 -- Inventory -- January 20, 1815; no total; JARRETT GILLIAM, JNO. GILLIAM, JAS. WAUGH. Recorded: , January 20, 1817.
Book 5, Page 631 -- Division -- $4010.40 and to nine legatees. To RICH. BURKS, son of DAVIS(D?)--land next to RODERICK MC CULLOCH and JNO. GILLIAM--also Bedford tract on Reed Creek; to CORNL. ROACH--mansion house above RICH. and N. Manson; to GEO. ROACH--60 acres at DAVIES' old mill and James River island; to BENJ. KELLY--75 acres Medow lot; to HENRY ROACH--97 3/4 acres next to mansion house and N. Manson; heirs of JNO. ROACH--60½ acres known as Mill Field; to CHAS. ROACH--108½ acres known as TOOLEY's Field; to DANL. PEYTON--100 acres--LOUISE's place and PEYTON owes estate; to WM. ROACH--145 acres where he lives and laid off for him in father's lifetime. January 20, 1817. AMBR. RUCKER, JAS. LEE, RICH. BURKS, CHAS. WINGFIELD.
Book 5, Page 665 -- Administrators Account -- by both administrators from 1815--GEO. ROACH for tobacco; names of WM., CHAS., HENRY, CORNL. and DAVID J. ROACH. November 18, 1817. THOS. N. EUBANK, JNO. ELLIS, NATHAN D. BURKS.

GEO. ROACH -- Book 6, Page 676 -- Administrators Bond -- SARAH ROACH, THOS. N. EUBANK, WM. ROACH, August 21, 1826, for SARAH ROACH.
Book 8, Page 2-9 -- Division and plat by THOS. N. EUBANK, JOSIAH ELLIS, and WM. H. MC CULLOCH, January 19, 1833. Mansion house tract of 186 acres--46 acres and island of 23 acres to MRS. SALLY ROACH, her dower lot; to SUSAN SHOEMAKER, wife of NICHL. SHOEMAKER; to SARAH GILLIAM, infant of MARY GILLIAM, deceased--slaves; island in James River; mansion house tract; both sides Wilderness Creek and next to ARTHUR L. DAVIES, THOS. N. EUBANK, JNO. MITCHELL, HENRY L. ROACH, WM. ROACH, RICH. BURKS, JNO. PRYOR, surveyor. Recorded: February 18, 1833.

HENRY ROACH -- Book 8, Page 320 -- October 23, 1832; June 17, 1833. Witnesses: JAS. and JNO. D. DAVIS, JAS. GILLIAM. WM. C. MORRIS renounced administrator and JAS. DAVIS qualified. Bondsman: WM. C. MORRIS. My two grandchildren, MARY and ELIZ. WALKER, infants of my deceased daughter, SALLY WALKER; son, CHAS. LEWIS ROACH; son, HENRY LANDON ROACH--130 acres deed of gift; daughter, POLLY ROACH; grand-children: CHAS. and ELIZ. MITCHELL, infants of daughter, NANCY MITCHELL, deceased, who got 72 acres in her lifetime; grandson, JNO. HENRY HANCOCK, son of ELIZ., who married WM. HANCOCK--when he is 21 or with heirs; daughter, AMANDA D. MORRIS (or MORRISS)--one-half of where I live--if no issue; daughter, ELVIRA JANE ROACH--one-half of where I live and house. Executor: WM. C. MORRISS and trustee for infants.
Book 9, Page 6 -- Plat and Division -- both sides Wilderness Creek and one mile from Fluvanna River and four miles from WAUGH's ferry; joins THOS. N. EUBANK, JARRETT GILLIAM's heirs; JNO. MITCHELL; HENRY L. ROACH--325 acres. Devised by HENRY ROACH to daughters, AMANDA D. MORRISS and ELVIRA JANE ROACH. Surveyed for them, November 26, 1833, by JNO. PRYOR. ELVIRA got house and 167½ acres and AMANDA got 157½ acres. November 19, 1834. MARTIN PARKS, NELSON C. DAWSON, BEVERLY DAVIES.
Book 9, Page 64 -- Inventory -- September 14, 1833 -- $315.97. THOS. N. EUBANK, WM. M. GILLIAM, JAS. GILLIAM. The name of HENRY L. ROACH is used as an adjoining ovner. HENRY L. ROACH is indexed with Administrators Account in Book 6, Page 764, but I have checked a number of books in vain for this data.

JNO. ROACH -- Book 5, Page 527 -- Administrators Bond -- AMY ROACH and THOS. N. EUBANK, November 20, 1815, for AMY ROACH.
Book 5, Page 633 -- Division order -- November, 1815. THOS. MORRIS, JAS. WARE, MARTIN PARKS. Recorded: January 20, 1817. To heirs of HENRY ROACH--60½ acres assigned to JNO. ROACH's heirs in division of ASHCRAFT ROACH's estate; WM. ROACH, guardian for three of orphans.

MRS. SALLY ROACH -- Book 11, Page 96 -- Administrators Bond -- NICHL. SHOEMAKER, CHAS. L. DAVIES, W. ANTHONY RICHESON, January 16, 1843, for NICHL. SHOEMAKER.

MRS. SALLY ROACH (cont.) -- Book 11, Page 262 -- Inventory -- order
of 1843; no total; THOS. N. EUBANK, HAZAEL WILLIAMS, JNO. D. DAVIS,
JAS. GILLIAM. January 20, 1843.
Book 11, Page 284 -- Sale -- January 27, 1843: $303.70.
Book 11, Page 308 -- Dower of slaves of MRS. SALLY ROACH from estate
of husband, GEO. ROACH. Order of December 29, 1844; lots to NICHL.
SHOEMAKER and THOS. WRIGHT; SHOEMAKER agrees to take mansion house
and 46 acres and WRIGHT agrees to take ROACH island--23 acres.
February 17, 1845. JAS. DAVIS, THOS. N. EUBANK, HAZAEL WILLIAMS.

CORNELIA T. ROANE -- Book 8, Page 244 -- Guardians Bond -- EDWD. A.
CABELL, WM. R. ROANE, WM. TURNER, August 20, 1832, for EDWD. A.
CABELL as guardian of CORNELIA T. ROANE, daughter of WM. R. ROANE.

ELIZ. ROANE -- Book 8, Page 336 -- Administrators Bond -- THOS. A.
HOLCOMBE, August 19, 1833; no bondsman.
Book 8, Page 439 -- Administrators Account -- from January 20, 1834;
received of KENNON SMITH, administrator of BURWELL SMITH, a bank
dividend for four years and bank stock from JNO. MARX and Son.
October 20, 1834. JNO. THOMPSON, JR., M. H. GARLAND.

ELIZ. R. ROANE -- Book 10, Page 155 -- Guardians Bond -- WM. P. SISSON
and WINSTON WOODROOF, September 16, 1839, for WM. P. SISSON as guardian
of ELIZ. R. ROANE, daughter of CHRISTOPHER ROANE.

JAS. B. (M) ROANE -- Book 8, Page 353 -- Guardians Bond -- THOS. A.
HOLCOMBE and JNO. WARWICK, September 16, 1833, for THOS. A. HOLCOMBE
as guardian of JAS. and RO. ROANE, orphans of WM. R. ROANE.
Book 8, Page 442 -- Guardians Account -- from August 26, 1833; bank
stock surrendered to your guardian, WM. CLAIBORNE, August 10, 1834.
CHAMP CARTER, WM. S. CLAIBORNE.
Book 8, Page 432 -- Guardians Bond -- WM. S. CLAIBORNE, CHAS. B.
CLAIBORNE, JOS. K. IRVING, October 20, 1834, for WM. S. CLAIBORNE
as guardian of JAS. M. ROANE, WM. R., VA. and SARAH ROANE, orphans
of WM. R. ROANE, deceased.
Book 10, Page 288 -- Administrators Bond -- WM. S. CLAIBORNE and
JOS. K. IRVING, November 16, 1840, for WM. S. CLAIBORNE. This is
indexed for JASON ROSE.

ROBT. ROANE -- Book 8, Page 440 -- Guardians Account -- THOS. A.
HOLCOMBE from October, 1833. To JAS. ROANE for shoes; WM. S.
CLAIBORNE, guardian. October 20, 1834.
Book 11, Page 46 -- Guardians Account by CLAIBORNE from 1834. Tuition
and board in Caroline County; COL. ROANE's estate in Carles City;
JORDAN estate in Brunswick; grandmother's estate; also name of
JAS. M. ROANE, JR. and his account. Approved by WM. B. ROANE and
VA. E. and S. D. BOWEN. April 29, 1841. Ward died before age of
21 (JAS. M. ROANE). Recorded: April 18, 1842. D. S. EMMET and
RO. L. COLEMAN.

SARAH ROANE (E initial) -- Book 8, Page 438 -- Guardians Account --
C. L. MOSBY and also on same page is his account as guardian of
VA. ROANE. From October 26, 1833. Hack to Lynchburg for both wards--
$1.75; servant--75¢; MRS. J. A. ROYALL for board for you and servant
for half year--$75.00; DR. W. S. CLAIBORNE made guardian at my request;
dividends from KENNON SMITH, executor of BURWELL SMITH. October 20,
1834. JNO. W. YOUNG and WM. S. CLAIBORNE.
Book 11, Page 36 -- Guardians Account -- by CLAIBORNE from 1834;
MOSBY, former guardian; trip to Brunswick; Chas. City; Brunswick
for JORDAN estate; Chas. City bill of Chas. HILL answered. Money
from your grandmother's estate. February 24, 1842. D. S. EMMET;
RO. L. COLEMAN.
Book 12, Page 180 -- Guardians Account -- by CLAIBORNE; from 1842;
board and tuition to MRS. CABELL. Interest in your father's estate
from C. L. (S) MOSBY. May 30, 1849. FRANCIS W. V. SUTTON, SR.

VA. E. ROANE -- Book 8, Page 357 -- Guardians Bond -- October 21, 1833.
CHAS. L. MOSBY, WM. M. BURWELL--by THOS. A. HOLCOMBE, for CHAS. L.
MOSBY as guardian of VA. and SARAH ROANE, orphans of WM. R. ROANCE,
deceased.

VA. E. ROANE (cont.) -- Book 8, Page 438 -- Guardians Account --
from October 26, 1833 -- for VA. and SARAH. Page 439 is Guardians
Account for ELIZ. ROANE by HOLCOMBE; page 440 Guardians Account for
RO. or WM. RO. ROANE by HOLCOMBE; page 442 Guardians Account for
JAS. B. ROANE by HOLCOMBE; January 26, 1834.
Book 11, Page 40 -- Guardians Account -- by CLAIBORNE from 1834
for VA. and SARAH; VA. E. became wife of STEPHEN D. BOWEN--account
to 1840; property to BOWEN. February 23, 1842. L. S. EMMET and
RO. L. COLEMAN.

WM. B. ROANE -- Book 11, Page 322 -- Guardians Account -- by
CLAIBORNE from 1842. H. W. HEATH for tuition and board--also books--
$62.64; board to L. N. LIGON--$50.00; trip to Natural Bridge by
guardian--$9.00; your part of J. M. ROANE estate--$228.00; cash whilst
at University--$30 and $60. Ward of age; interest in estate of his
brother, JAS. ROANE, deceased. L. T. CASH and ALBERT BIBB.

WM. R. ROANE -- Book 8, Page 338 -- Administrators Bond -- THOS. A.
HOLCOMBE and JNO. WARWICK, August 19, 1833, for THOS. A. HOLCOMBE.
Book 8, Page 358 -- Inventory -- September 24, 1833--$5978.79.
PROSSER POWELL, JAS. L. LAMKIN, LEWIS L. BOWLING.
Book 9, Page 106 -- Sale -- September 26, 1833. Buyers: CHAS.
ROANE--$1386.72. Children took articles by permission of administrator:
JAS. M., WM. B., CORNELIA, R. T. VA. EPPES ROANE, LUCY CATH. ROANE,
MARY C. NORVELL, FAYETTE H. NORVELL. Page 112 slave sold--one given
to WM. S. CLAIBORNE, guardian of SALLY and WM. R. ROANE. CLAIBORNE as
husband of CORNELIA and guardian of VA. ROANE. Slaves given to children
by father and payments of legacies from grandparents and received by
WM. R ROANE for their lifetimes--or in his lifetime. August 17, 1835.
Book 9, Page 207 -- Administrators Account -- from August 26, 1833.
JNO. MAHONE--coffin for ELIZ.--$10.00; Guiguid for burial--$20.00;
Campbell County tickets; C. ROANE; J. BENAGH; WM. W. NORVELL, August 8,
1835. Page 211 account continued from December 18, 1834. Sale of
home tract to BENJ. B. TALIAFERRO. Recorded: December 21, 1835.
Book 11, Page 222 -- Estate Commitment to Sheriff -- on motion of
F. H. NORVELL, JAMES POWELL, Sheriff, February, 1844.
Book 11, Page 316 -- Administrators Bond -- WM. B. ROANE and WM. S.
CLAIBORNE, June 16, 1845, for WM. B. ROANE.

BENJ. ROBBINS -- Book 11, Page 57 -- Administrators Bond -- JAS. P.
COLEMAN and JOS. K. IRVING, June 21, 1842, for JAS. P. COLEMAN.

ELLIOTT ROBERTS -- Book 3, Page 89 -- April 8, 1788; September 1, 1788;
codicil of May 19, 1788. Witnesses to will: RICH. FARRAR, THOS.
FARRAR, JNO. COLE, CORNL. MURRILL; to codicil: RICH. FARRAR, THOS.
BICKNELL, THOS. FARRAR, CORNL. MURRILL, LEONARD PHILLIPS. Son,
ZACH.--Rockfish land next to MATT. HARRIS and JNO. MORRISON, deceased;
son, JNO.--Buck creek land bought of JOS. MONTGOMERY; son, MATT.;
son, HENRY--when of age; daughters: ELIZ. THOMAS, FRANCES ROBERTS,
SUSANNA and ANN ROBERTS; daughter, SARAH THOMAS--negroes in hands of
JNO. THOMAS. When youngest is of age and then names: ZACH., JNO.,
HENRY, MATT., ELIZ., FRANCES, SUSANNA and ANN. Executors: my wife,
ELIZ., and sons, ZACH., JNO. ROBERTS and my brother, HENRY ROBERTS.
Codicil revokes coming of age item and administrators may divide.
Book 3, Page 91 -- Administrators Bond -- HENRY, ZACH., JNO. ROBERTS,
October 6, 1788. Bondsman: WM. HARRIS and CHAS. IRVING.
Book 3, Page 101 -- Inventory -- L1398-10-0, February 28, 1789.
RICH. FARRAR, PETER LYON, BENJ. MOORE.

FREDERICK ROBERTS -- Book 16, Page 440 -- January 21, 1864; March 21,
1864. Witnesses: GARLAND POINDEXTER, JAS. W. HENSHAW, AMBROSE
SHEPHERD. R. A. WRIGHT declined to administrate. CAROLINE M.
ROBERTS qualified. Bondsmen: E. J. HILL and S. L. BURFORD. To wife,
CAROLINE M. and at death to children--if no heirs. Executor: RO. A.
WRIGHT.
Book 16, Page 465 -- Inventory -- $10,050.00; slaves etc. at $11,010.00.
GARLAND POINDEXTER, JOS. T. RAMSEY, AMBROSE M. SHEPHERD. March 25,
1854. Administrators Bond is page 457.

HENRY ROBERTS -- Book 4, Page 413 -- Administrators Bond -- ZACH.
ROBERTS, MATT. and WM. LEE HARRIS, September 16, 1805, for ZACH.
ROBERTS.

JNO. ROBERTS, SR. -- Book A, Page 20 -- Administrators Bond -- CHAS. P.
TALIAFERRO and STERLING CLAIBORNE, September 22, 1817, for CHAS. P.
TALIAFERRO.
Book A, Page 37 -- March 11, 1809; September 22, 1817. Witnesses:
JNO. BROWN, JR., RUTHY BROWN, JESSE RICHARDSON, WINSTON HAMBLETON, RO.
HAMBLETON. CHAS. P. TALIAFERRO qualified. Daughter, SUSANNA ROBERTS--
Amherst County land; daughter, SALLY ROBERTS--if either daughter is
without issue. JNO. RICHARDSON ROBERTS, a natural son of my deceased
daughter, POLLY ROBERTS. Executor: friend, JNO. BROWN, JR.

JNO. H. ROBERTS -- Book 11, Page 324 -- Commissioner of Revenue,
September 15, 1845. Bondsman: LINDSEY COLEMAN.
Book 11, Page 424 -- Estate Commitment to Sheriff -- July, 1846.
WM. M. WALLER, Sheriff.
Book 11, Page 441 -- Inventory -- $184.30. WM. M. WALLER, Sheriff,
September 4, 1846. JNO. M. PRICE, JNO. R. MC DANIEL, RO. PATRICK.
Book 11, Page 533 -- Sale -- September 4, 1846; no family names among
buyers. $164.00. JNO. WHITEHEAD, Deputy Sheriff.
Book 11, Page 554 -- Administrators Account -- by WALLER, from
September 25, 1846. Recorded: September 20, 1847.

MATT. ROBERTS -- Book 4, Page 412 -- Administrators Bond -- ZACH
ROBERTS and MATT. and WM. LEE HARRIS, September 16, 1805, for ZACH
ROBERTS.

NANCY ROBERTS -- Book 3, Page 283 -- Guardians Bond -- HENRY, JNO.,
and ZACH ROBERTS, October 21, 1793, for HENRY ROBERTS as guardian of
NANCY ROBERTS, orphan of ELLIOT ROBERTS.
Book 4, Page 423 -- so indexed, but not in 3 or 4.

NANNIE ROBERTS -- Book 6, Page 207 -- Guardians Bond -- THOS. D. HILL
and JNO. MC DANIEL, January 15, 1821, for THOS. D. HILL as guardian
of NANNIE ROBERTS, orphan of RO. ROBERTS.

ARCHER ROBERTSON -- so signed, but ROBINSON in document -- Administrators Bond -- ARTHUR F. and WM. R. ROBINSON, March 17, 1856, for
ARTHUR F. ROBINSON to administrate. S. F. ROBERTSON's name is also
signed at end.

ARCHIBALD ROBERTSON -- Book 9, Page 137 -- Administrators Bond --
MAURICE H. GARLAND and SAML. GARLAND, November 16, 1835, for MAURICE H.
GARLAND.
Book 9, Page 140 -- Inventory -- December 3, 1835 -- $17,081.30.
RICH. SHELTON, JNO. D. L. (S) RUCKER, DAVID PATTESON. Recorded
December 21, 1835.
Book 9, Page 293 -- Sale -- January 1, 1836; buyers: SARAH F.,
widow: $16,565.06. Recorded March 21, 1837.
Book 10, Page 290 -- Administrators Bond -- SAML. GARLAND and JNO. F.
HAWKINS, November 16, 1840, for SAML. GARLAND.

JAS. M. B. ROBERTSON and C -- Book 9, Page 257 -- Guardians Bond --
SARAH F. ROBERTSON, JNO. THOMPSON, JR., SAML. M. GARLAND and JAS. M.
BROWN, November 22, 1836, for SARAH F. ROBERTSON as guardian of
JAS. M. B., ARTHUR J. (I), ARCHIBALD, WM. B., JNO. B., and ANDREW D.
ROBERTSON, orphans of ARCHIBALD ROBERTSON.

JNO. B. ROBERTSON -- Book 19, Page 266 -- JNO. B. ROBERTSON substituted
trustee in deed of trust from RO. N. PENDLETON to SAML. M. GARLAND,
February 3, 1863. Sold by JNO. B. ROBERTSON on April 16, 1877--two
interests of 1/7th each devised by JOEL BETHEL, deceased, and bought
by RO. M. BETHEL. May 22, 1877. Recorded: July 16, 1877.

MATT. ROBERTSON -- Book 4, Page 505 -- January 5, 1808; February 15,
1808. Witnesses: JOS. C. ROBERTS, JNO. and WM. ROBERTSON. Son,
JAS.; daughter, SARAH; daughter, REBECCA ELDER; wife, CATH. Executors:
wife and my brother, THOS. ROBERTSON.

MATT. ROBERTSON (cont.) -- Book 4, Page 506 -- Administrators Bond --
CATH. and THOS. ROBERTSON and JAS. WOODS, February 15, 1808, for first
two.
Book 4, Page 507 -- Inventory -- note due by JAS. ROBERTSON, son of
THOS., February 23, 1808. RO. PAGE, JNO. PUGH, WM. SMITH.

REBECCA ROBERTSON -- Book 2, Page 199 -- August 14, 1784; November 1,
1784. Witnesses: THOS. BELL, ALEX. REID, ALEX. HENDERSON, JR. Son,
THOS.--240 acres where I live; daughters including MARY ROBERTSON.
Executor: son, THOS.
Book 2, Page 200 -- Administrators Bond -- November 1, 1784. THOS.
ROBERTSON; bondsman; ALEX. REID, SR.
Book 2, Page 226 -- Inventory -- November, 1784, order--L17-0-6.
THOS. BELL, JNO. MC CLURE, ALEX. HENDERSON. May 2, 1785.

ELIZ. ROBINSON -- Book 5, Page 564 -- Guardians Bond -- THOS. D. HILL
and ARMSTEAD RUCKER, February 19, 1816--MATT. LIVELY also signed.
THOS. D. HILL as guardian of ELIZ. ROBINSON, orphan of RO. ROBINSON,
deceased.

JNO. ROBINSON -- Book 3, Page 516 -- November 18, 1796; September 17,
1798. Handwriting by ZACH DAWSON and SAML. DAY. Sons, WM. and JNO.
ROBINSON, to administrate. Wife, LUCY; my children then living at
her death. SIMEON and JOS. are to be educated (schooled) until bound
out for trades until 21. My children: WM., STEPHEN, HARRY, DOLLY,
PHEBY, AGATHA, JNO., THOS., SIMEON, and JOS.
Book 4, Page 311 -- Administrators Bond -- WM. ROBINSON, JNO. ROBINSON,
WM. HUGHES, SAML. DAY, September 17, 1798, for WM. and JNO. ROBINSON.
Book 6, Page 654 -- Administrators Bond -- SIMEON A. ROBINSON, REUBEN
COX, WM. I. ISBELL, March 20, 1826, for SIMEON A. ROBINSON.

LUCY ROBINSON -- Book 5, Page 565 -- Guardians Bond -- HUGH NORVELL
and GEO. W. TAYLOR, February 19, 1816, -- CHAS. WINGFIELD also signed --
for HUGH NORVELL as guardian of LUCY, POLLY, and NANCY ROBINSON
(ROBERSON) orphans of RO. ROBERSON (sic). It is ROBERTSON.
Book 6, Page 625 -- August 27, 1823; October 17, 1825. Witnesses:
JAS. L. LAMKIN, WM. AKERS, SAML. TAYLOR. Lands to children; son,
WM., has bought interest of seven of my children: HENRY, THOS.,
LEWIS, JOS., and BEVERLY ROBERTSON and my daughters, POLLY MC DANIEL
and PHOEBE TENNERSON. My other children: STEPHEN, JNO., ROBT.,
AGNESS and SIMEON. Executor: GEO. MARKHAM. Signed as ROBINSON.

MARTHA ROBINSON (S initial) -- Book 6, Page 611 -- Guardians Bond --
JESSE BECK and SAML. SMITHSON, July 18, 1825, for JESSE BECK as
guardian of MARTHA S. ROBINSON, orphan of WM. ROBINSON.

WM. ROBINSON -- Book 6, Page 560 -- January 4, 1824; March 21, 1825.
Witnesses: GEO. EVANS MARKHAM, JAS. L. LAMKIN, JNO. GARLAND, JNO.
ALCOCK, DANL. and WM. DAY. "Having lived to attain a good old age."
Son, SIMEON W.--50 acres on Poplar Island--next to JAMES WADE;
daughters, LUCY HOLLANDSWORTH, ELIZ. WILLIAMS, CATHERINE TERRY;
home tract held by JESSE and me--understanding between BECK and me--
tract deeded to me by my mother--132 acres. BALDY MC DANIEL and
LODWICK MC DANIEL are to be trustees for my daughter, POLLY W.
ROBINSON, and for my daughter, SARAH JANE ROBERTSON (sic). He then
refers to daughters and there are some scrambled initials: MARTHA,
L. P., A. D., S. P. M.--very hard to decipher-- ROBINSON. Three last
named, if no issue. Executors: ALBON MC DANIEL and GEORGE MARKHAM.
Book 6, Page 563 -- Administrators Bond -- JNO. M. WILLIAMS and JAS. L.
LAMKIN, March 21, 1825, for JNO. M. WILLIAMS. Note: descendants
say that M. in WILLIAMS' name stands for MORGAN. He married ELIZ.
ROBINSON, daughter of WM.
Book 6, Page 600 -- Inventory -- $1176.57. June 16, 1825; JESSE
BECK, CHAS. MUNDY, WM. TURNER.
Book 6, Page 57 -- JNO. M. WILLIAMS, administrator, from April, 1825;
L. ROBINSON to WM. ROBINSON; coffin for MRS. ROBINSON; bond of SIMEON W.
ROBINSON. August 10, 1827. WM. WARWICK and DAVID HOFFMAN.

CHARLES RODES -- Book 4, Page 176 -- March 19, 1805; June 17, 1805.
Witnesses: HUDSON MARTIN, JR., WM. MARTIN, JOHN RODES, DILMUS JOHNSON.
Wife, ANNY (AMY?)--land to JOHNSON's "ole" shop and joins DAVID and
CHAS. RODES; son, CHARLES; son, DAVID, in trust of CHAS. YANCEY,
Albemarle; DAVID's children by wife, MARY, sister to said YANCEY;
my Albemarle land where grandson, THOS. MARTIN, lives; land bought
of WM. FOX in Amherst County on Meriwether and Indian Borders;
daughter, JANE GARLAND; daughter, ANNA MARTIN, in Kentucky; grandson,
CHARLES MARTIN; daughter, MARY MARTIN; daughter, LUCY, wife of
AZARIAH MARTIN--if any children; granddaughter, ANNY MARTIN, daughter
of ANNA MARTIN; granddaughter, AMY RODES; daughter of CHAS. RODES;
granddaughter, AMY RODES, daughter of DAVID RODES; executors: son,
CHAS.; and grandsons, CHAS. and THOS. MARTIN. Note: it is hard to
say whether it is ANNY or AMY for these women and girls.
Book 4, Page 197 -- Inventory -- L2690-8-9, October 12, 1805. NELSON
CRAWFORD, JR., PETER LEMOINE, JAS. S. BROOKS.
Book 4, Page 199 -- Albemarle Inventory -- no total; August 16, 1805.
ZECHOMAS YANCEY, MARSHALL DURRETT, JNO. PIPER, ZACH. EMMERSON.
Book 6, Page 605 -- Administrators Account -- THOS. MARTIN, administra-
tor: November 20 and 26, 1805; MRS. ANN MARTIN--her share to CHAS.
RODES and legacies of AZARIAH MARTIN and MRS. JANE GARLAND, CHAS.
YANCEY, trustee; JNO. H. RODES named; ANN RODES; some paid; CHAS. P.
and THOS. RODES. Buyers: JNO. H. and JAS. RODES; JNO. and JACOB
RUDIZELL. Total: $987.03½.

WM. ROGERS -- Book 9, Page 347 -- Refunding Bond -- WM. and CHAS.
ROGERS and EATON CARPENTER, September 19, 1837, to CORNL. SALE and
EATON CARPENTER, administrators of BENJ. CARPENTER--slaves divided
and WM. has received share. Witnesses: SAML. M. GARLAND, JAS. F.
TALIAFERRO, G. W. STAPLES, ABSALOM HIGGINBOTHAM, CHAS. TUCKER, AUSTIN
CARPENTER.

WM. A. ROGERS -- Book 11, Page 394 -- Power of Attorney by WM. A.
ROGERS, Albemarle County, to THORNTON D. ROGERS, Albemarle County,
to sign bond for THORNTON D. ROGERS as administrator of JOS. F.
BAXTER, June 18, 1846. Certified by Albemarle Justices of the Peace:
ALEX. POPE, ABELL, JNO. J. BOCOCK (BOWCOCK). Recorded: Amherst
County, July 26, 1846.

CHAS. ROSE, SR. (DR.) -- Book 4, Page 54 -- February 1, 1802;
October 18, 1802. Witnesses: JUDITH JORDAN, JNO. WALTERS or WATTERS,
JNO. PHILLIPS. SARAH ROSE qualified; bondsman: PATRICK ROSE, JR.,
JAS. WOODS, JNO. JORDAN. Wife, SARAH--VELIEVETT tract--1500 acres
and Pinna Woods--to build house at Believett--three youngest sons,
CHARLES, HENRY and HARRY; three youngest daughters: JANE, SARAANN
and MILLY ROSE; four oldest --: ELIZ. SCOTT, JNO. M., PATRICK and
ALEX. F. ROSE; six youngest to be educated. CLAYPOOL tract of 1000
acres; sister, PEGGY ROSE. Wife to administrate with friends,
PATRICK ROSE, SR. and JR., WM. S. CRAWFORD, JAS. WOODS.
Book 4, Page 116 -- Inventory -- medical books etc.; L1106-4-6; JNO. C.
CARTER, DANL. MC DONALD, DAVID CLARKSON, June 20, 1803.
Book 4, Page 367 -- Administrators Bond -- ALEX. B. ROSE, April 28,
1803. Bondsmen: ROBT. RIVES, PETER ROSE.

CHAS. ROSE, JR. -- Book 4, Page 83 -- April 6, 1803; April 18, 1803.
Witnesses: JNO. CHAMPE CARTER, NATHL. HILL, JR., EBENEZER HICKCOCK,
MATT. HIGHT, WM. HILL, JR. ALEX. B. ROSE qualified; bondsmen;
PATRICK ROSE, RO. RIVES. Of Roseeile (Rose Isle), Amherst County
(this tract is now in Nelson); cousin, MARIA MOORE ROSE; mother,
CATH. ROSE--one-third interest in my father's estate--JNO. ROSE,
deceased--father; Executor: brother, ALEX. B. ROSE.
Book 4, Page 132 -- Inventory -- L2307-8-0; JNO. THOMPSON, JAS.
DILLARD, CHAS. WATTS, September 18, 1803.
Book 4, Page 369 -- Administrators Bond -- SARAH ROSE, JNO. JORDAN,
PATRICK ROSE, JR., JAS. WOOD, June 21, 1803, for SARAH ROSE. Note:
this is DR. ROSE, but indexed for JR.

CHAS. C. ROSE -- Book 19, Page 220 -- Administrators Bond -- J. D.
PENDLETON, January 15, 1827, for J. D. PENDLETON.

CHAS. IRVING ROSE -- Book 7, Page 194 -- December 28, 1827; December 15, 1828. Witnesses: WM. S. CLAIBORNE, STERLING CLAIBORNE. Of Nelson County; brother, PATRICK ROSE to care for my mother. Executor: DR. HARRY J. ROSE (HENRY J. ?). He qualified; bondsman: THOS. J. WALKER; WILSON PRICE.

CHAS. R. ROSE -- Book 12, Page 411 -- Administrators Bond -- RO. A. COGHILL and SAML. M. GARLAND, August 18, 1851, for COGHILL. Book 12, Page 477 -- Inventory -- Six slaves; order of August, 1851; FRANCIS V. SUTTON, JR. WM. S. CLAIBORNE.

GEO. N. ROSE -- Book 9, Page 335 -- Administrators Bond -- THOS. N. EUBANK and JNO. THOMPSON, JR., September 18, 1837, for THOS. N. EUBANK.

H. J. ROSE -- Book 11, Page 122 -- Administrators Bond -- SARAH E. ROSE, JOS K. IRVING, SAML. M. GARLAND, EDMD. C. MOORE, PAULUS POWELL, November 23, 1842, for SARAH E. ROSE.

HENRY ROSE -- Book 1, Page 159 -- Administrators Bond -- HUGH and PATRICK ROSE, EDMD. WILCOX, LUNSFORD LOMEX, JNO. ROSE, March 5, 1770, for first two.
Book 1, Page 174 -- November 9, 1779 (someone has tampered with this and put ? by 1779 for it does seem to be an error); March 5, 1778. Witnesses: EDMD. WINSTON, JNO. FONTAINE, WM. FONTAINE. Goddaughter, CAROLINE ROSE, daughter of my brother, HUGH ROSE; sister, SUSANNAH LAWSON; sister, MARGARET ROSE. If brothers, HUGH, PATRICK and CHAS. will pay my just debts--all of my landed estate. Nephew, CHAS. ROSE, son of my brother, JNO. ROSE; my mother's dower--God grant that she may live long to enjoy it; friends not to go into mourning--unless it is part mourning. Executors: brothers: HUGH, PATRICK and CHAS.

HENRY J. ROSE -- Book 10, Page 346 -- April 3, 1841; May 17, 1841. Witnesses: WARNER JONES, HENRY L. DAVIES, JAS. A. ROSE. JOS. R. IRVING and WM. S. CLAIBORNE refused to qualify. SARAH E. ROSE quali- fied; bondsman: SAML. M. GARLAND, JOS. R. IRVING, JNO. THOMPSON, JR., EDMD. C. MOORE. Buildings to be completed on lot bought of MR. GARLAND; wife, SALLY; daughter, ANN. By will of ANN WALKER my son, FITZHUGH, is due one-third of land I sold to MR. HARRIS; son, CHAS., is due slave; son, HENRY; my four children. I am security for THOS. J. WALKER as commissioner to sell interest of his son, THOS. WALKER, in the SELMA estate; wife to maintain our children. Executors: friends: JOS. R. IRVING, WM. S. CLAIBORNE and to see that children are well brought up. Book 10, Page 359 -- Inventory -- $6764.50, June 21, 1841. V. MC GINNIS, JNO. A. (H) PHILLIPS, WM. H. KNIGHT.
Book 16, Page 52 -- so indexed, but it is Book 15, Page 52 -- Guardians Bond -- PAUL C. CABELL and R. A. COGHILL, January 17, 1859, for PAUL C. CABELL as guardian of HENRY J. ROSE; no parent set forth.

HUGH ROSE -- Book 1, Page 307 -- Sheriff, February 6, 1776; Bondsman: GABL. PENN, EDMD. WILCOX, JOS. CABELL, JNO. ROSE. Bond to GEO. III. Book 3, Page 328 -- October 16, 1794; January 19, 1795. Witnesses: RO. AUSTIN, THOS. WORTHAM. Codicil: witnesses: LANDON CABELL, RO. AUSTIN. Too weak to sign will--HENRY and Seven Islands land; daughters, JUDY, NANCY; son, RO. HENRY ROSE--Tye River tract; daughter, CAROLINE TURPIN; daughter, LUCY (SUKY ?); GUSTAVUS is to have Geddes--house where I now live (I have commented on this house before. It is now owned by "CLAIBORNE sisters"--several married--and I have been gra- ciously enteretained when my wife and I visited it); daughter, POLLY; my wife. Executors: PATRICK ROSE, WM. CABELL, JR., SAML. IRVINE, WM. CRAWFORD. Codicil: THOS. WORTHAM and wife to have plantation where they live.
Book 3, Page 329 -- Administrators Bond -- PATRICK ROSE, January 19, 1795, and WM. CABELL, JR. Bondsmen: RO. RIVES, JOS. BURRUS. Book 3, Page 354 -- Inventory -- January 22, 1795 L2674-5-6. BENAMMI STONE, GEO. PENN, JEREMIAH FRANKLIN.
Book 3, Page 452 -- Administrators Account -- from February 2, 1795, by administrators. REV. CHAS. CRAWFORD for sermon; JNO. JOHNSON, schoolmaster; Henry County lands; chancery--JORDAN's heirs; MARGARET ROSE's legacy; bond--HUGH ROSE and SUSANNAH MARTIN; widow; CAROLINE

HUGH ROSE (cont.) -- ROSE, GEO. GALASPIE for hire of slaves L8-8-0.
September 14, 1790; very long report of ten pages. JNO. ROSE,
executor of RO. ROSE; April 16, 1798. SAML. MEREDITH, W. WARWICK,
DAVID S. GARLAND.
Book 4, Page 200 -- Administrators Account -- by ALEX. P. ROSE and
WM. CABELL from March 20, 1798; SUSANNA MARTIN's execution paid by
MICAJAH CAMDEN; to CAROLINE M. ROSE--in hands of SAML. ROSE; RO. H.
ROSE's judgement--called later DR. June 25, 1805. SAML. MEREDITH,
DAVID S. GARLAND, JOS. BURRUS.

JAS. A. ROSE -- Book B, Page 21 -- Estate Commitment to Sheriff --
Tuesday, August 30, 1842; motion of JNO. WHITEHEAD; Sheriff: NELSON
CRAWFORD.

JANE ROSE -- Book 9, Page 420 -- February 7, 1838; April 10, 1838,
codicil; April 16, 1838. Witnesses: WM. P. READ, SALLY F. POWELL,
PAULUS POWELL; to codicil: WM. P. READ and MILLY J. GARLAND. SAML. M.
GARLAND qualified; bondsman: JOS. K. IRVING. My brother, JAS. A.
ROSE, owns mulatto slave, PATRICK, and executors to free him and give
him money and transport him to some free state. JOS. K. IRVING,
trustee for my grandson, THOS. IRVING WALKER--land in Patrick County,
Meadows of Dan tract--when 21. Daughter, SUSAN A. PRICE, if with
issue. Executors to buy old negro, JNO., owned by THOS. S. WALKER,
if price is reasonable, with sum from my father's estate. Codicil:
slave girl to be hired by JOS. K. IRVING. Executor: SAML. M. GARLAND.

COL. JNO. ROSE -- Book 4, Page 41 -- Inventory of COL. JNO. ROSE,
L3471-14-9, July 17, 1802/slaves and personal estate; JAS. MONTGOMERY;
JNO. C. CARTER; DAVID CLARKSON; DANL. MC DONALD.
Book 4, Page 62 -- Inventory -- L1613-2-5; December 20, 1802. FRANCIS
CRACRAFT, RO. MOSS, RO. BOWLING. Indexed for COLONIUS ROSE.

LUCINDA ROSE -- Book 4, Page 317 -- Guardians Bond -- CAROLINE
MATILDA ROSE and WM. CABELL, JR., September 16, 1797, for CAROLINE
MATILDA ROSE as guardian of LUCINDA and EMILY ROSE, orphans of HUGH
ROSE, deceased. I have pointed out before that the index here will
often record only one ward, but sometimes a good many will show in
bonds.

MILDRED ROSE (IRVING) -- Book 9, Page 359 -- Administrators Bond --
JAS. A. ROSE, HENRY J. ROSE, HOWELL L. BROWN, SAML. M. GARLAND, JOS. K.
IRVING, CHAS. B. CLAIBORNE, December 18, 1837, for JAS. A. ROSE.
Book 9, Page 362 -- July 6, 1835; December 18, 1837. Witnesses:
SAML. M. GARLAND, HENRY J. ROSE. Formerly MILDRED IRVING; son, JAS.
ALEX. ROSE; other children by first marriage were amply provided for
by first husband, CHAS. IRVING, deceased. JAS. ALEX. ROSE, issued
by second marriage, is to administrate.
Book 9, Page 373 -- Inventory -- $76.44. WM. MC CAUL, JONATHAN A,
STOUT, January 15, 1838.

PATRICK J. R. ROSE -- Book 8, Page 103 -- Administrators Bond --
WILSON N. PRICE and WM. H. GARLAND, June 20, 1831, for WILSON N.
PRICE.
Book 8, Page 104 -- March 27, 1831; June 20, 1831. Witnesses:
JAMES POWELL and JAS. A. ROSE. My five slaves in trust of my sister,
SUSAN A. P. PRICE, for support of my mother, JANE ROSE.

PAULINA (POLLINA) ROSE -- Book 4, Page 318 -- Guardians Bond --
CAROLINA MATILDA ROSE and WM. CABELL, JR., September 16, 1797, for
CAROLINA MATILDA ROSE as guardian of POLLINA ROSE, orphan of H. ROSE,
deceased. This is indexed for PAULINA nad POLLINA in data.

ROBT. S. ROSE -- Book 10, Page 62 -- October 3, 1835; August 28, 1835.
Witnesses: W. W. WATSON, Geneva (County, New York; Ontario); S. D.
TILLMAN and JAS. H. WOODS, same county. Recorded Amherst County,
Tuesday, November 20, 1838. Motion of JNO. THOMPSON, JR.; JANE L.
ROSE, executrix and sole legatee of New York, for JNO. THOMPSON to
administrate. Fayette, Seneca County, New York--daughter, MARY,
wife of RO. C. NICHOLAS; my six children; daughter, SUSAN; wife, JANE

ROBT. S. ROSE (cont.) -- LAWSON ROSE; my seven children (sic), if no
issue. Wife to administrate. Page 64 JNO. THOMPSON, JR. qualified--
date as above.

SAML. ROSE -- Book 1, Page 325 -- so indexed, but it is Book 3, Page
325 -- Guardians Bond -- SAML. IRVINE, JAS. CALLAWAY, JAS. PENN,
December 15, 1794, for SAML. IRVINE as guardian of SAML. ROSE, orphan
of HUGH ROSE, deceased.

PATRICK H. ROWSEY -- Book 15, Page 57 -- Inventory -- October 14, 1858.
JAS. M. MILLNER, administrator. RO. CARTER, WM. L. MILLNER, HARTWELL T.
PRYOR--$399.20. Recorded: February 21, 1859.
Book 15, Page 59 -- Sale -- October 14, 1858. THOS. B. and RO. GATEWOOD
buyers.
Book 16, Page 258 -- Administrators Account -- from October 14, 1858.
To the executor (?) of JNO. ROWSEY--$7.70; to JNO. ROWSEY--$6.00; to
LACY ROGERS for coffin--$5.00. April 20, 1863.

ABNER RUCKER -- Book 10, Page 205 -- January 24, 1837; February court,
1839, Fayette County, Kentucky. Witnesses: ALEX. P. CAMPBELL, PETER
TILTON. JAS. C. RODES, Clerk, February 15, 1839; recorded Amherst
County, March 16, 1840. THOS. A. RUSSELL, Presiding Judge of Fayette.
JAS. C. MC KENZIE and CHISWELL DABNEY qualified in Amherst County,
March 16, 1840, for JAS. C. MC KENZIE. Wife, NANCY--$1.00 for
unkindness to me; daughters, REBECCA and SALLY when of age; if they
leave me, and go to their mother after my kindness to them--$1.00
each. All of my children. Executor: DANL. MC PAYNE to divide
estate among my children. One is referred to RAILEY's fine work on
Woodford County, Kentucky, for more on this man and RUCKER family
data.

ALEX. M. RUCKER -- Book 18, Page 145 -- Administrators Bond -- EDWIN M.
WARE, GODFREY T. RUCKER, WM. L. MILLNER, November 20, 1871, for
EDWIN M. WARE.
Book 18, Page 233 -- Inventory and Sale -- no inventory total;
December 1, 1871; JAS. M. MILLNER, W. L. VAUGHAN, G. T. DAVIS. Sale:
$246.95 on same date; buyers: J. W., WM. R. G. T. and ELLEN RUCKER.
Book 18, Page 365 -- Administrators Account -- from November 20,
1871. Recorded: October 2, 1873.
Book 20, Page 213 -- Administrators Account -- from October 2, 1873;
recorded May, 1881. To G. T. RUCKER, ELLEN M. RUCKER, MAG E. SMITH.

AMBROSE RUCKER, SR. -- Book 4, Page 479 -- December 3, 1803; codicil,
January 21, 1807; December 21, 1807. Witnesses: JNO. COONEY, HENRY A.
CHRISTIAN, ANTHONY RUCKER, TINSLEY RUCKER. ISAAC RUCKER qualified;
bondsmen: ANTHONY RUCKER, DAVID TINSLEY, JNO. MC DANIEL, BENJ. RUCKER,
JR. Wife, MARY--where I live and 473 acres; Mt. plantation on Harris
Creek; son, AMBROSE; children and grandchildren; land formerly con-
tested by LUCAS and me. Son, ISAAC--Rockey Creek land; son, BENJ.--
where son, ISAAC, now lives; store houses and barns; heirs of son,
REUBEN, deceased; heirs of WINIFRED PLUNKET, deceased; heirs of PEGGY
MC DANIEL, deceased; to FRANKEY LEE and heirs; my MOLLY BURFORD (sic);
to ELIZ. MARR; to SOPHIA RUCKER, my daughter; to SOPHIA JENNINGS. He
names a SOPHIA RUCKER and does not designate her as daughter.
Daughter, CAROLINE HANSFORD; to MATILDA MARR; daughter, CHARLOTTE
RUCKER; daughter, SALLY MARR; my children and grandchildren. Children
of REUBEN RUCKER; of WINIFRED PLUNKET; of MARGARET MC DANIEL; MOLLY
BURFORD; FRANKEY LEE; AMBROSE and ISAAC RUCKER; SOPHIA JENNINGS;
CAROLINE HANSFORD; BETSY MARR; MATILDA MARR; SALLY MARR; CHARLOTTE
RUCKER; BENJ. RUCKER; and then SR. ANTHONY RUCKER; heirs of ISAAC
RUCKER, deceased. Begins new sentence with BENJ. RUCKER, SR.--my
Kentucky lands patent to me; grave lot reserved; Executors: wife,
MARY; sons, AMBROSE and ISAAC RUCKER. Margin: January 18, 1808;
handwriting by WM. WARE and THOS. MOORE. Codicil: wife and sons,
AMBR. and JNO. to administrate; residence tract to be sold and sum
divided. January 21, 1809. It is hard to separate children and
grandchildren in this will. Items are indexed SR. and JR. and hard
to separate.

AMBROSE RUCKER, SR. (cont.) -- Book 4, Page 481 -- Administrators
Bond -- ISAAC and ANTHONY RUCKER, DAVID TINSLEY, BENJ. RUCKER, JNO.
MC DANIEL, December 21, 1807, for ISAAC RUCKER.
Book 3, Page 259 -- Tobacco Inspector, Amherst Warehouse. December 17,
1792. Bondsman: AMBROSE RUCKER, JR.
Book 5, Page 69 -- Commissioners Revenue -- February 18, 1811.
Bondsman: JAS. WAUGH, JAS. TINSLEY, SAML. BURKS.
Book 5, Page 396 -- Tobacco Inspector, Amherst Warehouse, September 19,
1814. Bondsman: NELSON C. DAWSON.
Book 5, Page 549 -- Administrators Account -- by ISAAC RUCKER from
1818--REUBEN RUCKER for coffin; PLUNKETT heirs; B. RUCKER; CHARLOTTE
RUCKER; SOPHIA JENNINGS; AMBROSE RUCKER, son of REUBEN; bond of MARY
BURFORD; bond of TINSLEY RUCKER; bonds of RICH. H., ABSALOM, RICH.,
REUBEN, BENJ., JNO. RUCKER, A. PLUNKETT, ANTHONY RUCKER, JNO. H.
PLUNKETT, AMBROSE RUCKER, SR.; 68½ acres I bought; I. RUCKER, deceased;
executor of AMBR. RUCKER; expenses to Kentucky in 1808--$9.00; account
of ISAAC RUCKER, executor of AMBR. RUCKER. November 21, 1815. THOS.
CREWS, NELSON C. DAWSON, CHAS. MUNDY.

AMBROSE RUCKER, JR. -- Book 6, Page 28 -- Treasurer of School Board;
or Commissioners, September 21, 1818. Bondsman: RICH. BURKS.
Book 6, Page 253 -- Same, September 17, 1821. Bondsman: ISAAC
RUCKER.
Book 6, Page 298 -- Same, June 17, 1822. Bondsman: same.
Book 9, Page 61 -- Administrators Bond -- LINDSEY MC DANILE, WM.
MC DANIEL, AMBR. R. MC DANIEL, March 17, 1835, for LINDSEY MC DANIEL.
Book 10, Page 383 -- Estate Commitment to Sheriff -- June, 1839;
motion of GEO. MC DANIEL. Sheriff: EDMD. PENN.

ANTHONY RUCKER -- Book 3, Page 259 -- Tobacco Inspector, Amherst
Warehouse, December 17, 1792. Bondsman: AMBROSE RUCKER.
Book 3, Page 290 -- Same, September 16, 1793; bondsman: ISAAC RUCKER.
Book 3, Page 405 -- Same, September 19, 1796; bondsman: BENJ. RUCKER.
Book 3, Page 512 -- Same, October 16, 1797; bondsman: JOS. BURRUS.
Book 3, Page 518 -- Same, September 17, 1798; bondsman: BENJ. RUCKER.
Book 6, Page 210 -- April 20, 1820; codicil of July 14, 1820; codicil
of January 23, 1821; codicil of January 27, 1821; February 19, 1821.
Witnesses to will: JNO. COLEMAN, REUBEN D. RUCKER, EDWIN L. (S)
RUCKER, NATHAN D. RUCKER, DAVID TINSLEY, SR.; codicil one witnesses:
BETSY KNIGHT, NANCY KNIGHT, JAS. LONDON, MATT. KNIGHT, DAVID TINSLEY,
SR. Witnesses to codicil 2: ABSALOM RUCKER, WM. APPLEBURRY, ANTHONY
RUCKER, JR. Witnesses to codicil 3: WM. S (L) APPLEBURRY, DAVID
TINSLEY SR., BETSY and NANCY KNIGHT. NELSON C. DAWSON and AMBROSE
RUCKER qualified; bondsman: SPENCER NORVALL, RICH. BURKS, ELIAS
WILLS. Wife (RAILEY in Woodford Book, Kentucky County, says that she
was REBECCA BURGESS), page 383f--op. cited--125 acres inclusive;
BEEM's orchard; slaves; mulatto, JAS. GILBERT--three acres at corner
of my land for life; son, ABSALOM RUCKER--100 acres; land reserved
where the church stands for divine worship; six equal lots: son,
ABNER; son, ARMISTEAD; son, ABSALOM; daughter, AGNES OGDEN; children
of deceased daughter, ANN; children of deceased daughter, AMELIA
RICHESON; ABNER's part in trust until business between us about
Kentucky land on four mile creek is settled; also until AMELIA
RICHESON's children are of age or married. Executors: NELSON
CRAWFORD, SR., AMBROSE RUCKER, son of REUBEN, ISAAC RUCKER. Codicil:
160 acres for son, ABSALOM; have deeded 213 acres to BENJ. OGDEN--200
of it to my wife to make her equal with my children for certain
causes best known to myself; it is all that I intend for OGDEN to have
and he has no control over part going to my daughter, AGNES OGDEN and
children. Codicil: Revokes clause as to OGDEN and he gets equal part
with wife and children. Codicil: CAPT. JAS. WARE to proceed per
contract as to patent for invention for building a batteaux; if
successful, get one-half. Page 214 is Administrators Bond.
Book 6, Page 218 -- Inventory -- Many slaves; no total; March, 1821;
DAVID TINSLEY, SR., JNO. HANSARD, ISAAC TINSLEY, WM. MC DANIEL.
Book 6, Page 415 -- Curator Bond -- December 15, 1823, for SAML. M.
GARLAND; bondsman: ARCHIBALD ROBERTSON, EDWD. A. CABELL. This is
indexed AMBR. RUCKER, JR.

ANTHONY RUCKER (cont.) -- Book 6, Page 520 -- Account by GARLAND from January 8, 1824--plow horse for MRS. RUCKER; 25¢ bridge toll; negro hires; some retained by MRS. RUCKER. September 24, 1824. JNO. D. MURRELL, SAML. LANCESTER, D. S. MURRELL.
Book 6, Page 544 -- Inventory -- December 30, 1822--$7884.00 JESSE RICHESON, administrator de bonis non; CHAS. P. TALIAFERRO; WM. TURNER; THOS. D. HILL.
Book 8, Page 57 -- Administrators Account -- by JESSE RICHESON from 1829; CHAS. L. BARRET, ZA DRUMMOND. Recorded: July 21, 1830.
Book 8, Page 234 -- Estate Commitment to Sheriff -- motion of THOS. N. EUBANK and BENJ. TALIAFERRO. JESSE RICHESON administrator de bonis non July, 1832. NELSON DAWSON, Sheriff.
Book 8, Page 324 -- Inventory -- December 29, 1832; several totals; one for slaves by BEVERLY DAVIES, Deputy for Sheriff: $4455.00 Another of $4614.50, December 29, 1832, by WM. MC DANIEL, NATHAN D. RUCKER, MARTIN D. TINSLEY.
Book 9, Page 183 -- Administrators Account -- by DAWSON, late sheriff from 1832. JNO. J. PURVIS for MRS. RUCKER and slaves in her possession; HOLLINS' store account for widow; writ on A. T. RUCKER, PETER RUCKER, MARTIN PARKS. September 20, 1834. MARTIN D. TINSLEY, JNO. PRYOR, CHAMPE CARTER.
Book 10, Page 111 -- so indexed, but nothing there. ALFRED PERCY, JR. wrote an article on the batteaux in his Piedmont Apoc. and discussed the patent at some length. I regret his death and we were great friends. I am sorry that he did not get to examine the deeds and powers of attornies in deed book P which I have not released. Therein it is shown that BENJ. RUCKER was joint inventor with him. There is data showing the patent had been applied for and powers to various men in several states so that they could collect revenues due the inventors.

BENJ. RUCKER -- Book 4, Page 363 -- Sheriffs Bond -- so indexed, but not there.
Book 5, Page 19 -- Division of six lots of slaves; to THOS., BENNET, GIDEON RUCKER, SOPHIA BURRUS, LUCY MC DANIEL, JAS. RUCKER, MILLY BROWN, BENJ. BROWN, agent. Note six lots, but seven in division. REUBEN NORVELL, NELSON C. DAWSON, SPENCER NORVELL, October 17, 1810. Allotted per will.
Book A, Page 1 -- June 20, 1808; codicil of November 10, 1809; no probate date, but Administrators Bond is Page 4 for GIDEON RUCKER, THOS. and JAS. RUCKER, September 26, 1810; bondsman: ISAAC and REUBEN RUCKER, WM. TURNER, BENAMMI STONE. Witnesses to will: JNO. COONEY, RICH. RUCKER, ARMISTEAD RUCKER, ANTHONY RUCKER. Witneses to codicil: REUBEN NORVELL, NELSON C. DAWSON, JR., ANTHONY and REUBEN RUCKER. Son, JAS.--Campbell County on Black Water Creek near Lynchburg--560 acres; son, THOS., Amherst County land on Stovall and bought from various persons 1260 acres; son, GIDEON, two tracts on Rutledge--372 acres; daughter, LUCY MC DANIEL; daughter, MILLY BROWN; daughter, SOPHIA BURRUS; son, BENNETT RUCKER--750 acres where I live. Executors: sons, JAS., THOS. and GIDEON. Codicil: fears ambiguity as to some phrases--daughter, MILLY BROWN, had received sums; also sums to JAS., THOS., GIDEON, BENNETT, LUCY and SOPHIA.
Book A, Page 32 -- Administrators Account -- by three administrators-- accounts of BENNETT, R., BENJ. J. in data; division of October; April 26, 1815.

CHAS. H. RUCKER -- Book 11, Page 320 -- Sheriff, Deputy or Constables Bond -- June 16, 1845; bondsman: PETER RUCKER, STEPHEN BOWLES.
Book 11, Page 524 -- Constables Bond -- June 20, 1847. Bondsmen: PETER RUCKER, GEO. T. PLEASANTS.
Book 12, Page 178 -- same, June 18, 1849. Bondsmen: JAS. B. DAVIS, STEPHEN BOWLES.
Book 12, Page 417 -- Same, June 16, 1851. Bondsman: W. A. RICHESON.
Book 12, Page 530 -- Sheriffs Bond -- June 21, 1852. Bondsmen: JESSE RICHESON, by S. M. GARLAND; PETER RUCKER, by GARLAND; GEO. T. PLEASANTS; W. A. RICHESON.
Book 13, Page 360 -- Sheriffs Bond -- June 19, 1854. Bondsmen: same-- plus RO. A. COGHILL.

CLIFTON H. RUCKER -- Book 9, Page 432 -- January 26, 1838; May 21, 1838. Witnesses: JAS. MC DANIEL, JR., ELDRED R. PHILLIPS, AMBR. RUCKER. AMBROSE B. RUCKER qualified; bondsmen: EDWIN S. and NATHAN D. RUCKER--page 434. Two sons, WM. PARKS and JAMES STAPLES RUCKER--all Amherst County, Missouri, and any other land--when WM. is of age. When both are of age or without issue. My six brothers and two sisters: REUBEN D., EDWIN S., NATHAN D., MARY ANN D. RUCKER, ALFRED M. RUCKER, MARGARET M. WOODROOF, AMBROSE B. and GEO. M. RUCKER. My two sons are to be educated. Executors: brothers: EDWIN S., AMBROSE B., and GEO. M. RUCKER.
Book 9, Page 434 -- Guardians Bond -- AMBROSE B., EDWIN S., and NATHAN D. RUCKER, May 21, 1838, for AMBROSE B. RUCKER as guardian of WM. PARKS and JOS. STAPLES RUCKER, (seems to be JOS. STAPLES in will), orphans of CLIFTON H. RUCKER, deceased.
Book 10, Page 52 -- so indexed, as inventory -- not there; no index in book itself.
Book 13, Page 148 -- Administrators Account -- from March 21, 1838; paid ALFRED M. and ELIZ. RUCKER; Island taxes; cash of A. B. and JNO. RUCKER; enclosing graveyard. WM. P. RUCKER, AMBR. B. RUCKER as guardian of JAS. STAPLES RUCKER. Recorded: May 15, 1853.
Book 13, Page 374 -- Administrators Account -- from December 31, 1838-- AMBR. B. RUCKER; name of WM. P. RUCKER and Guardians Account for both orphans from 1838. Rent of Chase Island, 1852. Recorded: August 21, 1854.

CORA E. RUCKER and C -- Book 15, Page 495 -- Guardians Bond -- JNO. E. EDWARDS and HOWARD A. CLARK, November 19, 1860, for JNO. E. EDWARDS as guardian of CORA E. and MARY M. RUCKER, orphans of EDWIN S. RUCKER, deceased. Below is Administrators Bond by same men and date for HOWARD CLARK as administrator of EMILY S. RUCKER. CLARK appears as HOWSAN in some items.
Book 16, Page 156 -- Guardians Bond -- HOWSAN A. CLARK, SAML. T. CLARK, and EDWARDS, September 15, 1862, for HOWSAN A. CLARK as guardian of same orphans.
Book 16, Page 344 -- JNO. E. EDWARDS appears as guardian in account from November 20, 1869; expense to CH to qualify; account of GEO. M. RUCKER and WASH. J. RUCKER. Recorded: February 9, 1863.
Book 17, Page 399 -- Guardians Bond -- by CLARK from September, 1862. Tuition; cash of A. B. RUCKER; also account for MARY M.--trip to Farmville for both wards; cash of GEO. M. RUCKER. May 10, 1868.

EDWIN S. RUCKER -- Book 15, Page 211 -- Inventory -- July 18, 1859-- $2248.00; ZACH D. TINSLEY, DANL., H. RUCKER, E. L. SHELTON, NATHAN D. RUCKER, JAS. L. DUPUY.
Book 15, Page 215 -- Administrators Bond -- EMILY J. RUCKER, AMBR. B. RUCKER, SAML. T. CLARK, July 18, 1859, for EMILY J. RUCKER.
Book 15, Page 479 -- Administrator De Bonis Non -- October 15, 1860. RO. TINSLEY. Bondsman: ZACH D. TINSLEY.
Book 16, Page 92 -- Inventory -- November 26, 1860: $3449.75. A. R. WOODROOF, GEO. HYLTON, D. H. RUCKER.
Book 16, Page 141 -- Administrators de bonis non Bond -- July 21, 1862; C. DABNEY; bondsman: C. H. LYNCH, by SAML. GARLAND.
Book 16, Page 294 -- Administrators Account -- by EMILY J. RUCKER from May 26, 1859. Account of N. D. RUCKER, PATRICK's expenses to Prince Edward; account of WASH. J. RUCKER; account of A. B. RUCKER; WOODSON for tuition of children; bond of CHAS. H. RUCKER; account of WM. B. RUCKER; A. C. RUCKER's tobacco rent; subscription to build church at Amherst Courthouse (probably Episcopal, but I am not sure)-- $100.00; shoes for LUCY. Recorded: April 20, 1863; returned, August 15, 1852 (sic).
Book 19, Page 160 -- Administrators Bond -- JNO. B. ROBERTSON; bondsman: J. THOMPSON, April 17, 1876.
Book 19, Page 267 -- Administrators Account -- May 14, 1877--by ROBERTSON. Legatees: V. H., W. J. RUCKER, A. S. PORTER and wife, CORA, MARY, W. F. and A. B. RUCKER, assignee of HILTON RUCKER. Recorded: July 16, 1877.

ELIZ. RUCKER -- Book 5, Page 179 -- Guardians Bond -- ANDREW MOWLAND, JAS. WARE, WILLIS RUCKER, JNO. M. EDWARDS, September 21, 1812, for

ELIZ. RUCKER (cont.) -- ANDREW MOWLAND as guardian of ELIZ. RUCKER, orphan of ___.
Book 5, Page 138 -- Indexed as Administrators Bond, but nothing there nor in book index.
Book 13, Page 355 -- Administrators Bond -- June 19, 1854; RO. TINSLEY and GEO. HYLTON. Bondsman: AMBROSE B. and GEO. M. RUCKER.

EMILY J. RUCKER -- Book 17, Page 54 -- Administrators Account -- September 16, 1863. HOWSAN and CLARK; paid estate of A. B. RUCKER. Recorded: December 18, 1865.

EMILY S. RUCKER -- I think that this is for woman above, but the two items are so indexed.
Book 15, Page 495 -- Administrators Bond -- HOWARD A. CLARK and JNO. E. EDWARDS, November 19, 1860, for HOWARD A. CLARK. I have previously pointed out that CLARK is shown as HOWARD and HOWSAN.

HENRY P. RUCKER -- Book 5, Page 430 -- Guardians Bond -- ISAAC and AMBR. RUCKER, May 16, 1814, for ISAAC RUCKER as guardian of HENRY P., AMBROSE, ISAAC, WM. B. C. RUCKER, infants of ISAAC.
Book 6, Page 274 -- Indexed as Constables Bond -- not there.

HYLTON G. RUCKER -- Book 15, Page 452 -- Administrators Bond -- VALENTINE H. RUCKER and AMBR. C. TUCKER, October 15, 1860, for VALENTINE H. RUCKER.
Book 16, Page 308 -- Administrators Account -- from December 19, 1860. To Amherst County and A. B. RUCKER. Recorded: May 21, 1863.

ISAAC RUCKER -- Book 5, Page 371 -- Administrators Bond -- REUBEN RUCKER, AMBR. and RICH. RUCKER, August 16, 1813; also RICH. HARRISON and ARCHELAUS REYNOLDS for REUBEN RUCKER.
Book 9, Page 148 -- Estate Commitment to Sheriff -- December 21, 1835; motion of RO. TINSLEY; administrated by JOHN RUCKER. THOS. N. EUBANK, Sheriff.
Book 10, Page 35 -- Estate Commitment to Sheriff -- July, 1838; motion of WILL A. RICHESON, JNO. COLEMAN, Sheriff.
Book 11, Page 222 -- Estate Commitment to Sheriff -- April, 1844; motion of THOS. G. HILL. ISAAC RUCKER, deceased, and son of MOSES RUCKER. JAS. POWELL, Sheriff. This reminds me of a song which came out in my high school days, "Whose Izzy is he ? Is he yours or is he mine? I'm getting dizzy watching Izzy all of the time."

JANE RUCKER -- Book 5, Page 185 -- Guardians Bond -- NANCY and RICH. RUCKER, October 19, 1812, for NANCY RUCKER as guardian of JANE and SUSANNAH RUCKER, orphans of JNO. RUCKER, deceased. Also bondsmen were ARMISTEAD and REUBEN RUCKER.
Book 15, Page 326 -- May 27, 1860; August 20, 1860. Witnesses: RO. H. and JOS. R. CARTER, LUTHER R. DAVIS, WM. H. POWELL. CHAS. H. RUCKER qualified; bondsmen: W. L. MILLNER and THOS. WHITEHEAD. Son, CHAS. H.; daughter, ELIZ. P. MILLNER; grandsons, AMBROSE R. HENDERSON and WM. RUCKER PRYOR. My children: BRUNETTA TOLER, MARTHA E. HENDERSON, CHAS. H. RUCKER, ELIZ. P. MILLNER, MARY T. PRYOR, EDITH E. PRYOR, SARAH E. RHODES. Executor: son, CHAS. H. Page 459 for Administrators Bond.
Book 16, Page 24 -- Inventory -- December 29, 1860. GEO. W. STAPLES, MADISON HICKS, H. E. SMITH, BLUFORD MORRIS--$2791.25. Sale: $73.05. Recorded: July 21, 1861.

JNO. RUCKER -- Book 1, Page 529 -- December 1, 1779; September 4, 1780. Witnesses: AMBROSE RUCKER, WM. WHITTEN, REUBEN RUCKER. Planter; wife, ELEANOR--one-half of where I live; son, WM.--Bedford land on Elk Creek; son, GEO.--one-half of Bedford land; daughter, NELLY RUCKER; daughter, BETTY RUCKER; colt got by MILLER's horse; daughter, SUKEY COWARD; sons, JNO., ISAAC, JAS.; daughter, SARAH PENDLETON. Executors: wife; son, JAS.; son, JNO.; brother, ISAAC.
Book 2, Page 1 -- Inventory -- of Bedford estate: L78,407-6-3. November 6, 1780. GEO. MC DANIEL, DAVID TINSLEY, JNO. MC DANIEL. ":12 inventory by same men, May 7, 1781: L95-18-8.
Book 3, Page 436 -- Administrators Account -- from 1780--nine legatees

JNO. RUCKER (cont.) -- paid L75-13-10; from grandfather's estate,
JNO. RUCKER. Many RUCKER names: BENJ. ANTHONY, GEO., WM., MRS.
ELINOR RUCKER, JAS., ISAAC, COL. AMBROSE, PETER. Grandfather is
called The Elder. June 19, 1797. Three administrators.
Book 5, Page 175 -- Administrators Bond -- NANCY, WILLIS, ARMISTEAD
RUCKER, SAML. BURKS, REUBEN PENDLETON, JAS. WARE; July 20, 1812, for
first two.
Book 5, Page 186 -- Inventory -- $3989.76, November 16, 1812; SAML.
BURKS, WM. SHELTON, REUBEN PENDLETON.

JNO. D. L. RUCKER -- Book 8, Page 239 -- Guardians Bond -- RICH. F.
RUCKER and ELIHU TANDY, August 20, 1832, for RICH. F. RUCKER as
guardian of JNO. D. L. RUCKER, orphan of JNO. RUCKER, deceased.

LUCY E. RUCKER -- Book 15, Page 494 -- Guardians Bond -- VALENTINE H.
RUCKER, GEO. HYLTON, A. C. RUCKER, November 19, 1860, for VALENTINE H.
RUCKER as guardian of WILL and LUCY E. RUCKER, infants of EDWIN S.
RUCKER, deceased.
Book 17, Page 136 -- Guardians Account -- from February 5, 1861,
MISS O. P. TINSLEY for board and tuition; G. RUCKER's estate; MISS
CHARLOTTE MANSON for board and tuition; A. D. RUCKER for board; RUCKER
versus RUCKER; Bedford school expenses. Total estate: $2332.02.
July 16, 1866.

MARCELLUS P. RUCKER -- Book 16, Page 155 -- Administrators Bond --
ELIZ. T. RUCKER, NATHAN D. RUCKER, JAS. HIGGINBOTHAM, September 15,
1862, for ELIZ. T. RUCKER.
Book 16, Page 214 -- Inventory -- December 26, 1862--$2775.00; JAS. D.
HALL, JAS. HIGGINBOTHAM, JNO. V. WHEELER.

MARTHA A. RUCKER -- Book 11, Page 274 -- so indexed, but not there.
Not in 9, 10, 12, or 13.

MILDRED RUCKER -- Book 5, Page 434 -- Inventory -- four slaves:
$1425.00, April 18, 1814; WILL KNIGHT, REUBEN PENDLETON, JAS. PETTIT.

MOSES RUCKER -- Book 9, Page 60 -- Estate Commitment to Sheriff --
March 16, 1835; motion of PETER RUCKER. Sheriff: THOS. N. EUBANK.

NANCY W. RUCKER -- Book 5, Page 684 -- dower in estate of JNO. RUCKER,
deceased. Three slaves to her as widow: $2250; each legatee will
get $366.57; guardians. Commissioners: NELSON C. DAWSON, REUBEN
PENDLETON, DAVID TINSLEY, SR. May 20, 1817.
Book 6, Page 30 -- Administrators Bond -- TINSLEY RUCKER, NELSON C.
DAWSON, AMBR. RUCKER, September 21, 1818, for TINSLEY RUCKER.
Book 8, Page 176 -- Division: 577¼ acres; mill lot--52¼ acres
assigned to MRS. NANCY RUCKER during lifetime by her consent; 49 acres
to JANE E. RUCKER; 51 acres to MRS. MARTHA TANDY and MATT. WILLS;
63 acres to MRS. ELIZ. MORELAND; 74 acres to JNO. D. L. RUCKER;
100 acres and mansion house to WILLIS RUCKER; 66 acres to MRS. SUSAN
BROWN; 120 acres to RICH. F. RUCKER--both sides Mill Creek; border of
Harris Creek and both sides of road from Bethel to Amherst Courthouse;
joins DAVIND TINSLEY heirs; JNO. SHELTON; ARCHIBALD ROBERTSON and owned
by MRS. NANCY RUCKER. Note: first items are indexed for NANCY and
others for NANCY W.

PETER RUCKER -- Many Constables Bonds -- Book 8, Page 74 -- December 20,
1830; bondsman: RICH. L. ELLIS and RO. H. CARTER.
Book 8, Page 103 -- June 20, 1831; bondsman: WM. HAYNES, GODFREY
TOLER.
Book 8, Page 318 -- June 17, 1833; bondsmen: RICH. L. ELLIS and WM.
HAYNES.
Book 9, Page 79 -- June 15, 1835; bondsmen: same as above.
Book 9, Page 322 -- Same, June 19, 1839; bondsmen: ADDISON TALIAFERRO,
W. ANTHONY RICHESON.
Book 10, Page 135 -- Same, June 17, 1839; bondsman: THOS. C. GOODWIN.
Book 10, Page 355 -- Same, June 21, 1841; bondsman: GEO. T. PLEASANTS.
Book 11, Page 152 -- Same, June 19, 1843; bondsmen: JAS. MC DANIEL,
A. TALIAFERRO.

PETER RUCKER (cont.) -- Book 15, Page 314 -- Inventory -- January 2, 1860--$28,155.27. CHAS. H. RUCKER; administrator: EDWIN M. WARE. Commissioners: with BLUFORD MORRIS, RO. H. THORNTON, RO. H. CARTER, MARTIN D. TINLSEY.
Book 15, Page 323 -- November 22, 1859; Monday, December 19, 1859. Witnesses: RO.H. THORNTON, MARTIN D. TINLSEY, BLUFORD MORRIS. CHAS. H. RUCKER qualified. Wife, JANE; grandson, AMBROSE R. HENDERSON--until 21; son, CHAS. H., to be his trustee and to eeucate him; my children: BRUNETTA J. TOLER, MARTHA E. HENDERSON, wife of RO. B. HENDERSON, ELIZ. P. MILLNER, wife of WM. L. MILLNER--if heirs; MARY L. (S) PRYOR, widow of JNO. PRYOR, JR., EDITH E. PRYOR, wife of JAMES PRYOR, SARAH A. RHOADS, wife of REUBEN RHOADS--if heirs. Executor: son, CHAS. H.--then sets forth sums advanced to children.
Book 15, Page 469 -- Sale -- January 3, 1860; various heirs above were buyers--$2769.69½.
Book 15, Page 472 -- Sale -- September 1, 1860; land--207½ acres to JAS. N. PRYOR; two adjacent tracts to W. H. BARNES et al.--219 acres; RO. B. HENDERSON tract at $1960.45. EDWIN M. WARE, clerk of sale.
Book 15, Page 496 -- Refunding Bond -- WM. L. MILLNER and W. M. B. TOLER, bondsman to CHAS. H. RUCKER--October 12, 1860. MILLNER has received legacy in right of wife, ELIZ. P.

POLLY RUCKER -- Book 14, Page 6 -- Administrators Bond -- RO. H. THORNTON, JNO. D. DAVIS, H. W. QUARLES, July 16, 1855, for RO. H. THORNTON.
Book 14, Page 282 -- Administrators Account -- From December 31, 1855; sum from GEO. W. BURFORD's administrator. Recorded: Monday, May 18, 1857.

REUBEN RUCKER -- Book 2, Page 36 -- Administrators Bond -- AMBROSE RUCKER, GEO. MC DANIEL, ISAAC RUCKER, ANTHONY RUCKER, March 4, 1788, for first two.
Book 2, Page 46 -- Inventory -- May 4, 1782: 1196-6-6. JNO. JONES, REUBEN HARRISON, RICH. HARRISON.

RICH. RUCKER -- Book 5, Page 696 -- Administrators Bond -- BENJ. and ARMISTEAD RUCKER, ALEX. MARR, October 20, 1819, for BENJ. RUCKER.
Book 6, Page 125 -- Inventory -- February 21, 1820: $3570.37. CHAS. WINGFIELD, RICH. BURKS, GEO. W. TAILOR.
Book 6, Page 255 -- Administrators Bond -- ALEX. MARR and THOS. ALDRIDGE, October 15, 1821, for ALEX. MARR.
Book 9, Page 236 -- Estate Commitment to Sheriff -- August 15, 1835; motion of ALEX. M. RUCKER, unadministrated by ALEX. MARR; Sheriff: THOS. N. EUBANK.
Book 11, Page -- not there; nor in book index.

SALLY RUCKER -- Book 10, Page 364 -- December 1, 1840; July 19, 1841. Witnesses: SAML. C. GIBSON, WM. B. RUCKER, WM. H. BARNES, JOS. R. CARTER. WM. B. RUCKER qualified. Two brothers, WM. B. and JAS. W. RUCKER; estate of deceased father, GEO. RUCKER; sister, SUSAN B. THOMPSON; friend, MARGARET EUBANK; brother, JONATHAN RUCKER; executor: brother, WM. B. RUCKER.
Book 11, Page 19 -- Inventory -- $2850.00, August 9, 1841. RO.H. CARTER, SAML. C. GIBSON, THOS. A. EUBANK.
Book 12, Page 219 -- Administrators Account -- from 1841--coffin--$5.00; shroud--$6.02; clothing--Sunday suit for negroes--$12.50; legacy of SUSAN B. TOMSON (sic); NELSON A. THOMSON, administrator of MARTHA RUCKER, deceased; legacy of MARGARET EUBANK; paid to ELIZ. RUCKER; legacies of JO. and J. W. RUCKER, MR. JONATHAN RUCKER--your portion of SARAH RUCKER's estate--portion of land money of GEO. RUCKER's estate as shown by J. N. RUCKER and N. A. THOMSON. Slave inventory and division to WM. B. and JAS. W. RUCKER. November 18, 1848. RO. H. CARTER, WINSTON C. MANTIPLY, CHAS. L. BROWN.

WILBUR (ER) F. RUCKER -- Book 17, Page 118 -- Guardians Account -- VALINTINE H. RUCKER from April 11, 1861; estate of HYLTON G. RUCKER-- one-half; to ward, WILBER F.; RUCKER versus RUCKER; account of A. B. RUCKER, SR.; STEPHEN's account, 1864; recorded: July 16, 1866.
Book 16, Page 165 -- error in Master index; it is Book 18, Page 165 --

WILBUR (ER) F. RUCKER (cont.) -- Guardians Bond -- HENRY E. SMITH
and EDGAR WHITEHEAD, March 19, 1872, for HENRY E. SMITH as guardian
of WILBER F. RUCKER, orphan of EDWIN S. RUCKER, deceased.

WM. B. RUCKER -- Book 16, Page 121 -- December 27, 1860; Witnesses:
JOS. R. CARTER, WM. H. BARNES, JAS. M. WATTS; codicil of December,
1860, same witnesses; codicil of December 24, 1861; Witnesses:
JAS. M. MILLNER, A. R. WOODROOF, JOS. R. CARTER; February 17, 1862.
May 19, 1862, D. H. and A. B. RUCKER qualified. Wife, MARY ANN D.--
mansion house tract; BROWN tract surveyed by JNO. PRYOR--353 acres
plus; son, ADDISON C., may cultivate portion; son, DANL. H.--where he
lives--352 acres; daughter, SUSAN M. SMITH and husband, HENRY E.
SMITH--slaves and land--also northern part of Academy tract next to
JAS. M. WATTS--about 120 acres. Son, WM. A.--western part of land
south of Academy tract--about 100 acres. Executor: friend,
A. B. RUCKER and my son, D. H. RUCKER; codicil: no bond required
for executors. Codicil: son, ADDISON, money for slave hire and
eastern part of Mansion house tract about 100 acres. Executors:
above; if ADDISON C. married; if wife married; School House border
line; turnpike road; RO. H. CARTER's line and Brown tract included.
Administrators Bond is Book 16, Page 124.
Book 16, Page 475 -- Slave division, November 11, 1862--to SUSAN M.
SMITH, ADDISON C. RUCKER, WM. A. RUCKER. Commissioners: D. B.
CHEATWOOD, WM. H. BARNES, GEO. HYLTON.
Book 16, Page 504 -- Administrators Account -- Amounts from and to
ADDISON C. RUCKER; A. B. and WM. A. RUCKER, HENRY E. SMITH; account
of N. D. RUCKER; appraisal of JOS. C. CLARK's estate by order of
court. August 8, 1862; Recorded: June 20, 1864.

WM. PARKS RUCKER -- Book 9, Page 434 -- Guardians Bond -- AMBROSE B.
RUCKER, EDWIN S., NATHAN D. RUCKER, May 21, 1838, for AMBROSE B. RUCKER
as guardian of WM. PARKS and JAS. STAPLES RUCKER, orphans of CLIFTON H.
RUCKER, deceased.
Book 13, Page 158 -- Guardians Account-- from October 12, 1838; bond
paid to N. D. RUCKER; tuition to MRS. TERRILL and SAM IRVINE; bond to
ELIZ. RUCKER; tuition to L. EMMERSON; BELL RUCKER and Company; order
of G. M. RUCKER. Recorded: December 13, 1852, and signed by WM. P.
RUCKER.

WILLIS RUCKER -- Book 5, Page 185 -- An incomplete bond as to condi-
tions, but guardian appears: W. R., REUBEN, ARMISTEAD and RICH. RUCKER,
October 19, 1812--and seemingly for W. R. as guardian of WILLIS RUCKER.
It is just above one for NANCY, RICH., ARMISTEAD, and REUBEN RUCKER,
same date, for NANCY RUCKER as guardian of JANE and SUSANNA RUCKER,
orphans of JNO. RUCKER, deceased.

TANDY RUTHERFORD -- Book 17, Page 231 -- December 21, 1865; June 17,
1867. Witnesses: CHAS. T. COLEMAN, J. H. DUNCAN, W. L. DUNCAN
(WESLEY L. in data as to proof). CORNL. TYREE qualified; bondsman:
JNO. W. WHITTEN and RO. A. COGHILL, July 15, 1867; WM. A. TYREE
qualified with same bondsman. My "neace," JANE HOWEL, and others
likewise identified with same spelling; MILDRED PROFFITT; ANN MITCHELL;
children of deceased niece, MARY BURLEY; cousin, CORNL. TYREE; cousin,
BETHANIA TYREE; cousin, HANNAH C. A. TYREE; SALLIE E. WHITTEN; ANNIE
LILLIAN TYREE--to be left in hands of BETHANIA TYREE--and HANNAH TYREE;
cousins: JACOB TYREE;--in hands of same women as above; tobacco to be
sold and divided to TYREE family; Executors: CORNL. and WM. A. TYREE.
Administrators Bond is Book 17, Page 240 for WM. A. TYREE. Note:
WM. A. TYREE was minister and founder of Amherst Baptist Church around
1880--records are lost, but we have an old letter framed and with
1884 date telling that church will soon be ready for use. He also
ran an academy for boys just west of the village. CORNL. was active
as Baptist minister in Rockbridge. Recorded: of Administrators
Account, Book 17, Page 375 on September 8, 1868. From January 21,
1868. Legacies to SAML. L. TYREE, MARY A. MC KINNEY, ANNA LILLAIN
TYREE or LELIA, JACOB, BETHANIA, HANNAH TYREE, C. A. TYREE, unpaid
legacies of JANE HOWL, MILDRED PROFFITT, ANN MITCHELL, children of
MARY BURLEY, deceased; BETHANIA TYREE, HANNAH C. A. TYREE, ANNA L. (S)
TYREE. Paid SALLIE WHITTEN, MOLLIE J. TYREE, CORNL. TYREE, W. A. TYREE.

TANDY RUTHERFORD (cont.) -- Book 17, Page 521 -- Administrators
Account -- from 1868. Legacies paid to JANE HOWL, GEO. W. MITCHELL
for S. A. MITCHELL, H. J. BEASLEY for daughter, ELLA G. BEASLEY,
MILDRED PROFFITT--THOS. WHITEHEAD, attorney; HANNAH A. C. TYREE;
BETHANIA TYREE. December, 1869.
Book 18, Page 24 -- Administrators Account -- from January 1, 1870.
JACOB TYREE, legatee; BETHANIA TYREE for ANNIE L. (S) TYREE; legacies
not paid to JANE HOWL, MILDRED PROFFITT, ANN MITCHELL, children of
MARY BURLEY, BETHANIA and HANNAH A. C. TYREE. September 29, 1870.
Book 19, Page 47 -- Administrators Account -- from -- debt duit of
E. P. TUCKER and GEO. W. HENLEY. WM. A. TYREE, legacy; ANN L. TYREE,
ANN MITCHELL's lapsed legacy. Names of legatees: BETHANIA, HANNAH
A. C., MARY A. MC KINNEY, MARY JANE TYREE, SALLIE E. WHITTEN, ANNIE L.
TYREE, SAML. L. TYREE; August 16, 1875.

JNO. RYAN -- Book 2, Page 257 -- Administrators Bond -- WM. BIBB,
CALEB HIGGINBOTHAM, JNO. STAPLES, December 5, 1785, for WM. BIBB.

MARY E. S. RYAN -- Book 17, Page 469 -- indexed as 467 -- Trustees
account of ALBERT C. HARRISON, for her and children from January 1,
1858. PAULUS POWELL, administrator to CASH--payment on purchase of
Powellton Hotel property--20 acres. Sold to TALIAFERRO THOMPSON.
Recorded: June 21, 1869.

-S-

CORNL. SALE -- Book B, Page 58 -- April 17, 1855; August 22, 1856.
Witnesses: JNO. THOMPSON, JR. and DABNEY SANDIDGE. Nephew, LEWIS S.
CAMPBELL; to be trustee for PERMELIA FLOYD and children now or later
born--where she and her husband now live--100 acres; husband is SAML.
FLOYD--joins where I now live and bought from THOS. GOODRICH and wife.
L. S. CAMPBELL gets my land--qualified estate under my father's will.
Many slaves are named and wants them to get good treatment since they
helped me get my estate. Executor: LEWIS S. CAMPBELL.

FRANCIS SALE -- Book 9, Page 289 -- Estate Commitment to Sheriff --
March, 1837; motion of THOMAS GOODRICH--initial hard to decipher--O
or C?; JNO. COLEMAN, Sheriff.

JNO. SALE -- Book 5, Page 500 -- August 7, 1809; May 15, 1815.
Witnesses: BARNETT CASH, SAML. CASH, JAS. HIX. Wife, FRANCES;
daughter, MOLLY SALE who married CHAS. HOUCHIN and heirs. Executors
to save enough for visit to western country where she lives, if
necessary. Note: SWEENY treats a HOUCHIN from Amherst who discovered
Mammouth Cave in Kentucky. My other nine children: THOS., JNO.,
NANCY--wife of THOS. GOODRICH, CORNL., SAML., ELIS. M. who married
WILEY CAMPBELL, ALEX., ROBT., and MARTHEY SALE. If any dies without
issue. Executors: sons, THOS., CORNL. and SAML. SALE.
Book 5, Page 501 -- Administrators Bond -- THOS. and CORNL. made
bond; bondsmen: EDMD. WINSTON, BENJ. TALIAFERRO.
Book 6, Page 16 -- Inventory -- JNO. SMITH, EDMD. T. COLEMAN, ABSALOM
HIGGINBOTHAM--several totals, July 20, 1818. Executors as above.

NELSON SALE -- Book 16, Page 36 -- Administrators Bond -- LINDSEY
DAVIS and RO. W. SNEAD, February 18, 1861, for LINDSEY DAVIS.

PHOEBA SALE -- Book 5, Page 85 -- Guardians Bond -- JESSE JONES, RO.
RIVES, and CHAS. TALIAFERRO, October 21, 1811, for JESSE JONES as
guardian of PHOEBA SALE, orphan of JNO. SALE, deceased.

THOS. SALE -- Book 3, Page 289 -- so indexed, but nothing on him.
Book 3, Page 496 -- July 1, 1797; June 18, 1798 (blurred). Witnesses:
CHAS. TALIAFERRO, JNO. SALE. My wife, CLARY; daughters PEGGY ALSUP
and heirs; FRANCES SALE and heirs, but, if none, to daughters, BETSY
and POLLEY SALE. Grandsons, JAS. and REUBIN SALE and granddaughter,
BETSY SALE. Sons, JNO., THOS., WM., BENJ. and ANTHONY SALE. Proof
by CORNL. and SAML. SALE on February 18, 1799. WM. SALE qualified on
this date. Bondsmen: ROD. TALIAFERRO and WM. CLARKSON.

THOS. SALE (cont.) -- Book 3, Page 571 -- Inventory -- L1028-14 on
May 14, 1799. JNO. DUNCAN, JNO. SMITH, JNO. TALIAFERRO.

JAS. SALES -- Book 5, Page 567 -- Inventory -- $59.42, November 28,
1815. JNO. CRAWFORD, JNO. EUBANK, THOS. N. EUBANK. Recorded:
March 18, 1816.

THOS. SALES -- Book 6, Page 50 -- Guardians Bond -- HENRY LAINE and
THOS. N. EUBANK, December 21, 1818, for HENRY LAINE as guardian of
THOS. SALE, orphan of JNO. SALE. Note: s is put on in index, but
SALE used in data.

JANETTA C. SAMPSON -- Book 11, Page 253 -- Administrators Bond --
GEO. CARR, CHAS. T. COLEMAN, WINSTON MANTIPLY and JNO. E. SAMPSON,
December 16, 1844, for CARR.

JNO. P. SAMPSON -- Book 11, Page 68 -- Administrators Bond -- JNO. E.
SAMPSON, JANETTA SAMPSON, LINDSEY COLEMAN, EDMUND C. MOORE and
WARNER JONES, May 16, 1842, for first two to administrate.
Book 11, Page 91 -- Inventory -- August 29, 1842--$13,057.52--conveyed
by Deed of Trust by late JNO. P. SAMPSON to JNO. E. and JOS. T. SAMPSON
for benefit of JANETTA SAMPSON--JANETTA and JNO. E. SAMPSON, executors,
August 29, 1842. JNOA A. STOUT, V. MC GINNIS, DABNEY GOOCH, JNO.
WHITEHEAD.

SUSAN SAMPSON -- Book 11, Page 248 -- Guardians Bond -- JNO. ED.
SAMPSON, October 21, 1844, for JNO. ED. SAMPSON as guardian of SUSAN
SAMPSON, orphan of JNO. P. SAMPSON, deceased.

AMANDA P. SANDIDGE -- Book 14, Page 484 -- Guardians Bond -- S. B.
SANDIDGE and PAULUS E. SANDIDGE and JNO. W. MYERS, December 21, 1857,
for S. B. SANDIDGE as guardian of AMANDA P. SANDIDGE, orphan of
ANDERSON SANDIDGE.

AMMON SANDIDGE -- Book 15, Page 288 -- Guardians Bond -- HENRY E.
SMITH and JAS. P. COLEMAN, April 16, 1860, for HENRY E. SMITH as
guardian of AMMON SANDIDGE, orphan of ANDERSON SANDIDGE.

ANDERSON SANDIDGE -- Book 15, Page 251-2 -- pages so numbered --
Administrators Bond -- H. E. SMITH and WILLIS WHITE, November 21,
1859, for H. E. SMITH.

BELINDA SANDIDGE -- Book 16, Page 88 -- Administrators Account -- by
CHRISTOPHER C. and JNO. S. SANDIDGE, executors of DUDLEY SANDIDGE;
BELINDA is widow and she has delivered all property left her by
husband to execuotrs--slaves; crops etc. February 9, 1861.
Book 20, Page 445 -- May 16, 1865; June 18, 1883. Witnesses: HENRY
LOVING and SIMS BROCKMAN. Proved by HENRY LOVING, SR. and BROCKMAN's
handwriting proved by LOVING and J. W. HENLEY. Son, RICH. P. is to
administrate--all to him.
Book 20, Page 456 -- Administrators Bond -- RICH. P. SANDIDGE, July 16,
1883. Bondsman: W. B. HENLEY and WM. SANDIDGE. An earlier BELINDA
SANDIDGE shows Book 14, Page 566, Administrators Bond, EDWIN M. WARE
and J. P. MC DANIEL, May 17, 1858, for WARE.

BENJ. SANDIDGE -- Book 6, Page 146 -- Ordinary bond at home in county,
June 19, 1820. Bondsman: CORNL. SALE, GEO. W. HIGGINBOTHAM, CHAS.
TUCKER, ABSALOM HIGGINBOTHAM, WILLIS WHITE, ZACH DRUMMOND, ABSALOM
HIGGINBOTHAM, WILLIS WHITE, ZACH DRUMMOND, ABSALOM HIGGINBOTHAM,
November 16, 1829, for WHITE and ABSALOM HIGGINBOTHAM to administrate
estate--Book 7, Page 280.
Book 7, Page 307 -- Inventory -- $5213.46 CHAS. L. BARRET, CORNL.
SALE, DABNEY SANDIDGE.
Book 8, Page 1 -- Division and plat -- both sides Buffaloe and each
side of road from Buffaloe Springs to White Gap; adjoins THOS. GOODWIN,
J. D. TURPIN, WM. DEMPSEY, WM. TURNER, JNO. FLOOD, R. S. ELLIS,
LINDSEY BURKS, JNO. MORGAN, AARON HIGGINBOTHAM, LINDSEY DANDIDGE,
AMBR. TOMLINSON's heirs, Z. DRUMMOND, WM. LONG, JOS. DODD's heirs,

BENJ. SANDIDGE (cont.) -- JAMES GOVAN, JACOB PHILLIPS--1745 acres. To
MRS. ELIZ. SANDIDGE, widow--mansion house; BOB's tract to MRS. B. A.
MAHALA HUNT, wife of JNO. T. HUNT; Fork tract to ANDERSON SANDIDGE;
Tungate tract to MRS. POLLY HIGGINBOTHAM, wife of ABSALOM HIGGINBOTHAM;
Mill tract to LINDSEY SANDIDGE; Luck Mt. tract to MRS. NANCY BOURNE;
KIDD's tract to MRS. BETSY HIGGINBOTHAM, wife of AARON HIGGINBOTHAM;
Long Mt. tract to MRS. TABITHA WHITE, wife of WILLIS WHITE.   JNO.
PRYOR, surveyor.   CHAS. L. BARRET, DABNEY SANDIDGE, JNO. M. MORGAN,
commissioners.   June 21, 1830.
Book 8, Page 150 -- Administrators Account -- WILLIS WHITE from
1829--covenant of DABNEY SANDIDGE; rent of mill; account of RO.
SANDIDGE, JOSHUA SANDIDGE, debt of AARON HIGGINBOTHAM--$448.91.
CHA.S L. BARRET, commissioner.   November 23, 1831.
Book 8, Page 159 -- slave division to MRS. NANCY BOURNE, formerly
SANDIDGE; ELIZ. SANDIDGE, widow; JNO. T. HUNT who married MAHALA
SANDIDGE, daughter of BENJ.; ABSALOM HIGGINBOTHAM who married POLLY
SANDIDGE, daughter of BENJ.; ANDERSON SANDIDGE; WILLIS WHITE who
married TABITHA SANDIDGE, daughter of BENJ.; LINDSEY SANDIDGE; AARON
HIGGINBOTHAM who married ELIZ., daughter of BENJ.   Recorded: December 5,
1830.   CHAS. L. BARRET, JNO. MORGAN, CORNL. SALE.
Book 9, Page 185 -- Administrators Account -- ABSALOM HIGGINBOTHAM
from October 1, 1830; bonds of NANCY BOURNE, ANDERSON SANDIDGE, CLARY
SANDIDGE, wife of LINDSEY SANDIDGE, LINDSEY SANDIDGE, AARON HIGGINBOTHAM,
legacy to NANCY BOURNE; trip to Buckingham by WM. B. C. RUCKER; CORNL.
SALE as execuotr of JNO. MORGAN; mention of suit of WM. COLEMAN.
Legatees: ANDERSON SANDIDGE, NANCY BOURNE, AARON HIGGINBOTHAM, LINDSEY
SANDIDGE, ABSALOM HIGGINBOTHAM, WILLIS WHITE, administrator, and
JNO. T. HUNT.   July 17, 1835.   JNO. PRYOR, commissioner, and legatee.
Book 12, Page 77 -- Administrators Account -- by WILLIS WHITE from
June 30, 1845.   MRS. SANDIDGE, ANDERSON SANDIDGE, overseer; mention
of DABNEY, LINDSEY, and BENJ. SANDIDGE; deed to SAUNDERS.   Recorded:
December 18, 1848.

CHRISTOPHER C. SANDIDGE -- indexed for CHAS. F. -- Book 10, Page 334 --
Guardians Bond -- DUDLEY and DABNEY SANDIDGE, March 16, 1841, for
DUDLEY as guardian of CHRISTOPHER C. SANDIDGE--no parent set forth.
Book 17, Page 168 -- Administrators Bond -- SUSAN C. SANDIDGE and
J. M. WOODSON, August 20, 1866, for SUSAN.
Book 17, Page 225 -- Administrators Bond -- JAS. D. MARTIN and JACOB M.
WOODSON, May 20, 1867, for JAS. D. MARTIN.
Book 17, Page 233 -- Inventory -- May 30, 1867: $249.25.   HENRY
LOVING, THOS. D. COLEMAN, M. C. GOODWIN.
Book 17, Page 234 -- Sale: $263.50 MARTIN was sole buyer.   Recorded:
June 17, 1867.
Book 17, Page 530 -- Sale and Inventory -- with same total: and
Administrators Account by MARTIN, 1 July 1869.   Recorded: September,
1869.
Book 19, Page 146 -- Administrators Account -- by JAS. D. MARTIN,
administrator de bonis non, from July 1, 1869.   Debt due R. P. SANDIDGE.
Recorded February 22, 1876.
Book 19, Page 351 -- Administrators Account -- by MARTIN; recorded
July 17, 1878.   To widow and children, but no names set forth.

DUDLEY SANDIDGE -- Book 4, Page 583 -- Constables Bond -- February 20,
1809.   Bondsmen: WM. CAMDEN and JNO. SMITH.
Book 10, Page 335 -- Guardians Bond -- DUDLEY and DABNEY SANDIDGE,
March 16, 1841, for DUDLEY as guardian of his children: MARY E. and
ELIZ. M. SANDIDGE.
Book 15, Page 512 -- August 19, 1856; codicil of November 21, 1859;
January 21, 1861.   Witnesses to will: C. H. MASSIE and SIMS BROCKMAN;
to codicil: HENRY LOVING and BROCKMAN.   CHRISTOPHER C. and JNO. S.
SANDIDGE qualified.   Bondsmen: SAML. M. GARLAND, HENRY LOVING, THOS.
WHITEHEAD, RO. A. PENDLETON, J. F. SMITH, J. M. WOODSON.   Wife,
BELINDA--where I live; Long Mt. tract; my children: ANN SANDIDGE and
CHRISTOPHER C. SANDIDGE; execuotrs: sons, CHRISTOPHER C. and JNO. S.
SANDIDGE.
Book 16, Page 37 -- Inventory -- January 25, 1861; no total; HENRY
LOVING, T. B. ROYSTER, M. C. GOODWIN.

DUDLEY SANDIDGE (cont.) -- Book 16, Page 38 -- Agreement by heirs to
divide slaves. To CHRISTOPHER C., V. F. SANDIDGE, J. M. and ELIZ.
WOODSON, D. S. and ISABELLA M. WOODSON, E. P. and ROBT. M. JEFFRIES,
JNO. S., R. P. and W. D. SANDIDGE, SALLIE F. and EDWD. P. EVANS,
BELINDA SANDIDGE as trustee of ANN SANDIDGE; to E. P. JEFFRIES and wife;
WM. D. SANDIDGE, JNO. S. SANDIDGE, JACOB M. WOODSON and wife, EDWD. P.
EVANS and wife, V. F. SANDIDGE, DAVID WOODWON and wife, RICH. P.
SANDIDGE. In one place it is F. F. instead of V. F. Approved by
BELINDA SANDIDGE as trustee of CHRISTOPHER SANDIDGE. Signed by ENOCH P.
JEFFRIES. BELINDA as widow of DUDLEY SANDIDGE, REGINA M. JEFFRIES,
SALLIE F. EVANS.
Book 16, Page 88 -- Sale by C. C. and JNO. S. SANDIDGE as executors,
February 15, 1861; no total.
Book 16, Page 394 -- Administrators Account -- by execuotrs, February 1,
1861. To WM. D. SANDIDGE for coffin; Long Mt. tract. Recorded:
September 21, 1863. Note: WM. D. died in Confederate service,
December, 1861.
Book 17, Page 154 -- Administrators Account -- by same executors
from August 19, 1863. Amounts to B. and V. F. SANDIDGE, D. S.
WOODSON, B. DANDIDGE, trustee. Legatees: RICH. P., CHRISTOPHER C.,
J. M. WOODSON, JNO. S. SANDIDGE, E. P. EVANS, E. P. JEFFRIES; unable
to pay debts because there is no confidence in Confederate money.
Recorded August 20, 1866.
Book 18, Page 218 -- Administrators Account -- by JNO. S. SANDIDGE
from January 21, 1866; recorded August 19, 1872.
Book 18, Page 497 -- Administrators Account -- by same executor from
April 1, 1873; recorded June 17, 1873.
Book 20, Page 141 -- Administrators Account -- by same executor
from April 1, 1873; recorded June 17, 1873.
Book 20, Page 141 -- Administrators Account -- by same executor from
April 15, 1873; recorded March 15, 1880.
Book 20, Page 497 -- Inventory -- August 3, 1883: $21.20; R. SIMS,
BROCKMAN, ALBERT GANNAWAY, THOS. B. ROYSTER. Sale, August 3, 1883;
family buyers: JNO. S., MRS. S. (L) SANDIDGE, R. P. SANDIDGE.
Book 21, Page 4 -- Mansion house tract to widow for life; sold by
JNO. S. SANDIDGE, executor to TAYLOR BERRY, August 3, 1883--44½ acres.

ELIZ. SANDIDGE -- Book 11, Page 315 -- Administrators Bond -- WILLIS
WHITE and ABSALOM HIGGINBOTHAM, June 15, 1845, for WILLIS WHITE.
Book 11, Page 350 -- Sale by administrator, August 22, 1845; family
buyers--LINDSEY SANDIDGE, ANDERSON SANDIDGE; no total. Recorded
November 17, 1845.
Book 11, Page 353 -- Inventory -- June 20, 1845: $260.90; CORNL.
SALE, JNO. H. FUQUA, PATRICK DRUMMOND.

JNO. SANDIDGE -- Book 4, Page 78 -- December 6, 1796; February 21,
1803. Witnesses: BENJ. COLEMAN, JOS. MAGANN, JR., SAML. RUSSELL,
MOSES HALL. WM. and WALLER SANDIDGE qualified. Bondsmen: PULLIAM
SANDIDGE, PETER CARTER, WALKER ATKINSON, BENJ. SANDIDGE, TOS. MORRISON.
Daughters: MARY, RACHEL and AMY SANDIDGE; son, WALLER--land bought
from JNO. ROBERTS--180 acres and Luck Mt. tract; land bought from
NELSON CRAWFORD and Blanston Mt. survey. Children: WM., PULLIAM,
DOLLY HIGGINBOTHAM, MARY SANDIDGE, ANN HIGGINBOTHAM, LARKIN SANDIDGE,
BENJ. SANDIDGE, BETSY CARTER, ANNIS CHILDRESS, DELPHIA CARTER, RACHEL
SANDIDGE, AMY SANDIDGE, WALLER SANDIDGE--if any without issue.
Daughter, ANN HIGGINBOTHAM and children: DOLLY, FANNY, AGEY, WARNER,
BETSY and ANN HIGGINBOTHAM when of age. Daughter, DELPHIA CARTER,
deceased--her children or child: LARKIN GATEWOOD CARTER; daughter,
RACHEL SANDIDGE, when of age. Executors: sons, WM., LARKIN, and
WALLER SANDIDGE.
Book 4, Page 112 -- Inventory -- L1305-7-6, June 20, 1803. HENRY
BALLINGER, JOS. and BENJ. HIGGINBOTHAM.
Book 4, Page 343 -- Administrators Bond -- see will.
Book 5, Page 21 -- Administrators Account -- by executors from
October 29, 1803. To WM. HIGGINBOTHAM; son, BENJ.; legacy; JESSE
CHILDRESS; LARKIN SANDIDGE; G son of JOS. (sic); WM. SANDIDGE;
WARNER HIGGINBOTHAM; WALLER SANDIDGE; CHANDLER BOURNE; PULLIAM
SANDIDGE's heirs; THOS. MORRISON; BETSY HIGGINBOTHAM and BETSY SCHOL-
FIELD to use of estate; WM. HIGGINBOTHAM; P. S. and T. M. (sic).

JNO. SANDIDGE (cont.) -- Recorded June Court: NELSON CRAWFORD, BENJ.
TALIAFERRO, WM. WARE.

JNO. S. SANDIDGE -- Book 18, Page 210 -- Road commissioner in Temperance, June 19, 1872. Bondsman: THOS. WHITEHEAD.

LINDSEY SANDIDGE -- Book 17, Page 88 -- Administrators Bond -- HENRY E.
SMITH, ARTHUR WHITE, M. B. SANDIDGE, March 19, 1866, for HENRY E.
SMITH.
Book 17, Page 435 -- Trustee account of BENJ. J. RUCKER from November 29,
1855; distributees: B. J. RUCKER and wife, ELIZ; M. B. SANDIDGE;
ARTHUR WHITE and wife; N. B. SANDIDGE; T. H. RUCKER and wife, NANCY C. H.
RUCKER. Recorded: June 21, 1869.

MARY E. SANDIDGE -- Book 10, Page 335 -- Guardians Bond -- DUDLEY and
DABNEY SANDIDGE, March 16, 1841, for DUDLEY as guardian of MARY E.
and ELIZ. M. SANDIDGE--his children.

PULLIAM SANDIDGE -- Book B, Page 82 -- Estate Commitment to Sheriff --
August 21, 1859. Motion of ARTHUR F. ROBERTSON, administrator de bonis
non of ARCHIBALD ROBERTSON; M. C. GOODWIN, Sheriff.

SARAH T. SANDIDGE -- Book 10, Page 335 -- Guardians Bond -- DABNEY
SANDIDGE, RICH. CRAWFORD, JOEL SMITH, March 15, 1841, for DABNEY
SANDIDGE as guardian of his children: SARAH T. and WM. SANDIDGE.

WM. SANDIDGE -- Book 8, Page 22 -- June 26, 1830; September 20, 1830.
Witnesses: AARON H. MORRISON, JAS. F. TALIAFERRO, RICH. SMITH, JR.,
DABNEY HILL, MARBELL C. GOODWIN, BARNETT CASH, SAML. W. CHRISTIAN.
Son, DUDLEY--land formerly owned by EDMD. POWELL; sold by EDMD. POWELL
to JACOB SMITH and by him to me--by his executors. Son, DABNEY--my
blacksmith tools; my wife, TAMSEY; my daughter, OLIVE, deceased, who
married AMBR. MC DANIEL--her heirs get tract where AMBR. MC DANIEL
lives--known as Cotterel tract; I bought it from JAS. SHIELDS, ELIJAH
BROCKMAN and MOSES MARTIN. Slaves to OLIVE's children. DUDLEY and
DABNEY to be trustees of BYBIE tract of 200 acres bought from JNO.
MATTHEWS and to be used for my daughter, TAMSEY MOUNTCASTLE, and
children--and future ones. Granddaughter, LUCINDA MC DANIEL; grand-
daughter, TAMSEY MC DANIEL; granddaughter, SOPHIA MOUNTCASTLE.
Grandchildren: KEZIAH MOUNTCASTLE, REGINA MARIA, daughter of DUDLEY,
CHRISTOPHER COLUMBUS SANDIDGE, SARAH TAMSEY, daughter of DABNEY.
Executors: BENJ. TALIAFERRO, and my sons, DUDLEY and DABNEY SANDIDGE.
Book 8, Page 44 -- Administrators Bond -- Both sons qualified,
September 20, 1830. Bondsmen: CORNL. SALE and ZACH. DRUMMOND.
Book 12, Page 241 -- Administrators Account -- by both, December 30,
1830. Receipt from AMBR. R. MC DANIEL for his minor children by late
OLIVE MC DANIEL; LUCINDA R. MC DANIEL as heir, January 3, 1831.
Receipt of WM. H. MC DANIEL as heir, October 27, 1837; receipt of
JNO. HAYSLITT as guardian of TAMSEY MC DANIEL, now HAYSLITT, for
legacy after death of TAMSEY SANDIDGE, widow of WM. SANDIDGE. Receipt
of JNO. S. MC DANIEL as heir; also of DABNEY MC DANIEL, as heir,
October 27, 1837. These MC DANIEL and HAYSLITT items were witnessed
by JNO. B. DUNCAN. March 22, 1849, JNO. G. ROGERS, Glasgow, Kentucky,
witnesses for GIDEON MC DANIEL as child of AMBR. R. and OLIVE MC DANIEL.
He names CAPT. BENJ. TALIAFERRO and DUDLEY and DABNEY SANDIDGE as
executors. Receipt of May 15, 1849, by JNO. W. CASH who married
REBECCA MOUNTCASTLE, heir; receipt of RO. H. OGDEN, December 18, 1847--
part of bond by WM. TUCKER for land bought from estate as heir of
OLIVE MC DANIEL. JNO. S. MC DANIEL as heir of OLIVE MC DANIEL; JNO
HYASLITT as heir of OLIVE MC DANIEL. DUDLEY SANDIDGE for self and
children; receipt of AMBR. R. MC DANIEL, October, 1837, as guardian
of DABNEY H., LINDSEY D., GEO. and GIDEON MC DANIEL for land sold to
WM. TUCKER. Recorded: October 16, 1849.
Book 15, Page 163 -- January 18, 1858, motion of MRS. TAMSEY MOUNT-
CASTLE; SAML. G. CASH and wife, SOPHIA; JNO. W. CASH and wife,
REBECCA--consent of DUDLEY and DABNEY SANDIDGE, trustees of TAMSEY
MOUNTCASTLE, for a division of her slaves by R. W. SNEAD; J. A.
HIGGINBOTHAM; J. W. BROADDUS; B. T. HENLEY; and A. TALIAFERRO into
three parts to CASH heirs and her under will of WM. SANDIDGE.

WM. SANDIDGE (cont.) -- Book 18, Page 41 -- Notary Public -- February 20, 1871; Bondsman: HENLEY DRUMMOND.
Book 18, Page 83 -- Supervisor -- June 19, 1871. Bondsman: HENRY LOVING.
Book 18, Page 205 -- Supervisor -- TEMPERANCE SITT., June 17, 1872; Bondsman: HENLEY DRUMMOND.
Book 18, Page 341 -- Same, June 16, 1873.
Book 18, Page 432 -- Same, June 29, 1874; Bondsman: WM. KENT.
Book 19, Page 263 -- Same, June 29, 1877; Bondsman: JAS. M. MILLNER.
MRS. T. K. ROBERTS, daughter of late DR. ED. SANDIDGE, has a very valuable old paper in her possession: "This is to certify that WM. SANDIDGE, Soldier in CAPT. JAS. PAMPLIN's company of militia from the County of Amherst hath faithfully served his tower (sic) of duty and is hereby discharged. August 10, 1781. JAS. PAMPLIN, Captain." This was found in old family papers.

ROBT. SANGSTER -- Book 10, Page 167 -- August 27, 1839; November 18, 1839. Witnesses: WARNER JONES, WM. H. KNIGHT, WM. M. WALLER. SARAH SANGSTER qualified. Wife, SARAH; my children: JANE, MARGARET, ADELINE, MARTHA (MARIA) and SARAH. My daughter, MARY ANN, by first marriage. Book 10, Page 171 -- so indexed, but not here.

JNO. SAVAGE -- Book 8, Page 276 -- September 15, 1832; October 15, 1832. Witnesses: LA FAYETTE TIBBETTS, PLEASANT T. MALLORY, PATRICK H. GARLAND. Wife, ELIZ., to administrate.

ELIZ. SCHOFIELD -- Book 7, Page 8 -- This is poorly written and appears to be SMITHFIELD, but on page 9 it is as indexed. She is dead and served as administratrix of WM. SCOFIELD. Her administrator is ABRAM CARTER. Returned: June 19, 1827. CHAS. L. BARRET, WM. COLEMAN, NELSON CRAWFORD. WM. MITCHELL, step-son, and heir by will of WM. SCOFIELD--100 acres sold.

WM. SCHOFIELD -- Book 3, Page 191 -- November 8, 1790; July 4, 1791. Witnesses: MOSES HALL, MARY HALL, WM. HIGGINBOTHAM. Wife, BETTY; grandchildren and step-son, WM. MITCHELL. Executors: wife and JNO. SANDIDGE. BETTY qualified on probate date. Bondsmen: WM. MITCHELL and NELSON CRAWFORD.
Book 3, Page 212 -- Inventory -- no total; September 29, 1791. SAML. HIGGINBOTHAM, JNO. SANDIDGE, MOSES HALL.
Book 4, Page 16 -- Administrators Account -- from 1801 JOSIAH ELLIS, Sheriff. Returned: July 20, 1801. DANL. WARWICK and MARTIN PARKS.
Book 6, Page 109 -- Administrators Bond -- ABRAM CARTER; August 19, 1817; Bondsman: JNO. CRAWFORD. Formerly administered by BETTY SCHOFIELD, deceased.

ALEX. SCOTT -- Book 12, Page 476 -- Administrators Bond -- GEO. W. STAPLES and NELSON HICKS, February 17, 1851, for GEO. W. STAPLES.

EDWD. SCOTT (W initial) -- Book 17, Page 454 -- Guardians Bond -- RO. G. SCOTT and GEO. H. DAMERON, February 15, 1849, for RO. G. SCOTT as guardian of EDWD. W. SCOTT, over 14.

GEO. W. SCOTT -- Book 4, Page 515 -- Guardians Bond -- ISAAC SCOTT, JNO. COLEMAN, JACOB SCOTT, and WM. EVANS, May 16, 1808, for ISAAC SCOTT as guardian of his son, GEO. W. SCOTT.

ISAAC SCOTT -- Book 10, Page 260 -- June 13, 1840; July 20, 1840. Witnesses: WM. M. WALLER, CHAS. TUCKER, ANSEL MAYS. WIATT LONDON objected, but withdrew them on September 21, 1840. Wife, MARTHA; my eight children; daughter, MARTHA, gets one-fourth and rest to GEO.; RUTHA, wife of FLEMING SCOTT; ELIZ. MAYS; CATH. CARPENTER; MAHALA LONDON; SAML. D. and JNO. W. SCOTT. Bond of GEO. to D. and D. HIGGINBOTHAM. Executors: friends, CHAS. TUCKER and WM. M. WALLER.
Book 10, Page 279 -- WIATT LONDON, JNO. SCOTT, AUSTIN CARPENTER, JOEL MAYS, October 19, 1840, for WIATT LONDON.

JACOB SCOTT -- Book B, Page 17 -- Estate Commitment to Sheriff -- Friday, March 26, 1841; motion of NANCY HOLLOWAY. NELSON CRAWFORD, Sheriff.

SAML. SCOTT -- Book 4, Page 66 -- November 30, 1802; January 17, 1803. Witnesses: JACOB SCOTT, EZEK. GILBERT, ALEX. PENN. JOS. COWEN qualified. Bondsman: DAVID S. GARLAND. At my death, MRS. NANCY SHIELDS, to write to JOS. COWEN, Staunton--goods here and at Staunton. My mother and sisters in Ireland. COWEN is to administrate. Administrators Bond is page 362.

BENJ. E. SCRUGGS -- Book 12, Page 490 -- Order of August, 1851, to divide slaves owned by BENJ. E. SCRUGGS and MARTAH R. GILBERT as guardian of her daughters: ANN W. and MARTHA R. GILBERT, JR. Returned November 20, 1851; JNO. PRYOR, RO. H. CARTER, JOS. R. CARTER. Formerly those of F. W. GILBERT and -- GILBERT.

JNO. P. SCRUGGS -- Book 9, Page 60 -- Administrators Bond -- BENJ. P. WALKER and JOS. K. IRVING, March 17, 1845, for BENJ. P. WALKER. Book 9, Page 68 -- Inventory -- $52.36; ISAAC W. WALKER, JNO. DILLARD, CHAS. M. CHRISTIAN, April 3, 1835.

SUSANNAH SCRUGGS -- Book 3, Page 523 -- March 6, 1798; October 15, 1798. Witnesses: JNO. ROBERTSON, JNO. CA. SCRUGGS, MARTHA TOWNSEND. Grandson, SAML. SCOTT SCRUGG, to administrate and no bond required.

ELIZ. E. SEAY (nee JONES or JONE) -- Book B, Page 72 -- August 21, 1857; March 29, 1859. Witnesses: JNO. THOMPSON, JR., JOS. C. SMOOT, S. J. WIATT. THOMPSON refused to serve as administrator. Maiden name was ELIZ. E. JONES or JONE (?) and marriage contract in Fluvanna, September 17, 1839, and recorded in Amherst County. Slaves; my trustees, HUDSON and NOEL, assistants in contract; slaves to be freed; one in possession of DR. TWYMAN as security of husband's debts, but can be redeemed. Executor: JNO. THOMPSON, JR. Administrators Bond on same page for RO. M. BROWN; bondsman: JNO. THOMPSON, JR.
Book B, Page 92 -- Administrators Account -- by BROWN from March 29, 1859; slaves hired; Confederate tax. Recorded: August, 1866.
Book B, Page 84 -- Inventory -- Six slaves; no total; from $1000 to $250 in value. A. C. HARRISON, SAML. H. HENRY, WM. E. COLEMAN, 18 April 1859.

JNO. SEAY -- Book 10, Page 350 -- MARY G. SEAY, HARRIET R. PENDLETON, WM. G. PENDLETON, May 17, 1841, for MARY G. SEAY.
Book 10, Page 400 -- Inventory -- $922.50 WM. PETTYJOHN, NATHAN GUTHRIE, JNO. D. WILLS, July 7, 1841.
Book 11, Page 148 -- Administrators Account -- from October 16, 1841 burial by Duiguid--$20.00; paid November 18, 1841. DANL. DAY, WM. PETTYJOHN, September 23, 1842.
Book 11, Page 587 -- Administrators Account -- Administrator is now MRS. MARY G. NOWELL--seems to be NOEL and NORVEL. December 20, 1847. WM. PETTYJOHN and RO. RIDGWAY.

REUBEN SEAY -- Book 2, Page 221 -- Administrators Bond -- KEZIAH HANSBROUGH and JNO. LOVING, March 7, 1785, for KEZIAH HANSBROUGH.

VINCENT T. SETTLES -- Book 14, Page 82 -- Minister's bond; no denomination. September 17, 1853; Bondsman: RO. A. COGHILL and SAML. M. GARLAND. I happen to know that he was a Baptist.

FANNIE H. SHACKLEFORD -- Book 14, Page 588 -- FANNIE H. SHACKLEFORD and GEO. H. LAMBETH to JNO. W. SCHOOLFIELD, executor of MRS. FRANCES B. SHACKLEFORD--FANNIE has received $2000 by will of decedent. November 20, 1857.

MRS. FRANCES B. SHACKLEFORD -- Book 13, Page 448 -- July 24, 1852; Monday, February 19, 1855. Witnesses: CHAS. WINGFIELD, JNO. L. GOODWIN, EDWD. J. GOODWIN. Contested by ELIZA G. LAMBETH; GARLAND POINDEXTER and wife, JULIA ANN; HENRY H. MEREDITH and wife, MARY; W. G. H. BINGHAM. Consent to continue; JNO. W. SCHOOLFIELD qualified. Bondsman: HENRY H., BENJ. H. and A. C. LEWIS, 19 March 1855, administrator again produced will; proved by witnesses and admitted. Two bonds made by curator and as executor. Land where I live to be sold. Niece, FANNY SHACKLEFORD, lives with me; to JAS. T. BOYD of Kink (sic) and Quenn

MRS. FRANCES B. SHACKLEFORD (cont.) -- County; money for education of
STEPHEN POINDEXTER, son of GARLAND POINDEXTER; kind friends and
neighbors, ELIZ. and HARRIET RIDGWAY; friend, ANN QUARLES; cousin,
ELIZ. G. LAMBETH and son, JNO.; slave in hands of my cousin, MARY
MEREDITH, and her daughter, FANNY BOYED MEREDITH; ten slaves to be
freed, and, if possible, sent to Liberia on Coast of Africa; if they
consent--or to a free state. My cousin, NANCY GAINS, King and Queen
County; Methodist Episcopal Church South--for missions; executor:
friend, JNO. W. SCHOOLFIELD of Smythe County and CHISWELL DABNEY,
Lynchburg. Bonds are on page 451.
Book 13, Page 456 -- Sale -- March 7, 1855; long list; $1909.69.
N. H. and A. C. LEWIS were witnesses to sale.
Book 13, Page 462 -- Inventory -- $3674.80; recorded March 19, 1855.
Book 14, Page 36 -- Slave Inventory -- 51 by number and names; no
total; ages and sex. September 17, 1855.
Book 14, Page 52 -- Land Inventory -- $6500; March 19, 1855; CHAS. H.
RUCKER, WM. KENT, CHAS. WINGFIELD; land sold--page 53--548 acres bought
by JAS. MC GEE. Bondsmen: ARTHUR CONNELL and ALEX. SIMPSON--$7151.40.
Recorded November 20, 1855.
Book 14, Page 119 -- Curator Account -- from February 23, 1855;
Duiguid and Sons for burial of servant--$6.00; Lynchburg and Amherst
business trips; to CAROLINE, infirm negress for wood--$1.50; servant
for guardian wheat field--$1.00. Recorded: February 19, 1855.
Book 14, Page 325 -- Administrators Account -- from September 18, 1855--
subscription to Christian Advocate--67¢; many slave items; sundry
items furnished company to sit up with NANCY's "corps"--$2.50; 75¢
for servant to wait on NANCY. Recorded: September 17, 1855.
Book 14, Page 539 -- Administrators Account -- from August 31, 1856;
many slave items; legacy of FRANCES H. H. SHACKLEFORD. HENRY H.
LEWIS, agent for administrator. August 31, 1857.

GEO. SHACKLEFORD -- Book 11, Page 510 -- November 23, 1843; July 19,
1847. Witnesses: C. S. MOSBY, JNO. WILLIAMS. Wife, FRANCES B.;
my children: EDMUND L., JNO. H., WM. H., JAS. M., GEO., JR., TALIAFERRO
O. and JULIET E. HOCKDAY, wife of EDWIN J. HOCKDAY--all of Kentucky.
Executors: wife and EDMUND L., JNO. H. and WM. H.--three oldest sons.
Book 12, Page 28 -- Administrators Bond -- STERLING CLAIBORNE, ELIJAH
FLETCHER, WM. S. CLAIBORNE, November 15, 1847, for STERLING CLAIBORNE.
Book 12, Page 38 f -- Inventory -- November 18, 1843--$773.32. CHAS.
WINGFIELD, RO. RIDGWAY, LAFEYETT LAMBETH. Widow took possession of
property with administrator's permission. Witness: S. GARLAND.

THOS. SHANNON -- Book 1, Page 221 -- July 17, 1772; August court,
1772. Witnesses: GEO. BLAIN, JR., JNO. MC LINE (?), JNO. HERD, ANN
CROW. "Nephew," SARAH CROW; rest of WM. CROW's children; my cousin,
THOS. SHANNON, and his son, JNO. My brother, SAML's son, THOS.
Executors: SAML. SHANNON and JAS. REID.
Book 1, Page 223 -- Administrators Bond -- SAML. SHANNON, JAS. and
ALEX. REID, SAML. WOODS, August 3, 1772, for SAML. SHANNON.
Book 1, Page 225 -- Inventory -- no total; August 6, 1772. JAS.
DUNWOODY, RO. DUNWOODY, WM. SIMPSON.
Book 1, Page 449 -- Administrators Account -- October 22, 1778; JAS.
REID--cash in hands of SAML. SHANNON, one of executors. FRANCIS
MEREWETHER and MICHL. MC NEELY.

SARAH W. SHAW (Nee SANDERSON) -- Book 11, Page 72 -- April 27, 1842;
July 18, 1842. Witnesses: ALEX. MUNDY, PETER H. DILLARD, WM. J. C.
OLERTON (?). TIMOTHY SHAW qualified--bondsman: ALEX. MUNDY. My
husband, TIMOTHY SHAW; money from sale of land of my father, DANL.
SANDERSON; land bought from my brother, THOS. B. SANDERSON and next
to TARLTON WOODSON and WILLIS SANDERSON. Administrators Bond on
page 78.

CHRISTOPHER M. SHEEHAN -- Book 16, Page 98 -- Administrators Bond --
JNO. SHEEHAN and SAML. M. GARLAND, October 21, 1861, for JNO. SHEEHAN.
This is indexed: JNO. SHEEHAN.

E. E. SHELTON -- Book 16, Page 548 -- Guardians Bond -- BENJ. L.
SHELTON and RALPH C. SHELTON, 21 March 1864, for BENJ. L. SHELTON as

E. E. SHELTON (cont.) -- guardian of E. E., ELLIN R. W. R., EDGAR,
SHELTA B., H. B. and M. A. SHELTON--no parent set forth.

JNO. SHELTON, SR. -- Book 13, Page 232 -- February 12, 1849; November 23,
1853. Witnesses: EDWIN L. (S) RUCKER, JAS. MC DANIEL, SR., DAVID
PATTESON, WM. CLARK--aged and infirm--son, RICH--one-eighth and land
bought of ANDREW MORELAND and 100 acres from west end of where I
live--surveyed by COL. JNO. PRYOR in 1835; daughter, MARY W. SHELTON--
land and slaves; sons, EDWIN L. and RALPH C. SHELTON--trust set up
for them as trustees for my daughter, ELIZ. K. BURKS, wife of LEE H.
BURKS--free from his control and at her death to her living children.
Trust for daughter-in-law, SARAH H. R. SHELTON, wife of my son, JNO. P.
and free from his control. Family cemetery where JNO. P. lives and
bought from JAS. BENNET. Granddaughter, SALLY WILLIAMS SHELTON, only
child of my son, WM. SHELTON--her father in his lifetime. FARNSWORTH
tract to RALPH C.; sons, BENJ.--or BENJ. L. T. (?) SHELTON; contesting
heirs forfeit rights. Executors: sons, RICH., EDWIN L,, RALPH C. and
here it appears to be BENJ. L. (S) T. SHELTON.
Book 13, Page 245 -- Administrators Bond -- RALPH C. et al. with
RO. H. THORNTON for RALPH C. and EDWIN L. SHELTON to administrate.
Book 13, Page 327 -- Court order -- November, 1853; inventory; 32
slaves--$19,139.00. EDWIN L. RUCKER, WM. A. DEARING, THOS. R. TERRY,
WILEY CLARK. December 13, 1853.
Book 13, Page 388 -- Sale -- December 15, 1853; slave prices on page
393; total: $23,780.00.
Book 14, Page 411 -- Administrators Account -- by administrators from
December 15, 1853; very long to page 436; October 18, 1855.
Book 15, Page 265 -- Administrators Account -- by RALPH C.--from
March 31, 1856; very long to page 273.

JNO. JAS. SHELTON -- Book 8, Page 101 -- Constables Bond -- June 23,
1831. Bondsmen: JAS. SHELTON, JAS. M. DANIEL, SR. and JR., HENRY T.
PENDLETON--for JAS. J.--indexed JNO. J.
Book 8, Page 311 -- Same men June 20, 1833; called JNO. JAS. here.

JOSHUA SHELTON -- Book 5, Page 207 -- March 3, 1813; March 15, 1813.
Witnesses: RO. TINSLEY, WILLIS RUCKER, GABL. GOSNEY. Wife, POLLY--
mansion house and tract; brother, WM. SHELTON, and friend, COL. THOS.
MOORE, to administrate. WM. PENDLETON for attendance on me in illness;
my brothers and sisters: JNO.SHELTON, NANCY RUCKER, SALLY CHAPPEL,
ELIZ. LEE.
Book 5, Page 380 -- Administrators Bond -- WM. SHELTON, ARMISTEAD
RUCKER, PETER P. THORNTON, BENJ. RUCKER, September 20, 1813, for
WM. SHELTON.
Book 5, Page 575 -- Inventory -- $2633.17. February 19, 1816. RICH.
BURKS, JAS. HANSARD, SAML. BURKS.
Book 6, Page 74 -- Administrators Account -- from May 31, 1813--here
he is called JNO. and JOSHUA in various items. WM. PENDLETON's
legacy. June 21, 1819. REUBEN PENDLETON, JAS. DAVIS, MERIT W. WHITE.

MARY W. SHELTON -- Book 16, Page 417 -- 1861; witnessed on May 2, 1862
by ZACH D. TINSLEY and JNO. R. CUNNINGHAM. Probated January 18, 1864.
To be buried near dear parents; my sister, ELIZ. K. BURKS, and her
"ares"--if no issue; slaves to return to other heirs: SEATON B. or
NATHAN (?) BURKS; JNO. NAPOLEON BURKS, trustees. My sister's daughters;
ADALINE EMELA and MARTHA and ROBERTA BURKS--if no issue, then to other
heirs. Brothers: JACK, BENJ., RICH., RALPH, EDWIN;--a B before each
name--brother? BENJ.'s little daughter, MARY ANN; brother JACK's
daughters; then no punctuation: LUCY JANE SARAH VA and FANNY; if
JACK outlives his wife--all of BENJ.'s children--if no issue; nephew,
JNO. L. SHELTON, for education; to BENJ.--table bought from GEO. CURL;
sister, E. K. BURKS. $200 to St. Matthew's Episcopal Church; $100 to
wall in family cemetery at brother JACK's; $100 for burial and a head
"peace"--like my dear parents. Administrators: brothers: RICH.,
EDWIN, RALPH and BENJ.
Book 16, Page 429 -- Administrators Bond -- R. C. and BENJ. L. SHELTON,
February 15, 1864, for both.
Book 16, Page 460 -- Inventory -- March 24, 1864--$43,194.00. THOS. R.
LENY, ARCHIE COX, AMBR. C. RUCKER, JAS. F. PENDLETON.

RALPH SHELTON -- Book 6, Page 280 -- Guardians Bond -- JNO. SHELTON, BENNET A. CRAWFORD, March 18, 1822, for JNO. SHELTON as guardian of RALPH SHELTON, orphan of JNO. SHELTON.

RICH. SHELTON -- Book 6, Page 205 -- November 3, 1818; January 15, 1821. Witnesses: SAML. or LEMUEL P. MITCHELL, WM. PENDLETON, JAS. MC DANIEL, GEO. JONES, JAS. BENNETT, HENRY HAYNEY, JNO. SHELTON. Children of daughter, JANE ELLIS, deceased--blurred: JNO., CHAS., RICH. S. (L), PONECK (?), JOSHUA, POWHATAN ELLIS, NANCY HUNTER, JANE EUBANKS. May granddaughter, MARY MONTGOMERY, and infant daughters of MARY W. MONTGOMERY, deceased; son-in-law, GEO. LEE, who married my daughter, ELIZ., and children. My son, JNO. SHELTON--500 acres where he lives--next to DAVID and GEO. TINSLEY; JNO. CAMM; JAS. BENNETT; NELSON C. DAWSON. My daughter, SALLY CHAPPELL; daughter, NANCY RUCKER and dead or alive children: WILLIS, JANE E., ELIZ. L., MERELANET (?), SUSANNA T., RICH. F. and JNO. D. L. RUCKER. NEINEY's (?) children: MARTHA and JNO. M. WILLIS; infants of SALLY S. WILLIS, deceased, who was daughter of NANEY; MARY EDWARDS, daughter of NANCY to pay them their parts of what she may have received from estate of JNO. RUCKER, deceased. Land where JOSHUA SHELTON lived--down Millen (?) Creek to JNO. SHELTON's line in tract where I live. My nine (?) daughters; son, WM.--tract bought from RICH POWELL's estate; grandsons, RALPH SHELTON and RICH. F. RUCKER; daughter-in-law, POLLEY SHELTON, widow of my son, JOSHUA SHELTON. Administrators: DAVID TINSLEY, SR. and DAVID S. GARLAND and my son, WM.
Book 6, Page 207 -- Administrators Bond -- January 15, 1821. WM. SHELTON; bondsman; PETER P. THORNTON; RICH. HARRISON; RICH. BURKS; smae bond on page 209.
Book 6, Page 217 -- Administrators Bond -- DAVID S. GARLAND, March 20, 1821; bondsman: HILL CARTER.
Book 6, Page 534 -- Inventory -- no total, August 19, 1822; REUBEN PENDLETON, DABNEY T. PHILLIPS, MERRIT WHITE--indexed SMITH.

SARAH C. SHELTON -- Book 15, Page 53 -- Administrators Bond -- RALPH C. and B. L. SHELTON, January 17, 1859, for RALPH C. SHELTON--indexed as Guardians Bond.
Book 15, Page 216 -- Inventory -- July 18, 1859--$1242.00. SAML. R. WORTHAM, JNO. D. L. RUCKER, THOS. R. TERRY.

SARAH W. SHELTON -- Book 14, Page 77 -- Guardians Bond -- April 21, 1856. RALPH C. and EDWIN L. SHELTON for RALPH C. SHELTON as guardian of SARAH W. SHELTON, orphan of WM. SHELTON.
Book 15, Page 91 -- Guardians Account -- from April 21, 1856; tuition of ward to MARY E. SHELTON, Hollins Institute in part. Commissioner: JNO. S. ELLIS--from estate of WM. SHELTON--legacy left ward by JNO. SHELTON, deceased. Ward is due $3928.55.

VA. R. SHELTON -- Book 13, Page 394 -- Guardians Bond -- WILEY CLARK and TARLTON W. SHIELDS, November 20, 1854, for WILEY CLARK as guardian of VA. R. SHELTON, daughter of JNO. P. SHELTON.

WM. J. SHELTON -- Book 11, Page 154 -- Administrators Bond -- June 19, 1843. RALPH C. SHELTON, JNO. D. S. RUCKER, DAVID W. PATTESON for RALPH C. SHELTON.
Book 15, Page 186 -- Inventory -- $1023.50; December 18, 1843. JAS. M. MC DANIEL, RICH. F. RUCKER, WILLIS M. REYNOLDS, EDWIN S. RUCKER.

A. M. SHEPHERD, SR. -- Book 19, Page 372 -- Administrators Bond -- AMBR. M. SHEPHERD and JESSE E. ADAMS, October 21, 1878, for AMBR. M. SHEPHERD, JR.

AUGUSTINE SHEPHERD -- Book 3, Page 402 -- November 21, 1795; February 15, 1796. Witnesses: JNO. MC CLURE, THOS. ROBERTSON, ALEX. MC CLURE, FREDERICK PUGH. Wife, SARAH--plantation; Albemarle County tract next to RICH. WOODS; daughters: NANCY FOSTER, SUSANNAH, SARAH, HENRIETTA SHEPHERD when of age or married; son, AUGUSTINE--tract next to JNO. HAGGARD; daughter, MARY HAGGARD; NANCY FOSTER's husband in his lifetime; daughter, ANNIS WOODSON, has legacy from my father's estate. Executors: wife; son, AUGUSTINE; son-in-law, JNO. HAGGARD; friend, HUDSON MARTIN.

AUGUSTINE SHEPHERD (cont.) -- Book 3, Page 416 -- Administrators Bond --
SARAH and AUGUSTINE on probate date; Bondsman: JOS. SHELTON, JOS.
ROBERTS, BENJ. HARRIS. Same bond on page 287 of book 4.
Book 5, Page 480 -- Inventory -- no total; April, 1797; JNO. ROBERTS,
JNO. MC CLURE, THOS. ROBERTSON.

CHRISTOPHER SHEPHERD -- Book 10, Page 253 -- Administrators Bond --
DAVID SHEPHERD and SAML. M. GARLAND, August 19, 1840, for DAVID
SHEPHERD. Note: I erred in putting DAVID SHEPHERD--it is DAVID
SHEPHERD GARLAND as administrator.

DAVID SHEPHERD -- Book 2, Page 85 -- October 13, 1782; November 4,
1782. Witnesses: WIATT POWELL, WM. PENN, FRANCIS LEE. Margin:
Look in will for GABL. PENN, SAML. MEREDITH and AMBR. RUCKER--
affidavits. This seems to be an official marginal notation. Wife,
BETSY--lifetime interest in lands; DAVID SHEPHERD, son of my brother,
JNO.; SAML., son of my brother, DUBARTUS; my three brothers: AUGUSTINE,
JNO., and DUBARTUS. To DAVID and JAS. GARLAND--land; my sister,
JOHANNA WOODS; CHRISTOPHER ASHLING, son of my sister, FRANCES ASHLING;
children of deceased brother, WM. DAVID and JAS. GARLAND, sons of
WM. GARLAND. Brother of my wife--JAS. PENN. Executors: brother,
AUGUSTINE, and friend, GABL. PENN.
Book 2, Page 87 -- Administrators Bond -- AUGUSTINE SHEPHERD and
GABL. PENN on probate date. Bondsmen: SAML. MEREDITH, DANL. GAINES,
JNO. JONES.
Book 2, Page 96 -- Inventory -- L1425-1-6; November 26, 1782. GAINES
and MEREDITH and AMBR. RUCKER.
Book 2, Page 99 -- Division -- to widow, BETSY; DEBARTUS and AUGUSTINE
SHEPHERD as trustees of children of WM. SHEPHERD and sons of WM.
GARLAND: DAVID and JAS. GARLAND; to CHRISTOPHER ASHLING for son,
CHRISTOPHER; to JNO. SHEPHERD, WM. WOODS for wife, JOANA, AUGUSTINE
SHEPHERD as trustee of DAVID SHEPHERD, son of JNO.; DEBARTUS for his
son, SAML. December 21, 1782. SAML. MEREDITH, AMBR. RUCKER, JNO.
WEST.
Book 3, Page 182 -- Administrators Account -- by GABL. PENN from
September 11, 1778; cash delivered to you when going to Sweet Springs,
June, 1781; to ELIZ. SHEPHERD, JNO. SAVAGE as overseer, 1784. SAML.
MEREDITH, HUGH and PATRICK ROSE. June 7, 1791.
Book 9, Page 36 -- Administrators de bonis non Bond -- SAML. M.
GARLAND, January 19, 1835. Bondsmen: EDWD. A. CABELL and WM. M.
WALLER.

ELIZA SHEPHERD -- Book 10, Page 205 -- Guardians Bond -- JOS. RHOADS
and WM. B. TOLER, February 17, 1840, for JOS. RHOADS as guardian of
ELIZA SHEPHERD, orphan of WM. B. SHEPHERD, deceased.

ELIZ. C. SHEPHERD -- Book 12, Page 338 -- Administrators Bond --
AMBR. M. SHEPHERD, JAS. F. M. SHEPHERD, JAS. F. TALIAFERRO, RICH.
LANDRUM, December 16, 1850, for AMBR. M. SHEPHERD.
Book 12, Page 370 -- Inventory -- $5838.88 FRANCIS V. SUTTON, SR.,
THOS. G. BELL, RO. L. COLEMAN, April 21, 1851.
Book 12, Page 399 -- Sale -- January 22, 1851. Family buyers:
JAS. F. M., W (?) M., A. M. and ANN SHEPHERD. Total: $747.87 3/4.

HARRIET SHEPHERD -- Book B, Page 89 -- Administrators Bond -- AMBR. M.
SHEPHERD and RO. A. PENDLETON, Friday, March 22, 186-; last number
is left off in all items hereon for AMBR. M. SHEPHERD.

HARRIET M. SHEPHERD -- Book 11, Page 614 -- Estate Commitment to
Sheriff -- June, 1847; motion of JNO. THOMPSON, JR., JAS. L. LAMKIN,
Sheriff.

JAS. SHEPHERD -- Book 10, Page 249 -- Administrators Bond -- DAVID S.
and SAML. M. GARLAND, August 19, 1840, for DAVID S. GARLAND.

JAS. F. M. SHEPHERD -- Book 12, Page 527 -- Lunatick -- June 22, 1852.
RO. A. COGHILL and SAML. M. GARLAND for RO. A. COGHILL.
Book 14, Page 13 -- December 17, 1850; codicil December 17, 1850;
August 20, 1855. Witnesses: JNO. R. IRVING and PITT WOODROOF.

JAS. F. M. SHEPHERD (cont.) -- Handwriting by R. L. COLEMAN and THOS.
WHITEHEAD. Wife, ELEANOR, to administrate. Codicil: everything to
her.
Book 14, Page 50 -- Administrators Bond -- ELEANOR SHEPHERD and R. A.
COGHILL, November 19, 1855, for ELEANOR SHEPHERD.

PLEASANT SHEPHERD -- Book 10, Page 246 -- Administrators Bond --
DAVID S. and SAML. M. GARLAND, August 19, 1840, for DAVID S. GARLAND.

WM. SHEPHERD -- Book 8, Page 104 -- No date when written; June 20,
1831. Witnesses: GODFREY TOLER, JAS. J. TOLER, WM. TOLER. Wife,
MARY; son, HENRY; son, WM. B.--his wife and children; phrasing bad--
AMY SHEPHERD and children by my son, WM. B.
Book 8, Page 117 -- Administrators Bond -- WM. B. and HENRY SHEPHERD,
August 16, 1831, for WM. B. SHEPHERD.
Book 8, Page 129 -- Inventory -- August 26, 1831; $1308.12. LEE
MILLNER, PETER RUCKER, MURRY HENSON. Recorded: September 19, 1831.
Book 11, Page 403 -- Administrators Bond -- HENRY W. SHEPHERD and
JAS. MILLNER, March 16, 1846, for HENRY W. SHEPHERD.
Book 11, Page 411f -- Sale -- April 3, 1846, by HENRY as administrator.
ANN SHEPHERD was a buyer. JOS. R. CARTER, Clerk--$244.31. Recorded:
April 20, 1846.
Book 11, Page 412 -- Inventory -- March 25, 1846: $2640.70. PITT
WOODROOF, RO. H. CARTER, JOS. R. CARTER, PETER RUCKER.

WM. B. SHEPHERD -- Book 13, Page 367 -- Administrators Bond -- AMY
SHEPHERD, JNO. D. EUBANK, THOS. SHEPHERD, September 18, 1854, for
AMY SHEPHERD.

WM. H. SHEPHERD -- Book 14, Page 496 -- Guardians Bond -- PETER C.
SHEPHERD and H. E. SMITH, October 19, 1857, for PETER C. SHEPHERD as
guardian of WM. H. SHEPHERD, orphan of WM. B. SHEPHERD, deceased.

ALEX. SHIELDS -- Book 4, Page 379 -- Guardians Bond -- JAS. SHIELDS
and MICHL. WOODS, December 19, 1803, for JAS. SHIELDS as guardian of
ALEX. SHIELDS, orphan of JNO. SHIELDS, deceased.

JAMES SHIELDS -- Book 3, Page 362 -- Inventory -- Order of July, 1795:
L186-19-6. JNO.N. and SAML. REID; returned December 21, 1795.
Book 4, Page 82 -- Inventory -- L251-8-3; THOS. JONES, DAVID or
DANL. (?) CLARKSON, JR. November 16, 1802.
Book 4, Page 358 -- Administrators Bond -- RO. SHIELDS, DANL. MC DANIEL
and WM. JACOBS, October 18, 1802, for RO. SHIELDS.
Book 10, Page 52 -- Administrators Bond -- WILLIS R. PLUNKETT and
ABSALOM HIGGINBOTHAM, October 15, 1838, for WILLIS R. PLUNKETT.

JANE SHIELDS -- Book 3, Page 338 -- September 24, 1794; July 20, 1795.
Witnesses: SAML. REID, SUTY (?) REID, JNO. N. REID. Daughter,
RACHEL DOCK--someone has used pencil and put above: "DOAK"; sons,
JNO. and JAS. Body clothes to my granddaughters. Executors: ALEX.
REID and my son, JAS.
Book 3, Page 339 -- Administrators Bond -- JAS. SHIELDS and JNO. N.
REID, July 20, 1795, for JAS. SHIELDS.

JNO. SHIELDS -- Book 4, Page 59 -- Inventory -- no total; December 20,
1802. WM. JACOBS, DANL. MC DONALD, CHAS. JONES.
Book 4, Page 353 -- Administrators Bond -- RO. SHIELDS, JAS. WOODS,
JOS. MONTGOMERY, NELSON ANDERSON, September 20, 1802, for RO. SHIELDS.

NANCY SHIELDS -- Book 11, Page 223 -- Estate Commitment to Sheriff --
July, 1844; motion of JAS. POWELL, late sheriff. WM. M.--sheriff
(sic).
Book 11, Page 424 -- Ditto, June, 1846; JAS. POWELL, late sheriff;
powers revoked on motion of POWELL. WM. M. WALLER, Sheriff.
Book 11, Page 528 -- Sales -- February 27, 1846; JNO. WHITEHEAD,
Deputy for WALLER--$16.29.
Book 11, Page 438 -- Inventory -- no total; small; LINDSEY COLEMAN,
wm. BURFORD; September 20, 1847.
Book 11, Page 550 -- Administrators Account -- WALLER from February,

NANCY SHIELDS (cont.) -- 1846--$54.88. RO. M. BROWN, commissioner. January 20, 1847.

REBECCA SHIELDS -- Book 4, Page 380 -- Guardians Bond -- RO. SHIELDS and WM. JACOBS, December 19, 1803, for RO. SHIELDS as guardian of REBECCA SHIELDS, orphan of JNO. SHIELDS, deceased.

MARY SHINAULT -- Book 10, Page 78 -- Administrators Bond -- JNO. BURNETT, JNO. BARKER, JAS. DAVIES, February 18, 1839, for JNO. BURNETT.

NICHL. SHOEMAKER -- Book B, Page 65 -- JNO. JAS. OGDEN, WALKER R. OGDEN, CHAMPE OGDEN, RO. W. SNEAD, August 24, 1857, for JNO. JAS. OGDEN.
Book B, Page 67 -- Inventory -- September 5, 1857; no total, but long; JO R. ELLIS, J. Y. BARRETT, PETER FLOOD.
Book B, Page 75 -- Inventory and Sale and Administrators Account -- from August 22, 1857; Recorded: August 22, 1859.
Book B, Page 86 -- Administrators Account -- from August 23, 1858; MRS. SHOEMAKER; interest in SLEDD's land fund. Recorded November 3, 1859.
Book B, Page 88 -- Administrators Account -- from October 17, 1859; recorded: March 28, 1861.

WM. SHOEMAKER -- Book 5, Page 405 -- Minister's Bond -- Baptist; November 18, 1813. Bondsman: THOS. L. HOLLOWAY.

ROBT. R. SHRADER -- Book 12, Page 255 -- Administrators Bond -- JNO. JAS. SHRADER and JAS. L. COGHILL, April 15, 1850, for JNO. JAS. SHRADER.

SAML. SIMMONS -- Book 6, Page 281 -- Ordinary -- March 19, 1822, at Amherst Courthouse JNO. PRYOR, bondsman. I have commented on this tavern before--bitter fight a few years ago when old house was torn down for bank. RO. ALLEN had tavern thereon known as ALLEN's Tavern, but this name had been lost and it was known as the ROBERTSON House. Many wild tales as to age of building were circulated, but no proof was ever presented by the "aggufiers." To say the least, it was a monstrosity and was not in good repair at all. The beautiful bank building is quite an asset.

JNO. A. SIMPSON -- Book 7, Page 179 -- Inventory -- by LINDSEY COLEMAN, October 20, 1828.
Book 7, Page 193 -- Administrators Bond -- CHAS. P. TALIAFERRO and LYNE S. TALIAFERRO, December 15, 1828; CHAS. P. TALIAFERRO as coroner of county has become administrator of JNO. S. SIMPSON who has been found guilty of murder and has not surrendered himself.
Book 7, Page 223 -- Inventory -- January 20, 1829--$145.50; WM. BOURNE, JAS. S. HIGGINBOTHAM, JAS. OGDEN.
Book 8, Page 115f -- Administrators Account -- to THOS. COPPEDGE for MARY SIMPSON; HENRY RUCKER for WM. GILBERT; amounts from L. B. and AARON G. SIMPSON, July 19, 1831.
Book 8, Page 136 -- Administrators Bond -- RO. GARLAND and WM. MC DANIEL, October 17, 1831--GARLAND is now coroner and administrator-- found guilty of murder by inquest and has not surrendered himself.
Note: I do not want to be dogmatic, but believe that I have data--or have seen it--showing that SIMPSON killed a slave.

JULIUS SIMPSON -- Book 16, Page 187 -- Administrators Bond -- WM. L. SIMPSON, L. M. JONES, JAS. W. MILLNER and FRANCIS A. SIMPSON, November 17, 1862, for WM. L. SIMPSON.
Book 16, Page 200f -- Division of lands and slaves -- to MRS. SIMPSON--mansion house and garden--blank acres. To POWHATAN LAIN-- lower end of farm--no acres; WM. L. SIMPSON--ditto; JOS. SMITH-- ditto; LINDSEY M. JONES--ditto; FRANCES A. SIMPSON. Plat by JACOB D. PIERCE; slaves to same heirs. January 19, 1863. EDWIN M. WARE, RO. H. CARTER, RO. W. SNEAD.
Book 16, Page 201 -- Inventory by same men, December 1, 1862. Bond of POWHATAN LAINE, September 29, 1859. F. A. SIMPSON, WIATT GATEWOOD, WM. L. SIMPSON--slaves and rest of estate of $26,779.02. January 19, 1863.

JULIUS SIMPSON (cont.) -- Book 16, Page 206 -- Sale -- December 10, 1862--some of buyers: L. M. JONES, W. L. SIMPSON, F. A. SIMPSON, MRS. SIMPSON, P. LAINE. EDWIN M. WARE, Clerk. Returned January 19, 1863.
Book 16, Page 486 -- Administrators Account -- from November 21, 1862-- to MARGARET E. SIMPSON, widow; legatees: F. A. SIMPSON, LINDSEY M. JONES, POWHATAN LAINE and wife, JOS. SMITH, WM. L. SIMPSON. April 18, 1864.

L. D. SIMPSON -- Book 14, Page 439 -- September 4, 1857; Monday, October 19, 1857. Witnesses: JNO. W. SCOTT, RO. H. MAYS, TANDY S. TYLOR. Mother, NANCY SIMPSON; my sister, NANCY M. LIGGON; brother, WM. T. SIMPSON--trustee, SAML. M. GARLAND; my niece, FRANCES OLIVIA PATRICK, daughter of my deceased sister, ELIZ. JANE PATRICK; WM. T. to be trustee until she is 21 or married. Executors: WM. T. and MRS. NANCY SIMPSON.
Book 15, Page 459 -- Indexed Book 14, Page 459 -- Sale -- February 15, 1858. THOS. WHITEHEAD, administrator; WM. T. SIMPSON was a buyer,
Book 15, Page 579 -- Inventory -- January 21, 1858; also sale and same buyer as above.
Book 16, Page 47 -- Administrators Account -- by WHITEHEAD, December 5, 1860; WM. SIMPSON as buyer; paid D. PATTESON, administrator of L. P. SIMPSON. March 18, 1861.

LEWIS P. SIMPSON -- indexed as SAMPSON in some data -- Book 11, Page 415 -- Administrators Bond -- April 20, 1846: L. D. SIMPSON, HENRY L. DAVIES, H. S. (L) BROWN, CHAS. H. MASSIE, SAML. M. GARLAND for L. D. SIMPSON.
Book 11, Page 468 -- Inventory -- December 8, 1846--$3425.75. WM. D. MILES, ALLISON OGDEN, LEWIS S. CAMPBELL.
Book 11, Page 485 -- Sale -- December 22, 1846; NANCY, WM., L. D. and ELIZ. SIMPSON were buyers--$162.10.
Book 12, Page 163 -- Slave division: widow's share; L. D. SIMPSON received sums during testator's life and so has JNO. F. LIGGON who married MARGARET SIMPSON--note: L. D. calls her NANCY in his will. Percent shares to JNO. F. LIGGON and wife; L. D. SIMPSON; MARY FRANCES SIMPSON; WM. T. SIMPSON; WM. J. PATRICK as trustee for wife, ELIZ.-- late SIMPSON. March 12, 1849. SAML. M. GARLAND and RICH. POWELL.
Book 14, Page 518 -- Administrators Bond -- January 18, 1858. DAVID PATTESON and SAML. B. SCOTT for DAVID PATTESON.

MARY F. SIMPSON -- Book 15, Page 41 -- Inventory -- October 15, 1858; JAS. HIGGINBOTHAM, JOEL H. CAMPBELL, JNO. D. GILBERT--one negress at $1250 and 18 years of age.
Book 15, Page 61 -- Administrators Bond -- DAVID PATTESON and WM. KENT, September 20, 1858, for DAVID PATTESON.
Book 15, Page 229 -- Administrators Account -- from November 15, 1858. Reference to chancery suit, but not styled. Lots to JNO. LIGGON and wife, NANCY M., WM. SIMPSON, NANCY SIMPSON, LODWICH SIMPSON's admin-istrator, WM. J. PATRICK. Returned July 1, 1859. GEO. H. DAMERON, auctioneer. Evidently each one got $266.85 from slave sale, mention of her expenses from Lynchburg.

NANCY SIMPSON -- Book 16, Page 151 -- May 6, 1862; September 15, 1862. Witnesses: JAS. and CLIFTON HIGGINBOTHAM. SAML. GARLAND qualified; bondsman: RO. A. PENDLETON. She referred to deed of October 13, 1859, in Amherst County to free slaves and executor to use $300 to remove and settle them. Daughter, NANCY MARGARET LIGGON, wife of JNO. F. LIGGON, and heirs. Executor: SAML. M. GARLAND.
Book 16, Page 491 -- not indexed -- Administrators Account -- August 18, 1863; GARLAND reports that bond has been given for removal of slaves. Mention of MARGARET LIGGON and executor of WM. SIMPSON. To September, 1862.
Book 20, Page 272 -- Administrators Bond -- April 17, 1882: RO. M. BROWN, JR. and SR. for JR.--administrator de bonis non.

WM. SIMPSON -- Book 3, Page 22f -- Administrators Bond -- AGNES SIMPSON, DAVID SIMPSON, MOSES HUGHES, ALEX. HENDERSON, January 1, 1787 for AGNES SIMPSON.

WM. SIMPSON (cont.) -- Book 3, Page 32 -- Inventory -- April 2, 1787, L 822-7-8½ JNO. MURRILL, JR., THOS. MORRISON, JR., ALEX. HENDERSON.

WM. T. SIMPSON -- Book 16, Page 114 -- January 10, 1859; April 21, 1862. Witnesses: BENJ. S. (L) HOWL, JAS. A. KEETON, JAS. POWELL, JR., ALEX. GOOCH. Codicil: March 6, 1862 wherein he names RO. M. BROWN, administrator and witness by RO. A. PENDLETON and ALEX. GOOCH. $25 out of every $100 to RO. TINSLEY as trustee for slaves of my mother, NANCY SIMPSON, and given to her by deceased son, L. D. SIMPSON; TINSLEY also trustee for my niece, FRANCES OLIVIE PATRICK, daughter of WM. J. PATRICK, Campbell County--if no heirs; my sister, NANCY MARGARET LIGGON, and children, Powhatan County--apart from husband, JNO. F. LIGGON. Friend, RO. TINSLEY, to administrate.
Book 16, Page 121 -- Administrators Bond -- RO. M. BROWN and JNO. THOMPSON, JR. April 21, 1862, for RO. M. BROWN.
Book 16, Page 135 -- Inventory -- June 9, 1862; no tota; JAS. and JAS. S. HIGGINBOTHAM, JNO. D. GILBERT.
Book 16, Page 436 -- WM. T. SIMPSON versus FRANCIS O. PATTICK, Chancery, October 1862--SIMPSON's executors versus PATRICK's trustee--commissioner to report on sale of slave, GUSTAVUS. RO. M. BROWN, executor. TAYLOR BERRY, commissioner. September 21, 1863, mention of LIGGON and wife versus SIMPSON's executor. Children of MARY SIMPSON, legatees--scratched and on next page. Children of MARY SIMPSON: NANCY M. LIGGON and children; FRANCIS O. PATRICK, trustee. September 16, 1863.
Book 17, Page 124 -- TAYLOR BERRY made report -- June 16, 1866. Reference to Administrators Bond by BROWN. Recorded July 15, 1866.
Book 21, Page 81 -- Administrators Account -- by BROWN; suit of EWART's trustee versus --- MABRY versus PATTERSON in Buckingham County. Mention of former slaves: LUCY W., wife of JIM TYLER; INDIANA, wife of WESLEY DAVIS; MISSOURI, wife of JO MARTIN--each gets $23.03. MRS. LIGGON gets $103.65 and so did EWART's trustee.

MARMADUKE B. SISSON -- Book 11, Page 355 -- Administrators Bond -- RO. WINGFIELD, ALEX. MUNDY, JNO. DILLARD, December 15, 1845, for RO. WINGFIELD.
Book 11, Page 390 -- Inventory -- $4655.12½ LEWIS S. CAMPBELL, JOEL BETHEL, PETER F. CHRISTIAN. Returned: September 30, 1845. 12L167 so indexed, but nothing thereon.
Book 12, Page 201 -- Administrators Account -- from December 30, 1845 to MISS MAMIE L. SISSON, JNO. H. GREGORY and wife; wheat seeded at WALKER's plantation; MRS. MARY SISSON. JOEL BETHEL, SAML. M. GARLAND. August 20, 1849.

TARPLEY SISSON -- DARBLEY in one place -- Book 9, Page 254 -- Estate Commitment to Sheriff -- November, 1836. Motion of HENRY J. ROSE; THOS. N. EUBANK, sheriff.

GALVILLA SKINNER -- Book 11, Page 116 -- Guardians Bond -- WM. L. WATTS and JAS. GOING, March 20, 1843, for WM. L. WATTS as guardian of GALVILLA SKINNER, orphan of TALIPHARO SKINNER, deceased. Note: I have chased SKINNER family from upper New York where the name COURTLAND SKINNER is employed--TORY family, in main. My wife stems from a COURTLAND SKINNER who shows in Madison and Estill Counties, Kentucky. There is also a MEDAD SKINNER in data, but she does not stem from him. I am stymied in North Carolina where COURTLAND SKINNER married HANNAH REID or READ. MEDAD REID was on bond. Was this man out of the New York family? I have done no original research in North Carolina on REID or SKINNER lines, but was supplied this data by someone in North Carolina.

SALLY SLADEN -- Book 12, Page 250 -- Administrators Bond -- WM. I. ISBELL, RO. ISBELL, FREDERICK W. CABELL, November 19, 1849, for WM. I. ISBELL.

FRANCIS SLAUGHTER -- Book 10, Page 383 -- Estate Commitment to Sheriff, June, 1840; motion of SPOTSWOOD G. LOVING. WILL and CHAS. SPENCER lumped with motion as to estates of LUCY R. SPENCER and RO. RIVES. Sheriff: EDMD. PENN.

FRANCIS SLAUGHTER (cont.) -- Book 13, Page 182 -- Administrators
Bond -- FRANCIS H. BELL and CHAS. W. STATHAM, May 18, 1853, for
FRANCIS H. BELL.

ANN SLEDD -- Book 5, Page 197 -- August 31, 1812; January 18, 1813.
Witnesses: RICH. TANKERSLEY, WINSTON TANKERSLEY, JNO. GROOME, SAML.
COLEMAN, BLANSFORD HICKS. To my grandchildren--children of BARKSDALE
and LUCY SLEDD.
Book 9, Page 394 -- indexed as an inventory, but nothing thereon.

BELINDA SLEDD -- Book 5, Page 199 -- Guardians Bond -- JER. L. KELLEY
and THOS. GRISSOM, January 18, 1813, for JER. L. KELLEY as guardian
of BELINDA SLEDD, orphan of WM. SLEDD.

JAMES SLEDD -- Book 4, Page 399 -- Administrators Bond -- WM. SLEDD,
NICHL. VANSTAVERN, RICH. HARTLESS, February 18, 1805, for WM. SLEDD.

JNO. SLEDD -- this name does not appear in index and are indexed for
JAS. SLEDD -- Book 5, Page 52 -- Inventory -- L90-2-3, December 16,
1811; ROD. MC CULLOCH, THOS. MORRIS, JAS. WAUGH.
Book 5, Page 73 -- Administrators Bond -- JNO. and WM. SLEDD and
ARCHELAUS REYNOLDS, June 17, 1811, for JNO. SLEDD.
Book 6, Page 47 -- Guardians Bond -- SEATON SLEDD, WM. PETERS, WM.
TUCKER, November 16, 1818, for SEATON SLEDD as guardian of JNO.,
EDITHA, ELIZ., and JOSHUA SLEDD, orphans of WM. SLEDD.

SALLY SLEDD -- Book 5, Page 457 -- BENJ. CARTER and JNO. FLOOD,
September 18, 1814, for BENJ. CARTER as guardian of SALLY SLEDD,
orphan of WM. SLEDD. Also for SUSANNAH SLEDD--same parent.

SEATON SLEDD -- Book 6, Page 258 -- Guardians Bond -- SEATON SLEDD,
WM. PETER, BENJ. CARTER, WM. BATES, PETER CARTER, WM. WILMORE, PETER
MARTIN, October 15, 1821, for SEATON SLEDD as guardian of JNO.,
EDITHA, ELIZA, and JOSHUA SLEDD, orphans of WM. SLEDD.

WM. SLEDD, CAPT -- Book 5, Page 192 -- Administrators Bond -- JESSE
RICHESON, JNO. RICHESON, JNO. WARE and JNO. EUBANK, December 21,
1812, for JESSE RICHESON.
Book 5, Page 438 -- Inventory -- of CAPT. WM. SLEDD; December 31,
1812--$30,191.87. THOS. N. EUBANK, GEO. BROWN, PETER CARTER.
Book 5, Page 707 -- Administrators Account -- from March 16, 1815;
to MRS. LUCY SLEDD; to JNO. SLEDD; liquidation of estate of JAMES
HARTLESS; SEATON SLEDD's bond. Recorded March 11, 1818. JNO. WARE,
SR., WM. JOPLING, PETER P. THORNTON.

JAS. SMALL -- Book 1, Page 199 -- Administrators Bond -- ESTER SMALL,
EDWD. STEPHENSON, JNO. PUCKET, August 5, 1771, for ESTER SMALL.
Book 1, Page 201 -- Inventory -- Setpember 27, 1771; no total; JAS.
LACKEY, JAS. BARNETT.

ABRAHAM or ABRAM SMITH -- Book 4, Page 220 -- April 17, 1806; June 16,
1806. Witnesses: JOHNSON PHILLIPS, JOEL RAMSEY, JR. JAS. CAMDEN,
JR. JON. SMITH, son of ABRAM, and JAS. CAMPBELL qualified. Bondsmen:
WM. DUNCAN, GEO. CAMPBELL. Division to children before death--to
JAS. CAMPBELL, where he lives; son, ELIAS--old plantation; son,
JNO.--his old place and where he lives; also Piney River tract of
196 acres. JAS. CAMPBELL--196 acres on Tye; my three children.
My mulatto boy, JNO. NATHAN, born in 1797, to serve JAS. CAMPBELL
until 21 and then to be free.
Book 4, Page 268 -- Inventory -- no total; December 15, 1806. JNO.
and HENRY CAMPBELL, JESSE WRIGHT. Administrators Bond on Page 432.
Book 5, Page 9 -- Administrators Account -- by JNO. SMITH and JAS.
CAMPBELL--to legatees--not named. November 20, 1810. MICAJAH
CAMDEN, WM. MOORE, JAS. FULCHER, JNO. CAMPBELL.

CHAMPNESS SMITH -- Book 4, Page 190 -- October 1, 1805; October 21,
1805. Witnesses: RO. GRISSOM, RICH. PENDLETON, WM. PETERS, THOS.
COLEMAN, AMBR. RUCKER. Wife, ELIZ., until youngest child is 15;
children: AUSTIN, JNO., NANCY, HELLEY (?), POLLY, KITTY, BETSY,

CHAMPNESS SMITH (cont.) -- SALLY, and CHAMPNESS. Executors: wife and son, AUSTIN, and JNO. SMITH.
Book 5, Page 611 -- Administrators Bond -- JNO. SMITH and RO. TINLSEY, December 10, 1816, for JNO. SMITH.
Book 5, Page 651 -- Inventory -- $3121.25. March 17, 1817. RO. TINSLEY, SAML. B. DAVIES, JAS. TINSLEY, JNO. SMITH, acting executor.

CLARY SMITH -- Book 4, Page 257 -- June 24, 1806; September, 1806. Witnesses: WM. REED, JNO. MC KERSEY, ADAM REED, DANL. REED. PHILIP SMITH qualified; bondsmen: WM. CAMDEN, WM. WARE. Brother, PHILIP SMITH; JAS. SMITH; money for mare due from WM. SANDIDGE; feathers at DELPHY SMITH's; calf at JOS. HIGGINBOTHAM's; sister, MARY SMITH; bonds in hands of TALIAFERRO and LOVEN--JNO. and BENJ. TALIAFERO and WM. LOVEN (probably LOVING); cousin, BENJ. HIGGINBOTHAM; brother, WIATT SMITH; son, WM. SMITH. Executors: friends, BENJ. and JOS. HIGGINBOTHAM and PHILIP SMITH. Administrators Bond on Page 433.
Book 4, Page 268 -- Inventory -- December 15, 1806. HENRY BALLENGER, BENJ. and PULLIAM SANDIDGE.

FRANCIS SMITH -- Book 4, Page 339 -- Administrators Bond -- WM. ISBELL, WALTER CHRISTIAN, CHRISTOPHER ISBELL, October 19, 1801, for WM. ISBELL.

GEO. SMITH -- Book 9, Page 136 -- Administrators Bond -- LUCINDA SMITH, DON STOKELY, WM. ARMISTEAD, November 16, 1835, for LUCINDA SMITH.

HARRIET SMITH -- Book 5, Page 176 -- Guardians Bond -- ANSELM CLARKSON, BENJ. TALIAFERRO, HILL CARTER, August 17, 1812, for ANSELM CLARKSON as guardian of HARRIOTT and RICH. SMITH, orphans of WM. SMITH, deceased.

HENRY SMITH -- Book 5, Page 176 -- Guardians Bond -- RICH. and PHILIP SMITH, August 17, 1812, for RICH. SMITH as guardian of HENRY SMITH, orphan of WM. SMITH.
Book 8, Page 417 -- November 3, 1832; June 18, 1834. Witnesses: JOS. PENN, RICH. J. WAUGH, WM. H. KNIGHT. CHAS. PARSONS qualified; bondsman: WM. M. WALLER. Of Nelson County--old; son-in-law, CHAS. PARSONS; any sum due from War office as a Revolutionary soldier. Administrators Bond is page 418.

JACOB SMITH -- Book 4, Page 20 -- July 19, 1800; September 21, 1801. Witnesses: HENRY BALLINGER, JNO. CLARKSON, WM. WARE, JOS. HIGGINBOTHAM, and NELSON CRAWFORD qualified. Bondsmen: ANTHONY RUCKER, WM. CAMDEN. Son, PHILIP; son, JNO.--land conveyed to him by ZACH TALIAFERRO; children of my son, WM.: MILLY TOD, WIATT, HENRY, HARRIOT and RICH. SMITH--land on both sides Puppie Creek--joins where WM. SMITH formerly lived; Tobacco Row lines of mine; JNO. YOUNG, BENJ. TALIAFERRO, PHILADELPHIA SMITH, widow of WM., and children. Daughter, MARY SMITH; son, JAMES SMITH; daughter, CLARY SMITH; son, WIATT SMITH; son, RICH.; grandson, JACOB SMITH--land bought of EDMOND POWELL. Executors: WM. WARE, JOS. HIGGINBOTHAM, son of JOS., NELSON CRAWFORD. Administrators Bond on page 335.
Book 4, Page 24 -- Inventory -- at dwelling house, October 13, 1801; L145-12-9; JNO. SALE, BENJ. HIGGINBOTHAM, ELIJAH BUCKMAN.
Book 4, Page 579 -- Administrators Account -- WM. WARE from 1801. Calf of MARY SMITH; one of CLARY SMITH; accounts of RICH., WIATT, PHILIP, JNO., son of ABRAM, JAS. SMITH. L1377-19-11. CHAS. and JNO. TALIAFERRO, WM. SANDIDGE. Signed and approved by JAS., RICH., MARY, and PHILIP SMITH, executor of CLARY SMITH, and PHILIP SMITH. June 24, 1808. Witnesses: CHAS. and BENJ. TALIAFERRO.
Book 17, Page 177 -- Administrators Bond -- THOS. A. BARBOUR and SAML. M. GRALAND, September 17, 1866, for THOS. A. BARBOUR.
Book 17, Page 206 -- Inventory and Sale -- December 1, 1866; inventory; small; no total; C. F. BENNETT, JNO. D. GILBERT, JAS. M. OGDEN. Sale on same date--MRS. G. A. M. SMITH, buyer--$291.55.
Book 18, Page 6 -- Administrators Account -- by BARBOUR; report on sale above. From November 15, 1866; recorded: January, 1870.

JAS. P. SMITH -- Book 4, Page 448 -- Sale -- November 17, 1857--
$196.99, JAS. P. COLEMAN, administrator. Recorded: Monday, October 19,
1857; so recorded as to dates. Inventory, October, 1857--French
brandy, whiskey, Malaga wine, jars, decanters, tumblers, sugar box
and spoons, measures, funnel, good and common whiskey and rum--$182.72.
JAS. POWELL, WM. E. COLEMAN, J. H. MASON. If they sampled all of
this, I wonder that they ever agreed on a total.
Book 14, Page 451 -- Administrators Bond -- JAS. P. COLEMAN, JOEL F.
SMITH; September 21, 1857, for JAS. P. COLEMAN.

JAS. W. SMITH -- Book 6, Page 37 -- Constables Bond -- November 16,
1818; bondsman: WM. DUNCAN, CHAS. P. TALIAFERRO.
Book 6, Page 232 -- Same, June 18, 1821; second hundred; Bondsman:
WM. DUNCAN.
Book 6, Page 236 -- Same, June 21, 1819; bondsman: CHAS. P. TALIAFERRO.
Book 6, Page 598 -- Same, June 20, 1825; bondsman: JNO. and JACOB
SMITH.
Book 12, Page 232 -- Estate Commitment to Sheriff -- February, 1850;
motion of WILLIS GILLESPIE; LINDSEY COLEMAN, Sheriff.

JNO. SMITH -- Book 3, Page 395 -- Administrators Bond -- JOS. SMITH,
AUGUSTINE SMITH, RO. DINWIDDIE, September 19, 1796, for JOS. SMITH.
Indexed for JOS. SMITH.
Book 6, Page 265 -- Called Senior -- August 18, 1821; December 17,
1821. Witnesses: WM. SALE, RICH. SMITH, WM. DUNCAN, RO. H. COLEMAN.
WM. WALLER qualified; bondsman: HILL CARTER, JAS. W. SMITH. Wife,
SARAH--where I live; daughter, ELIZ. SMITH; daughter, NANCY SMITH--
her guardian and when 21 or married; daughter, POLLY SMITH--same;
sons, WM., EDWD. and RICH. and guardian. Sons, JAS. W. and JNO.
SMITH. Daughters, SALLY TUCKER and BELINDA SANDIDGE; son, JACOB.
Any minor children; division at end of four years. Slave to children
by lots and not to be sold. Executors: friends, DAVID S. GARLAND
and WM. WALLER and guardians of minors: WM., NANCY, EDWD. POLLY, and
RICH. SMITH. Administrators Bond on page 269.
Book 6, Page 669 -- Administrators Account -- by WALLER from 1822;
account of JAS. W. SMITH, JACOB, JNO. JR., SARAH, RICH., WM. SMITH.
JAS. W. as guardian of POLLY; EDWD.; and RICH. SMITH. Estate of
PHILIP SMITH, deceased; NANCY SMITH, legatee. June 1, 1826. LYNE S.
TALIAFERRO, HILL CARTER, CORNL. SALE.
Book 8, Page 54 -- Administrators Account -- from June, 1826: to
NANCY, WM., POLLY, EDWD. and RICH. SMITH--legacies by CHAS. TUCKER,
JNO. and JACOB SMITH--amounts due estate. May 1, 1830. CHAS.
TALIAFERRO, CORNL. SALE.
Book 12, Page 178 -- Inventory and Division -- lots to RICH. P. SMITH,
DUDLEY SANDIDGE, DABNEY SANDIDGE, G. MILES, C. TUCKER. Commissioners:
CHAS. A. PENN, JAS. F. TALIAFERRO, M. C. GOODWIN.
Book 12, Page 203 -- HAMILTON (HAMBLETON) BOYD and JNO. KINNIER,
August 20, 1849, for HAMILTON BOYD.
Book 12, Page 206 -- March 20, 1849; August 20, 1849. Witnesses:
ISAAC R. REYNOLDS, JO. V. HOBSON. HAMBLETON and BOYD qualified.
Mother, REBECCA; executors: friend, HAMILTON BOYD.
Book 12, Page 257 -- Inventory -- October 30, 1849: $716.25. WIATT
PETTYJOHN, NAPOLEON B. MAGRUDER, ISAAC R. REYNOLDS.
Book 13, Page 104 -- Administrators Account -- by BOYD from August 20,
1849; DR. HOBSON's bill; cash to REBECCA SMITH: $1852.93. Recorded
in Lynchburg, June 27, 1851.

JOS. SMITH -- Book 3, Page 579 -- April 3, 1798; December 16, 1799.
Witnesses: THOS. PANNELL, DILMUS JOHNSON, JOSIAH SMITH. "Antient";
son, THOS.; son, AUGUSTINE; son, WM.; daughters: SUSANNA FOX, JENEY
SMITH; sons, SAML. and JOSIAH; land on north side Rockfish; suit
between THOS. SMITH, deceased, and me; wife, MARY; equal division to
JOSIAH, SARA, JUDAY, and MARY SMITH. My son, JNO., deceased.
Executor: son, JOSIAH.

MARTIN SMITH -- Book 6, Page 256 -- Administrators Bond -- NICHL.
TURNER, AMBR. PLUNKET, and WM. TURNER, October 15, 1821, for NICHL.
TURNER.

MARTIN SMITH (cont.) -- Book 6, Page 276 -- Inventory -- Recorded
January 21, 1822; shown to us by administrator. JNO. DILLARD, WM.
TURNER, GEO. STAPLES.

MARY SMITH -- Book 10, Page 336 -- April 16, 1839; February 15, 1841.
Witnesses: JNO. THOMPSON, JR., JNO. F. TALIAFERRO, EDWD. B. TAYLOR.
Executor renounced administrator and JOEL SMITH qualified; bondsman:
HENRY L. DAVIES, WM. L. WALLER, DABNEY SANDIDGE, ADDISON TALIAFERRO.
Old slave, DICEY, is ancestor of all of my slaves and she is to be
supported. Aged and infirm brother, JAMES SMITH. Slaves--two boys
will be 25 on April 1, 1854--JNO. and CHAS.--to be freed and sent to
Ohio or some free state; hires to be saved for them. Slaves to
WM. T. SANDIDGE, son of DABNEY SANDIDGE; also to his daughter,
ELIZ. SANDIDGE; CHRISTOPHER SANDIDGE, son of DUDLEY SANDIDGE; nephew,
WIATT SMITH, son of my brother, WM. SMITH. HARRIET GILLESPIE, wife
of WILLIS GILLESPIE, and her children; brother, JAS. SMITH; slave,
REUBEN, to be sold for debts. MILDRED SANDIDGE, daughter of DUDLEY
SANDIDGE. Body servant, MARY, daughter of DICEY, gets freedom,
money, mare, furniture--for faithfulness. Nephew, JOEL SMITH, son
of WM.--where I live. Slaves to stay with my brother, JOEL SMITH.
Executors: friends: ADDISON TALIAFERRO and CHAS. MASSIE. Administra-
tors Bond is on Book 10, Page 338.
Book 10, Page 344 -- Inventory -- Many slaves; total is thus:
$12,396.00 and $500. March 19, 1841. CORNL. SALE, CHAS. A. PENN,
ALLISON OGDEN.
Book 11, Page 257 -- Administrators Account -- by JOEL SMITH from
January, 1840. JAS. POWELL, administrator of A. MARTIN; WIATT P.
SMITH; -- JOEL SMITH has delivered to CHRISTOPHER, ELIZ. and MILDRED
SANDIDGE, children of DUDLEY SANDIDGE, their guardian--five slaves;
also to WM. and SARAH SANDIDGE, children of DABNEY SANDIDGE, by
father--slaves; also to HARRIET GILLESPIE. December 16, 1844.
CORNL. SALE, JNO. H. FUQUA.
Book 20, Page 251 -- Guardians Bond -- LOUIS P. MORRIS and JNO. H.
PARR, January 16, 1882, for LOUIS P. MORRIS as guardian of MARY,
NANNIE, and MORRIS SMITH--it has been written over and is hard to
decipher and does not jibe with next item.
Book 21, Page 73 -- Guardians Account -- May 11, 1884--LEWIS MORRIS,
guardian of NANNIE, MOLLY (MARY) and MOSES SMITH--from JNO. H. PARR,
administrator of F. COGHILL. August 18, 1884. Page 251 is indexed
for MORRIS SMITH.

MILLY P. SMITH -- Book 6, Page 714 -- Administrators Bond -- RICH.
SMITH, JR., CHAS. MASSIE, DABNEY SANDIDGE, January 15, 1827, for
RICH. SMITH, JR. July 18, 1826; January 15, 1827. Witnesses:
JNO. B. DUNCAN and DABNEY SANDIDGE. Daughter, MARY E. SMITH--undivided
interest in my father's estate; debt due me from MAT. P. SMITH;
brother, RICH. SMITH, and friend, CHAS. P. TALIAFERRO, to administrate.
Book 7, Page 197 -- Inventory -- December 13, 1828--$838.50. DABNEY
SANDIEGE, CHAS. MASSIE, CHAS. P. TALIAFERRO.

PHILL SMITH -- Book 5, Page 470 -- August 22, 1814; November 21, 1814.
Witnesses: JNO. ROBERTSON, WM. HENLEY, JNO. SMITH, JR., JAS. W.
SMITH. JNO. SMITH qualified; bondsman: JNO. PENN, RICH. SMITH.
Daughter, RHODA WELCH; son, THOS. SMITH; son-in-law, ANDREW WELCH;
RHODA and children apart from ANDREW; if THOS. marries and alters
course of life--meanwhile in trust of executors. ELIZ. SMITH,
daughter of my nephew, JNO. SMITH. Executors: nephew, JNO. SMITH
and REV. WM. DUNCAN--both of Amherst County.
Book 6, Page 245 -- Administrators Account -- from March 17, 1810--
this does not jibe with date of probate in 1814, so must be another
man. Coffin in 1810--by THOS. GOODRICH; suit versus L. TALIAFERRO
in Mississippi territory; balance due heirs. Recorded August 24,
1821; LEONARD HENLEY, WM. SANDIDGE, EDMD. T. COLEMAN.

RICH. SMITH, SR. -- Book 9, Page 226 -- April 5, 1826; May 16, 1836.
Witnesses: BENJ. TALIAFERRO, R. HENLEY, HENRY J. ROSE. RICH. SMITH,
JR. qualified; bondsmen: DANL. L. COLEMAN and ADDISON TALIAFERRO.
Amherst County land; slaves freed and named; long dissertation on
removal, but may stay in Virginia and choose masters. Amounts to

RICH. SMITH, SR. (cont.) -- friends, DUDLEY and DABNEY SANDIDGE;
JAS. POWELL; CHAS. TUCKER. Nephew, JACOB SMITH, son of JNO. and
SARAH SMITH--three slaves; nephew, RICH. P. SMITH, JR. and RICH.
SMITH--both nephews; both to administrate. RICH. P. is also son of
JNO. and SARAH.
Book 9, Page 234-2 pages so numbered -- Inventory -- RICH. SMITH, JR.,
administrator, June 29, 1836: $7559.75. CHAS. MASSIE, W. L. DUNCAN,
TANDY RUTHERFORD.
Book 11, Page 424 -- Estate Commitment to Sheriff -- June, 1846;
motion of JAS. POWELL--unadministrated by RICH. SMITH. Sheriff:
WM. M. WALLER. Three items on this page: RICH. P. SMITH as to estate
of RICH. SMITH, JR., September, 1846, and one of July, 1846, but no
person named as making motions.

RICH. SMITH -- Book 6, Page 480 -- Guardians Bond -- JAS. W. SMITH,
JACOB SMITH, JESSE RICHESON, WM. DUNCAN, August 16, 1824, for JAS. W.
SMITH as guardian of RICH., EDWD. and MARY SMITH, orphans of JNO.
SMITH.
Book 7, Page 175 -- Guardians Bond -- JAS. W. SMITH, JACOB SMITH,
EDWD. SMITH, September 15, 1828, for JAS. W. SMITH as guardian of
RICH. SMITH, orphan of JNO. SMITH, deceased.
Book 8, Page 200 -- Constables Bond -- RICH. JR.--April 17, 1832.
Bondsmen: ADDISON TALIAFERRO, CHAS. MASSIE.
Book 8, Page 318 -- Same--JR., June 17, 1833; bondsmen: ADDISON
TALIAFERO and DABNEY G. RAY.
Book 9, Page 79 -- Same, June 15, 1835; bondsmen: CORNL. SALE, R. P.
SMITH.
Book 9, Page 317 -- Same, June 19, 1837; bondsmen: CHAS. MASSIE,
DANL. L. COLEMAN.
Book 11, Page 331 -- Administrators Bond -- NANCY SMITH, LINDSEY
COLEMAN, WIATT P. SMITH, JOEL F. SMITH, July 21, 1845, for NANCY SMITH.
Book 11, Page 341 -- Inventory -- $1243, September 12, 1845: C. A.
PENN, DABNEY SANDIDGE, CORNL. SALE.
Book 11, Page 424 -- Estate Commitment to Sheriff -- June, 1846;
motion of JAS. POWELL; WM. WALLER, Sheriff.
Book 11, Page 550 -- Administrators Account -- by WALLER--JR. here;
from May 1, 1847.
Book 13, Page 396 -- Administrators Bond -- RO. and ZACH. D. TINSLEY,
December 18, 1854, for RO. TINSLEY.

RICH. P. SMITH -- Book 12, Page 344 -- December 25, 1850; January 20,
1851. Witnesses: CHAS. H. MASSIE, HENRY LOVING, JACOB SMITH, WM.
TUCKER. Of lawful age; until my youngest child is 15; to be educated.
Wife, MARY T., to administrate.
Book 12, Page 363 -- Administrators Bond -- MARY T. SMITH, March 17,
1851. Bondsmen: WM. TUCKER, JACOB SMITH, C. A. PENN.
Book 12, Page 413 -- Inventory -- about 500 acres; slaves, May 9,
1851. CHAS. TUCKER, HENRY LOVING, JAS. M. GANNAWAY.

WM. SMITH -- Book 3, Page 445 -- May 27, 1797; October 16, 1797.
Witnesses: SAML. FARNKLIN, REUBEN HARRISON, PHILLIP SMITH, JR., JAS.
SMITH. My six children--until daughter, MILLEY POWELL SMITH, is of
age or married. Four sons, JOEL FRANKLIN, WIAT, HENRY FRANKLIN, and
RICH. SMITH--until RICH. is of age. Wife, PHILADELPHIA.
Book 3, Page 481 -- Inventory -- L339-14-0; January 20, 1798. JNO.
DUNCAN, CHAS. and BENJ. TALIAFERRO.
Book 4, Page 291 -- Administrators Bond -- JOEL FRANKLIN, JNO. SMITH,
PHILADELPHIA SMITH, PHILIP SMITH, REUBEN HARRISON, October 16, 1797,
for first three to administrate.

WIATT or WYATT SMITH -- Book 6, Page 711 -- Guardians Bond -- W. S.,
WM. P., ALFRED and BENJ. SMITH and JAS. POWELL, December 18, 1826,
for W. S. as guardian of PHILIP, MARTHA ANN, MOSES and JNO. SMITH,
orphans of WYATT SMITH.

WM. M. SMITHSON -- Book 6, Page 294 -- Constables Bond -- June 17,
1822; bondsmen: SAML. SMITHSON and CHAS. PALMORE.

CATH. SMOOT -- Book 10, Page 341 -- Guardians Bond -- THOS. SMOOT, LINDSEY COLEMAN, JNO. SMOOT, April 19, 1841, for THOS. SMOOT as guardian of WM. H., SARAH A., CATH. and JNO. SMOOT; no parent set forth, but on same page, same date, and men--THOS. SMOOT as guardian of PAULINA SMOOT, infant of THOS. SMOOT. Her bond is incorrectly indexed as Book 16, Page 341.

MOSES SNEAD -- Book 14, Page 44 -- Inventory -- DABNEY SANDIDGE, MARBLE C. GOODWIN, JNO. W. BROADDUS; no total; October 25, 1855.
Book 14, Page 46 -- Sale -- October 25, 1855; buyers: RO. W. SNEAD, B. T. HENLEY, D. P. (sic) for C. H. RUCKER, Sheriff and administrator-- $1301.76.
Book 14, Page 98 -- Slaves sold, December 25, 1855; bought by RO. W. SNEAD--$2345.00; B. T. HENLEY as above.

ROBT. W. SNEAD -- Book 16, Page 142 -- Sheriff, July 21, 1862; bondsmen: TAYLOR BERRY, RO. N. ELLIS, R. A. PENDLETON, CHAS. MASSIE, LINDSEY DAVIS, JAS. B. DAVIS, M. C. GOODWIN, RUFUS A. HIGGINBOTHAM, JNO. J. SHRADER, A. C. HARRISON, R. WM. SWANN, J. G. BARRETT, LANCELOT MINOR, J. DUDLEY DAVIS, JAS. P. COLEMAN.
Book 17, Page 36 -- Sheriff, September 18, 1865. Bondsmen: R. A. PENDLETON, GEO. H. DAMERON, SAML. M. GARLAND, RO. A. COGHILL, M. C. GOODWIN, A. C. HARRISON, R. M. TALIAFERRO, B. L. TALIAFERRO, R. A. HIGGINBOTHAM, LEO DANIEL, JR., JNO. J. SHRADER, ALFRED W. WILLIAMS, THOS. WHITEHEAD, JNO. S. SANDIDGE.

SUSANNAH SNEAD -- Book 10, Page 383 -- Estate Commitment to Sheriff -- October, 1839; motion of WM. WILLIS, EDMD. PENN, Sheriff.

JNO. SNIDER (SNYDER) -- Book 1, Page 397 -- September 13, 1774; December 1, 1777. Witnesses: JNO. PETER, DAVID and SARAH ENECKS (ENIX). SARAH testified on probate date and held until January 5, 1778, when others testified. To JNO. AARON--100 acres between my son, JNO., and son-in-law, GEO. COCKBURN; my wife, ELIZ.; at death to ELIZ. COCKBURN; to MARY and SARAH AARON; ANNA JONES; RACHEL BROWN. October 22, 1777--forgot when my will was "wrote"--Dutch Creek land-- sell and divide to my children. Executors: COL. JAS. NEVIL, CAPT. CORNL. THOMAS.
Book 1, Page 399 -- Administrators Bond -- JNO. BROWN and JULIAN NAIL, January 5, 1778, for JNO. BROWN.
Book 1, Page 458 -- Inventory -- L129-15-9; March 1, 1779. JAS. MATTHEWS, GROVES HARDING, WM. JOHNSON.

JNO. SORRELL -- Book 2, Page 140 -- March 25, 1780; September 1, 1783. Witnesses: TERISHA TURNER, BENJ. MOORE, EPHRAIM BLAINE, SAML. ANDERSON. Wife, MOLLY COLEMAN SORRELL--my land; daughter, KATY HOWARD; granddaughter, MARY ANN SNEAD and two oldest children, FRANCES and JNO. SNEAD; grandson, MARTIN DAWSON--as long as he is a Gospel preacher; grandsons, THOS. and WM. DAWSON; great-grandson, JNO. SORRELL DAWSON, son of my grandson, JNO. DAWSON and wife, SALLY--land on north side Hickory Creek. JNO. S. is to pay his brother, PLEASANT DAWSON, when of age, and brother, BENJ. DAWSON, when of age--sons of JNO. and SALLY DAWSON; also his brother, MARTIN DAWSON, when of age; great-granddaughter, SUSANNAH DAWSON, daughter of my grandson, JNO. DAWSON and wife, SALLY, when of age. Great-granddaughter, MARY DAWSON, daughter of JNO. and SALLY, when of age or married; great-granddaughter, PRISCILLA DAWSON, daughter of JNO. and SALLY DAWSON, when of age or married. Great-granddaughters, NANCY and BETSY DAWSON, daughters of JNO. and SALLY; grandson, JNO. DAWSON, son of MARTIN DAWSON and wife, PRISCILLA. Executors: grandsons, JNO. and MARTIN DAWSON and PETER LYONS.
Book 2, Page 143 -- Administrators Bond -- JNO. DAWSON and MARTIN DAWSON, JR., WM. HARRIS, JNO. LOVING, JR., JAS. TURNER, October 6, 1783, for J. and MARTIN DAWSON.
Book 2, Page 157 -- Inventory -- Two pages so numbered; no total; March 1, 1784. TERISHA TURNER, BENJ. MOORE, SAML. ANDERSON.

PHILLIP SOWELL -- Book 5, Page 421 -- December 23, 1809; February 21, 1814. Witnesses: WM. COLEMAN, SHEROD BUGG, N. SPENCER. JANE

PHILLIP SOWELL (cont.) -- SOWELL qualified. DAVID S. GARLAND refused to do so. Wife, JANE, and DAVID S. GARLAND to administrate.
Book 5, Page 428 -- Administrators Bond -- JANE SOWELL; bondsman: JNO. PENN.
Book 5, Page 429 -- Inventory -- March 21, 1814; LEONARD HENLEY and WM. DUNCAN.

ELIJAH SPARKS -- Book 6, Page 191 -- Minister's Bond -- no denomination; November 22, 1820--bondsman: MICAJAH PENDLETON, WM. ARMISTEAD. One would guess that he was a Methodist since PENDLETON was one and early temperance advocate.

FRANCIS W. SPENCER -- Book 3, Page 287 -- Tobacco Inspector, Swan Creek Warehouse, October 12, 1793; bondsman: REUBEN THORNTON, JNO. BOUSH.

LUCY R. SPENCER -- Book 10, Page 383 -- Estate Commitment to Sheriff -- June, 1840; motion of SPOTSWOOD G. LOVING, WILL and CHAS. SPENCER-- along with estates of RO. RIVES and FRANCIS SLAUGHTER. EDMD. PENN, Sheriff.

NORVELL SPENCER -- Book 5, Page 577 -- Administrators Bond -- LUCY R. SPENCER, RO. RIVES, STERLING CLAIBORNE, May 20, 1816, for LUCY R. SPENCER.
Book 5, Page 588 -- Inventory -- $8748.00; July 18, 1816. WM. KNIGHT, THOS. LANDRUM, MARTIN WILSON, WILLIS FRANKLIN.
Book 5, Page 603 -- Guardians Bond -- LUCY R. SPENCER, SAML. TURNER, September 16, 1816, for LUCY R. SPENCER as guardian of WM FRANCIS, CHAS. HENRY, LUCY JANE and SARAH ELIZ. NORVEL SPENCER, orphans of NORVELL SPENCER, deceased.
Book 6, Page 308 -- Administrators Bond -- LUCY R. SPENCER, CORNL. POWELL, GEO. GARRER, FRANCIS SLAUGHTER, July 15, 1822, for LUCY R. SPENCER.
Book 8, Page 156 -- Administrators Bond -- JNO. WHITEHEAD, WM. CAMP, WM. SPENCER, RICH. STEPHENS, November 21, 1831, for JNO. WHITEHEAD.
Book 8, Page 202 -- Inventory -- January 2, 1832: $5590.25; other items with no total; LAVENDER LONDON, WM. C. WINGFIELD, JNO. DILLARD.
Book 8, Page 286 -- Division -- October 7, 1831; DAVID S. GARLAND, PEYTON KEITH, JNO. DILLARD; COL. JNO. PRYOR, surveyor; plat page 287-589½ acres. Naked Creek. 183½ acres to SARAH E. N. SPENCER; 200 acres and mansion house to WM. SPENCER; FARRAR house lot of 206 acres to CHAS. H. SPENCER--only surviving children of NORVELL SPENCER. East side Naked Creek and road from stream to Geddes and both sides of Gedess Mt.--two miles from New Glasgow. Lines of PAUL C. CABELL, JOS. DILLARD, JAS. HIGGINBOTHAM, THOS. LANDRUM, STERLING CLAIBORNE, WM. MORGAN, SOPHIA CRAWFORD. I have remarked elsewhere that Geddes still stands and that I have been there.

SAML. SPENCER -- Book 3, Page 305 -- Tobacco Inspector, Swan Creek, March 17, 1794; Bondsman: R. THORNTIN, PLEASANT MARTIN.
Book 15, Page 329 -- February 16, 1860; July 10, 1860. Witnesses: BENJ. W. PHILLIPS, WM. R. CHRISTIAN, RICH. M. SEAY. Wife, SUSAN E.; my children--when yougest is 21. Wife to administrate.
Book 15, Page 447 -- Administrators Bond -- FRANCIS A. BLAIR, DAVID APPLING, JAS. D. WATTS, August 20, 1860, for FRANCIS A. BLAIR.
Book 15, Page 479 -- Inventory -- slaves, etc.; totals of $5250., $165, and $179. September 17, 1860. JAS. W. KEITH, DAVID APPLING, RICH. N. SEAY.
Book 16, Page 221 -- Administrators de bonis non Bond -- February 16, 1863, JACOB D. PIERCE, J. J. SHRADER for JACOB D. PIERCE.
Book 16, Page 360 -- Inventory -- June 15, 1863; slaves etc.: $12,730.00. DAVID APPLING, JESSE T. WOOD, RO. WM. WATTS.

SARAH SPENCER -- Book 8, Page 157 -- Guardians Bond -- RICH. STEPHENS, WM. CAMP, WM. F. SPENCER. November 21, 1831, for RICH. STEPHENS as guardian of SARAH SPENCER, orphan of NORVELL SPENCER.
Book 8, Page 424 -- Agreement recorded August 18, 1834: WM. F., CHAS. H. SPENCER, and RICH. STEPHENS, guardian of SARAH SPENCER to JNO. WHITEHEAD, administrator de bonis non of NORVELL SPENCER, as of

SARAH SPENCER (cont.) -- January 2, 1833--they are heirs of NORVELL SPENCER and of LUCY R. SPENCER; LUCY was administratrix of NORVELL SPENCER; debts of mother were for their benefit and WHITEHEAD is to pay them out of NORVELL SPENCER's estate.

WM. SPENCER -- Book 4, Page 280 -- Tobacco Inspector, Swan Creek; November 18, 1805. Bondsman: NELSON ANDERSON.
Book 4, Page 284 -- Same men and bond, October 20, 1806.
Book 5, Page 603 -- Guardians Bond -- LUCY R. SPENCER and SAML. TURNER, September 16, 1816, for LUCY R. SPENCER as guardian of WM. FRANCIS, CHAS. HENRY, LUCY JANE, SARAH ELIZA NORVELL SPENCER, orphans of NORVELL SPENCER.

JESSE F. SPINNER -- Book B, Page 110 -- Indexed for him. He was bondsman for BARNETT M. PAGE, administrator of NANCY KELLY, October 12, 1877. Of Bedford and gave powers to CHAS. L. ELLIS, October 1, 1877, to sign for him.

IDA SPOONER -- Book 9, Page 336 -- Guardians Bond -- WM. S. CRAWFORD and ELIJAH FLETCHER, September 18, 1837, for WM. S. CRAWFORD as guardian of IDA SPOONER, orphan of ELIZ. H. SPOONER, deceased.

THOS. H. SPOONER -- Book 9, Page 335 -- Guardians Bond -- for same men and date: THOS. H. as orphan of ELIZ. H. SPOONER, deceased.

ISAAC O. STANFIELD -- Book 17, Page 68 -- December 11, 1865; no probate date; double-checked. Witnesses: RO. A. PENDLETON and JNO. N. FOUKOWITZER. Wife, JANE, to administrate.

DAVID STAPLES -- Book 16, Page 79 -- February 19, 1861; September 16, 1861. Witnesses: SAML. P. COX, EDWIN C. HIGGINBOTHAM, WM. A. STAPLES. Wife, ELIZ; daughter, EMILY; my children: WM. A., NELSON C., POLLY ANN, JAS. M., DAVID T., BETSY ANN, EMILY ANN, FRANCES ANN, JULIA ANN; children of CYNTHIA ANN PLUNKETT, deceased; children of R. S. STAPLES, deceased. They are natives of Missouri and so is NELSON C.
Book 16, Page 80 -- Administrators Bond -- DAVID T. STAPLES, September 16, 1861. It is obvious that he liked the name, ANN.
Book 16, Page 110 -- Inventory -- October 5, 1861; store house and lot in Lynchburg on the canal; Mt. Airy and 80 acres--late residence; City View; two small islands near Chase Island and James River. $20,369.00; CHAS. H. RUCKER, H. F. BOCOCK, WM. KENT.
Book 16, Page 324 -- Administrators Account -- from July 2, 1861; tomb stone--$45.00; coffin--$15.00; barber for shaving corpse--$5.00; Campbell County taxes; EMILY STAPLES for bed cover for girl. January 30, 1863.
Book 16, Page 476 -- Administrators Account -- from August 20, 1862. To SALLEE STAPLES; 1862 Campbell County taxes; legacy of EMILY STAPLES; annuity of ELIZ. STAPLES; bond of FIDELIA STAPLES. Recorded: December 22, 1863.
Book 17, Page 102 -- Administrators Account -- from December, 1863; annuity of ELIZ. STAPLES. Legatees: WM. A., NELSON C., POLLY ANN, JAS. M., DAVID T., BETSY ANN, EMILY ANN, FRANCES ANN, JULIA ANN STAPLES; children of CYNTHIA ANN PLUNKETT and RO. S. STAPLES, deceased. Missouri legatees: NELSON C. STAPLES, trustee. JAS. M. HARRIS and WILLIS H. PLUNKETT, May 15, 1866.

EMMA J. STAPLES -- Book 15, Page 217 -- Guardians Bond -- September 19, 1859; WM. A. STAPLES and JOEL H. CAMPBELL, for WM. A. STAPLES as guardian of EMMA J. STAPLES, infant of W. A. STAPLES. I had a class-mate in Shelbyville, Kentucky, high school class of 1925 by name of EMMA STAPLES. Her family came from here.

GEO. W. STAPLES -- Book 11, Page 153 -- Constables Bond -- June 19, 1843; bondsmen: RO. W. WATTS and W. A. RICHESON.
Book 11, Page 319 -- Same, June 16, 1845; bondsmen: PETER RUCKER, RO. A. PENDLETON, SAML. STAPLES.
Book 11, Page 525 -- Same, June 21, 1847; bondsmen: PETER RUCKER and GEO. T. PLEASANTS.

GEO. W. STAPLES (cont.) -- Book 12, Page 176 -- Constables Bond --
June 18, 1849; bondsmen: DABNEY SANDIDGE, JNO. RHODES.
Book 12, Page 417 -- Same, June 16, 1851; bondsmen: DABNEY SANDIDGE,
M. C. GOODWIN.
Book 13, Page 364 -- Constables Bond -- Fourth District, elected
May 25, 1854; bondsmen: M. C. GOODWIN, J. L. JONES, E. P. TUCKER.

JEROME W. STAPLES -- Book 12, Page 228 -- Administrators Bond --
ARMISTEAD H. OGDEN, JAS. and WALKER R. OGDEN, November 19, 1850, for
ARMISTEAD H. OGDEN.
Book 12, Page 233 -- October 12, 1849; November 19, 1849. Witnesses:
CURTIS GILL, DILLARD H. PAGE, JAS. OGDEN. Son, ROBT., by first wife;
daughter, SARAH, by first wife; wife, LOUISA L. and her children:
BETTY ANN and LUCY ELLEN. Executor: friends, ARMISTEAD OGDEN.
Book 12, Page 468 -- Inventory -- November 23, 1849: $1211.00;
DILLARD H. PAGE, BENJ. CAMDEN, CHAS. TUCKER; small list at $8.50.
Headed by name of EDWIN STAPLES, but seems to belong to sales on
page 469. Sale, Recorded: November 17, 1851.
Book 14, Page 11 -- Sale and Administrators Account -- $365.00;
Administrators Account from April 21, 1849; to LOUISA STAPLES.
Recorded: August 20, 1855.
Book 15, Page 341 -- Division to RO. V. STAPLES and SALLY WOODSON,
formerly STAPLES, and wife of MATT. WOODSON. January 16, 1860:
B. T. HENLEY, JAS. W. HENLEY, RO. C. WILLSHER.

JNO. STAPLES -- Book 3, Page 290 -- Tobacco Inspector, Tye River,
November 19, 1793; bondsman: LUCAS POWELL.
Book 3, Page 406 -- Same, September 19, 1796; same bondsman.
Book 3, Page 420 -- March 29, 1797; June 19, 1797. Witnesses: W. B.
HARE and JAS. M. BROWN. Daughter, ELIZ.; son, WM.; daughter, JUDAH;
other children as of age: SAML., JNO., SALLY, AGATHA, AMY (ANNY?),
POLLY, JOS. My wife--; executors: WM. STAPLES and WM. WARWICK.
WM. WARWICK qualified. Bondsman: WM. B. HARE. JNO. wants younger
children to get better education than older ones, if estate allows.
Book 3, Page 447 -- Inventory -- L742-6-0, September 30, 1797:
ELISHA ESTES, WM. JOHNSON, ℍOS. BIBB, GEO. PURVIS. Indexed for JNO.
SMITH.
Book 4, Page 128 -- Administrators Account -- from 1797; account
of SAML. STAPLES, July 18, 1803. DAVID S. GARLAND, RO. RIVES, WILL
LOVING.
Book 4, Page 290 -- Administrators Bond -- WM. WARWICK and WM. B.
HARE, June 19, 1797.

JOS. STAPLES -- Book 4, Page 156 -- January 30, 1804; September 17,
1804. Witnesses: EZEK. GILBERT, WM. SMITH, JNO. LOVING, ALLEN BLAIR.
Wife, MARY--where I live; son, SAML.; children to be kept together
and labor on plantation; each gets horse when of age; daughter, ELIZ.
STAPLES; son, SAML., JOS., JNO., WM.; daughters: ELIZ., POLLY, SALLY,
POLLINA, NANCY. Executors: friends: JNO. and JOS. LOVING. Codicil:
plantation to be sold and one bought that is more convenient for
my wife's friends. Witnesses: JAS. M. BROWN, ALLEN BUGG, HENRY
CASHWELL.
Book 4, Page 507 -- Administrators Bond -- JNO. and JOSEPH LOVING,
February 15, 1808. Bondsmen: SHELTON CROSTHWAIT, SAML. GARLAND.
Book 6, Page 236 -- indexed as Constables Bond, but not thereon.
JOSE. STAPLES married MOLLY LOVING--bachelor and spinster, March 7,
1782. JNO. WRIGHT, surety. If anyone is interested in the Shelby
County, Kentucky, man, I suggest that the study begin with Deed
Book O, Page 61--herein MARY STAPLES, of Amherst County, for love
of son, JOS. STAPLES, Shelby County, Kentucky and $1.00 sells him
88 acres--her dower and from estate of his father, JOS. STAPLES.

MARGARET F. STAPLES -- Book 8, Page 354 -- Guardians Bond -- GEO.,
JAS., DAVID STAPLES, and ISAAC WALKER, September 16, 1833, for
GEO. STAPLES as guardian of MARGARET, MARTHA, MILDRED, ANN ELIZA
STAPLES, orphans of EDWD. STAPLES.
Book 8, Page 367 -- Guardians Bond -- LAWSON TURNER, November 18,
1833, as guardian of MARGARET F. STAPLES, orphan of EDWD. STAPLES.
Bondsmen: JNO. DILLARD, WM. KENT, A. PLUNKET.

MARGARET F. STAPLES (cont.) -- Book 9, Page 125 -- Guardians Bond --
for same man and ward, September 21, 1835.

MARY STAPLES -- Book 12, Page 255 -- Administrators Bond -- WM. M.
CABELL and MAYO CABELL, March 18, 1850, for WM. M. CABELL.

PAULINA STAPLES -- Book 5, Page 580 -- Guardians Bond -- JOS.
KENNEDY, May 20, 1816, as guardian of PAULINA STAPLES, orphan of
JOS. STAPLES. Bondsman: JESSE KENNEDY.

RO. STAPLES -- Book 15, Page 105 -- Guardians Account -- EDMD. P.
TUCKER, guardian of RO. and SALLIE STAPLES from March 14, 1858;
tuition to W. A. BROCKMAN; land rented. Recorded: August 12, 1858.

RO. V. STAPLES -- Book 13, Page 361 -- Guardians Bond -- SAML. G.
CASH, M. C. GOODWIN, JNO. W. CASH, JAS. M. GANNAWAY, June 19, 1854,
for SAML. G. CASH as guardian of RO. V. and SARAH C. E. STAPLES,
orphans of JENNIE STAPLES, deceased.
Book 16, Page 307 -- Administrators Bond -- M. B. WOODSON, JAS. M.
GANNAWAY, B. L. TALIAFERRO, April 20, 1863, for M. B. WOODSON.
Book 16, Page 443 -- Sale -- February 15, 1864; land sold to M. B.
WOODSON--$8025.00.

ROZANNA E. STAPLES -- Book 15, Page 159 -- Administrators Bond --
W. A. STAPLES, SAML. J. TURNER, JOEL H. CAMPBELL, April 18, 1859,
for W. A. STAPLES.

SALLIE PENN STAPLES -- Book 15, Page 203 -- Guardians Bond -- R. A.
COGHILL and P. C. CABELL, June 20, 1858, for R. A. COGHILL as guardian
of SALLIE PENN STAPLES; no parent set forth.

SAML. STAPLES -- Book 1, Page 320 -- Administrators Bond -- CHAS.
IRVING, CHAS. ROSE, EDMD. WILCOX, November 4, 1776, for CHAS. IRVING.
Book 1, Page 372 -- Inventory -- November --; Recorded: September 1,
1777 L206-12-3; plus items not added. WM. MARTIN, ABRAHAM WARWICK,
JNO. LOVING, JR.

SAML. STAPLES, JR. -- Book 1, Page 388 -- Administrators Bond --
JNO. STAPLES, WM. LOVING, JNO. LOVING, JR., October 6, 1777, for
JNO. STAPLES.
Book 1, Page 405 -- Inventory -- L18-3-0; January 10, 1778; recorded
March 2, 1778. WM. MARTIN, JNO. THURMOND, WM. FITZPATRICK.

SAML. D. STAPLES -- Book 11, Page 318 -- Constables Bond -- June 16,
1845. Bondsmen: PASCHAL RHOADS, NATHAN A. CASH, G. W. STAPLES.

WM. STAPLES, SR. -- Book 15, Page 321 -- March 2, 1852; codicil,
February 2, 1854; Tuesday, June 19, 1860. Witnesses: EDGAR WHITEHEAD,
ALEX. GOOCH; to codicil: LEO DANEIL, JR. and GEO. M. THOMAS. SAML. M.
GARLAND qualified; bondsman: WM. E. COLEMAN. If wife outlives me;
two grandchildren by deceased daughter, ELIZA ROBERTSON; to MELINDA
PARISH, free from husband; at her death, to GEO. W., WM. JR and children
of JNO. STAPLES, deceased: MELINDA, GEO. W., WM. JR. He refers to
MELINDA and my three sons by first wife; daugher, NANCY AKERS; JNO.,
WM. and SAML. ROBERTSON, children of deceased daughter, ELIZA ROBERTSON;
daughter, FRANCES TAPLES; children of deceased son, JEROME; son,
JOS.; son, SAML. D.; son, EDWD.; son, JAMES--nothing for reasons known
to me. Executor: friends, SAML. M. GARLAND. Administrators Bond is
page 332.

ALEX. M. STATON (THOS. is middle name) -- Book 16, Page 176 --
Guardians Bond -- SUSAN D. STATON, October 20, 1862, as guardian of
ALEX. THOS. STATON; no parent set forth.

ANDREW J. STATON -- Book 17, Page 3 -- Administrators Bond -- HENRY E.
SMITH and N. C. TALIAFERRO, December 19, 1864, for HENRY E. SMITH.

ANDREW M. STATON -- Book 16, Page 155 -- Administrators Bond -- RUFUS A.
HIGGINBOTHAM and HENRY LOVING, September 15, 1862, for RUFUS A.
HIGGINBOTHAM.

ANDREW M. STATON (cont.) -- Book 17, Page 1 -- Inventory -- September 23, 1862; no total; WILLIS and ARTHUR WHITE, L. S. CAMPBELL. Recorded: November 21, 1864. Sale, November 30, 1862; buyers: MRS. STATON, MRS. R. STATON, G. W. STATON: $486.80.

JNO. D. STATON -- Book 14, Page 484 -- Administrators Bond -- SUSAN N. STATON and W. W. STATON, December 21, 1857, for SUSAN N. STATON. Book 14, Page 560 -- Inventory -- at late residence, January 21, 1858: $306.25. JAS. R. A. HIGGINBOTHAM, SAML. G. CASH, JOAB W. WHITTEN.

THOS. STATON -- Book 2, Page 219 -- Administrators Bond -- ANN STATON and JOS. BALLINGER, March 7, 1785, for ANN STATON. Book 2, Page 227 -- Inventory -- no total; May 2, 1785. JNO. CHILDRESS, WM. HIGGINBOTHAM, JNO. WOOD, WM. HALL. Book 16, Page 124 -- Administrators Bond -- PARTHENIA L. STATON, May 19, 1862. Book 16, Page 143 -- Inventory -- July 11, 1862: $697.00; WILLIS WHITE, ED. J. DAVIS, A. G. GOOCH. Book 17, Page 223 -- Sale -- January 30, 1866; buyers: PARTHENY, M. T., WM., MRS. L. C., N., THOS., C. W., WM. P., G. W. STATON. No total. Recorded: June 1, 1867.

WM. STATON -- Book 2, Page 67 -- Administrators Bond -- LUCY STATON, JNO. PENN, GEO. MC DANIEL, July 1, 1782, for LUCY STATON. Book 2, Page 76 -- Inventory -- August 22, 1782; no total; WM. LEE, CHAS. REYNOLDS, JOS. DAWSON. Book 18, Page 164 -- Administrators Bond -- JNO. H. PARR and THOS. J. HIGGINBOTHAM, February 19, 1872, for JNO. H. PARR. Book 19, Page 457 -- Administrators Account -- February 17, 1879; expenses to and from Washington--$15.00; clothing for SUSAN A. STATON; pension claim.

AUGUSTINE STEEL -- Book 3, Page 140 -- February 8, 1790; June 7, 1790. Witnesses: RUCH HUDSON, SHEROD BUGG, ELISHA DENNIS. Grandson, JNO. HARRIS, son of my daughter, MARY HARRIS--70 acres where his parents live; daughter, BARBARY WILLIAMS; son, JNO.; daughter, CATH. WOOD; daughter, BETSY STEEL; daughter, SALLY STEEL; son, GEO. STEEL--youngest when of age. My four children: GEO., SALLY, NANCY and ABRAHAM STEEL. Executors: COL. HUGH ROSE and CAPT. LINDSEY COLEMAN--also as guardians of youngest children. To bind them out as they think proper. Book 3, Page 141 -- Administrators Bond -- HUGH ROSE and LINDSEY COLEMAN for both on probate date. Book 3, Page 149 -- Inventory -- no total; July 5, 1790; JER. FRANKLIN, RUSH HUDSON, SHEROD BUGG. Book 3, Page 300 -- indexed as Administrators Account, but not thereon. Book 3, Page 581 -- Administrators Account -- by COLEMAN from April 16, 1796. WM. WILLIAMS in chancery suit--costs versus STEEL heirs up to May, 1800; cost of land division. May 17, 1800. DAVID S. GARLAND, JAS. HIGGINBOTHAM, JNO. HILL.

NANCY STEEL -- Book 4, Page 315 -- Guardians Bond -- WM. WILLIAMS and SHEROD BUGG, October 15, 1798, for WM. WILLIAMS as guardian of NANCY STEEL, orphan of AUGUSTINE STEEL. Clerk notes that it was recorded September 17, 1798 (sic).

WM. E. STEENE, JR. -- Book 9, Page 360 -- Administrators Bond -- JUDITH STEEN and EDWD. TINSLEY, December 18, 1837, for JUDITH STEEN. Book 9, Page 375 -- Inventory -- $1555.00 plus items not figured. LUDWELL S. DAWSON, CHAS. M. DAWSON, WM. TUCKER, January 15, 1838. Book 10, Page 257 -- Administrators Account -- JUDITH ANN STEEN, administratrix from January 8, 1838; bond for three infants--one year; MISS TERRY for tuition for JULIAN--one of children. WM. J. and RALPH C. SHELTON, commissioners. August 18, 1840. Book 11, Page 29 -- Sale -- Town of Bethel, January 8, 1842; MRS. STEEN was a buyer. Book 11, Page 73 -- Administrators Account -- from August, 1840; three infants mentioned; JULIA's tuition to MISS TERRY; same commissioners. July 18, 1842.

WM. E. STEENE, JR. (cont.) -- Book 11, Page 242 -- Administrators
Account -- from January 8, 1842; three infants mentioned--ROWLAND P.
BURKS and D. PATTESON. Recorded: September 16, 1844.
Book 11, Page 424 -- Administrators Account -- from January 1, 1844;
Bedford County tickets; same commissioners. July 20, 1846.
Book 12, Page 87 -- Administrators Account -- from January 1, 1846;
three infants mentioned; same commissioners. May 15, 1849.
Book 12, Page 200 -- Inventory -- of slaves on order of December,
1848: $2401.11; widow, JUDITH ANN STEEN--one-third; rest not divided.
D. PATTESON and EDWIN S. RUCKER, August 20, 1849.
Book 12, Page 435 -- in Administrators Account -- from December, 1849;
JAS. LAMKIN, administrator. JUDITH hired slaves. July 21, 1851.
Book 12, Page 279 -- Slave Inventory -- September 19, 1849. EDWIN S.
RUCKER, JNO. CAMDEN, RO. W. WATTS; no total; May 20, 1850.
Book 12, Page 485 -- Administrators Account -- by JAS. L. LAMKIN,
Sheriff; bond of WM. P. SCOTT, guardian of JULIA ANN, EDWD. and GEO.
STEEN, January 19, 1852. I do not find Estate Commitment to Sheriff.
Book 14, Page 486 -- Inventory of Slaves -- on order of December,
1856. Motion of JOS. C. HENDRICK and wife, JUDITH, and EDWD. T.
STEEN: $3950.00. HENDRICK and wife got one-ninth. Divided to
EDWD. T. STEEN, WM. P. SCOTT as guardian of GEO. F. STEEN. December 31,
1856. WHITING DAVIES, GEO. P. HYLTON, ARTHUR B. DAVIES, ARCHELAUS
COX.

JAS. STEPHENS -- Book 3, Page 291 -- Tobacco Inspector -- Tye River,
November 18, 1793. Bondsman: WM. LEE HARRIS.
Book 3, Page 393 -- Same, September 19, 1796; bondsman: JNO. PENN.
Book 3, Page 407 -- Same, September 19, 1796; Bondsman: JNO. PENN.

EDWD. STEPHENSON -- Book 1, Page 86 -- Septmeber 17, 1766; October 6,
1766. Witnesses: WM. SIMPSON, JNO. THOMSON, FRANS. MERIWETHER. My
wife; oldest son, ROBT.--110 acres where he liveth; son, JNO.--123
acres ditto. Son, EDWD.--where I live; son, WM.--101 acres. Remainder
of where JNO. STEPHENSON now lives; son, JAMES; daughters: MARGET,
JANE, ELIZ. and MARY STEPHENSON--my four daughters until married.
Executors: sons, ROBT., JNO. and EDWD.
Book 1, Page 89 -- Administrators Bond -- JNO. and EDWD. qualified;
bondsman: ALEX. REID, JR., JNO. THOMSON, JNO. HENDERSON, DUNCAN
CAMERON, December 1, 1766.
Book 1, Page 107 -- Inventory -- January 27, 1767; no total; RO.
WEIR, DAVID MERIWETHER, JAS. DUNWOODY. Recorded: July 6, 1767.

JNO. STEWART -- Book 2, Page 190 -- Administrators Bond -- CHAS.
STEWART, JNO. STEWART, JER. TAYLOR, CHAS. ROSE, August 2, 1784, for
CHAS. STEWART.
Book 2, Page 192 -- April 14, 1784; August 2, 1784. Witnesses:
WIATT POWELL, WM. CHAPPEL, THOS. STEWART. Wife, ANN; my youngest
children to be educated; son, SAML.--three years of education; same
for sons, DAVID and RICH.; daughter, SALLY--two years. Children:
CHAS., JNO., JAS., ROBT., MARY, THOS., ELIZ., ANN--hard to decide as
to one or two here; SAML., DAVID, SALLY, RICH. and WM. STEWART.
Son, JNO.--3750 acres in Kentucky. Executors: sons, CHAS. and JNO.
Book 4, Page 459 -- Administrators Bond -- JNO. STEWART, WM. TEAS,
RO. NIMMO (MIMMO?), April 22, 1806, for JNO. STEWART.
Book 4, Page 462 -- Constables Bond -- January 21, 1803; bondsman:
SAML. SPENCER.

JNO. STILLWELL -- Book 10, Page 383 -- Estate Commitment to Sheriff --
February, 1841; surviving partner of WEBSTER and STILLWELL. EDMD.
PENN, Sheriff.

BENJ. STINNETT, SR. -- Book 1, Page 245 -- October 21, 1764; July 5,
1773. Witnesses: RICH. PETER, JAS. STINNETT, HANNAH PETER. Wife,
ELIZ.--where she now lives; son, WM.; daughter, SUSANNAH--when both
are of age; son-in-law, JOHN CHILDRESS. Executors: wife and son,
BENJ.
Book 1, Page 246 -- Administrators Bond -- ELIZ. STINNETT and RICH.
PETER, July 5, 1773, for ELIZ. STINNETT.
Book 1, Page 248 -- Inventory -- L28-9-11; September 6, 1773; NOELL
JOHNSON, JNO. WHITEHEAD, BENJ. NOEL.

HENRY STINNETT -- Book 13, Page 242 -- Guardians Bond -- MARBEL E.
STINNETT and WM. M. WARE, November 21, 1853, for MARBEL E. STINNETT
as guardian of HENRY, ROBT., and GEO. STINNETT, orphans of CHAS.
STINNETT.

SUSANNAH STINNETT -- Book 9, Page 289 -- Estate Commitment to Sheriff --
March, 1837; motion of JAS. WHITEHEAD; JNO. COLEMAN, Sheriff.

BENAMMI STONE -- Book 8, Page 170 -- Administrators Bond -- JAS. P.
GARLAND, JNO. HORSLEY, WILKINS WATSON, January 16, 1832, for JAS. P.
GARLAND.
Book 8, Page 171 -- December 15, 1823; codicil, September 30, 1824;
codicil, October 2, 1824; January 16, 1832. Witnesses to will:
S. GARLAND, JESSE MUNDY, BEVERLY DAVIES, ARTHUR B. DAVIES. Witnesses
to codicils: BEVERLY DAVIES, RICH. CRAWFORD, HENRY L. DAVIES. Far
advanced in life; aged and beloved wife, ELIZ.; son-in-law, JAS. P.
GARLAND, and wife, CATH.; son-in-law, ROBT. GARLAND, and wife,
NANCY--if she has issue. SPOTSWOOD GARLAND married my daughter,
POLLY--now dead, but she left one child--now dead. JAS. P. GARLAND
bought this one-third interest from SPOTSWOOD GARLAND and it is to
be charged versus him in settlement. Children of JAS. P. and CATH.;
JAS. P. holds bond and I permitted him to sell 71½ acres of my land
to JNO. H. SMITH so that he could better sell his own land. Valuable
religious books to be kept in family. Want no disputes, but, if so,
to be handled by DAVID S. GARLAND, HUDSON M. and SAML. GARLAND.
Administrators: wife, ELIZ.; and sons-in-law, RO. and JAS. P.
GARLAND. Codicil: RO. GARLAND is removed as administrator and JAS. P.
is to act; RO. and wife to get trust fund in hands of JAS. P. Codicil:
WM. M. WALLER is to assist JAS. P. GARLAND. WALLER declined and
JAS. P. GARLAND qualified; bondsmen--see page 170 above.
Book 8, Page 192 -- Inventory -- $4271.25; LINDSEY COLEMAN, A. B.
DAVIES, A. L. DAVIES, January 18, 1832. Note: STONE owned Hunting
Tower which was old home of GILBERT--see deeds in early books. This
house still stands and is not far from parsonage and is now owned
by MADISON SETTLE and wife, DABNEY. MADISON tells me that there are
several graves marked in cemetery near the house, but I have never
visited the graves.

GEO. STONEHAM -- Book 4, Page 448 -- Administrators Bond -- ELIJAH
MAYS, HEX. HARGROVE, LEWIS WHITE, PARMENAS BRYANT, August 19, 1807,
for ELIJAH MAYS.
Book 4, Page 472 -- Inventory -- September 24, 1807--L811-19-3;
STEPHEN WATTS, JAS. DILLARD, CHAS. WATTS.
Book 5, Page 199 -- Administrators Account -- from August 18, 1807;
bond of MARY STONEHAM, February 13, 1813. JAS. DILLARD, CHAS. WATTS,
WM. H. DIGGS. Note: see my abstract of Nelson County, Virginia,
will book A for interesting STONEHAM data.

HENRY STONEHAM (indexed SLOUCHIN) -- Book 6, Page 277 -- Administrators
Bond -- JNO. DILLARD, WM. ARMISTEAD, January 21, 1822, for JNO. DILLARD.

PLEASANT M. STORY -- Book 9, Page 37 -- Administrators Bond -- MARTHA
STORY(EY), JOEL. B. (R) FRAZER, JOS. E. STORY, January 19, 1835, for
MARTHA STORY(EY).
Book 9, Page 50 -- Inventory -- $217.50; D. STAPLES, REUBEN CARVER,
JACOB WOODSON, February 16, 1835.
Book 9, Page 366 -- Administrators Account -- from July 19, 1836.
Bond of P. STORY, JR.; bond to DAVID STAPLES, December 18, 1837.
JNO. DILLARD and DANL. DAY.

JONATHAN A. STOUT -- Book B, Page 29 -- Estate Commitment to Sheriff --
Tuesday, August 31, 1847; motion of S. M. GARLAND. Sheriff: JAS. L.
LAMKIN.

CAROLINE STOVALL -- Book 4, Page 322 -- Guardians Bond -- JER.
TAYLOR, SAML. HILL, THOS. STEWART, July 21, 1800, for JER. TAYLOR
as guardian of CAROLINE STOVALL, orphan of GEO. STOVALL, deceased.

GEO. STOVALL, JR. -- Book 1, Page 501 -- Administrators Bond -- ANNE
STOVALL and ARCHELAUS MITCHELL, October 4, 1779, for ANNE STOVALL.

GEO. STOVALL, JR. (cont.) -- Book 1, Page 514 -- Inventory -- October 10, 1779: L3975-3-0; JOS. CREWS, HENRY MC DANIEL, WM. WEBSTER. This man was quite prominent in early Amherst--see my order book items for 1766ff.

JAS. STOVALL -- Book 3, Page 204 -- June 22, 1787; October 3, 1791. Witnesses: JAS. CHRISTIAN, THOS. OGLESBY, RO. CHRISTIAN. Wife, MARY--where I live; son, GEO., when of age. My father's estate, which I have not received, in hands of THOS. STOVALL. Executors: wife, JNO. CHRISTIAN, SR., WM. BRADLEY. She qualified with BRADLEY as bondsman.
Book 3, Page 348 -- Inventory -- September 5, 1795. No total; JNO. CHRISTIAN, JNO. CHRISTIAN B, STEPHEN WATTS.

SOPHIA STRANGE -- Book 15, Page 250 -- Administrators Bond -- RO. and ZACH. D. TINSLEY, November 21, 1859, for RO. TINSLEY.
Book 16, Page 272 -- Administrators Account -- from November 21, 1859; THOS. STRQNGE and wife; MC DANIEL versus MC DANIEL in favor of WM. MC DANIEL's executor; execution by L. MC DANIEL. Recorded: April 20, 1863.

ANTHONY STREET -- Book 3, Page 135 -- August 29, 1788; June 7, 1790. Witnesses: MARTIN PARKS, WM. PARKS, JAS. CARY. Wife, ELIZ.; my four children: SAML., THOS., ELIZ. SMITH, FRANKEY HARRILL; my four grandchildren: ANTHONY COX, WM. COX, FRANKEY CRAWLEY, ELIZ. COX. Executors: friends: JNO. WIATT, RICH. SHELTON, RICH. POWELL, and wife, ELIZ. Administrators Bond is page 136: RICH. POWELL, RICH. HARRISON, ZACH. DAWSON for RICH. POWELL.
Book 3, Page 189 -- Inventory -- July 2, 1790; no total; PHILIP BURTON, JNO. HARRISON, GEO. MC DANIEL.
Book 3, Page 581 -- Error: AUGUSTINE STEEL item.

JOS. STRICKLIN -- Book 4, Page 169 -- May 10, 1804; February 18, 1805. Witnesses: WM. PERRY, JESSE PERRY, WM. EDMONDS. Wife, ABIGAIL-- where I live; daughter, SARAH HOWARD--100 acres in Rockbridge and known as Whitesides; daughter, HANNAH OWINGS--80 acres in Rockbridge on Little Mary; son, JOS.--90 acres in Rockbridge near Moor's Furnace in Mt. gap. Daughter, POLLY CARPENTER--Augusta land--three tracts; son, SAML.--land bought of WM. EDMONDS in County of Amherst; daughter, NANCY WITT; daughters: ABIGAIL and AMEY; son, ABIEL. Executors: wife and son, ABIEL, and friend, HAWES COLEMAN.

ANANIAS STUART -- Book 21, Page 171 -- Minister's Bond -- June 15, 1885; no data.

WM. SUDARTH, SR. -- Book 1, Page 4 -- December 25, 1761; April 5, 1762. Witnesses: LAWRENCE SUDARTH, MARTHA SUDARTH, GEO. TAYLOR, THEOPHILUS FAVER. Daughters: SARAH DENNY. AGNES WILLIBEY, CHARITY TATE, ELIZ. RAY. My three sons, JAS., WM. and LAWRENCE; youngest daughter, MARY SUDARTH, to administrate. She qualified--page 5 on probate date. Bondsmen: THEOPHILUS FAVER, CHAS. TATE, LAWRENCE SUDARTH.

KITTY SULLIVAN -- Book 4, Page 527 -- Guardians Bond -- JOSHUA SHELTON and NICHL. VANSTAVERN, July 19, 1808, for JOSHUA SHELTON as guardian of KITTY SULLIVAN, orphan of ROZELL SULLIVAN, deceased. Page 538 contains same bond.

DAVID SWANSON -- Book 5, Page 88 -- Constables Bond -- November 19, 1811; first hundred; bondsmen: WM. LEE and STERLING CLAIBORNE.

JNO. SWANSON -- Book 3, Page 540 -- March 13, 1799; April 15, 1799. Witnesses: JNO. CAMM, PEACHY FRANKLIN, ARCHELAUS MAYS. Daughter, JANE SWANSON, County of Carthness (?), Scotland--200 acres on Limekiln Creek; 86 acres on Elk Island Creek; 61 acres on Turkey Mt.--all in Amherst County; if she is dead, or no issue. Children of my brother, FRANS, and sister, ANN. Sons, DAVID, JOSEPH, JNO. and GABL.--400 acres on Buffaloe. Friend, DR. JAS. M. BROWN--where he recently built a dwelling house--one acre additional. Executor: DR. JAS. M. BROWN and DANL. MC DANIEL.

JNO. SWANSON (cont.) -- Book 4, Page 307 -- Administrators Bond --
JAS. M. BROWN and DANL. MC DANIEL qualified on probate date. Bondsman:
PHILIP GOOCH.

JOSEPH SWANSON -- Book 8, Page 355 -- September 5, 1833; September 21,
1833. Witnesses: MOSES PHILLIPS, ASAHAEL FRENCH. OTHO SWANSON
qualified; bondsman: SAML. M. GARLAND and EDMD. WINSTON. Wife,
SUSANNAH P. (?); my children: OTHO, WM., JNO. T.(?), JAS. M.,
CHAS. S., ELIZA J., LOUISA, JOSEPH, FRANCIS, and GEO. W. SWANSON.
Son, OTHO, is to administrate.
Book 8, Page 368 -- Inventory -- October 21, 1833: $559.75. JAS. D.
WATTS, MOSES PHILLIPS, WM. WRIGHT.

OTHELLO (OTHO) SWANSON -- Book 8, Page 416 -- March 19, 1834; June 16,
1834. Witnesses: JAS. D. WATTS, JAS. W. KEITH, WM. WRIGHT; proved
by KEITH and WRIGHT on June 19, 1834. SAML. M. GARLAND qualified;
bondsman: JOS. K. IRVING. Mother, SUSANNAH SWANSON; my brothers and
sisters; Amherst County land to me from my father to be sold and
money used to buy land more convenient for mother, brothers, and
sisters. Executor: friend, SAML. M. GARLAND. Administrators Bond
is on page 418.
Book 9, Page 124 -- Administrators de bonis non Bond -- September 21,
1835--SUSANNAH SWANSON, WASH HILL, and WM. SWANSON for SUSANNAH SWANSON.
This page is quite faded.

BETTIE W. SWISHER -- Book 23, Page 346 -- Same men and date for
SWISHER as guardian of his infant daughter, BETTIE W. SWISHER.

-T-

ADDISON TALIAFERRO -- Book 8, Page 431 -- Coroner -- September 15,
1834. Bondsmen: HENRY L. DAVIES, ZACH D. TINSLEY.
Book 17, Page 168 -- Sale in part -- R. M. TALIAFERRO, administrator,
December 14, 1865. Family buyers: R. M., A., J. M., R. P., B. L.,
N. D. Consent of heirs under the will: B. L.; N. L. as guardian of
N. D.; A. JR. EDITHA RICHARDS, HENRIANN TALIAFERRO. Returned
September 17, 1866. Note: will was recorded later; see below.
Book 17, Page 204 -- Inventory -- no total; November 28, 1865; JNO. W.
BROADDUS, JAS. M. TALIAFERRO, RUFUS M. HIGGINBOTHAM. Returned:
October 16, 1866.
Book 17, Page 227 -- Sale at Mansion house -- October 4, 1866. Family
buyers: B. L., R. M., A., N. D., HENRIANN TALIAFERRO. Returned
May 20, 1867.
Book 17, Page 257 -- Administrators Bond -- RICH. M. TALIAFERRO, RO. W.
SNEAD, B. L. and ADDISON TALIAFERRO, September 18, 1865, for RICH. M.
TALIAFERRO.
Book 19, Page 169 -- March 24, 1865; September 18, 1865. Witnesses:
JAS. M. TALIAFERRO, CHAS. F. COLEMAN. My woman, MARY, commonly
called MARY OGDON, and mulatto, NANCY, to be freed. My four sons:
son, NICHL., to be educated; my daughters; my lawfully begotten
grandchildren; daughter, EDITHA RICHARDS, wife of WM. A. RICHARDS;
negro girl to S. M. GARLAND--this has been scratched through--ARNOLD
"as part of her share."
Book 23, Page 286 -- Administrators de bonis non Bond -- September 19,
1892: SARAH B. TALIAFERRO. Bondsman: C. L. SCOTT.

BENJ. TALIAFERRO -- Book 7, Page 205 -- Sheriff -- January 19, 1829.
Bondsmen: LINDSEY COLEMAN, JNO. PENN, JESSE RICHESON, CORNL. SALE,
WM. BOURNE, ZACH DRUMMOND, WM. M. WALLER, JAS. L. LAMKIN, ARTHUR B.
DAVIES.
Book 7, Page 325 -- Sheriff -- January 18, 1830. Bondsmen: as above,
but JAS. F. TALIAFERRO in place of JNO. PENN.
Book 11, Page 416 -- June 22, 1844; June 15, 1846. Witnesses:
DAVID LOGAN, SAML. C. GIBSON, DABNEY SANDIDGE, WIATT P. SMITH. My
Staton Creek land on middle fork of Pedlar; my wife, MILDRED; daughter,
ROSA B., deceased, who was wife of WM. BOURNE, and her children;
daughter, LUCINDA, wife of MAYO DAVIES; daughter, MILDRED T. (?), wife
of LYNE S. TALIAFERRO; daughter, MARY A. M., wife of RICHESON HENLEY;

BENJ. TALIAFERRO (cont.) -- daughter, SARAH CATH., wife of JNO. C.
WHITEHEAD; daughter, ELIZ. M., wife of JNO. M. (W) BROADDUS; daughter,
BELINDA CAROLINE, wife of LEONARD CHILDRESS, and children. Executors:
sons-in-law, MAYO DAVIES and WM. BOURNE. My six daughters and children
of deceased daughter, ROSA B. BOURNE--if daughters have no issue; if
ELIZ. BROADDUS is without issue. Where I live.
Book 11, Page 434 -- Inventory -- June 16, 1846: $9433; Jas. and
Kanawha canal stock. CHAS. MASSIE, JOEL F. SMITH, JNO. H. FUQUA.
Book 11, Page 58 -- Administrators Account -- MAYO DAVIES and WM.
BOURNE, administrators from July 15, 1846. Tax on Nelson County land;
to J. C. WHITEHEAD to make equal to L. S. TALIAFERRO; to M. A. HENLEY;
heirs of R. B. BOURNE, M. DAVIES, WM. BOURNE; receipt to THOS. J.
OLD, E. E. BROADDUS, E. C. CHILDRESS, MR. TALIAFERRO, JAS. TALIAFERRO--
for estate business out of county. JNO. H. FUQUA, commissioner:
September 4, 1847.
Book 12, Page 211 -- Administrators Account -- by same executors from
15 November 1847; to BENJ. HENLEY, administrator of R. HENLEY,
account; $1.34 for trip to show land in mountains; MRS. TALIAFERRO for
farm expenses; legacy to A. M. HENLEY; CARY WHITEHEAD, C. B. SNEAD,
E. BROADDUS, LYNE S. TALIAFERRO; cash of B. T. HENLEY; JESSE RICHESON
bought mountain land. Commissioners: CHAS. H. MASSIE and JNO. R.
IRVINE. August 20, 1849. Also expense of WM. BOURNE and MAYO
DAVIES' executors.
Book 13, Page 287 -- Administrators Bond -- October 15, 1854; JAS. F.
TALIAFERRO and HENRY LOVING for JAS. F. TALIAFERRO.

COL. CHAS. TALIAFERRO -- Book 3, Page 504 -- July 13, 1791; June 18,
1798. Witnesses: DANL. TUCKER, SAML. HIGGINBOTHAM, LINDSEY COLEMAN.
Son, RICH; son, CHAS.; son, WM.; son, RODERICK--when of age for them;
Tobacco Mt. Row spur land on Puppie Creek along main road from WM.
HOWARD's; son, JNO.; son, JAS., when of age; sons, ZACH and BENJ.--
land bought of SAML. MARKSBURY; daughter, SARAH TALIAFERRO; daughter,
ROSE TALIAFERRO; at death of my wife. Executors: sons, CHAS., JNO.,
ZACH and BENJ. TALIAFERRO. They refused to qualify and WM. and
RODERICK TALIAFERRO did so; bondsmen: JNO. WARE, JNO. SMITH, THOS.
MORRIS.
Book 3, Page 526 -- Inventory -- L1461-4-4; LEONARD HENLEY, HENRY
BALLINGER, BENJ. HIGGINBOTHAM, December 13, 1798.
Book 3, Page 528 -- Division to WM., RODERICK and JAS. TALIAFERRO;
WM. LOVING who married SARAH TALIAFERRO. December 13, 1798. Same
commissioners as above.
Book 4, Page 311 -- Administrators Bond -- WM. and RODERICK TALIAFERRO,
September 17, 1798; see bondsmen above.
Book 6, Page 471 -- August 11, 1821; August 16, 1824. These are
indexed in part for COL. CHAS. TALIAFERRO. Witnesses: BENNET A.
CRAWFORD, GEO. N. ROSE, JNO. PRYOR, SAML. HANSBROUGH, JAS. F. TALIAFERRO.
Son, RICH. M.--346½ acres west of my house; son, ADDISON--532 acres
east of my house; son, BENJ. B.--where I live--468 acres; daughter,
NANCY COLEMAN; children of my deceased daughter, BELINDA COLEMAN:
LUCY C. and RO. L. COLEMAN; if no heirs; executors: three sons,
RICH. M., ADDISON, and BENJ. B. TALIAFERRO.
Book 6, Page 528 -- Inventory -- $3236.42, December 20, 1824. CORNL.
SALE, ORMUND WARE, CHAS. MASSIE.
Book 6, Page 541 -- Division -- December 28, 1824: to ADDISON
TALIAFERRO, LINDSEY, CAROLINE and LANDON COLEMAN; to BENJ. B.
TALIAFERRO. Recorded: 21 February 1825. CORNL. SALE, ORMUND WARE,
RICHESON HENLEY.
Book 6, Page 595 -- Division to CAROLINE and LANDON COLEMAN, children
of REUBEN COLEMAN, deceased. RO. A. PENN has married CAROLINE and
to draw slaves and pay LANDON COLEMAN to adjust accounts. April 18,
1825. RO. TINSLEY and WALTER B. BOSWELL.
Book 7, Page 96 -- Administrators Account -- by BENJ. B. TALIAFERRO
from 1824--to ADDISON TALIAFERRO, SILAS C. FREEMAN for preaching--
$5.00; to LYNE S. TALIAFERRO, JNO. PRYOR for schooling and shop
account; half of tobacco is mine; to CHAS. P. TALIAFERRO; ADDISON
and BENJ. B. TALIAFERRO, administrators. October 17, 1826: JNO.
PRYOR and JAS. P. (F?) TALIAFERRO.
Book 8, Page 383 -- Indexed for 583, an error -- Administrators
Account -- by BENJ. B. TALIAFERRO from November 10, 1826. Amounts to

COL. CHAS. TALIAFERRO (cont.) -- LYNE S. TALIAFERRO, JNO. FLOOD,
ELIJAH DAVIS, CHAS. P. TALIAFERRO--not termed heirs. May 16, 1829.
CHAS. MASSIE, commissioner. ADDISON TALIAFERRO's account as admin-
istrator. Page 284, from June 3, 1828. Amount received from CHAS. P.
TALIAFERRO. December 19, 1829. CHAS. L. BARRET, commissioner.

CHAS. P. TALIAFERRO -- Book 5, Page 182 -- Commissioner of Revenue --
October 19, 1812. Bondsman: HILL CARTER.
Book 5, Page 447 -- Three Sheriffs Bonds -- July 18, 1814. Bondsman:
HILL CARTER, BENJ. TALIAFERRO, BENJ. CHACKELFORD, DAVID S. GARLAND,
EDMD. WINSTON, JR.
Book 5, Page 514 -- Sheriffs Bond -- June 19, 1815; bondsman: HILL
CARTER, BENJ. TALIAFERRO, JAS. DILLARD, EDMD. T. COLEMAN, BEN
SHACKELFORD, J. M. BROWN, NELSON CRAWFORD.
Book 6, Page 488 -- Coroner -- September 20, 1824. Bondsmen: JAS. F.
and LYNE S. TALIAFERRO.

ELIZ. TALIAFERRO -- Book 6, Page 293 -- March 6, 1822; June 17, 1822.
Witnesses: CHAS. P. and SARAH TALIAFERRO. LYNE S. TALIAFERRO and
JAS. POWELL qualified. Bondsman: BENJ. TALIAFERRO. Bond due from
ZACH and HENLEY DRUMMOND. Son, LYNE S. TALIAFERRO; granddaughter,
ELIZA ANN BARRET. Executors: son, LYNE S., and friend, DR. JAS.
POWELL.
Book 6, Page 334 -- Inventory -- $268.12½; November 18, 1822. JNO. B.
DUNVAN, JACOB SMITH, JAS. H. SMITH. Administrators Bond is on page
349.
Book 6, Page 472 -- Additional Inventory -- of $120 by same committee
as other inventory, July 21, 1824.

JAS. F. TALIAFERRO -- Book 6, Page 230 -- Constables Bond -- June 18,
1821. Bondsman: ARTHUR B. DAVIES.

JNO. TALIAFERRO -- Book 6, Page 339 -- Administrators Bond -- CHAS. P.
TALIAFERRO, JAS. PENN, and LYNE S. TALIAFERRO, November 18, 1822, for
CHAS. P. TALIAFERRO.

JNO. B. TALIAFERRO -- Book 3, Page 337 -- May 2, 1795; July 20, 1795.
Witnesses: WM. JACOBS, JOS. BURGER, HEZ. WOOD. To MARTHA TAYLOR;
slave to be bought from my father, ZACH TALIAFERRO, and to be freed
when 11; brother, CHARLES--clothes and fiddle; two youngest sisters,
ANNE and FRANCES TALIAFERRO. Executors: DANL. MC DANIEL, RICH. and
CHAS. TALIAFERRO.
Book 3, Page 562 -- Administrators Account -- by MC DANIEL--to RICH.
TALIAFERRO, RO. RIVES and Company, Bent Creek store, 1797; WILSON
PENN, legatee; JOS. BURGHER--legatee ?; SAML. MEREDITH, JAS. DILLARD,
DAVID S. GARLAND, May 4, 1797. WILSON PENN married one legatee and
THOMPSON WATKINS married one. HENLEY DRUMMOND, agent for WATKINS
or WATKIN. There is no B initial with this item:
Book 4, Page 514 -- Administrators Bond -- BETSY TALIAFERRO, CHAS.
TALIAFERRO, WM. LOVING, BENJ. and CHAS. T. TALIAFERRO, May 16, 1808,
for BETSY to administrate.

LYNE S. TALIAFERRO -- Book 6, Page 599 -- Constables Bond -- June 20,
1825; bondsmen: CHAS. L. BARRET, CHAS. P. TALIAFERRO.
Book 7, Page 26 -- Constables Bond -- June 19, 1827; same bondsmen
for two years in 2nd Hundred.

MILDRED T. TALIAFERRO -- Book 13, Page 244 -- Administrators Bond --
MAYO DAVIES, HENRY L. DAVIES, JAS. F. TALIAFERRO, November 21, 1853,
for MAYO DAVIES.
Book 13, Page 323 -- Inventory -- No total; January 18, 1854. CHAS.
MASSIE, M. C. GOODWIN, JNO. R. IRVINE.
Book 14, Page 163 -- Sale -- December 20, 1853; JAS. M. and JAS. F.
TALIAFERRO were buyers, September 15, 1856. Second list and no
total and same date: JAS. F. TALIAFERRO was a buyer.

NANCY TALIAFERRO -- Book 4, Page 215 -- April 19, 1806. NANCY
releases claim as widow of WM. TALIAFERRO. THOS. N. EUBANK, JNO.
EUBANK, JR., JNO. EUBANK, committee.

R. M. TALIAFERRO -- Book 17, Page 218 -- Treasurer of Amherst
County--November 19, 1866; report on Orange and Alexandria Railroad.
Book 17, Page 286 -- another report as above, December 14, 1867.
Book 18, Page 417 -- Notary Public -- May 18, 1874. Bondsman: N. D.
TALIAFERRO.
Book 19, Page 432 -- February 13, 1879; see N. D. above.
Book 21, Page 405 -- Administrators Bond -- HENRY A. TALIAFERRO and
SALLIE B. or A.--so signed--April 18, 1887, for HENRY A. TALIAFERRO.
She gave power of attorney to CHAS. L. ELLIS and is called MRS.
SALLIE A.

RODERICK TALIAFERRO -- Book 4, Page 584 -- Constables Bond -- June 19,
1809. Bondsman: CHAS. L. BARRET and CHAS. TALIAFERRO. Signed
ROD. L., but RICH. L. at top.
Book 8, Page 148 -- indexed as inventory, but not there.

SALLIE B. TALIAFERRO -- Book 20, Page 117 -- Trustee account by
R. M. TALIAFERRO from 15 March 1869, to June 21, 1880. 87 acres on
Rutledge bought by H. A. TALIAFERRO December 20, 1877; rent on land
on railroad; 26 or 27 acres bought by J. F. DAVIS, January 1, 1880;
recorded: October 18, 1880.

WM. TALIAFERRO -- Book 4, Page 192 -- October 1, 1805; October 21,
1805. Witnesses: CHAS. P. TALIAFERRO, WM. SANDRIDGE (sic), SAML.
CASH. January 20, 1806, BENJ. TALIAFERRO qualified; bondsman: CHAS.
TUCKER. October 21, 1806, COL. CHAS. TALIAFERRO qualified. Bondsman:
NELSON CRAWFORD. Son, JNO. EUBANK TALIAFERRO when of age; my wife.
Executors: brothers: CHAS., JNO., BENJ. and RODERICK TALIAFERRO.
Book 4, Page 214 -- Inventory -- 17 February 1806; L 352-16-10; no
committee named.
Book 4, Page 215 -- Renunciation of will by widow, NANCY N., April 19,
1806. Witnesses: THOS. N. EUBANK--JNO. EUBANK SR. and JR.
Book 4, Page 426 -- Administrators Bond -- for BENJ. TALIAFERRO.
Book 4, Page 426 -- Administrators Bond -- for CHAS. TALIAFERRO.
Book 6, Page 365 -- Administrators Account -- by both administrators
from 1806. To NANCY TALIAFERRO; bond of ZACH and WM. TALIAFERRO;
to PHILIP SMITH, TALIAFERRO and LOVING, P. TALIAFERRO, BENJ. TALIAFERRO.
March 14, 1823. NELSON CRAWFORD, WM. JOPLING, DABNEY SANDIDGE.

WM. H. TALIAFERRO -- Book 18, Page 349 -- Administrators Bond --
FRANK TALIAFERRO and HENRY LOVING, August 18, 1873, for FRANK TALIA-
FERRO.

ZACH TALIAFERRO -- Book 3, Page 419 -- February 22, 1797; July 19,
1797. Witnesses: WM. HORSLEY, JOS. HORSLEY, NATHL. OFFUTT. Wife,
JUDITH--mill and distillery and property got by her in marriage;
land on Tye; three sons, CHAS., WARREN and BURKENHEAD TALIAFERRO--
1275 acres in Georgia which GEN. ELIJAH CLARK and MAJOR JAS. SHEPHERD
are bonded to make title to me. Son, WILLIAM--land on Horsley. My
following children: RICH., ANN WATKINS, CHAS., FRANCES PENN, WARREN
and BURKENHEAD. Executors: sons, ZACH., RICH., CHAS. and WARREN
TALIAFERRO.
Book 3, Page 565 -- Inventory -- no total; August 23, 1797. JNO.
CHRISTIAN SR. and JR., JNO. HORSLEY.
Book 3, Page 586 -- Administrators Account -- by RICH. TALIAFERRO
from July, 1797. WILSON PENN for saddle for wife; to JNO. TALIAFERRO;
JOS. and MARTHA HORSLEY's note; Buckingham Sheriff; to CHAS. and
JUDITH TALIAFERRO; JNO. HORSLEY for leading lines. October 16, 1800.
JOS. BURRUS, SAML. MEREDITH, DAVID S. GARLAND.
Book 4, Page 290 -- Administrators Bond -- RICH. TALIAFERRO, July 19,
1797. Bondsmen: DANL. MC DANIEL, WM. JACOBS.

JNO. TANKERSLEY -- Book 11, Page 114 -- Administrators Bond -- GEO. T.
PLEASANTS and SAML. WATTS, March 20, 1843, for GEO. T. PLEASANTS.
Book 11, Page 121 -- Inventory -- April 12, 1843--$1600.70; A. B.
DAVIES, JOS. R. CARTER, S. (L) D. BOWEN.
Book 11, Page 158 -- Sale -- April 20, 1843; no family names: $264.00½.
Book 11, Page 328 -- Administrators Account -- from April, 1843; rent
paid to NANCY N. ELLIS. JNO. PRYOR, commissioner, June 16, 1845.

JNO. TANKERSLEY (cont.) -- Book 11, Page 594 -- Administrators
Account -- March, 1847; JNO. PRYOR as above. A. HADEN for making
coffin--$5.00; PHILIP THURMOND hired slaves; chancery suit of
TANKERSLEY versus TANKERSLEY. Burial expenses: $17.95. WM.
GILLASPIE bought a slave. Recorded: December 20, 1847.

RICH. TANKERSLEY -- Book 6, Page 136 -- Administrators Bond -- JAS.
TANKERSLEY, HUGH NORVEL, and JNO. TANKERSLEY, February 21, 1820, for
JAS.
Book 11, Page 220 -- Administrators Bond -- JNO. C. NOELL and WM.
HIX, April 15, 1844, for JNO. C. NOELL.

DAVID H. TAPSCOTT -- Book 13, Page 464 -- Administrators Bond --
JNO. T. ELLIS, RICH. P. ELLIS, JNO. THOMPSON and SAML. M. GARLAND,
March 20, 1855, for JNO. T. ELLIS.
Book 13, Page 518 -- Inventory -- $4528.73, July 16, 1855. RO.
TINSLEY, LEO DANIEL, JR., EDGAR WHITEHEAD.
Book 14, Page 88 -- Sale -- November 16, 1856 at farm: $1267.05.
Recorded: Monday, April 21, 1856.
Book 14, Page 92 -- Sale -- on May 29, 1855. $1287.25. Two negroes:
SHADRACK and BUNVELL were among buyers.
Book 14, Page 98 -- Sale -- of negroes at courthouse, March 17, 1856.
SHADRACK was among those sold. MUSTALPHA and ANN and child were
others sold. BOB was to be put on block, but it was alleged that he
was free. Chancery to investigate. Recorded: Monday, April 21, 1856.

GEO. TATE -- Book 18, Page 314 -- February 20, 1863; June 16, 1873.
Witnesses: JOS. PEETER and JAS. A. CAMPBELL. ISABELLA TATE, widow,
qualified. Appraisers: Z. CECIL, W. H. MOUNTCASTLE, J. CAMPBELL,
WM. WRIGHT, J. PORTER. Daughter, HANNAH E. MORRISON; wife, ISABELL,
to administrate. Administrators Bond is on page 317.

MARY TATE -- Book 9, Page 67 -- Guardians Bond -- THOS. BARBER and
WM. MC DANIEL, March 17, 1835, for THOS. BARBER as guardian of MARY,
LEIGHTON, and WADDY TATE, orphans of HENRY TATE, deceased.

PATSY TATE -- Book 10, Page 160 -- Administrators Bond -- THOS.
BARBOUR and JOS. EWERS, October 21, 1839, for THOS. BARBOUR to
administrate estate of PATSY TATE, late YANCEY.

JAS. TAYLOR -- Book 11, Page 240 -- Refunding Bond -- JAS. TAYLOR,
JAS. C. BECK, and JNO. RHODES to JESSE MUNDY, administrator of JESSE
BECK, deceased, September 16, 1844. TAYLOR ahs received legacy in
right of wife, SUSANNAH, daughter of JESSE BECK.

JAS. W. TAYLOR -- Book 16, Page 151 -- Administrators Bond -- R. N.
ELLIS and RO. W. SNEAD, August 18, 1862, for R. N. ELLIS.

SALLY TAYLOR -- Book 16, Page 196 -- February 23, 1855; codicil of
July 13, 1855; December 15, 1862. Witnesses to will: THOS. G. HILL,
JNO. M. SPEED, WM. KENT. To codicil: PAULUS POWELL, THOS. G. HILL,
WM. KENT. ELIZA CREWS qualified and C. DABNEY renounced will. This
was done on February 28, 1855, but no witnesses present and continued
to January 19, 1863, when KENT and HILL proved it. SETH WOODROOF
was bondsman for ELIZA CREWS. Slave, WM. HENRY JEFFERSON, freed and
$100 to enable him to remove to Liberia of a free state. Servant,
FRANCES, gets lot above quarry lot on public road--she has been freed.
Niece, ELIZA CREWS--three acres and house and lot--if no issue, then
to my friend, CHISWELL DABNEY, Lynchburg, and he is to administrate.

SAML. TAYLOR -- Book 6, Page 748 -- Administrators Bond -- ELIZ.
TAYLOR and THOS. R. TERRY, March 19, 1827, for ELIZ. TAYLOR.

THOS. TAYLOR -- Book 6, Page 208 -- Administrators Bond -- SAML.
TAYLOR and REUBEN PENDLETON, January 15, 1821, for SAML. TAYLOR.
Book 10, Page 36 -- Administrators de bonis non Bond -- August 21,
1838, for WM. I. ISBELL; bondsman: RO. ISBELL.

VIRGINIA (VIRGIN) TAYLOR -- Book 3, Page 363 -- Administrators Bond --
GEORGE and WM. CABELL, October 21, 1795, for GEORGE CABELL; it is

VIRGINIA (VIRGIN) TAYLOR (cont.) -- VIRGIN here.
Book 3, Page 393 -- Inventory -- VIRGINIA here--L72-0-0. March 29,
1796. PHIL JOHNSON, THOS. JOHNSON, JNO. ROBINSON.

ANTHONY W. TEMPLIN -- Book 10, Page 385 -- Refunding Bond -- by A. W.
TEMPLIN, turstee, and JOS. PETTYJOHN, July 27, 1841, to WILKINS
WATSON, executor of EDWARD WATSON--EDWD in will gave two slaves to
his granddaughter, MARIA WATSON, now MARIA TEMPLIN. In codicil
TEMPLIN was made trustee and acknowledges delivery of slaves.
Witness: RO. TINSLEY.

HENRY TENNISON -- Book 3, Page 39 -- January 24, 1786; June 4, 1787.
Witnesses: JNO. ROBINSON, WM. ROBINSON, JNO. ROBINSON, JR. Son,
JNO.; daughter, SUSANNA GRESHAM and her heirs; son-in-law, THOS.
GRESHAM. He qualified on probate date; bondsman: JNO. CRAWFORD.
Book 3, Page 47 -- Inventory -- June 14, 1787 L22-11-9; JNO. ROBINSON,
ISAAC and ANTHONY RUCKER.

JNO. TENNISON -- Book 3, Page 307 -- Administrators Bond -- GEO.
MC DANIEL, JR. and AMBR. RUCKER, September 15, 1794, for GEO. MC DANIEL,
JR.

WM. O. TERRELL -- Book 15, Page 311 -- May 24, 1860; Monday, June 18,
1860. Witnesses: JAS. D. WATTS, THOS. J. COOKE, SAML. SCOTT. WM. W.
MINOR qualified; bondsman: W. G. CARR and FRANKLIN MINOR. WM. W.
MINOR, Albemarle County, trustee for my aunt, LUCY C. TERRELL; to
RICH. H. CARR and MARGARET RANDOLPH MINOR, both of Albemarle County.
Executor: WM. W. MINOR. Administrators Bond is page 320 and SAML.
SCOTT was attorney-in-fact for bondsman.
Book 15, Page 451 -- Inventory -- $7319.55; negro claimed by DR. JAS.
ROGERS of Albemarle. 400 acres bought by JAS. D. WATTS, June 18,
1860. FA. A. BLAIR, DAVID APPLING, R. W. SEAY.
Book 15, Page 580 -- Inventory -- Bond of SABNEY MINOR for benefit of
WM. W. MINOR, SR. (?), RICHMOND T. MINOR, February 1, 1852; transferred
to WM. O. TERRELL, February 1, 1860. Bond of DABNEY, JAS. and
WM. T. MINOR, FRANKLIN MINOR; claims versus estate of father of WM. O.
TERRELL--the late RICHMOND TERRELL. Bond of DR. WM. G. CARR,
Albemarle; bond of FRANKLIN BARKSDALE, W. G., R. E. G. CARR, and
WM. W. MINOR, Albemarle. Certified in Albemarle by GEO. CARRY (?);
recorded, Amherst County, November, 1860.
Book 16, Page 492 -- Sale -- August 21, 1860.
Book 16, Page 495 -- Administrators Account -- from June 18, 1860;
to J. D. WATTS for land; to MISS LUCY C. TERRELL, R. H. CARR, MARGARET
MINOR, LUCY C. TERRELL was life tenant and died June 23, 1863.
Book 16, Page 500 -- legatee acount by WM. W. MINOR, trustee; account
of LUCY C. TERRELL from May 18, 1861--one-half to her and one-half
to R. H. CARR; CARR's account as legatee from June 23, 1863; bond of
J. O. CARR, M. R. MINOR, legatee. SAML. H. HENRY could not examine
accounts because of connections with Confederate army. Legacy of
LUCY C. TERRELL and at death to RICH H. CARR and MARGARET RANDOLPH
MINOR. Recorded May 16, 1864. If I mistake not, the name of RICHMOND
TERRELL is an old one. I have looked at TERRELL book in days past
because my wife's ancestor, JOSHUA HUDSON, is mentioned in will of
RO. TERRELL in Orange. The book has JOSHUA's name wrong, as I
remember.

DAVID W. TERRY -- Book 10, Page 397 -- DAVID W. TERRY and WM. BECK,
November 16, 1841, to JEEW MUNDY, administrator of JESSE BECK; TERRY
has received his share of estate.

JNO. TERRY -- Book 9, Page 301 -- Administrators Bond -- RACHEL TERRY
and ADDISON TALIAFERRO, April 17, 1837, for RACHEL TERRY.
Book 9, Page 330 -- Inventory -- $4633.75; July 26, 1837; recorded
August 21, 1837. GEO. T. PLEASANTS, PETER P. THORNTON, RO. H. CARTER.
Book 9, Page 332 -- additional security bond on Administrators Bond
by RACHEL. Bondsmen: JAS. R. CARTER, PETER P. THORNTON, HENRY W.
QUARLES. August 21, 1837.

VELINIUS A. TERRY -- Book 15, Page 320 -- THOS. R. TERRY and WILEY CLARK, June 18, 1860, for THOS. R. TERRY to administrate estate of VELIRIUS A. TERRY.

WM. TERRY -- Book 7, Page 43 -- Administrators Bond -- THOS. TUCKER and WM. HAYNES, October 18, 1827, for THOS. TUCKER.
Book 7, Page 88 -- Inventory -- November 6, 1827--$123.42. WM. HAYNES, GIDEON C. GOODRICH, WIATT DUNCAN.
Book 8, Page 255 -- Administrators Account -- by TUCKER from March 25, 1828; WM. J. THURMOND, trustee, August 15, 1829. WM. JOPLING, ORMUND WARE, JNO. PRYOR.

PETTIS THACKER -- Book 5, Page 627 -- Administrators Bond -- AMBR. RUCKER, ELIAS WILLS, JAS. LEE and REUBEN PENDLETON, January 20, 1817, for AMBR. RUCKER.
Book 6, Page 119 -- Inventory -- $7658.15; February 21, 1820. PLEASANT DAWSON, CHAS. WINGFIELD, ARCHELAUS REYNOLDS.
Book 6, Page 134 -- Division and plat of 424 acres; to JEMIMA JENKINS, AMOS THACKER, SALLY BURFORD, TEMPEY THACKER, ELIZ. CREWS; also slaves etc. Harris Creek land. Nothing to JOEL THACKER for he had received money from land sales and refused to render an account. Same committee as for inventory February 20, 1820. Deed data shows that some of these heirs went to Kentucky.

SARAH THACKER -- Book 10, Page 289 -- Administrators Bond -- WM. BURFORD, CHAS. MAYS, WM. A. BURFORD, November 16, 1841, for WM. BURFORD.

MISS TEMPY (TEMPIS) THACKER -- Book 5, Page 630 -- Idiot Bond -- January 20, 1817, for AMBR. RUCKER and JAS. LEE as her committee. Bondsmen: CHAS. WINGFIELD, RICH. BURKS.
Book 6, Page 48 -- Administrators Bond -- REUBEN NORVELL and JAS. POWELL, November 19, 1818, for REUBEN NORVELL.
Book 6, Page 55 -- Administrators Bond -- AMOS THACKER, AMBR. RUCKER, JAS. LEE, CHAS. WINGFIELD, JNO. MERRITT, February 15, 1819, for first two.
Book 6, Page 84 -- Administratros Account -- by RUCKER and JAS. LEE for MISS TEMPY THACKER as her committee from January 30, 1817--board for one year; her part of father's estate. November 7, 1817. Deceased: July 31, 1819, report. NELSON C. DAWSON, ELIAS WILLS, CHAS. WINGFIELD.
Book 6, Page 118 -- NELSON C. DAWSON, JAS. L. LAMKIN and CHAS. WING-FIELD, February 21, 1820--slaves sold and division to five legatees. Land to be sold. AMOS THACKER, administrator.

ALSON THOMAS -- Book 13, Page 26 -- Baptist Minister's Bond -- November 15, 1852. Bondsmen: JNO. C. WHITEHEAD, ZA DRUMMOND.

CORNL. THOMAS -- Book 1, Page 289 -- June 1, 1775; October 2, 1775. Witnesses: SAML. JORDAN CABELL, THOS. MARTIN, JR., BENJ. JORDAN, LUCY CHILDERS, JESSE ALLEN, NICHL. CABELL. To wife--use of my house-- west side of porch to be divided by two rooms with part of my kitchen. Son, JNO.--land above Pedlar, when 21; sons, NORBORN and CORNL. If my wife dies with issue by me; my three daughters at days of marriages. At my mother's death--slaves due me. Executors: friends, JAS. NEVIL, JNO. HENDERSON, JR., JOS. CABELL, DAVID CRAWFORD.
Book 1, Page 291 -- Administrators Bond -- JAS. NEVIL, JNO. HENDERSON, JR., JOS. CABELL, DAVID CRAWFORD, NICHL. CABELL, THOS. JOPLING, HUGH ROSE, JNO. DAWSON, JACOB SMITH, October 2, 1775, for NEVIL, HENDERSON, JOS. CABELL and CRAWFORD.
Book 1, Page 299 -- Inventory -- very long; no total; February 5, 1776. JAS. HIGGINBOTHAM, ROD. MC CULLOCH, JACOB SMITH.
Book 1, Page 328 -- Division: committee as above. Recorded: February 3, 1777. Six lots to JNO. THOMAS; JNO. WOOD who married ELIZ. THOMAS--one two are named herein.

HENRY A. THOMAS -- Book 14, Page 255 -- Administrators Bond -- JNO. W. BROADDUS and RO. W. SNEAD, February 16, 1857, for JNO. W. BROADDUS.
Book 14, Page 280 -- December 31, 1856; February 16, 1857. Witnesses:

HENRY A. THOMAS (cont.) -- RO. H. CARTER, ELIZ. A. HAWKINS. Daughter,
LUCY W. THOMAS--where I live; my wife. Executor: JNO. W. BROADDUS.
Book 14, Page 385 -- Sale -- February 18, 1857. A. T. and A. F.
THOMAS were buyers. No total; recorded: June 15, 1857.

LUCY THOMAS -- Book 1, Page 348 -- Guardians Bond -- JNO. HENDERSON,
JR., EDMD. WILCOX, THOS. JOPLING, May 5, 1777, for JNO. HENDERSON, JR.
as guardian of LUCY THOMAS, orphan of CORNL. THOMAS, deceased.

MARY E. THOMAS -- Book 14, Page 57 -- Administrators Bond -- S. M.
GARLAND and R. A. COGHILL, January 21, 1856, for S. M. GARLAND.
December 14, 1854; January 21, 1856. Witnesses: JNO. L. FRENCH and
TANDY L. TYLER. Proved by FRENCH on probate date and by FRENCH,
February 18, 1856. All to my friend, SAML. M. GARLAND to support my
husband, GEO. M. THOMAS. Nothing is to go to W. H. TYLER, wife of
CHILDREN or to SAML. H. THOMAS, wife or children. My husband knows
reasons and this is satisfactory to both of us.
Book 14, Page 144 -- Sale -- February 1, 1856; $698.75. Recorded:
Monday, March 17, 1856.
Book 14, Page 149 -- Inventory -- $572.75. WM. P. WOODROOF, DANL. W.
JENNING, JNO. L. TURNER. Recorded: Monday, March 17, 1856.
Book 14, Page 230 -- Curator's Account -- by GARLAND from February,
1856; to G. M. THOMAS; recorded: Saturday, November 23, 1856.

NORBORN THOMAS -- Book 3, Page 77 -- Guardians Bond -- DAVIS CRAWFORD,
WM. CRAWFORD, THOS. POWELL, Minor, June 2, 1788, for DAVIS CRAWFORD
as guardian of NORBORN THOMAS, orphan of CORNL. THOMAS.

JNO. THOMPSON -- Book 10, Page 247 -- Administrators Bond -- DAVID S.
and SAML. M. GARLAND, August 19, 1840, for DAVID S. GARLAND.

JNO. THOMPSON, JR. -- Book 8, Page 98 -- Clerk of Superior Court --
June 4, 1831; Bondsman: THOS. N. EUBANK, JNO. HORSLEY, WM. M. WALLER,
S. M. GARLAND, CHAMPE CARTER, RO. TINSLEY.
Book B, Page 1 -- Clerk of Superior Court -- April 10, 1832; Bondsman:
JNO. HORLSEY. Witness: CHAMPE CARTER.
Book 19, Page 173 -- September 23, 1872; July 18, 1876. Produced by
HENRY LOVING; handwriting by R. A. COGHILL and R. A. PENDLETON.
HENRY LOVING qualified. Of great age; to be buried in Nelson County
at birthplace--Farmer's Joy, at feed of parents, JNO. and REBECCA
THOMPSON (initial E for her); Amherst Quarry stone to be used for
stones at graves. I am interested in the quarry. Elder brother,
JAS. P. THOMPSON, McMinnisville, Tennessee, is financially embarrassed
by bond of his son-in-law--his children. My great nephew, JNO. BAKER
HULL, son of my niece, S. R. HULL, wife of RO. HULL, Baltimore--when
21; his brother, HENRY HULL; nephew, LUCAS THOMPSON, son of my brother,
WM. W. THOMPSON; nephew, JNO. T. BROWN; to MOLLIE R. LUCAS, wife of
A. W. LUCAS; law books to JNO. T. BROWN; to MRS. CATH. MUIR and her
brother, J. W. DIBBRELL--items bought at sale of her brother's estate;
wife of J. W. DIBBREL is now dead. Brother's daughter, REBECCA VOORHIES
and husband, DR. F. F. VOORHIES and any children. Friend, MRS. D. P.
SHRADER and husband; sister, REBECCA E. P. DAVIES; nephew, GEO. D.
CROSTHWAIT or children; brother WILLIAM's two youngest daughters:
MARTHA and ELLEN; niece, ALICE L. THOMPSON and her sisters; State
property and bank speculation of 1872--intend to execute deed within
few days to JAS. R. GILMER, HENRY LOVING and H. M. BELL. I believe
it to be of great value. My relative, HENRY LOVING, is to administrate.
It may be asked why nephew, JNO. T. BROWN, was not appointed, buy
many years of experience needed. He is given $1000.00 to assist.
Note: The VOORHIES home still stands on south end of village and
belongs to WATTS family. They found an old distillery account book
for Nelson County in an ice house and it is very interesting. It
evidently belonged to father of JNO. THOMPSON, JR.
Book 19, Page 176 -- Administrators Bond -- HENRY LOVING, July 18,
1876.
Book 19, Page 285 -- Inventory -- A. C. HARRISON, BENJ. BROWN, TAYLOR
BERRY, $40,999.92. Goochland tax on land in
Book 19, Page 32 -- Administrators Account -- and West Virginia land
tax; to ALICE L. THOMPSON, March 18, 1878.

JNO. THOMPSON, JR. (cont.) -- Book 22, Page 466 -- Decree of April 12, 1888: THOMPSON's executors versus GILMORE, administrator; JASPER HOWSE, special surveyor to determine true lines of ROD. MC CULLOCH tract. Orizinal surveys obtained from ZACH TALIAFERRO, LAUGHLIN MC LEAN and ROD. MC CULLOCH tracts. Assisted at times by CAPT. J. F. WILSON, State Mining Company and MR. LOVING, executor. BARNETT's 1870 survey--very interesting; fire had destroyed timber: Brown's Creek; old stumps; MC CULLOCH survey was not correct and several errors are given. Plat shows MC LEAN tract owned by THOMPSON estate; top of Blue Ridge shown to one side; slag quarry; MC CULLOCH's tract of 400 acres by patent and 493 acres survey; part of TALIAFERRO tract is owned by Virginia Slate Mining Company--4442 acres. Judge appears "to have been nonsensually counseled." Plaintiff's title confirmed: Virginia Slate is to pay plaintiff. Recorded: October 12, 1888. JNO. THOMPSON, JR. was very active in this county as a study of deed books will show. He lived in the old DAVIES (or known as WEBSTER home now) on south main and near the VOORHEIS place across the street. It became the HIGGINBOTHAM Academy in later years. He gave the land on which the Amherst Baptist Church and parsonage now stand.

JNO. J. THOMPSON -- Book 16, Page 128 -- Administrators Bond -- RO. A. COGHILL and RO. A. PENDLETON, June 15, 1862, for RO. A. COGHILL.

PLEASANT THOMPSON -- Book 13, Page 286 -- Administrators Bond -- JAS. M. GANNAWAY and LITTLEBERRY TUCKER, December 19, 1853, for JAS. M. GANNAWAY.
Book 13, Page 329 -- Inventory -- January 3, 1854: $320.28. HENRY CAMPBELL, LAWSON CAMPBELL, WIATT TUCKER, JR.
Book 13, Page 386 -- Sale -- January 3, 1854; LUCY THOMPSON was buyer: $318.62. SHELTON H. WRIGHT, Clerk of Sale.
Book 13, Page 508 -- Administrators Account -- from January 7, 1854; cash of MRS. LUCY THOMPSON. Recorded: September 17, 1855.
Book 14, Page 286 -- Administrators Account -- from October 1, 1853; bond of LUCY THOMPSON; recorded: May 19, 1857.

REBECCA E. THOMPSON -- Book 10, Page 168 -- January 23, 1839; November 20, 1839. Witnesses: JNO. THOMPSON, JR., RO. M. BROWN, CAROLINE E. THOMPSON. Having attained three score years and ten--to be buried at Farmer's Joy in Nelson County by side of deceased husband, JNO. THOMPSON; daughter, MILDRED HERNDON; single daughters: REBECCA E. and JANE M. B. THOMPSON; other children have received estates from their father. Son, WM.; others are married and settled. Executors: son, JNO., JR. and LUCAS P. THOMPSON.

RO. THOMPSON -- Book 3, Page 71 -- September 26, 1787; April 7, 1788. Witnesses: JAS. RAINS, JAS. BOWLING, THOS. WATT. My six last children--Kentucky land--about 1451 acres; daughter, JENNY SIMMONS-- 200 acres; son, MITCHELL--300 acres; daughter, MARGARET THOMSON (sic)-- 200 acres; son, DAVID--250 acres; son, JNO.--250 acres; son, NELSON-- 251 acres; granddaughter, MILDRED ARCHE THOMSON, when of age; my wife, KATH., to administrate. My first children: MARY MARSHALL, JOSIAH, ROBT., PATIENCE SMITH, BARTLELL, RHODA WATKINS, BENAJAH, ANN MORRIS. CATH. (sic) qualified. Bondsman: WM. BIBB and HEZ. HARGROVE.
Book 3, Page 78 -- Administrators Bond -- JNO. MULLINS, WM. WALTON, JNO. CLARKSON, June 2, 1788, for JNO. MULLING--"if any will is produced."
Book 3, Page 79 -- Inventory -- April 18, 1788: L237-12-8; JAS. WILLS, LUCAS POWELL, WM. BIBB.
Book 3, Page 103 -- Inventory -- June 1, 1789, of RO. THOMPSON of Albemarle. L143-0-3; BERNARD BROWN, JNO. MAUPIN, THOS. TARMAN.

JAS. F. THORNTON -- Book 9, Page 259 -- Indexed Constables Bond: not there.
Book 9, Page 323 -- Constables Bond -- June 17, 1837; Bondsmen: PETER P. THORNTON, DANL. L. COLEMAN.
Book 10, Page 134 -- Same, June 17, 1839; Bondsmen: HENRY W. QUARLES, PETER P. THORNTON.
Book 19, Page 218 -- Administrators Bond -- JAS. M. MILLNER and JESSE L. MILLNER, bondsmen. February 19, 1877.

JAS. F. THORNTON (cont.) -- Book 19, Page 280 -- Inventory -- March 6, 1877: $263.05; WM. W. FOSTER, ISAIAH PRYOR, M. B. SANDIDGE; Sale, March 6, 1877--P. P. D.; G. D. and JAS. W. THORNTON were buyers--$199.50.
Book 19, Page 389 -- Administrators Account -- September 29, 1879.

MARY THORNTON -- Book 12, Page 518 -- August 30, 1850; February 16, 1852. Witnesses: A. B. DAVIES, JNO. HAMNER. Proved by HAMNER on probate and May 17, 1852, by DAVIES. Sons, WM., JAS., RO. H.; daughters: JANE HANNAH; if son, WM., has no issue; granddaughters, LUCY and ELIZ. QUARLES--if no issue or when married.
Book 12, Page 526 -- Administrators Bon -- RO. H. and JAS. F. THORNTON, HENRY W. QUARLES and RO. N. ELLIS, June 21, 1852, for RO. H. THORNTON.
Book 14, Page 589 -- Slave Inventory -- June 29, 1852; JAS. R. CARTER, RO. H. CARTER, PLEASANT MITCHELL. Special bequests to WM. L. THORNTON and the two QUARLES girls; other heirs: JAS. F. and RO. H. THORNTON, JANE C. HANNAH. Same committee. July 19, 1858.

PETER P. THORNTON -- Book 5, Page 231 -- Constables Bond -- 21 June 1813. Bondsman: HILL CARTER.
Book 5, Page 516 -- Same, 19 June 1815; bondsman: A. B. DAVIES.
Book 5, Page 699 -- Same, 17 June 1817; bondsman: JAS. FULCHER.
Book 5, Page 628 -- Commissioner of Revenue -- 20 June 1817; bondsman: AMBR. RUCKER.
Book 6, Page 208 -- Same, 15 January 1821; bondsman: STERLING CLAIBORNE.
Book 6, Page 273 -- Same, 21 January 1822; bondsman: WM. M. WALLER.
Book 6, Page 332 -- Same, 21 October 1822; bondsman: MARTIN PARKS.
Book 6, Page 409 -- Same, 18 November 1823; bondsman: A. B. DAVIES.
Book 6, Page 496, 626, 697 -- Same men on 15 November 1824; 17 October 1825; 15 October 1826.
Book 7, Page 174 -- Commissioner Revenue -- 15 September 1828; EDMD. WINSTON, WM. M. WALLER.
Book 7, Page 273 -- Same, 21 September 1829; bondsman: WM. M. WALLER.
Book 8, Page 45 -- Same, 20 September 1830; bondsman: RO. TINSLEY.
Book 8, Page 135 -- Same men, 19 September 1831.
Book 8, Page 351 -- Commissioner Revenue -- 16 September 1833; bondsman: HENRY L. DAVIES.
Book 8, Page 431 -- Same, 15 September 1838; bondsman: STERLING CLAIBORNE.
Book 9, Page 123 -- Same, 21 September 1835; bondsman: STERLING CLAIBORNE.
Book 9, Page 247 -- Same men, 19 Septmeber 1836.
Book 9, Page 333 -- Same, 18 September 1837; bondsman: CHAMPE CARTER.
Book 10, Page 48 -- Same, September 17, 1838; bondsman: HENRY W. QUARLES.
Book 10, Page 155 -- Same, 16 September 1839; bondsman: ZACH DRUMMOND.
Book 10, Page 264 -- Same, 21 September 1840; bondsman: HENRY W. QUARLES.
Book 10, Page 384 -- Same men on 20 September 1841.
Book 11, Page 238 -- Same, 16 Setpember 1844; bondsman: HENRY W. QUARLES and HENRY L. DAVIES.
Book 14, Page 228 -- Administrators Bond -- 15 December 1856, for RO. H. THORNTON. Bondsmen: JAS. F. THORNTON, JNO. A. MOSELY, J.R. MABEN.
Book 14, Page 593 -- Inventory -- 22 January 1857--$11,226.30. R. N. ELLIS, JOS. R. CARTER, RO. H. CARTER.
Book 18, Page 325 -- Administrators Account -- EDMD. J. SMITH for coffin--$10.00; January 30, 1857 date. Heirs: JAS. F. THORNTON for support of old slave; W. S. THORNTON, RO. H. THORNTON, children of FRANCIS QUARLES and wife, BELINDA A.--both deceased; JANE C. HANNAH. 19 May 1873.

PETER P. THORNTON, JR. -- Book 9, Page 78 -- Constables Bond -- 15 June 1835. Bondsmen: PETER P. THORNTON and FRANCIS E. QUARLES.

PHILIP THORNTON (indexed for, but it is PHILIP THURMOND) -- Book 5, Page 78.

REUBEN THORNTON -- Book 4, Page 297 -- Administrators Bond -- ANTHONY
THORNTON and RO. RIVES, 17 June 1798, for ANTHONY THORNTON to
administrate estate of REUBEN THORNTON.

WM. S. THORNTON -- Book 10, Page 366 -- Constables Bond -- July 19,
1841. Bondsmen: JAS. F. THORNTON, HENRY W. QUARLES.
Book 11, Page 150 -- Same, June 19, 1843; bondsmen: PETER P. THORNTON,
HENRY W. QUARLES.
Book 17, Page 27 -- Administrators Bond -- JAS. F. THORNTON, RO. H.
THORNTON, JAS. W. PHILLIPS, March 24, 1865, for JAS. F. THORNTON.
Book 17, Page 226 -- Plat and division; no location set forth; joins
JNO. BROWN, H. M. WOODROOF, heirs of BELINDA QUARLES, JAS. F. THORNTON--
212 acres--42 acres to heirs of JANE C. HANER, deceased (HANNAH in
other data), JAS. F., RO. H. THORNTON; heirs of BELINA QUARLES. Land
was devised by PETER P. THORNTON to his son, WM. S. THORNTON.
November 19, 1866. RO. H. CARTER, JOEL BOWLES, HENRY WHITE.

JUDITH THURMOND -- Book 6, Page 292 -- Administrators Bond -- WM.
THURMOND, WM. TURNER, CHAS. PALMORE, DABNEY HILL, May 20, 1822, for
WM. THURMOND.

LUCY THURMOND -- Book 8, Page 97 -- JNO. THOMPSON, ADDISON TALIAFERRO,
CORNL. SALE, and TANDY JONES, May 16, 1831. First two as trustees
for estate conveyed in trust by WM. THURMOND, deceased, for benefit
of LUCY THURMOND and children.

PHILIP THURMOND -- Book 4, Page 141 -- September 5, 1803; December 19,
1803. Witnesses: P. GOOCH, PHILIP LOCKHART, MATT. TUCKER. Proved
on probate by GOOCH and January 16, 1804 by LOCKHART. JUDITH THURMOND
qualified; bondsmen: WM. SLEDD, WM. THURMOND. Of Lexington Parish;
all of my children; daughter, JUDITH; daughter, SALLY WARE; son, WM.;
daughter, ELIZ. RUCKER; daughter, MARY M. MC CABE; son, PHILIP; my
unfortunate children: FRANKEY and THOS. When JUDITH marries; wife
to administrate along with CHAS TUCKER and son, PHILIP. Note:
JUDITH was a TUCKER and some of family went to Georgia--deed data.
Book 4, Page 293 -- Administrators Bond -- by JUDITH; see above in
will.
Book 4, Page 410 -- Administrators Bond -- JUDITH again qualified,
August 19, 1805, Bondsmen: CHAS. TUCKER and PHILIP THURMOND.
Book 5, Page 5 -- Inventory -- August 23, 1810: $1370.81. WM.
JOPLING, EDMD. GOODRICH, JNO. EUBANK.
Book 5, Page 78 -- Administrators Bond -- PHILIP THURMOND, August 23,
1810; bondsman: JNO. RICHESON.

RICH. THURMOND -- Book 5, Page 432 -- Administrators Bond -- WM. D.
HILL, ELIZ. THURMOND, HARRISON HUGHES, February 21, 1814, for HILL.
Note: this name of RICH. drives the researcher wild. I have set
forth my futile search for parents of HENDERSON THURMAN of Madison
County, Kentucky, who married MARY ANN GILLESPIE. There was a RICH.
in census of Madison who could fit as his father. Another was in
Washington County, Kentucky and on and on they are found.

WM. THURMOND -- Book 5, Page 70 -- May 20, 1811; WM. has been sen-
tenced to two years in penitentiary. JNO. TUCKER and ELIAS WILLS are
made trustees. I think that he killed a slave.
Book 8, Page 95 -- Administrators Bond -- PHILIP THURMOND, JR., MARTIN
N. DAWSON, WM. TURNER, May 16, 1831, for JR.
Book 8, Page 105 -- Slave Inventory -- of $2547.76. WM. HAYNES, THOS.
TUCKER, FRANCIS A. K. DAVIES--in trust to LUCY THURMOND et al. May 20,
1831.
Book 8, Page 267 -- Trustee account by WM. J. THURMOND. Lynchburg
suit; THURMOND versus WILLS; bacon sold to PHILIP THURMOND, JR.;
received of RICH. JONES' estate amounts to LUCINDA and PHILIP THURMOND.
Apirl 15, 1832. WM. SHELTON, THOS. N. EUBANK, PETER P. THORNTON.
Book 4, Page 43 -- Estate Commitment to Sheriff -- April 1, 1851;
Sheriff: JNO. D. DAVIS.

JAMES TILFORD -- Book 3, Page 43 -- June 4, 1787--only date. Witnesses:
HENLEY DRUMMOND, MAJOR DOWEL. Wife--land; sons, ANDREW; DAVID--93 acres

JAMES TILFORD (cont.) -- in Amherst County of July, 1769, and signed
by BOTETOURT. Three youngest daughters, executors: NICHL. MORAN and
DAVID TILFORD; sons, JNO., JAS., JOS., and SAML. Daughters: MARY,
MARGARET and RACHEL. MORAN qualified; bondsmen: DAVID TILFORD and
NICHL. WREN, but DAVID is to administrate, too.
Book 3, Page 69 -- Inventory -- L219-6-11, February 4, 1788. HENLEY
DRUMMOND, MAJOR DOWELL, EDMD. COUGHFFEE (COFFEY).
Book 4, Page 10 -- November 13, 1799; June 15, 1801. Witnesses:
DANL. M. DONALD, DAVID CLARKSON, NICHL. MORAN. Sons and daughters
to be educated. Executors: NICHL. MORAN and JNO. MASTERS. MASTERS
qualified; bondsman: JAS. MONTGOMERY.
Book 4, Page 15 -- Inventory -- July 18, 1801: L342-11-0; DANL.
MC DONALD, JNO. JACOBS, WM. COFFEY.

BETSY ANN TILLER -- Book 8, Page 175 -- Guardians Bond -- CALM SEAY
and JAS. D. WATTS, March 19, 1832, for CALM SEAY as guardian of BETSY
ANN TILLER, orphan of WM. TILLER, deceased.

ELIZA TILLER -- Book 7, Page 216 -- Guardians Bond -- RICH. LANDRUM
and WM. H. KNIGHT, March 19, 1829, for RICH. LANDRUM as guardian of
ELIZA and SOPHIA TILLER, orphans of WM. TILLER, deceased.

LUCY JANE TILLER -- Book 6, Page 426 -- Guardians Bond -- CHAS. H.
CHRISTIAN, SAML. CHRISTIAN, SAML. R. DAVIES, December 15, 1823, for
CHAS. H. CHRISTIAN as guardian of LUCY TILLER, orphan of WM. TILLER.
Book 6, Page 492 -- Guardians Bond -- JNO. ALCOCK, PEYTON KEITH,
JACOB SCOTT, August 19, 1824, for JNO. ALCOCK as guardian of LUCY
JANE TILLER, orphan of WM. TILLER, deceased.

SOPHIA TILLER -- Book 6, Page 449 -- Guardians Bond -- as of Book 6,
Page 426 above: CHAS. H. CHRISTIAN, guardian of WM. TILLER's orphan
ELIZA TILLER is also named in this bond as an orphan of WM. TILLER.
Book 9, Page 156 (indexed for 136) -- Guardians Account -- by RICH.
LANDRUM as guardian of MISS SOPHIA and MISS ELIZA TILLER from
December 21, 1830; cash to CAMM SEAY, January 30, 1835. LINDSEY
COLEMAN, RO. PATRICK, committee.

WM. TILLER -- Book 5, Page 183 -- Administrators Bond -- WM. TILLER
and DAVID S. GARLAND, October 19, 1812, for WM. TILLER.
Book 5, Page 196 -- Inventory -- $12.00; December 30, 1812. THOS.
APLING, JAS. TYREE, JOS. KENNEDY.
Book 5, Page 604 -- Inventory -- $636.77. ALLEN BLAIR, WM. CASHWELL,
THOS. APLING. September 16, 1816.
Book 6, Page 425 -- Guardians Bond -- JNO. ALCOCK and LEWIS LAINE,
December 15, 1823, for JNO. ALCOCK as guardian of WM., RICH., and
ELIZ. ANN TILLER, orphans of WM. TILLER.
Book 6, Page 473 -- Administrators Bond -- JNO. ALCOCK and GILES
DAVIDSON, August 16, 1824, for JNO. ALCOCK.
Book 6, Page 542 -- Inventory -- $747.43; bill of injunction by CHAS. H.
CHRISTIAN--slave, JNO., sold January 21, 1824, to ALCOCK. Eighty acres
bought by RICH. LANDRUM; bondsmen: CHAS. H. and SAML. D. CHRISTIAN.
CHAS. H. CHRISTIAN bought the slave, JNO.; bondsmen: SAML. D. CHRISTIAN
and RICH. LONDON for $570. Recorded: February 21, 1825. THOS.
APLING, JONAS PIERCE, LEWIS LAYNE.
Book 7, Page 104 -- Administrators Account -- by ALCOCK from March 31,
1816 (?): MRS. CHRISTIAN, late widow of TILLER; tuition to GEO. W.
HIGGINBOTHAM; for picking cotton--367 pounds; clothing and schooling
for BETSY ANN TILLER, infant daughter of WM. TILLER; school books
for children; tuition to WM. BLAIR. CHAS. H. CHRISTIAN and wife,
FRANCES, late widow of TILLER. November 19, 1827. DAVID S. GARLAND,
THOS. APLING, LEWIS LAYNE.

LEWIS TINDALL -- Book 6, Page 8 -- Ordinary Bond -- June 15, 1818;
bondsman: JNO. ALLEN. Note: this is probably the LEWIS TILDEN
indexed for Book 5, Page 8, but nothing thereon.

MARTHA JANE TINDALL -- Book 6, Page 722 -- Guardians Bond -- LEWIS
TINDALL and WM. PAMPLIN, February 19, 1827, for LEWIS TINDALL as
guardian of MARTHA JANE LEWIS TINDALL, orphan of LEWIS TINDALL. This

MARTHA JANE TINDALL (cont.) -- could be MATILDA, but is indexed as above.

ANSON TINSLEY -- Book 11, Page 375 -- Estate Commitment to Sheriff -- April, 1845; motion of WM. MC DANIEL; WM. M. WALLER, Sheriff.

BANISTER TINSLEY -- Book 7, Page 210 -- Orders of Bedford and Amherst Count courts to divide his lands. Widow, MILLEY TINSLEY, gets Bedford land; JUDAH BURKS, formerly TINSLEY, gets Amherst County tract joining Bethel and ROBINSON; JOS. TINSLEY--Amherst County tract on Dairy Branch and jions ALEX. TINSLEY and THOS. CLEMENTS--also mention of Harris Creek and TINSLEY's Mill; JOSHUA TINSLEY gets Amherst County tract next to A. TINSLEY; ABSALOM TINSLEY gets Bedford tract; MARTHA TINSLEY--ditto. November 27, 1828. NATHL. STRANGE and RO. STRANGE of Bedford; THOS. CLEMENTS of Amherst County. Plat of Amherst County tracts on page 211-124 acres on Harris.

CHAS. E. TINLSEY -- Book 14, Page 483 -- Guardians Bond -- JNO. DUDLEY DAVIS and GEO. HYLTON, December 21, 1857, for JNO. DUDLEY DAVIS as guardian of CHAS. E. TINSLEY, infant of NELSON TINSLEY, deceased.

DAVID TINSLEY -- Many tobacco inspector bonds at Amherst Warehouse.
Book 4, Page 235 -- January 21, 1799; bondsman: THOS. MOORE.
Book 4, Page 242 -- November 18, 1799; bondsman: JNO. and JOSHUA TINSLEY.
Book 4, Page 276 -- September 17, 1804; bondsman: REUBEN PENDLETON.
Book 4, Page 280 -- September 16, 1805; bondsman: ISAAC TINSLEY.
Book 4, Page 511 -- Same, September 25, 1807; bondsman: ISAAC RUCKER.
Book 4, Page 533 -- September 19, 1808; bondsman: JOSHUA TINSLEY.
Book 4, Page 591 -- September 18, 1809; bondsmen: GEO. and JOSHUA TINSLEY.
Book 5, Page 27 -- September 16, 1811; bondsman: AMBR. RUCKER.
Book 7, Page 156 -- Will of DAVID TINSLEY, SR. April 7, 1826; codicil of May 9, 1826; codicil of January 5, 1827; May 19, 1828. Witnesses to will: AMBR. RUCKER, JAS. BENNET. To first codicil: JAS. BENNET, JNO. T. TINSLEY, ZACH. D. TINSLEY. To second codicil: BENNET and AMBR. RUCKER. ROBT. and EDWD. TINSLEY qualified; bondsmen: WILL MC DANIEL and WM. M. WALLER. Aged and infirm; grandson, DAVID TINSLEY, son to GEORGE--for dutiful attention to me in my old age--slave boy, RANDAL; daughters have had sums; daughter, MATILDA MC KANE; sons have had sums and land to live upon; all of their debts are released; sons, DAVID and EDWD.--Raspberry Neck tract where EDWD. lives; son, GEO.-- 159 acres--58 of it bought of LINDSEY TINSLEY--houses and where he lives and in his possession for many years; son, ANSON--158 acres to include 58 acres bought of GEO. H. BURFORD and next to his tract bought from PHILIP BURFORD; GEO.; EDWD. and ANSON get the Mill on Harris; they have improved it; TINSLEY's Mill and my interest to GEO. and ANSON--about 20 acres; heirs of my daughter, SELUDA BUSBY; daughters, LUCY TINSLEY, NANCY BURFORD, MATILDA MC KANE, RUTHA BURFORD and children; granddaughter, NANCY DAVIDSION, daughter of PEGGY HAMM, deceased; NANCY--formerly HAMM--heirs if any; EDWD. TINSLEY who married my daughter, LUCY--my son, GEO., is on his note to Bank of Virginia; EDWD. has removed from state and GEO. is liable for about $900--LUCY's part to be charged with it. Executors: sons, GEO. and EDWD. and friend, RO. TINSLEY. Codicil: ANSON's land is to include my house, barn and orchard. Codicil: have given my son, DAVID, a slave at $375; SELUDA BUSBY's heirs a slave at $400; daughter, LUCY TINSLEY, a slave at $300; daughter, NANCY BURFORD--one at $370; daughter, RUTH BURFORD--one at $350; son, EDWD.--one at $388.40; granddaughter, NANCY DAVIDSON--one at $375.00.
Book 7, Page 161 -- Administrators Bond
Book 7, Page 167 -- Inventory -- June 11, 1828; $2700.57. NELSON C. DAWSON, PROSSER POWELL, JAS. BENNETT.
Book 7, Page 297 -- Division -- NANCY DAVIDSON, NANCY BURFORD--90 acres on Miller's Branch; 80 acres and house where late JNO. TINSLEY lived to heirs of SELUDA BUSBY; LUCY TINSLEY--125 acres on Bethel road; RUTH BURFORD--110 acres on upper creek lot; 125 acres of lower creek lot to MATILDA MC KANE--also 57 acres in which DAVID, SR. had dower and bought of widow of PHILIP BURFORD; 158 acres to GEO. TINSLEY;

DAVID TINSLEY (cont.) -- 158 acres and mansion house to ANSON TINSLEY; Harris Creek mill to GEO. and ANSON; land on JAS. to DAVID, JR. and EDWD. TINSLEY--below Bethel. Plat on 298--main tract on west side of Harris and both sides of road from Amherst Courthouse to Bethel and next to JNO. SHELTON and ARCH. ROBERTSON--894 acres. SELUDA married MATT. BUSBY--gets tract of JNO. TINSLEY, deceased. LUCY married GEO. TINSLEY--note: in will it is EDWD. and this is correct. EDWD. shows in deeds data as being in Kentucky. Summary on page 300f: lands and slaves: DANL. L. BURFORD, GEO. and EDWD. TINSLEY (wife LUCY, AMBR. BURFORD and wife, NANCY, DAVID TINSLEY, heirs of SELUDA BUSBY, MATILDA MC KANE, EDWD. TINSLEY, NANCY DAVIDSON. Committee: PROSSER POWELL, JNO. PRYOR, J. PETTYJOHN. December 11, 1829. I have not traced the mill, but believe that site of old Cash Mill on Harris--just below where my son, THURMAN BLANTON DAVIS, lives with wife, MARY GAYLE (nee PETTYJOHN) is the place.
Book 8, Page 27 -- Administrators Account -- by EDWD. and RO. TINSLEY from 1828; to GEO. TINSLEY for keeping Old Mill, a slave, for one year; executors as trustees of RUTH BURFORD, DANL. L. BURFORD for division expenses; division to EDWD. TINSLEY and wife; GEO. TINSLEY's bond for division and same for ZACH TINSLEY; AMBR. BURFORD and wife on division bond; DAVID TINSLEY--debt to testator and to him as heir to heirs of SELUDA BUSBY; THOS. NORVELL; bondsman: SPENCER NORVELL, for slaves to BUSBY heirs and to THOS. H. SNEAD for same, December 10, 1829. WILKINS WATSON, A. B. DAVIES, committee.
Book 8, Page 28 -- RO. TINSLEY's account -- Bedford County business from 1828; sum from executors of JNO. TINSLEY; tax versus GEO. TINSLEY; P. POWELL's dinner when he came to divide estate and commissioners failed to meet--25 cents; bond of NELSON TINSLEY. December 11, 1829. Committee as above.
Book 8, Page 29 -- EDWD. TINSLEY's Account -- from May 31, 1828; mill expenses; GEO. TINSLEY, heir; A. RUCKER's trustees and bond of EDWD. and GEO. to them; debt of AMBR. RUCKER--collected of DABNEY by RO. TINSLEY and paid to EDWD. TINSLEY in part of JNO. in Bedford versus RO. TINSLEY et al.; DAVID TINSLEY, JR.--overseer in 1829; REBECCA RUCKER--1829 amount; list of debts due. December 10, 1829; same committee.
Book 8, Page 72 -- Refunding Bond -- December 20, 1829, by DAVID and GEO. TINSLEY to EDWD. and RO. TINSLEY. DAVID has received slave under will.
Book 8, Page 74 -- Refunding Bond -- by AMBR. BURFORD and GEO. TINSLEY to executors, December 11, 1839; BURFORD has received amount.
Book 8, Page 76 -- Refunding Bond -- to executors, December 20, 1830, by GEO. S. (?) TINSLEY for legacy. Bondsman: AMBR. BURFORD.
Book 8, Page 163 -- Refunding Bond -- by MATILDA MC CANE, WM. H. TINSLEY and REUBEN COX, October 29, 1831, for MATILDA--two slaves received.
Book 8, Page 288 -- Account by RO. TINSLEY from 1828; account of ALEX. TINSLEY, MATILDA MC CANE, GEO. TINSLEY, EDWD. TINSLEY and wife, LUCY. November 19, 1832. Committee: W. S. CRAWFORD.
Book 8, Page 291 -- Refunding Bond -- of EDWD. TINSLEY of Kentucky; WM. H. TINSLEY and REUBEN COX to same executors. December 14, 1831. EDWD. has received legacy in right of wife, LUCY.
Book 10, Page 38 -- RO. TINSLEY's account from December 31, 1832; court of appeals suit; debt of A. TINSLEY by B. MC CAREY. Committee: LINDSEY COLEMAN; Recorded: August 20, 1838.
Book 11, Page 129 -- Account by RO. and EDWD. TINSLEY, September term, 1843: SAML. M. GARLAND, commissioner. To RUTH BURFORD, GEO. TINSLEY, NANCY BURFORD, WILLIS DAVIDSON and wife, NANCY, ANSON TINSLEY, AMBR. BURFORD and wife, EDWD. TINSLEY; account paid to SYLVESTER BURFORD; M. BUSBY for enclosing graveyard; DAVID TINSLEY; BANISTER TINSLEY's administrator; paid J. MILLER and trustees; suit of MC DANIEL versus DAWSON; heirs of SELUDA BUSBY; to GEO. TINSLEY; MATILDA MC KAIN; LUCY TINSLEY; DAVID and ANSON TINSLEY; EDWD. TINSLEY; NANCY BURFORD; ANSON BURFORD--trustee for RUTH BURFORD and children; suit in Botetourt; DAVIS TINSLEY was legatee of GEO. MC DANIEL and suit of WM. MC DANIEL may reduce amounts. May 15, 1843.
Book 12, Page 307 -- RO. TINSLEY's account from 1845. Botetourt and Amherst suits; amount to heirs: GEO., DAVID and LUCY TINSLEY; MATILDA MC CAIN; heirs of SELUDA BUSBY; NANCY BURFORD; RUTH BURFORD's

DAVID TINSLEY (cont.) -- trustee; WILLIS DAVIDSON and wife, NANCY;
ANN TINSLEY; EDWD. and RO. TINSLEY; DAVID TINSLEY; ANSON BURFORD as
trustee of RUTH BURFORD; EDWD. TINSLEY. September 16, 1850.
Book 22, Page 49 -- August 17, 1887; February 20, 1888. Witnesses:
V. MC GINNIS and SIDNEY FLETCHER. Wife, MARGARET ELIZ.; son, SAML.
EDWIN; dwelling and family burial ground. Joins TALIAFERRO THOMPSON
on main road--beyond blacksmith shop; daughter VIRGINIA's line--given
heretofore to her. Son, SCOTT TINSLEY; my three children; wife to
administrate.
Book 22, Page 63 -- Administrators Bond -- ELIZ. M. TINSLEY, March 19,
1888. Inventory of April 10, 1888; no total; not large. Signed
MARGARET E. TINSLEY, administratrix. SIDNEY FLETCHER, TALIAFERRO
THOMPSON, COLUMBUS CAMPBELL, committee.

EDWARD TINSLEY -- Book 2, Page 56 -- Administrators Bond -- WM.,
ISAAC and DAVID TINSLEY, May 6, 1782, for WM. TINSLEY.
Book 2, Page 81 -- Inventory -- Many slaves: L497-10-0; personal:
L669-4-11. BENJ. and A. RUCKER; GEO. MC DANIEL, September 22, 1782.
Book 2, Page 118 -- ELIZ. PENDLETON's account and that of WM. TINSLEY;
land in Orange sold to PORTER; account of RICH. VERNON; account of
EDWD. TINSLEY; ISAAC TINSLEY; JNO. TINSLEY; DAVID TINSLEY; JOSHUA
TINSLEY; JOS. JOHNS; COL. AMBR. RUCKER; WM. TINSLEY to be paid in
tobacco--one-tenth to each account. Summary on page 125. EDMD.
WINSTON; JNO. PENN; RICH. SHELTON.
Book 15, Page 207 -- No date when written; codicil of September 14,
1858; July 18, 1859. Witnesses to will: SPOTSWOOD H. COX and
ARCHELAUS COX. RO. TINSLEY qualified; bondsmen: Z. D. TINSLEY,
MARTIN D. and DAVID TINSLEY. Daughter, JUDITH A. HENDRICKS; daughter,
LUCY J. RUCKER and children; daughter, SARAH SHELTON; daughter,
NANCY M. POWELL; daughter, FRANCES J. SCOTT; daughter, VA. P. LOVE;
sons, CHAPMAN J. and EDWD. M. TINSLEY--these two have not received
sums. Six daughters and families; Bethel tract of 400 acres and lots
in Bethel on the ferry road. Land where NANCY M. POWELL lives with
JUDITH A. where JAS. POWELL lives. One acre for burial ground and
to have stone wall. Eight parts: to RO. TINSLEY for daughter,
JUDITH A. HENDRICKS--free from husband--her children; I was her
bondsman when she was JUDITH A. STEEN, administratrix of WM. STEEN--
Bethel land; 2. JNO. D. L. RUCKER as trustee of children of deceased
daughter, LUCY J. RUCKER--when they are of age; 3. RO. TINSLEY as
trustee of my daughter, SARAH SHELTON, and her daughter, SALLIE WILLIAMS
SHELTON. 4. RO. TINSLEY as trustee for my daughter, NANCY M. POWELL.
5. RO. TINSLEY as trustee of my daughter, FRANCES J. SCOTT, and
children--her son, EDWD. SCOTT. 6. MONROE LOVE as trustee for my
daughter, VA. P. LOVE and children. 7. RO. TINSLEY as trustee for
my son, EDWARD M. TINSLEY--if no issue. 8. RO. TINSLEY as trustee
for my son, CHAPMAN J. TINSLEY. Executor: son, RO. TINSLEY.
Codicil; have conveyed land at Bethel to JUDITH and HENDRICKS and
NANCY M.: POWELL and families.
Book 15, Page 216 -- Administrators Bond -- See will.
Book 15, Page 337 -- Inventory -- September 7, 1859--396 acres Channel
Island tract; CHAPMAN J. TINSLEY, trustee; JNO. D. L. RUCKER; Bethel
town and rerry (?) lot--$19,654.66. JNO. PRYOR, ARCHELAUS COX,
EDWD. FLETCHER, GEO. H. DAMERON. Recorded: March 9, 1860.
Book 16, Page 226 -- Administrators Bond -- GEO. H. DAMERON, SAML. R.
WORTHAM, WM. P. SCOTT, February 16, 1863, for GEO. H. DAMERON.

ELIZ. TINSLEY -- Book 8, Page 88 -- Administrators Bond -- MAURICE H.
GARLAND and SAML. GARLAND, March 24, 1831, for MAURICE H. GARLAND.
Book 8, Page 310 -- Estate Commitment to Sheriff -- March, 1833;
motion of BOYD MILLER, administrator of unadministrated estate:
EDMD. WINSTON, Sheriff.

FREDERICK TINSLEY -- Probably FRED. J. of next item -- Book 7, Page
330 -- Guardians Bond -- WM. MC DANIEL and LINDSEY MC DANIEL, March 18,
1830, for WM. MC DANIEL as guardian of FREDERICK TINSLEY, orphan of
GEO. M. TINSLEY, deceased.

FREDERICK J. TINSLEY -- Book 12, Page 277 -- Administrators Bond --
CALVIN BENNETT and JAS. BENNETT, July 15, 1850, for CALVIN BENNETT.

FREDERICK J. TINSLEY (cont.) -- Book 12, Page 351 -- Inventory --
$93.50; THOS. BARBOUR, C. MC IVER and JOS. EWERS, August 3, 1850.
Sale, $113.85; recorded: January 20, 1851. Administrators Account
from July 15, 1850. To JOSHUA D. TINSLEY; amount from DAVID TINSLEY.
Recorded: January 16, 1852.
Book 13, Page 142 -- Administrators Account -- from April 21, 1852.
RO. TINSLEY--attorney fee. Recorded: October 17, 1853.

GEO. M. TINSLEY -- Book 7, Page 150 -- Administrators Bond -- RO.
and GEO. TINSLEY, March 17, 1828, for RO. TINSLEY.
Book 7, Page 165 -- Inventory -- April 4, 1828: $2771.13; NELSON
DAWSON, GEO. W. PETTYJOHN, MATT. WILLS.
Book 8, Page 3 -- Guardians Bond -- WM. MC DANIEL and AMBR. MC DANIEL,
June 21, 1830, for WM. MC DANIEL as guardian of GEO. M. and CHARLOTTE
ANN TINSLEY, orphans of GEO. M. TINSLEY, deceased.
Book 8, Page 10 -- Guardians Bond -- WM. and LINDSEY MC DANIEL,
August 17, 1830, for WM. MC DANIEL as guardian of ELIZA TINSLEY,
orphan of GEO. M. TINSLEY, deceased.
Book 8, Page 34 -- Administrators Account -- by RO. TINSLEY from 1828;
to JAS. D. JOHNS for his part of tobacco; ALFRED TINSLEY as overseer
and his part of tobacco and legacy; bond of NELSON TINSLEY; to LUCY
and FREDERICK TINSLEY; MILLNER COX's administrator; JAS. D. JOHNS as
legatee; administrator of BANISTER TINSLEY; ANDERSON TINSLEY as
legatee; JAS. D. JOHNS and wife, FRANKEY, daughter of GEO. M. TINSLEY;
to CALVIN F. BENNETT and wife, LUCY, daughter of GEO. M. TINSLEY;
to ELIZABETH TINSLEY; ALFRED and FREDERICK TINSLEY for support;
GEO. M. TINSLEY for his support of ALFRED for one year; to ANN TINSLEY.
Committee: LINDSEY COLEMAN, A. B. DAVIES. June 22, 1830.
Book 8, Page 138 -- Administrators Account -- by RO. TINSLEY from
June 23, 1830. BANISTER TINSLEY's administrator mentioned; WIATT
BAILEY and wife--costs; ANDERSON TINSLEY--amounts deposited under
decree; ELIZ. EUBANK; LUCY BENNETT; JAS. D. JOHNS and wife, FRANKEY;
CALVIN BENNETT and wife, LUCY; ELIZA TINSLEY; to FREDERICK; GEO. M.;
and ANN TINSLEY--WM. MC DANILE, guardian of ANN. Recorded: October 17,
1831.
Book 12, Page 301 -- Administrators Account -- by RO. TINSLEY from
September 23, 1831. Suits in Lynchburg and Amherst Counties; to
JOHNS and wife; CALVIN BENNETT and wife; HAZAEL WHEAT and wife, ELIZA;
FREDERICK J. and GEO. M. TINSLEY; to CHAS. B. GWATHAN and wife,
CHARLOTTE ANN; to ALFRED TINSLEY. Recorded: September 16, 1850.

ISAAC TINSLEY -- Book 15, Page 310 -- Administrators Bond -- A. F. and
JNO. B. ROBERTSON, April 16, 1860, for A. F. ROBERTSON.

ISAAC TINSLEY, JR. -- Book 6, Page 462 -- Administrators Bond --
ARCHIBALD ROBERTSON and SAML. GARLAND, June 24, 1824, for ARCHIBALD
ROBERTSON.

JAS. ALEX. TINSLEY -- Book 9, Page 137 -- Guardians Bond -- JNO. T.
TINSLEY and WILLIS M. REYNOLDS, November 16, 1835, for JNO. T.
TINSLEY as guardian of JAS. ALEX., MARTHA ANN, and MARTHA JANE TINSLEY,
infants of JNO. T. TINSLEY. Note: two MARTHAs are so named.
Book 10, Page 45 -- Administrators Bond -- RO., ZACH D. and MARTIN D.
TINSLEY, September 17, 1838, for RO. TINSLEY.
Book B, Page 10 -- Administrators Bond -- RO. TINSLEY and WM. HOBSON,
April 5, 1838, for RO. TINSLEY.
Book B, Page 13 -- Estate Commitment to Sheriff -- September 1, 1840;
RO. TINSLEY has died; Sheriff: EDMD. PENN.

JNO. TINSLEY -- Book 5, Page 657 -- May 5, 1816; July 21, 1817.
Witnesses: R. TINSLEY, EDWD. TINSLEY, JR., DAVID TINSLEY, SR., JNO.
HUNTER, JAS. DUNN. RO. TINSLEY qualified; bondsmen: REUBEN PENDLETON,
DAVID and GEO. TINSLEY. Five children of deceased daughter, FRANCES
HARRISON: POLLY, SALLY, JNO., CHAS. and NANCY when of age. Where I
live to be sold. Son, EDWD.; daughter, ELIZ. WEST; son, ANTHONY G.;
daughter, SALLY SLEDD; son, ROBT.; daughter, LUCY FOWLER; son, OLIVER;
son, JAS.; FRANCES HARRISON, deceased; son, LINDSEY TINSLEY. They have
received land shares. Executor, son, ROBT. TINSLEY. Administrators
Bond is page 668.

JNO. TINSLEY (cont.) -- Book 6, Page 169 -- Inventory -- $4687.30.
SAML. C. BURKS, GEO. TINSLEY, ARMSTEAD RUCKER. August 4, 1820.
Book 6, Page 376 -- Administrators Account -- from November, 1816.
Inspectors at Bethel; seven legatees; note of GEO. TINSLEY; EDWD.;
OLIVER, and LINDSEY TINSLEY; LUCY FOWLER; RO. TINSLEY; ANTHONY G.
TINSLEY; ELIS. WEST; SALLY SLEDD; children of FRANCES HARRISON,
deceased. Note: he refers to seven legatees, but more are named.
August 18, 1823. SAML. BURKS, AMBR. RUCKER, DABNEY WARE.

JOSHUA TINSLEY -- Book 6, Page 291 -- Administrators Bond -- GEO. M.
and ALEX. TINSLEY, May 22, 1822, for both. Bondsmen: ISAAC, GEO. L.
(S) and BANISTER TINSLEY.
Book 6, Page 363 -- Inventory -- No total, 17 March 1823; many slaves.
AMBR. RUCKER, WM. SHELTON, DABNEY WARE, SPENCER NORVEL, SR.
Book 7, Page 46 -- Slave Inventory and division -- shares to ALEX.
TINSLEY, JNO. HUTCHESON, THOS. CLEMONS, WIAT W. BAILEY, BANISTER
TINSLEY, GEO. M., ANDERSON TINSLEY, MERRIT M. WHITE. Mansion house
tract; eight lots drawn. All legatees are of age. January 25, 1823.
AMBR. RUCKER, SPENCER NORVELL, WM. TURNER, committee.

LUCY TINSLEY -- Book 7, Page 205 -- Guardians Bond -- ALFRED TINSLEY
and JAS. BENNETT, January 19, 1829, for ALFRED TINSLEY as guardian
of LUCY TINSLEY, orphan of GEO. M. TINSLEY, deceased.
Book 11, Page 340 -- Administrators Bond -- MILTON BUSBY, ZACH D.
TINSLEY, ARCHELAUS COX, August 18, 1845, for MILTON BUSBY.

PARMELIA TINSLEY -- Book 12, Page 519 -- February 24, 1852; April 19,
1852. Witnesses: JAS. W. BROWN, CALVIN F. BENNETT. Wife of ALEX.
TINSLEY; son, CHAS. WASH. TINSLEY; son, JOSHUA TINSLEY; daughter,
RHODA, wife of MAURICE MORRIS--deed of lean in Amherst County; money
in hands of AMBR. B. RUCKER, Lynchburg; land to RO. TINSLEY in trust
for support of my husband. My three children. Executor: RO. TINSLEY.
Book 12, Page 567 -- Administrators Bond -- ZACH D. TINSLEY and RO.
TINSLEY, August 19, 1852, for ZACH D. TINSLEY.
Book 13, Page 1 -- Inventory -- October 18, 1852; $1634.62½; CALVIN F.
BENNETT, JOS. EWERS, CHRISTOPHER MC IVER.
Book 13, Page 298 -- Administrators Account -- from October 26, 1852;
amounts to RO. TINSLEY, trustee of R. MORRIS, CHAS. W., RO. and
JOSHUA TINSLEY. August 8, 1853.
Book 16, Page 432 -- Administrators Account -- from October 26, 1852.
Recorded: October 19, 1863.

RO. TINSLEY -- Book 8, Page 99 -- Clerk of court for seven years
from last Monday of July next. June 20, 1831. Bondsmen: JAS.,
ZACH D. TINSLEY, WM. M. WALLER, DABNEY SANDIDGE, LINDSEY COLEMAN,
CORNL. SALE.
Book 9, Page 333 -- Clerk of Superior Court, September 4, 1837.
Bondsmen: JAS. TINSLEY, JNO. THOMPSON, JR., WM. C. CHRISTIAN.
Book 11, Page 304 -- Clerk of Superior Court -- August 31, 1844.
Bondsmen: JAS. WARWICK, ZACH. D. TINSLEY. Circuit Superior Court.
Book 12, Page 471 -- Clerk of Circuit Court -- September 3, 1851.
Bondsman: ZACH D. TINSLEY.
Book 16, Page 106 -- March 12, 1859; January 20, 1862. Handwriting
by C. DABNEY and RO. M. BROWN. ELIZA L. TINSLEY qualified. Wife and
marriage contract--Buffaloe tract and homeplace to wife, ELIZA L.
Would free slaves, but wife needs them; to be freed at her death.
Friend and relative- ZACH D. TINSLEY, and sons. Other slaves freed
and to be settled in some free state with families; probably Ohio.
Slave, NELSON, is very capable and will make good. If not to Ohio,
then to Liberia. Some years ago had burial plot of my parents enclosed
of wood; enclose for four graves--wife, unless she objects, in stone
or iron railing. Friend, SAML. H. HENRY, to administrate. $1000 fee
to be paid and he may use it to educate his son; my law books to him.
He is to attend to slave matter and wife is also to administrate.
Book 16, Page 108 -- Administrators Bond -- see will.
Book 16, Page 469 -- M. H. WHARTON, May 16, 1864, for M. H. WHARTON.
Book 20, Page 225 -- Administrators Bond -- ELIZA L. WHARTON and JAS. R.
GILLIAM, December 19, 1881, for ELIZA L. WHARTON.
Book 21, Page 389 -- Administrators de bonis non Bond -- March 21, 1887,

RO. TINSLEY (cont.) -- TAYLOR BERRY and H. C. JOYNER for TAYLOR BERRY.

WM. TINSLEY -- Book 4, Page 191 -- Guardians Account -- JNO. TINSLEY, guardian of WM. TINSLEY, son of WM., from June 28, 1800; to school master, THOS. W. GOOCH, January 1803; JOSIAH and JAS. HARRISON for expenses; RO. TINSLEY for land rent; bond of BATTAILE HARRISON, August 16, 1805. Committee: THOS. MOORE, RICH. POWELL, RICH. HARRISON.
Book 4, Page 325 -- Guardians Bond -- JNO. TINSLEY and MOSES RUCKER, October 20, 1800, for JNO. TINSLEY as guardian of WM. TINSLEY, orphan of WM. TINSLEY, deceased.
Book 4, Page 394 -- Guardians Bond -- AMBR. RUCKER, son to R-(sic), MIN (sic), JAS. WAUGH, REUBEN PENDLETON, November 19, 1804, for AMBR. RUCKER as guardian of W. TINSLEY, orphan of WM. TINSLEY, deceased.
Book 5, Page 182 -- August 23, 1812; October, 1812. Witnesses: SAML. K. JINNINGS, CHAS. WINGFIELD, WM. L. BURKS. JAMES WAUGH and MARTIN PARKS qualified. Wife, SUSANNAH; niece, MARY COLIN PARKS and heirs; my mother, SARAH WAUGH. Executors: friends, JAS. WAUGH and CAPT. MARTIN PARKS.
Book 5, Page 209 -- Inventory -- December 14, 1812: L553-2-5½, Recorded: May 17, 1813. BENJ. SHACKELFORD, JAS. DAVIS, EDMD. GOODRICH.
Book 5, Page 560 -- December 22, 1809; February 19, 1816. Witnesses: JNO. HANSARD, ARMISTEAD RUCKER, RICH. BURKS, WM. EDMUNDS, ALEX. TINSLEY, MATHY (?) KNIGHT, LINZA BURKS. ELIZ. and ISAAC TINSLEY qualified. Wife, BETTY--260 acres where I live; sons, ISAAC, JAS., REUBEN; daughter, MILLY HAYNES and heirs; daughter, NANCY HUGHES. Executors: wife, brother, DAVID TINSLEY, and my son, JAS. TINSLEY.
Book 5, Page 562 -- Administrators Bond -- BETSY and ISAAC TINSLEY, RICH. BURKS, JNO. HANSARD, ARMISTEAD RUCKER, February 19, 1816, for first two to administrate.
Book 5, Page 571 -- Inventory -- March 14, 1816; $4917.53½, EDMD. WINSTON, JR., RICH. BURKS, ARMISTEAD RUCKER.
Book 6, Page 101 -- Administrators Bond -- JAS., RO., and REUBEN TINSLEY, November 16, 1819, for JAS. TINSLEY.
Book 6, Page 106 -- Administrators Bond -- ISAAC TINSLEY, MERRIT M. WHITE, RICH. BURKS, November 16, 1819, for ISAAC TINSLEY.
Book 6, Page 108 -- Administrators Bond -- JAS. TINSLEY, NICHL. HARRISON, RICH. HARRISON, November 16, 1819, for JAS. TINSLEY.
Book 6, Page 127 -- Administrators Account -- ISAAC TINSLEY, acting executor; shop account of EDWD. TINSLEY; cash from JAS. TINSLEY, February 18, 1820; hire of negroes as agreed by heirs. Committee: REUBEN NORVELL, DABNEY WARE, AMBR. RUCKER, EDMD. WINSTON.

WM. TINSLEY, JR. -- Book 3, Page 138 -- Administrators Bond -- SALLY TINSLEY, JNO. TINSLEY, RICH. POWELL, June 7, 1790, for SALLY TINSLEY.
Book 3, Page 155 -- Inventory -- Done in 1790 and recorded February 7, 1791; not total. PHILIP BURTON, RICH. HARRISON, ANTHONY RUCKER.

JNO. TOMLIN (X by mark for TOMLIN, but bond reads TOMLINSON) -- Book 15, Page 61 -- January, 1859; February 21, 1859. Witnesses: H. E. SMITH, WM. H. MC DANIEL. NANCY TOMLIN qualified. Wife, NANCY, to administrate; my single daughters: NANCY, PATSY and MARY. Administrators Bond is Page 66.

AMBROSE TOMLINSON -- Book 6, Page 368 -- January 12, 1820; July 21, 1823. Witnesses: ABRAM CARTER, WM. CARTER, WM. DUNCAN. Wife, MARY-- 285 acres where I live; also 19 acres adjoining and part of Tongate tract; 50 acres on south side and leading to JNO. RICHESON's; slaves; daughter, ELIZ.; my nine children: ELIZ., JNO., MARY, ANN, deceased, AMBR., JAS., JOICE, and DAVID--nine set forth, but only eight named. He then refers to eight of my children and names only seven: ELIZ. is not named. WM.--where he lives. Executors: friends, WM. and JAS. TOMLINSON, SR. and JR.; CHAS. MARTIN, November 20, 1823, for WM. and JNO. TOMLINSON to administrate.
Book 6, Page 438 -- Inventory -- Many slaves; $4988.00; SAML. HANS- BROUGH, HENRY P. RUCKER, CORNL. SALE; additional inventory; no total; Recorded: February 16, 1824; JESSE RICHESON is on second inventory.
Book 6, Page 621 -- Administrators Account -- WM. and JAS. TOMLINSON from December 19, 1823. To JNO. TOMLINSON, DAVID, W., DAVID JR., JAS.

AMBROSE TOMLINSON (cont.) -- and ELIZ. TOMLINSON. Recorded:
September 19, 1825.
Book 6, Page 592 -- Administrators Bond -- ISAAC RUCKER, CHAS. L.
BARRETT, JAS. W. SMITH, March 26, 1825, for ISAAC RUCKER.
Book 17, Page 194 -- January 22, 1866; October 15, 1866. Witnesses:
SAML. RICHESON, THOS. D. WATTS, JAS. S. RICHESON. Children: ADDISON,
ANN WRIGHT, JAS., MARY MARTIN, FANNY RAMSEY; heirs of PRESTON TOMLINSON;
heirs of MANSON TOMLINSON; my three children: SARAH TOMLINSON,
PHOEBA ALLEN and EDWD. TOMLINSON are to care for my wife, MARY.
Executor: SAML. RICHESON.
Book 17, Page 201 -- Administrators Bond -- SAML. and JAS. S. RICHESON,
November 19, 1866, for SAML. RICHESON.

AMBROSE TOMLINSON, JR. -- Book 14, Page 299 -- Administrators Bond --
RUFUS A. HIGGINBOTHAM and JAS. HIGGINBOTHAM, March 16, 1857, for
RUFUS A. HIGGINBOTHAM.
Book 15, Page 87 -- Inventory -- No total; sale, $626.40; buyers:
MRS. TOMLINSON, JNO., JR., JNO. D.; bond of LUCY J. TOMLINSON and bonds
of JNO. and JAS. D. TOMLINSON. Committee: JNO. W. JENNINGS, JAS.
CLEMENTS, THOS. M. GOODWIN--THOS. J. M. GOODWIN. Recorded: February 21,
1859.
Book 16, Page 240 -- Administrators Account -- from August 16, 1858;
paid H. E. SMITH, administrator of L. J. TOMLINSON with interest from
July 16, 1858; bond of MRS. LUCY J. TOMLINSON for sale items; amount
of estate at death of his wife, LUCY J.; HENRY E. SMITH, guardian of
children of A. TOMLINSON, JR. Recorded: November 16, 1860.

DAVID TOMLINSON -- Book 14, Page 173 -- Administrators Bond -- HENRY E.
SMITH and RO.H. CARTER, September 15, 1856, for HENRY E. SMITH.

LUCY J. TOMLINSON -- Book 14, Page 437 -- Administrators Bond --
HENRY E. SMITH and JNO. W. JENNINGS, October 19, 1857, for HENRY E.
SMITH.
Book 15, Page 531 -- Administrators Account -- from November 8, 1857:
$535.77. Recorded: May 21, 1860.

MARGARET TOMLINSON -- Book 14, Page 450 -- Guardians Bond -- HENRY E.
SMITH and JNO. W. JENNINGS, October 19, 1857, for HENRY E. SMITH as
guardian of MARGARET, HARRIET, DOROTHY, JNO. J. and -- TOMLINSON,
orphans of AMBR. TOMLINSON, deceased.

MARY TOMLINSON -- Book 8, Page 8 -- Administrators Bond -- WM. H.
GARLAND and WM. M. WALLER, June 21, 1830, for WM. H. GARLAND. This
is indexed for GARLAND.

MARCUS B. TONEY -- Book 11, Page 517 -- Guardians Bond -- WM. H. C.
TONEY, WM. B. and THOS. J. TERRY, March 15, 1847, for WM. H. C. TONEY
as guardian of MARCUS B. TONEY, orphan of ELIZ. P. (?) TONEY, deceased.

CHAS. TOOLEY -- Book 2, Page 50 -- Administrators Bond -- ELIZ. TOOLEY
and GEO. PERRY, May 6, 1782, for ELIZ. TOOLEY.
Book 2, Page 64 -- Inventory -- L129-18-3, June 3, 1782. JOSIAH
JOPLING, LEE HARRIS, ABNER WITT.

JNO. TOOLEY (TULE in one item) -- Book 4, Page 78 -- August 4, 1801;
February 21, 1803. Witnesses: RICH. POWELL, MERRIT WHITE, THOS.
MOORE, REUBEN PENDLETON. To ARTHUR WHITE and heirs; slaves etc. and
he is to administrate.
Book 5, Page 700 -- TULE here--October 9, 1817; January 20, 1818.
Witnesses: ROYLIN BYAS, JAS. BEYUS--very poor spelling here--wife,
POLLY; $1.00 each to JAS., GEORGE (JORGE), NANCY and LANDON and equal
shares of what I have on place at my death.

HENRY TRENT -- Book 3, Page 397 -- December 27, 1793; October 17, 1796.
Witnesses: MICAJAH GOODWIN, ARCHELAUS MITCHELL, JR., CHAS. CARTER.
Son, JNO. B.--where I live; daughter, EADY MITCHELL--John's Creek
land next to James River; daughter, PATTY CALLAWAY; granddaughter,
NANCY GILES; son, OBADIAH H.; son, JNO. HENRY TRENT--or JNO. B.(?),
when of age; grandsons: ALEX. and HENRY TRENT; THOS. MITCHELL is to

362

HENRY TRENT (cont.) -- keep slaves three years and deliver to JNO. B.
TRENT--when ALEX. and HENRY TRENT are of age. Executors: OB. HENRY
TRENT, AMBROSE RUCKER, THOS. MOORE.
Book 3, Page 413 -- Inventory -- No total, February 20, 1797; DAVID
TINSLEY, RICH. POWELL, JOSHUA SHELTON.
Book 3, Page 542 -- Administrators Account -- by JNO. B. TRENT from
1796; OB. H. TRENT by will; property shares to heirs L2-7-13; April 22,
1799. NELSON C. DAWSON, RICH. POWELL, REUBEN PENDLETON, DAVID TINSLEY.
Book 4, Page 294 -- Indemnifying Bond -- June 17, 1796 by JNO. B.
TRENT and SAML. PARISH to DUDLEY CALLAWAY; CALLAWAY is on his bond
as administrator.
Book 4, Page 300 -- Administrators Bond -- JNO. B. TRENT, SAML.
HILLS, ZACH DAWSON, NELSON C. DAWSON, MOSES RUCKER, THOS. MITCHELL,
DUDLEY CALLAWAY, December 19, 1796, for JNO. B. TRENT.

WM. TROTTER -- Book 2, Page 166 -- February 27, 1784; May 3, 1784.
Witnesses: SAML. DENNEY, CHAS. TATE, WM. ALLIN. All to ELINOR
COFFEY; executor: SAML. S. DINNY.
Book 2, Page 168 -- Administrators Bond -- SAML. DINNEY, CHAS. TATE,
WM. ALLIN, May 3, 1784, for SAML. DINNEY.
Book 2, Page 198 -- Inventory -- L 0-16-9 CHAS. TATE, CHAS. TERTAIN,
WM. ALLIN; October 4, 1784.

C. N. TUCKER -- Book 16, Page 176 -- Administrators Bond -- CHAS. H.
TUCKER and JAS. M. GANNAWAY, October 20, 1862, for CHAS. H. TUCKER.
Book 16, Page 218 -- Inventory -- No total; November 5, 1862: JAS. M.
GANNAWAY, L. S. CAMPBELL, REUBEN B. WARE.

CALIFORNIA TUCKER -- Book 14, Page 213 -- Guardians Bond -- PAMELA M.
TUCKER, WILKERSON D. TUCKER, WM. P. WILSHER and RO. C. WILSHER,
November 17, 1856, for PAMELA M. TUCKER as guardian of CALIFORNIA
TUCKER, orphan of WM. TUCKER, deceased. Two pages here have same
number.

CHAS. TUCKER -- Book 3, Page 415 -- This is indexed for him, but he
is guardian of FERDINAND LEIGH, orphan of WM. LEIGH.
Book 5, Page 39 -- Inventory -- L930-19-0; November 5, 1811. WM.
SANDIDGE, BARTLETT CASH, EDMD. T. COLEMAN.
Book 5, Page 76 -- Administrators Bond -- WM. and CHAS. TUCKER,
MICAJAH CAMDEN, HENRY CAMDEN, HENRY HILL, August 21, 1811, for first
two.
Book 5, Page 636 -- Administrators Account -- from 1811; to PETER
CASH for JESSE CASH--balance due from his interest in land; JOS. PHILIPS
for paling graveyard. To heirs: not named. Recorded: February 17,
1817. HILL CARTER, JNO. SMITH, EDMD. T. COLEMAN.

CHAS. J. TUCKER -- Book 9, Page 90 -- Guardians Bond -- NANCY TUCKER,
JAS. W. COPPEDGE, July 20, 1835, for NANCY TUCKER as guardian of
CHAS. J. TUCKER, orphan of JNO. TUCKER, deceased.
Book 11, Page 123 -- Guardians Bond -- WM. and CHAS. TUCKER, May 15,
1843, for WM. TUCKER as guardian of CHAS. J. TUCKER, orphan of JNO.
TUCKER.
Book 11, Page 224 -- Guardians Account -- by NANCY TUCKER from
January 1, 1837; tuition through 1843; cash of CHAS. TUCKER. Recorded:
June 17, 1844.
Book 12, Page 91 -- WM. TUCKER's account from 1844; DILLARD, trustee;
paid ward in full on December 18, 1848, and recorded same date.

CLAIBORNE TUCKER -- Book 7, Page 40 -- Guardians Bond -- CHAS., THOS.,
and WIATT TUCKER, October 15, 1827, for CHAS. TUCKER as guardian of
CLAIBORNE TUCKER, orphan of JNO. TUCKER.

DANL. TUCKER -- Book 4, Page 425 -- Administrators Bond -- JUDITH
TUCKER, WM. HARRIS, WM. LEE HARRIS, WM. H. DIGGS, WM. and LINDSEY
COLEMAN, JR., MATT. HARRIS and REUBEN HARRIS, January 20, 1806, for
JUDITH TUCKER.
Book 4, Page 625 (but it is 621) -- Inventory -- March 14, 1806;
recorded March 19, 1810; DAVID S. GARLAND, JNO. PENN, SR., LEONARD
HENLEY; no total.

DRURY TUCKER -- Book 4, Page 25 -- Inventory -- L2533-0-0; October 23, 1801. LEONARD HENLEY, RO. HOLLOWAY, JNO. SMITH.
Book 4, Page 27 -- February 4 (?), 1798; September 21, 1801.
Witnesses: GEO. DILLARD, HENRY CAMDEN, CHAS. BURRUS, BEVERLY WILLIAM-SON. DANL. TUCKER qualified; October 19, 1801; bondsmen: JNO. PENN, AMBR. RUCKER, JR. Son, ISAAC; son, LITTLEBERRY; son, ZACH; son, PLEASANT. Wife, FRANKEY; my eleven children: MARY DOUGLAS, WM., DANL., MARTHA RUCKER, MATT. TUCKER, MILLY HARRISON, RO. TUCKER, ISAAC, LITTLEBERRY, ZACH and PLEASANT TUCKER. Executors: friends, DANL. and LITTLEBERRY TUCKER.
Book 4, Page 114 -- Administrators Account -- from November 9, 1801; cash paid for eggs at funeral; just above is item for 1 3/4 gallons of whiskey so it must have been a lavish "wake." MRS. BRAZTON's suit in Richmond; FRANCES TUCKER, widow; certified by LITTLEBERRY TUCKER; eleven heirs. Committee: DAVID S. GARLAND, JNO. PENN, LEONARD HENLEY. Recorded: September 19, 1803.
Book 4, Page 119 -- Division to widow, FRANKEY; and eleven legatees: PLEASANT, MATT., TUCKER, GEO. DOUGLAS for wife, MARY, RO. TUCKER, RICH. HARRISON for wife, MILLY, DANL. TUCKER, ISAAC TUCKER, WM. TUCKER, LITTLEBERRY TUCKER, GEO. TUCKER and wife, MARTHA, ZACH TUCKER. November 30, 1801. Committee: DAVID S. GARLAND, LEONARD HENLEY, JNO. MC DANIEL.
Book 4, Page 415 -- Insane Bond -- November 20, 1798; DANL. and LITTLEBERRY TUCKER; bondsman: JAS. DILLARD, RICH. HARRISON, MAJOR HENRY STONEHAM, WM., ZACH, and PLEASANT TUCKER.
Book 4, Page 333 -- Administrators Bond
Book 5, Page 89 -- Administrators Bond -- WM. COLEMAN, MATT. TUCKER, WILKINS WATSON, RICH. HARRISON, January 20, 1812, for WM. COLEMAN.
Book 5, Page 113 -- so indexed, but not there.
Book 5, Page 171 -- Inventory -- $2433.33; July 4, 1812; DAVID S. GARLAND, JNO. LONDON, WM. CAMDEN.
Book 15, Page 493 -- July 19, 1860; March 19, 1860. Witnesses: RO. C. WILSHER, JAS. M. GANNAWAY, N. A. CASH, RO. N. STAPLES. HENRY LOVING qualified; bondsmen: JAS, F. TALIAFERRO, S. S. HARRIS. Old and feeble; executors: son, LITTLEBERRY TUCKER, and HENRY LOVING; if wife is alive at my death--121 acres where I live; my other children; daughter, SUSAN, deceased, and her children; my living daughters.
Book 16, Page 504 -- Administrators Account -- by LOVING from April 26, 1863--coffin--$10.00; amounts to CHAS. and LITTLEBERRY TUCKER. Recorded: May 15, 1864.

EDMUND P. TUCKER -- Book 14, Page 154 -- Sheriffs Bond -- July 21, 1856; bondsmen: RO. C. WILSHER, G. W. HENLEY, A. TALIAFERRO, S. C. GIBSON, W. D. TUCKER, B. T. HENLEY, CHAS. H. MASSIE, M. C. GOODWIN, JNO. S. TUCKER, SAML. M. GARLAND.
Book 17, Page 323 -- April 24, 1868, account by THOS. W. WHITEHEAD, trustee for E. P. and GEO. W. HENLEY, under two deeds of trust--war interrupted business--two tracts sold--from March 18, 1858 to BETTIE L. TUCKER--63 acre tract; storehouse and mill. Recorded: June 15, 1868.
Book 18, Page 384 -- Surveyor Bond -- December 15, 1873; bondsmen: SAML. M. GARLAND, H. E. SMITH.
Book 19, Page 26 -- Same, June 15, 1875; bondsman: HENRY SMITH.
Book 19, Page 444 -- Surveyor -- June 16, 1879; bondsmen: SAML. M. GARLAND, WM. TUCKER, CORNL. STINNETT.
Book 19, Page 444 -- Same, June 18, 1883; bondsmen: R. A. PENDLETON, E. B. MC GINNIS.
Book 22, Page 169 -- Administrators Bond -- WILKINS WATSON and EDWD. A. WATSON, October 15, 1888, for WILKINS WATSON.
Book 22, Page 305 -- Inventory -- December 4, 1888; E. A. BURKS, WM. MC DANIEL, R. HENLEY--$56.70; sale, December 4, 1888; no total; FRANCES TUCKER was a buyer.
Book 23, Page 238 -- Administrators Account -- from August 31, 1888; to W. B. HENLEY for motion to qualify as administrator; recorded May 16, 1892.
Book 22, Page 413 -- April term, 1889; WATSON versus TUCKER; C. S. SCOTT, attorney was appointed guardian of IDA L. TUCKER and NANNIE LEONARD BIBB. Commissioners: E. S. WARE, S. K. WILSHER, L. P. TYREE to divide 487 acres; S. G. JOHNSON and WM. A. MC DANIEL appointed by

EDMUND P. TUCKER (cont.) -- heirs since TYREE and WILSHER didn't
attend. June, 1889. RO. A. PENDLETON and JNO. B. ROBERTSON, surveyors--
633 plus acres--lots to NANNIE L. BIBB, E. A. TUCKER, ISA L. TUCKER,
plat on headwaters of Franklin Creek. Lines of J. A. WARE, P. H.
DRUMMOND, ED. DRUMMOND. Divided to children and grandchildren of
W. P. TUCKER.

JOHN TUCKER -- Book 7, Page 44 -- Administrators Bond -- CHAS. TUCKER,
EATON CARPENTER, WM. TUCKER, September 17, 1827, for CHAS. TUCKER.
Book 7, Page 80 -- Inventory -- $1523.25; BARTLETT CASH, JAS. W. SMITH,
November 19, 1827.
Book 9, Page 147 -- Dower to NANCY TUCKER, Indian Creek tract. Lines
of WM. WALLER, JULIA ANN CRAWFORD, ABRAHAM MARTIN, JR. 73 acres; plat;
slaves. September 7, 1829. BARTLETT CASH, CORNL. SALE, WM. M. WALLER.
Book 9, Page 355 -- Administrators Account -- from October 2, 1827
books for JNO. TUCKER; bond of WM. M. WALLER, administrator of RO.
MAYS, H. TUCKER for crying negroes, NANCY TUCKER, cash from WIATT
TUCKER, January 12, 1837. CORNL. SALE, ABSALOM HIGGINBOTHAM, WM. M.
WALLER.
Book 12, Page 59 -- Administrators Account -- from October 16, 1838--
JNO. TUCKER is dead; defense of estate of CHAS. TUCKER, deceased, in
Thurmond versus WILLS et al. Recorded: July 17, 1848.

JNO. J. TUCKER -- Book 9, Page 220 -- Guardians Bond -- CHAS. and
WM. TUCKER, March 21, 1836, for CHAS. TUCKER as guardian of JNO. J.,
ELIZ. D. TUCKER, orphans of JNO. TUCKER, deceased.

JNO. W. TUCKER -- Book 16, Page 410 -- Minister's Bond -- December 21,
1863; no denomination. Bondsmen: JNO. W. HOWARD, JAS. GARLAND.
Book 17, Page 43 -- Same, December 18, 1865; bondsman: LEWIS S.
CAMPBELL.

JUDITH TUCKER -- Book 8, Page 163 -- Inventory -- November 23, 1831:
$244.12½. ED. A. CABELL, JNO. PENN, WM. HENLEY.

MARY JANE TUCKER -- Book 9, Page 349 -- Guardians Bond -- WM. A.
RICHESON, JESSE RICHESON, PETER RUCKER, November 20, 1837, for WM. A.
RICHESON as guardian of MARY JANE, RO., MARTHA, THOS. and AMELIA
TUCKER, orphans of THOS. TUCKER, deceased.

MATT. TUCKER -- Book 6, Page 658 -- Administrators Account -- by JAS.
DILLARD, late sheriff, from 1820--$5.00 for coffin; JNO. COLEMAN,
commissioner. Recorded: March 21, 1821.

REBECCA JANE TUCKER -- Book B, Page 21 -- Estate Commitment to Sheriff --
Saturday, March 26, 1842; motion of HENRY M. ESTILL; unadministrated
by NELSON CRAWFORD in next motion in Book B, Page 29 by ESTILL and
put in hands of present sheriff, JAS. L. LAMKIN, August 27, 1847;
Friday.
Book 12, Page 432 -- Administrators Account -- by LAMKIN from February,
1848. Recorded: July 21, 1851.
Book B, Page 60 -- Administrators de bonis non Bond -- JAS. L. COGHILL
and RO. B. TUCKER, September 3, 1854 for JAS. L. COGHILL; LAMKIN gives
account. Recorded: September 6, 1865.

ST. GEO. TUCKER -- Book 5, Page 81 -- Guardians Bond -- WM. COLEMAN
and REUBEN COLEMAN, September 16, 1811, for WM. COLEMAN as guardian
of ST. GEO. TUCKER, orphan of DANL. TUCKER, deceased. Deed data
shows ST. GEO. in Kentucky.

SARAH E. TUCKER -- Book 16, Page 74 -- Guardians Bond -- JNO. S.
TUCKER, B. L. TALIAFERRO, April 15, 1861, for JNO. S. TUCKER as
guardian of SARAH E., CHAS. W., M. A., W. LEWIS C. and C. C. TUCKER--
hard to decipher names correctly; no parent set forth; indexed for
Book 15, Page 74.
Book 23, Page 467 -- June 1, 1899; Monday, July 17, 1899. Witnesses:
W. T. WARE, C. C. GILL. Daughter, NETTIE LOWRY waited on me during
my illness; granddaughter, ESTHER LOWRY; four children of my daughter,
BETTY WILMER; my three children: RO. LEE, EDLOE and NETTIE LOWRY.
Executor: C. T. SMITH.

SUSAN TUCKER -- Book 7, Page 39 -- Guardians Bond -- CHAS., MATT.
and THOS. TUCKER, October 15, 1827, for CHAS. TUCKER as guardian of
SUSAN TUCKER, orphan of JNO. TUCKER.

SUSANNAH TUCKER -- Book 6, Page 405 -- September 18, 1823; November 17,
1823. Witnesses: WM. GATEWOOD, ABRAM CARTER. THOS. TUCKER qualified;
bondsmen: WM. TUCKER and ABRAM CARTER. My children, since the death
of my husband, THOS. TUCKER; granddaughter, SUANNA PRYOR; if no issue;
her brothers and sisters. My daughter, ELIZ. PRYOR, and her daughter,
ELIZ. PRYOR. My daughter, SALLY PRYOR, and children. My granddaughter,
JANE PRYOR. (Note: it should be SUSANNAH PRYOR above.) Executors:
THOS. TUCKER and JESSE RICHESON.
Book 6, Page 455 -- Inventory -- May 17, 1824; JESSE RICHESON, WM.
COLEMAN, PETER CARTER.
Book 8, Page 260 -- Administrators Account -- from July 7, 1824;
calico for JUDITH MARTIN; hinges and nails for graveyard; funeral
expenses and dinner for company at my own expense--$15.00; Corn sold
to WM. TUCKER, August 17, 1829; JNO. PRYOR, WM. JOPLING, ORMUND WARE.

THOS. TUCKER -- Book 3, Page 585 -- November 23, 1800; October 20,
1800--so recorded in book. Witnesses: BENJ. COLEMAN, JNO. RICHESON,
JNO. WARE, ELIZ. TUCKER. Daughter, SALLY PRYOR; money due from ZACH
TALIAFERRO; wife, SUSANNAH--land; my four children: JAS., JUDITH,
WM. and THOS. to be educated; if no issue, then to my daughter,
TUCKER. Wife and my brother, CHAS., are to administrate. CHAS.
qualified; bondsmen: JNO. SMITH and BENJ. COLEMAN--page 325 of book 4
and bears date of October 20, 1800.
Book 4, Page 12 -- Inventory -- L533-15-4, July 29, 1801. JNO. WARE,
ZACH SHOEMAKER, WM. SLEDD.
Book 5, Page 88 -- Administrators Bond -- SUSANNA TUCKER, December 16,
1811; bondsmen: ZACH SHOEMAKER, WM. TUCKER.
Book 9, Page 340 -- Administrators Bond -- WM. A. RICHESON, JESSE
RICHESON, RO. H. CARTER, October 16, 1837, for WM. A. RICHESON.
Book 10, Page 102 -- Inventory -- January 8, 1838: $6385.31; debt
due from estate of TURNER. JOS. R. CARTER, LEE MILLNER, PITT WOODROOF,
January 8, 1838.
Book 10, Page 163 -- Administrators Account -- by RICHESON from
October 17, 1837; to JNO. DAVIS, son of JNO.; NANCY C. WATTS; JNO. D.
CRAWFORD, son of JNO.; WM. TUCKER. Commissioner: WM. L. SAUNDERS,
October 21, 1839. I do not think that these payments are to heirs--
only accounts due.

WM. TUCKER -- Book 14, Page 150 -- November 1, 1853; Monday, August 18,
1856. Witnesses: CHAS. B. MASSIE, RO. L. COLEMAN, JAS. P. COLEMAN.
WM. and WIATT TUCKER qualified; bondsmen: H. LOVING, RO. W. SNEAD,
R. S. PENDLETON, G. W. CARTER. Wife, PERMELIA--settlement of
November 1, 1853. Sons, WM. and WIATT--800 acres in four tracts;
daughter, ELIZ. HIGGINBOTHAM--SAML. C. GIBSON and JAS. GANNAWAY,
trustees--if any children; daughter, SALLY MC DANIEL, and children;
PLEASANT STORY for my daughter, MARY, and children: children of
deceased son, CHAS.--STORY to be trustee; my infant daughter,
CALIFORNIA; daughters apart from husbands. Executors: sons, WM. and
WIATT TUCKER.
Book 14, Page 218 -- Inventory -- No total; October 23, 1856; RO. W.
SNEAD, A. TALIAFERRO, WM. SANDIDGE; sale, same date: buyers: W. D.
and executors; ROLIN TUCKER; no total. Slave inventory; page 216;
no total; furniture to two heirs, October 6, 1856; R. W. SNEAD,
M. C. GOODWIN, CHAS. H. MASSIE.
Book 17, Page 443 -- April 9, 1868; July 19, 1869. Handwriting by
LEONARD DANIEL, JR. and GEO. H. DAMERON. G. A. R. TUCKER qualified;
bondsmen: RO. M. BROWN and WM. E. COLEMAN. My four children: MARY
BURFORD--deed of record to where she lives--her last two children:
ELLER and EMMER; to WM. D. and children, BISHOP and EMPRESS--50 extra,
when 18; GUSTAVUS is to be agent; $50 to Ordaner and other children
under care of their mother until 18; GUSTAVUS A. R., SUSIE M., W. L.
and MA IA (?)--to be received by their parents, if any left; give
MARIA TURPIN $100; divide fairly to all grandchildren; GUS is due
most at present; divide furniture; ANNIE knows what is left; your
father and then names of MARY and WM. D., ANNIE MARIAH and GUSTAVUS;

WM. TUCKER (cont.) -- several notes due--one on S. L. BURFORD.
Book 17, Page 515 -- Inventory -- JACOB H. ROBINSON, RO. L. WALDRON,
JNO. B. TILDEN, September 7, 1869; found at home of SAML. POINDEXTER,
JR. Lynchburg. Certified there by JNO. T. MERRILL, Notary Public.
September 7, 1869. Recorded: Amherst County, September 20, 1869.
Book 18, Page 178 -- Administrators Account -- by G. A. TUCKER,
November, 1871. Legatees: MARY BURFORD, ANN M. POINDEXTER, WM. D.
TUCKER, G. A. R. TUCKER; list on page 180: ELLA and EMMA BURFORD;
OTIS R. TUCKER; WLATER S. TUCKER; GRISWOLD M. TUCKER--all males are
sons of WM. D. TUCKER. EMPRESS and NINA TUCKER are daughters of
WM. D. TUCKER. ANN M. POINDEXTER and daughter, OREANA POINDEXTER;
G. A. R. TUCKER and children; W. LAWRENCE and MARY JANE TUCKER;
railroad freight on remains and grave; to ELLA J. BURFORD per WM. A.
BURFORD; WALTON (it is WALTER above) S. TUCKER; daughters of ANN M.
POINDEXTER: OREANA, MARY E., ROSA, JENNIE; and sons, WM. L. and RO.
LEE. SUSAN M. TUCKER, daughter of G. A. R. TUCKER; guardian of
ELLA J. BURFORD, OTIS R. TUCKER, son of WM. D. TUCKER; WALTER S. and
GRISWOLD M. TUCKER; G. A. R. as trustee for his children. Very long.
Book 19, Page 153 -- Administrators Account -- August 12, 1875;
expenses to Georgia and return; to W. D.; OTIS R.; WALTER L.; G. A. R.
as trustee of G. M.; C. E. and N. D. TUCKER and self as legatee and
guardian of SUSIE N. TUCKER; to MARY J. and W. L. TUCKER; to ANN M.
POINDEXTER and as trustee of MARY E.; ROSA and JENNIE; WILLIS S.;
OREANN; and RO. LEE POINDEXTER; G. A. R. TUCKER, SR. as guardian of
G. A. R., JR.; children of G. A. R. TUCKER: SUSIE M., JR., W. L.
and M. J. TUCKER. Recorded March 20, 1876.
Book 21, Page 86 -- Inventory -- September 19, 1844; L. P. TYREE,
JOS. H. MASSIE, W. SANDIDGE.
Book 21, Page 98 -- Curator, JAS. S. SANDIDGE, September 15, 1884;
bondsmen: TAYLOR BERRY and R. A. COGHILL.
Book 21, Page 138 -- Inventory -- not in previous one, December 1,
1884; by same men as page 86: $11.25; sale, December 1, 1884; buyers:
CHAS., JNO. W., JAS., MRS. ANN, MISS MILLY TUCKER: $361.33.
Book 21, Page 285 -- Account by SANDIDGE from August 24, 1884; March 4,
1886; to W. J., CHAS. A., WM. J. TUCKER; cash of JNO. W. TUCKER;
legacies in 1885 to JNO. W. and MARY ANN TUCKER; recorded: May 18,
1886.

WYATT TUCKER -- Book 8, Page 15 -- Administrators Bond -- This is an
item for GABL. PAGE; see.
Book 14, Page 99 -- August 24, 1848; Monday, May 19, 1856. Witnesses:
JAS. MILLNER, SR., JNO. R. IRVINE, JAS. BROWN. One-half in trust to
WILKERSON D. TUCKER for my daughter, MARY F. HILL, wife of THOS. G.
HILL, and children; my son, WILKERSON D., if no issue.
Book 14, Page 142 -- Administrators Bond -- WILKERSON D. TUCKER, EDMD. P.
TUCKER, JAS. S. TUCKER, A. TALIAFERRO, HENRY L. DAVIES, June 16, 1856,
for WILKERSON D. TUCKER. He is called WM. D. inbond, but is signed
WILKERSON D.
Book 14, Page 186 -- Sale -- October 8, 1856; buyers: CHAS., W. D.,
P. L.(S); no total; Recorded: October 20, 1856.
Book 14, Page 219 -- Inventory -- Many slaves; no total, October 6,
1859; buyers: W. D., CHAS., J. S., WYATT, WM., ROLAND and CHAS. J.
TUCKER.

JNO. TURBIT -- Book B, Page 82 -- Estate Commitment to Sheriff --
August 27, 1859; motion of GEO. W. LATHAM; Sheriff: M. C. GOODWIN.

ELIZ. JANE TURNER -- Book 9, Page 25 -- Guardians Bond -- GEO. H. and
LAWSON TURNER, THOS. HUTCHESON, December 15, 1834, for GEO. H. TURNER
as guardian of ELIZ. JANE TURNER, oprhan of RICH. TURNER, deceased.

FLEMING TURNER -- Book 4, Page 337 -- Guardians Bond -- JNO. and SAML.
TURNER, October 19, 1801, for JNO. TURNER as guardian of FLEMING
TURNER, orphan of STEPHEN TURNER.

FRANCIS W. TURNER -- Book 4, Page 338 -- Guardians Bond -- JNO. and
SAML. TURNER, October 19, 1801, for JNO. TURNER as guardian of
FRANCIS W. TURNER, orphan of STEPHEN TURNER.

MAJOR HENRY TURNER -- Book 7, Page 276 -- Administrators Bond --
LAWSON, GEO. L. TURNER, GEO. STAPLES, JAS. S. HIGGINBOTHAM, STEPHEN B.
and WM. TURNER, November 16, 1829, for first two.
Book 7, Page 277 -- September 29, 1828; November 16, 1829. Witnesses:
JESSE MUNDY, CHAS. MUNDY, JAS. S. DILLARD, SAML. WOODSON. Daughter,
SALLY DAWSON; son, WM.; daughter, PATSY GREGORY; daughter, POLLY D.
OMOHUNDRO; son, JAS. S.; son, HENRY; son, STEPHEN B.; son, LAWSON;
son, GEO.; daughter, RUTH STONE; daughter, NANCY B. CARVER; wife,
RACHEL; grandson, JAS. H. TURNER; son, TERISHA; son, SAML.; heirs of
deceased daughter, ELIZ. GREGORY.
Book 7, Page 340 -- Inventory -- $3143.25, of MAJOR HENRY TURNER,
December 1, 1829. GEO. STAPLES, JESSE BECK, JNO. WARWICK.
Book 8, Page 381 -- Administrators Account -- by both administrators:
Superior Court of Lynchburg and certified to Amherst County; legacies
of MARTHA GREGORY, TERISHA TURNER, HENRY TURNER, M. H. GARLAND, E. P.
OMOHUNDRO, JAS. S. TURNER, GEO. N. GREGORY, B. P. BALDER, REUBEN
CARVER, S. (L) B. TURNER, SAML. TURNER, WM. TURNER, JAS. S. TURNER;
bond of HEZ. STONE and GHOS. GRAVES to estate. January 1, 1833.
JOS. S. DILLARD and JESSE MUNDY, committee.

JAS. TURNER -- Book 4, Page 223 -- November 24, 1805; June 15, 1806.
Codicil, January 31, 1806. Witnesses to will: WM. LEE HARRIS, JOS.
PHILLIPS. Witnesses to codicil: ALEX. ROBERTS. Wife, REBECCA--where
I live; son, WM., when of age; daughters: NANCY, MILDRED, JUDITH,
LUCY and PATSY; son, JNO.--150 acres where he lives; my mill--LYONS'
old mill which I bought of the LYONS' estate: SAML. ANDERSON's line
to spring branch of TERISHA TURNER--land called BAILEY's on both
sides of Rockfish; son, JAS.; daughter, ELIZ. PHILLIPS--200 acres in
Kentucky. Rest of Kentucky land to be sold and divided to daughters,
REBECCA AUSTIN, NANCY, MARY TURNER, SUSANNAH DAMRON, MILDRED, JUDITH,
LUCY, and PATSY--hard to separate names here. Son, JAS., what he
owes me as executor of my son, STEPHEN, and suit in Amherst County.
Executors: friends, BENJ. HARRIS, WALTER LEAKE and SAML. MURRELL of
Albemarle and BENJ. DAWSON of Kentucky.
Book 4, Page 429 -- Administrators Bond -- WALTER LEAKE and WM. LEE
HARRIS, June 18, 1806, for WALTER LEAKE.
Book 4, Page 450 -- Inventory -- No total; July 20, 1807; JNO. MOSELY,
MATT. HARRIS, WM. H. MOSELY.
Book 5, Page 177 -- Administrators Account -- to JNO. TURNER; will
expenses; bond of TERISHA TURNER; JAS.; NANCY; MILLY TURNER. August 17,
1812.

JNO. L. TURNER -- Book 9, Page 274 -- Guardians Bond -- WM. KENT,
LEWIS R. REYNOLDS, DAVID STAPLES, December 19, 1836, for WM. KENT as
guardian of JNO. L. TURNER, orphan of WM. T. (?) TURNER, deceased.
Book 17, Page 106 -- Inventory -- May 15, 1866: $866.00. POWHATAN
WINGFIELD, J. H. CAMPBELL, JAS. M. JOYNER, R. N. PENDLETON.

LUCY TURNER -- Book 4, Page 478 -- Guardians Bond -- JNO. GRAVES,
JOS. SHELTON, DAVID S. GARLAND, DABNEY CARR, RO. ANDERSON, November 17,
1807, for JNO. GRAVES as guardian of LUCY TURNER, orphan of JAS.
TURNER, deceased.

MARTHA TURNER -- Book 8, Page 245 -- Guardians Bond -- August 20,
1832, for JNO. P. HUDSON and WM. TURNER for JNO. P. HUDSON as guardian
of MARTHA TURNER, orphan of WM. T. TURNER, deceased.

MARTHA F. TURNER -- Book 23, Page 251 -- January 18, 1887; June 20,
1892. Witnesses: JNO. W. and THOS. B. PLEASANTS, D. H. RUCKER.
Motion of CHAS. E. NICHOLAS, executor named, who qualified. Appraisers:
JNO. PLEASANTS, R. H. EUBANK, R. N. ELLIS, WM. DODD, WM. TUCKER.
Niece, MATTIE S. NICHOLAS; great nephew, STEPHEN TURNER NICHOLAS--when
21; children of MATTIE; sister, AMERICA WATTS. Executors: CHAS. E.
NICHOLAS. Administrators Bond is page 265.

MARY TURNER -- Book 7, Page 327 -- Guardians Bond -- JAS. F. and
NATHAN TURNER, February 15, 1830, for JAS. F. TURNER as guardian of
his infant daughter, MARY TURNER.

MILDRED F. TURNER -- Book 11, Page 11 -- Guardians Bond -- JNO. L.
TURNER and DANL. DAY, February 21, 1842, for JNO. L. TURNER as guardian
of MILDRED F. TURNER, orphan of RICH. TURNER, deceased.

NATHAN H. TURNER -- Book 9, Page 344 -- July 17, 1837; deposition of
WARNER JONES, M.D.--two hours before death, NATHAN H. TURNER called
upon WM. WOODROOF and JAS. W. KEITH to witness and stated that wife
was to have everything; at her death, to the children. Died on
morning of June 19th last. ELIZA TURNER qualified; bondsmen: WARNER
JONES, WM. S. and JNO. F. TURNER.
Book 9, Page 378 -- Inventory -- $3933.25; January 15, 1838. JAS. W.
KEITH, MOSES PHILLIPS, LANDON A. PROFFITT.

PATSY TURNER -- Book 4, Page 490 -- Guardians Bond -- HENRY WRITTEN-
HOUSE, TERRY TURNER, WM. BAILEY, December 21, 1807, for HENRY
WRITTENHOUSE as guardian of PATSY TURNER, orphan of JAS. TURNER.

REBECCA C. TURNER -- Book 4, Page 258 -- July 21, 1806--renounces will
of husband, JAS. TURNER, and claims dower. Witnesses: MATT.
LANKFORD, WM. H. LEIGH, DUNMORE DAMERON.
Book 24, Page 127 -- January 11, 1888; February 3, 1891. Handwriting
by CAMILLUS CHRISTIAN. Executors named qualified. I do not note use
of initial C for this later will. January 11, 1888; February 13,
1891. Son, SAML. J.; my three daughters; all of my children and heirs
of any who may have died. Probated in Lynchburg; recorded Amherst
County, January 23, 1911.

RICH. TURNER -- Book 8, Page 178 -- February 20, 1832; March 19, 1832.
Witnesses: D. STAPLES, CHAS. MUNDY, WM. S. GREGORY. Wife, SARAH;
son, JON. L.; daughter, CASSANDRA, when of age; daughter, MARY WOOD;
son, GEO.; daughter, ADALINE; daughter, LUCY ANN; daughter, ELIZA
JANE; son, SAML.; son, WM.; daughter, FRANCES; daughter, AMANDA.
Executors: WM. TURNER and WM. KENT; son, JNO. L., when of age.
Page 180 is Administrators Bond for executors named. Bondsmen:
WILLIS M. REYNOLDS, THOS. HUTCHINSON, WM. PETTYJOHN.
Book 8, Page 229 -- Inventory -- July 16, 1832; $4506.81. D. STAPLES,
JOS. L. DILLARD, REUBEN CARVER.
Book 14, Page 346 -- Administrators de bonis non Bond -- May 18, 1857:
SAML. J. and JNO. L. TURNER for SAML. J. TURNER.
Book 14, Page 387 -- Inventory of estates of RICH. and SARAH TURNER;
SARAH, widow of RICH., June 15, 1857. WM. A. STAPLES, RO. C. MARTIN,
JESSE MUNDY. SARAH: $236.50; RICH.: $8127.50.
Book 16, Page 244 -- SAML. TURNER's account from January 1, 1858;
MRS. TURNER's part until death and date of January 1, 1858; hire of
slaves from death of life tenant, May 30th to date. One-eleventh to
each of these: SAML. J. TURNER, JESSE WOOD and wife, MARY--SAML. J.
TURNER, assignee; JNO. BAILEY and wife, LUCY A.--SAML. J. TURNER
assignee; GEO. H. TURNER; WM. G. HARLANE and wife, ADELINE; E. B. MAYS
and wife, CASSANDRA; WM. R. TURNER, JNO. L. TURNER, GEORGE W. HOWL
and wife, FRANCES, JAS. C. TAYLOR and wife, AMANDA, ELIZ. J. MAYS.
Recorded: February 21, 1859.

SALLY TURNER -- Book 9, Page 46 -- Guardians Bond -- TANDY JONES and
CHAS. MASSIE, February 16, 1835, for TANDY JONES as guardian of SALLY
and BETSY TURNER, orphans of WM. T. (S) TURNER, deceased.
Book 10, Page 153 -- Guardians Bond -- WM. KENT and DAVID STAPLES,
August 19, 1839, for WM. KENT as guardian of same ward.
Book 10, Page 238 -- someone erred; nothing thereon.
Book 10, Page 353 -- Inventory -- February 20, 1841, $1887.00; JAS. L.
LAMKIN, THOS. HUTCHINSON.
Book 10, Page 309 -- Administrators Bond -- WM. KENT and DAVID STAPLES,
February 15, 1841, for WM. KENT; also Administrators Account from
February, 1841. Duiguids--funeral bill: $20.00 legatees due $912.24;
Recorded: November 1, 1843; GEO. DILLARD, commissioner.

SAML. TURNER -- Book 7, Page 271 -- Administrators Bond -- JOHN and
JAS. DILLARD, JAS. D. WATTS, JNO. S. DILLARD, NATHAN H. TURNER,
August 17, 1829, for JNO. DILLARD.

369

SAML. TURNER (cont.) -- Book 7, Page 274 -- July 29, 1829; September 21,
1829. Witnesses: JAS. POWELL, PEYTON KEITH, LUCY R. SPENCER. Son,
WM., if he marries; son, JNO., if no heirs; son, NATHAN, if he married;
son, SAML., ditto; son, JEFFERSON; daughter, NANCY; son, STEPHEN, if
he married. E. A. CABELL, JR. and P. C. CABELL, trustees for MARY D.
TURNER, daughter of my son, JNO. Son-in-law, JNO. DILLARD; to SAML.
TURNER DILLARD. Executors: son, WM., and son, JNO. and son-in-law,
JNO. DILLARD. JNO. DILLARD qualified, September 22, 1829; bondsmen:
JAS. and JOS. DILLARD, WM. TURNER, MOSES PHILLIPS--Book 7, Page 276.
Book 7, Page 281 -- Division of three tracts. 1. Jas. River into
three tracts and Tye land into three; plat on 282 204 acres; 2. Mansion
house tract on Tye; 699 acres. 3. Luck Mt. 264 acres. Luck Mt.
not so valuable, but has compensations. James River tract shows
lines of GEO. STAPLES, JAS. DILLARD, MUNDY, CHAS. S. --. Children
and legatees: WM. S., JNO. F., SAML. and NATHAN TURNER, JNO. DILLARD
who married NANCY TURNER, EDWD. A. CABELL as trustee of STEPHEN
TURNER, PEYTON KEITH as guardian of JEFF. TURNER; Lot 1 or upper
river tract to NATHANIEL TURNER; middle tract drawn by JNO. DILLARD;
lower river to SAML. TURNER; mansion house by PEYTON KEITH as guardian
of JEFF. TURNER; middle mansion tract to JNO. F. TURNER; Tye River
to EDWD. A. CABELL as trustee of STEPHEN TURNER; Luck Mt. drawn by
WM. S. TURNER, November 9, 1829. HENRY H. WATTS, JNO. DILLARD, SR.,
LINDSEY COLEMAN. Next plat of James banks about two miles below
STAPLES' Mill and directly at upper end of DILLARD's Island; joins
GEO. STAPLES, JAS. DILLARD, CHAS. MUNDY. Plat--all in Amherst County
except small portion of northeast corner in Nelson; both sides Tye
and Camp Creeks. Joins EDWD. A. CABELL, PEYTON KEIGH, TERISHA
TURNER, JNO. DILLARD, MRS. SOPHIA CRAWFORD. Luck Mt.; head br. of
Horsley and south border of Buffaloe. Joins JNO. FLOOD, JNO. BURKS,
GODFREY TOLER, WM. DEMPSEY, BENJ. SANDIDGE, deceased--about 1½ miles
from Buffaloe Springs. Recorded: November 16, 1829.
Book 7, Page 303 -- Inventory -- Many slaves; JAS. HIGGINBOTHAM;
JAS. D. WATTS; WM. WRIGHT, November 16, 1829. JNO. DILLARD has had
inventory: $16,495.26; pending controversy about will.

SARAH TURNER -- Book 4, Page 274 -- November 14, 1806; February 15,
1807. Witnesses: SAML. TURNER, WM. F. LEIGH, LEONARD MAWYEAR.
Proved by SAML. and WM. H. TURNER. All of my children except MARY
LONDON--she gets household goods, etc. Grandson, TERISHA TURNER, is
now living with me. He and JNO. J. DAWSON are to administrate.
Book 14, Page 307 -- Administrators Bond -- SAML. J. and JNO. L.
TURNER, May 18, 1857.
Book 14, Page 387 -- see RICH. TURNER for joint inventory. May 25,
1857.

STEPHEN TURNER -- Book 4, Page 8 -- April 29, 1799; June 12, 1801.
Witnesses: RO. RIVES, CHAS. YANCEY, JOS. TURNER, JESSE HIGGINBOTHAM,
JNO. JOHNSON. Wife, SARAH, where I live--given to me by SAML. SPENCER
and patent to him--less than 300 acres. Son, FRANCIS W. L.; son,
TERISHA; my six sons: SAML., TERISHA, JNO., JAS., FLEMING and
FRANCIS W. L. (S) TURNER. TERISHA gets where he lives--NN side of
Tye to CABELL's line and slaves, JACK, FILL, HARRY and WILL JOHN.
400 acres bought of BLAKEY, to JAS. TURNER--Seven Creek; 400 and 300
acres on both sides of Piney held by HAY, to FLEMING; 382½ bought of
BATES; Daughter, MARY TRUITT; daughter, ELIZ. STEPHENS; daughter,
SALLY STEPHENS; daughter, NANCY TINDALL. Doubts have arisen as to
legitimacy of my children herein named from having married with my
present wife who was sister of my first wife, deceased. I have lived
with her for forty years. All of my estate was acquired by honest
and frugal policy.
Book 4, Page 331 -- Administrators Bond -- JNO., TERISHA, and SAML.
TURNER qualified, June 15, 1801. Bondsmen: JAS. MURPHY, STEPHEN
WATTS, NELSON ANDERSON, RO. RIVES.
Book 18, Page 32 -- January 5, 1857; December 19, 1870. Witnesses:
FRANCIS A. BLAIR, DAVID APPLING; codicil and witnesses: H. E. SMITH,
R. C. APPLING. Wife, MARTHA F., formerly WATTS; friend, JAMES D.
WATTS, to administrate. Codicil: have survived JAS. D. WATTS and
BLAIR. Wife to administrate. HENRY SMITH qualified. Bondsmen:
JNO. W. and PHILIP PLEASANTS, JAS. W. PLEASANTS, JAS. N. PRYOR, DANL. H.
RUCKER, JNO. R. CUNNINGHAM; page 33.

STEPHEN TURNER (cont.) -- Book 18, Page 42 -- Inventory -- on order
of December, 1870: $347.00; JNO. W. PLEASANTS, JNO. R. CUNNINGHAM,
LOUIS P. PLEASANTS; carryover total brings it to $498.50, at late
residence. Recorded: January 13, 1871. Note: codicil bears no
data as to when written.

STEPHEN TURNER, JR. -- Book 3, Page 330 -- Administrators Bond -- JAS.
TURNER, JR., JOS. ROBERTS, January 19, 1794, for JAS. TURNER, JR.
Book 3, Page 376 -- Administrators Account -- March 13, 1795; planta-
tion called Miles BAILEY's; due estate: L60-14-2; inventory: L25-2-0.
JNO. DIGGS, WM. HARRIS, JOS. SHELTON, February 15, 1796; also inventory
on October 31, 1795 by JOS. SMITH, BENJ. PAIN, ZACH FORTUNE.

TERISHA TURNER -- Book 4, Page 34 -- May 7, 1793; April 19, 1802.
Witnesses: JNO. DAWSON, GEO. MORRIS, MARTIN DAWSON, BENJ. PAYN,
BENJ. MOORE, OBADIAH MOORE, JOSEPH SMITH. Acneint; sons, JAS. and
STEPHEN--700 acres in Granville County, North Carolina and in hands
of STEPHEN; son, JNO.--519 acres on FRY's branch; son, HENRY, 519
acres on Porage; son, WM.--519 acres near JNO. and HENRY; daughter,
MARY LONDON; daughter, SARAH STOVALL; wife, SARAH, where I live and
100 acres on Briery fork in Albemarle; son, GEO., if no issue; son,
WM.--land near BENJ. DAWSON's spring branch. Executors: sons, HENRY
and WM.
Book 4, Page 111 -- Inventory -- L654-11-0, December 8, 1802; JNO. S.
DAWSON, PETER LYON, ZACH ROBERTS.
Book 4, Page 344 -- Administrators Bond -- HENRY and WM. TURNER,
April 19, 1802; Bondsmen: STEPHEN WATTS, HENRY ROBERTSON, BENJ.
PAYNE.
Book 5, Page 60 -- Administrators Bond -- TERISHA TURNER, WM. LEE
HARRIS, HENRY TURNER, JAS. MURPHY, June 18, 1810, for TERISHA TURNER;
no testator is named, but indexed for TERISHA TURNER.

WM. TURNER -- Book 9, Page 24 -- September 23, 1834; October 20, 1834.
Witnesses: JNO. D. WILLS, THOS. HUTCHESON, HENRY D. WARWICK. Wife,
grandson, JNO. L.--son of deceased son, WM. T.--when of age; Executors:
friends, WM. KENT and JESSE MUNDY.
Book 9, Page 25 -- Administrators Bond -- WM. KENT, November 20, 1834,
Bondsmen: EDMD. WINSTON, WILLIS H. REYNOLDS.
Book 9, Page 49 -- Inventory -- February 16, 1835; $265.00; blacksmith
tools. D. STAPLES, WM. PETTYJOHN, JAS. DAVIS.
Book 9, Page 331 -- July 1, 1829; August 21, 1837. Witnesses: JESSE
MUNDY, E. P. OMOHUNDRO, SAML. TURNER. Son, WASH. R., when of age; my
three brothers: STEPHEN B., LAWSON and GEO. TURNER: land in Fluvanna
on Bee branch and joins JOS. WOOLING. Executors: brothers, STEPHEN B.
and LAWSON TURNER.
Book 20, Page 259 -- Administrators Bond -- S. H. TURNER and HENRY
LOVING, JR., February 20, 1882, for S. H. TURNER.
Book 20, Page 286 -- Inventory -- March 3, 1882; no total; RO. A.
KENT, W. S. HOWL, S. J. BAILEY, STEPHEN H. TURNER, administrator.
Sale, March 3, 1882; SAML. J., JNO., GEO. H., ANDREW, JORDAN TURNER--
buyers. $273.67.

WM. F. TURNER -- Book 9, Page 75 -- Estate Commitment to Sheriff --
June 17, 1835; motion of LUCY A. TURNER; left unadministrated by WM.
TURNER, deceased. Sheriff: THOS. N. EUBANK.
Book 9, Page 328 -- Administrators Account -- by EUBANK, late sheriff
from January 1, 1831: $247.41. Recorded: August 21, 1837. LINDSEY
COLEMAN, JONATHAN A. STOUT.

WM. R. TURNER -- Book 9, Page 346 -- Guardians Bond -- GEO. H. and
SAML. J. TURNER, ALFRED MAYS, November 20, 1837, for GEO. H. TURNER
as guardian of WM. R. TURNER, orphan of RICH. TURNER, deceased.

WM. S. TURNER, JR. -- Book 13, Page 31 -- June 8, 1851; December 20,
1852. Witnesses: JAS. S. PENDLETON, JR., ANN L. WATTS, RO. A.
COGHILL. Wife, FRANCES JANE, to administrate. Daughter, MARY E.
DILLARD, wife of JNO. Q. A. DILLARD; my children; daughter, MARY, shall
come in final distribution in hatch pot with my other children.
Book 13, Page 32 -- Administrators Bond -- FRANCES J. qualified;

WM. S. TURNER, JR. (cont.) -- December 20, 1852.
Book 13, Page 33 -- Guardians Bond -- RO. A. COGHILL and RO. A.
PENDLETON, December 20, 1852, for RO. A. COGHILL as guardian of WM. S.
TURNER, orphan of NATHAN H. TURNER.
Book 13, Page 82 -- Inventory -- $15,259.25; JAS. D. WATTS, MOSES
PHILLIPS, A. L. FOGUS; recorded: March 21, 1853.
Book 14, Page 521 -- Refunding Bond -- by WM. S. TURNER, September 17,
1855; bondsman: JAS. W. PHILLIPS. To CHAS. H. RUCKER, Amherst
County Sheriff and administrator of EDWIN WOODROOG; RUCKER has paid
legacy to WM. S. TURNER.

WM. T. TURNER -- Book 6, Page 690 -- Administrators Bond -- WM. TURNER
and WM. DAY, September 17, 1826, for WM. TURNER.
Book 6, Page 705 -- Inventory -- $1191.00; November 20, 1826; CHAS.
MUNDY, CHAS. PALMORE, DANL. DAY.

CHAS. TYLER -- Book 12, Page 32 -- Estate Commitment to Sheriff --
October, 1848; motion of MATILDA J. TYLER, widow; Sheriff: JAS. L.
LAMKIN.
Book 12, Page 80 -- Inventory -- November 17, 1848; GEO. MARKHAM, THOS.
ALLEN, WILLIS WHITE.
Book 12, Page 107 -- Sale -- November 17, 1848; mention of lands in
Delaware; buyers: JULIAN, ELIZ., WM. H., MATILDA P. (J above) TYLER,
widow.
Book 12, Page 254 -- Administrators Bond -- THOS. J. (G) ROWSEY, JAS. F.
THORNTON, April 15, 1850, for THOS. J. (G) ROWSEY.
Book 12, Page 281 -- Administrators Account -- by LAMKIN late sheriff,
from November 17, 1848; bonds of ELIZ., MATILDA P., widow; JULIANNA
TYLER; WM. H. TYLER. Commissioners: D. H. TAPSCOTT, LEONARD DANIEL,
WM. E. COLEMAN. Recorded: September 16,1850.
Book 12, Page 481 -- Administrators Account -- by ROWSEY from April 15,
1850; to MATILDA P. NOEL; bond of ZA. DRUMMOND. Recorded: October 20,
1851.

DANL. TYLER -- Book 3, Page 385 -- Administrators Bond -- DANL. TYLER
and EM. EVANS, June 20, 1795, for DANL. TYLER to administrate estate
of CHAS. TYLER. Indexed for DANL.

ELIZ. TYLER -- Book 12, Page 150 -- Administrators Bond -- LAWSON G.
TYLER and P. G. JOINER, February 19, 1849, for LAWSON G. TYLER.

JNO. TYLER -- Book 8, Page 48 -- Administrators Bond -- ELIZ. TYLER,
CHAS., LAWSON G., and JNO. TYLER, November 15, 1830, for ELIZ. TYLER--
no date when will was written; probated, November 15, 1830. Witnesses:
RICH. WILSON, RO. PATRICK, JNO. H. CHRISTIAN, JOS. A. KEETON. Wife,
ELIZ.; my children: GEO. G., LAWSON G., CHAS., TANDY, WM. H., JNO.,
ONEY HUCKSTEP, PATSY W. BRIDGE; granddaughter, ANN M. TYLER--two years
of education and support while with her grandmother or until married.
LAWSON G. and CHAS. TYLER are to direct wife when they see anything
wrong in way she manages.
Book 8, Page 133 -- Inventory -- $1694.00; slaves, etc.; RO. WINGFIELD,
JOS. KYLE, THOS. WINGFIELD.
Book 10, Page 187 -- Refunding Bond -- December 16, 1839. JNO.
TYLER and JAS. G. CHRISTIAN, to JOSEPH PETTYJOHN, administrator of
CHAS. WILSON, RICH. WILSON, father of CHAS., has since died.
Book 12, Page 166 -- Inventory -- April 16, 1849; $769.00; RO.
WINGFIELD, JOS. KYLE, JAS. H. JOINER.
Book 12, Page 170 -- Administrators de bonis non Bond -- March 19,
1849. LAWSON G. TYLER and PETER G. JOINER for LAWSON G. TYLER.

JULIMMER TYLER -- Book 12, Page 226 -- Guardians Bond -- THOS. J.
ROWSEY and LAWSON G. TYLER, November 19, 1849, for THOS. J. ROWSEY
as guardian of JULIMMER TYLER, orphan of CHAS. TYLER, deceased. This
item is not indexed.

RICH. TYLER -- Book 14, Page 384 -- Guardians Bond -- THOS. J. ROWSEY
and LAWSON G. TYLER, June 15, 1857, for THOS. J. ROWSEY as guardian
of RICH., PATARA F., and ALBERT TYLER, orphans of CHAS. TYLER,
deceased.

FANNIE TYREE -- Book 15, Page 509 -- November 25, 1860; December 17, 1860. Witnesses: JNO. H. WATTS, EDWD. A. BURKS. Sisters: BETHEMIA and HANNAH TYREE; interest in where my mother lives. Brother, SAML. L. TYREE; niece, SALLY E. WHITTON; nephew, CHAS. J. TYREE; nephew, LUCAS P. TYREE; sister, MARY A. MC KENNEY; nephew, JAS. J. FRANKLIN; niece, MARY J. TYREE; brother, WM. A. TYREE; brother, JACOB TYREE; sisters: MARTHA WHITTON and two daughters, MARY J. TYREE and SALLY E. WHITTON. JACOB's children: WM., DORAH (SARAH?), and BETHEMIA TYREE. Executor: brother, WM. A. TYREE.
Book 16, Page 29 -- Administrators de bonis non Bond -- February 18, 1861; JNO. WASH WHITTEN, TALIAFERRO STINNETT, for JNO. WASH WHITTEN.
Book 16, Page 74 -- Inventory -- three slaves; $930.00; W. A. RICHESON, JNO. H. WATTS, TALIAFERRO STINNETT, Arpil 15, 1861.

GEO. P. TYREE -- Book 16, Page 470 -- Administrators Bond -- NELSON SEAY and J. P. COLEMAN, May 16, 1864, for NELSON SEAY.

JACOB TYREE SR. -- Book 4, Page 22 -- October 6, 1796; September 21, 1801. Witnesses: WM. PHILLIPS, HUDSON M. GARLAND, PHILIP GOOCH, BARNET OWEN, GABL. PAGE, POLLY OWEN. My wife, MARY; daughters: NANCY WOOD, MARY BAILEY; son, WM.--where I live on Pitt branch; daughter, SARAH RUTHERFORD; daughter, FANNY TINSLEY; son, JACOB; daughter, JANE GIBSON; granddaughter, BETSY TURNER; JACOB GINSON, husband of daughter, JANE; orphans of ISRAEL HARMON. Executors: WM. TYREE and JACOB JR. This next will seemingly is for JR.
Book 11, Page 487 -- August 11, 1844; codicil, August 31, 1846; April 19, 1847. Handwriting by JNO. WHITEHEAD, CHAS. MASSIE, TANDY RUTHERFORD, JACOB TYREE JR.--must be grandson of old SR. above. JR. qualified. Bondsmen: CHAS. H. MASSIE, DABNEY SANDIDGE. Wife, MARTHA; our single children; daughter, JANE W. DAVENPORT and children; daughter, MARY A. FRANKLIN and children; son, SAML. L. TYREE; daughter, BETHEMIA; daughter, HANNAH TYREE; daughter, FRANCES S. (L) TYREE; son, CORNL.; son, JACOB; son, WM. A. If any single daughters move out of state; otherwise to live with brothers. Executors: friends, CHAS. MASSIE and sons, CORNELIUS, JACOB and WM. A. Codicil: daughter, JANE W. DAVENPORT has died; have bought where I live from RICH. L. ELLIS; wife, MARTHA, to enjoy it; JANE W. DAVENPORT left three children--when of age. My single daughters: BETHEMIA, HANNAH and FRANCES.
Book 11, Page 509 -- Inventory -- $5270.00; W. L. DUNCAN, DAVID TINSLEY, WM. LAVINDER.
Book 11, Page 519 -- Administrators Bond -- April 19, 1847; JACOB JR. Bondsmen: DABNEY SANDIDGE, CHAS. H. MASSIE.
Book 12, Page 213 -- Administrators Account -- from May 8, 1847. To JNO. H. TYREE for money loaned testator; interest in negroes of SAML. H. ALLEN of Tennessee; July 16, 1849. WESLEY L. DUNCAN, RO. L. HENLEY.
Book 16, Page 96 -- Administrators Bond -- RO. L. COLEMAN and RO. A. COGHILL, October 21, 1861, for RO. L. COLEMAN.
Book 16, Page 228 -- Administrators de bonis non Bond -- March 16, 1863: WM. A. TYREE and TANDY RUTHERFORD for WM. A. TYREE.
Book 20, Page 399 -- Administrators Bond -- C. J., L. P., JNO. S. TYREE, February 19, 1883, for C. J. TYREE.
Book 21, Page 7 -- Inventory -- March 9, 1883: $148.00; JAS. CLEMENTS, G. W. DODD, W. A. CHOCKLEY, C. J. TYREE.
Book 21, Page 212 -- Trustee Account -- by H. C. JOYNER, sheriff for children from December 31, 1884; land rented to GEO. W. DODD, JR. Recorded: August 17, 1885; and rented to WM. J. TYREE.

JAS. T. TYREE -- Book 16, Page 358 -- so indexed, but not found in books checked.

JNO. W. TYREE -- Book 14, Page 391 -- Guardians Bond -- SAML. H. MC KINNEY, JNO. S. BASS, JNO. W. MC KINNEY, JESSE T. DUIGUID, REUBEN H. STATON, WM. R. MC KINNEY, August 17, 1857, for SAML. H. MC KINNEY as guardian of JNO. W., MARIA W., CHAS. D., ANNA L. (S), THOS. M. RO. L. (S), SAML. JOS. and ACHILLES D. TYREE, orphans of ACHILLES D. TYREE, deceased.

JNO. W. TYREE (cont.) -- Book 24, Page 86 -- April 25, 1904;
October 23, 1907. Witnesses: E. F. CAMPBELL, D. BLACKWOOD, GEO. H.
RAY, JR. To ACHILLES D. TYREE, JR., IDA W. and JOS. S. TYREE,
children of my brother, ACHILLES D. TYREE--when of age.

RICH. J. TYREE -- Book 13, Page 48 -- January 17, 1853. CHAS. S.
MC KINNEY, JNO. W. MC KINNEY, GEO. S. DUIGUID, SAML. TYREE, REUBEN H.
STATON for CHAS. S. MC KINNEY as guardian of RICH. J., etc.--see No.
239 as orphans of ACHILLES D. TYREE, deceased. Did RICH. die between
this date and next bond of 1857?

-V-

CLARY VANHORN -- Book 4, Page 378 -- Guardians Bond -- HIRAM MC GINNIS
and JNO. LOVING, November 2, 1803, for HIRAM MC GINNIS as guardian of
CLARY VANHORN, orphan of BENJ. VANHORN. This is indexed for CLARY
VAUGHAN.

L. C. VASS -- Book 16, Page 36 -- Minister's Bond -- February 18,
1861. Bondsman: A. F. ROBERTSON. SAML. GARLAND, Clerk. No denomination is set forth.

CORNL. VAUGHAN -- Book 1, Page 218 -- Guardians Bond -- JOS. EDWARDS,
ISAAC WRIGHT, PHILIP THURMOND, August 3, 1772, for JOS. EDWARDS as
guardian of CORNL. VAUGHAN, orphan of MARTIN VAUGHAN, deceased.
Book 2, Page 23 -- August 20, 1779; September 3, 1781. Witnesses:
JNO. MERRITT, WM. CARTER, MARY ANN WARE. Brother, JNO. VAUGHAN;
sister, ANN EDWARDS; sister, MARY ANN VAUGHAN; my wife, ANN.
Administrators: wife and friend, PETER CARTER. CARTER qualified
with bondsmen: NOELL JOHNSON, JOS. DILLARD.
Book 2, Page 27 -- Inventory -- December 3, 1781: L 119-19-6. EDWD.
WARE, ISAAC WRIGHT, CHAS. TALIAFERRO.

WM. VAUGHAN -- Book 3, Page 514 -- Tobacco Inspector -- at Tye River
Warehouse, November 20, 1797. Bondsmen: GEO. LOVING, WM. TEAS;
governor appointed him, October 5, 1797.

ABRAHAM VENABLE -- Book 9, Page 148 -- Estate Commitment to Sheriff --
motion of FREDERICK H. MURRELL, December 21, 1835; Sheriff: THOS. N.
EUBANK; RO. TINSLEY, clerk.

JOS. VENABLE -- Book B, Page 20 -- Estate Commitment to Sheriff --
Wednesday, September 1, 1841. Motion by MURRELL as above. Sheriff:
NELSON CRAWFORD.
Book 12, Page 62 -- Estate Commitment to Sheriff -- May term, 1849.
Sheriff: LINDSAY COLEMAN.

JOSIAH VENABLE -- Book 6, Page 27 -- Administrators Bond -- PETER P.
THORNTON, BENJ. TALIAFERRO, WM. SHELTON, August 17, 1818, for PETER P.
THORNTON.
Book 6, Page 32 -- Inventory -- August 28, 1818: $2341.62. BENJ.
and JAS. F. TALIAFERRO, WM. SALE.
Book 7, Page 234 -- Administrators Account -- to MRS. VENABLE for
sugar and coffee--$2.00, April 21, 1828. GIDEON C. GOODRICH, JOS. R.
CARTER, RO. C. CARTER.
Book 9, Page 168 -- Administrators Account -- from April 19, 1828 to
December 21, 1835.

MARY VENABLE -- Book 6, Page 47 -- Guardians Bond -- JANE VENABLE and
PETER P. THORNTON, November 16, 1818 for JANE VENABLE as guardian of
MARY and ELIZ. VENABLE, orphans of JOSIAH VENABLE.

RICH. J. VENABLE -- Book 6, Page 37 -- Guardians Bond -- PETER P.
THORNTON and WM. DUNCAN, November 16, 1818, for PETER P. THORNTON
as guardian of JOS. M., ABRAM L. and RICH. J. VENABLE, orphans of
JOSIAH VENABLE. This is indexed for JOSIAH M. VENABLE.

POLLY VEST -- Book 6, Page 448 -- Guardians Bond -- THOS. LAINE, ISAAC RUCKER, and BENJ. B. DAWSON, March 20, 1824, for THOS. LAINE as guardian of POLLY, SALLY, LEVI and BETSY VEST, orphans of JNO. VEST. This is indexed for POLLY VENABLE.

JNO. VIA -- Book 3, Page 4 -- August 17, 1781; March 6, 1786. Witnesses: DANL. and MILLY PERROW, ELIZ. EVENS. My four sons; daughters, SUSANNAH and MARY ANN VIA. One should consult my deed abstracts for more VIA data wherein sons are identified: Book H, Page 235.
Book F, Page 117 -- GIDEON, DAVID, JNO. and WM. VIA.

WM. VIA -- Book 12, Page 362 -- Administrators Bond -- JAS. W. KEITH and STERLING CLAIBORNE, March 17, 1851, for JAS. W. KEITH.
Book 7, Page 324 -- Administrators Bond -- according to index.
Book 12, Page 362 -- Inventory -- but they show nothing. The indexer must have really been in his cups when he worked on V's for I have found many errors.

-W-

ABIGAIL HARDWICH WADE -- Book 1, Page 486 -- Guardians Bond -- RICH. BALLINGER and FRANCIS SATTERWHITE, July 5, 1779, for RICH. BALLINGER as guardian of ABIGAIL HARDWICK WADE, orphan of PEARCE WADE.

CLARY WADE -- Book 1, Page 485 -- DAVID WOODROOF and JAS. PAMPLIN, July 5, 1779, for DAVID WOODROOF as guardian of CLARY WADE, orphan of PEARCE WADE.

JER. WADE -- Book 1, Page 492 -- Guardians Bond -- BALLENGER WADE and RICH. BALLENGER, August 2, 1779, for BALLENGER WADE as guardian of JER. WADE, orphan of PEARCE WADE.

JNO. WADE -- Book 3, Page 45 -- February 15, 1785; July 2, 1787. Witnesses: JAS. MC ALEXANDER, JR., ALEX. and JNO. MC ALEXANDER. Son, DAWSON; wife, ELIZ.; son, JESSE; daughter, ELINOR SHASTEEN; ELIZ. WADE qualified; bondsmen: SAML. DENNY.
Book 3, Page 60 -- Inventory -- L23-10-0; CHAS. TATE, JNO. and ALEX. MC ALEXANDER, September 1, 1787.

LUCRETIA WADE -- Book 1, Page 485 -- Guardians Bond -- RICH. BALLINGER and FRANCIS SATTERWHITE, July 5, 1779, for RICH. BALLINGER as guardian of LUCRETIA WADE, orphan of PEARCE WADE, deceased.

PEARCE WADE -- Book 1, Page 161 -- December 13, 1769; March 5, 1770. Witnesses: JNO. DAWSON, THOS. WATTS, BOYCE EADSON. Wife, ELIZ.--where I live; daughter, SUSANNA; when my youngest child is of age; daughter, ELIZ.; daughter, ABIGAIL HARDWICH. Executors: AMBR. RUCKER, RICH. PETER, RICH. SHELTON, JAS. CREWS.
Book 1, Page 166 -- Administrators Bond -- JNO. HARDWICK, DANL. GAINES, JOS. MAGANN, BALLINGER WADE, May 7, 1770, for JNO. HARDWICK.
Book 1, Page 172 -- Inventory -- no total, but long; June court, 1770: JNO. BURFORD, BATTAILE HARRISON, JAS. CREWS.
Book 1, Page 487 -- Administrators Account -- from 1769; to SUSANNAH WADE for keeping the mill; dower land to ELIZ. WADE; tuition for children paid to JNO. MERRITT and JONATHAN JOHNSON; to BALLINGER WADE; building widow's house; miller's house; July 4, 1774. DANL. GAINES, RICH. SHELTON, AMBR. RUCKER, BENJ. RUCKER.
Book 3, Page 5 -- JNO. HARDWICK and EDMD. WINSTON to secure BALLINGER WADE, administrator of PEARCE WADE, March 6, 1786. This is indexed JNO. HARDWICK.

ANN F. WALKER -- Book 9, Page 92 -- May 20, 1835; July 30, 1835. Witnesses: ROD. L. WATTS, AGNES CHRISTIAN, CHAMPE CARTER. HENRY J. ROSE qualified; brother, PETER WALKER; sister, SUSAN WALKER; uncle, JAS. POWELL; debt due my father's estate; debt of DR. HENRY J. ROSE; sister, SALLY E. ROSE; niece, ELIZA JANE WALKER; to DR. ROSE as token for medical services--money; nephew, CHAS. ROBT. ROSE--slave and child,

ANN F. WALKER (cont.) -- but she may choose to be sold to owner of her
husband; nephew, WM. FITZHUGH ROSE; where DR. ROSE dwells; executor:
brother-in-law, DR. HENRY J. ROSE.

CORNL. WALKER -- Book 11, Page 344 -- Minister's Bond -- Protestant
Episcopal Church; August 18, 1845. Bondsmen: HENRY L. DAVIES, SAML. M.
GARLAND.

ISAAC WALKER -- Book 10, Page 207f -- September 30, 1837; codicil,
September 30, 1839; March 16, 1840. Witnesses to will: JNO. JOHNS,
J. M. WEST, WM. DUIGUID CHRISTIAN, R. D. PALMER, same for codicil.
ELIZ. WALKER qualified; bondsmen: BENJ. P. WALKER, SAML. J. WALKER, and
SAML. BRANCH. Wife, SARAH ELIS. WALKER; son, SAML. BRANCH WALKER when
of age--to be liberally educated. Nephew, ISAAC W. WALKER, son of my
brother, SAML. J. WALKER--when 21; MISS LUCY ELAM to be supported--
while single--and living with my wife. Wife to administrate. Codicil:
If son dies before 21; to wife and my brothers: SAML. J. and BENJ. P.
WALKER.
Book 10, Page 239 -- Inventory -- May 22, 1840: at his house; many
slaves: $15,651.25. ALEX. MUNDY, STEPHEN CHRISTIAN, WM. DILLARD.
Book 11, Page 332 -- Administrators Account -- by REUBEN D. PALMER from
January 1, 1844; ribbons for MISS ELAM. BRYANT NOWLIN, commissioner:
February 1, 1845.
Book 11, Page 588 -- Administrators Account -- by PALMER from 1845;
certified in Appomattox County, December 31, 1846; recorded Amherst
County, December 20, 1847.
Book 12, Page 198 -- Administrators Account -- by PALMER from 1846;
JAS. G. PATTERSON, commissioner; recorded March 21, 1849.
Book 13, Page 284 -- Administrators Account -- by PALMER from
December 31, 1850; executor did not appear to settle accounts within
time set by new code; recorded November 26, 1850.
Book 13, Page 426 -- Administrators Account -- by ELIZ. WALKER who has
married REUBEN D. PALMER who presents account from September 20, 1850;
store account of RO. K. WALKER; "skerclings" for starting over the
mountains to work: $1.00; recorded December 18, 1854.
Book 14, Page 29 -- Administrators Account -- by PALMER from July 1,
1854; to S. B. WALKER, ISAAC W. WALKER, R. K. WALKER's agent. Marriage
is again set forth and SAML. B. WALKER is the only child. Recorded
September 17, 1855.
Book 14 -- ISAAC WALKER -- acutally 13 above; so indexed.
Book 12, Page 459 -- Administrators Account -- by PALMER in right of
his wife, ELIZ.; date of May 22, 1857--marriage (?); gave bond,
March 16, 1840; bondsmen: SAML. J. WALKER, SAML. BRANCH, SR.; from
December 31, 1848; MISS LUCY ELAM's name appears several times; trip
to Roanoke. Recorded: October 20, 1851.

JOEL WALKER -- Book 3, Page 402 -- July 24, 1794; June 20, 1796.
Witnesses: GEO. HYLTON, RO. PAMPLIN. This is a confusing will: wife,
ELIZ. DEBTS ; and then -- wife, MARY WALKER; living daughter, ELIZ.
DEBTS; executors; friends: WM. DEBTS, WM. THOMELL (?), NATHL. LANCASTER.

RO. WALKER -- Book 6, Page 466 -- January 30, 1824; codicil, June 26,
1824; July 19, 1824. Witnesses: JAS. POWELL, JNO. PENN, RO. A. PENN;
to codicil: JAS. COLEMAN, JNO. PENN. AJAX and WIATT P. WALKER qualified; bondsmen: JAS. POWELL, A. B. DAVIES, JNO. PENN, HENRY L. DAVIES.
Personal and real property bought of WIATT POWELL to be kept during
lifetime of MRS. SARAH POWELL; all of my children; sons, PETER and
AJAX; daughters: ANN FRANCES, SUSAN, SARAH ELIZ., WIATT and THOS.
Executors: sons, AJAX and WIATT; codicil: son, PETER, trustee for
his children. Administrators Bond is page 468.
Book 6, Page 483 -- Inventory -- Many slaves; $8536.17. LINDSEY
COLEMAN, CHAS. L. BARRET, JNO. PENN, September 20, 1824. Page 569
additional inventory and Administrators Bond by AJAX WALKER, March 21,
1825. Bondsmen: A. B. DAVIES, PAUL C. CABELL, H. L. DAVIES.

SAML. B. WALKER -- Book 10, Page 211 -- Guardians Bond -- ELIZ. and
BENJ. P. WALKER, SAML. BRANCH by BENJ. P. WALKER, March 16, 1840, for
ELIZ. WALKER as guardian of SAML. B. WALKER, orphan of ISAAC W. WALKER.
Book 11, Page 611 -- Guardians Account -- by REUBEN D. PALMER in right

SAML. B. WALKER (cont.) -- of his wife, ELIZ., December 20, 1847.
Committee: WM. L. (S) DUIGUID, DAVID PATTESON, RO. HUNTER.
Book 12, Page 199 -- Guardians Account -- by PALMER from December 31,
1846; August 20, 1849. Committee: DUIGUID, JAS. G. PATTESON, JESSE T.
DAVIDSON.
Book 12, Page 451 -- Administrators Account -- by PALMER in right of
his wife, ELIZ., who is mother of his ward; she qualified, March 16,
1840; tuition accounts from December 31, 1848; recorded: October 20,
1851.
Book 13, Page 288 -- Guardians Account -- by PALMER from December 31,
1850; $60 for starting to college; watch repair to JNO. P. WRIGHT;
HENRY D. F. FLOOD for use of college scholarship; for starting to
Military Institute and stage fare to Lexington. Recorded: Saturday,
November 26, 1853.
Book 13, Page 424 -- Guardians Account -- by PALMER from December 31,
1852.
Book 14, Page 33 -- Guardians Account -- from December 31, 1853;
RO. K. WALKER, agent and store account. Your father's estate; refer-
ence to ELIZ., his mother as guardian and married PALMER. Recorded:
May 21, 1855.

SARAH ELIZ. WALKER -- Book 8, Page 44 -- Guardians Bond -- THOS. J.
WALKER and JNO. PENN, September 20, 1830, for THOS. J. WALKER as
guardian of SARAH ELIZ. WALKER, orphan of RO. WALKER.

THOS. J. WALKER -- Book B, Page 30 -- Estate Commitment to Sheriff --
Wednesday, March 29, 1848; motion of HUMPHREY GILBERT, JAS. L. LAMKIN,
Sheriff.

WM. WALKER -- Book 18, Page 242 -- Inventory -- no total; September 16,
1872. J. J. DILLARD, S. B. WALKER, JNO. C. MUNDY. Indexed WATSON.

WM. R. WALKER (or WM. B.?) -- Book 6, Page 519 -- Administrators
Bond -- HENRY L. ROACH and THOS. N. EUBANK, November 19, 1824, for
HENRY L. ROACH.

DAVID G. WALLER -- Book 16, Page 177 -- Administrators Bond -- WM. M.
WALLER, SAML. M. WALLER, SAML. M. GARLAND, October 20, 1862, for
WM. M. WALLER.
Book 16, Page 220 -- Inventory -- November 21, 1862; no total;
S. S. (L) HARRIS, JNO. S. TUCKER, JAS. F. TALIAFERRO.
Book 17, Page 145 -- Administrators Account -- March 19, 1866; recorded:
May 28, 1866; bond of MRS. SUSAN DAVIS, S. G. WALLER, SAML. M. WALLER;
decedent was Confederate soldier and killed in battle in 1862; admin-
istrator was also in Confederate army and "but little at home."

ELIZ. WALLER -- Book 6, Page 668 -- Administrators Bond -- WM. M.
WALLER and HILL CARTER, June 20, 1826, for WM. M. WALLER.

THOS. M. WALLER -- Book 16, Page 177 -- Administrators Bond -- WM. M.
WALLER, SAML. M. GARLAND, SAML. M. WALLER, October 20, 1862, for
WM. M. WALLER.
Book 16, Page 219 -- Inventory -- no total; November 20, 1862; SAML. H.
HARRIS, JNO. L. TUCKER, JAS. F. TALIAFERRO.
Book 17, Page 161 -- Administrators Account -- May 29, 1866; recorded:
June 27, 1866; amount to SAML. G. WALLER or S. G. WALLER.

WM. MACON WALLER -- Book 11, Page 298 -- Sheriffs Bond -- February 17,
1845; bondsmen: JNO. WHITEHEAD, M. C. GOODWIN, BENJ. B. TALIAFERRO,
RO. A. COGHILL, ABRAHAM MARTIN, LEWELLEN T. CASH, RICH. CRAWFORD, E.
FLETCHER, CHAS. H. MASSIE, RO. A. PENDLETON, RO. M. BROWN, DANL. L.
COLEMAN.
Book 11, Page 379 -- Sheriffs Bond -- March 16, 1846; bondsmen:
WHITEHEAD as above; M. C. GOODWIN, JAS. B. DAVIS, E. FLETCHER, RICH.
CRAWFORD, BENJ. T. TALIAFERRO, ADDISON TALIAFERRO, H. L. DAVIES.
Book B, Page 34 -- September 14, 1847; Setpember 1, 1849; Handwriting
by JOS. K. IRVING and RO. TINSLEY. SAML. M. GARLAND qualified;
bondsmen: HOWELL L. BROWN, DAVID H. TAPSCOTT, ZACH DRUMMOND, ADDISON
TALIAFERRO, JNO. THOMPSON, JR., MARBELL C. GOODWIN, RO. A. PENDLETON,

WM. MACON WALLER (cont.) -- PAULUS POWELL. My wife; children to be
educated--when of age or daughters married. Daughters: LUCY ANN GOVAN
and husband, ARCHIBALD GOVAN; daughter, ELIZ. M. DUVAL and husband,
ALEX. DUVAL; daughter, FANNY M. CALDWELL and husband, REV. MR. DAVID
CALDWELL; my mansion house tract; friends of many years to administrate:
DR. THOS. MASSIE, Nelson County; JNO. THOMPSON, JR., SAML. M. GARLAND
and to be guardians.
Book 12, Page 186 -- Administrators Account -- SAML. M. GARLAND,
executor, received of CHAS. TUCKER, amount due WALLER as administrator
of JNO. SMITH; amount from RICH. SMITH who has become owner of tract
and bought interest of JACOB, JAS. W., JNO. and EDWD. SMITH; amount
from DUDLEY SANDIDGE on SMITH's account. Recorded: September 20,
1849. This man was quite prominent in Amherst County and lived in
area of Lowesville.

JAS. WALSH (indexed WASH) -- Book 12, Page 326 -- Administrators Bond --
GEO. H. DAMERON, JNO. WASH, PETER JOINER, November 18, 1850, for
GEO. H. DAMERON.
Book 13, Page 170 -- Administrators Account -- from November 20, 1850;
paid to JNO. WALSH. Recorded: May 16, 1853. Note: I have decided
to indent every other number to save space for this work is rather
long.

ELIZ. WALTON -- Book 10, Page 191 -- ELIZ. WALTON, RICH and RO. WALTON
to JOS. PETTYJOHN, administrator of CHAS. WILSON. RICH. WILSON, father
of CHAS., had died and Estate Commitment to Sheriff, JNO. COLEMAN,
July 9, 1839. Witness: JNO. P. WILSON

J. B. WALTON -- Book 24, Page 168 -- October 1, 1898; Friday, April 24,
1914. Witnesses: THOS. WHITEHEAD, JR. and I. (J) P. WHITEHEAD. Wife,
FRANCES A., to administrate.

BENJ. WARD (indexed WOOD) -- Book 1, Page 2 -- Administrators Bond --
HENRY KEY and JNO. HARVIE, December 7, 1761, for HENRY KEY. Inventory,
L4-12-6; March 1, 1762: RICH. TANKERSLEY, WM. BIBB, JACOB BROWN.

FERREL WARD (indexed WAUGH) -- Book 17, Page 274 -- Administrators
Bond -- WM. H. WARD, HARMON ERDMOUS (?), JAS. M. ALLEN, R. A. PENDLETON,
December 18, 1865, for WM. H. WARD.

BELINDA WARE -- Book 5, Page 528 -- Guardians Bond -- WM. JOPLING,
CHAS. TALIAFERRO, ABRAM CARTER, November 20, 1815, for WM. JOPLING as
guardian of ORMOND and BELINDA WARE, orphans of WM. WARE.

BETSY WARE -- Book 4, Page 421 -- Guardians Bond -- WM. LONNLIN, ALEX.
MC ALEXANDER, ZACH FORTUNE, November 18, 1805, for WM. LONNLIN as guard-
ian of BETSY WARE, orphan of RO. WARE, deceased.
Book 6, Page 12 -- October 30, 1818; November 16, 1818. Witnesses:
RICH. EUBANK, JNO. S. CARTER, ABRAM CARTER. WM. JOPLING and MADISON
WARE qualified; bondsman: ABRAM CARTER. My mother, PATSY WARE; my
heirs: JNO. WARE, SALLY JOPLING, MADISON WARE, BELINDA SANDIDGE, ORMUND
WARE, PERLINA WARE. Executors: WM. JOPLING and MADISON WARE.
Administrators Bond is on page 38.

EDWARD WARE -- Book 3, Page 9 -- June 1, 1779; July 3, 1786. Witnesses:
PETER CARTER, ROD. MC CULLOCH, ELIZ. MC CULLOCH. To MARK WARE and
children; to JAS. POWELL--400 acres where he lives; to WM. POWELL--ditto
as to 214 acres; to JNO. POWELL--ditto as to 400 acres; to EDWD. POWELL--
ditto as to 200 acres where I live and 351 acres on Pedlar on Rich Mt.;
to ELIZ. JOPLIN--200 acres next to M. (?) HIGGINBOTHAM; to ANNE CAMP-
BELL--land next to GORDON; SARAH WARE--same; wife, LETTIS; EDMUND
POWELL (EDWD. above). Executors: JAS. WILLIAMS, EDWD. and JNO. POWELL.
Book 3, Page 11 -- Administrators Bond -- WM. and JAS. WARE, THOS.
LUCAS, JNO. CRAWFORD, July 3, 1786, for first two to administrate.
Book 3, Page 19 -- Inventory -- no total; October 2, 1786. CHAS.
TALIAFERRO, SAML. HIGGINBOTHAM, PETER CARTER. Note: For years I have
tried in vain to connect this MARK WARE with my sister-in-law, SALLY
WARE, who married by brother, BERNARD BYRD DAVIS. She knows that she
descended from a MARK WARE who came into area of Pendleton County,

EDWARD WARE (cont.) -- Kentucky. She has a sister, LETTY WARE, who
was in my high school class in Shelbyville and she married JNO. MOUNT.
Family tradition also has it that SALLY is descended from GEN. GREENE
of Revolution, but we are unable to establish this either.

EDWIN M. WARE -- Book 7, Page 118 -- Guardians Bond -- NANCY WARE,
GEO. A. JOPLING, WM. CORNELIUS, and WM. HAYNES, January 21, 1828, for
NANCY WARE as guardian of EDWIN M. WARE, orphan of MADISON WARE.
Book 7, Page 173 -- Guardians Bond -- NANCY WARE and THOS. N. EUBANK,
August 18, 1828, for counter security to protect JOPLING.
Book 21, Page 159 -- Road Surveyor -- Magruder's Precinct, June 15,
1885; bondsman: JNO. P. BEARD.

JAS. WARE -- Book 4, Page 519 -- Surveyor -- July 16, 1808; bondsmen:
REUBEN PENDLETON, DAVID TINSLEY, NICHL. HARRISON.
Book 5, Page 440 -- Ordinary at house in county; February 21, 1814;
bondsman: JAS. GARLAND.
Book 5, Page 667 -- Same, July 21, 1817; bondsman: RICH. HARRISON.
Book 6, Page 138 -- Same, May 15, 1820; bondsman: BENNETT A. CRAWFORD.
Book 6, Page 390 -- Same, June 17, 1823; bondsman: WM. ARMISTEAD.

JNO. WARE -- Book 4, Page 440 -- Guardians Bond -- CHAS. SMITH and
JAS. WOODS, January 19, 1807, for CHAS. SMITH as guardian of JNO.
WARE, orphan of RO. WARE, deceased.
Book 8, Page 435 -- Estate Commitment to Sheriff -- October, 1834;
motion of RICH. ELLIS. Sheriff: EDMD. WINSTON.
Book 15, Page 286 -- Administrators Bond -- W. M. and JNO. M. WARE,
April 16, 1860, for W. M. WARE.

JNO. D. WARE -- Book 7, Page 217 -- Constables Bond -- March 16, 1829;
bondsman: JNO. PENN and R. N. EUBANK.
Book 7, Page 243 -- Same, June 15, 1829; bondsmen: R. N. EUBANK and
DABNEY SANDIDGE.
Book 8, Page 102 -- Same, June 20, 1831; bondsmen: EUBANK and WM. H.
GARLAND.

JOS. V. WARE (ARTHUR GAGES WARE tells me that the V stands for VALEN-
TINE) -- Book 16, Page 455 -- Guardians Bond -- E. S. WARE, GEO. HYLTON,
and ELIZ. A. WARE, March 21, 1864, for E. S. WARE as guardian of JOS. V.
WARE; no parent set forth. I note that I refer to this item in No. 49,
but seem to have erred.
Book 24, Page 173 -- November 17, 1913; October 15, 1914. Handwriting
by E. B. MC GINNIS, R. H. DRUMMOND and F. S. TINSLEY. Daughter,
ELIZ. C. WARE; wife, MALLISA F. WARE. His marriage bond clears up his
parentage: Book 2, Page 153 of marriages--November 23 bond; ceremony
of 25th November, 1868. Groom: JOS. V. WARE; resident of Amherst
County; son of R. B. and ELIZA WARE; farmer; officiant, REV. THOS. H.
CAMPBELL. Bride: MELISSA F. GILL--both parties were single and 21
years of age--resident of Amherst County; daughter of CURTIS GILL and
wife, ELIZ. CURTIS GILL married ELIZ. MARTIN--page 379 of first
register: 7 January 1843. Security or witness: ABRAHAM MARTIN.
Return on page 484 for same date.

MADISON WARE -- Book 6, Page 297 -- April 14, 1822; June 17, 1822.
Witnesses: ORMUND WARE, WILL JOPLING, JOS. R. CARTER. RICH JONES
qualified; bondsmen: CHAS. C. CARTER, LINDSEY MC DANIEL. Wife,
NANCY--where I live; son, EDWIN; executor: friend, RICH. JONES.
Administrators Bond is page 293.
Book 6, Page 320 -- Inventory -- July 11, 1822: $1290.30; JOS. R.
CARTER, ABRAM CARTER, WM. PRYOR.
Book 6, Page 408 -- Administrators Account -- JNO. M. MC DANIEL gave
account from November 20, 1823; estate of RICH. JONES for board and
clothing of NANCY and son, EDWIN WARE; slave hired to JNO. WARE;
execution on BETSY WARE and WM. WARE; Board for five years for NANCY
and EDWIN. March 18, 1829. Committee: THOS. CREWS, JAS. GARLAND,
JAS. POWELL.
Book 8, Page 114 -- Administrators Account -- by JONES from 1822;
plantation and slave expenses from May to end of crop season; board
for NANCY and EDWIN from May 11th at $80.00 per year. Recorded:

MADISON WARE (cont.) -- June 7, 1828. Committee: PETER P. THORNTON, JOS. R. CARTER, JNO. PRYOR.

MANSFIELD WARE -- Book 6, Page 238 -- Constables Bond -- June 21, 1819; bondsman: DABNEY WARE.
Book 6, Page 349 -- Same; March 17, 1823; bondsmen: same.
Book 6, Page 361 -- Same, June 16, 1823; bondsman: JAS. FULCHER.

MARGARET WARE -- Book 14, Page 478 -- May 23, 1856; Monday, January 18, 1858. Witnesses: WM. M. WARE, EDWIN M. and JNO. J. WARE. Son, EDWD. R. to administrate and care for my husband, JNO. WARE; my other children.

MARY WARE (indexed for MARGARET WARE) -- Book 14, Page 517 -- Administrators Bond -- RO. M. BROWN and THOS. M. WHITEHEAD, January 18, 1858, for RO. M. BROWN.
Book 14, Page 564 -- Administrators Bond -- EDWIN M. WARE and JAS. P. MC DANIEL, May 17, 1858, for EDWIN M. WARE.

NANCY WARE -- Book 13, Page 86 (indexed Book 12, Page 86) -- Administrators Bond -- RO. M. BROWN and RO. WHITEHEAD, March 21, 1853, for RO. M. BROWN.
Book 13, Page 502 -- Administrators Account -- from March, 1853; Chancery: LUCAS versus PENDLETON; distributed to her ten children.

O. WARE -- Book 14, Page 565 -- Administrators Bond -- EDWIN M. WARE and JAS. P. MC DANIEL, May 17, 1858, for EDWIN M. WARE.

PATSY WARE -- Book 7, Page 32 -- Administrators Bond -- ORMUND WARE, August 20, 1827; bondsman: THOS. N. EUBANK.
Book 7, Page 89 -- Inventory -- $673.49, December 17, 1827; CHAS. P. TALIAFERRO, BENJ. B. TALIAFERRO, JOS. R. CARTER.

PAULINA WARE -- Book 5, Page 532 -- Guardians Bond -- JNO. WARE, WM. JOPLING, THOS. EUBANK, November 20, 1815, for JNO. WARE as guardian of PAULINA WARE, orphan of WM. WARE, deceased.

REUBEN B. WARE -- Book 16, Page 444 -- Administrators Bond -- EDWIN S. WARE, March 21, 1864; bondsmen: GEO. HYLTON, HENRY LOVING, ELIZA A. WARE.
Book 17, Page 10 -- Inventory -- Order of March, 1864: $29,700; HENRY LOVING, DANL. D. CHRISTIAN, WILKERSON WARE, January 12, 1865.
Book 17, Page 248 -- Real Estate Division -- July 23, 1867; EDMD. P. TUCKER, Surveyor--245 acres; widow, ELIZA A. 51 acres and mansion house; JOS. H. HIGGINBOTHAM and wife, HECTOR A. 44 acres; JOS. W. WARE, 43½ acres; EDWIN S. WARE 48 3/4 acres; JAS. R. WARE, 60 3/4 acres; plat on Indian Creek; east side Scott's Mr. Lines: JESSE WRIGHT, JNO. H. CHRISTIAN, main road, JOEL C. MAYS.
Book 17, Page 420 -- AF (?) and Sale -- slaves liberated by Presidential decree; buyers at sale: E. S., J. V., E. A., T. W., WILKERSON, J. R. WARE: $807.57; December 10, 1867. T. W. WARE for corn; J. J. WARE for tobacco; to ELIZA A., E. S., JNO. V., J. R. WARE and JOS. A. HIGGINBOTHAM; ELIZA A. as guardian of J. R. WARE. Note: REUBEN B. WARE married in Nelson County, page 36 of first register: ELIZA A. CUNNINGHAM, January 25, or 15--blurred; REES CUNNINGHAM, Security. Good sketch of CUNNINGHAM family in Hardesty and Brock.

THOS. WARE -- Book 1, Page 441 -- Guardians Bond -- JAS. HENDERSON and ALEX. MILLER, October 5, 1778, for JAS. HENDERSON as guardian of THOS. WARE, orphan of RO. WARE, deceased.

WM. WARE -- Book 4, Page 548 -- Sheriffs Bond -- November 15, 1802; bondsmen: NELSON CRAWFORD, JOSIAH ELLIS, CHAS. TALIAFERRO, NELSON ANDERSON, JESSE JOPLING, JAS. JOPLING, WM. CAMDEN, JNO. SMITH.
Book 5, Page 216 -- January 13, 1809; June 21, 1813. Witnesses: REUBEN NORVELL, THOS. CREWS, MICAJAH CAMDEN. Codicil, October 30, 1811. Witnesses: ABRAHAM CARTER. Proved by NORVELL, CREWS, CAMDEN and CARTER and oaths of CHAS. CRAWFORD and CORNL. SALE. JNO. WARE and WM. JOPLING qualified; bondsmen: CHAS. CRAWFORD, LEONARD HENLEY, NELSON

WM. WARE (cont.) -- CRAWFORD, ABRAM CARTER. Liberty for other executors to join. Wife, PATTY; son, ORMUND; sons, MADISON, JNO.--where he
lives--mansion tract; WM. HORSLEY's line; top of Piney Hill; LAWLESS'
old house; the road; land bought of ARCHIBALD BURDEN; top of the mountain; line of TINSLEY RUCKER. Land to NANCY W. RUCKER; daughter,
SALLY JOPLING--land next to WM. PRYOR--one-half conveyed to WM.
JOPLING; daughter, PERMELIA POWELL; granddaughter, NANCY W. RUCKER,
when of age--daughter of TINSLEY RUCKER; daughters, BETSY, LUCINDA
WARE; son, MADISON, when of age; son, ORMUND, when of age; daughter,
BELINDA WARE; daughter, PERLINA WARE--to finish education. Land bought
of ISAAC WAUGH (?) estate. Executors: brother, JNO. WARE, NELSON
CRAWFORD, WM. JOPLING. Administrators Bond is page 220. Codicil:
I have since bought tract of CHAS. TALIAFERRO: Buffaloe and Pedlar on
dividing ridge; to JNO.; Burden tract ot ORMUND and SALLY JOPLING.
Book 5, Page 441 -- Inventory -- of COL. WM. WARE, December 2, 1813;
CHAS. TALIAFERRO, JNO. CRAWFORD, WM. PRYOR. June 20, 1814.
Book 6, Page 197 -- Constables Bond -- December 18, 1820; bondsman:
AMBR. RUCKER, DABNEY WARE.
Book 6, Page 398 -- Administrators Account -- JNO. WARE and WM.
JOPLING from 1813; MADISON WARE, WM. WARE, JNO. JR. and SR., ORMUND
WARE; 46 acres sold to THOS. LAINE; BELINDA WARE; PAULINA WARE; PATSY
WARE; MRS. WARE; SALLY JOPLING; PERMELIA POWELL: $12,481.66. March 25,
1822. BENJ. TALIAFERRO, AMBR. RUCKER, JNO. PRYOR, CHAS. L. BARRET,
NANCY W. RUCKER, heir, states that mother has received share. Nine
shares mentioned; October 20, 1823.

JAS. WARREN -- Book 1, Page 137 -- February, 1769; July 3, 1769.
Witnesses: ELEAZER and RALPH LEMASTER and SARAH LEMASTER; recorded:
August 7, 1769, when ELEAZER attested. JOHN WHITTELL qualified, but
MATT. WHITTELL declined to serve; bondsmen: MATTHEW WHITTELL, AMBR.
JONES, JAS. GOSSETT. Son, JNO.; daughter, ELIZ. WHITTELL--178 acres
between COL. BRAXTON and CHRISTIAN's orphans. Executors: JNO. and
MATT. WHITTELL.
Book 1, Page 143 -- Inventory -- L60-18-6, August 31, 1769. RO. and
DRURY CHRISTIAN, HENRY BELL. Page 148 they report additional inventory
of L2-4-0; November, 1769.

LARKIN WARREN -- Book 16, Page 157 -- Administrators Bond -- RO. N.
ELLIS and RO. W. SNEAD, September 15, 1862, for RO. N. ELLIS.

RO. WARREN -- Book 1, Page 146 -- Administrators Bond -- PEARCE WADE,
JOSHUA FOWLER, BATTAILE HARRISON, September Court, 1769, for PEARCE
WADE.
Book 1, Page 154 -- Inventory -- L12-19-1 3/4; RICH. PETER, JNO. DAWSON,
JAS. CREWS, CALEB WATTS, March 5, 1770; exhibited by ELIZ. late widow.

M. C. WARRINER -- Book 24, Page 210 -- May 11, 1912; Monday, July 7,
1916. Witnesses: W. H. KENT and W. WARD HILL. My wife--to administrate, WM. KINCKLE ALLEN.

ABRAHAM WARWICK -- Book 4, Page 598 -- April 12, 1808; May 16, 1808.
Witnesses: ELISHA ESTES, WM. DIXON; proved by DIXON, July 17, 1809.
Wife, AMY--where I live--436 acres and where my son, WM., lived some
years ago; daughter, SALLY TALIAFERRO, wife of ZACH TALIAFERRO; daughter,
POLLY MARTIN, wife of EDWD. MARTIN; three children of son, BEVERLY,
deceased; NELSON R. (B?), JUDITH L. (S) and CANDIA G. WARWICK--equal
to what they received from estate of HENRY MARTIN, deceased, and from
their father. Grandson, NATHAN HARDING; my son, JAS.; my daughter,
ELIZ. WILLS--apart from husband; my sons, JAS., WM., JNO., DANL.,
ABRAHAM B. and to administrate ABRAHAM B.--where he has built; grand-
daughter, LUCINDA B. WARWICK.
Book 11, Page 176 -- Administrators Bond -- JNO. WARWICK, STERLING
CLAIBORNE, CHAS. L. MOSBY, November 22, 1843, for JNO. WARWICK.
Book 11, Page 222 -- Estate Commitment to Sheriff -- August, 1843;
JAS. POWELL, Sheriff.
Book 11, Page 274 -- Inventory -- many slaves; $44,295.00 (?); WM. S.
and JNO. H. LOVING, FLOYD L. WHITEHEAD. August 29, 1843.
Book 11, Page 288 -- Slave dower of AMEY WARWICK, deceased. December 14,
1844; sold by JNO. WARWICK: $2796.00; shares to heirs of LUCINDA B.

ABRAHAM WARWICK (cont.) -- WILLS; heirs of POLLY MARTIN; balance to five brothers of will, but JAS. is dead; January 15, 1845. RO. TINSLEY, EDMD. PENN, H. L. BROWN.

AMY WARWICK -- Book 11, Page 288 -- Sale of 13 negroes; dower--she is deceased; December 14, 1843; public auction by JNO. WARWICK, administrator of ABRAHAM WARWICK; sold to A. B. and D. WARWICK: $3015.00--less charges of $219.00; to heirs of LUCINDA B. WILLS; less legacy--of POLLY MARTIN, deceased; to JAS., WM., JNO., DANL., and A. B. WARWICK, January 15, 1845; RO. TINSLEY, EDMD. PENN, H. L. BROWN.

GEO. W. WARWICK -- Book 12, Page 207 -- Guardians Account -- by A. D. READ from April 28, 1842; bond paid F. A. WARWICK; allowance of W. WARWICK's will for acting as guardian; to MRS. F. A. WARWICK; READ as guardian of infants of WM. WARWICK, deceased: $4777.58, but GEO. W. is only one named in account. August 21, 1849.

JNO. WARWICK -- Book 6, Page 158 -- Sheriffs Bond -- August 22, 1820; bondsmen: DAVID S. GARLAND, HILL CARTER, THOS. N. EUBANK, CHAS. MUNDY. Book 6, Page 242 -- Same men, August 20, 1821. Book 6, Page 307 -- Collector's Bond -- July 15, 1822; bondsmen: CARTER and MUNDY above. Book 11, Page 577 -- February 23, 1848; March 20, 1848. Witnesses: WM. DILLARD, JNO. P. WILSON, JESSE MUNDY, HENRY L. DAVIES. The future condition of my slaves has long been a subject of anxious concern with me; all are to be freed as soon as crops are saved and annual hires terminated. Applies to all not previously sent to some free state during his lifetime: Indiana (sic) is his choice. Slaves are to have his estate after payment of debts and executors are to provide comfortable clothing, outfits, and travel expenses and settlement in new homes as funds will permit. Faithful and confidential servant, FREDERICK, wife, LUCY, and children; NICEY and three youngest children are to remain upon that part of my plantation now occupied by FREDERICK for his lifetime; if they don't choose to remove to freedom--houses to be set apart for them. Land described to new fence near LEMUEL TURNER; to Glade Road as meanders to LEWIS S. CAMPBELL--200 acres with stock; provisions, and outfit to cultivate. Hopes that executor will treat them as friends and not as slaves for FREDERICK is very infirm and family is helpless. $1000 to be put in trust and at his death, to be used to send family to some free state. $30 per year out of fund to FREDERICK for faithful services to me. After settlement in some free state, executor is to sell land and use proceeds for fund for the two families. Executors: DAVID PATTESON, JR., JAS. F. ROYALL, CAPT. SAML. MC CORCLE, and CHAS. L. MOSBY, Lynchburg. Two old servants, CALIPH and JNO., are infirm and unable to support selves in a free state--to live on boundary of FREDERICK's land; if they outlive him, money to be set aside for them. Note: this will has been cited in at least one Virginia history book. Book 12, Page 44 -- Inventory -- $1415; April 17, 1845; JNO. P. WILSON, LEWIS S. CAMPBELL, JOEL BETHEL. Book 12, Page 126 -- Administrators Bond -- DAVID PATTESON, 20 March 1848.

LUCINDA B. WARWICK -- Book 4, Page 490 -- Guardians Bond -- ABRAHAM BLUFORD WARWICK and LANDON CABELL, December 21, 1807, for ABRAHAM BLUFORD WARWICK as guardian of LUCINDA B. WARWICK, orphan of BEVERLY WARWICK.

MARCELLUS S. WARWICK -- Book 13, Page 287 -- Commissioner's Bond -- December 19, 1853. Bondsmen: GEO. W. WARWICK made bond as committee for him since MARCELLUS S. is a lunatic and bondsmen: THOS. J. WARWICK by S. M. GARLAND. Book 13, Page 472 -- Account from December 19, 1853--lunatic account by GEO. W.; to T. J. WARWICK, Asylum Treasurer: $204.00. Recorded: Monday, February 19, 1855. Book 14, Page 308 -- Account from January 1, 1855; to Asylum; dower negroes; Recorded: February 28, 1857. Book 14, Page 365 -- Same; tax; from January 1, 1856. March 27, 1857.

MARCELLUS S. WARWICK (cont.) -- Book 15, Page 117 -- Same from January 4, 1858; Amherst County land tax on James River tract. January 28, 1859. Book 15, Page 501 -- Same from February 14, 1857; to Asylum, $204.00; May 21, 1860.
Book 16, Page 262 -- Same from January 3, 1860; 982 acres transferred from R. WARWICK's estate: $2123.43; Asylum payments; investments may be affected by political troubles through which we are passing, April 20, 1863.
Book 16, Page 366 -- Same from February 5, 1861; to Asylum, July 20, 1863.
Book 16, Page 94 -- Same from January 5, 1863; Bedford ticket.
Book 17, Page 98 -- Same from February 10, 1865; account of S. P., T. J. (?) WARWICK, GEO. W. for his brother, MARCELLUS S.; money lost in general wreck of all deposits: $2306.25 May 20, 1867.
Book 17, Page 321 -- Same from January 1, 1867; Lynchburg ticket; June 9, 1868.

ROBT. D. WARWICK -- Book 14, Page 208 -- February 13, 1854; Monday. April 20, 1857. Witnesses: SAML. SCOTT, RO. A. COGHILL. DANL. WARWICK qualified; bondsman: HENRY LOVING, May 18, 1857. JAS. WARWICK qualified same date; bondsmen: HENRY LOVING, R. A. COGHILL. Father, DANL. WARWICK; my brother, JAS.; estate in Amherst County; Nelson and Richmond; father and brother to administrate.
Book 14, Page 214 -- Administrators Bond for DANL.
Book 14, Page 348 -- for JAS.
Book 14, Page 397 -- Inventory -- May 8, 1857; long slave list: $73,094.00; CHAS. TUCKER, JNO. L. TUCKER, DAVID G. WALLER.

RO. M. WARWICK -- Book 9, Page 338 -- Administrators Bond -- LOUISA B. WARWICK and DAVID J. WARWICK, October 16, 1837, for LOUISA B. WARWICK.
Book 9, Page 414 -- Inventory -- $5866.87; January 18, 1838. H. L. LANGHORNE, WASH. APPERSON, CREED TAYLOR.
Book 9, Page 499 -- indexed as sale, but there is no such page in this book.

WM. WARWICK -- Book 8, Page 240 -- June 8, 1831; August 20, 1832. Handwriting by ELIJAH FLETCHER and JNO. BULLOCK. Monday, June 17, 1833, administrators renounced administrator: JNO. M. OTEY qualified; bondsman: PASCHAL BURFORD, ARMISTEAD OTEY, JACOB KENT. Wife, FRANCES A.; four sons: REUBEN B., GEO. W., THOS. J., MARCELLUS S.--400 acres where I live; sons, RO. and DANL.--slaves; son of my wife, ADOLPHUS D. READ--I was his guardian; slave hired to STITH MEAD; my interest in estate of REUBEN BLAKEY, deceased--see STITH MEAD deeds and wife, PRUDENCE. B. F. D.--Granddaughters, ADALINE and MARTHA WINFREE; two little daughters of my daughter, ANSOLETTE SAUNDERS--house occupied by them with their father, DAVID SAUNDERS; my son, RO. M. 300 acres where he lives and bought from estate of PHILIP JOHNSON; house and lot in Lynchburg near JAS. GILLIAM and occupied by A. HATCHER; interest in estate of my father, ABRAHAM; son, DANL.--400 acres next to house occupied by STITH MEAD and joins JNO. M. WILLIAMS and C. DABNEY; tenement in Lynchburg occupied by TURNER and KERR; if my wife has child--when eldest is 21; four oldest sons to administrate: WILLIAM SIDNEY, CORBIN, ABRAHAM and JNO. MARSHALL; youngest son to be educated.
Book 8, Page 323 -- Administrators Bond
Book 8, Page 377 -- Inventory -- November 7, 1833; long; many slaves; no total; JAS. LEE, H. S. LANGHORNE, JNO. M. WILLIAMS and sale, November 15, 1833; MRS. F. A. WARWICK and R. M. WARWICK were buyers; HENRY DUNINGTON, auctioneer. Sale reported in Lynchburg. November 29, 1833; JNO. R. D. PAYNE, J.P.
Book 10, Page 305 -- Administrators de bonis non Bond -- December 21, 1840. DANL. J. WARWICK; bondsmen: JNO. M. OTEY by SAML. M. GARLAND.
Book 10, Page 370 -- Administrators Account -- by OTEY from June 21, 1833; funeral $20.00; to widow and children; tuition for R. WARWICK to JNO. CARY; real estate division expenses; tuition to CARPENTER for GEO. and THOS. WARWICK; Amherst County and Campbell taxes; guardian expenses for OTEY; farm and mill in Amherst County; cash of JNO. M. WARWICK; D. J. WARWICK; tuition for REUBEN to CARY and FRANK CARR; books for children: WM., VICTOR (VINTOR?), REUBEN; pocket money in Richmond; A. D. READ's expense to Princeton; GEORGE's medical bill

WM. WARWICK (cont.) -- in Philadelphia; pocket money for GEO. and expenses returning to Princeton. C. L. MOSBY, committee. July 19, 1841.
Book 11, Page 446 -- Administrators de bonis non Bond -- ADOLPHUS D. READ, September 21, 1846; bondsmen: DANL. J. and GEO. W. WARWICK.

JNO. WATERS -- Book 1, Page 313 -- Administrators Bond -- FRANCES WATERS, BENJ. WRIGHT, JOSIAH ELLIS, WM. HARRIS, July 1, 1776, for FRANCES WATERS.
Book 1, Page 322 -- Inventory -- January Court, 1777 L26-13-1; DANL. BURFORD, JR., JOS. DAWSON, MARTIN DAWSON.

ALEX. WATSON -- Book 5, Page 526 -- Administrators Bond -- ELIZ. WATSON, WILKINS WATSON, RO. RIDGWAY, September 18, 1815, for ELIZ. WATSON.
Book 5, Page 593 -- Inventory -- $3447.05; ELIAS WILLS, WM. TURNER, JESSE BECK, July 15, 1816.
Book 5, Page 700 -- Administrators Bond -- JNO. WILLS, ELIAS WILLS, WM. TURNER, February 18, 1818, for JNO. WILLS.
Book 6, Page 25 -- Administrators Account -- by ELIZ. WATSON, alias E. WILLS, from 1813; to ELIAS WILLS for work and waggoning; support for self and three children for three years, August 15, 1818; JNO. LONDON, WM. TURNER, JESSE BECK.
Book 6, Page 361 -- Guardians Account -- so indexed, but not there.
Book 7, Page 289 -- Guardians Bond -- JAS. L. LAMKIN and JOS. PETTYJOHN, November 16, 1829, for JAS. L. LAMKIN as guardian of ALEX. and MARIA WATSON, orphans of ALEX. WATSON.
Book 9, Page 201 -- Guardians Account -- from November 16, 1829; IRVINE for tuition; DR. OWENS--medical bill; December 21, 1835: A. B. DAVIES, JNO. THOMPSON, JR.
Book 9, Page 365 -- Guardians Account -- from January 12, 1836, by late guardian, JAS. L. LAMKIN. A. B. DAVIES, October 16, 1837.

EDWD. WATSON -- Book 5, Page 671 -- Guardians Bond -- JNO. D. WILLS and ELIAS WILLS, August 18, 1817, for JNO. D. WILLS as guardian of EDWD.; MARIAH and ALEX. WATSON, orphans of ALEX. WATSON, deceased. This page is fading rapidly. B. F. D.
Book 10, Page 178 -- April 6, 1836; codicil, March 21, 1837; codicil, October 17, 1837; June 6, 1838; December 16, 1839. Witnesses to will: A. B. DAVIES, J. P. GARLAND; to codicils: H. L. DAVIES, J. P. GARLAND, A. B. DAVIES. WILKINS WATSON qualified; bondsmen: A. B. and H. L. DAVIES, JAS. E. HORNER. Son, WM.; daughter, NANCY LACKEY; grandsons, EDWIN and ALEX. WATSON, sons of my deceased son, ALEX.; his daughter, MARIA WATSON--get land where JNO. WILLS lives; also benefit of decree in my name versus JNO. A. SIMPSON or his estate for value of my slave, LONDON, killed by SIMPSON. If MARIA has no issue; granddaughter, POLLY LACKEY; son, WILKINS WATSON; land bought under decree versus SIMPSON. Codicil: grandson, ALEX--in trust of grandson, EDWIN. Codicil: son, WM., has had sums and to make no claims. Land has been deeded to ALEX. and EDWIN WATSON and MARIA TEMPLIN, formerly WATSON. Codicil: MARIA has married ANTHONY TEMPLIN and he is to hold slave for her.
Book 10, Page 182 -- Administrators Bond
Book 10, Page 198 -- Inventory -- $9648.66. December 28, 1839; J. PETTYJOHN, JAS. P. GARLAND, JNO. H. ROBERTS; list of bonds due estate; no total, February 17, 1840.
Book 10, Page 220 -- Refunding Bond -- May 4, 1840, by EDWIN WATSON and JOS. PETTYJOHN, bondsmen, to WILKINS WATSON for slave delivered to EDWIN. Witness: RO. TINSLEY.

EDWIN WATSON -- Book 6, Page 350 -- Guardians Account -- by JNO. D. WILLS, EDWIN, infant orphan of ALEX. WATSON from 1819; hire of slaves; widow's share deducted; estate not yet divided. March 19, 1823.

JAS. WATSON -- Book 4, Page 55 -- June 27, 1802; September 20, 1802. Witnesses: JACOB WOOD, RO. ALLEN. Proved by ALLEN; October 18, 1802, by WOOD. March 24, 1803, MATT. WATSON qualified; bondsmen: EDWD. WATSON and ANTHONY DIBRELL. Wife, PATTY, and our daughters: FANNY and KITTY; son, MATT.--where I live; while FANNY and KITTY are single; to LUCY MAJORS--Kentucky land to which I may be entitled; rest of

JAS. WATSON (cont.) -- Kentucky land to my five youngest children:
JAS., MATT., WILMOUTH DIBRELL, wife of ANTHONY DIBRELL, FANNY and KITTY.
Executors: son, EDWD. and MATT. and ANTHONY DIBRELL.
Book 4, Page 122 -- Inventory -- $2540.98; June 25, 1803; JNO.
MC DANIEL, JAS. PENDLETON, JOS. HIGGINBOTHAM.
Book 4, Page 365 -- Administrators Bond
Book 5, Page 517 -- Administrators Bond -- MAACAH (sic) WATSON, WM.
WATSON, JAS. P. GARLAND, July 17, 1815, for first two.
Book 5, Page 582 -- Inventory -- December 19, 1815: $1259.65; DRURY
BELL, GILES DAVIDSON, MICAJAH PENDLETON.

MARIA L. WATSON -- Book 8, Page 45 -- Guardians Account -- from
January 1, 1813, by JNO. D. WILLS; board and schooling; to ALEX.
WATSON to equalize division; same to EDWIN WATSON, February 9, 1819.
Page 46 is account for ALEX. WATSON; June 22, 1830. A. B. DAVIES, RO.
TINSLEY, WM. BOURNE.
Book 9, Page 205 -- Guardians Account -- from January 1, 1831; CREASY's
shoes; DUNNINGTON for whipping slave; 50¢; cash paid you by trustees,
GEO. W. PETTYJOHN, C. DABNEY, ALEX. WATSON--payment; November 17, 1835;
A. B. DAVIES, JNO. THOMPSON, JR.
Book 6, Page 351 -- Administrators Account -- from 1819; infant
orphans of ALEX. WATSON--account also for ALEX. Recorded: March 19,
1823; slave hires; LINDSEY COLEMAN, WM. BOUREN, A. B. DAVIES.

WILKINS WATSON -- Book 14, Page 207 -- July 12, 1856; August 25, 1856;
October 20, 1856. Witnesses: J. M. COBBS, J. P. GARLAND (will and
codicil); to codicil: J. POWELL, SAML. M. GARLAND. Produced by JAS. E.
HORNER and DANL. E. WATSON. ELIZ., widow, contested November 17,
1856, admitted for contest. Decemberl 1 16, 1856, COBB and JAS.
GARLAND, testified and admitted. HORNER and DANL. E. WATSON qualified.
Executors to sell where I live; my children: WILKINS, EDWIN, LILLY
VA.--when married or 21; if wife refuses, dower to her; all of my chil-
dren; my three infants. Executors: son, DANL. E. and son-in-law,
JAS. E. HORNER and to be guardians; no bond required.
Book 14, Page 227 -- Administrators Bond -- December 16, 1856.
Book 14, Page 400 -- Guardians Bond -- ELIS. Z., E. P. TUCKER, GEO. W.
HENLEY, JAS. M. GANNAWAY, August 18, 1857, for ELIZ. A. WATSON as
guardian of three infants.
Book 14, Page 440 -- Inventory -- 424½ acres near Amherst County
Courthouse; bond of D. J. CAMERON (unknown); Deed of Trust, JAS. E.
HORNER, trustee, November 21, 1854, after death of testator - for
infants; Monday , October 19, 1857.
Book 14, Page 448 -- Crop Sale -- $302; Monday, October 19, 1857.
Book 14, Page 517 (two pages so numbered) -- Administrators Bond --
JAS. E. HORNER and SAML. MURPHY, January 18, 1858, for JAS. E. HORNER.
Book 15, Page 167 -- Trustee Account -- by HORNER for children from
17 November 1856; MRS. WATSON's suit versus him. May 16, 1859.
Book 16, Page 519 -- Administrators Account -- November 4, 1857 by
both administrators; to G. A. and LUCY J. WATSON; enclosing graveyard;
WATSON's executor versus E. A. WATSON; March 20, 1864.
Book 20, Page 6 -- Administrators de bonis non Bond -- January 19,
1880; TAYLOR BERRY; bondsman: RO. A. COGHILL.
Book 21, Page 122 -- Assistant Assessor -- District 1; bondsmen:
WILKINS T. WATSON, BENJ. B. BROWN, E. A. WATSON. February 16, 1885.

CALEB WATTS -- Book 6, Page 686 -- December 14, 1825; September 18,
1826. Witnesses: WM. ARMISTEAD, BENJ. R. DAWSON, WM. A. TERRELL,
WM. H. PARKS; wife; sons: WM., JNO.; friend, GEO. BURKS, son of DAVIS;
my sons, CHAS., SAML.; daughter, JANE MAGANN and heirs; son, CURTIS;
sons, JOS., MITCHELL, JAS.; daughters, PAMEILIA WRIGHT, ELIS. BROWN,
ANNA BROWN and children. Executors: GEO. BURKS above; sons, CURTIS
and SAML. WATTS.
Book 6, Page 707 -- Administrators Bond -- CURTIS WATTS, HARRISON
WRIGHT, BENJ. R. DAWSON, WM. H. MC CULLOCH, November 20, 1826, for
CURTIS WATTS.
Book 6, Page 733 -- Inventory -- February 19, 1821: $1744; MARTIN
PARKS, JNO. TALBOT, JAS. DAVIS.
Book 8, Page 65 -- Curators Bond -- November 17, 1830: SAML. WATTS,
LINDSEY MC DANIEL, BENJ. R. DAWSON--unadministrated by CURTIS WATTS,
late administrator.

CALEB WATTS (cont.) -- Book 8, Page 72 -- Inventory -- $1348.50; MARTIN
PARKS, NELSON C. DAWSON, BENJ. R. DAWSON.
Book 8, Page 130 -- Administrators Account -- by CURTIS WATTS from
July 17, 1826--amount from SUSAN WATTS; September 19, 1831. PETER P.
THORNTON, WM. SHELTON.
Book 9, Page 5 -- Administrators Account -- by SAML. WATTS from 1831;
CALEB WATTS' part of tobacco 1832; CURTIS WATTS--witness fee; WM.
HOLLAND for making coffin--$8.00; cash to JANE MEGANN. March 17, 1834.
HENRY W. QUARLES, EDMD. PENN.

CATH. WATTS -- Book 8, Page 340 -- August 19, 1833; CATH. renounced
will of late husband, HENRY H. WATTS. Witnesses: NELSON D. WINGFIELD,
JESSE MUNDY.
Book 12, Page 226 -- Motion of JOS. PETTYJOHN and JESSE MUNDY to show
why counter security should not be given. They are bondsmen for CATH.
to administrate estate of HENRY H. WATTS; summons waived and administrator revoked; Estate Commitment to Sheriff, LINDSEY COLEMAN, December
ter, 1849.
Book 12, Page 232 -- Power of Attorney -- by CATH., to son, CHAS. M.
WATTS; debt due me as administrator de bonis non of HENRY H. WATTS
in Nelson County Superior Court from estate of STEPHEN WATTS to my
late husband, HENRY H. WATTS. Witnesses: JOS. PETTYJOHN, JAS. LAMKIN.
Book 17, Page 38 -- Administrators Bond -- November 20, 1865, by
BEVERLY P. MORRIS and CHAS. M. WATTS for BEVERLY P. MORRIS to administrate.

HANNAH WATTS -- Book 3, Page 130 -- February 19, 1790; April 5, 1790.
Witnesses: JOS. BURGER, MARY BURGER, WINNEFORD MORAN. Natural
daughter, ELIZ.--all owed to me by SHADRACK WATTS. Executor: JESSE
CLARKSON. He qualified on probate date; bondsman: DAVID CLARKSON.

HENRY WATTS -- Book 5, Page 184 -- Guardians Bond -- DAVID S. GARLAND
and EDMD. PENN, October 19, 1812, for DAVID S. GARLAND as guardian
of HENRY WATTS and wife, ELIZ., orphan of GEO. DILLARD. This is so
written. B. F. D.

HENRY H. WATTS -- Book 8, Page 293 -- November 13, 1832; January 21,
1833. Witnesses: WM. DILLARD, JOS. S. CLARK, NELSON D. WINGFIELD,
JNO. L. (S) DILLARD. CHAS. MUNDY qualified; bondsmen: ALEX. and JESSE
MUNDY; JOS. PETTYJOHN. Wife, CATH.--guardian of children until 21 or
married--"unless bonded out at school." Three children by first
marriage when of age or when youngest, ANN, shall marry; ELIZ.; EDWIN
and ANN MARIA--legacy from their grandfather, PENN; my seven living
children: ELIZ., EDWIN, ANN, STEPHEN, CHAS., JESSE and MARY--if no
issue. Executors: friends, CHAS. and ALEX. MUNDY, JAS. D. WATTS,
JNO. DILLARD.
Book 8, Page 330 -- Inventory -- $9814.70; GEO. STAPLES, WILLIAM
DILLARD, CHAS. M. CHRISTIAN, July 15, 1833.
Book 8, Page 412 -- Administrators Account -- by CHAS. MUNDY; accounts
of MARY R. CHRISTIAN; tuition to W. M. YATES; boat and watermen items;
hats for sons--$6.00; JNO. H. TARDY; CATH. WATTS for family expenses;
ANN's tuition to WALTER YATES; funeral--$10.00. May 19, 1834. JNO.
and JOS. DILLARD, D. STAPLES.
Book 9, Page 23 -- Slaves to MRS. CATH. WATTS, widow. November 19,
1835. WM. and JOS. S. (L) DILLARD; ISAAC W. WALKER.
Book 10, Page 118 -- Administrators Account -- by EDMD. WINSTON,
administrator de bonis non, from May 19, 1834; to S. LOVING, executor
of STEPHEN WATTS; bond of JAS. WATTS; SILAS P. VAWTER, trustee; cash
to EDWIN; C. E. WATTS; bond for children--three oldest; to ANN M. WATTS;
E. H. WATTS; claim versus BENJ. WATTS; Nelson County suit; when ANN is
of age or married; her school expenses; account with CATH., widow,
from August 7, 1834; saddle and bureau for ELIZ.; four youngest and
three oldest children. January 19, 1839. WM. J SHELTON, commissioner.
Book 11, Page 531 -- Administrators de bonis non Bond -- CATH. WATTS,
JOS. PETTYJOHN, ALEX. MUNDY, June 21, 1847, for CATH. WATTS.
Book 12, Page 253 -- Administrators de bonis non Bond -- JOS. PETTYJOHN,
January 22, 1850; bondsman for CATH. WATTS.
Book 12, Page 412 -- Administrators Account -- by CATH. from 1847;
dower; D. STAPLES, commissioner, January 19, 1850.

386

HENRY H. WATTS (cont.) -- Book 12, Page 441 -- Administrators Account --
from 1850; legatees: not named; see next item. RO. M. BROWN, com-
missioner. July 26, 1851.
Book 13, Page 18 -- Administrators Account -- from 1851, May 18.
Legatees: CATH. WATTS, widow; LEWIS STAPLES and wife, ELIZ.; EDWIN
WATTS; RO. M. JENNINGS and wife, ANN; STEPHEN; CHAS.; JESSE and MARY
WATTS. WATTS versus WATTS; EDMD. WINSTON, former administrator.
September 20, 1852.
Book 18, Page 63 -- Administrator de bonis non Bond -- B. P. MORRIS
and STEPHEN WATTS, January 16, 1871, for B. P. MORRIS.

JESSE A. WATTS -- Book 14, Page 212 -- Administrators Bond -- CHAS. M.
WATTS and ALEX. MUNDY, December 15, 1856, for CHAS. M. WATTS.
Book 14, Page 296 -- Inventory -- same date; DAVID PATTESON, HENRY L.
DAVIES, G. A. R. TUCKER; no total, but interesting list of dental and
medical books and instrumental list.

MORTON SIMS WATTS -- Book 12, Page 129 -- Guardians Bond -- JAS. D.
WATTS and WM. DILLARD, May 15, 1848, for JAS. D. WATTS as guardian of
his infant son, MORTON SIMS WATTS.

NANCY WATTS -- Book 18, Page 37 -- December 11, 1865; January 16, 1871.
Witnesses: PHILIP ST. GEO. TUCKER, V. H. RUCKER. ALBERT D. WATTS
qualified, March 20, 1871. Love all of my children, but have lived
with son, ALBERT D., since husband's death--sole legatee.
Book 18, Page 65 -- Inventory -- in with that of SAML. WATTS.
Book 18, Page 67 -- Sale -- with that of SAML. WATTS.

RO. W. WATTS -- Book 12, Page 575 -- Constables Bond -- October 18,
1852; bondsman: PAULUS POWELL.
Book 13, Page 91 -- Same, September 25, 1852; bondsmen: PAULUS POWELL,
ED. J. DAVIS, JNO. CRIS NOEL, M. D. GOODWIN.
Book 14, Page 361 -- Trustee account by HENRY SMITH from December 20,
1854; SMITH bought slave and her child and executed Deed of Trust.
WATTS in financial straits; balance to go to his wife, MARY ANN WATTS,
but debts exhausted it. April 8, 1857.
Book 15, Page 282 -- Minister's Bond; no denomination; December 19,
1859; bondsman: JAS. D. WATTS.
Book 17, Page 38 -- Same, November 20, 1865; bondsman: W. D. TURNER.
I suspect that he was a Methodist since most of the family belong to
that group. B.F.D. I might add here that I made an error in the
PETTYJOHN lineage of my daughter-in-law, MARY GAYLE. I stated that she
descended from JNO. P. PETTYJOHN and second wife, nee WATTS, but I have
learned that she stems from JNO. P. PETTYJOHN's first wife, nee OLD.

SAML. WATTS -- Book 14, Page 586 -- November 4, 1852; Monday, August 16,
1858. Witnesses: ZACH D. TINSLEY, EDWIN S. RUCKER, JNO. R. CUNNINGHAM.
ALBERT D. WATTS qualified. (This man is an ancestor of MARY GAYLE
PETTYJOHN who married my son, THURMAN BLANTON DAVIS); bondsman: W. A.
DEARING. Wife, NANCY; son, ALBERT D.--313 acres where I live; all of
my children except SAML. C. and MARTHA ANN, wife of WILKERSON WARE--
they have received shares; same for son, RODERICK L.--given sums on
May 20, 1851. Executor: son, ALBERT D.; Administrators Bond is
page 587.
Book 15, Page 36 -- Inventory -- Bond of NELSON S. WATTS: $12,841.51;
ZACH D. TINSLEY, EDWIN S. RUCKER, BENJ. L. SHELTON, September 20, 1858.
Book 15, Page 283 -- Administrators Account -- from August 23, 1858;
recorded: January 14, 1860.
Book 16, Page 280 -- Administrators Account -- from October 21, 1859;
to E. BROWN, legatee; from CALEB WATTS' estate; legacy of JNO. BROWN;
February 18, 1861.
Book 18, Page 64 -- Inventory -- Friday, March 31, 1871: $7491.50;
followed by inventory of $10.00 for NANCY WATTS, S. W. MASON, M. H.
GARLAND, Z. D. TINSLEY; May 15, 1871.
Book 18, Page 66 -- Sale -- March 31, 1871; JNO., JANE, A. D.; also
NANCY's sale: $12.56 along with SAML's at $742.45. Recorded: June 19,
1871.

THOS. WATTS -- Book 3, Page 522 -- Inventory -- October 15, 1798;
ROD. MC CULLOCH, JNO. BURKS, PETER P. THORNTON.

THOS. WATTS (cont.) -- Book 4, Page 224 -- Administrators Account --
CALEB WATTS, administrator; September, 1798; WM. WATTS, overseer;
returned January 7, 1806; recorded: June 16, 1806.
Book 4, Page 295 -- Administrators Bond -- CALEB WATTS, JAS. HARRISON,
DUDLEY CALLAWAY, WM. ANGUS, June 17, 1798, for C. W. PETTYJOHN family
tradition has it that CALEB was son of THOS. WATTS, but I have no
other proof other than this circumstantial evidence herein. MARY GAYLE
PETTYJOHN's father is named THOS. WATTS PETTYJOHN. His mother was
BELLE W., daughter of ALBERT D. WATTS.

THOS. BROWN WATTS -- Book 16, Page 100 -- April 24, 1861; November 18,
1861. Handwriting by JNO. C. MUNDY and RO. W. WATTS. AMERICA V. WATTS
qualified. December 16, 1861; bondsmen: DAVID APPLING and JAS. M.
WATTS. Father, JAS. D. WATTS; aunt, AMERICA V. WATTS; cousin, SALLY C.
APPLING; AMERICA V. to administrate; when SALLY APPLING is 21 or
married--to be educated.
Book 16, Page 117 -- Inventory -- Monday, December 16, 1861; division
of slaves to A. V. WATTS and S. C. A. APPLING (sic), JAS. D. WATTS,
JAS. W. KEITH, LEWIS E. TURNER, committee. Inventory, January 30, 1862:
$550.00.

WYATT WATTS -- Book 12, Page 28 -- Administrators Bond -- LUDWELL and
ROD. L. WATTS, November 15, 1847, for LUDWELL WATTS.
Book 12, Page 372 -- Inventory -- of WIATT WATTS; order of November,
1847; ARCHIBALD REYNOLDS, HAZAEL WILLIAMS, ELLOT WORTHAM, JNO. D. DAVIS;
recorded: April, 1851.
Book 12, Page 412 -- Sale -- November 9, 1849; WATTS buyers: LUDWELL,
NANCY, MARY (?), WM. S. (P) THORNTON, Clerk of Sale. May 19, 1851.

MARY H. WAUGH -- Book 8, Page 302 -- October 13, 1832; February 18,
1833. Witnesses: THOS. B. ROYSTER, GEO. W. KNIGHT. WM. H. KNIGHT
qualified; bondsman: JOS. STAPLES. Wife of RICH. J. WAUGH and formerly
MARY H. KNIGHT. Conveyed and recorded April 18th last all estate to
my brother, WM. H. KNIGHT, with reservations noted and now exercise
them. Husband and brother to bury me; my aunt, JANE DAWSON; rest to
my husband. Brother to be administrator.

RICH. J. WAUGH -- Book 6, Page 604 -- Constables Bond -- June 21, 1825;
bondsmen: LUCAS P. THOMPSON, CHAS. L. BARRET.
Book 7, Page 27 -- Same, August 19, 1827; bondsmen: HILL CARTER,
WM. H. KNIGHT.
Book 7, Page 248 -- Same; bondsmen: HILL CARTER, GEO. W. HIGGINBOTHAM.
Book 8, Page 101 -- Same, June 20, 1831; bondsmen: WM. H. KNIGHT,
HENRY J. ROSE.

RODERICK WAUGH -- Book 15, Page 261 -- No data when written: probated,
Monday, January 16, 1860. Proved by JNO. PRYOR and T. GILLESPIE.
J. DUDLEY DAVIS qualified; bondsman: JAS. B. DAVIS. Wife, EDITHA ANN;
nephew, WM. H. WAUGH, son of THOS. WAUGH; friend, EVERETT MILTON
GILLESPIE; brother, NICHL. WAUGH; executor; friend, CHAS. L. (S)
DAVIS and PEMBROKE E. WAUGH.
Book 15, Page 285 -- Inventory -- January 28, 1860; 100 acres: $263.16;
JAS. D. DAVIS, TARLTON W. CHILDES or CHILES, RO. N. ELLIS, W. L. DAVIS,
J. DUDLEY DAVIS, administrator.

THOS. WAUGH -- Book 6, Page 491 -- Administrators Bond -- RODERICK
and NICHL. WAUGH, October 18, 1824, for both.
Book 6, Page 564 -- Inventory -- Bedford County, done, November 12,
1824; recorded Amherst County, March 21, 1825: WM. and ALEX. REYNOLDS,
BARNARD RUCKER. Amherst County inventory: $6041.17; many slaves;
November 25, 1824; WM. H. MC CULLOCH, THOS. N. EUBANK, GEO. MORRIS.
Recorded as above.

CUTHBERT WEBB -- Book 1, Page 460 -- June 11, 1777; November 2, 1778.
Witnesses: BENJ. and THOS. MILES, WM. COX. Of Albemarle County;
wife, MARY; all of my children; executors: wife and my brother,
THEODORICK WEBB. Wife present at probate, but further proof on
April 5, 1779.
Book 1, Page 461 -- Administrators Bond -- THEODORICK WEBB, JOS. and

CUTHBERT WEBB (cont.) -- NICHL. CABELL, April 5, 1779, for THEODORICK
WEBB. The two miles attested in November.
Book 1, Page 462 -- Administrators Bond -- MARY WEBB, JAS. MATTHEWS,
JAS. TULERY, April 5, 1779, for MARY WEBB.

RO. WEIR or WIER -- Book 1, Page 208 -- January 18, 1772; July 6,
1772. Witnesses: WM. IRVIN, CHAS. YANCEY, ALEX. HENDERSON, FRANCIS
TURNER. Wife, MARTHA; children--JNO. excepted 60 acres; if he dies
before maturity; daughter, ELIZ.--until married; AGNES, ANDREW, RO.,
THOS., MARTHA ANN--no punctuation so could be two daughters; ESTHER--
as they come of age. If any sons choose to learn trade, they are to be
bound out at 18; lands I live on; JNO. to stay with mother until 21
and support children. Executors: THOS. STEWART and brother-in-law,
CHOS. BELL. Codicil: 100 acres on northern end may be sold.
Book 1, Page 210 -- Administrators Bond -- THOS. BELL and SAML. WOODS,
May 6, 1772, for THOS. BELL.
Book 1, Page 226 -- Inventory -- L72-1400, September court, 1772;
ALEX. REID, JNO. MORRISON, ALEX. MILLER.
Book 3, Page 35 -- so indexed, but not there.
Book 3, Page 180 -- Administrators Account -- from March 2, 1772;
legatees: ANDREW, RO., ANDREW for sister, ELIZ., JAS. HENDERSON,
guardian of THOS. WEIR, ELIZ. WEIR, SAML. YOUNG who married ANN WEIR,
April 18, 1791; JNO. DIGGS, NATHL. CRAWFORD, WM. HARRIS.
Book 3, Page 315 -- June 1, 1794; October 20, 1794. Witnesses:
WILLIAM BRIDGEWATER, JNO. STAPLES, BENJ. BRYANT. Wife, MARY; all of
my children: JNO., BETSY, ANDREW; expected child--if a daughter; land
to be sold when she is 18. Executors: wife and brother-in-law, CHAS.
MASSIE; brother, THOS. WEIR; and friends, HUDSON MARTIN and THOS.
MORRISON.
Book 3, Page 358 -- Inventory -- MARY WIER, acting executrix; no
total; THOS. MORRISON, THOS. TALTON (?), JAS. MORRISON. December 21,
1795.

JNO. WELSH (WILSH) -- Book 3, Page 150 -- June 13, 1790; September 6,
1790. Witnesses: WM. JACOBS, JAS. EDMONDS, NATHL. TILMOND JONES.
Wife, MARGET (sic); to administrate and at her death, JAS. EDMOND is
to administrate. EDMONDS qualified; bondsman: JOS. WELSH.
Book 3, Page 171 -- Inventory -- L36-15-6; Febr-ary 7, 1791. KILLIS
WRIGHT, WM., THOS. and CHAS. LAINE.

FRANCIS WEST -- Book 3, Page 300 -- Inventory -- 16 June 1799; L76-12-
7½; WM. THOMPSON, DANL. PROFFITT, JNO. BALL. This item was found in
page search, but was not indexed. I had the clerk to do so. There
is a paucity of WEST data in will books, but deed books show a great
deal on the family here and in Kentucky. I am jotting down a few
references in deed books: A:34; E:271, 334, 341; F: 246, 248, 461,
536ff; G:209; H:183f; I:12, 58, 105, 131, 134, 237; K:84, 61, 326.
These were done for a distant kinsman of my wife's, DR. MALCOLM HARRIS,
who lives at West Point, Virginia, and is author of the fine book on
Louisa County. My wife is not a WEST descendant, but DR. HARRIS' son
married into the family. At least he suspects it since he can trace
to a DANDRIDGE SPOTSWOOD WEST of Amherst County who donated the land
for the Oronoco Church of the Brethren. DR. WEST tells me that there
is a stone in the church graveyard for this man. He married a COLE, as
I recall. There is also WEST data in Nelson.

JAS. WEST -- Book 4, Page 312 -- Administrators Bond -- FRANCIS WEST
and JNO. MATTHEWS, October 15, 1798, for FRANCIS WEST.

JAS. WHITE -- Book 2, Page 126 -- Administrators Bond -- SARAH WHITE,
ISAAC RUCKER, ANTHONY RUCKER, WM. CHAPPLE, August 4, 1783, for SARAH
WHITE.
Book 2, Page 131 -- Inventory -- L194-4-6; September 1, 1783. JOHN
STEWART, JOS. CREWS, WIATT POWELL.

MERRITT M. WHITE -- Tobacco Inspector Bonds -- Book 5, Page 526 --
Amherst Warehouse, November 20, 1815; bondsman: RICH. BURKS.
Book 5, Page 605 -- September 16, 1816; bondsman: same.
Book 6, Page 163 -- September 18, 1820; bondsman: JAS. DAVIS.

MERRIT M. WHITE (cont.) -- Book 6, Page 252 -- September 17, 1821; bondsman: JAS. POWELL.

NANCY M. WHITE -- Book 11, Page 448 -- Guardians Bond -- HENRY A. WHITE and OLIVER P. JONES, October 19, 1846, for HENRY A. WHITE as guardian of NANCY M. WHITE, orphan of WM. WHITE, deceased.

BARTHOLOMEW WHITEHEAD -- Book 16, Page 440 -- July 22, 1854; codicil: 2 August 1860; 18 May 1861. Probated 21 March 1864. Witnesses to will: ALEX. GOOCH, LEO DANIEL, JR. Witnesses to codicil 1: RO. A. PENDLETON, ALEX. GOOCH, S. M. GARLAND; to codicil 2: STERLING CLAIBORNE and S. M. GARLAND. WESLEY E. DUNCAN refused to qualify; ELIZ. WHITEHEAD qualified; bondsman: STERLING CLAIBORNE. Wife, NANCY; children: ELIZ., POLLY, CATH. WHITEHEAD, SALLY WRIGHT. Land to ELIZ., POLLY, CATH. Sons, GEO., JAS. and BARTHOLOMEW WHITEHEAD. Executor: friend, WESLEY E. DUNCA. Codicil 1: SALLY WRIGHT has had her share and so has CATH.: to ELIZ. and POLLY; CATH. free from husband and to any issue at her death. Codicil 2: POLLY has died; to ELIZ. at POLLY's request. Administrators Bond is page 456.

BARTLETT WHITEHEAD -- Book 3, Page 316 -- Guardians Bond -- MOSES WRIGHT, BENJ. CAMDEN, JNO. SMITH, October 20, 1794, for MOSES WRIGHT as guardian of BARTLETT WHITEHEAD, orphan of JNO. WHITEHEAD.

BURCHER WHITEHEAD -- Book 5, Page 466 -- Administrators Bond -- JNO. and RICH. WHITEHEAD, October 17, 1814, for JNO. WHITEHEAD.
Book 5, Page 469 -- August 24, 1814; October 17, 1814. Witnesses: G. SAND, CHAS. DUNCAN, WM. KIDD. Until youngest daughter, MARY JANE, is 18 or married; wife, NANCY; my eight children: JNO., PINCY (?), SALLY, WM., ELIZ., FLOYRRO, SYBELL, MARY. JNO. has had horse and furniture; when others are married or 21, to get same. Executors: son, JNO. and wife, NANCY.
Book 5, Page 486 -- Inventory -- December 5, 1814: $1355.13; JAS. SMITH, LEONARD HENLEY, WILKINS WATSON.

CARY WHITEHEAD -- Book 3, Page 257 -- Guardians Bond -- JNO. SMITH and JNO. CAMDEN, December 17, 1792, for JNO. SMITH as guardian of CARY WHITEHEAD, orphan of JNO. WHITEHEAD.
Book 4, Page 631 -- Guardians Account -- from September 16, 1794; amount from BURCHER WHITEHEAD, administrator of JNO. WHITEHEAD; recorded: July 16, 1810. Indexed for CARY SMITH. There is also an Administrators Account as to JNO. WHITEHEAD here by BURCHER WHITEHEAD; recorded as for the other item.

JNO. WHITEHEAD -- Book 3, Page 52 -- Administrators Bond -- SARAH WHITEHEAD and JNO. SCOTT, September 3, 1787, for SARAH WHITEHEAD.
Book 3, Page 70 -- Inventory -- L337-1-9; JNO. PENN, WM. CAMDEN, CORNL. SALE, October 23, 1787.
Book 3, Page 219 -- Administrators Bond -- BURCHER WHITEHEAD and WM. CAMDEN, April 16, 1792, for BURCHER WHITEHEAD. Indexed for BURCHER WHITEHEAD.
Book 3, Page 238 -- Administrators Bond -- for same men, July 16, 1792; unadministrated by SARAH WHITEHEAD, deceased.

MARY K. WHITEHEAD -- Book B, Page 65 -- Administrators Bond -- THOS. WHITEHEAD and RO. M. BROWN, August 24, 1857, for THOS. WHITEHEAD.

JER. WHITTEN -- Book 1, Page 414 -- Administrators Bond -- WM. WHITTEN (WHITTING), JNO. WHITTEN (ditto) and JER. WHITTEN, April 7, 1778, for WM. WHITTEN.
Book 1, Page 429 -- Inventory -- no total, April 20, 1778; NEAL MC CANN, JNO. SLEDD, ZACH TAYLOR.
Book 4, Page 40 -- Inventory -- L377-6-11; July 19, 1809; no committee named.
Book 4, Page 345 -- Administrators Bond -- WM. WHITTEN, LACKIE BYAS, EDWD. SANDERSON, April 19, 1802, for WM. WHITTEN.

JOAB W. WHITTEN -- Book 16, Page 192 -- Administrators Bond -- JAS. CLEMENTS and A. TALIAFERRO, December 15, 1862, for JAS. CLEMENTS.

JOAB W. WHITTEN (cont.) -- Indexed for JACOB W. WHITTEN.
Book 17, Page 171 -- Inventory -- December 20, 1862: $609.00; WILLIS
WHITE, JNO. W. JENNINGS, ARTHUR WHITE; recorded: August 9, 1864.
Book 17, Page 236 -- Administrators Account -- from December 15, 1862;
received of MARY F. WHITTEN on sales to date; February 25, 1865, and
June 15, 1866.

MATT. WHITTEN (another index error; so indexed, but for NANCY WHITTEN).

NANCY WHITTEN -- Book 4, Page 361 -- Guardians Bond -- JAS. FRANKLIN,
LITTLEBERRY WHITTEN, WM. NOEL, JAS. BYAS, November 15 1802, for JAS.
FRANKLIN as guardian of NANCY WHITTEN, orphan of JER. WHITTEN.

TABITHA WHITTEN -- Book 4, Page 363 -- Guardians Bond -- WM. WHITTEN
and HENRY CAMDEN, January 17, 1803, for WM. WHITTEN as guardian of
TABITHA WHITTEN, orphan of JNO. WHITTEN.

ELIZ. WHITTINGTON -- Book 10, Page 383 -- Estate Commitment to Sheriff --
EDMD. PENN, Sheriff; motion of OBADIAH HENDERSON, December court, 1840.

FRANCIS J. WHITTINGTON -- Book 10, Page 359 -- Guardians Bond --
DANL. DAY and JAS. E. WHITTINGTON, June 31, 1841, for DANL. DAY as
guardian of FRANCIS J. WHITTINGTON, orphan of STARK B. WHITTINGTON,
deceased.

MARTHA V. WIATT -- Book 7, Page 230 -- Guardians Bond -- CHISWELL
DABNEY and EDMD. WINSTON, April 20, 1829, for CHISWELL DABNEY as guardian of MARTHA V. WIATT, orphan of THOS. WIATT, deceased.

SALLY WICKASHAM -- Book 8, Page 334 -- Administrators Bond -- AMBR.
PLUNKET, WM. and LINDSEY MC DANILE, July 15, 1833, for AMBR. PLUNKET.

CHAS. WILSHER -- Book 14, Page 6 -- Guardians Bond -- July 16, 1855.
WM. P. WISHER, CHAS. H. MASSIE, SAML. GARLAND for WM. P. WILSHER as
guardian of CHAS. and PERMELIA G. WILSHER, orphans of LAWSON G. WILSHER.

JAS. L. WILSHER -- Book 13, Page 524 -- Guardians Bond -- RO. C.
WILCHER, EDMOND P. and WM. D. TUCKER, M. C. GOODWIN, July 16, 1855, for
RO. C. WILCHER as guardian of JAS. L., SARAH M. and STAFFORD R.
WILCHER, orphans of LAWSON G. WILCHER. I am employing spellings as
given.

JOS. W. WILSHER -- Book 2, Page 51 -- April 23, 1777; May 6, 1782.
Witnesses: PETER and ANN JOINER, SARAH EVINS. Wife, BARBARY--land;
sons: CHAS. and JNO. W.--land; daughter, SARAH WILCHER.
Book 2, Page 53 -- Administrators Bond -- BARBARY WILSHER and JNO.
EDWARDS, JR., May 6, 1782, for BARBARY WILSHER.
Book 2, Page 69 -- Inventory -- August 4, 1782: 142-7-6; PETER
HENDRIXSON, JNO. CHRISTIAN, NOTLEY MADDOX, JNO. EDMUNS.

LAWSON G. WILSHER -- Book 11, Page 216 -- Administrators Bond --
PARMELIA WILCHER, C. A. PENN, CHAS. MASSIE, DANL. COLEMAN, WARNER
JONES, February 17, 1844, for PARMELIA WILCHER. Note: page 293 of
marriages: May 11, 1827, LQWSON G. WILSHER and PAMELIA (PERMELIA) M.
GOOCH; parent or guardian of wife: GIDEON GOOCH, LUCY GOOCH was one
of securities.

NANCY WILCHER -- Book 9, Page 21 -- Division, December 7, 1833; to
children and heirs of NANCY WILCHER, CHAS. MUNDY, J.P.--PETER RUTHER-
FORD, guardian of SARAH A., JANE W. and MILDRED A. WILCHER, children
of NANCY; lot ot JOS. M. GARNER and wife, SARAH A. Committee: JOS.
KYLE, DRURY CHRISTIAN, JONAS PIERCE. Note: next item shows that
NANCY and SARAH are the same.

SARAH WILSHER -- Book 8, Page 137 -- Administrators Bond -- PETER
RUTHERFORD, TANDY RUTHERFORD, JAS. PAMPLIN. October 17, 1831, for
PETER RUTHERFORD.
Book 8, Page 144 -- Guardians Bond -- PETER RUTHERFORD and LAVENDER
LONDON, October 17, 1831, for PETER RUTHERFORD as guardian of SARAH,

SARAH WILSHER (cont.) -- JANE, and MILLY WILCHER, orphans of SARAH
WILCHER. Sale; inventory and division, September 19, 1831; ten slaves
at $2950 to each heir--$983.33--SARAH A., JANE W., MILDRED A. WILCHER,
children of SARAH (formerly RUTHERFORD). Originally TYREE as shown
by data; April 28, 1798--JACOB TYREE, security, for JOS. WILSHER and
SALLY RUTHERFORD, widow. See Deed Book H, Page 558. June 21, 1798--
JACOB sells slave to JOS. WILCHER--love for daughter, SARAH.

JNO. C. WILCOX -- Book 10, Page 250 -- Administrators Bond -- SAML.
WATTS and BENJ. B. TALIAFERRO, August 17, 1840, for SAML. WATTS.

THOS. WILCOX -- Book 5, Page 224 -- Inventory -- February 27, 1813;
HENRY TURNER, WM. TURNER, JESSE BECK; returned: June 21, 1813.

WINFFIELD WILCOX -- Book 5, Page 203 -- Administrators Bond -- WINIFRED
WILCOX, JNO. C. WILCOX, JAS. MARR, RICH. JONES, February 15, 1813, for
WINIFRED WILCOX. Note: name of testator is blank in bond, but indexed
for WINGFIELD WILCOX.

WINIFRED WILCOX -- Book 10, Page 215 -- Administrators Bond -- SAML.
WATTS, JNO. R. MC DANIEL, GEO. W. OLD, Apri. 20, 1840, for SAML. WATTS.
Book 13, Page 84 -- Administrators Account -- by GEO. W. OLD from
November, 1840; eight legatees and division, but no names. JNO. PRYOR,
commissioner. Recorded: October 19, 1852.

ELIZ. WILLIAMS -- Book 5, Page 68 -- Guardians Bond -- LARKIN MAYS
and GEO. MAYS, January 22, 1811, for LARKIN MAYS as guardian of ELIZ.
WILLIAMS, orphan of WM. WILLIAMS.

JNO. M. WILLIAMS (descendants state that M. stood for MORGAN) -- Book 17,
Page 174 -- October 29, 1849; codicil: February 22, 1855; codicil:
January 20, 1860; September 17, 1866. Witnesses: C. DABNEY, JESSE J.
SALMONS, SHUZ (?) LATHAM, WM. L. FAIR, L. E. WILLIAMS. Witnesses to
codicil 1: JNO. M. SPECK, J. J. LANGHORNE, C. DABNEY; to #2: WM. Q.
SPENCE, C. W. PRICE, C. DABNEY. ELIZ. A. WILLIAMS qualified; bondsman:
CHAS. W. (N) WILLIAMS. Wife, ELIZ. A.; seven youngest children--
420 acres; daughter, ELIZ. M. EDWARDS and children--where she and
husband live and joining MRS. SHACKELFORD; OPossum Island road. Sons,
JAS., ALFRED, WESLEY--good plain ENGLISH education for three youngest--
ADOLPHUS N., MARY JANE, LORENZO D., RO. R., HENRY C., THOS. S., CHAS. W.,
LORENZO D. to have enough to finish professional education. Wife to
administrate. Codicil 1: RO. R. has his share. Codicil 2: RO. R. is
to share in estate. Administrators Bond is page 176.
Book 23, Page 305 -- THOS. S. WILLIAMS qualified, October 17, 1892;
bondsman: STEPHEN ADAMS. Note: I erred in putting this bond also
for item before this one. See ROBINSON data for family of ELIZ. A.

JNO. WESLEY WILLIAMS -- Book 14, Page 298 -- October 13, 1853; Monday,
April 20, 1857. Witnesses: THOS. WHITEHEAD, ALFRED WILLIAMS. Proved
by them, May 18, 1857. Wife, MARGARET, and children. Executor:
father-in-law, GEO. T. PLEASANTS.
Book 15, Page 288 -- Administrators Bond -- ALFRED M. WOODROOF;
December 19, 1859; bondsman: A. R. WOODROOF, EDGAR WHITEHEAD.
Book 16, Page 96 -- Inventory -- slaves: $5300 etc.; total: $12,549.13,
October 21, 1861, by administrator.
Book 16, Page 334 -- Administrators Account -- from December 22, 1859;
bond of R. R. WILLIAMS, 1856; recorded: June 15, 1863.

LEWIS E. WILLIAMS -- Book 7, Page 172 -- Constables Bond -- August 18,
1828; bondsman: JNO. M. WILLIAMS, CHRISTOPHER J. TIMBERLAKE.
Book 7, Page 243 -- Same, June 15, 1829; bondsman: JNO. M. WILLIAMS,
WM. Y. WINTON.
Book 8, Page 100 -- Same, June 20, 1831; bondsmen: JNO. M. WILLIAMS,
BENJ. NORVELL.
Book 8, Page 333 -- Same, July 15, 1833; bondsmen: JNO. M. WILLIAMS,
CHAS. PALMORE.

POLLY WILLIAMS -- Book 5, Page 376 -- Guardians Bond -- JNO. MITCHELL,
EDWD. TAYLOR, September 20, 1813, for JNO. MITCHELL as guardian of

POLLY WILLIAMS (cont.) -- POLLY WILLIAMS, orphan of WM. WILLIAMS, deceased.

BEVERLY WILLIAMSON -- Book 4, Page 265 -- June 17, 1806; September 15, 1806. Witnesses: EDMD. LANIER, MOSES MARTIN, SUDAH (?) WILLIAMSON, EDMD. WILLIAMSON, EDMD. WILLIAMSON. ALEX. SALE, qualified; bondsmen: JAS. SHIELDS, BENJ. TALIAFERRO. Wife, LIZA--land bought of JOEL CASH--except 29 acres next to MUSE; right hand of ridge path; grand-daughter, CAROLINE WILLIAMSON SALE, when of age; my children or heirs--not to pay board and wife is to keep and support them. Executors: RO. RIVES, ALEX. SALE.

Book 4, Page 269 -- Inventory -- L990-4-6; BARTLETT CASH, JNO. SMITH, LEONARD HENLEY; January 19, 1807. Administrators Bond is page 436. Book 4, Page 509 -- Administrators Account -- from November 17, 1806; bond of EDMD. WILLIAMSON; LUDD WILLIAMSON; THOS. WILLIAMSON--overseer; ELIZ. WILLIAMSON; WM. BOURNE for tuition; POLLY and JNO. WILLIAMSON. June 15, 1818; CHAS. P. TALIAFERRO; D. SHEPHERD, JNO. SMITH.

ELIZ. WILLIAMSON -- Book 12, Page 254 -- Administrators Bond -- WILL S. (L) FAIR and RO. GRAY, March 19, 1850, for WILL S. (L) FAIR.

MARTHA WILLIAMSON -- Book 5, Page 519 -- Guardians Bond -- CORNL. SALE, SAML. CASH, ABRAM HIGGINBOTHAM, July 17, 1815, for CORNL. SALE as guardian of MARTHA WILLIAMSON, orphan of BEVERLY WILLIAMSON.

RACHEL WILLIAMSON -- Book 11, Page 222 -- Estate Commitment to Sheriff -- October, 1843; motion of JAS. F. TAYLOR; JAS. POWELL, Sheriff.

RO. WILLIAMSON -- Book 5, Page 518 -- Guardians Bond -- EDMD. T. COLEMAN and CORNL. SALE, July 15, 1815, for EDMD. T. COLEMAN as guardian of POLLY and RO. WILLIAMSON, orphans of BEVERLY WILLIAMSON. Book 5, Page 691 -- Guardians Bond -- BENJ. TALIAFERRO, JNO. ELLIS, ALEX. SALE, May 20, 1817, for BENJ. TALIAFERRO as guardian of same ward: RO.--above.

HUGH WILLOUGHBY (WILLABEE) -- Book 1, Page 136 -- July 20, 1768; June 5, 1769. Witnesses: THOS. BICKNELL, CHARITY and SARAH WILLABEE. Wife, AGNES--when youngest child is of age. Executors: JAS. NEAVEL, Gent.; WM. MARTIN, gunsmith. Produced by wife; NEVIL and MARTIN declined to serve; wife qualified. Bondsmen: CHAS. TATE and LAWRENCE SUDDOTH.

CAPT. MATT. WILLS -- Book 10, Page 35 -- Administrators Bond -- JNO. M. WILLS and JAS. MC DANIEL, JR.; July 16, 1838, for JNO. M. WILLS. Book 10, Page 82 -- Inventory -- CAPT. MATT. WILLS; $12.00; order of July, 1838; recorded: March 15, 1839; WM. J. SHELTON, EDWIN SHELTON, WILLIS M. REYNOLDS.

MATT. J. WILLS -- Book 8, Page 238 -- Guardians Bond -- ELIHU TANDY and W. P. SISSON, August 20, 1832, for ELIHU TANDY as guardian of MATTHEW J. WILLS, orphan of JNO. D. WILLS, deceased.

PATSY WILLS -- Book 10, Page 384 -- Estate Commitment to Sheriff -- May 18, 1841; motion of WILLIS M. REYNOLDS; NELSON CRAWFORD, Sheriff.

ZACH. WILLS -- Book 5, Page 464 -- Administrators Bond -- THOS. ALDRIDGE and MICAJAH CAMDEN, October 17, 1814, for THOS. ALDRIDGE.

WILSHER--see WILCHER data for this variation in spelling.

BENJ. WILSON -- Book 5, Page 483 -- Administrators Bond -- JER. WILSON and STERLING CLAIBORNE, January 16, 1815, for JER. WILSON.

CHAS. WILSON -- Book 9, Page 49 -- Administrators Bond -- JOS. PETTYJOHN and JNO. P. WILSON, February 16, 1835, for JOS. PETTYJOHN. Book 9, Page 103 -- Inventory -- February 25, 1835: $411.90¾; JAS, S. HIGGINBOTHAM, THOS. MILES, RO. PATRICK. Book 10, Page 176 -- Administrators Account -- from February 7, 1835; HUCKSTEP versus WILSON; proper items certified as to amounts for every

CHAS. WILSON (cont.) -- distributee, but nothing in account: WILKINS
WATSON versus JONATHAN A. STOUT; September 26, 1839.

HORACE WILSON -- Book 10, Page 190 -- HORACE WILSON versus JAS. S.
HIGGINBOTHAM, July 9, 1839; to JOS. PETTYJOHN, administrator of CHAS.
WILSON, deceased; RICH. WILSON, father of CHAS. WILSON, has since
died and Estate Commitment to Sheriff, JNO. COLEMAN.

JNO. P. WILSON -- Book 10, Page 194 -- Refunding Bond -- by JNO. P.
WILSON and RO. WALTON, October 24, 1839, to JOS. PETTYJOHN--facts set
forth as above, Book 10, Page 190.
Book 17, Page 21 -- October 1, 1862; February 20, 1865. Witnesses:
SAML. M. GARLAND, RO. A. PENDLETON, ADOLPHUS PETTICOLAS, JNO. D. GILBERT.
RICH. W. WILSON qualified. Brother, HORACE WILSON; nephew, RICH.
WALKER WALTON; nephews: WM. HENRY, JNO. JAS., WALKER WILSON and
FIELDEN B. TYLER; niece: SARAH ANN, ELIZA MARION, MARY CATH. and
MARIA LOUISA TYLER. Brother, RICH. WALKER WILSON, Amherst County
land; to administrate; Lynchburg bank account. Administrators Bond
is page 22.

NATHL. WILSON -- Book 6, Page 93 -- Administrators Bond -- CHAS. L.
BARRET and STERLING CLAIBORNE, September 20, 1819, for CHAS. L. BARRET.
Book 6, Page 110 -- Inventory -- $384.71; November 12, 1819. WM. HENS-
LEY, ISAAC RUCKER, JAS. CRAWFORD.
Book 6, Page 336 -- Administrators Account -- from November 1, 1819;
bond of RACHEL WILSON, July 18, 1822. NELSON CRAWFORD, SAML. HANS-
BROUGH, JOS. R. CARTER.
Book 6, Page 559 -- Administrators Account -- from 1822; JAS. S.
PENDLETON, JOS. STAPLES, JAS. ROSE; February 22, 1825.

RICH. WILSON -- Book 5, Page 203 -- Constables Bond -- January 31, 1803;
bondsman: BENJ. RUCKER.
Book 5, Page 231 -- Same, June 21, 183; bondsman: JNO. COLEMAN.
Book 10, Page 74 -- February 1839; Estate Commitment to Sheriff; motion
of DAVID S. GARLAND; JNO. COLEMAN, Sheriff.
Book 10, Page 81 -- Inventory -- $30.00; April 15, 1849; WM. D. MILES,
JAS. S. HIGGINBOTHAM, RO. PATRICK.

FRANCES L. WINGFIELD -- Book 15, Page 262 -- June 24, 1858; January 16,
1860. Witnesses: ALEX. MUNDY, PLEASANT S. DAWSON. February 20, 1860,
proved by MUNDY and held over and proved by P. S. BROWN. Wife of
NATHAN A. WINGFIELD; prenuptial contract of 1848 and recorded in
Amherst County; to MARY J. LANDRUM, wife of STEPHEN J. LANDRUM; to
FELICIANNA A., STEPHEN J. LANDRUM; graveyard where I live in trust.
Trustees: COL. WM. DILLARD, JNO. JAS. DILLARD, T. W. DILLARD; lands
to support my husband, but they may discontinue at any time. At
husband's death, to FELICIANNA A. LANDRUM and children and to STEPHEN
J. LANDRUM and wife, MARY, if any children. Executors: STEPHEN J.
and WM. J. LANDRUM.

GEO. M. WINGFIELD -- Book 16, Page 400 -- Minister's Bond -- September 21,
1863; bondsman: HENRY W. QUARLES; no denomination.

MARTHA WINGFIELD -- Book 8, Page 352 -- Administrators Bond -- RO.
WINGFIELD, THOS. WINGFIELD, JONAS PIERCE, ALEX. MUNDY, September 16,
1833, for RO. WINGFIELD. This is indexed for MARTHA, but is Administrators Bond for estate of NATHAN WINGFIELD.

MATT. WINGFIELD -- Book 1, Page 449 -- Administrators Bond -- THOS.
WINKFIELD (sic) and SAML. ALLEN, December 7, 1778, for THOS. WINKFIELD.
Book 1, Page 484 -- Inventory -- April 16, 1779: L70-1-6. GEO.
HILTON, SAML. ALLEN, JAS. PAMPLIN.

NANCY WINGFIELD -- Book 8, Page 285 -- Administrators Bond -- RO.
WINGFIELD, ALEX. MUNDY, THOS. WINGFIELD, JONAS PIERCE, December 17,
1832, for RO. WINGFIELD.
Book 8, Page 385 -- Inventory -- December 5, 1843; several slaves--
$3361.76. WILEY CAMPBELL, PETER F. CHRISTIAN, JOS. KYLE.

NATHAN WINGFIELD -- Book 4, Page 35 -- November 4, 1801; June 21, 1802.
Witnesses: WILEY CAMPBELL, WM. BOWMAN, PETER PIERCE. NANCY WINGFIELD
qualified. Bondsmen: JOS. DAVENPORT, JNO. WINGFIELD, Wife, ANN;
children: ELIZ. DAVENPORT, ANN, MARY, SARAH, THOS., WM., RO., JNO.
and PATSY WINGFIELD. Wife to administrate.
Book 4, Page 46 -- Inventory -- $1423.33, September 13, 1802. CHAS.
CHRISTIAN, JNO. CHRISTIAN B., JOEL CAMPBELL.
Book 4, Page 349 -- Administrators Bond
Book 13, Page 243 -- Minister's Bond -- November 21, 1853; bondsman:
WM. DILLARD; no denomination.

RO. WINGFIELD -- Book 7, Page 12 -- Constables Bond -- June 18, 1827;
bondsmen: JONAS PIERCE, THOS. STRANGE.
Book 15, Page 65 -- Administrators Bond -- ELIZ. C. WINGFIELD,
22 February 1859; bondsman: A. C. HARRISON.
Book 15, Page 160 -- Inventory -- April 11, 1859; slaves; no total;
JNO. S. TURNER, RO. N. PENDLETON, JOEL H. CAMPBELL.

SARAH WINGFIELD -- Book 14, Page 88 -- Administrators Bond -- CHAS. B.
REYNOLDS, EDWD. L., GEO. W. and JNO. W. PETTYJOHN, March 17, 1856, for
CHAS. R. REYNOLDS and EDWD. L. PETTYJOHN.
Book 14, Page 157 -- Sale -- March 20, 1856; SAML. WINGFIELD was
buyer; land and slaves sold. Returned: April 17, 1856; mansion
tract Winston tract; MERRITT tract--338; 17; 49; 89; 33; 66; 1; 13--
various acreages amounts of $1989.09 and $1144.22. E. J. HILL, JNO. L.
GOODWIN, N. B. MAGRUDER.
Book 14, Page 161 -- Inventory -- no total.

WM. F. WINGFIELD -- Book 9, Page 127 -- Guardians Bond -- NELSON D.
WINGFIELD and NICHL. GUTHRIE, October 19, 1835, for NELSON D.
WINGFIELD as guardian of his infant son, WM. F. WINGFIELD.

EDMD. WINSTON -- Book 8, Page 300 -- Sheriffs Bond -- February 18,
1833; Bondsmen: JNO. PENN, JNO. THOMPSON, JR., CORNL. SALE, JAS.
MC DANIEL, JR., WM. DILLARD, JAS. D. WATTS, JO PENN, SAML. M. GARLAND.
Book 8, Page 393 -- Same, February 18, 1834; bondsmen: RICH. L. ELLIS,
JNO. PENN, S. M. GARLAND, WM. M. WALKER, HENRY T. (?) PENDLETON, JAS.
MC DANIEL, JR., JO PENN, HOWELL L. BROWN (I conducted services for a
MRS. HOWELL BROWN on what is called in Virginia, Easter Monday, and
in her home is portrait of this HOWELL L. BROWN, done by some
Kentuckian.) This was first service in new Amherst Funeral Chapel.
B.F.D.

GEO. WISE -- Book 11, Page 78 -- Administrators Bond -- CATH. WISE
and ELIJAH L. CHRISTIAN, August 15, 1842, for CATH. WISE.

JANE WITT -- Book 3, Page 396 -- Administrators Bond -- JANE WITT and
JOS. ROBERTS, September 19, 1796, for JANE to administrate estate
of LITTLEBERRY WITT. Another of those index goofs.

JNO. WITT. Book 2, Page 34, -- December 4, 1781; March 4, 1782.
Witnesses: ABNER, DAVID and WM. WITT, JNO. REID, JNO. PUCKET. Seven
first sons born to my wife, LUCY; daughter, LUCY; sons, WM., LITTLE-
BERRY, GEO. and ELISHA.
Book 2, Page 35 -- Administrators Bond -- JNO. and ABNER WITT, March 4,
1782, for JNO. WITT.
Book 2, Page 77 -- Inventory -- September 2, 1782; ALEX. REID, JR.,
WM. BARNETT, SAML. LACKEY.

LITTLEBERRY WITT -- Book 3, Page 493 -- Inventory -- L128-5-0; JANE
WITT, administratrix--see above for bond; January 18, 1797. ALEX.
REID, ALEX. MC ALEXANDER, WM. BARNETT, RO. HANDY.

JNO. W. WOLDRIDGE -- Book 15, Page 46 -- Guardians Bond -- SIMS
BROCKMAN and R. H. DRUMMOND, November 15, 1858, for SIMS BROCKMAN
as guardian of JNO. W. WOLDRIDGE, orphan of HENRY WOLDRIDGE, deceased.

ALEX. WOOD -- Book 6, Page 190 -- Administrators Bond -- JNO. EWERS
and CABELL WOOD, October 16, 1820, for JNO. EWERS and CABELL WOOD.
Bondsman: ABRAM EWERS, RICH. WOOD.

ALEX. WOOD (cont.) -- Book 6, Page 191 -- Inventory -- $141.09½; JOS. DILLARD, YOUNG HAWKINGS, FARNCIS SLAUGHTER, November 11, 1820.
Book 9, Page 7 -- Administrators Account -- by CABELL WOOD from August 9, 1820; recorded: November 19, 1834.
Book 9, Page 20 -- Administrators Account -- by EWERS from December 24, 1824; JESSE and JUDITH WOODS mentioned. Recorded: August 2, 1834. MOSES PHILLIPS, JAS. D. WATTS, JNO. ALLCOCK.

CABELL WOOD -- Book 16, Page 119 -- Inventory -- Thursday, February 27, 1862: $413.75. WM. RIDGWAY, NICHL. WAUGH, RO. HENDERSON. Same is recorded again in Book 16, Page 225.
Book 16, Page 392 -- Administrators Account -- OLIVER C. WOOD, administrator from 2/17/1862; itmes for widow; cash lent on return from MANAPHIM (?); to BETSY WOOD; to widow--not named--one-third only and rest--one-fourth each to OLIVER C. WOOD, ELIZ. MITCHELL, JAS. WOOD and AMERA (?) ANN WOOD. Recorded: September 21, 1863.

JAS. WOOD -- Book 4, Page 299 -- Coroner -- March 22, 1796; bondsmen; JOS. SHELTON and JAS. BROOKS.
Book 5, Page 406 -- August 30, 1813; January 17, 1814. Witnesses: AJCOB TYREE, JOS. SEAY, PETER and TANDY RUTHERFORD. NANCY WOOD, ELIJAH STATON; JAS. WOOD qualified; bondsmen: LEROY CAMDEN, JACOB TYREE. Wife, NANCY; son, JACOB; children, if any, of son, JNO.; my other children: LUCY STATON, JEMIMAH DICKSON, KESURAH DICKSON, NANCY DICKSON, SAML., WM., JAS. and BETSY WOOD. Executors: wife, ELIJAH STATON, JAS. WOOD.
Book 5, Page 419 -- Inventory -- amount not clear--L2806016 or $'s? RO. WALKER, WM. DUNCAN, JOE (?) NOEL; order of January, 1814. Recorded: February 21, 1814.

JUDITH WOOD -- Book 9, Page 308 -- Refunding Bond -- by JUDITH WOOD and SARAH EWERS to THOS. EWERS, administrator of JNO. EWERS, December 30, 1835; JNO. gave by will one-sixth to JUDITH WOODS, subject to life estate of his widow. Widow and heirs agreed to division and JUDITH received $257.77.

SALLY WOOD -- Book 3, Page 41 -- Guardians Bond -- MARY WOOD and ABRAHAM and JNO. LEMASTER, June 4, 1787 for MARY WOOD as guardian of SALLY; MARY and JNO. WOOD, orphans of JNO. WOOD.

SARAH WOOD -- Book 11, Page 402 -- January 7, 1846; March 16, 1846. Witnesses: ALEX. S. WOOD, WILLIS A. WOODS, MOSES H. PHILLIPS. DAVID APPLING refused to serve. JESSE T. (F) WOOD qualified; bondsman: DAVID APPLING. Nephew, JESSE T. WOOD and his son, DANL. ABRAHAM. Executor: friend, DAVID APPLING.

SUSAN WOOD -- Book 8, Page 400 -- Administrators Bond -- LUDWELL L. DAWSON and GEO. MARKHAM, March 17, 1834, for LUDWELL L. DAWSON.

WM. WOOD -- Book 3, Page 40 -- Guardians Bond -- MARY WOOD and ABRAHAM LEMASTER, June 4, 1787, for MARY as guardian of WM. WOOD, orphan of JNO. WOOD.

CORNELIA J. WOODROOF -- Book 16, Page 200 -- Guardians Bond -- JNO. J. and ALFRED M. WOODROOF, January 19, 1863, for JNO. J. WOODROOF as guardian of CORNELIA J. WOODROOF; not parent set forth.

DAVID WOODROOF, SR. and JR. -- Book 5, Page 491 -- Administrators Bond -- JNO. MC DANIEL and JAS. MARR, March 20, 1815, for JNO. MC DANIEL--JR. here.
Book 5, Page 497 -- Inventory -- L991-17-6, April 17, 1815; ARMISTEAD RUCKER, JOS. HIGGINBOTHAM, JAS. PENDLETON, DAVID TINSLEY SR. and JR.
Book 5, Page 633 -- SR. here -- March 15, 1813; February 17, 1817. Witnesses: NELSON DAWSON, EDMD. L. WOODROOF, TOM HARRISON, RO. WALKER, JNO. MC DANIEL, THOS. CREWS qualified; bondsmen: REUBEN COLEMAN, AMBR. RUCKER. Wife, CLARY--where I live; my heirs--JNO. TAYLOR excepted; son, WM.--where I live on both sides of Lynch road; grandson, JNO. TAYLOR; daughters of my deceased son, THOS.: MATILDA and AMANDA; grandsons: JNO. TALIAFERRO and HILL. My heirs: JNO.,

DAVID WOODROOF, SR. and JR. (cont.) -- DAVID JR., JESSE, WM. WOODROOF
and NANCY HARRISON and fatherless children above cited. Executors:
son, DAVIS, JNO. MC DANIEL, RICH. POWELL SR., RO. WALKER, THOS. CREWS.
Book 5, Page 644 -- Inventory -- Seven legatees; JNO. T. HILL for
T. WOODROOF's children; DAVID WOODROOF's children; JESSE WOODROOF;
NANCY HARRISON; WM. and JAS. WOODROOF; JNO. WOODROOF. March 17, 1817.
DAVID TINSLEY, JNO. WARWICK, CHAS. MUNDY.
Book 6, Page 441 -- Administrators Account -- for JR's. estate. JNO.
MC DANIEL, administrator, from March 15, 1815. To JUDITH WOODROOF,
RICH POWELL for tuition, RICH. SR. mentioned, HENRY BROOKS for
tuition, to JAS. WOODROOF, cash from WM. WOODROOF: JESSE WOODROOF
for oats and nails, DRS. POWELL and GILBERT; December 30, 1822. JNO.
LONDON, WM. BOURNE, PHILIP LIVELY.
Book 4, Page 456 -- SR. -- Administrators Account -- by THOS. CREWS
from March 19, 1817; to MRS. WOODROOF; JESSE and WM. WOODROOF;
NICHL. HARRISON; JAS. WOODROOF; JNO. WOODROOF's children; DAVID
WOODROOF's children; THOS. WOODROOF; bond of WIATT WOODROOF; April 14,
1824. T. S. HOLLOWAY, CHAS. P. TALIAFERRO, WM. BOURNE.
Book 6, Page 693 -- Administrators Account -- by CREWS from April,
1819; to MRS. WOODROOF for 1817; NICHL. HARRISON--his share; JESSE
WOODROOF, JNO. T. HILL, THOS. WOODROOF, ADVID, JAS., WM, and JNO.
WOODROOF. July, 1826. WM. BOURNE, WILKINS WATSON, LINDSEY COLEMAN.

EDMUND WOODROOF (L initial) -- Book 9, Page 98 -- Refunding Bond --
November 9, 1833, by EDMUND L. WOODROOF and LINDSEY MC DANIEL,
administrator of JESSE WOODROOF. EDMUND has received his share of
estate from administrator.

EDWIN WOODROOF -- Book 14, Page 521 -- Refunding Bond -- by WM. S.
TURNER and JAS. W. PHILLIPS to CHAS. H. RUCKER, Sheriff and administrator of EDWIN WOODROOF, September 17, 1855; TURNER has received share
of estate.

ELIZA WOODROOF -- Book 8, Page 135 -- Guardians Bond -- WM. P. WOODROOF
and DABNEY P. GOOCH, 1 October 1831, for WM. P. WOODROOF as guardian
of ELIZA WOODROOF, orphan of WM. WOODROOF, deceased.

MRS. ELIZ. WOODROOF -- Book 15, Page 444 -- Inventory -- no total;
June 2, 1860; WM. and SAML. J. TURNER and illegible name.
Book 17, Page 72 -- indexed for EDWIN WOODROOF -- Administrators
Account -- by M. C. GOODWIN, Sheriff; January 21, 1861. A. C.
HARRISON, commissioner in WOODROOF versus WOODROOF; dalay because of
hostilities--created general suspension of business; amounts to
TIPTON H. WOODROOF; due by judgement versus M. H. WHARTON, administra-
tor of RO. TINSLEY; 49 acres sold; S. L. BURFORD for burial--$20.00.
Recorded: March 5, 1866. Some earlier items.
Book 6, Page 499 -- Administrators Bond -- WALTER B. BOSWELL and
DABNEY P. GOOCH, and HENRY L. DAVIES, November 16, 1824, for WALTER B.
BOSWELL.
Book 9, Page 98 -- Refunding Bond -- by ELIZ. WOODROOF; bondsman:
DANL. O. BASS; July 20, 1835, to LINDSEY MC DANIEL, administrator of
JESSE WOODROOF. MC DANIEL paid legatees, October 20, 1834--to ELIZ.
in own right and as guardian of her four children: HIRAM, MARTHA,
TIPTON and SUPRE (?) WOODROOF. This is indexed ELIZA.

GEO. N. WOODROOF -- Book 13, Page 226 -- Administrators Bond --
THOS. B. ROYSTER and ABSALOM HIGGINBOTHAM, August 13, 1853, for
THOS. B. ROYSTER.
Book 15, Page 611 -- Administrators Account -- from August 14, 1854;
to ELIZA. J. COBBS, widow; WM G. WINTER and wife; WM. J. LIMBACK and
wife; claim of RICH. E. WALKER versus estate as of March 24, 1840,
was rejected; WALKER is later called RICH. G.; June 23, 1860, signed
by ELIZA J. COBBS. RO. TINSLEY, attorney, filed Interogatus order,
order of February 20, 1860.

HARDIN WOODROOF (not indexed) -- Book 1, Page 13 -- Guardians
Account -- March 7, 1763, by JAS. NEVIL, guardian; from JNO. WOODROOF,
administrator of DAVID WOODROOF; HARDIN is DAVID's orphan.

HIRAM WOODROOF -- Book 8, Page 433 -- Guardians Bond -- ELIZ. WOODROOF, LINDSEY MC DANIEL, DANL. BASS, October 20, 1834, for ELIZ. WOODROOF as guardian of HIRAM, MARTHA JANE, TIPTON H. and SUPRE W. WOODROOF, orphans of JESSE WOODROOF, deceased.
Book B, Page 82 -- Estate Commitment to Sheriff -- March, 1860; motion of T. C. (?) WOODROOF; M. C. GOODWIN, Sheriff.

J. A. WOODROOF -- Book 16, Page 199 -- Guardians Bond -- JNO. J. and ALFRED M. WOODROOF, January 19, 1863, for JNO. J. WOODROOF as guardian of J. A. WOODROOF; no parent set forth.

CAPT. JESSE WOODROOF -- Book 7, Page 337 -- February 28, 1830; April 19, 1830. Witnesses: J. POWELL, JNO. H. WATTS, NATHAN D. RUCKER. LINDSEY MC DANIEL qualified. Bondsmen: JAS. OGDEN, SAML. WATTS, WM. MC DANIEL. My wife, four yountest children: HIRAM, MARTHA, TIPTON and SOIPRE (?)--where I live. My children: EDMD., SUSAN DAWSON, FRANCES DAWSON; my seven children and name of SUPRE. Executors: LINDSEY MC DANIEL and PROSSER POWELL.
Book 8 Page 11 -- Inventory -- of CAPT. JESSE WOODROOF; five horses claimed by HARDIN WOODROOF as property of HIRAM WOODROOF, his grandson--given by HARDIN to HIRAM: $1220.00, August 17, 1830; WM. MC DANIEL, WM. KNIGHT, EDMD. WINSTON.
Book 8, Page 246 -- Administrators Account -- from April 27, 1830; JNO. H. WATTS--his part of wheat; HORACE WILSON and DANL. B. DAILEY for tuition fees; MRS. WOODROOF; to THOS. J. BOYD (legatee?); NELSON S. WATTS--part of tobacco; account of PITT WOODROOF, August 23, 1832: A. B. DAVIES, JAS. P. GARLAND, EDMD. WINSTON.
Book 9, Page 51 -- Administrators Account -- from May 26, 1832; PITT WOODROOF for leather; ELIZ. WOODROOF, FRANCES L. DAWSON for making clothes for DICK and LEWIS; ELIJAH FLETCHER, assignee of EDMD. L. WOODROOF; BENJ. R. DAWSON, guardian of his children; February 16, 1835. EDMD. PENN and EDMD. WINSTON.

MARY WOODROOF -- Book 7, Page 249 -- Guardians Account -- LINDSEY MC DANIEL from July 24, 1822; cash sent you by HENRY; by PITT WOODROOF and W. WOODROOF, May 9, 1829. EDMD. WINSTON, J. P. GARLAND, WM. BOURNE.
Book 10, Page 90 -- Guardians Bond -- WM. P. WOODROOF and WILEY CAMPBELL, March 21, 1839, for WM. P. WOODROOF as guardian of MARY WOODROOF, orphan of WM. WOODROOF, deceased.

NANCY WOODROOF -- Book 5, Page 580 -- Guardians Bond -- SAML. HEISKELL, WM. WOODROOF, JAS. PENDLETON, BENJ. HARRISON, November 18, 1817, for SAML. HEISKELL as guardian of NANCY, POLLY, WINSTON and PITT WOODROOF, orphans of DAVID WOODROOF, deceased.

PITT WOODROOF -- Book 11, Page 179 -- Coroner, January 15, 1844; bondsmen: ZA DRUMMOND, SAML. HEISKELL.
Book 11, Page 219 -- Minister's Bond -- Methodist Episcopal Church; December 19, 1842; bondsmen: JNO. R. MC DANIEL, WINSTON WOODROOF.
Book 21, Page 408 -- Administrators Bond -- S. J. BAILEY and LENA M. WOODROOF, May 16, 1887, for S. J. BAILEY.
Book 22, Page 428 -- Administrators Account -- from February 21, 1887; recorded: June 16, 1890.

PITT WOODROOF, JR. -- Book 21, Page 457 -- Inventory -- $425; account versus P. P. and W. A. WOODROOF; S. J. BAILEY, administrator; C. J. TURNER, W. J. HOWL, CLIFTON B. WOODROOF; sold privately by administrator. Recorded: August 15, 1887.

POLLY WOODROOF -- Book 6, Page 224 -- Guardians Bond -- THOS. H. BASS and RICH. HARRISON, November 23, 1820, for THOS. H. BASS as guardian of POLLY WOODROOF, orphan of DAVID WOODROOF.
Book 6, Page 299 -- Guardians Bond -- LINDSEY MC DANIEL and SAML. HEISKELL, May 25, 1822, for LINDSEY MC DANIEL as guardian of same orphan.

RHODA WOODROOF -- Book 6, Page 342 -- DABNEY T. PHILLIPS and WM. SHELTON, December 16, 1822, for DABNEY T. PHILLIPS as guardian of RHODA WOODROOF, orphan of WM. WOODROOF.

RICH. WOODROOF -- Book 1, Page 1 -- Guardians Bond -- JAS. NEVIL and
JNO. REID, August 3, 1761, for JAS. NEVIL as guardian of RICH. and
HARDIN WOODROOF, orphans of DAVID WOODROOF.
Book 1, Page 14 -- Guardians Account -- cash of JNO. WOODROOF,
administrator of DAVID WOODROOF; March 7, 1763.
Book 2, Page 28 -- Guardians Account -- for HARDING - sic - and RICH.
WOODROOF; two bonds by WM. and LUCAS POWELL. L40-0-0; December 3, 1781.

SARAH ANN WOODROOF -- Book 6, Page 338 -- Guardians Bond -- DABNEY T.
PHILLIPS and WM. SHELTON, December 16, 1822, for DABNEY T. PHILLIPS
as guardian of SARAH ANN WOODROOF, orphan of WM. WOODROOF.

SETH WOODROOF -- Book 6, Page 341 -- Guardians Bond -- ARCHELAUS
REYNOLDS, JNO. D. WILLS, JAS. PETTIT, December 16, 1822, for
ARCHELAUS REYNOLDS as guardian of SETH WOODROOF, orphan of JESSE
WOODROOF.
Book 24, Page 134 -- August 2, 1875; August 10, 1875. Lynchburg;
recorded in Amherst County July 18, 1911. Witnesses: JNO. Q. ADAMS,
D. T. C. PETERS. Of Lynchburg; SAML. R. DAWSON, trustee for my half-
sister, MRS. FRANCES DAWSON; at her death, to educate DAWSON's
children. Friend and partner, WM. Q. SPENCE--ANDERSON debt due me
and in litigation in Superior Court of Appeals. My connection,
NANCY GEORGE PETTYJOHN; at death to her children--nieces, ELIZ. and
RHODA RIDGWAY; my connection, MRS. MARIA JOHN PETTYJOHN and children;
nephews: CHAS., JESSE and JOS. PETTYJOHN; cousin, JAS. C. FOWLER;
brother, SUPRA C. WOODROOF. Two quarry lots in Amherst County near
CREWS--three acres--to ISHAM and JNO. HENRY WADDELL; four acres of
superior land in Amherst County near Lynchburg--formerly that of
O'BRIAN; Lynchburg property; island in James. Executors: WM. Q.
SPENCE and JNO. W. DANIEL--residue to them. Young friend, JNO. W.
GEEINER--$50 extra per month for close attention to business until
banking business of WOODROOF and SPENCE closes business.

SOPHIA WOODROOF -- Book B, Page 46 -- Administrators Bond -- WM. P.
WOODROOF and SAML. M. GARLAND, 22 August 1853, for WM. P. WOODROOF.

THOS. WOODROOF -- Book 5, Page 9 -- Inventory -- April 2, 1810;
L269-9-6; THOS. CREWS, WM. MC DANIEL, HENRY BROWN.
Book 5, Page 14 -- Administrators Bond -- DAVID WOODROOF, JNO.
MC DANIEL, NICHL. HARRISON, February 19, 1810, for DAVID WOODROOF.
Book 5, Page 685 -- Administrators Account -- to SARAH ALLEN--legatee?;
JNO. LONDON; THOS. CREWS; CHAS. MONDAY, commissioner. March 15,
1817. This is followed by one: amounts to MRS. WOODROOF; CAPT. D.
WOODROOF's account; WM. and JAS. WOODROOF's names are seen; THOS.
LANDRUM for his son, NELSON; paid to JNO. MC DANIEL.

WM. WOODROOF -- Book 6, Page 147 -- Order at home in county, June 19,
1820; bondsman: SAML. HEISKELL.
Book 6, Page 327 -- Inventory -- no total; JNO. MC DANIEL, WM.
MC DANIEL, WM. R. ROANE, August 21, 1822.
Book 10, Page 203 -- Administrators Bond -- WM. H. KNIGHT, RO. L.
COLEMAN, February 17, 1840, for WM. H. KNIGHT.
Book 10, Page 254 -- Administrators Account -- by CHAS. MUNDY, late
sheriff from 1826; slave sold under decree, Lynchburg Chancery. A. B.
and HENRY L. DAVIES; recorded: August 18, 1840.

WM. P. WOODROOF -- Book 11, Page 102 -- Refunding Bond -- WM. P.
WOODROOF and ALEX. M. CAMPBELL, December 21, 1842, to LEWIS S.
CAMPBELL, administrator of WILEY CAMPBELL; division under will at
end of year of testator's death. WOODROOF has received slaves in
right of wife.
Book 19, Page 274 -- Administrators Bond -- JOEL H. CAMPBELL and
W. ALEX. WOODROOF, August 20, 1877, for JOEL H. CAMPBELL.
Book 19, Page 345 -- Inventory -- RO. BETHEL, B. W. CHILDRESS, RICH.
WINGFIELD, August 21, 1877: $188.60; recorded: March 8, 1878; sale
$180.60; JNO., DAVIE and JOEL F. WOODROOF buyers; plus farm items at
$123.45. Recorded: April 22, 1878.
Book 19, Page 451 -- Administrators Account -- from August 20, 1877;
December 8, 1877; recorded: June 18, 1879.

WILLIE P. WOODROOF -- Book 16, Page 199 -- Guardians Bond -- JNO. J.
and ALFRED M. WOODROOF, January 19, 1863, for JNO. J. WOODROOF as
guardian of WILLIE P. WOODROOF; no parent set forth.

WINSTON WOODROOF -- Book 6, Page 183 -- Guardians Bond -- JNO.
MC DANIEL and THOS. CREWS, November 20, 1820, for JNO. MC DANIEL as
guardian of WINSTON and PITT WOODROOF, orphans of DAVID WOODROOF,
deceased.

WYATT WOODROOF -- Book 3, Page 441 -- Inventory -- L196-16-10½,
September 2, 1797; AMBR. and ISAAC RUCKER, JNO. WIATT.
Book 4, Page 313 -- Administrators Bond -- DOROTHA WOODROOF, W. LEE
HARRIS, JNO. HARRIS and WM. H. DIGGES, July 17, 1797, for DOROTHA
WOODROTHA WOODROOF.

BETSY WOODS -- Book 4, Page 421 -- Guardians Bond -- EDWD. PAGE and
JOS. SHELTON, March 18, 1805, for EDWD. PAGE as guardian of BETSY
WOODS, orphan of RICH. WOODS.
Book 6, Page 12 and 38 -- are indexed for her, too, but are for
BETSY WARE.

JAS. WOODS -- Book 2, Page 13 -- April 12, 1781; June 4, 1781.
Witnesses: JNO. OGLESBY, JAS. OGLESBY JR., JESSE OGLESBY, JAS. MC LAIN.
Planter; wife, BARBARA; grandson, JAS. WOODS--150 acres where I live;
next to 200 acres higher up the river; 100 acres next to where SAML.
WOODS, deceased, lived; 400 acres in Albemarle next to HUGH ALEXANDER
Mill tract; my other grandchildren: WM. MARY, MARGARET, BARBARA,
ELIZ. and JANE WOODS. If grandson, JAS., dies before 21 or marriage.
Executors: friends, WM. SIMPSON SR. and grandson, JAS. WOODS.
Book 2, Page 15 -- Administrators Bond -- JAS. WOODS, MICHL. MC NEELY,
DAVID SHELTON, WM. HARRIS, JNO. POPE, MATT. HARRIS, JOS. ROBERTS on
probate date for JAS. WOODS.

RICH. WOODS -- Book 4, Page 249 -- Tobacco Inspector -- Camden's
Warehouse, February 15, 1802; bondsman: JNO. CHRISTIAN, Buffaloe.
Book 7, Page 32 -- Administrators Bond -- JESSE and CABELL WOOD,
August 20, 1829, for JESSE WOOD.

SAML. WOODS -- Book 2, Page 5 -- January 8, 1781; February 5, 1781.
Witnesses: JAS. BROOKS, ALEX. REID, JR., WM. SMALL, JNO. DAVIS, JOS.
SMITH. Wife, SARAH, where I live; also tract bought of THOS. PATTON
on Rockfish; eldest son, JAS.--350 acres in Albemarle and next to
HENRY KERR and ALEX. FRETWELL; son, WM.--land next to Rockfish Meeting
House and formerly that of WM. PATTON and WM. CROW; my mill and
Quarter--formerly that of RO. and EDWD. STEPHENSON, DAVID CLARK, WM.
CLARK and LANGSDON DEPRIEST--to be newly built; when WM. is of age;
education of my three youngest daughters; my five daughters when of
age or married; son, JAS., has estate left him by his grandfather
and me; executors: GABL. PENN and FRANCIS MERIWETHER, JAS. BROOKS,
JAS. WOODS JR., WM. WOODS. "Leave JANE, HANNAH, ELIZ. and WM. DUNNON"
until of age; if my wife has a child.
Book 2, Page 8 -- Administrators Bond -- JAS. BROOKS, ALEX. REID, JR.,
JNO. LOVING, WM. HARRIS, JOS. HIGGINBOTHAM MORRISON, WM. BARNETT, JOS.
ROBERTS, SAML. LACKEY, ALEX. MILLER, February 5, 1781, for JAS. BROOKS.
Book 2, Page 105 -- Inventory -- MICHL. MC NEELY, WM. BARNETT, THOS.
MORRISON, JR.; very long; no total; June 2, 1783.
Book 5, Page 108 -- Administrators Account -- from 1781; to WM., MISS
POLLY, JAS. WOODS; Albemarle sheriff; board for youngest children;
WM. WOODS' militia expenses; Augusta Clerk; MISS PEGGY WOODS; COL.
JNO. WOODS; board of MISS POLLY and PEGGY; account of RICH. WOODS; to
FREDERICKSBURG for iron for the mill; washing for three youngest
children, February 1783. JNO. SHIELDS for schooling three youngest
girls; callico for MISS BARBARA and JENNY; Bedford Clerk; rent of
Meeting House place, 1783; bond of WM. WOODS, 1783; books, etc.;
WM. WOOD, JR.; JAS. WOODS for MISS POLLY and PEGGY; land on Long
Island of Holston--BRADLEY's--sold to WM. COCKE and ELISHA WALKER;
one tract called RICHARD's Claim; FRANCIS MONTGOMERY for SMITH Wood
Mill; shoe buckles for youngest girls; bibles for MISS BARBARA and
JANE; to JAS. WOODS SR.; MISS BETSY; rent of PATTEN's plantation;

SAML. WOODS (cont.) -- legacy of wife; tuition for three youngest
girls; Albemarle taxes; house on CLACK's place; interesting rent
items for 1783 and 1784; TROTTER's executors; RICH. WOODS; board of
three youngest girls at dancing school; their board for 1781; SAML.
GAY for tuition in 1785; The Merchant Mill; Executor versus estate
of LUKE HAMILTON; shoes for BARBARA and JENNY; board for them and
BETSY; 100 acres in Augusta bought by WATERSON in 1786; JAS. WOODS
for his sisters 1786; JAS. WOODS for shoe leather for girls; bridles
for BARBARA and JANE; mill and still rent; JNO. DAVENPORT rented
place called CLAUD's, 1787; shoes for PEGGY; sundries for both girls;
Long Island of Holston which J. WOODS got; his trip to Holston;
clerk of Sullivan; Buckingham ticket; GEO. MARTIN for cow for wife,
BARBARA, 1797; JOS. MONTGOMERY for clothes for his wife; North Carolina
trip relative to Long Island and Holston; data in hands of MAJOR
WALTON by decedent; to western lands--900 miles; appearance before
North Carolina legislature "seting" at Hill's--1792; several trips
and reference to dispute over lands; had to buy two riding horses;
Tennessee land--1500 acres which I had located; grants; ½ to COL.
KING for his trouble; 750 acres to heirs; a British debt and trip to
Manchester; Bedford judgement; sale: L7007-16-0, April 5, 1781,
November 13, 1782; credits taken from testator's books--p. 156--long
and many names; dispute between administrator and heirs--too much for
building mill and not enough allowed for tobacco. Till 1796, but
no month or day. JNO. ROSE, NATHAN CRAWFORD, HUDSON MARTIN.

ANN WOODSON -- Book 11, Page 180 -- Guardians Bond -- WASH. KNIGHT
and LEWIS MAYS, January 15, 1844, for WASH. KNIGHT as guardian of
ANN WOODSON, orphan of E. WOODSON, deceased.

CHAS. WOODSON -- Book 9, Page 125 -- Estate Commitment to Sheriff --
September 21, 1835; motion of STEPHEN DAVIDSON; Sheriff: THOS. N.
EUBANK.

JUDITH F. WOODSON -- Book 14, Page 157 -- April 14, 1856; Monday,
June 18, 1856. Witnesses: JAS. POWELL, ZACH BOWLES, WM. P. WOODROOF.
PETER F. and DRURY CHRISTIAN qualified--where I live on river low
ground--PRYOR's line where it struck river; NIXON's road. Brother,
PETER CHRISTIAN; tract for children of deceased brother, JAS. G.
CHRISTIAN; brother, DRURY CHRISTIAN's children; MARY ELIZ.--daughter
of JAS. G. CHRISTIAN--if no issue; his other children; JUDITH ANN,
daughter of DRURY CHRISTIAN--if no issue--his other children; brother,
WALTER L. CHRISTIAN; executors: WALTER L., PETER F. and DRURY
CHRISTIAN.
Book 14, Page 142 -- Administrators Bond -- see will.
Book 14, Page 242 -- Inventory -- $7626.18; October 11, 1856. WM. P.
WOODROOF, ZACH BOWLES, JAS. W. DILLARD.

JUNIUS WOODSON (so indexed, but it is LINIAS) -- Book 6, Page 479 --
Guardians Bond -- SARAH WOODSON, WM. I. ISBELL, CHRISTOPHER ISBELL,
August 26, 1824, for SARAH WOODSON as guardian of LINIAS, ELIZA ANN
and JNO. WOODSON, orphans of JNO. WOODSON, deceased.

W. A. WOODSON -- Book 16, Page 424 -- Baptist Minister's Bond --
January 18, 1864; bondsman: ZACH D. TINSLEY.

PETER WOODWARD -- Book 10, Page 251 -- Administrators Bond -- August 19,
1840: DAVID S. and SAML. M. GARLAND for DAVID S. GARLAND.

THOS. WOODY -- Book 2, Page 174 -- Administrators Bond -- MARY WOODY
and WM. WRIGHT JR., June 7, 1784, for MARY WOODY.
Book 2, Page 217 -- Inventory -- no total; RO. and JAS. WRIGHT, CHAS.
STATHAM; March 7, 1785.

ELLIOTT WORTHAM -- Book 7, Page 242 -- Constables Bond -- June 15,
1829; bondsmen: GEO. BURKS and JAS. DAVIS.
Book 8, Page 166 -- Same, February 20, 1832; bondsmen: JAS. and
CHAS. L. DAVIS.
Book 8, Page 177 -- Same, June 17, 1833; bondsmen: JAS. DAVIS,
RICH. L. ELLIS.

FRANCES D. WORTHAM -- Book 13, Page 447 -- Guardians Bond -- JNO. D. DAVIS and MILTON M. PARKS, January 15, 1855, for JNO. D. DAVIS as guardian of FANNY D. WORTHAM, orphan of NANCY B. WORTHAM, deceased.

RICH. B. WORTHAM -- Book 13, Page 448 -- Guardians Bond -- Same parties and date as above for JD as guardian of RICH. B. WORTHAM, orphan of NANCY B. WORTHAM.

AUGUSTINE WRIGHT -- Book 1, Page 360 -- Administrators Bond -- ALCEY WRIGHT, MOSES HUGHES, JNO. BALL, JNO. EDMONDS, July 7, 1777, for ALCEY WRIGHT.
Book 1, Page 378 -- Inventory -- L410-0-9; August 10, 1777; WM. SPENCER, JOS. DILLARD, RICH. ALCOCK.
Book 3, Page 504 -- so indexed as division, but nothing thereon.

BARTHOLOMEW WRIGHT -- Book 23, Page 344 -- Administrators Bond -- JOS. S. CLAVIN and SARAH C. CLAVIN, February 20, 1893, for JOS. S. CLAVIN.

BENJ. WRIGHT -- Book 3, Page 454 -- March 20, 1799; October 21, 1799. Witnesses: GEO. GILLESPIE, JR., LEWIS and ALEX. GILLESPIE. Eighty acres where I live to son, JESSE; my wife, ELIZ.; my children: FEEBE GOODE, MOSES WRIGHT, ELIZ. CAMDEN, ONEY CAMDEN, MARTHA HOUCHINS, SUSANNAH MASSEY, SALLY CAMPBELL, MATILDA CASH, JESSE WRIGHT--five shares only to daughter, MARY HOUCHIN. Executors: JNO. MASSEY, JESSE WRIGHT.
Book 3, Page 574 -- Inventory -- L281-15-6; February 17, 1800; NOTLEY MADDOX, JNO. CAMPBELL, GEO. GILLESPIE.
Book 4, Page 23 -- Administrators Account -- by JESSE WRIGHT October 19, 1801. JOEL FRANKLIN, BARTLETT and HOWARD CASH, committee.
Book 4, Page 286 -- Administrators Bond -- JNO. MASSIE, JESSE WRIGHT, GEO. CAMPBELL, JNO. CAMDEN, October 21, 1799, for first two.

BETSY WRIGHT -- Book 6, Page 603 -- Guardians Bond -- JNO. VIA and LEWIS LAYNE, June 20, 1825, for JNO. VIA as guardian of BETSY WRIGHT, over 14, orphan of DOCIA WRIGHT.

FRANCIS WRIGHT -- Book 1, Page 110 -- December 9, 1766; September 7, 1767. Witnesses: DAVID WOODROOF, JNO. WATERS, ANNA WATERS. Oldest son, BENJ.; daughter, ANNER WATTERS; daughter, ELIZ. MORRIS; daughter, MARY SHELTON; son, THOS.; sons, JOHN and ISAAC. Executors: sons, ISAAC and JNO.--they qualified; bondsman: DAVID WOODROOF; JOB and PETER CARTER.
Book 1, Page 120 -- Inventory -- September 7, 1767: L168-0-0; RICH. SHELTON, DAVID WOODROOF, RICH. POWELL. Recorded: May 2, 1768.

ISAAC WRIGHT -- Book 4, Page 465 -- February 17, 1803; September 21, 1807. Witnesses: EDWARD CARTER, CHAS. CRAWFORD, THOS. N. EUBANK, JNO. EUBANK. January 18, 1808, ABRAM CARTER qualified; bondsman: GODFREY TOLER. Wife, SUSANNAH--100 acres and house; daughters: HANNAH and MOLLY BROWN--six shillings to MOLLY as her mother has had her legacy before; daughters: SUSANNAH NOWLIN and NANCY CARTER; sons, JESSE, ISAAC, MORRIS, ISAAC (named twice), ELLIS, BENNETT, JNO. and NELSON. Executors: RICH. L. ELLIS, JNO. ELLIS, NELSON CRAWFORD, THOS. H. ELLIS, JNO. SHELTON. Page 496 Administrators Bond--see above.
Book 4, Page 515 -- Inventory -- February 29, 1808 L438-3-6; JNO. RICHESON, WM. JOPLING, EDMD. GOODRICH. Note: poor writing and son, BENNETT, above could be BENJ.
Book 5, Page 444 -- from August, 1808; cash to JNO. E. WRIGHT; bond of SUSANNAH BECKLEY; cash to MARIA WRIGHT; JESSE WRIGHT; legacy to SUSANNAH NOWLIN; saddle for SUSANNAH WRIGHT; MRS. WRIGHT for dower lands; MARINE (?) WRIGHT. October 5, 1813. PETER P. THORNTON, NELSON CRAWFORD, THOS. N. EUBANK, GODFREY TOLER. Land sold to WM. PRYOR.

JESSE K. WRIGHT -- Book 14, Page 497 -- Committee report by RO. H. PROFFITT, from December 31, 1852; board and washing for one year; land money; JESSE K. WRIGHT, deceased. Recorded: November 16, 1857.

JORDAN WRIGHT -- Book 4, Page 151 -- Inventory -- L459-12-0; June 26, 1804; JOS. LOVING, SAML. EDMUNDS JR., ACHILLES WRIGHT, SAML. EDMUNDS SR.
Book 4, Page 383 -- Administrators Bond -- LEVINA WRIGHT and CHAS. BURKS, June 19, 1804, for LEVINA WRIGHT.

NELSON WRIGHT -- Book 4, Page 491 -- Guardians Bond -- ABRAM CARTER and WM. WARE, December 21, 1807, for ABRAM CARTER as guardian of NELSON WRIGHT, orphan of ISAAC WRIGHT, deceased.

RHODA WRIGHT -- Book 10, Page 49 -- Guardians Bond -- JAS. CAMPBELL, JNO. W. BROADDUS, GEO. CAMPBELL, September 17, 1838, for JAS. CAMPBELL as guardian of RHODA WRIGHT, orphan of BENJ. WRIGHT.

RICH. WRIGHT -- Book 4, Page 397 -- Administrators Bond -- PARMENAS WRIGHT and GEO. MURPHY, February 18, 1805, for PARMENAS WRIGHT.

RICH. JORDAN WRIGHT -- Book 6, Page 77 -- Guardians Bond -- CHAS. M. BURKS and GEO. BURKS, June 15, 1819, for CHAS. M. BURKS as guardian of RICH. JORDAN WRIGHT; no parent set forth.

SHELTON H. WRIGHT -- Book 16, Page 175 -- Administrators Bond -- JAS. M. GANNAWAY, LAWSON CAMPBELL, RO. A. COGHILL, October 20, 1862, for JAS. M. GANNAWAY.
Book 16, Page 213 -- Inventory -- November 26, 1862: $2409. SIMS BROCKMAN, JNO. S. and WIATT TUCKER.
Book 18, Page 117 -- Administrators Account -- from September 27, 1862; paid A. J. WRIGHT by WM. H. WRIGHT. Recorded: Monday, September 18, 1871.

WALKER WRIGHT -- Book 23, Page 154 -- Guardians Bond -- Same men and date for R. C. CHILDRESS as guardian of WALKER WRIGHT, infant daughter of BETTIE WRIGHT, deceased.

WM. WRIGHT -- Book 12, Page 438 -- Administrators Bond -- JAS. D. WATTS and WM. DILLARD, September 15, 1851, for JAS. D. WATTS.
Book 12, Page 461 -- Inventory -- September, 1851, order: $3508.23. DAVID APPLING, MOSES PHILLIPS, JNO. W. JENNINGS; also notes due of $3608.48. Recorded: October 20, 1851.
Book 12, Page 474 -- February 27, 1851; September 15, 1851. Witnesses: JAS. D. WATTS, DAVID APPLING. Daughter, MARY J. PURVIS; daughter, ELIZA W. PROFFITT; daughter, MILDRED T. GRIFFIN; sons, WM. A., JESSE K.--if he married; MARY J.--credit of sum when she went to western country. Executors: son, WM. A., and son-in-law, GEO. M. PURVIS and son-in-law, RO. H. PROFFITT.
Book 13, Page 125 -- Administrators Account -- December 14, 1852; Sale; JESSE K. WRIGHT was buyer; slaves divided to GEO. M. PURVIS and wife, MARYJ.; RO. H. PROFFITT and wife, ELIZA; JNO. A. GRIFFIN and wife, MILDRED T.; WM. A. and JESSE K. WRIGHT (PROFFITT as trustee for JESSE K.). Recorded: May 19, 1853.

-Y-

NELLY YANCEY -- Book 10, Page 388 -- Administrators Bond -- THOS. BARBOUR and HOWARD MARTIN, September 20, 1841, for THOS. BARBOUR.

GEO. WHITEFIELD YOUNG -- Book 6, Page 39 -- Guardians Bond -- PHILIP LIVELY, STERLING CLAIBORNE, JAS. W. SMITH, November 16, 1818, for guardian (not specified) of GEO. W. YOUNG, orphan of JNO. YOUNG, deceased.
Book 6, Page 439 -- Guardians Bond -- CHAS. L. BARRET, LYNE S. TALIAFERRO, BENJ. B. TALIAFERRO, December 16, 1822, for CHAS. L. BARRET as guardian of same ward. See JNO. YOUNG for middle name of orphan.

JAS. YOUNG -- Book 1, Page 205 -- Administrators Bond -- SAML. WOODS, JNO. HARVIE, April 6, 1772, for SAML. WOODS.

JAS. YOUNG (cont.) -- Book 1, Page 207 -- Inventory -- May 4, 1772; L7-7-0; WM. SMITH, THOS. GRIFFIN, JAS. STEVENS.

JNO. YOUNG -- Book 5, Page 649 -- Wife, NANCY; my five children: JNO. WICKLIFF YOUNG, SARAH HURT (HUNT?) YOUNG, SUSANNAH YOUNG who married PHILIP LIVELY; HIRAM YOUNG; and GEO. WHITEFIELD YOUNG--if any dies without issue and when of age. Administrators: three friends, BENJ. TALIAFERRO, LEWIS HENRY DUNCAN and WM DUNCAN. April 15, 1817; May 20, 1817. Witnesses: CHAS. P. TALIAFERRO, LYNE S. TALIA-FERRO, JAS. F. TALIAFERRO.
Book 5, Page 690 -- Administrators Bond -- WM. DUNCAN, BENJ. TALIA-FERRO, GEO. TUCKER, May 20, 1817, for WM. DUNCAN.
Book 6, Page 486 (indexed incorrectly as Book B, Page 486; 494) -- Administrators Account -- and BENJ. TALIAFERRO gives it from May 3, 1817; recorded September 24, 1824. JNO. B. DUNCAN, CORNL. SALE, DABNEY SANDIDGE; closing of blacksmith shop.
Book 6, Page 494 -- Administrators Account -- by DUNCAN--JNO. W. YOUNG for funeral and advance to WM. YOUNG. Note: I have seen data somewh-re--perhaps in GEO. BRAXTON TAYLOR's Va. Baptists--stating that JNO. W. YOUNG was a prominent Baptist minister in Amherst County. B.D.

JNO. W. YOUNG -- Book 5, Page 630 -- Constables Bond -- January 20, 1817; bondsman: CHAS. P. TALIAFERRO for two years.
Book 5, Page 697 -- Same men to GOV. JAS. P. PRESTON, June 17, 1817; constables bond.

SALLY YOUNG -- Book 6, Page 41 -- Guardians Bond -- WM. DUNVAN and STERLING CLAIBORNE, and JAS. W. SMITH, November 16, 1818, for WM. DUNVAN as guardian of SALLY and HIRAM YOUNG, orphans of JNO. YOUNG.

BELKNAP, Edward 88
BELOW, Hannah 170
  Len 238
BELLOW, Easter 238
BELL, Ann E. 13
  Bolling 13,14
  Chas. 13,389
  Chas. Christian 13
  D. 13
  David 13
  Delilah S. 13
  Drury 13,14,66,144,176,
  177,272,289,385
  Eliz. 14
  Francis H. 330
  Frank Lee 13
  George 13
  G. H. 14
  Geo. H. 13,14
  Hannah 13
  Henry 8,13,64,65,66,68,
  107,381
  Henry D. 13
  Henry Duke 13
  H. M. 351
  Jno. 194
  Jno. P. 13
  Mary Duke 13
  Mary V. 13
  Patrick M. 13
  P. B. 14
  Robt. 13
  Sally 14
  Sally Ware 13
  Saml. 13
  Samuel 13
  Sarah 13
  Sophia 14
  Stiley 14
  Stilla W. 14
  S. W. 14
  Thos. 303,389
  Thos. G. 325
  Wm. F. 13
  Wm. L. (S.) 14
BENAGH, J. 301
BENG, M. L. 145
BENNET, Jas. 323,324,356,
  358,360
BENNETT, Betsy 31
  Calvin 14,358,359
  Calvin F. 14,19,298,359,
  360
  C. F. 331
  Charlotte Ann 14
  Eliz. 14
  Geo. M. T. 14
  James 14,31
  James M. 14
  Jas. 14,31
  Jno. 107
  Lucy 359
  Sarah E. 14
  Rich. 195,196
BERASFORD, John 11
BERKLEY, Mrs. 243
BERKELEY, R. C. 243
BERNARD, Jenny 146
BENARD, Jinney 145
BERNARD, Mary 146
BERRFORD,...11
  Mary 11
BERROW, Danl. 276
BERRY, Albert 252
  Asa 282
  Harriet J. 159
  Harriet Jane 159
  Marville L. 207
  M. L. 29,291
  Taylor 14,33,39,73,90,
  132,158,222,244,298,318,
  329,335,351,361,367,385
BETHEL, Alcey 28

BETHEL cont'd:
  Amanda C. 14
  Cornelia 15
  Frances 14
  Hudson M. 14
  Jane 14
  Jno. 123
  Joel 14,15,48,50,131,161,
  226,287,302,327,382
  John 28
  Joshua S. 14
  Mary B. 14
  Mildred 14,15,49
  Ro. 399
  Robert 15
  Robt. 15
  Robt. M. 14
  Ro. M. 302
  Thos. H. 15
  Thos. Howard 14
  William 15
  W. J. 251
  Wm. J. 14
BETTS, Edwd. C. 50
BEVERLY, Chas. 15
  James 15
  Saml. 15
BEVLEY, Elix. 15
  Matterson 15
BEYUS, Jas. 362
BIAS,...292
  Cornelius 38
  James 38
  Jas. 293
  Joel 38
  Larkin 118
BIBEY, Edmund 178
BIBB, Albert 301
  Arthur 290
  Baxter H. 16
  Benj. B. 15,113,244
  Chas. 15
  Chas. M. 16
  Cyrus T. 16
  Eliz. 15,228
  Elizabeth L. 15
  Harriet E. 15
  Henry 16
  J. 16
  James 15,16
  James M. 16
  Jas. 16,209
  Jas. Sr. 149
  Jno. 16,87,131,195
  John 15,16
  J. R. 243
  Josephine 290
  Joshua 16
  Leroy 71
  Lucy Jane 15,16
  Margaret 15
  Martin 15,16,36,113,194
  Martin J. 15
  Martin T. 15
  Mary Ellen 15
  Nancy 15,113
  Nancy C. 15
  Nannie L. 365
  Nannie Leonard 364
  Peggy 15
  Perlina F. 16
  Polly 173
  R. C. 15,117,291
  Ro. B. 16
  Ro. C. 290,291
  Robert Bennett 15
  Robert C. 16
  Ro. C. 15,16,32,113,222
  Russell 113
  Sally 15
  Sarah 16
  Temperance 16
  Thos. 15,16,87,114,147

BIBB cont'd:
  Thomas 15,16
  Tos. 338
  W. C. 16
  William 15,16
  Wm. 15,16,221,295,315,
  352,378
  Wm. C. 16
  Wm. H. 15,16,291
BICKNALL, Anna 16
  James 16
  John 16
  Mary Ann 16
  Micajah 16
  Ruth 16
  Saml. 16
  Thos. 16
  William 16
  Wm. Jr. 16
BICKNELL, Maryan 15
  Thos. 393
BIGG, Gallatin M. 177
BILLY,...134
BINGHAM, W. G. H. 321
BISHNELL, Wm. 8
BISHOP, Luman 228
BITTS, Edwd. C. 50
BLACK, Joseph Lindsey 17
  Madison 228
BLACKMORE, John 17
BLACKWOOD, D. 374
BLAIN, Alex 150
  Geo. 245,254
  Geo. Jr. 322
  Rachel 17
BLAINE, Ephraim 251,335
  Geo. 17
  Jane 252
BLAIR,...138
  Alex 18
  Alexander F. 17
  Alex. C. 17
  Alex F. 17,18
  Allen 17,18,19,28,123,
  204,210,290,355,388
  Ann S. 19
  Eliz. 19
  Emily F. 17
  F. 17,91
  F. A. 91,122
  Fa. A. 349
  Francis A. 17,18,91,122,
  336,370
  Francis Allen 17
  Geo. A. 17,18,
  Gilla 17
  James 17
  James Colbard 19
  J. 211
  Jno. S. 17,18,19,153
  John S. 17,196
  J. S. 17
  Joseph 19
  Lucinda 18
  Lycurgus 18
  Mary 19
  Mary A. 17
  Mary Ann 17,18,19
  Mildred 19
  Nancy 18,211
  Polly 17,18
  Sophronia 18
  W. 211
  William 17,18
  William H. 18
  Winston 17,196
  Winston S. 18
  Wm. 19,355
  Wm. H. 17,18,211
BLAKE, B. 143
BLAKEMORE,...17
BLAKEY, Reuben 383
BLAND, Abell 19

BRIAR, Green 75
BRIDGE,...67
  Patsy W. 372
BRIDGLAND, Alex 62
BRIDGWATER, Chas. 230
  Hannah 199
  Jonathan 24
  Nathaniel 24
  Nathl. 98
  Saml. 24,71,158,199
  William 24,389
  Wm. 24
BRIGHTWELL, Chas. 65
BRINKHOLDER & BAILEY 252
BROADUS, Ellen T. 202
  Jno. W. 69
BROADDUS. Jno. 205
  E. 345
  E. E. 345
  Eliz. 345
  Jno. M. 48,345
  Jno. W. 4,46,49,58,153,
  155,160,161,164,165,202,
  205,210,228,231,261,335,
  344,345,350,351,403
  J. W. 164,165,319
  Wm. H. 194
BROCKMAN, E. 164
  Elijah 25,319
  Elizabeth 25
  F. D. 25
  Florence 25
  Florence A. 277
  Flouence 25
  Frances 25
  Jno. 53,75,127
  John 25
  Margaret 25
  Matilda 25
  R. Sims 318
  Sims 25,226,227,274,316,
  317,395,403
  W. A. 25,339
  William 25
  Willis A. 277
  Wm. 25
BROKENBROUGH, Austin 143
BROMHEAD, Benj. 267
BROOKS, Henry 397
  James 25
  Jas. 214,230,296,396,400
  Jas. S. 304
  Margaret 25
  Maria 25
  Rober 25
  Robt. 25
BROUGH, Catherine 49
BROWN, A. A. 113
  A. B. 165
  Abram B. 25
  Alex. 27,115
  Allett 26
  Andrew 47
  Anna 385
  Arthur Davies 96
  B. 74,171
  B., Jr. 77
  Benj. 45,69,74,79,87,92,
  127,129,137,171,172,218,
  219,270,283,309,351
  Benjamin, Jr. 25
  Benj. B. 385
  Benj. Jr. 25
  Benj. J., Jr. 57
  Betsy 26
  Bernard 352
  Chandler 62
  Charles 26
  Charles W. 26
  Charles Warren 25
  Chas. L. 8,56,69,92,98,
  138,154,226,227,240,272,
  313

BROWN, cont'd:
  Chas. S. 92
  Chas. W. 26
  C. L. 227
  E. 387
  Elis 385
  Eliz. 129
  Eliz. H. 87,129
  E. S. 279
  F. 20
  Fielding 4,27,193
  Fielding T. 26,264
  Geo. 330
  Geo. M. 27,50,52,153
  Hannah 402
  Henry 10,26,27,52,57,62,
  100,183,185,399
  Henry L. 25,26
  H. D. 135
  H. L. 80,129,133,135,165
  240,284,382
  Howell 26,129,268
  Howell D. 135
  Howell L. 26,87,220,268,
  284,306,377,395
  Howel S. 6
  H. S. 2,328
  Jacob 378
  James 26,28
  James M. 26,28
  James Murray 26
  James W. 3,4
  Jane 26
  Jas. 293,367
  Jas. M. 40,85,157,170,
  272,273,302,338,343,344
  Jas. Murray 27,124
  Jas. W. 3,360
  Jeremiah 27
  Jesse 27
  J. M. 346
  Jno. 26,27,56,62,335,354
  387
  Jno. M. 126,217
  Jno. P. 27,73
  Jno., Sr. 26
  Jno. T. 25,26,351
  Jocob 26
  Joe S. 4
  John 26,27
  John M. 26,27
  John Mat. 25
  John W. 27
  Jos. 111,210,214,264
  Joseph 26,27,28
  Joseph S. 27
  Jos. C. 3
  Jos. S. 3,222
  J. P. 27
  J. R. 230
  J. Thompson 197
  J. T. Thompson 74
  Maurice 26
  Martin 3,27
  Mary 27,138
  Mary E. 25
  Mary Jane 171,172
  M. E. 25
  Milly 26,242,309
  Molly 25,402
  Mordecai 88
  Paul 57
  Phebe 22,27
  P. S. 394
  Rachel 27,335
  Ro. 30,69,96
  Ro. L. 289
  Robt. L. 7
  Ro. H. 67
  Ro. M. 17,26,27,30,31,42
  50,57,69,75,77,92,94,95
  96,98,100,106,117,119,
  125,133,148,152,181,192

BROWN, Ro. M. cont'd: 216,
  221,239,260,263,268,321
  327,329,352,360,366,377
  380,387,390
  Ro. M., Jr. 117,328
  Ro. M., Sr. 328
  Ruth 27
  Ruthy 302
  Sally C. 25
  Sarah 26
  Sarah A. 226
  Sarah P. 27
  Stark 27
  Susan 26,312
  Susanna 26
  Thomas A. 28
  Thomas R. 28
  Thompson 26
  Thos. 28
  Thos. A. 27,64
  Thos. L. 95
  William 27
  Willis 28
  Wm. 194
  Wm. L. 35
BROWNING, James A. 28
  Jas. A. 28
  William H. 28
BRUMHALL, Thos. 162
BRYAN, Ann Rooking 29
  Benj. 29
  John Letcher 29
  Sarah Jane 28
  Virginia Petzer 29
  William 29
  Wm. 29
  Wm. M. 28,29
BRYANT, Amos 80,119
  Anderson 29
  Ann Pakiss Rooking 29
  Benj. 389
  Eliz. 18
  Jos. 281
  Pamelia 29
  Parmenas 16,29,342,352
  Peremenas 28
  Spottswood 55
  William 29
  Wm. 29,81
  Wm. O. 204
BRYDIE, Alex 237
  Eliz. 220
BUCHANAN, David 29
BUCK, Jno. 157
BUCKLEY, William L. 29
BUCKMAN, Elijah 331
BUCKNALL, Thos. 36
BUCKNER, Aylett H. 57
BUGG, Allen 36,338
  Sherod 29,184,185,335,
  340
BULLOCK, Jas. 27
  Jno. 383
BUNTING, Jas. 293
BURCH, Nelson 219
BURDEN, Archibald 381
BURFORD, Alfred 29
  Amanda 30
  Amanda G. 29,32
  Ambr 357
  Ambr. R. 258
  Ambrose 24,30,31,32,186
  Ambrose R. 31,209
  Anson 174,358
  Ann M. 29
  Archibald 31
  Archs. 30
  Betsy 123
  Caroline 12,30,31
  Catherine 30
  Dan Jr. 267
  Danl. 19,32,144,212,238
  Daniel 30,31

BURFORD cont'd:
  Danl. F. M. 30
  Danl. L. 19,31,357,384
  Delilah 30
  Editha 31
  Eliz. 32,33
  Eliza Ann 30
  Eliz. L. 15
  Emma 367
  Emmer 366
  Ella 367
  Ella J. 367
  Eller 366
  Floyd 30
  Geo. H. 30,154,356
  George 31
  Geo. W. 313
  Gustovus 30
  Hugh A. 29
  Jackson 29
  Jackson L. 29,32,73
  James 30,31,32
  James C. 30,31
  James N. 30
  James S. 31
  Jas. 26,359
  Jas. N. 210
  Jas. R. 258,259
  Jno. 148,375
  Jno. L. 73,265
  John 29,30,31
  John L. 15,30,31,32
  Josephine 33
  McCalphin 31
  Margaret 235
  Martha 30
  Martha Ann 31
  Mary 31,32,366,367
  Mary E. 29,32
  Matilda 30,32
  Molly 307
  Nancy 30,32,356
  N. Jackson 33
  Paschal 383
  P. Benj. 33
  Philip 30,31,32,33,356
  P. D. 33
  Polly 31,32
  Powhatan 30,31
  Reubeen 31,32,123
  Rich. 30
  Robt. 31
  Ruth 356,357,358
  Rutha 356
  Ruthy 32
  Sally 31,350
  Sarah 15,32,33
  Silverster L. 270
  S. L. 89,279,298,301,
  367,397
  Susan 32,33
  Susan J. 83
  Sylvester 30,31
  Sylvester L. 4,83,298
  Sylvester M. 279
  Sylvester S. 32,89,103,
  239
  Synthy H. 32
  Themuthis 30
  Thos. H. 30
  V. F. 33
  Vincent 33
  Vincent F. 32,139
  V. T. 31
  W. C. 31,33
  William 31,32
  Wm. 30,31,32,78,123,264
  265,326,350
  Wm. A. 12,32,124,350,367
  Wm. C. 32,33,42
  Wm. J. 32
BURGER, Jos. 346,386
  Mary 386

BURGESS, Rebecca 308
BURGHER, Jos. 247,346
BURRUS, Chas. 271
  Jos. 271,273,274,275,308
  Sophia 309
BURGORD, William 31
BURK, Jno. 387
  Jos. 49
  Mary Ann 49
BURKE, Jno. 13
BURKS,...272
  A. B. 34
  Abraham F. 33
  Adaline Emela 323
  A. C. 34
  Adaline 33,126
  Afred 142
  Alex 91,202
  Alexander 34
  Alex. H. 60,202
  Alex. R. 91
  Alfred C. 53
  Andrew J. 34
  Anne 143
  Bettie W. 202,203
  Caroline M. 34,36
  Charles 33
  Charles F. 35
  Charles M. 33,88
  Charles Z. 34
  Chas. 25,33,34,35,88,101
  149,158,403
  Chas. C. 56
  Chas. L. 35
  Chas. M. 33,126,403
  Chas. Sr. 174
  Chas. Z. 34,35,91
  Cicero 34
  C. M. 33
  David 33,34,35
  David J. 96
  David, Jr. 33
  David, Sr. 33,174
  E. A. 364
  Edward 35
  Edward A. C. 34
  Edwd. A. 373
  E. K. 323
  Eliz. 33,100
  Eliz. K. 323
  Elizabeth 35
  Eliz. B. 35
  Ellen T. (Broadus) 202
  Emily 34
  Geo. 33,34,35,97,100,142
  248,249,251,256,385,401,
  403
  Geo. A. 34,100
  Geo. B. 248
  Geo. G. 34
  Geo. P. 142
  George 33,34,35
  Henry 34
  Jack 34
  James 35
  James M. 34
  Jane 33,34,35
  J. D. 35
  Jno. 34,100,101,149,370
  Jno. Napolean 323
  Jno. P. 36
  J. P. 33
  John 33,34,35
  Jos. L. 64
  Josiah C. 33
  Judah (Tinsley) 356
  Lee H. 323
  Levinsia 33
  Lindsey 33,34,316
  Linza 293,361
  M. A. C. 34
  Mag 77
  Marcel 34

BURKS cont'd:
  Marcus 34,35
  Marcus A. 36
  Marcus A. C. 36
  Margaret 35
  Marshall 35
  Martha 323
  Martin P. 36
  Mary 33,35,68,103
  Mary Cash 35
  Mary F. 35
  Mary Talor 142
  Milisent 33
  Minerva Jane 35
  Nancy 33,34,35,143
  Nancy C. 33,126
  Nancy G. 35,248
  Nancy M. 34
  Nathan 323
  Nathan D. 299
  Nathaniel D. 35
  Obedience 33
  Palpatine 34,35
  Phebe 33,34
  Polly 35
  R. 151
  Rachel 35,104
  R. H. 33
  Rich. 31,33,34,35,151,
  158,162,175,265,299,313,
  323,324,361,389
  Richard 33,35
  Rich. H. 33,162,244
  R. M. 34
  Roberta 323
  Robt. H. 35
  Rowland 34,35
  Roland P. 35,176,241
  Rowling 35
  Saml. 33,34,35,36,40,45,
  68,96,142,151,158,162,
  176,266,286,288,308,312,
  323,360
  Saml. C. 36,202,360
  Saml. Jr. 36
  Sarah 34
  Sarah Ann 35
  Sarah Jane 34,36
  Susannah 35
  William 34
  Willis 34,235
  Wm. 34,35,36,147
  Wm. H. 67
  Wm. L. 35,36,269,361
BURRESS, John B. 36
  Permelia 85
  Sarah 85
BURRUS,...10
  Carolus 36
  Charles 36,37
  Chas. 364
  David 117
  Eliz. 36
  Elizabeth 7
  Jno. C. 85
  Jos. 36,37,45,61,72,76,
  85,167,177,184,194,195,
  196,213,214,244,305,306
  Joseph 2,36,37
  Pamelia 36,37
  Permelia 36
  Peter 49
  Pickett 36
  Salley 37
  Sally 36
  Sarah 37
BURLEY, Eliz. 150,211
  J. 30
  Mary 314,315
  N. 173
  Nathl. 18
  Uriah 192,193,258
  Wm. T. 210

CASH cont'd:
  Rebecca R. 148
  Reuben 59,60,217
  Robt. 58,59,61
  Rosanna 59
  Ruth 59,61
  Sally 141
  Saml. 61,80,315,347,
  393
  Saml. D. 58
  Saml. G. 58,61,286,319,
  339,340
  Sarah 61
  Sarah H. 58
  S. G. 33,148
  S. M. 59,60
  Sophia 61,319
  Stanley M. 59
  Stephen 59,60,61
  Stephen P. 51
  Susan 61
  Tabitha 59
  Tamsey 61
  Thos. 61,217
  Will M. 59
  William P. 58
  Willis 58
  Wm. 52
  Wm. M. 59,60,61
CASHWELL, Ann 53
  Betsy 62
  Catherine 62
  Charity 62
  Eliz. 61
  Fanny 155
  Henry 47,62,238,338
  Jas. 207
  Jas. A. 53
  Jas. H. 21,53,54,56,62,
  207,210
  Jas. M. 155
  Jno. 21,62,240,252
  Judith 62,155
  Mildred 62
  Milly 62
  N. 155
  Nancy 54,210
  Peter 21,22,61,62,80,
  149,155,170
  Peter Jr. 62
  Peter Sr. 62
  Powhatan C. 62
  Rachell 62
  William 62
  Wm. 62,275,355
CAULWELL, David 75
CAVEL, Jos. Cabell 294
CATHERMUIR, Mrs. 351
CAWFLIN, Eliz. 84
  Benj. 73,84
  Jas. Benj. 73,84
  Keziah 84
CAWTHRONE, Antonetta 62
  Gilemena 62
  Jane 62
  Louisa 62
  Lulina 62
  Mary 62
  Mary Ann 62
  Nancy 83
  Robt. 62
CECIL, Z. 348
CEENAULT, Thos. 191
CHACKELFORD, Benj. 346
CHAPAN, Ro. 63
CHAPLAIN, B. 178
CHAPLIN, E. H. 95
CHAPMAN, Caroline 75
CHAPPEL, Sally 323
  Wm. 341
CHAPPELL, Sally 324
  Wm. 139
CHAPPLE, Wm. 389

CHARTER, Champe 78
CHASE, Wm. R. 252,253
CHASKEY, Jas. 63
  Patsy 63,72
CHAZNALL, Alex 219
CHEATHAM, Jonathan 7
  Josiah 7
  Manerva 63
  Menerva 63
  Minerva 63
  Silas 63
CHEATWOOD, Anne E. 63
  Anne Eliz. 63
  Daniel 63
  Danl. 63,132,146,219,284
  Danl. A. 284
  Frances 63,281
  Hiram 63,177,270,283,284
  285
  Hyrum 63
  Levina 63
  Levisa 63
  Louivinia 63
  Mary Frances 63
  Sally 63
CHEEK, Wm. 144
CHENAULT, Ann 63
  Christopher 23
  Thomas 63
CHESTNUT, Jno. 216
CHEWNING, A. G. 209
CHICK, Mary R. 171
CHILDERS, Ann 199
  Lucy 350
CHILDES, Tarlton W. 388
CHILDRES, Mary 137
CHILDREE, Benj. 199
CHILDRESS, Anna 201
  Annis 318
  Belinda Caroline 345
  B. W. 217,219,399
  Benj. 63,156,157,158,201
  Benj. W. 201
  E. C. 345
  Jesse 318
  John 341
  Jno. 340
  Jos. 52,64,77
  Joseph 63
  Leonard 345
  Leonard H. 63,64,161,165
  Lucy 64,255
  Mary 164,165
  Pink 64
  Peggy 184
  Polly 63
  R. C. 403
  Royal 63
  Thos. 64
CHILDS, Tarlton 248
  Tarlton W. 282
CHILES, Eliz. 162
  Tarlton W. 388
CHISNAL, Alex 219
CHISNALL, Alex 210
CHISNEL, Alex 207
CHRIST, Saml. 68
  Scott 68
CHRISTIAN, A. 279
  Abner 13,14,65,66,68,
  145,,146
  Agnes 64,69,70,375
  Agness 67
  Alex 64
  Andrew J. 67
  Anthony 64
  Anne 166
  Ann E. 70
  Ann Eliza 69,70
  Asa 67
  Asa W. 67
  Betsy 64,68
  Camillus 369

CHRISTIAN cont'd:
  C. H. 240
  Charles Burks 64
  Chas. 13,64,66,67,68,77
  90,131,136,183,187,206,
  218,395
  Chas. B. 64,65,77
  Chas. Edward 65
  Chas. F. 183
  Chas. H. 66,67,69,109,
  131,168,228,285,355
  Chas. L. 64,65,67,68,14
  Chas. M. 14,67,68,69,1C
  146,206,281,321,386
  Chas. W. 64,70,190
  Courtney 68
  Cordelia W. 211
  D. 67
  Danl. 67,191,215
  Danl. D. 380
  Danl. F. 62,67,269
  D. F. 67
  Drury 6,8,14,65,66,67,
  68,69,136,144,145,146,
  247,391,401
  Edmond 64
  Edmonia 64
  Edmund 69,70
  Edmund D. 70
  Elijah 65,67,180,193
  Elijah L. 64,65,67,218,
  395
  Elijah S. 65
  Elisha 67
  Eliz. 65
  Eliza A. 64
  Eliz. Ann Murray 65,66
  Eliz. H. 66
  Eliz. Harvey 66
  Elvira M. 211
  Emily Frances 65
  Frances 64,69,209
  Frances A. 64,65,69
  Frances Ann 65
  Frances C. 66
  Eliz. 66,68
  Geo. 64,66,68,70,193,2
  Geo. H. 64,67
  Geo. M. 64
  Geo. W. 69,70,95,211,2
  Helen 64
  Henry 29,66,285
  Henry A. 307
  James 68
  Jane L. 130
  Jas. 13,23,66,68,69,10
  343
  Jas. B. 68,108
  Jas. G. 6,65,66,67,69,
  144,152,372,401
  Jas. (Grisham) 67
  J. G. 67
  Jno. 8,13,65,66,67,68,
  77,78,145,146,181,187,
  210,276,343,391,400
  Jno. B. 5,66,67,68,136
  343,395
  Jno. C. Jr. 5
  Jno. F. 65,67
  Jno. H. 60,65,181,217,
  228,372,380
  Jno. J. 67
  Jno. Jr. 5,77,347
  Jno. L. 67
  Jno. S. 108
  Jno. Sr. 343,347
  Jno. Wesley 65
  John 65,68
  Judith 67
  Judith L. 67
  Lucy 66,68,269,270
  Lucy J. 66
  L. W. 206

COFFEY, Averilla 73
Chas. E. 97
Danl. R. 97
Edmd 296,355
Elinor 363
Henry 73
H. L. 73
Jas. 135
Mary F. 73
P. J. 73
Peter J. 73
Wm. 355
COFFIN,...86
COFFLIN, Andrew Jackson
73
Eliz. 73
Harriet Ann 73
Jno. Benj. 73
M. J. B. 73
Wm. Joseph 73
COFFLAND, Jas. 33
COFLIN, Ann 73
Eliz. 73
J. B. 73
Jas. B. 73
Jos. 73
Louis B. 73
Wm. 73
COFFLIN, Benj. 84
COFFMAN, Jacob 175
COGHILL, F. 333
James Lindsey 73
Jas. L. 327,365
J. L. 73
Lindsey 73,155
Mary 73
Mary J. 73
Nancy 73
Nancy R. 297
R. A. 42,124,133,148,
182,187,209,297,,326,
339,351,367
Rich. 73
Ro. 73,83,148,179,240
Ro. A. 8,11,14,16,19,
23,33,34,39,54,60,80,83
91,100,102,146,148,149,
158,172,177,187,208,
221,225,226,227,232,
237,244,256,265,268,269
270,271,278,284,289,290
292,305,309,314,321,325
335,352,371,372,373,377
385,403
Robt. 23
Robt. A. 2,8,73
To. A. 91
V. McGinnis 34
COLE,...389
Jno. 251,301
Rebecca 251
COLEMAN, Benj. 9,26,45,49
79,318,366
Belinda 345
Berry 74,78,79
Betsy Ann 74
Betty 75,80
Betty Ann 75,80
Betty F. 77
Betty Floyd 74
Brockman 75,113
Caroline 75,79,345
Caroline Co. 76
Chas. T. 77,78,314,316
Chas. P. 344
Colonel Wm. 80
Cornelia P. 79
D. 78
Daniel L. 75,78,80
Danl. 75,76,77,78,113,
165,186,196,273,391
Danl. L. 4,145,164,186,
261,272,273,274,286,333

COLEMAN, Danl L. cont'd:
334,352,377
Dnal L. 53
Duke 75,113
Edwd 63
Edwd J. 273
Edmd 113
Edmd T. 64,75,238,271,
315,333,346,363,393
Edmund T. 75,77,78,86,
113
Eliz. 76,77,78,157
Eliz. Breckinridge 6
Eliza 79
Eliza Alderson 79
Frances 78,79,217
Frances R. 76,78,172,217
F. R. 79
Geo. 38,41,76,78
Geo. L. 76,77
Geo. T. 186
Harry Ann 75
Hawes 106,110,158,180,
252,295,343
Henry Landon76
Hugh 222
Hugh N. 222
Hugh Nelson 210
J. 78
Jam 151
James 74
James P. 74
Janetta 77
Janetta E. 77,78
Jannetta E. 77
Jas. 76,77,78,123,215,
376
Jas. D. 75,80
Jas. P. 42,74,75,77,79,
102,113,126,175,182,183,
187,221,260,264,265,272,
273,301,316,332,335,366
Jesse 77,78
John 77
Jno. 10,16,26,31,62,65,
75,76,78,79,80,81,85,
107,139,146,160,183,199,
204,205,233,241,255,259,
281,284,291,308,311,315,
342,365,378,393,394
Jno. D. 74
Jno. Daniel 77,79,80
Jno. R. 77,79
Jos. 78
Joseph 105
J. P. 182,184,217,373
J. R. 77
Judith 76
Judy 79
L. 78
Lewis 123,153
Lin. 76
Lindsey 10,13,17,44,52,
67,69,75,76,77,78,79,80,
87,88,93,104,112,115,119
128,135,162,179,184,185,
204,213,220,239
Jno. 139
Landon 345
Leroy 277
Lindsey 264,271,273,274,
275,282,285,286,302,316,
326,327,332,334,335,340,
342,344,345,355,357,359,
360,370,371,374,376,385,
386,397
Lindsey Jr. 363
Littlebery 74,77,78
Lucy 77,78,79
Lucy C. 345
Margaret 79
Margaret H. R. 78
Margaret R. 79

COLEMAN cont'd:
Mary 75,76,78
Mary C. 75,78
Mary E. 77
Mary F. 78,79
Mary T. 78
Mary Frances 79
Mary T. 79
Mildred 75,76
Milley 78
Milian 79
Millie 79
Million 77
Milly Rose 71
Minerva 63
Nancy 77,78,150,157,345
Nelson 107
Nicholas 77
P. C. 77
Peter 22
Polly 76
Polly W. 43
Reuben 65,75,76,78,79,80
220,276,345,365,396
Rich. M. 186
Ro. 75,78,113,149,214,
274,275
Ro. C. T. 71
Robt. 36,76,77,79,176
Robt. L. 46
Ro. H. 78,332
Ro. L. 23,24,26,30,54,59
60,75,76,77,79,80,96,113
130,149,185,186,211,222,
227,272,294,301,325,345,
366,373,399
Ro. Landon 79
Rol. L. 272,300
Rufus 230
S. 77
Sally 77,78,79
Sally W. 79
Saml. 76,78,191,215,277,
330
Saml. L. 76,273
Sarah 79
Sarah A. W. 79
Seaton 222
Silas 63
Spilsby 77,78,79
Thos. 75,76,77,78,79,80,
151,157,194,227,276,277,
282,330
Thos. B. 76
Thos. D. 80,317
Thos. P. 76
Thos. Taylor Daniel 74
Tom 151
W. E. 25,39,133,139
William 63
Winston 140
Wm. 44,75,76,77,78,79,80
115,119,138,224,233,317
320,335,363,364,365,366
Wm. A. 80
Wm. E. 33,69,78,80,126,
132,137,139,169,187,264,
272,321,332,339,372,366
Wm. Ed. 63
COLEMAND, Sarah W. 74
Reuben 21
COLWELL, Saml. 229
CONNELL, Arthur 322
CONNER, Jas. 127
Danl. 40
John 275
COOKE, Thos. J. 349
COONEY, Jno. 76,105,210,
238,307,309
COONS, W. E. 28
COOPER, Charlote 80,81
Courtney 80
Jane 80

COOPER cont'd:
Nathan 81
Phillip 80,81
Robt. 81
COPPEDGE, Chas. 81,294
Jas. H. 208
Jas. W. 2,363
Lewellen 140
Martha A. 140
COPPIDGE, Chas. 81
Nancy 81
Thos. 81,327
Thos. Jr. 81
CORDER, Kenndolph 28
CORNELIUS, Edwin 81
Eliz. 81
Elvira 81
Geo. 81
Geo. Washington 81
Lucy 81
Salés 4
Thos. 81
Wm. 81
COOEMAN, Jno. 253
COORBENE, John N. 25
COTTRAL, Lydda 61
COTTRELL, Gilbert 81
Jno. 245
Susanna 81
Thomas 81
Thos. 81
Wm. 81
COUGHFFEE, Edmd. 355
COULTER, Frances 72
COUNEY, Jno. 207
COURTS, Sarah 43
COWARD, Sukey 311
COWEN, Jos. 321
COX, A. 69,71,89
Achs. 83
Achillis 83
Anthony 343
Archelaus 81,82,83,103,
341,358,360
Archelus 30
Archie 323
Ben 82
Benj. 81
Caroline 81,83
Caroline M. 203,206
Clary 81,82
Edward 81
Edward L. 82,106
Eliz. 82,83,343
Eliza 69
Fletcher 82
Frances 174
Geo. 82
Jno. 81,82,83,271
Juliann 30
Margaret 81,82
Martha 82,83
Martha Ann 83
Mary Ann 81
Mary E. 82
Milner 81,82
Millner 359
Milnor 175
Nancy 82,103,104
Pasty 83
Patsy 271
P. C. 83
P. G. 83
Radford 83
Rebecca 258
Reuben 81,82,83,254,258,
269,271,303,357
Reuben N. 206
Rich. 82
Rich. N. 258
Robt. W. 83
Ro. H. 215
Reuben 8,243

COX cont'd:
Sally 20
Saml. P. 83,337
Sarah 82
Spotswood 82,83
Spotswood H. 81,82,83,
358
Thos. M. 124,256
T. W. 9
Wm. 81,82,83,343,388
Wm. Fletcher 82
Wm. Henry 258
Wm. P. 82
Wm. R. 82,83
Wm. Radford 83
Valentine 81
Wyatt 8,82,83
COY, Danl. 124
CRAFT, Michl. 46
CRACRAFT, Francis 306
CRAFT, Rebecca 83
Rebecca A. 83
Wm. 83
CRANK, C. H. 281
G. H. 91
CRAWFORD,...27,232
Alex P. 83,86
Ann 220
Anne 83,84,110
B. 85
B. A. 85
Ben 230
Benj. 84
Bennett 84
Bennet A. 324,345
Bennett A. 45,85,86,204,
379
Champe 135
Chas. 54,83,84,85,95,177
380,402
Rev. Chas. 305
D. 85
D., Jr. 84
David 52,54,57,59,84,85,
93,95,100,205,251,350
David, Jr. 84,134
David, Sr. 84
Davis 351
E. 86
Edmd. 207
Edmund 86
Eliz. 86,93,94
Eliz. H. 86
Frances 84
Gabriella 86
Gabriella S. 83,86
Hannah H. 85
Hugh Nelson 86
James 85
Jas. 394
Jno. 35,57,76,85,93,95,
153,234,242,243,286,316,
349,378,381
Jno. D. 29,86,160,229,
256,366
Joel 84,132
Joell 166
John 84,85
Julia Ann 83,365
Julian 86
Julianna 86
Lucy 86
Margaret 86
Maria Antonietta 125
Mary 84
Molly Ann 36
Mrs. 86
Na 85
Natham 8,84,85,86
Nathan 110,158,180,241,
294,295,401
Nathan, Jr. 93
Nathl. 107,389

CRAWFORD cont'd:
Nelson 9,11,20,22,26,40,
45,50,52,54,83,85,86,93
94,95,118,129,144,153,
160,167,230,233,242,247,
256,292,294,297,306,318,
319,320,331,346,347,365,
374,380,,381,393,394,402
Nelson C. 21,308
Nelson, Jr. 215,304
Nelson, Sr. 215
Peter 83,84
Reuben 38,85,128,272
Rev. Chas. 274
Rich. 24,85,86,211,319,
342,377
Sarah 84,86,132
Sophia 83,86,272,273,336
370
Susannah 84
Thos. 83,84
Vanstroup 86
Van Trump 26
William 220
William S. 85
William Sid 86
Wm. 56,84,85,86,128,138,
220,272,305,351
W. S. 3,4,36,87,112,198,
199,220,237,273,357
Wm. S.41,83,85,86,93,95,
123,135,170,192,220,238,
247,255,271,304,337
Wm. Sid 109,125,288
Wm. Sidney 127
CRAWLEY, Franky 343
CREASY, Chas. 87,195
Eliza W. 175
Jordan 110,243
Lucinda P. 239
Mary F. 239
CRENSHAW, Alfred V. 240
CREW, Thos. 176,177
CREWS, Archelaus 174
Elix 278
Eliz. 350
Eliza 348
Gedeon 64,87,237
Gideon 97,273
Jas. 30,81,375
Jno. 72,81,87,186
Jos. 20,73,84,87,186,389
343
Jos. Jr. 87
Martha 31
Mary 87
Milly 30
Nancy 127
N. F. T. 128,174
Sally 87,88
Sarah 87
Thos. 61,65,78,79,86,87,
88,107,127,128,129,220,
273,287,288,308,378,380,
396,397,399,400
CRISP, Lucy 87
Wm. 15,87,131
CRISTIAN, Jno. H. 134
CROBKMAN, W. A. 277
CROCKAN, Wm. 73
CROCKETT, Laura V. 246
CROUCH, Saml. 212
Sarah 87
CROUCHER, Mary 87
Molly 88
Saml. 88
Sarah 87,88
Thos. 87,88
Wm. 87,88
CROUTCHER, Molly 87
Sally 87
Thos. 87
CRUTCHER, Saml. 212

DAVIES cont'd:
Jno. N. 93,94
Jno. Y. 95
Landon 94
Laura B. 92,94
Laura Beverly 92,94
Lucinda 344
Lucy 94
Mary F. 93,94,96
Mary Frances 93
Mayo 93,95,164,344,345,
346
Michl. Clayton, Jr. 93
Moses 185
N. 92
N. C. 85,94
Nichl. 85,92,93,94,95
Nichl. C. 92,93,94,95,
96
Nichl. Clayton 94
Nicholas 94,95
Nicholas C. 93,94,95
Rebecca E. P. 95,351
Roderick 95,204
Ro. J. 105
Rosey 13
Sally R. 95,120
Sally W. 87,129
Saml. B. 331
Saml. Boyle 94
Saml. P. 43
Saml. R. 92,93,95,128,
204,249,355
Sarah 95
Sarah A. 94
Sarah Ann 93,96
Sarah B. 92
Sarah M. 95,96,165
Sarah W. 95,96,101,129
S. R. 93
Susan M. 92
Whiting 92,93,94,95,96,
104,177,248,265,266,341
Whiton 94
Wm. B. 93,95,96,120,122
182
Wm. J. 20
Wm. M. 93,94,277
DAVIESS, Saml. R. 115,118
DAVIS, A. B. 91
Abram Henson 99
Addie E. 99
A. L. 91
Ann 99
Ann C. 128
Arthur 94
Arthur B. 287
Austin M. 160
Baxter 179
Benedictor 242
Benj. 98,101
Betty 236
Bernard Byrd 378
Bigby 99
Caroline Lewis 96
Chas. 13,96,100,101,102
118,228
Chas. C. 237
Chas. L. 97,228,234,248
250,251,293,294,388,401
Chas. LEwis 96
C. L. 249
Claudia 99
David 98,99,100,101
Ed. J. 340,387
Edward J. 97
Ed. P. 33
Elijah 155,250,251,346
Eliz. 85,97,98,100,101,
234
Eliza Ann 97
Fielding 98,99
Frances 179

DAVIS cont'd:
Geo. 96
Geo. D. 100,239,274
George 101
G. T. 307
Hannah 98,100,101
Harrison 94
Henry L. 264
H. S. 98
Indiana 329
Isaac 36,98
Isham 97,100,242
Israel 97
J. 101
J. Bigby 99
Jabez 101
James 97,98,99
James L. 98,99
Jane 179,199,216
Jas. 32,33,38,54,93,96,
97,98,100,117,118,121,
142,143,152,215,234,235,
248,261,295,299,323,361,
371,385,389,401
Jas. B. 38,102,142,158,
248,250,309,335,377,388
Jas. D. 388
Jas. Hopkins 179
Jas., Jr. 98
Jas. L. 98,99
Jean 101
Jesse 98
J. D. 53,118,249
J. Dudley 36,100,101,118
119,135,175,244,335,388
J. F. 347
Jno. 7,33,56,80,94,97,98
100,101,119,143,215,216,
366,400
Jno. A. 38
Jno. B. 98
Jno. C. 98
Jno. D. 2,35,38,96,97,98
101,104,109,117,118,119,
126,142,208,237,248,249,
250,266,297,299,300,313,
388,402
Jno. Dudley 97,100,118,
119,122,356
Jno. E. 97
Jno. Fulton 99
Jno. H. 101
Jno. Luther 99
Jno. M. 97
Jno. N. 248
Jno. T. 34,100
John 98,99,142,143,179,
216
John Fulton 99
John Luckey 99
John Luther 99
Jos. Sr. 46
Joshua 97
Lewis 29,96,97,98
Lindsey 38,102,142,248,
250,251,335
Linsey 315
Luther R. 98,99,311
Macajah 100
Madison 142
Margaret 101,116
Mary 97,98,215
Mary E. 164
Mary Eliz. 98
Mary Jane Millner F. 242
Matilda 100
Mildred 97,98,100
Mildred Miller 183
Milla 57
Millie 100
Mitilde 100
Nancy 96,97,100
Nathaniel 97,100

DAVIS cont'd:
Nathl. 100
Nelson 100
Philip 116
Phillip 98,100,101,293,
294
R. E. P. 95
Richard 97
Ro. 100,242
Robt. 100,101
Roderick 95
Ro. J. 40
Sally 98,101,248
Sallie Jane 120
Saml. 96,97,98,100,101,
166
Sarah 100
Sarah W. 101
Sophronia A. 99
Sophronia C. 99
Susan 377
Susan Frances 96
Susan M. 95
Susannah 101
Terza 7
Theodicia 100
Thedosha 100
Thos. 97,98
Thos. Isaac 99
Thos. Morriss 96
Thurman Blanton 241,278,
279,295,357,387
Stage 101
Va. 102
Va. M. 102
Virginia 102
W. 100,215
Wesley 329
Will L. 97
Winifred 101
W. L. 100,215,388
W. S. 215
Wm. 97,98,101,102
Wm. D. 98,99,250
Wm. Daniel 98,102
Wm. H. 102
Wm. L. 97,104
Wm. Ludwell 96
Wm. W. 97
DAWSON, Adaline 102
Alex Lewis 102
Ann 102
Ben 102
Benj. 102,104,105,335,
368
Benj. B. 375
Benj. R. 102,103,104,
385,386,398
Betsy 103,105,335
Caddis 104
Caddis B. 104
Caroline 102
Cath. 102
Charity 102
Chas. 103,104
Chas. M. 340
Churchwell 103,105
Churchwell P. 102,104
Editha 239
Eddy 267
Edmd. 398
Elijah 104
Eliz. 54,103,104
Eliza Jane 2,102
Fanny Caroline 102
Fleming 184
Francis 102,398,399
Francis Caroline 102
Frances L. 398
Geo. H. 71
Geo. W. 189
H. C. 124
Hudson 63

DAWSON cont'd:
J. 335
Jane 74,102,388
Jas. 102
Jennie 72
Jesse 104
Jno. 102,105,147,246,
251,252,286,335,350,
371,375
Jno. J. 370
Jno. S. 103,252,335,371
Jno. Sorrell 335
John 7,103
Jonathan 103,105
Jonathan R. 105
Jos. 81,102,214,340,384
Joseph 103
Judith 142
L. 80
L. L. 83
Lewis 22,45,103,104
Lucy 103,104
Lucy Ann 102
Ludwell 102,103
Ludwell L. 83,103,396
Ludwell S. 257,340
M. 120
Martin 29,102,103,104,
105,251,267,275,286,293
296,335,371,384
Martin Jr. 335
Martin M. 102
Martin N. 102,104,137,
293,294,354
Mary 103,105,184,335
Mary D. 35
Mary J. 104
Mary Jane 104
Mildred 104
Milly 184
Nancy 37,335
Nancy Burton 104
N. C. 151
Nelson 23,38,46,103,104
105,118,124,140,186,247
309,359,396
Nelson C. 22,30,31,36,
38,45,83,92,103,104,105
114,123,142,147,148,174
186,187,194,195,212,234
235,240,243,259,266,286
288,299,308,309,312,324
350,356,363,386
Nelson Carter 104
Nelson C. Jr. 103,104
Nelson Jr. 103
Nelson C. Sr. 104
P. (?). 3
Peggy 35,104
Pleasant 30,31,38,83,90
102,103,104,105,186,187
234,296,335,350
Pleasant S. 394
Priscilla 103,335
Robt. 214
Russell 35
Sally 335,368
Saml. G. 104
Saml. Irvine 103
Saml. J. 102,104
Saml. K. 103,104
Saml. R. 399
Sidney M. 104,105
S. K. 103
Sorrel 103
Susan 102,398
Susannah 335
Thomas 103
Thos. 104,105,196,335
Wm. 99,102,104,105,267,
335
Wm. B. 105
Wm. O. 105

DAWSON, cont'd:
Zach 36,103,104,105,195,
213,214,235,266,303,343,
363
DAY, Danl. 32,33,97,100,
105,106,135,150,152,277,
303,342,369,372,391
Daniel 12,188
Ezek. 73
Ezekiel 105
Jno. 105
Martha 239
Rebecca 106
Saml. 105,241,303
Samuel 106
Salomon 105
Solomon 5,135,241
Wm. 5,30,31,32,102,105,
152,188,218,303,321,372
DEAN, Lucy 233
Polly 233
DEANE, Capt. 279
J. C. 278,279
Rhoda H. 279
DEARMON, Thos. H. 237
DEARING, Jane E. 106
W. A.. 387
Wm. A. 323
William A. 106
DEBTS, Eliz. 376
Wm. 376
DEMASTER, Geo. E. 32
DEMPSEY, Evelina 296
Janna 237
Seaton Y. 106
Westley G. 106
William M. 106
Wilson 106
Wilson M. 106,212
Wm. 106,316,370
Wm. M. 106
DENT, Salley Lee 44
DENNIS, Elisha 185,340
Eliz. 184
DENNEY, Saml. 363,375
DENNY, Sarah 343
DEPRIEST, Ann 114
Jno. 114,131,132,221
Langdon 132,230
Langsdom 400
Wm. 114,229
DIBRELL, Anthony 76,384,
385
DIBBRELL, J. W. 351
DIBRELL, Sarah O. 106
Wilmouth 385
DICKERSON, Mary A. 58
Thomas 242
Thos. 88
Thos. Sr. 161
Thruston 230
Willis 57
Willis E. 57
DICKEY, Cath. 106
Eliz. E. 105
Eliz. H. 106
Jane 106
DICKINSON, Willis E. 226
DICKSON, Eugene 36
Jemimah 396
Kesurah 396
Lucretia 255
Nancy 396
Wm. 255
DIGGES, Jno. 63,106,245
Wm. H. 199,400
DIGGS, Eliz. 106
Jno. 252,371,389
J. S. 134
W. H. 39
Wm. H. 39,76,106,205,342
363
DIGUST, Jas. 241

DIKSON, Wm. 255
DILLARD, Alfred T. 117,
222
C. C. 43,46
Drury 65
Eliz. 107,109
Eliza 107
Francis 109
F. T. W. 91
F. W. 204
Geo. 13,36,38,44,57,76,
87,107,109,112,137,177,
203,210,214,271,272,274
275,364,369,386
George 129
I. 293
James 36,108
Jane 107,108
Jas. 13,64,65,66,84,107
109,138,145,166,185,216
218,219,234,346,353,364
365,369,370,342
Jas. B. 91
Jas. F. 219
Jas. H. 170
Jas. Jr. 66
Jas. J. Jr. 108
Jas. L. 241
Jas. M. 7,109,254
Jas. S. 63,107,108,110,
234,254
Jas. Sr. 108
Jas. T. 284
Jas. W. 109,401
J. J. 377
Jno. 27,32,65,68,108,
109,133,170,1771,185,
189,193,196,197,203,205
207,211,214,218,219,233
239,254,271,272,273,281
285,290,321,329,333,336
338,342,369,370,386
Jno. A. 109
Jno. J. 66,91,109,274
Jno. Jas. 107
Jno. L. 386
Jno. S. 369,286
Jno. Sr. 68,171,370
Jno. Q. A. 197,371
John 369
John Jas. 239
Jos. 58,62,76,78,86,107
108,169,204,210,254,336
370,374,386,396,402
Jos. L. 107,108,369
Jos. P. 108
Jos. S. 108,368
J. T. 219
Lucy 109,273
Martha 109
Mary 65,109
Mary E. 109,371
Nancy F. 109
O. D. 169
Peter H. 109,322
Q. A. 109
Sally 65
Saml. F. 109
Saml. T. 109
Saml. Turner 370
Stephen 109
Stephen T. 109
Terisha 239
Terisha W. 109
Terry W. 204
Thos. 107
T. W. 66,109,206,219
W. 91,204
William 386
Willis H. 109
Wm. 64,65,66,68,70,91,
108,109,136,157,189,197
204,206,208,209,219,...

GARLAND cont'd:
Jane M. 133
Jas. 44,117,132,133,134,
150,157,214,239,263,325,
365,379,385
Jas., Jr. 133
Jas. P. 86,128,132,133,
134,171,176,177,185,188,
240,275,276,286,342,384,
385,398
Jno. 133,303
Jno. R. 134
Jno. Richard 133
J. P. 72,247,384,385,398
Landon C. 39,133
L. C. 133
Letitia 132
L. F. 39
Louisa 133
Louisa F. 39
Mary 134
Maurice 117,134,190
Maurice H. 134,189,207,
297,302,358
M. H. 300,368,387
M. J. 133
Milly 294
Milly J. 306
Nancy 135,342
Nathl. 135
Panthea Ann 133
Patrick H. 320
Patrick Henry 238
P. H. 133
Polly 342
P. P. 133,134
Preston 132
Preston H. 132,133,134,
135
Ro. 134,222,268,327,342
Robt. 135,342
S. 1,322,342
Saml. 26,33,36,45,46,80
109,117,132,133,135,145,
157,183,186,189,190,207,
212,229,240,265,287,289,
302,328,342,358,359,374,
391
Saml. H. 59,271
Saml., Jr. 134
Saml. L. 27,37,121,304
Saml. M. 2,6,10,15,19,23
25,26,32,34,38,39,51,58,
68,71,74,77,80,82,88,92,
96,100,101,109,110,112,
115,117,122,124,125,126,
129,131,132,133,134,136,
139,144,145,155,159,163,
165,168,169,171,172,177,
186,190,192,193,203,204,
206,208,209,215,217,222,
228,232,233,235,239,240,
245,246,254,258,259,262,
265,270,273,274,278,283,
287,294,302,305,306,308,
309,310,317,321,322,325,
326,328,329,331,335,339,
344,348,351,357,376,377,
378,385,390,394,395,399,
401
Saml. Meredith 239
Saml. M., Sr. 134
S. M. 77,148,153,286,298
342,344,351,395
Sp. 39
Spostwcod 276
Spotswood 43,77,128,144,
276,281,342
Thos. 132,134
W. H. 133
William H. 6
Wm. 132,133,134,135,325
Wm. H. 73,133,134,135,..

GARLAND, Wm. H. cont'd:
240,250,362,379
Wm. Henry 238
Wm. P. 134
Wm. PP 268
GARLICK, Jno. C. 135
GARNER, Benj. F. 136
Caroline 136
Jos. 136
Joseph M. 136
Jos. M. 136
Mary 136
Oney 109,136,219
GARRETT, Sally 174
GARRISON, William 7
GARTH, Jno. 137,247
GARVIN, Benj. F. 136
Jas. M. 136
Lucy 174
Nancy 136
Perline 136
Thos. J. 136
GATEWOOD, Amey 136
Ann 122
Dolley 136
Dudley 47,193,275
Edmun 136
Foster 136
James 27,47
Jas. 47
Judith 136
Larkin 8,65,274,276
Margaret 122
Nancy 136
Ransom 33
Reuben 136
Ro. 307
Sarah 136
Thomas B. 15
Thos. 136
Thos. B. 290,307
Wiatt 15,16,112,290,291,
327
William 136
Wm. 136,229,366
Wm., Sr. 122
GAY, Saml. 401
GAYLE, Mary (Pettyjohn)
357
GENTRY, Harmon 258
GEEINER, Jno. W. 399
GEORGE, Landerick 136
Ro. 136
Robt 136
Sarah 136
GEOGORGY, Henry 232
Henry T. 232
GEOGORY, Jno. 15,16
GIBBS,...160
Jno. 159
GIBSON, Ballard E. 118,137
B. E. 137
Ed. B. 137
Edwd. 137
Elvira 137
Isaac 137
Jacob 137,154
Jane 373
Jane A. 98
Jas. A. 137
Jno. 137
Jno. E. 137
Jno. G. 137
Jos. 263
Louisa A. R. 137
Martha W. 137
M. H. 137
Saml. C. 75,80,98,126,
165,313,344,366
S. C. 98,137,164
W. B. 137
Wm. H. 137
W. W. 137

GILBERT,...342
Amerly 139
Ann 140
Anne 138,139
Ann Stark 139
Ann W. 137,321
Chas. Anthony 139
Clifton L. 139,140
Doctor 177
E. B. 56,113,117,137,139
E. L. 25,140
Eliz. 137,139
Ezek. 137,138,139,272,
321,338
Ezek. B. 137,138,140,142
Ezekiah 137
Ezekial 180
Ezekiel 137,138
Ezekiel B. 113
Ezek. L. 138
Fannie C. 138,139
Fanny 139
F. C. 139
Frances C. 140
Frances W. 139
F. W. 137,321
Geo. 88,138,139
George 138
Henry 9,88,138,139,193
Henry C. 138
Humphrey 377
Jas. 139,308
Jas. L. 140
Jas. S. 140
J. D. 138,139
Jno. D. 138,139,140,260,
328,329,331,394
Jno. Wiatt 138,139
Josiah 138
Josias 138
Judith 139,152
Judith C. 140
Ludlow 139
Mariah 139
Martha 137
Martha C. 139
Martha P. 138
Martha R. 137,139,321
Martha R., Jr. 321
Martha Rookins 140
Mary 138,139
Mary J. 138
Mary J. P. 137,139,140
Mary Wyatt 139
Maude C. 138
Maurice 138,139
Olivia E. 140
P. M. 140
Powhatan 138,140
Powhatan M. 138,139
Rich. 138,139
Richard 138,139
Ro. N. 140
Sally 139
Saml. C. 119
Sophia 139
Sophia A. 140
Sophia H. 137,139
Thos. 138,139
Thomas 139
Wilmouth 139,140
W. W., Jr. 139
Wm. 138,139,216,327
Wm. W. 140
GILES, Nancy 362
Wm. B. 130
GILISBIE, Philip 141
GILL, C. C. 365
Curtis 130,140,338,379
Eliz. 379
Hannah 140
Melissa F. 379
Rowlet 140

HOPKINS, cont'd:
  William 179
  Wm. 179
HOPPER, Eliz. 115
  Geo. 115,116
HOPSON, Martha 64
HORCHENS, Edwd. 163
HORNER, Jas. E. 384,385
  Jno. 70
HORRALL, Eliz. 21
  Wm. 21
HORSLEY, Eliz. 180
  Hector 180
  Jno. 3,5,40,112,139,180,
  276,283,285,293,342,347,
  351
  Jno. Jr. 14,66,285
  John 180
  Jos. 180,347
  Joseph 180
  Judah 180
  Martha 180,347
  Nichl. 180
  Nicholas 180
  R. 180
  Ro. 220
  Robert 180
  Robt. 3,180
  Saml. 180
  William 3,180
  William Andrew 180
  Wm. 13,22,34,35,112,130,
  180,205,276,347,381
HOUCHIN, Chas. 315
HOUCHINS, Martha 402
HOUGHTON, Thos. B. 187
HOWARD, Claiborne 229
  Geo. 68
  Jno. W. 365
  Katy 335
  Sally 229
  Sarah 343
  Wm. 29,193,345
HOWEL, Jane 314,315
HOWELL, Eliz. 9
  Thos. 225
HOWL, Absalom 69,181,182,
  283
  Absalom J. 181,182
  Absalom Jr. 181
  Anne 180
  Benj. 181
  Benj. F. 181,182
  Benj. F. Jr. 232
  Benj. S. 329
  Cath. 181
  Catherine 181
  Catherine B. 182
  Eliz. 181,182
  Elizabeth 182
  Frances 369
  Geo. 181
  Geo. W. 116,181
  George W. 369
  Jane 181
  Jane W. 181
  Jas. 182
  Jno. 181
  Jno. J. 182
  Jno. Jas. 181
  John James 181
  Michael 181
  Michl. C. 181,182
  Rebecca 181,182
  Robt. 182
  Ro. Patrick 181
  W. J. 398
  W. S. 371
HOWLE, Rebecca 182
HOWSE, Jasper 352
HUCHESON, J. 107
  Thos. 218
HUCKSTEP, Anna 183

HUCKSTEP, cont'd:
  Anne 182
  Eliza Ann 183
  F. A. 182
  Fannie 89
  Geo. C. 182,183
  Geo. H. 89,182
  Jennie 89
  Lucy T. 182
  Oney 372
  Oney D. 183
  Richard 182
  Richard C. 183
  Saml. 131,182,239
  Samuel 183
  Virginia 182
HUCSTEPT, Amey 240
HUDSON, Alex 185
  Ann 140,183,184,266
  Bennett 159,183,184,185,
  226
  Betsy 185
  Chas. C. 173
  David 183
  Drury 5
  Edmund 183,185,186
  Eliz. 187
  Frances 183,185
  Geo. 32,159,183,184,185,
  186
  George 184
  Geo. W. 81
  Horatio 184
  Jas. 185
  Jno. 130,184,185,186
  Jno. P. 185,186,368
  Joseph 184
  Joshua 76,140,183,184,
  185,275,349
  Joshua Sr. 184,185
  Joshua Jr. 184
  Lillian H. 223
  Lewis D. 184
  Lucy 43,141,183,184,185
  M. 185
  Martha 185
  Micajah 183,184,226,227
  Mrs. 277
  Nancy 140,184
  Pamelia 183,185
  Parmelia 60
  Paulus 185
  Permelia 185,186
  R. 185
  Reuben 183-186
  R. J. 223,281
  Robt. 183-185
  Robt. Jefferson 186
  Ruch 340
  Rush 184,185,340
  Rush Jr. 184
  Rush Sr. 185
  Sallie 186
  Saml. 186
  Sarah 171,185
  Shelton 185,186
  Sophia 186
  Susan 186
  Susannah 20
  Willis 184
  Wm. W. 186
  W. W. 183
HUGHES, Avery Amanda 186
  D. S. G. 186
  Eliz. 8
  Fanny 186
  Harrison 31,83,162,186,
  264,354
  Jas. 295
  Jno. P. 90
  L. H. 186
  Maria W. 186
  Moses 9,294,328,402

HUGHES, cont'd:
  Nancy 361
  Orlander 186
  Rich. A. 90
  Schuyler 186
  William 186
  Wm. 31,81,83,186,303
HUGHS, James 295
  Jno. 195
HUGHSON, Otis 187
HULVER, Ephraim 100
HULL, Henry 351
  Jno. Baker 351
  Ro. 351
  S. R.351
HUME, Eliz. 9
HUMPHREY, Eliz. 25
  David 135
HUMPHREYS, Louise F. 134
HUNT, B. A. Mahala 317
  Benj. T. 187
  Bennett Ann Mahala 187
  Jno. A. 36
  Jno. S. 187
  Jno. T. 317
  Jno. Vicor 1878
  John 187
HUNTER, Cath. 187
  David 44,45,46,187
  Geo. 187
  Isaac 187
  Jno. 359
  Maria Louisa 187
  Margaret 187
  Nancy 324
  Ro. 377
  Robt. 187
  Wm. J. 187
  Wm. Jr. 187
HUNTLEY, Jas. O. 281
HUNTON, Wm. 187
HURT, Eliza H. 105
  G. 117
  S. C. 100
HUTCHENSON, John 188
  Thos. 367,369
HUTCHERSON, Ann 187,188
  Eleanor 187,188
  Eliz. 187,188
  Jno. 187,188
  Joshua 187,188
  Lucinda 187,188
  Lucy 187,188
  Permelia 187,188
  Permely 187
  Thos. 97,218,263
HUTCHESON, Ann 188
  Catherine 188
  Chas. 188,189
  Ellender 187
  James 188
  Jas. 100,188
  Jas. A. 189
  Jesse 97,188
  Jesse F. 97
  Jno. 189,360
  Jno. J. 188
  Lucy 188
  Pelina 188
  Saml. 188
  Sarah Ann Elinda Perme
  188
  Thomas 188
  Thos. 1,8,12,98,175,18
  371
  William 189
  Wm. 189
HUTCHINS,...188
HUTCHINSON, Jno. 187
  Jno. J. 238
  Joshua 188
  Thomas 188
HUSKILL, Daniel 187

JOPLING, cont'd:
  Josiah 63,101,158,199,
  245,362
  Josiah Bridgwater 199
  Martha 199
  Ormund 381
  Ralph 63,199
  Sally 199,378,381
  Sarah 199
  Sudannah 199
  Susannah 199
  Thomas 1
  Thos. 1,82,101,157,199
  350,351
  Thos. Jr. 3
  Thos. J. Jr. 63
  Thos. Sr. 3,63
  Will 15,26,57,120,142,
  198,293,379
  Wm. 71,81,85,151,160,
  162,199,233,277,285,297
  347,354,366,378,380,381
  402
JORDAN,...300
  Benj. 350
  Jno. 304
  Judith 304
JORDON, Jas. T. 270
  Samla. 41
JORDAN, W. C. 91
  Wm. 5,79,276,277
JOURDAN, Thos. 264
JOYNER, H. C. 208,361,373
  Houston C. 203
  Jas. H. 203
  Jas. M. 368
  Sophia B. (Tiller) 203
  Wm. 181
JURDAN, Thos. 71
JURRIL, Thos. 196
JUTT, Jno. 57

KAHOE, Nee 59
KEATON, Jas. A. 181
KEER, Henry 400
KEETON, Jas. A. 182,329
  Jos. A. 372
KEITEN, Danl. W. 182
KEITH, Cary Ann 232
  Geo. H. 149
  James W. 203
  Jas. 17,187,203
  Jas. W. 3,6,17,18,70,
  187,203,211,232,284,289
  290,336,344,369,375,388
  Marshall M. 203
  Nc 11
  Peyton 3,4,5,6,14,17,18
  28,112,123,145,183,203,
  289,290,336,355,370
  Sarah 203
  Thos. 203
  Wm. P. 203
KELLY, Benj. 299
  Jesse 204
  Mary 206,223
  Nancy 204
  Wm. 204
KELLEY, Jer. L. 330
KELLUS,...125
KEMP, S. V. 40
KENADY, Jos. 3
KENT, Donald 206
  Eliz. L. (Turner) 206
  Eliz. R. 206
  Cordon 206
  Jas. R. 206
  Jno. T. 204,206
  Mary 204
  Mary A. 206
  Mary C. 204,206
  Ro. A. 371
  Sallie Rhuehammer 206

KENT, cont'd:
  Sally Ann 204
  W. 181,185
  William H. 206
  Wm. 5,6,20,32,50,57,72,
  102,106,108,116,147,148,
  186,188,189,193,204,213,
  218,232,257,262,268,279,
  287,290,320,322,328,337,
  338,348,368,369,371
  Wm. H. 105,206
KENNEDY,...3
  Cyntha 203
  Eliz. 204
  Jesse 109,203,204,339
  Jos. 146,204,244,339,355
  Joseph 204
  Mary 204
  Nicholas 204
  Susan 204
  Susanna 203
  Thos. 140
KENNERLEY, Jos. 194
KENNERLY, Jos. 104
KENNEY, Jordon M. 122
  N. C. 274
KENSEY, Ann 28
  Eliza A. 28
KEMPER,...206
KEPPUS, Wm. 205
KERR, Edward 252
  Hamilton 253
KEY, Anne 16
  Belinda 242
  Henry 1,8,9,115,230,242,
  378
  John Jr. 9
  Martin 223
  Mary 8
  Rachel 156
  Tandy 179
KEYTON, Jas. A. 181
KIDD, Amanda M. 205
  Amy 205
  Anna H. 205
  Caroline M. 205
  Jiniah 205
  Jno. J. 205
  Jno. Norman 205
  Juriah 205
  Obedience 205
  Ro. 205
  Ro. I. 205
  Ro. J. 205
  Ruth 205
  Tandy K. 194
  Wm. 205,390
  Wm. C. 205
KIDMEADE, Rich. 20
KINCAID, Ro. 157
  Ro. J. 157
KINEY, C. 80
KINNEY, Chesley 80
  Nichl. 176
KINNIER, Jno. 332
KING, Anna 242
  Col. 401
  Dorcas 191
  Ezek. C. Jr. 134
  Jno. 252
  Joseph 191
  Martha E. 257
  Walter 41
KINGSOLVING, Betsy 214
  Geo. 214
  Geo. W. 214
KIPPERS, Jno. 205
  Wm. 205
KIRKPATRICK, Saml. C. 246
KLOAZ, Marie 184
KNIGHT, Bessie M. 206
  Betsy 308
  Betsy Ann 205

KNIGHT, cont'd:
  Butler E. 237
  Chas. M. 205,206,207
  Edna F. 205
  Eliz. 154,205,208
  Elizabeth 154
  Fayette 208
  Fannie E. 207
  Geo. W. 205,388
  Henry 153,205
  Jno. M. 110
  Lucinda 205,218
  Margaret 205
  Mathy 361
  Mary 205
  Mary H. 388
  Mary J. 205
  Matt. 58,308
  Matthew 205,207
  matthew L. 206
  Nancy 308
  Nellie T. 206
  Signora F. 205
  Sophia 205
  Sophia (Hill) 207
  Sophia W. 205
  Sophia W. (Hill) 206
  Susan 205
  Susan B. 205
  Stephen H. 205
  Wash 401
  Will 312
  Will H. 46
  W. L. 56
  Wm. 16,44,46,136,139,175
  183,191,205,215,216,253,
  260,261,273,286,336,398
  Wm. H. 3,4,18,27,73,112,
  130,143,144,171,173,175,
  176,214,240,255,305,320,
  331,355,388,399
  Wm. L. 209
  Wm. M. 110,206
  Wm. Henry 205
KNOWEL, Barbara 42
KYLE, Andrew M. 89
  Bettie Walker 171
  Betty W. 171
  David 68,171,172,173,206
  David Sr. 206
  Geo. W. 206
  Hiram C. 14,192,197,287
  James C. 206
  Jno. 206
  Jno. S. 57,206,240,281
  Jos. 6,48,63,67,69,110,
  122,130,136,145,150,181,
  182,206,219,263,283,284,
  285,372,391,394
  Jos. Jr. 206
  Jos. Sr. 206
  Joseph Jr. 206
  Joseph Sr. 206
  Laura Ann 171
  Legus M. 206
  Matthew 206
  Ro. 15,255
  Robt. R. 206
  Ro. R. 15
  Rowland 206
  Sophia 68
  Sophia N. 66
  Wm. 255

LANCASTER, Jno. 166
  Mary 208
  Nathl. 376
LACKEY, Adan 267
  Andrew 207
  Eve 7,207
  Hannah 207
  James 207
  Jas. 330

PARKS cont'd:
  Arthur Wilson 265
  Benj. 267
  Betty 265
  Beverly 265
  Charley 265
  Chas. M. 265
  Edwd. 265
  Elis 266
  Eliz. 266
  Eliz. G. 266
  Eliz. M. 265
  Eldred 265
  Eldred B. 265
  Gaines M. 266
  Gaines W. 249,265,266
  Granville P. 265,266
  Granville T. 266
  G. W. 265
  Jinnie 265
  Jno. 266,267
  Jno. M. 248,249,265,266
  Lucy A. 266
  Margaret N. 266
  Margaret 266
  Martin 33,35,56,93,95,
  96,104,118,152,174,228,
  234,251,265,266,267,353
  361,385,386
  Mary 36,103,104,267
  Mary C. 33,266
  Mary Colin 361
  Mary Jane 266
  Milisent 33
  Milton M. 101,118,266,
  402
  Nancy 33,266
  Nell 267
  Peggy 36
  Perlina 93
  Robt. 187
  Saml. G. 33,104
  Sarah 267
  Sarah Anne 266
  Sarah F. 267
  Sarah J. 98
  Sarah Jane 101
  Tabitha 267
  Thos. 52,191
  Va. A. 265
  Walden B. 267
  Weldon B. 94,248
  Wm. 33,266,267
  Wm. H. 266,385
  Wm. P. 104
PARR, Geo. F. 201
  Jas. Hyter 201
  Jno. H. 80,201
  Jos. H. 224
  Margaret E. 201
  Martha A. (Blunt) 201
  Thos. W. 201
  Willie R. 201
  Wm. 174,186,201,223
PARRICK, David 267
  Henry 267
  Joyce 267
  Zephanie 267
PARISH, Saml. 363
PARSON, Nancy 152
PARROCK,...267
PARSONS, Eliz. 267
  Jno. Jno. 267
  Nancy 120
  Patsey 120,152
  Sally 267
  Sarah 81
PARSON, Tandy 267
PATRICK, Chas. 46,48
  Eliz. 267
  Gerremiah 255
  R. 267
  Ro. 283,355,372,393

PATRICK, cont'd:
  Robt. 181,267
  Wm. J. 267
PATTEN, Jno. 86,254
  Sarah 86
PATTERSON, David 89,90,182
  188,387
  Eliz. 238
  Jamestown 255
  Jno. 143
  Jno. V. 29
  Jos. G. 376,377
  Mary 103
  Nancy 229
  Reuben 180
  Reuben B. 180
  Sally 16
PATTESON, B. 58
  Chas. 66
  Chas. J. 267
  Chas. N. 221
  Chas. P. 267
  D. 28,92,218
  David 121,188,249,377
  D. R. 40
  Eliz. 238
  Eliz. A. 267
  Ella H. 267
  Geo. 29,73,267
  Jno. 267
  Jno. H. 103
  Sarah A. 267
  Skylor 267
  Va. L. 267
  Va. S. 267
  Wm. N. 267
PATTON, Alex 229,230,251,
  268
  Jane 268
  Thos. 252,268,400
  Wm. 400
PAXTON, Saml. 160
  Thos. 249
PAYN, Benj. 371
PAYNE, Annie Carter 56
  Benj. 246,371
  D. M. C. 239
  Geo. M. 220
  Jno. R. D. 39
PEARCE, Jacob 168
PEASLEY, Rev. Mr. 256
PEEL, Hugh 143
PEETER, Jos. 348
PENDLETON,...90,241,253
  Adelade 271
  Adelaide 2,74
  Anne G. 98,101
  Ann Maria 268,270
  Betta 271
  Bettie 270
  Benj. 271
  C. 73
  Cath. 268,271
  Catherine 2
  Chas. F. 244
  Edmund 98,101,268,271
  Eliz. 271,284,358
  Eliza J. 268
  Eliza Jane 271
  Franka 271
  Frances 132
  Francis 270
  Francis A. 268
  Harriet 268,269
  Harriet R. 256
  Henry S. 62
  Henry T. 69,269,276,,277
  395
  H. T. 270
  Isaac 271
  Jacob D. 270
  Jacoby 270
  James 269

PENDLETON, cont'd:
  Jane Rose 269
  Jas. 87,124,176,236,268
  269,270,271,396,398
  Jas. C. 2
  Jas. D. 98
  Jas. Dudley 101
  Jas. S. 1,74,133,143,
  144,173,185,238,239,268
  269,270,271,284,286,287
  394
  Jas. Sr. 268
  Jas. S. Jr. 2,271,371
  J. J. 269
  J. L. 102,273
  John 269,271
  Jos. 87
  Jno. 238,268,269,270,
  286
  Jr. 269
  J. R. 269
  J. S. 58,102,148,227
  Louisa E. 270
  Louisa J. 98,101
  Lucy 270
  Lucy A. 74
  M. 53,293
  Martha 132
  Martha G. 269
  Martha M. 132
  Maru Jane Ann 214
  Mary 269,270,271
  Mary E. 269
  Mary Frances 256,269
  Mary Jane Ann 214
  Micajah 3,5,13,18,65,98
  117,180,269,270,276,385
  Mildred 270
  Nellie S. 270
  Ollie 270
  Patsey 81
  Patsy 269,271
  Pen 270
  P. L. 274
  R. 103
  R. A. 58,59,80,90,102,
  269,286,287,351,364,378
  Reuben 1,2,31,82,104,
  132,133,174,197,199,247
  263,264,269,270,271,287
  288,348,350,356,359,361
  362,363,379
  Reubin P. 269
  Rich. 151,269,270,271,
  277
  Rich. Jr. 269
  Rich. Prichard 151
  R. N. 269,368
  Ro. 270
  Ro. A. 11,28,33,34,43,
  72,74,77,105,133,135,
  158,159,168,175,177,194
  208,211,214,232,237,256
  260,262,263,270,271,284
  352,365,372,377,390,394
  Robt. 270
  Robt. A. 2
  Ro. N. 118,269,270,395
  R. S. 366
  Sallie 270
  Saml. 270
  Sarah 271
  Sarah D. 98
  Susan F. 98,101
  Wm. 81,186,190,269,270,
  271
  Wm. C. 133
  Wm. G. 2,107,124,238,
  286
  Wm. Sr. 271
PEN, Mary 276
  Thos. 276
PENN,...242,284

RICHESON, cont'd:
Thos. 297,298
Thos. Petticus 297
Varland 229,297
Va. E. 298
W. A. 77,90,192,204,,231
286,297,298,309,337,373
W. Anthony 299,312
Will A. 311
Wm. 44
Wm. A. 32,42,69,112,149,
204,239,297,298,365,366
Wm. Anthony 56
RIDGWAY, Eliz. 298,322,399
Eliz. C. 298
Harriet 298,322
Mary 298
Polly 278
Ro. 23,30,39,83,186,212,
213,278,279,298,322,384
Rhoad A. 298
Rhoda 399
Rhoda A. 298
Robt. 5,298
Sally J. 298
Thos. 31,68
Wm. 396
Ro. 321
RIDDLE, David 237
RIGHT, Jno. 245
RIGHTS, Wm. 245
RICKETTS, Jane 298
Matt 298
Thos. 298
RILEY, Miles 292
RINE, Austin B. 221
Nancy 221
RIPPTOE, Peter 166
RIVES, Aliy 291
Henry 38
Margaret 41
Nathan 287
Nathl. 288
R. 4,8
Ro. 8,39,41,102,128,154,
158,222,237,256,291,304,
305,315,329,336,338,346,
354,370,393
Robt. 298,304
RIVER, James 9
Rachel Tye 133
Ro. 61,263
Robt. 298
RLLIS, Jno. 293
ROACH, Amanda 299
Amy 298,299
Ashcraft 100,298,299
Chas. 299
Chas. Lewis 299
Cornl. 299
David D. 299
David J. 299
Eliz. 299
Elvira 299
Elvira Jane 142,299
Geo. 299
Henry 298,299
Henry L. 299,377
Henry Landon 299
Jno. 298,299
Louise 299
Polly 299
Sallya 251,299,300
Sarah 143,299
Wm. 54,142,2293,298,299
ROADS, Ann 296
Edwd. 296
Reuben 161,296
ROANE, C. 301
Chas. 301
Christopher 300
Col. 300
Cornelia 301

ROANE cont'd:
Cornelia T. 300
Eliz. 300,301
Eliz. R. 300
Jas. 300,301
Jas. B. 300,301
Jas. M. 300,301
Jas. M. Jr. 300
J. M. 301
Lucy Cath. 301
Ro. 300,301
Robt. 300
R. T. Va. Eppes 301
Sally 301
Sarah 300,301
Sarah E. 300
Va. 300,301
Va. E. 300,301
Wm. 172,301
Wm. B. 172,300,301
Wm. R. 23,188,300,301,
399
W. R. 175
ROANCE, Wm. R. 300
ROBARDS, Henry 1,199
Jos. 207
ROBERSON, Arthur 289
Benj. 289
Ro. 303
Stephen 155
ROBERTS, Alex 98,103,368
Alvin P. 77
Alvin Prince 77
Ann 301
Caroline M. 301
Elliott 301,302
Eliz. 301
Frances 301
Frederick 301
Henry 199,292,301,302
Henry Ann 22
Jane 180
Jas. 229
Jno. 11,301,302,318,325
Jno. H. 11,96,129,158,
240,275,287,302,384
Jno. Jr. 66,302
Jno. Richardson 302
Jno. Sr. 20,302
Jos. 20,52,54,71,97,166,
229,254,295,371,395,400
Joseph 26,158
Jos. H. 239
Matt 301,302
Nancy 34,302
Nannie 302
Polly 302
Rich. M. 78
Ro. 302
Sally 56,302
Susanna 229,301,302
T. K. 320
W. A. 239
Wm. 14
Wm. H. 22
Zach 103,106,199,282,
301,302,371
Zachariah 7
ROBERTSON,...158,327
A. 26,27,263
A. F. 28,359,374
Andrew D. 302
Arch 357
Archer 302
Archibald 26,302,308,
312,319,359
Arthur F. 319
Arthus F. 286
C. 302
Cath. 302,303
D. P. 102
Eliz. 174
Eliza 339

ROBERTSON, cont'd:
Henry 371
James Murray 26
Jas. 302,303
Jas. M. B. 302
Jno. 235,302,321,333,339
Jno. B. 114,134,235,270,
286,302,310,359,365
John 28
John R. 28
Jos. C. 302
Louisa B. 74
Mary 303
Matt 302,303
Rebecca 303
Ro. 303
Roda 26
Saml. 339
Sarah 302
Sarah F. 302
Sarah Jane 303
S. F. 302
Thos. 123,302,303,324,
325
Wm. 191,302,339
Wm. B. 302
ROBBINS, Benj. 301
ROBINSON, A. D. D. 303
Agatha 303
Agness 303
Arthur F. 302
Beverly 303
Dolly 303
Eliz. 174,303
Eliza A. 392
Harry 303
Henry 303
Jacob H. 367
Jno. 303,349
Jno. Jr. 349
Jos. 303
L. 303
Lewis 303
L. P. 303
Lucy 178,303
Martha 303
Martha S. 303
Mrs. 303
Nancy 174,303
Pheby 303
Polly 303
Polly W. 303
Ro. 303
Robt. 174,303
Sarah E. 68
Simeon 303
Simeon A. 303
Simeon W. 303
S. P. M. 303
Stephen 303
Thos. 303
Wm. 257,303,349
Wm. R. 302
RODES, Amy 304
Ann 304
Anny 304
Charles 304
Chas. 46,304,329
Chas. P. 304
David 304
Jas. C. 307
Jas. 304
Jno. 84
Jno. H. 304
Jno. T. 32,192
John 304
J. T. 97
Mary 304
Thos. 304
ROGERS,...171
Benj. 59,214
Chas. 51,304
Chas. C. 50

www.ingramcontent.com/pod-product-compliance
Lightning Source LLC
Chambersburg PA
CBHW021842020426
42334CB00013B/156